YEARBOOK OF EUROPEA

YEARBOOK OF
EUROPEAN LAW

27

2008

EDITORS

P. EECKHOUT
Professor of European Law
King's College London

T. TRIDIMAS
Sir John Lubbock Professor of Banking Law
Queen Mary College, University of London

ASSISTANT EDITOR
J. A. GUTIERREZ-FONS

BOOK REVIEW EDITOR
G. DE BÚRCA

OXFORD
UNIVERSITY PRESS

OXFORD
UNIVERSITY PRESS

Great Clarendon Street, Oxford OX2 6DP

Oxford University Press is a department of the University of Oxford.
It furthers the University's objective of excellence in research, scholarship,
and education by publishing worldwide in

Oxford New York

Auckland Cape Town Dar es Salaam Hong Kong Karachi
Kuala Lumpur Madrid Melbourne Mexico City Nairobi
New Delhi Shanghai Taipei Toronto

With offices in

Argentina Austria Brazil Chile Czech Republic France Greece
Guatemala Hungary Italy Japan Poland Portugal Singapore
South Korea Switzerland Thailand Turkey Ukraine Vietnam

Oxford is a registered trade mark of Oxford University Press
in the UK and in certain other countries

Published in the United States
by Oxford University Press Inc., New York

British Library Cataloguing in Publication Data

Data available

Library of Congress Cataloging in Publication Data

Data available

Typeset by Newgen Imaging Systems (P) Ltd., Chennai, India
Printed in Great Britain
on acid-free paper by
Antony Rowe, Chippenham, Wiltshire

ISBN 978–0–19–956269–5

1 3 5 7 9 10 8 6 4 2

Editorial Committee

Contents

SURVEY

REVIEWS OF BOOKS

Abbreviations

AC	Appeal Cases
AETR	Accord européen relatif au travail des équipages des véhicules effectuant des transports internationaux par route (also ERTA)
AG	Advocate General
A-G	Attorney General
AJCL	*American Journal of Comparative Law*
AJIL	*American Journal of International Law*
All ER	All England Law Reports
Art/s	Article/s
ASIL	*American Society of International Law*
BJE	*Bulletin des juristes européens*
BVerfG	Bundesverfassungsgericht
BYIL	*British Year Book of International Law*
CA	Court of Appeal
Camb LJ	*Cambridge Law Journal*
CAP	Common Agricultural Policy
CDE	*Cahiers de droit européen*
CEN	Comité Européen de Normalisation
CENELEC	Comité Européen de Normalisation Électrotechnique
CESR	Committee of European Securities Regulators
CFI	Court of First Instance of the European Communities
CFSP	Common Foreign and Security Policy
Ch	Chancery Division of the High Court
Chap	Chapter
Cie	Compagnie
CIL	*Contemporary Issues in Law*
CISA	Convention Implementing the Schengen Agreement
CLP	*Current Legal Problems*
CLR	Commonwealth Law Reports
CM/Cmnd	Command Paper
CML Rev	*Common Market Law Review*
CMLR	Common Market Law Reports
Colum J Eur L	*Columbia Journal of European Law*
Colum L Rev	*Columbia Law Review*
COM	European Commission Documents

CPAS	Public Centre for Social Assistance (Centre Public d' Assistance Sociale)
CPR	Civil Procedure Rules
CPS	*Comparative Political Studies*
Crim L Rev	*Criminal Law Review*
CUP	Cambridge University Press
CYELS	*Cambridge Yearbook of European Legal Studies*
CYIL	*Canadian Yearbook of International Law*
DÖV	*Die Öffentliche Verwaltung*
DVBl	Deutsches Verwaltungsblatt
EAEC	European Atomic Energy Community
EBLR	*European Business Law Review*
(EC) Bulletin	Bulletin of the European Communities
ECBA	European Criminal Bar Association
ECE	Economic Commission for Europe
ECHR	European Convention on Human Rights
ECJ	European Court of Justice
ECLR	*European Competition Law Review*
ECrtHR	European Court of Human Rights
ECR	European Court Reports
EC Treaty	Treaty of Rome
EEA	European Environmental Agency
EEA	European Economic Area
EEC	European Economic Community
EELR	*European Environmental Law Review*
EFSA	European Food and Safety Authority
EFTA	European Free Trade Area
EHRR	European Human Rights Reports
EIPR	*European Intellectual Property Review*
EIRR	European Industrial Relations Reports
EJCL	*European Journal of Comparative Law*
EJCCL & CJ	*European Journal of Crime, Criminal Law and Criminal Justice*
EJIL	*European Journal of International Law*
EJLR	*European Journal of Law Reform*
EJPR	*European Journal of Political Research*
ELJ	*European Law Journal*
EL Rev	*European Law Review*
EOAR	European Ombudsman Annual Report
EP	European Parliament
EP (or PE) doc	European Parliament document

EPL	*European Public Law*
ETS	European Treaty Series
EUConst	*European Constitutional Law Review*
EuGRZ	*Europäische Grundrechte-Zeitschrift*
EUI	European University Institute
EuR	*Europarecht*
Euratom	European Atomic Energy Community
EuZW	*Europäische Zeitschrift für Wirtschaftsrecht*
EWCA Civ	England & Wales Court of Appeal (Civil Division)
EWHC (Admin)	England & Wales High Court (Administrative Court)
Ex	Exchequer Cases
FAO	Food and Agriculture Organization
FEOGA	Fonds européen d'orientation et de garantie agricole (European agricultural guidance and guarantee fund)
FIDE	Federation of European Law Associations
GATT	General Agreement on Tariffs and Trade
GATS	General Agreement on Trade in Services
GG	Grundgesetz
GmbH	Gesellschaft mit beschränkter Haftung
Harv Int'l LJ	*Harvard International Law Journal*
HL	House of Lords
HRLJ	*Human Rights Law Journal*
HR Rev	*Human Rights Review*
ICLQ	*International and Comparative Law Quarterly*
IMF	International Monetary Fund
Int.Rev Penal L	*International Review of Penal Law*
JCER	*Journal of Contemporary European Research*
JCLS	*Journal of Corporate Law Studies*
JCMS	*Journal of Common Market Studies*
Jean Monnet WP	Jean Monnet Working Paper
JEI	*Journal of European Integration*
JEPP	*Journal of European Public Policy*
JINTCRJ	*Journal of International Criminal Justice*
JLS	*Journal of Legal Studies*
Juris	*Juristen Zeitung*
KritJ	*Kritische Justiz*

LIEI	*Legal Issues of European Integration*
Lloyd's Rep	Lloyd's Law Reports
LPA	*Les Petites Affiches*
LQR	*Law Quarterly Review*

MEP	Member of the European Parliament
MJ	*Maastricht Journal of European and Comparative Law*
Mod L Rev/MLR	*Modern Law Review*
MP	Member of Parliament

n	footnote
NATO	North Atlantic Treaty Organization
NGO	Non-Governmental Organization
NJW	*Neue Juristische Wochenschrift* (German Law Journal)
nyr	not yet reported

OECD	Organisation for Economic Co-operation and Development
OEEC	Organisation for European Economic Co-operation
OEIL	Legislative Observatory
OJ	Official Journal (of the European Communities)
OJLS	*Oxford Journal of Legal Studies*
OJ Eng Sp Ed	Official Journal of the EC, English Special Edition (pre-1973)
OLAF	European Anti-Fraud Office (l'Office européen de lutte anti-fraude)
OUP	Oxford University Press

PDO	Protected Designations of Origin
PL	*Public Law*
PLI	Popular legislative initiative

QB	Queen's Bench Division of the High Court

RDE	*Rivista di Diritto Europeo*
RDP	*Revue du Droit Public*
RDUE	*Revue du Droit de l'Union Européene*
Rec	*Recueil de la jurisprudence de la Cour de justice des Communautés européennes*
REDC	*Revista Española de Derecho Comunitario*
REEI	*Revista Electronica de Estudios Internacionales*
REP	*Revista de Estudios Politicos*
Rev Econ Stud	*Review of Economic Studies*

Rev Sc Crim	*Revue de Science Criminelle et de Droit Penal Comparé*
RFDUC	*Revista de la Facultad de Derecho de la Universidad Complutense de Madrid*
RFDUL	*Revista da Faculdade de Direito da Universidade de Lisboa*
RIDC	*Revue internationale de droit comparé*
RMC	*Revue du Marché Commun*
RMCUE	*Revue du Marché Commun et de l'Union européenne*
RTDE	*Revue trimestrielle de droit européen*
s	section
SPS agreement	Agreement on the Application of Sanitary and Phytosanitary Measures
TBT	Agreement on Technical Barriers to Trade
TEC	Treaty Establishing the European Community
TEU	Treaty on European Union/Maastricht Treaty
ToA	Treaty of Amsterdam
ToN	Treaty of Nice
TRIPS	Agreement on Trade-related Aspects of Intellectual Property Rights
UCLAF	Anti-Fraud Coordination Unit (Unité de Coordination de la Lutte Anti-Fraude)
UN	United Nations Organization
UNESCO	United Nations Educational, Scientific and Cultural Organization
UNTS	United Nations Treaty Series
Vill L Rev	*Villanova Law Review*
WHO	World Health Organization
WLR	Weekly Law Reports
WTO	World Trade Organization
Yale LJ	*Yale Law Journal*
YbIEL	*Yearbook of European Environmental Law*
YEL	*Yearbook of European Law*
ZaöRV	*Zeitschrift für ausländisches öffentliches Recht und Völkerrecht*
ZHR	*Zeitschrift für das gesamte Handelsrecht und Wirtschaftsrecht*

ARTICLES

Creation's Final Laws: The Impact of the Treaty of Lisbon on the 'Final Provisions' of Earlier Treaties

*Gavin Barrett**

I. Introduction

Some of the most critically important provisions of the existing constitutive treaties of the European Union are to be found in their so-called final provisions—which deal with fundamental matters varying from the means by which the Treaty in question should be amended[1] to what should be done if the Treaty sets an objective but fails to provide the necessary legal powers to achieve it.[2] The purpose of this article is to examine the most significant changes which the Treaty of Lisbon effects to such provisions—more specifically, to the 'Final Provisions', which have been located up until now in Title VIII of the Treaty on European Union,[3] and to the 'General and Final Provisions' to be found in Part VI of the Treaty establishing the European Community (the EC Treaty).

Of the amendments effected by the Treaty of Lisbon to the Final Provisions of the Treaty on European Union, the most significant are four in number. In the order in which these are dealt with by the Treaty of Lisbon itself, they are (1) the conferring of legal personality on the European Union; (2) the alteration of the steps required to be taken in order to amend the Treaties in the future; (3) provision being made for the possibility of Member States leaving the Union;

---

* Senior Lecturer and President's Research Fellow, School of Law, University College Dublin, Visiting Scholar, Institut des Hautes Études Européennes, Université Robert Schuman, Strasbourg. Readers should note that in this analysis, references made to Article numbers in both the Treaty on European Union and the Treaty on the Functioning of the European Union refer to the final such numbers—in other words, they take into account the renumbering which is to be effected by Article 5(1) of the Treaty of Lisbon. The writer's thanks are expressed to the organizers and participants both in a research colloquium hosted by the Dublin European Institute on 29 April 2008 and in a Malta European Studies Association seminar held at the European Documentation and Research Centre, University of Malta on 19 June 2008, at both of which events the opportunity was provided to discuss some of the ideas outlined in more detail in this article.

[1] See Article 48 of the Treaty on European Union.
[2] See Article 308 of the Treaty Establishing the European Community.
[3] To be renumbered Title VI by Article 1(54) of the Treaty of Lisbon.

and (4) the expansion of the jurisdiction of the European Court of Justice, which is effected by the removal from the Final Provisions of the Treaty on European Union of the restrictions in this regard which have been found there up to now. It is proposed, in addition, to look at (5) the most significant amendment of the General and Final Provisions of the Treaty on the Functioning of the European Union, which is the amendment of the so-called 'flexibility' clause (which enables the taking of action at European level where this is necessary to attain a stipulated objective, but the necessary powers have nonetheless not been provided for doing so).

II. A First Change: The Conferring of Legal Personality on the European Union

The new Article 47 of the Treaty on European Union,[4] will provide simply that 'the Union shall have legal personality'. The entry into force of this provision will bring to an end the peculiar situation which exists at present—viz, that legal personality under international law has for long been expressly conferred at Treaty level on the European Community[5]—and indeed on the European Atomic Energy Community[6]—but only in the most elliptical and implicit manner on the European Union—an organization of which the European Community forms the most important component part.

The reasons for the failure—until now—to recognize expressly the legal personality of the Union at Treaty level (either in addition to, or in exclusion to that of the Communities) stem (as with many of the more idiosyncratic features of European integration) from historic Member State concerns about sovereignty, which originally led to a reluctance to acknowledge the reality that the creation of the European Union involved the setting up of an international organization in its own right at all.[7]

Perhaps paradoxically, legal personality has nonetheless for long been conferred in implicit fashion on the European Union. An international organization can only conclude international agreements if it has legal personality—and, since the coming into force of the Treaty of Amsterdam in May 1999, Article 24 of the existing Treaty on European Union has been viewed as conferring power on the Union to conclude international agreements both in the common foreign and

---

[4] To be inserted by Article 1(55) of the Treaty of Lisbon. Note also the provision of Article 282 of the EC Treaty that 'in each of the Member States, the Community shall enjoy the most extensive legal capacity accorded to legal persons under their laws' is replaced by a provision in Article 335 of the Treaty on the Functioning of the European Union in which the Union is conferred with this right.

[5] Under Article 281 of the EC Treaty, to be repealed by Article 2(280) of the Treaty of Lisbon.

[6] See Article 184 of the Euratom Treaty.

[7] See in this regard JC Gautron, 'Article I-7' in L Burgorgue-Larsen, A Levade, and F Picod (eds), *Traité établissant une Constitution pour l'Europe—Tome I* (Bruylant, 2007) 118.

security policy field and in the field of police and judicial cooperation in criminal matters.[8] As Hartley has put it, 'Article 24 does not expressly confer legal personality on the Union, but the Council and the Member States must have regarded it as doing so by implication.'[9]

The historical origins of the new Article 47 lie in the recommendations made regarding the contents of the now-defunct Constitutional Treaty made by Working Group III of the Convention on the Future of Europe (which, it will be recalled, was the body which produced the first draft of the Constitutional Treaty).[10] Working Group III—which was chaired by former Italian prime minister Giuliano Amato—was asked to consider, inter alia, the consequences of the taking of two separate steps—(a) an explicit recognition of the Union's legal personality; and (b) a merger of the Union's legal personality with that of the Community. The Working Group came out in favour of the taking of both steps. Much of the impetus, in particular for the taking of the latter step—that of creating a single personality for the Union—as opposed to having a legal personality *both* for the Community and the Union—derives from the final report of Working Group III.[11]

Overall, the net effect of the changes which the Treaty of Lisbon will bring about may be explained as follows:[12] there are at present three organizations in the European Union framework which have legal personality—the European Community, the European Atomic Energy Community and the European Union. In the wake of the coming into force of the Treaty of Lisbon, the legal personalities of the European Union and the European Community will be

---

[8] In the latter respect, by virtue of Article 38 of the Treaty on European Union. For examples of agreements under Article 24, see the Agreement between the Union and the Federal Republic of Yugoslavia approved by Decision 2001/352/CFSP ([2001] OJ L125/1 (5.5.2001)) and between the Union and the Former Yugoslav Republic of Macedonia approved by Decision 2001/682/CFSP ([2001] OJ L241/1 (11.9.2001)). Note that a brief but useful discussion of what the issue of what legal personality involves for an international organization is to be found in the working paper, *Note on effects on making Union legal personality explicit and on the merger of Union and Community legal personalities* (WD 001—WG III, Convention on the Future of Europe, Brussels, 13 June 2002).

[9] See T Hartley, *The Foundations of European Community Law* (6th edn, OUP, 2007) 158. See also JC Piris, *The Constitution for Europe—A Legal Analysis* (Cambridge University Press, 2006) 60–61. Piris points not only to the repeated use of Article 24 of the EU Treaty, but also the treatment by third countries of the European Union as an active subject of international law (cf, however, in this regard, Gautron, n 7 above at 120) and the fulfilment of Union of all the criteria set out by the International Court of Justice in its Advisory Opinion of 11 April 1949 on the international personality of the United Nations, *Reparation for Injuries Suffered in the Service of the United Nations ('Reparation Case')* [1949] ICJR 174. See further in this regard, S Marquardt, 'La capacité de l'Union européenne de conclure des accords internationaux dans le domaine de la coopération policière et judiciaire en matière pénale' in G de Kerchove and A Weyembergh (eds), *Sécurité et justice: enjeu de la politique extérieure de l'Union européenne* (Institut d'Études Européennes, Université de Bruxelles, 2003) at 179.

[10] The conclusions of Working Group III on Legal Personality are to be found on the Internet at: <http://register.consilium.eu.int/pdf/en/02/cv00/00305en2.pdf>.

[11] See P Norman, *The Accidental Constitution* (2nd edn, EuroComment, 2005) at 67. Amato was also one of two vice-chairmen of the Praesidium, the steering committee of the Convention.

[12] See in this regard, JC Piris, n 9 above at 60–61.

fused into one (ie that of the European Union).[13] The European Atomic Energy Community, in contrast, will retain its own separate legal personality. The decision to retain Euratom's separate legal personality apparently has its roots in the desire to avoid jeopardizing the political acceptability of the Lisbon Treaty by bringing the thorny question of nuclear power into the equation.[14]

Insofar as concerns the idea of expressly conferring legal personality on the Union at all is concerned, its main advantage seems to be that this step will facilitate the conclusion by the European Union of agreements in *all* areas in which it has competence and not merely those in the limited fields covered to date by Article 24 of the Treaty on European Union.[15] There are other consequences however. Working Group III summarized its views of the advantages in the following way:

> the explicit conferral of legal personality on the Union heightens its profile on the world stage. The Union thus becomes *a subject of international law*—alongside the Member States but without jeopardising their own status as subjects of international law—and would as a result be able to avail itself of all means of international action (right to conclude treaties, right of legation, right to submit claims or to act before an international court or judge, right to become a member of an international organisation or become party to international conventions, eg the ECHR, right to enjoy immunities), as well as to bind the Union internationally.[16]

Insofar as concerns the idea of doing away with a situation in which the Union and the Community have *separate* personalities, the clearer profile which the Union will have in the wake of the conferring of a single legal personality 'not only in relation to third States, but also vis-à-vis European citizens' is certainly one positive aspect of this.[17] In advocating a single personality for the Union,

---

[13] By virtue of the coming into force of Article 47 of the Treaty on European Union, expressly conferring legal personality on the Union, and the repeal of Article 281 of the EC Treaty, which has heretofore conferred legal personality on the European Community.

[14] This would have created difficulties in particular in securing Green support for the Lisbon Treaty. (See generally on this issue JC Gautron, n 7 above. Interestingly, considerations relating to ratification difficulties (though of a different nature) constituted the main reason for the creation of a European Atomic Energy Community in the first place. (See generally in this regard, the discussion by F Duchêne, *Jean Monnet: The First Statesman of Interdependence* (Norton, 1994) of the agreement and ratification process of the Euratom Treaty).

[15] Indeed the creation of a single legal personality for the Union may be regarded as having facilitated the creation under the Treaty of Lisbon of a single general procedure for the negotiation and conclusion of international agreements (as to which see Article 218 of the Treaty on the Functioning of the European Union, to be inserted by Article 2(173) of the Treaty of Lisbon).

[16] See paragraph 19 of the Working Group's final report. Obviously, however, for the purposes of the European Union's own legal order, any such actions will have to be exercised within the scope of another rule expressly endorsed under the Treaty of Lisbon—the principle of conferral (as to which see Article 5(1) and (2) of the Treaty on European Union as inserted by Article 1(6) of the Treaty of Lisbon). The impact of this rule (as well as the exception thereto constituted by Article 352 of what is to become the Treaty on the Functioning of the European Union) is returned to in the text below.

[17] See paragraph 11 of the Final Report of Working Group III on the Convention on the Future of Europe, summarizing in this regard the positions of the Legal Services of the European Parliament, Council, and Commission.

Working Group III was anxious to state its view that taking such a step would not *per se* necessarily entail any change in the allocation of competences between the Union and the Member States.[18] It is certainly also true that the mere conferral of legal personality on the European Union alone does not provide any answer to the question of the legal nature of the European Union, since a variety of entities varying from international organizations to confederal and federal entities have enjoyed such status.[19] And yet, conferring a single legal personality on the Union does facilitate certain other reforms. Hence, for example, Working Group III argued that retaining the Union's present three-pillar structure would be 'anachronistic' in the wake of the creation of a single legal personality. The creation of a single personality for the Union may thus be regarded as being a stepping stone to the creation of the single-pillar union now envisaged in the Treaty of Lisbon.[20]

III. A Second Change: The Alteration of the Procedures for Amending the Treaties

A second significant amendment effected by the Treaty of Lisbon to the Final Provisions of the Treaty on European Union consists of the introduction of altered procedures for amending the constitutive Treaties.[21] At present, the procedure for amending the Treaties is set out in Article 48 of the Treaty on European Union. It is this procedure which was used in the adoption and ratification of the

---

[18] See Final Report of Working Group III, at paragraph 20 thereof.

[19] The question of the true nature of the European Union is a major subject in its own right. One interesting recent view in this regard is that of Piris, who has described the European Union as a 'partially federal union', to be distinguished clearly from a federal state (Piris, n 9 above at 192 *et seq*). See further by the same writer on the same topic, 'The European Union: Towards a New Form of Federalism' in B Markesinis and J Fedtke (eds), *Patterns of Regionalism and Federalism* (Hart Publishing, 2005).

[20] See Final Report of Working Group III, at paragraphs 3 and 14 thereof. Norman has stated that consideration of the EU's legal personality 'triggered quite wide-ranging thought about the final shape of the constitutional treaty'. (See P Norman, n 11 above at 68.)

[21] There is, it should be said, a question as to whether the Member States need to adhere to Article 48 at all (although cf the view expressed by the Court of Justice in Case 43–75 *Defrenne v Sabena* [1976] ECR 455 at paragraph 58 thereof that the amendment procedure had to be adhered to). (See generally concerning this debate, Hartley, n 9 above at 88–89 and the articles cited therein.) However, the point will probably remain an academic one, because until now, the terms of Article 48 have always been adhered to, and the Member States would be unlikely to depart from a specifically agreed procedure of this nature. (Cf, however, Hartley, who has pointed out that the now-defunct European Coal and Steel Community Treaty was amended without the procedures laid down in it having been complied with both by the Saar Treaty of 27 October, 1956 and by the Convention on Certain Institutions Common to the European Communities of 25 March, 1957, and that the validity of these amendments was never questioned.) The constitutive treaties, it should be noted, however, may also be amended by accession treaties, and were most recently amended pursuant to the 2005 Treaty of Accession of Romania and Bulgaria to the European Union, which entered into force on 1 January, 2007.

Amsterdam and Nice Treaties and which is in the process of being deployed in relation to the Lisbon Treaty.

Under Article 48 as it stands prior to the Treaty of Lisbon changes, any Member State Government or the Commission is entitled to submit proposals to the Council for the amendment of the Treaties on which the Union is founded. If the Council, after consulting the European Parliament and, where appropriate, the Commission,[22] then delivers an opinion in favour of calling an intergovernmental conference[23] such a conference is convened by the President of the Council for the purpose of determining by common accord the amendments to be made to those Treaties.[24] The amendments then enter into force after being ratified by all the Member States in accordance with their respective constitutional requirements.

This procedure does not differ hugely from what international law would require in any case were there no Article 48.[25] In practice, implementing its requirements is a lengthy, drawn-out process, too cumbersome to be used every time a technical provision in the treaties needs to be amended and lacking both transparency and (arguably) sufficient susceptibility to democratic input and control. The Article 48 amendment procedure became the object of particular concern in the wake of the protracted, bad-tempered resolution of the negotiations on the Treaty of Nice under the French Council presidency in December 2000, the outcome of which, while it sufficed to facilitate the enlargement process, had more than an element of the *ad hoc* about it, and certainly did not address anywhere near all the issues which needed resolution for a more long-term settlement at European level.[26]

Article 1(56) of the Treaty of Lisbon therefore substitutes the entire text of the current Article 48 of the Treaty on European Union with a view to setting out a new method—or rather, new *methods*—for amending the Treaties in the future.

---

[22] The European Central Bank was also required to be consulted in the case of institutional changes in the monetary area.

[23] Ie, a conference of representatives of the governments of the Member States.

[24] Although not explicitly mentioned in the text of Article 48 up to now, the Council decision in this regard is taken by a simple majority vote of the Member States—one of the very few places in the European Union legal structure where such a vote (rather than a unanimous or qualified majority vote) is required. (Under Article 205(1) of the EC Treaty, save as otherwise provided in the EC Treaty, the Council is required to act by a majority of its Members. However, in all but very rare cases, it is otherwise provided by the EC Treaty.)

[25] In international law, a treaty between States is amended by the agreement of a subsequent contrary Treaty. Article 48 imposes additional requirements in this regard. One difference, as shall be seen in the text below, is the existence under Article 48 of a role—albeit merely a consultative one—for the European Parliament, as well as a consultative role (where appropriate) for the Commission and (in the case of institutional changes in the monetary area) the European Central Bank. See generally, T Hartley, n 9 above at 88.

[26] Hence the Declaration on the Future of the Union adopted and annexed to the Final Act of the 2000 intergovernmental conference. (Available at the time of writing at: <http://europa.eu.int/eur-lex/lex/en/treaties/dat/12001C/pdf/12001C_EN.pdf> at p 84 thereof.)

The new 'amendment procedure' will replace the old single lane road for Treaty change with a four-lane motorway for Treaty amendment.[27] In the first place (constituting, it might be said, the slow lane) there will be the so-called 'ordinary revision procedure',[28] which could alternatively be referred to as the 'main' or 'solemn' procedure for amending the Treaty. The new 'ordinary' procedure will be like the present Article 48 procedure—but with some additions tacked on. The idea of these extra elaborations is to address concerns about the opaqueness and lack of transparency in the current procedure. Secondly (constituting the fast lanes for Treaty revision) there will be three separate so-called 'simplified revision procedures'[29] (referred to, for the sake of convenience in this article, as the first simplified revision procedure and the (less extensive) second and third simplified revision procedures). Each of these 'simplified revision procedures' constitutes an effort to provide an accelerated procedure compared to the rather lumbering 'ordinary' amendment process—regarded as too cumbersome for technical amendments, especially in the wake of the additional elements which the Treaty of Lisbon inserts into this process.

It is proposed to explain briefly and in turn each of the new procedures. But before doing so, we may pause briefly to explain the most important limits to each and all of them. To date, the existing Article 48 has itself been doubly respectful of State sovereignty in that it imposes a requirement that all amendments to the Treaties be agreed upon 'by common accord'—in other words, unanimously—and then accepted by their national Parliaments (*via* the requirement that amendments be ratified by each Member State in accordance with its constitutional procedures). This may be contrasted with eg, the United Nations Charter, amendments to which come into force—for all members of the United Nations—when they have been adopted by a vote of two thirds of the members of the General Assembly and ratified in accordance with their respective constitutional processes by two thirds of the Members of the United Nations, including all the permanent members of the Security Council.[30] Under the Treaty of Lisbon, it is a case of *plus ça change, plus c'est la même chose*. Thus, although the Article 48 procedure is replaced by a number of separate procedures under the Lisbon reforms, none of the new procedures deviate in substance from this double-unanimity requirement.[31] All three of the simplified revision procedures

---

[27] One should perhaps not take the motorway analogy too far—as will shortly be seen, there is plenty of scope for traffic on the new four-lane route to move at a fairly slow pace.

[28] Article 48(1) to be inserted by Article 1(56) of the Treaty of Lisbon.

[29] Ibid.

[30] Article 108 of the Charter of the United Nations. See Hartley, n 9 above at 88 and more generally, B de Witte, 'Rules of Change in International Law: How Special is the European Community?' (1994) 25 NethYIL 299.

[31] It is interesting to note that Article 101(1)(b) of the ill-fated 'Penelope' working document produced by the European Commission on 4 December 2002 (described as a 'Contribution To A Preliminary Draft Constitution Of The European Union' and available at the time of writing at: <http://ec.europa.eu/economy_finance/emu_history/documents/treaties/Penelope%20pdf_en.pdf>) suggested that revisions of the Principles or Fundamental Rights in that Constitution be

are notable for their effective maintenance of a power to veto Treaty amendments not only in the hands of all Member States but also on the part of their national Parliaments. This double-veto factor seems likely to provide the single most significant obstacle to the deployment of any of them. A highly cautious approach can therefore be said to have been adopted at Lisbon. The added value in efficiency terms of each of the three simplified revision procedures will largely be confined to eliminating the need for an intergovernmental conference, and avoiding the addition of the requirement of a Convention.[32]

A. The Proposed Ordinary Revision Procedure

The proposed ordinary revision procedure is an enhanced and extended form of the existing Article 48 procedure.[33] Under this proposed ordinary revision procedure, the process of revision of the Treaties is now to take place in four steps. The first step—as under the existing Article 48—will be that any Member State Government or the Commission will be able to submit to the Council proposals for the amendment of the Treaties. Post-Lisbon, however, and for the first time, the European Parliament is also to have this right.[34] This will mark an upgrade of the role of the European Parliament, which although it has influenced and stimulated Treaty reform in the past,[35] has never had the capacity to initiate it formally.

The proposals will now have to be submitted to the European Council by the Council and national Parliaments have to be notified of them.[36] Again, this represents some change. Neither the European Council nor national Parliaments

adopted by the European Council by a majority of five-sixths of its members and would enter into force when five-sixths of the Member States had completed the procedures required by their constitutional rules for its adoption. The Convention on the Future of Europe, however, opted in favour of a requirement of unanimous agreement for Treaty amendment, followed by unanimous ratification, a choice which the 2004 intergovernmental conference which agreed the Constitutional Treaty adhered to and the 2007 intergovernmental conference which agreed the Lisbon Treaty also followed.

[32] As to which, see further below.

[33] Grard has thus referred to 'une logique juridique internationale, intergouvernementale, qu'un maquillage constitutionnel ne saurait masquer'. (See L Grard, 'Article IV-443' in L Burgorgue-Larsen, A Levade, and F Picod (eds), n 7 above, 796 at 799.)

[34] See generally Article 48(2) to be inserted by Article 1(56) of the Treaty of Lisbon.

[35] The draft Treaty establishing the European Union which was adopted by a large majority by the European Parliament in 1984 (with Altiero Spinelli acting as the rapporteur) is credited with the introduction of the term 'European Union' into political discourse, and was one factor—albeit not the main one—which led to the signature of the Single European Act in 1986. The membership of the Convention on the Future of Europe which produced the first draft of the Constitutional Treaty included 16 members of the European Parliament and 16 alternate members (not counting MEPs such as Ireland's Proinsias de Rossa who also participated but as a representative of the Oireachtas) in addition. Thus three MEPs acted in this capacity in the 2007 intergovernmental conference which led to the Treaty of Lisbon. See in this regard, A Duff, *True Guide to the Treaty of Lisbon* (Alliance of Liberals and Democrats for Europe) (available at the time of writing at: <http://www.alde.eu/fileadmin/files/Download/True-Guide-NEW.pdf>) at p 14 thereof.

[36] Article 48(2) as inserted by Article 1(56) of the Treaty of Lisbon.

had any explicit role under the original version of Article 48, although it can scarcely be doubted that heads of State and Government—the members of the European Council[37]—kept a close eye on the process of Treaty reform. Of course, national Parliaments would always have been involved later in the process of ratification, but their being made aware of the *initial* proposals—even if this is a limited level of involvement—certainly represents an improvement on the *status quo* in terms of openness and democratization.[38]

The Member States were careful at Lisbon to stipulate that these proposals might, inter alia, serve either to increase or to reduce the competences conferred on the Union in the Treaties. This stipulation, however, merely highlights something which has always been true in any case of Treaty reform initiated under Article 48.

The second step in the new amendment process will be that if the European Council, after consulting the European Parliament and the Commission, adopts by a simple majority a decision in favour of examining the proposed amendments, the President of the European Council will be required to convene a Convention. The Convention—composed of representatives of the national Parliaments, the Heads of State or Government of the Member States, of the European Parliament and of the Commission[39]—will examine the proposals for amendments and to adopt by consensus a recommendation to an intergovernmental conference.

Ironically, in spite of the general approval which has greeted the idea of incorporating a convention-type body in any future process of European Union Treaty reform, the intergovernmental conference that agreed the Lisbon Treaty was not itself preceded by a convention. Sufficient reason may have existed for this: the vast bulk of the Treaty of Lisbon merely repeats what is to be found in the (defunct) 2004 Constitutional Treaty. Thus it could be argued that a convention would simply have found itself going over the same ground as the earlier Convention. Should the Treaty of Lisbon enter into force, such a decision to dispense with a convention when engaging in Treaty reform will—wisely, it is submitted—remain a possibility, although—equally wisely—it will be less likely to be a step taken with quite the same degree of ease as it was in relation to the Treaty of Lisbon. Hence under the proposed new Article 48, it is provided that the European Council may decide by a simple majority not to convene a convention 'should this not be justified[40] by the extent of the proposed amendments'. In this case, the European Council is to define the terms of reference

---

[37] Togther with the President of the Commission. See Article 4 of the Treaty on European Union as it presently stands.

[38] See for a general study of national Parliaments and the European Union, G Barrett (ed), *National Parliaments and the European Union: The Constitutional Challenge for the Oireachtas and Other Member State Legislatures* (Clarus Press, 2008).

[39] Under the proposed new Article 48(3). The European Central Bank is also to be consulted in the case of institutional changes in the monetary area.

[40] Presumably—although this is not stated explicitly—in the European Council's view.

for an intergovernmental conference.[41] However, this decision may be reached only after obtaining the consent of the European Parliament. Any risk that the European Council might overuse, for the sake of political convenience, its discretion to leapfrog the convention stage is thus deliberately checked by giving the European Parliament a veto over the taking of this step. Philadelphia-style conventions seem likely to be with us to stay in any process of Treaty revision, therefore.

Provision for the possibility of having a convention is new to the Treaty on European Union—and yet, for the most part, it is not at all new to the European Union, constituting as it does merely the codification of existing practice. As is well known, such was the disillusion with the operation of the old Article 48 procedure in the wake of the 2000 intergovernmental conference which led to the adoption of the Treaty of Nice, that in drafting the (ultimately abortive) Constitutional Treaty of 2004, Member States—eager to make the process more user-friendly and transparent—immediately began the search for a new, or at least improved, way of doing things. A ready alternative model—or, more accurately, a supplementary procedure which could be grafted onto the requirements of the Article 48 procedure—presented itself in the form of the Convention which had been presided over by the former German President, Roman Herzog and which had worked from December 1999 until October 2000, drafting the Charter of Fundamental Rights of the European Union.

As a result, the Convention on the Future of Europe was established under the December 2001 Laeken Declaration of the European Council. This existence of this Convention—which deliberated from 2002 to 2003—was thus not the result of any legal obligation, but rather was based on a European Council decision. It was made up of 105 members, drawn from the national Parliaments of Member States and candidate countries, the European Parliament, the European Commission, and representatives of governments or of heads of State. The Convention was chaired by former French president Valéry Giscard d'Estaing and concluded its work in July 2003 having produced a draft Treaty establishing a Constitution for Europe. The ratification process of the Constitutional Treaty was ultimately to grind to a permanent halt in the wake of the 'no' votes during the ratification processes in France and the Netherlands in May and June 2005. However, the general feeling was that notwithstanding this setback, the experiment of grafting the convention method itself onto the Article 48 procedure had—even if not entitled to be entirely exempt from any criticism[42]—at least been a considerable improvement on the existing Article 48 process, and a process

---

[41] Ibid.

[42] The Convention was not as successful as it might have been in increasing public awareness of the process of Treaty reform. In addition, the manner in which its President, Valéry Giscard d'Estaing exercised his function gave rise to some complaints. Notwithstanding such criticisms, however, it is clear that the Convention's ultimate conclusions constituted a compromise which attracted overwhelming support from its membership.

which should be maintained—and this is just what the insertion of the foregoing provisions into the Treaty on European Union is intended to do.

The third step in the process in the proposed 'ordinary revision procedure' will be that a conference of representatives of the governments of the Member States is to be convened by the President of the Council for the purpose of determining by common accord the amendments to be made to the Treaties. The fourth and final step will be that the amendments are to enter into force after being ratified by all the Member States in accordance with their respective constitutional requirements. For better or for worse, neither step three nor four represents a change from the existing provision in Article 48.

Two final general observations may be made in relation to the ordinary revision procedure. The first is that the Member States have taken care to ensure that even in the wake of the Lisbon Treaty coming into force, they will remain very much in control of this main procedure for revising the Treaties. Hence the main powers in the ordinary revision procedure lie with those institutions in which Member State interests are most vigorously defended—viz, the European Council and the Council of Ministers. Other bodies gain only the right to submit proposals for amendments to the Treaties,[43] to be notified of such proposals,[44] or to be consulted on whether they should be examined,[45] or (in the case of the Convention, should one be convened), to make recommendations to an intergovernmental conference.[46] The European Parliament's rights, in particular, are confined to (a) submitting proposals for the amendment of the Treaties (a right held equally by the Commission and the government of each Member State),[47] (b) the right to be *consulted* on a non-binding basis on whether any proposal for the amendment of the Treaties should be examined,[48] (c) a right to insist on the convening of a Convention,[49] and (d) the right (the importance of which should not be underestimated) to have its representatives participate in any such Convention.[50] Parliament's consent is *not* required, in contrast, either in relation to the vital decision for the holding of the intergovernmental conference, or—even more vitally—as a precondition for the entry into force of amendments

[43] As with the European Parliament and the Commission, under Article 48(2) of the Treaty on European Union to be inserted by Article 1(56) of the Treaty of Lisbon.
[44] As in the case of national Parliaments, under Article 48(2) of the Treaty on European Union to be inserted by Article 1(56) of the Treaty of Lisbon.
[45] Article 48(3) (first indent) of the Treaty on European Union to be inserted by Article 1(56) of the Treaty of Lisbon.
[46] Ibid.
[47] Article 48(2) of the Treaty on European Union to be inserted by Article 1(56) of the Treaty of Lisbon.
[48] Article 48(3) (first indent) of the Treaty on European Union to be inserted by Article 1(56) of the Treaty of Lisbon.
[49] Article 48(3) (second indent) of the Treaty on European Union to be inserted by Article 1(56) of the Treaty of Lisbon.
[50] Article 48(3) (first indent) of the Treaty on European Union to be inserted by Article 1(56) of the Treaty of Lisbon.

agreed by that conference. Although there is a considerably increased role both for the European Parliament and for national Parliaments[51] in the proposed ordinary procedure of Treaty revision, the Member States will undoubtedly continue to occupy centre stage in relation to Treaty reform.

The second observation relates to the retention of the requirement not alone of the unanimous consent of all of the Member States for Treaty amendments under the ordinary revision procedure, but the additional requirement of *ratification* by all of the Member States in accordance with their respective constitutional requirements. The maintenance of this latter requirement was politically understandable and perhaps even necessary to ensure ratification of the Lisbon Treaty. In the long term, however, how practical such an approach will continue to be seems questionable. In a European Union of 27-plus Member States, ratification—at least if accompanied by a referendum—has demonstrated itself to be a highly unpredictable process.[52] It may have been a more sustainable long-term provision for the Member States to provide that in any future ratification process a Treaty ratified by an overwhelming majority of States would enter into force in those States in which it had been ratified, with the dissenting State or States free to exit from the Union or negotiate some kind of external association arrangement.[53] It is clear, however, that the inclusion of such a provision in Article 48 would have been a highly politically controversial inclusion.[54] On the

---

[51] Who it should be noted, also have the right to have representatives participate in any such Convention. See Article 48(3) (first indent) of the Treaty on European Union to be inserted by Article 1(56) of the Treaty of Lisbon.

[52] With the electorates of Denmark, Ireland, the Netherlands, and France having produced negative opinions on Treaties before having either changed their minds (which is what happened in Denmark as regards the Treaty of Maastricht, and Ireland, as regards the Treaty of Nice) or agreeing—via their elected representatives—to a roughly similar compromise (which is what occurred subsequent to the 2005 rejection of the constitutional Treaty in Dutch and French referendums). At the time of writing, the fate of the Treaty of Lisbon itself now hangs in the balance after the decision of the Irish electorate in a referendum held on 12 June 2008 to decline to facilitate its ratification.

[53] Compare the approach used for the ratification of the 1787 United States Constitution under which—controversially at the time—only nine of the 13 States were required to ratify the Constitution in order for it to enter into force. Rhode Island, which had refused to send delegates to the Constitutional Convention in Philadelphia actually rejected it in a popular vote in 1788 before then changing its mind and ratifying the Constitution (the last of the original 13 States to do so in 1790).

As noted above, Article 101(1)(b) of the ill-fated 'Penelope' working document produced by the European Commission on 4 December 2002 (described as a 'Contribution To A Preliminary Draft Constitution Of The European Union' and available at the time of writing at: <http://ec.europa.eu/economy_finance/emu_history/documents/treaties/Penelope%20pdf_en.pdf>) suggested that revisions of the Principles or Fundamental Rights in that Constitution would enter into force when five-sixths of the Member States had completed the procedures required by their constitutional rules for its adoption.

[54] The Convention rejected the suggestion that a Member State might be required to leave the European Union for any reason. (See the (rejected) suggestion for amendment of Article I-59 of the draft Constitution made by Convention members Brok, Szajer, Akcam, Van Der Linden, Lamassoure, Brejc, Demetriou, Figel, Liepina, Santer, Kelam, Kroupa, Tajani, Almeida, Garrett, Altmaier, Kauppi, Lennmarker, Maij-Weggen, Rack, and Vilen on behalf of the EPP Convention

other hand, the retention of the twin requirements of unanimous agreement on Treaty revisions and unanimous ratification will continue to create a danger of paralysis in the constitutional development of the Union and continue to make Treaty reform for the entire area of the European Union depend on the outcome of a referendum held in any one of the Member States where such a plebiscite is possible or required (instead of, as seems more reasonable, making the nature of that Member State's involvement with the European Union depend on any such referendum).[55] As matters stand, the new version of Article 48(5) deals with the issue of recalcitrant Member States merely by providing that if, two years after the signature of a treaty amending the Treaties, four fifths of the Member States have ratified it and one or more Member States have encountered difficulties in proceeding with ratification, the matter shall be referred to the European Council. This effective postponement of the effort to agree on a solution is substantively identical to the provision dealing with the matter that was found in the Constitutional Treaty.[56] In the short to medium term, such a failure to map out any solution may be tolerable. In the long term, however, an alternative approach to requiring unanimous ratification of Treaty change may be needed to avoid permanent constitutional paralysis in the European Union as a whole.

B. Proposed Simplified Revision Procedures

Apart from the so-called ordinary revision procedure, the revised Article 48 also makes provision for three separate so-called simplified revision procedures for amending the Treaties. From the theoretical standpoint, all of these are of interest in that they confer a form of *Kompetenz Kompetenz* on the European Union in that, for the first time they empower an institution of the Union itself—viz, the European Council[57]—to amend the Treaties.[58] However, the change will have little or no impact in practice since the Member States have maintained a careful grip on the amendment of the Treaties. This is because the choice of the institution most concerned in the amendment process, the European Council is an arena for

---

Group, at p 3 thereof (available online at the time of writing at: <http://european-convention.eu.int/Docs/Treaty/pdf/46/46_Art%20I%2059%20Brok%20EN.pdf>).

[55] Unanimous ratification of the Treaty of Lisbon is probably only feasible, because only one Member State in the Union, Ireland, intends to have a referendum on the Treaty of Lisbon itself.

[56] Article IV-443(4) of the Constitutional Treaty. The origins of this provision appear to be in a paragraph inserted by the Praesidium during the drafting by the Convention on the Future of Europe of the draft Treaty establishing a Constitution for Europe, submitted to the European Council in Rome on 18 July 2003. (See P Norman, n 11 at 181).

[57] For an analysis of the evolving role of the, European Council, see JP Jacqué, 'Article I-21' and 'Article I-22' in L Burgorgue-Larsen, A Levade, and F Picod (eds), n 7 above at 298 and 306.

[58] See in this regard, eg L Grard, 'Article IV-443' in L Burgorgue-Larsen, A Levade and F Picod (eds), n 7 above at 809.

the promotion of Member States' own individual interests, and the requirement of unanimity applies in relation to the deployment of any of the simplified revision procedures. It is proposed to deal briefly with each of the three simplified revision procedures separately.

(i) *The First Simplified Revision Procedure*

At least part of the European Union's success has derived from its pursuit of exalted objectives by mundane-seeming methods. The integration process which has evolved into the European Union already involved a combination of lofty, even sublime goals ('the maintenance of peaceful relations', 'the elimination of the age-old opposition of France and Germany', 'the federation of Europe'[59] and 'ever closer union among the peoples of Europe'[60]) and banal-seeming means (including Treaty rules regulating the market in everything from coal and steel to banking and insurance services[61] to—perhaps taking an extreme example— 'edible meat offal' and 'oil seeds and oleaginous fruit'[62]). The existing process of amendment of the constitutive treaties—now lengthened, it should be remembered, by the 'Convention' provisions which are to be inserted by the Treaty of Lisbon—has always been an awkward and cumbersome means of amending highly technical provisions of the constitutive Treaties, and the case for a simplified revision process for at least some of the provisions which are of lesser importance has for long been strongly arguable. Prior at least to the 2004 intergovernmental conference, however, Member State willingness to address the matter was less evident. In fairness, such unwillingness may have been motivated by the difficulty of locating precisely the dividing line between provisions which are significant enough to merit requiring the full 'convention plus intergovernmental conference' treatment and those on which a speedier process should be capable of being deployed. The Treaty of Lisbon—following the example of the defunct Constitutional Treaty—seeks to resolve this issue, with what we may call the first simplified revision procedure: a new Article 48(6) is inserted in the Treaty on European Union, designed to facilitate easier amendment of the Treaty provisions concerning issues more technical than constitutional in nature.[63] This measure implicitly categorizes the provisions of the Treaties as measures of one of two different levels of importance.

---

[59] See regarding all of these the Schuman Declaration of 9 May 1950, reproduced at: <http://europa.eu/abc/symbols/9-may/decl_en.htm>.

[60] See Article 1 of the Treaty on European Union.

[61] See Article 51 of the Treaty Establishing the European Community.

[62] See in this regard Annex I to the Treaty establishing the European Community and Article 32 of the Treaty.

[63] The first simplified revision procedure originated in the 2004 intergovernmental conference which agreed the Constitutional Treaty and has much in common with a proposal made by the Irish Presidency during the negotiations. (See concerning the history of this provision, L Grard, 'Article IV-443' in L Burgorgue-Larsen, A Levade, and F Picod (eds), n 7 above at 815–817.)

Where has the dividing line been drawn? This requires some explanation. Until now, the text of the EC Treaty has been divided into six parts. Part One is entitled 'Principles'. Part Two is entitled 'Citizenship of the Union', but will be rechristened 'Non-discrimination and citizenship of the union' by the Lisbon Treaty.[64] Part Three carries the title 'Community policies' but will be renamed 'Union policies and internal actions'.[65] Part Four is entitled 'Association of the overseas countries and territories'. Part Five (which will be renumbered Part Six[66]) deals with the institutions of the Union but is now to be rechristened 'Institutional and financial provisions'.[67] Part Six (now to be renumbered Part Seven[68]) is entitled 'General and final provisions'. A new Part Five, entitled 'external action by the union' is also to be added under the Treaty of Lisbon.[69]

After the coming into force of the Treaty of Lisbon, amendments of six Parts thereof—viz, Parts One, Two, Four, Five, Six and Seven of the EC Treaty (or the Treaty on the Functioning of the European Union, as it will then be known[70]) will continue to require the deployment of the ordinary revision procedure, outlined above. It is the provisions of Part Three alone which will be capable of being subjected to the first simplified revision procedure.

It is worth pausing briefly to consider Part Three. In terms of its total number or words and pages, this Part certainly accounts for a fair proportion of the physical bulk of the EC Treaty. Thus, for example in the existing (pre-Lisbon) consolidated text, it accounts for 77 pages out of 320 pages of Treaties and Protocol text.[71] On the other hand, the legal importance of a document is obviously not determined by its length,[72] and it is true that the overwhelming bulk of the provisions of Part Three consist of material which, however important it might be, is of a kind which would be unlikely to find its way into any national constitution. The Community policies dealt with under Part Three have up to now been a broad range of areas some of which are highly integrated,[73] others of which are less so,[74] and others which are hardly integrated at all and in which the Union plays a relatively minor support role.[75] Titles covering the following subject areas are to be found in Part Three: free movement of goods (to be supplemented

[64] Article 2(31) of the Treaty of Lisbon.
[65] See Article 2(39) of the Treaty of Lisbon.
[66] See Article 2(177) of the Treaty of Lisbon.
[67] Article 2(177) of the Treaty of Lisbon.
[68] See Article 2(279) of the Treaty of Lisbon.
[69] See Article 2(154) of the Treaty of Lisbon.
[70] See Article 2(1) of the Treaty of Lisbon.
[71] Consisting of 186 pages of Treaty text and 134 pages of Protocol text. In the consolidated version of the Treaties published in the Official Journal of the European Union (OJ Vol. 51 C115 (9 May 2008)), Part Three occupies a near-identical proportion of 78 pages of a total of 316 pages of Treaty and Protocol text.
[72] A point perhaps best illustrated by the example of United States Constitution, which is a mere seven articles long, albeit now supplemented and altered by 27 amendments.
[73] Such as the rules concerning the free movement of goods.
[74] Such as the rules on asylum and immigration.
[75] Such as the rules on education, public health, and culture.

under Lisbon by a Title on internal market rules generally);[76] agriculture (to be amended, under the Lisbon Treaty, to the more accurate 'agriculture and fisheries'[77]); free movement of persons, services and capital; visas, asylum, immigration and other policies related to the free movement of persons (to be replaced under Lisbon by a broader Title *sub nom* 'area of freedom, security and justice'); transport; common rules on competition, taxation and the approximation of laws; economic and monetary policy; employment; the common commercial policy (a Title which, however, is to be removed from Part Three by the Treaty of Lisbon and so will not be capable of being amended by the first simplified revision procedure[78]); customs cooperation; social policy, education, vocational training and youth (a Title which will be retitled simply 'social policy' by the Treaty of Lisbon[79] and supplemented by two Titles on the European social fund,[80] and on education, vocational training, youth and sport, respectively[81]); culture; public health; consumer protection; trans-European networks; industry; economic and social cohesion (to be retitled 'economic, social and territorial cohesion' by the Treaty of Lisbon[82]); research and technological development (to be amended, under the Lisbon Treaty to 'research and technological development and space'[83]); the environment; development cooperation (a Title which, however, is to be removed from Part Three by the Treaty of Lisbon and so will not be capable of being amended by the first simplified revision procedure[84]); and economic, financial and technical cooperation with third countries (again, a Title which is to be removed from Part Three by the Treaty of Lisbon and so will not be capable of being amended by the first simplified revision procedure[85]). New Titles on energy,[86] tourism,[87] civil protection[88] and administrative cooperation[89] are also to be added to Part Three by the Treaty of Lisbon. All of the foregoing will be capable of being amended *via* the deployment of the first simplified revision procedure.

The first simplified revision procedure will operate as follows after the coming into force of the Treaty of Lisbon.[90] In the first place, the Government of any

---

[76] See Article 2(40) of the Treaty of Lisbon.   [77] Article 2(46) of the Treaty of Lisbon.
[78] Under Article 2(112) of the Treaty of Lisbon, the Title 'common commercial policy' is to be moved to Part Five of the Treaty on the Functioning of the European Union (which deals with the Union's external action).
[79] See Article 2(114) of the Treaty of Lisbon.
[80] Article 2(121) of the Treaty of Lisbon.   [81] Article 2(123) of the Treaty of Lisbon.
[82] Article 2(130) of the Treaty of Lisbon.   [83] Article 2(135) of the Treaty of Lisbon.
[84] Under Article 2(145) of the Treaty of Lisbon, the Title 'development cooperation' is to be moved to Part Five of the Treaty on the Functioning of the European Union (which deals with external action by the Union).
[85] Under Article 2(146) of the Treaty of Lisbon, the Title 'economic, financial and technical cooperation with third countries' is to be moved to Part Five of the Treaty on the Functioning of the European Union (which deals with external action by the Union).
[86] Article 2(147) of the Treaty of Lisbon.   [87] Article 2(148) of the Treaty of Lisbon.
[88] Article 2(149) of the Treaty of Lisbon.   [89] Article 2(150) of the Treaty of Lisbon.
[90] See generally the proposed new Article 48(6) of the Treaty on the European Union, substituted by Article 1(56) of the Treaty of Lisbon.

Member State, the European Parliament or the Commission will be entitled to submit to the European Council proposals for revising all or part of the provisions of Part Three. Once this happens, the European Council—acting by unanimity after consulting the European Parliament, the Commission, and the European Central Bank in the case of institutional changes in the monetary area—may adopt a decision amending all or part of the provisions of Part Three of the Treaty on the Functioning of the European Union. The decision is not to enter into force until it is approved by the Member States in accordance with their respective constitutional requirements.

The procedures—although less rigorous than those of the old Article 48, and, obviously, those of its replacement (with its additional requirement of a convention) will still represent a formidable obstacle to amendment of the Treaties where they apply. In the first place, notwithstanding proposals to relax the requirements of unanimity made in the course of the 2004 intergovernmental conference, the Member States insisted on retaining the requirement of unanimity in this context, an agreement that was held to at Lisbon. This gives each one of the currently 27 Member States an effective veto over any change. Moreover, the coming into force of the decision has also been made dependent on securing the approval of the decision by Member States in accordance with their constitutional requirements—which will involve at the very least Parliamentary ratification in all States and in Ireland, for example, could conceivably involve a referendum.[91]

Hence the most onerous features of the old Article 48 revision procedure—the requirement of a unanimous vote, followed by Parliamentary approval—remain under the first simplified revision procedure. Because of this it may be said—at least in relation to the most technical rules whose amendment is facilitated—that it is doubtful if the relaxation which the first simplified revision procedure involves has gone as far as its underlying rationale seemed to demand. (It may be noted that the Member States have also cautiously stipulated that an amending decision under Article 48(6) shall not increase the competences conferred on the Union in the Treaties, which is obviously a major restriction on the use of the new procedure.[92]) However, the requirement of the convening of an intergovernmental conference (and a convention) is at least dispensed with, and also the technical requirements of a formal ratification process. Once the approval of the last Member State takes place, the decision to amend the Treaties under the simplified procedure may enter into force.

The first simplified revision procedure is a general one, applying, as has been noted above, Part Three of the Treaty on the Functioning of the European Union. Side by side with it exist a number of similar but more narrowly-targeted

---

[91] See in this regard the Supreme Court decision in *Crotty v An Taoiseach* [1987] IR 713, [1987] ILRM 400.

[92] Article 48(6), third sub-paragraph of the Treaty on the European Union.

revision procedures, which allow the amendment of individual Treaty provisions. Versions of at least some of these are already to be found in the existing Treaties.[93] Some of them, however, are new, although they correspond for the most part to similar provisions which were to be found in the now-defunct Constitutional Treaty.[94] In four of the latter cases[95] amendment of primary legislation has been

[93] See Article 25(2) of the Treaty on the Functioning of the European Union (as amended by Article 2(38) of the Treaty of Lisbon) (corresponding to Article III-129, sub-paragraph 2 of the Constitutional Treaty and corresponding to Article 22(2) of the existing EC Treaty) which concerns adding to the rights of EU citizens; Article 126(14), sub-paragraph 2 (as amended by Article 2(90) of the Treaty of Lisbon) of the Treaty on the Functioning of the European Union (corresponding to Art III-184(13), sub-paragraph 2 of the Constitutional Treaty and Art 104(14) of the existing EC Treaty) which permits the replacement of the Protocol on the Excessive Deficit Procedure; and Article 308, sub-paragraph 3 of the Treaty on the Functioning of the European Union (as amended by Article 2(255) of the Treaty of Lisbon) (corresponding to Art III-393, sub-paragraph 4 of the Constitutional Treaty and Article 266, sub-paragraph 3 of the existing EC Treaty).

[94] See Article 83(1), sub-paragraph 3 of the Treaty on the Functioning of the European Union (as inserted by Article 2(67) of the Treaty of Lisbon) (corresponding to Article III-271(1) sub-paragraph 3 of the Constitutional Treaty) which concerns extending the list of crimes in relation to which minimum rules regarding definitions and sanctions can be laid down; Article 86(4) of the Treaty on the Functioning of the European Union (as inserted by Article 2(67) of the Treaty of Lisbon) (corresponding to Article III-274(4), sub-paragraph 3 of the Constitutional Treaty) which concerns extending the powers of the European Public Prosecutor's Office to include serious crime having a cross-border dimension; Article 129(3) of the Treaty on the Functioning of the European Union (as substituted by Article 2(93) of the Treaty of Lisbon and corresponding to Article III-187(3) of the Constitutional Treaty) which, in conjunction with Article 40.1 of the Protocol on the Statute of the European System of Central Banks and of the European Central Bank (corresponding to Article 40.1 in the equivalent Protocol which was annexed to the Treaty establishing a Constitution for Europe) permits the amendment of the Statute of the European System of Central Banks and of the European Central Bank; Article 281, sub-paragraph 2 of the Treaty on the Functioning of the European Union (as substituted by Article 2(226) of the Treaty of Lisbon and corresponding to Article III-38, sub-paragraph 2 of the Constitutional Treaty) which permits amendment of the Statute of the Court of Justice; Article 107(2)(c) of the Treaty on the Functioning of the European Union (as amended by Article 2(77) of the Treaty of Lisbon and corresponding to Article III-167(2)(c) of the Constitutional Treaty, which permits the eventual ending of the exemption from State aids rules of certain areas of the Federal Republic of Germany affected by the former division of Germany); Article 98 of the Treaty on the Functioning of the European Union (as amended by Article 2(73) of the Treaty of Lisbon and corresponding to Article III-243 of the Constitutional Treaty, which permits the eventual ending of the exemption from common transport area rules of certain areas of the Federal Republic of Germany affected by the former division of Germany); Article 355(6) of the Treaty on the Functioning of the European Union (corresponding to Article IV-440(7) of the Constitutional Treaty) which permits the adoption of a decision amending the status, with regard to the Union of certain Danish, French, or Netherlands countries and territories; and Article 40.2 of the Protocol on the Statute of the European System of Central Banks and of the European Central Bank, (corresponding to Article 40.2 in the equivalent Protocol which was annexed to the Treaty establishing a Constitution for Europe) which concerns the amendment of Article 10(2) of the same Protocol regarding voting rights in the Governing Council of the European Central Bank.

[95] Viz, Article 129(3) of the Treaty on the Functioning of the European Union (as substituted by Article 2(93) of the Treaty of Lisbon and corresponding to Article III-187(3) of the Constitutional Treaty) which, in conjunction with Article 40.2 of the Protocol on the Statute of the European System of Central Banks and of the European Central Bank permits the amendment of the Statute of the European System of Central Banks and of the European Central Bank; Article 281, sub-paragraph 2 of the Treaty on the Functioning of the European Union (as substituted by Article 2(226) of the

made possible using qualified majority vote in Council, apparently the only place where this is allowed under the Treaty of Lisbon reforms.

(ii) Second and Third Simplified Revision Procedures—An Introduction

Two further simplified revision procedures over and above those applying to Part Three of the Treaty on the Functioning of the European Union are laid down by the new Article 48(7).[96] These second and third simplified revision procedures are sometimes referred to as general *passerelle* clauses. *Passerelle* clauses are a subset of simplified revision procedures. They are passages along which the rules concerning European Union decision-making procedures can be changed in an accelerated fashion.[97] They constitute a route on which decision-making procedure stipulated in the Treaties (viz, unanimity or a special legislative procedure) can be transformed to a less heavy or cumbersome process (viz, qualified majority vote, or the ordinary legislative procedure) without going through the ordinary process of Treaty amendment. The image conjured up by the term *'passerelle'* is thus one of a convenient bridge, or shortcut, leading from a place of cumbersome, awkward procedural requirements to a place where procedural requirements are less burdensome. *'Passerelle'* clauses are not new to the Treaty of Lisbon. Several of them are to be found in the existing Treaties.[98] Such clauses have been well described as often being what has remained of unsuccessful attempts in previous intergovernmental conferences to switch from unanimity to qualified majority voting, a consolation prize to those who had pleaded in favour of qualified majority voting[99]—but who did not get it because the introduction of majority voting into the area in question was regarded as too much of a trespass on national sovereignty at the time of the intergovernmental conference in question.

What is new about the Treaty of Lisbon scheme is therefore not the existence of *passerelle* clauses, but rather that this *passerelle* system has been generalized

Treaty of Lisbon and corresponding to Article III-381, sub-paragraph 2 of the Constitutional Treaty) which permits amendment of the Statute of the Court of Justice; and Article 107(2)(c) of the Treaty on the Functioning of the European Union (as amended by Article 2(77) of the Treaty of Lisbon and corresponding to Article III-167(2)(c) of the Constitutional Treaty which permits the eventual ending of the exemption from State aids rules of certain areas of the Federal Republic of Germany affected by the former division of Germany); and Article 98 of the Treaty on the Functioning of the European Union (as amended by Article 2(73) of the Treaty of Lisbon and corresponding to Article III-243 of the Constitutional Treaty which permits the eventual ending of the exemption from common transport area rules of certain areas of the Federal Republic of Germany affected by the former division of Germany). Note that the first two cases concern Protocols only. (See more generally, Piris, n 9 above at 127–129.)

[96] Ie, to be inserted by Article 1(56) of the Treaty of Lisbon.

[97] Ie, compared to the ordinary procedure for amendment of the Treaties.

[98] See further the text below relating to the second and third simplified revision procedures individually.

[99] Piris, n 9 above at 125.

through the creation of the second and third simplified revision procedures. The bridge or *passerelle* has been widened. The Member States were probably emboldened in agreeing to the expansion of the system by the knowledge that in practice the *passerelles* in the existing Treaties have tended hardly ever to be used.[100] As regards the prospects of the new generalized *passerelle* clauses being used should the Treaty of Lisbon be adopted, this is likely to vary according to the subject area concerned. Dogged opposition by particular Member States to anything but unanimous voting insofar as concerns certain issues eg, indirect taxation[101] makes it seem unlikely that the *passerelles* will ever be used in relation to the decision-making rules on this issue. There are other provisions of the Treaties, however, where continued adherence to the existing modalities of decision-making procedures already seems somewhat anomalous and, it may be suggested tentatively, may be less likely to continue to be defended indefinitely.[102]

Historically, both the second and the third simplified revision procedures derive their origins in the Convention on the Future of Europe,[103] the body which produced the first draft of the Constitutional Treaty, although the systemizing idea of affixing the label 'simplified revision procedures' to the general *passerelle* clauses—and thereby (correctly) classifying them as a subset of rules designed to ease the amendment of certain provisions of the Treaties—stems from the 2004 intergovernmental conference which agreed the final text of the Constitutional Treaty.[104] Both the idea of generalized *passerelle* clauses and their new name were subsequently retained in the Lisbon Treaty.

It should be noted that under the Treaty of Lisbon, the general *passerelles* to qualified majority voting and co-decision made up of the second and third simplified revision procedures are to exist side by side with several sectoral *passerelles*. Some of these sectoral *passerelles* are the same as, or modified versions of *passerelles*

---

[100] One significant deployment of a *passerelle* procedure was that effected under Article 67(2) (second indent) of the EC Treaty by Council Decision 2004/927/EC of 22 December 2004 providing for certain areas covered by Title IV of Part Three of the Treaty establishing the European Community to be governed by the procedure laid down in Article 251 of that Treaty ([2004] OJ L396/45 (31.12.2004)). Under this decision, the Council (at the request of the European Council at the time the latter adopted the Hague Programme 'Strengthening Freedom, Security and Justice in the European Union') applied the co-decision procedure to the adoption of measures relating to border controls and frontier checks on persons, freedom of travel for third country nationals for periods of up to three months, the balancing of efforts of Member States in receiving refugees and displaced persons, and immigration policy insofar as this covers illegal immigration and residence.

[101] In relation to which see Article 113 of the Treaty on the Functioning of the European Union (as amended by Article 2(79) of the Treaty of Lisbon).

[102] See eg, Article 103(2) of the Treaty on the Functioning of the European Union, under which the European Parliament's role in the adoption of certain legislation in the competition law field continues to be confined to a consultative one.

[103] See Article I-24(4) of the draft Treaty establishing a Constitution for Europe, submitted to the European Council in Rome on 18 July 2003 (available online at the time of writing at: <http://european-convention.eu.int/docs/Treaty/cv00850.en03.pdf>).

[104] See Article IV-444 of the Treaty establishing a Constitution for Europe.

which exist under the existing Treaties.[105] Some of the sectoral *passerelles* are new, however.[106]

The deployment of the generalized *passerelles* which are the second and third simplified revision procedures is subjected to a number of restrictions. In the first place (as is the case with all three of the simplified revision procedures), each and every Member State is given an effective veto over any such deployment, since the European Council decision to switch to qualified majority voting or co-decision,[107] as the case may be, must be unanimous.[108]

Secondly, the European Parliament is also given a power of veto over any deployment of the second or third simplified revision procedures, since it is stipulated that the decision to switch to qualified majority voting or co-decision, as the case may be, can only be reached after obtaining the consent of the European Parliament. The Parliament's consent, moreover, must 'be given by a majority of its component members', and not merely a majority of those members who vote, which would be an easier requirement to meet.[109] This requirement distinguishes the second and third simplified revision procedures from the first, in relation to which the European Parliament is given the right only to be consulted. (In relation to potentially more radical reforms involved in the first simplified revision procedure, the Member States evidently wished to retain exclusive effective control of the right to amend the Treaties.)

The third and most innovative restriction on Treaty amendment *via* the second and third simplified revision procedures is that any initiative taken by the European Council to switch to qualified majority voting or co-decision, as the

---

[105] See Article 153(2), sub-paragraph 4 of the Treaty on the Functioning of the European Union (as amended by Article 2(116) of the Treaty of Lisbon). This provides for the possibility of the application of co-decision in the social policy field and corresponds to Article 137(2), sub-paragraph 3 (last line) of the existing EC Treaty (and Article III-210(3), sub-paragraph 2 of the now-defunct Constitutional Treaty). Note also Article 192(2), sub-paragraph 2 of the Treaty on the Functioning of the European Union (as substituted by Article 2(144) of the Treaty of Lisbon). This provides for the possibility of the application of qualified majority voting in the environmental field and corresponds to Article 175(2), sub-paragraph 2 of the existing EC Treaty (and Article III-234(2), sub-paragraph 2 of the Constitutional Treaty).

[106] See Article 312(2), sub-paragraph 2 of the Treaty on the Functioning of the European Union (as inserted by Article 2(261) of the Treaty of Lisbon) which provides for the possibility of the application of qualified majority voting for the adoption of the multiannual financial framework (and corresponds to Article I-55(4) of the now-defunct Constitutional Treaty); Article 81(3), sub-paragraph 2 of the Treaty on the Functioning of the European Union as substituted by Article 2(66) of the Treaty of Lisbon, which provides for the possibility of the application of co-decision (the 'ordinary legislative procedure') to family law with cross-border implications (which corresponds to Article III-269(3), sub-paragraph 2 of the Constitutional Treaty); and Article 333 of the Treaty on the Functioning of the European Union as inserted by Article 2(278) of the Treaty of Lisbon which provides for the possibility of the application of both co-decision and qualified majority voting in the context of enhanced cooperation (and which corresponds to Article III-422 of the Constitutional Treaty).

[107] Referred to as the 'ordinary legislative procedure' in the text of the Treaties as they would appear subsequent to their amendment by the Treaty of Lisbon. See eg, Article 48(7) of the Treaty on European Union (as inserted by Article 1(56) of the Treaty of Lisbon).

[108] Article 48(7), fourth sub-paragraph of the Treaty on the European Union.

[109] Ibid.

case may be, is required to be notified to the national Parliaments. If a national Parliament makes known its opposition within six months of the date of such notification, the decision shall not be adopted. On the other hand, in the absence of opposition the European Council may adopt the decision.[110]

A fourth and final restriction is that both the second and third simplified revision procedures are to be precluded by a specific Treaty provision[111] from being applied to a number of particularly sensitive provisions of the Treaty on the Functioning of the European Union,[112] which are thus immunized from the application of the general *passerelle* clauses.

Overall, the second and third simplified revision procedures may be said to involve an easier and a more rapid means of treaty amendment of the Treaties than does the ordinary revision procedure. They should also provide a quicker route to amendment than the first simplified revision procedure, since changes under the second and third simplified revision procedures (unlike the first) are not stipulated to require approval by the Member States in accordance with their respective constitutional requirements before entering into force.[113] The efficiency advantages of the second and third simplified revision procedures may be summarized by saying that both eliminate any need for (a) both an intergovernmental conference (required under the ordinary revision procedure) and a convention (now to become, at least in the normal run of events, part and parcel of the ordinary revision procedure); and (b) either a ratification process (required under the ordinary revision procedure) or a Member State procedure of approval in accordance with its constitutional requirements (required in the case of the first simplified revision procedure) are dropped here. On the other hand, as has been seen, the considerable hurdle of the requirement of a unanimous vote of the Member States in favour of Treaty amendment remains. So too does the newly-created hurdle of national Parliamentary acceptance of any Treaty changes. This new role for national Parliaments is clearly intended to restore what is lost to them (and to the democratic process) in the dropping under the second and third simplified revision procedures of any requirement of a Member State ratification or approval process. Thus even if national Parliaments lose their heretofore-enjoyed

---

[110] See generally Article 48(7), third sub-paragraph of the Treaty on the European Union.

[111] Article 353 of the Treaty on the Functioning of the European Union as inserted by Article 2(290) of the Treaty of Lisbon.

[112] Article 311, third and fourth sub-paragraphs of the Treaty on the Functioning of the European Union (as inserted by Article 2(259) of the Treaty of Lisbon) which deals with the Union's providing for its own resources; Article 312(2), first sub-paragraph of the Treaty on the Functioning of the European Union (as inserted by Article 2(261) of the Treaty of Lisbon) which deals with the adoption of a multiannual financial framework; Article 352 of the Treaty on the Functioning of the European Union (as substituted by Article 2(289) of the Treaty of Lisbon) which is the flexibility clause dealt with elsewhere in this article, and Article 354 of the Treaty on the Functioning of the European Union (as substituted by Article 2(291) of the Treaty of Lisbon) which deals with suspension of rights resulting from membership of the Union.

[113] Note however that the Article 48(7) sub-paragraph 3 role for national Parliaments will involve a minimum delay of six months to permit Parliaments to make known their opposition.

role under national law in ratifying any treaty amendment where the second or third simplified treaty revision procedure is applied, they gain a roughly equivalent right directly from primary European Union law in the form of the Article 48(7) power given to each and every individual national Parliament to veto Treaty change under the second simplified revision procedure. It should be noted that in order to come into play this right must be positively exercised by the national Parliament, however.[114] The consequences of the failure of any national political system to facilitate such an exercise are unstipulated.

(iii) Some Further Observations Specifically on the Second Simplified Revision Procedure

The membership of what has become the European Union has expanded in size from six to 27 Member States and is likely to expand yet further. With the addition of each new Member State the difficulty increases of arriving at any decision that the Treaties require to be taken by unanimity. Member State consciousness of this point has meant that every amending Treaty from the Single European Act to the Treaty on European Union to the Treaty of Amsterdam to the Treaty of Nice to the Treaty of Lisbon has sought to increase the level of qualified majority voting at Council level and to reduce the level of voting by unanimity. Notwithstanding the gradual spread of majority voting, the number of decisions which will involve a Treaty-imposed requirement of a unanimous Council vote even after the Treaty of Lisbon enters into force remains strikingly high, with each instance involving the danger that the Union will be unable to exercise its competence to act in the relevant policy area. Faced with the seemingly inevitable need to amend any Treaty legislative basis requiring a unanimous Council vote if it is ever seriously proposed to attempt to deploy that provision (and yet confronted by an inability to secure agreement on the elimination of unanimity voting in these areas), the Member States accepted, inter alia, the compromise of the second simplified revision procedure. This simplified revision procedure is to apply where either the Treaty on the Functioning of the European Union or Title V of the Treaty on European Union[115] provides for the Council to act by unanimity in a given area or case. The relevant provision stipulates that the European

---

[114] Which, one presumes, must be given an opportunity to express such opposition by its national Government. Note that the French Constitution has recently been amended to facilitate the expression of such opposition by the French Parliament. (See in this regard the new Article 88.7 which was inserted in the French constitution on 4 February 2008, and a copy of which may be seen online at the time of writing at: <http://vge-europe.eu/index.php?post/2008/02/06/Traite-de-Lisbonne-%3A-le-Congres-adopte-la-revision-de-la-Constitution-prealable-a-la-ratification>). A requirement of referendum at national level is not replaced by it, although there would be nothing to prevent a Member State making its Parliamentary vote depend on a positive outcome in a referendum.

[115] Title V, in the wake of the coming into force of the Lisbon Treaty, will concern 'general provisions on the union's external action and specific provisions on the common foreign and security policy'. (See Article 1(23) of the Treaty of Lisbon.) The provisions of Article 48(7) with regard to Title V succeed Articles I-40(7), III-300(3) and III-300(4) of the Constitutional Treaty.

Council may adopt a decision authorizing the Council to act by a qualified majority in that area or in that case.[116]

Two specific limits and restrictions on the possibility of using the second simplified revision procedure exist (ie, over and beyond those which were listed in
the text above as applying to both the second and the third simplified revision
procedure). One of these has already been noted: it consists of the rule that the
second simplified revision procedure may be used to authorize the use of qualified majority voting only in those cases where unanimity is stipulated by the
Treaty on the Functioning of the European Union or by Title V of the Treaty
on European Union.[117] A further restriction of scope exists in that the second
simplified revision procedure may not be used to authorize the use of qualified
majority voting in relation to decisions with military implications or those in the
area of defence.[118]

Beyond what has already been said, how does the second simplified revision
procedure compare with the first? It is far shallower in impact in one respect,
since (unlike the first) it applies only in relation to the single question of the voting mechanism which applies where the Council acts. This shallowness of application probably explains the Member States' willingness to allow the European
Parliament a veto over its deployment. On the other hand, it is broader than
the first simplified revision procedure in the sense that it applies (unlike the first
procedure) across the text of the Treaty on the Functioning of the European
Union and that of Title V of the Treaty on European Union.

(iv) Some Further Observations Specifically on the Third
Simplified Revision Procedure

What may be called the third simplified revision procedure will apply where the
Treaty on the Functioning of the European Union provides for legislative acts to
be adopted by the Council in accordance with a so-called 'special legislative procedure'. Article 48(7) provides that where this is the case, the European Council
may adopt a decision allowing for the adoption of such acts in accordance with
the so-called 'ordinary legislative procedure'.

This requires some explanation. From the time of the coming into force of the
Treaty of Lisbon, what is now referred to as the co-decision procedure—in other
words, the joint adoption by the European Parliament and the Council of a regulation, directive or decision on a proposal from the Commission—is to be rechristened the 'ordinary legislative procedure' to reflect its pre-eminence and preferred
status as a legislative method.[119] Other methods of legislation will continue to

---

[116] Article 48(7), sub-paragraph 1 of the Treaty on the European Union.
[117] Ibid.   [118] Ibid.
[119] Article 289(1) of the Treaty on the Functioning of the European Union as inserted by
Article 2(236) of the Treaty of Lisbon. The new Article 289(1) notes that this procedure is defined
in Article 251.

exist, however. in particular, the old assent and consultation procedures. Hence, the description 'special legislative procedure' is to be used to describe the specific cases which will continue to be provided for by the Treaties, in which the adoption of a regulation, directive, or decision will be by the *Council* with the participation of the European Parliament.[120]

The third simplified revision procedure is a *passerelle* clause which simplifies further switches away from such special legislative procedures in favour of the use of co-decision (or the 'ordinary legislative procedure'), and thereby continuing the trend which has prevailed since the introduction of co-decision by the Treaty of Maastricht (a trend which has evolved because co-decision is regarded as the most democratically acceptable means of law-making in a Union in which a need for some form of majority voting within the Council is dictated by efficiency concerns.)

Beyond what has already been said, how does the third simplified revision procedure compare with the other two? Like the second simplified procedure, it can be deployed to one effect only—in this case, to amend a legislative procedure. Obviously, therefore, it is less 'deep' than the first simplified procedure in this respect. Once again (as with the second simplified revision procedure) this probably explains the Member States' willingness to allow the European Parliament a veto over its deployment. In terms of the Treaties to which it applies, it occupies the middle ground of the three procedures, broader than the first, narrower than the second, in that it applies only across the text of the Treaty on the Functioning of the European Union and nowhere else. It has no application in relation to the Treaty on European Union.

IV. A Third Change: The Possibility of a Member State Withdrawing From the European Union

One of the most significant, and to some extent, also controversial Articles to be inserted into the Treaty on European Union is the new Article 50.[121] As with many fundamentally significant legal provisions, its core—Article 50(1)—is deceptively short, consisting of the mere 17 words 'any Member State may decide to withdraw from the Union in accordance with its own constitutional

---

[120] Or by the European Parliament with the participation of the Council, although this is a more rarely-occurring phenomenon. See generally Article 289(1) of the Treaty on the Functioning of the European Union as inserted by Article 2(236) of the Treaty of Lisbon.

[121] To be inserted by Article 1(58) of the Treaty of Lisbon. Piris gives some indication of the general ambivalence about what is to become Article 50 in his observation that 'whether such a provision constitutes an advance or a setback may be assessed differently.' (JC Piris, n 9 above at 130). See further in relation to the antecedent provisions of Article 50, R Friel, 'Secession from the European Union: Checking Out of the Proverbial "Cockroach Motel"' (2004) 27 Fordham International Law Journal 590 and by the same writer, 'Providing a Constitutional Framework for Withdrawal from the EU: Article 59 of the Draft European Constitution' (2004) 53 ICLQ 407.

requirements'.[122] Whatever its future practical effects, what Article 50 says about the nature of the European Union should not be underestimated. It has been pointed out that a right of withdrawal normally exists in confederations of states but never in federal states. Piris has used this to conclude that 'this provision on withdrawal could be seen as clarifying a basic issue, ie that the Union is actually a voluntary association between states which remain sovereign as to the question of whether or not they remain in that association'.[123] It is in the light of considerations such as this, and not just its likely future effects, that the true significance of Article 50 needs to be assessed.

Under the Treaties in their pre-Lisbon form, the existence of any such right had always been left deliberately unstated as a matter of Community or Union law. It is true that under the 1969 Vienna Convention on the Law of Treaties,[124] the normal rule in international law is that the termination of a treaty or the withdrawal of a party may take place at any time by consent of all the parties after consultation with the other contracting States.[125] This can scarcely be regarded as determinative, however, since in its earliest rulings the Court of Justice established that Community law was not mere international law.[126] At a relatively early stage, the Court also indicated that another relevant feature of international law—the rule of reciprocity—does not apply within the Community legal order, holding that 'a Member State cannot under any circumstances unilaterally adopt, on its own authority, [measures in violation of the Treaty] designed to prevent any failure on the part of another Member State to comply with the rules laid down by the Treaty'[127]—much less suspend its enforcement of or indeed denounce the Treaty on this basis. Furthermore, a number of other factors could be said to appear to be leaning against a right of withdrawal. Hence, albeit somewhat ambiguously, certain Treaty provisions make reference to the Treaties having been concluded for an 'unlimited period'.[128] Others refer to the 'irreversible' character of the movement to the

---

[122] Article 50(1) of the Treaty on European Union to be inserted by Article 1(58) of the Treaty of Lisbon.

[123] Piris, n 9 above at 130. This is consonant with the characterization by the same writer of the European Union as 'partially federal union' as opposed to a state. (Piris at 192, and see also by the same writer, 'The European Union: Towards a New Form of Federalism' in B Markesinis and J Fedtke (eds), *Patterns of Regionalism and Federalism* (Hart Publishing, 2005)).

[124] Which is generally taken, despite its post-EC Treaty origins, to represent customary international law. (See authorities cited by Hartley, n 9 above.)

[125] Or, alternatively, in conformity with the provisions of the Treaty in question, although, as will already have been noted from the text above, that alternative does not apply prior to the coming into force of the Treaty of Lisbon, no such provision having been made in the existing Treaties.

[126] See in this regard the rulings of the European Court of Justice in Case 6/64 *Costa v ENEL* [1964] ECR 585 and Case 26–62 *NV Algemene Transport- en Expeditie Onderneming van Gend & Loos v Netherlands Inland Revenue Administration* [1963] ECR 1, in both of which judgments the autonomy of the Community legal order was clearly asserted.

[127] Case 232/78 *Commission v France* [1979] ECR 2729.

[128] The existing Article 51 of the Treaty on European Union and Article 312 of the EC Treaty state that the respective Treaties are concluded 'for an unlimited period'. However, this assertion is

third stage of economic and monetary union, into which the Community is provided to have 'irrevocably' entered on 1 January 1999.[129] Certain dicta of the Court of Justice also merit mention in this regard. Hence, it had been asserted by the European Court of Justice in *Costa v ENEL*—one of its earliest and most important rulings—that 'the transfer by the states from their domestic legal system to the community legal system of the rights and obligations arising under the treaty carries with it a *permanent* limitation of their sovereign rights.'[130] Last but not least, the level of political and economic commitment involved in entry to and membership of the Community—in addition to the very nature of a project envisaging 'ever closer union'[131]—might have been argued to lean against the intended existence of a legal entitlement on the part of any Member State simply to walk away from its Treaty commitments.[132]

On the other hand, numerous factors could also be cited in favour of the existence of a right of withdrawal. Such a right, as has already been mentioned, is the norm under international law. Furthermore, the Treaties have never expressly *excluded* a right of withdrawal. Again, such a right could also be argued to be inherent in the sovereignty of the Member States.[133] In practice, notwithstanding the language used in the Treaties adverted to in the text above, the Member States have frequently acted as if they regarded themselves as having the right of withdrawal from the process of European integration. Hence the June 1975 referendum in the United Kingdom on the question of whether the United Kingdom should remain in the Common Market was clearly predicated on the assumption of the existence of the right of that State to leave should it wish.[134] In 1985,

---

ambiguous: it could be interpreted as a statement merely of the indefinite duration of the Treaties' continuation in force in the absence of their repudiation by their signatory States, rather than a commitment on the part of any Member State to permanent membership.

In favour if this interpretation, it should be noted that the relevant provisions will continue to exist in the wake of the coming into force of the Treaty of Lisbon, notwithstanding the creation of a right of withdrawal (although, of course, they are renumbered).

[129] See in this regard the Protocol on the transition to the third stage of economic and monetary union annexed to the Treaty establishing the European Community in 1992.

[130] As with the Treaty provisions just discussed, there seems to be a certain degree of ambiguity in such remarks however.

[131] See the Preamble of the Treaty on European Union (both in its pre- and post-Lisbon format).

[132] See the concerns in this regard expressed by Mr Elmar Brok, one of the European Parliament representatives in the Convention on the Future of Europe Contribution, in E Brok, 'The Constitution of the European Union' (CONV 325/1/02 REV1, 6 December 2002). See also the (rejected) suggestion for amendment of Article I-59 of the draft Constitution made by Convention members Brok, Szajer, Akcam, Van Der Linden, Lamassoure, Brejc, Demetriou, Figel, Liepina, Santer, Kelam, Kroupa, Tajani, Almeida, Garrett, Altmaier, Kauppi, Lennmarker, Maij-Weggen, Rack, and Vilen on behalf of the EPP Convention Group, at p 3 thereof (available online at the time of writing at: <http://european-convention.eu.int/Docs/Treaty/pdf/46/46_Art%20I%2059%20Brok%20EN. pdf>).

[133] See R Mehdi, 'Article I-60' in L Burgorgue-Larsen, A Levade, and F Picod (eds), n 7 above 735 at 739.

[134] For a good general study of the relationship of the United Kingdom and the European Union, see H Young, *This Blessed Plot* (2nd edn, Papermac, 1999).

Greenland (admittedly a region rather than a Member State)[135] actually did
secede from the then European Communities. And the ruling of the German
Federal Supreme Court in its famous Maastricht judgment—although of course
it represented the views of the judicial branch of government of one Member
State only—famously asserted that Court's view that the Member States were,
as it put it, 'the "masters of the Treaties", which have established their adherence
to the Union Treaty concluded "for an unlimited period"...with the intention
of long-term membership, but could also ultimately revoke that adherence by a
contrary act.'[136]

Of course, the reality is and always has been that should any Member State
decide that it no longer wishes to remain part of the Union, the Union has never
had any means at its disposal to prevent this from happening, even in the event
of its wishing to. The argument could thus be made that this being so, the adoption of Article 50 will constitute less a concession to intergovernmentalism than
a mere recognition of reality at Treaty level.[137] The powerful position of the
Member States, and the limits of the law, have been demonstrated occasionally
by incidents such as the famous pursuit by de Gaulle's France of its 'empty chair'
policy from July 1965 to January 1966, notwithstanding its Treaty obligations,
and less spectacularly, by Sweden's declining to enter the third and final stage
of economic and monetary union, notwithstanding the absence of any Treaty
derogation having been negotiated by it in this regard on its accession to the
European Union in 1995.[138]

However, the question does pose itself of why the Member States have now
agreed at Lisbon to enshrine such a right in the Treaty on European Union, particularly if the Member States always assumed the existence of an unstated right
of withdrawal, and given the potential such a provision might have for increasing centrifugal pressures on the Union. The drafting history of the Article
suggests answers: Article 50 is a word-for-word reproduction of an Article in the

---

[135] Greenland has the constitutional status of a self-governing Danish province, rather than that
of a Member State. See regarding the secession of Greenland, the Treaty amending, with regard to
Greenland, the Treaties establishing the European Communities ([1985] OJ L029 (01.02.1985)).
Danish secession followed on a 1979 referendum organized by the regional government in which the
electorate had shown themselves to be hostile to continued involvement in the then Communities.

[136] Paragraph 55 of the ruling of the Court, cited from the translation of this judgment found at
[1994] 1 CMLR 57 at 91 thereof. The *Bundesverfassungsgericht* is not the only national court to have
arrived at this conclusion, however. Hence, for example, in its judgment of 6 April, 1998 in the case
of *Carlsen and others v Prime Minister* (I 361/1997, UfR 1998, 800) the Danish Supreme Court, the
Højesteret, delivered a similar ruling. (See in relation to this case, K Høegh, 'The Danish Maastricht
Judgment' (1999) 24 ELR 80.)

[137] Mehdi, n 133 above at 744.

[138] Swedish non-entry to the eurozone has been facilitated by its deliberate failure to meet the
entry conditions through its non-participation in the Exchange Rate Mechanism. In a referendum
held in 2003, the Swedish electorate rejected the idea of entry to the eurozone. See generally in relation to the legal conditions governing entry into the third stage of economic and monetary union,
G Barrett, *EMU—The Third Stage. An Examination of the Treaty and non-Treaty Basis of Economic and
Monetary Union* (Institute of European Affairs, 1997).

Constitutional Treaty, the text of which was originally inserted by the Convention on the Future of Europe. According to the Convention's steering committee, the Praesidium, an Article 50-type provision is now necessary for three reasons.

In the first place, such an Article clarifies the legal situation. This is a not over-persuasive ground given that the pre-existing situation has prevailed for half a century without occasioning any apparent difficulty.[139]

Secondly, the argument is made that 'the existence of a provision to that effect is an important political signal to anyone inclined to argue that the Union is a rigid entity which it is impossible to leave'.[140] To put this another way, by virtue of Article 50, a reminder is intended to be issued that membership of the Union is, as one writer has put it, the outcome of a freely-consented to decision, and not a sentence to imprisonment in a penal colony.[141] Article 50 is meant to confront opponents of the European Union of the ongoing reality of democratic acceptance in each and every Member State of that State's membership of the European Union. It clarifies that membership of the Union is an ongoing freely-made choice (the logic being that the contrary can not be convincingly be argued to be the case if each Member State retains an expressly-stated right to leave the Union). Such a reminder has been argued to have been more urgent by the need to reassure the peoples of the central and eastern European Member States of the European Union, most of whom were involved in the past into international arrangements not of their populations' choosing.[142]

Thirdly, such an Article, it is asserted, 'allows the introduction of a procedure for negotiating and concluding an agreement between the Union and the Member State concerned setting the arrangements for withdrawal and the framework for future relations'.[143] Sections (2) to (4) of Article 50 are concerned with this and are examined below.

It has also been suggested that the Article 50 withdrawal mechanism might present a useful tool to facilitate dealing with what in a future European Union of up to 33 Member States is a potential dilemma (although one which the Union has never yet had to face)—viz, the question of how the Union should cope with a single Member State which finds itself enduringly unable to reach agreement with other Member States on the future direction of the Union.[144] Discussions of this issue occurred during the debates on the corresponding provision in the Constitutional Treaty in the Convention on the Future of Europe. The suggestion

---

[139] See Annex 2 to Draft Constitution, Volume I—Revised text of Part One (communicated by Praesidium to the Convention) (CONV 724/1/03 REV 1 ANNEX 2) (Brussels, 28 May 2003) at p 131 thereof (available online at the time of writing at: <http://register.consilium.eu.int/pdf/en/03/cv00/cv00724-re01en03.pdf>).

[140] Ibid.

[141] Mehdi, n 133 above at 739 (author's translation).

[142] Ibid.

[143] Annex 2 to Draft Constitution, Volume I—Revised text of Part One (communicated by Praesidium to the Convention), n 139 above.

[144] JC Piris, n 9 above at 129. Mehdi, n 141 above at 738.

of inserting a provision in the Treaty that not alone voluntary withdrawal, but also involuntary exclusion—ie, expulsion—of a Member State should be made possible (on the limited grounds of reasons which now justify suspension of membership) was rejected by the Convention.[145]

Article 50 seems unlikely to be invoked in the foreseeable future. In what is more than a half-century since the beginnings of what has evolved into the European Union, during which time a multitude of political and economic crises have been weathered by both the Union and its Member States, no Member State has ever found it to be in its interests even to contemplate seriously secession, let alone to withdraw. The hope of the drafters of Article 50 seems to be that the serious economic and political disadvantages of taking such a drastic step—which presumably would also entail exit from monetary union for countries which take part in that—will continue to guarantee for the foreseeable future that Article 50 of the Treaty on European Union will not be invoked by any Member State.[146] It can only be hoped that this calculation is correct and that time ultimately proves unfounded the trenchantly-expressed fears expressed by Convention members who opposed the adoption of such a provision that 'such an explicit exit clause could allow Member States to blackmail the Union, paralyse its decision-making processes and even endanger the stability of the Union' and 'would also give a wrong political signal with regard to the required mutual solidarity in the Union'.[147]

---

[145] See the (rejected) suggestion for amendment of Article I-59 of the draft Constitution made by Convention members Brok, Szajer, Akcam, Van Der Linden, Lamassoure, Brejc, Demetriou, Figel, Liepina, Santer, Kelam, Kroupa, Tajani, Almeida, Garrett, Altmaier, Kauppi, Lennmarker, Maij-Weggen, Rack, and Vilen on behalf of the EPP Convention Group, at p 3 thereof (available online at the time of writing at: <http://european-convention.eu.int/Docs/Treaty/pdf/46/46_Art%20 I%2059%20Brok%20EN.pdf>). This failure to provide the Union with 'equality of arms' in this respect, eg in the event of grave violations of Union values, has been criticised by some. (See, eg K Kaddous, 'Article IV-446' in L Burgorgue-Larsen, A Levade, and F Picod (eds), n 7 above at 826–827). As Kaddous has observed, other prominent international organizations provide for such a right of expulsion. Under Article 8 of the Statute of the Council of Europe, any member of the Council of Europe which has seriously violated its Article 3 duty to accept the principles of the rule of law and of the enjoyment by all persons within its jurisdiction of human rights and fundamental freedoms, and collaborate sincerely and effectively in the realization of the aim of the Council may be requested by the Committee of Ministers to withdraw from that organization. Under Article 6 of the Charter of the United Nations, a member of the United Nations which has persistently violated the principles contained in the Charter may be expelled from the United Nations Organisation by the General Assembly upon the recommendation of the Security Council.

It should be noted that since the coming into force of the Treaty of Amsterdam in 1999, a procedure has existed for the suspension of a Member State's rights under the Treaties for a serious and persistent breach of the principles of liberty, democracy, respect for human rights and fundamental freedoms or the rules of law. The possibility of suspension will continue to apply in the wake of the coming into force of the Treaty of Lisbon. (See Article 7 of the Treaty on European Union as amended by Article 1(9) of the Treaty of Lisbon.)

[146] In support of such a calculation, it seems likely that self-interest has played a significant role in ensuring that no Member State has ever withdrawn from the European Union. See for arguments relevant in this regard A Milward, *The European Rescue of the Nation-State* (2nd edn, Routledge, 2000).

[147] See the (rejected) suggestion for amendment of Article I-59 of the draft Constitution made by Convention members Brok, Szajer, Akcam, Van Der Linden, Lamassoure, Brejc, Demetriou, Figel, Liepina, Santer, Kelam, Kroupa, Tajani, Almeida, Garrett, Altmaier, Kauppi, Lennmarker,

The Procedure for Withdrawing from Membership of the Union

The remaining five sections of Article 50, sections (2) to (6), deal with the modalities of such a withdrawal—in essence, what one might call the divorce procedures—in the event of this Article ever being invoked by a Member State.[148] Specifically, what is to happen is that a Member State which decides to withdraw is to notify the European Council of its intention. In the light of the guidelines then provided by the European Council,[149] the Union is required to negotiate and conclude an agreement with that Member State which both sets out the arrangements for the State's withdrawal, and takes account of the framework for its future relationship with the Union. The procedure to be adopted in this situation is to involve the Commission submitting recommendations to the Council, which is then to adopt a decision authorizing the opening of negotiations and to nominate the Union negotiator or the head of the Union's negotiating team.[150] The agreement is to be concluded on behalf of the Union by the Council, acting by a qualified majority (excluding the State in question).[151] (In this connection, however, a qualified majority is defined unusually as comprising at least 72% of the members of the Council, representing at least 65% of the population of the States.[152]) Furthermore, the consent of the European Parliament must first be obtained, giving this institution a veto over the agreement.

Maij-Weggen, Rack, and Vilen on behalf of the EPP Convention Group, at p 3 thereof (available online at the time of writing at: <http://european-convention.eu.int/Docs/Treaty/pdf/46/46_Art%20I%2059%20Brok%20EN.pdf>). Mehdi has referred to the risk of blackmail inherent in such a provision by observing that it puts an instrument in the hands of the more powerful States in particular, the use of which becomes more credible to the extent that it is explicitly envisaged by the fundamental law of the Union. (See R Mehdi, 'Article I-60' in L Burgorgue-Larsen, A Levade, and F Picod (eds), n 7 above at 745.)

[148] See generally regarding the negotiation of the original version of the withdrawal procedure, Mehdi, n 133 above at 744–748.

[149] It is important to note that for all the purposes described in the next two paragraphs, the member of the European Council or of the Council representing the withdrawing Member State is not to participate in the discussions of the European Council or Council or in decisions concerning it. (See Article 50 (4) of the Treaty on European Union to be inserted by Article 1(58) of the Treaty of Lisbon.)

[150] Article 218(3) of the Treaty on the Functioning of the European Union (to be inserted by Article 2(173) of the Treaty of Lisbon). Under Article 50(2) of the Treaty on European Union (to be inserted by Article 1(58) of the Treaty of Lisbon), the agreement in question is required to be negotiated in accordance with Article 218(3).

[151] Article 50 stipulates expressly that the member of the European Council or of the Council representing the withdrawing Member State is not to participate in the discussions of the Council or in the decision concerning it in this regard. (Article 50(4) of the Treaty on European Union (to be inserted by Article 1(58) of the Treaty of Lisbon).)

[152] Article 238(3)(b) of the Treaty on the Functioning of the European Union (as inserted by Article 2(191) of the Treaty of Lisbon). (Article 238(3)(b) is made applicable in this context by the second sub-paragraph of Article 50(4) of the Treaty on European Union (to be inserted in that Treaty by Article 1(58) of the Treaty of Lisbon).)

Negotiations are not to be permitted to drag on indefinitely: there is to be no question of a Member State's desire to leave the Union being stymied by the failure, deliberate or otherwise, by the Union to reach agreement with it. Thus under Article 50, finality is ensured *via* a provision that the Treaties are to cease to apply to the State in question from the date of entry into force of the withdrawal agreement or, failing that, two years after the notification to the European Council of its intention to withdraw from the European Union—unless the European Council, in agreement with the Member State concerned, unanimously decides to extend this period.[153]

Article 50 specifically contemplates that a State which withdraws from the Union might possibly change its mind and ask to rejoin. If it does, however, it must submit itself to the same formal procedures as any other applicant State— that laid down in Article 49 of the Treaty on European Union, which requires, inter alia, the unanimous agreement of the Council of Ministers, in addition to the consent of the European Parliament (acting by a majority of its component members).[154]

V. A Fourth Change: An Expanded Jurisdiction for
the European Court of Justice

Apart from the fact of its rejection (as regards most decision-making at European level) of the paralyzing embrace of unanimity voting which prevails in most international systems,[155] and the democratic input provided by the European Parliament, one of the most telling differences between what has been termed

---

[153] Article 50 (3) of the Treaty on European Union as inserted by Article 1(58) of the Treaty of Lisbon. The member of the European Council or of the Council representing the withdrawing Member State is not to participate in the discussions of the European Council or in the decision concerning it in this regard. (Article 50(4) of the Treaty on European Union (to be inserted by Article 1(58) of the Treaty of Lisbon).)

[154] Article 50(5) of the Treaty on European Union (to be inserted by Article 1(58) of the Treaty of Lisbon).

[155] See in relation to the effect of unanimity in international organisations, the revealing anecdote in J Monnet, *Mémoires* (Fayard, 1976) at 113–114. The risk and high cost of exclusion from an ultimate European settlement may provide States with a sufficient incentive to negotiate (if not always to ratify) on a unanimous basis *Treaty* reform at European Union level—but does not provide sufficient motivation to ensure efficient decision-making on a daily basis in relation to secondary legislation at European Union level, especially in a Union with 27 Member States—hence the need (at least formally) for majority voting, and the possibility of being outvoted, to be the prevailing rule. Another interesting exception concerning the stultifying effects of a requirement of unanimity voting is the World Trade Organisation (WTO) which maintains a requirement of unanimous agreement among Member States on the fundamental rules it espouses. Again, the explanation for the non-collapse of this system appears to lie in the real danger of exclusion from full integration into the world trading system of States who do not agree with the majority view regarding the appropriate course of action for the WTO, combined with the high cost of such exclusion.

until now the Community system and the traditional intergovernmental method has been the judicial role provided by the European Court of Justice

The Court of Justice, in particular through its enunciation of key doctrines ranging from the autonomy of Community law to supremacy to direct effect, indirect effect, and State liability has played a key role in shaping the nature of the Community legal order, ensuring the rule of law and vital features of the Community legal system ranging from its uniformity throughout the territories of the Member States to the fact that Member States are held to the commitments which they undertake at European level. The role which the Court has played has been important in terms of regulating relationships between Member States. But it has also been important in terms of the protection of the individual under Community law.

As European Union-level competences have spread into new policy areas— some of them, such as justice and home affairs, areas of great sensitivity insofar as individual rights are concerned—the necessity for an appropriate degree of judicial control to be established and maintained over both Union and Member State action has grown more urgent than ever. Nonetheless, the necessary trust to allow this to happen has taken some time to build up. The beginnings of cooperation in the justice and home affairs area at European Union level, although wrapped in the mantle of European Union activity, were in reality largely intergovernmental in nature,[156] and only the passage of time and the benefit of experience—as well as successive Treaty amendments[157]—has had a sufficiently persuasive effect to enable a gradually increased role to be permitted to the European Court of Justice.

One of the most significant of the existing final provisions of the Treaty on European Union has been Article 46, which has limited the applicability in the context of that Treaty of the provisions concerning the European Court of Justice set out in the three Community Treaties (viz, the EC Treaty, the Euratom Treaty, and until its expiry on 23 July 2002, the European Coal and Steel Community Treaty). Up until now, Article 46 has provided that the various provisions of these Treaties concerning the powers of the Court of Justice and their exercise would apply only to (a) those provisions of the Treaty on European Union which amended the original Community provisions;[158] (b) the Treaty on European Union's provisions on police and judicial cooperation in criminal matters[159]— but only under the conditions provided for by the existing Article 35 (which, inter alia, requires Member States to opt in to the jurisdiction of the Court of Justice

---

[156] See generally regarding this period: G Barrett, *Justice Cooperation in the European Union* (Institute of European Affairs, 1997).

[157] In the justice and home affairs area, the Treaty of Amsterdam was a key point of evolution here. See G Barrett, 'Justice and Home Affairs—an Overview' in B Tonra, *Amsterdam—What the Treaty Means*, (Institute of European Affairs, 1998), and 'Justice Cooperation in the European Union After Amsterdam', Contemporary Issues in Irish Law and Politics (Vol 2, 1998) at 239.

[158] Article 46, sub-paragraph 1 of the Treaty on the European Union.

[159] Ie, the provisions of Title VI of the Treaty on European Union in its present form.

to give preliminary rulings[160]); (c) the Treaty on European Union's provisions on enhanced cooperation,[161] (subject to certain modifications);[162] (d) the provision of the Treaty on European Union concerning protection by the Court of fundamental rights insofar as the Court had jurisdiction under Community Treaties or the Treaty on European Union;[162a] (e) the purely procedural stipulations of the Treaty on European Union article which ensures respect for the Treaty's founding principles;[163] and (f) the Treaty's final provisions.[164] The provisions of the Treaty on European Union concerning the common foreign and security policy, nowhere mentioned in this list, fall completely outside the jurisdiction of the Court at present.

While the restrictions on the jurisdiction of the Court of Justice provided for by Article 46 of the existing Treaty on European Union are not by any means the only restrictions on that jurisdiction under the existing Treaties,[165] they are certainly the most significant.

The existing Article 46 of the Treaty on European Union is simply to be deleted when the Treaty of Lisbon comes into force,[166] although it should be noted that some of its restrictions are resurrected elsewhere in the amended Treaties. The most significant effect of this deletion will be that (subject to one exception[167]) the entire area of justice and home affairs will finally be brought under the jurisdiction of the Court of Justice—a step which seems an appropriate, welcome— and long overdue—increase in the protection of individual rights. It should also result in better enforcement of Member State obligations as this policy area will no longer be exempted from the possibility of Commission proceedings being brought for failure on the part of Member States to fulfil their legal obligations.[168]

---

[160] See Article 35(2) of the Treaty on European Union. Note also Article 35(5) according to which the Court has no jurisdiction to review the validity or proportionality of operations carried out by the police or other law enforcement services of a Member State or the exercise of the responsibilities incumbent on Member States with regard to the maintenance of law and order and the safeguarding of internal security, and the extremely limited scope for direct actions provided for in Article 35(6).

[161] Ie, the provisions of Title VII of the Treaty on European Union in its present form.

[162] More specifically, under the conditions provided for by Articles 11 and 11a of the Treaty establishing the European Community and Article 40 of the Treaty on European Union itself, as these both stand.

[162a] Currently, Article 6(2) of the Treaty on European Union.

[163] Ie, Article 7 of the Treaty on European Union as it now stands.

[164] Ie, Articles 46 to 53 of the Treaty on European Union.

[165] See, for example, the restrictions imposed by Article 230 of the EC Treaty concerning the Court's jurisdiction, even in the Community context, regarding direct actions. And note also the restrictions on the Court's jurisdiction under Title IV of the EC Treaty (which concerns visas, asylum, immigration and other policies related to free movement of persons).

[166] Article 1(54) of the Treaty of Lisbon.

[167] Article 276 of the Treaty on the Functioning of the European Union (as inserted by Article 2(223) of the Treaty of Lisbon). The Court of Justice of the European Union is to have no jurisdiction to review the validity or proportionality of operations carried out by the police or other law enforcement services of a Member State or the exercise of the responsibilities incumbent upon Member States with regard to the maintenance of law and order and the safeguarding of internal security.

[168] Viz, under Article 258 of the Treaty on the Functioning of the European Union (corresponding to Article 226 of the existing EC Treaty and Article III-360 of the Constitutional Treaty).

The expansion of the Court's judgment in this respect has thus been correctly characterized as 'good news for the rule of law, the uniform application of EU law and the protection of individual rights'.[169]

The deletion of the existing Article 46 will result in only a small (albeit significant) increase in the Court's jurisdiction in the common foreign and security field. This is because the Treaty of Lisbon inserts other provisions elsewhere in the Treaty on European Union,[170] the effect of which is to continue the exclusion of the Court from the common foreign and security policy field. A new exception, however is established: the Court is given jurisdiction to review the legality of decisions providing for restrictive measures against natural or legal persons.[171]

There are a range of other provisions of the Treaty of Lisbon which are of relevance to the Court of Justice, such as the increase in the scope for direct actions in which it is sought to annul acts of the Union both through the abolition of the onerous requirement of individual concern in order for natural or legal persons to bring a direct action before the Courts of the European Union challenging a regulatory act which is of direct concern to them,[172] and the increase in the number of possible defendants whose actions can be challenged.[173] Even the name of the judicial branch of the Union is to be changed. It is to become known as the Court of Justice of the European Union, and is to include the Court of Justice, the General Court (the new name for the Court of First Instance) and specialized courts (the new name for judicial panels).[174] However, a more in-depth examination of these and other innovations,[175] significant as they may be, falls outside

[169] Piris, n 9 above at 113–114. Although he was writing about the reforms which the Constitutional Treaty sought to effect, the same point holds good here.

[170] Article 24(1) of the Treaty on European Union as substituted by Article 1(27) of the Treaty of Lisbon, and Article 275 of the Treaty on the Functioning of the European Union as inserted by Article 2(223) of the Treaty of Lisbon (corresponding to Article III-376 of the now-defunct Constitutional Treaty).

[171] Ibid. The Court will also have what might be termed a 'border-policing role' in that Article 24(1) will also confer jurisdiction on the Court to monitor compliance with the rule that the common foreign and security policy is not to affect the application of the procedures and the extent of the powers of the institutions laid down by the Treaties for the exercise of those Union competences which are to be referred to in Articles 3 to 6 (new numbering) of the Treaty on the Functioning of the European Union.

[172] Provided the act in question does not entail implementing measures. See Article 263(4) of the Treaty on the Functioning of the European Union (as substituted by Article 2(214) of the Treaty of Lisbon and corresponding to Article III-365(4) of the Constitutional Treaty).

[173] Under Article 263(1) of the Treaty on the Functioning of the European Union (as amended by Article 2(214) of the Treaty of Lisbon and corresponding to Article III-365(1) of the Constitutional Treaty), the Court of Justice is empowered to review the legality of acts of bodies, offices, or agencies of the Union intended to produce legal effects vis-à-vis third parties.

[174] Article 19(1) of the Treaty on European Union (as inserted by Article 1(20) of the Treaty of Lisbon and corresponding to Article I-29(1) of the Constitutional Treaty).

[175] Note, eg Article 255 of the Treaty on the Functioning of the European Union (as inserted by Article 2(209) of the Treaty of Lisbon and corresponding to Article III-357 of the Constitutional Treaty) under which a panel is to be set up in order to give an opinion on candidates' suitability to perform the duties of judge and Advocate-General of the Court of Justice. Note also Article 281, sub-paragraph 2 of the Treaty on the Functioning of the European Union (as substituted by

the purview of this article, since their introduction is effected outside the final provisions of the Treaties.

VI. A Fifth Change: the Amendment of the So-Called 'Flexibility' Clause

Apart from the changes which it effects to the Final Provisions of the Treaty on European Union, the Treaty of Lisbon also effects a number of amendments to the General and Final Provisions of the Treaty Establishing the European Community (now, of course, to be rebranded the Treaty on the Functioning of the European Union). Of these amendments, the most important (and the only one it is proposed to examine here) is the generalization to Union level of the so-called 'flexibility clause'.

The legal system of the European Community has for long been based on the principle of conferral,[176] according to which the Community and its institutions have no inherent powers, but rather enjoy only those powers which have been conferred upon them.[177] With the coming into force of the Treaty of Lisbon, the express application of this principle will be expanded, and hence the limits of *Union* (rather than Community) competences provided to be generally governed by the principle of conferral.[178] The principle of conferral has always itself been subject to limits which restrict its impact, however.[179] One such broad limit has been provided for in the Treaty of Rome itself, in the form of the provision in Article 308 that:

Article 2(226) of the Treaty of Lisbon and corresponding to Article III-381, sub-paragraph 2 of the Constitutional Treaty) which permits amendment of the Statute of the Court of Justice. Piris, n 169 above at 113–115 provides a useful summary of amendments which would have been introduced had the Constitutional Treaty ever come into force and which corresponds largely with the changes which the Treaty of Lisbon now seeks to bring into effect.

[176] Otherwise referred to variously as the principle of limited powers, the principle of conferred powers or, in French, the principle of *'le principe d'attribution'*. See the existing Article 5 of the EC Treaty, (which was inserted with the coming into force of the Treaty of Maastricht in 1993) according to which 'any action by the Community shall not go beyond what is necessary to achieve the objectives of this Treaty' and Article 7 (the content of which has always formed part of Community law) according to which 'each institution shall act within the limits of the powers conferred upon it by this Treaty'. For an introduction to this general topic, see Hartley, n 9 above at 104–110.

[177] Under Article 3b(2) (to be inserted by Article 1(6) of the Treaty of Lisbon) under the principle of conferral, the Union is to act only within the limits of the competences conferred upon it by the Member States in the Treaties to attain the objectives set out therein.

[178] See Article 5(1) of the Treaty on European Union (to be inserted by Article 1(6) of the Treaty of Lisbon). Note also Article 7 of the Treaty on the Functioning of the European Union (to be inserted by Article 2(13) of the Treaty of Lisbon), according to which 'the Union shall ensure consistency between its policies and activities, taking all of its objectives into account and in accordance with the principle of conferral of powers.'

[179] See generally Hartley, n 9 above at 105–110.

if action by the Community should prove necessary to attain, in the course of the operation of the common market, one of the objectives of the Community, and this Treaty has not provided the necessary powers, the Council shall, acting unanimously on a proposal from the Commission and after consulting the European Parliament, take the appropriate measures.[180]

Although it seems to have given rise to a certain amount of controversy in at least one Member State, Denmark,[181] Article 308 has been a useful instrument in the Community's legislative toolbox, since if the Article did not exist, Member States would be forced to go through the cumbersome and time-consuming procedure required to agree and ratify an international treaty or convention regulating the problem in question.[182]

Because of the considerable scope it would otherwise give for circumventing Treaty restrictions of Community action, however, Article 308 has been subjected to considerable restrictions. Most famously, the Court of Justice held in its *ECHR*[183] ruling that what is now Article 308 could not:

serve as a basis for widening the scope of Community powers beyond the framework created by the provisions of the Treaty as a whole and, in particular, by those that define the tasks and the activities of the Community. On any view, Article [308] cannot be used as a basis for the adoption of provisions whose effect would, in substance, be to amend the Treaty without following the procedure which it provides for that purpose.[184]

On similar lines, measures taken under Article 308 must not be contrary to an express prohibition contained in the Treaty.[185] This would also seem to be a logical corollary of the latter sentence just quoted from the ruling of the Court. The

---

[180] See regarding this, *M Bungenberg, Article 235 nach Maastricht—Die Auswirkungen der Einheitlichen Europäischen Akte und des Vertrages über die Europäische Union auf die Handlungsbefugnis des Art. 235 EGV (1999)* (Germany: Nomos Verlagsgesellschaft, Baden-Baden, 1999), as analysed in R Schütze, 'Dynamic Integration—Article 308 EC and Legislation "in the Course of the Operation of the Common Market"' (2003) 23 OJLS 333, A Dashwood, 'The Limits of European Community Powers' (1996) 21 ELR 113, and G Marenco, 'Les conditions d'application de l'article 235 du traité CEE' [1970] RMC 147.

[181] See in this regard, K Høegh, 'The Danish Maastricht Judgment' (1999) 24 ELR at 82–85.

[182] Some idea of the relevant efficiencies of proceeding by way of treaties or conventions, on the one hand, and secondary legislation on the other, may be garnered from the fact that the Brussels Convention (the Convention of 27 September, 1968 on Jurisdiction and the Enforcement of Judgments in Civil and Commercial Matters) was agreed on 27 September, 1968, but did not enter into force until 1 February 1973—well over four years later. The Brussels Regulation (Council Regulation (EC) No 44/2001 of 22 December, 2000 on jurisdiction and the recognition and enforcement of judgments in civil and commercial matters) which superseded it was adopted on 22 December 2000 and entered into force on 1 March 2002—less than a year and three months later. If anything, the contrast is greater than this example indicates since Article 76 of the Brussels Regulation specifically provided for what was an unusually long period before the Regulation entered into force.

[183] Opinion 2/94 Accession by the Community to the European Convention for the Protection of Human Rights and Fundamental Freedoms [1996] ECR I-1759.

[184] Paragraph 30 of the ruling of the Court.

[185] See Hartley, n 9 above at 109.

normal requirement of respect for subsidiarity—which applies wherever the Community acts in areas which do not fall within its exclusive competence—has also applied up until now in relation to the use of Article 308.[186]

The wording of Article 308 itself has also imposed a series of restrictions on the use of the so-called 'flexibility clause', although these are of varying degrees of significance.[187] The first of these textual restrictions has been that the flexibility clause can at present be used only to attain one of the objectives of the Community—a long leash on the Community legislator, but not an infinitely long one.[188] The second textual restriction has been that action on the part of the Community has had to be 'necessary' to attain this objective, whatever it might be (a limit which the Court would be likely, were it ever called upon to do so, to apply lightly.[189]) The third textual restriction has been the requirement that this objective be attained in the course of the operation of the common market, again a fairly light requirement which seems to require merely that it be attained within the broad framework of the common market.[190] The fourth textual restriction on the deployment of Article 308 has been that the Treaty must not have provided the necessary powers, a requirement which has been deemed by the Court of Justice to preclude reliance on Article 308 where power to act is clearly conferred by another Treaty provision,[191] but nonetheless allows it to act where the power to act given elsewhere is unclear, uncertain or

---

[186] Subsidiarity may be defined as the requirement that in areas which do not fall within the exclusive competence of the Community (or *post* Lisbon, the Union), the Community (or *post* Lisbon, the Union) shall take action only if and in so far as the objectives of the proposed action cannot be sufficiently achieved by the Member States and can therefore, by reason of the scale or effects of the proposed action, be better achieved by the Community (or *post* Lisbon, the Union). (See Article 5 of the EC Treaty as it stands prior to the coming into force of the Treaty of Lisbon, and see Article 5(3) of the Treaty on European Union to be inserted by Article 1(5) of the Treaty of Lisbon which maintains substantially the same definition with some minor tweaking of the wording, in addition to a clause which calls attention to the point that achievement by the Member States in this regard includes achievement either at central level or at regional and local level.)

[187] See generally on this topic Hartley, n 9 above at 106–110.

[188] Existing Community objectives, as set out in Article 2 of the EC Treaty, are broad although not unlimited. (Contrast them, for example, with those set out in Article 2 of the Treaty on European Union, as it presently stands.) As Hartley points out, however, it may be possible to infer objectives from other provisions of the Treaty, since Article 308 makes no explicit mention of Article 2 (or any other provision of the Treaty). (Hartley, n 9 above at 106). Hartley himself takes the view that it is appropriate to infer objectives from Article 3 of the EC Treaty (which purports however to lists activities of the Community, rather than objectives).

[189] See its approach in relation to subsidiarity, as exemplified in cases such as Case C-233/94 *Germany v European Parliament and Council* [1997] ECR I-2405 (the 'Deposit Guarantee Directive' case), Case C-84/94 *United Kingdom v Council* [1996] ECR I-5755 (the 'Working Time Directive' case). See more generally, G de Búrca, 'The Principle of Subsidiarity and the Court of Justice as an Institutional Actor' (1998) 36 JCMS 217.

[190] The point is not unambiguous but see the Dutch and German language versions of the existing Article 308 (cited by Hartley, n 9 above at 107) and see also now the wording of Article 352(1) of the Treaty on the Functioning of the European Union to be inserted by Article 2(289) of the Treaty of Lisbon.

[191] See Case 45/86 *Commission v Council* [1987] ECR 1493 (the 'Tariff Preferences' case).

insufficient.[192] The fifth such restriction has been that the measures taken must be appropriate, which seems to be an invocation of the doctrine of proportionality (which, as a general principle of Community law would apply in any case[193]). What may be described as a sixth restriction has consisted of the procedure laid down by Article 308 for its use. Very importantly, this requires a proposal by the Commission, and less formidably (but nonetheless mandatorily[194]) consultation of the European Parliament and—again, crucially in practice—unanimity on the part of the Member States.

In practice, the level of use to which Article 308 has been put by the Community legislator has gone through a series of phases. From 1958 to 1972, during the first phase of the Community's existence, Article 308 was used on average a mere five times a year. This rose, however, from 1972 to 1986 to an average of 27 times a year, and from 1987 to 1993, to 30 times a year. In the wake of the coming into force of the Maastricht Treaty, as might be expected with the expansion in the legal bases available for legislative action, its use fell away to about 20 occasions each year.[195] Overall, Article 308 may be described as having produced a light stream of legislation, rather than a flood.

Analysing the Impact of Lisbon

Under the Treaty of Lisbon,[196] the single paragraph of text that presently makes up Article 308 is to be replaced by a new four-paragraph Article (renumbered Article 352).[197] The first paragraph extends Article 352 to the Union generally—with some modifications, looked at immediately below. The three new paragraphs both highlight pre-existing restrictions to the deployment of the 'flexibility clause' and add others which go beyond those which have just been seen to have applied to date in the Community context.

---

[192] See Case 8/73 *Hauptzollamt Bremerhaven v Massey-Fergusson GmbH* [1973] ECR 897.

[193] T Tridimas, *The General Principles of EU Law* (2nd edn, OUP, 2006) at chapter 3 thereof.

[194] Note in this regard the ruling of the European Court of Justice in Case 138/79 *Roquette Frères v Council* [1980] ECR 3333 and Case 139/79 *Maizena v Council* [1980] ECR 3393 according to which a measure adopted in disregard of a requirement of consultation would be void.

[195] See generally M Bungenberg, *Article 235 nach Maastricht—Die Auswirkungen der Einheitlichen Europäischen Akte und des Vertrages über die Europäische Union auf die Handlungsbefugnis des Art. 235 EGV (1999)* (Germany: Nomos Verlagsgesellschaft, Baden-Baden, 1999) as analysed in R Schütze, 'Dynamic Integration—Article 308 EC and Legislation "in the Course of the Operation of the Common Market"' (2003) 23 OJLS 333, especially at 335–337.

[196] See Article 2(289) of the Treaty of Lisbon.

[197] Note also what may be termed the mini-flexibility clause which is to be introduced by Article 77(3) of the Treaty on the Functioning of the European Union (as inserted by Article 2(65) of the Treaty of Lisbon), and under which, if action by the Union should prove necessary to facilitate the exercise of the right to move and reside freely within the territory of the Member States, and if the Treaties have not provided the necessary powers, the Council, acting in accordance with a special legislative procedure, may adopt provisions concerning passports, identity cards, residence permits, or any other such document. The procedure provided for is that the Council is to act unanimously after consulting the European Parliament.

Briefly, the new Article 352(1) will provide that:

if action by the Union should prove necessary, within the framework of the policies defined in the Treaties, to attain one of the objectives set out in the Treaties, and the Treaties have not provided the necessary powers, the Council, acting unanimously on a proposal from the Commission and after obtaining the consent of the European Parliament, shall adopt the appropriate measures. Where the measures in question are adopted by the Council in accordance with a special legislative procedure, it shall also act unanimously on a proposal from the Commission and after obtaining the consent of the European Parliament.

The most striking feature of this formulation is its continuity with the provisions of the existing Article 308. Four significant changes in the wording may be pointed out however. The first three of these are consequent on the new European Union-wide context in which Article 352 will operate post-Lisbon.[198]

Hence, first, the new Article 352(1) will apply where action by the *Union* (not, as up to now, the Community) is necessary to attain one of the *objectives set out in the Treaties* (not, as up to now, objectives of the Community). This broadens the scope of the new Article in two respects. First, and most obviously, it will confer a power on the Union as a whole and not merely, as up to now, on one part of it only.[199] Secondly, the objectives which will be capable of being attained *via* the deployment of Article 352(1) will be broader, since what will be referred to post-Lisbon will be the objectives of the *Union* rather than merely (as before) the objectives of the *Community*.[200] Post-Lisbon, the objectives of the Union (or at least most of them[201]) will be set out in Article 3 of the Treaty on European Union, which lists a set of objectives which are a mixture of (a) (somewhat reformulated) objectives set out until now in the EC Treaty, (b) (somewhat reformulated) objectives set out until now in the Treaty on European Union;[202] and (c) some new objectives.[203] The objectives listed in the second and third

[198] And not, as prior to the coming into force of the Lisbon Treaty, a merely European Community-wide context.

[199] Viz, up until now, on the Community.

[200] These have been set out up until now in Article 2 of the EC Treaty. The objectives of the European Union have been set out in Article 2 of the Treaty Establishing the European Union but prior to the coming into force of the Treaty of Lisbon have had no relevance for the purposes of the existing Article 308 of the EC Treaty.

[201] It may, as Hartley points out, be possible to infer other objectives from other provisions of the Treaties. (Hartley, n 9 above at 106.)

[202] Thus for example up until now (not entirely appropriately) the objective of maintaining and developing the Union as an area of freedom, security, and justice, in which the free movement of persons is assured, has been located in Article 2 of the Treaty on European Union. (See in relation to the post-Lisbon position in this regard, Article 3(3) of the Treaty on European Union (to be inserted by Article 1(4) of the Treaty of Lisbon)). Article 3(1)'s statement that 'the Union's aim is to promote peace, its values and the well-being of its peoples' is also new, even if the process of European integration has arguably always had the establishment and maintenance of peaceful relations betweeen European States as its core objective.

[203] Thus for example, the combating of social exclusion and discrimination and the promotion of solidarity between generations and protection of the rights of the child, all listed in Article 3(3) of the

elements of this mixture involve the main factors In the broadening of the scope of Article 352.

A second change consequent on the new European Union-wide context in which Article 308 will operate post-Lisbon is that what would otherwise become an excessively limiting factor that an objective be required to be attained 'in the course of the operation of the common market' is replaced by the less constrictive formulation that the objective be required to be attained 'within the framework of the policies defined in the Treaties'.

A third change in the wording of Article 352 is the reference to the EC Treaty not having provided the necessary powers being replaced by a reference to the *Treaties* not having done so. This actually represents a considerable broadening of a restriction on the use of the 'flexibility clause', since the situations in which the (post-Lisbon)Treaties provide for a power to act will obviously be far broader than those in which the (pre-Lisbon) EC Treaty alone did so. In each case in which such a power is provided for, the flexibility clause cannot be deployed.

A fourth major change which will be introduced by the Treaty of Lisbon—and one which is not directly consequent on the new European Union context of the operation of Article 352—is the introduction of a requirement to obtain the consent of the European Parliament (an institution which up to now has needed only to be consulted). This will give this institution a new right to veto any recourse to the flexibility clause, in the wake of the coming into force of the Treaty of Lisbon. This constitutes at the same time an increase in the level of democratic control which exists on the deployment of the 'flexibility' clause and a significant additional hurdle to be overcome should use be sought to be made of it.

So much for Article 352(1). Of the three extra paragraphs which are to be added to Article 352 by the Treaty of Lisbon,[204] one effectively merely highlights an existing restriction on the use to which the flexibility clause may be put.[205] One creates a major restriction on the scope of the Article's application,[206] and one in effect does both of these things—ie, it both highlights existing restrictions on the use of the 'flexibility clause' and creates a new restriction.[207]

Article 352(3) will provide expressly that measures based on the flexibility clause are not to entail harmonization of Member States' laws or regulations in cases where the Treaties exclude such harmonization. As has been seen in the text

Treaty on European Union (to be inserted by Article 1(4) of the Treaty of Lisbon), are new objectives. New objectives are also set out in the field of the common foreign and security policy, but as shall be seen presently, these are not relevant in the context of Article 308.

[204] Ie, by Article 2(289) of the Treaty of Lisbon.

[205] Viz, Article 352(3) of the Treaty on the Functioning of the European Union as inserted by Article 2(289) of the Treaty of Lisbon.

[206] Article 352(4) of the Treaty on the Functioning of the European Union as inserted by Article 2(289) of the Treaty of Lisbon. Although it must be remembered that this is in the context of an overall expansion in the scope of the flexibility clause.

[207] Article 352(2) of the Treaty on the Functioning of the European Union as inserted by Article 2(289) of the Treaty of Lisbon.

above, however, even under the existing Article 308, the correct view appears to be that measures adopted under the flexibility clause must not be contrary to an express prohibition contained in the Treaty.[208] Article 352(3) therefore merely seems to represent a codification of the pre-existing position.

Article 352(4) in contrast provides for major restrictions on the scope of application of Article 352. It stipulates that (a) Article 352 cannot serve as a basis for attaining objectives pertaining to the common foreign and security policy. Furthermore, (b) any acts adopted pursuant to Article 352 are to respect the limits set out in Article 40, paragraph 2 of the Treaty on European Union. The latter requirement means that acts under Article 352 are not permitted to affect either the application of procedures or the extent of institutional powers[209] concerning the exercise of Union competences under the Common Foreign and Security Policy Chapter of the EU Treaty.[210] The Member States have thus carefully ruled out the deployment of the flexibility clause in relation to matters coming within the common foreign and security policy. This is a highly significant restriction on the expansion of the scope of Article 352 to the European Union field generally.[211] It is one which—combined with the availability of a broad range of alternative legal bases—may have the effect of keeping any increase in the scale of deployment of Article 352 within moderate bounds.

Finally, the new Article 352(2) expressly requires the Commission to draw national Parliaments' attention to proposals based on Article 352, using the subsidiarity-monitoring procedure (a procedure introduced under the Treaty of Lisbon, which will be capable at least in theory, of producing consequences as serious as that of legislative initiatives being entirely blocked).[212] It has already been observed in the text above, however, that the normal requirement of subsidiarity has already applied up until now in relation to the use of Article 352. There is therefore nothing beyond declaratory value in the statement in Article 352(2) of the application of the subsidiarity principle in the context of the 'flexibility clause'. Article 352(2)'s linking-in of the mechanism for monitoring subsidiarity, however, undoubtedly constitutes an innovation under the Treaty of Lisbon. It is not, for all that, an innovation peculiar to Article 352, since a *general* obligation is now to be imposed in any case on the Commission (under Protocols

---

[208] See text above at n 185.   [209] Ie, laid down elsewhere in the Treaties.
[210] Viz, Chapter 2.   [211] Ie, from what up to now has been the Community field.
[212] Under Article 5(3) of the Treaty on European Union (to be inserted by Article 1(6) of the Treaty of Lisbon), national Parliaments are to ensure compliance with the principle of subsidiarity in accordance with the procedure set out in a Protocol on the application of the principles of subsidiarity and proportionality, which is to be annexed to the Treaty on European Union and to the Treaty on the Functioning of the European Union. See for an examination of the provisions on subsidiarity, G. Barrett, '"The King is Dead, Long Live the King": The Recasting by the Treaty of Lisbon of the Provisions of the Constitutional Treaty concerning National Parliaments' (2008) 33 ELR 66 at 73–84, and see more generally on the role of national Parliaments, G Barrett (ed), *National Parliaments and the European Union: The Constitutional Challenge for the Oireachtas and Other Member State Legislatures* (Clarus Press, 2008).

annexed to the Treaties by the Treaty of Lisbon"[213]) to forward all draft legislative acts originating from it directly to national Parliaments. The invocation by Article 352(2) of the subsidiarity-monitoring procedure is thus best characterized as a specific, highlighted example of a more broadly applicable obligation. Notwithstanding this, it is nonetheless an innovation, and one clearly potentially capable of rendering the use of Article 352 more difficult in political terms.

VII. A Conclusion of Sorts

It will be apparent from the foregoing that what are likely to be some of the most enduringly important amendments effected by the Treaty of Lisbon if and when this comes into force will consist of the alterations which it effects to the so-called final provisions of the existing constitutive treaties of the European Union. The ultimate impact of the envisaged changes will be revealed only if and when they come into force. However, it seems nonetheless appropriate to conclude with a few tentative comments on the proposed amendments discussed in this article.

It has been seen that the first amendment examined—that of the conferring of legal personality on the European Union—will constitute both a step likely to be of considerable practical impact and one which will enhance and clarify the profile of the Union at international level and within the Member States

As for the second amendment looked at—the alteration of the Treaty amendment process—this change will, insofar as the introduction of the 'ordinary revision procedure' is concerned, consolidate improvements made in practice in the transparency and inclusiveness of this process, and, insofar as the introduction of the 'simplified revision procedures' are concerned, will produce some degree of added efficiency, although the amendments made by the Treaty of Lisbon in this respect are strikingly conservative in nature. In addition, after the coming into force of the Lisbon Treaty (as before), the Member States will be left very firmly in the driving seat in the amendment process.

The third change—viz, the provision being made for the possibility of Member States leaving the Union—is one of considerable theoretical significance. Whether in practice, it operates (as its drafters hope) as a centripetal force on the European Union,[214] or (as is feared by those who opposed the inclusion of such a provision in the Treaties) an insidiously centrifugal force, or indeed whether it ends up making little difference at all is difficult to predict. It will at any rate operate in a context in which leaving the Union has always been viewed by the

---

[213] See Article 2 of the Protocol on the Role of National Parliaments in the European Union (to be annexed to the Treaty on European Union, to the Treaty on the Functioning of the European Union, and to the Treaty establishing the European Atomic Energy Community) and Article 4 of the Protocol on the Application of the Principles of Subsidiarity and Proportionality (to be annexed to the Treaty on European Union and to the Treaty on the Functioning of the European Union).

[214] Or, which amounts to the same thing, as a release valve for centrifugal pressures.

Member States simultaneously both as their continued entitlement and an utterly unattractive political and economic prospect

The fourth change—the expansion of the jurisdiction of the judicial branch of the Union, effected by the removal from the Final Provisions of the Treaty on European Union of the restrictions in this regard which have been found there up to now—will be of most significance in finally subjecting the justice and home affairs area to near-comprehensive control by the Court of Justice of the European Union. This is a welcome and long overdue reform, from a number of perspectives including that of individual rights, the rule of law and the need for uniformity of the European Union legal order.

Finally, the most significant amendment of the General and Final Provisions of the Treaty on the Functioning of the European Union, the amendment of the so-called 'flexibility' clause might be predicted to result in some expansion in the use of this device as a legislative basis. However, any such expansion is likely to be reined in by a number of factors, such as the existence of a broad range of alternative legal bases for legislation, the views which have been expressed by the Court of Justice concerning the limited circumstances in which the flexibility clause may be deployed and the various limitations written into the Treaty text concerning the deployment of Article 352. The end result seems likely to be that the 'flexibility clause' will continue to be the legal basis of a relatively small stream of legislation only, rather than a flood of European Union measures.

Finally 'Fit for Purpose'? The Treaty of Lisbon and the End of the Third Pillar Legal Order

Steve Peers[*]

I. Introduction

The EU's special rules on policing and criminal law (the 'third pillar') may be as hard to kill as the legendary Rasputin. First of all, the Treaty of Amsterdam transferred immigration, asylum, and civil law from the third pillar to the first pillar, but this seemed to give the remaining third pillar a new lease of life. Then the Constitutional Treaty intended to merge the third pillar in effect with the first, but could not finish the job, due its non-ratification.[1] For its part, the Court of Justice was able to wound the third pillar somewhat, but not fatally.[2] Next, the Commission's proposal for a transfer of the third pillar into the first pillar using the current Article 42 of the Treaty on European Union (TEU) received short shrift from the Member States' justice and home affairs ministries.[3] Finally, the June 2007 mandate for the Intergovernmental Conference that ultimately negotiated the Treaty of Lisbon initially tried to finish the job, but in the event the current third pillar rules on the Court's jurisdiction were maintained for a period of five years, and (in a hangover from the Constitutional Treaty) the legal effect of current third pillar measures has been preserved as well. Only when the last of the current third pillar measures has been replaced can it truly be said that the third pillar is finally dead.

Nevertheless, since it provides any new measures concerning policing and criminal law to be adopted after its entry into force will have to be adopted using (by and large) the normal 'Community' framework,[4] it is appropriate

[*] Professor of Law, University of Essex.
[1] [2004] OJ C310.
[2] See particularly Cases C-105/03 *Pupino* [2005] ECR I-5285 and C-176/03 *Commission v Council* [2005] ECR I-7879.
[3] COM (2006) 331, 28 June 2006.
[4] On questions of competence for all Justice and Home Affairs (JHA) matters under the new Treaty, see S Peers, 'Justice and Home Affairs Competences and Decision-Making after the Treaty of Lisbon', forthcoming.

to give the Treaty of Lisbon the credit for finally ending the third pillar legal regime. No one should mourn this peculiar institutional system, which lacked essential safeguards concerning judicial protection and moreover failed to ensure sufficient legitimacy or effectiveness upon EU action in this area. To borrow a phrase used by a former British Home Secretary, the system was not 'fit for purpose'.[5]

Having said that, since the transitional rules in the Treaty of Lisbon will entail a continued restriction for some time on the full jurisdiction of the Court and on the application of the full principles of the Community legal order to policing and criminal law acts, these rules are worthy of closer examination.[6] It can be seen that, despite their complexity, the transitional rules can be interpreted to ensure as smoothly as possible a transition from the Court's old jurisdiction to the new rules. And of course, the entry into force of the Treaty of Lisbon is anyway highly uncertain following the Irish referendum of June 2008.

II. Jurisdiction of the Court of Justice

A. Current Legal Position

At the outset, it is worth pointing out that the Treaty of Lisbon would end not only the special regime governing the Court's jurisdiction over the 'third pillar', but also the separate special regime governing the jurisdiction of the Court of Justice as regards immigration, asylum, and civil law (Title IV of the Treaty Establishing the European Community (TEC)). The Title IV jurisdiction is identical to the Court's 'normal' TEC jurisdiction, except that: references for a preliminary ruling can only be sent from 'final' courts; there is a limitation on the Court's jurisdiction as regards specified issues related to internal border controls; and the Court has a special jurisdiction to receive 'requests for interpretation' regarding Title IV or Title IV measures sent by the Commission, the Council, or Member States.[7]

In practice, the Court had by the time of writing received 31 references for a preliminary ruling, of which only four concerned immigration and asylum law;[8] and only two of those four cases were admissible.[9] Of the 27 civil law references,

---

[5] As regards judicial protection, see the author's critique in S Peers, 'Salvation outside the Church? Judicial Protection in the Third Pillar after the Pupino and SEGI judgments' (2007) 44 CML Rev 883. As regards effectiveness and legitimacy, see ibid.

[6] This paper is updated to 31 January 2008.

[7] Article 68 of the TEC.

[8] Cases C-45/03 *Dem'Yanenko* (order of 18 March 2004, unpublished); C-51/03 *Georgescu* [2004] ECR I-3203; C-241/05 *Bot* [2006] ECR I-9627; and C-465/07 *Elgafaji and Elgafaji*, pending.

[9] *Bot* and *Elgafaji and Elgafaji* (ibid).

12 had been decided,[10] 10 were still pending,[11] two were Inadmissible,[12] and three had been withdrawn.[13] The Court had also received five annulment actions,[14] along with 39 infringement actions, of which 16 had been decided,[15] 21 had been withdrawn,[16] and two were pending.[17]

Article 67(2) of the TEC provides that the Council 'shall' 'adapt' the provisions relating to the Court of Justice in Title IV 'after [a] period of five years' referred to as a 'transitional period' from the entry into force of the Treaty of Amsterdam, so by 1 May 2004. No such change had been agreed at time of writing, although a Commission proposal dating from June 2006 to apply the normal rules on the Court's jurisdiction has been under discussion.[18] In December 2007, however, the Council had respectively adopted and approved amendments to the Court's Statute and Rules of Procedure to provide for an emergency preliminary rulings procedure in JHA cases.[19]

The termination of this special regime by the Treaty of Lisbon is particularly welcome as it immediately ends the severe restrictions on the Court's jurisdiction,

[10] Cases C-443/03 *Leffler* [2005] ECR I-9611; C-1/04 *Staubitz-Schreiber* [2006] ECR I-701; C-473/04 *Plumex* [2006] ECR I-1417; C-234/04 *Kapferer* [2006] ECR I-2585; C-341/04 *Eurofood* [2006] ECR I-3813; C-103/05 *Reisch Montage* [2006] ECR I-6827; C-283/05 *ASML* [2006] ECR I-12041; C-386/05 *Color Drack* [2007] ECR I-3699; C-98/06 *Freeport*, judgment of 11 October 2007, not yet reported; C-435/06 *C*, judgment of 27 November 2007, not yet reported; C-68/07 *Sundelind Lopez*, judgment of 29 November 2007, not yet reported; and C-463/06 *FBTO Schadeverzekeringen*, judgment of 13 December 2007, not yet reported.

[11] Cases C-180/06 *Ilsinger*; C-462/06 *Glaxo SmithKline Beecham* (opinion of 17 January 2008); C-14/07 *Weiss und partner* (opinion of 29 November 2007); C-185/07 *Riunione Adriatica Di Sicurta v West Tankers*; C-339/07 *Deko Marty Belgium*; C-372/07 *Hassett*; C-420/07 *Apostolides*; C-444/07 *MG Probud*; C-523/07 *A*; and C-533/07 *Falco Privatstiftung*.

[12] Cases C-24/02 *Marseille Fret* [2002] ECR I-3383 and C-555/03 *Ryanair* [2004] ECR I-6041.

[13] Cases C-387/04 *Donath*; C-175/06 *Tedesco*; and C-413/07 *Haase*.

[14] Cases C-257/01 *Commission v Council* [2005] ECR I-345; C-540/03 *EP v Council* [2006] ECR I-5769; C-77/05 *UK v Council*, judgment of 18 December 2007, not yet reported; and C-133/06 *EP v Council*, pending (opinion of 27 September 2007).

[15] Cases C-454/04 *Commission v Luxembourg*, 2 June 2005; C-449/04 *Commission v Luxembourg*, 21 July 2005; C-462/04 *Commission v Italy*, 8 September 2005; C-448/04 *Commission v Luxembourg*, 8 September 2005; C-476/04 *Commission v Greece*, 17 November 2005; C-455/04 *Commission v UK*, 23 February 2006; C-102/06 *Commission v Austria*, 26 October 2006; C-48/06 *Commission v Luxembourg*, 7 December 2006; C-72/06 *Commission v Greece*, 19 April 2007; C-4/07 *Commission v Portugal*, 27 September 2007; C-5/07 *Commission v Portugal*, 27 September 2007; C-3/07 *Commission v Belgium*, 8 November 2007; C-59/07 *Commission v Spain*, 15 November 2007; C-34/07 *Commission v Luxembourg*, 29 November 2007; and C-57/07 *Commission v Luxembourg*, 6 December 2007; and C-58/07 *Commission v Spain*, 14 February 2008 (all cases unreported).

[16] Cases C-460/04 *Commission v Netherlands*; C-474/04 *Commission v Greece*; C-515/04 *Commission v Belgium*; C-516/04 *Commission v Belgium*; C-450/04 *Commission v France*; C-461/04 *Commission v Netherlands*; C-451/04 *Commission v France*; C-47/06 *Commission v Luxembourg*; C-75/06 *Commission v Portugal*; C-51/07 *Commission v Luxembourg*; C-91/07 *Commission v Italy*; C-104/07 *Commission v Italy*; C-29/07 *Commission v Greece*; C-79/07 *Commission v Malta*; C-86/07 *Commission v Italy*; C-87/07 *Commission v Malta*; C-389/06 *Commission v Belgium*; C-37/07 *Commission v France*; C-30/07 *Commission v Hungary*; C-496/06 *Commission v Germany*; and C-192/07 *Commission v Germany*.

[17] Cases C-485/06 *Commission v Germany* and C-216/07 *Commission v Germany*.

[18] COM (2006) 346, 28 June 2006.

[19] [2008] OJ L24/39 and 42.

which have obviously drastically reduced the number of cases reaching the Court as regards immigration and asylum, which had moreover been retained in breach of the obligation to change the system as set out in Article 67(2) of the TEC.[20]

As for the third pillar, the regime currently governing the Court's jurisdiction was first set out in the original TEU, and then amended by the Treaty of Amsterdam. Before the original TEU, Member States agreed on Protocols to two civil law Conventions (the Brussels Convention on civil and commercial jurisdiction, and the Rome Convention on conflict of law in contract) which provided for jurisdiction for the Court to interpret those Conventions following a reference from a final court or an appeal court in any Member State.[21] In the original TEU period, Article K.3.2(c) of the TEU provided an option for the Council to confer jurisdiction upon the Court to interpret third pillar Conventions, on a reference for a preliminary ruling from national courts or to settle disputes between Member States (or between Member States and the Commission) regarding the interpretation or disputes regarding the application of the Conventions. This option was taken up in six of the eight policing and criminal law Conventions agreed between 1993 and 1999.[22]

Following the Treaty of Amsterdam, the current rules governing the Court's third pillar jurisdiction are set out in Article 35 of the TEU. This Article provides for Member States to opt in to the Court of Justice's jurisdiction over preliminary rulings as regards most third pillar acts adopted after the entry into force of the Treaty of Amsterdam (Framework Decisions, Decisions, and Conventions, but not Common Positions). Seventeen Member States have opted in,[23] and one of these Member States have chosen the further option to limit the ability to refer questions to its final courts only.[24] It is also left to Member States to decide, by means of provision in their national law, whether final courts are obliged to send questions. Next, the Court of Justice has jurisdiction over annulment actions brought by the Commission or Member States. Finally, the Court has jurisdiction over dispute settlement proceedings against Member States brought by the Commission (as regards Conventions) or by other Member States (as regards all

---

[20] See generally S Peers, 'The Jurisdiction of the Court of Justice over EC Immigration and Asylum Law: Time for a Change?' in Toner, Guild, and Baldaccini (eds), *Whose Freedom, Security and Justice? EU Immigration and Asylum Law and Policy* (Hart, 2007) 85.

[21] For details, see S Peers, *EU Justice and Home Affairs Law* (OUP, 2007) 354, and subsequently the Decision on Romanian and Bulgarian accession to the Rome Convention and its Protocols ([2007] OJ L347/1).

[22] The exceptions were the extradition Conventions of 1995 and 1996 which have never entered into force. The Court was also given jurisdiction to interpret two civil law Conventions adopted during this period (the service of documents Convention and the Brussels II Convention): but these Conventions never entered into force, since they were replaced by EC Regulations after the entry into force of the treaty of Amsterdam. See generally Peers, ibid, 17–18.

[23] [2008] OJ L70/23. They are the first 15 Member States, except the UK, Denmark, and Ireland, and later Hungary, the Czech Republic, Latvia, Lithuania, and Slovenia, from among the Member States joining in 2004 and 2007.

[24] Spain.

third pillar measures). There is a limitation of the Court's jurisdiction in Article 35(5) of the TEU: the Court 'shall have no jurisdiction to review the validity or proportionality of operations carried out by police or other law enforcement authorities of a Member State or the exercise of responsibilities incumbent upon Member States with regard to the maintenance of law and order and the safeguarding of internal security'.

In practice, by the time of writing, the Court had received 16 third pillar references,[25] with two annulment actions brought by the Commission against third pillar acts,[26] and no dispute settlement proceedings. Among other things, the Court confirmed that it has no jurisdiction over damages actions against the EU institutions, but that it did have jurisdiction to receive references concerning the validity of Common Positions, even such measures as should arguably have been adopted in a different form.[27] It also ruled that it had jurisdiction to interpret the Articles of the TEU where necessary to determine the validity of third pillar acts.[28] Additionally, the Court received a challenge by a Member State to an act of Eurojust, the EU's prosecutors' agency, which it ruled inadmissible,[29] although a number of staff disputes against Europol and Eurojust have been brought before the EU courts;[30] the cases against Europol are the only cases concerning pre-Amsterdam third pillar measures which have reached the EU courts. The Court has also confirmed that the rules governing third references are the same (leaving aside Member States' opt-outs) as the rules applying to Article 234 of the TEC.[31]

B. The Treaty of Lisbon

In the Treaty of Lisbon, as in the Constitutional Treaty, the Court's 'normal' jurisdiction is extended to JHA matters, with the sole remaining limit on the

---

[25] As regards the 'double jeopardy' rules of the Schengen Convention, there have been 12 references. There have been judgments in eight of these cases: C-187/01 and C-385/01 *Gözütok and Brugge* [2003] ECR I-1345; C-469/03 *Miraglia* [2005] ECR I-2009; C-436/04 *van Esbroek* [2006] ECR I-2333; C-467/04 *Gasparini* [2006] ECR I-9199; C-150/05 *Van Straaten* [2006] ECR I-9327; C-288/05 *Kretzinger,* judgment of 18 July 2007, not yet reported; and C-367/05 *Kraaijenbrink,* judgment of 18 July 2007, not yet reported. Two cases have been withdrawn (Cases C-491/03 *Hiebeler* and C-272/05 *Bowens*), and two are still pending (Cases C-297/07 *Bourquain* and C-491/07 *Turanksy*). On other issues, there have been four references: Cases C-105/03 *Pupino* [2005] ECR I-5285, C-303/05 *Advocaten voor de Wereld* [2007] ECR I-3633, C-467/05 *Dell'Orto* [2007] ECR I-5557, and C-404/07 *Sos,* pending.

[26] Cases C-176/03 *Commission v Council* [2005] ECR I-7879 and C-440/05 *Commission v Council,* judgment of 23 October 2007, not yet reported.

[27] Cases C-354/04 P *Gestoras Pro Amnistia* [2007] ECR I-1579 and C-355/04 P *SEGI* [2007] ECR I-1657.

[28] *Advocaten voor de Wereld,* n 25 above.

[29] Case C-160/03 *Spain v Eurojust* [2005] ECR I-2077.

[30] See *JHA Law* (n 21 above), 19.

[31] See S Peers, 'Salvation outside the Church? Judicial Protection in the Third Pillar after the Pupino and SEGI judgments' (2007) 44 CML Rev 887–888.

Court's jurisdiction being the existing restriction regarding police cooperation.[32] Logically, this restriction must be interpreted the same way as the existing
restriction. Although the Court of Justice has not yet interpreted the existing
restriction, I have argued that it should be interpreted narrowly, so that it only
restricts the Court's jurisdiction to rule on the effect of the operational actions of
Member States' authorities, leaving the Court with jurisdiction to interpret the
underlying EU rules.[33]

While it can obviously be assumed that the Court's extended jurisdiction over
immigration, asylum, and civil law will take effect upon the entry into force of
the Treaty of Lisbon as regards pre-existing measures in these areas,[34] presum-
ing that the Court's jurisdiction has not already been extended in the meantime
in whole or part as regards Title IV of the TEC, the position is less clear-cut
as regards pre-existing third pillar measures. Such acts, according to both the
Constitutional Treaty and the Treaty of Lisbon, retain their legal effect until they
are amended, an issue considered further below.[35] Does it follow also that the
Court's 'old' jurisdiction remains applicable until the amendment of the pre-
existing measures? Neither the Constitutional Treaty nor the original draft of the
Treaty of Lisbon (as released in July 2007) addressed this issue explicitly.

Furthermore, there is no clear guidance from the jurisprudence of the Court as
regards the analogous issue of its continued jurisdiction to interpret the European
Coal and Steel Community Treaty (ECSC Treaty), and measures adopted pursuant to it, after that Treaty's expiry in 2002. The Court of Justice ruled in July
2007 that it continues to have jurisdiction to interpret ECSC measures, but
did not make clear whether that jurisdiction was based on the TEC, the ECSC
Treaty, both, or neither.[36]

This issue was ultimately addressed by the October 2007 draft of the Treaty
of Lisbon, and subsequently by the final text of that Treaty. Following discussions among legal experts, a new Article 10 was added to the Protocol on transitional provisions. Article 10(1) of the Protocol provides that, '[a]s a transitional
measure', the Court of Justice's current jurisdiction over third pillar measures
will continue to apply to third pillar acts adopted before the entry into force of

---

[32] New Article 240a (future Article 276) of the TFEU.

[33] See S Peers, 'Who's Judging the Watchmen? The Judicial System of the Area of Freedom,
Security and Justice' (1998) 18 YEL 337 at 409–412.

[34] However, it should be recalled that the immigration-related provisions of the Schengen
Information System (SIS) have not been allocated to the third pillar, and so remain by default in the
third pillar until the new EC legislation on this issue becomes applicable (Regulation 1987/2006
establishing SIS II: [2006] OJ L 381/4); at time of writing, it appears that SIS II will not begin operations until after the Treaty of Lisbon enters into force. However, it should be recalled that the existing
SIS has in the meantime been amended by EC legislation, which complicates matters (see Regulations
378/2004 and 871/2004, [2004] OJ L64/5 and L162/29, along with the Commission Decision on
the Sirene Manual: [2006] OJ L317). Furthermore, the Court can rule on whether application of SIS
infringes EC free movement law: Case C-503/03 *Commission v Spain* [2006] ECR I-1097.

[35] See section III.

[36] Case C-119/05 *Lucchini*, judgment of 18 July 2007, not yet reported, para 41.

the Treaty of Lisbon ('pre-existing measures'), for a period of five years after the entry into force of the new Treaty. After that point, according to Article 10(3) of the Protocol, the Court's new jurisdiction will apply to all pre-existing third pillar measures, presumably including pre-Amsterdam third pillar measures still in force on that date.

This clause means in particular that the Commission will not have power to bring infringement proceedings against Member States as regards alleged breaches of pre-existing measures during this transitional period,[37] and that Member States which presently limit or entirely rule out the Court's jurisdiction over references for a preliminary ruling will continue to do so during this period. In fact, the transitional restriction probably even has an impact as regards Member States which already permit all their courts and tribunals to refer third pillar questions to the Court of Justice,[38] and which furthermore require their 'final' national courts to do so, because this obligation upon final courts probably differs from the obligation to refer pursuant to Article 234 TEC as defined in *CILFIT*.[39] The application of the Court's 'normal' third pillar jurisdiction will also confirm that any national court in such a Member State is obliged to send questions on the validity of third pillar measures to the Court of Justice, in accordance with the *Foto-Frost* judgment.[40] It is arguable that such a rule does not presently exist in the third pillar, even for those Member States which have given all of their courts and tribunals the facility to refer cases.

As for annulment actions, the current limitation of standing to the [Council], the Commission and Member States as regards third pillar measures will be retained as regards pre-existing third pillar acts, but these restrictions will be almost entirely irrelevant following the entry into force of the Treaty of Lisbon, due to the two-month time-limit on bringing proceedings.[41] This limitation would have limited, if any, impact upon natural or legal persons, who would

[37] Indeed Article 10(1) of the Protocol makes express reference to the limitation upon the Commission's powers pursuant to Art 226 (future Article 258) of the TFEU. However, it should not be forgotten that the Commission has powers to bring disputes with Member States before the Court as regards all post-Amsterdam Conventions and, to some extent, pre-Amsterdam Conventions. The Commission has recently threatened for the first time to use such powers: see the second report on the Convention on the EU's financial interests (COM (2008) 77, 14 February 2008).

[38] Again Article 10(1) of the transitional Protocol states expressly that the Court's powers remain valid as regards Member States which have already accepted its preliminary rulings pursuant to the current Article 35(2) of the TEU. It is therefore wholly wrong to say that the Court will have *no* jurisdiction over pre-existing third pillar measures—just as it is wholly wrong to say that it lacks such jurisdiction at present.

[39] Case C-283/81 [1982] ECR 3415; see subsequently Cases C-99/00 *Lyckesog* [2002] ECR I-4839, C-224/01 *Kobler* [2003] ECR I-10239, and C-495/03 *Intermodal Transports* [2005] ECR I-8151.

[40] Case 314/85 [1987] ECR 4199; see subsequently Case C-461/03 *Gaston Schul* [2005] ECR I-10513.

[41] The limitation would have a limited relevance, though, where a measure was adopted just before the entry into force of the new Treaty and could otherwise have been subject to challenge pursuant to expanded rules on standing within a short period after the new Treaty entered into force. See by analogy Case C-273/04 *Poland v Council*, judgment of 23 October 2007, not yet reported (in particular

lack standing to bring direct actions against most third pillar measures in any event due to the 'direct and individual concern' requirement set out in Article 230 (future Article 263) of the TEC.[42] However, the restriction will rule out the Court's (direct) jurisdiction as regards damages claims for pre-existing third pillar acts during the transitional period.[43] Indeed, given that the five-year transitional period regarding the Court's jurisdiction matches the five-year time limit for bringing claims pursuant to the EC's/EU's non-contractual liability as set out in the Statute of the Court of Justice,[44] then the Court of Justice (or more precisely, the 'General Court' at first instance) will not, in principle, ever be able to entertain direct actions concerning the EU's non-contractual liability for pre-existing third pillar acts. It might be possible, however, for national courts to refer questions to the Court of Justice on this issue.[45]

Three points regarding this transitional restriction on the Court's jurisdiction need to be clarified. First of all, Article 10 of the transitional Protocol refers to maintaining the jurisdiction of the Court of Justice 'in the version in force before the entry into force' of the new Treaty. This does not specifically address the question of the Court's jurisdiction over measures adopted *before* the entry into force of the Treaty of Amsterdam, which, as noted above, significantly amended the legal regime applicable to the Court's third pillar jurisdiction. But, in the absence of any wording in the Treaty of Lisbon to indicate a contrary interpretation, it would make sense to apply Article 10 of the Protocol *mutatis mutandis* to such measures, including third pillar Joint Actions, which were not subject to the Court's jurisdiction at all.

Secondly, it should be emphasized that the Court of Justice, in the current legal framework, enjoys its normal *first pillar* jurisdiction over aspects of the third pillar—in particular where third pillar measures allegedly 'encroach' upon first pillar competences, and as regards staff cases and cases concerning administration of the EU budget.[46] This would obviously continue to be the case during the transitional period, so the EU Courts would, for instance, retain jurisdiction over non-contractual damages liability of the Union's pre-existing third pillar acts due to alleged encroachment into (current) first pillar competences.[47]

Thirdly, the question of 'mixed jurisdiction'—the overlapping application of different jurisdictional regimes—will continue to apply as long as the transitional

---

the Advocate General's Opinion), although the judgment did not ultimately rule definitively on this issue.

[42] It seems unlikely that the clarification of this rule as regards 'regulatory acts' in the Treaty of Lisbon will be very relevant within the third pillar context (see Article 2(214)(c) of the new Treaty).

[43] See Case C-355/04 P *SEGI* [2007] ECR I-1657.

[44] Article 46 of the Statute of the Court of Justice.

[45] See S Peers, 'Salvation outside the Church? Judicial Protection in the Third Pillar after the Pupino and SEGI judgments' (2007) 44 CML Rev 900–901. On the Court's jurisdiction over the EU's non-contractual liability in the event of the amendment of a pre-existing act, see below.

[46] See 'Salvation' (n 45 above), 902–908.

[47] See the Court of First Instance judgment in *SEGI*: Case T-332/02 [2004] ECR II-1647.

regime applies. Indeed, the unavoidable result of the transitional rules is that, during the transitional period, there will be mixed jurisdiction over different measures concerning the *same subject matter*, and so such issues may be more likely to arise in practice than they have already.[48] As I have argued before, the question of which jurisdictional regime to apply in such cases must be resolved by choosing the most favourable jurisdiction where, on the facts of the case, issues subject to different jurisdictional regimes of the Court are inextricably intertwined.[49] There is no reason to doubt that this principle should still be applied during the transitional period relating to the Court's third pillar jurisdiction. In fact, the purely transitional nature of the remaining restrictions on the Court's jurisdiction suggests the application of this principle *a fortiori*.

This brings us to a significant exception to the transitional limits on the Court's jurisdiction. Article 10(2) of the transitional Protocol specifies that the Court's normal (post-Lisbon) jurisdiction will apply following 'the amendment of' a pre-existing third pillar act, 'with respect to the amended act for those Member States to which that amended act shall apply'. A Declaration to the Treaty of Lisbon invites the Council, Commission, and EP 'to seek to adopt, in appropriate cases and as far as possible' within the five-year transitional period, 'legal acts amending or replacing' pre-existing third pillar measures.[50]

How much amendment of an act is necessary in order for Article 10(2) to apply? In the absence of any *de minimis* rule or any indication that acts are in any way severable as regards the Court's jurisdiction, this rule will apply where *any* amendment, no matter how minor, is adopted in respect of *any* pre-existing third pillar act, and it will apply to the entire pre-existing act following such an amendment. Indeed, the reference to 'the amended act' can only be understood as a reference to an entire act, as amended, and this interpretation is consistent with the transitional nature of the Protocol and its intention to ensure a transition to the Court's new jurisdiction as soon as possible. Put another way, Article 10(2) of the Protocol should not be interpreted narrowly because it is an exception to Article 10(1); rather Article 10(2) should be interpreted broadly because Article 10(1) is an exception to the basic rules of the Court's jurisdiction, and moreover a purely transitional exception. This interpretation also avoids the absurdity of having mixed jurisdiction over different provisions of the *same text*; if Member States had wanted such a bizarre result, they would surely have provided for it more expressly. Moreover, a *de minimis* threshold would necessarily be imprecise

---

[48] The 'mixed jurisdiction' issue has consistently been avoided by the Court whenever it has been raised or could have been been relevant: see Cases C-467/05 *Dell'Orto* [2007] ECR I-5557 and C-467/04 *Gaspardini* [2006] ECR I-9199, the order in Case C-276/06 *El-Youssfi* [2007] ECR I-2851, and Case C-503/03 *Commission v Spain* [2006] ECR I-1097. The point is relevant again in Case C-228/06 *Soysal*, pending.

[49] See S Peers, 'Who's Judging the Watchmen? The Judicial System of the Area of Freedom, Security and Justice' (1998) 18 YEL 397–399.

[50] Declaration 50 in the Final Act of the Treaty of Lisbon.

in the absence of any guidance as to how it would apply, and so would violate legal certainty.

There are two important aspects to this exception: the definition of 'amendment' and the date from which the revised jurisdiction of the Court of Justice applies. On the first point, which is also very important as regards the legal effect of measures and the opt-out rules,[51] sometimes it will be indisputably obvious when an act has been amended. For example, a Directive amending the Framework Decision on the European Arrest Warrant (EAW) to clarify one or more of the grounds for refusing to execute an EAW would clearly constitute an 'amendment' of that Framework Decision.[52] To cite a further example, the proposed Framework Decision which would amend the existing Framework Decision on terrorism to add some new offences would clearly constitute an 'amendment' to a pre-existing third pillar act, although it is likely that this particular proposal will be adopted before the entry into force of the Treaty of Lisbon, with the result that Article 10(2) of the Protocol would not become engaged.[53] Another example is the proposal to amend the Eurojust Decision,[54] which might be less likely to be adopted before the new Treaty enters into force and which would therefore have to be proposed again in the form of a Regulation under the new institutional framework, thereby engaging Article 10(2) of the Protocol once it is adopted.

But there are less obvious cases. For example, the Commission has proposed a Decision to replace the Europol Convention and its Protocols.[55] The Council plans to adopt this proposal by June 2008, before the Treaty of Lisbon enters into force;[56] but all of the measures implementing the current Europol Convention will then be replaced by measures implementing the Europol Decision by the end of 2009.[57] Would the adoption of replacement implementation measures (or the substantive amendment of existing those implementation measures which have already been replaced) after the entry into force of the Treaty of Lisbon entail the application of the Court's revised jurisdiction over the Europol Decision and all other implementing measures? Would it also entail the application of the Court's new jurisdiction over the Europol Convention, and its Protocols, and all measures implementing the Convention (at least to the extent that the latter had not

---

[51] On legal effect, see section III below. On opt-outs, see S Peers, 'In a world of their own? Opt-outs from EU Justice and Home Affairs Law and the Treaty of Lisbon', forthcoming.

[52] See Articles 3 and 4 of the Framework Decision ([2002] OJ L190/1), and the proposed Framework Decision amending this and three other Framework Decisions as regards *in absentia* trials: Council doc. 5598/08, 13 February 2008.

[53] COM (2007) 650, 6 November 2007.

[54] See the proposal in Council doc. 5613/08, 13 February 2008.

[55] COM (2006) 817, 20 December 2006.

[56] See the conclusions of the JHA Council, 12–13 June 2007. At time of writing, the Council had reached a 'general approach' on Chapters I to III and VI, VII, and IX of the proposal, at the JHA Councils of June, November, and December 2007.

[57] See the implementation plan regarding the transformation of Europol, in Council doc. 14590/07, 31 October 2007.

been replaced), given that after the formal adoption of the new Decision, the existing legal framework will still be applicable until 2010?[58]

Or would the Court's jurisdiction only apply to each (post-Lisbon) implementing measure as and when it is adopted—entailing 'mixed jurisdiction' for some implementing measures as compared to others, and as compared to the Europol Decision? Alternatively, it is possible that the parent Decision will be amended before some or all of its implementing measures are adopted. Similar questions arise in respect of the SIS II Decision and the Decision implementing the Prum Treaty as part of EU law, all of which provide for implementing measures.[59]

Questions about the definition of 'amendment' could also arise when some or all of a pre-existing act is repealed by an act adopted after the entry into force of the Treaty of Lisbon. Would the remaining pre-existing act (if that act is only partly repealed) now be subject to the newer jurisdiction of the Court of Justice? Would this equally apply to the provisions of the pre-existing act which have been repealed? Furthermore, would the former pre-existing act, if that act is fully repealed, be subject to the Court's newer jurisdiction? The latter two questions might seem moot, but it could be relevant if questions about the interpretation or validity of that pre-existing act, or the relevant provisions of it, are still pending at the time of its repeal, and/or if that act still remains valid in a small number of Member States, due to their opt-outs from an amendment to the pre-existing measure.

A particular question also arises in respect of the Schengen Convention, leaving aside the question of the amendment of the measures implementing that Convention. Should the Convention, for the purposes of Article 10(2) of the Protocol, be treated as a single measure or a package of distinct measures? So, for example, would an amendment to a provision of the Convention regarding mutual assistance trigger the Court's new jurisdiction as regards policing, and vice versa? Moreover, would an amendment to the first pillar provisions of the Convention trigger the application of the Court's new jurisdiction as regards the policing and criminal law provisions of the Convention?[60]

The answer to these questions surely be must be uniform at EU level, rather than left to national discretion.[61] The underlying principle should be to ensure an orderly and coherent transition to the Court's new jurisdiction, thereby avoiding 'mixed jurisdiction' to the extent possible. Applying this principle, parent acts and their implementing measures should progress from the old to the new jurisdictional rules as an *ensemble*, and the most logical point to trigger the application

[58] See Article 60 of the proposed Decision.

[59] See respectively [2007] L205/63 (SIS II Decision) and [2007] OJ C267/4 (proposed Decision implementing Prum Decision).

[60] For example, the proposed visa code (COM (2006) 403, 19 July 2006) might not be adopted until after the entry into force of the Treaty of Lisbon. The code would repeal a number of Articles of the Convention (Article 48 of the proposal).

[61] See, by analogy, the argument in S Peers, 'Who's Judging the Watchmen? The Judicial System of the Area of Freedom, Security and Justice' (1998) 18 YEL 386–387.

of the Court's new jurisdiction is the date of amendment of the *parent* measure, given that the implementing measures depend on the parent measure for their validity.

As for the repeal of part or whole of a pre-existing measure, considering that the underlying purpose of Article 10(2) of the Protocol is surely to avoid the risk of mixed jurisdiction within a single measure, there is no need to extend the Court's new jurisdiction to pre-existing measures which have been wholly or partly repealed by a post-Lisbon act. The position of Member States which opt out of such a post-Lisbon measure as regards the Court's jurisdiction is in any event protected by Article 10(2) of the Protocol, which makes it clear that the Court's new jurisdiction will only apply early in respect of pre-existing measures to those Member States which participate in post-Lisbon acts which amend such pre-existing measures. This opting-out rule applies regardless of whether the post-Lisbon measures confine themselves to repealing whole or part of the pre-existing measures, or whether the post-Lisbon measures make substantive additions to the text of the pre-existing measures.

Next, in the absence of any indication otherwise, the third pillar aspects of the Schengen Convention should be considered to be a single act for the purposes of Article 10(2) of the Protocol. However, it would surely be subverting the underlying intention of the Protocol to insist that amendment to the first pillar provisions of the Convention would trigger the application of the Court's new jurisdiction to the third pillar provisions of the Convention, given that the Article of the Protocol is confined in its application to the third pillar. Moreover, this would mean that the adoption of legislation (for example as regards visas) which some Member States do not (and presently *cannot*[62]) participate in would alter the jurisdiction of the Court as regards the policing and criminal law provisions of the Convention, without affording such Member States any opportunity to opt out of the Court's jurisdiction in that respect. Again, this would undercut the intention of the Protocol as regards protecting the position of such Member States in respect of the Court's jurisdiction.

Finally, what about the extension of a pre-existing measure by cross-reference? For example, what if the EU adopts a measure on the second phase of the European evidence warrant that does not as such amend the Framework Decision establishing the first phase of the evidence warrant,[63] but rather provides that certain rules

---

[62] See Cases C-77/05 and C-137/05 *UK v Council*, judgments of 18 December 2007, not yet reported.

[63] This assumes that the relevant Framework Decision will be adopted before the Treaty of Lisbon enters into force. The Council agreed in principle on this proposal in June 2006, but has not yet formally adopted it at time of writing; for the latest version of the agreed text, see Council doc. 13076/07, 21 December 2007. In the first phase of the evidence warrant, such warrants will only apply to existing evidence (see Article 4 of the agreed text of the Framework Decision). The Commission ultimately plans to present a proposal applying mutual recognition rules to all types of evidence (see the Annex to the working paper on the mutual recognition principle and criminal law, SEC (2005) 641, 20 May 2005).

in that Framework Decision (for example, the rules on the grounds to refuse to execute a warrant)[64] apply partly or wholly to the second phase warrants as established by the post-Lisbon act? In this case, the underlying obligations in the pre-existing act would not have been altered as such, and to that extent should not be regarded as amended.

This brings us to the second question: when Article 10(2) of the Protocol applies, when does the Court's new jurisdiction take effect? This question is, of course, easily answered as regards any wholly new obligations established by a post-Lisbon measure: while there is no obligation to implement such a measure until its date of transposition or taking effect, national courts can send any questions about that measure before its transposition date or taking effect in the event that the measure is transposed in advance of the deadline in that Member State,[65] and the Court will also have jurisdiction to rule on whether the Member State or national courts have seriously compromised the application of that measure before its transposition date or entry into effect.[66]

The real issue is when exactly the Court will obtain its new jurisdiction over any pre-existing act *which has now been amended*. There must be a uniform EU-wide answer to this question, for the reasons set out above.[67] Would the new jurisdiction apply from the date of adoption of the new measure, from its date of entry into force, from the date of its entry into effect or transposition deadline, or from when it is actually transposed by Member States? And, whatever date applies, would the Court's new jurisdiction apply immediately to cases concerning the pre-existing measure which are, at that date, pending?

In the absence of any clear indication of an answer to these questions from the text of the Protocol, the answers to these questions must be based on the principle that Article 10(2) of the Protocol aims to expedite the transition to the Court's new jurisdiction. Therefore it should follow that the Court's new jurisdiction shall apply as soon as the amended act *enters into force*, event if that act is not due for transposition or application for some months or years afterward. This would, inter alia, avoid the awkward question of when the Court's new jurisdiction would apply if different provisions of the act were due to enter into effect or were

---

[64] See Article 16 and 23(4) of the agreed text (ibid).

[65] Case C-66/96 *Hoj Pedersen* [1998] ECR I-7327.

[66] See in particular Cases C-129/96 *Inter-Environnment Wallonie* [1997] ECR I-7411 and C-212/04 *Adeneler* [2006] ECR I-6057. This assumes that the case law relating to Directives applies *mutatis mutandis* to other acts as necessary. It has been argued that the Court in *Pupino* was inconsistent with *Adeneler* on this point: see Loof, 'Temporal Aspects of the Duty of Consistent Interpretation in the First and Third Pillars' (2007) 32 ELR 888. However, the Court was not asked specifically to comment on this point in *Pupino*, which pre-dated the *Adeneler* judgment, and the Court's assumption that the relevant Framework Decision was applicable to the continued effects of pre-existing events can be explained by the application of new procedural rules to pending cases (see, as regards the same Framework Decision, paragraphs 47 and 48 of the judgment in Case C-467/05 *Dell'Orto* [2007] ECR I-5557).

[67] See the text at n 61 above.

due for transposition at different dates,[68] or if some Member States were granted a delay in application of some of the provisions of the amending measure.[69]

It might be objected that the Court's new jurisdiction should not apply until the amendments are fully applicable, so as to ensure consistency of the date of application of that jurisdiction as regards the old provisions of the amended act (which are still retained in force) and the new provision of that act. But this interpretation would substantially limit the practical effectiveness of Article 10(2), given that Directives are subject to a transposition period of (usually) two years and possibly more, and that it may be practically difficult to adopt many policing in criminal law measures in the two years after the new Treaty enters into force—thus delaying the impact of the Court's new jurisdiction over amended acts for about a full four years out of the five-year transitional period. This difficulty arises because: outstanding third pillar proposals and initiatives will lapse when the new Treaty enters into force; there may be insufficient time for the Commission to propose, and for the European Parliament (EP) and Council to agree and adopt, any fresh proposals before the EP elections in June 2009; and then there will be subsequent months of limited EU activity until late 2009 because it takes several months after an election before the EP is fully operational, and because the Commission is less active in the final months of an outgoing Commission's mandate and the first few months of a new Commission's mandate.

On the other hand, if the institutions agree on a strategy of readopting much of the pre-existing third pillar *acquis* without substantive amendments in the form of Regulations and Directives as soon as possible after the entry into force of the new Treaty, the Court will immediately gain its new jurisdiction over these 'new' measures. But in this scenario, the pre-existing measures affected by this fast-track strategy will simply be repealed, rather than amended, and so there will be no question of the Court exercising its new jurisdiction over the pre-existing measures in any event.[70] The argument still stands, therefore, that Article 10(2) will be deprived of much of its useful effect if it applies only as of the transposition deadline or entry into effect of post-Lisbon measures amending pre-existing measures.

What happens to cases pending before the Court of Justice or the national courts at the time when the new jurisdiction of the Court of Justice becomes applicable? As for cases pending before the Court of Justice, logically the Court's old jurisdiction will continue to apply if the cases were brought before the Court before the date on which its new jurisdiction over the relevant measure took effect. This is only relevant to dispute settlement proceedings between Member

---

[68] See, for instance, the Framework Decision on victims ([2001] OJ L82/1).

[69] For instance, see Article 33 of the Framework Decision on the European Arrest Warrant (n 52 above).

[70] This would be the case whenever (during the transitional period) any pre-existing measures are wholly repealed by new acts, rather than simply amended.

States, or between Member States and the Commission, for jurisdiction over references from national courts will be expanded, rather than contracted, once the Court of Justice's new jurisdiction takes effect. Retaining the Court's old jurisdiction for cases already pending before it does mean that references which are inadmissible because the referring national court lacked the jurisdiction to refer them will remain inadmissible. But it would always be open to the national court concerned to rescind its original reference and to make a fresh reference to the Court of Justice, which would now be admissible. If national procedural rules stand in the way of such a step, they should be set aside as a breach of EU law due to their restrictive effect on the ability of the national courts to send references to the Court.[71]

Where a case is pending before a national court at the time when the new rules on the Court of Justice's jurisdiction take effect, the new rules should immediately apply to the pending cases, unless the case solely concerns the interpretation of provisions which have been repealed (or replaced as regards their substance) by the amending act. This interpretation is justified, in the absence of any indication to the contrary in the text of the Protocol, because it best reflects the objective of Article 10(2) of the Protocol to ensure application of the new rules on the Court's jurisdiction as soon as possible.

An awkward question arises, however, as regards damages actions against the EU institutions. Does the application of the Court's new jurisdiction when an amending act is adopted give it jurisdiction to rule over the EU's damages liability in respect of the previous act? If so, does the five-year limitation period as regards the institutions' liability start to run as regards the previous act from the time of the application of the Court's new jurisdiction due to the adoption of the amending act? The logical answer should be that while the Court's jurisdiction over damages liability will now apply as regards the pre-existing acts which have now been amended (although not to any pre-existing provisions which have been repealed by the amending act), the five-year limitation on the institutions' liability as regards such acts must be calculated from the date of adoption of the *original* act, rather than the amending act, which will in many cases mean that the time limit has expired. Restarting the time limit applicable to the institutions' damages liability must be rejected because it would contradict the wording of the Statute of the Court.[72]

Article 10(3) of the Protocol specifies that the limitation on the Court's jurisdiction shall cease to have effect five years after the entry into force of the Treaty of Lisbon. This extinguishes any further need to define 'amendments' of a pre-existing act as far as the Court's jurisdiction is concerned, although the issue will remain relevant to the legal effect of pre-existing measures and to the various

---

[71] See by analogy Cases 6/71 *Rheinmuhlen* [1971] ECR 719, C-312/93 Peterbroek [1995] ECR I-4599, and C-430 and 431/93 *Van Schijndel* [1995] ECR I-4705.
[72] See n 44 above.

opt-outs over those measures.[73] This raises again the question of the effect of the Court's new jurisdiction on the cases pending before the Court itself or national courts when the new jurisdiction takes its full effect. The simple answer to that question is that cases pending at the time when Article 10(3) takes effect should be treated in the same way as cases which were pending at the time when Article 10(2) became applicable—as discussed above. But the application of the Court's jurisdiction over damages in this context is irrelevant in this context for, as noted above, by the end of the five-year transitional period in the Protocol, the five-year limitation for bringing proceedings for non-contractual liability will rule out the Court's jurisdiction over liability for pre-existing third pillar acts.

III. Legal Effect

A. Current Legal Position

As for the legal effect of third pillar measures, the Court of Justice has confirmed that, although Article 34 of the TEU rules out the direct effect of Framework Decisions, Framework Decisions are nevertheless subject to the principle of indirect effect, which requires national courts to interpret national law in light of the EU measure as far as possible, as long as such an interpretation does not aggravate a person's criminal liability as a matter of substantive criminal law.[74] In part, this principle is derived from the principle of loyal cooperation, which applies to the third pillar even though it is not expressly mentioned in the current Title VI of the TEU.[75]

The Court of Justice has also ruled that third pillar Common Positions have no legal effect on third parties.[76] However, the Court has not ruled on the legal effect of third pillar Conventions or Decisions, or on the legal effect of other third pillar measures adopted before the Treaty of Amsterdam (Joint Positions and Joint Actions). Nor has it ruled on whether the principle of supremacy applies in some form to the third pillar, on whether the EC principles concerning external competence apply, or on whether the EC principles on liability in damages, and more generally of effective remedies for breaches of EC law, apply to the third pillar.[77]

---

[73] See n 51 above. Indeed, the importance of defining 'amending acts' as regards the opt-outs is not confined to pre-existing third pillar measures, but applies to any case where a JHA measure is to be amended, regardless of whether that measure was adopted before or after the Treaty of Lisbon comes into force and regardless of whether that proposed amendment concerns policing and criminal law on the one hand or immigration, asylum, or civil law on the other.

[74] See Case C-105/03 *Pupino* [2005] ECR I-5285.

[75] See *Pupino*, ibid, and Case C-355/04 P *SEGI* [2007] ECR I-1657.

[76] *SEGI*, ibid.

[77] On all these issues, except external competence, see S Peers, 'Salvation outside the Church? Judicial Protection in the Third Pillar after the Pupino and SEGI judgments' (2007) 44 CML Rev 883, Spaventa, 'Opening Pandora's Box: Some Reflections on the Constitutional Effects of the

B. Treaty of Lisbon

Article 9 of the transitional Protocol provides that pre-existing third pillar measures (and foreign policy measures) shall retain their legal effect until they are 'repealed, annulled or amended' by measures adopted after the entry into force of the Treaty of Lisbon. This clause has its origins in one of the final provisions of the Constitutional Treaty,[78] which sought more generally to ensure the continued application of previous measures in light of the new legal framework of the Constitutional Treaty. While this provision has the primary purpose of guaranteeing the validity of these pre-existing measures,[79] it should also be interpreted, in the absence of a more specific provision on this issue, as preserving the distinct rules on the *legal effect* of pre-existing third pillar measures, in particular their lack of direct effect (at least as regards Decisions and Framework Decisions), until such as time as they are amended.

The definition of an 'amendment' for this purpose must surely be the same as in Article 10 of the Protocol, as discussed in detail above. This is because there is no indication to the contrary in the Protocol, and because a consistent interpretation of the two provisions would best accomplish the objective of ensuring a transition as smoothly as possible to the rules in the new Treaty. On the same grounds, Article 9, by analogy with Article 10, must surely 'transform' the legal effect of the pre-existing measures at the same time as Article 10 alters the Court's jurisdiction in respect of those measures[80]—which, as I argue above, should be the date of entry into force of the amending act. However, it should be noted that, as compared with the Court's new jurisdiction, there is no time limit for the application of the new rules on legal effect to all pre-existing third pillar measures. So some of those measures will possibly be subject to the old rules on legal effect for more than five years, and indeed potentially indefinitely, even though the Court will enjoy its full jurisdiction over them after five years. The pre-existing measures will also continue to have their prior legal effects in any Member States which opt out of the amending measures, while remaining bound by the pre-existing rules.[81]

If the Court of Justice is asked about the legal effect of pre-existing third pillar measures after the entry into force of the Treaty of Lisbon, it might be tempting for the Court to conclude that the 'Amsterdam era' of the third pillar was, in

---

Decision in *Pupino*' (2007) 3 Eur Const Law Review 5, and Lenaerts and Corthaut, 'Of Birds and Hedges: The Role of Primacy in Invoking Norms of EU Law' (2006) 31 ELR 287.

[78] Article IV-437 of the Constitutional Treaty.

[79] This explains the reference to annulment and repeal of those measures.

[80] Leaving aside the automatic application of the Court's new jurisdiction after five years as provided for in Article 10(3) of the Protocol, as there is no equivalent of this rule in Article 9 of the Protocol.

[81] See S Peers, 'In a world of their own? Opt-outs from EU Justice and Home Affairs Law and the Treaty of Lisbon', forthcoming.

hindsight, merely a transitional period between intergovernmentalism and the application of the Community method, and therefore to rule that as many EC law principles as possible govern pre-existing third pillar acts. This interpretation would also ensure greater consistency of application as between pre-existing and post-Lisbon acts in this field.

The Court may well have the opportunity to clarify these outstanding issues following the entry into force of the Treaty of Lisbon, by exercising the pre-existing jurisdiction that it will retain over pre-existing measures. The more that the third pillar legal order resembles the Community legal order, according to the Court's future judgments, the less important Article 9 of the Protocol will be and *vice versa*. As noted above, it is likely that some pre-existing measures will not be amended within the five-year transitional period, which (if correct) would mean therefore that the Court would have an extended opportunity to rule on the legal effect of such measures after that period.

IV. Conclusions

The current third pillar has been marked not just by a surprising degree of activism by the Court of Justice, but also by considerable concerns from some national courts about the compatibility of the EAW in particular with their national constitutions.[82] While an inextricable conflict between the EU and national legal orders was narrowly avoided in such cases, there could be a greater risk of such clashes in future, in light of the clarified competence, extension of qualified majority voting, stronger legal effect of EU measures, and enhanced jurisdiction for the Court of Justice in this area.

To avoid a paralysing conflict, it will first and foremost be up to the EU's political institutions to take sufficient account of the constitutional concerns of the Member States when considering legislation. But it will be furthermore up to the Court of Justice to take particular account of the concerns of national constitutional courts in its dialogue with them concerning future policing and criminal law measures. If the Treaty of Lisbon is ratified, we shall soon see how well the Court will be able to manage this sensitive task.

---

[82] See Mitsilegas, 'Constitutional Principles of the European Community and European Criminal Law', VIII European Journal of Law Reform 301; Mitsilegas, 'The Constitutional Implications of Mutual Recognition in Criminal Matters in the European Union', (2006) 43 CML Rev 1277; Komarek, 'European Constitutionalism andt he European Arrest Warrant: In Search of Contrapunctual Principles' (2007) 43 CML Rev 9.

How Fundamental are Fundamental Principles? Primacy and Fundamental Rights after Lisbon

*Lucia Serena Rossi**

I. The Primacy of EU Law and its Limits: A Gentlemen's Agreement

The primacy of European law over the laws of Member States is a well-known public secret which apparently is best not written into the European Treaties. This has been confirmed by the recent evolution from the Constitutional Treaty to the Lisbon Treaty with the over 40-year-old principle, finally codified by the former (and prior to that by the Giscard Draft), being deleted by the latter. In that context, politicians realised what lawyers were already aware of and, horrified, vetoed the codification of the principle.

It is peculiar that the most fundamental of the EU legal order's fundamental principles has never succeeded in attaining an explicit affirmation in the EC-EU founding treaties, despite their many revisions. Thus, the principle of primacy remains a judge-made rule which, nonetheless, ensures that EU law is recognized by all Member States as outweighing national laws.

Such a state of affairs, not particularly worrying for common law legal systems, is puzzling for many civil law countries where written Constitutions have been modified in order to recognize a principle that, apparently, cannot be ratified by all Member States.

A. Yes, but ... (Constitutional or Supreme Courts and the Concept of Primacy)

It is briefly worth recalling that supremacy has been introduced by the EU judicial system which itself comprises the ECJ and national Constitutional or Supreme Courts.

* Professor of EU Law, Director Interdepartmental Research Centre on EU LAW (CIRDCE) University of Bologna.

In light of the enduring silence of the Treaties, a long-distance dialogue between national Constitutional Courts and the ECJ has led the former to define their position as regards the delicate question of EU law in the national hierarchy of legal values.

It is important to note that the theoretical starting point was not identical in all the original members of the European Economic Community. Whilst France and Belgium recognized the supremacy of international treaties over subsequent national laws, other national Constitutions, which—as in Italy—had been adopted prior to the signature of the 1951 European Coal and Steel Community Treaty and 1957 EEC Treaty, did not contain similar provisions.

As is well known, in *Van Gend & Loos*[1] the ECJ qualified the European Community as 'a new legal order of international law for the benefit of which the states have limited their sovereign rights, albeit within limited fields, and the subjects of which comprise not only the Member States but also their nationals' and in *Costa-Enel*[2] it pronounced the primacy of EU law: 'Contrary to ordinary international treaties, the EEC Treaty has created its own legal system which ... became an integral part of the legal systems of the Member States and which their courts are bound to apply.'

The initial acceptance of such developments was not easy for the Italian Constitutional Court, especially in light of the fact that only a few months before (in the same case, ie *Costa-Enel*) it had stated that previous (European) rules could be repealed by later (Italian) legislation.[3] That being so, a few years later, in *Frontini*,[4] the same Court held that Article 11 of the Italian Constitution (which had originally been drafted with the United Nations in mind) allowed for the necessary limitations of sovereignty for membership of the European Community. Nevertheless, the Court considered that such a surrender of sovereignty could not be unlimited. In particular, Community rules could not outweigh the protection of the fundamental rights or the fundamental principles enshrined in the Italian Constitution. It was only with the *Granital*[5] case that the Italian Court finally recognized that, as prescribed by the ECJ in *Simmenthal*,[6] all national judges have a duty to set Italian law aside when it is incompatible with EU law without the need to request the authorization of the Constitutional Court. Nonetheless, it maintained the same exceptions set in *Frontini*: whenever the European rule infringes a fundamental principle of the Italian constitutional system or a fundamental right, it will be for the Constitutional Court to decide

---

[1] Case 26/62 [1963] ECR 1.

[2] Case 6/64 *Costa-Enel* [1964] ECR 585.

[3] See Corte Costituzionale Italiana, n 14/1974, para 14.

[4] See Corte Costituzionale Italiana, n 173/1983.

[5] See Corte Costituzionale Italiana, n 170/1984. See inter alia Gaja, 'New developments in a Continuing Story: the relationship between EEC Law and Italian Law' (1990) 27 CML Rev 83–95, Adinolfi, 'The Judicial Application of Community Law in Italy' (1998) 35 CML Rev 1313–1369.

[6] Case 106/1977 *Amministrazione delle Finanze dello Stato v Simmenthal SpA* [1978] ECR 629.

what rule should prevail.[7] Such exceptions were called '*counterlimits*' by those who considered EC primacy as a *limit* to the binding force of Italian law.

The idea that certain essential national values can defy EC law primacy was shared by other Constitutional Courts which re-affirmed their competence to assess conflicts between fundamental values and EU Law. Throughout the years, however, the primacy has gradually but universally been accepted as the rule, with national limits coming to be regarded as exceptions. Each Court, however, created its own theory, depending on the characteristics of its national Constitution.[8]

In *Solange I*[9] the German Constitutional Court held that the applicability of secondary Community law in the Federal Republic was subject to a fundamental rights review by the Bundesverfassungsgericht. Subsequently, in *Solange II*[10] it changed its stance, declaring that it would no longer control the compatibility of Community law with German fundamental rights, 'as long as the European Communities, and in particular the case law of the Court of Justice of the European Communities, generally ensured an effective protection of fundamental rights'.[11] Following some reserve in the *Maastricht Urteil*,[12] in the *Banana Case*[13] the same Court stated that its control would only apply if the EC protection of fundamental rights no longer functioned, a hypothesis that must not be evaluated in light of a single case, but of a wider perspective, revealing general structural deficits on the European level.[14] Consequently, the applicant must prove that European law, and the judgments handed down by the Court of Justice of the European Communities, have fallen below the standard of protection requested by the '*Solange II*' decision.

As regards the French Conseil Constitutionnel, we can see that it originally argued that a Community Act could not be transposed into French law if

---

[7] In the case *Fragd*, Corte Costituzionale Italiana, n 232/1989, a violation of the principle of due process by the Court of Justice (annulling regulations without retroactive effect) could have been envisaged. The Italian Constitutional Court went close to declaring such a violation, but diplomatically avoided doing so. After that judgement, the ECJ followed the Italian Court, changing its practice.

[8] See on this subject Besselink 'Entrapped by the Maximum Standard: on Fundamental Rights, Pluralism and Subsidiarity in the European Union' (1998) 35 CML Rev 629–680.

[9] Decision of the German Federal Constitutional Court of the 29 May 1974, BVerfGE 37, 279. This decision followed the ECJ judgment of 1970 in the Case 11/70 *Internationale Handelsgesellschaft mbH v Einfuhr- und Vorratsstelle für Getreide und Futtermittel*) [1970] ECR 1125. This would apply 'as long as the integration process has not progressed so far that the Community law also receives a catalogue of fundamental rights decided on by a parliament and of settled validity, which is adequate in comparison with the catalogue of fundamental rights contained in the Grundgesetz.'

[10] Decision of the German Federal Constitutional Court of 22 October 1986, BVefGE 73, 339–388.

[11] Decision of the German Federal Constitutional Court, cited above at n 9, paras 378–381.

[12] Decision of the German Federal Constitutional Court of the 12 October 1993, 2 BvR L 134/92 and 2159/92.

[13] Decision of the German Federal Constitutional Court of 7 June 2000, 2 BvL 1/97.

[14] Dieter H Scheuing, 'The Approach to European Law in German Jurisprudence' 5 German Law Journal No 6 2004, available online at: <http://www.germanlawjournal.com/article.php?id=446>.

inconsistent with an 'express provision of the French Constitution'.[15] Such an attitude was subsequently overturned to cover conflicts with the 'national identity of Member States inherent to their fundamental political and constitutional structures',[16] and finally 'rules and principles inherent to the French constitutional identity'.[17]

On the other hand, the Spanish Constitutional Court has drawn a distinction between the primacy of EU Law and the supremacy of the Constitution itself, with the latter being seen as hierarchically superior to the former.[18]

Where the national system does not provide for a Constitutional Court, the question has been settled by other Supreme jurisdictions. The House of Lords has rejected the doctrine of implied repeal for certain 'constitutional statutes' such as the 1972 European Community Act stating that due to their importance they may only be repealed or amended by Parliament's express intervention.[19] In the event of a contrast between EU legislation and fundamental or constitutional rights guaranteed by English law (this must probably also be read to comprise cases of incompatibility with other 'constitutional statutes'[20]), the question is whether the European Communities Act can be considered as wide enough to incorporate that measure into national law. The principle of EU law supremacy must therefore originate from, and be authorized by, Parliament. Such an authorization is not unconditional and absolute given that, according to English constitutional law, Parliament does not have the power to subordinate the doctrine of Parliamentary sovereignty to the principle of EU supremacy.

The above analysis could include a number of other Constitutional or Supreme Court doctrines[21] which accept the primacy of European law in different guises

---

[15] Décision n 2004–496 DC du 10 juin 2004, loi pour la confiance dans l'économie numérique.

[16] Décision n 2004–505 DC du 19 novembre 2004, Traité établissant une Constitution pour l'Europe, See Richards, 'The Supremacy of Community Law before the French Constitutional Court' 31 EL Rev 2006, 499–517.

[17] Décision n 2006–540 DC du 27 juillet 2006, Loi relative au droit d'auteur et aux droits voisins dans la société de l'information (DADVSI).

[18] Tribunal Constitucional Declaration of 13 December 2004.

[19] English and Wales High Court (Administrative Court), decision [2002] EWHC 195 Admin, *Thoburn v Sunderland City Council* (<http://www.bailii.org/ew/cases/EWHC/Admin/2002/195. html>). See S Boyron, 'In the Name of European Law: the Metric Martyrs case' (2002) 27 ELR 771–779; A Biondi, 'La supremazia dell'ordinamento comunitario e i "martiri del sistema metrico" nell'ordinamento inglese', Quaderni Costituzionali 2003 847–848.

[20] Lord Justice Laws, in *Thoburn v Sunderland City Council*, cited above at n 19, qualifies as of 'constitutional statutes' the Magna Carta, the Bill of Rights 1689, the Acts of Union 1707, the Reform Acts, the Human Rights Act 1998, the Scotland Act 1998, the Government of Wales Act 1998, and the European Communities Act 1972. Such statutes are, because of their constitutional importance, to be protected from implied repeal and, whilst not entrenched in English law, can only be repealed by the express intervention of Parliament.

[21] The Slovenian Constitution declares that international organizations to which the exercise of part of the sovereign rights is transferred must be based 'on respect for human rights and fundamental freedoms, democracy and the principles of the rule of law'. According to Ciril Ribičič, Judge of the Constitutional Court of the Republic of Slovenia, the Constitutional Court will not be allowed

but which, in principle, do not consider it as absolute. Therefore, it can be argued that each national legal order has taken a different path to accepting the primacy of European Law. The essential values to be preserved—and which might restrict the supremacy of EU law—are not interpreted in the same way throughout the Member States.

From this perspective, and if one considers that the European legal system and national Constitutions are distinct elements forming a single legal order (monistic approach), they would be interlocked in an odd hierarchy. At the summit we would find certain national constitutional fundamental principles with hierarchical superiority over European law. The latter would then itself have supremacy over non-fundamental national constitutional principles and ordinary national laws which would represent the lowest tier of the hierarchy. One should note that as the top fundamental principles are not identical, they would retain a national character and thus would need to be defined by the competent national Constitutional Court.

This representation could also be translated into a dualistic approach, without changing the final result. Even if the relationship were not considered as hierarchical but was based on an attribution of competences, the final word on the delimitation of such competences would be a prerogative of national Constitutional or Supreme Courts.

B. No, but... (The ECJ on Constitutional Values as Limits to Primacy)

As stated above, all Courts (national and/or European) seem to have developed their own theory on the supremacy of EU law. Nonetheless, a common element emerges: the protection of certain fundamental values is a potential limit to the supremacy of EU law.

That being so, the idea of what principles and what rights are so fundamental to prevent the application of Community law may have different interpretations when the unique parameter is the national Constitution.

The Court of Justice (ECJ and Court of First Instance (CFI)) have often explicitly rejected that national constitutional principles can limit the force of European law. This is apparent in *Kreil*,[22] where the principle of equality stemming from the Treaty was considered more important than the German 'constitutional' prohibition of enrolling women in the army. Moreover, in cases such as

---

to react in cases in which national interests in general are violated by EU law, but only for violations concerning human rights and fundamental freedoms, democracy, and the principles of the rule of law. See Implementing European Standards into the Case Law of the Constitutional Court, available online at: <http://www.us-rs.si/en/index.php?sv_path=3583,3367,3368,3379>.

[22] Case C-285/1998 *Tanja Kreil v Bundesrepublik Deutschland* [2000] ECR I-69.

Internationale Handelsgesellshaft,[23] *Dow Chemical*,[24] and *Gonnelli*,[25] the Court has reiterated that in so far as the EU Treaty contains (more or less explicit) derogations such as public policy, mandatory requirements etc, Member States cannot claim infringement of fundamental rights or principles formulated by their national Constitutions in order to reject the validity or binding effects of a Community measure. Finally, the Court has also held that a Member State cannot invoke provisions, practices, or situations present in its domestic legal order (including those resulting from the internal constitutional organization) to justify the failure to observe obligations arising under Community law.[26]

Notwithstanding its express refusal to confirm the existence of national constitutional limits, the ECJ has shown its willingness to grant them a substantial value rapidly developing the concept of 'essential principles' of the European legal order to assess the legality of Community Acts. Nonetheless, the reasoning adopted by the ECJ stood in stark contrast with that followed by national Constitutional Courts. In fact, as the EEC Treaty was originally conceived on a functional basis, the general category of fundamental rights received no mention, forcing the Court to refer to external sources: 'common constitutional traditions',[27] and the European Convention on Human Rights.[28]

[23] See ECJ in Case 11/70 *Internationale Handelsgesellschaft mbH v Einfuhr- und Vorratsstelle für Getreide und Futtermittel*) [1970] ECR 1125, para 3: 'The validity of a Community measure or its effect within a Member State cannot be affected by allegations that it runs counter to either fundamental rights as formulated by the constitution of that state or the principles of a national constitutional structure.'

[24] 'The validity of Community measures can only be judged in the light of Community law and, therefore, reference either to infringements of fundamental rights as formulated in the Constitution of a Member State or to the principles of a national constitutional structure cannot affect the validity of a Community measure or its effect in the territory of that State'. See ECJ Joined Cases 97/87 to 99/87 *Dow Chemical Iberica SA, and others v Commission of the European Communities* [1989] ECR 03165, para 38.

[25] See order of the CFI, Case T-231/02 *Gonnelli and AIFO v Commission of the European Communities* [2004] II-1051, para 57: 'Furthermore, in their observations on the objection of inadmissibility, the applicants cannot maintain that, to remedy this alleged lack of judicial protection, the Italian Constitutional Court could refrain from applying Community measures contrary to the fundamental rights proclaimed in the national Constitution since, in accordance with settled case-law, Community law has primacy over national law (Case 6/64 Costa [1964] ECR 614)'.

[26] See, inter alia, Case C-87/02 *Commission v Italy* [2004] ECR I-5975, para 38; Case C-102/06, *Commission v Austria*, not published in the ECR, para 9; Case C-212/06 *Government of the French Community and Walloon Government v Flemish Government*, not published in the ECR.

[27] See Case 11/70 *Internationale Handelsgesellschaft mbH v Einfuhr- und Vorratsstelle für Getreide und Futtermittel*) [1970] ECR 1125, para 12: '...fundamental rights form an integral part of the general principles of law, the observance of which it ensures in safeguarding these rights, the court is bound to draw inspiration from constitutional traditions common to the member states, and it cannot therefore uphold measures which are incompatible with fundamental rights recognized and protected by the constitutions of those states'.

[28] Case 4/73 *J Nold, Kohlen- und Baustoffgroßhandlung v Commission of the European Communities*) [1974] ECR 491, para 13: 'fundamental rights form an integral part of the general principles of law, the observance of which it ensures in safeguarding these rights, the court is bound to draw inspiration from constitutional traditions common to the member states, and it cannot therefore uphold measures which are incompatible with fundamental rights recognized and protected by the constitutions of those states. Similarly, international treaties for the protection of human rights on which the member states have collaborated or of which they are signatories, can supply guidelines which should be followed within the framework of community law.'

Although having rejected the idea that national Constitutions may formally limit EC law primacy, the ECJ seems to grant the former a substantial role as parameter of validity of Community acts. However, the reference to common constitutional traditions is not a mere *renvoi* as the Court tends to interpret such traditions in the light of the EC legal framework,[29] in an attempt to declare that they are also fundamental principles of the EU/Community. In *Hauer* the Court stated that common constitutional traditions are a 'source of inspiration' and international treaties 'can supply guidelines which should be followed within the framework of community law'.[30]

In more recent case law the Court simply, and almost mechanically, refers to common constitutional traditions without giving further details (for instance concerning the principle of retroactive application of more lenient penalties[31]).

The concept of common constitutional tradition is not to be understood as the sum of all the rules contained in national Constitutions, nor does the Court attempt to compare all Constitutions in order to determine a sort of minimum common denominator. The ECJ merely limits its evaluation to certain constitutions, starting with that of the claimant State and concluding that a certain principle is common to other Constitutions and, more importantly, that it is to be considered as a fundamental principle of the community legal order. By carrying out such an analysis, national constitutional values, once *external* to EC law, are *internalized*, becoming an integral part of the Community system.

Such a logic ensures that 'pride' is preserved. In fact, respect for national values is guaranteed without endangering the primacy of EC law, and the EC legal order appears to be a self-contained system. However, and above all, it is up to the ECJ to determine what should be considered 'fundamental' and/or 'common'. The Court, in fact, still refers to an 'EU' notion of fundamental rights, which embraces national Constitutions, the European Court of Human Rights (ECHR) and, of late, the Charter of Fundamental rights.

In recent years the Luxembourg judges have not hesitated to prioritize fundamental rights when weighing them against market freedoms. In certain cases, reference is explicitly made to the specific national Constitution at issue, as in

---

[29] Case 44/79 *Hauer v Land Rheinland-Pfalz* [1979] ECR 3727, para 14: 'the question of a possible infringement of fundamental rights by a measure of the community institutions can only be judged in the light of community law itself. The introduction of special criteria for assessment stemming from the legislation or constitutional law of a particular member state would, by damaging the substantive unity and efficacy of community law, lead inevitably to the destruction of the unity of the common market and the jeopardizing of the cohesion of the community.'

[30] Case 44/79, *Hauer*, ibid, para 15. See also Case 29/69 *Erich Stauder v City of Ulm—Sozialam* [1969] ECR 00419, para 7; Case C-274/99 *Bernard Connolly v Commission of the European Communities* [2001] ECR I-01611, para 37; Case C-283/05 *ASML (ASML Netherlands BV v Semiconductor Industry Services GmbH (SEMIS))* [2005] ECR I-12041, para 26.

[31] See Joined Cases C-387/02, C-391/02, and C-403/02, *Criminal Proceedings against Silvio Berlusconi and Others* [2005] ECR I-3565, paras 67 to 69; Case C-45/06 *Campina GmbH & Co, formerly TUFFI Campina emzett GmbH v Hauptzollamt Frankfurt (Oder)* [2007] I-2089, para 32; Case C-420/06 *Rüdiger Jager v Amt für Landwirtschaft Bützow*, not published in the ECR.

Schmidberger[32] and *Omega*.[33] Moreover, the ECJ seems eager to appear as a Constitutional Court and its case law concerning the protection of fundamental rights has sometimes been very radical. In *Carpenter*,[34] for example, the scope of the Treaty was clearly over-stretched in order to protect individual rights against a Member State.

If a common ground for the evaluation of fundamental rights is provided to all Member States by the European Convention of Human Rights (which according to the Court has a 'special significance in that respect'[35]), the same cannot be said for common constitutional traditions.

In particular, it is up to the Court to decide when a constitutional tradition can be qualified as 'common'. Constitutional values which, although very significant for one Member State, are not considered as common constitutional traditions, may not be worthy of regard for the ECJ.

In a few cases the ECJ has granted certain deeply-rooted national constitutional values special consideration, seemingly of a more substantial and political nature than a formal and legal one. In *Grogan*,[36] the Court succeeded (with a certain amount of difficulty) in interpreting the Common market (and its own jurisdiction) so as allow the Irish prohibition on abortion to limit the free movement of services and the fundamental right of expression.

In other cases the Court reconciles national constitutional principles and Community Acts by exploiting the flexibility allowed in the transposition of directives. In *Fazenda Pública*,[37] the Court was asked to determine whether, when

---

[32] Case C-112/00 *Eugen Schmidberger, Internationale Transporte und Planzüge v Republik Österreich* [2003] ECR I-5659 para 69: 'the Austrian authorities were inspired by considerations linked to respect of the fundamental rights of the demonstrators to freedom of expression and freedom of assembly, which are enshrined in and guaranteed by the ECHR and the Austrian Constitution', and para 74: 'Thus, since both the Community and its Member States are required to respect fundamental rights, the protection of those rights is a legitimate interest which, in principle, justifies a restriction of the obligations imposed by Community law, even under a fundamental freedom guaranteed by the Treaty such as the free movement of goods'.

[33] Case C-36/02 *Omega Spielhallen- und Automatenaufstellungs-GmbH v Oberbürgermeisterin der Bundesstadt Bonn* [2004] ECR I-9609, para 35: 'Since both the Community and its Member States are required to respect fundamental rights, the protection of those rights is a legitimate interest which, in principle, justifies a restriction of the obligations imposed by Community law, even under a fundamental freedom guaranteed by the Treaty such as the freedom to provide services'.

[34] Case C-60/00 *Mary Carpenter v Secretary of State for the Home Department* [2002] ECR I-6279.

[35] See, inter alia, Case C-260/89 *Elliniki Radiophonia Tiléorassi AE and Panellinia Omospondia Syllogon Prossopikou v Dimotiki Etairia Pliroforissis and Sotirios Kouvelas and Nicolaos Avdellas and others* [1991] ECR I-2925, para 41; Case C-274/99 *Bernard Connolly v Commission of the European Communitie* [2001] ECR I-01611, para 37; Case C-94/00 *Roquette Frères SA v Directeur général de la concurrence, de la consommation et de la répression des fraudes, and Commission of the European Communities* [2002] ECR I-9011, para 25; Case C-112/00 *Schmidberger*, cited above at n 32, para 71 and Case C-36/02, *Omega*, cited above at n 33, para 33.

[36] Case C-159/90 *The Society for the Protection of Unborn Children Ireland Ltd v Stephen Grogan and others* [1991] ECR I-4685.

[37] Case C-446/98 *Fazenda Pública v Câmara Municipal do Porto—Reference for a preliminary ruling: Supremo Tribunal Administrativo—Portugal* [2000] ECR I-11435.

faced with a national provision empowering the Minister of Finance to define significant distortions of competition on a case-by-case basis, the Portuguese Court should find that provision unconstitutional, for failure to comply with the principle that taxation must have a legal basis, or whether it should apply it by virtue of the fact that it complied with the Community Sixth Directive (which has primacy over national Constitutions). The Court considered that, since the Sixth Directive does not require that in transposing it Member States grant an administrative authority power to specify what is covered by the concept of 'significant distortions of competition', it is possible for the former to adopt other methods of transposition which are consistent both with the Directive and with a national Constitution. Similar reasoning has been applied with regard to the Swedish Constitution in *Unibet*.[38]

Finally, the Court has frequently evaluated what could generally be defined as 'constitutional cultures' of the Member States—when they are invoked as a means for avoiding the application of general common rules—with the same strict test of proportionality employed to assess mandatory requirements. This is apparent in the case law concerning language and protection of minorities (*Groener*,[39] *Mutsch*,[40] *Otto Bickel e Ulrich Franz*,[41] *Angonese*[42]), in some aspects of citizenship, such as the regulation of surnames (*Garcia Avello*[43]) or the conditions of the right to vote (*Eman Sevinger*[44]), where the weighing of the national interest is carried out with reference to the community principle of non-discrimination on grounds of nationality. Furthermore, in cases involving the organization of armies (*Sirdar*,[45] *Kreil*,[46] *Dory*[47]) the Court, although recognizing that Member States possess exclusive competence to regulate such a subject matter, analysed

[38] Case C-432/05 *Unibet (London) Ltd, Unibet (International) Ltd v Justitiekanslern* [2007] ECR I-2271.

[39] Case C-379/87 *Anita Groener v Minister for Education and the City of Dublin Vocational Educational Committee* [1989] ECR 3967. In this case Court accepted the Irish Minister for Education's refusal to appoint a Dutch art teacher who had failed a test intended to assess her knowledge of the Irish language on the ground that teachers have an essential role to play, not only through the teaching which they provide but also by their participation in the daily life of the school and the privileged relationship which they have with their pupils.

[40] Case 139/84 *Criminal Proceedings against Robert Heinrich Maria Mutsch* [1985] ECR 2681. According to the Court, the principle of free movement of workers requires that a worker who is a national of one Member State and habitually resides in another Member State be entitled to require that criminal proceedings against him take place in a language other than the language normally used in proceedings before the court which tries him if workers who are nationals of the host Member State have that right in the same circumstances.

[41] Case C-274/97 *Criminal Proceedings against Horst Otto Bickel and Ulrich Franz* [1998] I-7673.

[42] Case C-281/98 *Roman Angonese v Cassa di Risparmio di Bolzano SpA* [2000] ECR I-4139.

[43] Case C-148/02 *Carlos Garcia Avello v État belge* [2003] ECR I-11613.

[44] Case C-300/04 *MG Eman and OB Sevinger v College van Burgemeester en wethouders van Den Haag* [2006] ECR I-8055.

[45] Case C-273/97 *Angela Maria Sirdar v The Army Board and Secretary of State for Defence* [1999] ECR I-7403.

[46] Case C-285/98 *Tanja Kreil v Bundesrepublik Deutschland* [2000] ECR I-69.

[47] Case C-186/01 *Alexander Dory v Bundesrepublik Deutschland* [2003] ECR I-2479.

the consequences that such an organization could have on the community principle of gender equality in employment.

In conclusion, it may be argued that the primacy of European law and the hierarchy of supreme values are still founded on a sort of constitutional custom, or on what may be better defined as a *gentlemen's agreement*, ie a silent compromise among different co-existing theories relating to the foundations of the whole system. Although ambiguous, such a system appears to be effective. The judiciary of Member States and of the EU, albeit prepared to state their theoretical idea of hierarchy, carefully avoid its extreme practical application which would provoke a crisis of the whole system.

Fundamental principles remain a sort of grey area, where vagueness and flexibility are two sides of the same coin. A wise use of the judges' discretionary powers can create a common system of values, based on the awareness and mutual respect of diversities.

II. Codifying Primacy: Can Ambiguity be Abandoned?

The Constitutional Treaty, signed in Rome on 29 October 2004, expressly stated that primary law and law adopted by the institutions of the Union in exercising competences conferred on it (secondary law) have primacy over the law of the Member States (Article I-6).

In order to respond to the many criticisms that such a stipulation (already inserted into the Giscard Draft) had encountered, a Declaration was annexed to the Constitutional Treaty. The content of such a Declaration was rather ambiguous, providing that 'the Conference notes that Article I-6 reflects existing case law of the Court of Justice of the European Communities and of the Court of First Instance'. It seems that the primary objective was to exclude ECJ competence in the CFSP. However, it also paved the way for an 'ECJ-like' idea of primacy of EU law (which, as we have seen, is not readily reconcilable with that advanced by national Constitutional or Supreme Courts).

That being so, the above was offset by Article I-5, according to which the Union must respect the national identities of Member States, inherent in their fundamental political and constitutional structures, inclusive of regional and local self-government and their essential State functions. The fact that the Charter of Fundamental Rights was part of the Constitutional Treaty could also have been regarded as a further guarantee of national fundamental values as, in so far as they were mirrored by the Charter, they gained new strength vis-à-vis incompatible secondary EU law.

Nonetheless, for many Member States this was more alarming than reassuring.[48] The mere codification of the principle of primacy within a Treaty qualified

---

[48] This effect of the word 'Constitution' had been foreseen by Dashwood, 'The Relationship between the Member States and the European Union/European Community' (2004) 41 CML Rev 335–381.

as *constitutional* not only provoked the indignation of certain ill-informed politician but was also paradoxical for national Constitutional Courts.

Throughout the short life (or quasi-life) of the Constitutional Treaty, many new judgments on the relationship between national Constitutions and the Treaty were delivered, in a sort of *actio finium regundorum,* reaffirming the ultimate sovereignty of national Constitutions' basic principles. A few examples are the Spanish and French Constitutional Court decisions on the Constitutional Treaty itself.[49]

In the same period, Constitutional judgments relating to the Framework Decision on the European Arrest Warrant show that even when faced with the same problem, single Constitutional Courts may react differently. As the prohibition to extradite citizens is considered as a fundamental principle by many Constitutions, the question of constitutional consistency of the Framework Decision was raised before several national Constitutional Courts, leading to numerous different solutions. The Polish and Cypriot Courts, although maintaining that it could be infringed by the Framework Decision, concluded that, in light of the importance of the latter's aims, the national Constitution was to be amended.[50] The German Bundesverfassungsgericht decided that it was the German law incorrectly implementing the Framework Decision (and not the Framework Decision itself) that should be declared unconstitutional. The Belgian Court questioned the compatibility of the Framework Decision with fundamental rights, asking the ECJ for a preliminary ruling. The latter concluded as to an absence of violation.[51]

One of the real (and again paradoxical) effects of the aborted Constitutional Treaty has been that of bringing the issue of supreme values of the EU legal order to the fore. The codification of the gentlemen's agreement between judges proved to be too challenging, even 40 years after *Costa-Enel.*

Finally, as a result of the de-constitutionalisation process, all references to primacy have been erased from the text of the Lisbon Treaty. Only a Declaration of the Conference (n 17 above) recognizes that, in accordance with well settled case law of the Court of Justice, 'the Treaties and the law adopted by the Union on the basis of the Treaties have primacy over the law of Member States, under the conditions laid down by the said case law'.

Furthermore, the Conference has inserted an Annex containing the Opinion of the Council Legal's Service on the primacy of EC law of 22 June 2007,[52] according to which 'it results from the case law of the Court of Justice that primacy of EC law is a cornerstone principle of Community law. According to the Court, this principle is inherent to the specific nature of the European Community'.

---

[49] See Conseil constitutionnel, 19.1.2004, dc n 505/2004, Tribunal Constitucional, 13.12.2004 (1/2004).

[50] On the Polish judgment, see comment of Leczykiewicz, (2006) 43 CML Rev 1181–1191.

[51] Case C-303/05 *Advocaten voor der Wereld VZW v Leden van de Ministerraad* [2007] ECR I-3633.

[52] Opinion of the Council Legal Service 11197/07 (JUR 260).

The opinion further states that 'the fact that the principle of primacy will not be included in the future treaty shall not in any way change the existence of the principle and the existing case law of the Court of Justice'.

The legal force of these documents is weak. On the one hand, Declarations are non-binding acts, that can nevertheless be used as secondary means of interpretation. On the other hand, opinions of the Legal service of the Council are internal acts, which may give rise to some external effects only in so far they are part of the Declaration itself. Whilst a Declaration is better than nothing, it is clearly insufficient to overcome the inherent ambiguities expressed above.

As already stated, the Constitutional Treaty established an equilibrium between primacy (Article I-6) and the respect of national systems (Article I-5). Whilst the Lisbon Treaty relegates primacy to a Declaration, it preserves the safeguards to national identities. The new Article 4 of the Treaty on European Union (TEU) sketches the relations between the EU and national legal systems, combining three different principles. The logical succession of such principles is probably also intended as a legal one. First comes the classic international law principle confirming that competences not conferred upon the Union by the Treaties remain with Member States. Then, the obligation for the EU to respect the equality of Member States and their national identities, inherent in their political and constitutional fundamental structures as well as their essential State functions.

Lastly, we find what has always been the cornerstone of the relations between the Community and its Member States: the duty of loyal cooperation, with the final specification of the duties of Member States. Such a duty has been recognized by the ECJ as being mutual, operating in both directions.

As a result of the process of 'provisional constitutionalization' and subsequent 'de-constitutionalization', the principle of supremacy of EU law is still concealed, whilst its limits have been reinforced and openly affirmed.

In comparison with the current Treaties, a new obligation emerges for the EU to respect fundamental identities, constitutional structures, and essential functions of the Member Sates. Such an obligation must be observed by the EU when acting *within* its competences. The consequence is that all legislation contrasting with the fundamental constitutional structures of Member States could be annulled on grounds of violation of the Treaty.

A question arises as to whether the case law of the ECJ on constitutional values (mentioned above) can still be considered valid. In future, should constitutional traditions not common to Member States deserve higher respect or can they—when invoked against fundamental freedoms or other EU principles—still be limited by a proportionality test? Will the Lisbon Treaty change the current situation? Once again, the final word rests with the Court.

It is worth stressing that the Italian Constitutional Court has recently reaffirmed the primacy of EU law, qualifying it as 'constitutional', while other international treaties, notably the ECHR, are merely 'sub-constitutional'.[53] As a consequence whilst Italian judges may not disapply Italian laws contrary to an international Convention without requesting a preliminary constitutional ruling, they may, on the contrary, directly apply European law, calling upon the Constitutional Court only in cases involving conflicts with fundamental principles of the national Constitution. Such a strongly pro-European judgment was certainly unexpected, especially in light of the fact that the new Article 117 of the Italian Constitution (introduced by the 2001 revision[54]) does not distinguish EU legislation from international treaties, both being described as limiting the legislative powers of the Italian State and Regions. It seems that the Italian Court has interpreted the new constitutional provision in connection with Article 11 of the Constitution in order to confer a privileged status to EU law.[55] Nonetheless, if a conflict should arise between an EU rule and a fundamental principle of the Constitution, primacy can neither be automatically recognized nor granted, the final choice being left to the Constitutional Court. In cases of conflict between EU legislation and the European Convention, on the other hand, such a judgment would seem to acknowledge that Italian judges must apply the former, setting the latter aside.

Generally speaking, after Lisbon the principle of primacy may not necessarily be weakened. By appearing as a lesser threat for national constitutional identities, it might be more readily accepted by Constitutional and Supreme Courts.

III. Fundamental Rights after Lisbon

The described process of de-constitutionalization has also concerned the Charter of Fundamental Rights which, in the meantime and by virtue of several ECJ judgements,[56] has acquired the status of soft law.[57]

The Charter was undoubtedly the most—if not the only—really 'constitutional' part of the Constitutional Treaty and for this reason it has formally been removed from the Lisbon Treaty and included in a new Declaration adopted in Strasbourg on 12 December 2007 by the three EU legislative institutions.[58]

---

[53] See Corte Costituzionale Italiana, ns 348/2007 and 349/2007.

[54] Legge costituzionale 18/10/2001, n 3 (GU, n 248 del 24 ottobre 2001): 'Legislative powers shall be vested in the State and the Regions in compliance with the constitution and with the constraints deriving from EU legislation and international obligations.'

[55] See also Corte Costituzionale, n 39/2008.

[56] See Case C-13/05 *Sonia Chacón Navas* [2006] ECR I-6467; Case C-432/05 *Unibet (London) Ltd, Unibet (International) Ltd v Justitiekanslern* [2007] ECR I-2271.

[57] The Charter has been frequently employed in the legal reasoning not only by the Advocates General, the CFI, and more recently also by the ECJ, but also by national judges. For a monitoring of such a case law, see the Observatory on Fundamental Rights, available online at: <http://www.europeanrights.eu/index.php?lang=eng>.

[58] This time, unlike the 2000 Nice Declaration, the Council of Ministers was represented at the highest level.

Paradoxically, the fact that the Charter has been disembodied from the Treaty may have positive effects, in so far as it is more handy and readable for citizens whilst still maintaining its symbolic force (after all, it remains a constitutional idea). Of course, legal problems may arise as it is no longer part of the Treaty. How could the Charter be amended? Should the new procedure for ordinary revision be applied? Certainly it seems difficult to imagine that the Charter could be amended without a new Convention.

In any case the Charter represents a major step for citizens as fundamental rights finally become visible and transparent and will not continue to be a complicated secret for insiders. The Charter is a sort of *habeas corpus*, which can be invoked either to demand the annulment of acts of the EU institutions or against Member States which violate fundamental rights when implementing EU law (or when acting within the scope of the Treaty).[59] The first case is particularly important, as neither national Courts nor the ECHR may annul a Community/ Union act. In this context, the Charter not only clarifies the situation but it also reduces the wide discretionary powers of the ECJ to decide what rights are fundamental and their scope. Finally, it raises the level of fundamental rights in the EU by defining the ECHR (as well as the national constitutions[60]) as a minimum standard.

The Lisbon Treaty gives full legal value to the Charter. A new Article 6 of the TEU affirms (paragraph 1) that the Charter 'shall have the same legal value as the Treaties', specifying that it does not extend the competences of the European institutions. Although the Charter is not encompassed in a Protocol, its legal status is similar to that of Protocols, which, according to international law, have 'the same value of the Treaty' to which they pertain. For this reason the Court of Justice is competent to interpret and apply it. The same Article establishes that the rights, freedoms and principles within the Charter shall be interpreted in accordance with the general provisions in Title VII of the latter and with due regard to the so called 'Praesidium explanations', setting out the sources of those provisions, which are now referred to in the Preamble of the Charter. Paragraph 2 establishes that the Union shall accede to the ECHR.

Finally, Article 6 (paragraph 3) reminds that 'fundamental rights, as guaranteed by the European Convention for the Protection of Human Rights and Fundamental Freedoms and as they result from the constitutional traditions common to the Member States, shall constitute general principles of the Union's law.'

---

[59] See LS Rossi, 'Constitutionnalisation de l'Union européenne et des droits fondamentaux' (2002) Rev Trim Dr eur, pp 22–53.

[60] See Article 53 of the Charter, and for some remarks on the latter, see Liisberg, 'Does the EU Charter of Fundamental Rights Threaten the Supremacy of Community Law?' (2001) 38 CML Rev 1171–1199.

Reading paragraphs 1 and 3 of the new Article 6, a difference can be noticed between the Charter, which is binding and linked to specific means of interpretation, and the 'classic' category of fundamental rights, as they emerge from common constitutional traditions, and/or the ECHR. Such a differentiation may seem useless as the Charter was declared (and declares itself, see Preamble) to be a simple codification of existing fundamental rights, as settled in the ECHR and in common constitutional traditions. Nevertheless, it becomes particularly significant if one considers the opting out of the United Kingdom and Poland. Although the force of the Charter is limited as far as their legislations are concerned, these States are still fully engaged by the general principles of EU law envisaged by the Court of Justice, such as the protection of human rights.

It could be questioned whether the ECJ enjoys the same discretionary power in interpreting the Charter and general fundamental rights. On the one hand, the ECJ is the only official interpreter of the Charter, but it must respect both the Praesidium Explanations and the limits fixed by the Charter itself. It can also be expected that in the future the Court will interpret the Explanations in a more general perspective.

On the other hand, even if in principle the Luxembourg Court is not the only judge of general principles, as it cannot ignore what the ECHR and national Constitutional Courts state with regard to the European Convention and national Constitutions respectively, it may have more room for interpreting those principles. As seen above, the ECJ tends to transform them into internal values, to be applied in light of the EU system. Some limits to its discretionary power could arguably stem from the new Article 4 and, in the future, from the accession of the EU to the ECHR, which is established by Article 6 but subordinated to a problematic decision by unanimity.

It is likely that the Court will use the Charter as a term of reference and as a list of fundamental rights, nevertheless continuing to refer to the other sources. The geographical limits to the scope of the Charter (due to the opting-outs) will probably compel the Court to keep the broader category of general principles alive, as an autonomous source of fundamental rights.

The British and Polish opting-outs, referred to in the Protocol, n 30, raise numerous questions. The *consideranda* of such a Protocol state that Article 6 of the Treaty on European Union requires that the Charter be applied and interpreted strictly by the courts of Poland and of the United Kingdom. Interpretation must be in accordance with the Explanations referred to in that Article, and with the Charter itself, provided that the latter merely grants visibility to rights, freedoms, and principles already recognized by the Union, without creating new rights or principles.

Article 1 establishes that 'the Charter does not extend the ability of the Court of Justice of the EU, or any court or tribunal of Poland or of the United

Kingdom, to find that the laws, regulations or administrative provisions, practices or action of Poland or of the United Kingdom are inconsistent with the
fundamental rights, freedoms and principles that it reaffirms. In particular,
and for the avoidance of doubt, nothing in Title IV of the Charter creates justiciable rights applicable to Poland or the United Kingdom except in so far as
Poland or the United Kingdom has provided for such rights in its national law.'
The reference to Title IV only seems to be inserted by way of exemplification,
meaning that the opt-out is general. It is not very clear, however, how one must
reconcile this provision with the fact that soon after the same Protocol reaffirms that 'references in this Protocol to the operation of specific provisions of
the Charter are strictly without prejudice to the operation of other provisions
of the Charter', provided that there is no other reference to specific provisions
of the Charter.

The reasons for such opting-out are probably linked to concerns that national
judges may widen the binding force of the Charter, using an interpretation by
analogy so as to cover domestic laws outside the scope of EU legislation. In fact,
in Italy some judges already draw inspiration from the Charter, expressly referring to it in order to solve disputes of a purely domestic nature.

The picture is completed by two confusing Declarations issued by Poland.
According to the first one, 'the Charter does not affect in any way the right of
Member States to legislate in the sphere of public morality, family law, as well as
the protection of human dignity and respect for human physical and moral integrity.' By virtue of the second Declaration, Poland asserts that, having regard to
the traditional social movement of 'Solidarity', it fully respects social and labour
rights, as established by EU law, and in particular those reaffirmed in Title IV of
the Charter of Fundamental Rights of the European Union.

From a legal standpoint, the consequences of the Protocol and the Declarations
are not very significant as all Member States are bound by the Treaties to respect
fundamental rights when implementing EU rules. Moreover, the fact that the
Charter 'does not extend' the power of the ECJ and national Courts to declare
that a national provision is inconsistent with the rights referred to in the Charter,
implies that their existing competence is preserved and not restricted.

Conversely, from a political and symbolic point of view, the British and Polish
opt-outs have relevant effects. The Charter could have represented a first common identity core of a constitutional nature in so far as it expresses values that
may be considered as shared by all Member States. Unfortunately, in light of the
above the Union is characterized by a real identity deficit; it is difficult to see how
the Charter could play such a role.

That being so, it must be recognized that a major step forward has been made.
By granting the Charter legal status, the Treaty of Lisbon ensures its transformation from soft law into hard law.

Moreover, although the Lisbon Treaty may not improve the protection of fundamental rights when compared with the Constitutional Treaty, it will definitely have such an effect if judged against the Treaty of Nice.

First of all, it establishes the accession of the EU to the ECHR (which is however subordinated to a unanimous decision and therefore not trouble-free).[61] Such an accession entails a further step forward in the protection of fundamental rights, as well as a more complex articulation of judicial remedies.[62] In any case, the accession agreement should be negotiated with great caution, in an attempt to strike a balance between two competing requirements: on the one hand, the preservation of the autonomy of the EU legal order and on the other hand the need to allow the Strasbourg Court to interpret the ECHR without altering the relations between Member States and the European system. Protocol No 8 annexed to the Lisbon Treaty imposes the conservation of certain specific characteristics of the Union and Union law, in particular with regard to the Union's participation in the control bodies of the European Convention, as well as the mechanisms for identifying the subject (EU/Member States) to whom applications have to be addressed. The accession agreement shall ensure that the competences of the Union or the powers of its institutions are not affected and shall also preserve the situation of Member States derogating from the European Convention and reservations made by Member States. Finally, any dispute concerning the interpretation or application of the EU Treaties shall only be settled by the resolution mechanisms included therein.

Secondly, it must be borne in mind that the Treaty of Lisbon provides for a new list of fundamental values of the EU. Article 2 of the TEU, which is broader than Article 6 of the current EU Treaty, includes among 'the fundamental values of the Union, which are common to the Member States', the respect for human dignity, freedom, democracy, equality, the rule of law and respect for human rights, including the rights of persons belonging to minorities, as well as pluralism, non-discrimination, tolerance, justice, solidarity and equality between women and men. These values are equally binding for the EU and Member States. As regards the latter, the new Article 7 of the TEU establishes a procedure of suspension of the rights of Member States responsible for a serious and persistent breach of the values referred to in Article 2. Such values also form the essential core of a European identity and for this reason must be shared by all the States wishing to accede to the EU (as prescribed by Article 49 of the TEU). Similarly, they

---

[61] By effect of the Lisbon Treaty also the judicial protection of the individual rights is improved, as far as the conditions they have to fulfil in the procedures of legality review for some non-legislative acts concerning them directly even if not individually.

[62] On the current relations between ECJ and the European Court. see Douglas-Scott, 'A Tale of Two Courts: Luxembourg, Strasbourg and the Growing European Human Rights Acquis' (2006) 43 CML Rev 629–665.

represent a guideline for EU external relations, as clearly stated by new Articles 3, para 5[63] and 21 of the TEU,[64] introduced by the Lisbon Treaty.[65]

IV. New Challenges: How Fundamental are Fundamental Rights?

Undoubtedly, fundamental rights embody a major part of the fundamental principles of the EU. They also limit the effects of EU legislation in so far as, on the one hand, the respect of domestic constitutional rights by EU institutions is seen by Member States as a filter for the primacy of EU law and, on the other hand, the Court of Justice may declare an act of the EU institutions to be null where there is a violation of fundamental rights.

Considering that throughout the years the EU system for the protection of fundamental rights has made important strides forward, and that in the future a further level of control will be established by the Strasbourg Court, one may

---

[63] 'In its relations with the wider world, the Union shall uphold and promote its values and interests and contribute to the protection of its citizens. It shall contribute to peace, security, the sustainable development of the Earth, solidarity and mutual respect among peoples, free and fair trade, eradication of poverty and the protection of human rights, in particular the rights of the child, as well as to the strict observance and the development of international law, including respect for the principles of the United Nations Charter.'

[64] '1. The Union's action on the international scene shall be guided by the principles which have inspired its own creation, development and enlargement, and which it seeks to advance in the wider world: democracy, the rule of law, the universality and indivisibility of human rights and fundamental freedoms, respect for human dignity, the principles of equality and solidarity, and respect for the principles of the United Nations Charter and international law. The Union shall seek to develop relations and build partnerships with third countries, and international, regional or global organizations which share the principles referred to in the first subparagraph. It shall promote multilateral solutions to common problems, in particular in the framework of the United Nations. 2. The Union shall define and pursue common policies and actions, and shall work for a high degree of cooperation in all fields of international relations, in order to: (a) safeguard its values, fundamental interests, security, independence and integrity; (b) consolidate and support democracy, the rule of law, human rights and the principles of international law; (c) preserve peace, prevent conflicts and strengthen international security, in accordance with the purposes and principles of the United Nations Charter, with the principles of the Helsinki Final Act and with the aims of the Charter of Paris, including those relating to external borders; (d) foster the sustainable economic, social and environmental development of developing countries, with the primary aim of eradicating poverty; (e) encourage the integration of all countries into the world economy, including through the progressive abolition of restrictions on international trade; (f) help develop international measures to preserve and improve the quality of the environment and the sustainable management of global natural resources, in order to ensure sustainable development; (g) assist populations, countries and regions confronting natural or man-made disasters; and (h) promote an international system based on stronger multilateral cooperation and good global governance. 3. The Union shall respect the principles and pursue the objectives set out in paragraphs 1 and 2 in the development and implementation of the different areas of the Union's external action covered by this Title and by Part Five of the Treaty on the Functioning of the European Union, and of the external aspects of its other policies. The Union shall ensure consistency between the different areas of its external action and between these and its other policies.'

[65] For a comprehensive descriptions of the multi-faceted significance of the Fundamental rights in the EC policies, see Lenaerts, 'Fundamental Rights in the European Union' (2000) 25 ELR 575–600.

question whether national Constitutional or Supreme Courts will give up their role as watchdogs of fundamental domestic principles. The answer seems to be in the negative, at least from a short-term perspective.

First of all, a contrast could arise between national values and European values (be it from Brussels or from Strasbourg) leading national courts to refuse the primacy of a European rule not because it entails a standard of protection which is lower than the domestic one but because it sets a standard which is considered too high. An example could be the right to establish a family, or the interpretation of gender discrimination as including sexual orientation, an area in which both the Strasbourg Court (*EB*[66]) and the Luxembourg Court (*Tadao Maruko*[67]) have recently assumed very liberal positions. Recognizing the possibility for homosexuals to adopt children or conferring legal effects to unions involving people of the same sex (or, even more radically, to polygamist unions) may still be perceived by some Member States as conflicting with core domestic constitutional traditions.

Secondly, a new challenge is increasingly stemming from issues related to public security. The sphere of action and competences of the EU in the area of freedom, security and justice will be enhanced by effect of the Lisbon Treaty, with the latter providing for the use of the same legal basis and instruments applicable to the internal market. Although respect for fundamental rights and the different legal systems and traditions of Member States is clearly stated in Article 67 of the Treaty on the Functioning of the European Union (TF), such conflicts may become particularly disruptive and dangerous for the coherence of the system.

A relevant example is provided by the black lists concerning suspect terrorists, enacted by a decision of the Sanction Committee of the UN Security Council and demanding States to freeze the assets of the persons listed therein. Subsequent acts of the EU (common positions) and of the EC (regulations or decisions) take the necessary implementing measures, which raise the question of the violation of the applicants' fundamental rights (property rights, statement of reasons, right to be heard and fair trial). In these cases a conflict may arise among different standards of fundamental rights and diverging ideas regarding the extent to which derogations to fundamental rights may be allowed for security reasons.

Initially, in *Yusuf,* and *Kadi*,[68] the CFI declared that the EU is bound to observe the resolutions of UN bodies, regardless of the fundamental principles

---

[66] See ECHR, the case of *EB v France*, App no 43546/02.

[67] See ECJ, Case C-267/06 *Tadao Maruko v Versorgungsanstalt der deutschen Bühnen*, not published in the ECR.

[68] See Case T-306/01 *Yusuf* (*Ahmed Ali Yusuf and Al Barakaat International Foundation v Council of the European Union and Commission of the European Communities*) [2005] ECR II-3533, and Case T-315/01 *Kadi* (*Yassin Abdullah Kadi v Council of the European Union and Commission of the European Communities*) [2005] ECR II-3649. The CFI assessed the question of competence, finding that the combination of Articles 60, 301, and 308 of the EC Treaty may provide a legal basis for adopting sanctions against individuals (given that the EC Treaty only provides for sanctions against States). This is disputable since the provisions enacted can hardly be considered as 'necessary for the good functioning of the internal market' (according to the prescription of Article 308 of the EC Treaty).

of the EC and the ECHR. Such a duty derived from the fact that obligations of Member States of the United Nations under the Charter of the United Nations clearly prevail over all other obligations of domestic or international treaty law (including, the ECHR[69]). Although not a member of the United Nations, according to the Court the EU must not infringe the duties imposed on its Member States. Consequently, it is bound to adopt all the measures necessary to enable its Member States to fulfil the said obligations. Nevertheless, the Court found that it would be competent to indirectly review the lawfulness of decisions of the Security Council on the basis of *jus cogens*, which is binding on all subjects of international law, including the organs of the United Nations, but concluding that the freezing of funds does not infringe the standard of universal protection of the fundamental rights of the human person covered by *jus cogens*.

Since the aforementioned judgements and EU procedures have been strongly criticized,[70] subsequent decisions of the CFI and of the ECJ have tried to soften the reasoning under many profiles, ensuring that a minimum level of protection is guaranteed to claimants. In *Chafiq Ayadi* and *Faraj Hassan*,[71] the CFI stressed that the respect of fundamental rights must allow national judges to exclude homes, cars or everyday consumers goods from the list of assets to be frozen. In *Othman*[72] it granted the applicant a sum of money necessary to pay for legal aid.

A new attitude focusing on the rights of defence of applicants has recently been confirmed by the Court of Justice and the CFI. In *Organisation des Modjahedines du Peuple d'Iran*[73] the CFI annulled a Council's decision for the first time.[74] This judgment also draws a fundamental distinction between the

---

[69] Primacy extends to decisions contained in a resolution of the Security Council, in accordance with Article 25 of the Charter of the United Nations, under which the Members of the United Nations are bound to accept and carry out the decisions of the Security Council.

[70] See the 'Dick Martin Introductory Memorandum', 19 March 2007, presented to the Parliamentary Assembly of the Council of Europe (available online at: <http://www.statewatch.org/news/2007/may/coe-marty-un-lists.pdf>). On the many legal questions raised by such a case law, see Nettesheim, 'U.N. Sanctions against Individuals: a Challenge to the Architecture of the European Union Governance' (2007) 44 CML Rev 567–600.

[71] See Case T-253/02 *Chafiq Ayadi v Council of the European Union* [2006] ECR II-2139; Case T-49/04 *Faraj Hassan v Council of the European Union and Commission of the European Communities* [2006] ECR II-52.

[72] See order of the CFI in the Case T-318/01 *Omar Mohammed Othman v Council of the European Union and Commission of the European Communities* [2002] OJ C68/13.

[73] See Case T-228/02 *Organisation des Modjahedines du peuple d'Iran v Council of the European Union* [2006] ECR II-4665.

[74] In that case the UN Security Council resolution did not individuate itself the names of the persons to be sanctioned, so leaving a discretionary power to the EU and EC institutions. For this reason, the institutions were expected to apply the fundamental guarantees of the applicants, such as the right to be heard and the duty to state the reasons of the act. The CFI however annulled only the EC decision but affirmed the impossibility of annulling a JHA Common Position. In this judgment the Court also held that, as a rule, the safeguard relating to the obligation to state reasons provided for by Article 253 of the EC Treaty is fully applicable in the context of the adoption of a decision to freeze funds under the contested regulation. The Court has inferred from that principle, interpreted in the light of the case law, that the statement of reasons for an initial decision to freeze funds must at least make actual and specific reference to the reasons why the Council considers, having regard to

first application of a freezing measure, which requires a 'surprise effect' in order for it to be effective, and the decision to maintain such a measure: the right to be heard of the victim should be contextual in the first case and preliminary in the second. In *Ocalan-PKK*[75] the ECJ annulled a decision of the CFI (on the grounds of manifest error). In *SEGI* and *Gestoras*[76] the ECJ declared that when individual rights are affected, judicial review of Justice and Home Affairs (JHA) common positions is possible as regards annulment and preliminary rulings.[77] The same trend is visible in recent case law, highlighting the tight connection which exists between the duty to state reasons and defence rights. In *Stichting-Al Aqsa*,[78] *Kongra-Gel*,[79] and *Ocalan*[80] certain Council decisions freezing assets were annulled in so far as they failed to state reasons. In *Sison*,[81] the CFI not only annulled a Council decision for failure to state reasons but also clarified the duties of the EU/EC institutions to respect fundamental rights when UN provisions leave them discretionary powers.[82] The Court also considered that the breach of the applicant's rights of defence may, in principle, be sufficiently serious for European institutions to incur liability (although the Court found that in the present case there was no proof of a direct causal link between the measures adopted and the alleged losses).

Finally, the recent Opinions of Advocate General Poiares Maduro in *Kadi* and *Al Barakaat*[83] state that the EC regulations in issue, which implement UN decisions, breach the applicants' rights to property and fair trial/judicial review and must therefore be annulled.

---

the precise information or material in the relevant file available to it, that a decision has been taken by a competent authority of a Member State in respect of the person concerned, unless overriding considerations concerning the security of the Community and its Member States, or the conduct of their international relations, militate against it.

[75] See Case C-229/05 P *Osman Ocalan, on behalf of the Kurdistan Workers' Party (PKK) and Serif Vanly, on behalf of the Kurdistan National Congress (KNK) v Council of the European Union* [2007] ECR I-439.

[76] See Case C-354/04 P *Gestoras Pro Amnistía and Others v Council of the European Union* [2007] ECR I-1579 and Case C-355/04 P *Segi and Araitz Zubimendi and Aritza Galarraga v Council of the European Union* [2007] ECR 1657.

[77] See also Case C-117/06 *Gerda Möllendorf, Christiane Möllendorf-Niehuus,* not published in the ECR, where the ECJ dealt for the first time with the rights of third parties, which may be jeopardized by the application of freezing measures.

[78] See Case T-327/03 *Stichting Al-Aqsa v Council of the European Union,* not published in the ECR.

[79] See Case T-253/04 *Kongra-Geland others v Council of the European Union,* not published in the ECR.

[80] Case T-229/02 *Osman Ocalan v Council,* [2008] not published in the ECR.

[81] Case T-47/03 *Jose Maria Sison v Council of the European Union,* not published in the ECR.

[82] According to this judgment the Council must carry out a periodic review of the measures (at least twice a year) in order to ascertain whether they are still necessary.

[83] See the Opinions of AG Poiares Maduro in the Case T-315/01 *Kadi* (*Yassin Abdullah Kadi v Council of the European Union and Commission of the European Communities*) [2005] ECR II-3649, and in the Case C-415/05 P *Al Barakaat Foundation v Council of the European Union and Commission of the European Communities,* pending case.

The ECJ is now called upon to decide whether to follow the suggestions of Advocate General Maduro. Such a decision is not straightforward as the issue at stake is not simply to 'soften' the previous case law, but to reverse it. To this end, the Court may employ the classic proportionality test in an attempt to find the right balance between the obligation to respect UN sanctions and the exigency of applying them with the least prejudice of fundamental rights.

The decision also involves problems relating to the hierarchy of fundamental principles and fundamental rights. Is loyalty to the UN system the top constitutional priority of the EU and of its Member States? Must the EU really implement Acts on which adoption it has no say and which infringe its own fundamental principles?

As the EU is not a member of the UN, the source of its duties towards the latter are still to be found in the TEU itself, notably in the principle of loyal co-operation with EU Member States. Therefore, if the Member States' Supreme or Constitutional Courts decide that the UN sanction system violates fundamental rights, the ECJ and CFI would necessarily be bound to follow the national Courts. It is worth recalling that on 24 April 2008 the British High Court invalidated the asset-freezing regime implementing the UN Security Council Resolutions because it was adopted by the Government bypassing the Parliament.

On the other hand, given that, as Advocate General Maduro has remarked, the principle of loyal co-operation works both ways, Member States are called upon to respect the fundamental values of the EU and to voice their concerns before the Security Council of the UN. The former must therefore question whether complying with the UN sanctions system is more important than respect for those rights which are considered fundamental by national constitutions and by the ECHR, and which lay behind the very idea of a European identity.[84]

In any case it could be helpful to recall what the Court stated in *Burgoa*.[85] It is true that according to Article 307 of the TCE rights and obligations arising from international agreements concluded before the entry into force of the Treaty between one or more Member States on the one hand, and one or more third countries on the other, are not affected by the provisions of the Treaty. Nevertheless, such an Article only implies a duty on the part of the institutions of the community not to impede the performance of the obligations of Member States which stem from a prior agreement and does not bind the Community itself to implement the latter. In other words, the principle of loyal co-operation may compel the EU not to preclude (for instance on the ground of free movement

---

[84] For different opinions about the idea of fundamental rights as core identity of the European Union, see Von Bogdandy, 'The European Union as a Human rights Organizations? Human Rights and the Core of the European Union' (2000) 37 CML Rev 1307–1338; Eeckout, 'The EU Charter of Fundamental Rights and the Federal Question' (2002) 39 CML Rev 945–994; Dutheil De La Rochère, 'The EU and the Individual: Fundamental Rights in the Draft Constitutional Treaty' (2004) 41 CML Rev 345–354.

[85] See Case 812/79 *Attorney General v Juan C Burgoa* [1980] ECR 2787.

of capital) the effect of national measures implementing the Security Council decisions. But it cannot oblige the EU to itself adopt provisions (moreover in matters where its competence is questionable[86]) infringing its own fundamental principles.

V. Concluding Remarks

In the current stage of European integration, the question of what principles are really fundamental in the EU becomes increasingly important. Fundamental principles in fact may limit the primacy of EU legislation (when they are considered by national judges) or affect the legality of the latter (when assessed by the ECJ).

Every national constitutional system has its own fundamental principles; likewise, the EU has also developed its own. But, as the national constitutional orders are strictly interlocked with the EU system, those principles reflect each other as in a hall of mirrors, with a continuous external-internal intertwining. Though they may still be separately identified, the borderline between them is fading and a process of convergence is underway (the Charter of Fundamental Rights being the first manifestation).

To date, cases of potential conflict have been avoided by the judges on the grounds of a tacit gentlemen's agreement. After Lisbon, in spite of the enhanced protection of fundamental rights and of national constitutional traditions, fundamental principles remain a sort of grey area, where vagueness and flexibility are two sides of the same coin.

If ambiguity may facilitate a constitutional *modus vivendi* within the borders of the Union, it may nonetheless become dangerous when the EU system of values, as well as the national ones, are confronted with external challenges. Threats to fundamental rights and to fundamental principles should lead Member States to jointly reflect on what is really fundamental for Europeans.

---

[86] Even after the Treaty of Lisbon coming into force, as the new explicit EU competence in this matters (provided for by the new Article 61H of the TF) will be not exclusive, Member States will retain the national competence of implementing the Security Council decisions, being not obliged to do it by using the legislative framework of the EU if this is not necessary fot the purposes of Article 61.

Supr[i]macy *à la Française*: Another French Exception?

*Xavier Groussot**

Though the *Conseil d'Etat* has, in the past, been reluctant to welcome the principle of supremacy, its recent jurisprudence demonstrates that it has drastically changed its stance and seeks, instead, appeasement and judicial dialogue with the Court of Justice. The *Conseil constitutionnel* with its doctrine of '*réserve de constitutionnalité*' has clearly influenced the administrative judge. These decisions of the French national courts should be read and understood in light of the recent legislative and jurisprudential developments at both EU and national levels. Are these decisions unique in the European legal landscape? Or do they reflect, instead, a general movement of cooperation? Against this background, the French decisions will be put in the context of *discursive legal pluralism*. By establishing the supremacy of European law, the Court of Justice has launched, indeed, a discursive process with the national courts.[1] This dialogue is not only vertical but also horizontal, ie between the national courts (both internally and externally). It is argued in this essay that the Constitutional Treaty, the *European Arrest Warrant* saga, and the case law of the Court of Justice in the context of fundamental rights have accelerated this process of cooperation and dialogue. Finally, this article argues against the need for a liberal approach towards legal pluralism by taking seriously into account the risk of constitutional cataclysm in the situation where a national court would invalidate EU legislation. It thus insists on the need for preventing constitutional conflicts. This article is divided into two parts. The first part analyses the concept of supremacy. Supremacy is studied in light of fundamental rights and judicial *kompetenz-kompetenz*. The different views of the Court of Justice and the highest national courts in Europe as to the reach of supremacy are thoroughly discussed. The second part focuses on the examination of the most recent French decisions and stresses their close link with *discursive legal pluralism*.

* Associate Professor of EU Law, Lund University.
[1] See KJ Alter, *Establishing the Supremacy of European Law: The Making of an International Rule of Law in Europe* (OUP, 2001).

I. Epistemology of Supr[i]macy

A. Supremacy or Primacy?

With the EU Reform Treaty and the eradication of the 'C' word, one could say that the 'terminology-issue' is of crucial importance in the European legal order. Notably, the Lisbon Treaty has also rubbed out the 'primacy' clause (Article I-6 Constitutional Treaty) included in the *feu* Constitutional Treaty. It is only in the Annex of the Reform Treaty that includes the Opinion of the Council Legal Service on the primacy of EC law:

> It results from the case-law of the Court of Justice that primacy of EC law is a cornerstone principle of Community law. According to the Court, this principle is inherent to the specific nature of the European Community. At the time of the first judgment of this established case law (Costa/ENEL, 15 July 1964, Case 6/64) there was no mention of primacy in the Treaty. It is still the case today. The fact that the principle of primacy will not be included in the future shall not in any way change the existence of the principle and the existing case-law of the Court of Justice.

Similarly to Article I-6 of the Constitutional Treaty, this Opinion does not expressly enunciate the prevalence of EC law over the national constitutions of the Member States. The formulation, therefore, differs from the case law of the Court of Justice in terms of clarity. Also like in the Constitutional Treaty, the word 'primacy' is used instead of 'supremacy'. It appears clear that 'primacy' has become a trendy word. But is it a better wording than 'supremacy'? And, does it boast a different meaning?

Weatherill has expressed the view that 'supremacy' should be preferred to 'primacy' since it reflects a more orthodox terminology in the English language.[2] Moreover, it is true that the Anglo-Saxon doctrine and the Advocates General have often referred to 'supremacy'. As an aside, we locate a 'supremacy clause' in the US Constitution (Article VI, paragraph 2) that clearly establishes the prevalence of the constitution over all types of States' laws. However, when it comes to the judgments of the Court of Justice, the Kirchberg judges have only referred once to 'supremacy' in the *Walt Wilhelm* case.[3] The Court of Justice prefers to rely instead on 'primacy' as it is clear from the recent *I-21 Germany* and *Lucchini* cases.[4] In my view, this is not so strange since the Court of Justice's rulings are always drafted in French where the standard formulation is '*primauté*'. It is also

---

[2] S Weatherill, Memorandum, Select Committee on European Union, House of Lords, submitted on 5 October 2003.
[3] Case 14/68 *Walt Wilhelm* [1969] ECR 1, para 5. Cited in FC Mayer, 'The European Constitution and the Courts', in A von Bogdandy and J Bast, *Principles of European Constitutional Law* (Hart, 2006) 281, at 292.
[4] See eg, Joined Cases C-392/04 and C-422/04 *I-21 Germany* [2006] ECR I-8559 and Case C-119/05 *Lucchini* [2007] ECR I-6199.

worth remarking that the typical wording is '*primauté*' within the French doctrine, and this even before the Constitutional Treaty and its Article I-6.

It has been suggested that a distinction may be established between primacy
and supremacy.[5] Arguably, this division is useful since it points to the non-hierarchical nature of the interrelation between EU law and national law. In that sense,
Mayer has stated that 'an intelligent primacy principles takes the concerns of the
Member States seriously and accommodates them, but without undermining the
integrity of the European legal order and the European Court of Justice'.[6] To put
it differently, it may be said that the use of 'primacy' instead of 'supremacy' reflects
a certain legal pluralist perception of the relationship between the European and
national legal orders. This proposition is seducing. Yet one may think that the
distinction is unnecessary since 'primacy' has no fixed meaning.[7] Indeed, primacy appears either absolute by reading the Court of Justice's case law or conditional (non-absolute) if one examines judgments of the highest national courts in
Europe. In this essay, 'primacy' and 'supremacy' are used interchangeably.

B. Primacy, Fundamental Rights, and Judicial
Kompetenz-Kompetenz

The paradigms of supremacy and fundamental rights are closely connected.
Indeed, the acceptance of the principle of supremacy by the national courts has
traditionally been linked to the level of protection afforded by the fundamental
rights elaborated by the European Court of Justice. In other words, a national
court may be reluctant to recognize the supremacy of Community law if it
assumes that EU fundamental rights do not sufficiently protect the individuals.
Such an approach was made clear already in 1974 by the German Constitutional
Court in the *Solange I* case.[8] Since then, fundamental rights have developed tre-
mendously through the jurisprudence of the Court of Justice, which has clearly
played a crucial and proactive role. The culmination came with the EU Charter of
Fundamental Rights (CFR) which, inter alia, codifies the case law of the Court of
Justice. This Charter will become binding with the entry into force of EU Reform
Treaty. However, it is worth noting that, unfortunately, the CFR remains quasi-
invisible. Indeed, it does not form an integral part of the Lisbon Treaty, such as
with the Part II of the Constitutional Treaty. Instead, a mere reference is made
in a Treaty provision and the full text is buried in an Annex. In doing so, that
goes clearly against the main objective of the Convention which has drafted the
Charter, ie ensuring the visibility of the EU fundamental rights for the citizens.

---

    [5] FC Mayer, 'Supremacy-Lost?' (2005) 6 German Law Journal, no 11, at p 2.
    [6] Ibid, at p 6.
    [7] JH Reestman, 'Primacy of Union Law' (2005) 1 EuConst 104. The author distinguishes
between an existential and a more pragmatic reading of primacy.
    [8] Decision of 29 May 1974, *Internationale Handelsgesellschaft*, BVerfGE 37, [1974] 271 CMLR
540.

The CFR may have repercussions on the principle of supremacy. In that sense, Article 53 of the Charter could pose a threat to the supremacy of EU law.[9] More precisely, there might be a risk of multiplication of conflicts between domestic constitutional norms and Union law that would, consequently, increase the proclivity of the national courts to review the acts of the Union. This 'terror thesis' was rightly set aside by Liisberg who has undertaken a wide analysis of the drafting history of Article 53 of the CFR as well as a detailed comparison of similar provisions in international and US federal instruments (Article 53 of the ECHR entitled 'safeguard for existing human rights', Article 27 of the declaration of Fundamental Rights and Freedoms entitled 'degree of protection', and the Ninth Amendment of the US Constitution). The conclusion suggested a limited legal significance for Article 53 of the CFR.[10] The aim of Article 53 is to clarify that the EU Charter of Fundamental Rights does not replace national constitutions and does not jeopardize the existence of higher standards of protection at the domestic level.

In addition, it should be noted that Poland and the UK have opted out from the application of the CFR. The opting-out protocol excludes jurisdiction of the Court of Justice and national courts with regard to the Charter, thus making its provisions unenforceable and denying their direct effect. Yet, the CFR may be rendered indirectly legally binding through the case law of the Court of Justice and its general principles of Community law. The *Viking Line* and *Laval* cases which have recently recognized the right of collective action as a fundamental right on the basis of, inter alia, Article 28 of the CFR are, in my view, the starting point of a long debate touching upon the primacy of EU law in relation to fundamental rights litigation.[11]

Also, it is worth remarking here that the issues of *kompetenz-kompetenz (La compétence de la compétence)* and primacy are strongly interrelated; and it is often difficult to dissociate them. As to the concept of *kompetenz-kompetenz*, it is important to draw a distinction between legislative and judicial *kompetenz-kompetenz*. Legislative *kompetenz-kompetenz* can be described as the power to determine the legitimate scope of competence.[12] This constitutional competence-competence

---

[9] According to Article 53, '[n]othing in this Charter shall be interpreted as restricting or adversely affecting human rights and fundamental freedoms as recognized, in their respective fields of application, by Union law and international law and by international agreements to which the Union, the Community or all the Member States are party, including the European Convention for the Protection of Human Rights and Fundamental, and by the Member States' constitutions'. Declaration 12 explains that '[t]his provision is intended to maintain the level of protection currently afforded within their respective scope by Union law, national law and international law'. In other words, the CFR does not endanger the level of protection afforded, for instance, by the national constitutions.

[10] JB Liisberg, 'Does the EU Charter of Fundamental Rights Threaten the Supremacy of Community Law?' (2001) 38 CML Rev 1171, at 1198.

[11] Case C-438/05 *Viking Line* [2007] ECR I-10779 and Case C-341/05 *Laval* [2007] I-11767.

[12] J Shaw, 'Europe's Constitutional Future' [2005] PL, 132, at 142. See also, I Pernice, 'Multilevel Constitutionalism in the European Union' (2002) 27 ELR 511, at 519.

is intricately related to the existence of an autonomous European legal order
and to the question whether the EU institutions boast legislative competence-
competence. It seems accepted by the major part of the doctrine that the
European Union does not have this power since whatever the powers attributed
by the Treaties they are derived from the Member States' delegation.[13] This is the
principle of attributed powers.[14] Furthermore, it should be noted that the Federal
Constitutional Court in the *Maastricht* case made clear that the Member States
remain the Masters of the Treaty.[15] In a similar vein, during the accession of
Sweden, the Government Bill underlined that it is the Member States, not the EC
institutions, which decide in the Union how far the cooperation shall extend and
what competence the EC institutions shall be given.

By contrast, judicial *kompetenz-kompetenz* raises the issue of who is to decide
the limits of Community competence.[16] More precisely, which court, from the
Court of Justice or the national court, has the final say to decide on the scope
of these competences and to determine whether the Community has acted *intra
vires*. In other words, who is the final arbiter of the validity of Community legislation? Or who has the ultimate authority in testing EU law? At first sight, it appears
that the EC Treaty confers exclusive jurisdiction to the Court of Justice. In that
sense, Article 230 of the EC Treaty states expressly that a direct action before the
Court of Justice can be based on the lack of competence. This situation is illustrated by the *Tobacco Directive* case, where the Court of Justice found that the
Directive was invalid due to the choice of a wrong legal basis.[17] Also, Article 234
of the EC Treaty empowers the national courts to make a preliminary ruling on
the validity of Community acts. As stated in the *Foto-Frost* case,[18] the effectiveness and uniformity of Community law would be put into jeopardy if the national
courts were authorized to decide on the validity of Community legislation. This
essay will emphasize that the exclusive jurisdiction of the Court of Justice has been
contested by the national courts, though avoiding a direct altercation.

One may also consider that the principle of primacy constitutes a two-fold
concept due to the type of obligations resulting from its application.[19] Indeed,
primacy entails both positive and negative obligations for the national courts. On

---

[13] For more developments see A Dashwood, 'The Relationship between the Member States and
the European Union/European Community' (2004) 41 CML Rev 335.

[14] See the EU Reform Treaty and the taxonomy established in relation to competences.

[15] W Hassemer, 'Case-law of the Federal Constitutional Court of Germany regarding the
Position of Constitutional Courts Following Integration into the European Union', in the *Position of
Constitutional Courts Following Integration into the European Union*, Conference September–October
2004, Bled, Slovenia, 106.

[16] P Craig, 'Report on the United Kingdom', in A Slaughter et al. (eds), *The European Courts and
the National Courts* (Hart, 1997), 195, at 206.

[17] See eg, Case C-376/98 *Germany v Parliament and Council* [2000] ECR I-8419.

[18] Case 314/85 *Foto-Frost* [1987] ECR 4199.

[19] M Claes, *The National Courts' Mandate in the European Constitution*, thesis 10 June 2004,
Maastricht, at p 475. The author considers the principle of supremacy as dual. She makes a distinction between ordinary and ultimate supremacy.

the one hand, the national courts are under an obligation to set aside any domestic legislation that conflicts with EC law (positive supremacy). This obligation is mostly undertaken by ordinary courts and exists even in the circumstances of a conflict with constitutional legislation. On the other hand, the national courts are under an obligation not to uphold domestic constitutional law in order to invalidate EC legislation (negative supremacy). This obligation is mostly undertaken by constitutional courts and results from the exclusive jurisdiction of the Court of Justice in assessing the validity of EU law. The non-respect of this obligation would create what Craig has called a *nuclear problem* or what Weiler and Haltern have denominated a *Mutual Assured Destruction*.[20] This view has been recently contested by liberal legal pluralism. We shall come back to this in the last part of this essay.

Finally, it appears clear that the issues of judicial *kompetenz-kompetenz* and (negative) supremacy are closely related. The obligation for the national court not to uphold national constitutional norms gives the answer to who is the final arbiter of the validity of Community law, that is to say the Court of Justice.[21] From the perspective of European law, the answer is easy to give. However, there is another view voiced by (many?) national supreme/constitutional courts that do not fully agree with the exclusive jurisdiction of the Court of Justice and claim their jurisdiction to apply their own constitutions.

C. Absolute Primacy—The Court of Justice View

As seen previously, primacy entails two types of obligations for the national courts, that is to say an obligation to set aside conflicting national norms and an obligation not to uphold constitutional provisions. These lines of case law reflect a monist conception of EU law based on a clear and absolute hierarchy of the Community norm over national law. The founding Treaties do not explicitly refer to the supremacy of the Community legal order over the domestic orders. As is well known, the Court of Justice in *Costa v Enel* established strongly the *lex superior* principle.[22] In this respect, the Court argued that 'by creating a Community of unlimited duration, having its own institutions, its own personality, its own legal capacity of representation on the international plane, and more particularly, real powers stemming from a limitation of

---

[20] JHH Weiler and K Haltern, 'Constitutional or International? The Foundations of the Community Legal Order and the Question of Judicial Kompetenz-Kompetenz', in A Slaughter et al. (eds), *The European Courts and the National Courts* (Hart, 1997) 331, at 362.

[21] The principle of supremacy is strongly connected with the issue of competence. Indeed, if the EU institutions take an act but lack the appropriate competence, this act must be declared *ultra vires*. In this situation, the principle of supremacy is evidently not applicable. Furthermore, the effects of supremacy are different according to the competence at issue. For instance, exclusive competence leads to a strict application of the pre-emption principle. In that sense, it may also be said that pre-emption precedes supremacy *(a contrario* see *Simmenthal,* para 18).

[22] Case 6/64 *Costa v Enel* [1964] ECR 585.

sovereignty or a transfer of powers from the States to the Community. The Member States have limited their sovereign rights, albeit within limited fields, and have thus created a body of law which binds both their nationals and themselves'. The Court of Justice clearly posits the autonomy and specificity of the European legal order. Primacy is explicitly seen as an essential '*corollary*' of this new legal entity. And it results from the jurisprudence that this principle established the prevalence of Community law over all types of national law (even constitutional law). This line of reasoning is, arguably, transposable to the third pillar.[23] But is primacy really a principle since it bears the hallmark of a rule—conclusiveness?

The application of primacy has consequences especially for the national courts. In *Simmenthal,* the Court of Justice established obligations for both the Member States (legislature) and the national courts which are justified by the need to ensure the effectiveness of Community law.[24] As to the former, the Court established the pre-emptive effect of Community law which precludes the adoption of national legislative measures that would be incompatible with Community provisions. Arguably, pre-emption precedes supremacy. As to the latter, the Court considered that the principle of precedence (supremacy) renders automatically inapplicable any provision of national law conflicting with Community law.[25] In other words, the national courts, which must apply Community law in its entirety and protect rights conferred on individuals, are under an obligation to set aside the domestic legislation (prior or subsequent to the Community rule) contrary to Community law.[26] It is not only for the constitutional courts to set aside, but also the ordinary courts must fulfil this obligation resulting from the principle of supremacy.[27]

Importantly, the obligation to set aside conflicting national norms does not necessarily lead to the abrogation of the national legislation.[28] This interpretation is confirmed by the *IN.CO.GE* case, where the Court of Justice favoured the inapplicability of the national measure.[29] By contrast, in *Factortame,* the Court of Justice was confronted with the question whether it should set aside a rule preventing a national court seized of a dispute falling within the scope of Community law from granting interim relief. The Court, referring to the *Simmenthal* judgment, stated that, '[a]ny provision of a national legal system and any legislative, administrative or judicial practice which might impair the effectiveness of Community

---

[23] K Lenaerts and T Corthaut, 'Of Birds and Hedges: The Role of Primacy in Invoking Norms of EU Law' (2006) 31 ELR 287.

[24] Case 106/77 *Simmenthal II* [1978] ECR 629.   [25] Ibid, paras 17–18.

[26] Ibid, paras 20–21. See also Case C-347/96 *Solred* [1998] ECR I-937, para 30, and Case C-144/04 *Mangold* [2005] ECR I-9981, para 77.

[27] FG Jacobs, 'The Evolution of the European Legal Order' (2004) 41 CML Rev 303, at 315.

[28] A Dashwood, 'The Relationship between the Member States and the European Union/European Community' (2004) 41 CML Rev 335, at 378.

[29] Joined Cases C-10 and C-22/97 *IN.CO.GE* [1998] ECR I-6307. See also, Case C-198/01 *Consorzio Industrie Fiammiferi* (CIF) [2003] ECR I-8055, para 53.

law by withholding from the national court having jurisdiction to apply such law the power to do everything necessary at the moment of its application to set aside national legislative provisions [...] are incompatible'.[30] The Court found an obligation for the national court to set aside obstructive national rules which prohibit the conferral of a suitable remedy. Accordingly, this obligation stems not only from the principle of effectiveness, but also from the application of the principle of loyalty (Article 10 of the EC Treaty) in order to ensure the legal protection which derives from the direct effect of Community law.[31] In the end, it is worth noting that the House of Lords abrogated the national rule prohibiting the granting of interim injunctions against the Crown.

Also, it should be stressed that the primacy of Community law applies to the constitutions of the Member States. The Court, in *Internationale Handelsgesellschaft*, stressed the need to ensure the uniformity and efficacy of Community law in all the Member States. Indeed, it would be a tremendous step-back if the States were allowed to use their domestic constitutions in order to circumvent the Community obligations.[32] The Court ruled that 'the validity of a Community measure or its effect within the Member States cannot be affected by allegations that it runs counter to either fundamental rights as formulated by the constitution of that State or the principles of a national constitutional structure'.[33] To put it in a nutshell, there is an obligation for the national courts and the Member States not to invoke constitutional provisions against the enforcement (application) of Community law or the validity of Community legislation. Absolute primacy constitutes an existential condition of the Community legal order by guaranteeing its autonomy, uniformity, and effectiveness.

First of all, there is a duty for the Member States not to use constitutional provisions to justify the non-respect of the obligations resulting from primary and secondary Community law. As to primary law, *Commission v Luxembourg*, a case concerning Article 48 of the EC Treaty and the national requirement for posts in the public service involving the exercise of powers, provides a good example.[34] The Grand Duchy of Luxembourg invoked Article 11 of the Constitution, according to which only a Luxembourg national may occupy civil and military posts, in order to discard the application of Community law. It argued that it constitutes a supreme rule of domestic law that precludes the breach of obligations alleged by the Commission. The Court stated with force that 'recourse to provisions of the domestic level systems to restrict the scope of the provisions of Community law would have the effect of impairing the unity

---

[30] Case C-213/89 *Factortame* [1990] ECR I-2433, para 20.   [31] Ibid, para 19.

[32] Case 11/70 *Internationale Handelsgesellschaft* [1970] ECR 1125.

[33] Ibid, para 3.

[34] Case C-473/93 *Commission v Luxembourg* [1996] ECR I-3207. See also Case 149/79 *Commission v Belgium* [1980] ECR 3881.

and efficacy of that law'.[35] The same type of reasoning is applicable to the implementation of secondary law, eg Directive.[36]

Secondly, there is an obligation not to uphold national (constitutional) provisions against the acts of institutions in order to declare their invalidity. The Court of Justice, as seems to follow from the *Internationale Handelsgesellschaft*, was thus concerned by the fact that the national courts may review EC law in light of their own constitutional law. In the words of the Court, 'recourse to the legal rules or concepts of national law in order to judge the validity of measures adopted by the institutions of the Community would have an adverse effect on the uniformity and efficacy of Community law. In fact, the law stemming from the Treaty, an independent source of law, cannot because of its very nature be overridden by rules of national law, however framed, without being deprived of its character as Community law and without the legal basis of the Community itself being called into question.'[37] This last sentence reflects very clearly the existential character of primacy for the European legal order.

In the wake of this ruling, the Court of Justice made it clear in *Foto-Frost* that it had exclusive jurisdiction to rule on the validity of Community acts. It appears important to look at the reasoning of the Court in more detail.[38] Before entering into the reasoning, it is worth noting that Article 234(1)(b) of the EC Treaty provides the individual applicant with an indirect action to challenge the validity of Community acts. According to the said Article, the national courts can refer questions to the Court of Justice concerning the validity and interpretation of acts of the institutions of the Community. In that regard, the Court remarked that Article 234 of the EC Treaty (ex 177) does not settle the question whether national courts may declare invalid the acts of the institutions.

Then it considers two situations. On the one hand, the national courts may consider the validity of Community acts and, if they consider that the grounds put forward are unfounded, they may reject them and conclude that the measure is valid. On the other hand, the national courts do not have the power to declare acts of the Community institutions invalid. In that regard, the Court assessed the purpose of the preliminary ruling procedure and stressed that the powers conferred by Article 234 of the EC Treaty are meant to ensure that Community law is applied uniformly by national courts. According to the Court, '[t]hat requirement of uniformity is particularly imperative when the validity of a Community act is in question. Divergences between courts in the Member States as to the validity of Community acts would be liable to place in jeopardy the very unity

---

[35] Ibid, paras 37–38.
[36] See Case C-285/98 *Kreil* [2000] ECR I-69. In this case, Article 12 A of the Basic Law barred women from serving in military positions involving the use of arms and was thus contrary to Directive 76/201 which is declared applicable to employment in the public service.
[37] *Internationale Handelsgesellschaft*, n 32 above, para 3.
[38] Case C-314/85 *Foto-Frost* [1987] ECR 4199.

of the Community legal order and detract from the fundamental requirement of legal certainty.'[39]

Thus, in the second situation, the Court of Justice has the exclusive jurisdiction to declare acts of the Community invalid.[40] This is primarily justified by the need to avoid divergences between the (supreme/constitutional) national courts which would have the effect of impairing the unity of the Community legal order. The Court of Justice, in analysing the text of Article 234 of the EC Treaty and its own place in the preliminary ruling procedure, resorts to the argument of effectiveness. According to the Court, the coherence of the system requires that the power to declare act invalid must be reserved to the Court of Justice since Article 234 gives exclusive jurisdiction to the Court of Justice. By referring to Articles 20 and 21 of the Statute of the Court of Justice (concerning the participation of the Community institutions in the proceedings, supply of information by the institutions, and Member States not participating in the proceedings), the Court is considered to be in the best position to decide on the validity of Community acts.[41]

The *Foto-Frost* case is a strong ruling. It is clear, simple, persuasive as well as pedagogical. Interestingly, the argument of effectiveness, used in the *Simmenthal* case, is now completed by the argument of uniformity.[42] This judgment thus provides a sound integrating element for effectiveness and uniformity. It is without doubt that the Court of Justice has judicial *kompetenz-kompetenz.* However, this approach has been challenged and there have been problems in some Member States in reconciling Community law with the provisions of their national constitutions. Arguably, in a Europe composed of 27 Member States the risk of divergences is higher and thus the necessity to have one single Court (the Court of Justice) to decide on the validity of Community acts is vital. The extension of qualified majority voting in the recent Treaties points towards the same conclusion. The Community legal order would be undermined if provisions of national constitutional law could be used, by the national courts, to invalidate Community measures or as exceptions to the enforcement of Community law.[43] In certain instances, the national courts have been reluctant to recognize the exclusive jurisdiction of the Court of Justice regarding the validity of Community acts and the primacy of Community law over national constitutional law.

[39] Ibid, para 15.

[40] Ibid, para 19. For national courts and application for interim measures, see Case C-465/93 *Atlanta* [1995] ECR I-3761. The national court can grant interim relief. It must have serious doubts as to the validity of the Community measure and must have referred the measure for a preliminary ruling.

[41] Ibid, paras 17–18.

[42] See House of Lords, 'The Future Role of the European Court of Justice', 6th report, 2004, para 63.

[43] V Skouris, 'The Position of the European Court of Justice in the EU Legal Order and its relationship with National Constitutional Courts', in 'The Position of Constitutional Courts Following Integration into the European Union', Conference September–October 2004, Bled, Slovenia, 37.

D. Conditional Primacy—The View(s?) of the National Courts

The national courts have reacted differently to the ultimate judicial *kompetenz-kompetenz* of the Court of Justice. Importantly, most of the national courts do not see any objection to the exclusive jurisdiction of the Court of Justice. However, some national courts have claimed jurisdiction to review Community acts and it should be pointed out that no courts have expressly acknowledged the ultimate authority of the Court of Justice.[44] Indeed, national constitutions of some Member States have been framed in such a way that the final constitutional, legislative and judicial authority lies in the Member State. Consequently, as rightly put by Denza, '[n]ational courts have made clear that their own mandate is ultimately based on their own constitution, that the supremacy of European Community law is accepted because it has been given effect by national constitutional modalities, and that national constitutions may under extreme circumstances impose limits on it'.[45]

The Federal Constitutional Court (FCC) in Germany provides a good illustration as to the reactions of a national court against the principle of supremacy and the related issue of the exclusive jurisdiction (judicial *kompetenz-kompetenz*) of the Court of Justice. Those issues have arisen mainly in the context of fundamental rights and the division of competences. The assertion by the Court of Justice, in *Internationale Handelsgesellschaft*, that Community law is superior to the national law of the Member States—even their constitutional law—was the trigger of the national court's rebellion, which reacted against the evident lack of human rights within EC law in the *Solange* cases.[46] Notably, the possibility to control the compatibility of Community law in the light of fundamental rights guaranteed by national constitutional law was already invoked by the FCC in 1967.[47]

The 'spectre' of the lack of fundamental rights' protection reappeared in the wake of the Maastricht Treaty. The *Maastricht* decision of the FCC, also known as the *Brunner* case,[48] exemplifies the persistent interest of the German constitutional court regarding the issue of basic rights. This decision, however, did not focus essentially on the human rights issue, but mainly concerned

---

[44] See House of Lords, 'The Future Role of the European Court of Justice', 6th report, 2004, para 65.

[45] Ibid, para 67. Going further, this reasoning is also applicable to the Netherlands which gives a supra-constitutional value to EU law.

[46] Decision of 29 May 1974, *Internationale Handelsgesellschaft*, BVerfGE 37, 271, [1974] CMLR 540; Decision of the 22 October 1986, BVerfGE 73, 339, [1987] 3 CMLR 225. See for an overview of the debate, B de Witte, 'The Past and Future Role of the European Court of Justice in the Protection of Human Rights', in P Alston (ed), *The EU and Human Rights* (OUP, 1999), 859, at 863–864; M Kumm, 'Who is the Final Arbiter of Constitutionality in Europe? Three Conceptions of the Relationship between the German Federal Constitutional Court and the European Court of Justice' (1999) 36 CML Rev 351, at 364.

[47] *Bundesverfassungsgericht*, 18 October 1967, *BVerfGE* 22, 233.

[48] *Bundesverfassungsgericht,* 12 October 1993, *Brunner,* BVerfGE 89, 155, in [1994] 1 CMLR 57.

the question of legislative competence and democratic legitimacy.[49] The FCC reviewed the Treaty of Maastricht in light of the Basic Law and found that it was not contrary to the democratic principles since the German Parliament preserved competences of substantial importances. In that respect, the German Court stressed that the Member States are the Masters of the Treaties. In the '*Banana* case' (2000), the FCC confirmed that the protection of fundamental rights was sufficient, and that it will not automatically adjudicate a complaint challenging the validity of a Community act in the light of the Basic Law.[50] To phrase it differently, the idea of cooperation renders superfluous the case-by-case control by the national constitutional court.

The reactions from the national courts regarding primacy and judicial *kompetez-kompetenz* are not only limited to Germany. For instance, the *Carlssen* case of the Danish Supreme Court has followed the same line of reasoning as the FCC in the *Maastricht* case.[51] The Court seems to consider that it is the duty of the Danish Supreme Court to act as the ultimate watchdog of the Danish Constitution. According to Rasmussen, national courts have 'the final say' under Danish constitutional law. In a situation, where the Supreme Court disagrees with the ruling of the Court of Justice as to the validity of a Community act, it would have to say so.[52] Also, it is worth remarking that the Italian Constitutional Court has reacted to the principle of primacy because of the low fundamental rights standard. Indeed, the *Corte Costituzionale* in *Frontini and Pozzani* (1973) accepted the supremacy of Community law with the reservation that Community institutions may never violate one of the fundamental principles of the Italian Constitution.[53] The national judges reiterated their reservation in the *Granital* case (1984),[54] when they renounced their privilege to

---

[49] The *Maastricht* case may be interpreted as a mere restatement of the *Solange II* case. In other words, the German court does not exercise its jurisdiction regarding fundamental rights so long as the Community protection is essentially equivalent to the German Constitution. Another interpretation might be that the *Solange II* formula (no jurisdiction so long as) is replaced in order to become jurisdiction exercised in a relationship of co-operation with the Court of Justice in the field of fundamental rights.

[50] See BVerfGE 102, 147. In the *Banana* case, which dealt with the Regulation 404/93, German undertakings alleged breaches of Articles 12 and 14 of the Fundamental Law, concerning the right to property, the right to freely exercise a professional activity and the principle of equality. The Court explicitly relied on the *Solange II* formula and linked it with the *Maastricht* decision. The interesting part of the judgment lies in the interpretation of the requirements for constitutional complaints regarding secondary Community law. In that respect, the control of constitutionality of secondary Community law, in conformity with Article 100 of the Fundamental Law, is granted only if detailed motivations prove that the Community law measure does not guarantee the minimum level of protection of fundamental rights.

[51] *Carlsen v Prime Minister*, judgment of 6 April 1998 [1999] 3 CMLR 854.

[52] House of Lords, 'The Future Role of the European Court of Justice', 6th report, 2004, para 68.

[53] *Corte Costituzionale*, 27 December 1973, No 183, in 18 Giur.cost (1973) 2401, see also in 10 RTDE 1974, 148.

[54] *Corte Costituzionale*, 8 June 1984, No 170, in 29 Giur.cost (1984) 1098, see also in (1985) 21 RTDE, 414.

declare the national constitutional law incompatible with Community law in light of the *Simmenthal II* jurisprudence (1978).

In the UK, the debate has, essentially, focused on the question of Parliamentary sovereignty and the extent to which Parliament may, by the terms of the European Communities Act 1972 (the ECA 1972), have abrogated its authority. The adoption of the ECA 1972 led, generally, to profound modifications in the UK domestic legal order, eg concerning interpretation and remedies.[55] To quote, Lord Denning, 'when we come to matters with a European element, the Treaty is like an incoming tide. It flows into the estuaries and up our rivers. It cannot be held back. Parliament has decreed that the Treaty is henceforth to be part of our law. It is equal in force to any statute.'[56] The traditional approach of Parliamentary sovereignty has recently been reaffirmed by Lord Justice Laws in *Thoburn*.[57] Lord Justice Laws emphasized that the foundation for all Community competence was English law, since the supremacy of EU law is conditioned by the Parliament which may explicitly repeal the ECA 1972 (constitutional statute which cannot be impliedly repealed). In other words, the relationship between the EU and UK legal orders rests within the domestic law/legislature/Parliament. This view appears to be confirmed in a report of the House of Lords.[58] Based on section 2 of the ECA 1972, the UK courts must respect the principle of supremacy. However, primacy may conflict to a certain extent with the constitutional principle of Parliamentary sovereignty (supremacy) and the Parliament could explicitly adopt a provision that should take effect in spite of section 2 of the ECA 1972.

In Spain, the Constitutional Tribunal in December 2004 considered the ultimate supremacy of the national constitution without overtly confronting the primacy of EC law. Indeed, dealing with the accession to the Constitutional Treaty, the *Tribunal Constitucional* maintained that there was no rivalry between the primacy of Community law and the principle of supremacy as proclaimed in the Spanish Constitution since they constitute categories of different orders.[59] In a nutshell, primacy does not cause the invalidity of a conflicting rule; whereas supremacy concerns the hierarchy between rules and the inferior contradicting

---

[55] See concerning interpretation, A Arnull, 'Interpretation and Precedent in European Community Law', in M Andenas and F Jacobs (eds), *European Community Law in the English Courts* (OUP, 1998), 115; JA Usher, *General Principles of EC Law* (Longman, 1998), at 140–144; concerning remedies, see C Boch, *EC Law in the UK* (Longman, 2000), at 127–149.

[56] *Bulmer v Bollinger* [1974] 2 All ER 1226.

[57] Lord Justice Laws in *Thoburn v Sunderland City Council* [2002] 1 CMLR 1461, para 59 (*Metric Martyrs* Case). For comments on the *Metric Martyrs* case, see G Anthony, 'Clustered Convergence? European Fundamental Rights Standards in Irish and UK Public Law' [2004] PL 283; A O'Neill, 'Fundamental Rights and the Constitutional Supremacy of Community Law in the United Kingdom after Devolution and the Human Rights Acts' [2002] PL 724.

[58] House of Lords, 'The Future Role of the European Court of Justice', 6th report, 2004, paras 83–84.

[59] See CB Schutte, '*Tribunal Constitucional* on the European Constitution. Declaration of 13 December 2004', (2005) 1 EuConst, 281, at 288.

rule should be annulled.[60] More recently, the *European Arrest Warrant* (EAW) cases litigated in various Member States offer interesting illustrations of the limitations put by the national courts on an absolute vision of the primacy of EU law. The FCC, in 2005, declared void national measures implementing the European Arrest Warrant Framework Decision on the ground that they violate Article 16.2 of the Basic Law.[61] This provision ensures the protection of German citizens from extradition since there exists a special association between the legal system and the citizen and, in theory, the principle may not be excluded from this democratic association. It is in the light of this Article that the FCC mentioned the citizenship provision enshrined in the Constitutional Treaty (Article I-10 of the Constitutional Treaty) and, in that sense, reaffirmed the rank of the Basic Law.

Notably, the position of the FCC was followed by the Cyprus Supreme Court (CSC) which also invalidated national measures implementing EU legislation in a similar context.[62] In Poland, the Constitutional Tribunal (PCT) in April 2005 came to the same conclusion by considering that the national measure implementing EU law was contrary to Article 55 of the Constitution and thus should be annulled.[63] However, the position of the PCT was slightly different from the FCC and the Cyprus Supreme Court since it took into account the potential effects of the decision on the EU legal order and gave an 18-month transitional period to the legislature for amending the Constitution. In that sense, it may be said that the decision of the PCT was 'EU-friendly'.[64] Also, it is worth remarking that the positions of the Czech Republic Constitutional Court and the Belgian *Cour d'arbitrage* (Constitutional Court) were quite different in the *EAW* cases.[65] The Czech Republic Constitutional Court made used of the principle of construction and thus applied the *Pupino* case.[66] The *Cour d'arbitrage*, on the other hand, made a preliminary ruling to the Court of Justice on the validity of the Framework Decision.[67] Overall, it should be noted that the highest courts did not test directly the EU legislation (the Framework Decision) but the national

---

[60] For developments, see R Alonso García, 'The Spanish Constitution and the European Constitutions: the Script for a Virtual Collision and Other Observations on the Principle of Primacy', (2005) 6 German Law Journal. Interestingly, the author described the distinction as unnecessary and to a certain extent confusing. In addition, it is arguable that the distinction made by the Tribunal is rather close from concepts such as primacy in application and primacy in validity established in German law.

[61] BVerfGE 2236/04, 18 July 2005.

[62] Judgment No 294/2005, 7 November 2005.

[63] Judgment of 27 April 2005 in Case P 1/05. See also Judgment of 11 May 2005 on the Accession Treaty. The PCT strongly reaffirmed the supremacy of the national Constitution.

[64] See A Albi, 'Supremacy of EC Law in the New Member States: Bringing Parliaments into the Equation of Co-operative Constitutionalism' (2007) 3 EuConst25, at 39; J Komárek, 'European Constitutionalism and the European Arrest Warrant—In Search of the Contrapunctal Principles' Limits' (2007) 44 CML Rev 9, at 12.

[65] Czech Constitutional Court, 3 May 2006; Judgment No 124/2005 of the *Cour d'arbitrage*, 13 July 2005. The Belgian court has been renamed *Cour constitutionnelle* in May 2007.

[66] Ibid, *Cour d'arbitrage*. See T Vandamme, 'Prochain Arrêt: La Belgique !' (2008) 4 EuConst 127.

[67] Case C-303/05 *Advocaten voor de Wereld* [2007] ECR I-3633.

implemented measures. The Framework Decision has never been declared invalid by a national court.

These findings prompt a number of conclusions. First of all, it must be pointed out that the challenge to the primacy of EU law (and exclusive jurisdiction of the Court of Justice) by the highest national courts has mainly taken place in the context of constitutional provisions (fundamental rights and specific provisions such as in the *EAW* cases) and legislative competences. In the former category, the risk of constitutional conflict is practically quasi-inexistent since the national constitutions are usually modified before the adoption of new Treaties. In other words, the national constitutions are *prima facie* in conformity with EU law. If the amendment is impossible due to the deeply rooted nature of the constitutional provision, an 'opt-out' protocol always remains possible.[68] Furthermore, the CFR, which represents a high standard of protection, will acquire legally binding force with the entry into force of the EU Reform Treaty for 25 out of 27 Member States. It appears thus doubtful that fundamental rights could nowadays constitute an area where the principle of primacy might be stalwartly put into question. It may be safely argued that the reactions of the national courts in the field of fundamental rights have influenced to a large extent the Court of Justice jurisprudence. The *modus operandi* is closer to a cooperative dialogue between the national courts and the Court of Justice than a head-on confrontation.

Finally, it must be made clear that the national judicial authorities do not contest the competence of the Court of Justice to control the validity of Community law, but its exclusive jurisdiction to declare it invalid. Though in theory some of the highest national courts play down the exclusive jurisdiction of the Court of Justice, in practice they have never invalidated a Community act. Indeed, national courts would think, rethink and cogitate at length before coming to such conclusions that would result in a crisis endangering the uniformity of Community law and lead to the assured destruction of the relationship between the two legal orders. This type of extreme situation has, fortunately, been avoided by the Court of Justice in taking very seriously the preliminary questions on validity and also in establishing a healthy judicial dialogue with the national courts. Also, the attitude of the national courts in the *European Arrest Warrant* cases reflects the necessity to avoid a direct altercation. Discursive legal pluralism is making its way in Europe. But is it the same in France? Or is there a stronger constitutional resistance towards the primacy of EU law?

II. Constitutional Resistance and Discursive Legal Pluralism

In times where 40 French academics have called for a revolt against EU law in an open letter to the President of the French Republic, where the *peuple français*

---

[68] This is clearly illustrated by the abortion clause for Ireland.

has rejected the Constitutional Treaty, and where both the *Conseil constitution-nel* and the *Conseil d'Etat* have given key decisions on the reach of the principle of primacy of EC law, it appears necessary to analyse in closer detail the attitude of French courts. *Le Droit communautaire est-il en péril?* Do the rulings of French national courts reflect a clear rebellious attitude towards EU law and, in particu-lar, the jurisprudence of the European Court of Justice? Or, do they welcome, instead, its reception by scrupulously respecting the duty of sincere cooperation? It is argued that though the *Conseil d'Etat* has, in the past, been reluctant to welcome the principle of primacy, the recent jurisprudence demonstrates that it has drastically changed its stance and seeks, instead, appeasement and judicial dialogue with the Court of Justice. The *Conseil constitutionnel* with its doctrine of '*réserve de constitutionnalité*' has clearly influenced the administrative judge. Against this background, the rulings of the French courts will be analysed in the light of *discursive legal pluralism*.

A. Ex-ante Constitutional Review by the *Conseil Constitutionnel*

(i) *The Decisions on the Implementation of EU Secondary Legislation by National Measures*

The recent ruling of the *Conseil d'Etat* in *Arcelor*[69] clearly follows the pos-ition of the *Conseil constituionnel* established in various decisions concerning the implementation of Community Directives and the Constitutional Treaty. In that respect, the Decisions of the *Conseil constitutionnel* (CC) given dur-ing the summer 2004 (10 June, 1 July, and 29 July 2004) are of particular importance.[70] In its Decision 2004–496 of 10 June 2004, *confiance dans l'économie numérique*, the CC recognized, 12 years later after its amendment for the ratification of the Maastricht Treaty, the importance of Article 88–1 of the Constitution.[71] By using this provision instead of Article 55 of the Constitution, the CC acknowledged the specificity of Community law. This Article reflects the recognition by the legislature of both the *acquis communau-taire* and the constitutional nature of the French participation in the European construction.[72] By consequence, the CC considered that the implementation of a directive in an internal law results from a constitutional obligation which

---

[69] CE Ass, 8 February 2007, *Société Arcelor Atlantique et Lorraine*, Req No 287110.

[70] Decision no 2004–496 DC, 10 June 2004, *Loi pour la confiance dans l'économie numérique*, Decision no 2004–497, 1 July 2004, *Loi relative aux communications numériques et aux services de communication audiovisuelle*, Decision no 2004–498, 29 July 2004, *Loi relative a la bioéthique*.

[71] P Mazeaud, 'L'évolution de la jurisprudence du Conseil constitutionnel sur les lois de trans-position des directives', in *L'administration française et l'union européenne: Quelles influences? Quelles stratégies?*, rapport public du Conseil d'Etat, 2007, 398.

[72] J.E Schoettl, 'Primauté du droit communautaire: l'approche du Conseil constitutionnel', in *L'administration française et l'union européenne: Quelles influences? Quelles stratégies?*, rapport public du Conseil d'Etat, 2007, 379, at 382.

should not be impeded unless it is contrary to an explicit provision of the Constitution. This is the so-called '*réserve de constitutionnalité*'.[73] It may be said that secondary Community legislation is placed under the constitutional protection of Article 88–1.

In its Decision 2004–498, the CC shed light on the scope of the '*réserve de constitutionnalité*'. Here, the CC had to assess whether Article 17 of the bioethical legislation, which implements an EU Directive, was contrary to a constitutional provision (Article 11 of the Declaration of Article 1789).[74] At the end, it found that the freedom of expression is both guaranteed at the national level by Article 11 of the Declaration of 1789 and at the Community level by a general principle of Community law on the basis of Article 10 of the ECHR (paragraph 6). By consequence, the CC declared itself incompetent since the implementation of the Directive did not constitute an obstacle to an express and specific constitutional provision. In addition, it is worth remarking that in 2006 the CC modified the formulation of the '*réserve de constitutionnalité*' by stating that the implementation of a Directive should not conflict with a rule or principle inherent to the French constitutional identity. This wording, arguably, transpires the text of Article I-5 of the Constitutional Treaty.

To conclude, it appears that the CC implicitly recognizes that the principle of primacy of Community law applies in the internal legal order (this is based on Article 88–1 of the Constitution) unless there are contrary and specific constitutional provisions. Put differently, in the absence of an explicit and contrary constitutional provision reflecting the French constitutional identity, the CC recognizes the application of the *Foto-Frost* doctrine in the sense that only the Court of Justice, through preliminary ruling, may declare Community law invalid in light of the competences defined by the Treaty and the fundamental rights guaranteed by Article 6 of the Treaty on European Union.[75] At first glance, the Court of Justice appears thus as the final arbiter of Community law in the context of competences and fundamental rights. This decision, however, constitutes a limited exception to the exclusive jurisdiction of the Court of Justice to control the (in)validity of Community acts.[76]

---

[73] This approach is also confirmed by two decisions of 2006: Decision No 2006–540 DC, 27 July 2006 *Loi transposant la directive sur les droit d'auteurs*, and Decision No 2006–543 DC, 30 November 2006, *Loi transposant les directives gaz et électricité*.

[74] In its Decision No 2004–497, 1 July 2004, *Loi relative aux communications numériques et aux services de communication audiovisuelle*, the CC clarified the scope of the previous jurisprudence by stating that the necessary character of the legislative provision should be assessed in light of the unconditional and precise character of the Directive.

[75] See paragraph 4, DC 2004–498 and paragraph 7 DC 2004–496.

[76] The constitutional review by the CC under Article 54 of the Constitution seems to apply only in relation to international agreements and thus not in relation to EU secondary law. The testing would remain limited to the national measure implementing the EU legislation. See also Article 61 of the Constitution.

(ii) *The Position of the Conseil Constitutionnel on the Constitutional Treaty (Primacy Clause)*

The scope and limits of the primacy of EU law with the domestic legal order are also appreciated in the Decision 2004–505 of 19 November 2004 on the Constitutional Treaty. In addition, it gives us a piquant example as to the relationship and reconciliation between the primacy clause and Article I-5(1) of the Constitutional Treaty. The Decision proposes an extensive reasoning as to the scope of Article I-6 of the Constitutional Treaty, codifying the principle of primacy and its relationship with Article I-5 concerning the national constitutional autonomy.[77] The main question at stake is whether the French Constitution should be amended in order to ratify the Constitutional Treaty. The CC analysed, inter alia, the scope and object of the primacy clause in Union law. First, the CC focused on the nature and denomination of the Constitutional Treaty as well as its relationship with the national Constitution. In this respect, it stressed that the Constitutional Treaty remains an international Treaty and pointed out that the label (designation) of this new Treaty does not modify the position of the French Constitution, which remains at the apex of the internal judicial order, in the hierarchy of norms. Interestingly, this finding is expressly based on Article I-5 of the Constitutional Treaty.[78]

Then, regarding more specifically the reach of the supremacy principle, the CC emphasized once again the specificity of the Community legal order vis-à-vis the international legal order. The CC referred to the principle of primacy, which is enshrined in Article I-6 of the Constitutional Treaty and considered that it stems from a declaration annexed to the Treaty that the principle of supremacy has the same scope as before. Notably, the CC made reference, once again, to Article I-5 of the Constitutional Treaty, according to which the national identity of the Member States inherent to their basic political and constitutional structures should be respected. To conclude, the CC stressed that it results from all the provisions of the Constitutional Treaty and notably from Articles I-5 and I-6, that the Constitutional Treaty does not modify the nature of the European Union and the scope of the principle of primacy. Consequently, the inclusion of Article I-6 of the Constitutional Treaty shall not lead to an amendment of the French Constitution.[79]

At the end of the day, it appears that the principle of primacy, which is for the first time expressly included in a Treaty, is not contrary to the French Constitution. A strict application of Article I-6 of the Constitutional Treaty (principle of primacy) would oblige all the administrative and judicial authorities to set aside any national provision, even constitutional, contrary to the application and

---

[77] See reasoning of the French CC in Decision No 2004–505 DC of 19 November 2004. See also Decision No 2007–560 DC of 20 December 2007.
[78] Ibid, paras 9–10.   [79] Ibid, paras 11–13.

implementation of Union law. Furthermore, it would preclude all national courts to have recourse to national constitutional provisions in order to determine the validity of a Community measure. Understood in that sense, the admission of the constitutionality of Article I-6 would contradict the decisions of the CC made during the summer of 2004 and should have led to the amendment of the Constitution. As seen before, the CC has implicitly recognized that the principle of primacy of Community law applies in the internal legal order (this is based on Article 88–1 of the Constitution) unless there are contrary and specific constitutional provisions. This is the so-called '*réserve de constitutionnalité*'.[80]

However, the CC does not seem to consider that an extensive interpretation of Article I-6 of the Constitutional Treaty would conflict with the French Constitution since the primacy clause must be read in conjunction with other provisions of the Constitutional Treaty. In this respect, it results from Article I-5 of the Constitutional Treaty and the common intention of the parties reflected by the *travaux préparatoires* at the signature, that this Treaty does not modify the nature of the European Union.[81] In particular, Article I-5 of the Constitutional Treaty ensures the respect of the national judicial traditions. More precisely, it states that the Union must respect the identity of the Member States inherent to their basis political and constitutional structures. Thus, it may be said that the scope of Article I-6 of the Constitutional Treaty appears to be limited by the preceding provision concerning national constitutional autonomy (Article I-5 of the Constitutional Treaty).

(iii) *The Position of the Conseil Constitutionnel towards General Principles of Community Law*

It appears, now, important to analyse the position of the CC towards Community law and, more precisely, its general principles. In the *Maastricht I* decision,[82] the CC, using the formulation of the Court of Justice recognized the *sui generis* nature of the Community legal order (*'ordre juridique propre'*). Thus, the constitutional judge acknowledged the impact of the Community legal order into the domestic system. Notably, the CC remarked that Article F(2) of the Treaty on European Union (now Article 6(2)) explicitly refers to the general principles of Community

---

[80] In the absence of an explicit and contrary constitutional provision, the CC recognizes the application of the *Foto-Frost* doctrine in the sense that only the Court of Justice, through preliminary ruling, must control the validity of Community law in the light of the competences defined by the Treaty and the fundamental rights guaranteed by Article 6 of the Treaty on European Union. This decision constitutes a limited exception to the exclusive jurisdiction of the Court of Justice to control the validity of Community acts. The disadvantages of this '*réserve de constitutionnalité*' are negligible since they touch upon only very few areas (laïcité, égalité d'accès aux emplois publics). Extrapolating on a possible conflict, it is doubtful that the EU legislator would adopt measures that jeopardized, say the principle of secularity (*laïcité*).

[81] The principle of supremacy is also considered as already included in Article 88(1) of the Constitution.

[82] CC, No 92–308 DC, 9 April 1992.

law and stresses the important role of national courts in the application of the said Article.[83] In that regard, it could be argued that the CC recognized the obligation for the domestic jurisdiction to respect the general principles of Community law. Also, one might state that the general principles of Community law, as part of the Community legal order, appear hierarchically equal to the EC Treaty and, as such, influence the national legal order.

The Constitutional Courts in Austria,[84] Spain,[85] and Germany,[86] have made express references to the general principles of Community law. As explained by Flauss, the refusal of the CC to take explicitly into consideration the general principles of Community law constitutes a political choice.[87] Indeed, the acceptance of the general principles of Community law by the CC may reflect a certain 'communitarisation' of the constitutional norms.[88] It would make the Court of Justice appears as the supreme and final constitutional adjudicator. This choice might also be explained by resorting to three judicial arguments (lack of fundamental rights protection in EU law, lack of similar scope between the general principles of Community law and the general principles of constitutional law, and lack of preliminary references by the CC).

First, it has been argued that the EU is marked by an incomplete system concerning the protection of fundamental rights.[89] In other words, the fundamental rights protected by the general principles of Community law are few and scattered.[90] One may disagree with such an assertion. Such reasoning resembles that given by the Federal Constitutional Court in the early years. The situation has drastically changed. Consequently, this assertion, in my view, lacks full convincing force, since fundamental rights protection, nowadays, can be deemed rather strong and fully-fledged. The EU Charter of Fundamental Rights also constitutes a strong element against the 'lack of protection' thesis. Second, the basic problem is that certain general principles recognized in Community law do not constitute constitutional principles for the CC in the internal legal order. This is the situation with the principles of legal certainty,[91] legitimate expectations,[92]

---

[83] Ibid, '*Maastricht I* case', para 18.

[84] See Belgian and Spanish reports of the London FIDE Conference (2002).

[85] Constitutional Tribunal, 28 February 1994 (58/1994). The Tribunal declared sexual discrimination unconstitutional by applying the Court of Justice case law. Interestingly, Article 20(2) of the Spanish Constitution, to a certain extent, obliges the Tribunal to take Community jurisprudence into consideration. More recently, the Constitutional Tribunal made explicit reference to the Charter of Fundamental Rights.

[86] BVerfGE, 28 November 1992, 85/191. The FCC referred to the case law of the Court of Justice concerning discrimination.

[87] JF Flauss, 'Principes généraux du Droit communautaire dans la jurisprudence des juridictions constitutionnelles des États membres', in *Droits nationaux, droit communautaire: influences croisées* (CERIC, 2000) 49, at 54.

[88] Ibid, at 51.   [89] Ibid, at 57.

[90] L Favoreu, 'La constitution française et le droit communautaire', in *Droits nationaux, droit communautaire : influences croisées* (CERIC, 2000) 77, at 77.

[91] CC, No 95.339 DC, 28 December 1995.

[92] CC, No 96.385 DC, 30 December 1996.

and transparency.[93] Third, there is no direct dialogue between the CC and the Court of Justice since there is no preliminary ruling from the CC.

Finally, in 2004, the CC made an explicit reference to the general principles of Community law.[94] In the so-called *décision bioéthique*, the CC had to assess whether Article 17 of the bioethical legislation, which implements an EU Directive, was contrary to a constitutional provision (Article 11 of the Declaration of Article 1789). In the end, it found that the freedom of expression is both guaranteed at the national level by Article 11 of the Declaration of 1789 and at the Community level by a general principle of Community law on the basis of Article 10 of the ECHR (paragraph 6). This explicit reference may be seen as the upshot of the impact of the EU Charter of Fundamental Rights. This assertion appears true in light of the decision of the CC as to the constitutionality of the Treaty establishing a Constitution for Europe.[95] As seen before, after a thorough analysis of the EU Charter of Fundamental Rights, the CC concluded that there is no need to modify the national Constitution.

B. Ex-post Control by the Conseil d'Etat

Article 55 of the Constitution establishes a hierarchy of norms between international law and the French national legal order. This Article states that, '*[t]reaties and international agreements which have been lawfully ratified or approved shall, as from the date on which they are published, take precedence over Laws, subject to the requirement that the other contracting parties apply the treaties or agreements in question*'. In a nutshell, the international agreement must be ratified, published, and subjected to the principle of reciprocity. According to Vedel, the direct content of Article 55 concerns the resolution of conflicting norms. It means that a judge confronted with such a conflict must remove the internal statute contrary to the international treaty.[96] In 1975, the Court of Cassation recognized the primacy of Community law over a later French statute.[97] The reasoning was based on Article 55 of the French Constitution. Touffait, in his conclusions, advised that the reasoning should not be based on Article 55 in order to assert the primacy of Community law over national law, since it would imply that the position of Community law into the national legal order depends solely on the Constitution. In that sense, it might be contended that the general prosecutor had already determined the potential normative conflict between Community law and the wording of Article 55 of the Constitution. Very late,

---

[93] CC, No 93.335 DC, 21 January 1994.

[94] Decision No 2004–498, 29 July 2004, *Loi relative a la bioéthique*, para 6.

[95] See n 77 above, Decision No 2004–505, *Traité établissant une Constitution pour l'Europe*. See also Decision No 2007–560, *Traité de Lisbonne*.

[96] G Vedel cited in L Potvin-Solis, *L'effet des jurisprudences européennes sur la jurisprudence du Conseil d'Etat français*, LGDJ (1999) 422.

[97] Cass. Ch. mixte, 24 May 1975, *Sté des Cafés Jacques Vabre* [1975] 2 CMLR 336.

in 1989, the *Conseil d'Etat* (CE) in *Nicolo*, following the *commissaire du gouvernement* (CG) Frydman, affirmed the primacy of the international convention over a prior domestic statute (*loi postérieure*),[98] thus abolishing the so-called theory of the '*loi-écran*' (veil-statute).

It is worth noticing here that the theory of 'veil-statute' leads to affording supremacy to the domestic statute over international conventions by impeding the ordinary judge in discarding the domestic law. The said theory was established, in the late sixties, by the '*Semoules* case'.[99] Next, the CE considered in *Boisdet* that a Community Regulation prevailed over the French Law.[100] In *Rothmans*, the administrative judge considered that the refusal by the French ministry, based on a decree[101] and a statute,[102] to allow cigarette manufacturers to increase the price of their products was contrary to the 'tobacco Directive' of 19 December 1992.[103] Consequently, it annulled the decision of the French Minister. In light of the administrative jurisprudence, the hierarchy between the Constitution and the international treaties remains to be determined. However, this difficult issue appears to be tackled by the CE in the *Sarran* case and further clarified by the recent *Arcor* case in the specific field of EU law.[104]

Article 55 of the French Constitution asserts the superiority of international treaties over domestic statutes. It does not, however, refer explicitly to the Constitution. Arguably, the wording of this provision seems to indicate a hierarchy favourable to the French Constitution. The administrative jurisprudence has confirmed such a view. In *Koné*, a principle of constitutional law prevailed over international law.[105] Further, in *Aquarone*, the CE refused to make internal custom prevail over domestic constitutional law.[106] Notably, in the *Sarran* case, the CE made clear that the domestic Constitution takes precedence over the International Treaty. It appears, thus, important to analyse such a case in more detail and, particularly, in the light of Community law. *In casu*, the applicant brought an action before the Council of State invoking the illegality of a decree that had been adopted on the basis of Article 76 of the French Constitution providing for consultation of the population of New Caledonia. Sarran and Levacher argued that Articles 3 and 8 of the decree were contrary to the Articles 2, 25, and 26 of the ICCPR and Article 14 of the ECHR. The CE held that:

[98] CE Ass, 20 October 1989, *Nicolo*, RFDA 1989, 813. See J Dutheil de la Rochère, 'The Attitude of French Courts Towards ECJ Case Law', in D O'Keeffe and A Bavasso (eds), *Judicial Review in European Union Law* (Kluwer, 2000), 417, at 420–422.

[99] CE, 1 March 1968, *Syndicat General des Fabricants de Semoules de France* [1970] CMLR 395.

[100] CE, 24 September 1990, *Boisdet*, AJDA 1990, 906.

[101] Decree of the 10 December 1976.

[102] Statute of the 24 May 1976.

[103] CE, 28 February 1992, *SA Rothmans International France and SA Phillip Morris France*, AJDA 1992, 210.

[104] CE Ass, 30 October 1998, *Sarran et Levacher et autres*, AJDA 1998, 1039. See also CE, 30 July 2003, *Association Avenir de la langue française*, Recueil Lebon 2003, 347.

[105] CE Ass, 3 July 1996, *Koné*, Recueil Lebon, 255.

[106] CE Ass, 6 June 1997, *Aquarone*, RGDIP 1997, 1053.

Considérant que si l'article 55 de la constitution dispose que les traités ou accords régulièrement ratifiés ou approuvés ont, dès leur publication, une autorité supérieure à celle des lois sous réserve, pour chaque accord ou traité, de son application par l'autre partie, la suprématie ainsi conférée aux engagements internationaux ne s'applique pas, dans l'ordre interne, aux dispositions de nature constitutionnelle, qu'ainsi, le moyen tiré de ce que, le décret attaqué, en ce qu'il méconnaîtrait les stipulations d'engagements internationaux régulièrement introduits dans l'ordre interne, serait par le même contraire à l'article 55 de la constitution, ne peut lui aussi qu'être écarté.

On the one hand, this paragraph ('*considérant*') has been appraised as *obiter dictum* since the CE could have invoked its incompetence to disregard the application of the French Constitution.[107] On the other hand, it has been assessed that such a very clear statement constituted the *ratio decidendi* of the judgment.[108] Regardless, it is clear from the case that the CE emphasized the superiority of the constitutional dispositions over the international treaties. These dispositions of a constitutional nature include the written Constitution but also the constitutional principles developed by the CC. Further, it might be argued that all the international conventions are concerned since, *in casu*, the CE found that the Constitution prevailed over the ICCPR and the ECHR.[109] The CE asserted the superiority of the Constitution over international norms. The supremacy conferred by Article 55 of the Constitution to international conventions does not apply, in internal law, to dispositions of a constitutional nature. In practice, this means that it is impossible to plead before an administrative court that a constitutional disposition is contrary to an international convention.

This case clearly illustrates the conflict between the legal orders.[110] The supreme administrative court clearly established a theory of 'Constitution écran' ('veil-constitution'). In other words, being hierarchically superior, the Constitution appears immune from judicial review by an international norm (more particularly a Community norm). Rephrasing Flauss, to give an absolute character to the supremacy of the constitutional norm over the conventional norm constitutes, without doubt, an eminent dogmatic option which is apparently excessive.[111] By contrast, the other solution would have allowed the ordinary judge to review the Constitution in light of an international norm ('*contrôle de conventionnalité de la Constitution*').

---

[107]   F Chaltiel, 'Droit constitutionnel et droit communautaire', RTDE 1999, no 3, 395, at 404.

[108]   See JF Flauss, 'Contrôle de conventionnalité et contrôle de constitutionnalité devant le juge administratif' (1999) RDP 919.

[109]   Ibid, at 931.

[110]   F Chaltiel, n 107 above, at 404. See also Decision No 2004–496 DC, 10 June 2004, *Loi pour la confiance dans l'économie numérique,* Decision No 2004–669, 1 July 2004, *Loi relative aux communications numériques et aux services de communication audiovisuelle,* Decision No 2004–498, 29 July 2004, *Loi relative a la bioéthique,* Decision No 2006–540 DC, 27 July 2006, *Loi transposant la directive sur les droit d'auteurs),* and Decision No 2006–543 DC, 30 November 2006, *Loi transposant les directives gaz et électricité.*

[111]   JF Flauss, n 108 above, at 927.

Finally, it seems clear that the CE in the *Sarran* case reasserts its overriding interest and role in protecting the French Constitution and, thus, appears as its guardian.[112] This case might thus lead to serious problems, especially, in relation to Community law. To put it differently, there is a risk of conflict between constitutional and Community norms. Indeed, according to the Community jurisprudence,[113] Community law prevails over national law even constitutional law. In practice, such a conflict is very improbable. How can one assess the reaction of the CE in the context of EC law? This decision appears to me as *prima facie* negative since it goes against Community (case) law. Notwithstanding this, it is worth emphasizing, once again, that the *Sarran* case does not explicitly apply to the Community legal order.

In February 2007, the CE in *Arcelor* decided a significant case which provides a new approach departing from the theory of veil-constitution and reconciling the principle of supremacy of EC law with the supremacy of the French Constitution.[114] In this case, Arcelor and other plaintiffs challenged the decree 2004–832 implementing Directive 2003/87 after the President, the prime ministers, and other competent ministers had refused to repeal it. The applicants argued that the national measure (decree) infringed different principles (the right to property and to trade freely and the principle of equality) guaranteed by the French Constitution. In an exciting opinion, the *CG* (Mattias Guyomar) advised the CE to follow the decisions of the CC concerning national measures implementing secondary Community legislation and thus to adopt a restrictive interpretation of the so-called *réserve de constitutionnalité*. Notably, the *CG* emphasized that the solution adopted by the CC is in harmony with the jurisprudence established by various national courts in other Member States of the European Union such as in Spain (Declaration given on 13 December 2004 by the Constitutional Tribunal), Germany (the *Solange II* and *III* cases of the FCC) and Italy (*Fragd* decision of the Constitutional Court). Furthermore, he stressed the danger of a '*cavalier seul*' (lone rider) when a general movement of judicial cooperation is clearly discernable between the supreme national courts of the Member States and the Court of Justice. Also, the *CG* considered that the recent ruling of the European Court of Human Rights (EctHR) in *Bosphorus*,[115] establishing a presumption of equivalence in the context of fundamental rights, is symptomatic of this broad and new wave of judicial cooperation. In the end, The CG underlined that the '*dialogue des juges*' should be preferred to the '*guerre des juges*'.[116] The CE followed the *CG*. In its operative part (*considérant de principe*), the national court

---

[112] C Richards, 'Sarran et Levacher: Ranking Legal Norms in the French Republic' (2000) 25 ELR 192.

[113] Case 11/70 *Internationale Handelsgesellschaft* [1970] ECR 1125.

[114] See n 69 above.

[115] Judgment of 30 June 2005, *Bosphorus Airways v Ireland*, Application No 45036/98.

[116] As noted by the CG, the expression '*dialogue des juges*' had been used 20 years ago by Bruno Genevois.

referred first to Articles 55 and 88–1 of the Constitution. According to the CE, Article 88–1 imposes a constitutional obligation to implement Directives. Then, the CE established very clear and detailed guidelines on how to assess the validity of a national measure implementing Community law when the parties argue a breach of fundamental rights enshrined in the Constitution. In that regard, the highest administrative court emphasized that the control of constitutionality of the national measure implementing the Directive must be exercised by having recourse to a specific method in the situation where the national measures implement unconditional and precise provisions, ie provisions having direct effect.[117] At the outset, the administrative judge must establish whether the alleged constitutional principle is also protected, both in nature and scope, by the general principles of Community law as interpreted by the (most recent) case law of the Court of Justice. Indeed, the general principles of Community law should guarantee, by their application, the effective respect of the constitutional disposition or principle. If there is such a protection, the administrative judge must scrutinize the national measure in the light of the general principles of Community law. In the absence of doubts as to the validity of the act, the national judge should discard the argument; in the contrary situation, he/she should refer a question on validity to the Court of Justice. If there is no such a protection (absence of a general principle of Community law), the national judge must directly examine the constitutionality of the implementing measures. Notably, the CE, in the circumstances of the case, considered that the alleged rights to property and trade and the principle of equality also constitute general principles of Community law which are protected in the same way in the French Constitution.

To conclude, one may venture to say that the operative part of the ruling appears very well articulated and thus contrasts with the laconic formulation generally used by French courts in drafting judgments. In that sense, it may be said that the *Arcelor* case also has an informative and pedagogical purpose for the lower administrative judges when they (will) examine the validity of the national measures implementing Community law. Therefore, this case, arguably, established a (horizontal) judicial dialogue at the national level. In addition, it is worth noting that the CE considered that there might be a problem of validity of the Directive in relation to the principle of equality and decided in March 2007 to refer a question to the Court of Justice.[118] Another (vertical) dialogue is here established, this time

---

[117] See C Charpy, 'The Status of (Secondary) Community Law in the French Internal Order: The Recent Case-Law of the *Conseil Constitutionnel* and the *Conseil d'Etat*' (2007) 3 EuConst 436, at 462. The author considers that this leads to the abandonment of the theory of the screen Act of Parliament and opens the door to (*a posteriori*) constitutional review of Acts of Parliament by ordinary French courts, until now the exclusive competence of the CC.

[118] Case C-127/07 *Société Arcelor Atlantique et Lorraine*, lodged on 5 March 2007. As put by the national court: is Directive 2003/87/EC of 13 October 2003 valid in the light of the principle of equal treatment, in so far as that Directive makes the greenhouse gas emission allowance trading scheme applicable to installations in the steel sector without including in its scope the aluminium and plastic industries?

with the Court of Justice through the use of the preliminary ruling procedure. Importantly, this case does not constitute an isolated example of the increasing cooperation of the CE with the Court of Justice. In December 2006, in *De Groot*, the CE departed from its previous jurisprudence (*ONIC*[119]) and recognized an extensive interpretation of the authority of preliminary rulings.[120]

C. Discursive Legal Pluralism and the Prevention of Constitutional Conflicts

(i) Vous Avez Dit Discursive Legal Pluralism?

Legal pluralism has become very popular in the doctrinal vernacular and different *courants* of constitutionalism may be identified.[121] One of them, *multi-level constitutionalism* or *Verfassungsverbund* (compound of constitution) originates from Germany and more precisely from the theory of Pernice.[122] European and national constitutional law constitute two levels of a unitary system. The essence of multi-level constitutionalism is based on the non-hierarchical relationship between the EU and national legal orders. Another branch can be called *liberal legal pluralism* and finds its roots in the writings of Kumm.[123] The author considers two scenarios in cases where a national court might invalidate EU secondary legislation: the *Cassandra scenario* and the *Pangloss scenario*.[124] The *Cassandra scenario* is based on the prophecy and fear of a major constitutional cataclysm in such a situation. The *Pangloss* scenario views the risk of constitutional explosion as more or less inexistent and refutes the domino effect of such an attitude. Kumm considers that there are solid grounds to deem that the second scenario comes closer to depict probable events than the first and argues for a residual and subsidiary role to be given to the national courts as ultimate arbitrators of fundamental constitutional commitments.[125]

By contrast, *discursive legal pluralism* offers a framework for preventing the constitutional conflicts. Maduro has established a set of (contrapuntal) principles which forms the basis of this theory and aims at ensuring the coherence of the system.[126] The hallmark of his theory is based on dialogue: a horizontal discourse (between national courts) and a vertical discourse (between the Court of Justice

---

[119] CE, 26 July 1985, *ONIC*, Req No 42204.

[120] CE, 11 December 2006, *De Groot en Slot Allium,* Req No 234560.

[121] For an extensive classification of the different branches of constitutionalism, see M Avbelj, 'Questioning EU Constitutionalism' (2008) 9 German Law Journal, No 1.

[122] I Pernice, 'Multilevel Constitutionalism in the European Union' (2002) 27 ELR 511.

[123] M Kumm, 'The Jurisprudence of Constitutional Conflict: Constitutional Supremacy in Europe before and after the Constitutional Treaty' (2005) 11 ELJ 262.

[124] Ibid, at 291–293.

[125] Ibid, at 304. The author proposes that national court may give precedence to their specific and essential constitutional provisions for striking EU legislation.

[126] MP Maduro, 'Contrapunctal Law: Europe's Constitutional Pluralism in Action', in N Walker (ed), *Sovereignty in Transition* (Hart, 2003) 501.

and the national courts). In addition, *discursive legal pluralism* takes into consideration the so-called *institutional choice* and thus views the question of ultimate authority not only as a question of legal sovereignty but also as closely linked to political sovereignty.[127] Finally, *discursive legal pluralism* takes very seriously the risk of constitutional cataclysm in the event of a national court invalidating an EU secondary legislation. We may call that the *Martin's scenario*. This pessimistic scenario appears to me closer to describing a likely event for multiple reasons.

First of all, there are no valid reasons to rule out that a *race to the bottom* would happen.[128] It is tenable to argue that the *EAW* cases demonstrate that a domino effect is highly probable. Furthermore, it would make no sense to base the source of validity of EU law at the domestic level when there is a bridge based on domestic constitutional arrangement permitting EU law to travel in order to play its (supreme) role in the national legal order.[129] Also, this situation will destroy the integrity of Article 234 of the EC Treaty by blurring the separation of functions between the Court of Justice and the national courts. Going further, it could be contended that if a national court invalidates EU secondary legislation, then the Court of Justice should have the possibility, in turn, to nullify national legislation. Symmetry should be respected in order to ensure the coherence of the system. This is, of course, an unworkable situation. Finally, the growing uses of qualified majority voting as well as enlargement have clearly increased the risk of constitutional frictions. As to the new Member States, it is not a secret that most of them boast very powerful constitutional courts using a system of ex-post constitutional review.[130] Concerning qualified majority voting, the German 'Banana' case has offered a perfect example of the palpable tension. The risk of threat is very high.[131] We should prevent the *Martin's scenario*. Conflicts on the meaning and range of primacy cannot be resolved by requiring the Court of Justice and the domestic courts to jettison their claim. Compromise is necessary and the dialogue is of the essence.

(ii) On Vertical and Horizontal Dialogues

Dialogue is indispensable between the Court of Justice and the national courts. To begin with, it should be noted that the national courts are the preferred

[127] See for developments, A Albi, 'Supremacy of EC Law in the New Member States: Bringing Parliaments into the Equation of Co-operative Constitutionalism' (2007) 3 EuConst 25, at 39; J Komárek, 'European Constitutionalism and the European Arrest Warrant—In Search of the Contrapunctal Principles' Limits' (2007) 44 CML Rev 9, at 12.

[128] Ibid.

[129] S Weatherill, Memorandum, Select Committee on European Union, House of Lords, submitted on 5 October 2003.

[130] MP Maduro, 'Contrapunctal Law: Europe's Constitutional Pluralism in Action', in N Walker (ed), *Sovereignty in Transition* (Hart, 2003), at 508–509. According to author, in a situation where of ex-post constitutional judicial review is lacking, the possibility of conflict between EU acts (other than treaties) and national constitutions is, to a large extent, eliminated.

[131] See n 50 above.

interlocutors of the Court of Justice. This assertion appears true by considering the special and crucial role given to the preliminary ruling procedure in the European legal order. In a similar vein, the national courts are the *'power-house'* of EU law.[132] Indeed, the local courts enforce Community law by applying the principle of construction (indirect effect) and Member State liability; and—more generally—are entrusted with ensuring the legal protection which citizens derive from Community law, eg in the context of national procedural autonomy (effectiveness/equivalence) and human rights. This transfer of power is vital in order to ensure the efficacy of the system since the Court of Justice cannot obviously take all the 'enforcement' burden. This delegation also means an increased discretion given to the national courts to assess, for instance, the proportionality of national measures in free movement or/and fundamental rights' cases.[133]

The importance of this accommodating dialogue has been recognized both by the national courts and the Court of Justice. Already, in the *Maastricht* decision, the Federal Constitutional Court pointed out the need of a *'relationship of cooperation'* in the context of fundamental rights.[134] As an aside, this case shows that an indirect dialogue is established between the Court of Justice and the national constitutional courts even when no preliminary rulings procedure is made available.[135] The same remark applies to, for instance, Italy,[136] France,[137] and Spain.[138] It is worth noting that the French CC justified the absence of direct dialogue by the nature of the *ex-ante* system of constitutional review. Interestingly, the CC has also stressed that it depends on the ordinary national courts to refer, by way of preliminary ruling, to the Court of Justice, as the occasion arises.

The judicial discourse is also established or encrypted within the Court of Justice case law relating to the (effective) judicial protection of individuals. In that respect, it is worth recalling the *UPA* case where the Court of Justice stated that:

in accordance with the principle of sincere cooperation laid down in Article 5 of the Treaty [new Article 10 of the EC Treaty], national courts are required, so far as possible, to interpret and apply national procedural rules governing the exercise of rights of action in a way that enables natural and legal persons to challenge before the courts the

[132] D Edward, 'National Courts—the Powerhouse of Community Law' (2002) 5 CYELS 1.

[133] MP Maduro, 'Contrapunctal Law: Europe's Constitutional Pluralism in Action', in N Walker (ed), *Sovereignty in Transition* (Hart, 2003), at 528–529.

[134] FC Mayer, 'The European Constitution and the Courts', in A von Bogdandy and J Bast, *Principles of European Constitutional Law* (Hart, 2006), at 312–313.

[135] The FCC has never made a preliminary ruling to the Court of Justice. See also, FCC, 5 August 1998, BVR 264/98. The situation is different with the constitutional courts in Austria (Case C-144/99 *Adria-Wien Pipeline* [2001] ECR I-8365) and Belgium (*Cour d'arbitrage Belge*, Case No 6/97, 19 February 1997).

[136] Case No 536/95, 29 December 1995. No longer since April 2008; see Case No 103/08.

[137] Case No 2006–540 DC, 27 July 2006, *Loi transposant la directive sur les droit d'auteurs*.

[138] Case No 28/1991, 14 February 1991.

legality of any decision or other national measure relative to the application to them of a Community act of general application, by pleading the invalidity of such an act.[139]

Notably, the Court in 2007 has delivered in the *Segi* case the same type of (subliminal?) message in relation to the judicial protection of individuals within the third pillar.[140] The case established a duty of loyal cooperation for the national courts within Union law. In addition, the *Unibet* case affirms once again the importance of the national courts in the context of national procedural autonomy.[141] This new trend appears to reinforce the dialogue between the national courts and the Court of Justice.

The spirit of conciliation also arises from the jurisprudence of the Court in the field of fundamental rights. The Court of Justice appears ready to respect the specific constitutional identity of the Member States.[142] At least, this is my reading of the *Omega case,* in which the Court balanced the right to dignity (Article 1 of the German Basic Law) with the freedom to provide services.[143] It is interesting to note that the Court in *Laval* made an explicit reference to the importance of the right to collective action enshrined in the Swedish Constitution.[144] This is not really the style of the Court to make such an observation in relation to the general principles of Community law. Moreover, it appears that the Court of Justice has given discretion to the national courts in applying the proportionality test.[145] As put clearly in *Viking Line*, 'it is ultimately for the national court, which has sole jurisdiction to assess the facts and interpret the national legislation, to determine whether and to what extent such collective action meets those requirements'.[146] The domestic court is explicitly

[139] Case P C-50/00 *UPA v Council* [2002] ECR I-6677, para 42.

[140] Case C-355/04 P *SEGI v Council* [2007] ECR I-1657, para 38.

[141] Case C-432/05 *Unibet* [2007] ECR I-2271, paras 38–39, '[u]nder the principle of cooperation laid down in Article 10 EC, it is for the Member States to ensure judicial protection of an individual's rights under Community law... it is for the domestic legal system of each Member State to designate the courts and tribunals having jurisdiction and to lay down the detailed procedural rules governing actions for safeguarding rights which individuals derive from Community law.'

[142] Extrapolating on a possible conflict in relation to French law, it is doubtful that the EU legislator would adopt measures that jeopardized, say, the principle of secularity (*laïcité*). Yet one might imagine a conflict concerning a national measure falling within the scope of EU law in the context of fundamental rights. For instance, a national from a Member State working in France in the public administration, could be impeded, according to domestic legislation (law on religious signs), to work because he/she is wearing an ostensible religious sign, eg Sikh man or Muslim woman. This conflict might be the object of a preliminary ruling to the Court of Justice on the interpretation of free movement of workers and freedom of religion/expression. The Court of Justice would have to solve a conflict between a very strong constitutional principle (principle of secularity [*laïcité*]) and the fundamental rights enshrined in the Union legal order. The Court in this situation would certainly use a wide margin of appreciation for the Member State, acknowledging thus the 'density' of the constitutional principle.

[143] Case C-36/02 *Omega* [2004] ECR I-9609.

[144] See *Laval*, para 92, n 11 above.

[145] See *Viking Line*, paras 80–85, n 11 above. The Court of Justice may, however, provide guidance.

[146] Ibid, para 85.

seen as the ultimate arbiter of the validity of national law in the context of EU fundamental rights. Besides, in *Advocaten voor de Wereld*, a preliminary ruling on validity of the EAW Framework Decision, the Court has confirmed the need for dialogue and concession within the third pillar.[147] Indeed, it appears clear that the Court of Justice has given a wide margin of appreciation to the Member States in the third pillar and, in the same way, confirmed the importance of fundamental rights for limiting Member State action in this area. Put in the context of the *EAW* saga—which can be perceived in itself as a horizontal discourse between the highest courts—this ruling of the Court of Justice could be seen as fitting perfectly with *discursive legal pluralism*. Indeed, as outlined by Sarmiento, the decision of the Court of Justice confirmed the Czech approach and gave some support to the German and Cypriot cases by confirming the Member State's wide discretion in third pillar matters.[148] The upshot of all this is that a spirit of dialogue and compromise emerges from this multi-level system of European constitutionalism. But can we draw such a conclusion in light of the French decisions?

(iii) *Judicial Dialogue and the French Decisions*

With the decisions of summer 2004 and the consecration of the doctrine of '*réserve de constitutionnalité*', it appears that the CC implicitly recognizes that the principle of primacy of Community law applies in the internal legal order unless there are contrary and specific constitutional provisions.[149] Put differently, in the absence of conflict with a rule or principle inherent to the French constitutional identity, what Mazeaud, President of the CC, calls *l'essentiel de la République*, the CC recognizes the application of the *Foto-Frost* doctrine in the sense that only the Court of Justice, through preliminary rulings, may declare Community law invalid in light of the competences defined by the Treaty and the fundamental rights guaranteed by Article 6 of the Treaty on European Union.[150] At first glance, the Court of Justice appears thus as the final arbiter of Community law in the context of competences and fundamental rights. This decision, however, constitutes a limited exception to the exclusive jurisdiction of the Court of Justice to control the (in)validity of Community acts. The principle of primacy is welcomed. However, there is no general acceptance of absolute primacy as viewed by the Court of Justice; the European principle is thus not fully embraced. The same conclusion holds true in relation to the CE. Since the *Arcelor* case, the CE is now in line with the jurisprudence of the

---

[147] Case C-303/05 *Advocaten voor de Wereld* [2007] ECR I-3633.

[148] See D Sarmiento, 'European Union: The European Arrest Warrant and the Quest for Constitutional Coherence', International Journal of Constitutional Law, Advance Access published online on 3 January 2008.

[149] This is the formulation used by the CC in 2004 and it may be seen as controversial. In 2006, the CC made reference to the French constitutional identity. The CC was certainly influenced by the wording of Article I-5 of the Constitutional Treaty. The CE makes use of another formulation which refers to the 'level of protection'.

[150] See paragraph 4, DC 2004–498 and paragraph 7, DC 2004–496.

CC. This constitutes a manifestation of horizontal discourse which ensures, in fact, the coherence of the national system. In a similar vein, the *Arcelor* case reflects a new stance of the administrative judge vis-à-vis EU law and constitutes, notably, a very didactic decision establishing a test to be applied by the administrative judge when confronted with an alleged violation of national constitutional norms by measures implementing secondary Community legislation. In comparison to its previous jurisprudence, it may be said that the CE accepts the judicial dialogue with the Court of Justice. As rightly stressed by the *CG* in *Arcelor*, a general trend of judicial cooperation is clearly discernable between the supreme national courts of the Member States and the Court of Justice. It results from this movement that the primacy of Community law is co-existing peacefully with the Constitution. This legal pluralism was also reflected by the text of the Constitutional Treaty which though codifying the principle of primacy (Article I-6 of the Constitutional Treaty) does not explicitly mention the prevalence of Community law over national constitutional law. Furthermore, Article I-5 of the Constitutional Treaty emphasized the importance of national constitutional autonomy and had to be read in conjunction with Article I-6 of the Constitutional Treaty.

Recent years have also been marked by key rulings (*SNIP*, *Freymuth*, and *Arcelor*) concerning EU fundamental rights (general principles of Community law) which clearly welcome them in the French legal order.[151] The CE in *SNIP* considered that the general principles have an equal status in the legal hierarchy to the EC Treaty and concluded that the general principles of Community law are norms which prevail over national statutes. In this sense, it confirms that the general principles constitute a '*super-légalité communautaire*'.[152] By recognizing the primacy of the general principles of Community law, the CE follows the path opened in 1989 by the *Nicolo* case[153] and, in addition, brings more coherence to the review system in the context of European remedies. More precisely with regards to the latter, it allows national courts to review the national statute, not only in light of the ECHR, but also in connection with the general principles of Community law.[154] Thus, it reinforces the '*judicial arsenal*'[155] of the CE. However, a strict dichotomy between Community law matters and purely internal situations results from the *Freymuth* jurisprudence. To put it differently, the administrative judge establishes a '*réserve de nationalité*' as to the application

---

[151] CE, 9 May 2001, *Freymuth,* Req No 210944; CE, 3 December 2001, *Syndicat national de l'industrie pharmaceutique et autres (SNIP)*, RFDA 2002, p 166.
[152] G Isaak, *Droit communautaire général* (7th edn, Armand Colin, 1999), at 160, D Simon, *Le système juridique communautaire* (PUF, 1997), at 254.
[153] See n. 98 above.
[154] See AL Valembois, 'La prévalence des principes généraux du droit communautaire sur la loi nationale, à propos de l'arrêt du Conseil d'Etat du 3 décembre 2001, Syndicat national de l'industrie pharmaceutique et autres', AJDA 2002 Chroniques, 1219.
[155] Ibid.

of the general principles of Community law and is thus not ready to accept their spill-over within purely internal matters. Finally, it seems clear from *Arcelor* that a dialogue is established with the Court of Justice in relation to its jurisprudence on fundamental rights and the examination of national measures implementing secondary legislation. The administrative judge must establish whether the alleged constitutional principle is also protected, both in nature and scope, by the general principles of Community law as interpreted by the (most recent) case law of the Court of Justice.

Indeed, the general principles of Community law should guarantee by their application the effective respect of the constitutional disposition or principle. The dialogue is also visible within the constitutional jurisprudence. Indeed, for the very first time in 2004, the CC made an explicit reference to EU fundamental rights (general principles of Community law). It may be said that EU fundamental rights are now part of the so-called *bloc de constitutionnalité*.[156] The CC has also underlined the importance of Article 88 of the Constitution, instead of Article 55, and has thus recognized the specificity of the EU legal order.[157] More generally this line of jurisprudence marks, in my view, the general acceptance—and thus the implied recognition of its level of protection—of the fundamental rights case law as elaborated by the Court of Justice. The vertical dialogue is here more subtle. Finally, it can be safely argued that there is no French exception as to the application of primacy. The decisions of the CC and CE enter clearly within a general movement of cooperation and dialogue. *Discursive legal pluralism* is making its way into European constitutionalism.

---

[156] C Charpy, 'The Status of (Secondary) Community Law in the French Internal Order: The Recent Case-Law of the *Conseil Constitutionnel* and the *Conseil d'Etat*' 3 EuConst (2007) 436, at 462.

[157] In *Arcelor*, the CE referred both to Articles 55 and 88 of the Constitution. In *Nicolo* and *Sarran*, the cases were based on Article 55. The use of Article 88 can also be seen as a sign of *discursive legal pluralism* since the CC and CE recognize the specificity of the EU legal order.

Procedural Overview and Substantive Comments on Articles 226 and 228 EC

*Stine Andersen**

I. Summary

This article takes stock of the general EC infringement procedure established under the EC Treaty, Articles 226 concerning failure to apply and enforce Community law, and 228 concerning failure to take the necessary measures to comply with a judgment of the European Court of Justice (ECJ), ie, repetitive infringements. The aim of the article is two-fold. First, it accounts for the procedural steps involved in the light of pertinent case law and secondly, it appraises the procedure against contemporary international law and international relations compliance theory. It is demonstrated that the European Community (EC) infringement procedure is primarily based on non-coercive consensus-building and problem-solving. Nonetheless, it proposes a durable procedural framework for awarding pecuniary sanctions. Specifically, Article 228 of the EC Treaty concerning Member State failure to comply with a judgment of the ECJ remedies some of the drawbacks international lawyers have pointed out characterize sanctions, viz, matters pertaining to (i) mobilization, (ii) legitimacy, (iii) maintenance of sanctions, and (iv) boycotts versus fines. Thus, it is maintained, the European Commission has been granted a tool to put sustained pressure on defaulting Member States while maintaining them in a process towards compliance and this in a manner which does not undermine the treaty regime's legitimacy.

* Stine Andersen, assistant attorney at Kammeradvokaten (Legal Adviser to the Danish Government)/Law Firm Poul Schmith. The views expressed are those of the author. This article is based on a chapter from my doctoral dissertation 'The Commission's Role in Ensuring Member State Compliance with Community Law' defended in 2007 at the European University Institute, Florence. I wish to thank Gráinne de Búrca and Christian Joerges for their very helpful comments and suggestions on earlier drafts. The usual disclaimer applies. stine.andersen@eui.eu.

II. Introduction

The EC[1] has been conceptualized within the terms of various frameworks including those of public international law and constitutional law. However it is most often referred to as a third and *sui generic* entity.[2] Though the legal foundations of the European (Economic) Community are 'instruments of international law',[3] significant differences persist in terms of organization and authority. It is the special features of supranationalism such as the institutionalisation of *autonomous* legislative, judicial and executive powers which set the EC apart from other international organizations. Lawyers and students of international relations concerned with enforcement of supranational and international law have of course considered comparable themes across regimes, including deterrence, norm internalization, persuasion, the significance of statal long-term and short-time self-interest, the extent to which federal experiences can be relied upon, etc. In particular, one condition underpins international law in general as well as the EC in particular, that is, the lack of a definitive central authority,[4] or an identifiable sovereign,[5] to back legal commands by force vis-à-vis sovereign states.[6] The EC Member States have the primary responsibility of giving effect to the *acquis Communautaire*.[7] In political terms, the government and national Parliaments[8] are accountable and in technical and legal terms, the governments and myriad administrative and judicial authorities. As compared with many international law regimes in which

---

[1] Until the entry into force of the Maastricht Treaty, the European *Economic* Community. This article is only concerned with the EC pillar of the European Union, ie the EC Treaty.

[2] Bruno de Witte enquires whether 'Community law *is* still a branch of international law' taking the procedures for its amendment as an analytical point of reference. B de Witte, 'Rules of Change in International Law: How Special is the European Community?', in LANM Barnhoorn and KC Wellens (eds) *Diversity in Secondary Rules and the Unity of International Rules* (Martijn Nijhoff Publishers, 2005). It is concluded that '[o]n a global evaluation, the rules of change of the European Community...remain closely modelled on the traditional rules of international law.'

[3] AA Levasseur and RE Scott, *The Law of the European Union—A New Constitutional Order* (Carolina Academic Press, 2001) 341.

[4] Compare the discussion on national and international law in *Black and White Taxicab & Transfer Co v Brown and Yellow Taxicab & Transfer Co* 276 US 518, 533 (1928) (Dissenting opinion). See also R Fisher, *Improving Compliance with International Law* (University Press of Virginia, 1981) 11–12.

[5] *Southern Pacific Co v Jensen* 244 US 205, 222 (1917) (Dissenting opinion).

[6] See discussion by C Joerges in M Zürn and C Joerges (eds), *Law and Governance in Postnational Europe. Compliance Beyond the Nation-State* (Cambridge University Press, 2005) 262–266.

[7] According to Article 10 of the EC Treaty, Member States shall take all appropriate measures to ensure fulfilment of the obligations arising from the Treaty or resulting from action taken by the institutions of the Community. See also the answer given by Mr Fischler on behalf of the Commission to Written Question P-1052/2000 [2001] OJ 72E (06.03.2001), pp 17–18. The Member State remains responsible regardless of possible delegation of implementation power to for instance a federal or regional level of government. See Cases C-96/81 *Commission v Netherlands* [1982] ECR I-1791, 97/81 *Commission v Netherlands* [1982] ECR I-1819, Joined Cases 227/85, 228/85, 229/85 and 230/85 *Commission v Belgium* [1988] ECR 1, para 9 and in 131/88 *Commission v Germany* [1991] ECR I-825, para 71.

[8] The Commission/Internal Market addresses Member State Parliaments directly in recognition of their critical role in 'correct and timely transposition'. See Recommendation from the Commission on the transposition into national law of Directives affecting the internal market, SEC 2004/918 final, 12.7.2004, para 4.

enforcement is a matter to be addressed and settled between treaty-signatories, a distinct feature of the EC system is the existence and function of the European Commission (the Commission) with autonomous powers to monitor Member State compliance and, significantly, to engage judicially binding sanctions.[9] With the establishment of the (E)EC Treaty, the signatories agreed to institutionalize supervision by the Commission in addition to the judicial review undertaken by the Court of Justice of the European Communities (the ECJ or the Court), thereby introducing an explicit third party.[10] Thus the Commission has, in somewhat vague terms, a duty, to 'ensure that the provision of... [the EC] Treaty and the measures taken by the institutions pursuant thereof are applied'.[11] It is the guardian of the Treaty. The task is generally exercised within the legal framework of Articles 226 (Article 169 EEC) and 228 EC (Article 171 EEC), ie the general Community infringement procedure.[12] It is, however, not exclusive. Thus, a range of additional *lex specialis* procedures have been established in the EC Treaty.

Article 226 of the EC Treaty concerns failure to apply and enforce Community law, while Article 228 concerns failure to take the necessary measures to comply with a judgment of the ECJ, ie repetitive infringements. Both procedures contain a two-stage administrative phase and a judicial phase, however, only Article 228 allows for Member State sanctions.[13] Thus, the legal construction distinguishes between compliance with treaty obligations, 'first order compliance', and compliance with judgments of the treaty regime's dispute settlement body, 'second order compliance'.[14] The basics of the principal tool available to the Commission for

---

[9] Article 211 of the EC Treaty. The Security Council is strictly speaking an autonomous institution with supervisory as well as sanctioning powers. Because of its composition and decision-making procedures, I do not include the Council and its subsidiary sanctioning and monitoring branches in my categorization of independent institutions. There are a number of monitoring bodies within the realm of the UN some of which give interpretive guidance. The Human Rights Committee is one example. It issues general comments to signatories of the International Covenant on Civil and Political Rights based on reports submitted by the States (Article 40). The committee does not have judicial recourse but may, on request, attempt to mediate between disputing States (Articles 41 and 42).

[10] FV Kratochwil, *Rules, Norms, and Decisions: on the Conditions of Practical and Legal Reasoning in International Relations and Domestic Affairs* (Cambridge University Press, 1989), 181–182.

[11] Article 211 of the EC Treaty.

[12] In this paper, the 'infringement procedure' refers to both Article 226 and Article 228 of the EC Treaty. At times the Commission uses the notion to denote both provisions. See, eg Commission Official web page: <http://europa.eu.int/institutions/comm/index_en.htm>. On occasion the Commission uses it to address Article 226 of the EC Treaty. See, eg Commission Communication on Better Monitoring of the Application of Community Law, COM/2002/725 final, p 3, n 3. The objective of the EC infringement procedure is to 'prevent' them 'from failing in their obligations under the Treaty. See in this regard, Case 249/81 *Commission v Ireland* [1982] ECR 4005.

[13] In the Reform Treaty the Commission shall not issue a reasoned opinion before bringing a Member State before the Court of Justice under Article 260 TFEU (Article 228 EC). Furthermore, the Commission may request sanctions already under Article 258 TFEU (Article 226 EC) for initial failure to transpose directives into domestic law.

[14] See generally R Fisher, *Improving Compliance with International Law* (Charlottesville: University Press of Virginia, 1981) for this distinction. It should be noted that Fisher is not concerned with Community law. Although I refer to the distinction, nothing else of the author's general theoretical framework is implied. A differentiation similar to the one between EC Member State failure to observe Community law, on the one hand, and failure to comply with a judgment of the ECJ on

carrying out its supervisory function have remained largely unchanged with the one exception of the sanctions mechanism inserted in the Treaty of Maastricht.[15] It should be noted that the EC Treaty explicitly empowers Member States to initiate direct infringement proceedings.[16] Article 227 of the EC Treaty is seldom invoked, and it is remarkable that a mere handful of cases have been referred to the Court since the signing of the Rome Treaty.[17] Nevertheless, the maintenance of the legal and thus political ability to pursue infringements constitutes a safeguard for the Member States attributing independent supervisory powers to the Commission. It has been vital for the establishment of statal confidence in a system which primarily relies on third-party monitoring and which allows the Commission full discretion in deciding whether to pursue infringements.

The article proceeds as follows. First, it discusses the notions of enforcement, compliance and effectiveness.[18] Secondly, it describes the procedural steps of the EC infringement procedure and reviews pertinent case law. Finally, it analyses the procedure in view of the international law compliance theory. It does so in order to explain and better understand the purpose and function of the procedural steps and the role of the Commission, and to bring out the distinct features of the institutional designs and organizational rules which have made it a particularly robust enforcement mechanism.

III. Supranational Enforcement

A. Article 226 EC

(i) Enforcement

In its literal meaning, enforcement is the process of increasing the strength of something,[19] to compel observance or fulfilment of an obligation.[20] Some

the other is made within the WTO Dispute Settlement Understanding Article 21 on Surveillance of Implementation of Recommendations and Rulings and Article 22 on Compensation and Suspension of Concessions. 'The DSU rules . . . recognize the different legal and political dimensions of such "follow-up disputes" by providing for recourse to arbitration procedures with short deadlines.' See EU Petersmann, 'Justice as Conflict Resolution: Proliferation, Fragmentation and Decentralization of Dispute Settlement in International Trade' EUI WP, LAW No. 2004/10, p 40. See also p 24.

[15] Treaty on European Union signed in Maastricht on 7 February 1992, entered into force on 1 November 1993.

[16] Article 227 of the EC Treaty.

[17] Cases 141/78 *France v UK* [1979] ECJ 2923, C-388/95 *Belgium v Spain* [2000] ECR I-3123, and C-145/04 *Spain v UK* [2006] ECR I, n.y.r., stand as exceptions to the rule. The statistics on direct infringement proceedings should be seen against the background of a well-established practice of Member State intervention in direct actions initiated by the Commission together with the Member State right to submit observations in preliminary ruling proceedings as foreseen in Article 23 in the Protocol on the Statute of the Court of Justice, [2002] OJ C325 (24.12.2002), pp 167–181.

[18] On these notions, see also AJ Gil Ibáñez, *The Administrative Supervision and Enforcement of EC Law* (Hart, 1999).

[19] *Oxford English Dictionary Online* (OUP, 2004), para 1.

[20] Ibid, para 5. K Carter, 'New Crimes against Peace? The Application of International Humanitarian Law Compliance and Enforcement', in Canadian Council on International Law

authors employ enforcement in a more generic sense as 'the process of compliance-generation, independent of the means (ie coercion or management) chosen'.[21] In the further text, enforcement refers to all action undertaken by the Commission, formally as well as informally, in view of Articles 226 and 228 of the EC Treaty irrespective of whether it is done in a cooperative, persuasive, or coercive fashion or in a combination thereof.

(ii) Compliance and Effectiveness

The Member States' obligation to take the appropriate measures to ensure fulfil-ment of Community law and to facilitate the achievement of the Community's tasks is unambiguous. However, the notions of compliance and effectiveness deserve brief consideration. Compliance refers to conduct in conformity with a specified rule.[22] Carter adds that the notion implies more than merely acting in accordance with a given norm. There is an additional indication of 'consensual conformity'.[23] The author thus suggests that norm-conforming behaviour which has been brought about by sheer coercion should not be included in the standard conception of compliance. This would be some variety of 'conformity for instru-mental reasons'.[24] Even if absolute compliance is not reached, law itself and also institutional designs may yield some behavioural change. Young maintains that non-compliance is 'when actual behaviour departs significantly from prescribed behaviour'.[25] Thus, absolute compliance is not a gauge for a successful regime. On the contrary, both in domestic, federal, and international law regimes, a cer-tain degree of failure is, and has to be, accepted[26] and perhaps it is more useful to ask whether tolerable levels of law-deviance are maintained.[27] The normative expectation of compliance with Community law is rising however, encouraged by the successful attainment of integration objectives and the deepening and broadening of the regime.[28]

and The Markland Group (eds), *Treaty Compliance: Some Concerns and Remedies* (Kluwer Law International, 1998), 2.

[21] M Zürn, 'Law and Compliance at Different Levels', in Michael Zürn and Christian Joerges (eds), *Law and Governance in Postnational Europe, Compliance beyond the Nation-State* (Cambridge University Press, 2004), 7, n 8.

[22] K Raustiale and A Slaughter, 'International Law, International Relations and Compliance', in W Carlsnaes, T Risse, and BA Simmons (eds), *Handbook of International Relations* (SAGE, 2002), 539. R Fisher, *Improving Compliance with International Law* (University Press of Virginia, 1981) 20.

[23] K Carter, n 20 above, at 2.

[24] K Raustiale and A Slaughter, n 22 above, at 539.

[25] O Young, *Compliance and Public Authority: A Theory with International Implications* (Johns Hopkins University Press, 1979), 3.

[26] See, eg R Fisher, n 22 above.

[27] Compare A Chayes and A Handler Chayes, *The New Sovereignty: Compliance with International Regulatory Agreements* (Mass, Harvard University Press, 1995), 17.

[28] G Tesauro, 'Remedies for Infringement of Community Law by Member States', in Walter van Gerwen and Manfred Zuleeg (eds), *Sanktionen als Mittel zur Durchsetzung des Gemeinschaftsrechts*, (Bundesanzeiger, 1996) 18.

A particular feature of the general Community infringement procedure is that of *negotiated compliance*. The Commission as an administrative organ is not generally 'empowered to determine conclusively, by opinions formulated pursuant to Article 169 of the EC Treaty or by other statements of its attitude under that procedure, the rights and duties of a Member State'.[29] The infringement procedure, however, leaves room for informal bilateral problem resolution between the Commission and a Member State about the manner in which the Member State shall fulfil its Community obligations,[30] or rather, how it can arrange itself in a manner acceptable to the Commission. This is a consequence of the Commission's unqualified discretion to terminate proceedings throughout the administrative phase.[31] The function of the Commission reaching friendly settlements has characteristics resembling those of the ECJ, namely that of 'settling litigation that arises on the occasion of the application of the legislative rules to individual cases or specific categories of cases'[32] and the Commission thus undertakes a quasi-judicial role. However, and vitally, the practice of negotiated compliance does not imply final settlement. Any such informal understandings are devoid of authoritative significance and the ECJ is by no means bound by their substantive content.[33] The doctrines of supremacy,[34] direct effect,[35] and Member State liability[36] are important parts of the story. As the Court notes, 'vigilance of individuals concerned to protect their rights' constitutes 'an effective supervision in addition to the supervision entrusted by Article 169 (now Article 226) and 170 (now Article 227) to the diligence of the Commission and of the Member States'.[37] With the establishment of the doctrines of direct effect, supremacy and, more recently, of Member State liability, the ECJ has developed a constitutional framework in which citizens monitor and enforce Member State compliance thereby complementing the Commission in its role as guardian of the Treaty. National courts have thus come to play an indispensable role in enforcing Member State compliance within their domestic jurisdictions.[38] Although the doctrines function independently of the Community infringement procedure, they should be mentioned briefly in relation to the practice

[29] Cases 142 and 143/80 *Amministrazione delle Finanze dello Stato v Essevi SpA and Carlo Salengo* [1980] ECR I-1413, para 18.

[30] For an overview of various conceptual distinctions between bargaining and negotiation made in international relations literature, see C Jönsson, 'Diplomacy, Bargaining and Negotiation', in Carlsnaes, Risse, and Simmons, *Handbook of International Relations* (SAGE, 2002), 218.

[31] Case C-212/98 *Commission v Ireland* [1999] ECR I-8571, para 12.

[32] K Lenaerts, Some Reflections on the Separation of Powers in the European Union (1991) 28 CMLR 11–35, at 12.

[33] Article 220 of the EC Treaty.

[34] Case 6/64 *Costa v ENEL* [1964] ECR 585.

[35] Case 26/62 *van Gend & Loos* [1963] ECR 1.

[36] In the case, the Court reasoned liability to be 'inherent in the system of the [EC] Treaty.' Cases C-6/90 and C-9/90 *Francovich v Italy* [1991] ECR I-5357, para 35.

[37] Case 26/62 *van Gend en Loos* [1963] ECR 1, at 13.

[38] The national courts may seek interpretive guidance from the ECJ under Article 234 of the EC Treaty.

between the Commission and the Member States of reaching friendly agreements and the significance thereof. Specifically, because a Commission opinion does not amount to an authentic interpretation, a Member State which acts in accordance with a friendly agreement is not necessarily *sensu stricto* substantively complying. Thus, friendly settlements obtained bilaterally are immaterial for the interpretation domestic courts undertake when private individuals challenge a Member State. These courts are obliged to give full effect to Community law.[39] Furthermore, the ECJ may come to rule on the matter through the preliminary referral procedure under Article 234 of the EC Treaty if necessary to enable the national court to give judgment or where any such question is raised in a case pending before a court or tribunal against whose decisions there is no judicial remedy under national law. Member State liability does constitute a deterrent to infringements and is by some considered a type of sanction,[40] although it is linked to the protection of individuals and reparation of loss and damage caused by a Member State breach[41] rather than to enforcement. Significantly, supremacy and particularly the doctrine of direct effect contribute to blurring the interface between domestic law and Community law and they constitute part of a sophisticated set of compliance pressures on Member States from below and above. The Commission has actively campaigned to raise citizen awareness of the possibility of challenging Member States before national courts and to bring actions for State liability.[42] In addition to the gains decentralized enforcement yields *per se* in terms of general compliance, it also adds to the bargaining position of the Commission during the prejudicial phase. The fact that Member States may be held liable before national courts constitutes an important impetus for genuine, substantive compliance and ensures that friendly understandings do not effectively amount to a Member State refuge. The Commission does seem to employ the principles of direct effect and Member State liability in addition to the general pressure the Commission can exercise in processes of bilateral compliance negotiations and bargaining.[43] It, thus, recommends to '[s]tudy, jointly with the Member States, the possibilities for improving means of *settling*

---

[39] Case 14/83 *von Colson* [1984] ECR 1891, para 26.

[40] See, eg W van Gerven and M Zuleeg, 'Einführung in die Problemstellung', in Walter van Gerven (ed), *Remedies and Sanctions for the Enforcement of European Community Law* (Bundesanzeiger, 1996) 12.

[41] Case C-224/01 *Gerhard Köbler v Österreich* [2003] ECR I-n.y.r., para 45.

[42] Individuals may submit complaints directly to the Commission. Although the Commission acknowledges the significance of what is essentially a means to detect infringements, it stresses that it has no formal or informal obligations to pursue potential infringements brought to its knowledge. See Commission Communication to the European Parliament and the European Ombudsman on relations with the complainant in respect of infringements of Community law, COM/2002/141 [2002] OJ C244 (10/10/2002), p 2. See also A Slaughter, A Stone Sweet, and JHH Weiler (eds), *The European Court and National Courts—Doctrine and Jurisprudence: Legal Change in its Social* Context (Hart Publishing, 1998) on the significance of decentralized enforcement, and further A Burley and W Mattli, 'Europe before the Court: A Political Theory of Legal Integration' (1993) IO 47:1, 41–76.

[43] Suggestive is Case 43/75 *Defrenne* [1976] ECR 455.

disputes amicably and *national redress procedures*'.[44] Likewise, the Commission reminds Member States of their legal obligations publicly[45] thereby creating a public expectation of implementation and informing individuals on their rights stemming from the *acquis*.

Like domestic and federal legal systems, international treaty regimes will inevitably display some non-compliance and there are scholars who maintain that there is no evidence that international[46] and European[47] levels of compliance are necessarily lower. The number of direct infringement cases under Article 227 is not suggestive of the true level of compliance. First, the number of direct infringement proceedings should be seen against the backdrop of a well-established practice of Member State intervention in direct actions initiated by the Commission together with the right to submit observations in preliminary ruling proceedings as foreseen in Article 23 of the Protocol on the Statute of the Court of Justice.[48] Secondly, Member States may be reluctant to initiate cases due to reasons of political discretion.

The administrative and judicial phases foreseen in Articles 226 and 228 EC taken together constitute a mechanism by which the Commission can intensify pressure on a Member State to change its behaviour. Audretsch thus notes that persistence is anticipated with a gradual increase of the cost of violation.[49] Parallel to this intensification there is an actual diminution of cases.[50] This inverse relationship between Commission pressure and apparent Member State compliance, as suggested in Audretsch's comment when read together with the Commission compliance breakdowns, calls for further clarification. The Commission does possess extensive information on Member State compliance obtained primarily through complaints, but also via Member State transposal notifications, or lack thereof,[51] and where foreseen in secondary legislation through direct control by

---

[44] Commission Staff Working Paper; Recommendations for the Improvement of the Application of Community Law by the Member States and Its Enforcement by the Commission. September 2001, p 3 (underscoring in the original text). Compare Maduro, who holds that 'EU law is the product of discourse among the actors of a broad European legal community'. M Poiares Maduro, 'Contrapunctual Law: Europe's Constitutional Pluralism in Action', in N Walker (ed), *Sovereignty in Transition* (Hart Publishing, 2003), 520.

[45] Commission Communication on Better Monitoring of the Application of Community Law, COM/2002/725, p 8.

[46] MK Bulterman and M Kuijer (eds), *Compliance with Judgments of International Courts* (Martinus Nijhoff Publishers, 1996), 39.

[47] See M Zürn and C Joerges (eds), *Law and Governance in Postnational Europe, Compliance beyond the Nation-State* (Cambridge University Press, 2004).

[48] Protocol on the Statute of the Court of Justice [2002] OJ C325 (24.12.2002), pp 167–181. See furthermore G Bebr, *Judicial Control of the European Communities* (Stevens & Sons Limited, 1962), 168 *et seq.* who notes that the right of intervention is unimpaired.

[49] See, eg HAH Audretsch, *Supervision in European Community Law* (Amsterdam: Elsevier Science Publishers BV, 1986), 410–411.

[50] See furthermore, R Rawlings, 'Engaged Elites: Citizen Action and Institutional Attitudes' in C Kilpatrick, T Novitz, Skidmore (eds), *Commission Enforcement, The Future of Remedies in Europe* (Hart Publishing, 2000), 273.

[51] There are examples where no Member State has replied within the notification deadline. An example is Directive 2000/53/EC of the European Parliament and of the Council of 18 September

the Commission.[52] This enables it to make statistical and analytical assessments on compliance within the various Community policy areas.[53] In the EC enforcement literature, infringement proceedings under Articles 226 and 228 of the EC Treaty have commonly been employed as indicators of real levels of Member State compliance with Community law. A 2007 breakdown by procedural stage of Article 226 proceedings shows that 1,760 letters of formal notice and 423 reasoned opinions were issued and 211 cases referred to the ECJ under Article 226. A grand total of 84 cases had been referred to the ECJ for failure to comply with a judgment of the court under Article 228. However, the indicators should be read with caution. Although there are policy areas where statistics arguably indicate acceptable or particularly good compliance records,[54] the qualitative and quantitative state of compliance is difficult to measure. Significantly, the Commission is at 'liberty to decide whether or not to bring the matter before the Court' before as well as after issuance of a reasoned opinion.[55] Therefore the gradually decreasing number of cases pending, as seen in the Commission's annual reports on application of Community law, merely reflects termination decisions adopted by the Commission. Significantly, this discretionary power is unqualified and the statistical reports do not reveal the Commission's reasoning. At times, termination reflects the fact that the Commission considers that its initial infringement assertion was factually or legally ill-founded or new jurisprudence may have altered the legal interpretation upon which the Commission initially based its proceedings. Moreover, facts are often only fully brought to light during the administrative phase and it may turn out that the Member State is complying. To recap, termination of infringement cases does not necessarily reflect a behavioural change, although friendly settlements according to the Commission usually are due to changes in national legislation.[56] A recent study by Falkner et al systematically looks at enforcement patterns at the State level however only pertaining to a few selected secondary law acts.[57] The authors examined the success and failure of

2000 on end-of-life vehicles 2000/53/EC, referred to in written question by Chris Davies (ELDR) to the Commission [2003] OJ C110 E (08.05.2003), p 56.

[52] See, eg Council Regulation (EC) No 2371/2002 of 20 December 2002 on the conservation and sustainable exploitation of fisheries resources under the Common Fisheries Policy [2002] OJ L358 (31.12.2002), pp 59–80, Article 27.

[53] See the Annual Reports on Monitoring the Application of Community Law annually issued by the Commission. The reports are made in response to European Parliament Resolution of 9 February 1983 and Declaration No 19 annexed to the Maastricht Treaty signed on 7 February 1992. The Commission explicitly refers also to the 'the general public and economic operators.' See: <http://europa.eu.int/comm/secretariat_general/sgb/droit_com/index_en.htm#infractions>.

[54] M Zürn and C Joerges (eds), *Law and Governance in Postnational Europe, Compliance beyond the Nation-State* (Cambridge University Press, 2004), at 2, notes that compliance records are in some respects higher than that of comparable enforcement of German federal law. See furthermore SM Schwebel, 'Commentary in the European Communities', in MK Bulterman and M Kuijer (eds), *Compliance with Judgments of International Courts* (Martinus Nijhoff Publishers, 1996), 39.

[55] Case C-212/98 *Commission v Ireland* [1999] ECR I-8571, para 12.

[56] Single Market News, No 33, April 2004, p 5.

[57] G Falkner, O Treib, M Hartlapp, S Leiber, *Complying with Europe: EU Harmonisation and Soft Law in the Member States* (Cambridge University Press, 2005).

implementation by looking at application and enforcement in addition to formal transposition and their survey reveals remarkably low degrees of perfect compliance within the established time limits and considerable variations between the then 15 Member States. In their explanatory analytical framework, the authors operate with 'different worlds of compliance' under the categories 'a world of law observance',[58] 'a world of domestic politics',[59] and 'a world of neglect'[60] none of which accounts for defection as a rational choice. The Commission has likewise initiated sector-specific studies at the level of selected Member States. One such survey concerned implementation of Article 15(2) of the EC Royalty and Interest Directive[61] and was conducted by the International Bureau of Fiscal Documentation (IBFD).[62] Other studies again suggest that 'systemic variation across functional domains' occur too.[63]

Finite executive resources do not allow the Commission to pursue strict top-down enforcement and even less so absolute enforcement of Community legislation.[64] Moreover, applying 'priority criteria reflecting the seriousness of the potential or known failure to comply with the legislation',[65] the Commission far from pursues all cases of presumed non-compliance brought to its attention, hence, a pending caseload might simply reflect a particular Commission compliance strategy or priority.[66] Finally, any temporary increases in cases brought before the ECJ in accordance with Article 226 of the EC Treaty is partially to be seen in the context of the substantive and geographical expansion of Community law.[67]

Effectiveness is another central notion in the Commission's rhetoric. In its most literal sense, effectiveness can be understood as making a law operative and the European Council has defined effectiveness as *full* implementation and enforcement by Member States.[68] Some scholars promote a less quantitative approach to effectiveness and emphasizes the *sui generis* nature of the notion in its particular

---

[58] Finland, Sweden, Denmark.

[59] Germany, UK, Austria, the Netherlands, Spain, and Belgium.

[60] Greece, Portugal, Luxembourg, France, Ireland and Italy.

[61] Council Directive 2003/49/EC of 3 June 2003 on a common system of taxation applicable to interest and royalty payments made between associated companies of different Member States [2003] OJ L157 (26.06.2003), pp 49–54.

[62] Can be seen at: <http://ec.europa.eu/taxation_customs/resources/documents/common/publications/studies/survey_IR_dir.pdf>.

[63] PM Haas, 'Compliance with EU Directives: Insights from International Relations and Comparative Politics' (1998) Journal of European Policy 5:1, 17–37.

[64] Compare, eg N Lebessis and J Paterson, 'Evolution in Governance: What Lesson for the Commission? A first Assessment', European Commission, Forward Studies Unit, Working Paper 1997, p 24.

[65] Commission Communication COM/2002/725, p 11.

[66] Mendrinou notes that 'infringement procedures are of great value for a tentative estimation of the extent of state non-compliance'. Maria Mendrinou, 'Non-Compliance and the European Commission's Role in Integration' (1996) Journal of European Public Policy 3:1, 1–22.

[67] Report by the Working Party on the Future of the European Communities' Court System, 19 January 2000 (Due Report), p 2.

[68] Statement of European Council, Bull EC 6–1990, 18–21, n 4, concerning the area of environmental law.

EC context.[69] More generally, Raustiala and Slaughter draw attention to the conceptual distinction between compliance and effectiveness in regime theory. They phrase effectiveness as, for instance, 'the degree to which a rule induces changes in behaviour that further the rule's goals; improves the state of the underlying problem; or achieves its policy objective'. Effectiveness is, thus, not automatically equal to a high level of compliance, although, as the authors acknowledge, 'more compliance is better'.[70] Where a supranational obligation matches domestic law from the beginning, compliance does not *per se* reflect a particularly effective treaty regime.[71] Dehousse et al. thus suggest that effectiveness can be read as more than a merely substantive or procedural notion, but as 'multi-directional processes of reaction and adaptation, potentially involving political and legal processes and changes in organizations'.[72] Snyder emphasizes that the notion of effectiveness also reflects power struggles, value choices and strategy considerations and consequently has implications of a political nature.[73] At first sight, there is an obliquity between the Commission's general obligation to monitor Member State compliance as foreseen in Article 211 of the EC Treaty[74] and its broad discretion whether to initiate and maintain infringement proceedings.[75] However, the practice of negotiated settlements indeed shows that the Commission may pursue objectives of effectiveness rather than of absolute compliance. This leaves the Commission a margin of manoeuvre to carry out a task which is essentially of a semi-political nature.

IV. Procedural Clarifications

A. Article 226 EC[76]

(i) *The Prejudicial Phase*

If the Commission suspects that a Member State is non-compliant, it may set the infringement procedure in motion by issuing a letter of formal notice. This

---

[69] See AJ Gil Ibáñez, *The Administrative Supervision and Enforcement of EC Law* (Hart, 1999), 12; F Snyder, 'The Effectiveness of European Community Law. Institutions, Processes, Tools and Techniques' (1993) MLR 56, 19–54, 24–27; and HAH Audretsch, *Supervision in European Community Law* (Elsevier Science Publishers BV, 1986), 350.

[70] K Raustiala and A Slaughter, 'International Law, International Relations and Compliance', in W Carlsnaes, T Risse, and BA Simmons (eds), *Handbook of International Relations* (SAGE, 2002).

[71] LR Helfer and A Slaughter, 'Why States Create International Tribunals: A Response to Professors Posner and Yoo' (2005) *California Law Review* 93, 28.

[72] R Dehousse, C Joerges, G Majone, and F Snyder, 'Europe after 1992, New Regulatory Strategies', EUI Working Paper, LAW No. 92/31. See F Snyder, n 69 above, at 19.

[73] F Snyder, *New Directions in European Community Law* (Weidenfeld & Nicholson, 1990), 3. See also at 22–25.

[74] 'In order to ensure the proper functioning and development of the common market, the Commission *shall*: … ensure that the provisions of this Treaty and the measures taken by the institutions pursuant thereto are applied […]' (emphasis added).

[75] Case C-474/99 *Commission v Spain* [2002] ECR I-5293, para 25.

[76] See generally, M Brealey and M Hoskins, *Remedies in EC Law: Law and Practice in the English and EC Courts* (Sweet & Maxwell, 1998).

is a first written warning whereby the Member State is invited to submit its observations on facts and rules. When the Commission considers the response to be inadequate and the Member State has not altered its behaviour in a satisfactory manner, the Commission may follow up with a reasoned opinion. A literal interpretation suggests that the Commission is obliged to deliver a reasoned opinion when it considers a Member State to be in default. Somewhat puzzlingly, this obligation is made dependant on the Commission's own view,[77] which has made it subject to some early academic consideration. The ECJ has now clarified that the Commission's discretion to further a case at this point in time is unqualified.[78] This flexibility enhances the pressure on Member States to correct unintended wrongful implementation, thus the Commission will not have to bring Article 226 of the EC Treaty in full into operation in cases of one-offs. This procedure starting with a 'warning letter' guarantees Member State interest in submitting observations and constitutes an essential procedural guarantee in accordance with the doctrine of *audi alteram partem*.[79] The Member State is given the opportunity to outline its stand on the facts and legal assessment thereof to the Commission for further consideration.[80] The underlying purpose is moreover to restrain the Commission so that it cannot alter, or extend, its complaints in a later reasoned opinion. This should not be understood in a literal sense and there is no requirement of identical wording where the subject matter has not been materially modified.[81] Whereas the first principle is a rule-of-law requirement, the second is of a pragmatic nature. At this early stage the Commission may not possess all the information required in order to make a compliance appraisal and the initial contact with a Member State may be in the interest of further information gathering in order to assess better actual Member State behaviour and is a low-cost remedy against benign non-compliance.

The Court of Justice has consistently confirmed the Commission's exclusive competence to decide on the initiation of infringement procedures.[82] Because the Commission enjoys discretionary power and is free to initiate proceedings, individuals are precluded from any right to compel it to adopt a reasoned opinion or to bring an action for annulment against a Commission refusal to

[77] HAH Audretsch, *Supervision in European Community Law* (Amsterdam: Elsevier Science Publishers BV, 1986), 35. See furthermore Paul Craig and Gráinne de Búrca, *EC Law: Text, Cases, and Materials* (3rd edn, OUP, 2003), 407.

[78] HAH Audretsch (1986), 35.

[79] Case 31/69 *Commission v Italy* [1970] ECR 25, para 13. Koen Lenaerts and Dirk Arts, 'Action for Infringement of Community Law by a Member State' in K Lenaerts, D Arts, and R Bray (eds), *Procedural Law of the European Union* (Sweet & Maxwell, 1999), 100–101.

[80] Case C-279/94 *Commissionn v Italy* [1997] ECR I-4743, para 15.

[81] Case C-280/02 *Commission v France* [2004] I-8573, paras 29 and 30.

[82] Joined Cases T-479/93 and T-559/93 *Commission v Giorgio Bernardi* [1994] ECR II-01115, 'Where an action is brought by a natural or legal person for a declaration of failure to act, in that by not initiating infringement proceedings against a Member State the Commission has failed, in breach of the Treaty, to take a decision, that action is inadmissible.'

take action against a State.[83] However, the Commission is naturally at liberty to institutionalize in-house rules for its handling of complaints against Member States and it may allow greater citizen influence. Indeed public legitimacy claims have been raised against the Commission's lack of procedural recognition of private complainants and the absence of a clearly defined policy for its use of discretion.[84] This point will be dealt with in more detail elsewhere in the article. Finally, individual members and civil servants of the Commission are restricted by Article 287 of the EC Treaty, which requires them 'not to disclose information of the kind covered by the obligation of professional secrecy.'[85]

In the preliminary opinion issued in the shape of a letter of formal notice, the Commission shall delineate the issue of its complaint. The objective is two-fold. First, some degree of concretization is required to enable the State to prepare its defence. Secondly, by pointing out in detail what the Commission considers incorrect, the Member State stands a better chance of altering its behaviour and thereby avoiding that the Commission make a referral to the Court.[86] This is in accordance with the purpose of the pre-litigation phase, namely to enable an amicable settlement whereby the Member State can conform to its Treaty obligations.[87] The responsive nature of the phase is played down in some cases. See, for instance, Case C-159/94 *Commission v France* in which the Court states that the 'purpose of the prelitigation procedure provided for by Article 169 of the Treaty is to enable the Member State to comply of its own accord with the requirements of the Treaty or, if appropriate, to justify its position'.[88] Where a case has not been settled in an informal fashion, the Commission still succeeds in communicating its awareness of a possible violation thereby raising pressure on the Member State. In its reasoned opinion, the Commission requests the Member State to take the measures necessary for it to comply. In doing so, the Commission has to observe a certain degree of specificity as to the subject matter of the application to the Court of Justice, and make a 'coherent and detailed statement of the reasons which led the Commission to conclude that the State in question failed to fulfil one of its obligations under the Treaty'.[89] This requirement does, however, not amount to an obligation to specify what the Commission regards to be the measures and

---

[83] Case T-182/97 *Smanor SA v Commission* [1998] ECR II-271.

[84] See R Rawlings, 'Engaged Elites: Citizen Action and Institutional Attitudes' in C Kilpatrick, T Novitz, P Skidmore (eds), *Commission Enforcement, The Future of Remedies in Europe* (Hart Publishing, 2000), at 268.

[85] See also PJ Gorge Kapteyn and P van Themaat Verloren (LW Gormley, edn ed), *Introduction to the Law of the European Communities after the Coming into Force of the Single European Act* (Kluwer Law International, 1989), 208.

[86] Case C-476/98 *Commission v Germany* [2002] I-9855, para 47.

[87] The Court has consistently held that this is the purpose of the procedural design of the pre-litigation phase. Cases C-207/96 *Commission v Italy* [1997] ECR I-6869, at para 17, and C-96/95 *Commission v Germany* [1997] ECR I-1653, at para 22. For a discussion thereof, see Opinion of Advocate General Alber in Case C-185/96 *Commission v Greece* [1998] I-6601.

[88] Case C-159/94 *Commission v France* [1997] I-5815, para 103.

[89] Case C-289/94 *Commission v Italy* [1996] ECR I-4405, para 16.

actions necessary to bring the concrete infringement to an end,[90] as some scholars have suggested.[91] This should be understood in view of the circumstance that the Court issues *declaratory judgments.* Member States have an obligation to give effect to Community law; however this may on the whole be done in numerous ways. The fact that the Court merely declares compliance or failure to fulfil an obligation corresponds to this functional division of powers. However, it also implies that the Court cannot consider fictive facts and, hence, it would not be able to address the Commission's non-binding suggestions on how to comply.[92] Moreover, because a question concerning the measures required for the implementation of a judgment under Article 226 of the EC Treaty does not form part of the subject-matter of such a judgment, the ECJ has held, 'such a question cannot form the subject-matter of an application for interpretation of a judgment'.[93] Reasoned opinions are merely party contentions. Only if the Commission wants to make failure to adopt measures to enable the infringement complained of to be remedied the subject matter of its action shall it specify those measures in its reasoned opinion.[94] Charges which have not been included in the reasoned opinion are inadmissible at the stage of proceedings before the Court.[95] Finally the situation may arise that the Member State significantly alters its behaviour after the time limit laid down by the Commission in its reasoned opinion expires, but before the Commission makes a referral to the Court. This may effectively render a judgment redundant. In such a situation, the Commission enjoys discretion as to whether it wishes to issue a revised reasoned opinion, which takes the changed circumstances into consideration.[96] Advocate General Ruiz-Jarabo Colomer dubs the period following the issue of a reasoned opinion a 'period of grace' because the Commission undertakes not to start legal proceedings while the Member State retains the option to alter its behaviour. After this period, he cautions, 'dialogue gives way to action'.[97]

(ii) Time Limits

The EC Treaty does not lay down time limits for a Member State to respond to warning letters and reasoned opinions. It is, however, established case law that Member States shall be given an opportunity to comply and that the Member

---

[90] Cases C-328/96 *Commission v Austria* [1999] I-7479, para 39, and C-247/89 *Commission v Portugal* [1991] ECR I-3659, para 22.

[91] K Lenaerts and D Arts, 'Action for Infringement of Community Law by a Member State' in K Lenaerts, D Arts, and R Bray (eds), *Procedural Law of the European Union* (Sweet & Maxwell, 1999), 102: 'The Commission also may—or possibly must—set forth the measures which need to be taken in order to bring the infringement to an end.'

[92] See differently K Lenaerts, n 91 above, at 102.

[93] Case C-503/04 *Commission v Germany* [2007] n.y.r., para 16.

[94] Case C-394/02 *Commission v Greece* [2005] ECR I-4713, para 23.

[95] Case C-305/03 *Commission v Luxembourg* [2006] ECR I-1213.

[96] Case C-177/03 *Commission v France* [2004] ECR I-11671.

[97] Opinion of Advocate General Ruiz-Jarabo Colomer in Case C-362/01 *Commission v Ireland* [2002] I-11433, para 21.

State's right of defence has to be respected.[98] Time limits are significant in the judicial phase for the reason that the ECJ appraises Member State conduct or omission 'prevailing in the Member State at the end of the period laid down in the reasoned opinion'.[99] What constitutes a reasonable and sufficient time limit should be understood in view of both objective and subjective circumstances. Cases of emergency are one example of the former.[100] On the subjective side, the Court has taken into account whether the Member State was already familiar with the Commission's stand.[101] Likewise, time limits of one month have been considered reasonable in situations where a Member State has objected to the Commission's allegations of a breach consistently.[102] Whereas the ECJ cannot prolong the time limit set by the Commission, the Commission itself may upon Member State request decide to make a suspension.[103] The Commission is not required to act within a particular period of time.[104]

(iii) The Judicial Phase

The Commission has final recourse to the Court. Contrary to the somewhat ambiguous Treaty text, which suggests that the Commission is obliged to issue a reasoned opinion, the Treaty explicitly states that the Commission *may* bring a matter before the ECJ. The Commission does not have to demonstrate specific interest in bringing an action. This should not be conceived of as a Commission right, but rather a consequence of the Commission's particular function 'in the general interest of the Community'.[105] The Court does not interfere with the Commission's decision on the appropriateness of launching a complaint and thus it cannot demand a withdrawal.[106] It may happen that a Member State alters its legislation during the pre-litigation period and also subsequent to the Commission bringing action. This does not mean that the Commission must drop the case. Thus the Commission may impute its complaints to the new circumstances in the course of the proceedings as long as the subject-matter of the dispute remains the same.[107] The Court has, however, exclusive power to interpret Community law

[98] Case C-473/93 *Commission v Luxembourg* [1996] ECR I-3207, para 19.
[99] Joined Cases C-20/01 and C-28/01 *Commission v Germany* [2003] I-3609, para 32.
[100] Case 293/85 *Commission v Belgium* [1988] ECR 305, para. 14: 'account must be taken of all the circumstances of the case. As a general rule the Commission operates with a 60 days' deadline for Member State response to a reasoned opinion. See, eg: <http://europa.eu.int/comm/internal_market/en/update/score/score2.htm>.
[101] Case 85/85 *Commission v Belgium* [1986] ECR I-1149, para 13.
[102] Case C-247/89 *Commission v Portugal* [1991] ECR I-3659, para 25.
[103] Case 16/84 *Commission v Netherlands* [1985] ECR I-2355, para 10.
[104] Case C-96/89 *Commission v Netherlands* [1991] ECR I-2461.
[105] Joined Cases C-20/01 and C-28/01 *Commission v Germany* [2003] I-3609, para 29.
[106] Cases C-236/99 *Commission v Belgium* [2000] ECR I-5657, para 28, and C-383/00 *Commission v Germany* [2002] ECR I-4219, para 19.
[107] Case C-177/04 *Commission v France* [2006] ECR I-2461, para 39 with analogy to Case C-42/89 *Commission v Belgium* [1990] ECR I-2821, para 11, which concerned Article 226 of the EC Treaty.

and appraise Member State conduct.[108] In a recent ruling, the Court tried whether Ireland had taken all the measures necessary to ensure a correct implementation of a whole range of directive provisions. Thus rather than examining compliance with individual obligations it found a 'large-scale administrative problem'.[109]

The purpose of the application to the Court is to identify the complaints which the Court is requested to rule upon[110] and it should include a synopsis of the factual and legal matters upon which the Commission will base its case.[111] As a guarantee in the interest of the Member State, the subject matter of the dispute must be restricted to that of the reasoned opinion.[112] However, if the subject-matter of the proceedings as defined in the reasoned opinion has simply been limited, the ECJ notes, there is no requirement that the operative part of the reasoned opinion and the form of order sought in the application to the Court should be identical.[113] Adjudication is foreseen to be an *ultima ratio*[114] and the number of infringement proceedings initiated that reach the ECJ is relatively small.[115] Because a failure to comply is determined by reference to the situation existing at the end of the period laid down in the reasoned opinion,[116] subsequent changes are immaterial.[117]

An infringement can be neither clear nor manifest. The ECJ is not concerned with the nature or seriousness of an infringement[118] and it does not consider whether a Member State has been acting *in culpa*.[119] Judgments according to Article 226 of the EC Treaty by the ECJ are of a purely declaratory nature. Thus, '[e]ither there is a failure to fulfil obligations and the Court can merely find accordingly, or there is none, and the action must be dismissed.'[120] A ruling

---

[108] Articles 7, 220 of the EC Treaty and Cases 142 and 143/80 *Amministrazione delle Finanze dello Stato v Essevi SpA and Carlo Salengo* [1980] ECR I-1413, para 18.

[109] In Case C-494/01 *Commission v Ireland* [2005] ECR I-03331. For an analysis of the judgment, see P Wennerås, 'A New Dawn for Commission Enforcement under Articles 226 and 228 EC: General and Persistent (GAP) Infringements, Lump Sums and Penalty Payments', (2006) 43:1 CMLR 31–62.

[110] Case 347/88 *Commission v Greece* [1990] ECR I-4747, para 28.

[111] Case 159/94 *Commission v France* [1997] I-5815, para 105.

[112] Case 3/96 *Commission v Netherlands* [1998] I-03031, para 18.

[113] Case 441/02 *Commission v Germany* [2006] ECR I-3449, para 61.

[114] Case 20/59 *Italian Government v High Authority* [1960] ECR 325.

[115] The ECJ delivered 166 rulings under Article 226 of the EC Treaty in 2005. The report and the statistical breakdowns can be found at: <http://ec.europa.eu/community_law/eulaw/pdf/XXIII_rapport_annuel/23_rapport_annuel_en.htm>.

[116] Cases C-142/01 *Commission v Italy* [2002] ECR I-4541, para 8, and C-435/99 *Commission v Portugal* [2000] ECR I-11179, para 16.

[117] Case C-211/02 *Commission v Luxembourg* [2003] ECR I-2429, para 6.

[118] Case C-359/93 *Commission v Netherlands* [1995] ECR I-157, para 14.

[119] This is not necessarily the case with implementation of EC structural funds where financial entitlement can be made conditional on compliance. See, eg the culpability-considerations in Regulation No 1655/1999 laying down general rules for the granting of Community aid in the field of trans-European networks [1999] OJ L197 (29.07.1999), pp 1–7. 'Except where the Member States and/or the implementing authority provide proof that they were not responsible for the irregularity, the Member State shall be liable in the alternative for reimbursement of any sums unduly paid.'

[120] Opinion of Advocate General Mischo in Case C-78/00 *Commission v Italy* [2001] ECR I-8195, para 65.

under Article 226 may by clarifying the Member States' obligations certainly allow headway for citizens who wish to challenge a Member State before national courts.[121] However, as Advocate General Stix-Hackl remarks 'the rights accruing to individuals derive, not from that judgment, but from the actual provisions of Community law having direct effect in the internal legal order'.[122] Because the objectives and effects of the infringement procedure are different from proceedings before a national court, the 'existence of the remedies available through the national courts [and significantly the access for national judges to make prejudicial references under Article 234 EC] cannot prejudice the bringing of an action under Article 226 EC'.[123]

(iv) Burden of Proof

The burden of proof rests with the Commission under the general infringement procedure.[124] Nonetheless, the Court has emphasized, a Member State cannot merely deny a failure to comply if the Commission produces 'sufficient' evidence. In that case the Member State must 'contest substantively and in detail the information produced and the consequences thereof'.[125] Otherwise, the Court may consider that the charges have indeed been demonstrated. This implies that the Member State must give details on how a particular law is applied.[126] This obligation is based upon a reading of the fidelity clause in Article 10 of the EC Treaty in conjunction with Article 211 of the EC Treaty.[127]

(v) Fidelity Clause

The principle of loyal cooperation applies to the Member States and also to the Commission as a Community institution.[128] Although the principle is judiciable the Court has held that it serves no purpose to rule upon this general obligation in addition to the question of non-compliance.[129] There may however be distinct occurrences of disloyalty in relation to infringement proceedings that can

---

[121] See Paul Craig and Gráinne de Búrca, *EC Law: Text, Cases, and Materials* (2nd edn, OUP, 1998) 329.

[122] Opinion of Advocate General Stix-Hackl in Case C-426/98 *Commission v Greece* [2001] I-2793 with reference to Joined Cases 314/81, 315/81, 316/81, and 83/82 *Procureur de la République* [1982] I-4337, para 15.

[123] Case C-508/03 *Commission v UK* [2006] ECR I-03969, para 71.

[124] See generally K Lenaerts and D Arts, 'Action for Infringement of Community Law by a Member State' in K Lenaerts, D Arts, and R Bray (eds), *Procedural Law of the European Union* (Sweet & Maxwell, 1999), 107.

[125] Case C-272/86 *Commission v Greece* [1988] ECR I-4875, summary and paras 30 and 31.

[126] K Lenaerts (1999), n 124 above, at 108.

[127] In addition, the Court may require Member States and the Commission to 'produce all documents and to supply all information which the Court considers desirable' in the judicial phase. See Protocol of the Statute of the Court of Justice, Article 24. This can be found online at: <http://www.curia.europa.eu/en/instit/txtdocfr/txtsenvigueur/statut.pdf>.

[128] Article 10 of the EC Treaty and Joined Cases C-63/90 and C-67/90 *Portugal and UK v Council* [2002] ECR I-5073, para 52.

[129] Case C-392/02 *Commission v Denmark* [2005] ECR I-9811, para 69.

be pursued before the Court. When the Commission ends infringement proceedings because it considers an infringement to have been terminated or it has
reached a satisfactory understanding on how the State shall fulfil its specific obligations in understanding with the Member State, such agreements shall take
place in respect of the principle of loyal cooperation. A Member State can be
held in breach of Article 10 of the EC Treaty in a separate case if it merely complies under the concrete threat of judicial recourse but fails to continue to comply
when the Commission has terminated its proceedings.[130]

B. Article 228(2) EC

(i) Introductory Remarks on Member State Liability

In its ruling *Francovich v Italy*, the Court ruled that Member State liability is
'inherent in the system of the [EC] Treaty'.[131] The judgment strengthened what
the ECJ had recognized in *van Gend & Loos*, when establishing the doctrine of
direct effect, namely that for there to be 'an effective supervision in addition to the
supervision entrusted by Articles 169 (now Article 226) and 170 (now Article 227)
of the EC Treaty to the diligence of the Commission and of the Member States',
requires 'vigilance of individuals to protect their rights'.[132] Together the two
judgments form part of ECJ case law that maximizes the effectiveness of supranational obligations through national procedures thereby obliterating the opposition between domestic and Community law. The doctrine of liability is useful
to keep in mind when discussing sanctions. Although the principle of Member
State liability is essentially linked to reparation of loss and damage caused by
the breach to nationals, ie protection of individuals,[133] it constitutes a pecuniary incentive to comply or, in other terms, a deterrent to infringements. Direct
effect implies that actions before national courts, to some extent, can complete
the Commission's task under Article 226 of the EC Treaty. Member State liability carries a similar promise with regards to Article 228 of the EC Treaty.

   Empirically, the doctrine of direct effect and the principle of Member State
liability corroborate Roger Fisher's general assumption that international law
norm-internalization through national courts is an important promoter of compliance.[134] The range of conditions for establishing direct effect[135] and Member

---

[130] Case C-374/89 *Commission v Belgium* [1991] ECR I-367, paras 14–16.
[131] Cases C-6/90 and C-9/90 *Francovich v Italy* [1991] ECR I-5357 para 35.
[132] Case 26/62 *van Gend & Loos* [1963] ECR 1, 13.
[133] Case C-224/01 *Gerhard Köbler v Österreich* [2003] ECR I-0, para 45.
[134] R Fisher, *Improving Compliance with International Law* (University Press of Virginia, 1981).
See also A Burley and W Mattli, 'Europe before the Court: A Political Theory of Legal Integration'
(1993) 47:1 International Organisation, 41–76, at 41: '[T]he Court created a pro-Community constituency of private individuals by giving them a direct stake in promulgation and implementation of
Community Law.'
[135] See, eg Case 148/78 *Publico Ministero v Ratti* [1979] ECR 1–1629 at 1651.

State liability[136] does, however, limit the dissuasive effect in certain policy areas, thereby minimizing the mechanism's general capacity to induce Member State compliance. In addition, some argue that actors in the private sector may hesitate to challenge a Member State anxious that it could have negative ramifications on, for example, their market prospects.[137] However this point should not be overstated as market actors on the whole have the upper hand when they threaten national authorities with legal proceedings or to consult the Commission.

(ii) Early Community Deliberations on Enforcement and The Maastricht Amendment

Participation in the economic and political Community has become significant for modern European statehood. Conversely, partial or absolute expulsion carries great promise as a deterrent to non-compliance.[138] The idea of Community sanctions was contemplated at a relatively early point in the European Economic Community's history.[139] At a later occasion Spinelli and the European Parliament too envisaged that the European Council should be conferred powers to impose penalties on a Member State in the event of serious and persistent violation of democratic principles or fundamental rights by a Member State. The sanctions could take the form of suspending the rights deriving from the application of part or the whole of the Treaty provisions to the State in question and its nationals without prejudice to the rights acquired by the latter. Moreover, according to the proposal, the sanctions could go as far as suspending participation by the State in question in the European Council, the Council of the Union, and any other organ in which that State is represented as such.[140] The proposal was in stark contrast to the procedure in place under Article 171 of the EEC Treaty as it was then, which provided no other remedy than obtaining a declaratory judgment that a Member State had failed to comply with a judgment of the Court and the option of initiating new infringement proceedings under Article 169 of the EEC Treaty (Article 226 of the EC Treaty) in case of continual non-compliance. Literature on international law enforcement suggests expulsion to be too potent a general sanction[141] and there are several reasons why it appears inappropriate as a general enforcement tool in the case of the EC.

---

[136] Cases C-6/90 and C-9/90, *Francovich v Italy* [1991] ECR I-5357, para 40.

[137] Final Report of the Committee of Wise Men on the Regulation of the European Securities Markets, 15 February 2001 (the Lamfalussy Committee), p 40.

[138] Compare A Chayes and A Handler Chayes (1995) on interdependence and the significance of membership in international treaty regimes.

[139] G Tesauro, 'Remedies for Infringement of Community Law by Member States', in W van Gerwen and M Zuleeg (eds), *Sanktionen als Mittel zur Durchsetzung des Gemeinschaftsrechts*, (Bundesanzeiger, 1996), 19–20.

[140] Draft Treaty Establishing the European Union [1984] OJ C77/33 (19.3.1984), pp 44–55, Article 44.

[141] A Chayes and A Handler Chayes, n 27 above, at 69 and 107.

First, compliance with the *acquis Communautaire* is not based on reciprocity,[142] which the potential introduction of membership sanctions would arguably suggest. Secondly, the collective interest in the functioning and maintenance of the overall treaty regime also implies that neither exclusion nor isolation constitute optimal responses to less serious instances of non-compliance with Community obligations. Article 7 of the Treaty on European Union (TEU) does provide a legal basis for suspension of Member State rights including voting rights; a sanction principally of a political nature leaving the Court of Justice a residual role of judicial review of the Council decision. The graveness of this sanction is reflected in the material scope of the provision covering 'principles of liberty, democracy, respect for human rights and fundamental freedoms, and the rule of law'.[143] Because the application of Article 7 of the TEU is limited to serious and *persistent* breaches, it was not applicable in the only case to date where the Council genuinely contemplated invoking it.[144]

It may of course be argued that exclusion can take several, and also informal, forms. The Commission for instance adheres to the assumption that Member States are concerned about national reputation to the extent that it influences their behaviour. In the Commission's internal rules of procedure it is, therefore, stipulated that warning letters should normally not be accompanied by publicity, in order to allow the Member State to comply without losing face. However, at the other end of the scale, ie at the stage of a reasoned opinion or application to the Court of Justice, the Commission does a lot of press work to increase pressure on the Member States.[145] Hence, the Commission uses political stigmatization connected with the infringement procedure in a strategic manner to increase the cost of the alleged violation. The strategy is known from international law practice and theory and is based on an assumption of State interdependency, or rather on State inter-linkages. Significantly, States are perceived as particularly

---

[142] Opinion of Advocate General Léger, Case C-5/94 *Hedley Lomas* [1996] ECR I-2553, para 27, 'Nothing is more alien to Community law than the idea of a measure of retaliation or reciprocity proper to classical public international law.' See also Joined Cases 90/63 and 91/63 *Commission v Luxembourg and Belgium* [1964] ECR 625, at 631. According to Case C-11/95 *Commission v Belgium* [1996] ECR I-4115, para 37: 'it is settled case-law that a Member State cannot unilaterally adopt, on its own authority, corrective or protective measures designed to obviate any breach by another Member State of rules of Community law'. Some argue that recourse to self-help as a principle of general international law would be compatible with the Community regime if another Member State consistently refused to comply with a ruling under Article 228 of the EC Treaty. See HAH Audretsch, *Supervision in European Community Law* (Amsterdam: Elsevier Science Publishers BV, 1986), 139.

[143] See reference in Article 7 of the TEU to Article 6(1) of the TEU and Article 309 of the EC Treaty. See furthermore P Craig and G de Búrca, *EC Law: Text, Cases, and Materials* (3rd edn, OUP, 2003).

[144] The Council members were concerned about the political developments within Austrian politics. However no genuine breach of the principles of Article 6(1) of the TEU existed. See G de Búrca, 'Beyond the Charter: How Enlargement has Enlarged the Human Rights Policy of the European Union' (2004) Fordham International Law Journal 27, 679–714, at 697.

[145] Electronic Interview, DG Fish, Legal Unit.

vulnerable to exposure and shaming. The suggestion that non-compliance may entail political costs has received some attention from a Community perspective.[146] However the argument of effectual sanctioning of non-compliance in the form of exclusion from solidarity and cooperation in a political sense, ie during the legislative processes, is arguably less strong in the Community than in many international treaty regimes. Firstly, it is difficult to assess the extent to which Council actors are conscious about compliance issues[147] or willing to address the matter during the diplomatic pre-decisional phase. Secondly, diplomatic sanctioning by other Member States of a notoriously recalcitrant Member State is not likely to happen in a consistent manner in the legislation bargaining process often characterized by shifting informal alliances determined by national priorities. Member States with shared policy interests may, however, also turn out to follow the same compliance pattern. Hence common features of their compliance patterns will presumably not influence their concerted policy formations. On a different note, there is of course a real risk that non-compliance will deter the Council members and also Member State governments from taking new and deep commitments.[148] Finally, as pointed out by Koh, loss of reputation presupposes that the non-compliant State 'defies a mutually accepted interpretation of the treaty norm'.[149]

In its Draft Treaty Establishing the European Union from 1984, the European Parliament proposed 'jurisdiction of the Court to impose sanctions on a Member State failing to fulfil its obligations under the law of the Union'.[150] Previous political reluctance to strengthen centralized enforcement mechanisms in this way has by and large been explained with reference to the obstacle of national sovereignty.[151] Audretsch notes that sanctions would amount to more than 'certain sacrifices of sovereignty', thus entailing the creation of 'a real federal power'.[152] Following the Maastricht Treaty signed on 7 February 1992 and entering into force on 1 November 1993, the Commission may request the Court to impose a lump sum or penalty payment on a Member State in addition to a declaration

---

[146] HAH Audretsch, n 142 above, at 227. For a discussion of Member State reputation with a specific focus on the EC Internal Market, see Jonas Tallberg, *European Governance and Supranational Institutions—Making States Comply* (Routledge, 2003). For a critique that State concern as to reputation is an unambiguous assumption, see GW Downs and MA Jones, 'Reputation, Compliance and International Law' (2002) Journal of Legal Studies 31:1, 95–114.

[147] See, eg answer given by the Council to Written Question E-66/03 by Carlos Bautista Ojeda (Verts/ALE) to the Council. Fisheries conflicts between Spain and Portugal. 'The Council is not aware of the incident which occurred recently involving Spanish fishermen and a Portuguese Navy vessel.'

[148] Compare GW Downs, D Rocke, and P N Barsoom 'Is the Good News about Compliance Good News for Cooperation?' (1996) IO 50, 379–406.

[149] H Koh, 'Why Do Nations Obey International Law? (1997) Yale Law Journal 106, at 2639 with reference to A Chayes and A Handler Chayes (1995).

[150] Draft Treaty Establishing the European Union [1984] OJ C77/33 (19.3.1984), pp 44–55, Article 43.

[151] K Alter, 'Who are the "Masters of the Treaty"?: European Governments and the European Court of Justice' (1998) IO 52:1, 121–147, p 127.

[152] HAH Audretsch (1986), at 140.

that it has failed to comply with a ruling under Article 226 of the EC Treaty.[153] A lump sum is a 'single sum of money that serves as complete payment'[154] and penalty payments are sums of money to be paid periodically from the date the Court awards them until the Member State breach has been brought to an end. Commentators were puzzled to learn that it was the traditionally anti-federalist UK which eventually proposed the insertion of a pecuniary penalty provision in the EC Treaty.[155] One possible explanation is that the UK was fearful that non-compliance would undermine the internal market and that its own record of compliance was relatively good.[156] Further, there had been an incremental growth in the number of repetitive infringements in a five-year period leading up to the Maastricht IGC. A more general explanation might be found in the perception of Community law. When the House of Lords in 1983 for the first time deliberated on the status of Community law vis-à-vis national law, the *acquis* was addressed as a 'subject matter of an international obligation'.[157] Such conceptualization would not seem entirely apt at present and given the span of Community law, the cost of defection should outweigh concerns that sanctions have a federal appearance. Further, a comparative study on implementation of Community law based on interviews with national civil servants, first published in 1988, suggests that national administrations 'do not consider the Community law implementation of the Community substance of directives as the application of foreign imposed law'.[158] If Community norms at the implementation stage are perceived as part of national law *per se,* the demands articulated by the Commission under Articles 226 and 228 of the EC Treaty should not be interpreted as meddlesome. Whereas the ECJ endorsed the UK proposal, somewhat surprisingly the Commission was sceptical. More generally, it held that the principle of Member State liability should be strengthened and codified in the Treaty thereby invigorating decentralized enforcement instead of the infringement procedure. The Commission voiced concern over the fact that repetitive infringement often expressed a lack of resources and that imposing pecuniary sanctions would merely aggravate the cause of non-compliance. Additional and more concrete problems in terms of making sanctions effective were brought up. Timmermans notes that in 'reading the Commission's contribution to the Conference in this respect one gets the

---

[153] The wording is identical to that of Article 143 of the Treaty establishing the European Atomic Energy Community, 25 March 1957 (Euratom Treaty).

[154] *The American Heritage Dictionary of the English Language* (4th edn, Houghton Mifflin Company, 2004). See: <http://dictionary.reference.com/browse/lump sum>.

[155] J Tallberg, *European Governance and Supranational Institutions—Making States Comply* (Routledge, 2003), 77.

[156] J Tallberg, ibid, and Maria Mendrinou, 'Non-Compliance and the European Commission's Role in Integration' (1996) Journal of European Public Policy 3:1, at 14.

[157] P Mead, 'The Obligation to Apply European Law: Is Duke Dead?' (1991) 16 ELR 490–501, at 491.

[158] H Siedentopf, 'The Implementation of Directives in the Member States', in H Siedentopf and J Ziller (eds), *Making European Policies Work* (SAGE, 1988), 178.

impression that the Commission did not consider the Introduction of a sanction mechanism a priority'.[159]

It is notable that sanctions have been imposed only a handful of times since Article 228 of the EC Treaty entered into force more than a decade ago. The Commission has however indicated that a greater application of sanctions can be anticipated. Although the Commission initially made most use of its power to request sanctions in areas of environmental and social affairs, it does consider it a generally applicable instrument,[160] which is also evidenced by more recent referral practice[161] and reminders of the penalty provision are as a rule included in letters of notice and reasoned opinions under Article 228.[162] A Commission request for fines is a procedural requirement for the Court to award sanctions, however, the Court has exclusive powers to impose a penalty and to rule on the amount. Recent jurisprudence from the ECJ has provided important points of procedural clarification on Article 228(2), on the powers of the Court and the Commission respectively and the possibility of imposing periodic and lump sum penalties cumulatively. The following sections set out a procedural overview of Article 228(2) with reference to relevant jurisprudence.

(iii) Dates of Relevance

When examining whether a Member State has failed to take the necessary measures to comply with a judgment under Article 226 of the EC Treaty, the Court of Justice considers the situation on expiry of the date set by the Commission in its reasoned opinion under Article 228 of the EC Treaty.[163] In relation to the possible imposition of a penalty payment, it is the date on which the Court examines the facts that is relevant.[164] If the State has brought itself into compliance before Court proceedings are initiated and the facts having been verified, the Member State no longer risks sanctioning.

(iv) Lump Sum and Penalty Payments—Exclusive or Complementary

Article 228(2) of the EC Treaty reads that the Commission shall 'specify the amount of the lump sum *or* penalty payment to be paid by the Member State concerned which...[it] considers appropriate in the circumstances' (emphasis added). The Commission initially took the standpoint that periodic penalty

---

[159] CWA Timmermans, 'Commentary', in MK Bulterman and M Kuijer, *Compliance with Judgments of International Courts* (The Hague, Martinus Nijhoff Publishers, 1996), 115.

[160] 19th Annual Report on Monitoring the Application of Community Law (2001), COM 2002/324 [2002] OJ C224 (10.10.2002), p 14.

[161] 21st Annual Report on Monitoring the Application of Community Law (2003), COM 2004/1638, Annex A, pp 7–9.

[162] 11th Annual Report on Monitoring the Application of Community Law (1993), COM/94/500, 29.3.1994.

[163] Case C-177/04 *Commission v France* [2006] ECR I-2461, para 20.

[164] Cases C-177/04 *Commission v France* [2006] ECR I-2461, para 21, and C-304/02 *Commission v France* [2005] ECR I-0, para 31.

payments were 'more appropriate than lump sum payments as a means of achieving the essential objective of infringement proceedings, namely . . . compliance at the earliest possible opportunity'.[165] The underlying rationale was that penalty payments are forward looking. The position should be seen against the background that the Commission seemingly understood the two sanction types mentioned to be mutually exclusive, as a strict literal interpretation of Article 228 would suggest.

Applying a broad and teleological interpretation, Advocate General Geelhoed in his opinion in Case C-304/02,[166] recommended that France be ordered to pay *both* a lump sum and a penalty payment.[167] The opinion prompted the Court to re-open the oral procedure allowing the parties and other Member States to express their views and France to prepare a new defence. In that the Commission had initially requested the Court to order France to pay a pecuniary penalty, the question arose as to whether the Court could deviate from the penalty type considered most appropriate by the Commission. Several governments argued that such an interpretation would be incompatible with the principles of legal certainty, predictability, transparency and equal treatment.[168] Germany argued further that the ECJ, as opposed to the Commission, lacked the 'political legitimacy necessary to exercise such a power in a field where assessments of political expediency play a considerable role' and argued that given the extensive nature of the power it would be against the 'general principle of civil procedure common to all the Member States that courts cannot go beyond the parties' claims'.[169] First, the Court stated, the judicial procedure under Article 228(2) is *sui generis* and cannot be compared to civil procedure principles.[170] Secondly, the Court made a definite distinction between the administrative and judicial phases of Article 228. Whereas the Commission operates in a political realm in which it benefits from unfettered discretion, the ECJ on the contrary enjoys absolute jurisdiction under Article 228(2). Thus questions of appropriateness of fines and suitability are entirely within the Court's judicial function once a case has been referred to it.[171]

---

[165] 13th Annual Report on Monitoring the Application of Community Law (1994), COM 96/600 [1996] OJ C303 (14.10.1996), p 1. See also Information from the Commission—Memorandum on Applying Article 171 of the EC Treaty [1996] OJ C242 (21.8.1996), pp 6–8. The illegitimate French ban on British beef made the Commission consider the option of a lump sum fine. See 20th Annual Report on Monitoring the Application of Community Law (2002), COM 2003/669, p 9.

[166] Opinion of Advocate General Geelhoed [2004] in Case C-304/02 *Commission v France* [2005] ECR I-0, para 38.

[167] In the second round of submissions, the Commission and the Danish, Netherlands, Finnish, and UK Governments answered in the affirmative to the question of the possibility of imposing both a penalty payment and a lump sum. The French, Belgian, Czech, German, Greek, Spanish, Irish, Italian, Cypriot, Hungarian, Austrian, Polish, and Portuguese Governments argued against such an interpretation.

[168] France, Belgium, Denmark, Germany, Greece, Spain, Ireland, Italy, the Netherlands, Austria, Poland, and Portugal. The Commission and the Czech, Hungarian, and Finnish Governments answered in the affirmative.

[169] Case C-304/02 *Commission v France*, para 88.   [170] Ibid, para 91.

[171] Ibid, para 103.

In considering periodic penalty payments a tool to 'Influence future conduct',[172] it may be contemplated whether lump sum payments are a sanction to punish past conduct.[173] In his opinion, Advocate General Colomer rejects such interpretation. '[T]he payment of a lump sum . . . must . . . be regarded as a means of obtaining ultimate compliance and not as a penalty which serves to punish . . . unlawful conduct or still less as a form of compensation.'[174] The Advocate General built his argument on the assumption that the Court cannot deviate from the type of sanction proposed by the Commission, which would consequently decide the nature of the sanction. As noted above, it is now clear that the ECJ is not bound in this sense. The qualification of lump sum fines as non-punitive is nonetheless correct as confirmed in the 2005 case against France. The penalties have *distinct functions*, but serve the *identical objective* of inducing compliance with a judgment.[175] The purpose of penalty payments is one of 'inducing a Member State to put an end as soon as possible to a breach which, in the absence of such measure, would tend to persist'.[176] Implied in this formulation is a requirement that penalty payments must be purposively justified. Lump sums are 'based more on assessment of the effects on public and private interests of the failure . . . to comply'[177] with emphasis on the duration of the breach. The two functions are thus of coercion and deterrence respectively and they should be employed according to their particular capacity to meet those purposes consistent with the circumstances of a given case.[178] Community sanctions are not based on some sort of liability consideration.[179] Yet, in making the lump sum fine operational the ECJ has made certain that a State is no longer guaranteed a net benefit of the treaty violence, which is the case when penalty payments are applied in isolation, due to the fact that a State is liable from the date of delivery of the second judgment. The time passing from initiation of the infringement procedure for failure to comply with a judgment of the Court to the consecutive judgment would thus be cost-free without a lump sum penalty in cases where a Member State complies after referral has been made to the ECJ yet before judgment is given. This systemic deficiency has now been remedied.[180] The Commission has consequently changed its practice

---

[172] Case C-387/97 *Commission v Greece* [2000] EC 2000 I-5047, para 41.

[173] Levente Borzsak, 'Punishing Member States or Influencing their Behaviour or iudex (non) calculat?' (2001) Journal of European Law 13, 235–262.

[174] Opinion of Advocate General Alber in Case C-387/97 *Commission v Greece* [2000] I-5047, para 30.

[175] Case C-304/02 *Commission v France* [2005] ECR I-0, para 80 in conjunction with para 84.

[176] Ibid, para 81.   [177] Ibid.   [178] Ibid.

[179] Cases C-177/04 *Commission v France* [2006] ECR I-2461, para 60, and C-304/02 *Commission v France* [2005] ECR I-0, para 91. Stephen Weatherill, 'Addressing Problems of International Implementation in EC Law', in C Kilpatrick, T Novitz, and P Skidmore, *The Future of Remedies in Europe* (Hart Publishing, 2000), at 103 qualifies it as a 'constitutional deficiency in the EC system' that gains stemming from non-compliance 'will not be clawed back.' For a similar critique, see also HAH Audretsch, *Supervision in European Community Law* (Elsevier Science Publishers BV, 1986), at 141.

[180] In its Communication from the Commission—Application of Article 228 of the EC Treaty, SEC/2005/1658, the Commission explains that it will 'from now include' both types of sanctions

and it no longer withdraws its action automatically.[181] However, given the lack of absolute monitoring and because of the discretion the Commission enjoys in pursuing infringements, this does by no means imply that a State will necessarily 'suffer enough from the punishment that the net benefit will not be positive'[182] if one considers every infringement taking place.

(v) *Method of Calculation*

For reasons of transparency, the Commission has issued two communications, in 1996 and 1997, concerning its use of Article 228 of the EC Treaty and approach to calculating fines. They have now been replaced in view of subsequent jurisprudence.[183] The method of calculating penalty payments proposed by the Commission allows for variation consistent with the seriousness of the infringement, the duration of the infringement and the need to ensure that the penalty functions as a deterrent to further infringements. A flat-rate amount of 600 euros per day is now index-linked to a GDP deflator, rounded off and multiplied by a coefficient scaling from 1 to 20 reflecting the seriousness of the breach and with a coefficient between 1 and 3 depending on the duration of the infringement. Where appropriate, the Court acknowledges that immediate Member State compliance may be difficult to achieve. This will be reflected in the coefficient reflecting the duration.[184] To ensure the effectiveness of the penalty, the final amount is multiplied by a coefficient supposed to match the Member State's ability to pay based upon its GDP and Council votes.[185] This geometric mean-based so-called 'n' factor is, eg, 0.58 for Estonia and 25.40 for Germany.[186] The Court has taken the three basic measures on board. However, being a judicial organ with an ultimate adjudicative authority, the Commission propositions are merely considered to

---

in its applications to the ECJ. See point 10.3. There may be situations where the Commission will exclusively ask for a lump sum to be imposed. See point 10.5.

[181] Commission MEMO/05/482, Financial Penalties for Member States who fail to comply with judgments of the European Court of Justice: European Commission Clarifies rules, Brussels, 14 December 2005, p 5.

[182] Compare Downs et al. who presuppose State behaviour to be rooted in strict rationalist self-optimization, see GW Downs, D Rocke, and P N Barsoom 'Is the Good News about Compliance Good News for Cooperation?' (1996) IO 50, 385. The authors are not specifically concerned with sanctions within the EC context. For an account of game theory and collective action theory underpinning an economic enforcement understanding, see Jonas Tallberg, 'Paths to Compliance: Enforcement, Management, and the European Union' (2002) IO 56:3, 609–643, 611–612.

[183] Information from the Commission—Memorandum on Applying Article 171 of the EC Treaty [1996] OJ C242 (21.08.1996), pp 6–8, and Information from the Commission—Method of Calculating the Penalty Payments Provided for Pursuant to Article 171 of the EC Treaty [1997] OJ C63 (28.02.1997) have thus been replaced by Communication from the Commission—Application of Article 228 of the EC Treaty, SEC/2005/1658.

[184] The Commission has likewise acknowledged that it takes more time and energy to bring some infringements to an end than others.

[185] The Council votes are politically determined and hence do not necessarily reflect genuine ability to pay.

[186] Communication from the Commission—Application of Article 228 of the EC Treaty, SEC/2005/1658, point 18.1.

be 'useful point[s] of reference'[187] and are in their entirety without binding effect to the Court's exercise of discretion.[188]

As a rule, the Commission proposes a minimum fixed lump sum payment established on the basis of the 'n' factor. For Estonia this basic amount is 290,000 euros and for Germany, say, it is 12,700,000 euros.[189] Besides, the Commission operates with a method of calculation resembling the approach it takes to penalty payments by 'multiplying a *daily amount* by the *number of days the infringement persists* between the date of delivery of the judgment under Article 226 and the date the infringement comes to an end, or, failing compliance, the date of delivery of the judgment under Article 228'.[190] The Commission will propose the second amount if it exceeds the minimum lump sum. In the only case in which the Court has awarded a lump sum fine so far the amount came to 20,000,000 euros, whereas the Commission supported by Advocate General Geelhoed had proposed a significantly larger lump sum of 115,522,500 euros.[191]

(vi) Frequency

Initially, the Commission advocated the imposition of periodic payments on a daily basis. The Court however discarded the assumption that periodic payments should necessarily be imposed with respect to each day's delay[192] as was the case in the first judgment, Case C-387/98 *Commission v Greece.* Having regard to the particular circumstances in *Commission v Spain,* the Court of Justice decided that the imposition of a pecuniary penalty should be on an annual basis.[193]

(vii) When the Infringement Comes Closer to an End—Adjustability

The Court makes an undifferentiated judgment on the question of compliance and rules unilaterally on the size of the fine. It is clear that 'the importance of immediate and uniform application of Community law means that the process of compliance must be initiated at once and completed as soon as possible'.[194] In his opinion of 1999, AG Colomer raised the question of how to respond to gradually remedied infringements.[195] This is an issue of importance in view of the general Community principle of proportionality, which requires that fines

[187] Cases C-387/97 *Commission v Greece* [2000] EC 2000 I-5047, para 92, and C-278/01 *Commission v Spain* [2003] ECR I-14141, para 52.
[188] Cases C-387/97 *Commission v Greece* [2000] EC 2000 I-5047, para 89, and C-278/01 *Commission v Spain* [2003] ECR I-14141, para 41.
[189] Communication from the Commission—Application of Article 228 of the EC Treaty, SEC/2005/1658, p 9.
[190] Ibid, point 21.
[191] Case C-304/02 *Commission v France* [2005] ECR I-n.y.r., para 116.
[192] Information from the Commission—Method of Calculating the Penalty Payments Provided for Pursuant to Article 171 of the EC Treaty [1997] OJ C63 (28.02.1997), para 1.
[193] Case C-278/01 *Commission v Spain* [2003] ECR I-14141, para 46.
[194] Case C-387/97 *Commission v Greece* [2000] ECR I-5047, para 82.
[195] Opinion of Advocate General Colomer in Case C-387/97 [1999] ECR I-3475.

be proportional to a given breach and appropriate in view of a case's circumstances.[196] The question was addressed in *Commission v Spain*, where it was
acknowledged that awarding a static fine would potentially be inappropriate to
the circumstances and non-proportionate to the breach. It has now been clarified that the amount can decrease and, thus, take account of gradual progress.[197]
With that judgment the ECJ established a more nuanced conception of compliance relevant to the penalty payment in preference to the absolute distinction
between compliance and non-compliance advocated by the Commission.[198] In
the concrete case, which concerned an obligation to ensure the quality of inshore
bathing water[199] the gradation was made contingent on the percentage of bathing
areas in compliance with the given directive.[200] The particular type of obligation
and also the access to control the measure deemed central to the penalty amount
were fairly plain in this case. It must be anticipated that compliance with various
other types of obligations will be far more problematical to monitor fully and in
particular to grade.

(viii) A Commission Duty to Specify Indicatively which Measures to be Taken

The Court's judgments are of a declaratory nature[201] and thus restricted to affirm-
ing whether or not a Member State is complying. On this note, the ECJ, supported
by the Commission, has itself proposed that it should be empowered to clarify
specifically what measures a Member State should take in order to comply, albeit
unsuccessfully.[202] The open-ended character of its judgments notwithstanding, it
is assumed that the Court may suggest how a State *can* comply. Indeed, the wide
Member State discretion to determine how to fulfil its Community obligations
in accordance with the doctrine of proportionality, but also the particular style of
much Community law essentially being diplomatic craftsmanship may compli-
cate law abidance. In cases where penalty payments have been awarded, the question of when the Member State is complying becomes of paramount significance.

The Commission has no general powers to appraise Member State conduct[203] and consequently no authority to reach a binding decision that an

---

[196] Case C-278/01 *Commission v Spain* [2003] ECR I-14141, para 52.

[197] Ibid, para 49.

[198] On this distinction, see furthermore opinion of Advocate General Mischo in Case C-278/01
Commission v Spain [2003] ECR I-14141, para 77.

[199] Council Directive 76/160/EEC of 8 December 1975 concerning the quality of bathing water
[1976] OJ L31 (05.02.1976), pp 1–7.

[200] Case C-278/01 *Commission v Spain* [2003] ECR I-14141, para 50.

[201] Opinion of Advocate General Alber in Case C-260/98 *Commission v Greece* [2000] I-6537,
para 76: 'proceedings for failure to fulfil Treaty obligations seek a declaration of principle on the content of the rules of Community law.'

[202] CWA Timmermans, 'Commentary', in MK Bulterman and M Kuijer, *Compliance with
Judgments of International Courts* (Martinus Nijhoff Publishers, 1996), at 116.

[203] Cases C-393/98 *Ministério Público and António Gomes Valente v Fazenda Pública* [2001]ECR
I-1327, para 18, 142 and 143/80 *Amministrazione delle Finanze dello Stato v Essevi SpA and Carlo
Salengo* [1980] ECR 1413, para 16.

infringement has been brought to an end. There are circumstances that suggest that an *obligation* for the Commission to specify indicatively the Member State measures, which it considers to be necessary, might emerge from the growing jurisprudence on Article 228(2) of the EC Treaty. In particular, the broadening of the Commission's *de facto* discretionary powers and the reversed burden of retaining judicial review where the Commission fails to terminate a penalty payment,[204] but also the mutual duty of loyal cooperation applying to the EC institutions and the Member States should be considered.[205] Such an obligation, akin to a 'rule of law' requirement, would reduce the potential arbitrary treatment of a Member State which is paying Community fines. The Commission Legal Service has now issued an in-house note clarifying that it shall be notified to Member States in reasoned opinions, exactly what they are expected to do to be considered to have terminated the infringement.[206] Given that the indications do not amount to acts of authoritative interpretation, they have no bearing on private individuals' ability to challenge a Member State before national courts and direct Member State infringement proceedings under Article 227 of the EC Treaty.

(ix) Member State Failure to Pay

Fines under Article 228(2) of the EC Treaty are paid to 'the Community own resources', an account of the Commission, and qualifies as 'other revenue'.[207] No powers of collection have been conferred upon the Commission in the Treaty. However, it is not entirely clear whether that makes the system wholly dependent upon Member State willingness or whether the EC budgetary rules allow the Commission to offset the amount.[208] Member States are liable for interest on payments behind schedule.

(x) Burden of Proof

The burden of proof rests with the Commission and continues to do so after the amendment of Article 228 of the EC Treaty. This means that it is for the Commission to provide evidence that a Member State has failed to observe its obligations, however, it is 'for the Member State concerned to challenge in substance and in detail the information produced and its consequences'.[209]

[204] Compare Article 228 of the EC Treaty and Article 232 of the same Treaty (failure to act).

[205] Article 10 of the EC Treaty.

[206] Interview, Commission, 2004.

[207] Article 269 of the EC Treaty and Council Decision 2000/597/EC [2000] OJ L253 (7.10.2000), pp 42–46.

[208] Article 88 of the European Coal and Steel Community Treaty (ECSC) explicitly allowed for suspension of Community payments or inter-State corrective measures. This step required approval by 2/3 of the Council votes.

[209] Cases C-304/02 *Commission v France* [2005] ECR I-0, para 56, and C-365/97 *Commission v Italy* [1999] ECR I-7773, para 84–87.

C. Confidentiality

Although the preliminary investigations and the consecutive conciliatory phase of the administrative phases of Articles 226 and 228 of the EC Treaty allow infringements to be dealt with bilaterally and somewhat discretely between the Commission and the Member States, the Commission brings up a number of infringement cases in the committee consisting of the Permanent Representatives of the Member States (COREPER).[210] It should be recalled that the Council and, hence, COREPER is not empowered to exert influence on the compliance obligation at this point. The practice of taking the matter out of the Commission's and the concrete Member State's immediate sphere serves as a means to exert peer pressure. Another instrument, which has emerged as a political routine of the Commission, is that of informing the broader public about pending cases in order to put compliance pressure on the malefactor. This serves instrumental objectives of exposure and stigma, in addition to informing citizens of potential rights and liability claims enforceable before national courts.

Despite these practices, the Commission has an interest in maintaining the procedure as one of confidentiality and especially so because Article 226 merely provides the Commission with a 'warning procedure'.[211] Secrecy thus enables the Commission to exert pressure on a Member State by threats of disclosure. The system has however given rise to a number of citizen complaints pertaining to transparency. Stressing that dialogue, transparency, and legal rights in supranational enforcement are important conditions for citizen trust in the Community, the European Ombudsman has advocated citizen rights in the administrative phase of Article 226 such as access to documents where a complainant is affected, right to be heard, and compulsory explanation why a case has been terminated. The Ombudsman did so with reference to the Charter of Fundamental Rights of the European Union. Citizen right of access to the central EU institutions' documents was established as a general rule with the Amsterdam IGC[212] and in 1994, the Commission issued a decision concerning public access to its documents with a view to 'giv[ing] effect to the principle of the widest possible access for citizens to information with a view to strengthening the democratic character of the institutions and the trust of the public in the administration'.[213] However, Article 226 comprises no citizen rights in addition to the Commission's self-imposed institutional obligations towards complainants.[214] The Commission reform of its enforcement working methods of 1998 implied a policy objective of 'greater

---

[210] According to Article 207 of the EC Treaty, the Committee may adopt procedural decisions in cases provided for in the Council's Rules of Procedure.

[211] Joined Cases 2/62 and 3/62 *Commission v Luxembourg and Belgium* [1962] ECR 793, 430.

[212] Article 255 of the EC Treaty.

[213] Case T-309/97 *The Bavarian Lager Company Ltd v Commission* [1999] II-03217, para 36.

[214] 16th Annual Report on Monitoring the Application of Community Law [1998] OJ C354 (7.12.1999), pp 1–192, para 1.2.

transparency' and above all the Commission now notifies citizens before closing a file.[215]

In 2000, the Commission drew up a proposal for a regulatory framework concerning access to documents of the European Parliament, the Council and the Commission. The document recognized broad rights of access, but also set out clear priorities of confidentiality.[216] Notably, the administrative phase of Article 226 was considered exempt from the general rights of access for two reasons. One was set out directly and one was set out tactfully in the explanatory memorandum. First, the Commission maintained that public access to the infringement proceedings and their preliminary phases 'could significantly undermine the protection of the public interest'.[217] There is no specific exemption of documents relating to the general infringement procedure in the finally adopted Regulation 1049/2001 regarding public access to European Parliament, Council and Commission documents. However, the Commission may continue to deny access to a document where disclosure would undermine the protection of the 'public interest'.[218] The Court shed light on this notion in Case T-309/97 *The Bavarian Lager Company* where it examined the Commission's Decision of 1994 on public access to Commission documents, which contained a similar clause.[219] In the ruling, the Court noted that the general rule of citizen access to documents is to some extent countervailed by Member State expectations of 'confidentiality from the Commission during investigations which may lead to an infringement procedure'.[220] The underlying rationale is that the purpose of the infringement, namely to find an amicable settlement, may otherwise be hampered. It is not certain whether jurisprudence dictates absolute and unconditional seclusion of documents pertaining to Article 226. This may be the reason why the Commission proposed an explicit rule in this regard. In the ruling in *The Bavarian Lager company*, the Court applied a teleological interpretation of the infringement procedure and stated that the purpose was to 'enable the Member State to comply of its own accord with the requirements of the Treaty or, if appropriate, to justify its

---

[215] Commission Communication COM/2002/141, pp 3–6.

[216] Proposal for a Regulation of the European Parliament and of the Council regarding public access to European Parliament, Council and Commission documents, COM/2000/30. The proposal was eventually adopted as Regulation (EC) No 1049/2001 of the European Parliament and of the Council of 30 May 2001 regarding public access to European Parliament, Council and Commission documents [2001] OJ L145 (31.5.2001), pp 4348. See also Richard Rawlings and Carol Harlow, 'Accountability and Law Enforcement: the Centralised EU Infringement Procedure' (2006) 31 ELR 447–475.

[217] Commission proposal COM/2000/30.

[218] Regulation (EC) No 1049/2001 of the European Parliament and of the Council of 30 May 2001 regarding public access to European Parliament, Council and Commission documents [2001] OJ L145 (31.5.2001), pp 43–48, Article 4.

[219] Commission Decision of 8 February 1994 on public access to Commission documents [1994] OJ L46 (18.02.1994), pp 58–61.

[220] Cases T-309/97 *The Bavarian Lager Company Ltd v Commission* [1999] ECR II-03217, para 46, and T-105/95 *WWF UK v Commission* [1997] ECR II-313, para 63.

position'.[221] This could be taken to mean, *a contrario,* that secrecy only applies to some situations. By the time a case has been ruled upon by the ECJ, the Member State can no longer comply voluntarily and interest in the proper conduct of the pre-litigation procedure has arguably ended. That the Council and the European Parliament did not finally endorse the Commission's proposal regarding an explicit clause may have some signalling effect.[222] However, the ultimate version can be rooted in non-political considerations as to good legislative practice. Thus, if Article 226 is already exempted by the notion of 'public interest', it would create confusion to introduce *lex specialis* provisions to such effect.[223]

The Commission's second justification for secrecy appears in the explanatory memorandum of the 2000 legislative proposal, which sets out that the interest at stake is its own. The Commission considers its 'space to think'[224] out of the public eye a prerequisite for high-quality policy formation. The Commission is an autonomous institution, which defines its policies in collective deliberation and under collegial responsibility.[225] This is the case generally and also in its supervisory function,[226] which likewise is an area where the Commission drafts principled policy formation. Exactly in its supervisory function, there is considerable potential for the Commission to manifest a political role and consequently adopt interpretations and pursue cases in line with its own preferences. If carried out in full transparency, the practice of semi-legal, semi-political conciliation between the Commission and Member States would, however, display the Commission's credibility as guardian of the Treaty from a citizen perspective and potentially also elicit critical responses from Member States not involved in a given dispute. This could bar the College from displaying sensitivity to the political and practical obstacles in the Member States, which may otherwise influence its decision to advance a case.

It is clear that the Community interest in obtaining a solution at the prejudicial stage prevails over citizen interests in transparency and public access to documents.[227] Article 226 is not a rigid, legalistic procedure, but rather one of

---

[221] Case T-309/97 *The Bavarian Lager Company Ltd v Commission* [1999] II-03217, para 46.

[222] Compare COM (2000)30/final/2, Article 4(1)(a) with Regulation (EC) No 1049/2001 of the European Parliament and of the Council, Article 4(1)(a).

[223] One risk being that codifying some rules suggests an exhaustive listing.

[224] COM/2000/30/final/2, explanatory memorandum para 4.

[225] Case C-191/95 *Commission v Germany* [1998] ECR I-5449, para 39.

[226] According to Case C-1/00 *Commission v France* [2001] ECR I-09989, paras 79–80 the principle of collegiality is based on the equal participation of the Commissioners in the adoption of decisions, from which it follows, in particular, that decisions should be the subject of collective deliberation. A decision to bring infringement proceedings must be the subject of collective deliberation by the college of Commissioners.

[227] It should be remembered that citizens in some situations can pursue infringements directly and hence do not rely fully upon Commission action. '[O]wing to their very nature and their place in the system of sources of Community law, regulations operate to confer rights on individuals which the national courts have a duty to protect.' (Case C-379/04 *Richard Dahms GmbH v Fränkischer Weinbauverband e V* [2005] ECR I-8723, para 13.) '[W]herever the provisions of a directive appear, as far as their subject-matter is concerned, to be unconditional and sufficiently precise, those provisions

confidential, political negotiation and it can usefully be thought of as a tool of diplomatic dispute resolution albeit with ultimate judicial recourse.

V. The EC Infringement Procedure in Perspective

A. Managing Non-compliance

A preliminary remark on the scope of this section should be made here concerning the methodologically distinct questions of enforcement and effectiveness. The focus here is solely on the manner in which the law structures the interaction between the Member States in default and the Commission acting as a semi-diplomatic, semi-legal institutional actor. The section does not attempt to assess the extent to which sanctions and the threat thereof have brought about compliance in the concrete cases or generally. The sections proceed as follows. The first part analyses the EC infringement procedure in view of managerial compliance theory and the number of defined successive stages it prescribes. In the second part, the particular procedural and institutional features that make EC treaty-based sanctions viable will be examined.

Whereas enforcement theorists adhere to sanctions as part of a coercive enforcement strategy which is ultimately assumed to compel observance, management theorists in turn advocate capacity building, formal and informal dispute settlement, and continuous adaptation of treaty norms.[228] In short, the managerial approach aims at consensual observance of treaty norms through discourse. The penultimate stage comprises of threats to invoke the regime's dispute settlement mechanisms or actual recourse whilst the final stage consists of mere considerations as to the legitimacy of the treaty provision itself.[229] The processes up to and including the penultimate stage and their logic of succession resemble the general Community infringement procedure as stipulated in Article 226 of the EC Treaty. Abram Chayes and Antonia Handler Chayes build their managerial approach on a variation of state-interdependency. With the explanatory notion of the 'New Sovereignty', they seek to distance themselves from the traditional mega-language of sovereignty and the centrality of nation-States as ultimate authorities.[230] This is, at least theoretically speaking, a mode whereby States act to realize national objectives unhindered by the influence of other States and

---

may, in the absence of implementing measures adopted within the prescribed period, be relied upon as against any national provision which is incompatible with the directive or in so far as the provisions of the directive define rights which individuals are able to assert against the State.' (Joined Cases C-6/90 and C-9/90 *Francovich v Italy* [1991] ECR I-5357, para 11.)

[228] A Chayes and A Handler Chayes, n 27 above, ch 2.

[229] Ibid, at 7.

[230] 'Traditionally, sovereignty has signified the complete autonomy of the state to act as it chooses, without legal limitation by any superior entity,' (Ibid, at 26.)

without external interference. It is exactly the inadequacy of autonomous action to achieve, for example, economic and security ends that provokes the claim that 'sovereignty no longer consists in the freedom of States to act independently, in their perceived self-interest, but in membership of and reasonably good standing with the regimes that make up the substance of international life.'[231] The sovereignty notion itself is questioned and its actual significance recast. From the starting point that dependency on other States has increased and that transnational interaction has become crucial for the realization of domestic policy objections, Chayes and Chayes maintain that membership and good standing with other participants of transnational treaty regimes constitutes a fundamental gauge of contemporary statehood. Therefore, they hold, States are in principle willing to comply. The authors' contrasting of sovereignty and interdependency is germane to the history of the EC.

Chayes and Chayes suggest three main causes why non-compliance nevertheless occurs, namely, ambiguous treaty language, capacity problems including lack of knowledge and comprehension of treaty obligations and excessively short transposition periods.[232] These factors, all present in the Community compliance picture, will be briefly commented on before I compare Article 226 of the EC Treaty with the main components of managerialism. Significantly, the Commission considers lack of knowledge and substantive comprehension of Community provisions to be a considerable source of non-compliance.[233] The EC Council has also on several occasions raised the issue that implementation suffers from overly complicated or unclear legal drafting[234] and, in 2002, the Commission launched an action plan on 'a strategy for further coordinated action to simplify the regulatory environment' with a view to making Community law more readily understandable.[235] Excessively short transposition deadlines, the time factor, explain some infringements. The Commission however also cautions that overly long transition periods 'can deprive directives of their effect'.[236]

(i) Cooperation

Literature on market governance, in particular theories of self-regulation, suggests that regulatees faced with only one deterrence option are more likely to be

---

[231] Ibid, at 27.   [232] Ibid, at 15.

[233] See, eg answer given by Mr Bolkestein on behalf of the Commission to Written Question P-2950/00 [2001] OJ C89E (20.03.2001), p 26 in the area of public procurement. '[T]he Commission also believes that non-compliance is to a large extent caused by a lack of knowledge and understanding of the rules.'

[234] Conclusions of the European Council summits at Lisbon (23–24 March 2000), Stockholm (23–24 March 2001), Laeken (8–9 December 2001) and Barcelona (5–16 March 2002).

[235] Communication from the Commission, Action plan 'Simplifying and Improving the Regulatory Environment' of 5/6 2005.

[236] White Paper on Governance, Preparatory work, 'Recommendations for the Improvement of the Application of Community Law by the Member States and its Enforcement by the Commission', September 2001, p 5.

in opposition and that enforcement approaches founded on punishment bear the risk of undermining a cooperative position where it is motivated by a sense of responsibility.[237] This line of thought is also present in the managerial approach. Prohibitory rules enforced in a hasty and pre-emptory manner are considered likely to be counterproductive. Instead the authors perceive treaties and regimes as 'institutions for the management of an issue area over time'[238] and this framework includes also a strategy to manage failures to comply. The dual role of the Commission as both policy initiator and guardian of the Treaty supports a reading of the general Community infringement procedure as a subset of a coherent scheme to manage certain policy areas over time.

Infringement proceedings frequently concern politically sensitive matters and the tone of the interaction may harden during the negotiations. However, the Commission characterization of the procedure as one of an 'adversarial nature'[239] merits reappraisal. A ruling by the Court of Justice is of a purely declaratory nature; the principle of loyal cooperation applies to the Commission as a Community institution and not merely to the supervisees;[240] the judicial phase of Article 226 does not imply a culpability test and, significantly, the burden of proof in infringement procedures lies with the Commission alone.[241] Thus, there is no presumption of non-compliance in the procedural design of Article 226.[242] Given the somewhat soft powers of the Commission, a contextual understanding of the enforcement mechanism and the implied function of the Commission suggests a role as a loyal cooperator endorsing and assisting national compliance. Overt violations of treaty obligations aside, and these seldom occur, the pre-litigation and also the judicial phases are more usefully thought of as forums for clarification. This is both in relation to substantive questions and to Member State behaviour. Where it becomes apparent that a Member State has misread its obligations or failed to conform to them, it shall loyally arrange itself in accordance with the obligation.[243] In its 22nd Annual Report on Compliance, the Commission itself underscores that the purpose of the general infringement procedure in general and of the pre-litigation phase in particular, is to encourage voluntary compliance. Thus, as a complement to its treaty-based enforcement measures, the Commission has encouraged Member State cooperation through non-binding arrangements and thereby expanded the scope for cooperative

---

[237] I Ayres and J Braithwaite, *Responsive Regulation: Transcending the Deregulation Debate* (OUP, 1992), at 19.

[238] A Chayes and A Handler Chayes, n 27 above, at 227–228.

[239] Commission Communication COM/2002/725, p 5.

[240] Case 2/88 *Zwartveld* [1990] ECR I-489, para 18.

[241] Cases 96/81 and 97/81 *Commission v Netherlands* [1982] ECR 1791. See, however, Case 272/86 *Commission v Greece* [1988] ECR I-4875, para 21 clarifying that where the 'Commission has produced sufficient evidence…[it is] incumbent on…[the Member State] to contest substantively and in detail the information produced and the consequences thereof.'

[242] Case C-287/03 *Commission v Belgium* [2005] ECR I-03761, para 27.

[243] This general obligation is codified in the fidelity clause in Article 10 of the EC Treaty.

interaction.[244] The Commission thus redefines the infringement procedure as one of cooperativeness and portrays its role as that of a supervisor by focusing on its capacity to accommodate and assist Member States' compliance.

The distinction between compliance and effectiveness set out above is useful to have in mind when comparing the managerial approach *towards* compliance and the EC infringement procedure. Central is a range of activities that take treaty norms as a point of reference rather than perceiving them as pre-fixed obligations to be imposed in a rigid manner. That the Court of Justice issues declaratory judgments, suggests a need for interpretive clarification and an assumption that States will meet the terms voluntarily. The Commission does presume, implicitly[245] and explicitly,[246] that Member States are generally willing to comply[247] and it asserts that judicial recourse is 'not the only nor necessarily the most efficient way to ensure compliance'.[248] In practice, endeavours to ensure compliance do rest primarily on informal and formal approaches, in accordance with the purpose of the pre-litigation phase, which is to ensure a friendly agreement. The range of ancillary compliance approximation measures institutionalized unilaterally by the Commission[249] and some on the initiatives of the European Parliament,[250] includes 'benchmarking, peer pressure, annual reporting on implementation of Community law',[251] SOLVIT-programmes[252] as well as naming and shaming. These instruments and practices are continuously evaluated and adapted.[253] Other soft tools have become available thanks to secondary legislation.[254]

---

[244] 22nd Annual Report from the Commission on Monitoring the Application of Community Law (2004), COM 2005/570, p 3.

[245] For instance by setting up 'package meetings' where Member States are provided an opportunity to voluntarily conform to their Community obligations.

[246] The Commission's understanding of most non-compliance as being benign appears from interviews conducted by Börzel in 2001 with Commission functionaries from a range of Directorate Generals. TA Börzel, 'Guarding the Treaty. The Compliance Strategies of the Commission', in TA Börzel and RA Cichowski, *State of the European Union Volume 6: Law Politics and Society* (OUP, 2003), 207.

[247] This defining starting point permeates the managerial model. See A Chayes and A Handler Chayes (1995) and H Koh (1997).

[248] 'Implementation of EU Environmental Law: Survey Highlights Serious Shortcomings', IP/04/1038, Brussels, 19 August 2004.

[249] See, eg Commission score boards.

[250] See, eg the annual reports on monitoring the application of Community law issued by the Commission.

[251] Commission paper, 'Towards the Enlarged Union—Strategy Paper and Report of the European Commission on the Progress towards Accession by each of the Candidate Countries', COM/2002/700 final, p 25.

[252] In the area of Internal Market, the SOLVIT arrangement provides individuals an opportunity to alert national or local administrations about alleged non-compliance. The administration is foreseen to bilaterally contact the relevant counterpart in the Member State causing problems to seek a resolution. Compared to Article 227 of the EC Treaty, SOLVIT provides for non-adversarial, practical solutions.

[253] Commission Communication COM/2002/725, p 6.

[254] See, eg Decision No 3052/95/EC of the European Parliament and of the Council of 13 December 1995 establishing a procedure for the exchange of information on national measures

Together these formal and informal procedures resemble core elements of the managerial model. Pursuing Court action is, however, a significant part of the overall monitoring regime,[255] and the Commission recognizes it as a vital feature of the procedure.[256]

(ii) *Identification and Justification*

Active management starts with identifying infringements[257] and the Commission has classified behaviour it considers to be particularly grave. The three main categories of infringements are prioritized in the following order: (a) infringements that undermine the foundations of the rule of law, (b) infringements that undermine the smooth functioning of the Community legal system, and (c) infringements consisting in the failure to transpose or the incorrect transposal of directives.[258] Rapid changes in situations may render obligations inapt and themselves be a cause of non-compliance. The Commission urges that *ex post* evaluation is a useful tool to identify shortcomings and argues that, where appropriate, review clauses should be included in legislative acts.[259] This enables the Commission to issue legislative proposals when a provision is non-operational or needs amendment.

The procedural structure starting with a 'warning letter', guarantees Member State interest in submitting its observations. It also allows for an exchange of interpretations of particular provisions, jurisprudence, etc, and, significantly, it prevents the Commission from acting as a vindicative prosecutor by automatically initiating the infringement proceedings. It thus compels the parties to seek out pre-judicial conflict solution during the preliminary as well as the consecutive conciliatory phase.

(iii) *Technical Assistance*

At the Community level technical assistance is provided for instance through package meetings involving also national civil servants at the expert level. The reciprocal nature of Article 10 of the EC Treaty arguably entails that Member States can request assistance from the Commission.[260]

---

derogating from the principle of the free movement of goods within the Community [1995] OJ L321 (30.12.1995), p 1–5, Article 9.

[255] See, eg Second Forum on Implementation and Enforcement of Community Environmental Law, *Intensifying our Efforts to Clean Urban Waste Water,* closing remarks of Commissioner Wallström, p 2. More generally, see Commission Communication COM/2002/725, pp 10–12.

[256] Answer given by Mr Prodi on behalf of the Commission to Written Question P-3784/2002 [2003] OJ C280E (21.11.2003), p 29.

[257] A Chayes and A Handler Chayes, n 27 above, at 110.

[258] Commission Communication COM/2002/725, p 11.

[259] Communication from the Commission, Action plan 'Simplifying and Improving the Regulatory Environment' of 5/6 2005, p 8 and Part IV.

[260] Case 94/87 *Commission v Germany* [1989] ECR I-175, para 9. Note that the case concerns State aid. See furthermore Case 2/88, *Zwartveld* [1990] ECR I-489, para 18.

(iv) *Discourse and Persuasion—Elitist Settlements*

The general Community infringement procedure as well as the managerial approach attributes a central role to structured discourse.[261] When presumed infringements stem from conflicting interpretations by the Commission and the Member State, the administrative phases consist of exchanges of arguments and expositions[262] rather than technical advice. Elitist settlements can differ considerably from a hypothetical ruling had the Commission referred the case to the ECJ and they do not influence the material obligations of the Member State.[263] However, the possibility for a given Member State to negotiate a favourable understanding with the Commission constitutes an incentive to engage in bilateral dialogue. The method of recurring exchanges based on facts and law resembles the 'iterative process of discourse' central to managerialism.[264] The aim of this problem-solving exercise is to obtain a *practical* elimination of defections and the consequences derived thereof[265] whereby the Commission might manage to generate behavioural changes on the side of the Member States. Consideration of 'Member States' responses, arguments and, where appropriate, intentions of rectifying the situation' are decisive to Commission follow-up action.[266] It is of course highly significant that this negotiation takes place in the shadow of formal adjudication. The Commission, thus, has a notable advantage throughout the process given that it decides on the advancement of the case.

(v) *Dispute Settlement*

Although adjudication is foreseen as an *ultima ratio*[267] and only a relatively small number of infringement proceedings initiated are referred to the ECJ, formal dispute settlement constitutes a significant element of Article 226 of the EC Treaty. First, awareness that there is a final, impartial body to undertake normative interpretation and to appraise Member State conduct restricts the scope for idiosyncratic and non-cooperative conduct by the parties. This is negotiation in the shadow of law. Secondly, as seen from case law on, for instance, the EC freedoms, there are a significant number of provisions that leave ample room for genuine

---

[261] Compare A Chayes and A Handler Chayes, n 257 above, at 229.

[262] At least from Commission side given the obligation to set out in the reasoned opinion 'a coherent and detailed statement of the reasons which persuaded the Commission that the State concerned had failed to fulfil one of its obligations under the Treaty.' See Case C-247/89 *Commission v Portugal* [1991] ECR I-3659, para 22.

[263] Cases C-393/98 *Ministério Público and António Gomes Valente v Fazenda Pública* [2001] ECR I-1327, para 18, C-142 and 143/80 *Amministrazione delle Finanze dello Stato v Essevi SpA and Carlo Salengo* [1980] ECR 1413, para 16.

[264] Compare A Chayes and A Handler Chayes, n 257 above, at 25.

[265] See Case 70/72 *Commission v Germany* [1973] ECR 813.

[266] Answer given by Mr Flynn on behalf of the Commission to Written Question E-3681/97 [1997] OJ C158 (25.5.1997), p 176.

[267] Case 20/59 *Italian Government v High Authority* [1960] ECR I-325.

interpretational doubt.[260] This matter of legal indeterminacy is not unique to EC law. In a regime based on the rule of law, some disputes will inevitably call for final clarification.

(vi) Transparency

Whereas the Member States have engaged in the Community on the 'basis of reciprocity',[269] compliance with the *acquis communautaire* does not rest on reciprocity.[270] The immediate purpose of ensuring compliance is twofold. First, to obtain the collective benefits that sparked off the institution of the Treaty. The second and interrelated purpose is to ensure that no parties exploit the others' faithful cooperation and thereby make loyal Member States bear the costs of others' temptation to free-ride. That Member States are concerned about the costs of complying in a defective enforcement milieu, can be seen from the proceedings before the Court where Member States invoke other treaty parties' failure to comply,[271] although such arguments have no legal bearings on their own commitment to comply. Weatherill points out that the possible implications of such Member State apprehension, taken together with the lack of access to corrective measures, may be serious in addition to being very hard to detect. Thus, he notes, there is an inherent risk of directives, and framework directives in particular, giving incentives to 'a more subtle form of retaliation based on reduction in domestic costs of compliance'.[272] Weatherill's point transcends isolated instances of non-compliance. Rather, he is concerned with the intrinsic risk of competitive under-implementation. This practice is furthered by uncertainty as to whether other Member States derive advantage from opportunistic behaviour to the detriment of Member States that satisfy their Treaty obligations.[273] 'Gold-plating' by adding 'layers of complexity and red-tape' when transposing directives, is one way the Member States can do so.[274] As already stressed, because the Commission has no authority of interpretation and because it often

---

[268] K Lenaerts, D Arts, and R Bray (eds), *Procedural Law of the European Union* (Sweet & Maxwell, 1999), 84: 'The "finding" serves principally to enforce the actual application of Community law ... The action may also be used as a means of determining the exact nature of the obligations of a Member State in the event of differences of interpretation of Community law.'

[269] Case 6/64 *Costa v ENEL* [1964] ECR I-585, para 3.

[270] Cases C-142/01 *Commission v Italy* [2002] ECR-4541, para 7, and C-163/99 *Portugal v Commission* [2001] ECR I-2613, para 22.

[271] The concern is not only raised by the Member States. See, eg the European Parliament on competitive disadvantages for companies established in Member States that genuinely comply. See also European Parliament Own-Initiative Report, Towards a Strategy on the Prevention and Recycling of Waste, INI/2003/2145, 20/04/2004.

[272] S Weatherill, 'Addressing Problems of International Implementation in EC Law' in C Kilpatrick, T Novitz, and P Skidmore (eds), *The Future of Remedies in Europe* (Hart Publishing, 2000), 113.

[273] Weatherill, ibid.

[274] Handling the Process of Producing and Implementing Community Rules: Report of the Working Group 'Better Regulation' (Group 2c) May 2001 (White Paper on European Governance, Work Area no 2).

does not have full information on the facts of law in a Member State, its procedural breakdowns merely reflect the work of the Commission as an investigatory body.[275] Transparency in this regard can function to deter States from considering non-compliant behaviour in the first place. Member State obligations to make transposition notifications serve an objective of prevention and, at least in formal terms, succeed to a significant extent although it is certainly difficult to assure substantive implementation.[276] In addition, transparency can serve as a means of mutual reassurance of compliance and thereby persuade other States to undertake genuine implementation. However, although the Commission's statistical breakdowns may constitute a source of information, which enables the Member States to monitor one another, the practice of publicity may also have negative repercussions for the overall compliance situation. Börzel has suggested that the serious compliance deficit identified by the Commission is indeed a hypocritical artefact.[277] Insofar as her assessment is correct, the Commission's complaints that Member States do not comply satisfactorily may indeed cause the same Member States to perceive some of their peers as free-riders. If the reaction to the Commission's public shaming and negative compliance assessments is non-compliance as a means of tacit retaliation or self-protection, the Commission's shaming strategy risks becoming a self-perpetuating cause of non-compliance.

(vii) *Preliminary Conclusion*

It has been demonstrated that the general Community infringement procedure relies on an instrumental logic similar to that of the managerial theory of enforcement. Chayes and Chayes foresee the range of prescribed measures and activities to 'separately and in intricate combination press toward compliance'.[278] Similarly, the various *de facto* and *de jure* phases of the EC infringement procedure have isolated functions, but they form part of a comprehensive enforcement strategy intended to anticipate compliance. Snyder thus suggests that the pre-judicial compliance negotiation and adjudication should be considered as

---

[275] The exception to this is naturally cases where a Member State infringement is established by the Court.

[276] By 11 February 2008 an average of 99.32% of directives had been notified by the 27 Member States. <http://ec.europa.eu/community_law/directives/directives_communication_en.htm> provides a link to the 'Situation on 11 February 2008 statistical break-down', p 1. See, however, Handling the Process of Producing and Implementing Community Rules: Report of the Working Group 'Better regulation' (Group 2c) May 2001, p 17: 'Late transposition ought to be the exception: it is almost the rule.' The Commission automatically institutes infringement proceedings whenever Member States fail to communicate transposition measures in time. See answer given by Mrs Wallstrom on behalf of the Commission to Written Question no E-2477/02 [2003] OJ C110E (08.05.2003), p 56.

[277] T Börzel, 'Non-compliance in the European Union: Pathology or Statistical Artefact?' (2001) Journal of European Public Policy, 8:5, 803–824.

[278] A Chayes and A Handler Chayes, n 27 above, at 110.

complementary forms of dispute settlement.[279] Significantly, the administrative and judicial phases provide forums for discursive interaction where treaty norms are interpreted and Member States induced to make the necessary behavioural changes in order to conform to their obligations. Aiming at non-punitive friendly settlements, voluntary Member State compliance may take place at any point of the process. Key words in this respect are argumentation, technical and legal exposition, persuasion, pressure through exposure and juridical recourse. A number of features of Article 226 of the EC Treaty suggest an assumption of voluntary compliance and that defection should be managed rather than sanctioned. Among those are the non-coercive nature of the enforcement tools, the significance attached to discourse and to technical assistance, the purely declaratory effect of rulings from the dispute settlement body and the assumed effect of shaming. In this section it has however also been cautioned that the Commission can be part of the cause of non-compliance if it does not use its shaming strategies with prudence. The shift towards a more cooperation-based approach seems laudable in this regard.

B. Sanctioning Non-Compliance

More recently, both political scientists and lawyers have, not surprisingly, questioned a rigid understanding of the managerial and enforcement models as necessarily mutually exclusive. Thus, Koh finds support in domestic enforcement practices that discourse leading to compliance can take place in the shadow of sanctions—and often succeed exactly because the two strategies complement each other[280] and Tallberg sees the EU as an example of how the two approaches successfully function *in concerto*.[281] Whereas, this article maintains, the managerial model usefully explains the legal framework of Article 226 of the EC Treaty, the Commission, however, also consider the shadow of sanctions to have a more general dissuasive effect increasing the general efficacy of the infringement procedure.[282] Moreover, it argues, Member States comply rapidly with Community obligations when there is the pressure of a fine payment.[283]

[279] F Snyder, 'The Effectiveness of European Community Law. Institutions, Processes, Tools and Techniques' (1993) MLR 56, 30.

[280] H Koh, 'Why Do Nations Obey International Law? (1997) Yale Law Journal 106, 2599–2659. See R Fisher, *Improving Compliance with International Law* (University Press of Virginia, 1981), 7, for a sceptical comment on the appropriateness of applying domestic compliance theories to compliance with international obligations and in particular analogues to domestic criminal law.

[281] J Tallberg, *European Governance and Supranational Institutions—Making States Comply* (Routledge, 2003), 14 and 143 *et seq.*

[282] See, eg Fourteenth Annual Report on Monitoring the Application of Community Law (1996) COM 97/299 [1997] OJ C332 (03.11.1997), p 1.

[283] Answer given by Mrs Wallstrom on behalf of the Commission to Written Question E-2776/01 [2002] OJ C134E (6.06.2002), pp 25–26. See also S Weatherill, 'Addressing Problems of International Implementation in EC Law', in C Kilpatrick, T Novitz, and P Skidmore, *The Future of Remedies in Europe* (Hart Publishing, 2000), at 93, on adding teeth to the procedure.

That is to say, they comply before the Court has delivered a second judgment under Article 228 of the EC Treaty. Although this is naturally difficult to validate in that the Commission does not openly document its practice of friendly settlements, the position suggests an instrumental logic built on a presumption of non-compliance to be overcome by force. Moreover, it would corroborate empirical evidence from international treaty regimes which suggests that economic coercion is more successful at the stage of threat than at the phase of implementation.[284] The indications given in Commission compliance records would, however, also be somewhat in opposition to assumptions shared by a vast number of theorists against the usefulness of sanctions.[285] In the following section, the system of pecuniary sanctions under Article 228 will be set out and discussed in the light of managerialism. It is argued that the procedural structure of Article 228 proposes a way of incorporating sanctions into a managerial process leading towards compliance and this in a manner which does not undermine the regime's legitimacy.

The two dominant strands within contemporary compliance theory, namely the enforcement and managerial approaches, rely on rational choice theory[286] and on a 'constructivist logic of appropriateness'[287] respectively. A stern critique of treaty-based sanctions has been voiced by the originators of managerialism, namely Abram Chayes and Antonia Handler Chayes. Interestingly, the deficiencies they point out are to some extent remedied under the EC sanctioning mechanism. Thus the discrepancy between the managerial traits of the general infringement procedure on the one hand, and the view expressed by the Commission that sanctions constitute an effective asset amongst their instruments for ensuring compliance, on the other, is less puzzling than it appears at first.

(i) Mobilization

A main obstacle to having sanctions imposed is often the need to mobilize the sanctioning treaty parties, ie problems of collective action. Each national decision is likely to be taken in view of a broad range of dispersed interests and pressures of

[284] See generally, C Morgan and A Miers, 'When Threats Succeed: A Formal Model of the Threat and Use of Economic Sanctions', 95th Annual Meeting of the American Political Science Association, Atlanta, Ga, 1999, p 16 and, specifically related to Article 228 of the EC Treaty, the answer given by Mrs Wallstrom on behalf of the Commission to Written Question E-2776/01 [2002] OJ C134E (6.6.2002), pp 98–99.

[285] S Weintraub (ed), *Economic Coercion and US Foreign Policy: Implications of Case Studies from the Johnson Administration* (Westview Press, 1982), 23; G Clyde Hufbauer and JJ Schott, *Economic Sanctions Reconsidered: History and Current Policy* (Institute for International Economics, 1990), 2; Jean Amphoux, 'Recours en constatation des manquements des États, les traités CEE et Euratom' (1969) Droit des Communautés Européennes, 1042–1088.

[286] Compare, eg Downs et al. (1996).

[287] K Raustiale and A Slaughter, 'International Law, International Relations and Compliance', in W Carlsnaes, T Risse, and BA Simmons (eds), *Handbook of International Relations* (SAGE, 2002), 548.

an economic and political nature among which, ensuring compliance *per se* will not necessarily prevail.[288] The members of the EC Commission College, however, may not pursue partisan interests and the College as a unit does not suffer comparable constrictions.

(ii) Legitimacy

A second problem is that of assembling and maintaining the consensus 'necessary for the legitimacy of sanctions'.[289] In the context of centralized Community enforcement, the decision to initiate proceedings, the question of assembling, lies with the Commission as an institution set up to protect and promote Community interests as a whole.[290] The Commission acts in the interest of the Community[291] and it draws on *general* political approval by the regime parties. Legitimacy considerations might arise in relation to the way the Commission exercises its discretion first, in making a second referral to the ECJ and secondly, as to the amount of the fines proposed. The former, ie the matter of intermittent sanctioning practice, is, however, a consequence of the anti-legalistic nature of Article 228 of the EC Treaty as foreseen by the legislator and confirmed by the Court of Justice. Rather than meticulously prescribing how the Commission shall observe its monitoring obligations, the procedure leaves room for the Commission to pursue ends by other means than a rigid rule-centred approach.[292] The latter issue is counteracted by the considerable guarantees[293] on the side of the defaulting Member States established by the Court of Justice and in particular the principle of proportionality.

(iii) Maintaining the Sanction

Under multilateral sanctioning schemes, continual consensus as a prerequisite for maintaining a sanction until the point of compliance comes down to the sum of political willingness of the sanctioning States. Community sanctions are not dependent upon any such consensus. Where a sanction takes the form of a periodic penalty payment it will be imposed from delivery of the second judgment until the infringement has been terminated. Significantly, this is a legal rather than political assessment.

---

[288] A Chayes and A Handler Chayes, n 27 above, at 64.

[289] Ibid.

[290] A Dashwood and R White, 'Enforcement Actions under Articles 169 and 170 EEC' (1989) 14 ELR 288–412, 389.

[291] Article 213 of the EC Treaty and CWA Timmermans, 'Judicial Protection against Member States', in D Curtin and T Heukels (eds), *Institutional Dynamics of European Integration. Essays in Honour of Henry G. Schermers. Volume II* (Martinus Nijhoff Publishers, 1994), 397.

[292] F Snyder, 'The Effectiveness of European Community Law. Institutions, Processes, Tools and Techniques' (1993) MLR, 30.

[293] See in particular the premises of Case C-278/01 *Commission v Spain* [2003] ECR I-14141.

(iv) Boycotts versus Fines

Chayes and Chayes' objections against economic sanctions primarily relate to sanctions in the form of boycotts, which are likely to place the heaviest burdens on parties least able to meet them. This latent dysfunction together with the general risk of evasion, they argue, will often feed 'pressure for relaxation of the sanctions',[294] which in turn undermines the sanctions' effectiveness. There are significant differences between the aforementioned type of sanction and that foreseen in the EC Treaty. Article 228(2) prescribes a positive amount to be paid without any further implications for the defaulting State. In addition, the Member State's ability to pay measured in GDP[295] constitutes a core variable of the fine amount.[296] Finally the principle of legality foreseen in Article 7 and ECJ precedents suggest that a non-compliant Member State cannot negotiate a friendly settlement with the Commission after a judgment has been delivered in accordance with Article 228 of the EC Treaty[297] and the compliance process, thus, enters a more technical phase without distracting interventions by the Commission or the other Treaty parties.

The equilibrium between actual non-compliance and the amount to be paid established by the ECJ allows for appreciation not only of full compliance, but also gradual progress.[298] This supports the interpretation put forward by General Advocate Michos that the objective of the penalty provision is to constitute 'une incitation positive de nature, conformément à la raison d'être de l'astreinte, à encourager l'État membre à s'exécuter dans les délais les plus brefs possibles'.[299] Thus the penalty provision, rather than creating deadlock situations, also rewards smaller behavioural changes.

(v) Preliminary Conclusion

The managerialist critique of treaty-based sanctions, in particular of their effectiveness and legitimacy, should be read in their proper context, viz, in relation to the general 'characteristics of the international system'[300] and not necessarily those of the EC, which is often characterized as a *tertium quid*. Thus, to question Chayes and Chayes' conclusions with reference to the EC infringement procedure does not seriously address the core premises of their critique. Nevertheless, there

---

[294] A Chayes and A Handler Chayes, n 27 above, at 66.

[295] For a critical account of the method of calculation, see MA, Theodossiou, 'An Analysis of the Recent Response of the Community to Non-compliance with Court of Justice Judgments: Article 228(2) E.C.' (2002) 27 ELR 25–46.

[296] Case C-278/01 *Commission v Spain* [2003] ECR I-14141, para 52.

[297] Cases C-142 and C-143/80 *Amministrazione delle Finanze dello Stato v Essevi SpA and Carlo Salengo* [1980] ECR 1413, para 18, and C-278/01, *Commission v Spain* [2003] ECR I-14141.

[298] Case C-278/01 *Commission v Spain* [2003] ECR I-14141, para 49.

[299] Opinion of Mr Advocate General Mischo in Case C-278/01 *Commission v Spain* [2003] ECR I-14141, para 98.

[300] A Chayes and A Handler Chayes, n 294 above, at 67.

are good reasons for examining the merits of the EC procedure by comparing it
to international law compliance theory. Significantly, the EC Treaty proposes a
procedural architecture where sanctions are not an arbitrary consequence of the
relative strength of the regime participants and where proportional fines put sustained pressure on the defaulting State. Because the sanctioning mechanism does
not stymie the normal relations between the State and the Treaty-regime, ie the
State's rights of participation remain intact as do all its general obligations, the
Community does not face some of the negative economic and political implications often connected with sanctions.

VI. Conclusion

In addition to providing a procedural summary of the general EC infringement
procedure, this article has examined and explained the steps involved under
Articles 226 and 228 of the EC Treaty using the established international law
compliance theory of managerialism and its critique. Whereas the subsections
contain numerous and detailed conclusions, this closing section will summarize some more policy-oriented conclusions and comment on the viability of the
Community infringement procedure. It is difficult to quantify Member State
compliance with Community law either generally or on a sector basis. This is in
part, because the Member States enjoy various degrees of discretion when giving effect to Community law hence compliance can take many forms. The first
section started out by discussing the notions of compliance and effectiveness. It
was maintained that the Commission's role is not so much to guarantee absolute
compliance; rather, it shall detect and address problems with implementation,
application and enforcement and it does so in a selective manner. Whereas the
degree of obligation is incontestably high within the Community, the element of
precision is more subtle. That is to say, the objectives of law can have a significant
degree of precision and still leave a broad margin of discretion concerning *how*
to give law effect. In the specific Community context this flexibility amounts
to a substantive virtue with a constitutional expression, namely the doctrine of
proportionality. Moreover, it has a procedural dimension under Community
enforcement. Thus the corresponding powers of the Commission as well as the
Court, as central institutional players and the procedural design of the infringement procedure acknowledge the degree of *flexibility* as to the manner in which
Community law is given effect. Accordingly, although the EC is characterized by
unprecedented autonomous powers, there are few examples of powers that can
be employed without a high degree of appreciation of the Member States either
directly or indirectly, including in the enforcement phase. The Commission enjoys
unfettered legal and political leeway to set out general and particular criteria for
pursuing infringements. This reflects that the Commission's role as guardian of

the Treaty is primarily one of identifying domestic impediments to the realization of Community law and to assist Member States in bringing about the necessary measures to give full effect to Community law. Thus, during the systemic series of exchange of factual and interpretive arguments, practical support and, occasionally, political pressure, the Commission's role can usefully be described and analysed in terms of effectiveness. The second section provided a procedural overview of Articles 226 and 228 of the EC Treaty. For the Member States, the case law sets out the boundaries of their procedural guarantees. For the Commission the case law is decisive to the procedure's instrumentality and to the potential significance of sanctions as a functional remedy against non-compliance. The principal starting point of the general infringement procedure presumes willingness on the part of the Treaty participants to comply and assumes that infringements are primarily to be overcome through discursive, problem-solving processes in which the Commission is to assist the Member State. The Commission is only empowered to employ a coercive approach in cases of manifest disobedience with infringements already ascertained by the ECJ in the judicial phase of Article 226. At this point, the general compliance expectation has been gravely upset. Thus, sanctions are not foreseen as an immediate response to infringements, but as a last resort where the various stages of Article 226 have been used. The ECJ has established a strict separation between the administrative and judicial phases of Article 228. Whereas the Commission enjoys broad and semi-political discretion throughout the administrative phase, the ECJ has unfettered discretion after a case has been referred to it for a judgment both with regards to the initial awarding of sanctions, the sanctioning type, the amount, and the frequency with which periodic penalties are imposed. Moreover, the ECJ has taken a noticeably strict stance on failure to comply under Article 228, including imposing both lump sum and penalty payments on its own motion and also awarding sanctions in situations, where the Commission no longer requested so. In the concluding section, it was maintained that although the EC polity cannot satisfactorily be conceptualized in terms of international law, the infringement procedure in isolation can usefully be analysed drawing on international law compliance theory. Specifically, it concerns a matter between an international (or rather, supranational) organization and a State and it relies primarily on confidential, bilateral, diplomacy. The comparative approach generates new insights into why the general infringement procedure is a particularly robust mechanism. The real significance of Article 228(2) is its capacity to bolster the interactive process of discourse and problem solving between the Commission and a given Member State in the period prior to actual judgment. However, when such an approach fails, the supervisor can fall back on sanctions without compromising basic considerations of legitimacy and effectiveness while retaining the State in a constructive process of engagement towards compliance.

Developing an Ever Closer Union between the Peoples of Europe? A Reappraisal of the Case Law of the Court of Justice on the Free Movement of Persons and EU Citizenship

Síofra O'Leary*

I. Introduction

Tucked away in the first recital of the preamble of the Treaty of Rome is a reference to the Member States' determination to lay the foundations of 'an ever closer union among the peoples of Europe'. This determination has endured several Treaty amendments and remains, to this day, at the heart of the preamble of the Treaty of the European Communities (EC Treaty) and the mission statement which the latter contains. It has long been thought that, through its case law, in particular that on the free movement of persons, the Court of Justice has contributed in no small measure to this process of creating an ever closer union. Writing on the free movement of workers prior to the conclusion of the Maastricht Treaty in 1992, the late Judge GF Mancini observed that '[i]f it can be said to be a good thing that our Europe is not merely a Europe of commercial interests, it is the Judges [of the Court of Justice] who must take much of the credit.'[1]

In subsequent years, the Member States added a further resolution to the Treaty preamble to establish a citizenship common to nationals of their countries. To this effect, Part Two of the EC Treaty establishes citizenship of the Union and endows the beneficiaries of that status with a series of rights and obligations. Every person holding the nationality of a Member State is a citizen

* Référendaire at the Court of Justice of the European Communities and Visiting Lecturer at the College of Europe, Bruges. The views expressed in this article are purely personal to the author.

This article was first presented as a paper at a seminar organised by the Europa Institute, University of Edinburgh, to celebrate the 50th anniversary of the Treaty of Rome. The author thanks Professor Jo Shaw and Dr Niamh Nic Shuibhne.

[1] See GF Mancini, 'The Free Movement of Workers in the Case Law of the European Court of Justice', in D O'Keeffe and D Curtin (eds), *Constitutional Adjudication in European Community and National Law* (Butterworths,1992) 68.

of the Union. This status, which is complementary to Member State nationality, permits EU citizens, inter alia, to enjoy rights of free movement and residence, subject to limitations and conditions contained in the Treaty and in secondary legislation; to vote and stand for election in European Parliament and municipal elections in the Member State in which they reside; to enjoy diplomatic and consular protection in third States in which their Member State of nationality is not represented, and to petition the European Parliament, apply to the Ombudsman and write to the EC institutions and receive an answer in one of the official languages of the EC.[2] Furthermore, Article 17(2) of the EC Treaty provides that EU citizens 'shall enjoy the rights conferred by this Treaty and shall be subject to the duties imposed thereby'. The jurisprudence the Court is in the process of developing on the basis of these EU citizenship provisions appears to borrow heavily from its existing free movement case law and the perception, once again, is of the Court contributing further and favourably to the creation of the ever closer union mentioned above.[3]

The purpose of this article is to explore the relationship between the Court's case law on the original provisions of the EEC Treaty on the free movement of persons and secondary legislation adopted thereunder and its more recent judicial output on EU citizenship. Following a review of the foundations of the Court's case law on the free movement of persons and, specifically, of workers, the article considers whether a degree of cross-pollenisation is occurring in the case law concerning these two distinct but related fields. The article explores, in particular, whether principles developed by the Court specifically with reference to EU citizenship are feeding back into the case law on the free movement of persons. The possible justification for and effects of this cross-pollenisation in the case law on the rights of EU citizens, whether economically active or inactive, are examined. Should a distinction continue to be made, as it once was, between these two categories, or indeed between further sub-categories, of migrants? Given the present thrust of its case law on the free movement of persons, can the Court still be regarded as contributing to the process of creating the ever closer union referred to above? The focus will be on recent decisions on migrant workers and on the bulk of the case law generated by the provisions on EU citizenship to date, case law which deals with issues relating to rights of residence, the principle of non-discrimination on grounds of nationality and EU citizens' entitlement, on that basis, to social benefits in host Member States or, in the case of returning migrants, in their Member States of origin.

---

[2] Articles 18–21 of the EC Treaty, respectively.

[3] See, inter alia, K Lenaerts, 'Union Citizenship and the Principle of Non-discrimination on Grounds of Nationality', in *Festskrift til Claus Gulmann* (Thomson, 2006) 289, 290.

II. The Court of Justice and the Free Movement of Persons—A Review

A. Delimiting the Personal Scope of the Free Movement of Persons

Prior to the introduction of EU citizenship, the enjoyment of rights of free movement and residence directly conferred by the EC Treaty was limited to those Member State nationals who performed or were involved, to some extent, in the performance of an economic activity. The Court's jurisprudence recognized the right of Member State nationals to enter and reside in the territory of other Member States, but only for the purposes intended by the Treaty—in other words those specified in Articles 39 (workers), 43 (establishment), and 49 (services) of the EC Treaty.[4] Migrant workers, the self-employed, providers and, over time, recipients of services, students, and job-seekers were all declared to come within the personal scope of EC law and were thus the beneficiaries of EC rights to free movement and non-discrimination on grounds of nationality, subject admittedly, in some cases, to temporal[5] or other limitations.[6] In the specific context of Article 39 of the EC Treaty, the Court was vehement that the concepts of worker and employed person, which define the field of application of this fundamental freedom, must receive an autonomous Community definition and not a restrictive one at that. The rules on the free movement of workers cover the pursuit of effective and genuine activities, to the exclusion of activities on such a small scale as to be regarded as purely marginal and ancillary. As long as their work is genuine and effective, even part-time workers and those who claim financial assistance payable out of the public funds of the host Member State in order to supplement their income, cannot be excluded from the personal scope of the free movement provisions,[7] nor should they, in principle, be denied the material benefits accruing thereunder.

---

[4] See Case 43/75 *Royer* [1976] ECR 497, para 31.

[5] See, as regards job-seekers, the approval of temporal limitations in Case C-292/89 *Antonissen* [1997] ECR I-745, para 21.

[6] See, as regards students, recognition of a right of residence to pursue vocational studies subject, however, to the legitimate interests of the Member States: Case C-357/98 *Raulin* [1992] ECR I-1027, para 39, or, as regards job-seekers, their limited right to rely on the principle of non-discrimination on grounds of nationality to gain access to substantive benefits available to workers: Case 316/85 *Lebon* [1987] ECR 2811. For a detailed account of the case law on the personal scope of Articles 39, 43, and 49 of the EC Treaty, see, inter alia, S O'Leary, *The Evolving Concept of Community Citizenship* (Kluwer, 1996); A Van der Mei, *Free Movement of Persons within the European Community* (Hart, 2003), and R White, *Workers, Establishment and Services in the European Union* (Hart, 2004).

[7] Cases 53/81 *Levin* [1982] ECR 1035, paras 12–17, and 139/85 *Kempf* [1986] ECR 1741, paras 14–15. Recently reiterated in Case C-10/05 *Mattern and Citokic* [2006] ECR I-3145, paras 18–23. It is for the national court alone, when assessing the facts, to determine whether the work is genuine and effective. It must base its examination on objective criteria and assess, as a whole, all the circumstances of the case relating both to the nature of the activities concerned and the employment relationship in issue: Case C-413/01 *Ninni-Orasche* [2003] ECR I-13187, para 27.

B. Free Movement and the Principle of Non-discrimination on Grounds of Nationality

By attaching considerable prominence to the principle of non-discrimination on grounds of nationality, applying that principle to both direct and indirect forms of discrimination and, eventually, prohibiting even indistinctly applicable restrictions of or obstacles to free movement, the case law of the Court on the free movement of persons has clearly had an impact on national social welfare provision. That impact can best be summed up with reference to three important developments, all essentially Court driven. The Court insisted that, although the Community may not have powers in a particular field of social policy, that does not mean that the EC exceeds the limits of its competence solely because the exercise of its jurisdiction in the field of free movement affects measures adopted in pursuance of Member State policies in those fields.[8] Thus, even where Member States retain social policy competence, they must nevertheless comply with EC law when exercising their powers. The Court also held that the principle of non-discrimination on grounds of nationality in Article 12 of the EC Treaty required generally that persons 'in a situation governed by EC law' be placed on a completely equal footing with nationals of the (host) Member State. Those in a situation governed by EC law included not only those residing in the host Member State but also, at least as regards certain treatment or benefits, those who were merely visiting and who were thus (potential) recipients of services.[9]

C. Entitlement to Social and Tax Advantages

Most importantly, with reference to that same principle of non-discrimination on grounds of nationality, the Court interpreted widely the range of substantive social benefits to which those who had availed of free movement could be entitled in the Member State of residence and/or employment. In particular, pursuant to Article 7(2) of Regulation 1612/68, migrant workers and, as it subsequently transpired, their family members,[10] were entitled to 'those [social] advantages by means of which the migrant worker is guaranteed [. . .] the possibility of improving his living and working conditions and promoting

---

[8] See, for examples, Cases 9/74 *Casagrande* [1975] ECR 773 (national education policy); 65/81 *Reina* [1982] ECR 33, para 15 (national demographic policy), and C-186/87 *Cowan* [1989] ECR 195 (rules of criminal procedure).

[9] See Case C-186/87 *Cowan* and the comments of F Schockweiler, 'La portée du principe de non-discrimination de l'article 7 du Traité CEE' (1991) Rivista di Diritto Europeo 3, 24.

[10] The restrictive stance initially adopted in Case 76/72 *Michel S* [1973] ECR 457, para 9 ('the benefits referred to by Article 7(2) of Regulation No 1612/68 are to benefit the workers themselves') was revised in Case 32/75 *Cristini* [1975] ECR 1085, para 13 ('in view of the equality of treatment which the provision seeks to achieve, the substantive area of application must be delineated so as to include all social and tax advantages, whether or not attached to the contract of employment, such as reductions in fares for large families').

his social advancement'.[11] The Court shunned a narrow textual interpretation of this provision, which would have limited it to workers and equality in relation to employment-related benefits,[12] in favour of a broad interpretation of the Regulation's personal and material scope, in accordance with its purpose and spirit. Member State nationals were not to be dissuaded from exercising their free movement by the prospect of being excluded from benefits, including social welfare provision, in the host Member State and, furthermore, the inclusion of migrant workers into the host Member State was to be encouraged and facilitated precisely by providing them with the same benefits available to that Member State's own nationals.[13] As one commentator on Article 7(2) of Regulation 1612/68 correctly observed, the causal link between the extension or denial of a particular benefit to migrant workers and their families and the consequences for mobility was not subjected to exhaustive scrutiny.[14] When migrant workers and their families relied on Article 7(2) of Regulation 1612/68 in order to justify their entitlement to social or educational benefits, they were not required to demonstrate their integration into the host society. Indeed, the receipt of the benefits in question was seen as a means to promote that integration.[15] When the Court did consider a Member State justified in its refusal of a particular benefit it was usually because the applicant did not come within

---

[11] See Cases 39/86 *Lair* [1988] ECR 3161, para 20, and 137/84 *Mutsch* [1985] ECR 2681, paras 16–17, for this broad definition. For a more restrictive definition, albeit the one normally cited, see Case 207/78 *Even* [1979] ECR 2019, para 22: '[Social advantages] are those which, whether or not linked to a contract of employment, are generally granted to national workers primarily because of their objective status as workers or by virtue of the mere fact of residence on the national territory and the extension of which to workers who are nationals of other Member States therefore seems suitable to facilitate their mobility within the Community.' Travel reductions for large families (Case 32/75 *Cristini* [1975] ECR 1085), social security allowances for handicapped dependent adults (Case 63/76 *Inzirillo* [1976] ECR 2057), State pensions guaranteed to old persons (Case 261/83 *Castelli* [1984] ECR 3199), unemployment benefit (Case 94/84 *Deak* [1985] ECR 1873), minimum subsistence allowances (Case 249/83 *Hoeckx* [1985] ECR 973), maintenance grants and tuition fees (Case 39/86 *Lair*), study finance (Case C-337/97 *Meeusen* [1999] ECR I-3289), child-raising allowances (Joined Cases C-245/94 and C-312/94 *Hoever and Zachow* [1996] ECR I-4895), and State-subsidized child-birth loans to low income families (Case 65/81 *Reina*), to name but a few, all constitute social advantages to which migrant workers and their family members are entitled, subject to the same conditions as nationals of the host Member State.

[12] See D O'Keeffe, 'Equal Rights for Migrants: the Concept of Social Advantages in Article 7(2), Regulation 1612/68' (1986) YEL 91, 95.

[13] In the context of Article 43 of the EC Treaty, see Cases C-334/94 *Commission v France* [1996] ECR I-1307, paras 21–22; C-63/86 *Commission v Italy* [1988] ECR 29, or C-168/91 *Konstantinidis* [1993] ECR I-1191. In the context of Article 49 of the EC Treaty, see Case C-186/87 *Cowan*.

[14] See O'Keeffe (n 12 above), 106. K Lenaerts and T Heremans, 'Contours of a European Social Union in the Case law of the European Court of Justice' (2006) 2 European Constitutional Law Review 101–115, 103, suggest that the social rights which were extended to migrant workers were those which added to the functionality of their right to freedom of movement and residence. This argument can be accepted only if it is recognized that almost everything was considered as capable of promoting their free movement and residence.

[15] See, for example, with respect to access to education, Joined Cases C-389/97 and C-390/97 *Echternach and Moritz* [1989] ECR 723, para 35 (albeit this particular case related to Article 12 of Regulation 1612/68).

the personal scope of the free movement provisions.[16] Exceptionally, the Court sometimes considered that the benefit in question did not qualify as a social advantage[17] or, in the case of a benefit requested by a family member, that it had not been proved that the requested benefit would benefit the migrant worker himself.[18] Thus, any concerns of Member States regarding entitlement of non-national migrants to the wide range of social benefits caught by Article 7(2) of Regulation 1612/68 were met, not by insistence on a real or genuine link with the Member State granting the benefit, but via the definition of worker and, specifically, the requirement that the activity exercised must be genuine and effective.[19]

It has been argued, with reference to the Court's developing EU citizenship case law, that whether or not a Member State may subject the grant of certain benefits to a residence requirement, or any other condition that may play to the disadvantage of nationals of other Member States, depends on the nature of the benefit.[20] Lenaerts suggests, for example, that it is reasonable to allow a Member State to require a link with its employment market as far as a job-seeker's allowance is concerned, but that such a link is not reasonable for a child-raising allowance which, as for any other social assistance benefit, may be reserved to those lawfully resident in the host Member State. Similarly, in the context of Article 49 of the EC Treaty, Dougan and Spaventa indicate that equal treatment may be limited to benefits which can be directly linked to enjoyment of the economic services which a recipient of services may have entered the territory of a Member State to receive.[21] While this sort of differential treatment with reference to the type of

---

[16] Case C-43/99 *Leclere* [2001] ECR I-4265, paras 59–61.

[17] Case 207/88 *Even*, paras 23–24, where the Court held that benefits based on a scheme of national recognition of hardship experienced by nationals in the service of their country did not fulfil the essential characteristics of social advantages.

[18] Case 316/85 *Lebon* [1987] ECR 2881, paras 12–13.

[19] For explicit confirmation that this category of migrant did not have to establish the existence of such a link, see Case C-258/04 *Ioannidis* [2005] ECR I-8275, para 33: 'the dependant children of migrant workers who are residing in Belgium derive their right to a tideover allowance from Article 7(2) of Regulation No 1612/68 *regardless of whether in that situation there is a real link with the geographic employment market concerned.*' See also A Van der Mei, 'Union Citizenship, Freedom of Movement and the Fear for 'Social Tourism', in H Schneider, *Migration, Integration and Citizenship*, Vol I (Forum Maastricht, 2005) 107–122, and S Giubboni, 'Free Movement of Persons and Social Solidarity' (2007) 13 ELJ 360–379, 363.

[20] See Lenaerts, n 3 above, at 304, who compares the approach of the Court in Cases C-138/02 *Collins* [2004] ECR I-2703, and C-209/03 *Bidar* [2005] ECR I-2119, where the applicants were seeking, respectively, a job-seeker's allowance and a student loan, with that in Case C-274/96 *Bickel*, where the applicant sought the right to use the German language in criminal proceedings in a region of a Member State, Italy, where German could be used by members of the resident population. See also C Barnard 'EU Citizenship and the Principle of Solidarity', in M Dougan and E Spaventa (eds), *Social Welfare and EU Law* (Hart, 2005) 158, 172.

[21] M Dougan and E Spaventa, '"Wish You Weren't Here"...New Models of Social Solidarity in the European Union' in Dougan and Spaventa, ibid, 180–218, 196 and 208, distinguish between benefits arising from a State's exercise of its public order duties, those which arise out of a State's choice to foster non-solidaristic objectives and those which reflect a link of solidarity between the community and the individual.

benefit being sought may be justifiable in the context of economically inactive migrants whose residence or mere presence on the territory of the Member State granting the benefit may be short-term or even fleeting, the case law on the free movement of migrant workers provides little or no support for such an approach. In fact, the Court's case law on frontier workers seemed to indicate that social advantages, including those of a social assistance nature, are generally exportable, so that frontier workers can rely on Article 7(2) of Regulation 1612/68 to request benefits, both contributory and non-contributory, not from their Member State of residence, but from their Member State of employment.[22]

The Court has discussed the legitimacy of a link between claimants, the benefits they seek and the social environment of the Member State from which the benefit is sought. However, these discussions have been almost exclusively in the context of Regulation 1408/71, which itself provides clear rules on its material scope and on entitlement to benefits on grounds of residence, as well as rules providing that certain benefits are not exportable.[23] The restrictive cases on entitlement to social and tax advantages under Regulation 1612/68, of which there are very few, appear primarily influenced by the fact that the claimant had ceased his or her occupational activity. In *Leclere*, for example, the applicant was a Belgian national, resident in Belgium, who had been employed in Luxembourg and who was thus a frontier worker, contributing, when in employment, to the Luxembourg social security scheme. Following an accident at work, he received a Luxembourg invalidity pension, although he continued to reside in Belgium. After the birth of his child, the applicant was refused a child-raising allowance. Leaving aside questions relating to Regulation 1408/71 and its relationship with Regulation 1612/68, the Court held, with reference to the latter, that a person, such as the applicant, in receipt of an invalidity pension from his Member State of employment but residing in a different Member State, is not a worker within the meaning of Article 7(2). He does not enjoy rights attaching to the status of worker—such as the right to equal treatment as regards entitlement to social and tax advantages—unless they derive from his previous professional activity. *Leclere* thus appears to contradict other case law on Article 7(2) of Regulation 1612/68, which suggests that entitlement to social and tax advantages can survive the termination of the employment relationship,[24] that those advantages

---

[22] See Cases C-57/96 *Meints* [1997] ECR I-6689, para 50, and C-237/97 *Meeusen*. While the first case concerned a work-related benefit and could be read as not calling into question residence requirements for social assistance type benefits, in the second case, concerning precisely that type of benefit, the Court held that the residence requirement imposed was unlawful. See further H Verschueren, 'The Relationship Between Regulation (EEC) 1612/68 and Regulation (EEC) 1408/71 Analysed Through European Court of Justice Case Law on Frontier Workers' (2004) 6 European Journal of Social Security 7–32, and Van der Mei, n 6 above.

[23] See, for example, Cases 313/86 *Lenoir* [1988] ECR 5391, or C-20/96 *Snares* [1997] ECR I-6057, paras 42–43. See also O'Keeffe, n 12 above, at 110–111: 'Exclusion from the scope of the social security regulation will depend on the nature and purpose of the minimum income benefit claimed, whereas those mostly lose their importance in the case of a claim based on Article 7(2).'

[24] Case 39/86 *Lair*.

are not restricted to benefits directly related to employment,[25] and that they can be exportable.[26] However, this restrictive approach can arguably be explained by two factors which do not detract from the generally expansive approach the Court has adopted on this provision of Regulation 1612/68 and do not provide grounds for suggesting migrant workers' entitlement to social benefits is dependant on separate proof of a link with the host Member State or the Member State providing the benefit. On the one hand, since the Court concluded that the benefit in question was not exportable pursuant to Regulation 1408/71, it may not have been willing to provide an alternative route for its exportation on the basis of Regulation 1612/68.[27] On the other, the birth of the applicant's child and, therefore, the event giving rise to his claim to the social advantage in his former Member State of employment, took place after his employment relationship had ended.[28] While these two factors may not entirely justify the severity of the Court's decision, they go some way to explaining why this exceptional case does not detract from the general rule.

D. The Impact of the Free Movement Provisions on National Social Welfare Provision

Thus, prior to the introduction of EU citizenship, the impact of EC law on the free movement of persons on social welfare provision by Member States was considerable. The Court was regarded as contributing to, even driving, the process of transforming these provisions of the Treaty of Rome on the free movement of persons into an incipient form of European citizenship.[29] Indeed, before the Single European Act (SEA) and long before Maastricht, Amsterdam, Nice and the ill-fated Constitution, it was suggested that discrimination, whether direct or indirect, with regard to any welfare benefit, against an EC national lawfully resident in a host Member State would be regarded as unlawful by the Court, unless the purpose of the benefit was wholly exceptional and inextricably connected in some way with nationality.[30] The Court was occasionally charged with having

---

[25] Case 63/76 *Inzirillo*, para 21.   [26] Case C-57/96 *Meints*, para 50.

[27] Article 42(2) of Regulation 1612/68 provides that: 'This Regulation shall not affect measures taken in accordance with Article 51 of the Treaty.' The provisions of Regulation 1408/71 take precedence, as a *lex specialis*, over the provisions of Regulation 1612/68. See, however, Case C-287/05 *Hendrix* [2007] ECR I-6909, discussed further below.

[28] See also Case C-33/99 *Fahmi* [2001] ECR I-2415, where the facts of the case, albeit unclear, suggested similar circumstances arose.

[29] See, inter alia, GF Mancini, *Democracy and Constitutionalisation in the EU* (Hart, 2000) 10, referring notably to Case C-186/87 *Cowan*, and R Plender, 'An Incipient Form of European Citizenship', in FG Jacobs (ed), *European Law and the Individual* (North Holland, 1976) 50.

[30] See J Steiner, 'The Right to Welfare: Equality and Equity under Community Law' (1985) 10 ELR 21, 41. For examples of such exceptional cases, see Cases 207/78 *Even*, regarding a scheme providing additional pension benefits for former soldiers who had served in the allied forces in the Second World War; and C-315/94 *De Vos* [1996] ECR I-1417, regarding the payment of supplementary retirement contributions for those engaged in compulsory military service.

extended Member States' and perhaps individuals' obligations towards migrant workers and their families far beyond the limits originally agreed. It was argued even then that if Member States were to be required to provide unanticipated and costly benefits, whether in the form of educational grants or long-term social assistance, for all legitimately resident migrant workers and their families, equity required some sharing of the, essentially financial, burden.[31]

How did Member States respond to this extension of their obligations to nationals from other EU Member States? After all, the growth of modern welfare States following the Second World War and the assumption of new economic and social responsibilities by the State had resulted in the use of immigration controls with a view to restricting the entry and residence of non-nationals. Underpinning the entitlement of citizens to the benefits offered by welfare States were notions of solidarity, social justice, and redistribution; notions which were not intended to work to the advantage of everyone.[32] Social solidarity—involving the subsidisation of the needs of one group in society by another—was essential to the adoption and legitimacy of national measures of social protection and social assistance. As several commentators have observed, such solidarity derived essentially from the existence of a common identity, forged through shared social, cultural, and historical experiences and institutional and political bonds, expressed most readily in the form of nationality and citizenship.[33] National welfare systems also relied on the principle of territoriality. By restricting benefits to those in their territory, States could exert the necessary control over the mechanics of their welfare systems.[34] Thus, to benefit from the provision of welfare one had to belong in some sense to the society or polity conferring the benefits and the usual corollary of a right to benefits was an individual duty to contribute to the financing of the benefit system.[35] Faced with a Court driven breach of their welfare systems, Member States defended the imposition of minimum threshold periods of employment and/or residence before entitlement to welfare benefits kicked in or argued for temporal limitations of Court judgments extending social welfare entitlement. The Court's response was uncompromising—nationality or residence conditions or conditions relating to a minimum duration of employment could not be imposed exclusively on nationals of other Member States, and even habitual residence tests applicable to nationals and non-nationals alike were,

---

[31] Steiner, ibid, 41 and N Green et al. (eds) *The Legal Foundations of the Single Market* (OUP, 1991), 175–193, in the specific context of the free movement of students.

[32] See, in this respect, M Walzer, *Spheres of Justice* (1983) 31: 'the idea of redistributive justice presupposes a bounded world; a group of people committed to dividing, exchanging and sharing social goods, first of all among themselves.'

[33] See, in particular, Dougan and Spaventa, n 20 above, and T Faist, 'Social Citizenship in the European Union: Nested Membership' (2001) 39 JCMS 37.

[34] Lenaerts and Heremans, n 14 above.

[35] See further, O'Leary, n 6 above; A Van der Mei, n 6 above; S O'Leary, 'Solidarity and Citizenship Rights in the Charter of Fundamental Rights of the European Union', in G De Bùrca (ed), *EU Law and the Welfare State: In Search of Solidarity* (Hart, 2005) 54–60, and Dougan and Spaventa (n 20 above).

in some instances, suspect.[36] As for temporal limitations, they were possible only in exceptional cases and were not justifiable simply with reference to the financial consequences which might ensue for a Member State from a preliminary ruling.[37] As illustrated above, the number of cases where the Court regarded a Member State as justified in its refusal of a social benefit requested by a resident migrant worker or non-resident frontier worker pursuant to Regulation 1612/68 were few and far between.

Despite this, there seemed little *real* resistance to the Court's view of the Member States' obligations towards the beneficiaries of free movement. There was, after all, no equivalent in the field of the free movement of persons of the *Barber* protocol which Member States had annexed to the Treaty on European Union (TEU) in 1992 to limit the effects of a judgment of the Court on equal pay and pensions. Indeed, while the Member States were busy drafting that protocol, they were equally involved in inserting the EU citizenship provisions into the same Treaty. While the rights conferred by that status were expressly subject to limitations and conditions, the Member States must have reflected on what the political, never mind the legal and constitutional, resonance of the establishment of this status would be. Reasons for the lack of resistance to Court of Justice case law on the free movement of persons may have been, firstly, that, from the point of view of the numbers migrating, the situation was far from critical at the time.[38] Secondly, apart from students, of those who did exercise their rights to free movement and residence, the vast majority were either contributing to the host economy in some way, through the provision or receipt of services, or were contributing tax revenue in the host Member State as a result of the economic activities in which they were engaged as employed or self-employed persons.[39] As a result, they were, in the main, net-contributors to the welfare systems in which they were claiming or might claim entitlement to benefits. The right of residence of job-seekers was subject to a temporal limitation and the Court ensured that

---

[36] See, for example, Case 249/83 *Hoeckx*, where the Court held that a minimum subsistence allowance constituted a social advantage within the meaning of Article 7(2) Regulation 1612/68 and that an additional residence requirement for non-nationals was discriminatory. It took an infringement action (Case C-326/90 *Commission v Belgium* [1992] ECR I-5517) to secure the removal of this residence condition from Belgium law. See the fate of habitual residence conditions in Cases C-185/96 *Commission v Greece* [1998] ECR I-6601 (benefits for large families), C-299/01 *Commission v Luxembourg* [2002] ECR I-5899 (guaranteed minimum income), and C-90/97 *Swaddling* [1999] ECR 1075 (income support in the context of Regulation 1408/71).

[37] Cases 309/85 *Barra* [1988] ECR 355, paras 13 and 14 and, subsequently, in the context of Articles 18 and 12 of the EC Treaty, see below C-184/99 *Grzelczyk* [2001] ECR I-6193, para 52.

[38] By the mid-1990s, Eurostat, Statistics in Focus. Population and Social Conditions, 2/1996, estimated that 5.5 million Member State nationals resided in a Member State other than their own.

[39] If one reads the case law on students and trainees, it is clear that their inclusion within the personal scope of application of the EC Treaty was based, at least partly, on their role as future economic actors and, therefore, future contributors of tax and social insurance. See, for example, Case 66/85 *Lawrie-Blum* [1986] ECR 2121, paras 18–19. In addition, the expectation was that they would remain in the host Member State for a limited period and their rights of residence and right not to be discriminated against were limited accordingly: see, for example, Case C-357/89 *Raulin*, paras 34, 39.

even during that limited period their right to equal treatment did not extend to costly social welfare benefits.[40] Similarly, students, another group of EC nationals who tangentially benefited from the existing free movement provisions could not rely on the principle of equal treatment with reference to the whole range of welfare benefits available in the host Member State.[41] The rationale behind these restrictions and limitations was the need to guard against what was the at least perceived threat of benefit tourism, whereby Member State nationals and their family members might avail of the free movement provisions solely or primarily with a view to enjoying more favourable welfare provision in the host Member State. Essentially, however, at that time, although the migration of economically active EU nationals to other Member States may have required that changes be made as regards the host Member State's provision of certain social benefits, neither the numbers of those migrating nor their purpose for doing so fundamentally challenged the essential organisational principles of national welfare systems.[42]

III. Something Old, Something New, Something Borrowed...—The Case Law on EU Citizenship

In principle, economically inactive Member State nationals had no right to free movement and residence until the adoption of three Residence Directives in 1990, which preceded the introduction of the provisions on EU citizenship by the Maastricht Treaty.[43] Even then, the Directives made the enjoyment of such rights subject to fulfilment of two important conditions, namely the possession by the applicants for residence of medical coverage in respect of all risks in the host Member State and sufficient resources to prevent them and/or their families becoming a burden on public funds in the host Member State.

---

[40] Case 316/85 *Lebon*, para 26. Cf Case C-85/96 *Martínez Sala* [1998] ECR I-2709, para 32, where the Court seemed to overrule this aspect of *Lebon* by considering a job-seeker to be a worker within the meaning of Article 39 of the EC Treaty and Regulation 1612/68; and Dougan, 'The Workseeker as Citizen' (2001) 4 Cambridge Yearbook of European Legal Studies 93–132.

[41] See Case 197/86 *Brown* [1988] ECR 3205, where the Court held that maintenance grants did not come within the scope of application of the EC Treaty for the purposes of Article 12.

[42] See N Bernard, 'Between a Rock and a Soft Place: Internal Market versus Open Co-ordination in EU Social Welfare Law', in Dougan and Spaventa, n 20 above, at 261. The one exception in this regard may have been the costs entailed by the movement of students following Case 293/83 *Gravier* [1985] ECR 593, but those costs were at least minimized by limiting students' entitlement to equal treatment to *access* to vocational training.

[43] Subject, of course, to the aforementioned exceptions of students and recipients of services. See Directives 90/364 on the right of residence [1990] OJ L180/26; 90/365 on the right of residence for employees and self-employed persons who have ceased their occupational activity [1990] OJ L180/28; and 90/366 on the right of residence of students [1990] OJ L180/30, annulled and readopted as Directive 93/96 [1993] OJ L317/54. These Directives have since been repealed, with effect from 30 April 2006, by Directive 2004/38 on the right of citizens of the Union and their family members to move and reside freely within the territory of the Member States [2004] OJ L229/35.

It is this right of economically inactive EU citizens to move and reside freely within the territory of the Member States, now featured in Article 18 of the EC Treaty, which is central to the Court's development of the status of EU citizenship. This case law provides the focus for discussion of the impact of EU citizenship on national welfare provision and the steady dilution of Member State sovereignty when it comes to such provision.[44] It also affords a basis for the analysis of the relationship between the case law on the free movement of persons and that on EU citizenship. The Court's initial reluctance to depart from resolving migration problems on the basis of established provisions of the EC Treaty on the free movement of persons[45] was soon replaced by a willingness to interpret, sometimes with considerable gusto, the import and scope of the status of EU citizenship. Its oft-repeated mantra now refers to this status as 'destined to be the fundamental status of nationals of the Member States'.[46] Just as it had previously done with reference to the free movement of persons and services, the Court is incrementally constructing a line of jurisprudence which widens both the personal and material scope of application of the Treaty provisions on the free movement, residence, and non-discrimination entitlements of EU citizens. From key decisions handed down by the Court on EU citizenship in recent years—not least *Martínez Sala*, *Grzelczyk*, *Baumbast* and *D'Hoop*—a number of fundamental developments can be divined.[47]

A. The Importation of Free Movement Language into the Case Law on EU Citizenship

Firstly, this case law reveals to what extent the jurisprudence on EU citizenship is being constructed on the foundations already laid by the established jurisprudence on the free movement of persons. Provided they are lawfully resident in the host Member State or, in some cases, lawfully present, economically inactive Union citizens are entitled to equal treatment with that State's own nationals in accordance with Article 12 of the EC Treaty. The terminology of the Court in *Cowan*, to the effect that those in situations governed by EC law are entitled not

---

[44] For discussion of the development of the Court's case law on Article 18 of the EC Treaty and the potential impact of that provision on national welfare provision, see, variously, J Steiner, 'Social Security for EC Migrants' (1992) Journal of Social Welfare and Family Law 33, 46; S O'Leary, 'The Principle of Equal Treatment on Grounds of Nationality in Article 6 EC. A lucrative source of rights for Member State nationals?', in A Dashwood and S O'Leary (eds), *The Principle of Equal Treatment in E.C. Law* (Sweet and Maxwell, 1997) 105–136; J Shaw and S Fries, 'Citizenship of the Union: First Steps in the European Court of Justice' (1998) European Public Law 533–559; M Dougan and E Spaventa, 'Educating Rudy and the (Non) English Patient: A Double-Bill on Residency Rights Under Article 18 E' (2003) 28 ELR 699–712, and S Giubboni, 'Free Movement of Persons and Social Solidarity' (2007) 13 ELJ 360–379, 363.

[45] See, for example, Cases C-193/94 *Skanavi* [1996] ECR I-929; C-100/01 *Olazabal* [2002] ECR I-10981, or C-348/96 *Calfa* [1999] ECR I-11.

[46] Case C-184/99 *Grzelczyk*, para 31.

[47] For closer analysis of each of these cases and criticism of the Court's methodology, or lack thereof, see O'Leary (n 35 above), and K Hailbronner, 'Union Citizenship and Social Benefits' (2005) 42 CML Rev 1245–1267.

to be discriminated against on grounds of nationality, has been imported into the EU citizenship cases and the provisions on citizenship in turn expand what situations can be considered as being governed by EC law, despite periodic assurances by the Court to the contrary.[48] *Baumbast* provides another example of the effect of the importation of free movement rhetoric on the scope of application of the provisions on EU citizenship.[49] That decision, to the effect that Article 18 of the EC Treaty confers a right of residence directly on EU citizens, would have been unthinkable when EU citizenship was first established and indeed had been contested by several national courts and, on occasion, by the Commission itself.[50] However, the Court presented its decision on the nature of Article 18 as the inexorable conclusion of its preceding citizenship case law and depicted it as all the more inevitable by framing it with reference to the well-established judicial reasoning on the nature of the rights of free movement and residence pursuant to Articles 39, 43, and 49 of the EC Treaty.[51] However, it has been argued that reliance on a case like *Royer*, decided by the Court in the context of the provisions of Article 39 of the EC Treaty and Directive 68/360 on the free movement of workers, is only valid if it is assumed that the applicant is *lawfully* resident in the host Member State pursuant to EC law and that was precisely the question national courts were seeking to resolve in these early EU citizenship/residence cases.[52] Similar borrowing of the established language of free movement can be seen in cases like *Bickel* and *Schempp*, where the Court asserts that, even though the impugned discrimination or restriction may derive from an area of law for which the Member States and not the EC is responsible (rules of criminal procedure or direct taxation, for example), they may not breach Article 12 of the EC Treaty and the provisions of the Treaty on EU citizenship.[53]

B. The Material Scope of Application of the Principle of Non-discrimination in the Context of EU Citizenship

Secondly, when relying on the principle of non-discrimination on grounds of nationality under Articles 12 and, indirectly, 17 of the EC Treaty, EU citizens are not limited to those situations coming within the supposedly more restricted

---

[48] See, for example, Joined Cases C-64/96 and C-65/96 *Uecker and Jacquet* [1997] ECR I-3171, para 23: 'citizenship is not intended to extend the scope of the Treaty'.

[49] Case C-413/99 *Baumbast* [2002] ECR I-7091.

[50] See, for example, *R v Secretary of State for the Home Department, ex parte Vitale* [1996] All ER (EC) 461 and 941, at 955, and the conflicting submissions of the Commission in Cases C-378/97 *Wijsenbeek* [1999] ECR I-6207 and C-413/99 *Baumbast*, where it first supported and then opposed the respective applicants' arguments to the effect that Article 18 of the EC Treaty was directly effective.

[51] Case C-413/99 *Baumbast*, para 80, relying on Case 48/75 *Royer*, para 31: 'According to settled case law, the right of nationals of one Member State to enter the territory of another Member State and to reside there constitutes a right conferred directly by the EC Treaty or, depending on the case, by the provisions adopted to implement it.'

[52] See Shaw and Fries (n 44 above), 542.

[53] Cases C-274/96 *Bickel* [1998] ECR I-7637, and C-403/03 *Schempp* [2005] ECR I-6421.

scope of application of the EC Treaty provisions on citizenship. The Court's invocation of the prohibition of discrimination on grounds of nationality has been much bolder than that. EU citizens may rely on that principle with respect to all those benefits falling within the EC Treaty's material scope—in other words, the range of benefits covered by Regulation 1408/71 and, logically, those covered by Regulation 1612/68, not least the enjoyment of social and tax advantages pursuant to Article 7(2). Remarkably, the Court extended the scope of application of these pieces of secondary legislation to lawfully resident but economically inactive EU citizens without addressing the fact that the other conditions for eligibility (eg status as a migrant worker or family member of a worker) to the rights and benefits covered by this legislation were not, arguably, met by such citizens. In later citizenship cases, the Court has even interpreted the material scope of EC law in a manner which appears to contradict the express terms of EC secondary legislation on free movement, residence, and equal treatment.[54] As we shall see, it is the consequences of this broad application of the principle of non-discrimination which provides the most interesting territory in which to explore the issue of cross-pollenisation in the case law on the free movement of economically active and inactive EU migrants.

C. Conditions and Limitations on the Exercise of EU Citizenship Rights

Thirdly, as *Baumbast* revealed, Article 18(1) of the EC Treaty confers directly upon EU citizens the right to move and reside freely across Member States. The exercise, as distinct from the existence of this right of free movement and residence is subject to the limitations and conditions expressly included by the Member States in Article 18(1). Essentially, these boil down to the requirements concerning the possession of sufficient resources and full medical coverage laid down in the 1990 Residence Directives. These limitations and conditions must be applied by Member States in accordance with the general principles of EC law, not least, respect for fundamental rights and the principle of proportionality. In no case can withdrawal of a residence permit or refusal to renew one become the automatic consequence of an EU citizen who is a national of another Member State having recourse to the host Member State's social assistance system. The Court has stated that the beneficiaries of the right of residence must not become an *unreasonable* burden on the public finances of the host Member State but also that the 1990 Residence Directives are premised on *a certain degree of financial solidarity between nationals of a host Member State and nationals of other Member States*, particularly if the difficulties which a beneficiary of the right of residence

---

[54] See, for example, the interpretation of Article 3 of Directive 93/96 in Case C-184/99 *Grzelczyk*, para 39, or of Article 24 of Directive 2004/38 in Case C-209/03 *Bidar*, paras 43–44.

encounters are temporary.[55] The upshot of this case law is that the competent authorities in the host Member State must embark on a case-by-case assessment of an EU citizen's entitlement.[56] It will, presumably, be difficult for the competent authority to verify whether, in granting a benefit following an individual application, it is contributing to the creation of an unreasonable burden on that State's public finances.

D. Entitlement of EU Citizens to Social Benefits and the Requirement of a Real or Genuine Link

Fourthly, Articles 12 and 18 of the EC Treaty prohibit not just directly and indirectly discriminatory national rules, but also legislation which places EU citizens at a disadvantage as a result of exercising their right to free movement and residence in another Member State. Such rules are said to give rise to inequality of treatment, contrary to the principles which underpin the status of citizen of the Union, that is, the guarantee of the same treatment in law in the exercise of the citizen's freedom to move. They can be justified only if they are based on objective considerations independent of the nationality of the persons concerned and proportionate to the legitimate aim of the national provisions.[57] Member States may be entitled to restrict access to social benefits to those with a genuine link or a real and effective degree of connection with the host society.[58] However, exclusion from that Member State cannot be the automatic result of reliance on

---

[55] Case C-184/99 *Grzelczyk*, para 44. On the *Baumbast* proportionality test see Dougan, 'The Constitutional dimension of the case law on Union citizenship' (2006) 31 ELR 613. See also N Nic Shuibhne, 'Derogating from the Free Movement of Persons: When can EU Citizens be Deported?', in Dougan and Spaventa (n 20 above), at 210, who suggests that the Court's approach to date to the financial resources criteria in the 1990 residence directives is reminiscent of its general antipathy to economic rationales as the basis of derogations from the fundamental freedoms in the EC Treaty.

[56] The extent of this obligation becomes apparent in a case such as Case C-138/02 *Collins*, para 72, where, when discussing the legitimacy of a residence requirement for a job-seeker's allowance, fulfilment of the residence requirement being proof of a genuine link, the Court held: '[the application of a residence requirement] by the national authorities must rest on clear criteria known in advance and provision must be made for the possibility of a means of redress of a judicial nature. [. . .][T]he period [of residence] must not exceed what is necessary in order for the national authorities to be able to satisfy themselves that the person concerned is genuinely seeking work in the employment market of the host Member State.' For criticism of the burden this case law places on national authorities, see K Hailbronner, 'Union Citizenship and Social Rights', in E Guild and JY Carlier, *The Future of the Free Movement of Persons in the EU* (Bruylant, 2006) 65–78.

[57] See Cases C-224/98 *D'Hoop* [2002] ECR I-6191, paras 30–36 and C-224/02 *Pusa* [2004] ECR I-5763, paras 19–20. For discussion of migration discrimination and the non-discriminatory obstacles to free movement at issue in *D'Hoop*, see A Illiopoulos and H Toner, 'A new approach to discrimination against free movers?' (2003) 28 ELR 389–397.

[58] The terminology used to describe this link has varied. In Case C-138/02 *Collins*, the Court referred to a 'genuine link' (para 67) and a 'connection' (para 71) between the benefit applicant and the employment market of the host Member State. In Case C-258/04 *Ioannidis*, it referred to a 'real link' (paras 30 and 33), a 'real and effective degree of connection' (paras 31 and 33). In Case C-209/03 *Bidar*, the Court referred to a 'certain degree of integration into the society of [the host] State' (paras 57 and 59) and a 'sufficient degree of integration' into that society (para 60).

social benefits. Thus, Member State nationals may, by virtue of their status as EU citizens, have a *prima facie* entitlement to residence and/or equal treatment with respect to a whole range of social benefits but it is legitimate for the Member State from which the benefit is being sought to demand proof, at least as regards indirectly discriminatory conditions for or restrictions on entitlement to welfare provision, of a real and effective link with the territory in which the social benefit in question is being claimed. The objective behind the requirement of a real or genuine link is to ensure that the obligation of financial solidarity towards EU citizens is not, from the Member State's point of view, stretched beyond acceptable limits.[59]

IV. Signs of Cross-pollenisation in the Case Law on the Free Movement of Persons and EU Citizenship

A. EU Citizenship and the Material Scope of EC Law

One of the first things that emerges from an examination of the Court's case law on EU citizenship is that, while the establishment of EU citizenship was not intended to extend the material scope of EC law, the Court's interpretation of the consequences of the introduction of that status have led it to reassess certain aspects of its established case law on the free movement of persons. In the *Collins* case, for example, which is discussed in further detail below, in relation to a claim by a job-seeker to entitlement to equal treatment as regards a job-seeker's allowance, the Court held that 'in view of the establishment of citizenship of the Union and the interpretation in the case law of the right to equal treatment enjoyed by citizens of the Union, it is no longer possible to exclude from the scope of Article [39(2)] EC [...] a benefit of a financial nature intended to facilitate access to employment in the labour market of a Member State.'[60] The Court thereby overruled its limitation of the application of the principle of equal treatment to job-seekers in relation to access to employment only, a limitation which had been clearly stated in *Lebon* (albeit already implicitly called into question in a previous EU citizenship case, *Martínez Sala*). Equally, in *Bidar*, the establishment of EU citizenship led to a revision of the Court's earlier case law excluding from the scope of application of EC law, and thus from the scope of application of the principle of non-discrimination on grounds of nationality, grants or loans covering the maintenance costs of students.[61] In view of the introduction of citizenship of

---

[59] Whether the requirement of a genuine link will prove sufficient to prevent abuse and benefit tourism is another question, see K Hailbronner, 'Union Citizenship and Social Benefits' (2005) 42 CML Rev 1258.

[60] Case C-138/02 *Collins*, para 63. See also Case C-258/04 *Ioannidis*, para 22.

[61] Compare Cases C-209/03 *Bidar*, paras 31, 39–40 and one of the previous cases limiting the scope of application of Article 12 of the EC Treaty, 39/86 *Lair*, para 15.

the Union and the addition to the EC Treaty of a Chapter devoted, inter alia, to education and vocational training,[62] the Court held that the situation of a citizen of the Union who is lawfully resident in another Member State falls within the scope of application of the Treaty within the meaning of the first paragraph of Article 12 of the EC Treaty for the purposes of obtaining assistance for students intended to cover their maintenance costs. Clearly then, EU citizenship is not without its expansive effects on existing free movement case law. These examples, where citizenship has been used to broaden the scope of the non-discrimination principle, whether under Articles 12 or 39(2) of the EC Treaty, could be relied on as evidence of the Court's continued generous interpretation of free movement provisions and further proof of its contribution to the ever closer union.

B. The Free movement of Workers and the Real or Genuine Link

Where commentators have mainly expressed concern about the Court's case law on EU citizenship it has tended to be with regard to its actual or potential effect on the provision of social welfare in the Member States. The overall focus of these commentaries is on whether the Court's case law in this field, and its extension of social solidarity between EU citizens on the basis of Articles 12, 17, and 18 of the EC Treaty, may have a negative impact on the national provision of social welfare, on the organisation of national social welfare schemes and on the bonds of solidarity on which those schemes are traditionally based.[63] This section, rather than focusing on these macro juridical-political issues, concentrates on the micro level and, specifically, on whether the case law on EU citizenship may also be having a restrictive impact on established principles of EC law relating to the free movement of persons. Focusing on recent decisions of the Court on the free movement of workers, it emerges that concepts designed specifically with reference to freely moving, economically inactive EU citizens are being transposed to those economically active EU migrants whose rights predate the establishment of EU citizenship, derive from the original Treaty of Rome and have been safeguarded to date by an abundant and seemingly unassailable line of jurisprudence.

Of particular interest in this regard is the requirement of a genuine or real link which the Court introduced in cases where EU citizens were seeking access to social benefits on the basis of a combination of Articles 12, 17, and 18 of the EC Treaty and Regulation 1612/68. Requiring such a link is seen as a legitimate

---

[62] Case C-209/03 *Bidar*, paras 39–40.

[63] See, for early examples, the work cited in n 44 above and, more recently, Dougan and Spaventa, n 20 above. This debate is not exclusive to the case law on EU citizenship, however, but can equally be seen, for example, in connection with the Court's case law on Article 49 EC (see, for example, C Newdick, 'Citizenship, Free Movement and Healthcare: Cementing Individual Rights by Corroding Social Solidarity' (2006) 43 CML Rev 1645–1668. See also Lenaerts and Heremans, n 14 above, at 103, who examine both these strands of case law.

means for Member States to justify any differential treatment of or restrictions on EU citizens claiming benefits, its purpose being essentially to counteract the possibility of abuse and benefit tourism. However, as highlighted in a previous section summarizing key aspects of the jurisprudence on the free movement rights of economically active EU nationals, their performance of or involvement in an economic activity presupposed or provided proof of the existence of such a link. In general, social benefits were denied either because the applicant did not come within the personal scope of the free movement provisions or because the benefit in question was held not to constitute a social advantage. The genuine or effective link between the benefit applicant and the host Member State was demonstrated at an earlier stage when the competent authority determined whether he or she came within the personal scope of application of the existing Treaty provisions on free movement.[64] In a series of recent cases involving the free movement of workers, this genuine link has emerged as a requirement which Member States can also justifiably impose on migrant workers claiming indirect discrimination or restrictions as regards access to benefits either in their Member State of residence or, in the case of frontier workers, in their Member State of employment.

The first signs of this development can be seen in the *Collins* and *Ioannidis* cases. In *Collins*, the right of residence of the applicant, an Irish-American job-seeker, recently arrived in the United Kingdom, derived from Article 39 of the EC Treaty. The Court held, in relation to his request for a job-seeker's allowance, that in the light of the establishment of EU citizenship, such a benefit fell within the scope of application of Article 39(2).[65] Yet, despite finding itself within the personal and material scope of application of Article 39, when considering whether the impugned residence requirement for enjoyment of a job-seeker's allowance was objectively justified, the Court held that 'it is legitimate for the national legislature to wish to ensure that there is a *genuine link* between an applicant for an allowance in the nature of a social advantage within the meaning of Article 7(2) of Regulation No 1612/68 and the geographic employment market in question.'[66] It cited, in support of this proposition, the EU citizenship case, *D'Hoop*, which first spawned the genuine link requirement. In *Ioannidis*, another case involving

[64] This distinction between economically active and inactive EU citizens survives the adoption of Directive 2004/38. See the discussion by Barnard in Dougan and Spaventa (n 20 above), 166. Cf S Besson and A Utzinger, 'Introduction: Future Challenges of European Citizenship' (2007) 13 European Law Journal 573–590, 587, who argue that the *ratio legis* of the 2004 Directive was to do away with any distinction between different categories of EU migrants.

[65] Case C-138/02 *Collins*, para 63. Note that the Court held that the applicant was not a worker for the purposes of Article 7(2) of Regulation 1612/68 (para 32). However, referring to Case C-171/91 *Tsiotras* [1993] ECR I-2925, para 8, which in turn referred to Case C-292/89 *Antonissen*, it clearly regarded him as a worker within the meaning of Article 39 of the EC Treaty (para 36).

[66] Case C-138/02 *Collins*, para 67. According to the Court in *Collins* (para 70), the existence of such a link may be determined, in particular, by establishing that the person concerned has, for a reasonable period, in fact genuinely sought work in the Member State in question. That period cannot exceed what is necessary for the national authorities to be able to satisfy themselves that the person concerned is genuinely seeking work in the employment market of the host Member State (para 72).

a job-seeker, this time a Greek national, educated mainly in Greece, who was resident in Belgium and seeking a tideover allowance while seeking employment, the national court referred questions on the basis of Articles 12, 17, and 18 of the EC Treaty, which the Court answered with reference to Article 39 of the EC Treaty. According to the Court, it is contrary to that provision of the Treaty for a Member State to refuse such an allowance to a job-seeker on the sole ground that he had completed his secondary education in another Member State. Citing *D'Hoop* once again, the Court considered that a single condition concerning where an applicant's education was accomplished was too general and exclusive in nature and favoured an element which, in the circumstances, was not necessarily representative of *a real and effective degree of connection* between the applicant for the allowance and the employment market of the host Member State. The significance of *Ioannidis* lies, as in *Collins*, not in its final outcome, but in the Court's willingness to countenance arguments justifying differential treatment of resident EU nationals based on the existence of a genuine link, despite the fact that the applicants in question came within the personal scope of Article 39 of the EC Treaty and the right to equal treatment which they were asserting derived equally from that provision.[67]

These particular cases could be distinguished by virtue of the fact that the benefit applicants in question were job-seekers and hence, at least for the time being, formed part of the economically inactive category of EU citizens for which the genuine link was designed. Indeed the tideover allowance at issue in *D'Hoop* and again in *Ioannidis*, was a job-seeker's allowance by another name. Furthermore, while the Court in *Collins* distanced itself from the finding in *Lebon* to the effect that job-seekers could rely on equal treatment only with reference to access to employment and not as regards entitlement to social and tax advantages, it framed its decision with reference to Article 39(2) of the EC Treaty and not Article 7(2) of Regulation 1612/68, which could suggest that the logic of established case law relating to that latter provision was not being called into question.[68]

However, signs are that the Court is not content to limit the transposition of the genuine link requirement to job-seekers. In a subsequent series of cases on Article 39 of the EC Treaty and Regulation 1612/68, some Advocates General continued to argue for the application of this requirement in relation to migrant workers and their arguments appear to have found sympathetic ears in the Court.[69] The *Hartmann* and *Geven* cases stemmed from the refusal by a Member State to grant a social benefit—a child-raising allowance which had already been

[67] See the Opinions of the Advocates General in Cases C-212/05 *Hartmann*, C-213/05 *Geven*, and C-287/05 *Hendrix*. In Case C-258/04 *Ioannidis*, contrast the approach of the Court with that of its Advocate General who, at paras 53–64 of his Opinion, dismissed the relevance of the provisions of Article 39 of the EC Treaty and resolved the case solely with reference to Article 12, in conjunction with Article 17 of the EC Treaty.

[68] See, however, Case C-287/05 *Hendrix*, para 53, which equates these two provisions.

[69] Ironically, the first Advocate General to argue explicitly in favour of application to migrant workers of the genuine link requirement—Advocate General Geelhoed in Case C-212/05

deemed a social advantage within the meaning of Article 7(2) of Regulation 1612/68[70]—to frontier workers who worked but did not reside in the Member State from which the benefit was being claimed. At the material time, German law made the grant of this social advantage to civil servants conditional on their residence in Germany. Apart from civil servants, frontier workers employed in Germany but residing in another Member State could claim the allowance on condition that they were engaged in more than 'minor employment'.[71]

At the heart of these cases was the question whether the German residence and minor employment requirements were in conformity with Article 7(2) of Regulation 1612/68 and could be objectively justified.[72] The Court's reasoning in these cases should give rise to concern. In *Hartmann*, in response to the arguments of the German Government that the child-raising allowance in question was limited to persons who, through their choice of residence, have established a real link with German society, the Court held that since the German legislation allowed workers not employed in the German civil service to benefit from the allowance, even if they were not resident, provided their employment was not minor, residence could not be regarded as 'the only connecting link with the Member State concerned'. Instead, 'a substantial contribution to the national labour market also constituted a valid factor of integration into the society of that Member State.' Since Mr Hartmann (through whom the right of the spouse to

Hartmann—also argued that the distinction between the free movement of workers and the freedom to move on the basis of EU citizenship should not be blurred (see paras 34 and 38 of his Opinion).

[70] See Case C-85/96 *Martínez Sala*, para 26.

[71] Mr Hartmann (Case C-212/05) was a German civil servant, married to an Austrian and resident in Austria. The German child-raising allowance was requested by his wife. Mrs Geven (Case C-213/05) was a Dutch national, resident in the Netherlands, but employed in Germany in minor employment. Her weekly working time varied between 3 and 14 hours. Under German law, employment is minor if it is regularly exercised for less than 15 hours a week and monthly remuneration does not exceed a particular threshold. Minor employment is not a stranger to the Court. In Cases C-317/93 *Nolte* [1995] ECR I-4625 and C-444/93 *Megner and Scheffel* [1995] ECR I-4741, German minor employees claimed that German rules excluding them from social security entitlement were incompatible with Directive 79/7/EEC of 19 December 1978 on the progressive implementation of the principle of equal treatment for men and women in matters of social security ([1979] OJ L6/24). The Court in those cases drew inspiration from case law on the definition of worker pursuant to Article 39 of the EC Treaty to conclude that the minor employees in question, despite the reduced numbers of hours worked, were part of the 'working population' and thus came within the personal scope of Directive 79/7.

[72] The Advocate General's preferred solution in the *Hartmann* case was that, since the applicant had moved to *reside* and not to *work*, he did not qualify as a worker under Article 39 of the EC Treaty. Given the Court's decision in Case C-152/03 *Ritter-Coulais* [2006] ECR I-1711, paras 31–32, the wording of the fourth recital of Regulation 1612/68—the right of freedom of movement must be enjoyed 'without discrimination by permanent, seasonal and frontier workers [...]'—and the fact that the Court has held that frontier workers can rely on Article 7 of Regulation 1612/68 (Case C-57/96 *Meints*, para 50)—it would have been odd indeed for the Court to follow his reasoning and to exclude this particular frontier worker from the personal scope of application of Article 39. While he proposed to transpose the genuine link requirement from the case law on EU citizenship to that on Article 39 and Regulation 1612/68 in *Hartmann*, in *Geven* he followed the traditional path, examining objective justification and proportionality and concluding that the minor employment requirement was disproportionate in the circumstances.

the allowance derived) was working full-time in Germany, he and his wife could not be refused the allowance in question simply because he was not resident there. The Court thus rejected the grounds for proving a genuine link advanced by the host Member State (residence) in favour of a different means of proving such a link with the society of that State (a substantial contribution to the national labour market). However, the fact that a migrant worker worked full-time or part-time was never previously considered relevant when it came to consideration of their entitlement not to be discriminated against as regards entitlement to social advantages or the justification and proportionality of a decision refusing such an advantage. Furthermore, the applicant in *Hartmann* was a German national, resident since his marriage in Austria, but prior to that in Germany, working in the German civil service, with two children, who are, presumably, dual German/Austrian nationals. In those circumstances, it is difficult to see why, even in the absence of an escape clause such as that provided by the fact that the German legislation did not regard residence as the only basis for establishing the required link with Germany, the Court felt the need to examine whether a sufficient link with German society existed at all. Of course, if the Court had referred to these factors when characterizing the link, it risked indicating to Member States that they could justify differential treatment of resident and non-resident workers with reference to a link derived essentially from their nationality of that State, which would not be compatible with EC law.

The decision in *Geven* is even more striking. The national court had held in that case that the applicant was in a genuine employment relationship allowing her to claim the status of migrant worker for the purposes of Regulation 1612/68. The Court held, however, that the fact that the applicant did not have a 'sufficiently substantial occupation' in the Member State concerned is capable of constituting a legitimate justification for a refusal to grant the social advantage at issue. In this respect, it recalled that social policy is, in the current state of EC law, a matter for the Member States, who have a wide margin of discretion in exercising their powers. The legislature of the Member State of employment *could reasonably consider* that the exclusion from the allowance in question of non-resident workers in minor employment constitutes a measure that is appropriate and proportionate, having regard to the objective pursued.[73] However, Mrs Geven was a migrant worker within the meaning of Article 39 of the EC Treaty and Regulation 1612/68. The national court, whose competence it is to determine if the individual's work is genuine and effective, had found, as a question of fact, that her work fulfilled

---

[73] Note, however, that in Case C-213/05 *Geven*, the Court assessed the proportionality of the decision to exclude the applicant from the benefit in question with reference to the German legislature's aim to grant the benefit only to those with a sufficiently close link with German society (ie the objective identified in paragraph 29 of the judgment) when it should arguably have assessed its proportionality with reference to the purpose of the benefit itself, namely to allow parents to care for their children by giving up or reducing their hours of employment (ie the objective identified in paragraph 21 of the judgment).

these criteria. If her work was genuine and effective, it follows from the Court's own case law that it was not marginal and ancillary. It seems odd, therefore, that the Court would rely on the insufficiently substantial nature of her occupation to justify a residence requirement for entitlement to the social advantage in question. Furthermore, as regards proportionality, the Court resurrected the most lenient test imaginable, a test previously heavily criticized and confined almost exclusively to justification by Member States of differential treatment of male and female workers in the field of social security.[74] A Member State, according to this test, must merely show that they were *reasonably entitled* to consider that the measure adopted is appropriate and proportionate. The Court in *Geven* did not consider or, in the alternative, direct the national court to consider, whether it was disproportionate to rely on the criterion of minor employment when in fact certain workers would be excluded from entitlement despite working at the limit of the minor employment threshold and, therefore, despite working hours almost equivalent to those of a part-time worker.[75] It did not consider the question of proportionality with reference to the applicant's eligibility for a similar benefit in her Member State of residence. Nor did it discuss whether it was logical to make entitlement to a social benefit dependant on a requirement of more than minor employment when the benefit in question was intended precisely to allow the recipient to cease work or reduce their working hours significantly.[76]

The judgments in *Hartmann* and *Geven* appear to depart from the Court's traditional approach to migrant workers, case law on restrictions of free movement, and objective justification of such restrictions and the entitlement of migrant workers to social advantages. Both decisions are confirmation, beyond the narrower confines of the case law on job-seekers, that Member States when deciding whether to grant social advantages can require the applicant migrant worker to demonstrate a real link with or a sufficient degree of integration in the Member State concerned. As explained above, previous refusals of social

---

[74] See Cases C-317/93 *Nolte* and C-444/93 *Megner and Scheffel*.

[75] Contrast the application of the principle of proportionality in Case C-213/05 *Geven* with that in a recent EU citizenship case, Case C-192/05 *Tas-Hagen* [2006] ECR I-451, para 38: 'a criterion requiring residence cannot be considered a satisfactory indicator of the degree of connection of applicants to the Member State granting the benefit when it is liable [...] to lead to different results for persons resident abroad whose degree of integration into the society of the Member State granting the benefit is in all respects comparable.'

[76] This logical weakness in the more than minor employment condition did not escape the attention of the referring court or the Advocate General—see para 40 of his Opinion in Case C-213/05 *Geven*. Compare also the reasoning of the Court in the latter case with that in Case C-135/99 *Elsen* [2000] ECR I-409, paras 24–26. In that case, the Court rejected the Commission's argument to the effect that a French frontier worker, working in Germany, lacked a sufficiently close link with the latter State to claim entitlement to a particular social security benefit: 'as regards the taking into account, for the purposes of old-age insurance, of unbroken periods of child-rearing following the birth of her child, [the applicant] worked exclusively in Germany and was subject, as a frontier worker, to the German legislation when the child was born. Thus a close link can be established between the periods of child-rearing concerned and the periods of insurance completed in Germany by virtue of her occupational activity in that state.'

advantages which were regarded by the Court as justified centred on the fact that the applicant did not fall within the personal scope of the free movement rules, or that the benefit being sought did not constitute a social advantage. In a few cases concerning frontier workers, where the question of residence conditions and the exportability of social advantages arose, the Court examined the proposed objective justification and the proportionality of the impugned national rules with respect to that justification and concluded that the conditions imposed by the Member State of employment were disproportionate in the light of the objective pursued.[77] This established approach to objective justification and proportionality seemed no longer to hold sway in *Hartmann* and *Geven*.

Can *Hartmann* and *Geven* be dismissed as isolated incidents, based on reasoning limited to the particular circumstances of frontier workers? Or are these decisions evidence of the fact that one of the consequences of the 'mainstreaming' of the provisions on EU citizenship may be a reversal or, at the very least, an alteration, of the traditional scale of values fixed by the EC Treaty authors and the EC legislator regarding economically active and inactive migrants and their families?[78] Various other decisions of the Court also appear to suggest that, in its rush to confirm EU citizenship as the fundamental status of the nationals of the Member States, the Court's case law now appears frequently and surprisingly restrictive with reference to claims brought pursuant to Article 39 of the EC Treaty and Regulation 1612/68.[79] There is a general blurring of the distinction between the economically active and inactive without the provision of a coherent framework within which to deal with the claims of either in the future. It is no doubt a good thing that the Court has begun to come to grips with the meaning and scope of the EU citizenship provisions, but it seems odd that the development of that status is at the expense of established case law on the free movement of persons. In *Ninni-Orasche*, a case involving a migrant worker, the Court insisted, in accordance with its case law in *Lair*, that for a former worker to enjoy equal treatment on the basis of Article 7(2) of Regulation 1612/68 as regards the benefit of a student assistance system, there had to be continuity between their previous occupational activity and the studies pursued.[80] The maintenance of this aspect of *Lair* in *Ninni-Orasche* contrasts sharply with the Court's disavowal of another part of that decision dealing with maintenance grants in *Bidar*, a case decided with reference to Articles 12 and 18 of the EC Treaty. Similarly, in the *Baldinger* case, the Court held, in line with its previous decisions in *Even* and *De Vos*, that Article 39 and Regulations 1408/71 and 1612/68, specifically Article 7(2) of the

---

[77] See, for example, Cases C-57/96 *Meints* and C-237/97 *Meeusen.*

[78] See further D Martin, 'De Martínez Sala à Bidar. Les paradoxes de la jurisprudence sur la libre circulation des citoyens', in E Guild and JY Carlier, *The Future of the Free Movement of Persons in the EU* (Bruylant, 2006) 160–170, and S Giubboni, n 19 above.

[79] See Martin, ibid, 165 *et seq.*

[80] Case C-413/01 *Ninni-Orasche*, para 35. The Court did concede an exception with respect to those workers forced by involuntary unemployment to undergo occupational retraining.

latter, do not preclude national legislation which refuses to grant an allowance in favour of former prisoners of war on the ground that the applicant did not hold the nationality of the Member State involved when the application was made.[81] The Court was unmoved by the Commission's argument to the effect that the criterion for differentiating between Austrian nationals—whether or not they held Austrian nationality *at the time of their application*—was disproportionate. Yet, in *Tas-Hagen*, a case decided with reference to Article 18(1) EC, the Court held that a residence condition applied by the Netherlands to civilian victims of war was disproportionate as it was based solely *on the date on which the application for the benefit is submitted* and as such was not a satisfactory indicator of the degree of attachment of the applicant to the society granting the benefit.[82] What justified this more stringent application of the principle of proportionality to an EU citizen's request for a war-related benefit as compared to the requests made by EU migrant workers?

The Court Reports throw up further examples of a restrictive approach to migrant workers when compared to that now reserved to their economically inactive citizen counterparts. The applicant in the *Hendrix* case was a Dutch national, resident in Belgium but working in the Netherlands, who was seeking to avail of provisions of Dutch law dispensing employers of the obligation to pay handicapped workers the minimum wage on the grounds that the State would provide for the necessary top up. Entitlement to this social benefit is dependant on residence in the Netherlands, which is why the applicant was said not to qualify.[83] The Advocate General, referring almost exclusively to case law on EU citizenship, affirmed that entitlement to a social benefit can, as a matter of principle, be subject to the requirement of a link or attachment to the host Member State. She argued that the impugned residence condition in *Hendrix* was evidence of such a link to the social and economic environment of the Member State from which the benefit was requested. The Court, for its part, indicated that the applicant was a migrant worker and that the benefit in question was a social advantage. It also recalled that, on the basis of established case law, Member States may not make payment of a social advantage dependent on the condition that recipients are resident in the national territory of the Member State. However, unlike in *Meints* and *Meeusen*, the original frontier workers' cases mentioned previously, the Court was not

---

[81] Case C-386/02 *Baldinger* [2004] ECR I-8411, paras 18–19. The applicant was originally an Austrian national who took Swedish nationality after having moved there in later life. He had served in the German armed forces and been taken as a prisoner of war. The Court observed that the allowance which he sought from the Austrian authorities and which was denied him on account of his nationality is provided to former prisoners of war who prove that they underwent a long period of captivity, in testimony of national gratitude for the hardships they endured and is thus paid as a quid pro quo for the service they rendered to their country. It held that such an allowance is excluded from the material scope of Regulation 1408/71 (by virtue of Article 4(4)) and does not fall within the category of social advantages in Article 7(2) of Regulation 1612/68.

[82] Case C-192/05 *Tas-Hagen*, paras 34–39.

[83] Case C-287/05 *Hendrix*, Opinion of Advocate General Kokott of 29 March 2007.

willing to indicate to the national court whether or not the application of a residence condition to this particular applicant was lawful. Instead, the operative part of the judgment states that Article 39 of the EC Treaty, Article 7 of Regulation 1612/68, and the relevant provisions of Regulation 1408/71, do not preclude legislation which provides that a benefit such as this may be granted only to persons resident on the national territory.[84] According to the Court, the benefit in question is closely linked to the socio-economic situation in the Netherlands, since it is based on the minimum wage and the national standard of living. However, the Court did call on the national court, with reference to the principle of 'interprétation conforme' and a proviso in the national legislation allowing the waiver of the residence condition if it gave rise to unfairness, to ensure that such unfairness did not occur. In this regard it referred the national court to the fact that the worker in question had maintained all of his economic and social links to his Member State of origin. But what does this mean? Does it simply mean that the residence condition in *Hendrix* should be considered unlawful when applied to national workers, resident in another Member State but still working in their Member State of origin? If so, then for many if not most frontier workers, application of the residence condition would appear to be lawful. This result contrasts with the solution reached by the Court in *Trojani*.[85] Despite the fact that the applicant in that case was not a migrant worker, contributed in no significant economic manner to the Member State in which he resided, and derived no right of residence from EC law, since he appeared to be lawfully resident under Belgian law, he could rely on Article 12 of the EC Treaty in order to be granted a social assistance benefit. Once again, residence and EU citizenship trump employment as a basis for entitlement to social benefits and the Court seeks, for the citizen, solutions which it no longer consistently or creatively seeks for migrant workers.[86]

V. Conclusions

The Court's constructive interpretation of the EU citizenship provisions is undoubtedly to be applauded and the fact that there is a certain degree of

---

[84] Given that the benefit in *Hendrix* was a special non-contributory benefit and, as such, was not exportable under the provisions of Regulation 1408/71, the Court's decision to examine Article 7(2) of Regulation 1612/68 is, in any event, unusual, if not incorrect. Having concluded that it was a non-exportable benefit under the first regulation all that remained for it to do was to examine the validity of that non-exportability with reference to the provisions of Article 39 of the EC Treaty.

[85] Case C-456/02 [2004] ECR I-7573.

[86] For further comparisons of EU citizenship and free movement cases see Martin (n 78 above) and, in particular, his discussion of Cases C-109/01 *Akrich* [2003] ECR I-9607 and C-200/02 *Chen* [2004] ECR I-9925. Note that, as a legal precedent, *Akrich* should perhaps be handled with care given the subsequent decisions in Cases C-1/05 *Jia* [2007] ECR I-1 and C-291/05 *Eind* [2007] ECR I-719. See also G Davies, 'The High Water Point of the Free Movement of Persons: Ending Benefit Tourism and Rescuing Welfare' (2004) 26 Journal of Social Welfare and Family Law 211–222, who justifies the Court's new, restrictive approach on practical grounds.

cross-pollenisation in the case law on economically inactive and active EU citizens is to be expected. Nevertheless, it is surprising that the case law in the latter field is being negatively impacted by the expansion of the rights of the former category of migrants. The Court's established case law on the free movement of persons has generally been applauded for the clear and structured framework it provided for transnational migration in the EU and for recognizing that such migration must be guaranteed in compliance with the principles of liberty and dignity. In this respect alone, the Court has contributed favourably to the creation of the ever closer union. Given that the EC has not only an economic but also a social purpose,[87] it was to be hoped and could have been expected that the Court would, over time, also strengthen the social dimension of EU citizenship. What this article criticizes is not this trend in the Court's case law on EU citizenship, or the growing assimilation of the position of economically active and inactive EU citizens, albeit a clear and coherent basis for its decisions is always a good idea, particularly given the requirement of uniformity which Article 234 of the EC Treaty is intended to serve. What should give rise to concern is the Court's failure, whether intentional or inadvertent, to prevent the nascency of EU citizenship exerting a negative influence on the central tenets of the established case law on the free movement of persons, case law without which, the provisions of the EC Treaty on citizenship would have been unthinkable.

With reference, in particular, to the recent case law examined in the closing sections of the article, if the Court has decided that social assistance can and must generally be made conditional on a link with the territory of the Member State granting the benefit, then it will have to clarify what exactly that link must constitute. Should it be based, for example, on employment or on residence? Cases like *Hartmann*, *D'Hoop*, and *Hendrix* suggest that the applicant's possession of the nationality of the Member State granting the benefit should largely suffice. However, does this not allow Member States to differentiate with reference to the very criterion—nationality—which may give rise to the discrimination which the provisions of the EC Treaty, secondary legislation, and the case law of the Court have been seeking to root out for decades? *Geven* suggests that an employment link is insufficient, or that it may be, in some cases, depending on the nature of the benefit being claimed or the specific employment circumstances of the claimant. However, this means that national authorities and, ultimately, the Court of Justice, may have to engage in a case-by-case assessment of whether denial of a benefit is reasonable given the individual circumstances of the claimant and the characteristics of the benefit. What is wrong with the Court's recent case law on the free movement of persons is not its confirmation of the genuine link requirement, but the automatic transposition of that requirement to a category of migrants who never previously had to justify such a link; their qualification as

---

[87] Recently confirmed in Case C-438/05 *Viking Line* [2007] ECR I-10779, para 79.

migrant workers providing sufficient proof that a link existed. It appears that in its attempts to assuage the concerns about the risks of benefit tourism expressed following its early EU citizenship decisions—concerns which may, correctly or incorrectly, have increased since 2004—the Court has adopted a one solution fits all approach and has failed to consider that EU citizens—economically active and inactive—may be equal but also different.

Limitations on Religion in a Liberal Democratic Public Order: Christianity, Islam, and the Partial Secularity of the European Union

*Ronan McCrea**

I. Introduction

European integration arose partly out of horror at the consequences of fascism and fear of its totalitarian counterpart, Soviet Communism. It is therefore unsurprising that the European Union (EU) has been committed, to an increasingly explicit degree, to the liberal democratic system of government throughout its history. The EU recognizes religion's potentially totalitarian aspects and therefore requires certain limits on religious influence over the law and politics as part of its commitment to the principles of liberal democracy. This paper shows how the Union has seen excessive religious influence in the legal and political arenas as a threat to the autonomy of the public sphere, to individual autonomy in the private sphere as well as to important values such as gender equality. It demonstrates how EU law and policies in relation to the enlargement of the Union and the integration of migrants have required applicant States and individual migrants respectively to indicate acceptance of limitations to religious influence over law and society as a condition of membership of, or residence in, the European Union. Thus, States have been required to maintain the autonomy of the public sphere from religious influence and to refrain from enacting legislation which enforces compliance with religious morality at the expense of individual autonomy to too great a degree. Similarly, migrants have been required to indicate their commitment to liberal principles such as gender equality and individual self-determination in matters of sexuality, even when such principles contradict their religious beliefs. EU law has, therefore, sanctioned far reaching State interference in the private sphere of beliefs and opinions in the order to protect the general principle of the autonomy of the individual in the private sphere. Furthermore, the Union's attempts to impose

* PhD Candidate, European Institute, London School of Economics, Barrister.

these limitations on religion have been complicated by the partial and contested nature of the secularity of the public orders of its own Member States. Muslim-majority States like Turkey have been required to forswear any desire to introduce religious elements into its law while Muslim migrants have been asked to give explicit assurances in relation to their acceptance of liberal values in relation to issues of gender and sexuality. On the other hand the Union has been mark-edly reluctant to interfere with the important symbolic and institutional roles held by certain culturally entrenched Christian denominations in many Member States despite the fact that many such denominations, most notably the Catholic Church, continue to intervene in political matters and to influence legislation in areas such as the family, abortion, and homosexual equality both at Member State and EU levels. The Union's attempts to protect its liberal democratic values from religious threats coupled with its explicit reluctance[1] to tamper with the evolving and sensitive arrangements surrounding Europe's culturally-entrenched denominations have therefore led to a situation which is discriminatory in that 'outsider' religions such as Islam are held to more demanding standards of secu-larity than 'insider' religions such as mainstream Christianity.

II. Enlargement and Religion in the Public Sphere

Since the Reformation and Enlightenment, relations between religious institu-tions and those of the State have been characterized in Europe by a gradual decline in religious power and the establishment of the legal and political supremacy of the institutions of the modern State.[2] Although religious institutions continue to play a role in law-making, including at EU level, religious bodies have much lower political impact than in other areas of the world. The limited nature of religious influence over legal norms in Europe is shown by the fact that, even in relation to the law governing what Casanova terms 'lifeworld' issues (namely those relat-ing to the beginning and end of life, family and sexuality) which are the highest political priority for mainstream European religions[3] and which embodied the largely conservative approach of the Abrahamic religions to a significant degree as recently as 60 years ago, liberal norms of personal autonomy, privacy, and equal-ity have become increasingly dominant. This approach embodies the arguably Western notion of religion as a largely private matter with limited influence over

---

[1] See Declaration 11, annexed to the Treaty of Amsterdam [1997] OJ C340/0308 (10.11.1997).
[2] See J Casanova, *Public Religion in the Modern World*, (University of Chicago Press, 1994), at ch 1, especially 21–23 and 37. See also A Ferrari, 'Religions, Secularity and Democracy in Europe: for a New Kelsenian Pact', Jean Monnet Program, NYU School of Law, Paper No 3/05 at: <http://www.jeanmonnetprogram.org/papers/05/050301.html>.
[3] See for instance the address of Pope Benedict XVI to the European People's Party of 30 March 2006, full text at: <http://www.vatican.va/holy_father/benedict_xvi/speeches/2006/march/documents/hf_ben-xvi_spe_20060330_eu-parliamentarians_en.html>.

law and political life and contrasts markedly with the situation in much of the rest of the world,[4] most notably the Islamic world[5] where religious principles continue to exercise a much greater influence over certain areas of law.[6]

A. Enlargement, Conditionality, and Human Rights

Even prior to 1989, it was clear that the criteria for inclusion in the Community amounted to more than adoption of a market economy. As far back as the 1960s, the Community was stressing the importance of respect for democratic principles and human rights in assessing Greece's application for membership.[7] From the 1970s onwards human rights achieved an increasing prominence in the Community.[8] Following the collapse of Communism, the speed with which newly liberated countries sought membership of the Union, meant that European institutions were required to make explicit the criteria which would be used to determine who could and could not become a member of the Community. The resulting 'Copenhagen Criteria' were outlined in that city at the European Council of June 1993.

The criteria specified that:

Membership requires that candidate country has achieved stability of institutions guaranteeing democracy, the rule of law, human rights and respect for and, protection of minorities, the existence of a functioning market economy as well as the capacity to cope with competitive pressure and market forces within the Union.[9]

The act of setting out such explicitly political criteria represented a recognition by Member States that a State which was economically eminently suitable for membership would not be permitted to join the Community unless it showed a

---

[4] P Berger and G Weigel (eds), *The Desecularization of the Modern World: Resurgent Religion and Modern Politics* (Erdemans Publishing Company and Public Policy Center, 1999).

[5] B Lewis, *The Crisis of Islam: Holy War and Unholy Terror* (Phoenix, 2003) 14–17.

[6] Private consensual sexual behaviour continues to be regulated by the criminal law to a significant extent in many largely Muslim societies. For instance, homosexuality remains a crime in the largely Muslim countries of Afghanistan, Algeria, Bahrain, Bangladesh, Iran, Iraq, Lebanon, Libya, Malaysia, Mauritania, Morocco, Oman, Pakistan, Somalia, the United Arab Emirates, and Yemen. See: <http://www.gaylawnet.com/>. In relation to the greater level of religiosity found in societies outside Europe, see P Norris and R Inglehart, *Sacred and Secular: Religion and Politics Worldwide* (Cambridge University Press, 2004).

[7] For an account of how democracy and human rights moved from implicit to explicit conditions of EU membership, see H Sjursen 'Enlargement in Perspective: The EU's Quest for Identity', Paper given as part of the European Institute Research Seminar series, at the London School of Economics, 24 May 2006.

[8] See the 1977 Tripartite Declaration on Human Rights of the Parliament, Council and Commission, 5 April 1977 ([1977] OJ C103 (27.4.1977)). This process continued into the 1990s with direct reference being made to the European Convention on Human Rights in the Amsterdam Treaty and with the adoption of a Bill of Rights for the EU in the Nice Treaty. See also the series of rulings the ECJ in cases such as *Stauder v City of Ulm–Sozialamt* [1969] ECR 419 through to *ERT* Case [1991] ECR I 2925.

[9] See: <http://europa.eu/scadplus/glossary/accession_criteria_copenhague_en.htm>.

commitment to certain ideals (democracy, protection of human rights etc) adherence to which was deemed necessary for the proper functioning of the European polity. These criteria have played a prominent role, not only in the enlargement process but also in the Union's view of itself. The Maastricht Treaty gave this process constitutional status stating in Article 6 that the Union was 'founded on the principles of liberty, democracy, respect for human rights and fundamental freedoms, and the rule of law' and pledging in the same article to respect the principles of the European Convention on Human Rights. The Copenhagen Criteria themselves have, according to both academic commentators and the Commission itself, also been turned into principles of European constitutional law.[10] The European Commission is charged with assessing whether candidate countries meet these conditions. It makes a recommendation to the Member States who must unanimously decide to open negotiations.[11] Formal accession negotiations have never been opened by the Union with a State that has not been judged by the Commission to be in compliance with the Copenhagen Criteria.

The criteria themselves do not, on their face, appear to mandate any particular approach to management of the relationship between religion, law, and politics. However, at certain moments in the accession process, the EU has indicated that adherence to the criteria and the liberal democratic values underlying them requires limitations on the role played by religion and religious norms in law-making.

B. Romania and Homosexuality

In 1996, the Romanian legislature amended Article 200 of the Penal Code to criminalize private homosexual acts and outlawed membership of gay and lesbian organizations. This law was strongly supported by the Romanian Orthodox Church with a former foreign minister identifying ecclesiastical opposition as a key factor behind the retention of the law.[12] The Romanian Government

[10] See the Commission Regular Report of 2002 COM(2002)700 which states 'since the entry into force of the Treaty of Amsterdam in May 1999, these [political] requirements have been enshrined as constitutional principles in the Treaty on European Union.' See also C Hillion, 'The Copenhagen Criteria and Their Progeny', in C Hillion (ed), *European Enlargement: A Legal Approach* (Hart Publishing, 2004), where it is argued that 'The novelty of the Copenhagen criteria also lies in the way the obligations they embody have been enforced: their gradual "constitutionalisation" has resulted in them being applied more strictly' and that 'One may suggest that the political conditionality has been implicit in the Community legal order from the very outset, and made progressively more explicit' at 3–4.

[11] Article 49 of the Consolidated Versions of the Treaty on European Union and the Treaty Establishing the European Community [2006] OJ C321 E/35 (29.12.2006). See 'How Does a Country Join the EU', European Commission, DG Enlargement, available at: <http://ec.europa.eu/enlargement/questions_and_answers/background_en.htm>.

[12] See 'It's Still No Breeze for Gays, Even Diplomatic Ones', in *The New York Times*, 17 October 2001. Note in particular the comments of former Foreign Minister Mircea Geoana attributing key importance to the Orthodox Church in the debate over decriminalization.

attempted to repeal Article 200 in 1998, but this was rejected by Parliament after a vociferous campaign by the Orthodox Church. Church officials referred to gays and lesbians as 'the ultimate enemy' and 'Satan's army' and accused legislators of being 'scared by the huge European pressures'.[13] Again in September 2000, the Orthodox Church intervened forcefully appealing to legislators not to amend Article 200. Acknowledging the European dimension to the controversy Archbishop Nifon stated that he did not 'believe that European Union integration hinges on the [homosexuality] issue'.[14]

At the time of the announcement of the Copenhagen Criteria in June 1993, the EU had no competence in relation to sexual orientation discrimination.[15] Neither had criminalization of homosexuality been raised as an issue in any previous enlargement.[16] However, notwithstanding this lack of internal competence or consensus amongst Member States,[17] the Union embraced the repeal of laws criminalizing homosexual activity as part of the accession process. Importantly however, it did so on the grounds that such laws constituted an interference with the human rights of gays and lesbians. In its 1998 report on Romania's progress towards accession, the Commission noted that a proposal to reform the penal code which included a proposal to decriminalize homosexuality had been rejected by the Romanian Parliament[18] and that there were 'reports of inhuman and degrading treatment by the police, especially of Roma, children, homosexuals and prisoners' by the police. These references were made in the section of the report dedicated to 'Human Rights and the Protection of Minorities' and not in the section which covered 'Democracy and the Rule of Law' indicating that the Commission saw the matter as a question of interference with the fundamental rights of a minority rather than a structural question relating to the role of religious norms in legislation.

The European Parliament was also particularly active on this issue. In September 1998, it adopted a resolution calling on Romania and Cyprus to abolish their anti-homosexual legislation. The resolution 'deplored the refusal of the Romanian Chamber of Deputies to adopt a reform bill presented by the

---

[13] See Florian Buhuceanu 'ACCEPT Country Report on the Status of LGBT', online at: <http://www.globalgayz.com/romania-news.html>.

[14] See 'Romanian Orthodox Church Denounces Homosexuality', Reuters News Agency, 13 September 2000, online at: <http://www.ilga.org>.

[15] The Amsterdam Treaty of 1997 did widen the scope or the Union's ability to legislate against discrimination to include discrimination on grounds of sexual orientation, but such legislation required unanimity in the Council and was not enacted until late in the year 2000 (Council Directive 2000/78/EC of 27 November 2000 establishing a general framework for equal treatment in employment and occupation (OJ L303)).

[16] Homosexual acts were illegal in Scotland and Northern Ireland at the time of the accession of the United Kingdom in 1973. A similar prohibition was part of the law of the Republic of Ireland until July 1993.

[17] Ibid.

[18] See Section 1.2 of 'Regular Report from the Commission on Romania's Progress towards Accession', online at: <http://ec.europa.eu/enlargement/archives/pdf/key_documents/1998/romania_en.pdf>.

Government to repeal all anti-homosexual legislation provided by Article 200 of the penal code'.[19] It also specifically linked the issue of decriminalization to the question of accession expressing the Parliament's refusal to 'give its consent to the accession of any country that, through it legislation of policies, violates the human rights of lesbians and gay men'.[20] The Parliament repeated these sentiments in subsequent resolutions in March 2000 and July 2001.[21] In the summer of 2001, the Parliament's Intergroup for Lesbian and Gay Rights held a hearing on the situation of lesbians and gays in the accession States. These activities contributed to an increase in pressure on the Commission to take a more proactive stand in relation to the issue of homosexuality and enlargement.[22] Like the Commission, the Parliament's resolutions were phrased solely in terms of the implications of criminalization for the human rights of gays and lesbians and did not address the controversy's religious aspects.

In remarks to the European Parliament in September 2001, the Commissioner responsible for Enlargement Gunter Verheugen stated that he wished to make it clear that the Commission would continue to press for human rights and non-discrimination in enlargement negotiations, including on grounds of sexual orientation.[23] The Commissioner's representative to the Intergroup on Gary and Lesbian Rights further stressed that there would be 'no flexibility' on this issue on the part of the Commission. Commissioner Verheugen was even more explicit in a letter sent to the International Lesbian and Gay Association in which he stated the applicant States would be expected to accept the elimination of discrimination based upon sexual orientation and that '[e]qual treatment of gays and lesbians is a basic principle of the European Union'.[24] In December 2001 faced with the determined opposition of the Orthodox Church and conscious of its failure to push decriminalization through the Parliament on the previous occasion, the Romanian Government resorted to an emergency ordinance to amend Article 200 and finally decriminalized homosexuality.[25]

European institutions had therefore succeeded in forcing the Romanian authorities to remove from their statute book a legal measure which enshrined in the criminal law religiously-influenced norms against homosexuality. They had done so in the face of a vociferous and popular campaign by religious leaders of

---

[19] Res. B4-0824 en 0852/98, adopted 17 September 1998. See in particular paragraph F.
[20] Ibid, para J.
[21] Res. A5-0223/2001, adopted 5 July 2001, paragraphs 80 and 83, and Res. A5-0050/2000, adopted 16 March 2000, paragraphs 59 and 60.
[22] See J Sweibel 'Gay and Lesbian Rights and EU Enlargement', online at: <http://www.eumap.org/journal/features/2002/april02/gaylesbeu>.
[23] Quoted in Sweibel, ibid.
[24] See International News Report 'Anti-Gay Nations May Not Join European Union' Rex Wockner, 31 July 2001, online at: <http://gaytoday.badpuppy.com/garchive/world/073101wo.htm>.
[25] Government Emergency Ordinance no 89/2001. The Romanian also introduced an ordinance to enact a law prohibiting discrimination (including discrimination on grounds of sexual orientation) (Government Ordinance no 137/2000). For details, see: <http://www.accept-romania.ro/news.htm>, entry of 1 February 2002.

Romania's State church in favour of retaining the law. However, despite this, the Union saw the issue not as a primarily religious one but as a question of human and minority rights. It was to take a somewhat different approach in its dealings with Turkey.

C. Turkey and Adultery

In the autumn of 2004, the Turkish Government presented its overhaul of the criminal code to Parliament as part of its attempt to win the backing of the European Council (scheduled for later that year) for the opening of accession negotiations with the EU. Despite the limited nature of EU competence in this area, it was the criminal law as it related to the 'lifeworld' issues of gender and sexuality that received the greatest attention.[26] Indeed as *Deutsche Welle* newspaper noted 'with pressure from the EU, women's rights groups were able to outlaw rape in marriages and get old fashioned terms like "chastity", "honor" and "moral" out of criminal law books'.[27] However, despite the fact that the Turkish Constitutional Court had abolished the crime of adultery in 1996 (on the grounds that it unfairly penalized women),[28] the 2004 reforms proposed that it be recriminalized. Prime Minister Erdogan defended the measure on the grounds that the law represented a 'vital step' towards preserving the family and 'human honour'. He further argued that although Turkey wanted to join the EU it did not have to adopt its 'imperfect' Western morals.[29] Although several EU Member States retained laws criminalizing adultery until relatively recently,[30] the European Commission reacted strongly to this proposal with the Commission's official spokesman stating that the proposal 'certainly cast doubts on the direction of Turkey's reform efforts and would risk complicating Turkey's European prospects'.[31] Certain Member States also expressed reservations with UK Foreign Secretary Jack Straw asserting that the proposal 'would create difficulties for Turkey'.[32] However, although Turkish women's groups

---

[26] See 'Turkey Changes Laws to Meet EU Standards' *Deutsche Welle*, 1 September 2004, online at: <http://www.dw-world.de/dw/article/0,2144,1314044,00.html>.

[27] Ibid.

[28] See 'Verheugen Warns Turkey on Adultery Law' *Deutsche Welle*, 10 September 2004, online at: <http://dw-world.de/dw/article/0,1564,1324102,00.html>.

[29] Quoted in 'Turkey's Adultery Ban Splits the Nation' *The Age* newspaper, 7 September 2004, online at: <http://www.theage.com.au/articles/2004/09/06/1094322712399.html?from=storylhs>.

[30] Irish law criminalized adultery until 1981, French law until 1975 and Austrian law until 1997. In the United States, 23 States have similar laws. See K Gajendra Singh, 'EU-Turkish Engagement: A Must for Stability of the Region', South Asia Analysis Group Papers, online at: <http://www.saag.org/papers12/paper1127.html>.

[31] See 'Adultery Fault Line with EU' *Turkish Daily News,* 18 September 2004, available online at: <http://www.turkishdailynews.com.tr/archives.php?id=37707>.

[32] See 'Turkey Backs off Plan to Outlaw Adultery', Associated Press, 14 September 2004, available online at: <http://www.wwrn.org/article.php?idd=7164&sec=36&con=54>.

had been amongst those most strongly opposed to the law,[33] the EU response did not stress the impact of the law on women or ideas of gender equality. Instead the response of Günther Verheugen, the Commissioner with responsibility for the Enlargement process, consisted of an uncompromising attack on the proposal which focused on the need to separate religious from legal norms. The Commissioner described the proposal to criminalize adultery as 'a joke' and that he '[could] not understand how a measure like this could be considered at such a time'. While stating that he was not 'defending adultery', Verheugen went on to note that it was important that 'Turkey should not give the impression . . . that it is introducing Islamic elements into its legal system while engaged in a great project such as the EU'.[34] The Commissioner further characterized such a move as completely out of step with Europe and as unacceptable to the EU.[35]

According to Commissioner Verheugen therefore, the feature of the proposed changed which was most unacceptable to the EU was not the repression of adultery. After all, the EU has very limited competence in this area and the Commissioner made it clear that he was 'not defending adultery'. What was out of step with European values and inconsistent with membership of the EU was to attempt to introduce 'Islamic elements' into the legal system. Faced with this reaction from the Commission and certain Member States, the proposal was withdrawn within a matter of days.[36]

D. A Difference in Approach?

Therefore, the manner in which the Copenhagen Criteria have been interpreted by the institutions of the EU means that a measure of respect for a private zone of autonomy within which the individual citizen is free to define his or her own sexual existence without being forced to adhere to religious norms, is seen as a fundamental requirement of accession to the Union. As the EU's own practice of consulting extensively with religious organizations shows, this does not require a complete removal of religious influence from the law-making process. However, such influence has to be constrained by the principles of personal autonomy, political pluralism and the respect for privacy rights. Accordingly, while religious bodies are welcome to contribute to the law-making process, religious dogma cannot determine the content of such laws, particularly when the demands of such dogma are inconsistent with the autonomy of the individual to determine

---

[33] See 'Verheugen Warns Turkey on Adultery Law' *Deutsche Welle*, 10 September 2004, available online at: <http://dw-world.de/dw/article/0,1564,1324102,00.html>.

[34] Ibid.

[35] See 'EU Warns Turkey Not to Recriminalize Adultery' D Wes Rist, 8 March 2005, available online at: <http://jurist.law.pitt.edu/paperchase/2005/03/eu-warns-turkey-not-to-recriminalize.php>.

[36] n 32 above.

his or her identity and private conduct. As the case studies show, these principles were applied to both Romania and Turkey as part of the Enlargement process.[37]

However, there remain striking differences in the approaches adopted by the Commission in dealing with the two countries. In both cases religious elements in societies with a single dominant religion (Sunni Islam and Orthodox Christianity respectively) had succeeded in pressuring the Government into attempting to enact (or to retain) legislation giving religiously-influenced norms, which condemned certain private sexual behaviour, the force of law. In the Romanian case, the EU viewed this solely as a question of the human right of gays and lesbians to be left alone by the State. In the Turkish case however, the proposal was seen not as a human rights issue or even an issue of privacy, but was instead framed as an issue of the general relationship between religion and the law. While the problem with the Romanian law was that it violated gay and lesbian human rights, the problem with the Turkish legislation was, according to the Commission, that it appeared to be 'introducing Islamic elements into its legal system'. Despite the leading role played by the Orthodox Church in the campaign to retain Article 200, Romania was never warned against introducing 'Orthodox elements' into its legal system and the systemic relationship between the Orthodox Church and the Romanian State was assumed to by the EU to be in accordance with acceptable norms. The attempt to criminalize adultery, on the other hand, was viewed as emblematic of a wider potentially systemic problem in the relationship between the law and religion in the Turkish State. A right to be free from religiously inspired rules was upheld for 'sinners' in both Romania and Turkey to be sure, but the manner in which EU framed its demands that this right be respected differed markedly.

E. Sexual Orientation Discrimination, A European Norm?

The difference in approach may of course be explained by the fact that homosexuality had already been the subject of debate within the Union for some years during which time a distinctive EU norm in relation to gay and lesbian rights had emerged. Although the Union's acquisition of substantive powers in relation to sexual orientation discrimination post dated the controversy in relation to Romania,[38] its institutions had since the early 1980s been debating and formulating an approach to the issue of gay and lesbian rights which by 1998 had, in certain respects, become relatively liberal. By 1998, outright criminalization

---

[37] This analysis is further supported by the limited case law in this area. In EFTA Surveillance Authority Decision 336/94 it was held that restrictions imposed by Member States on slot-machines could not be justified solely on religious grounds, while the rulings of the Court of Justice in Case C-260/04 *Commission v Italy* (para 35) and Case C-65/05 *Commission v Greece* make it clear that 'religious factors' can be taken into account by Member States exercising their margin of appreciation in regulating gambling.

[38] See n 15 above.

had been condemned by the European Court of Human Rights, the European Parliament had voiced its support for gay and lesbian equality on several occasions, and the Treaties had been amended so as to enable the Union to legislate in this area. There had been no similar process in relation to the laws regulating adultery which had not been the subject of any debate at EU level nor had adulterers either organized themselves or been recognized as a minority group to the same degree as gays and lesbians. It is therefore arguable that the Union's characterization of the Romanian issue solely in terms of its human rights implications arose from the fact that the Union had already established a common approach on this issue under which discrimination against gays and lesbians was seen as a violation of human rights. This certainly chimes with Commissioner Verheugen's statement in the summer of 2001 that 'equal treatment of gays and lesbians is a basic principle of the European Union'.[39] As Romania was seeking to join a polity which increasingly defines itself as a 'Community of Values', a failure to decriminalize homosexuality could be seen as a failure to adhere to the common value that the Union had established in relation to sexual orientation. An attempt to criminalize adultery did not involve such an established value and was therefore approached in a different manner from that of the criminalization of homosexuality.

However, despite the Commissioner's assertion that equal treatment of homosexuals was 'a basic value of the European Union', in the period in which the Commission was dealing with the issue of Article 200 of the Romanian Penal Code, acceptance of the principle of equal treatment of gays and lesbians in the EU was in fact quite limited. In its 1997 decision in *Grant v South West Trains*,[40] the ECJ specifically ruled that discrimination on grounds of sexual orientation was not prohibited by the Treaty and that gay and lesbian equality was not a fundamental principle of EU law. Indeed at paragraph 31 of the judgment the Court specifically stated:

While the European Parliament, as Ms Grant observes, has indeed declared that it deplores all forms of discrimination based on an individual's sexual orientation, it is nevertheless the case that the Community has not as yet adopted rules providing for such equivalence.

While the Treaty of Amsterdam did provide the Union with competence to legislate in this area, it could only do so on the basis of unanimity and did not do so until late 2000. Even when it did finally act in this area, the EU deferred significantly to religious sensibilities giving religious bodies (including institutions such as healthcare and educational establishments whose purposes were not exclusively religious) scope to continue to discriminate on the basis of sexual orientation in

[39] See International News Report 'Anti-Gay Nations May Not Join European Union' Rex Wockner, 31 July 2001, online at: <http://gaytoday.badpuppy.com/garchive/world/073101wo.htm>.
[40] Case C-249/96 *Grant v South West Trains* [1998] ICR 449, 17 February 1998.

the Employment Directive[41] and allowing Member States not to recognize civil
partnerships between same sex couples in the 2004 Citizenship Directive.[42] A
norm relating to the equality of sexual orientations had not therefore, been definitively embraced by the Union at the time during which it pressured Romania to
decriminalize homosexuality and was, at most, emergent and subject to continuing dispute.

(i) Religion in General or Islam?

A second explanation for the difference of approach outlined above is that the
EU saw, in the attempt by the Turkish authorities to criminalize adultery, something very different from that which they saw in the efforts of Romanian leaders to retain the ban on homosexuality. More specifically, the criminalization of
adultery may have been seen as representative of a wider desire to increase the
influence of religion over the Turkish State to a degree which might threaten the
liberal democratic order. The idea that a failure to maintain religious influence
within certain bounds represents a potential threat to the liberal democratic order
and is inconsistent with European citizenship, is seen in other contexts. As will
be shown below, both the law of the EU and of certain Member States in relation
to migration as well as the case law of the European Court of Human Rights suggest that the according to religious precepts of an overly influential role in public
life represents a threat to the liberal democratic system of government and to the
rights of others to freedom from religion. Furthermore, in both cases the law has
been applied in such a way that suggests that this threat is seen as being present to
a greater degree in Islam as opposed to other religions.

Turkey is, of course, a secular state, however many in Turkey perceive this
secularity to be under threat.[43] The army in particular has intervened on several
occasions to 'defend' the country's secular system from what it sees as the threat
of Islamic movements. The Turkish Government which sought to criminalize
adultery was made up of the AKP or Justice and Development Party. The AKP is
the successor to the Welfare Party (*Refah Partisi*) a party which had been forced
out of office in 1997 by the Turkish military and later banned for threatening the
secular nature of the Turkish Republic.

The AKP's Islamist past has meant that although it now portrays itself as a
moderate conservative party which supports democratic principles, it has been
viewed with extreme suspicion both by Turkey's secular elite and by some EU
Governments. This past may have caused the EU (along with many in Turkey)

---

[41] Council Directive 2000/78/EC of 27 November 2000 establishing a general framework for
equal treatment in employment and occupation, Art 4(2).

[42] Directive of the European Parliament and the Council 2004/58/EC of 29 April 2004 on the
right of citizens of the Union and their family members to move and reside freely within the territory
of the Member States, Arts 2(2)(b) and 3(2)(b).

[43] See for example E Özbudun, *Contemporary Turkish Politics: Challenges to Democratic
Consolidation* (Lynne Rienner Publishers, 2000).

to view the attempt to criminalize adultery as part of a wider strategy aimed at increasing the role of Islam in public life in Turkey and undermining the secular nature of the State. Of course, many current EU Member States are far from officially secular, with official State churches and close institutional and financial links between certain denominations being a prominent feature of the European constitutional landscape. Moreover, explicitly Christian parties are part of governments in several EU States such as Germany, Sweden, and the Netherlands. However, EU law has tended to see in Islam a greater threat to the liberal democratic order than other religions. Seen in this way, Commissioner Verheugen's statement that Turkey could not afford to give the impression that it was 'introducing Islamic elements into its legal system' can be seen as reflecting a view on the part of the EU that an Islamically-influenced legal system might fail to respect the degree of personal autonomy and respect of the right to privacy required by the liberal democratic European order.

The compatibility of Islam with Western liberal democracy has been the subject of much debate in recent years. The role played in Islam by the Sharia with its interventionist and conservative approach to issues of gender and sexuality, has been a prominent aspect of discussion in this area. Those who assert that a degree of incompatibility exists have focused on two main aspects. The first relates to the low level of secularization experienced by largely Muslim societies. In a protracted process beginning with the Enlightenment and Reformation, the major Christian denominations in Europe, either voluntarily or after protracted conflict, have accepted significant limitations on the scope of religious authority in relation to matters of public policy.[44] Lewis argues that this process has not occurred to the same extent in the Muslim majority countries (which also provide many of Europe's immigrants). Such societies are he believes 'still profoundly Muslim, in a way and in a sense that most Christian countries are no longer Christian'.[45] The second (and possibly related) argument asserts that mainstream Islamic theology is incompatible with the secular State and the notions of personal autonomy and distinction between public and private morality underlying the liberal democratic project. Joffé argues that 'representative democracy is seen as alien to Islam'[46] and that 'the holistic nature of normative Islamic society does not accept the premise of the socio-political atomism that is implicit in the democratic and capitalist projects'.[47] Gabriel notes that 'in modern Western societies many matters that are considered as more liable to moral scrutiny and

---

[44] See J Casanova, *Public Religion in the Modern World*, (University of Chicago Press, 1994), at ch 1, especially 21–23 and 37. See also A Ferrari, 'Religions, Secularity and Democracy in Europe: for a New Kelsenian Pact', Jean Monnet Program, NYU School of Law, Paper No 3/05 at: <http://www.jeanmonnetprogram.org/papers/05/050301.html>.

[45] B Lewis, *The Crisis of Islam: Holy War and Unholy Terror* (Phoenix, 2003) at 14.

[46] G Joffé 'Democracy, Islam and the Cult of Modernism', in *Democratization* Vol 4, No 3, Autumn 1997 at 134. Quoted in Van Ham P van Ham, *European Integration and the Postmodern Condition* (Routledge, 2001) at 211.

[47] Ibid.

judgment rather than legal Investigation' but that such matters 'are still within the ambit of law in Islamic societies'.[48] In a similar vein Lewis and Roy argue that 'few [...] practising Muslims are interested in a privatized faith as it is experienced by most Western Europeans and sometimes advanced as a model for Muslims'.[49] All of these views point to a potential incompatibility between Islam, as a faith based on an all-encompassing system of holy law (the Sharia) and the liberal democratic system acceptance of which is a prerequisite for EU membership. Indeed, the influential Muslim theologian Tariq Ramadan has argued that to require European Muslims to adopt the Western 'privatized' approach to religion effectively requires Muslims to 'be Muslim without Islam' and that such an approach is based on 'a widespread suspicion that to be too much a Muslim means not to be really and completely integrated into the Western way of life and its values'.[50] However, the idea that Islam is in some way incompatible with the modern State or liberal democracy is, notwithstanding its high levels of popular support,[51] highly controversial, with many commentators arguing that such views are tainted with orientalism and even racism.[52]

The truth or otherwise of these assertions is not for this work to address. What is important for our purposes is to note that the campaign by the Romanian Orthodox Church to retain legislation criminalizing homosexuality was viewed as an individual instance of interference by the State (albeit largely at the behest of religious authorities) with the privacy rights of a minority group. The attempt by the formerly Islamist governing party of Turkey to enact legislation criminalizing adultery was, on the other hand, seen as representative of a far wider and more serious issue; the maintenance of the more general limitations on Islamic influence over the legal system which were seen as necessary for Turkey to remain eligible

---

[48] T Gabriel, 'Is Islam against the West?', in R Geaves, T Gabriel, Y Haddad, and J Idleman Smith (eds), *Islam and the West Post 9/11* (Ashgate, 2004) at 15.

[49] JS Fetzer and JC Soper, *Muslims and the State in Britain France and Germany* (Cambridge University Press, 2005) at 150 summarizing the arguments made by Lewis in *Islam and the West* (OUP, 1993) at 173–186, and O Roy in *Vers un islam européen* (Editions Esprit, 1999) at 89–103.

[50] T Ramadan, *To Be a European Muslim* (Islamic Foundation, Leicester, 1999) at 184–185

[51] A poll of French citizens done for the newspaper *Le Monde* in November 1989 showed that two thirds of French people had a very negative view of Islam. See S Allievi, 'Relations between Religions', in B Maréchal (ed), *Muslims in the Enlarged Europe: Religion and Society* (Koninlijke Brill NV, 2003) at 323. A 1990 poll showed that 65% of Swedes had a negative view of Islam and 88% considered it to be incompatible with the democratic system (ibid). A Pew Research poll in 2006 interviewed some 14,000 people in 13 countries across the world. European respondents showed very high levels of hostility towards and fear of, Islam. Relations between Muslims and Westerners were seen as 'generally bad' by 70% of Germans, 66% of French people, 61% of Spaniards, and 61% of British people. Clear majorities in Germany, Britain, and Spain also agreed that there was 'a conflict between being a devout Muslim and living in a modern society' (although a large majority of French respondents rejected this view). High percentages of respondents in all countries stated that they considered Muslims to be fanatical (Spain 83%, Germany 78%, France 50%, and Britain 48%) (See 'The Great Divide: How Westerners and Muslims View Each Other' *Pew Research Foundation*, released 22 June 2006, available online at: <http://pewglobal.org/reports/display.php?ReportID=253>).

[52] See R Geaves, 'Who Defines Moderate Islam "post" September 11?', in R Geaves, T Gabriel, Y Haddad, and J Idleman Smith (eds), *Islam and the West Post 9/11* (Ashgate, 2004) at 66.

for EU membership (the introduction of 'Islamic elements' into the Turkish legal system being seen by the Commission as *ipso facto* inconsistent with its desire to join the Union). This objection to 'Islamic elements' contrasts strikingly with the acceptance by the Union of the specific invocation of Christian influence in the constitutions of EU Member States such as Ireland, Germany, and Spain whose constitutions, to varying degrees name the Christian God as a source of fundamental values or authority. Indeed the Government of the German State of Baden-Württemberg justified the retention of crucifixes in State schools, despite a ban on the Muslim headscarf on the grounds that human rights, democracy, and German constitutional values derive from Christian norms.[53] If anything, the difference in treatment has become even clearer in more recent times. In May 2007, Enlargement Commissioner Olli Rehn, while discussing Turkish membership in the European Parliament, stated that 'if a country wants to become a member of the EU, it needs to respect the principle of democratic secularism, part of our Copenhagen Criteria' thus identifying secularism as a part of the Criteria for the first time.[54] The Commissioner's statement was supported by Dr Hannes Swoboda MEP, a Vice-President of the Party of European Socialists, despite his acknowledgement that there was no common approach to secularism amongst existing Member States and that the Union had not stressed secularism in previous Enlargements.[55] Thus the approach of the EU to these issues seems, at least in part, to be influenced by notions of a potential incompatibility between Islam and the values of liberal democracy which view Islamic influence over the legal system as more threatening to the European public order than Christian influence.

(ii) *The European Convention on Human Rights, Islam, and Militant Democracy*

The perception that Islam and the role of Sharia therein are inconsistent with the notions of personal autonomy, privacy, and pluralism which underlie the European public order is also to be seen in several of the decisions of the European Court of Human Rights whose decisions, while not part of EU law, are very influential in determining the scope the Union's human rights obligations.[56] Most notably, in the case of *Refah Partisi and Others v Turkey*[57] the Grand Chamber of the Strasbourg court upheld the dissolution of the predecessor of Erdogan's AKP

---

[53] J Klausen, *The Islamic Challenge: Politics and Religion in Western Europe*, (OUP, 2005) at 177. Irish abortion law is also arguably heavily influenced by Catholic teaching in this matter.

[54] Olli Rehn, European Commissioner for Enlargement, Open Debate on Enlargement, European Parliament Foreign Affairs Committee, Brussels, 7 May 2007, Reference SPEECH/07/287, 7 May 2007, available online at: <http://europa.eu/rapid/pressReleasesAction.do?reference=SPEECH/07/287&format=HTML&aged=0&language=EN&guiLanguage=en>.

[55] See 'Democratic Secularism is a Copenhagen Criterion for Turkey', *Turkish Daily News*, 10 May 2007, available online at: <http://www.turkishdailynews.com.tr/article.php?enewsid=72817>.

[56] See Case C-540/03 *Parliament v Council* [2006] ECR I-05769.

[57] *Refah Partisi and Others v Turkey* (2003) 37 EHRR 1.

by the Turkish Constitutional Court on the grounds that it was a 'centre of activities contrary to the principle of secularism'.[58] The European Court's judgment reflected a profound fear of the political nature of Islam and made, in debates in which euphemism normally plays such a dominant role, strikingly clear pronouncements in relation to the role of Sharia and Muslim values in European political life.

In 1995, the *Refah Partisi* won the largest number of votes (22%) in the Turkish general election. It subsequently entered into a coalition government with another party and its leader became prime minister. In May 1997 the Principal State Counsel at the Court of Cassation brought proceedings in the Turkish Constitutional Court to dissolve Refah, on the grounds that it was '*a centre of activities against the principle of secularism*'. The application cited acts and speeches by leaders and members of the party which were alleged to show that the party aimed to introduce Sharia law and a theocratic regime both of which were said to be incompatible with a democratic society.[59]

Refah applied to the European Commission on Human Rights in May 1998. In July 2001, the Chamber of the Court held by four votes to three that there had been no violation of Article 11 of the Convention (which protects the right of freedom of association) and (unanimously) that no separate claim arose under Articles 9, 10, 14, 17, or 18.[60] Refah's lawyers appealed this decision to the Grand Chamber of the Court which unanimously held that the actions and speeches which formed the basis of the decision of the Turkish Court showed the party to have a long-term aim of setting up a regime based on Sharia. It further found that such a system would be incompatible with the democratic values of the Convention and that the opportunities which Refah had to put such policies into practice meant that its dissolution could be considered to have met a 'pressing social need' and to have been within the restricted margin of appreciation afforded to Contracting States in this area.

The degree to which the Court viewed an Islamist political orientation as threatening to the European political order is shown by the fact that on the three previous occasions on which the Strasbourg institutions had been called upon to rule on the compatibility of the decision by the Turkish authorities to dissolve a political party (all non-religious parties), it found a violation of the Convention in each case.[61] Furthermore, it noted that the dissolution of a political party was

---

[58] Ibid, para 12.

[59] See the summary of the facts of the case available at the Court's website at: <http://www.echr.coe.int/Eng/Press/2003/feb/RefahPartisiGCjudgmenteng.htm>.

[60] Ibid.

[61] See C Moe, 'Refah Partisi and Others v Turkey' *The International Journal of Not-for-Profit Law*, Vol 6 Issue 1, September 2003, available online at: <http://www.icnl.org/jounral/vol6iss1/rel_moeprint.htm>. The cases in question are: *United Communist Party of Turkey and Others v Turkey* (133/1996/752/951), 30 January 1998; *Socialist Party and Others v Turkey* (20/1997/804/1007), 25 May 1998; *Freedom and Democracy Party (ÖZDEP) v Turkey* (Application no 23885/94), 8 December 1999.

'a drastic measure' and that such severe measures could be used 'only in the most serious cases'.[62] The Court noted that democracy was the 'only political model contemplated by the Convention and, accordingly, the only one compatible with it'.[63] It also appears to endorse the Rawlsian model of church–State relations in stating that it had 'frequently emphasized the State's role as the neutral and impartial organizer of the exercise of various religions' and characterizing the adoption of such a role as a *'duty'*.[64] Recalling previous decisions in which it had upheld limitations on the right to wear an Islamic headscarf in certain contexts[65] the Court declared that in the Turkish context:

the Convention institutions have expressed the view that the principle of secularism is certainly one of the fundamental principles of the State which are in harmony with the rule of law and respect for human rights and democracy. An attitude which fails to respect that principle will not necessarily be accepted as being covered by the freedom to manifest one's religion.[66]

Accordingly, the political order upheld by the Convention may require religions to adapt and submit to secular government in order to be covered by the protection provided to religion under the Convention system. The Convention instruments may therefore refuse even to recognize as religious (for the purposes of the protection of Article 9), a movement which, like some interpretations of Islam, does not recognize the legitimacy (and supremacy within its sphere) of the secular State. In taking such an approach the Court seems to adopt a singularly 'Western' view of religion. As Esposito points out, the notion of religion as a system of personal beliefs as opposed to a comprehensive phenomenon 'integral to politics and society' is both 'modern and Western in origins'.[67] Moreover, he argues that such a view of religion causes secularist Westerners to view religions which do not adhere to such an approach, as 'incomprehensible, irrational, extremist, threatening'.[68]

The Court went on to declare explicitly its belief in the incompatibility of Sharia with democracy and human rights and in particular those parts of Islamic law dealing with the status of women. In paragraph 123 of the judgment it stated that it:

considers that sharia, which faithfully reflects the dogmas and divine rules laid down by religion, is stable and invariable. Principles such as pluralism in the political sphere or the constant evolution of public freedoms have no place in it. [...] It is difficult to declare one's respect for democracy and human rights while at the same time supporting a regime

---

[62] Case C-540/03 *Parliament v Council* [2006] ECR I-05769, para 133.
[63] Ibid, at para 86.   [64] Ibid, at para 91.
[65] *Dahlab v Switzerland*, Application no 42393/98, judgment of 15 February 2001, and *Yanasik v Turkey*, Application no 14254/89, Commission decision of 6 January 1993, DR 74.
[66] Case C-540/03 *Parliament v Council* [2006] ECR I-05769, para 93.
[67] J Esposito, *The Islamic Threat: Myth or Reality* (OUP, 2002) at 199.
[68] Ibid, at 198.

based on sharia, which clearly diverges from Convention values, particularly with regard to its criminal law and criminal procedure, its rules on the legal status of women and the way it intervenes in all spheres of private and public life in accordance with religious precepts. In the Court's view, a political party whose actions seem to be aimed at introducing sharia in a State party to the Convention can hardly be regarded as an association complying with the democratic ideal that underlies the whole of the Convention.[69]

The Court further endorsed its essentially 'Western' definition of religion and its view of limitations on the public role thereof as a necessary part of the European public order stating that 'freedom of religion, including the freedom to manifest one's religion by worship and observance, is primarily a matter of individual conscience,' and that 'the sphere of individual conscience is quite different from the field of private law'.[70]

The degree to which Islamic religious law is identified as incompatible with the European public order envisioned by the Convention is striking. While elements of the Court's reasoning could be applied to religion in general, it is nevertheless clear that the danger to the democratic human rights based order protected by the Convention was seen by the Court as coming from Islam. The judgment specifically problematizes Sharia and notes specific elements of Islamic law which its sees as incompatible with the ideals of the Convention.[71] In particular the judgment highlights the manner in which it believe Sharia violates the key Convention norms of privacy and personal autonomy ('it intervenes in all spheres of private and public life in accordance with religious precepts') and pluralism ('Principles such as pluralism in the political sphere have no place in it').[72]

Not only was Sharia considered to be incompatible with European values, as Boyle points out the Refah party was dissolved not for actual attempts to introduce Islamic law 'but rather because of what it might do, should it, at some point in the future, become the outright party in power'.[73] The threat posed by a party which was thought to harbour concealed desires to introduce Islamic Law was therefore considered by the Court to be such that the 'drastic' measure of dissolving a political party which had won a plurality of votes in the most recent election was justified. In upholding the dissolution of a political party which had recently won a fair and free election on the grounds that its Islamic ideology represented

[69] n 57 above, para 123.

[70] Ibid, at para 128.

[71] While explicitly Christian political parties in existing Member States may, due to the influence of their religious texts, have an similarly conservative approach to sexual morality, a desire to introduce biblical sexual morality into the secular law has not been attributed to them by European institutions.

[72] Such an all-encompassing nature which is also clearly inconsistent with the recognition of a zone of freedom from religion which the EU required of both Romania and Turkey. The Court also noted at paragraph 125 that Turkey had previously experienced 'an Islamic theocratic regime' during the Ottoman period.

[73] K Boyle, 'Human Rights, Religion and Democracy: The Refah Party Case' Essex Human Rights Review, Vol 1 No 1.

a threat to the democratic order, the Court of Human Rights not only appeared to embrace the highly controversial notion of 'militant democracy'[74] but also appeared to give implicit credence to the notion of the existence of a degree of incompatibility between political religion in general, political Islam in particular, and the liberal democratic system on which the Council of Europe is based. The views of the Court of Human Rights on these questions have the potential to influence the approach of EU institutions to these matters to a significant degree.[75] Furthermore, the Strasbourg Court's approach in this area is strikingly similar to the approach adopted by the EU to the adultery issue where the legislation in question was viewed as being representative of broader but concealed desires to introduce 'Islamic elements' into the Turkish legal system.

The notion that EU law perceives Islam to be potentially threatening towards both the notion of privacy and personal autonomy as well as the liberal democratic order more generally does not rely merely on extrapolation from the approach of the institutions of the Council of Europe. It is also to be seen in developments in the law of migration both of the Union itself of individual EU Member States which are the subject of the second set of case studies in this chapter.

III. Migration, Integration, and the EU

This section will assess the development of the law of the EU governing migration and the rights of long-term residents from non-EU countries. It will show how the EU law in these areas increasingly demands explicit reassurances from individual migrants that they are personally committed to liberal democratic values. It will then examine similar developments in the law governing citizenship and the integration of migrants at Member State level (with particular emphasis on developments in the Netherlands and Germany) in order to show how emerging trends at this level have influenced and been facilitated by the Union's law in this area.

In recent years, the question of the integration of immigrant communities has been particularly prominent in European politics. Much of this concern has centred on a perceived incompatibility between what are seen as the liberal democratic values of Europe societies and the more intensely religious and conservative values adhered to by some Muslim immigrant communities. Kofeman has noted that the increased diversity of migration to Europe has led European States to create more complex systems which differentiate between migrants on

---

[74] See for instance: P Macklem, 'Militant Democracy, Legal Pluralism and the paradox of Self-determination' International Journal of Constitutional Law (2006) 4(3), 488–516, P Harvey, 'Militant Democracy and the European Convention on Human Rights' ELR (2004) 29(3), 407–420, M Kocak and E Orucu, 'Dissolution of Political Parties in the Name of Democracy: Cases from Turkey and the European Court of Human Rights' European Public Law (2003) 9(3), 399–423.

[75] See 'Democratic Secularism is a Copenhagen Criterion for Turkey', *Turkish Daily News*, 10 May 2007, available online at: <http://www.turkishdailynews.com.tr/article.php?enewsid=72817>. See also Case 540/03 *Parliament v Council* [2006] ECR I-05769.

the basis of their mode of entry and legal status and which grant differential access to civil, economic, and social rights on this basis.[76] This section argues in addition to distinguishing between migrants on the basis of mode of entry and legal status, the migration law of both the EU and several Member States has begun to differentiate between migrants on the basis of their adherence to certain values, with those who fail to hold certain 'European' values being disfavoured in relation to the granting of citizenship and residence rights. Furthermore, just as the Commission sought a wider and more exacting standard of a-religiosity from Muslim Turkey than from Christian Romania, the migration laws of Member States and the EU have been applied to a greater degree to Muslim than non-Muslim immigrants.

This section further argues that one of the key 'European' values in question is the acceptance of limitations on the public role of religion and of the legitimacy of a zone of inidividual freedom from religion and its prescriptive norms. It suggests that just as the EU saw a threat to 'European norms' in the attempt by the Turkish Government to criminalize adultery, EU migration and integration law, having been influenced by emerging trends at Member State level, sees the failure of *individual* immigrants to adhere to such norms (particularly in relation to gender and sexuality where the views of devout Muslims diverge most notably from those of indigenous Europeans), as a threat to personal autonomy, to the liberal democratic order, and to the rights of others. Under this view, the holding of private views becomes a matter of concern for the State which justifies the penalization of the holding of such beliefs through withholding benefits such as citizenship or residence rights. Thus, in order to protect the privacy rights of personal autonomy of individual citizens, the Union either interferes with, or facilitates efforts by individual Member States to interfere with, the private views and conduct of individual (generally Muslim) immigrants. This making of 'windows into men's souls' problematizes not merely Islam, but individual Muslims who are required to demonstrate a personal commitment to certain ideas and whose private views and behaviour become public matters. Like the European Court of Human Rights' embrace of the notion of 'militant democracy' such an approach has the potential to undermine, to a degree, the private/public distinction which such laws are intended to protect.

A. The Union's 'Basic Principles on Integration'

In recent times both migration policy statements and substantive Community legislation in this area have increasingly emphasized the need for migrants to adopt 'European values' and have viewed a failure to do so as a threat to European societies. Although less explicit than the measures adopted in the Netherlands

---

[76] E Kofmann, 'Contemporary European Migrations: Civic Stratification and Citizenship' (2002) 21 Political Geography 1035.

and parts of Germany (which will be discussed below), the output of Community institutions has nevertheless, in common with the emerging law in these Member States, clearly seen a failure to restrict the public role of religious principles (particularly in relation to gender and sexuality) as a potentially threatening phenomenon which can be the subject of regulation in the interests of disempowered groups and the development of European society as a whole.

In 2003 the Commission began to monitor the integration policies of Member States through its 'Synthesis Report on National Integration Policies'.[77] The European Council of June 2003 added to this development by stressing the need for the 'issue of the smooth integration of legal migrants into EU societies [to be] further examined and enhanced'.[78] The conclusions also stated that:

> integration policies should be understood as a continuous, two-way process based on mutual rights and corresponding obligations of legally residing third-country nationals and the host societies.[79]

However, the later development of this principle of mutuality indicates that dilution of the principle of freedom from religion is not what the Union had in mind in endorsing such mutuality. The conclusions of the European Council held at Brussels on the 4 and 5 November 2004 called for the establishment of 'the common basic principles underlying a coherent European framework on integration' which were to 'form the foundation for future initiatives in the EU'.[80] It then set out a list of basic minimum elements of such principles. This basic minimum restated the conclusion of the Thessaloniki Council that integration was 'a continuous, two-way process' and stressed 'frequent interaction and intercultural dialogue'.[81] However, it supplemented these rather multicultural principles with an assertion that integration also 'implies respect for the basic values of the EU and fundamental human rights'.[82] The delineation of the precise relationship between these potentially conflicting principles was left for the Justice and Home Affairs Council.

The Justice and Home Affairs Council met later the same month and, in a meeting chaired by Dutch Immigration Minister Rita Verdonk, agreed on the content of the 'Common Basic Principles for Immigrant Integration in the European Union'.[83] The principles noted that 'the precise integration measures a society chooses to implement should be determined by individual Member States' but also stated the Union's interest in the issue, noting that 'The failure of an individual Member State to develop and implement a successful integration policy can have in different ways adverse implications for other Member States and the

---

[77] '2003 Synthesis Report on National Integration Policies' Annex 1 to 'Communication on Immigration, Integration and Employment' COM (2003) 336 Final, p 44 *et seq.* (section 2.6).

[78] Council of the European Union, Thessaloniki European Council, 19 and 20 June 2003, Presidency Conclusions 11638/03 POLGEN 55, at para 9.

[79] Ibid.   [80] Ibid.   [81] Ibid.   [82] Ibid.

[83] See Press Release, 2618th Council Meeting, Justice and Home Affairs, Brussels, 19 November 2004, 14615/04 (Presse 321).

European Union.'[84] In a theme that would become more explicit in the principles themselves, it stated that such failure 'can have impact [sic] on the economy and the participation at [sic] the labour market, it can undermine respect for human rights [...] and it can breed alienation and tensions within society'.[85] The invocation of the State interest in the promotion of respect for human rights as a relevant factor in relation to immigrant integration is particularly relevant as this interest provides the basis for the interference with the religious beliefs and cultural practices of individual immigrants which the principles on integration authorize.

The principles themselves clearly endorse a model of immigrant integration under which the religious beliefs of immigrants, in so far as they may affect the freedom from religion of others or the evolution of society in undesirable directions, are seen as a legitimate subject of State regulation. The first principle restates the conclusion of the Thessaloniki and Brussels Council that 'Integration is a dynamic, two-way process of mutual accommodation by all immigrants and residents of Member States.'[86] However the explanation provided by the Council for this principle makes it clear that what is envisaged is not a process of mutual transformation of political, legal, and cultural values. The explanation states that:

the integration process involves adaptation by immigrants, both men and women, who all have rights and responsibilities in relation to their new country of residence. It also involves the receiving society, which should create the opportunities for the immigrants' full economic, social, cultural and political participation.[87]

Therefore, integration is seen as a process of adaptation on the part of immigrants coupled with facilitation on the part of the native population. Native populations are required to facilitate the participation of immigrants in their societies but are not required to adapt their own values or culture. Immigrants, on the other hand, are under an obligation to engage in a process of 'adaptation ... in relation to their new country of residence.'[88]

The second principle makes this point even more clearly. It states that 'Integration implies a respect for the basic values of the European Union.'[89] The explanation states that:

Everybody resident in the EU must adapt and adhere closely to the basic values of the European Union as well as to Member State laws. The provisions and values enshrined in European Treaties serve as both baseline and compass, as they are common to the Member States.[90]

The adherence to the values of the EU is therefore categorized as an individual duty to which residents must adapt if necessary. The explanation goes on to assert that:

Member States are responsible for actively assuring that all residents, including immigrants, understand, respect, benefit from and are protected on an equal basis by the full

---

[84] Ibid, at 16.   [85] Ibid.   [86] Ibid, at 19.   [87] Ibid.
[88] Ibid.   [89] Ibid.   [90] Ibid.

scope of values, rights, responsibilities, and privileges established by the EU and Member State laws. Views and opinions that are not compatible with such basic values might hinder the successful integration of immigrants into their new host society and might adversely influence society as a whole.[91]

There are a number of important features of this principle. First, while the Member States are required to ensure that all residents (and not just immigrants) understand and respect the Union's basic values, a failure to adhere to these values on the part of immigrants is seen as more serious on the basis that such a failure will 'hinder their integration into their new host society' and 'might adversely influence society as a whole'. Adherence to the Union's basic values is seen under these principles as an important part of the society which the Union and its Member States are trying to build. More importantly, the principles make it clear that it is the holding of 'views and opinions that are not compatible with such basic values' which constitutes the threat to immigrant integration and the construction of the kind of society desired by the Union and its Member States. The mere holding of such views therefore generates a sufficient State interest to justify regulation by the law of the Member State or the Union. This approach clearly chimes with the approach of the Governments of the Netherlands and certain German States outlined below which sees in the ongoing adherence to religiously-influenced conservative attitudes to sexuality and gender by certain immigrant communities, a threat to the continued acceptance of key values. The idea that the promotion of certain values is an important goal of the State is also seen in other principles. Principle 5 notes the importance of education to immigrant integration and states that:

Transferring knowledge about the role and working of societal institutions and regulations and transmitting the norms and values that form the binding element in the functioning of society are also a crucial goal of the educational system.[92]

Having defined individual adherence to certain views, opinions, and values as an important goal for the State and as a potential site of legal regulation, the crucial question becomes how far the duty to accept such values should prevail over the rights of migrants to cultural and religious freedom. Principle 8 has a definite answer. It states that:

The practice of diverse cultures and religions is guaranteed under the Charter of Fundamental Rights and must be safeguarded, unless practices conflict with other inviolable European rights or with national law.[93]

The requirement of respect for diverse religions and culture is therefore specifically subordinated to the need to protect 'other inviolable European rights' or 'national law'. This notable rejection of multiculturalism's preference for group rights over individual rights and its aversion to the imposition of host society standards

---

[91] Ibid.   [92] Ibid, at 21.   [93] Ibid, at 23.

on migrant communities is made even more explicit in the accompanying explanation which states:

Member States [...] have a responsibility to ensure that cultural and religious practices do not prevent individual migrants from exercising other fundamental rights or from participating in the host society. This is particularly important as it pertains to the rights and equality of women, the rights and interests of children, and the freedom to practice or not to practice a particular religion.[94]

The explanation also expresses a preference for the use of non-coercive measures as a means of 'addressing issues relating to unacceptable cultural and religious practices that clash with fundamental rights' but goes on to state that 'however, if necessary according to the law, legal coercive measures can also be needed.'[95] The Union's policy framework for the integration of immigrants therefore, specifically subordinates the religious autonomy of individual migrants to the need to protect European basic values and the fundamental rights of others. While not naming any religion in particular, the framework does deliberately emphasize issues such as the equality of men and women which have been prominent in debates around the practice of Islam in Europe.[96]

B. The Refugee, Long-Term Residents, and Family Reunification Directives

Although the basic principles are not binding, the ideas underpinning them are clearly visible in the 'hard law' enacted by the EU in this area. Indeed, the principles themselves are specifically referred to in the preamble to the Directive establishing minimum standards for the granting of refugee status which anticipates the establishment of such principles in paragraph 36 which states that:

The implementation of the Directive should be evaluated at regular intervals, taking into consideration in particular [...], the development of common basic principles for integration.'[97]

---

[94] Ibid.   [95] Ibid.

[96] This decisively non-multicultural approach and the importance of the idea of limitations on the public role of religion in this area have been further underlined by the statements of Commissioner Fratini in relation to the controversy which erupted in relation to the publication of cartoons by the Danish newspaper *Jyllands Posten* which were perceived as being insulting towards the prophet Muhammed by many Muslims. While recognizing that '*it is important to respect sensitivities*' the Commissioner went on to state: '*Equally, we have reaffirmed that our European society is based on the respect for the individual person's life and freedom, equality of rights between men and women, freedom of speech and a clear distinction between politics and religion. We have said clearly and loudly that freedom of expression and freedom of religion are part of Europe's values and traditions, and that they are not negotiable*' (emphasis added). See the interview with Commissioner Fini in Equal Voices Issue 18 June 2006 published by the European Monitoring Centre on Racism and Xenophobia (EUMC). Available online at: <http://eumc.eu.int/eumc/index.php?fuseaction=content.dsp_cat_content&catid=4498115372af1>.

[97] Council Directive 2004/83/EC of 29 April 2004 on minimum standards for the qualification and status of third country nationals or stateless persons as persons who otherwise need international protection and the content of the protection granted [2004] OJ L304/0012–0023 (30.09.2004).

This section will show how in a number of directives relating to the legal status of immigrants, EU law has defined a failure on the part of individual immigrants to indicate acceptance of key liberal democratic values, as a threat to key public policy goals, particularly the right of individuals to live their lives in ways which conflict with religious doctrine. In particular, the directives in question legitimize actions on the part of individual Member States which seek to penalize those immigrants who fail to indicate their acceptance of limitations on the influence of religious principles on law and public policy and their acceptance of liberal democratic values such as pluralism and individual autonomy. Under this approach, the private views of immigrants become a legitimate site of State regulation notwithstanding the Union's commitments to freedom of conscience.

Two directives in particular have been distinctly marked by the decidedly non-multicultural ideas on which the basic principles are based. In September 2003, the Council adopted a Directive on the right to family reunification of third country nationals residing in the EU.[98] The preamble of the Directive states that 'Member States should give effect to the provisions of this Directive without discrimination on the basis of sex, race, colour, [...] religion or beliefs, political or other opinions.'[99]

This would seem to indicate that the religious or political views of those seeking family reunification are not a basis on which such a benefit could be refused. However, the provisions of the Directive to which this non-discrimination principle apply, indicate that such views can indeed be taken into account by Member States in considering applications under this directive. Paragraph 11 of the preamble states that:

the right to family reunification should be exercised in proper compliance with the values and principles recognised by the Member States, in particular with respect to the rights of women and children; such compliance justifies the possible taking of restrictive measures against applications for family reunification of polygamous households.

While the issue of polygamy is singled out, it is nevertheless made clear that the need to comply with 'the values and principles recognised by the Member States' applies across the board.

The general grounds for refusal of family reunification are set out in the directive. Paragraph 14 of the preamble states that:

the person who wishes to be granted family reunification should not constitute a threat to public policy or public security. In this context it has to be noted that the notion of public policy and public security covers also cases in which a third country national belongs to an association which supports terrorism, supports such an association or has extremist aspirations.

---

[98] Council Directive 2003/86/EC of 22 September 2003 on the right of family reunification [2003] OJ L251/12 (3.10.2003).

[99] Ibid, preamble to the Directive at para 5.

Thus it is made clear that merely supporting an organization which supports terrorism or holding certain political views ('extremist aspirations') can be sufficient grounds for the refusal of family reunification. The substantive article of the directive dealing with refusal of applications for family reunification (Article 6) does not specifically mention the holding of extremist opinions as a ground for refusal stating instead that 'Member States may reject an application [...] on grounds of public policy, public security or public health'[100] and that 'when taking the relevant decision, the Member State shall consider, [...], the severity or type of offence against public policy or public security committed by the family member, or the dangers that are emanating from such a person.'

Taken together paragraph 14 of the preamble and the provisions of Article 6 endorse the view that the holding of certain opinions by migrants is seen as a threat to either public security or to public policy both of which are seen as dependent on the continued attachment of citizens to the liberal democratic system. This approach lies at the heart of recent changes in immigration law and policy at Member State level which are outlined below. References to the rights of women in paragraph 11 of the preamble further support the view that such policies are necessary for the protection of certain groups who may be victimized should the 'extremist' worldview of certain migrants increase its influence in the host society.

As well as endorsing the notion of private opinions of migrants as a valid subject for State regulation, the Directive also contains measures designed to facilitate Member State efforts to encourage integration on the part of their migrant populations. Article 4(1) provides that Member States may require children over the age of 12 satisfy 'a condition for integration provided for by existing legislation on the date of implementation of this Directive'. This is supplemented by a more general provision in Article 7(2) which provides that 'Member States may require third country nationals to comply with integration measures, in accordance with national law'—thereby protecting the religion-related measures taken at Member State level outlined below. The compatibility of certain cultural/religious practices with the aim of greater integration is directly addressed in Article 4(5) which states that '[i]n order to ensure better integration and to prevent forced marriages Member States may require the sponsor and his/her spouse to be of a minimum age, and at a maximum 21 years, before the spouse is able to join him/her.'

Articles 4(1), 4(5) and 7(2) were all absent from the Commission's initial draft of the Directive but were included at the behest of certain Member States. Germany and Austria pushed strongly for Articles 4(1) and (along with the Netherlands) 7(2) which were inserted in September 2001[101] and November

---

[100] Ibid, Art 6(1).
[101] See Council document 12022/01 of 24 September 2001, see also K Groenendijk, 'Legal Concepts of Integration in EU Migration Law' European Journal of Migration and Law (2004) Vol 6 No 2 at 119.

2002,[102] respectively. Article 4(5) was inserted during the final stage of negotiations in February 2003 by the Dutch and German Governments.[103] These three Member States have, as will be shown below, taken a leading role in changing domestic immigration law in such a way that Muslim migrants in particular are required to give assurances that they are willing to place limits on the public and political role of their religion as a prerequisite for the granting of residence or citizenship rights.

These provisions have proved highly controversial. As noted above, many of the provisions which permitted the imposition of integration requirements were introduced by the Council at a very late stage in the legislative process. Indeed the insertion of the relevant provisions came so late that Parliamentary debates on the subject had focused almost exclusively on the question of the acquisition of competence in the native languages of Member States by immigrant populations. Furthermore, Article 4(6), which enabled Member States to place an age limit of 15 years on applications for reunification as minor children, was inserted after the consultation of the European Parliament which had advocated a less restrictive approach.[104] In December 2003, the Parliament applied to the Court of Justice to annul certain aspects of the Directive which, it alleged, violated the right to respect for family life and the non-discrimination principle both of which were asserted to form part of the general principles of law protected by the Court.

The Parliament did not seek the annulment of the Directive as a whole, but sought instead to have the provisions allowing for the imposition of integration conditions (along with a further provision allowing Member States up to three years to process applications) struck down and severed from the rest of the Directive which was to remain in force. The specific provisions challenged by the Parliament were:

- The final subparagraph of Article 4(1) enabling Member States to require that a child aged over 12 who arrives independently from the rest of his/her family, meet an integration condition before he or she is granted entry and residence.

- Article 4(6) which allows Member States to request that applications under the Directive for reunification of minor children be submitted before the child reaches the age of 15.

- Article 8 which enables Member States to provide a waiting period of no more than three years between the making of an application and the issuing of a permit.[105]

---

[102] See Council document 14272/02 of 26 November 2002. For an account of the disputes amongst Member States in relation to this measure, see Groenendijk, ibid, at 119–120.

[103] See Council document 6912/03 of 28 February 2003. See also Groenendijk, ibid.

[104] The Rapporteur backed the idea of language integration, but balked at the idea that failure to meet it could result in a refusal of a permit. See the report of Baroness Ludford MEP (COM (2001)127-C5–0250/2001–2001/0074(CNS)) (A5–0436/2001).

[105] Case C-540/03 *Parliament v Council* [2006] ECR I-05769.

The Advocate General advised the Court to dismiss the application on the grounds that it was not possible to sever the impugned provisions without altering the substance of the Directive and thereby trespassing on the territory of the Community legislature. In relation to the merits she found that the failure to consult the Parliament in relation to Article 4(6) rendered its adoption by the Council void[106] (though this point had not been argued by the Parliament's lawyers and was not taken up by the full court). She also found that Article 8 potentially permitted a situation where Member States could violate the fundamental rights of applicants under the Directive by applying a waiting period of up to three years and that it was therefore contrary to Community law.[107] Most importantly for our purposes, the Advocate General upheld paragraph 4(1) as a proportionate means through which Member States can pursue their legitimate desire to 'to integrate immigrants as fully as possible'.[108]

The Grand Chamber of the Court issued its judgment at the end of June 2006.[109] The Court resolved the admissibility question by holding that:

> the fact that the contested provisions of the Directive afford the Member States a certain margin of appreciation and allow them in certain circumstances to apply national legislation derogating from the basic rules imposed by the Directive cannot have the effect of excluding those provisions from review by the Court of their legality as envisaged by Article 230 EC.[110]

and that the issue of severability could only be resolved by consideration of the substance of the case.[111]

As noted above, the European Court of Human Rights has adopted a very particular approach to the issue of Islam and liberal democracy. In its ruling in relation to the Family Reunification Directive, the Court of Justice went out of its way to stress the importance of the role played by the European Convention of Human Rights in the determining the substance of the general principles which form part of EU law and which are upheld by the ECJ.[112]

Thus, the European Convention of Human Rights (ECHR) was recognized by the Court as being of special significance in the determination of the substance of the human rights norms protected in EU law. Furthermore, in its analysis of the provisions of the Directive impugned by the Parliament, the Court showed a striking degree of deference to the decisions of the Strasbourg court. The judgment noted that the preamble to the Directive states that it: 'respects the fundamental rights and observes the principles recognised in particular in Article 8 of the European Convention for the Protection of Human Rights and Fundamental Freedoms and in the Charter of Fundamental Rights of the European Union'.[113]

Although it failed to ask the Court to annul Article 7(2) of the Directive which allows Member States to impose integration conditions on third country

---

106 Ibid, para 59.   107 Ibid, para 105.   108 Ibid, paras 112 and 113.
109 Ibid.   110 Ibid, para 22.   111 Ibid, para 29.
112 Ibid, para 35.   113 Ibid, para 38.

nationals, the Parliament argued that, in relation to the right to family life of
applicants under the Directive:

a condition for integration does not fall within one of the legitimate objectives capable
of justifying interference, as referred to in Article 8(2) if the ECHR, namely, national
security, public safety, the economic well-being of the country, the prevention of health
of morals and the protection of the rights and freedoms of others.[114]

which seemed to indicate a somewhat wider objection to such measures. The Court
explicitly relied on several rulings of the Strasbourg Court in coming to its decision
not to annul the relevant parts of the Directive. In particular it noted the decisions in
Sen v the Netherlands, Gül v Switzerland, and *Ahmut v the Netherlands* from which
it concluded that Article 8 'may create positive obligations inherent in effective
"respect" for family life' and that 'regard must be had to the fair balance that has to
be struck between the competing interests of the individual and of the community
as a whole; [in relation to which] the State enjoys a margin of appreciation'.[115]
    It found that Article 4(1) of the Directive merely partially preserved this mar-
gin of appreciation in circumstances where a child over 12 arrives independently
of the rest of his or her family. Accordingly:

the final subparagraph of Article 4(1) of the Directive cannot be regarded as running
counter to the right to respect for family life. In the context of a directive imposing precise positive obligations on the Member States, it preserves a limited margin of appreciation for those States which is no different from that accorded to them by the European
Court of Human Rights.[116]

The Court specifically endorsed the compatibility of integration conditions with
the ECHR in paragraph 66 where it stated that: '[i]t does not appear that such
a condition is, in itself, contrary to the right to respect for family life set out
in Article 8 of the ECHR... In any event, the necessity for integration may fall
within a number of legitimate objectives referred to in Article 8(2) of the ECHR.'
This does not however indicate that Member State discretion in this area is unfettered as the Court points out in paragraph 70:

The fact that the concept of integration is not defined cannot be interpreted as authorising the Member States to employ that concept in a manner contrary to general principles
of Community law, in particular to fundamental rights. The Member States which wish
to make use of the derogation cannot employ an unspecified concept of integration, but
must apply the condition for integration provided for by their legislation existing on the
date of implementation of the Directive in order to examine the specific situation of a
child over 12 years of age arriving independently from the rest of his or her family.[117]

The Directive does therefore act as a kind of 'stand still' measure with Member
States being unable to introduce further restrictions in this area. However the
stand still provision as the Court made clear, applies only in relation to the

---

[114] Ibid, para 42.   [115] Ibid, para 54.
[116] Ibid, para 62.   [117] Ibid, para 70.

relatively narrow area of the Directive and does not affect the right of individual States to introduce other restrictive measures in the immigration arena in general. Moreover, the idea of compulsory integration, including a duty to adhere to 'European' or national values (which was already a feature of national legislation in certain Member States), was not of itself contrary to Community law.

The Grand Chamber also rejected the Parliament's arguments in relation to Article 4(6) on the basis that an age limit on applications interfered with family life and was discriminatory. The Council argued that encouraging immigrant families to bring their children at a young age in order to facilitate their integration was a legitimate objective under Article 8(2) of the ECHR.[118] The Court held that 'It does not appear that the contested provision infringes the right to respect for family life set out in Article 8 of the ECHR as interpreted by the European Court of Human Rights' and that the fact that Article 5(5) of the Directive requires Member States to take the best interests of the child into account meant that: 'Article 4(6) cannot be regarded as running counter to the fundamental right to respect for family life.'[119]

Article 8 of the Directive was upheld on similar grounds. The Court held that the provision:

preserves a limited margin of appreciation for the Member States by permitting them to make sure that family reunification will take place in favourable conditions, after the sponsor has been residing in the host State for a period sufficiently long for it to be assumed that the family members will settle down well and display a certain level of integration. Accordingly, the fact that a Member State takes those factors into account and the power to defer family reunification for two or, as the case may be, three years do not run counter to the right to respect for family rights set out in particular in Article 8 of the ECHR as interpreted by the European Court of Human Rights.[120]

The judgment is notable in several respects. First, the ECJ endorses integration of immigrant communities as a legitimate objective which can be pursued by States under Article 8(2) of the ECHR. It seems willing to uphold relatively substantial interferences with the Article 8 rights of immigrants in order to enable Member States to pursue the integration policies which they see fit. Moreover, the Court's heavy reliance on the judgments of the Strasbourg Court in order to determine the content of the Union's fundamental rights guarantees may prove important for the future development of the EU law as it relates to the interaction of questions of religion, integration, and the right of States to require adherence to certain religion-related norms from individual immigrants. The primary reason given by the Court for upholding the three impugned provisions of the Directive was that each complied with Article 8 of the ECHR as interpreted by the Strasbourg Court. The ECJ judgment therefore appears to indicate that legislation which appears to comply with the standards set down by

---

[118] Ibid, para 79.   [119] Ibid, para 90.   [120] Ibid, para 98.

the Strasbourg court will, almost inevitably, not be found to be in violation of the fundamental rights norms which form a part of EU law. The judgment in the *Refah Partisi* case indicates that the Court of Human Rights is willing to uphold extensive interferences with ECHR rights in order to defend the liberal democratic order from what it sees as the threat of political Islam. Should EU law follow this approach, interference by Member States with rights to religious liberty and to privacy in the defence of 'European' values is unlikely to fall foul of EU human rights norms.

The approach adopted by the Council in relation to the Family Reunification Directive has been repeated in a second directive which established the rights of third country nationals who are long-term residents of the EU.[121] Like the Family Reunification Directive, the preamble to the Long-term Residents Directive which was adopted in late 2003, contains a paragraph noting that Member States should not discriminate, inter alia, on grounds of religious or political beliefs in giving effect to the Directive.[122] However, it also subordin-ates this duty to a requirement that third country nationals seeking to use the terms of the Directive 'should not constitute a threat to public policy or public security'.[123] Article 5(2) of the Directive specifically states that 'Member States may require third country nationals to comply with integration conditions, in accordance with national law'.

Article 6 provides the grounds on which long-term resident status may be refused. It states that 'Member States may refuse to grant long-term resident sta-tus on grounds of public policy or public security.'[124] Member States therefore, can refuse long-term resident status on the ground that the applicant is a threat to public policy or public security. At the same time, Article 5 makes it clear that applications may be refused if integration conditions are not met. A failure on the part of migrants to integrate is, as a permissible ground for refusal of status under ground 6, therefore seen as a threat to either public policy or public secur-ity. Furthermore, Article 9(3) makes it clear that long-term resident status can be withdrawn from those who constitute a threat to public policy while Article 12 permits the expulsion of such people provided they are shown to constitute 'an actual and sufficiently serious threat to public policy or public security'.[125]

As with family reunification, the requirement contained in Article 5(2) was not present in the Commission's initial draft of the legislation but was inserted by Member States. Indeed, at the insistence of the Austrian and German Governments the phrase 'integration measures' was strengthened to 'integration conditions' in order to emphasize that failure to adhere to such conditions could

---

[121] Council Directive 2003/109/EC of 25 November 2003 concerning the status of third country nationals who are long-term residents [2004] OJ L16/44 (23.1.2004).

[122] Ibid, para 5 of the preamble.

[123] Ibid, para 9. Paragraph 21 also mentions public policy and public security as relevant factors along with public health.

[124] Ibid, Art 6(1).   [125] Ibid, Art 12(1).

potentially result in a refusal of the relevant permit.[126] The Court of Justice's ruling in relation to the Family Reunification Directive make it unlikely that such provisions will be held to fall foul of the Union's human rights commitments.

Therefore, in the light of both the statement of basic principles and the ruling of the ECJ in the family reunification case, the directives passed in this area clearly provide space within EU law for Member States to take active steps to regulate the religious views of individual migrants and to refuse concrete legal benefits to those migrants whose views do not adhere to the fundamental values of the Union or individual Member State. By categorizing a failure on the part of such migrants to adhere to the fundamental values of the Union as a threat to public policy and/or public security, EU legislation provides justification for laws aimed at limiting the degree to which those who adhere to conservative religiously-influenced norms in relation to gender and sexuality can either attempt or even simply desire to enshrine such norms in public policy. As Groenendijk points out, previous migration-related legislation in the Union had focused on integration primarily as something which could be encouraged by enhancing the residence status of immigrants and providing for equal treatment. Regulation 1612/68 for instance (which enshrines free movement of EU citizens) does not allow for any integration tests and restricts language examinations to situations where a knowledge of the language of the relevant Member State is necessary to carry out the relevant employment.[127] However, since 2003, EU law has increasingly adopted an approach under which 'the lack of integration or the assumed unfitness to integrate are grounds for refusal of admission to the country'.[128] The heavy reliance by the Court of Justice on the jurisprudence of the Court of Human Rights in order to determine the limitations that the fundamental rights norms of the EU will place on such a policy substantially lessens the likelihood of large scale interference with this policy on the part of the ECJ.

IV. Developments at Member State Level

A. The Netherlands

The increasing emphasis placed by EU law on integration and adoption of 'European Values' by immigrants has occurred against a background of similar developments at Member State level. In recent years several Member States have radically overhauled their approach to migrant integration and have placed the question of religion at the centre of such changes. The approach of the Netherlands to these issues of religion, migration, and citizenship has been extremely influential. The Netherlands is a country with a libertarian and egalitarian approach to

---

[126] See K Groenendijk, 'Legal Concepts of Integration in EU Migration Law' European Journal of Migration and Law (2004) Vol 6 No 2, at 122–123.
[127] Ibid, at 116.   [128] Ibid, at 113.

questions of sexuality. Prostitution and pornography are tolerated while same sex marriage has been legal since 2001. It also has a Muslim population of over one million (out of a total of approximately 16 million). A series of events occurred in the late 1990s and early 2000s involving the murders of and death threats against figures such as Pim Fortuyn, Theo van Gogh, and Ayaan Hirsi Ali, who were severely critical of Muslim attitudes towards gender, sexuality, and freedom of expression.

These trends and events led to a situation where 'old-style multiculturalism' was as Fukuyama says, 'widely seen as a failure in Holland'.[129] Dutch Government policy changed radically to deal with these concerns. In 2000, 2002, and 2003, legislative changes were introduced which required applicants for naturalization to indicate their 'integration' into Dutch society by means of a series of exams examining knowledge of Dutch society and the Dutch language.[130] Worries that the 'importation' of spouses by Muslim immigrants from their countries of origin was hampering integration efforts led to an increase in the minimum age after which spouses could benefit from family reunification. Tighter rules were introduced providing that religious preachers from abroad had to attend integration courses in which Dutch values would be explained to them. Most strikingly, a new test for immigrants with accompanying explanatory video was introduced in 2006.

The immigration test required immigrants to answer a series of questions about the Netherlands such as its provincial structure and the role of the monarchy. It also requires immigrants to show an awareness of Dutch norms in relation to sexual liberalism and gender equality. Questions in the exam ask how people should react if the see two men kissing or whether hitting women or female circumcision are acceptable practices.[131] Those who wish to sit the exam are required to take extensive language classes and are sent an instructional video which shows footage of topless bathing and a same-sex couple kissing. Those who pass the test will be required to swear allegiance to Holland and its constitution within five years.

The claim that the test is aimed at Muslims is strengthened by the fact that immigrants from non-European 'Western' countries such as the United States, Canada, and Australia are exempt.[132] Muslim groups severely criticized the proposal. The Islamic Human Rights Commission, a British-based organization, described the

---

[129] F Fukuyama 'Europe vs. Radical Islam', in Policy Review, 27 February 2006.

[130] Royal Decree of 14 April 2002, *Staatsblad* 2002, no 197, Royal Decree of 15 March 2003, *Staatsblad* 2003, no 118, Royal Decree on the entry in to force of the Act of 21 December 2000, *Staatsblad* 2000, no 618.

[131] See 'The Civic Integration Exam Abroad', published by Immigratie-en Naturalisatiedienst (the Dutch Immigration and Naturalisation Service), available online at: <http://www.ind.nl/en/Images/bro_inburgering_tcm6–105967.pdf>. In particular, see page 23 which specifies that in addition to EU citizens, American, Canadian, Australian, New Zealand, Japanese, Norwegian, and Swiss nationals are exempt from the test. See also 'Holland Launches the Immigrant Quiz' *The Sunday Times*, 12 March 2006, available online at: <http://www.timesonline.co.uk/article/0,,2081496,00.html>.

[132] 'Dutch Immigration Kit Offers a Revealing View' *The New York Times*, 17 March 2006, available online at: <http://www.iht.com/articles/2006/03/16/news/dutch-5852942.php>.

test as 'Islamophobic' and said that it sent out a message that 'Muslims are not only unwelcome ... but those that are already [in the Netherlands] do not conform to a uniform idea of what should be a citizen' [sic].[133] It also alleged that 'this type of treatment denies primarily Muslims, but in fact also many others, the rights to freedom of religion, belief and expression and political thought.'[134] Dutch theologian Karen Steenbrink of Utrecht University also criticized the video on the grounds that it was 'offensive to Muslims' and noted that topless bathing is in fact 'rarely seen in the Netherlands'.[135] Emecmo, a group which represents Moroccans in the Netherlands described the video as provocation rather than education and said it was clearly intended to stop Muslim immigration.[136] This was denied by the Government. Rita Verdonk, the then immigration minister, asserted that 'It is important to make clear demands of people. They need to subscribe to our European values, respect our laws and learn the language.'[137]

Religion in general and Islam in particular have therefore been prominent elements in the debate around the new Dutch policy in relation to immigration. While part of the overall objective of these measures has been to decrease immigrant numbers (visa fees were also significantly increased), the central role accorded to gender and sexuality in the measures adopted demonstrates that an equally important objective of the policies in question has been to make acceptance of sexual liberalism, gender equality, and the restriction of religious influence on public policy into prerequisites of Dutch citizenship. While it is clearly unable to determine the political and religious views of established citizens, the Dutch Government has made it clear that, in so far as immigrants are concerned, Dutch citizenship is available only to those who are willing to accept these values or who are, at the very least, willing to place limitations on their desires to see religious norms hostile to such values reflected in public policy. The tests clearly make the holding of certain views by individual migrants the subject of a degree of State regulation. The focus on requiring acceptance of gay relationships or the freedom of women to wear revealing clothing indicates that what is being sought is acceptance on the part of individuals of the right of others to engage in conduct thought sinful by many religions (most notably mainstream Islam). A failure to adhere to such libertarian values can result in a denial of the right to live in the Netherlands.

As both the exemption of 'Western' immigrants from the tests and the reactions of Muslim leaders show, these requirements are either aimed at or prove

---

[133] See Arzu Merali of the Islamic Human Rights Commission quoted at: <http://www.islamweb. net/ver2/archive/article.php?lang=E&id=123732>, 6 April 2006.

[134] Ibid. The film however received the backing of Mohammed Sini, chairperson of Islam and Citizenship (a national Muslim organization) who described homosexuality as 'a reality' and who called on immigrants 'to embrace modernity'. See 'Netherlands Issues Immigration Test' *Washington Times*, 16 March 2006, available online at <http://www.washingtontimes.com/world/20060315–100027-7407r_page2.htm>.

[135] Ibid.   [136] See n 129 above.

[137] See 'Europe Raises the Bar for Immigrants' *The Boston Globe*, 22 May 2006, available online at: <http://www.boston.com/news/world/europe/articles/2006/05/22/europe_raises_bar_for_immigrant/>.

most challenging for, Muslim immigrants and represent an implicit but clear assertion by the Dutch Government that adherence to the values of many of the current incarnations of the Islamic religion are incompatible with Dutch citizenship. As Klausen's research has shown, even amongst otherwise moderate Muslims, many do find it difficult to accept the concept of gay rights,[138] yet this is exactly what the Dutch Government now requires them to do on pain of denial of the right to immigrate to the Netherlands. Under this approach, the protection of the personal autonomy and freedom from religion of Dutch gays and lesbians is seen as requiring a degree of interference with the personal autonomy of those who cannot or will not confine their disapproval of homosexuality to the private sphere.

B. Germany

The Dutch approach to these issues has been very influential both on the policies of other Member States and on the approach of EU policy and legislation in this area. In Germany, changes in the nationality laws which came into force on 1 January 2000 loosened the link between blood line and nationality but made 'proof of commitment to the values of the Basic Law'[139] a prerequisite of citizenship. There is at least some evidence that elements of Islamic belief and practice are seen as potentially inconsistent with these values. Klausen has noted how the requirement has been 'a sticking point' for many German Muslims. Moreover, the federal agency for the protection of the Constitution (*Bundesamt für Verfassungsschutz*) has blacklisted Milli Görüs, one of the largest Muslim organizations in Germany, describing it as an 'Islamist' organization whose social work amongst the young is 'disintegrative . . . anti-democratic and anti-Western'.[140]

The CDU Federal minister for the Interior Wolfgang Schäuble praised the new Dutch immigration regulations saying that Germany 'can learn from the Netherlands'.[141] Under German law individual States have power to assess

---

[138] Klausen's survey of European Muslims who were actively engaged in civic life (a group which she acknowledges to be made up of a disproportionate number of moderate and more Western-oriented Muslims) also showed little evidence of an acceptance of sexual liberalism amongst this group. Even interviewees who expressed views which were otherwise liberal were unequivocal in their opposition to greater toleration of homosexuality, with some going as far as suggesting that no secular State had the right to impose toleration of gays and lesbians on Muslims (J Klausen, *The Islamic Challenge: Politics and Religion in Western Europe* (OUP, 2005). (See the interview with young Danish Imam at pages 15 and 16, the opposition of the Muslim Council of Britain to gay rights at page 34, the description of the opposition of 'the voluntarists' to all gay rights at page 92). Hussein attributes some of the decline in support for the Labour Party amongst British Muslims to the Blair Government's support for gay rights legislation (D Hussein, 'The Impact of 9/11 on British Muslim Identity', in R Geaves, T Gabriel, Y Haddad, and J Idleman Smith (eds), *Islam and the West Post 9/11* (Ashgate, 2004) at 120.

[139] Ibid, at 21.   [140] Ibid, at 43.

[141] See 'Testing the Limits of Tolerance' *Deutsche Welle*, 16 March 2006, available online at: <http://www.dw-world.de/dw/article/0,2144,1935900,00.html>.

whether potential citizens truly accept the principles of the Basic Law to which federal law requires them to sign an oath of allegiance. The State of Baden-Württemberg was the first to use these powers to propose a citizenship which examined the compatibility of the values of aspirant citizens with 'German values'. It was quickly followed by the State of Hesse which proposed a similar examination. Tests in both States were again clearly aimed at assessing the degree to which Muslims were willing to separate religious attitudes towards gender and sexuality to the private sphere and to accept liberal notions of individual self-determination. Indeed in Baden-Württemberg the State Government explicitly mentioned Muslims as the targets of the new policy.[142] Questions in the Hesse examination for example, asked immigrants 'A woman should not be allowed to move freely in public or travel unless escorted by a close male relative. What is your standpoint on this?' and 'What possibilities do parents have to influence their sons' or daughters' choice of partner? Which practices are forbidden?'[143] Similarly, the Baden-Württemberg test asked questions relating to forced marriage ('What do you think of the fact that parents forcibly marry off their children?'), homosexuality ('Does the holding of office by open homosexuals disturb you?'), and women's rights ('Do you think that a woman should obey her husband and that he can beat her if she is disobedient?').[144] Both tests also focus on other issues seen as particularly relevant to Muslims. The Hesse test examine attitudes towards Israel ('Explain the term "Israel's right to exist"') and Holocaust denial ('If someone described the Holocaust as a myth or a fairytale, how would you respond?'),[145] while the Baden-Württemberg exam asked whether the September 11th hijackers were 'terrorists or freedom fighters'.[146]

As in the Netherlands, the proposals were severely criticized for interfering with private attitudes and stereotyping Muslims.[147] Volker Beck, a leading member of the Green Party, noted that the anti-gay attitudes of Baden-Württemberg's (Christian) interior minister meant that 'he himself would probably fail the test'.[148] The Federal Parliament took up the issue in February 2006 with the CDU minister for integration policy Maria Böhmer noted how 'the United States gives courses in the constitution, history, culture and values of the country'.[149] In May 2006, the Federal and State Governments worked out a series of guidelines which fall short of introducing a Federal immigration test but which includes an 'integration course' which will focus on 'the German constitution and German

---

[142] See 'New Rules for Muslims in German State Blasted' *Deutsche Welle,* 5 January 2006, available online at: <http://www.dwworld.de/dw/article/0,2144,1840793,00.html>.
[143] See: 'Becoming German: Proposed Hesse Citizenship Test' *Der Spiegel,* 5 September 2005 available online at: <http://service.spiegel.de/cache/international/0,1518,415207,00.html>.
[144] See n 142 above.   [145] Ibid.
[146] See 'Europe Raises Bar for Immigrants' *Boston Globe,* 22 May 2006, available online at: <http://www.boston.com/news/world/europe/articles/2006/05/22/europe_raises_bar_for_immigrants/>.
[147] See 'How To Be a German' *Inter Press Service News Agency,* 31 May 2006, available online at: <http://www.ipsnews.net/news.asp?idnews=33203>.
[148] See n 142 above.   [149] See n 143 above.

values such as gender equality.'[150] Two years later in June 2008, the Federal Government introduced a citizenship test which required applicants to demonstrate knowledge of German legal and political structures. Although the test did not itself address issues of conscience and religion, it left in place the requirement that potential citizens demonstrate a commitment to upholding the values of the German constitution.[151]

C. Other Member States

The French Government has adopted a similar approach. As far back as the year 2000, the Government began to seek assurances from Muslim groups in relation to their commitment to 'French Values'. In January of that year the minister for the interior Jean Paul Chevènment concluded an agreement with Muslim organizations which sought to establish principles on which a structured relationship with State institutions could be based. The French Government proposed that all Muslim groups participating in the exercise would be obliged to sign up to a statement of 'Fundamental Principles'[152] which:

Solemnly confirmed their attachment to the fundamental principles of the French Republic and especially [...] to freedom of thought and religion, to Article 1 of the Constitution which affirms the secular character of the Republic and the respect this principle accords to all beliefs and finally to the provisions of the law of 9 December 1905 concerning the separation of the churches and the State.[153]

Other religious groups were not required to make similar declarations. Chevènment justified this targeting of Islam on the grounds that the country was faced with an 'exceptional' situation and that unlike Christianity, Islam:

has experienced neither the Renaissance nor the Reformation. Certainly, Islam does distinguish between the religious and temporal domains. However, there is no shortage of Muslims to show that this distinction calls for a level of coordination [between the

---

[150] See n 147 above.

[151] See 'Germany to Introduce Controversial New Citizenship Test' *Der Spiegel,* 11 June 2008, available online at: <http://www.spiegel.de/international/germany/0,1518,559021,00.html>.

[152] See S Ferrari, 'The Secularity of the State and the Shaping of Muslim Representative Organizations in Western Europe', in J Cesari and S McLoughlin (eds) *European Muslims and the State* (Ashgate, 2005) at 16–17. The statement was called '*Principes et fondements juridiques régissant les rapports entre les pouvoirs publics et le culte musulman en France*' and is available at: <http://www.pourinfo.ouvaton.org/immigration/dossierchenement/chevenment.htm>. Cesari also notes that: 'Many Muslim representatives considered the request to sign this declaration a demonstration of suspicion'; see J Cesari, 'Islam in France: The Shaping of a Religious Minority', in Y Yazbeck Haddad, *Muslims in the West from Sojourners to Citizens* (OUP, 2002) at 40.

[153] Ferrari, ibid. My own translation. The original French version reads: 'confirment solennellement leur attachement aux principes fondamentaux de la République française et notamment [...] à la liberté de pensée et à la liberté de religion, à l'art. 1 de la constitution affirmant le caractère laïcque de la République et respect par celle-ci de toutes les croyances et enfin aux dispositions de la loi du 9 décembre 1905 concernant la separation des Eglises et de l'Etat'.

two domains] and consequently permanent involvement of religion in the temporal sphere.[154]

Cesari notes that several Muslim organizations considered that this request showed that they were viewed with suspicion by the French authorities.[155]

In 2003, media attention in relation to the question of the role of Islam in French society focused on a law to ban the wearing of 'ostentatious' religious symbols in public schools which was widely seen as targeting the Muslim headscarf. However, in the course of proposing this ban to Parliament, the then Prime Minister, Jean-Pierre Raffarin placed the issue of the headscarf into the wider context of immigration, citizenship, and common values saying 'Integration is a process that presupposes a mutual wish to [integrate], a shift towards certain values, a choice of a way of life, a commitment to a certain view of the world proper for France.'[156] At the same time he announced that the Government would be introducing a 'contract' for immigrants under which learning the French language and 'attachment' to France and French values would be preconditions for the granting of residence permits.[157] The announcement of measures to encourage immigrants to adopt French values at the same time as legislation targeting the headscarf on the basis of its incompatibility with secular values was being introduced, gives the clearest possible indication of the thinking of the French authorities. Along with their colleagues in other EU Member States, they viewed (rightly or wrongly) elements of Islam (and in particular those relating to gender and sexuality), as incompatible with native values. Furthermore, the solution to such incompatibility lay in the adoption by immigrant communities of the secular values whose acceptance was to become a prerequisite of citizenship. Thus in a move which certain commentators have seen as at least partly prompted by the importance accorded to integration in the EU directives on long-term residents and family reunification,[158] France amended its 1945 law to require immigrants to satisfy a condition of 'Republican Integration'.[159]

---

[154] My own translation. The original French version is: 'à la différence du christianisme, n'a connu ni la renaissance ni la Réforme. Certes, l'Islam distingue le domaine religieux et le domaine mondain. Mais il ne manque pas de musulmans pour faire observer que cette distinction appelle une coordination et, par conséquent, une implication permanente du religieux dans le mondain' (from speech of Minister Chevènment of 28 January 2000 available online at: <http://www.pourinfo.ouvaton.org/immigration/dossierchenement/chevenment.htm>. See Ferrari, ibid.

[155] Many Muslim representatives considered the request to sign this declaration a demonstration of suspicion and lack of trust, a quote from J Cesari, 'Islam in France: The Shaping of a Religious Minority', in Y Yazbeck Haddad, *Muslims in the West from Sojourners to Citizens* (OUP, 2002) at 40.

[156] J Klausen, *The Islamic Challenge: Politics and Religion in Western Europe* (OUP, 2005) at 176.

[157] Ibid, at 123–124. These measures were introduced in April 2006.

[158] See S Barbou des Places and H Oger, 'Making the European Migration Regime: Decoding Member States' Legal Strategies' European Journal of Migration and Law (2004) Vol 6 No 4, at 361.

[159] See article 6(3) of Loi no. 2003–1119 du 26 novembre 2003 relative à la maîtrise de l'immigration, au séjour des étrangers en France et à la nationalité, *Journal Officiel* no 274, 27 novembre 2003.

The trend towards incorporating an acceptance of the idea of the right of freedom from religion as part of citizenship can also be seen in other Member States. In 2002 for example, Austria introduced a compulsory 'Integration Agreement' as part of reforms of its Aliens Act,[160] while in 2005 Britain introduced a 'Life in the UK Test' which examines the knowledge of applicants for British citizenship of British values, culture, and history. Included in the tests are questions probing acceptance of principles such as gender equality and importance of tolerance.[161] In late 2006, the then Prime Minister Tony Blair stressed the importance of these principles in a speech in which he criticized a 'new and virulent form of ideology associated with a minority of our Muslim community' and warned migrants that 'our tolerance is part of what makes Britain, Britain. Conform to it; or don't come here.'[162]

These laws have focused on actual or perceived resistance amongst Muslim populations to gender equality and sexual liberalism which have become emblematic of wider fears around the willingness of some Muslims to respect the notion of an individual right to a zone of freedom from religious norms. The response of some European Governments has been to stipulate acceptance of liberal values in these areas as a prerequisite of citizenship in order to test the willingness of Muslim immigrants to renounce any desire to use religious precepts as a basis for public policy (on the basis that it is in relation to areas such as gender and sexuality that religiously inspired views are strongest) and to accept the kind of limitations on public religion which have evolved in Europe over recent centuries. These countries see in the religious views of certain migrants a threat to the liberal a-religious nature of their societies and the rights to privacy and individual self-determination which such societies uphold. Their desire to protect this liberal a-religiosity (which is seen as important both culturally and as a means to protect certain groups such as women and homosexuals), renders the private views of potential citizens and residents a legitimate subject of legal regulation. Therefore, the linking of acceptance of the principle of freedom from religion to the granting of citizenship or residence rights, potentially interferes, in the name of protecting the privacy and autonomy of one set of individuals, with the privacy and autonomy of those who hold views which are condemnatory towards the conduct of others.

These developments have influenced EU law in this area in two ways. First, EU legislation has been careful not to impinge upon the ability of Member States to regulate the religious beliefs of migrants.[163] Second, in both substantive

---

[160] Ibid, at 360.

[161] See: 'Core British Values', BBC News, 17 May 2006, available online at: <http://news.bbc.co.uk/2/hi/programmes/politics_show/4988946.stm>, and also 'New UK Citizenship Testing Starts, BBC News, 1 November 2005 available online at: <http://news.bbc.co.uk/2/hi/uk_news/politics/4391710.stm>.

[162] See: 'Conform to Our Society Says PM', *BBC News*, 8 December 2006, available online at: <http://news.bbc.co.uk/2/hi/uk_news/politics/6219626.stm>.

[163] See the provisions of the Family Reunification and Long-term Residents Directives allowing for the imposition of integration conditions by individual Member States above.

legislation[164] and in its broader statements of policy,[165] the Union has endorsed the view of a failure to adopt certain 'European Values' and to confine one's religious convictions to the private sphere, as a threat to public policy justifying legal intervention. Furthermore, EU law has in turn influenced national laws with certain Member States using what has been termed the 'alibi' of restrictive European legislation in relation to integration matters to introduce such an approach into national law.

V. Conclusion

The EU therefore appears to have decided that certain limitations on religious influence over law and politics are necessary elements of membership of the Union. In particular, it has evidenced a concern that certain kinds of religion might pose a threat to core elements of a liberal democratic public order such as pluralism in the public sphere as well as to the key liberal democratic values of personal autonomy, equality, and respect for privacy. The history of the Crusades and Inquisition as well as more contemporary examples such as law and government in modern day Saudi Arabia and Iran, show that religion can both provide the basis for many serious violations of human rights and exercise a degree of control of the political and personal spheres which is incompatible with liberal democratic values. As the judgment of the Court of Human Rights in *Refah* rightly pointed out, the enactment of 'divine' law as the basis of the legal system is inconsistent with the openness to change and pluralism necessary in the liberal democratic system. As a self-declared 'Community of Values', the EU is entitled and possibly obliged to ensure that those States that seek to join it impose the limitations on religious influence over law and politics necessary for liberal democratic values to thrive and, as shown by its dealings with Romania and Turkey, it has used the Copenhagen Criteria on Enlargement to do so.

In the area of immigration, the approach of the Union has shown similar concerns. It has encouraged Member States to require migrants to the Union to indicate that they accept the primacy of liberal values over the conservative, interventionist, and arguably patriarchal approaches of many religions to issues of gender and sexuality as a prerequisite to the granting of residence rights or citizenship. This approach does involve a significant degree of interference with religious liberty and with the private views of individual migrants. However, in an approach analogous to the 'Militant Democracy' espoused by the Court of Human Rights in *Refah*, the Union has permitted Member States to interfere with private views and individual autonomy in order to secure respect for these principles in relation to issues such as gender and sexuality. Indeed, in the context

---

[164] See discussion of the grounds for refusing status in the Directives above.
[165] See Press Release, 2618th Council Meeting, Justice and Home Affairs, Brussels, 19 November 2004, 14615/04 (Presse 321).

of migration, States regularly select migrants on the basis that they have certain desirable traits (the youthful, highly skilled and those with cultural or ethnic ties to certain States are often granted favourable treatment under immigration laws). It is not therefore, inherently objectionable for EU Member States to select migrants on the basis of commitment to certain basic values.

However, the manner in which the Union has upheld these limitations on religion is deeply problematic. Both in relation to Enlargement and migration EU law and policy has treated Islam as inherently less compatible with liberal democratic norms than the Christian denominations which are more culturally and historically entrenched at Member State level. This attitude is seen both in the different approaches adopted by the Union in its dealings with Romania and Turkey and in the selective application of values tests to Muslim migrants. It is also seen in the wider European (as opposed to EU) context in the judgment of the Court of Human Rights in *Refah* and the requirement imposed on French Muslim groups that they indicate a commitment to the French form of secularism as a condition of the establishment of a structured relationship with the French State. The Union's approach in these areas appears based on the notion that Islam is inherently disposed towards authoritarianism and sexism to a greater degree than other religions. As noted above, many commentators think that this is in fact the case and that Islam is less compatible with Western liberalism than other faiths. However, even if this were true, the Union's method of dealing with such concerns would still be fundamentally flawed. Rather than setting out standards with which all religions must comply, the EU has chosen to assume compatibility between Christianity and the model of liberal democracy to which the Union attached while subjecting Muslims to rigorous examination of their secular bona fides. It may well be that were uniform standards to be applied across the board, Muslims would struggle to a greater degree than adherents of other religions to reconcile themselves with the limitations on religious influence over law and society inherent in the EU's version of liberal democracy. Indeed, given that the contemporary relationship between religion and the State in Europe is to a large degree the result of the accommodation which emerged between the Christian Churches and the European secular State following centuries of conflict, it would be surprising if adherents of mainstream European Christian denominations did not find it easier to reconcile the demands of the liberal democratic State with those of their religion. However, to apply these standards either to Muslims alone, or to Muslims to a greater degree than Christians is to view both religions as monolithic blocs,[166] to deny the individuality of individual believers, and thus to engage in direct discrimination.

[166] Indeed several commentators have noted that rejection of 'live and let live' privatized religion is not restricted to Muslim immigrants by any means, but is in fact prevalent amongst immigrants of many religions. See G Davie 'Religion in Britain: Changing sociological assumptions' Sociology, 34/I: 113–128. She further argues that the difference in attitude to religion of native Europeans and immigrant communities 'has led to persistent and damaging misunderstandings' (ibid). See also

The failure of the Union to apply these limitations on religious influence in a uniform way to various religious denominations is indicative of the contradictions at the heart of the European approach to religion. Europe has developed a very secularized political order in which religious groups exercise less influence than in almost all other areas of the world and where adherence to religious morality in areas such as sexual behaviour has, to a great degree, become a matter for individual decision and not regulation by the State.[167] These limitations on religious influence have emerged out of a centuries-long process of conflict and accommodation between the Christian Churches and European States. This process has been largely incremental and partial and its terms are still contested. In most Member States for example, certain Christian denominations have retained important symbolic, cultural, and institutional roles while many denominations continue to seek to influence the law in areas related to religiously important questions such as abortion, marriage, and sexual morality. This contested and evolutionary settlement is also historically specific to Europe. It has allowed certain religions to retain official roles which far exceed their actual influence and has allowed Churches to retain a certain political role albeit one which is moderated by implicit assumptions about the nature of the relationship between religion and the State (most notably the State's supremacy in the temporal arena). These very features make it ill-suited to deal with the consequences of a more multicultural age in which religions whose attitudes to the role of religion in law and politics have not been shaped by the same experiences of those of mainstream European Christianity play an increasing role in European life.

Europe is entitled to uphold the limitations on religion which are inherent in its liberal democratic and egalitarian system. Certain religions, including Islam, may represent a threat to those values and the Union, as a 'Community of Values', is entitled to require that States who wish to join such a community uphold limitations on religious influence necessary for such values to survive. The adherents of certain religions, such as Islam, may find that the membership of the European political and legal order requires them to adjust to a degree of secularity to which mainstream versions of their faith either object or are unaccustomed. However, the imposition of such standards by means of values tests for migrants or the removal of 'Islamic elements' from the Turkish legal system involves an approach which differs significantly from the evolving, contested, and partial nature of the secularity which characterize Europe's relations with its 'native' Christian denominations. Accordingly, the Union is faced with three choices: it can adopt a multicultural approach and prioritize the religious and cultural freedom of migrants at the expense of its liberal values. This approach however would appear

---

P Norris and R Inglehart, *Sacred and Secular: Religion and Politics Worldwide* (Cambridge University Press, 2004).

[167] See C Crouch, 'The Quiet Continent: Religion and Politics in Europe', in D Marquand and RL Nettler (eds), *Religion and Democracy* (Blackwell Publishers, 2000).

to be unpalatable to European electorates who have given strong support to parties campaigning against just such policies in recent years. It can, as it appears to have been doing to date, apply more secularist standards to newer religions and require their adherents to sign up to the supremacy of liberal values in a range of areas while allowing the adherents of more historically and culturally entrenched religions to accommodate themselves to secularist and liberal principles (in so far as their religions may be incompatible with such principles) in a gradual and incremental fashion and in such a way that the institutional and symbolic role of such religions in the public sphere is retained. This approach however is clearly discriminatory in that it involves the application of standards to the adherents of different religions in a partial and unequal manner. Furthermore, it risks deepening suspicion amongst Muslims that the Union's moves to uphold certain values are merely a smokescreen for a more discriminatory, nativist agenda. A third option involves the upholding of liberal democratic values through requiring explicit acceptance of limitations on religious influence over the public and private spheres from adherents of all religions. Such an approach may indeed prove to be more difficult for adherents of those religions, such as Islam, which did not participate in the historical struggles which established the basic contours of settlement between religion and the State in Europe. However, it would also call into question the privileges retained by certain religions as a result of the partial and incremental nature of the secularization that has occurred in most European countries. Such an approach has been seen in the German State of Berlin where concerns around the wearing of the Muslim headscarf by female civil servants led to a ban on all religious symbols in public buildings.[168] This however would involve a significant shift in the predominant European approach to religion which has to date been characterized in many countries by an attachment to and recognition of the cultural and symbolic role of certain denominations in national life. The EU has to date shown no inclination to do so, indeed at the time of the Amsterdam Treaty it explicitly declared that it would not interfere with the status of churches at national level.[169] Accordingly, the Union's approach to religion is likely to remain one which is notably less restrictive of culturally entrenched religions such as Christianity than 'outsider' religions such as Islam.

---

[168] Germany's former Federal President Johannes Rau warned that banning the headscarf would lead to widespread secularization of German public life. See '*Religionsfreiheit heute—zum Verhältnis von Staat und Religion in Deutschland*', Rede von Bundespräsident Johannes Rau beim Festakt zum 275, Geburtstag von Gotthold Ephraim Lessing in der Herzog-August-Bibliothek zu Wolfenbüttel. wolfenbüttel, 22 January 2004, available online at: <http://www.bundespraesident.de>, and also news report at: <http://news.bbc.co.uk/2/hi/europe/3421937.stm>. This view was echoed by a member of the Bundestag interviewed in Klausen's *The Islamic Challenge* that the presence of large numbers of Muslims in Europe was in fact pushing the continent towards greater secularism and separation of church and State (n 138 above, at 179).
[169] See Declaration 11, annexed to the Treaty of Amsterdam [1997] OJ C340/0308 (10.11.1997).

Commercial Gambling without Frontiers: When the ECJ Throws, the Dice is Loaded

*Dimitrios Doukas and Jack Anderson**

I. Introduction

Almost a decade ago, the European Court of Justice (ECJ) held that the EC Treaty provisions on the free movement of services do not preclude national legislation that reserves to certain prescribed bodies the right to take bets on sporting events.[1] In line with previous jurisprudence, the ECJ's judgment in *Zenatti* was predicated on the (Italian) legislation in question being justified by a socio-political concern regarding the harmful effects of commercial gambling and, concomitantly, that the accompanying restrictions were not disproportionate to that fundamental policy objective. In November 2003, the ECJ was again called upon to consider the compatibility with the Treaty of Italian legislation, which, on pain of criminal sanctions, prohibited the provision of betting services for sporting events without licence.[2] In *Gambelli*, the Court had to examine whether the legislation at issue was not only an obstacle to the freedom to provide cross-border services, but also whether it constituted a restriction on the freedom of establishment. The ECJ held that it was a matter for the national courts to determine whether such legislation was in terms of underlying policy and application, a justified and proportionate measure within the meaning of Articles 43 and 49 of the EC Treaty. Subsequently, the *Corte Suprema di Cassazione* found that the statutory scheme governing sports betting in Italy complied with Community law.[3]

* Dimitrios Doukas and Jack Anderson are Lecturers in Law at the School of Law, Queen's University, Belfast. The authors wish to thank Professor Catherine Barnard (University of Cambridge) for her valuable comments and help, Professor Stephen Weatherill (University of Oxford) for his feedback, and Dr Rita de la Feria (Oxford University Centre for Business Taxation) for her suggestions. The usual disclaimer applies.
[1] Case C-67/98 *Questore di Verona v Diego Zenatti* ('*Zenatti*') [1999] ECR I-7289.
[2] Case C-243/01 *Criminal Proceedings against Piergiorgio Gambelli and Others* ('*Gambelli*') [2003] ECR I-13031.
[3] Corte Suprema di Cassazione (Sezioni Unite Penali), Judgment No 111/04 of 26 April 2004 ('*Gesualdi*'), available online at: <http://www.ictlex.net/index.php/2004/04/26/cass-su-sent-11104/>.

In 2007, the regulation of betting on sporting events in Italy came before the ECJ for a third time.[4] This article critically analyses the *Placanica* case and reviews the issues raised, principally in terms of the impact they might have for domestic, commercial gambling legislation generally throughout the Community. This article contends that, although the ECJ now appears to be of the unequivocal view that the free movement provisions of Articles 43 and 49 of the EC Treaty must be interpreted as precluding a regulatory regime similar to that established in Italian law, careful analysis of the *Placanica* judgment and its aftermath demonstrates that Member States still enjoy significant freedom to restrict, or even prohibit, commercial gambling. The article discusses, on the one hand, the Member States' continuing discretion to enact such regulatory measures and the limits of that discretion—namely, the need to genuinely and consistently serve public interest justifications and comply with the principle of proportionality. On the other hand, it assesses the efficacy of the Court's approach in response to the reality of the rapid expansion of cross-border gambling services within the EU. For the purposes of this article, gambling services denote any service that involves wagering a stake with monetary value in games of chance. Commercial gambling is defined as encompassing profit-driven undertakings, such as casino gaming and sports betting, in their primary and electronic form, as well as semi-private and (national) public lotteries, which have as their underlying objective the promotion of benevolent causes.

This article is structured in four parts. Firstly, the established case law of the ECJ with respect to the manner in which Member States can derogate in matters of commercial gambling from the fundamental freedoms of services and establishment is outlined. Second, the current state of Community law concerning national restrictions on commercial gambling, according to the *Placanica* judgment and its aftermath, is examined. The third section highlights the inadequacy of the current piecemeal approach—usually by way of ECJ preliminary rulings or decisions on infringement actions—with regard to the putative establishment of an internal market in commercial gambling. It also illustrates the continuing fragmentation of the sector manifested in the divergent national regulatory regimes and the transparently inconsistent manner in which such regimes adapt to the limitations set on the Member States' discretion by the Court. Accordingly, it is suggested that a Community harmonization of national laws on commercial gambling would appear to be the more durable approach. The fourth section makes proposals for such a harmonization measure within the contextual technological reality that commercial gambling now operates *sans frontières*.[5]

Subsequently, the Italian Council of State (Consiglio di Stato) expressed itself in the same direction; see Judgments No 5203/2005 of 1 March 2005 and No 5898/2005 of 14 June 2005.

[4] Joined Cases C-338/04, C-359/04, and C-360/04 *Criminal Proceedings against Massimiliano Placanica, Christian Palazzese and Angelo Sorricchio* ('*Placanica*') [2007] ECR I-1891.

[5] The cross-border dimension to commercial gambling does, of course, creep beyond the boundaries of the EU. Note the comments in the Opinion of AG Colomer in *Placanica*, ibid, at [149] and

That final section discusses two basic models of harmonization, with the former being based on mutual recognition, and the latter on the country of origin principle and re-regulation. It is argued that the latter is more likely to effectively overcome the existing fragmentation of the gaming market and, equally, might have the capacity to respond to the conspicuous growth of remote and cross-border gambling activities within the EU.

II. The Dice is Rolled: Existing Case Law and Analysis

In *Schindler*, the ECJ considered the economic nature of the operation of lotteries, and acknowledged them as service provided to the purchasers of lottery tickets who are given the opportunity to participate in a game of chance with the hope of winning.[6] Accordingly, the Court held that the importation of lottery advertisements and tickets into a Member State (in this instance, the UK) with a view to the participation by residents of that State in a lottery operated in another Member State (Germany) fell within the scope of Articles 49–50 of the EC Treaty.[7] It followed that contemporary British legislation (prior to the introduction of the National Lottery in 1993), prohibiting the holding and promotion of lotteries and the sale of lottery tickets, should be regarded as a *prima facie* obstacle to the freedom of cross-border services.[8] In this, the ECJ applied the broad 'obstacles approach' of its *Säger* formula,[9] which encapsulates within the net of Article 49 any measure liable to prohibit or otherwise impede the activities of service providers established and lawfully operating in other Member States.[10] Further, the Court alluded to the fact that, although the British provision applied without distinction, it wholly precluded lottery operators from other Member States from promoting their lotteries and selling their tickets, either directly or through independent agents, in the UK.[11] Nonetheless, the ECJ was prepared to accept that, in view of the peculiar nature of lotteries, the Treaty provisions on the freedom to provide services would not necessarily preclude national legislation, such as the contested one, which barred access to the national market

the judgments of the EFTA Court in Case E-1/06 *EFTA Surveillance Authority v Norway*, 14 March 2007 and Case E-3/06 *Ladbrokes Ltd v the Government of Norway*, 30 May 2007; both available online at: <http://www.eftacourt.lu/>.

[6] Case C-275/92 *Her Majesty's Customs and Excise v Gerhart Schindler and Jörg Schindler* ('*Schindler*') [1994] ECR I-1039, at [25]–[29] and [33].
[7] Ibid, at [22]–[24] and [37].   [8] Ibid, at [45].
[9] Case C-76/90 *Säger v Dennemeyer* ('*Säger*') [1991] ECR I-4221, at [12].
[10] *Schindler*, n 6 above, at [43]. See generally, D Doukas, 'Untying the Market Access Knot: Advertising Restrictions and the Free Movement of Goods and Services' (2006–07) 9 Cambridge Yearbook of European Legal Studies 177–215, at 190, 196–197, and 200.
[11] *Schindler*, ibid, at [31]–[32] and [44].

in toto, provided it was not discriminatory.[12] This was the only limit set to the 'sufficient degree of latitude' permitted by the Court to each Member State in assessing the necessity of restricting or prohibiting lotteries activities on its territory in order to protect consumers and the social order.[13] Consequently, the Court did not examine the proportionality of the measure but held that because the objectives of the British legislation were underwritten largely by a concern for protection against the societal excesses of gambling, the inherent restrictions of that non-discriminatory statutory scheme were justified, and compatible with Article 49.[14]

Schindler raises three recurrent points of interest: the expansion of its operative principles to other forms of betting and gaming, the 'peculiarity' of lotteries and gambling generally, and the nature and extent of the public interest considerations justifying the restriction of such activities. Firstly, in *Läärä*[15] and *Zenatti*,[16] the operative principle in *Schindler* was extended to other forms of betting and gaming—respectively, the operation of slot machines and sports betting. Second, the 'peculiar' nature of gambling is usually a reference to the fact that, although national lotteries and gambling outlets have long been a reliable and lucrative source of income for many Member States, the inherently addictive nature of gambling means that it can have damaging social consequences and promote secondary criminality.[17] Third, in *Schindler* the ECJ noted that the public interest considerations underpinning the UK legislation in question—the prevention of crime, moral and cultural concerns regarding gambling excess, and the desire to direct gambling profits towards benevolent causes—were, despite their paternalistic nature, compatible with Article 49.[18] However, in *Schindler* the Court did not apply any proportionality test.[19]

From a thematic perspective, the primary focus of subsequent case law has been on the stated issue: the degree to which national legislation can justify restrictions on the provision of gambling services.[20] For instance, in *Läärä*, a case concerning Finnish legislation that granted monopoly rights to operate slot machines to a single licensed public body, the ECJ held that such exclusivity did not constitute a violation of the EC Treaty provisions relating to freedom to provide services

---

[12] Ibid, at [59] and [61].   [13] Ibid, at [61] and [62].

[14] Ibid, at [58], [60], and [63].

[15] Case C-124/97 *Markku Juhani Läärä and Others v Kihlakunnansyyttäjä (Jyväskylä) and the Finnish State* ('*Läärä*') [1999] ECR I-6067.

[16] *Zenatti* [1999] ECR I-7289.

[17] For a historical overview of the 'peculiar' nature of gambling in the UK, see D Miers, *Regulating Commercial Gambling: Past, Present and Future* (OUP, 2004).

[18] *Schindler* [1994] ECR I-1039, at [57]–[63].

[19] Contrast Case C-76/90 *Säger* [1991] ECR I-4221, at [15], and Case C-384/93, *Alpine Investments BV v Minister van Financiën* ('*Alpine Investments*') [1995] ECR I-1141, at [45].

[20] See generally, *Study of Gambling Services in the Internal Market of the European Union—Final Report of 14 June 2006* (prepared by the Swiss Institute of Comparative Law for the European Commission), 1st Part, Legal Study, ch 2, at pp 965–991, available online at: <http://ec.europa.eu/internal_market.services/gambling_en.htm>.

because the justifications underpinning the Finnish statutory scheme were motivated by public interest concerns that mirrored those in *Schindler*.[21] In addition,
and again echoing the *Schindler* authority, the *Läärä* judgment reiterated that it
is for the Member States alone to assess the level of protection that they intend to
provide in the context of the overriding policy aims.[22]

Going a step further than in *Schindler*, the ECJ in *Läärä* emphasized that any
restrictive measures must not only be public interest oriented, they must also
abide by the principle of proportionality.[23] In brief, such measures must appropriately guarantee the achievement of their underlying objectives, and must not
go beyond what is necessary to attain them.[24] However, given the discretion left
to national authorities in the relevant field, the mere fact that a Member State
opts for a system of protection distinguishable in stringency from that of another
Member State, does not affect the proportionality appraisal of the national provisions at issue.[25] Moreover, the Court recognized that limited authorization of
gaming on an exclusive basis could be justified by the need to protect consumers
and maintain order in society, as it had the advantage of confining the exploitative human passion for gambling to controlled channels. This prevented the risk
of crime and fraud, and allowed the use of the resulting profits for public interest purposes.[26] In the specific instance of the Finnish monopoly, which secured
the collection by the State of the net (and lucrative) proceeds from licensed slot
machines in Finland, the ECJ acknowledged that the revenue raised by the State
could just as easily have been obtained by other means, such as taxation of the
activities of operators authorized on a non-exclusive basis. Nevertheless, given
the risk of associated crime and fraud, the strict regime in place constituted the
most efficient means of restraining the lucrative nature of gaming activities.[27] In
that overall context, conferring exclusive rights on a public body instead of, for
instance, adopting regulations imposing a code of conduct on private operators,
did not, in the Court's opinion, appear to be disproportionate.[28]

In *Zenatti*, the defendant was acting as an intermediary in Italy for an English
company specializing in the taking of bets on sporting events. Unlike *Schindler*,
the legislation at issue did not totally prohibit the taking of bets in the manner
outlined but reserved to certain licensed bodies the right to organize betting.[29]

[21] The concerns included issues of public health, consumer protection, the prevention of crime
and charitable beneficiaries: *Läärä* [1999] ECR I-6067, at [31]–[33].
[22] Ibid, at [35] citing *Schindler* [1994] ECR I-1039, at [61].
[23] Ibid, at [31] and [33].
[24] Ibid, citing Case C-288/89 *Stichting Collectieve Antennevoorziening Gouda and Others v
Commissariaat voor de Media* [1991] ECR I-4007, at [13]–[15].
[25] *Läärä*, ibid, at [35]–[36]. Cf Case C-384/93 *Alpine Investments* [1995] ECR I-1141, at [51],
and Case C-262/02 *Commission v France ('Loi Evin')* [2004] ECR I-6569, at [37].
[26] *Läärä*, ibid, at [33] and [37].
[27] Ibid, at [40]–[41].   [28] Ibid, at [39] and [42].
[29] Unlicensed activity violated Article 4 of Law No 401 of 13 December 1989 (GURI No 294 of
18 December 1989), potentially attracting criminal sanction pursuant to Article 718 of the Italian
Penal Code; *Zenatti* [1999] ECR I-7289, at [5].

Consistently, the ECJ held that the fundamental freedom to provide services did not preclude the Italian statutory scheme because that scheme was underpinned by policy objectives intended to limit, in a proportionate manner, the harmful societal effects of excess sports gambling.[30] Arguably, *Zenatti* both expanded and refined the previous case law. Firstly, and with respect to the Italian legislation at issue, its overriding public interest considerations—the prevention of the damaging individual and social consequences relating to excess gambling—were coloured by a specific concern to permit betting only to the extent to which it might be socially useful and conducive to the proper conduct of competitive sports.[31] Second and more importantly, the Court in *Zenatti* refined the *Läärä* guidelines on the assessment of proportionality. It did this in two ways.

The ECJ confirmed that the scope of regulatory protection that a Member State intends to provide in its territory could, within the context of the legislation's objectives, fall within a margin of appreciation that reflects the particular social and cultural attitudes of that Member State to gambling.[32] That reinforces the point made in *Läärä* that the mere fact that a Member State has chosen a system of protection distinguishable from that adopted by another Member State should not affect the proportionality appraisal of the adopted provisions.[33] As regards that proportionality appraisal, the Court reiterated its finding in *Läärä* that limited authorization of gambling through a licensing regime or the granting of exclusive rights had significant social advantages when it came to controlling the exploitative excesses of gambling and its associated criminality.[34] Equally, the ECJ recognized that the resulting profits from limited authorization could contribute significantly to the financing of public interest activities.[35] Nevertheless, in *Zenatti*, and taking its lead from Advocate General Fennelly, the Court was at pains to point out that such a limitation was acceptable only if it reflected a concern to bring about a 'genuine diminution' in gambling opportunities and that the resulting 'benevolent' profits were redistributed, not as the elemental justification for the restrictive strategy, but as an incidentally beneficial consequence of that policy.[36] Crucially, and in mitigation, the ECJ held that it remained a matter for the national court to verify whether that element of the proportionality appraisal was satisfied by the national legislation in question.[37]

For those seeking the liberalization of cross-border gambling in the EU, their disappointment with the *Schindler/Zenatti* approach was exacerbated by its application in *Anomar*.[38] In that case, the Portuguese legislation at issue was as

[30] *Zenatti* [1999] ECR I-7289, at [38].   [31] Ibid, at [30].

[32] Ibid, at [33]. Cf *Schindler* [1994] ECR I-1039, at [61] and *Läärä* [1999] ECR I-6067, at [35].

[33] *Läärä*, ibid, at [36].   [34] Ibid, at [39]–[42] and *Zenatti* [1999] ECR I-7289, at [35].

[35] *Zenatti*, ibid.

[36] Ibid, at [36]. Note Opinion of AG Fennelly in ibid, at [32]. Cf *Schindler* [1994] ECR I-1039, at [60].

[37] *Zenatti*, ibid, at [37].

[38] Case C-6/01 *Associação Nacional de Operadores de Máquinas Recreativas (Anomar) and Others v Estado português* ('*Anomar*') [2003] ECR I-8621.

succinct as it was restrictive: gambling was confined to authorized casinos only, and gaming outside duly authorized areas was deemed an offence punishable by a period of imprisonment.[39] The underlying general application of the legislation was equally concise—the right to operate games of chance or gambling was reserved to the Portuguese State.[40] Applying its two-step test of public interest justification and proportionality, the ECJ found that, although the Portuguese legislation impeded the free movement of services, it was not in breach of Article 49 of the EC Treaty.[41] Its justifications—social policy, prevention of fraud, protection of consumers and gamblers—were of a recognized, genuinely motivated nature as clearly reflected in the legislature's intention in enacting the provision.[42] Again, the decision how best to pursue those objectives was a matter falling within the latitude allowed to the national authorities, subject, in this instance, to the Member State's historical, cultural, and moral attitude to gambling and games of chance.[43] In appraisal of its proportionality, the Portuguese legislation could not be precluded merely because other Member States had chosen differing, less restrictive regulatory systems.[44]

Post-*Anomar*, it appeared that only in circumstances where national legislation on gambling was either discriminatory or lacking clear social policy objectives or disproportionate with regard to its objectives, would it be deemed incompatible with the free movement of services. Admittedly, in *Lindman* just such a set of discriminatory and disproportionate circumstances arose.[45] Under Finnish law, although winnings from games of chance were generally exempt from Finnish income tax, the exemption did not apply to gambling winnings earned in another Member State by Finnish nationals and residents.[46] In the present case, a Finnish national's winnings in a Swedish lottery were taxed in Finland on the ground that it was impossible for the Finnish authorities to tax foreign operators that offered gambling services from abroad. In brief, the contention was that if the winnings from gambling organized abroad were not chargeable to tax in Finland, taxpayers in Finland and the organizers of games of chance abroad, such as the Swedish lottery operator in question, would share a tax advantage.[47] According to the ECJ, the fact that organizers of gambling activities established in Finland were subject to tax did not alter the manifestly discriminatory character of the contested legislation, which, in effect, left Finnish taxpayers with little prefer-

---

[39] Decree-Law No 422/89 (Diário da República, I, No 277 of 2 December 1989).

[40] *Anomar*, ibid, at [7]–[8]. For background, see the case note by G Straetmans in (2004) 41 CML Rev 1409–1428.

[41] *Anomar*, at [65]–[66] and [75].   [42] Ibid, at [72]–[74].

[43] Ibid, at [87]–[88] and [78]-[79], and consistent with *Schindler* [1994] ECR I-1039, at [61]; *Läärä* [1999] ECR I-6067, at [35]; and *Zenatti* [1999] ECR I-7289, at [33].

[44] *Anomar*, at [78]–[81].

[45] Case C-42/02 *Diana Elisabeth Lindman* ('*Lindman*') [2003] ECR I-13519.

[46] Article 85 Inkomstskattelagen (1535/1992) (Income Tax Law) and Article 2 Lotteriskattelagen (552/1992) (Law on Tax on Games of Chance).

[47] *Lindman*, ibid, at [4]–[5] and [15].

ence other than to participate in domestic lotteries.[48] The Finnish Government, whilst admitting that its tax laws were in that respect discriminatory in nature, contended that they were justified by public interest concerns relating to excess gambling, which, according to an intervention by the Norwegian Government, was clearly detrimental to public health.[49] That plea notwithstanding, the ECJ held the statutory scheme to be incompatible with Article 49 for lack of any evidence as to its appropriateness and proportionality.[50]

In terms of the overall debate on cross-border gambling in the EU, *Lindman* is largely distinguishable to its (income tax) facts and is conspicuous by the directly discriminatory nature of the contested national measure. The ECJ's judgment in *Gambelli*,[51] delivered a week earlier, is doubtless of more general application. Nevertheless, the Court in *Lindman* did make one significant contribution to the proportionality appraisal of national gambling legislation. It reminded Member States that, as a general principle of Community law, national legislation restricting the fundamental freedoms must prove by means of concrete analysis— statistical or otherwise—that the restrictions in place are commensurate to its objectives.[52] Thus, in the specific sense of provisions on gambling, any restrictive measures would have to be shown to be underpinned by a particular causal relationship between the gravity of the risks connected with excess gambling and the participation by nationals and residents of that Member State in such activities, including those organized in other Member States.[53]

Moving onto *Gambelli*, the case was—in terms of factual background, judicial approach, and outcome—very much a matter of *Zenatti* revisited. Criminal proceedings were instigated against Mr Gambelli and others on an accusation of having illegally collected and transmitted betting data on behalf of, and in agency for, a UK sports betting firm. Extant Italian legislation prohibited, on pain of criminal sanctions, the pursuit of such activities without licence or authorization of the State. The statutory scheme at issue was essentially a monopolistic State licensing regime with the rules governing invitation to tender for Italian betting licences making it impossible for capital companies quoted on regulated markets of other Member States to obtain licences.[54] The ECJ held that the scheme constituted a restriction on the freedom to provide services and on the freedom of establishment.[55] The Court explained that the statutory scheme made it impossible for

---

[48] Ibid, at [21]–[22].   [49] Ibid, at [23]–[24].   [50] Ibid, at [25]–[27].

[51] *Gambelli* [2003] ECR I-13031.   [52] *Lindman* [2003] ECR I-13519, at [25].

[53] Ibid, at [26], the Finnish Government disclosing no statistical evidence to that effect. On that point, see generally, T Verbiest, 'French and Belgian Views on European Gambling Regulation', in A Littler and C Fijnaut (eds), *The Regulation of Gambling—European and National Perspectives* (Martinus Nijhoff Publishers, 2007) 126–159, at 130.

[54] Under Legge Finanziaria (Finance Law) No 388 of 23 December 2000 (GURI Supplemento ordinario No 302 of 29 December 2000), authorization to organize betting was granted exclusively to licence holders or those otherwise authorized by law. Unlicensed activity violated Article 4 of Law No 401 of 13 December 1989 (GURI No 294 of 18 December 1989), attracting criminal sanctions.

[55] *Gambelli* [2003] ECR I-13031, at [59].

a British bookmaker to obtain an Italian licence for betting activities, and set up agencies in Italy for that purpose.[56] In addition, the measures impeded both the cross-border provision of betting services either directly, via the Internet, or through intermediaries in Italy, and the freedom of residents in Italy to receive such betting services.[57] In illustration, the Court noted that the actions of any individuals in Italy—who from their home connected via the Internet to a bookmaker established in another Member State, and placed their bets, using their credit card to pay—might attract criminal liability.[58]

Consistent with the *Zenatti* approach to restrictions on the free movement in the field of gambling,[59] the ECJ in *Gambelli* reiterated that, ultimately, it was a matter for the Italian courts to determine whether such restrictive legislation could, in the context of compatibility with Articles 43 and 49 of the EC Treaty, be seen to be non-discriminatory; could be justified on public interest considerations and could satisfy the various criteria of the proportionality appraisal laid down in previous case law.[60] Even so, it is important to note that the ECJ was anxious to circumscribe the discretion enjoyed by national authorities. The Court required expressly that any restrictions on gaming and betting activities based on public interest grounds would necessarily have to have the capacity to limit the stated activities in a consistent and systematic manner.[61] In this, the Court referred to the expansive (and lucrative) betting and gaming policy pursued by the Italian State, and held that, '[i]n so far as the authorities of a Member State incite and encourage consumers to participate in lotteries, games of chance and betting to the financial benefit of the public purse, the[y] . . . cannot invoke public order concerns relating to the need to reduce opportunities for betting in order to justify measures such as those at issue in the main proceedings.'[62]

In April 2004, the Italian Supreme Court held that Italy's commercial gambling legislation, and its underlying policies, were compatible with EC law.[63] The Court explained that, in the light of *Gambelli*, the expansive betting and gaming policy pursued by the Italian State contradicted only the public interest objective of preventing incitement to squander on gaming; however, it was not incompatible with the public policy objective of prevention of fraud and crime by channelling the exploitable passion for gambling into a controlled system of operators, as acknowledged in *Zenatti*.[64] The Italian Supreme Court affirmed the

---

[56] Ibid, at [45]–[49].   [57] Ibid, at [51]–[55] and [57]–[58].
[58] Ibid, at [56].   [59] *Zenatti* [1999] ECR I-7289, at [37].
[60] *Gambelli* [2003] ECR I-13031, at [64]–[66], [70]–[71], and [75].
[61] Ibid, at [62] and [67]. Cf also *Zenatti* [1999] ECR I-7289, at [36], and A Littler, 'Has the ECJ's Jurisprudence in the Field of Gambling Become more Restrictive when Applying the Proportionality Principle?', in A Littler and C Fijnaut (eds), *The Regulation of Gambling—European and National Perspectives* (Martinus Nijhoff Publishers, 2007) 15–40, at 34–37 and 39.
[62] *Gambelli*, ibid, at [68]–[69].
[63] *Gesualdi*, Corte Suprema di Cassazione (Sezioni Unite Penali), Judgment No 111/04 of 26 April 2004. See also the Opinion of AG Colomer in *Placanica* [2007] ECR I-1891, at [35]–[44].
[64] *Gesualdi*, ibid, at [11.2.3] to [11.2.5], citing *Zenatti* [1999] ECR I-7289, at [35].

proportionality of the restrictions on the freedoms of establishment and services resulting from the Italian licensing scheme, by relying on the wide discretion left to Member States to decide for more or less rigorous controls in the field of gambling.[65] It added that the licensing system was not discriminatory, since the exclusion of quoted companies from the tender procedure applied equally to both domestic and foreign operators.[66] The Italian Supreme Court further declared the criminal sanctions prescribed by Italian legislation for engaging in unauthorized games of chance to be proportionate restrictions on the free movement provisions. It regarded them as falling within that Member State's discretion to ensure a more incisive level of protection of the public order, by adopting more or less rigorous preventive criminal measures; ordinary courts could therefore not declare the criminal sanctions to be incompatible with EC law without exceeding the limits of their power.[67]

Two years later that statutory scheme was referred once more to the ECJ. A detailed review of the case law follows. In the immediate, it is suggested that this further reference was not surprising, and for two reasons. Firstly, a fundamental issue remains as to whether the principle of proportionality is observed having regard to the severity of the prohibition (breach of which attracts criminal liability, potentially of a retrospective nature, for both the providers and recipients of such services), and which makes it impossible in practice for lawfully constituted domestic undertakings or operators from other Member States to carry on economic activity in the Italian betting and gaming industry.[68] In *Gambelli*, the ECJ had drawn two 'red lines' on the proportionality appraisal of the contested Italian legislation, namely the fact that consumers were encouraged to participate in betting organized by licensed national bodies, and that the service providers from other Member States, who were already subject to a regulation entailing controls and penalties in their country of establishment, were already operating through lawfully constituted intermediaries in Italy.[69]

The second reason for the unsurprising nature of the *Placanica* reference, is more straightforward: in the context of commercial gambling, to what extent may Community fundamental freedoms be curtailed and constrained—there being little argument that currently such freedoms *are* significantly curtailed in Italian law—for the sake of the public interest concerns about the human passion for gambling and fears concerning associated, secondary criminality?

---

[65] *Gesualdi*, ibid, at [12], citing *Läärä* [1999] ECR I-6067, at [36], *Zenatti*, at [34], and *Anomar* [2003] ECR I-8621, at [79].

[66] *Gesualdi*, ibid, at [13].

[67] The Italian Supreme Court added that for the same reason both itself and the Italian Constitutional Court had regarded the criminal sanctions in question as constitutionally permissible restrictions on the freedom of economic activity enshrined in Article 41 of the Italian Constitution: *Gesualdi*, ibid, at [12].

[68] Note the Opinion of AG Colomer in *Placanica* [2007] ECR I-1891, at [133].

[69] *Gambelli* [2003] ECR I-13031, at [72]–[73].

In colloquial terms, given that the (tax revenue) stakes were so high, was the (legislative) dice loaded from the start? The Italian example demonstrates that, because of the latitude enjoyed by Member States in the field of gambling, a plausible, non-economic, public interest objective, such as the prevention of crime and fraud, may be used as a pretext to justify a national restrictive scheme, which serves primarily, albeit not exclusively, State economic interests and budgetary considerations.

III. The Dice is Loaded: The Placanica Panacea and its Aftermath

A. The *Placanica* Judgment

In *Placanica*, the ECJ was called for the third time in eight years to rule on the compatibility with EC law of the Italian legislation, which prohibits, on pain of criminal penalties, participation in the organization of gambling, including the collection of bets, without the possession of a licence and a police authorization.[70] Stanley, a betting and gaming company incorporated under English law, duly licensed in the UK and quoted on the London stock exchange, had been prevented from applying for a licence for organizing betting activities in Italy due to the earlier Italian licensing rules, which excluded companies quoted on regulated markets from the tender procedure. Instead, Stanley operated in Italy through agencies, run by its contracted intermediaries, where bettors could electronically place their bets with the British bookmaker. Three of the Italian intermediaries were prosecuted for taking part in a betting activity without the requisite prior licence or police authorization.[71]

As in *Gambelli*, the ECJ repeated that national legislation, such as the one at hand, which prohibited the pursuit of gaming and betting activities without prior licence or authorization, constituted a *prima facie* restriction on both freedom of establishment and freedom to provide services.[72] In particular, it restricted the right of a company established and lawfully operating in another Member State to provide its services to bettors in Italy and set up agencies there in order to facilitate this cross-border service.[73]

The Court, in confirming its established case law in the field of commercial gambling, held that such restrictions could be justified on grounds of overriding general interest, such as protection of consumers as recipients of services,

---

[70] For a concise outline of the statutory scheme at issue, see *Placanica* [2007] ECR I-1891, at [3]–[4] and [6]–[10] and, more generally, F Portolano and Y Pecoraro, 'The Italian Legal Framework on Gambling: A Growing Market' (2007) 18(6) Entertainment Law Review 199–204.

[71] *Placanica*, ibid, at [20]–[24], [26], and [29].

[72] Ibid, at [42], approving *Gambelli* [2003] ECR I-13031, at [46] and [58]–[59].

[73] *Placanica*, ibid, at [43]–[44].

prevention of fraud and incitement to squander on gaming, and maintenance of the public and social order.[74] It reiterated the wide margin of discretion enjoyed by national authorities in determining both the level of protection of these interests and in setting their policy objectives in the betting and gaming sector, in view of the moral, religious, and cultural aspects of gambling, and its harmful personal, financial, and social consequences.[75] This includes the freedom of Member States to totally prohibit or partially restrict gambling activities and establish (more or less) stringent control mechanisms relevant to that end.[76] In addition, the ECJ once more alluded to the limits of the discretion, which arise from the principles of proportionality and non-discrimination. In short, the Court reiterated that national authorities must be aware that any restrictive measures in the field of gambling cannot be regarded as compatible with the free movement provisions on establishment or services unless they are suitable, do not go beyond what is necessary for the attainment of the objectives pursued, and are applied without discrimination.[77]

As regards the subjection of betting and gaming activities to a licensing system, allowing only a limited number of operators to be active in the field, the Court distinguished between two objectives that might come into question. On the one hand, the reduction of gambling opportunities and, on the other hand, the prevention of the exploitation of gambling activities for criminal or fraudulent purposes by channelling them into a controlled system.[78] The ECJ explained that, although the former objective could in theory justify a limitation on the number of gambling operators, it could not provide a valid ground for the contested national legislation, because the latter did not reflect any concern to bring about a genuine diminution of gambling opportunities and limit activities in that field in a consistent and systematic manner.[79] In this, the Court noted that the Italian legislature was pursuing a policy of expanding betting and gaming activities, with a view to increasing tax revenue.[80] At the same time, the ECJ held that the licensing system at hand could, in principle, be regarded as an efficient mechanism for attaining the second objective, ie combating criminality by controlling the activities of operators in the betting and gaming sector.[81] It added that a policy of controlled expansion in this sector might be wholly consistent with the objective of drawing players away from clandestine to authorized and regulated gambling. The Court acknowledged that this objective could

---

[74] Ibid, at [46], approving *Schindler* [1994] ECR I-1039, at [57]–[60]; *Läärä* [1999] ECR I-6067, at [32]–[33]; *Zenatti* [1999] ECR I-7289, at [30]–[31]; and *Gambelli* [2003] ECR I-13031, at [60] and [67].

[75] *Placanica*, ibid, at [47]–[48].

[76] See *Schindler*, ibid, at [60]–[62]; *Läärä*, ibid, at [35]–[36]; *Zenatti*, ibid, at [33]–[34]; and *Gambelli*, ibid, at [63].

[77] *Placanica,* ibid, at [48]–[49].   [78] Ibid, at [52].

[79] Cf *Zenatti* [1999] ECR I-7289, at [35]–[36] and *Gambelli* [2003] ECR I-13031, at [62] and [67].

[80] *Placanica,* ibid, at [53]–[54].   [81] Ibid, at [57], first limb.

be achieved only if authorized operators represented a reliable and attractive alternative to illegal activities. This might necessitate the offer of an extensive range of games, advertising on a certain scale and the use of new distribution techniques.[82]

Although the Court built upon its earlier case law in order to refine the limits set to the Member States' discretion to regulate gambling, once again it confined itself to a theoretical recognition of the legitimacy of the objective of preventing the abuse of gambling for criminal or illegal purposes. Invoking the insufficiency of the facts available before it, the ECJ avoided assessing the proportionality of the Italian licensing system for the betting and gaming sector or at least the suitability of the limitation on the total number of licences available under Italian law in realizing the above aim. Instead, it left the final decision on the matter to the national court along with the assessment of the proportionality of the relevant restrictions.[83] The ECJ did not follow the opinion of Advocate General Colomer, who had suggested that the system of prior authorization prescribed by the Italian legislation was not based on objective criteria, in such a way as to circumscribe the national authorities' discretion; rather it allowed revocation of licence in the event of 'misuse by the licensee' without further details and it provided no comprehensive list of the criteria for refusing authorization.[84]

As regards the initial exclusion by Italian law of companies quoted in the regulated markets from the tender procedure for the award of licences in the betting and gaming sector, the Court noted that this continued to produce legal effects despite the 2003 legislative amendment, which had opened the procedure to all companies. This was because the licences already awarded in 1999 were valid for six years and renewable for another six years, while no new call for tenders had taken place.[85] The ECJ affirmed its finding in *Gambelli* that such an exclusion from the tender procedure constituted a restriction on the freedom of establishment, even if it applied without distinction to all quoted companies regardless of their Member State of establishment.[86] It followed logically that the lack of foreign operators among licensees could be attributed to the fact that the Italian rules made it impossible in practice for quoted companies from other Member States to obtain a licence.[87]

In line with the 'obstacles approach' underlying the *Säger* formula,[88] Advocate General Colomer explained that companies established in other Member States were more adversely affected by the restrictions at hand, since, if they wished to participate in the tender procedures for licences, they had to adapt their internal structure, with the result that they had no real possibility of establishing

---

[82] Ibid, at [55].   [83] Ibid, at [57], second limb, and at [58].
[84] Opinion of AG Colomer in *Placanica*, ibid, at [122].
[85] *Placanica*, ibid, at [61].   [86] *Gambelli* [2003] ECR I-13031, at [48].
[87] *Placanica*, ibid, at [61].   [88] *Säger* [1991] ECR I-4221, at [12].

themselves in the Member State imposing the restrictions.[89] He also noted the adverse impact on intermediaries, who were prohibited, on pain of criminal penalties, from providing services to bookmakers established in another Member State, who were in turn unable to establish themselves or obtain a licence to pursue their activity in Italy.[90]

In stark contrast to its approach to the licensing system, the Court was anxious to review the proportionality of the blanket exclusion of quoted companies from tendering. More categorically than in *Gambelli*, it declared the measure as going beyond what was necessary for the attainment of the objective of combating criminality in gambling. It adopted the opinion of Advocate General Colomer that this objective could be achieved by alternative means of monitoring the accounts and activities of operators in the betting and gaming sector, which would be less restrictive for the free movement provisions on establishment and services.[91] In support of its conclusion, the ECJ observed that the contested measure had been repealed by the Italian legislature in 2003, without having been replaced by any other measures.[92] It followed that the Court applied a strict proportionality test, the outcome of which was independent of the question whether the exclusion of quoted companies applied in fact in the same manner to operators established in Italy and those in other Member States.[93]

This was an indirect but clear response of the ECJ to the *Gesualdi* judgment of the Italian Supreme Court, which had found the Italian legislation excluding companies quoted on the stock exchange from the tender procedure to be compatible with the fundamental freedoms.[94] Moreover, it is striking that it did not suffice for the ECJ to declare the measure in question as a disproportionate restriction on the freedom of establishment and the free movement of services.[95] Although the Court acknowledged that it was for the national legislature to remedy the ongoing effects of the unlawful exclusion of certain gambling operators from tenders by laying down detailed procedural rules for the protection of rights derived from EC law, the Court went on to suggest appropriate remedies to the problem. These included the revocation and redistribution of old licences, or the award by public tender of an adequate number of new licences. In the meantime, it held that no sanctions should be imposed on operators unlawfully barred from the licensing procedure.[96]

---

[89] Opinion of AG Colomer in *Placanica*, at [118]. Cf *Schindler* [1994] ECR I-1039, at [43], *Zenatti* [1999] ECR I-7289, at [27] and *Anomar* [2003] ECR I-8621, at [65].

[90] Opinion of AG Colomer in *Placanica*, ibid, at [120].

[91] Ibid, at [125] and [127]. Such an alternative could be the gathering of information about the quoted companies' principal shareholders or representatives. Cf *Gambelli* [2003] ECR I-13031, at [74]–[75].

[92] *Placanica*, ibid, at [62].   [93] Ibid.

[94] Corte Suprema di Cassazione (Sezioni Unite Penali), Judgment No 111/04 of 26 April 2004. See also the Opinion of AG Colomer in *Placanica*, ibid, at [42] and [44].

[95] *Placanica* [2007] ECR I-1891, at [64].

[96] Ibid, at [63]. Cf Joined Cases C-392/04 and C-422/04 *i-21 Germany GmbH and Arcor AG & Co KG v Bundesrepublik Deutschland* [2006] ECR I-8559, at [57].

As regards the requirement of prior police authorization prescribed by the Italian licensing rules on betting and gaming, the ECJ recognized that such a measure, which ensured *ex ante* control and ongoing supervision, was, in principle, suitable to achieve the objective of preventing operators in that field from getting involved in criminal or illegal activities.[97] However, since in the present case police authorization presupposed possession of a licence, it inevitably inherited the defects of the licensing procedure. Accordingly, the Court suggested that any legal action taken by Italian authorities, for lack of police authorization, against persons who, contrary to EC law, would have been unable to obtain a licence (such as the British bookmaker and his intermediaries) was not compatible with the Treaty.[98]

In a similar vein, the ECJ decided on the question of the proportionality of the criminal penalties prescribed by the contested legislation for the pursuit of gambling activities without prior licence or police authorization; a question which had been left open in *Gambelli*.[99] The Court made it clear that a Member State may not impose a criminal penalty for failure to complete an administrative formality, where such failure is attributable to the Member State.[100] Therefore, the Italian authorities could not apply criminal penalties to any operators in the betting sector, who had been refused the award of a licence or police authorization in breach of Community law, because this would constitute a disproportionate restriction on the free movement provisions of Articles 43 and 49 of the EC Treaty.[101] Advocate General Colomer added that the harsher penalty imposed by Italian legislation for encroachment on betting reserved to the State, or entities such as the Italian National Olympic Committee (CONI) or the National Union for the Improvement of Horse Breeds (UNIRE) or their licensees, had less to do with crime prevention than with the economic importance of gambling for the public purse.[102] He further suggested that a penalty, which involved incarceration for up to three years, was disproportionate to the legitimate aim pursued, in view also of the promotion of betting by the State.[103] Self-evidently, such a conviction meant a criminal record, which made it impossible for convicted operators to obtain the requisite police authorization and pursue any activity in the field of betting.[104]

In sum, in *Placanica*, Advocate General Colomer's suggestion that the ECJ no longer avoid an in-depth examination of the consequences of the fundamental freedoms for the betting and gaming sector[105] was only partly followed, with regard to certain, and not all, aspects of the contested national legislation;

[97] *Placanica* [2007] ECR I-1891, at [65].
[98] Ibid, at [66]–[67]. See also Opinion of AG Colomer in *Placanica*, at [123].
[99] *Gambelli* [2003] ECR I-13031, at [73].
[100] *Placanica*, ibid, at [69] with reference to Case 5/83 *Criminal proceedings against HG Rienks* [1983] ECR 4233, at [10]–[11].
[101] *Placanica*, ibid, at [70]–[71].   [102] Opinion of AG Colomer in *Placanica,* at [136].
[103] Ibid, at [141] and [143].   [104] Ibid, at [142].
[105] Ibid, at [1] and [105]–[107].

namely the exclusion of certain forms of companies from the tendering procedures and the accompanying sanctions imposed on such companies for operating without a licence. Nevertheless, the strict proportionality test of that part
of the national rules, which the Court for the first time carried out itself, should
not be underestimated. In contrast, the ECJ left the assessment of the proportionality of the overall licensing system to the national court,[106] and did not
even rule out that a national policy of expanding and promoting the gambling
opportunities offered by a *de jure* or *de facto* State monopoly operator could be
wholly justified by the objective of channelling gambling passion into a controlled system.[107] Finally, neither did the Court examine the question of the
proportionality of the restrictions imposed on the bettors' freedom to receive
services insofar as they could be prosecuted, for the obvious reason that, unlike
Gambelli, the question was raised in criminal proceedings against a bookmaker's agents.[108]

On the one hand, the ECJ in *Placanica* expanded the 'red lines' drawn from
the principles of proportionality and non-discrimination, which Member States
are not allowed to cross in prohibiting or restricting gambling activities. It thus
regarded as incompatible with the Treaty the blanket exclusion of a certain type of
companies from the licensing procedure, and the concomitant sanctions against
those companies for operating without the necessary licence. On the other hand,
the Court seemed anxious to preserve the latitude allowed to the Member States
and their national courts in assessing the necessity and proportionality of the
national gambling schemes on public interest grounds. Thus, the ECJ's approach
appears to remain loaded in favour of the national margin of appreciation, albeit
within certain limits.

B. The Italian Horse-race Betting Case

Most recently, the ECJ adopted a clearer position with regard to the proportionality of the Italian licensing system for horse-race betting.[109] In the stated case,
the Commission brought infringement proceedings against Italy—challenging
the renewal by the Italian legislature before 2003 of the (329) old licences for
horse-race betting granted by UNIRE without a competitive tendering procedure as an alleged breach of Articles 43 and 49 of the EC Treaty.[110] Relying on
earlier case law concerning the transparency duty of public authorities granting
concessions, the Court held that the complete failure of Italian authorities to
invite competing bids for the purpose of granting licences for horse-race betting
operations infringed the general principle of transparency and the obligation to

---

[106] *Placanica*, ibid, at [57]–[58].   [107] Ibid, at [55] and [57].
[108] Cf Opinion of AG Colomer in *Placanica*, ibid, at [102].
[109] Case C-260/04 *Commission v Italy* ('*Horse-race Betting*') [2007] ECR I-7083.
[110] Ibid, at [4]–[8] and [12].

ensure a sufficient degree of advertising. It thus constituted a restriction within the meaning of Articles 43 and 49.[111]

The ECJ then had to consider whether such a restriction could be justified on the grounds of the express derogations of Articles 45–46 of the EC Treaty or reasons of overriding general interest acknowledged in *Gambelli* and *Placanica*, such as consumer protection, prevention of fraud and incitement to squander on gaming, and the preservation of public order.[112] The Court confirmed the limits set by the principles of proportionality and non-discrimination to the Member States' discretion to decide on the policy objectives and the level of protection in the betting and gaming sector.[113] The ECJ noted that the renewal of the old licences for horse-race betting was part of the Italian Government's strategy to increase the network of betting outlets, which also included the award of (671) new licences by means of invitations to tender. However, and crucially, the Italian authorities failed to demonstrate how the renewal of the existing betting licences without a tendering procedure could be justified and proportionate with regard to the objective pursued—the need to discourage clandestine operations. According to the Court, such a measure was not appropriate and went beyond what was necessary in order to preclude operators in the horse-race betting sector from engaging in criminal or fraudulent activities.[114] In line with established case law, the ECJ also dismissed the economic reasons put forward by the Italian Government (such as the need to ensure continuity, financial stability, and a proper return on past investments for licence holders) as possible grounds of justification for such a restriction on the fundamental freedoms.[115] Although the ECJ in the Italian horse-race betting case appears to have drawn clearer limits to the Member States' discretion to subject betting and gaming to a licensing system, its approach remained in principle loaded in favour of the national (albeit circumscribed) margin of appreciation. Thus, the Court seems ready to declare incompatible with the Treaty only manifest excesses of that discretion, which involve manifestly discriminatory or disproportionate national measures.

C. Electronic Games that are Not by Nature Games of Chance

A more thorough and rigorous proportionality test than the one applied to national bans or restrictions on commercial gambling seems to be applied by the ECJ to national measures restricting access to recreational games, which

[111] Ibid, at [23]–[25], citing Case C-324/98 *Telaustria and Telefonadress* [2000] ECR I-10745, at [61]–[62], and Case C-458/03 *Parking Brixen* [2005] ECR I-8585, at [48]–[49].
[112] *Horse-race Betting*, ibid, at [26]–[27] citing *Gambelli* [2003] ECR I-13031, at [60] and *Placanica* [2007] ECR I-1891, at [45]–[46].
[113] *Horse-race Betting*, ibid, at [28]–[29] citing *Gambelli*, ibid, at [64]–[65] and *Placanica*, ibid, at [48]–[49].
[114] *Horse-race Betting*, ibid, at [30]–[34] and [36].
[115] Ibid, at [35], citing Case C-35/98 *Verkooijen* [2000] ECR I-4071, at [48], and Case C-388/01 *Commission v Italy* [2003] ECR 1–721, at [22].

are not by nature games of chance. For instance, the Court held that the outright prohibition in Greece, on pain of criminal and administrative sanctions, of the installation and operation of electrical, electromechanical, and electronic games—including technical recreational games and computer games but excluding recreational games of skill—in any public or private premises other than casinos was in breach of the free movement provisions on goods, establishment, and services.[116] The Greek authorities claimed that due to technological developments the games in question were easily convertible into games of chance, which were illegal outside casinos. Moreover, they argued that the situation had become impossible to police, leading to serious social problems, such as the players' addiction, the squandering of money, the illegal enrichment of those involved in the operation, installation or trade of electronic games, and the loss of considerable tax revenue. Their defence also observed that less restrictive measures, which had been applied in Greece between 1996 and 2000, had proven ineffective.[117]

Relying on the *Dassonville* formula,[118] the ECJ regarded the ban as a measure having equivalent effect because it was liable to lead to a decrease in the volume of imports in gaming machines lawfully manufactured and marketed in other Member States, and had in fact led to a halt in the importation of gaming machines intended for installation in places other than casinos.[119] The *prima facie* inclusion of the ban within the net of Article 28 of the EC Treaty appears correct. However, as the measure stipulated where and by whom the electronic games in question could be installed and operated,[120] it would arguably have been more consistent with the *Keck* formula to regard the contested ban as a measure concerning 'certain selling arrangements', which might have in fact a more adverse impact on the marketing of imported goods.[121]

The Court acknowledged that the ban could in principle be justified by overriding reasons relating to the public interest, such as the protection of consumers and the maintenance of social order.[122] Nonetheless, it distinguished the present

---

[116] Case C-65/05 *Commission v Greece* ('*Electronic Games*') [2006] ECR I-10341.

[117] Ibid, at [20]–[21] and [32].

[118] Case 8/74 *Procureur du Roi v Benoît & Gustave Dassonville* ('*Dassonville*') [1974] ECR 837, at [5].

[119] *Electronic Games* [2006] ECR I-10341, at [29]–[30].

[120] See Case C-20/03 *Criminal Proceedings against Burmanjer and Others* ('*Burmanjer*') [2005] ECR I-4133, at [26], and Case C-441/04 *A-Punkt Schmuckhandels GmbH v Claudia Schmidt* ('*A-Punkt*') [2006] ECR I-2093, at [16]–[17]. See also AG Jacobs in Case C-412/93 *Société d' Importation Edouard Leclerc-Siplec v TF1 Publicité and M6 Publicité* ('*Leclerc-Siplec*') [1995] ECR I-179, at [45].

[121] See Joined Cases C-267 and 268/91 *Criminal Proceedings against Bernard Keck and Daniel Mithouard* ('*Keck*') [1993] ECR I-6097, at [16]–[17]. See also Case C-254/98 *Schutzverband gegen unlauteren Wettbewerb v TK-Heimdienst Sass GmbH* ('*TK-Heimdienst*') [2000] ECR I-151, at [25]–[26] and [29], and Case C-322/01 *Deutscher Apothekenverband eV v 0800 DocMorris NV and Jacques Waterval* ('*DocMorris*') [2003] ECR I-14887, at [73]–[76].

[122] *Electronic Games* [2006] ECR I-10341, at [31]–[33] and [38].

case from *Schindler*[123] and *Läärä*,[124] where it had allowed Member States a very wide discretion to restrict, or even prohibit, gambling activities given the high risk of crime and fraud and the damaging individual and social consequences of excess gambling. Unlike the national measures examined in *Schindler* and *Läärä*, the contested ban concerned electronic and electromechanical games, which were not by nature games of chance because they were not played for the prospect of winning a sum of money. Consequently, the ECJ applied a stricter proportionality test than the one applied in the field of gambling, and concluded that the measure in question was disproportionate.[125] It explained that the Greek authorities could have had recourse to less restrictive, technical, and organizational measures (such as the addition of special protection systems to the gaming machines suggested by the Commission, so that recreational games cannot be converted into games of chance) and could have ensured that these were correctly and effectively implemented in order to achieve the objectives pursued.[126]

The prohibition on operating electronic and electromechanical games in premises other than casinos, and games on computers available in undertakings providing Internet services, was further regarded as an obstacle to the freedom of establishment and the free movement of services. Relying on the market access test,[127] underlying its *Säger*[128] and *Gebhard*[129] formulas, the ECJ explained that such a measure was liable to make more difficult, or even completely prevent, the exercise by operators from other Member States of their right to establish themselves in Greece.[130] Furthermore, the measure constituted a barrier to the freedom to provide services on the ground that the concept of services encompassed both the operation of gaming machines, regardless of whether or not it was separable from their manufacture, importation, or distribution,[131] and the cross-border provision of information society services.[132] On the same grounds as those established in relation to Article 28 of the EC Treaty, the Court considered the contested legislation as a disproportionate restriction on the free movement provisions of Articles 43 and 49 of the EC Treaty.[133] The ECJ thus accepted

---

[123] *Schindler* [1994] ECR I-1039, at [58]–[60].

[124] *Läärä* [1999] ECR I-6067, at [33]–[42].

[125] *Electronic Games* [2006] ECR I-10341, at [35]–[37] with reference to *Läärä*, ibid, at [17]. Cf T Stein, 'Die Entwicklung der europäischen Glücksspielrechtsprechung und deren Auswirkung auf den deutschen Lotteriemarkt' (2002) 13 Europäisches Wirtschafts- und Steuerrecht 416–424, at 417 and 422.

[126] *Electronic Games*, ibid, at [39]–[41] and [17].

[127] Ibid, at [48]–[49]. Cf D Doukas, 'Untying the Market Access Knot: Advertising Restrictions and the Free Movement of Goods and Services' (2006–07) 9 Cambridge Yearbook of European Legal Studies 177–215, at 187–189, 197 and 200.

[128] *Säger* [1991] ECR I-4221, at [12].

[129] Case C-55/94 *Reinhard Gebhard v Consiglio dell' Ordine degli Avvocati e Procuratori di Milano* ('*Gebhard*') [1995] ECR I-4165, at [37].

[130] *Electronic Games* [2006] ECR I-10341, at [51]–[52].

[131] Ibid, at [53] citing *Anomar* [2003] ECR I-8621, at [56] and [75].

[132] Ibid, at [54] citing *Gambelli* [2003] ECR I-13031, at [54].

[133] Ibid, at [55]–[56].

the arguments of the Commission that the objectives pursued could have been attained by more specific tangible measures, which controlled, sanctioned or prevented the conversion of recreational games into games of chance, and did not take the form of a general prohibition with an adverse impact on other economic activities not linked to games of chance.[134]

IV. National Regulatory Regimes: Time to Put their Cards on the Table

It is evident from the case law that the future regulation of gambling in the internal market will have to attempt to reconcile both vertical and horizontal compatibility issues. In a vertical sense, the issue is, as illustrated, one of the compatibility of national regulatory regimes with the fundamental freedoms of services and establishment. In this sense, it is of importance to note that, despite the parameters set on the latitude of Member States in the field of gambling by the case law of the ECJ, there is a residual and general reluctance in the practice of the Community judicature and national courts, to question the Member States' discretion.[135] That reticence was illustrated in the English High Court in June 1999, where in reliance upon the wide discretion left to Member States in this field, that Court found that the prohibition of a lottery operator established in Liechtenstein (an EFTA country) from operating in the UK was not in breach with Article 49 of the EC Treaty.[136] Moses J noted that the UK authorities retained the 'sufficient degree of latitude' acknowledged in *Schindler*, to determine how best to protect lottery participants and social interests more generally. He added that the legislative requirements in Liechtenstein were not equivalent to those required of the licensed operator in the UK (Camelot) under the National Lottery Act 1993, and were inadequate to address the risks for consumers, which the UK Government considered important.[137]

In a horizontal sense, the focus must be on the manner in which the statutory schemes of individual Member States conflict with each other, thus affecting the functioning of the internal market of gambling—and associated, commercial, charitable, and sporting—services. The number of instances in which provisions

---

[134] Ibid, at [45].

[135] Note T Stein, 'Die Entwicklung der europäischen Glücksspielrechtsprechung und deren Auswirkung auf den deutschen Lotteriemarkt' (2002) 13 Europäisches Wirtschafts- und Steuerrecht 416–424, at 423.

[136] *R v Secretary of State for the Home Department ex p International Lottery in Liechtenstein Foundation and Electronic Fundraising Company plc* [1999] 3 CMLR 304.

[137] For commentary, see A Littler, 'Has the ECJ's Jurisprudence in the Field of Gambling Become more Restrictive when Applying the Proportionality Principle?', in A Littler and C Fijnaut (eds), *The Regulation of Gambling—European and National Perspectives* (Martinus Nijhoff Publishers, 2007) 15–40, at 27, and D Miers, 'A British View of European Gambling Regulation', in A Littler and C Fijnaut (eds), ibid, 81–126, at 101–102.

of national law concerning gambling may conflict with EC law or the law of other Member States is bound to increase, especially because of the regulatory schemes of some Member States, most notably and recently in the UK,[138] which provide for the award of licences for cross-border provision of gambling services.[139] More immediately, clear inconsistencies arise in the manner in which national regulatory schemes adopt and adapt to the public interest justifications and the proportionality appraisal criteria outlined by the ECJ. Examples of these inconsistencies are illustrated with reference to the domestic arrangements of the Netherlands and Germany with the underlying, recurring theme being that, in the absence of minimum harmonization, the reticence inherent in the current piecemeal approach of the Commission and the ECJ to commercial gambling is ultimately self-defeating.

According to a recent European Commission report, with the exception of the new Member States, restrictive national legislative measures on commercial gambling are based, at least implicitly, on some manifested concern for public, social, and moral order.[140] Nevertheless, as the report highlights, in those Member States where the relevant legislation has been challenged, 'the analysis of EC law compatibility effectuated by them [ie the national authorities and courts] so far is often not that exhaustive and at times even rather poor.'[141] Moreover, with respect to the public interest justifications advanced in national legislation, the stated provisions often do nothing more than list several justifications without any attempt to rationalize or reconcile such individual justifications. The regulatory scheme operating in the Netherlands provides an interesting case study in this regard.

A. The Netherlands

Article 1(a) of the Act on Games of Chance of 1964 prohibits the organization of games of chance in the Netherlands unless the operator is validly licensed by the Dutch authorities.[142] Article 1 also states that Dutch consumers who knowingly participate in illegal games of chance, or those intermediaries who promote participation in foreign games of chance on Dutch territory, may face criminal

---

[138] On 1 September 2007, the Gambling Act 2005 came into force giving effect to the British Government's liberalizing proposals for reform of the law on gambling. The Act contains a new regulatory system to govern the provision of all gambling in Great Britain, other than the National Lottery and spread betting. The Act introduces a unified regulator for gambling in Great Britain, the Gambling Commission, and a new licensing regime for commercial gambling to be conducted primarily by the regulator; see further: <http://www.gamblingcommission.gov.uk/>.

[139] For instance, Malta, Slovenia, Slovakia, Estonia, or Latvia. See generally, S Walz, 'Gambling um *Gambelli*?—Rechtsfolgen der Entscheidung *Gambelli* für das staatliche Sportwettenmonopol' (2004) 15 Europäische Zeitschrift für Wirtschaftsrecht 523–526, at 523.

[140] Study of Gambling Services in the Internal Market of the European Union—Final Report of 14 June 2006 (prepared by the Swiss Institute of Comparative Law for the European Commission), 1st Part, Legal Study, ch 2, at 984–987.

[141] Ibid, at 984.   [142] Wet op de Kansspelen ([1964], OJ 483), as amended.

sanction.[143] In essence, the Dutch statutory scheme is a State-sponsored oligopoly: not only must an applicant licensee comply with a series of strict requirements, but also at present only Dutch registered undertakings are licensed to provide commercial gambling services.[144] As revealed in Parliamentary debates on various minor amendments to the principal Act, the public interest justifications underlying the Dutch regulatory scheme are based on the need to counteract the addictive nature of gambling, broader consumer protection issues, and the prevention of secondary criminality.[145]

In December 2005, the Administrative Court of Breda had to consider what, in effect, was an appeal against a refusal to grant a casino gaming licence.[146] The Court held that pursuant to the guidelines laid down by the ECJ in *Gambelli*, public interest justifications underpinning restrictive measures on commercial gambling must not only be 'coherent and systematic' in objective, interpretation and application but also they must be *shown* to be so. In this instance, until such time as the relevant licensing authority could provide concrete evidence of the coherence of its restrictive regime—based on the requirements of Article 27h.1 of the Act on Games of Chance of 1964—the Court held the measures in question (the State monopoly held by Holland Casino) to be incompatible with Article 49 of the EC Treaty. Despite the clarity of that decision, it does not however present a true view of the (continuing) restrictiveness of Dutch jurisprudence on the provision of commercial gambling services.

In February 2005, the Dutch Supreme Court, in line with the Italian *Corte Suprema di Cassazione*, refused to interpret *Gambelli* as a legal catalyst for the liberalization of cross-border betting in the Community.[147] In the present case, the English-based gaming entity, Ladbrokes, was attempting to establish a business whereby it could accept online bets from customers based in Holland. Ladbrokes highlighted a *lacuna* in the Act on Games of Chance: there was no specific provision in the Act addressing online games of chance. The Dutch Supreme Court held however that, consistent with previous jurisprudence, interactive online gaming, or any promotional games of chance, for free or otherwise, not explicitly regulated must in any event comply with general principles of Dutch gaming law,

---

[143] Articles 1(c) and 1(b) of the Act on Games of Chance of 1964 as underwritten by the respective criminal penalties in Articles 31 and 32 of that Act.

[144] For an overview, see Study of Gambling Services in the Internal Market of the European Union, 1st Part, Legal Study, n 140 above, ch 1, at 645–650.

[145] See generally, J Franssen and R Budik, 'The Netherlands', in M Balestra and A Cabot (eds), *Internet Gambling Report* (7th edn, River City Group, 2004) at 434.

[146] Administrative Court of Breda 02.12.2005 (No 03/1868 WET) *Compagnie Financière Régionale BV v Ministers van Justitie en Economische Zaken*. See M Arendts, 'A View of European Gambling Regulation from the Perspective of Private Operators', in A Littler and C Fijnaut (eds), *The Regulation of Gambling—European and National Perspectives* (Martinus Nijhoff Publishers, 2007) 41–52, at 50, and Study of Gambling Services in the Internal Market of the European Union, 1st Part, Legal Study, n 140 above, ch 1, at 625 and 650.

[147] Dutch Supreme Court 18.02.2005 (No C03/306HR) *Ladbrokes v Lotto*, and Study of Gambling Services in the Internal Market of the European Union, ibid, at 646.

If such games of chance were addressed to Dutch consumers.[148] It followed, that Ladbrokes would, according to the Supreme Court, have to be licensed in order to carry on its stated activities, and, in the absence of same, its acts would have to be considered *per se* unlawful.

There is a glaring and uncomfortable inconsistency inherent in that specific finding and the Dutch statutory scheme more generally. In August 2003, the National Sports Totalisator Foundation (NSTF) was granted the right to offer an online or SMS version of its lottery games within its current licence. Participation in that interactive online Lotto was only possible with a Dutch bank account or credit account number, and NSTF was the only entity to be granted such a right. Subsequently, the Dutch authorities refused to issue a private applicant with a licence to promote a SMS lottery game. That refusal was challenged on the grounds that pursuant to ECJ case law, public interest justifications for restrictive commercial gambling regimes should not be considered valid when public sector gaming operators freely advertise their services or regularly introduce new games.[149] That argument was rejected, with the Dutch court in question holding that the increase in the offer of games by such an operator was not inconsistent with a restrictive gambling policy, as it still served the objective of channelling consumers into gambling services of an explicitly regulated nature, thus constituting a countermeasure against illegal gambling. In this, the court noted that because the proposed SMS game at issue specifically targeted 18–24 year olds, it would undermine the struggle against gambling addiction in the Netherlands.

There is little consistency in this approach. It appears that in the Netherlands the public interest justifications regarding the protection of consumers, gamblers, and minors, is, when needed, drawn as a veil to cover what is effectively a State oligopoly in the provision of commercial gambling services. The true nature of Dutch law regulating commercial gambling is revealed in a recent draft law that proposes to permit interactive Internet gaming on an experimental and provisional basis.[150] The measure's Explanatory Memorandum reiterates the fundamental objectives of Dutch law in this regard: counteracting illegal online gambling, preventing addiction, and protecting the interests of consumers and minors.[151] Nevertheless, the manner in which this objective is to be fulfilled is highly restrictive and again appears to flout the requirements of Article 49 of the

---

[148] See, for example, Arnhem Court of Appeal 23.11.2004 (No AR 7476, 2004/287–9 KG) *Interwetten Cyprus and others v Nationale Sporttotalisator and others*, and *Study of Gambling Services in the Internal Market of the European Union*, ibid, at 646.

[149] 's Gravenhage (The Hague) District Court 01.04.2005 (No AWB 04/382 BESLU) *Stichting Exploitatie de Nederlandse Staatsloterij v Staatssecretaris van Financiën and Stichting de Nationale Sporttotalisator*, and *Study of Gambling Services in the Internal Market of the European Union*, ibid, at 652.

[150] Amendment of the Act on Games of Chance, containing temporary provisions on games of chance via the Internet, TK 2005–2006, 30362, no 2. See generally, *Study of Gambling Services in the Internal Market of the European Union*, ibid, at 634–637.

[151] The Explanatory Memorandum, TK 2005–2006, 30362, no 3, at p 2.

EC Treaty. The proposed legislation will ensure that only a single exclusive online gaming licence will be issued for the Netherlands, and that this will be granted to the current sole casino gaming licensee: apparently, only Holland Casino, as an experienced provider of gaming services, can be trusted to control and monitor online gaming in the manner required by Dutch gaming policy.[152] Furthermore, future online gaming licences will *de facto* be exclusive to Dutch entities given the strict conditions attached to the granting of such licences. These requirements, which effectively ensure that only Dutch operators can realistically hope to provide such services, include requirements regarding software and website design; off-line registration procedures; predicating participation in such activities on having a Dutch bank account and compliance with Dutch law against money laundering.[153]

It is of note that the Dutch Council of State (*Raad van State*), which is consulted on all draft legislation, has criticized the proposed measure in light of its (in)compatibility with EC law.[154] Central to the criticism is one simple point: the proposed measure will allow consumers, from the comfort of their own homes, to participate in online gaming. In participative and legislative terms, this (potentially) facilitates an especially marked increase in the supply of lawful gaming services in the Netherlands. Accordingly, how can this specific expansion in supply be seen as consistent with the generally restrictive Dutch policy on gaming and betting?[155] In other words, in practice, Dutch gaming policy ensures that preferred gaming operators in the Netherlands can continue to expand their gaming products and to carry out aggressive marketing campaigns in support of such promotions. It follows that it is difficult to see how the public interest justifications given in support of such a policy are little more than a legal veil under which the principal aim of Dutch legislators—raising revenue from commercial gambling—can continue unabated.[156]

B. Germany

In March 2006, that tension between the social and fiscal interests inherent in commercial gambling was brought to the attention of the German Federal Constitutional Court.[157] Under section 284 of the Criminal Code, unauthorized public games of chance are a criminal offence in German federal law. The regulation of authorized gaming is, with the limited exception outlined in the

---

[152] Ibid, at 3–4.   [153] Ibid, at 6–8.

[154] Advies Raad van State en nader rapport, TK 2005–2006, 30362, no 4.

[155] Ibid, at 2. See further Study of Gambling Services in the Internal Market of the European Union, ibid, 1st Part, Legal Study, ch 1, at 636 and 655–656.

[156] See generally N Huls, 'Dutch Gambling Law and Policy: An Untenable Parochial Approach', in A Littler and C Fijnaut (eds), *The Regulation of Gambling—European and National Perspectives* (Martinus Nijhoff Publishers, 2007) 69–79.

[157] BVerfG, 1 BvR 1054/01, judgment of 28 March 2006, BVerfGE 115, 276, available online at: <http://www.bverfg.de/entscheidungen/rs20060328_1bvr105401en.html>.

Racing Betting and Lottery Act of 8 April 1922, a matter for the various Länder. In July 2004, the Länder adopted a minimum uniform regulatory framework for the entire Federal Republic.[158] The fundamental objectives of that State Lottery Treaty are to prevent excessive gambling, to channel the natural gambling passions of the population in a controlled manner, to protect minors, and to ensure that associated revenues can be used to fund beneficial public projects.[159] In the stated case, the complainant operated as a bookmaker in Munich under the Racing Betting and Lottery Act of 1922. In July 1997, she sought to expand her business in order to facilitate sports betting within the rest of the EU. The Bavarian State authorities refused the application. Subsequently, the bookmaker lodged a constitutional complaint challenging the refusal on the ground that the Bavarian statutory scheme on commercial gambling violated her fundamental right of occupational freedom under Article 12(1) of the German Constitution (Basic Law).[160] In holding that the constitutional complaint was well-founded, the German Federal Constitutional Court undertook a careful and useful application of the proportionality appraisal criteria, and in particular the consistency requirement,[161] set out by the ECJ in *Gambelli*.[162]

By way of background, the regulation of commercial gambling in Bavaria operates on a State-sponsored, oligopoly basis.[163] The Bavarian State Lottery Act complied with the objectives set out in the pan-Länder Treaty of July 2004 and was underwritten by the criminal sanctions contained in section 284 of the Federal Criminal Code. The Constitutional Court held that the Bavarian scheme was incompatible with Article 12(1) of the Basic Law, not *per se* because it restricted and reserved the organization of sports betting to a State-sponsored monopoly, but because the legislation in question did not at the same time adequately ensure that its underlying objectives—ostensibly, an attempt to control addictive behaviour—were substantially realized.[164] Consequently, the monopolistic nature of the Bavarian scheme, as underpinned by criminal sanctions, was

---

[158] Staatsvertrag zum Lotteriewesen in Deutschland (State Treaty on Lotteries in Germany), Bavarian Law Gazette 2004, 230. See generally, C Pelz and CT Stempfle, 'Nationales Glücksspielverbot vs. Internationale Glücksspielfreiheit—Aus für das Staatsmonopol?' (2004) 7 Kommunikation & Recht 570–576.

[159] State Treaty on Lotteries in Germany, ibid, ss 1–4.

[160] This right has already been interpreted to include the organization of gambling by private operators. See BVerfG, 1 BvR 539/96, judgment of 19 July 2000, available online at: <http://www.bverfg.de/entscheidungen/rs20000719_1bvr053996.html>.

[161] BVerfG, 1 BvR 1054/01, n 157 above, at [136] and [144]. See C Koenig and S Fechtner, 'EG-Wettbewerbsrecht versus staatliches Glücksspielmonopol?' (2006) 17 Europäisches Wirtschafts- und Steuerrecht 529–536, at 529 and 533–535, and M Arendts, 'A View of European Gambling Regulation from the Perspective of Private Operators', in A Littler and C Fijnaut (eds), *The Regulation of Gambling—European and National Perspectives* (Martinus Nijhoff Publishers, 2007) 41–52, at 49–51.

[162] *Gambelli* [2003] ECR I-13031, at [67]–[69].

[163] See Article 2 of the Act on Lotteries and Bets Organised by the Free State of Bavaria of 29 April 1999 (Bavarian Law Gazette 1999, 226).

[164] BVerfG, 1 BvR 1054/01, n 157 above, at [79].

disproportionate in nature and in application, and not a justified restriction on the fundamental right of occupational freedom under Article 12(1) of the German Constitution.

In a practical manner, the Constitutional Court pointed out that contemporary research could not definitively assess the addictive potential of fixed-odds sports betting,[165] though it was clear that fixed odds were less susceptible to fraud and cheating.[166] In addition, despite the possibility that sports betting might have a corruptive influence on sport, the Court acknowledged that participation in sports betting remained largely a matter of 'pure recreation and entertainment'.[167] Of added importance was the Court's interpretation of Bavaria's public interest revenue rationale in creating a betting monopoly. In operation, such a goal must be supported by clear evidence that goes beyond a means of revenue raising *simpliciter* and demonstrates, for instance, the schemes by which such revenue assists in combating gambling addiction.[168] The Court emphasized that the organization of the contested monopoly did not reflect a genuine and consistent orientation to the goal of combating gambling passion and addiction.[169] It explained that the methods and the large scale of marketing and advertising used were not designed to channel the existing gambling passion towards State betting, but rather to stimulate and encourage people to bet; they thus resembled the financially effective marketing of a socially acceptable, or even positively valued, leisure activity.[170] Besides, the extensive network of agencies, taking the form of newspaper and tobacco shops or other small businesses proximate to consumers, and the possibility of placing sports bets via the Internet or by mobile phones, made sports betting a normal and easily accessible activity of everyday life.[171] In summary, although the Constitutional Court fully acknowledged a State's right to create a betting monopoly, it found that:

... in its present structure, as shaped by both statute and practice, the state betting monopoly created in Bavaria is a disproportionate encroachment on occupational freedom. Citizens who are interested in working in this area can reasonably be expected to suffer the effects of the exclusion of commercial betting by private betting shops—which is subject to criminal sanctions—only if the existing betting monopoly serves to avoid and avert gambling addiction and problematic gambling behaviour, *not only on paper*, but as specifically implemented in practice.[172]

It therefore called the national (federal or Länder) legislature to reform the existing scheme by the end of 2007, either by regulating the State monopoly in a way that ensures effective combating of gambling addiction, or by allowing and regulating the organization of sports betting by private operators under the control

---

[165] Ibid, at [99]–[101].   [166] Ibid, at [103]–[104].
[167] Ibid, at [102].   [168] As opposed to merely 'skimming off funds', ibid, at [107]–[110].
[169] Ibid, at [132].   [170] Ibid, at [133]–[136].
[171] Ibid, at [137]–[139].   [172] Ibid, at [119].

of the State.[173] A restructuring of the State monopoly in conformity with the Constitution would require a limitation of advertising to mere information about betting possibilities, a careful selection of distribution and marketing channels (including a ban on linking betting opportunities to TV broadcasts of sporting events), and independent supervisory bodies, sufficiently distant from the public-revenue interest of the State.[174]

In August 2006, the German Federal Competition Authority decided that the maintenance of the State monopoly of lotteries could not be justified, and declined to apply the judgment of the Federal Constitutional Court on sports betting by analogy to the lotteries sector. It suggested that the lotteries monop-oly should be interpreted in conformity with EC law, so that it allows Länder to restrict, on public policy basis only, the (online) activities of State lotteries from another Land, or of private operators licensed in another Member State.[175] This decision was confirmed by the Düsseldorf Appeals Court,[176] and partly by the Federal Court of Justice, which however held that EC law did not preclude German Länder from subjecting to prior authorization or even *ex ante* prohibit-ing the Internet activities of a State lottery licensed in another Land on public policy grounds.[177]

The Dutch and German experiences provide a microcosm of the EU-wide situ-ation with respect to commercial gambling. And the picture is one of inconsist-ency. On the one hand, the Dutch Government seems content to continue with a restrictive monopolistic approach to all forms of gambling even though the recent expansion into interactive Internet gambling is clearly at odds with the policy justifications underlying its restrictive gaming regime generally. On the other hand, the German Federal Constitutional Court has warned its Länder that, although monopolistic statutory schemes are not necessarily repugnant to the Basic Law, their underlying justificatory objectives must be proportionate in nature and must be seen to be proportionate in application.

---

[173] Ibid, at [148]–[149] and at [155]–[156]. Cf M Arendts, 'A View of European Gambling Regulation from the Perspective of Private Operators', in A Littler and C Fijnaut (eds), *The Regulation of Gambling—European and National Perspectives* (Martinus Nijhoff Publishers, 2007) 41–52, at 51–52, where it is questioned whether a State monopoly with such limited marketing and sales can be a viable option.
[174] BVerfG, 1 BvR 1054/01, ibid, at [150]–[154].
[175] Bundeskartellamt, B10–92713–Kc-148/05, Decision of 23 August 2006. C Pelz and CT Stempfle, 'Nationales Glücksspielverbot vs. Internationale Glücksspielfreiheit—Aus für das Staatsmonopol?' (2004) 7 Kommunikation & Recht 570–576, at 574–576, who argue for an appli-cation of this principle to the whole gaming and betting sector in Germany.
[176] OLG Düsseldorf, VI–Kart 15/06, and VI–Kart 15/06(V), judgments of 23 October 2006 and of 8 June 2007. See C Koenig and S Fechtner, ‚EG-Wettbewerbsrecht versus staatliches Glücksspielmonopol?' (2006) 17 Europäisches Wirtschafts- und Steuerrecht 529–536, at 529–530.
[177] Bundesgerichtshof (BGH), KVR 31/06, judgment of 8 May 2007, available online at: <http://juris.bundesgerichtshof.de/cgi-in/rechtsprechung>. See also M Winkelmüller, 'The German Sports Betting Market in Flux: Germany Faced by New Statutory Provisions and ECJ Rulings', (2008) 19 Entertainment Law Review 28–34.

In line with the requirements set out by the Constitutional Court's ruling, the Länder adopted the State Treaty on Games of Chance in Germany, which entered into force on 1 January 2008 and repealed the State Treaty on Lotteries.[178] This maintained the prerogative of the State (Länder) authorities to authorize the operation of games of chance—thus keeping intact the State monopolies—and prohibited the organization or distribution of such games on the Internet.[179] It also allowed advertising for games of chance, though only in the form of mere information about the possibility of participating in licensed games. On the other hand, it prohibited any stimulating or misleading advertising, advertising on TV, via the Internet or other telecommunications media, and advertising addressed to minors or other target groups that might be at similar risk of addiction.[180] Finally, it required domestically licensed operators to confine players to responsible gaming.[181]

At present, the unpredictable manner in which the Member States' authorities and courts interpret the compatibility of their statutory gambling schemes with the fundamental freedoms of the EC Treaty, and the relevant ECJ case law, is unsatisfactory. It is noteworthy that, in at least five post-*Gambelli* judgments, the Supreme Courts of the Netherlands, Italy, Belgium, Finland, and Sweden all confirmed that the national restrictive schemes were in conformity with EC law.[182]

In contrast, on 10 July 2007, the French *Cour de Cassation* overturned a decision by the Paris Court of Appeal that had upheld the fine imposed against Zeturf, a Malta-based provider of online betting services on horse races taking place in France. The French Supreme Court contested the compatibility with EC law of the State monopoly of horse-race betting in France, entrusted to the *Pari Mutuel Urbain* (PMU), and referred the case to the Paris Court of Appeal, asking it to determine, on the basis of concrete evidence, whether the French scheme complied with proportionality and did not in fact simply serve as a means of revenue-raising for the State.[183] In a similar vein, on 18 January 2008, the Court of Appeal of Versailles, examining an appeal against criminal proceedings brought against Mr Bookmaker, a provider of online lottery and betting services licensed in Malta, issued an order requesting additional information that would allow it to determine whether French legislation complied with EC law and the relevant

---

[178] Staatsvertrag zum Glücksspielwesen in Deutschland (State Treaty on Games of Chance in Germany), Hessen Law Gazette 2007 (I), 841, available online at: <http://www.uni-hohenheim.de/gluecksspiel/staatsvertrag/Ausfuehrungsgesetze/Hessen.pdf>.

[179] Ibid, at s 4.   [180] Ibid, at s 5.

[181] Ibid, at s 6. See H Schöttle, 'Online-Glücksspiele und der Glücksspiel-Staatsvertrag' (2008) 11 Kommunikation & Recht 155–160.

[182] See T Veenstra, 'State Licensed Lotteries and Toto Companies in the Legal and Political Debate in the European Union', in A Littler and C Fijnaut (eds), *The Regulation of Gambling—European and National Perspectives* (Martinus Nijhoff Publishers, 2007) 53–67, at 57.

[183] See European Betting and Gaming Association (EBGA), 'France's Supreme Court Challenges Gaming Monopoly', available online at: <http://www.eu-ba.org/en/press/135>. See also C Rohsler, 'The Beginning of the End?' (2007) 6 World Online Gambling Law Report 16.

ECJ case law.[184] Meanwhile in Germany, the Administrative Courts of Cologne, Stuttgart and Giessen have referred a number of preliminary questions to the ECJ on the compatibility of the State-sponsored monopoly on sports betting and lotteries with the freedoms of services and establishment.[185] Pending those preliminary references, the Stuttgart Administrative Court recently granted a stay of execution against a ban imposed on the operations of the intermediary in Germany of a sports betting operator licensed in Malta.[186] By contrast, the Administrative Court of Appeals in Baden-Württemberg held that EC law did not preclude the ban in Germany on advertising for (including the sponsorship of the VfB Stuttgart football club by) *betandwin*, a bookmaker licensed in the UK-dependent territory of Gibraltar.[187]

Moreover, it is not surprising that the Commission has recently initiated infringement proceedings against a number of Member States, including Austria, Denmark, France, Greece, Finland, Germany, Hungary, Italy, the Netherlands, and Sweden, challenging the compatibility of various aspects of their national gambling regimes with EC law.[188] The Commission has also opposed a French Bill, which aims to block payments to online gaming operators proscribed by the French authorities, including operators duly licensed in other Member States, and thus to discourage consumers in France from participating in any other online games than the ones offered by the monopoly holders in France (*la Française des Jeux* and *PMU*).[189]

It is contended that this piecemeal approach will continue unless legislative intervention, in the form of minimum harmonization, is initiated at EC level. Equally, the Dutch and Bavarian examples illustrate implicitly why Member States will continue, in matters of commercial gambling, to flout the boundaries of, and exploit their discretion to derogate from the fundamental freedoms of the EC Treaty; and the reason is straightforward—the massive amounts of revenue at

---

[184] See European Betting and Gaming Association (EBGA), 'EBGA Welcomes Decision by French Criminal Court', available online at: <http://www.eu-ba.org/en/press/263>.

[185] Case C-409/06 *Winner Wetten GmbH v Mayor of Bergheim* [2006] OJ C326/25, Case C-316/07 *Markus Stoss v Wetteraukreis* [2007] OJ C269/16, Case C-358/07 *Kulpa Automatenservice Asperg GmbH v Land Baden-Württemberg* [2007] OJ C269/19, Case C-359/07 *SOBO Sport & Entertainment GmbH v Land Baden-Württemberg* [2007] OJ C269/19, Case C-360/07 *Andreas Kunert v Land Baden-Württemberg* [2007] OJ C269/20, Case C-409/07 *Avalon-Service-Online-Dienste GmbH v Wetteraukreis* [2007] OJ C283/14, and Case C-410/07 *Olaf Amadeus Wilhelm Happel v Wetteraukreis* [2007] OJ C283/14.

[186] VG Stuttgart, 4 K 213/08, judgment of 28 February 2008, available online at: <http://www.aufrecht.de/urteile>.

[187] Verwaltungsgerichtshof (VGH) Baden-Württemberg, 6 S 2020/06, judgment of 27 August 2007, available online at: <http://www.justizportal-bw.de>.

[188] See Press Releases IP/07/909 of 27/06/2007, IP/07/360 of 21/03/2007, IP/06/1362 of 12/10/2006, IP/06/436 of 04/04/2006, IP/08/118 of 31/01/2008, IP/08/119 of 31/01/2008, and IP/08/330 of 28/02/2008, available online at: <http://ec.europa.eu/internal_market/services/gambling_en.htm>.

[189] See European Betting and Gaming Association (EBGA), 'European Commission Opposes Payment Blocking in France', available online at: <http://www.eu-ba.org/en/press/296>.

Doukas and Anderson

stake. It is estimated that the turnover figures of commercial gambling run in the billions of euros.[190] That share of the pot is, in all probability, the principal reason why access by private operators, especially those from other Member States, to the gambling market of a Member State is prevented or otherwise impeded. It is why State monopolies rather than independent statutory bodies are the regulatory mechanism of choice, and it explains why, under current law, the interplay of public interest objectives and State fiscal interests will continue to be skewed in favour of the latter to the detriment of the integration of national markets in the services concerned, and thus to the detriment of the establishment and functioning of the internal market.[191]

V. The Need for Harmonization: From a Game Reserve to a Gaming Market

Despite the efforts of the ECJ to strike a balance between the protection of gambling in the context of the fundamental freedoms and the national discretion to impose restrictions on public interest grounds, the 'EU gambling market' still remains a 'game reserve' for the exploitation of the Member States.[192] The adverse impact of the divergences in national laws regulating gambling activities on the establishment and the smooth functioning of the internal market of gambling or associated services (such as media, sports, or tourism)[193] would make a strong case for the need of harmonization, and the competence of the Community[194] on the basis of Articles 95 or 47(2) and 55 of the EC Treaty. It is respectfully submitted that harmonization in this field could follow one of two models.

---

[190] In 2003, the five largest sectors of the EU gambling market—lotteries; casino gaming; machine gambling; sports betting and bingo—generated gross revenues of approximately €51,500 million; see *Study of Gambling Services in the Internal Market of the European Union—Final Report of 14 June 2006* (prepared by the Swiss Institute of Comparative Law for the European Commission), Executive Summary, at p xxxvi and, more generally, 2nd Part, Economic Study, at chs 3–4.

[191] Cf C Pelz and CT Stempfle, 'Nationales Glücksspielverbot vs. Internationale Glücksspielfreiheit—Aus für das Staatsmonopol?' (2004) 7 Kommunikation & Recht 570–576, at 575–576, and T Stein, 'Die Entwicklung der europäischen Glücksspielrechtsprechung und deren Auswirkung auf den deutschen Lotteriemarkt' (2002) 13 Europäisches Wirtschafts- und Steuerrecht 416–424, at 424.

[192] Stein, ibid, at 416.

[193] See Study of Gambling Services in the Internal Market of the European Union, n 190 above, Executive Summary, at p iv.

[194] Cf Case C-376/98 *Germany v European Parliament and Council* ('*Tobacco Advertising*') [2000] ECR I-8419, at [83]–[86], [95] and [101]; Case C-491/01 *R v Secretary of State for Health, ex p British American Tobacco (Investments) Ltd and Imperial Tobacco Ltd* ('*Tobacco Labelling*') [2002] ECR I-11453, at [60]–[61] and [74]–[75], and Case C-380/03 *Germany v European Parliament and Council* ('*Tobacco Advertising II*') [2006] ECR I-11573, at [36]–[38]. *Contra* M Sura, *Die grenzüberschreitende Veranstaltung von Glücksspielen im europäischen Binnenmarkt* (Nomos, 1995) at 239 *et seq.*

The first model would be based on the model adopted by the 'Television without Frontiers' Directive 89/552,[195] ie the 'Member State of origin' principle,[196] inherent also in the original Commission Proposal[197] that preceded the Services Directive,[198] combined with re-regulation through minimum harmonization of national rules on gambling activities.[199] These would include rules on the licensing of service providers, the content, quality and promotion of gambling services, and the protection of the public interest objectives at stake, such as the protection of consumers as service recipients, the prevention of crime, fraud or incitement to squander, and the maintenance of the public and social order. The aim of the proposed Directive would be to eliminate obstacles to the freedom to provide cross-border gambling services arising from disparities existing between the national laws on the pursuit of gambling activities. It would therefore lay down minimum rules for gambling services emanating from and intended for reception within the Community, and in particular in another Member State.

Accordingly, providers of gambling services would, in effect, be subject only to the national laws of their home Member State, including rules on access to and exercise of a gambling activity—in particular the behaviour and liability of the provider; and the quality, content, or promotion of gambling services. The Member State of origin would be primarily responsible for ensuring that any operator established on its territory complies with the national law applicable to gambling activities and with the provisions of the Directive.[200] On the other hand, Member States could not restrict, for reasons falling within the co-ordinated fields, gambling services provided on their territory by operators established in another Member State, unless there were exceptional circumstances for derogations,[201] mainly justified by a serious breach of the provisions of the Directive on the protection of consumers or the public order, and the prevention of crime and fraud. Thus, the principal regulator of the gambling activity

---

[195] Council Directive 89/552/EEC of 3 October 1989 on the coordination of certain provisions laid down by law, regulation or administrative action in Member States concerning the pursuit of television broadcasting activities, [1989] OJ L298/23, as amended by Directive 97/36/EC of the European Parliament and the Council of 30 June 1997, [1997] OJ L202/60, and by Directive 2007/65/EC of the European Parliament and the Council of 11 December 2007, [2007] OJ L332/27.

[196] Opinion of AG Colomer in *Placanica* [2007] ECR I-1891, at [144] and [147]–[148]. Cf P Larouche, 'A View from the Outside', in A Littler and C Fijnaut (eds), *The Regulation of Gambling—European and National Perspectives* (Martinus Nijhoff Publishers, 2007) 1–7, at 5.

[197] Article 16 of Proposal for a Directive of the European Parliament and of the Council on services in the internal market, COM(2004)2 final/3 (the 'Bolkenstein' Proposal). Article 18(1)(b) of the Proposal provided for a temporary derogation from the application of the country of origin principle to gambling until 2010.

[198] Directive 2006/123/EC of the European Parliament and of the Council of 12 December 2006 on services in the internal market, [2006] OJ L376/36.

[199] See generally, C Barnard, *The Substantive Law of the EU—The Four Freedoms* (2nd edn, OUP, 2007) at 384 *et seq.*

[200] Cf Articles 2(1) and 3(6) (*ex*-Article 3(2)) of Directive 89/552.

[201] Cf Article 2a of Directive 89/552.

would be the home Member State, and the presumption would be that the host
Member State could not impose additional rules or requirements unless there
were strong reasons exceptionally justifying derogations. The home Member
State could impose more detailed or stricter rules than the ones provided by the
Directive only on gambling operators established in its territory.[202] With regard
to providers of services established in other Member States, stricter rules could
exceptionally only be imposed if they did not amount to a double control, additional to the one already carried out in the Member State of origin, and did not
prevent the provision of gambling services as such.[203]

On the one hand, such a model would appear to be more likely to respond to
the increasing growth and sophistication of the gambling market within the EU.
That growth includes the emergence of new forms of remote gambling via the
Internet, through mobile telephone services, or through interactive TV wagering.
It would also entail the fusion of remote with land-based gambling, not only in
branding and marketing (including the use of contracted data transmission centres), but also in the context of retail outlets (such as Internet sports cafés offering
the possibility of gambling on remote sites).[204] A harmonization measure based
on home country control was also suggested by Advocate General Colomer in
Placanica.[205] It would have the advantage of opening up the market in gambling
services, while at the same time affording a uniform minimum level of protection
to the public interest objectives currently pursued by the national licensing or
exclusive rights systems of the Member States, such as protection of consumers
and public policy, and prevention of crime and fraud.[206] This would satisfy the
need to prevent an exploitation of the human passion for gambling acknowledged by the ECJ.[207] It is also true that even in Member States with a high level of
liberalization in the gambling sector, such as the UK, national legislation is based
on the principle of unstimulated demand, which requires that the offer of games
of chance should respond to the existing play instinct, but not increase it.[208]

[202] Cf Article 3(1) of Directive 89/552.
[203] On cross-border TV broadcasting, see Joined Cases C-34 to 36/95 *Konsumentombudsmannen (KO) v De Agostini (Svenska) Förlag AB and TV-Shop i Sverige AB* ('*De Agostini*') [1997] ECR I-3843, at [34] and [38].
[204] Study of Gambling Services in the Internal Market of the European Union, n 190 above, Executive Summary, at xxxv *et seq*. xl–xli and xliii. See also P Kerstens, 'Gambling Policy—The EU Dilemma', in A Littler and C Fijnaut (eds), *The Regulation of Gambling—European and National Perspectives* (Martinus Nijhoff Publishers, 2007) 9–13, at 9–11.
[205] He argued for a harmonization of national rules on gambling on the model of the (then draft) Directive on Services. See Opinion of AG Colomer in *Placanica* [2007] ECR I-1891, at [128]–[130], [132], [144], and [147]–[148], with reference to Opinion of AG La Pergola in *Läärä* [1999] ECR I-6067, at [36], and COM (2004)2 final/3, n 197 above.
[206] Cf M Arendts, 'A View of European Gambling Regulation from the Perspective of Private Operators', in A Littler and C Fijnaut (eds), *The Regulation of Gambling—European and National Perspectives* (Martinus Nijhoff Publishers, 2007) 41–52, at 52.
[207] Cf S Walz, 'Gambling um *Gambelli*?—Rechtsfolgen der Entscheidung *Gambelli* für das staatli-che Sportwettenmonopol' (2004) 15 Europäische Zeitschrift für Wirtschaftsrecht 523–526, at 523.
[208] See T Stein, 'Die Entwicklung der europäischen Glücksspielrechtsprechung und deren Auswirkung auf den deutschen Lotteriemarkt' (2002) 13 Europäisches Wirtschafts- und Steuerrecht 416–424, at 419.

On the other hand, such a model would exempt operators licensed in their Member State of establishment from the requirement of also obtaining a licence from the national authorities of another Member State, in order to provide their gambling services in that State.[209] This would allow gambling operators to choose freely their Member State of establishment, which, although it might give rise to a tax competition between Member States,[210] would not constitute an abuse of the freedom of establishment, in line with the *Centros* authority.[211] It would further mark the end of any outright bans on gambling activities in the form of any *de jure* or *de facto* State monopoly or any monopolistic position for private operators (eg national lotteries) currently existing in the Member States.[212] Hence, such a model would undoubtedly seem extremely difficult to reconcile with the discretion traditionally enjoyed by Member States to regulate, restrict, or even prohibit gambling activities in their territory, and their latitude to set their policy object-ives and determine the level of protection to be afforded in this field.[213] Given the acute sensitivity of such activities, from a moral and cultural viewpoint, and their serious social and financial repercussions, it would appear most unlikely, under the current state of EC law, that Member States would readily consent to opening the market in gambling services in a manner that would allow for exten-sive cross-border competition or relatively unconstrained remote gambling.[214] Doubtless, given the number of the Member States involved, a qualified majority would be extremely difficult to achieve. Added to this, it is uncertain whether such a proposal could be passed in the European Parliament given the serious concerns recently voiced by the latter about a possible deregulation of the gam-bling market.[215]

Admittedly, it was the specific nature of the relevant activities, 'which entail implementation by Member States of policies relating to public policy and consumer protection',[216] and significant lobbying pressure,[217] that led to the

---

[209] Cf Study of Gambling Services in the Internal Market of the European Union, n 190 above, Executive Summary, at xv.

[210] Cf T Veenstra, 'State Licensed Lotteries and Toto Companies in the Legal and Political Debate in the European Union', in A Littler and C Fijnaut (eds), *The Regulation of Gambling—European and National Perspectives* (Martinus Nijhoff Publishers, 2007) 53–67, at 64.

[211] See Case C-212/97 *Centros Ltd v Erhvervs- og Selskabsstyrelsen* ('*Centros*') [1999] ECR I-1459, at [17]–[18], [20], [27], and [29], and Case C-167/01 *Kamer van Koophandel en Fabrieken voor Amsterdam v Inspire Art Ltd* ('*Inspire Art*') [2003] ECR I-10155, at [95]–[98].

[212] Cf Study of Gambling Services in the Internal Market of the European Union, n 190 above, Executive Summary, at p xvi.

[213] See Walz, n 207 above, at 526.

[214] Cf Study of Gambling Services in the Internal Market of the European Union, Executive Summary, ibid, at xlvi. See also Opinion of AG Gulmann in *Schindler* [1994] ECR I-1039, at [85] and [112]–[114].

[215] Report of the Committee on Culture and Education of the European Parliament entitled 'Towards an EU Policy on Sport' ('Mavromatis Report') of 31 March 2008, and European Parliament Resolution of 8 May 2008 on the White Paper on Sport, P6_TA(2008)0198, at [87] and [89], both available online at: <http://www.europarl.europa.eu>.

[216] Recital (25) of Preamble to Directive 2006/123/EC.

[217] Part of this pressure was exerted by the European sports federations, which warned of a sub-stantial decrease in income for sports and education or employment from state licensed national

exclusion of gambling, including lottery and betting transactions, from the scope of the recent Services Directive.[218] While it cannot be disputed that the greater the choice and offer, the greater the incitement to squander and the risks for the public interests at stake,[219] the national concerns could be balanced by the proposed re-regulation through minimum safeguards against addiction to, or abuse of, gambling for criminal or fraudulent purposes. While re-regulation was not possible in the context of the general Directive on Services, given the broad and unidentified nature of services covered,[220] it is feasible and indispensable in the context of a specific harmonization measure on cross-border gambling. In fact, the common threads and the largely similar considerations underlying the national licensing systems can—despite their individual disparities and varying levels of liberalisation—provide a common ground for regulating the gaming market at Community level.[221]

An alternative could be a harmonization model based on the mutual recognition principle, inherent in the ECJ case law, and also in the final version of the Directive on Services,[222] after this was grafted from the 'country of origin' principle prescribed in the original *Bolkenstein* Proposal.[223] The emphasis would thus be shifted from the home Member State of the provider, as the principal regulator of a cross-border provision of services, to the principal power of the host Member State to impose restrictions.[224] Under the mutual recognition principle, in its (judicially applied) non-absolute form, home State control could only

lotteries. See D Miers, 'A British View of European Gambling Regulation', in A Littler and C Fijnaut (eds), *The Regulation of Gambling—European and National Perspectives* (Martinus Nijhoff Publishers, 2007) 81–126, at 84, and J Shaw, J Hunt, and C Wallace, *Economic and Social Law of the European Union* (Palgrave MacMillan, 2007) at 159.

[218] Article 2(2)(h) of Directive 2006/123/EC. Cf T Verbiest, 'French and Belgian Views on European Gambling Regulation', in A Littler and C Fijnaut (eds), *The Regulation of Gambling—European and National Perspectives* (Martinus Nijhoff Publishers, 2007) 126–159, at 133–138.

[219] S Walz, 'Gambling um *Gambelli*'—Rechtsfolgen der Entscheidung *Gambelli* für das staatliche Sportwettenmonopol' (2004) 15 Europäische Zeitschrift für Wirtschaftsrecht 523–526, at 524–525.

[220] See C Barnard, *The Substantive Law of the EU—The Four Freedoms* (2nd edn, OUP, 2007) at 401.

[221] Cf Opinion of AG Colomer in *Placanica* [2007] ECR I-1891, at [130]; Opinion of AG Gulmann in *Schindler* [1994] ECR I-1039, at [1]; and Opinion of AG Alber in *Gambelli* [2003] ECR I-13031, at [118]. Cf also P Kerstens, 'Gambling Policy—The EU Dilemma', in A Littler and C Fijnaut (eds), *The Regulation of Gambling—European and National Perspectives* (Martinus Nijhoff Publishers, 2007) 9–13, at 10–11, and T Stein, 'Die Entwicklung der europäischen Glücksspielrechtsprechung und deren Auswirkung auf den deutschen Lotteriemarkt' (2002) 13 Europäisches Wirtschafts- und Steuerrecht 416–424, at 416 and at 417–420.

[222] Article 16 of Directive 2006/123/EC.

[223] Article 16(1) and (2) of Proposal for a Directive of the European Parliament and of the Council on services in the internal market, COM(2004)2 final/3.

[224] Account only being taken of the protection provided in the home country. See C Barnard, *The Substantive Law of the EU—The Four Freedoms* (2nd edn, OUP, 2007) at 401–406. Cf J Flower, 'Negotiating European Legislation: The Services Directive' (2006–07) 9 Cambridge Yearbook of European Legal Studies 217–238, at 232–235, and C Barnard, 'Unravelling the Services Directive' (2008) 45 CML Rev 323–394.

prevail in the absence of a sufficiently compelling basis for host State control.[225] Accordingly, gambling operators could enjoy the freedom to provide their services in a Member State other than their home Member State. The host country could, notwithstanding that freedom, in principle impose its own requirements and restrictions on access to or the exercise of a gambling activity in its own territory, provided that such rules did not involve any discrimination on grounds of nationality or establishment in another Member State,[226] and were justified on public interest grounds and satisfied the principle of proportionality.[227] In this context, the host country could and should take into account the protection already afforded to the public interest objectives in question by the laws of the Member State of origin of the gambling operators,[228] so as to avoid creating unjustified double burdens.[229] The only requirements that the host Member State would, by definition, be precluded from imposing on the services provided by gambling operators from other Member States would be a requirement of establishment in its territory; authorization from the competent national authorities of the host country; or a ban on the setting up of infrastructure in its territory, necessary for the provision of services.[230]

The only common denominator between the two models would be the harmonization of the rules on the freedom of establishment of providers of gambling services, and especially their subjection to a licensing or prior authorization system. Any such national system should be applied in a non-discriminatory manner and be based on objective, clear, and non-discriminatory criteria and requirements, which are justified on public interest grounds, comply with proportionality, and provide full guarantees of impartiality and transparency. This would preclude national authorities from exercising their power in an arbitrary manner.[231] Besides, authorization for a new establishment should not involve duplicate controls, equivalent or essentially comparable as to their purpose, to those which a provider is already subject to in the same or another Member State.[232]

It is true that the second model, which would in principle allow every Member State to impose its own restrictions on gambling services within the limits of EC law,[233] would broadly reflect the established case law of the ECJ under Article 49

[225] See S Weatherill, 'Pre-emption, Harmonisation and the Distribution of Competence to Regulate the Internal Market', in C Barnard and J Scott (eds), *The Law of the Single European Market—Unpacking the Premises* (Hart Publishing, 2002) 41–73, at 45.

[226] Cf Article 16(1) of Directive 2006/123/EC.

[227] Cf Article 16(1) and (3) of Directive 2006/123/EC.

[228] Cf C Barnard, *The Substantive Law of the EU—The Four Freedoms* (2nd edn, OUP, 2007) at 404–406.

[229] See further P Craig and G de Búrca, *EU Law—Text, Cases and Materials* (4th edn, OUP, 2007) at 843.

[230] Cf Article 16(2)(a)–(c) of Directive 2006/123/EC.

[231] Cf Articles 9(1), 10(1)–(2), 12(1)–(2), and 13–15 of Directive 2006/123/EC.

[232] Cf Article 10(3) of Directive 2006/123/EC.

[233] Cf Articles 30(1)–(2) and 31(1) of Directive 2006/123/EC. See also P Larouche, 'A View from the Outside', in A Littler and C Fijnaut (eds), *The Regulation of Gambling—European and National Perspectives* (Martinus Nijhoff Publishers, 2007) 1–7, at 6–7.

of the EC Treaty.[234] Unlike the country of origin approach, which would establish a strong presumption of illegality of any restrictive measures adopted by
the host Member State, under the model based on mutual recognition, this presumption of illegality would be much weaker,[235] as the wide discretion of each
Member State to regulate gambling activities in its own territory would constitute the rule.[236] As such, the second model would inevitably inherit the basic
criticism attracted by the general Directive on Services: appearing inadequate to
remove obstacles to the free movement of gambling services and thus unlikely to
affect the extant fragmentation of the relevant market.[237] Accordingly, it might
be criticized for being a mere restatement of the established case law and affording legislative authority to the pragmatic compromise developed by the ECJ in
the field of services over the years.[238]

Nonetheless, despite its frailties, such a harmonization measure in the field of
gambling services would, it is argued, enhance legal certainty.[239] It could better circumscribe the discretion enjoyed by national authorities because it has the
potential to go beyond the caution shown by the Court on certain issues, such
as the objectivity of the criteria of a national licensing system in the betting and
gaming sector, a question which was left open in *Placanica*. More importantly,
affording legislative authority to the minimum legal standards established by the
Court would ensure uniform and due implementation across the Community.[240]
This would be more beneficial to the internal market of gambling services than
piecemeal judgments delivered by the ECJ on specific questions raised by individual national courts or the Commission in infringement proceedings against
individual Member States, which are, in practice, followed fitfully by national
jurisdictions.[241]

Overall, and in consideration of the inherent drawbacks of the second model,
the first harmonization model, based on the home country principle and re-regulation, appears more likely to strike the right balance between free movement in
the legitimate, albeit heavily regulated, gambling sector and the protection of the
public interests at stake. It could effectively overcome the barriers arising from

---

[234] Note Barnard, n 228 above, at 405.   [235] Ibid, at 405–406.

[236] Discussed by J Shaw, J Hunt, and C Wallace, *Economic and Social Law of the European Union* (Palgrave MacMillan, 2007), at 158, and T Stein, 'Die Entwicklung der europäischen Glücksspielrechtsprechung und deren Auswirkung auf den deutschen Lotteriemarkt' (2002) 13 Europäisches Wirtschafts- und Steuerrecht 416–424, at 422.

[237] Shaw et al., ibid, at 159–160.

[238] Ibid, at 159, and P Craig and G de Búrca, *EU Law—Text, Cases and Materials* (4th edn, OUP, 2007) at 843–844.

[239] Cf P Kerstens, 'Gambling Policy—The EU Dilemma', in A Littler and C Fijnaut (eds), *The Regulation of Gambling—European and National Perspectives* (Martinus Nijhoff Publishers, 2007) 9–13, at 12.

[240] Cf S Walz, 'Gambling um *Gambelli*?—Rechtsfolgen der Entscheidung *Gambelli* für das staatli-che Sportwettenmonopol' (2004) 15 Europäische Zeitschrift für Wirtschaftsrecht 523–526, at 524.

[241] Note D Miers, 'A British View of European Gambling Regulation', in A Littler and C Fijnaut (eds), *The Regulation of Gambling—European and National Perspectives* (Martinus Nijhoff Publishers, 2007) 81–126, at 82.

divergent national laws, and successfully face the reality of the rapid expansion of remote and cross-border gambling activities thanks to modern technology, and particularly the Internet, which has shattered, and does not recognize, traditional geographical boundaries.[242] Moreover, such a model could put an end to the legal *lacuna* left by the Directive 2000/31 on e-commerce,[243] which, although it established the country of origin principle for information society services, expressly excluded from its scope 'gambling activities which involve wagering a stake with monetary value in games of chance, including lotteries and betting transactions'.[244] It could further fill the gap left in consumer protection by Directive 2005/29/EC on unfair commercial practices, which applies without prejudice to national authorization regimes, including rules relating to gambling activities.[245]

In a broader sense, and given the moral, cultural, social, and economic particularities of gambling that justify the discretion of Member States to pursue their policies in this field,[246] it has been disputed whether Community action would be consistent with the principle of subsidiarity (Article 5(2) of the EC Treaty).[247] In fact, this was the underlying reason why the Community had abandoned its initial initiative to regulate the gambling sector following the December 1992 European Council in Edinburgh,[248] and had not put forward any harmonization proposals until the end of the 1990s.[249] However, given the existing fragmentation

---

[242] See further, the comments of A Littler, 'Has the ECJ's Jurisprudence in the Field of Gambling Become more Restrictive when Applying the Proportionality Principle?', in A Littler and C Fijnaut (eds), *The Regulation of Gambling—European and National Perspectives* (Martinus Nijhoff Publishers, 2007) 15–40, at 17 and 19–21, Kerstens, n 239, at 11, and C Pelz and CT Stempfle, 'Nationales Glücksspielverbot vs. Internationale Glücksspielfreiheit—Aus für das Staatsmonopol?' (2004) 7 Kommunikation & Recht 570–576, at 570.

[243] Directive 2000/31/EC of the European Parliament and of the Council of 8 June 2000 on certain legal aspects of information society services, in particular electronic commerce, in the internal market ('Directive on e-commerce'), [2000] OJ L178/1.

[244] Ibid, Art 1(5)(d), third indent. See Opinion of AG Colomer in *Placanica* [2007] ECR I-1891, at [145]. See also Littler, n 242 above, at 20–21, Miers, n 241 above, at 83, and J Hörnle, 'Country of Origin Regulation in Cross-border Media: One Step beyond the Freedom to Provide Services?' (2005) 54 ICLQ 89–126.

[245] See Recital (9) of Preamble and Article 3(8) of Directive 2005/29/EC of the European Parliament and of the Council of 11 May 2005 concerning unfair business-to-consumer commercial practices in the internal market, [2005] OJ L149/22.

[246] See *Schindler* [1994] ECR I–1039, at [60], *Gambelli* [2003] ECR I-13031, at [63], and *Placanica* [2007] ECR I-1891, at [47].

[247] See T Veenstra, 'State Licensed Lotteries and Toto Companies in the Legal and Political Debate in the European Union', in A Littler and C Fijnaut (eds), *The Regulation of Gambling—European and National Perspectives* (Martinus Nijhoff Publishers, 2007) 53–67, at 62–63 and 65. Cf P Kerstens, 'Gambling Policy—The EU Dilemma', in A Littler and C Fijnaut (eds), ibid, 9–13, at 10, and T Stein, 'Die Entwicklung der europäischen Glücksspielrechtsprechung und deren Auswirkung auf den deutschen Lotteriemarkt' (2002) 13 Europäisches Wirtschafts- und Steuerrecht 416–424, at 416–417.

[248] See Conclusions of the Presidency of the European Council—Edinburgh, 12 December 1992, Annex 2 to Part A: Subsidiarity, Examples of the Review of Pending Proposals and Existing Legislation, available online at: <http://www.europarl.europa.eu/summits/edinburgh/a2_en.pdf> p 31. See also Miers, n 241 above, at 105.

[249] See Council Response to Written Question No 3068/98, [1999] OJ C142/80.

of the gambling market into differing national regimes, the compatibility of a Community harmonization measure could be defended on similar grounds as the ones upheld by the ECJ in the *Tobacco Labelling* case.[250] The objective of the proposed measure is to eliminate the barriers raised to free movement within the internal market by the differences that still exist between the Member States' laws on the pursuit of gambling activities, while ensuring a high level of consumer protection in accordance with Article 95(3) of the EC Treaty. Such an objective cannot, it is argued, be sufficiently achieved by the Member States individually, as illustrated by the multifarious development of national laws, and calls for action at Community level.[251]

This approach would be in line with the rationale underlying the Community harmonization in the acutely sensitive field of broadcasting, and the recent Directive 2007/65 which extended the scope of the Directive 89/552 to all audiovisual media services, including those provided on-demand.[252] According to the relevant Commission's Proposal, there would be a real risk of barriers to the free movement and of legal uncertainty if, with the emergence of on-demand audiovisual services, Member States were to derogate from the country of origin principle for public policy reasons with the effect that such services would be subject to non-harmonized rules in different Member States.[253]

The proposed harmonization model would also respond to the need to review the Directive on e-commerce, already acknowledged by the Commission.[254] Referring to the complaints received from companies engaged in cross-border online gambling activities excluded from the scope of Directive 2000/31, the Commission explained that operators established in a Member State, and providing sports betting services via the Internet, are currently required by other Member States (eg, Denmark, Germany, Italy, and the Netherlands) to bar access to their services by the residents in those countries.[255] It added that the new, more liberal, regulatory schemes introduced by several Member States with regard to online gambling, entail the risk of regulatory fragmentation and distortions of competition.[256]

A final issue may be raised as to the appropriateness of the subjection of all commercial gambling activities to the same rules, since not all forms of games of

---

[250] *Tobacco Labelling* [2002] ECR I-11453, at [181]–[183].

[251] Ibid.   [252] Article 1 of Directive 2007/65/EC.

[253] Proposal for a Directive of the European Parliament and of the Council amending Council Directive 89/552/EEC, COM(2005)646 final, Explanatory Memorandum, at p 9. Cf Recitals (7) and (27) of Preamble to Directive 2007/65/EC.

[254] Report from the Commission to the European Parliament, the Council and the European Economic and Social Committee—First Report on the application of Directive 2000/31/EC, 21 November 2003, COM(2003)702 final.

[255] Ibid, at pp 19 and 21.

[256] Ibid, at p 21. See also Commission Decision 2005/752/EC of 24 October 2005 establishing an expert group on electronic commerce, [2005] OJ L282/20. Cf T Verbiest, 'French and Belgian Views on European Gambling Regulation', in A Littler and C Fijnaut (eds), *The Regulation of Gambling— European and National Perspectives* (Martinus Nijhoff Publishers, 2007) 126–159, at 130–133.

chance entail the same level of risk.[257] Admittedly, although, for example, fixed-odds sports betting may have a lesser addiction potential than 'genuine' casino and machine gambling, one cannot underestimate the serious risks involved which are very likely to arise if the former is practised at a larger scale and if organizers become insolvent, or gamblers and organizers engage in criminal or fraudulent activities.[258] The only distinction that should always be made in the context of the proposed re-regulation is the one already adopted by the ECJ between commercial gambling activities and recreational games, which are not by nature lucrative games of chance.[259]

VI. Conclusions

Commercial gambling as a cross-border economic activity is protected by the free movement provisions, primarily on services and establishment but also on goods. However, its scope of protection is considerably constrained because of the wide discretion generally enjoyed by Member States to regulate, restrict, or even prohibit gambling activities in their territory on public interest grounds. The ECJ has been anxious to refine the limits set to the discretion of national authorities in this field by the principles of proportionality and non-discrimination. It has therefore required that the national legal regimes appropriately, genuinely, and consistently limit gambling activities. The national regimes must be transparent by providing, for instance, for a tendering procedure for the licensing of gambling. They must also be substantiated by concrete evidence about the causal link between the gravity of the risks of excess gambling and the participation in gambling services, especially those provided from other Member States.

Nevertheless, the Court seems generally to avoid engaging in a rigorous review of the compatibility of the national licensing systems with the EC Treaty, and in principle leaves the assessment of their proportionality to national courts. In this context, it has not ruled out the possibility that even a national policy of expansion of the gambling opportunities, offered by a *de jure* or *de facto* State monopoly operator, might be justified by the need to channel gambling passions into a controlled system. On the other hand, the ECJ has been anxious to be seen to apply a more rigorous proportionality test to measures that seem to manifestly exceed the limits of the national discretion in this field. These measures include directly discriminatory taxation of winnings from gambling in another Member State; a blanket exclusion of certain companies from the tendering procedure; the

---

[257] Cf T Stein, 'Die Entwicklung der europäischen Glücksspielrechtsprechung und deren Auswirkung auf den deutschen Lotteriemarkt' (2002) 13 Europäisches Wirtschafts- und Steuerrecht 416–424, at 423.

[258] Note further the comments in BVerfG, 1 BvR 1054/01, judgment of 28 March 2006, BVerfGE 115, 276, at [100]–[106].

[259] See '*Electronic Games*' [2006] ECR I-10341, at [45] and [55]–[56].

accompanying sanctions imposed on them for operating without the requisite prior authorization; a renewal of existing licences without a tendering procedure; or a total ban on the operation outside casinos of recreational electronic games, which are not by nature lucrative games of chance.

Thus, despite the limits set by the ECJ case law, Member States still enjoy substantial latitude in determining their policy objectives and the level of protection in the gaming sector. The Court's deferential approach to this latitude allows Member States, in principle and in practice, to maintain the *de jure* or *de facto* monopolistic or oligopolistic organization of their national gambling markets, and caters for the overall reticence of national courts to question the compatibility of the existing national regimes with EC law. This has resulted in clear inconsistencies in the manner in which the various national gambling statutory systems adopt and adapt to the criteria established by the ECJ with regard to their public interest justification and the assessment of their compliance with the principles of proportionality and non-discrimination. The Community's piecemeal approach to cross-border commercial gambling, by avoiding any harmonization and leaving it to the ECJ to decide upon specific points of conflict between national gambling laws and EC law, perpetuates the current fragmentation of the gambling market in the EU. Bluntly, the EU gambling market remains a game reserve for the exploitation of Member States.

The adverse impact of the divergences in national gambling laws with respect to the establishment and the functioning of the internal market of gambling and associated services makes a strong case for Community harmonization. This should be based on the country of origin principle and re-regulation through minimum harmonization of national rules on commercial gambling activities. That approach would include rules on the licensing of service providers, the content, quality, and promotion of gambling services, and the protection of the public interest objectives at stake. Such a model would be more beneficial to the internal market than the mutual recognition model, inherent in the case law of the ECJ and the Directive on Services, which, in any event, does not apply to gambling. It would be more likely to strike the right balance between free movement in the legitimate, albeit heavily regulated, gambling sector and the protection of the public interest. It could effectively overcome the barriers arising from divergent national laws, and successfully face the reality of the rapid expansion of remote and cross-border gambling activities facilitated by modern technology, and particularly the Internet.

Binding the EU to International Human Rights Law

Israel de Jesús Butler* and Olivier De Schutter**

I. Introduction

For almost 40 years, human rights have received protection within the legal order of the European Union (EU). Despite the absence of any specific mandate in the Treaties, the European Court of Justice (ECJ) took the initiative of developing these rights as general principles of Community law as part of its attempt to establish the legitimacy of EC law and its claim to supremacy in the face of objections from the constitutional courts of certain Member States.[1] This development was subsequently endorsed by the other institutions of the EU (then still the European Communities),[2] and, following the Treaty of Maastricht on the European Union, by the Member States themselves.[3] In 2000, the EU raised the visibility of the human rights acquis for its citizens by proclaiming a Charter of Fundamental Rights.[4] The Charter has undoubtedly brought about a shift in the culture of the institutions of the Union. The European Parliament now systematically checks whether the legislative proposals on which it deliberates comply with the rights, freedoms, and principles of the Charter.[5] The Commission announced its intention to verify the compatibility of its proposals with the Charter in 2001.[6] In 2005, it adopted a Communication clarifying the methodology it

---

* City Solicitors' Educational Trust Lecturer in EU Law at Lancaster University.
** Professor at the University of Louvain (UCL) and at the College of Europe (Natolin); Visiting Professor, Columbia University (2007–08).

[1] Case 29/69 *Stauder v City of Ulm* [1969] ECR 419; Case 11/70 *Internationale Handelsgesellschaft v Einfuhr- und Vorratsstelle Getreide* [1970] ECR 1125.

[2] Joint Declaration by the European Parliament, the Council and the Commission Concerning the Protection of Fundamental Rights and the European Convention for the Protection of Human Rights and Fundamental Freedoms [1977] OJ C103/1 (27.04.77).

[3] See Article 6(2) of the Treaty on European Union (TEU) ([2002] OJ C325 (24.12.02).

[4] The Charter was solemnly proclaimed by the Presidents of the European Parliament, the Council and the Commission on 7 December 2000 [2000] OJ C364/1 (18.12.2000).

[5] See Article 34 of the Rules of Procedure of the European Parliament, 16th edn, July 2006, available online at: <http://www.europarl.europa.eu/omk/sipade3?PUBREF=-//EP//NONSGML+RULES-EP+20060703+0+DOC+PDF+V0//EN>.

[6] SEC(2001) 380/3.

would use for this purpose.[7] The revised guidelines for the preparation of impact assessments now pay greater attention to the potential effects of different policy options on the guarantees in the Charter.[8] The Reform Treaty, signed at Lisbon on 13 December 2007, will contain a reference to the Charter—in the amended form in which it was proclaimed on the same day—thus confirming its status as a legally binding instrument for the institutions of the Union and for the Member States when they implement Union law.[9]

These developments are both important and welcome. It is not our purpose here, though, to describe them in any detail. Nor shall we seek to illustrate their shortcomings insofar as they seek to ensure that, within the legal order of the EU, fundamental rights will not be violated. Overall, as a result of this impressive list of achievements, the Union clearly deserves to be seen as a model for other international organizations.[10] We note, however, that these developments remain internal to the Union. They do not result in any form of external supervision being exercised over the Union's institutions. And they are related to, but not in any way dependent on, the international human rights treaties to which the Member States are party.[11] The most optimistic of observers might consider these developments as paving the way towards greater recognition by the Union that it is bound to comply with international and European human rights law. However, there exist several problems with this view. Firstly, the Charter of Fundamental Rights does not necessarily replicate the breadth of rights protected by the range of human rights treaties to which the Member States are already party. Thus, there is a risk that even if the institutions are effective in ensuring that legislative proposals do not violate the rights contained in the EU Charter of Fundamental Rights, they may still conflict with other rights that the Member States have undertaken individually to guarantee. Secondly, the approach of the Union institutions to human rights is purely negative. They admit that EU law should

[7] Communication from the Commission, Compliance with the Charter of Fundamental Rights in Commission legislative proposals. Methodology for systematic and rigorous monitoring, COM(2005) 172 final of 27.4.2005.

[8] SEC(2005)791, 15.6.2005. Although the new guidelines are still based, as the former impact assessments (see Communication of 5 June 2005 on Impact Assessment, COM(2002)276), on a division between economic, social, and environmental impacts, the revised set of guidelines, fundamental rights are included under these different rubrics. Indeed, a specific report was commissioned by the European Commission (DG Justice, Freedom and Security) to EPEC (European Policy Evaluation Consortium) in preparation of the revised guidelines: see EPEC, *The Consideration of Fundamental Rights in Impact Assessment. Final Report*, December 2004, 61 pages.

[9] Article 6(2) of the TEU, as amended by the Treaty of Lisbon amending the Treaty on European Union and the Treaty establishing the European Community, signed at Lisbon, 13 December 2007 ([2007] OJ C306/1 (17.12.07)) (referring to the EU Charter of Fundamental Rights in the revised form it has been proclaimed, in a revised form, on 12 December 2007 ([2007] OJ C303/1 (14.12.07)).

[10] See eg with regard to human rights obligations on the UN, A Clapham, *Human Rights Obligations of Non-State Actors* (OUP, 2006) 109–137.

[11] The term 'international human rights treaty' should be taken to refer to a treaty that sets out a series of human rights parties are under a duty to guarantee. In general most human rights treaties will derive from (and often expand on) the catalogue of rights set out in the UN's Universal Declaration of Human Rights, 1948 (GA Res 217 A (III), 10.12.48).

not violate human rights standards, but they refrain from imposing a duty on the institutions to undertake activities that promote and protect human rights. Thirdly, there exists a significant risk that nurturing human rights standards in isolation from the standards that develop, evolve, and crystallize under the supervision of the United Nations and Council of Europe may be counter-productive. Such a situation may lead the institutions of the Union to develop their own standards, marginalizing the pre-existing *acquis* binding on its Member States, and potentially resulting in a lowering of the level of protection of human rights in the policy domains transferred to the Union.

In this article, we make the case for placing the Union under the supervision of United Nations and Council of Europe monitoring bodies. We present a variety of mechanisms through which such supervision could be organized. We share the optimistic view that, in time, this development is inevitable: the more the Union comes to share the attributes of a sovereign State, the more it shall have to enter into the kinds of agreements through which, like its Member States themselves, it will commit itself to the promotion and protection of human rights in all matters falling under its jurisdiction. If the Union is to be truly 'founded' on human rights then these must be the same rights as those to which all or most of its Member States have committed themselves through the United Nations and the Council of Europe. However, there is no time to lose in this: for as long as the Union fails to recognize that it must comply with international human rights law and submit to the supervisory mechanisms established under the relevant instruments, it exposes its citizens to the inadequacies of the lesser protection available in its internal regime. The propagation of separate human rights regimes for the Union and the Member States will create confusion among the latter as to the scope of their obligations and may provide them with a pretext for ignoring their international undertakings in the areas in which they have transferred powers to the Union.

This article will, firstly, highlight the need for external international supervision of the Union by explaining the current shortcomings of human rights protection at the internal level. We argue that the failure of the European Union to recognize its obligations under the international law of human rights leads to an interpretation of human rights which is narrower than that already accepted by its Member States and third States; that it creates difficulties for the uniform application of EU law; and that it may result, finally, in a lowering of the level of protection for individuals. Second, we explore the different techniques by which the Union could strengthen its links to the human rights standards developed within the Union Nations or the Council of Europe. We examine the possibility of accession by the EU to international or European human rights instruments. We also review alternatives to accession, namely supervision of the European Union by the relevant monitoring bodies established under those instruments even in the absence of formal membership of those Treaties. Before concluding we suggest how the Union could comply with international human rights law despite lacking a general competence to protect and promote human rights.

II. The Shortcomings of the Current Internal EU
Human Rights Regime

In the current state of EU law, fundamental rights are protected by the ECJ, through the vehicle of the general principles of law which the Court ensures respect for on the basis of Article 220 of the EC Treaty. Inspiration for the general principles is to be drawn from treaties to which the Member States are party, in particular the European Convention on Human Rights, and the constitutional traditions of the Member States. This development in the case law was subsequently recognized in the EU Treaty (Article 6(2)) which mandates the Union to 'respect' human rights as embodied in the general principles. More recently, the EU Charter of Fundamental Rights sets out what the Member States consider to reflect the current *acquis* of rights, freedoms, and principles that the EU is bound to observe. As confirmed most recently by the Preamble to the Protocol on the Application of the Charter of Fundamental Rights of the European Union to Poland and to the United Kingdom: 'the Charter reaffirms the rights, freedoms and principles recognized in the Union and makes those rights more visible, but does not create new rights or principles'. The Charter was to make visible the existing *acquis* of the Union in this field; it was not to invent a new catalogue of rights.

As a result of this evolution, the general principles of law, developed by the ECJ on the basis of the international human rights treaties to which the Member States are parties or on which they have collaborated and of the constitutional traditions common to the Member States, co-exist with the EU Charter of Fundamental Rights as two separate sources of human rights in the EU legal order. The Charter does not purport to 'freeze' the expansion of the body of substantive human rights accepted in EU law. The ECJ is entitled to develop these principles beyond what the Charter expressly recognizes, where a particular right fits the required criteria, as the bodies of international or domestic human rights law evolve. This much can be derived from Article 6(3) of the EU Treaty as amended by the Reform Treaty, along with Article 53 of the Charter.[12] However, even if the ECJ is free to expand the substantive body of recognized general principles, the Reform Treaty does not empower the Court to further expand the scope of application of EU law. Implicit in this is the view that human rights obligations are

---

[12] According to Article 6(3) of the EU Treaty, the Union is bound to respect fundamental rights 'as guaranteed by the [European Convention on Human Rights] and as they result from the constitutional traditions common to the Member States', as general principles of Union law. Article 53 of the Charter reads: 'Nothing in this Charter shall be interpreted as restricting or adversely affecting human rights and fundamental freedoms as recognised, in their respective fields of application, *by Union law* and international law and by international agreements to which the Union, the Community or all the Member States are party, including the European Convention for the Protection of Human Rights and Fundamental Freedoms, and by the Member States' constitutions' (emphasis added).

negative in nature: human rights, as embodied in the general principles, must be respected when the institutions of the Union or the Member States implementing Union law adopt certain measures. The Charter does not expand the competence of the EU; nor does it permit the Court to require the EU to take positive action to promote the standards it contains.[13]

There are three limits to these developments of the emerging system of protection of human rights in the EU. First, while the potential exists to expand the body of rights accepted by the ECJ to reflect developments in international and domestic law, we note that the Court has ignored a large body of international human rights treaties to which the Member States are party. This is difficult to justify in principle and may threaten the uniform application of EU law. We suggest, instead, that all human rights treaties to which Member States are party—even those not ratified by all the Member States—should be taken into consideration as if these treaties were binding upon the Union itself. Second, we note that if the ECJ bases itself in international human rights law, it will be obliged to adopt the internationally accepted doctrine that human rights may impose positive as well as negative obligations. Human rights should not simply be seen as limits on which measures the EU may adopt. Rather, the protection and promotion of human rights should be seen as objectives to be achieved by the exercise of the competences which have been conferred upon the Union. Third, we note that grounding the Union's human rights regime in internationally recognized standards should lead the EU to cooperate with the monitoring bodies established under those treaties and make use of their findings.

A. The Court's Use of International Human Rights Instruments

When asked to identify certain fundamental rights as worthy of protection, the ECJ currently examines whether the right in question is included, either in the European Convention on Human Rights, whose 'special significance' it has long recognized in its case law,[14] or in another international instrument for the protection of human rights which the Member States have all agreed to. The canonical formula used by the Court is that it 'draws inspiration [...] from the guidelines supplied by international instruments for the protection of human rights on

---

[13] See the Declaration concerning the Charter of Fundamental Rights of the European Union appended to the Reform Treaty.

[14] Case C-260/89 *ERT* [1991] ECR I-2925, para 41; Opinion 2/94 *Accession of the European Community to the European Convention for the Safeguard of Human Rights and Fundamental Freedoms* [1996] ECR I-1759, para 33; Case C-274/99 P, *Connolly v Commission* [2001] ECR I-1611, para 37; Case C-94/00 *Roquette Frères* [2002] ECR I-9011, para 25; Case C-112/00 *Schmidberger* [2003] ECR I-5659, para 71; Case C-36/02 *Omega* [2004] ECR I-9609, para 33. Article 6(2) of the EU Treaty only refers to the European Convention on Human Rights, neglecting a reference to other human rights treaties to which the Member States have collaborated on or signed (an omission retained by the Reform Treaty in Article 6(3) of the EU Treaty, as amended).

which the Member States have collaborated or to which they are signatories'.[15]
In practice, however, its use of sources other than the European Convention on
Human Rights has been parsimonious and selective. The 1966 International
Covenant on Civil and Political Rights (ICCPR) has been put before the ECJ as
a source of inspiration for recognizing a general principle on several occasions.[16]
While the Court superficially recognizes its significance it has not been possible
to find a case where it has actually relied upon its provisions.[17] In the *Grant* case,
it went so far as to deny the significance of a decision on the merits of a case delivered by the UN Human Rights Committee (HRC) which accepted that discrimination on the basis of sex contained in the ICCPR could include discrimination
on the basis of sexual orientation.[18] Perhaps the furthest that the ECJ has come to
drawing on other instruments has been in its decision of *Parliament v Council*[19]
where the European Parliament was seeking to annul certain provisions of the
2003 Family Reunification Directive.[20] The Court noted that:

> . . . the International Covenant on Civil and Political Rights is one of the international
> instruments for the protection of human rights of which it takes account in applying the
> general principles of Community law. [. . .] That is also true of the Convention on the
> Rights of the Child [. . .] which, like the Covenant, binds each of the Member States.[21]

The Court went on largely to rely on Article 8 of the European Convention
on Human Rights and the accompanying case law of the European Court of
Human Rights concerning family reunification. It made no further reference to
the ICCPR. While the Court did draw on the Convention on the Rights of the
Child (CRC)[22] this only occurred once in the decision and only as a means of
supplementing its consideration of the European Convention on Human Rights.
Arguably the CRC only received consideration because, unlike the European
Convention on Human Rights, it deals extensively with the rights of the child.
Given this Treaty's significance (it has 193 parties, with only USA and Somalia
not having ratified it)[23] and the fact that the European Court of Human Rights
itself draws on its provisions[24] one might have expected the ECJ to make greater

---

[15] Case 4/73 *Nold KG v Commission* [1974] ECR 491. The wording has not evolved greatly. See eg
Case C-94/00 *Roquette Frères* [2002] ECR I-9011.

[16] 999 UNTS 171.

[17] Case C-249/96 *Grant v South West Trains Ltd* [1998] ECR I-621, para 44 relating to ICCPR,
Art 2(1); Case C-60/92 *Otto BV v Postbank NV* [1993] ECR I-5683, para 11 relating to ICCPR,
Art 14; Case 374/87 *Orkem v Commission* [1989] ECR 3283, para 31 relating to ICCPR, Art 14.

[18] *Grant*, ibid, para 46.

[19] Case C-540/03 *Parliament v Council* [2006] ECR I-5769.

[20] Council Directive 2003/86/EC of 22 September 2003 on the right to family reunification
([2003] OJ L251/12).

[21] Paragraph 37 of the judgment.   [22] 1577 UNTS 3 (signed on 20 November 1989).

[23] See 'Multilateral Treaties Deposited with the Secretary-General' (ST/LEG/SER/E/19), or:
<http://www.ohchr.org/english/countries/ratification/4.htm>.

[24] See eg European Court of Human Rights *Mayeka & Mitunga v Belgium* Application no
13178/03, 12.10.06, where the European Court of Human Rights drew on the CRC in a case concerning family reunification.

use of the Treaty. Furthermore, the Court completely dismissed the significance of the 1961 European Social Charter (ESC) despite the several provisions it contains of direct relevance to the issues raised in the case and the fact that all the Member States are party to the original 1961 Treaty.[25] The ECJ appears to have altered its dismissive attitude towards the ESC in the *Laval* and *Viking* cases decided in December 2007, where it accepted 'the right to take collective action, including the right to strike', as part of the general principles of Community law, since it is 'recognised both by various international instruments which the Member States have signed or cooperated in, such as the European Social Charter... to which, moreover, express reference is made in Article 136 EC—and [ILO] Convention No 87 concerning Freedom of Association and Protection of the Right to Organise [of 1948]... and by instruments developed by those Member States at Community level or in the context of the European Union, such as the Community Charter of the Fundamental Social Rights of Workers [of 1989], which is also referred to in Article 136 EC, and the Charter of Fundamental Rights of the European Union'.[26] What led to this change of opinion concerning the status of the European Social Charter is not stated.

Several observations on the approach of the Court can be made. First, despite occasionally acknowledging the relevance of treaties other than the European Convention on Human Rights, it has been extremely rare for the ECJ to draw on any other instrument. What emerges from the cases is that the Court will rely primarily on the European Convention on Human Rights and while it may draw on other treaties to complement its analysis (*Parliament v Council*), it may not draw on them where they appear to go beyond the European Convention on Human Rights (*Grant*), except where there appears to be some support for this in the EC or EU Treaty (*Laval* and *Viking*). The two occasions when it has relied on other treaties—in relation to the CRC and the ESC—may either be considered exceptional, or signal an evolution in the Court's practice. These cases have in common that the rights referred to in the CRC and the ESC were also contained in the Charter of Fundamental Rights. It may be that the Court, therefore, will

---

[25] CETS 035. See Articles 7, 16, 17, and 19 of the ESC. As to the ESC, it stated (at para 107): 'So far as concerns the Member States bound by these instruments, it is also to be remembered that the Directive provides, in Article 3(4), that it is without prejudice to more favourable provisions of the European Social Charter'. The Joint Opinion of AG Jacobs (delivered 18.1.99, at para 146) in the *Albany*, *Brentjens*, and *Drijvende Bokken* cases (which dismisses the legal value of the ESC) may offer some explanation for the Court's attitude. The Court itself expressed no view on this in its decisions. (Case C-67/96 *Albany International BV* ECR [1999] I-5751; Joined Cases C-115/97, C-116/97, and C-117/97 *Brentjens' Handelsonderneming BV v Stichting Bedrijfspensioenfonds voor de Handel in Bouwmaterialen* [1999] I-6025, and Case C-219/97 BV *Maatschappij Drijvende Bokken v Stichting Pensioenfonds voor de Vervoer- en Havenbedrijven* ECR [1999] I-6121.)

[26] Case C-438/05 *International Transport Workers' Federation, Finnish Seamen's Union v Viking Line ABP, OÜ Viking Line Eesti*, n.y.r., para 43 (judgment of 11 December 2007); and Case C-341/05, *Laval un Partneri Ltd v Svenska Byggnadsarbetareförbundet, Svenska Byggnadsarbetareförbundets avd. 1, Byggettan, Svenska Elektrikerförbundet*, n.y.r., para 90 (judgment of 18 December 2007). See in particular the seemingly decisive Opinion of AG Mengozzi, para 78.

begin to move beyond the European Convention on Human Rights, but may only undertake audacious sorties into international human rights law under cover of the Charter. Even if this emerges to be the case, hitherto the Court has relied on treaties other than the European Convention on Human Rights either not at all or sporadically. Two problems result from this situation. First, as they are currently developed in an incremental manner by the ECJ the fundamental rights included among the general principles of law it ensures respect for are detached from international human rights law. Second, the selectivity of the ECJ in its references to international human rights treaties constitutes a potential threat to the uniform application and supremacy of Union law.

B. The Dissonance between Union Law and International Human Rights Law

As we have seen, the European Convention on Human Rights while it has accorded a 'special significance' to the European Convention on Human Rights, the Court has comparatively neglected other international human rights instruments—even those to which all its Member States are party. As illustrated above by the Court's treatment of the case law of the HRC in the *Grant* case, the ECJ has been reluctant to go beyond the guarantees established in the European Convention on Human Rights and the case law of the European Court of Human Rights when developing the general principles of law. In contrast, there is no shortage of cases illustrating the willingness of the ECJ to study the details of the case law of the European Court of Human Rights in order to apply the European Convention on Human Rights in accordance with that authoritative interpretation.[27] Nevertheless, the Member States are all party to a significant number of human rights treaties created under the aegis of the UN, apart from the ICCPR and the CRC. These are, in particular, the 1966 International Covenant on Economic, Social and Cultural Rights;[28] the 1965 International Convention on the Elimination of All Forms of Racial Discrimination;[29] the 1979 Convention on the Elimination of All Forms of Discrimination Against Women;[30] and the 1984 Convention against Torture and Other Cruel, Inhuman or Degrading Treatment or Punishment.[31] Why the Court does not rely systematically on these instruments is unclear, given that they satisfy the criteria of the Court for 'discovering' general principles of law. Quite apart from a consistent neglect of these international instruments which all the Member States have collaborated on and joined, the *Grant* decision in particular underlines the lack

---

[27] For a detailed analysis, see O De Schutter, 'L'influence de la Cour européenne des droits de l'homme sur la Cour de justice des Communautés européennes', in G Cohen-Jonathan and J Fr Flauss (dir), *Le rayonnement international de la jurisprudence de la Cour européenne des droits de l'homme* (Bruylant-Nemesis, 2005) 189–242.

[28] 993 UNTS 3.   [29] 660 UNTS 195.
[30] 1249 UNTS 13.   [31] 1465 UNTS 85.

of faith that the Court places in the interpretations of international human rights law issued by the monitoring bodies responsible for supervising the correct implementation of these treaties. In dismissing out of hand the case law of the HRC, the Court stated that it 'is not a judicial institution' and that its findings 'have no binding force in law'.[32] This understanding of the role of the Human Rights Committee ignores the generally accepted view that the UN monitoring bodies exercise a 'quasi judicial' function,[33] and that their interpretation of the treaties they are tasked to supervise should be treated as authoritative. Even though the parties have not expressly undertaken to regard the decisions of these bodies as legally binding, they are not without legal weight.[34] The Court further noted that the HRC's understanding of sex discrimination to include discrimination on the basis of sexual orientation 'does not in any event appear to reflect the interpretation so far generally accepted of the concept of discrimination based on sex which appears in various international instruments concerning the protection of fundamental rights'.[35] This illustrates a failure to appreciate the nature and status of the ICCPR as well as the role of the HRC. In a very real sense, international human rights law is what the HRC and the other UN monitoring bodies say it is. The UN Charter, which obliges its members to promote and protect human rights, does not attempt to elaborate the meaning of 'human rights' and instead relies on separate treaties to give the term concrete meaning.[36] However, the UN sponsored human rights treaties noted above represent the legally binding expression of human rights as they feature in the UN Charter, to which all the

---

[32] Case C-249/96 *Grant v South West Trains Ltd* [1998] ECR I-621, para 47.

[33] Traditional judicial dispute settlement is understood to refers to dispute settlement by a body of formally elected judges on the basis of evidence submitted by the parties, including the examination and cross examination of witnesses in oral hearings and the delivery of a judgment with which the parties have expressly committed themselves to comply. Quasi-judicial dispute settlement refers to dispute settlement by a body of independent experts who consider the evidence and arguments of the parties by reference to law (though does not necessarily hold oral hearings) and delivers findings which states have not expressly accepted as binding. See H Steinberger, 'Judicial Settlement of International Disputes', in R Bernhardt (ed), *Encyclopaedia of Public International Law* (Max Planck, 1981) 120; H Steiner, 'Individual Claims in a World of Mass Violations: What Role for the Human Rights Committee?', in P Alston and J Crawford (eds), *The Future of UN Human Rights Treaty Monitoring* (Cambridge University Press, 2000), 15, 29–30.

[34] The Human Rights Committee and the Committee on the Elimination of Racial Discrimination have stated that by consenting to the individual petition procedure, the State parties to the respective treaties have agreed to act upon their findings as to the existence *vel non* of a violation. 'Bearing in mind that, by becoming a party to the Optional Protocol, the State party has recognized the competence of the Committee to determine whether there has been a violation of the Covenant or not and that, pursuant to article 2 of the Covenant, the State party has undertaken to ensure to all individuals in its territory and subject to its jurisdiction the rights recognized in the Covenant, and to provide an effective and enforceable remedy in case a violation has been established, the Committee wishes to receive from the State party . . . information about the measures taken to give effect to the Committee's Views.' See eg HRC: *Sooklal v Trinidad and Tobago* Communication no 928/2000, para 7. Similarly, CERD: *LR v Slovakia*, Communication no 31/2003.

[35] *Grant* case (n 32 above), para 47.

[36] In particular, see UN Charter, Arts 55 and 56.

EU Member States have committed themselves.[37] It is the monitoring bodies of these treaties that are charged with explaining their meaning. The International Court of Justice,[38] but also increasingly national courts[39] and regional human rights protection bodies, including the European Court of Human Rights,[40] the Inter-American Court[41] and Commission of Human Rights,[42] and the African Commission on Human and Peoples' Rights,[43] base their understanding of human rights law on the interpretations given by these monitoring bodies. By continuing to ignore the significance of international human rights law the ECJ threatens the coherence and universality of human rights protection.

On this precise point, we may be currently witnessing an evolution in the position of the members of the European Court of Justice. In her opinion in *Parliament v Council* (discussed above) on the Family Reunification Directive,[44] AG Kokott refers explicitly to the case law of the European Committee of Social Rights, as a means of clarifying the meaning of the provisions of the ESC. However, this attitude remains exceptional and it is far from clear whether it will be followed by the judges themselves. Despite a Memorandum of Understanding now concluded between the Council of Europe and the EU, providing that reference should be made by the EU to case law elaborated in the context of the Council

---

[37] See eg ICCPR Preamble: 'The States Parties to the present Covenant ... Considering the obligation of States under the Charter of the Unites Nations to promote universal respect for, and observance of, human rights and freedoms ... Agree upon the following Articles ...'

[38] See eg, *Legal Consequences of the Construction of a Wall in the Occupied Palestinian Territory*, Advisory Opinion of 9 July 2004, ICJ Rep 2004, 136, at paras 109 and 112 where the ICJ interpreted the ICESCR and other UN human rights treaties by reference to views of their monitoring bodies. This attitude is unlikely to change in the future, especially considering that influential members of the International Court of Justice, such as its president Ms R Higgins and Mr B Simma, have been members of UN human rights treaty bodies.

[39] On the influence of the case law, including views adopted on individual communications, general comments, and concluding observations, of the UN human rights treaty bodies, see Committee on International Human Rights Law and Practice of the International Law Association, *Final Report on the Impact of the Work of the United Nations Human Rights Treaty Bodies on National Courts and Tribunals*, adopted at the 2004 Berlin Conference; and H Niemi, *National Implementation of Findings by United Nations Human Rights Treaty Bodies. A Comparative Study* (Institute for Human Rights, Abo Akademi University, December 2003), available online at: <http://www.abo.fi/instut/imr/norfa/Heli.pdf> (examining the national implementation of UN treaty body findings, including final views, concluding observations, and general comments, in Australia, Canada, the Czech Republic, Finland, Spain, and Sweden). See also, more generally, C Heyns and F Viljoen, *The Impact of the United Nations Human Rights Treaties on the Domestic Level* (The Hague: Kluwer Law International, 2002).

[40] See eg *Ergin v Turkey (No 6)*, 4/5/06, Application no 47533/99, paras 22–24.

[41] See eg *Case of the 'Juvenile Re-education Institute' v Paraguay*, 02/09/04, IACtHR Series C 112, para 161.

[42] See eg *Pinder v The Bahamas*, 15/10/07, IACommHR, Case 12.513, Report 79/07, paras 28–30.

[43] See eg *Legal Resources Foundation v Zambia* ACHPR, Communication no 211/98 (2001), paras 59, 63 and 70.

[44] Case C-540/03 *Parliament v Council* [2006] ECR I-5769. See para 74 of the opinion (after mentioning Article 19(6) of the ESC, which concerns the right to family reunification for migrant workers, AG Kokott refers to the fact that 'the European Committee of Social Rights, which supervises the implementation of the Social Charter, has to date, in its rulings, only accepted waiting periods of up to one year, and has rejected waiting periods of three years and more').

of Europe when developing human rights standards,[45] it is highly unlikely that the Court itself will engage in this practice. Prospects are even dimmer, of course, as regards other human rights monitoring bodies, established under UN human rights treaties or within the International Labour Organization (ILO).

Thus, the second problem to be highlighted is that the current approach of the ECJ to the incorporation of human rights standards within the general principles of law risks taking the EU down a path where the protection of human rights is not only narrower than the standards already recognized by the Member States through their treaty commitments, but also inconsistent and out of touch with the interpretations of recognized rights given by the monitoring bodies and applied and followed by national and international courts.

C. The Uniformity and Supremacy of EU Law vis-à-vis the Member States' International Undertakings

If the protection that the ECJ accords to human rights does not follow that which the Member States have individually undertaken in their treaty commitments, then inevitably action mandated by the EU will come into conflict with Member States' commitments under these treaties. This may raise a significant problem for the supremacy of EU law. If the ECJ fails to ensure respect for the rights contained in these treaties the national jurisdictions may decide—as they have in the past in relation to human rights guaranteed within their constitutions—that EU law must be 'disapplied' to the extent that compliance with these human rights obligations is required.[46] Nonetheless, even if the ECJ, for instance, were to incorporate into the general principles of Community law the idea that Member States were permitted on an individual basis to accord human rights higher standards

---

[45] Memorandum of Understanding between the Council of Europe and the European Union, adopted at the 117th Session of the Committee of Ministers held in Strasbourg on 10–11 May 2007, CM(2007)74 (10 May 2007) (hereinafter referred to a 'Memorandum of Understanding').

[46] This would follow if one were to accept the approach adopted by the Court of First Instance in the *Yusuf* and *Kadi* cases that human rights obligations deriving from the UN Charter take priority over EU law, and might be seen to follow from Articles 56 and 103 of the UN Charter. Case T-315/01 *Kadi v Council and Commission* [2005] ECR II-3649; Case T-306/01 *Ali Yusuf and Al Barakaat International Foundation v Council and Commission* [2005] ECR II-3533. On appeal, the ECJ, while it did not seem to go so far as the Court of First Instance, hypothesized that obligations derived from the UN Charter might take precedence over provisions of secondary EU legislation, but not primary legislation. Included in primary legislation were human rights as guaranteed by the general principles of Community law. See Joined Cases C-402/05 P and C-415/05 P *Kadi v Council and Commission* judgment of 3 September 2008 (not yet published), paras 301–308. On the relationship of EU to the international law of human rights, see further Ahmed and Butler, 'The European Union and Human Rights: An International Law Perspective' (2006) 17 European Journal of International Law 771. For a discussion on the difficulties relating to diverging standards of human rights protection within the national law of individual Member States and how national courts determine priority between laws protecting human rights and obligations under Community law, see Besselink, 'Entrapped by the Maximum Standard: On Fundamental Rights, Pluralism and Subsidiarity in The European Union' (1998) 35 CML Rev 629, 632–664.

of protection than recognized by the EU this would maintain the illusion of supremacy but sacrifice uniformity.[47] Conversely, in order to observe their obligations under EU law, States may be forced to ignore the obligations imposed on them under human rights treaties or ultimately to withdraw from such treaties. This situation is compounded in relation to those human rights treaties which are ratified only by some of the Member States. If, as its current case law would seem to suggest,[48] the ECJ is reluctant to make reference to such treaties, such situations could become more frequent in the future.

This problem may be approached as follows. Although all the Member States are currently party to a significant body of human rights treaties, not all of them were parties to these treaties before they joined the EU. Where a Member State has a conflict between EU law and other treaty commitments, the EC Treaty only allows deference to those treaty commitments where they were entered into before joining the Union. This is the case, for instance in relation to the ICCPR where only 18 of the current Member States were party before acceding to the EU.[49] Similarly, a number of Member States were parties to the Council of Europe Framework Convention on the Protection of National Minorities (Framework Convention) before joining the EU, but others joined later (e.g. the UK) and others still have not joined at all (e.g. Belgium, France, and Greece).[50] The relationship between Member States' commitments under EC law and their pre-existing international obligations is dealt with under Article 307 of the EC Treaty which reads:

> The rights and obligations arising from agreements concluded before . . . the date of their accession, between one or more Member States on the one hand, and one or more third countries on the other, shall not be affected by the provisions of this Treaty . . . To the extent that such agreements are not compatible with this Treaty, the Member State or States concerned shall take all appropriate steps to eliminate the incompatibilities established. Member States shall, where necessary, assist each other to this end and shall, where appropriate, adopt a common attitude.[51]

There are two notable features of Article 307. First, where a Member State comes to the EU with pre-existing commitments, the EU cannot require those Member

---

[47] Besselink, ibid, 674–678. He terms this the 'local minimum standard'.

[48] For instance, the Opinion of AG Kokott in *Parliament v Council* (note 44 above) stated (in para 76) that the Council of Europe Convention on Migrant Workers should not be taken account because at the time it had only been ratified by some Member States.

[49] Austria, Bulgaria, Cyprus, Czech Republic, Denmark, Estonia, Finland, Hungary, Latvia, Lithuania, Malta, Poland, Portugal, Romania, Slovakia, Slovenia, Spain, and Sweden. Seven of the remaining nine MS were all parties to the ICCPR by 1983, with Ireland and Greece acceding to the ICCPR in 1989 and 1997 respectively. See 'Multilateral Treaties Deposited with the Secretary-General' (ST/LEG/SER/E/19), or: <http://www.ohchr.org/english/countries/ratification/4.htm>.

[50] CETS 157. The treaty has 39 parties. For the status of ratifications, see: <http://conventions.coe.int/>.

[51] The ECJ has noted that this provision does no more than recognize the consequences, for the institutions of the Union, of the general public international rules on the conclusion of successive treaties: Case 10/61 *Commission v Italy* [1962] ECR 1.

States to default on their obligations to third States.[52] However, the Court has underlined that the 'duty of the Community institutions is directed only to permitting the member State concerned to perform its obligations under the prior agreement *and does not bind the Community as regards the non-member country in question*'.[53] This was recently reaffirmed by the Court of First Instance in the *Kadi* and *Yusuf* judgments with regard to compliance with Security Council Resolutions 1267 (1999), 1333 (2000), and 1390 (2002) obliging all UN members to execute certain restrictive measures against suspected members of the Al-Qaeda network and the Taliban.[54] Thus while the EU may not create obstacles to compliance by its Member States with pre-existing international obligations which they remain bound by, and which they may not derogate from simply by joining the EU, the EU itself is not bound vis-à-vis third parties in the international legal order. This creates an obvious problem: where an international human rights treaty imposes on a Member State obligations which cannot be reconciled with its obligations under EU law, compliance with these treaties may require a Member State to default on its obligations under EU law thus threatening the uniform application of EU law. This may result in obstacles to the establishment of, for instance, the internal market or to the area of freedom, security, and justice. EU law does allow a Member State to invoke its obligation to protect human rights, in order to impose restrictions on economic freedoms recognized under the EC Treaty.[55] In principle, such exceptions are only acceptable to the extent that the fundamental rights invoked are recognized as part of the EU legal order, among the general principles of law developed by the ECJ—which, we have seen, are drawn almost exclusively from the European Convention on Human Rights. There are borderline situations of course, for instance where—as in the *Omega Spielhallen* case of 2004[56]—national authorities invoke the particular significance they attach to a right, such as the right to human dignity, of

---

[52] The ECJ stated that Article 307 of the EC Treaty implied 'a duty on the part of the institutions of the Community not to impede the performance of the obligations of Member States which stem from a prior agreement': Case 812/79 *Attorney General v Burgoa* [1980] ECR 2787, at para 9.

[53] Ibid (emphasis added). See also, for a reaffirmation of this statement, Case T-184/95 *Dorsch Consult v Council and Commission* [1998] ECR II-667, para 74. For other examples where Article 307 of the EC Treaty was invoked, see Case C-324/93 *Evans Medical and Macfarlan Smith* [1995] ECR I-563, para 27; Case 10/61, *Commission v Italy* [1962] ECR 1; Case C-158/91 *Levy* [1993] ECR I-4287; and Case C-124/95 *Centro-Com* [1997] ECR I-81, para 56.

[54] See *Kadi*, para 192 and *Yusuf*, para 242 (CFI judgments), n 46, above. The CFI had to address the question whether the EU was bound to contribute to the implementation of the sanctions decided by the UN Security Council, under the resolutions referred to above. This was confirmed on appeal by the ECJ (n 46, above at paras 278–280) in so far as it affirmed that the Resolutions of the Security Council—while retaining their primacy in general international law—did not automatically bind the EU's institutions, nor oblige its Member States to act through the EU to implement them. Furthermore the disputed Resolutions could neither exclude the jurisdiction of the Court nor take precedence over primary EU legislation, including the general principles of law guaranteed by the ECJ.

[55] See eg Case C-368/95 *Familiapress* [1997] ECR I-3689 (para 24).

[56] Case C-36/02 *Omega Spielhallen- und Automatenaufstellungs-GmbH* [2004] ECR I-9609.

which different understandings coexist within the EU. But even in those cases, the specific national measure adopted in order to protect the value at stake will only be considered acceptable if the said value is shared among the different EU Member States, as would be demonstrated, for instance, by its inclusion in the EU Charter of Fundamental Rights.[57] In contrast, allowing a Member State to invoke, on a permanent basis, the need to ensure protection of a right included in an international agreement binding upon that State, but which is not part of the set of rights recognized among the general principles of law, would create a potentially threatening precedent for the uniform application of EU law.

The second feature of Article 307 is that where incompatibilities between EU and pre-existing human rights obligations are recognized to exist the Member States must take 'appropriate steps' to eliminate this incompatibility. This may necessitate the withdrawal by Member States from the human rights treaty in question. We have seen in the past instances where Italy and France have denounced ILO Conventions which conflicted with the requirements of gender equality under EC law.[58] But these were exceptional situations where the said conventions were based on the paternalistic approach to the protection of women typical of the first half of the twentieth century, rather than on the equal opportunities approach espoused under both EC law and international human rights law in the more recent period. It seems unthinkable, in contrast, that the Member States who are parties to the Framework Convention (noted above) would be obliged under EU law to denounce that instrument, for instance because the adoption of certain measures intended to protect and promote the rights of minorities would be considered to be in violation of the requirements of fundamental economic freedoms under the EC Treaty. In addition, it would prove politically embarrassing for the EU in its relations with third States targeted by the EU for human rights violations or where the EU imposes observance of human rights as conditions for

[57] See paragraph 34 of the judgment delivered in the *Omega* case : '... the Community legal order undeniably strives to ensure respect for human dignity as a general principle of law. There can therefore be no doubt that the objective of protecting human dignity is compatible with Community law, it being immaterial in that respect that, in Germany, the principle of respect for human dignity has a particular status as an independent fundamental right.'

[58] In Case C-158/91 *Lévy* [1993] ECR I-4287, the Court admitted that Article 234 EEC (now Article 307 of the EC Treaty, after amendment), could be an obstacle to sanctioning the State party to that Convention for not respecting Council Directive 76/207/EEC of 9 February 1976 on the implementation of the principle of equal treatment for men and women as regards access to employment, vocational training and promotion, and working conditions ([1976] OJ L39/40), on the point where an incompatibility existed. See on this point the Opinion of Tesauro AG of 16 January 1997 in Case C-197/96 *EC Commission v France* [1997] ECR I-1491, at 1491–1495. It is clear however that there is an obligation imposed on the EU Member States to remove the incompatibility—if necessary, by denouncing the pre-existing agreement—as soon as they have the opportunity to do so. See Case C-62/98 *Commission v Portugal* [2000] ECR I-5171, and, in the literature, Manzini, 'The Priority of Pre-existing Treaties of EC Member States within the Framework of International Law' 12 EJIL (2001) 781. France, for instance, denounced ILO Convention (No 89) of 9 July 1948 concerning Nightwork of Women Employed in Industry, in order to comply with Directive 76/207 (see Case C-345/89 *Stoeckel* [1991] ECR I-4047, and Case C-197/96 *Commission v France* [1997] ECR I-1489).

trade agreements.[59] Furthermore, the UN HRC has maintained that, absent an explicit provision to that effect, withdrawal from human rights treaties is, in fact, illegal or at least impossible, since human rights guarantees entered into by States devolve permanently to the national territory and the population.[60]

The scenario of a conflict between obligations under the Framework Convention and obligations under EU law is not purely hypothetical, as two examples may illustrate. Article 3(1) of Regulation 1612/68 on freedom of movement for workers[61] prohibits national rules, which 'though applicable irrespective of nationality, [have as] their exclusive or principal aim or effect... to keep nationals of other Member States away from the employment offered'. It further provides that this provision is not to 'apply to conditions relating to linguistic knowledge required by reason of the nature of the post to be filled'. In the *Groener* case the ECJ considered the legality of Irish domestic law restricting eligibility for certain teaching positions to individuals with an adequate knowledge of the Irish language. On the facts, the ECJ accepted the validity of the Irish rule. In view of the policy it pursued for the promotion of the Irish language, the requirement imposed on teachers 'to have an adequate knowledge of such a language must, provided that the level of knowledge required is not disproportionate in relation to the objective pursued, be regarded as a condition corresponding to the knowledge required by reason of the nature of the post to be filled within the meaning of the last subparagraph of Article 3(1) of Regulation No 1612/68'.[62] While the Court recognized that a Member State policy designed to maintain and promote the national language should in principle be recognized as pursuing a legitimate objective, it made clear that a wider-cast domestic policy would fall foul of EU law. If, for example, a Member State imposed language requirements unrelated to the post offered, the ECJ would interpret this as an unjustifiable protective measure restricting access to its employment market.[63] Whether such a narrow exception to the rule on free movement of workers may interfere with the full implementation by the Member States of their obligations under the Framework Convention to promote and protect minority languages within their territories remains to be seen.[64]

The litigation surrounding the Dutch law on the media (*Mediawet*) provides a second illustration. These cases presented the Court with the question whether

[59] See eg King, Toby 'Human Rights in European Foreign Policy: Success or Failure for Postmodern Diplomacy?' 10 EJIL (1999) 313.

[60] See further below.

[61] OJ, English Special Edition, 1968(II), 475.

[62] Case C-379/87 *Groener* [1989] ECR 3967, para 21.

[63] See the case of *Groener*, ibid, para 23. The imposition of such a condition would be assimilated to a situation such as that which arose in Case C-281/98 *Roman Angonese v Cassa di Risparmio di Bolzano* [2000] ECR 4139, which concerned the situation of an Italian national who applied to take part in a competition for a post with a private banking undertaking in Bolzano, but whose application was rejected because, although perfectly bilingual in Italian and German, he could not obtain a certificate of bilingualism issued by the public authorities of the province of Bolzano.

[64] Framework Convention, Arts 5, 9–12, 14.

the *Mediawet* restricted the freedom to provide audio-visual services contained in Articles 43–48 of the EC Treaty. The contested provisions included a prohibition on Dutch broadcasting corporations from investing resources into media services outside the Netherlands (to ensure funds were reinvested internally);[65] and restrictions on advertising contained in programming broadcast into the Netherlands from another Member State (to prevent excessive advertising and prevent dependency on advertising revenue from influencing programming).[66] The Court accepted that 'the Mediawet is designed to establish a pluralistic and non-commercial broadcasting system and thus forms part of a cultural policy intended to safeguard, in the audio-visual sector, the freedom of expression of the various (in particular social, cultural, religious and philosophical) components existing in the Netherlands' and found that these were legitimate objectives.[67] It found further that the restriction on investing in media services outside the Netherlands was justifiable,[68] but that the restrictions on advertising were not.[69] The distinction that may be drawn is that the latter restrictions were unacceptable because they effectively shielded Dutch broadcasting companies from competition from other Member States, whereas the former restrictions only had a tangible impact on national broadcasting companies in the Netherlands. Again this highlights that the ECJ may pay deference to a national policy to promote and protect cultural rights, but only to a limited extent and not where this policy has protectionist results. A Member State wishing to establish a more far reaching policy in conformity with obligations under the Framework Convention evidently risks conflict with EU law.

On the basis of these cases, it is easy to see why the present situation is unworkable. EU law as it stands will only permit Member States to prioritize human rights obligations which result in restrictive measures on the fundamental economic freedoms stipulated in the EC Treaty in limited circumstances. If EU law itself does not replicate the guarantees contained in international human rights law, a Member State will inevitably come into conflict with its EU obligations when giving effect to human rights treaties. As we know, the Member States may invoke the protection of fundamental rights in order to justify such restrictions, to the extent that such restrictions are non-discriminatory and proportionate.[70] But the margin of appreciation they are left in this regard may not be sufficient, at least where a Member State will seek not only to comply with its

---

[65] Case C-148/91 *Vereniging Veronica Omroep Organisatie v Commissariaat voor de Media* [1993] ECR 513.

[66] Case C-353/89 *Commission v Netherlands* [1991] ECR 4089; Case C-288/89 *Stichting Collectieve Antennevoorziening Gouda et al. v Commissariaat voor de Media* [1991] ECR 4007.

[67] *Vereniging*, ibid, paras 9–10; *Commission v Netherlands*, ibid, paras 3, 29, 30, 41, 42; *Stichting Collectieve* ibid, paras 22–24.

[68] *Vereniging*, ibid, para 15.

[69] *Commission v Netherlands*, paras 43, 48; *Stichting Collectieve*, paras 25, 30.

[70] Case C-112/00 *Schmidberger* [2003] ECR I-5659, para 71; Case C-36/02 *Omega* [2004] ECR I-9609, para 33.

human rights obligations, but also to adopt measures aimed at fulfilling human rights beyond the minimum requirement not to violate them. We will return to this problem in a moment. In addition though, and perhaps more importantly, allowing the Member States (under the conditions of non-discrimination and proportionality) to observe their pre-existing human rights obligations on a decentralized and individual basis may threaten the uniform application of EU law, a danger which would be even more pronounced with respect to treaties to which not all Member States are party, such as the Framework Convention. In the alternative, if we acknowledge that Article 307 requires Member States to remove incompatibilities between EU law and their pre-existing human rights commitments, we face the danger of Member States being led to withdraw from human rights treaties, which would be politically unacceptable and in certain cases contrary to international law. Neither of these outcomes is acceptable. The only means of resolving both of these problems is if the EU takes human rights treaties into account *as if it were directly obliged by them*, even in the case where not all Member States are party.[71] This would ensure that all the Member States will be treated equally and that the supremacy and uniform application of EU law will be preserved.[72]

D. Inspiring 'Respect' for Human Rights

The notion that human rights obligations impose more than a duty merely to refrain from violating human rights when action is taken is well established in international human rights law, including the case law of the European Court

---

[71] This is effectively the 'universalised maximum standard' advocated by Besselink, 'Entrapped by the Maximum Standard: On Fundamental Rights, Pluralism and Subsidiarity in The European Union' (1998) 35 CML Rev 670–674. This is not to say that Member States necessarily have to adopt common maximum standard domestic standards. The 'universal maximum standard' would form part of the *acquis communautaire* and therefore only apply to Member States insofar as they are implementing their obligations under EU law. It is conceivable therefore that individuals in Member States with lower standards of protection will find themselves better protected whenever their activities fall under the scope of EU law.

[72] Weiler (see Weiler 'Fundamental Rights and Fundamental Boundaries: On Standards and Values in the Protection of Human Rights', in Neuwahl and Rosas (eds), *The European Union and Human Rights* (Martinus Nijhoff, 1995) 51–76) argues against the introduction of a universal maximum standard based on the highest levels of protection found across the Member States because this risks ignoring the particularities inherent in different nations such that one State's high standards may be unrealistic, unacceptable, or irrelevant to another State. Weiler, rather, appears to call for the adoption of a single standard based on what the Community itself believes reflects an amalgamated and pan-European standard. However, he makes clear that this should not be regarded as a minimum common standard. Perhaps this standard is now embodied in the Charter of Fundamental Rights. At the same time Weiler argues that the ECJ should defer to domestic human rights standards which are higher than those recognized within EU law when called to adjudicate on particular cases. However, as outlined above, in practice, this is only permitted by the ECJ where interference with the EU's economic aims is minimal. Furthermore, Weiler's proposal would, again, undermine the uniform application of EU law.

of Human Rights.[73] The clearest expression of this has come from the UN Committee on Economic Social and Cultural Rights, responsible for monitoring the implementation of the International Covenant on Economic Social and Cultural Rights:

all human rights, impose . . . three types or levels of obligations on States parties: the obligations to respect, protect and fulfil. In turn, the obligation to fulfil contains obligations to facilitate, provide and promote.'[74]

It is well-established by the ECJ that 'respect for the fundamental rights which form an integral part of . . . general principles of law is a condition of the legality of Community acts'.[75] However, while it is not our intention to enter a discussion on the nature of positive obligations in international human rights law,[76] we note that the ECJ does not seem to have acknowledged that human rights obligations are not of themselves purely negative in nature. Consider the approach the Court adopted towards the Family Reunification Directive at issue in the *Parliament v Council* case. The Directive obliges a Member State to permit entry and residence, for the purposes of family reunification, to minors where the minor's sponsor is residing lawfully in the Member State and has been in possession of a residence permit for at least one year and has a reasonable prospect of achieving the status of permanent resident.[77] Article 4(1) permits a Member State to derogate from this rule by requiring children over the age of 12 to satisfy an 'integration' requirement—which is left to national authorities to define. Parliament argued that nothing in the Directive prevented the Member States from adopting 'integration' requirements that would conflict with the right to family reunification guaranteed by Article 8 of the European Convention on Human Rights, as well Article 24 of the ICCPR and the CRC more generally. The ECJ opined that Community law 'could . . . not respect fundamental rights if it required, or

[73]   See: A Mowbray, *The Development of Positive Obligations Under the European Court of Human Rights* (Hart Publishing, 2004); S Fredman, 'Human Rights Transformed: Positive Duties and Positive Rights' [2006] Public Law 498.
[74]   UN Committee on Economic, Social and Cultural Rights, *The Right to the Highest Attainable Standard of Health*, General Comment 14, UN Doc. E/C.12/2000/4, para 33 in *Compilation of General Comments*. See also UN Committee on Economic, Social and Cultural Rights, *The Right to Education (Article 13)*, General Comment No.13 UN Doc. E/C.12/1999/10 at para 46, UN Committee on Economic, Social and Cultural Rights, *The Right to Adequate Food* (Article 11), General Comment 12 UN Doc. E/C.12/1999/5, para 15. Tomasevski and Scott and Macklem also regard this typology as being developed for all human rights. See K Tomasevski, *Women and Human Rights* (Zed Books Limited, 1993) 107; C Scott and P Mecklem, 'Constitutional Ropes of Sand or Justiciable Guarantees? Social Rights in a New South African Constitution' 141(1) University of Pennsylvania Law Review (1992) 1, 73.
[75]   Case C-249/96 *Grant v South West Trains Ltd* [1998] ECR I-621, para 45; Opinion 2/94 *Accession by the Community to the European Convention on Human Rights* [1996] ECR I-1759, paras 34–35.
[76]   For a brief discussion of what this might entail for the EU, see Ahmed and Butler 'The European Union and Human Rights: An International Law Perspective' 17 European Journal of International Law (2006) 771.
[77]   See Council Directive 2003/86/EC, 22/9/03 [2003] OJ L251/12.

expressly or impliedly authorised, the Member States to adopt or retain national legislation not respecting those rights'.[78] The wording suggests that legislation will be invalid if it leaves scope for a Member State to exercise its discretion in such a way as to conflict with human rights guarantees. This is significant because it seems to recognize a positive duty on the Community to protect human rights by preventing their violation by a Member State when it implements EC law. In the same way that a national legislator would be failing in its duty to protect individuals' right to life if its legislation created a wide and vaguely worded exception to the crime of homicide, the EU would be at fault if its legislation did not prevent a Member State from interpreting the 'integration' requirements in such a way as to violate the right to family reunification. In the event however, the ECJ did not find that the Directive could be interpreted in such a way as to permit a Member State to set conditions of integration that conflicted with the right to family reunification, despite the fact that the Directive contained no indication of what those conditions might be. Furthermore, the principle expressed in the judgment, in the excerpt quoted above,[79] appears to be contradicted by the Court's assessment of Article 8 of the Directive. Here the Court concluded that 'while the Directive leaves the Member States a margin of appreciation, it is sufficiently wide to enable them to apply the Directive's rules in a manner consistent with the requirements flowing from the protection of fundamental rights'.[80] Thus, secondary legislation would be compatible with the requirements of fundamental rights insofar as it does not compel the Member States to violate such rights, even where it does not establish clear safeguards against such risk. This corresponds also with the position adopted by AG Kokott in her opinion in this case.[81] Her view was that the contested provisions of the Family Reunification Directive must be examined 'in order to determine *whether there is sufficient scope for them to be applied in conformity with human rights*'. Otherwise put 'Community provisions are compatible with fundamental rights if they are *capable of being interpreted in a way which produces the outcome which those rights require.* [...] [What] matters is not what rules Member States might be minded to adopt in order to take full advantage of the latitude which the contested provisions afford, but rather what rules Member States may lawfully adopt if the Community provisions in question are interpreted in conformity with fundamental rights.'[82] This suggests a much weaker standard of review: Community legislation will be valid as long as it can be interpreted in conformity with the general principles. The implication is that there is no requirement that Community law deny scope to a Member State to exercise its discretion under EU legislation in such a way as to violate human rights standards. The weaker standard of review is consistent with the approach in the *Lindqvist* case where the ECJ stated that it was for the national

---

[78] Case C-540/03 *Parliament v Council* [2006] ECR I-5769, para 23.
[79] See the text corresponding to the preceding note.
[80] Para 104.   [81] Para 79–82 deal expressly with this question.
[82] Para 79–82 of the opinion (emphasis added).

authorities to ensure that they did not adopt an interpretation of Community law that conflicted with the general principles of law, but that the Directive in question was not invalid merely for allowing a Member State discretion which could be exercised in this manner.[83] The approach thus adopted by the Court to reviewing EC legislation relies upon individual Member States being scrutinized on an *ad hoc* basis as particular cases emerge, either through preliminary references or enforcement actions by the Commission, which can hardly constitute a satisfactory solution. Thus the ECJ does ensure that the EU legislator respects human rights, but it does little to protect human rights, in that it does not require legislation to restrict the exercise of Member State discretion as a condition of its validity.

Were the Court to have developed its case law more in line with international human rights standards, where positive obligations are accepted as an inherent component of human rights, it would have allowed for greater levels of protection. It may be anticipated, however, that accession of the EU to the European Convention on Human Rights or the recognition of the binding status of the EU Charter of Fundamental Rights—both of which will be achieved or made possible by the adoption of the Reform Treaty—will lead the case law to develop in this direction. The Working Group on the incorporation of the Charter and of the accession of the Union to the European Convention on Human Rights (established under the Convention on the Future of Europe, which itself prepared the ground for the intergovernmental conference that agreed on the text of the Constitutional Treaty), were in agreement that accession to the European Convention on Human Rights or incorporation of the Charter would 'in no way modify the allocation of competences between the Union and the Member States'. Neither act would involve conferring new powers on the Union, including a general competence on human rights. However, this did not exclude the imposition of positive obligations on the EU. On the contrary, it was acknowledged that such positive obligations 'to take action to comply with the ECHR would arise', albeit 'only to the extent to which competences of the Union permitting such action exist under the Treaty'.[84] According to this view, while accession to the European Convention on Human Rights would not result in a transferral of supplementary powers to the Union, it might affect the exercise of any powers it has been attributed, to the extent that positive obligations to protect and fulfil human rights are imposed under the European Convention on Human Rights.

Similar positive obligations could be derived from the EU Charter of Fundamental Rights, or indeed from the fundamental rights recognized as general principles of law in the case law of the Court. In support of this one can point to Article 51 of the Charter and the appended explanatory note. Although

---

[83] Case C-101/01 *Lindqvist* [2003] ECR I-12971, paras 84–88.

[84] European Convention, Final report of Working Group II, doc. CONV 354/02 (22 October 2002), p 13 (footnote omitted).

Article 51(2) repeats that the Charter does not create new competences for the Union, Article 51(1) states that the institutions and the Member States in the implementation of EU law shall 'respect the rights, observe the principles and promote the application thereof in accordance with their respective powers', thereby suggesting that positive obligations may be derived from the Charter. This is reinforced by the prescription that application of the Charter must have 'due regard for the principle of subsidiarity', which again would suggest that the Charter will give rise to positive obligations on the EU to take action to promote human rights. Furthermore the explanatory note on this clause states that 'an obligation, pursuant to the second sentence of paragraph 1, for the Union's institutions to promote principles laid down in the Charter may arise only within the limits of these same powers'.[85] While couched in restrictive terms this actually acknowledges that the Charter might well impose a duty on the Union to exercise whichever powers it has been attributed in such a way as to ensure the effective protection and promotion of the rights contained therein.

The decision of the ECJ in *Parliament v Council* contains contradictory statements, and cannot be seen as a clear acknowledgement that the Union is under a positive obligation to protect human rights by inserting safeguards into legislation to limit discretion conferred on the Member States. If the pedigree of the general principles, as rights grounded in international law, had been recognized the imposition on the European legislator of a positive obligation to protect them when adopting a measure might have appeared self-evident. Of course, international human rights law acknowledges an obligation not merely to protect, but also to fulfil or promote human rights, and even if the *Parliament v Council* case hints that the Union may have to protect human rights, there is certainly no indication in the case law that the Union may have to promote human rights. In this vein the EU Network of Independent Experts on Fundamental Rights urged the Union to 'move away from a conception of the international obligations of the Member States in the field of human rights which see these obligations simply as imposing limits' on the Union. Rather the Union institutions must ask themselves 'which initiatives they could take, to favour [the implementation of human rights] ... by the Member States, where the Union has the required powers to act and where exercising these powers could truly add value to the protection of fundamental rights in the Union'. In addition to respect for human rights, they 'should be promoted, insofar as the institutions of the Union remain ... in the limits of the powers which have been attributed to them'.[86] If the Charter and the general principles reflect the international commitments common to the Member States then the rights therein should be interpreted in conformity with the scope and meaning accorded to those rights by those instruments. We return

---

[85] [2007] OJ C303/17 (14.12.07).

[86] EU Network of Independent Experts on Fundamental Rights, Report on the Situation of Fundamental Rights in the Union in 2003, January 2004, pp 30–31. For the sake of transparency, it should be noted that one of the authors (O De Schutter) was the main author of this report.

to the question of promoting human rights in the final section of the article. We now examine the different means through which the Union could remedy its disconnectedness from international human rights law.

III. Anchoring the Union in the International Law of Human Rights

While there are grounds for holding that the EU is already bound under international law to guarantee universally recognized human rights,[87] we are less interested here in exploring the question whether it has such obligations, than in the question of which tools could be used in order to improve the accountability of the EU for any human rights violations it commits. A number of possibilities exist for thus linking fundamental rights protected under EU law and the international law of human rights. The most far-reaching solution would be accession by the Union to international human rights treaties. Alternatively, the monitoring bodies established under the UN human rights treaties or the Council of Europe, could subject the Union to some form of supervision. We review both possibilities in the following section. We then discuss the implications which would follow from the acceptance of external supervision of the EU by monitoring bodies established under human rights treaties, focusing in particular on the question of positive obligations imposed on the EU.

A. Acceding to International Human Rights Treaties

The EU is not yet party to any treaty codifying human rights standards.[88] There are a number of treaties, however, to which the EU may become a party in the future. Among the human rights treaties concluded in the framework of the UN, the most immediate prospect for EU accession comes in the UN Convention on the Rights of Persons with Disabilities.[89] The Union has signed this and the Commission has indicated that it will become a full party to the Treaty alongside

---

[87] This issue was discussed at length in a previous publication which put forward different possibilities in this regard. See Ahmed and Butler, 'The European Union and Human Rights: An International Law Perspective' 17 European Journal of International Law (2006) 771.

[88] The EU is party to around 140 multilateral treaties, a list of which can be found online at: <http://ec.europa.eu/world/agreements/searchByType.do?id=2>.

[89] UN General Assembly resolution 61/106, 13/12/06. The European Community signed the treaty on 30 March 2007 along with 96 other parties. See 'Multilateral Treaties Deposited with the Secretary-General' available online at: <http://untreaty.un.org/ENGLISH/bible/englishinternetbible/bible.asp>. See also EU Press Release IP/07446, 30/3/07. The Commission took an active role in negotiating the treaty on behalf of the Union and the Convention makes explicit provision for accession by 'regional integration organisations' under Article 44. The Treaty makes no distinction in the range of obligations that would apply to such organizations stating that '[r]eferences to "States Parties" in the present Convention shall apply to such organizations within the limits of their competence.'

the Member States.[90] Among the treaties adopted in the framework of the Council of Europe, the accession of the EU to the European Convention on Human Rights shall be a priority following the entry into force of the Reform Treaty which, like the abandoned Constitutional Treaty,[91] mandates the EU to accede to the European Convention on Human Rights.[92] Furthermore, the 1997 Convention on Human Rights and Biomedicine provides for accession by the European Community,[93] as does the 1999 Amendments to the Convention for the Protection of Individuals with regard to Automatic Processing of Personal Data.[94] Once the EU ratifies or accedes to these human rights treaties[95] it will of course be subject to the range of obligations therein in the exercise of the competences it has been attributed. Execution of the substantive obligations will be overseen to a greater or lesser extent by the supervisory mechanisms established by these instruments. In this section, we offer a brief description of these mechanisms, to which, following accession, the EU would be subjected.

(i) *The UN Disabilities Convention*

The implementation of the Disabilities Convention, as the other core UN human rights treaties, will be overseen by a Committee of independent experts, called

[90] Vladimír Spidla (EU Commissioner for DG Employment and Social Affairs), 'Launch of the Year of Equal Opportunities' 2/4/07, SPEECH/07/218.

[91] ECJ Opinion 2/94 (Accession by the Community to the European Convention on Human Rights [1996] ECR I–1759), made clear that the EU would not have competence to accede to the European Convention on Human Rights without an amendment to the existing treaties to that effect. The aborted Treaty Establishing a Constitution for Europe, 16 December 2004, [2004] OJ C310/01, Art I–9(2) would have obliged the EU to accede to the European Convention on Human Rights.

[92] The Reform Treaty amends Article 6 of the TEU with a new Article 6(2) reading: 'The Union shall accede to the European Convention for the Protection of Human Rights and Fundamental Freedoms. Such accession shall not affect the Union's competences as defined in the Treaties.' See Treaty of Lisbon amending the TEU and ECT (CIG 14/07, 3/12/07). Protocol 14 to the European Convention on Human Rights (once it enters into force) will amend the Convention to expressly provide for accession by the EU; Article 17 of the Protocol will amend Article 59 of the Convention to this effect. See Protocol No 14 to the Convention for the Protection of Human Rights and Fundamental Freedoms, amending the control system of the Convention, CETS No: 194, 13/5/04.

[93] Convention for the protection of Human Rights and dignity of the human being with regard to the application of biology and medicine: Convention on Human Rights and Biomedicine, CETS No: 164, opened for signature in Oviedo on 4 April 1997.

[94] ETS No 108, 28/1/81. The right to protection of one's private life is articulated in: ICCPR, Art 17; ACHR, Art 11; European Convention on Human Rights, Art 8. Additional Protocol to the Convention for the Protection of Individuals with regard to Automatic Processing of Personal Data Regarding Supervisory Authorities and Transborder Data Flows, ETS No 181, 8/11/01. See Article 3(2).

[95] In addition, the EU may accede to a number of conventions adopted within the Council of Europe, but which are not human rights instruments *per se*, as understood in this article, although, by imposing on the State parties the adoption of certain measures, they may contribute to the protection of human rights. Examples are the Convention on the Protection of Children against Sexual Exploitation and Sexual Abuse (CETS No: 201, opened for signature in Lanzarote on 25 October 2007 (see Article 45(1))); or the Convention on Action against Trafficking in Human Beings (CETS No: 197, opened for signature in Warsaw on 16 May 2005 (see Article 42(1))).

the Committee on the Rights of Persons with Disabilities.[96] The Committee will have among its tasks the consideration of reports from parties to the Treaty, including the issuing of recommendations.[97] Reports on the progress made in implementing the Convention are expected from parties at regular intervals (at least every four years according to Article 35). As is the practice of the existing UN human rights treaty monitoring bodies,[98] the Disabilities Committee will—after reviewing its report and engaging in an oral dialogue with representatives of the EU—issue 'Concluding Observations' which will contain concrete indications for the Union on its general state of compliance with the Convention and recommend future changes on issues of concern to the Committee.[99] The assessments of the committees are based not only on the report provided by the party under examination but also on 'shadow' reports received from interested non-governmental organizations (NGOs) and information submitted by UN agencies.[100] This ensures that a more balanced account is presented to the Committee. While Concluding Observations are targeted at situations falling under the jurisdiction of each Party, the UN human rights treaty bodies also issue General Comments or Recommendations. These allow them to elaborate on the meaning and content of a particular right or set of obligations in the Treaty as guidance for parties.[101]

If the EU also becomes party to the Optional Protocol to the Disabilities Convention, individuals will be able to bring claims against the EU before the Disabilities Committee. After exhausting domestic remedies individuals may contact the Disability Committee with the substance of their complaint.[102]

---

[96] According to Article 34 of the Convention the members of the Committee are to be individuals of high moral standing and recognized competence in the area, elected by State parties with due regard for equitable geographical distribution.

[97] See Articles 35 and 36 of the Convention. These are commonly known as 'concluding observations' or 'concluding comments' among the UN human rights treaty monitoring bodies.

[98] These are: the HRC (monitoring the ICCPR, 1966, 999 UNTS 171); the Committee on Economic, Social and Cultural Rights (monitoring the International Covenant on Economic, Social and Cultural Rights, 1966, 993 UNTS 3); the Committee on the Elimination of Racial Discrimination (monitoring the International Convention on the Elimination of All Forms of Racial Discrimination, 1965, 660 UNTS 195); the Committee on the Elimination of Discrimination Against Women (monitoring the Convention on the Elimination of All Forms of Discrimination Against Women, 1979, 1249 UNTS 13); the Committee Against Torture (monitoring the Convention against Torture and Other Cruel, Inhuman or Degrading Treatment or Punishment, 1984, 1465 UNTS 85); the Committee on the Rights of the Child (monitoring the Convention on the Rights of the Child, 1989, 1577 UNTS 3); the Committee on Migrant Workers (monitoring the Convention on the Protection of the Rights of All Migrant Workers and Members of their Families, 1990, GA Res 45/158, 18/12/90). The documents issued by these bodies are available online at: <http://tb.ohchr.org/default.asp>.

[99] See eg Consolidated Guidelines for State Reports under the International Covenant on Civil and Political Rights, 26/22/01, CCPR/C/66/GUI/Rev2.

[100] A Clapham, 'UN Human Rights Reporting Procedures: an NGO Perspective', in P Alston and J Crawford, *The Future of UN Human Rights Treaty Monitoring* (Cambridge University Press, 2000) 175; Report of the UN Human Rights Committee 2006, Vol 1, A/61/40 (Vol. 1), para 14.

[101] See Article 29 of the Disabilities Convention. These general comments aim to provide general guidance for all the parties on the meaning of a provision in the Treaty.

[102] Optional Protocol, Art 2.

Proceedings are entirely written. However, they present an adversarial character in that both parties are provided the opportunity to provide responses to each others' arguments.[103] Once it has made a 'determination on the merits' the Committee may 'forward its suggestions and recommendations' to the parties to the dispute.[104] These may include a finding that there has been a violation of the Treaty, a direction to pay legal costs or damages, and a direction to take specific remedial action.[105] These are not of themselves legally binding upon the parties to the dispute but they do have some legal weight. The Human Rights Committee, which monitors compliance with the International Covenant on Civil and Political Rights, has maintained that its findings on individual cases are effectively binding on States because States have, firstly, committed themselves to offer a remedy to victims of violations and, secondly, have expressly delegated the task of finding violations to the Committee.[106]

(ii) *The European Convention on Human Rights*

Should the EU accede to the European Convention on Human Rights, it will become subject to the jurisdiction of the European Court of Human Rights.[107] The lack of a reporting system in the European Convention on Human Rights means that the European Court of Human Rights would not able to offer programmatic guidance on policy-formulation and promotional activities to the EU in the same way as the Disabilities Committee. However, this is a gap that might be filled by the Council of Europe's Commissioner for Human Rights, to which we return below.[108] In addition, while the European Court of Human Rights does not adopt statements expounding its understanding of the requirements of the Convention in general terms—as do the UN human rights treaty bodies—this function is to a certain extent fulfilled by the Committee of Ministers of the Council of Europe, through the adoption of recommendations.[109] The European Court of Human Rights is principally tasked with dealing with claims of individuals alleging violations

---

[103] See I Butler, *Unravelling Sovereignty: Human Rights Actors and the Structure of International Law*, (Intersentia, 2007) 123–131.

[104] Optional Protocol, Art 5.   [105] See Optional Protocol, Arts 4 and 5.

[106] See n 34, above.

[107] European Convention on Human Rights, Art 32.

[108] The institution of the Commissioner for Human Rights was established by Resolution (99)50 adopted by the Committee of Ministers on 7 May 1999 at its 104th Session, as a 'non-judicial institution to promote education in, awareness of and respect for human rights, as embodied in the human rights instruments of the Council of Europe' (Article 1 of the resolution). While the Commissioner for Human Rights may directly contact the governments of the Member States of the Council of Europe (Article 7 of the resolution), his mandate does not included addressing the EU, which is not a member of the Council of Europe. However, as we shall see, the Commissioner inevitably makes statements in relation to the EU since his mandate extends to any issues arising on the territory of any State member of the Council of Europe.

[109] See eg below, n 116. The European Court of Human Rights may deliver advisory opinions under Articles 47–49 of the European Convention on Human Rights, but it does not often exercise this function. The European Court of Human Rights delivered its first Advisory Opinion on 12 February 2008, on certain legal questions concerning gender balance in the composition of the lists of candidates submitted for the election of judges to the Court.

by the State (or in this case, the EU) though it may also receive inter-State complaints.[110] The judgments of the European Court of Human Rights are legally binding and the Committee of Ministers of the Council of Europe oversees their implementation.[111] The European Court of Human Rights may order the payment of financial compensation by the Party found to have violated the Convention, though more frequently it will merely find that a declaration of the existence of a violation is remedy enough. It will rarely give specific directions on how to remedy a violation,[112] leaving it to the Committee of Ministers to determine whether this has taken place and whether action has been taken to avoid systematic repetition of the violation in the future.[113]

(iii) *The Council of Europe Convention on Human Rights and Biomedicine, and the Convention for the Protection of Individuals with regard to Automatic Processing of Personal Data*

These two Conventions provide for the creation of consultative committees with fairly limited roles and similar composition: these are the 'Consultative Committee' created under the Convention for the Protection of Individuals with regard to Automatic Processing of Personal Data, and the 'Steering Committee on Bioethics' created under the Convention on Human Rights and Biomedicine. These committees may both make or respond to proposals relating to the amendment of the Treaty, respond to requests for clarification of the Treaty's terms and make proposals on how to better implement the Treaty.[114] The Consultative Committee is composed of both representatives of State parties, observers (who may be representatives of third States not parties to the Convention as well as intergovernmental organizations) and independent experts for the purposes of consultation.[115] The Consultative Committee has produced a series of

---

[110] European Convention on Human Rights, Arts 34 and 33 respectively.

[111] European Convention on Human Rights, Art 46.

[112] For an example of where this did occur, see European Court of Human Rights (Grand Chamber) *Assanidze v Georgia* (Application no 71503/01, 8/4/04).

[113] See eg Decisions Adopted by the Deputies of the Committee of Ministers, 997th (DH) meeting, 5–6 June 2007, CM/Del/Dec(2007)997.

[114] For the Convention on Data Protection, see Article 19. The Explanatory Report (para 87, available online at: <http://conventions.coe.int/Treaty/en/Reports/Html/108.htm>) to the Convention States: 'It was not held desirable that the committee should take the form of an international data protection authority. Nor was it considered appropriate to entrust to the committee the formal settlement of disputes arising over the application of the convention. Of course, the committee may help to solve difficulties arising between Parties.' For the Biomedicine Convention, see Article 32. According to Article 29 the Steering Committee or the parties may also request the European Court of Human Rights for an advisory opinion on the interpretation of the Treaty.

[115] See Consultative Committee of the Convention for the Protection of Individuals with regard to Automatic Processing of Personal Data (ETS No 108): Rules of Procedure, Articles 2–4. This document is available through the website of the Council of Europe at: <http://www.coe.int/t/e/legal_affairs/legal_co-operation/data_protection/background/T-PD_RULES.pdf>. For background on the committee, see: <http://www.coe.int/t/e/legal_affairs/legal_co-operation/data_protection/background/1Background.asp#TopOfPage>. The current committee is a merger of the original

(non-binding) recommendations to State parties elaborating detailed rules on the application of the Convention for the Protection of Individuals with regard to Automatic Processing of Personal Data to specific circumstances.[116]

Thus, the EU stands on the cusp of a new stage of human rights protection, in particular with regard to possible accession to the European Convention on Human Rights and the UN Disabilities Convention which are extensive in terms of the substantive rights that they guarantee. Holding the EU directly accountable to the monitoring bodies that operate under these treaties will constitute a long-overdue express recognition that the EU's extensive powers should be subject to review for compliance with human rights obligations by an entity that operates outside the EU's own self-referential 'system' of human rights protection. However, neither these two instruments, nor those instruments in combination with the Council of Europe Convention on Human Rights and Biomedicine and Convention for the Protection of Individuals with regard to Automatic Processing of Personal Data to which the EU may accede in the future, cover the entire range of international human rights protected through several other treaties elaborated under the aegis of the United Nations. The importance of these UN human rights treaties is evidenced by the fact that most or all of the EU Member States are parties to these instruments, thereby recognizing the significance of the rights they guarantee. For the reasons explained above, in addition, we believe that the EU should take into account all human rights treaties to which at least one EU Member State is a party, in order to avoid compromising either the commitments of that State under the said treaty, or the uniform application of EU law. Even if the EU is not bound, in the international legal order, by the treaties to which its Member States have acceded, at the very least it may be prohibitively costly, in both political and practical terms, to ignore them.

As we have seen, certain human rights instruments recently concluded within the UN and Council of Europe provide for the possibility of accession by the EU. This has been the case, in general, where certain competences have been conferred

---

consultative committee and a Project Group on Data Protection, which was a subsidiary body of the committee composed of experts. See also Explanatory Memorandum to Recommendation No R (2002) 9 of the Committee of Ministers to Member States on the protection of personal data collected and processed for insurance purposes, adopted by the Committee of Ministers 18 September 2002 at the 808th meeting of the Ministers' Deputies, available online at: <http://www.coe.int/t/e/legal_affairs/ legal_co-operation/data_protection/documents/international_legal_instruments/EM_R(2002)9_ EN.pdf>. On the Steering Committee, see 'Terms of Reference' in Steering Committee on Bioethics (CDBI), 'Information Document Concerning the CDBI', CDBI/INF (2007) 1 rev (available at: <http://www.coe.int/T/E/Legal_Affairs/Legal_co-operation/Bioethics/CDBI/>).

[116] It would appear that the majority of these are subsequently adopted by the Committee of Ministers which requests states parties to give effect to the recommendations in national law. For the Consultative Committee see: Recommendation No R (2002) 9 on the protection of personal data collected and processed for insurance purposes (18 September 2002). For a collection of these, see: <http://www.coe.int/t/e/legal_affairs/legal_co-operation/data_protection/documents/inter­national_legal_instruments/2Recommendations%20and%20resolutions%20of%20the%20 Committee%20of%20Ministers.asp#TopOfPage>. For the Steering Committee, see examples in 'Information Document Concerning the CDBI' (n 115 above).

upon the Union by its Member States in relation to the domain covered by the instrument concerned. We should move beyond the current practice, however. Accession of the EU should not be limited to treaties which have a direct overlap with areas of EU competence. Human rights obligations affect the exercise of all public power since it is through the exercise of their authority that States or other entities violate or uphold human rights. In this sense human rights cut across all areas of EU competence. Accordingly, accession by the EU to those treaties to which its Member States are party (partially or entirely) provides the best means of ensuring that the EU's competences are exercised in such a way as to give full effect to the obligations incurred by its Member States.

Indeed, were it not for the stipulations of human rights treaties, which traditionally are open to accession only by States, these precedents could be imitated in other areas in which the European Union has taken legislative action, thereby exercising competences it has been attributed by its Member States. Of course, in the absence of a general power of the Community or the Union in the field of fundamental rights,[117] the limits imposed on the exercise of the international powers of the Community or the Union are a serious obstacle to their accession to international instruments for the protection of human rights. However, even under the present definition of the external powers of the Union, accession to a number of international instruments in the field of human rights protection may be envisaged.[118] Just as the achievements of the European Community in the field of data protection have been deemed sufficient to envisage the accession of the Community to the Convention concluded on this question in the framework of the Council of Europe, similarly the *acquis* of EC law in the field of equal treatment between women and men and in the field of non-discrimination on grounds of race or ethnic origin would appear sufficient to identify a power of the Community to accede to the UN Conventions on the Elimination of All Forms of Discrimination against Women (CEDAW)[119] and on the Elimination of All Forms of Racial Discrimination (CERD).[120] It has also been argued that

---

[117] See on this the opinion delivered on 28 March 1996 by the European Court of Justice: Opinion 2/94, *Accession of the European Community to the European Convention for the Protection of Human Rights and Fundamental Freedoms* [1996] ECR I-1759, para 20. The Court stated in that opinion that the Community institutions do not have at their disposal a 'general power to enact rules on human rights or to conclude international conventions in this field', although it did not question that respect for human rights constituted a 'condition of lawfulness of Community acts': see paras 27 and 34 of the opinion. On this opinion, see, inter alia, O De Schutter and Y Lejeune, 'L'adhésion de la Communauté européenne à la Convention européenne des droits de l'homme. A propos de l'avis 2/94 de la Cour de justice des Communautés européennes', Cahiers de droit européen, 1996, 555; G Gaja, 'Opinion 2/94' (1996) 33 CML Rev 973.

[118] *Report on the Situation of Fundamental Rights in the European Union in 2003*, prepared for the EU Network of Independent Experts on Fundamental Rights, January 2004, at pp 19–20. Report available online at: <http://ec.europa.eu/justice_home/cfr_cdf/index_en.htm#>.

[119] 1249 UNTS 20378, adopted by UN Gen. Ass. Res. 34/180 of 18 December 1979. All the 27 Member States of the EU have ratified this instrument.

[120] 660 UNTS 9464, adopted by UN Gen. Ass. Res. 2106 A(XX) of 21 December 1965, and opened for signature at New York on 7 March 1966. All the 27 Member States of the EU have ratified this instrument.

the EU should accede to the 1996 Revised European Social Charter, adopted within the Council of Europe as a complement, in the field of economic and social rights, to the 1950 European Convention on Human Rights;[121] or to the Geneva Convention on the status of refugees of 28 July 1951.[122]

We may go one step further. The time may have come to question the classical approach to the question of the competence of international organizations to accede to international agreements, when the concerned agreements relate to the promotion and protection of human rights. It is well established that the competence of international organizations is a limited one: they may only act under the condition that, and insofar as, they have been attributed the power to do so by the Member States to which they owe their existence.[123] We may ask however, which implications follow for the accession of an international organization such as the EU to human rights treaties? By acceding to such instruments, the Parties undertake to respect certain minimal standards for the benefit of the persons under their jurisdiction, which implies in the first place that they will not adopt any measures which derogate from these standards. Insofar as the undertaking is purely negative (formulated as an obligation to abstain from), it is irrelevant whether or not the Party has the competence to take measures which implement the given standard. It is only where the undertaking is also to adopt certain measures—to fulfil positive obligations (to act)—that the question of competences may play a role. Once this interpretation is agreed upon, the prospect of the EU acceding to a wide range of human rights treaties becomes significantly easier to envisage.

B. Alternatives to Accession: Monitoring the EU through its Member States

Pending accession by the EU to human rights treaties, or as an alternative to accession, the monitoring bodies established under existing human rights treaties should develop tools to supervise the EU itself, and not only its Member States. This section discusses the possibility that the EU could be subject to direct

---

[121] The Revised European Social Charter of 3 May 1996 (ETS No 163) improves upon the original European Social Charter of 18 October 1961, by extending the list of rights protected. On the question of the accession of the EU to the Council of Europe Social Charter, see O De Schutter, 'Anchoring the European Union to the European Social Charter: The Case for Accession', in G de Búrca and B de Witte (eds), *Social Rights in Europe* (OUP, 2005) 111–152; and, for a more technical discussion, O De Schutter, *L'adhésion de l'Union européenne à la Charte sociale européenne* (EUI Working Paper LAW No 2004/11, 42 pages).

[122] 149 UNTS 2545.

[123] In its advisory opinion on *Legality of the use by a State of nuclear weapons in armed conflict*, the International Court of Justice stated that: '[...] international organizations [...] do not, unlike States, possess a general competence. International organizations are governed by the "principle of speciality", that is to say, they are invested by the States which create them with powers, the limits of which are a function of the common interests whose promotion those States entrust to them' (*ICJ Reports 1996*, 66, at 78 (para 25)).

scrutiny by the monitoring bodies responsible for supervising the implementation of human rights treaties to which EU Member States are parties. Our premise is that, if jurisdiction over certain situations is shared between the EU and its Member States, then monitoring of the Member States must be complemented with monitoring of the EU in those areas within its competence. The practice of certain monitoring bodies suggests a willingness on their part to extend their supervisory functions to States and intergovernmental organisations (IGOs) that are not themselves parties to their particular treaty but do exercise a degree of control over territory belonging to a State party. This existing practice forms the basis for suggesting more comprehensive engagement of the EU by the UN human rights treaty monitoring bodies, as well as by the Council of Europe monitoring bodies. We first describe such practice (a) and then examine whether it could be generalized (b).

(i) *The Existing Practice of Human Rights Monitoring Bodies*

One of the functions of the UN human rights treaty bodies is to receive and comment upon reports submitted periodically by the parties. In exercising this function, the HRC, responsible for the implementation of the ICCPR, has established two precedents that support the proposition that monitoring bodies could request the EU to submit to its supervision directly. In 1997, the exercise of sovereignty over the territory of Hong Kong reverted back to China from the United Kingdom. Under the terms of a Joint Declaration the United Kingdom and China agreed on the continued application of the ICCPR to Hong Kong, and in 1997 China notified the UN Secretary-General of its intention to report to the HRC in relation to Hong Kong.[124] The HRC had underlined in its 1996 Concluding Observations on the UK that '[o]nce the people living in a territory enjoy the protection of the rights under the International Covenant on Civil and Political Rights, such protection cannot be denied to them merely by virtue of dismemberment of that territory or its coming under the sovereignty of another State or of more than one State.'[125] Thus in the HRC's view, irrespective of any will on the part of China to submit to its supervision, the HRC was entitled to exercise its monitoring functions in respect of that territory, a point which it reiterated in its General Comment 26 on the 'Continuity of Obligations'.[126] Thus, the fact that

---

[124] See Report submitted by China in respect of Hong Kong, CCPR/C/HKSAR/99/1, 16/6/99, paras 1–5.

[125] Concluding Observations on the UK CCPR/C/79/Add.69, 18/11/96, para 4.

[126] China submitted its first report in relation to Hong Kong in 1999. For the report, see n 125, above and also see Concluding Observations on China (Hong Kong) CCPR/C/79/Add.117, 12/11/99. General Comment 26, 'Continuity of Obligations' (1997), in 'Compilation of General Comments Adopted by Human Rights Treaty Bodies', UN Doc. HRI/GEN/1/Rev7, 12/5/04, 172–173. The wording used by the HRC in the General Comment is: 'the rights guaranteed under the Covenant belong to the people living in the territory of a State party, and that once the people are accorded the protection of the rights under the Covenant, such protection devolves with territory and continues to belong to them, notwithstanding changes in the administration of that territory'.

China is not a party to the ICCPR is not an obstacle to the extension, to a territory administered by China, of the supervisory role of the HRC. Our second example is more recent and perhaps even more significant. In 2004, the HRC requested the UN Interim Administration Mission in Kosovo (UNMIK) to submit a report on the human rights situation in Kosovo in response to a submission of Serbia during consideration of its periodic report.[127] Kosovo is formally within the territory of Serbia, a party to the ICCPR, but has been administered by UNMIK since 1999. The HRC made this request of UNMIK after Serbia explained its inability to report on the implementation of the ICCPR in Kosovo given that authority over the territory lay in the hands of the UN. A similar approach has been taken in the European context where the Council of Europe has concluded agreements with NATO[128] and UNMIK[129] authorizing the Committee on the Prevention of Torture to access detention facilities run by these organizations for the purposes of supervising implementation of the European Convention for the Prevention of Torture.[130]

These examples are limited to situations where the territory of an existing State party to a treaty is actually being administered by another State or by an international organization. It might be objected that this situation is not comparable to that of the EU in relation to its Member States since the EU itself does not administer territory. Rather the EU relies on the authorities of the Member States to implement and enforce EU Law.[131] Nevertheless, since the EU Member States are bound to comply with the obligations imposed on them under EU law—from which it follows, as a matter of course, that EU law should be accorded supremacy over any national rules[132]—and since broad areas of competence have

[127] See Concluding Observations on Serbia, CCPR/CO/81/SEMO, 12/8/04; Concluding Observations on the report on Kosovo (Serbia) submitted by the United Nations Interim Administration Mission in Kosovo, para 4. See UN HRC Report 2005/2006, Vol I, A/61/40, 68.

[128] Press Release, 'Council of Europe Anti-Torture Committee gains access to NATO run detention facilities in Kosovo', 19/7/06. Available online at: <http://www.cpt.coe.int/documents/srp/2006–07-19-eng.htm>.

[129] Agreement between the UN Interim Administration Mission in Kosovo and the Council of Europe on technical arrangements related to the European Convention for the Prevention of Torture and Inhuman or Degrading Treatment or Punishment, 23/8/04. Available online at: <http://www.cpt.coe.int/documents/srp/2004–08-23-eng.htm>.

[130] European Convention for the Prevention of Torture and Inhuman and Degrading Treatment or Punishment, CETS No 126, opened for signature in Strasbourg on 26 November 1987.

[131] In this respect, the Member States are under a so-called 'duty of genuine' or 'loyal cooperation' derived from Article 10 of the ECT: 'Member States shall take all appropriate measures, whether general or particular, to ensure fulfilment of the obligations arising out of this Treaty or resulting from action taken by the institutions of the Community. They shall facilitate the achievement of the Community's tasks. They shall abstain from any measure which could jeopardise the attainment of the objectives of this Treaty.' On the meaning of Article 10, see: Case C-433/03 *Commission v Germany* [2005] ECR I-6985; Case C-105/03 *Pupino* [2005] ECR I-5285.

[132] This principle was articulated in Case 6/64 *Costa v ENEL* [1964] ECR 585: '... the law stemming from the Treaty, an independent source of law, could not, because of its special and original nature, be overridden by domestic legal provisions...without being deprived of its character as Community law and without the legal basis of the Community being called into question.'

been transferred to the EU, it is hard to deny that authority over the territory of Member States is at the very least shared with the EU.[133] Indeed the ECJ itself maintained very early on that there has indeed been a real transfer of sovereignty from the Member States to the EU.[134] The function of executing law and policy at the national level lies almost exclusively with the Member States' own administrative structure, but the function of determining the content of that law and policy is exercised jointly with the EU. Taking these considerations into account, it does not seem too far fetched to suggest that the monitoring bodies supervising those treaties to which the EU Member States are party, should also engage with the EU, not instead of, but as a complement to, their supervision of the Member States. The UN human rights treaties concerned include: the International Covenant on Civil and Political Rights, the International Covenant on Economic Social and Cultural Rights, the International Convention on the Elimination of All Forms of Racial Discrimination, the Convention on the Elimination of All Forms of Discrimination against Women, the Convention against Torture and Other Cruel, Inhuman or Degrading Treatment or Punishment, and the Convention on the Rights of the Child. It is arguably open to any of the committees supervising these treaties to engage with the EU in the same way as the HRC has with UNMIK and China on the basis of its joint rule over the territory of the Member States.

The proposition that the UN human rights treaty monitoring bodies could engage the EU directly over the fulfilment of obligations undertaken by its Member States is not without some precedent within the EU. The principal example is that of the UN's High Commissioner for Refugees.[135] Article 63 of the EC Treaty gives the EU competence to regulate matters relating to the 1951 Convention Relating to the Status of Refugees[136] and its 1967 Protocol.[137] All the

---

[133] Article 3 of the ECT lists 21 separate policy areas, while the TEU contains a further two in titles V and VI.

[134] 'By creating a community of unlimited duration, having its own institutions, its own personality, its own legal capacity and capacity of representation on the international plane and, more particularly, real powers stemming from a limitation of sovereignty or a transfer of powers from the states to the community, the member states have limited their sovereign rights, albeit within limited fields, and have thus created a body of law which binds both their nationals and themselves': Case 6/64 *Costa v ENEL* [1964] ECR 585.

[135] A further example is that of the Consultative Committee of the Convention on Personal Data discussed above (see above, nn 114–117 and accompanying text). The CPD Consultative Committee recently addressed the EU over a recent proposal for legislation in the area of privacy expressing its concerns at the planned Council Framework Decision. See Consultative Committee of the Convention for the Protection of Individuals with Regard to Automatic Processing of Personal Data (T-PD), T-PD-BUR (2006) 15 E FIN, 20/3/07, Paper Outlining the T-PD's Initial Remarks Concerning a Proposal for a Council Framework Decision on the Protection of personal Data Processed in the Framework of Police and Judicial Cooperation in Criminal Matters. This is also available as document of the Council of Ministers (Interinstitutional File: 2005/0202 (CNS), 8274/07, 5/4/072).

[136] 189 UNTS 150. Sometimes referred to as the 'Geneva Convention'.

[137] Protocol Relating to the Status of Refugees, 606 UNTS 267. Sometimes referred to as the 'New York Protocol'.

EU Member States are parties to both these instruments.[138] Among other things, these treaties establish guarantees of treatment for those who are accorded refugee status[139] as well as enshrining the principle of 'non-refoulement' which prevents an individual from being returned to their country of origin where they face a 'well-founded fear of being persecuted' on specified grounds.[140] In the context of its policy on visas and asylum, Article 63 obliges the Union to enact procedural and substantive provisions relating to individuals seeking asylum 'in accordance with' the 1951 Convention and its 1967 Protocol.[141] Although the EU has been criticized for the content of its secondary legislation in this area, it does nonetheless purport to set minimum standards for the Member States to follow modelled on those contained in the 1951 Convention and its 1967 Protocol.[142] Indeed, the legislation purports to go beyond these treaties to incorporate developments in the case law of the European Court of Human Rights, going beyond the protection of asylum-seekers to include other individuals in need of international protection.[143] However imperfectly the EU may be giving effect to the obligations of the 1951 Convention and 1967 Protocol incurred by the Member States, the legislation in this area establishes an important point of principle. Despite conferring on the Union the authority to establish a system of visas and entry requirements for third country nationals the Union has not purported to act as if it were free of the obligations that its Member States had previously undertaken

---

[138] 'Multilateral Treaties Deposited with the Secretary-General' available online at: <http://untreaty.un.org/ENGLISH/bible/englishinternetbible/bible.asp>.

[139] Chapter II of the 1951 Convention.   [140] 1951 Convention, Art 1(A)(2).

[141] See the secondary legislation: Directive 2003/9 laying down minimum standards for the reception of asylum seekers ([2003] OJ L31/18 (06.02.03)); Regulation 343/2003 establishing the criteria and mechanisms for determining the Member State responsible for examining an asylum application lodged in one of the Member States by a third-country national ([2003] OJ L50/1 (25.02.03)); Directive 2004/83 on minimum standards for the qualification and status of third country nationals or stateless persons as refugees or as persons who otherwise need international protection and the content of the protection granted ([2004] OJ L304/12 (30.09.04)); Directive 2005/85 on minimum standards on procedures in Member States for granting and withdrawing refugee status ([2005] OJ L326/13 (13.12.05)).

[142] K Hailbronner, 'Detention of Asylum Seekers' 9 European Journal of Migration and Law (2007) 159; A Maurer and R Parkes, 'The Prospects for Policy-Change in EU Asylum Policy: Venue and Image at the European Level' 9 European Journal of Migration and Law (2007) 173; C Phuong, 'Minimum Standards for Return Procedures and International Human Rights Law' 9 European Journal of Migration and Law (2007) 105; R Thomas, 'Assessing the Credibility of Asylum Claims: EU and UK Approaches Examined' 9 European Journal of Migration and Law (2006) 79.

[143] Directive 2004/83 sets out when 'persecution' will be deemed to have occurred using and expanding on the terminology of the 1951 Convention (compare Chapters III and IV of the Directive to Article 1 of the 1951 Convention). The Directive also establishes 'subsidiary' protection which purports to limit the circumstances when states may return a refugee beyond those established in the 1951 Convention (compare Directive Chapter VI to Article 1(F) of the 1951 Convention). This 'subsidiary' status is supposed to reflect the case law of the European Court of Human Rights which prohibits States from returning an individual to any state where they may suffer cruel, inhuman, or degrading treatment or punishment or torture, for whatever reason this may be. (See the Commission's proposal (COM(2001) 510 final, 5–6) and the EP's report (A5–0333/2002 FINAL, 8/10/02, 52)). It is questionable whether it actually achieves this given the list of circumstances where 'subsidiary status' may be denied (compare Article 17 of the Directiv to *Chahal v UK* ECHR 15/11/96, ECHR Reports 1996-V, para 82).

with respect to refugees. The Union implicitly acknowledges that it is bound by the international law in this area by its adoption of legislation that is overtly geared towards ensuring that treaty obligations are complied with in the context of its policy on visas and immigration.[144] This is confirmed by the relationship of the EU to the UN High Commissioner for Refugees, which is charged with 'providing international protection...to refugees'.[145] The 1967 Protocol places parties under an obligation to facilitate the Office of the High Commissioner for Refugees in supervising implementation of the two treaties, including providing information on the condition of refugees, the state of implementation and the law relating to refugees.[146] Although not making explicit reference to these obligations, Declaration No 17 accompanying the Amsterdam Treaty states that '[c]onsultations shall be established with the United Nations High Commissioner for Refugees and other relevant international organisations on matters relating to asylum policy.'[147] The Declaration has been put into effect through two exchanges of letters between the Commission and the UNHCR which provide for cooperation in developing EU policy in this area.[148] The UNHCR does not systematically monitor and report on compliance with the treaties in the same way as the HRC monitors the ICCPR. Rather than receiving reports from the EU or the Member States and issuing observations on compliance or receiving individual complaints, the role of the UNHCR is one of input into day-to-day policy formulation, in a relationship that has been described as one of partnership rather than lobbying,[149] and of expressing any concerns to the EU via, for example, letters to incoming presidencies.[150] One of the reasons for not producing

[144] The Council has stated that the 'aims of the Common European Asylum System...will be the establishment of a common asylum procedure and a uniform status for those who are granted asylum or subsidiary protection. It will be based on the full and inclusive application of the Geneva Convention on Refugees and other relevant Treaties.' See The Hague Programme: Strengthening Freedom, Security and Justice in the European Union [2005] OJ C53/01 (03.03.05).

[145] GA Res 428 (V), 14/12/50, Statute of the Office of the United Nations High Commissioner for Refugees, Annex, Article 1.

[146] 1967 Protocol, Arts II, III.

[147] Adopted by the Conference on the Amsterdam Treaty on then Article 73k (now Article 63) of the Treaty establishing the European Community [1997] OJ C340/134 (10.11.97). The Treaty of Lisbon amends Article 63 to state expressly that asylum policy 'must be in accordance with the Geneva Convention of 28 July 1951 and the Protocol of 31 January 1967 relating to the status of refugees, and other relevant treaties.'

[148] The agreement between the Commission and UNHCR giving effect to Declaration No 17 took the form of an exchange of letters of 15 February 2005, available online at: <http://www.unhcr. org/home/RSDLEGAL/42135cba4.pdf>. The text of the first exchange of letters of 6 July 2000 between Commissioner Vitorino and Mrs Ogata may be requested from the Brussels office of the UNHCR. Reference is made to it in many UNCHR documents including 'UNHCR Toolboxes on EU Asylum Matters', available online at: <http://www.unhcr.org/publ/PUBL/41b6d8694.html>.

[149] Interview with UNHCR Brussels Office official, 26/6/07.

[150] See 2005 and 2000 letters of exchange, UNHCR Toolboxes and eg, 'UNHCR's Recommendations for Portugal's European Union Presidency, July-December 2007', 15/6/07, available online at: <http://www.unhcr.org/protect/PROTECTION/4672a5a52.pdf>; 'The Hague Programme two years on: UNHCR's Recommendations to the German Presidency of the European Union January–June 2007', available online at: <http://www.unhcr.org/protect/PROTECTION/457ebab92.pdf>.

systematic assessments of the EU's state of compliance with the treaties is that much of the EU legislation relies on implementation and interpretation by the Member States.[151] Because of this the role of the national UNHCR offices in monitoring State compliance remains important and necessary.

The example of the partnership established between the EU and the UNHCR in the implementation in EU secondary legislation of the 1951 Geneva Convention and the 1967 New York Protocol illustrates the creative capacity of bodies responsible for monitoring or facilitating the implementation of human rights treaties, as well as a willingness on the part of the EU to cooperate. It is possible for such bodies to shift the emphasis of their work from the national to the EU level as greater authority is transferred from the Member States without the EU itself needing to become party to the treaties. In the area of visas, asylum, and immigration the EU expressly acknowledged that authority in this area could not be passed from the Member States without the existing obligations relating to refugees, and the UNHCR and EU have adapted to this by establishing a close relationship. But such formal recognition is not a prerequisite for the establishment, between the EU and other bodies, of similar forms of partnership.

(ii) Systematizing Existing Practice

Such arrangements as described above are informal. They are not conditional upon the EU acceding to the human rights treaties concerned. The are based on forms of voluntary cooperation between the EU and any supervisory bodies established under such treaties. We suggest that, in preparation for the formal accession of the EU to human rights treaties, such arrangements could be generalized across all human rights treaties to which the Member States have acceded. This is not a fantastical proposition. In fact, the EU has repeatedly demonstrated its willingness to facilitate the implementation of obligations imposed on its Member States under human rights treaties, by constructively engaging with the bodies in charge of supervising such treaties or by contributing to fora set up in order to clarify and develop the undertakings accepted under such treaties. For instance, while not party to the Council of Europe Convention for the Protection of Individuals with regard to Automatic Processing of Personal Data or its Protocol, the EU has participated in the formulation of recommendations as an observer to the Consultative Committee established under that Convention. The Proposal for a Council Framework Decision on the Protection of Personal Data Processed in the Framework of Police and Judicial Cooperation in Criminal Matters, which the European Commission presented in October 2005,[152] has taken the Data Protection Convention and relevant recommendations of the

---

[151] Interview with UNHCR Brussels Office official, 26/6/07.

[152] For the original text of the Commission's proposal, see Proposal for a Council Framework Decision on the protection of personal data processed in the framework of police and judical cooperation in criminal matters, COM(2005) 475 final, 4/10/05.

Consultative Committee as a point of reference.[153] Indeed, this practice of basing legislation proposed in the framework of the EU on the existing standards of the Council of Europe shall become a systematic practice in the future, as provided by the May 2007 Memorandum of Understanding between the Council of Europe and the European Union.[154] In the memorandum the EU acknowledges the 'Council of Europe as the Europe-wide reference source for human rights' and provides that the EU's institutions should take into account 'decisions and conclusions of its monitoring structures...where relevant'. It also provides for consultation and cooperation between the EU and the Council of Europe, including the Commissioner for Human Rights in order to ensure that EU law is coherent with human rights guarantees stemming from Council of Europe treaties.[155]

The EU has found other innovative solutions to ensure that its Member States can continue to cooperate with third States in the promotion and protection of human rights. In particular, the Council of Ministers has authorized the Member States to ratify treaties 'in the interest of the Community' which contribute to the protection of the rights of the child or the rights of migrant workers.[156] Such authorization is given where the subject areas covered by the agreements are considered to fall within areas of exclusive competence of the Union (thus ordinarily preventing the Member States acceding to these treaties),[157] although the treaties themselves only allowed for States to become parties.[158] Accession by the Member States has then been followed up by EU legislation largely giving effect to the terms of these treaties or expressly permitting the Member States to execute them in exception to the general rule established by EU law that Member States may not act in areas of exclusive EU competence.[159] These are examples of the

[153] Commission Proposal (n 152 above), 4, 6. See also the Commission's Impact Assessment accompanying the proposal (SEC(2005) 1241, 4/10/05), 12, 16.
[154] Ibid, 45.   [155] Memorandum of Understanding, paras 17–19.
[156] See Council Decision 2003/93/CE authorising Member States, in the interest of the Community, to sign the 1996 Hague Convention on Jurisdiction, Applicable Law, Recognition, Enforcement and Cooperation in respect of Parental Responsibility and Measures for the Protection of Children Council, 19/2/02 [2003] OJ L48/1 (21.02.03) (for the conclusion of the Convention of 19 October 1996 on Jurisdiction, Applicable Law, Recognition, Enforcement and Cooperation in respect of Parental Responsibility and Measures for the Protection of Children, reprinted in Hague Conference on Private International Law, Collection of Conventions (1951–2003), (2003), No 34); and Council Decision 2005/367/EC authorising Member States to ratify, in the interests of the European Community, the Seafarers' Identity Documents Convention of the International Labour Organisation (Convention 185), 14/4/05 [2005] OJ L136/1 (30.05.05) (for the conclusion of the Seafarers' Identity Documents Convention (Revised), 2003, ILO Convention 185, 19/6/03).
[157] Exclusive in the sense that while it was shared with between the Union and the Member States, the Union has adopted measures in these areas, thereby pre-empting action by the Member States. The background documents cited above refer to Case 22/70 *AETR* [1971] ECR 263.
[158] See: Report of the European Parliament on the proposal for a Council decision on authorising Member States to ratify in the interests of the Community the Seafarers' Identity Documents Convention of the International Labour Organization (Convention 185) A6–0037/2005, 10/2/05, 6–7; Council Decision 2003/93/CE, preamble, para 4.
[159] Council Regulation 2201/2003 ([2003] OJ L338/1 (23.12.03)) adopts a set of rules that reflect the rules set out in the 1996 Hague Convention, as well as the Convention of 25 October 1980 on

EU effectively attempting to incur obligations via its Member States where it cannot incur them directly, and then executing these obligations through secondary legislation. Although these treaties do not have monitoring mechanisms it may not be presumptuous to assume that in these circumstances a supervisory body would examine the EU directly as well as the Member States, since the latter would merely be executing EU legislation.

We argue that systematic engagement of the EU by those monitoring bodies which supervise the Member States (until such time that the EU accedes to these treaties in its own right) provides the best solution to ensuring consistency between the Union method of guaranteeing human rights and that existing in international human rights law. In this vein the EU Network of Independent Experts on Fundamental Rights proposed that 'in the fields which belong to the competences shared between the Union and the Member States, the Union could consider contributing to the preparation of the reports which the States must submit periodically to the committees created by the six main treaties of the United Nations in the field of human rights. The preparation of a report concerning specifically the contribution of the European Union to the implementation of the provisions contained in those treaties would present major advantages.' The group of experts went on to note that the very act of compiling such a report would create an important consciousness within the EU of the extent to which its existing competences may be used to give effect to human rights guarantees, as well as the degree to which it currently has an impact on human rights standards. This in turn could lead to more human-rights-aware policy formulation, in particular one which takes full account of the recommendations of the monitoring bodies, to ensure that the obligations the Member States incur through the EU facilitate and do not conflict with those they have incurred under these treaties.[160] The final section will now consider how international human rights obligations could be translated into EU policy.

IV. The Impact of Positive Obligations on the EU

As noted above, any flirtation between the EU and human rights law betrays a certain shyness. When discussing the general principles, accession to the European

---

the Civil Aspects of International Child Abduction (reprinted in Hague Conference on Private International Law, Collection of Conventions (1951–2003), (2003), No 28), to which all or most Member States were also party. For discussion of how the Regulation compares to the 1996 and 1980 Hague Conventions, see Commission Proposal for a Council Regulation concerning jurisdiction and the recognition and enforcement of judgments in matrimonial matters and in matters of parental responsibility, COM(2002) 222 final/2, 2002/0110 (CNS), 17/5/02. The Member States are authorized to make arrangements for seafarers in accordance with ILO Convention 185 in Annex VII, Section 3 of Regulation 562/2006 establishing a Community Code on the rules governing the movement of persons across borders ([2006] OJ L105/1 (13.04.06)).

[160] EU Network of Independent Experts on Fundamental Rights, Report on the Situation of Fundamental Rights in the Union in 2003, January 2004, p 21.

Convention on Human Rights or adoption of the Charter of Fundamental Rights, the EU institutions are quick to underline that the affair will do nothing to extend the existing competences of the Union. It is obviously a major concern that accepting or drawing on human rights as embodied in the treaties referred to above may lead the EU to act beyond its already wide powers. We now move to more detailed consideration of the nature of the positive obligations that international human rights law may impose on the EU to provide reassurance that while human rights law may bring about a change in the EU it will ask nothing of the EU that it cannot already give.[161]

As noted above, human rights impose on States, as correlative duties, obligations to respect, protect, and fulfil. The latter two may be classed as 'positive' obligations since they require the duty-holder to take positive action, rather than merely refrain from acting in such a way as to violate rights. The European Commission acknowledges that such positive obligations are incumbent upon the Union and can be realized within the existing competences of the EU:

> The EU's obligation to respect fundamental rights, including children's rights, implies not only a general duty to abstain from acts violating these rights, but also to take them into account wherever relevant in the conduct of its own policies under the various legal bases of the Treaties.[162]

The immediate objection that may be raised to this is the need to comply with the requirements of subsidiarity and proportionality. According to these principles, the EU may only act where individual action by the Member States would be insufficient to achieve the particular goal or may conflict with the requirements of the EC Treaty, and action by the Union has clear benefits. Furthermore, where it decides to act, the substance of those measures must be the least burdensome available to achieve the aims of the legislation in terms of the administrative and financial onus on the Member States or private actors. Thus framework directives are to be preferred to detailed directives or regulations.[163]

Such principles may be fully complied with by legislation aiming at protecting or fulfilling human rights. The Commission itself recognized as much in relation to the rights of the child:

> [N]otwithstanding the...lack of general competence, various particular competencies under the Treaties do allow [the Union] to take specific positive action to safeguard and promote children's rights. Any such action needs to respect the principles of subsidiarity and proportionality and must not encroach on the competence of the Member States.

---

[161] In support of this view, see eg J Weiler and P Alston, 'An "Ever Closer Union" in Need of a Human Rights Policy: The European Union and Human Rights', in P Alston (ed), *The EU & Human Rights* (OUP, 1999) 3, 23–24.

[162] Commission Communication, 'Towards an EU Strategy on the Rights of the Child', COM(2006) 367 final, 4/7/06, 8.

[163] See: Article 5 of the EC Treaty; Protocol on the application of the principles of subsidiarity and of proportionality, annexed to the EC Treaty by the Treaty of Amsterdam, para 6; Commission 'Report on Better Lawmaking 2003', COM(2003) 770 final.

A number of different instruments and methods can be envisaged, including legislative action, soft-law, financial assistance or political dialogue.[164]

Thus through what is labelled 'mainstreaming', the Commission acknowledged the cross-cutting nature of human rights and its capacity to take positive action on human rights in the context of all areas of its competence. What this would look like is now examined.

A. Human Rights in Areas of Exclusive Competence

Firstly, subsidiarity and proportionality need only be considered in areas of shared competence. Indeed, Union action is more obviously essential in those policy areas where competence is exclusive to the extent that Member States have lost their authority to act autonomously. For instance, with regard to the right to food guaranteed by the 1966 International Covenant on Economic Social and Cultural Rights (to which all EU Member States are party), the relevant treaty body has stated that the obligation to fulfil the right 'means the State must proactively engage in activities intended to strengthen people's access to and utilization of resources and means to ensure their livelihood, including food security... [W]henever an individual or group is unable, for reasons beyond their control, to enjoy the right to adequate food by the means at their disposal, States have the obligation to... [provide] that right directly. This obligation also applies for persons who are victims of natural or other disasters.'[165] Accordingly, to the extent that the EU has exclusive powers in formulating the Common Agricultural Policy, it should formulate policies that not only refrain from violating the right to food and prevent the Member States from doing so, but also create a climate of food security and supply food directly where exceptional circumstances interfere with access to food. The same would hold, for instance, for the adoption of economic sanctions in the framework of trade policy, in which the EU has an exclusive competence. Such sanctions should be carefully framed in order to avoid negative impact on the economic and social rights of the population in the targeted country.[166] Since this is an exclusive competence of the EU,[167] the principles of subsidiarity and proportionality have no role to play: the EU must exercise its powers in this area in a way which is compatible with the requirements of international human rights law.[168]

---

[164] Commission Communication, (n 162 above), 8.

[165] Committee on Economic Social and Cultural Rights, General Comment 12: The Right to Adequate Food, para 15, E/C.12/1999/5. Compilation of General Comments, n 74, above.

[166] UN Committee on Economic, Social and Cultural Rights, General Comment No 8 (1997): The relationship between economic sanctions and respect for economic, social and cultural rights, UN doc. E/1998/22.

[167] Article 254(2)) of the EC Treaty.

[168] For a related example, where the sanctions adopted by the EC were alleged to constitute a violation of the right to property under Article 1 of Additional Protocol No 1 to the European Convention

B. Human Rights in Areas of Shared Competence: The Duty to Protect

In areas of shared competence, it is difficult to assert that obliging the Union to *protect* human rights would violate subsidiarity or proportionality. As discussed above through the cases of *Linqvist* and *Parliament v Council*, it does not seem that the Union is currently under a duty to ensure that its legislation specifies how discretion conferred on the Member States should be exercised to minimize the risk of human rights violations. *Parliament v Council* contains contradictory dicta in this regard, but even where the Court asserts that such a duty does exist, its verification that the Family Reunification Directive provides adequate safeguards remains, at best, superficial. It is our view that the legislator should be placed under a duty to do all that is reasonable to prevent the risk that Member States may use discretion accorded to them under EU law in such a way as to violate human rights standards. Such an approach is consistent with subsidiarity since improved and *ex ante* guidance to the Member States is clearly to be preferred to the risk of the Member States' violations of human rights being the subject of *post hoc* infringment proceedings or litigation before national and European courts. And it conforms to the principle of proportionality since it will only restrict Member State discretion in such a way as to lessen the likelihood of them committing violations. The ECJ already reviews Member State legislation that implements Union law to verify compliance with the general principles of law.[169] However, this review is exercised *post hoc*, subject to the limits of the ECJ's jurisdiction and mostly dependent on the initiative of individual litigants seeking a remedy. This makes for inefficient verification that Member States are implementing EU law in conformity with the requirements of fundamental rights. Rather, imposing an *ex ante* duty on the Union to better delineate the discretion of Member States, thus decreasing the possibility of violations, offers individuals legal certainty and better protection of their rights as well as uniformity in the implementation of EU law. This is not to say that the EU should be at fault if ever a Member State interprets its discretion in a way that allows it to violate human rights standards, but this does not prevent the ECJ from developing an approach

of Human Rights, see *Bosphorus Hava Yolları Turizm ve Ticaret Anonim Sirketi v Ireland*, Eur Ct HR (GC), judgment of 30 June 2005, Application no 45036/98.

[169] This concerns not only the provisions of the Charter of Fundamental Rights (Article 51(1) of the Charter), but also the fundamental rights which are part of the general principles of Union law and the respect of which the ECJ controls on the basis of Article 220 of the EC Treaty, in all situations where the Member States implement European law (see, eg, the judgment of 13 July 1989 in Case 5/88 *H Wachauf* [1989] ECR 2609 (Recital 19); or the judgment of 3 December 1992 in Case C-97/91 *O Borelli SpA* [1992] ECR 6313 (Recitals 14 and 15)), where they make use of an exception provided by the treaties (judgment of 28 October 1975, Case 36/75 *Rutili* [1975] ECR 1219 (Recital 32); judgment of 18 June 1991, Case C-260/89 *ERT* [1991] ECR I-2925 (Recital 43)) or by the case law of the ECJ (judgment of 26 June 1997, Case C-368/95 *Familiapress* [1997] ECR I-3689 (Recitals 18 and 19); judgment of 12 June 2003, Case C-112/00, *Schmidberger*, Recitals 71 to 78)).

that tests whether legislation makes a reasonable effort to expressly pre-empt such a situation. In setting out the parameters of Member State discretion the legislator should, of course, draw on the standards referred to above, elaborated in human rights treaties to which some or all of its Member States are party, as well as the interpretations given to these treaties by their supervisory bodies. To an extent this is envisaged by the Memorandum of Understanding between the EU and the Council of Europe. But this practice should become the general rule, and be extended to include human rights treaties elaborated under the auspices of the UN and the ILO.

C. Human Rights in Areas of Shared Competence: The Duty to Fulfil

In areas of shared competence, it is quite easy to envisage the Union taking action to *fulfil* human rights without breaching the requirements of subsidiarity and proportionality. For instance, Articles 136 and 137 of the EC Treaty grant the Union certain powers in relation to employment policy. This area of competence clearly overlaps with the right to work contained in the ICESCR. The right to work does not entail an unconditional entitlement to gainful employment. Rather it establishes certain forms of protection for individuals who are in employment or have left employment, and obligations to promote entry into employment.[170] Under Article 137(2)(b) of the EC Treaty, the Union is empowered to adopt 'minimum requirements for gradual implementation' of rules relating to the labour market, such as the 'information and consultation of workers' (Article 137(1)(e)). Where it decides to adopt secondary legislation under this provision the EU could thus implement the obligation to fulfil the right to work which includes the obligation to undertake 'educational and informational programs to instill public awareness on the right to work'.[171] Similarly, the Union may also adopt minimum requirements relating to 'the integration of persons excluded from the labour market' (Article 137(1)(h)), and in this vein the right to work requires the adoption of measures to counter unemployment, including technical and vocational education to facilitate access to the employment market.[172] Thus where the Union decides to exercise its competence in a given area, it should ensure that it is exercised in such a way as to give maximum benefit to human rights promotion. It is not being argued that wherever the Community has shared competence it must act immediately with the aim of promoting human rights. Rather we argue that if the Community decides to act in an area of shared competence and determines that its proposed measures satisfy the tests of subsidiarity and proportionality it is

---

[170] See UN Committee on Economic, Social and Cultural Rights, General Comment No 18: The Right to Work (Article 6 of the International Covenant on Economic, Social and Cultural Rights), adopted on 24 November 2005, UN doc E/C.12/GC/18.
[171] General Comment, para 28.   [172] General Comment, paras 26–27.

difficult to see how integrating additional measures promotional of human rights could be objectionable.

D. The Need to Catalogue Competences

If one is to give effect to the proposition that the Union should protect and fulfil human rights, in addition to respecting them, when it exercises its powers this necessitates the cataloguing of Union competences and their relationship to Member States' human rights obligations. The Commission acknowledged this in relation to establishing a coherent approach to the rights of indigenous people noting the need for 'a systematic appraisal, firstly, of the large range of activities where concern for indigenous peoples is already taken into account, and secondly, of those activities which may have a potential impact on this group'.[173] The EU Fundamental Rights Agency is ideally placed to undertake a cataloguing of competences and their potential both to conflict with and fulfil particular human rights. This would provide the legislator with a systematic reference point when formulating and considering proposals. Such a competences/human rights data-base could supplement the Commission guidelines on verifying compliance of its proposals with the Charter of Fundamental Rights (noted in the Introduction). It would avoid the use of superficial and general statements that appear in pream-bular paragraphs of legislation, merely asserting compliance with human rights and encourage legislators to be more precise in their identification of the require-ments of human rights.[174] Furthermore, the Union could provide for systematic follow-up of legislation with a view to its revision where, for instance, it is clear that the Member States are abusing the discretion given to them for interpreta-tion or implementation.[175]

---

[173] Report from the Commission, 'Review of Progress of Working with Indigenous Peoples', COM(2002) 291 final, 11/6/02, 4.

[174] This would imply for instance that a directive on the right to family reunification restate the relevant norms of the international law of human rights in this field, defining clearly which limits the States may not ignore in the implementation of the directive; or that a directive on assistance in cases of transit for the purposes of removal by air makes explicit the exceptions to the obligation to assist imposed on the State of transit in such cases, which are imposed by the obligation for that State to respect internationally recognized human rights, including the interpretation thereof, for instance by the UN Committee Against Torture; or that the Working Time Directive details the rules which fol-low from the reading by the European Committee on Social Rights of the European Social Charter.

[175] See, eg, Article 17 of Council Directive 2000/43/EC of 29 June 2000 implementing the prin-ciple of equal treatment between persons irrespective of racial or ethnic origin [2000] OJ L180/22, (19.07.2000); Article 19 of Directive 2000/78/EC of 27 November 2000 establishing a general framework for equal treatment in employment and occupation [2000] OJ L303/16 (02.12.2000); Article 17 of Regulation (EC) No 1049/2001 of the European Parliament and of the Council of 30 May 2001 regarding public access to European Parliament, Council and Commission documents [2001] OJ L145/43 (31.05.01); Article 34(2) of the Framework Decision of the Council 2002/584/ JHA of 13 June 2002 on the European arrest warrant and the surrender procedures between Member States [2002] OJ L190/1 (18.07.02); Article 33 of Directive 95/46/EC of the European Parliament and of the Council of 24 October 1995 on the protection of individuals with regard to the processing of personal data and on the free movement of such data [1995] OJ L281/31 (23.11.95); or Article

V. Conclusion

In this article, we have presented the case for reinforcing the links between the EU and international human rights law. While the ECJ ensures that the Union does not violate human rights through its actions, its approach has several short-comings. The focus has been almost exclusively on the European Convention on Human Rights, ignoring the range of other human rights treaties to which all or some of the Member States are party. This has led the Union to be estranged from the universal human rights regimes established under the UN as well as other regional instruments. In consequence, the Union recognizes neither the range of rights nor the interpretation of rights accepted by its Member States (as well as significant numbers of third States) under these treaties. This has also led to a failure to understand the true nature of human rights as imposing positive as well as negative obligations. The reluctance of the EU to commit to international human rights standards may result in several negative consequences. First, where Member States attempt to implement their human rights obligations this may conflict with Union law. Permitting Member States human rights exceptions threatens the uniformity of EU law, which is more pronounced in relation to those treaties to which only some of the Member States are party. Second, Article 307 of the EC Treaty requires Member States to eliminate inconsistencies between pre-existing treaties with third States and EU law, which includes the denunciation of such treaties. This is not only politically embarrassing, but potentially illegal under international law. In this dysfunctional relationship between the EU and human rights, it is the individual that will suffer as human rights standards are lowered and legal uncertainty prevails.

We argue that the EU should embrace international human rights law by taking full advantage of the existing opportunities to join human rights treaties and collaborating with the monitoring bodies of those treaties to which its Member States are party. It has offered some small tokens of commitment to human rights through its collaboration with the UN High Commissioner for Refugees and by authorizing the Member States to ratify certain treaties on its behalf. We call for the systematization of such practices so that the EU may be guided directly by the recommendations and findings of the monitoring bodies that supervise the Member States. If the EU opens itself to international human rights law, it will realize the potential of its legislative and judicial role in protecting and promoting human rights beyond merely ensuring that these rights are respected. This is not to say that the EU can or should be transferred further competences allowing it to develop a full-fledged 'human rights policy'. Such a proposal would not

15 of the new instrument proposed in the Commission proposal for a Council Directive implementing the principle of equal treatment between women and men in the access to, and the provision of, goods and services, COM(2003)657 final.

only be politically infeasible. It would also be based on a misconception about which function human rights fulfil in a legal order: human rights are not a policy domain separate from the others, but a set of requirements which cut across all policy domains, and should guide the exercise of their powers by the public authorities whenever they act or have the competence to act. For now, we need to ensure that the powers that do exist in different policy areas are exercised in such a way as to respect, protect, and fulfil human rights. In this the legislator as well as the ECJ and the Fundamental Rights Agency have an important role. Both the legitimacy of the Union and its effectiveness will improve by moving in this direction.

Breaking the Taboo: National Minorities in the EC and the WTO Trade Regimes

*Thomas Burri**

When Captain James Cook returned to England from his second expedition to the South Pacific in 1775, he brought back from the island of Tonga the conception of 'tabu'.[1] In Tonga, tabu stood for a sacred or cursed deed (or an item) that was prohibited, such as 'fishing or picking fruits at certain seasons [, ...] prohibitions on talking to or touching chiefs [, ...] walking or traveling in certain areas, such as forests [...].'[2] The idea was picked up swiftly in England and caught on in most European languages. Today, tabu (or taboo) refers more broadly to 'a prohibition or restriction on words, forms of behaviour, etc, imposed by social custom.'[3] We will see in this paper that, in this sense, national minorities are tabu in international law in general, and particularly in international trade law. This paper attracts attention to this tabu, and, in this way, attempts to break it—or at least bend it.

The aim of this paper is twofold. First, it intends to clarify the relationship between national minorities and international trade regimes. For this purpose the paper focuses on the trade regimes established by the European Community (EC)[4] and the World Trade Organization (WTO) and their correlation with national minorities. This correlation has been neglected so far, because trade regimes are considered to belong to a different domain and to a different level than national minorities: the EC and the WTO primarily operate in the *economic* domain and they are centred on *States*, not on actors of sub-State origin such as transnational corporations, non-governmental organizations, or national minorities; whereas national minorities are said to belong to the *cultural* domain and

---

* LLM (College of Europe, Bruges), attorney at law (Zurich), lic.iur. (Basel). I am deeply grateful to Homburger AG, Zurich, for the generous scholarship for my studies at the College of Europe. My thanks go to Prof. Piet Eeckhout and Prof. Daniel Thürer. Contact: <Thomas.Burri@coleurope.eu>

[1] Encyclopaedia Britannica Online, *Taboo*, see: <http://www.britannica.com>, last visit: 3 May 2008 (see also the entry under *James Cook*).

[2] Encyclopaedia Britannica Online, *Taboo*, n 1 above.

[3] Judy Pearsall and Bill Trumble (eds), *Oxford English Reference Dictionary* (2nd edn, OUP, 2002) 1466.

[4] The term EC is preferred in this paper, because the paper focuses on trade regimes; however, where more precise or appropriate, the term European Union is used.

to operate on the *intra*-State level. This paper attempts to correct this widespread image. It shows that there are links between the EC and the WTO, on the one hand, and national minorities on the other and, in this way, attempts to add a further dimension to the common understanding of the EC and the WTO.

For the second aim, the EC and the WTO are looked at separately: the idea is to analyse and compare their general and, more specifically, their judicial approach to national minorities and to the issues these minorities face. Hence, after the general framework of the EC and the WTO, respectively, the case law of the European Court of Justice (ECJ) and the WTO dispute settlement bodies will be examined with regard to national minorities. The paper thus aims at showing differences between and similarities of the EC and the WTO. This approach has got much in common with the one of Weiler in his article 'Towards a Common Law of International Trade':[5] Weiler also examines the ECJ and WTO case law, but does so with regard to trade in goods.[6] A similar caveat as in Weiler's article therefore applies here.[7]

At the outset, one must point out that the WTO and the EC (and even more so the EU) are organizations of a different kind with different aims, mechanisms, and means. A simple transfer of EC mechanisms or institutions to the WTO is, in my view, not possible. The present WTO is not necessarily similar to the EC at an earlier stage. I strongly believe, though, that issues similar to the ones faced by the EC may one day arise in the WTO.[8] Hence, the one cannot afford to ignore the other: it seems crucial that the WTO learns from the experience made by and with the EC.[9] By highlighting differences between the EC and the WTO regarding national minorities, a contribution is made to this learning process and to the accumulation of experience. This is the main aim of this paper—an aim that is in a way inspired by Dunoff's call to trade scholars to examine more closely 'who is empowered and who is disempowered, under different conceptions of constitutionalism'.[10] Obviously, the present paper deals with a topic that is situated at the limits of the reach of the EC and the WTO. Unlike Weiler who analyses the core business of the Court of Justice and the WTO dispute settlement

---

[5] JHH Weiler, 'Epilogue: Towards a Common Law of International Trade', in JHH Weiler (ed), *The EU, the WTO, and the NAFTA—Towards a Common Law of International Trade?*, The Collected Courses of the Academy of European Law, vol IX/1 (OUP, 2000).

[6] For a similar approach in the domain of the environment, see J Scott, 'On Kith and Kine (and Crustaceans): Trade and Environment in the EU and WTO', in Weiler, ibid, 125.

[7] Of course, the method applied here as well as in Weiler's article has got its shortcomings: the social or political context of (minority) issues is ignored to a large extent because of the legal focus (see Weiler, n 5 above, 125).

[8] Note that this does not necessarily mean that there is a general 'convergence trend between the WTO and the EC' (Weiler, n 5 above, 202).

[9] This argument may also work vice versa (learning from WTO experience to the benefit of the EC).

[10] JL Dunoff, 'Constitutional Conceits: The WTO's "Constitution" and the Discipline of International Law' (2006) 17 EJIL (3) 673.

bodies (the case law in trade in goods),[11] this paper relies on a limited range of cases. References to national minorities and their concerns are often scarce and indirect. It is all the more important to bring them together and put them in a perspective (while of course avoiding speculation).

My main argument is as follows. I submit that it is *possible*, though *unlikely*, that national minority issues, as the Court of Justice had to address them, arise in the future before the WTO dispute settlement bodies (ie beyond the extent that this is currently the case for the latter). The reasons underlying this argument will become clear as they are developed throughout this paper. The argument is then made in detail in the concluding section.

The paper consists in seven sections. In sections I and II the following points will be addressed: the term national minority; the issues these national minorities are normally confronted with; and the basic correlation between these issues and trade regimes. Here the assumptions underlying the next two sections are clarified. In section III the EC's approach to these minority issues and in section IV that of the WTO is explained. Here the focus is on the legal regime as it is established inter alia by the founding documents. Sections V and VI are about national minority issues in case law: first the case law of the Court of Justice (among others *Parliament v Council* (linguistic diversity), *Bickel and Franz, Mutsch, Gouda, Angonese),*[12] then the case law of the WTO Panels and the Appellate Body (inter alia on *EC—Asbestos* and the *Softwood Lumber* disputes).[13] Section VII looks at the perspectives resulting from the analysis and gives the main argument in detail.

I. National Minorities

Finding a universally acceptable definition of the term 'national minority' seems to be no easy task. None of the authors that engaged in it was entirely successful in gaining widespread acceptance. While Capotorti's definition identified the relevant criteria, it failed to gain universal recognition.[14] Thus, it remains largely unclear which groups are the 'ethnic, religious or linguistic minorities' of Article 27

---

[11] See Weiler, n 5 above.

[12] Case C-42/97 *European Parliament v Council (linguistic diversity)* [1999] ECR I-869; Case C-274/96 *Bickel and Franz* [1998] ECR I-7637; Case 137/84 *Ministère Public v Mutsch* [1985] ECR 2681; Case C-288/89 *Stichting Collectieve Antennevoorziening Gouda and Others v Commissariaat voor de Media* [1991] ECR I-4007; Case C-281/98 *Angonese v Cassa di Risparmio di Bolzano* [2000] ECR I-4139.

[13] Case WT/DS135/AB/R *EC—Asbestos, European Communities—Measures Affecting Asbestos and Asbestos-Containing Products* [2001]; regarding the *Softwood Lumber* disputes, see n 112 below.

[14] F Capotorti, *Study on the Rights of Persons Belonging to Ethnic, Religious and Linguistic Minorities,* UN Doc E/CN.4/Sub.2/384/Add. 1–7, 1979, 568: 'A group, numerically inferior to the rest of the population of a State, in a non-dominant position, whose members—being nationals of the State— possess ethnic, religious or linguistic characteristics differing from those of the rest of the population and show, if only implicitly, a sense of solidarity, directed towards preserving their culture, traditions, religion or language.'

of the Civil Rights Covenant.[15] The drafters of the Framework Convention[16] gave up on defining the notion, though it is central to the agreement.[17]

This paper does not embark on the mission of finding *the* definition. Nevertheless, two comments are in order.

(i) From the absence of a commonly agreed definition results, of course, a certain uncertainty—but also flexibility which is needed for the implementation of certain agreements. It seems that it is sometimes better to live with and incorporate uncertainty.[18]

(ii) Although there is disagreement *in abstracto* as to the definition of the national minority, there is often agreement *in concreto* over whether a specific group is to be considered as a national minority or not. In other words, one cannot necessarily conclude from the lack of a definition to a lack of certainty in a specific instance. In Hungary, for instance, the law defines which groups qualify as national minorities;[19] in the Nordic countries the Sami are usually said to be a national minority; so are the Roma in European countries. In short, disputes over the qualification of groups as national minorities do arise, but not in each and every case. Often natural intuition or a definition of the law help in a specific case.

In light of the remaining uncertainty, this paper needs to clarify which groups it focuses on. Basically, 'national minority' shall be a minority that has been present in a State for a while and that is different from the majority in one or more important aspects (such as ethnicity, religion, or language). Hence, the focus will be on minorities that are sometimes called traditional or native, as opposed to immigrant or new minorities.[20] Only where explicitly noted the latter are also taken into consideration (because it seems useful). We shall not bother unduly with the

---

[15] UN Covenant on Civil and Political Rights, 16 December 1966, adopted by General Assembly resolution 2200A (XXI). Article 27 reads: 'In those States in which ethnic, religious or linguistic minorities exist, persons belonging to such minorities shall not be denied the right, in community with the other members of their group, to enjoy their own culture, to profess and practise their own religion, or to use their own language.'

[16] Framework Convention for the Protection of National Minorities, Council of Europe, February 1995, CETS no 157.

[17] The Framework Convention does not define the term 'national minority'. See the related issue of the Language Charter where the drafters decided to leave it to each party to define what a *minority* language is (European Charter for Regional or Minority Languages, Council of Europe, 5 November 1992, CETS no 148).

[18] This is an experience that natural scientists have made a long time ago. Cooney and Lang transpose these experiences from environmental sciences to the WTO: they match the WTO as a social system with ecosystems and argue convincingly that the WTO should not rely on purported scientific certainty, but rather include uncertainty by relying on a system of 'adaptive governance' (R Cooney and ATF Lang, 'Taking Uncertainty Seriously: Adaptive Governance and International Trade' (2007) 18 EJIL (3) (in particular p 551)).

[19] Articles 1(2) and 61(1) of Act LXXV of 1993 on the Rights of National and Ethnic Minorities, Hungarian Legislative Act, 1993.

[20] Von Bogdandy refers to them as 'autochthonous (native) or allochthonous (immigrated) minorities' (A von Bogdandy, 'The European Union as Situation, Executive, and Promoter of the

citizenship of members of a minority. Indigenous peoples are included in the scope. It is clear that some groups that are addressed in this paper as national minorities prefer another terminology and that the choices we make in this regard may appear as arbitrary.[21] However, this paper attempts to focus as much as possible on substantive issues and takes the liberty to disregard pure debates over nomenclature. The uncertainty resulting from this terminology is, whenever possible, mitigated by giving specific examples.

II. National Minorities, their Issues, and their *Trade* Issues

What are the issues national minorities face? We have elaborated a distinction between different minorities, following the lines of the issues they face, in detail elsewhere.[22] Suffice it here to sketch the three main groups minorities can be divided into according to this distinction. These groups may, of course, overlap.

(i) Minorities sometimes run the risk of being absorbed by the majority. The issue is then mainly that the minority's culture as such is endangered. We called this phenomenon a '*runaway integration*'[23] of the minority. This is often seen as the typical or classical minority issue. There are many examples, including the Ladins of South Tyrol or the German minority in Hungary (the so called Ungarndeutsche).

(ii) Other minorities experience a '*lack of integration*'.[24] The relationship between the majority and the minority is such that the characteristics that make the minority a minority are not tolerated and respected by the majority. One of the consequences is that the minority (and in particular individual members thereof) is discriminated against. Examples include the Roma in numerous European States or immigrated minorities (such as the Turks in Germany or immigrants from the Maghrib in France).

(iii) To the last group belong those minorities that have been living in a particular territory of a State for a long time. They have a strong identity and, accordingly, ask for some sort of self-determination. Their demands depend on the structure of the State: territorial autonomy, some type of advanced federalism, or

International Law of Cultural Diversity—Elements of a Beautiful Friendship' (2007) 13/07 *Jean Monnet Working Paper* 12).

[21] Quebecers, for instance, may prefer the term 'distinct society' (as in the proposed, but rejected constitutional amendment of 1987, section 2(1)b, to the Constitutional Act of 1867: 'The constitution shall be interpreted consistent with [...] the recognition that Quebec constitutes within Canada a distinct society.' (See the whole text of the amendment under: 1987 Constitutional Accord, at: <http://www.solon.org/Constitutions/Canada/English/Proposals/MeechLake.html>.)

[22] D Thürer and T Burri, 'Introduction: Minorities, Law, and Conflict Resolution', in D Thürer (ed), *Convivenza Tagungsband*, Zürich (2008, forthcoming), 6–11.

[23] Thürer and Burri, ibid, 7 of 13 (emphasis in original).

[24] Thürer and Burri, ibid, 6 of 13 (emphasis in original).

even independence are among them. These minorities typically have to face the same range of issues as a State. Depending on the level of integration, however, their needs are met to varying degrees by the different constituents of the state (central, regional, or even local authority). For lack of a better term we call them *autonomous minorities*[25] here, bearing in mind that not all of the groups thus included actually benefit from autonomy. Quebec, some of the constituent entities of Spain, or South Tyrol may be given as examples.

One might argue at this point that the link between national minorities as described above and trade regimes (ie the WTO or the EC) is not pertinent. Two comments must be made in this regard.

(a) First, it is quite obvious what the interests of *autonomous minorities* in trade regimes are: they are the same as a normal State's. There is obviously an economy in the territory of the minority with the usual imports and exports (to and from the rest of the state or countries abroad). Autonomous minorities therefore have a very basic interest in trade regimes. This trade interest establishes the link between autonomous minorities and trade regimes. This is sometimes overlooked, because the State of which the autonomous minority is part usually safeguards these interests of the minority on the international level. The minority's interests, much like the one of any sub-State entity, are thus hidden behind the façade of the State.

(b) The links between trade regimes and the first two minority groups (the ones suffering from an overdose or a lack of integration) are less obvious, but, in my view, still existing.[26] They are obscured by a conception of trade that is very common: trade means exporting goods. When goods are leaving a country, there are in general no minority characteristics that follow them. The fact that a good was produced by a minority is usually lost at the latest after the good has reached the (world) market. However, trade is not all about exporting goods. First, it is, of course, also about imports. When the focus is shifted from exports to imports of goods, it becomes clear that there may be obstacles to the import flow—obstacles introduced by the importing State to protect the interests of a national minority (such as language requirements). Second, trade is more and more about persons: persons moving to provide or receive services or even to work. Contrary to goods, minority characteristics of persons (such as their language or religion) do not just dissolve when a person moves from one place to another. Hence, members of minorities travelling for trade purposes or receiving persons who are on their trade ways inevitably establish a link between trade and national minorities. Of course,

---

[25] Thürer and Burri, ibid, 7–8 (however, without using this specific term).
[26] De Witte also points out that '[...] there may be occasional interference between the requirements of economic integration and national (or regional) policies of minority protection.' (B De Witte, 'Politics Versus Law in the EU's Approach to Ethnic Minorities' (2000) 4 EUI Working Papers 16).

concerns of these national minorities (at least the first two groups) are mainly cultural. But has there not been a long discussion about the cultural exceptions to free trade? Is not cultural diversity, as it is often advocated by minorities, necessarily linked to free trade? These links, only briefly sketched here, will become clearer, when the case law of the ECJ and of the WTO judicial organs is examined below.

Ergo, when examining the EC and the WTO below, we will have three guiding lines: (i) the layered structure of the States participating in the EC and the WTO.[27] We will inter alia focus on the role of regional (sub-State) entities, some of which are minority autonomy regimes; (ii) discrimination and integration issues regarding national minorities; (iii) issues of cultural diversity that arise within the examined trade regimes.[28]

III. The EC's Approach to National Minorities

There are two sides of EC minority protection: an internal and an external side. And they still do not resemble one another.[29] The internal (b) and the external (c) side are therefore addressed separately below. But first, the relationship between the Council of Europe and the EC regime in what regards minorities (a) needs to be clarified.

(a) If there is anything that may be called the European *acquis* of minority protection, the substance of it certainly stems from the Council of Europe.[30] It is not by coincidence that Thornberry and Estebanez's book *Minority Rights in Europe*[31] exclusively treats the Council of Europe. The two main instruments of the Council of Europe regarding minority protection have already been mentioned (the Framework Convention and the Language Charter).[32] Their implementation is monitored by expert committees. The European Charter on Local Self-Government[33] is of limited importance to national minorities in the sense of

---

[27] Political scientists would call this a focus on 'multilevel governance' (see, among many, L Hooghe and G Marks, *Multi-Level Governance and European Integration* (Rowman & Littlefield, 2001).

[28] However, this does not stretch the scope of this article as far as in von Bogdandy, n 20 above, where von Bogdandy attempts to treat all issues of cultural diversity in international law ('the international law of cultural diversity', see the title of the article). This paper remains focused on the cultural issues pertaining to national minorities.

[29] See von Bogdandy, n 20 above, 23–41.

[30] Note that the High Commissioner on National Minorities of the Organisation for Security and Co-operation in Europe also plays an important role.

[31] P Thornberry and MAM Estebanez, *Minority Rights in Europe*, (Strasburg, Council of Europe Publishing, 2004).

[32] See nn 16, 17 above.

[33] European Charter of Local Self-Government, Council of Europe, 15 October 1985, CETS no 122.

this paper, as it only marginally deals with regional self-government regimes.[34] The European Court of Human Rights plays an important role, in particular when handing down judgments on discrimination issues.[35] This brief list shows that the instruments and institutions of the Council of Europe address many minority issues. One is inclined to think that the EU can only afford not to deal with these issues, because the Council of Europe treats them. This burden sharing indicates that the EU should not be seen as a 'self-contained regime'.[36] The Union clearly does not exist in isolation of the Council of Europe. To the contrary, the two are closely interlinked.[37] But the EU has not, properly speaking, outsourced the task of addressing issues of minority protection to the Council of Europe: the EU is unable to delegate a task that it is itself in principle not competent to perform. Note also that membership in the Language Charter and the Framework Convention, for instance, differs significantly from membership of the EU.[38] One can safely say, though, that the EU relies in important regards on the work of the Council of Europe and that both organizations supplement each other.

(b) The EU has so far refrained from addressing minority issues inside its territory directly.[39] This is a consequence of three facts. The 'outsourcing' to the Council of Europe in this regard has already been mentioned. Second, the European Union which consisted of 15 Member States never knew as severe tensions along ethnic

---

[34] On the European Charter on Self-Government, see N Poulet, 'La dynamique des systèmes institutionnels en Europe: une stratégie à risque?', in H Pauliat (ed), *L'autonomie des collectivités territoriales en Europe—une source pontentielle de conflits?* (Limoges, pulim, 2004) 15, at 19–20, in particular on the influence of the charter on the countries of Eastern Europe. See also A Zardi, 'Démocratie locale et régionale en Europe d'aujourd'hui: le rôle et l'action du Conseil de l'Europe', also in Pauliat, 55, at 61–66, on the issues raised by a possible instrument regarding regional governance.

[35] See for instance Application no 43577/98 and 43579/98 *Nachova and others v Bulgaria* [2005] (alleged violation of non-discrimination (Article 14 of the ECHR) in conjunction with the right to life (Article 2 of the ECHR)); rejected by the European Court of Human Rights; for further reference, see D Thürer and B Dold, 'Keine Beweislastumkehr in Bezug auf Rassismus-Vorwürfe vor der Großen Kammer des EGMR im Fall Nachova u.a. gegen Bulgarien' (2005) 32 EuGRZ (22–23) 697–699. See also Protocol No 12 to the ECHR of 4 November 2000 (entered into force on 1 April 2005) on the general prohibition of non-discrimination (ie independent of any other human rights in the ECHR). Article 14 of the ECHR and Article 1(1) of Protocol No 12 explicitly mention that discrimination based on 'association with a national minority' is prohibited. However, note that few EU Member States, in particular among the 15 pre-enlargement EU Member States, have ratified Protocol No 12 (see the ratifications under: <http://conventions.coe.int/Treaty/Commun/QueVoulezVous.asp?NT=177&CM=8&DF=3/25/2008&CL=ENG>).

[36] See for instance, B Simma and D Pulkowski, 'Of Planets and the Universe: Self-Contained Regimes in International Law' (2006) 17 EJIL (3) 516: 'The legal system set up by the "Treaty establishing the European Community" bears very strong characteristics of self-containment.'

[37] The Union and the Council of Europe will even be closer linked, when the Union accedes to the ECHR according to Article 6.2 of the Lisbon Treaty on the European Union of 13 December 2007 (consolidated version, available at: <http://www.iiea.com/publicationx.php?publication_id=3>).

[38] Belgium, France, and Greece, for instance, are not parties to the Framework Convention, while most Western Balkan states, Norway, and Switzerland are.

[39] The European Parliament is an exception: it keeps on drawing attention to national minorities in its resolutions (see the list of resolutions in A von Bogdandy, 'The European Union as Situation, Executive, and Promoter of the International Law of Cultural Diversity—Elements of a Beautiful Friendship' (2007) 13/07 *Jean Monnet Working Paper* 12, p 36 (in fn 158)).

lines as some States in its neighbourhood.[40] Third, Member States' ideas about minority protection have differed considerably. Hence, it has been out of the question to hand over competences to the Union in this domain. Thus, the EU could and would only take an approach that is individualist, ie essentially based on a non-discrimination provision (Article 13 of the European Community Treaty (ECT)). Here again, the reference to national minorities is rather weak, as Article 13(1) of the ECT only mentions 'racial or ethnic origin'.[41] It is also worth noting that a non-discrimination approach is basically only apt to address lack of integration issues of national minorities (and not runaway integration issues).[42]

Yet, this is not the whole story. The collective dimension and the structural aspects of national minorities are taken into account in the Committee of the Regions. Its members must be politically responsible to a subnational constituent entity.[43] Among such subnational entities are also federal entities and autonomy regimes that have been established to the benefit of national minorities (or at least have a link to them). Of course, not each and every member of the Committee of the Regions represents the interests of a national minority. The members of the Committee of the Regions holding a mandate in the German Länder, for instance, can hardly be considered to do so.[44] Other members, though, hold mandates in subnational entities that are the structural manifestations of national minorities (for instance members from the Basque country, the German-speaking

[40] Bruno De Witte, 'Politics Versus Law in the EU's Approach to Ethnic Minorities' (2000) 4 *EUI Working Papers* 16, p 13: 'In the terms of reference for the project for which this paper was drafted, it was stated: "The EU of 15 is not unfamiliar to tension caused by ethnically-inspired conflicts, but until today such questions have rarely been lifted up to the Union level." This statement is quite correct [. . .].' One may, however, ask when such tensions are deemed to have reached the 'Union level'. Did the tensions in the suburbs of Paris of autumn 2005 reach that level? Today, the tensions caused by unsolved Roma issues must surely be considered to have reached the level of the European Union (all the more in light of the transnational nature of these issues).

[41] Article 13 of the ECT was elaborated in Council Directive 2000/43/EC implementing the principle of equal treatment between persons irrespective of racial or ethnic origin, 29 June 2000 [2000] OJ L180/22 (19.07.2000). For further reading on the EC's approach to non-discrimination, see E Ellis, *EU Anti-Discrimination Law*, (OUP, 2005).

[42] Note that the Lisbon Treaty on the Functioning of the European Union, 13 December 2007 does not substantially change this provision (see Article 10 in the consolidated version, available at: <http://www.iiea.com/publicationx.php?publication_id=3>). However, Article 2 of the Lisbon Treaty on the European Union (in the consolidated version), declares 'respect for human rights, including the rights of persons belonging to minorities' as a value on which the Union is founded (note the individualist, not collective approach: '*persons belonging* to minorities'). On the Charter of Fundamental Rights of the European Union, 7 December 2000 [2000] OJ C364/1 (18.12.2000), and its constitutional dimension, but not specifically on Article 21 (addressing discrimination on ground of 'membership of a national minority'), see P Eeckhout, 'The EU Charter of Fundamental Rights and the Federal Question' (2002) 39 CML Rev (5).

[43] Article 263(1)of the ECT: '. . . who either hold a regional or local authority electoral mandate or are politically accountable to an elected assembly . . .'. They may not be bound by instructions (Article 263(5) of the ECT).

[44] However, representing their constituent populations, the Länder may also take into account and represent the interests of national minorities (for instance the Länder Brandenburg and Saxony with the Sorbs, a German national minority).

community of Belgium, South Tyrol, or Corsica[45]). As these national minorities (mostly autonomous minorities in the sense of this paper) qualify as regions for the Committee of the Regions, they do enjoy a formal position in the EU. Hence the ECT gives them the possibility to take influence in the Union—be it still a limited influence, for the Committee of the Regions' powers are merely consultative. All other influence national minorities may have in the EU is either informal (ie exercised through lobbying efforts[46]) or mediated (ie channelled through the Member States and their governments).[47] Hence, we retain that there is a certain institutional representation of selected, mostly autonomous minorities: some limited consideration is given to national minorities in the structure of the EU.[48]

(c) 'Membership requires that the candidate country has achieved [...] respect for and protection of minorities, [...].'[49] This clause is the cornerstone of the external side of the EU's approach to minority protection. And in general it is the clearest display of the EU's interest in protecting minorities. The clause essentially states that minority protection is one of the criteria to be fulfilled by candidate States in order to be admitted to the EU. These criteria are the so-called Copenhagen criteria,[50] which embody the concept of 'conditionality':[51] accession to the Union is subject to certain conditions. This concept relies on the strong leverage which the EU had and still has when offering the accession perspective. Consequences of the application of this leverage include that

---

[45] As examples, the following current members of the Committee of the Regions may be listed: from the autonomous community of the Basque country: the president of the Basque Government (Juan José Ibarretxe Markuartu); from the German-speaking community of Belgium: the prime minister of the Government of the German-speaking community (Karl-Heinz Lambertz); from the autonomous province of Bolzano/Bozen/Bulsan (South Tyrol): the regional councillor/president of the autonomous province of Bolzano/Bozen/Bulsan (Luis Durnwalder); from the territorial collectivity of Corsica: the president of the assembly of Corsica (Camille de Rocca Serra).

[46] On lobbying in Brussels by subnational entities, see J Andriantsimbazovina, 'L'Union Européenne, les Etats membres et les collectivités infra-étatiques: l'interdépendance des niveaux de décision politiques', in H Pauliat (ed), *L'autonomie des collectivités territoriales en Europe—une source pontentielle de conflits?* (Limoges, pulim, 2004), 37, at 40–41.

[47] The existence of the Committee of the Regions is testimony to the reality that sub-State entities are indispensable to the implementation of European (and national) law—a reality which the Council of Europe grasped much earlier, in 1957, by establishing, so to speak, the older sister of the Committee of the Regions: the Conference of Local Authorities of Europe (which is today the Congress of Local and Regional Authorities).

[48] For the regional policies pursued by the EU, see T Cottier and C Germann, 'The WTO and EU Distributive Policy: the Case of Regional Promotion and Assistance', in J Scott and G De Búrca (eds), *The EU and the WTO: Legal and Constitutional Issues* (Hart, 2001), 185, at 190–197.

[49] Presidency Conclusions of the Copenhagen European Council, European Council, 21–22 June 1993, SN 180/1/93 Rev 1, no 7.A.iii) (p 13).

[50] These criteria were fixed at the Copenhagen European council of 21–22 June 1993. They were further detailed in the Commission's 'Agenda 2000' (European Commission, *Agenda 2000: For a Stronger and Wider Union*, EU Bulletin Supplement 5/97, 1997).

[51] On conditionality, among many, KE Smith, 'The Evolution and Application of EU Membership Conditionality', in M Cremona (ed), *The Enlargement of the European Union*, The Collected Courses of the Academy of European Law, vol XII/1 (OUP, 2003) 105.

all candidates ratified the Framework Convention;[52] that some of the candidate States introduced specific minority protection regimes; and that some of these States even went well beyond what the Copenhagen criteria or the Framework Convention would have demanded for compliance (for instance Hungary).

Two remarks need to be made regarding the external side of minority protection by the Union.

(i) With the fifth accession wave the external turned into an internal aspect: despite the leverage applied before accession, many minority issues remain unsolved within the Union. One particularly thinks of the challenges posed by the Roma. Will these issues be credibly addressed within the enlarged EU, or will they simply be ignored, because most of the pre-accession leverage is now lost?[53] This question can only be understood properly when looked at in a larger context. The question is a follow-up to the criticism raised shortly after the accession criteria were announced in 1993. The criticism alleged that the EU imposed stricter minority protection standards on States that desired to accede to the Union than on its own members. Many studies were then conducted on this problem of double standards.[54] It seems to me that the simple cause why this problem has not been properly addressed internally is a lack of political will of the Member States. Whether this political will could be mustered in the near future, is doubtful. That is why there is a considerable risk that minority protection as an internal EU policy issue will simply doze off.[55] However, two things are evident at the moment: first, it is clearly not enough to point to the fact that minority issues were more virulent in central and Eastern Europe than in the older Member States in order to justify the dual standard;[56] second, while the amendment to Article 6 of the TUE in Article 2 of the Lisbon Treaty on the EU[57] does make a contribution to the resolution of the dual standard problem, it does not seem to go far enough to effectively solve the problem.

[52] This also shows one of the typical bridges between the EU and the Council of Europe (see Smith, ibid, 105, at 116).

[53] On this question, see GN Toggenburg, 'A Remaining Share or a New Part? The Union's Role vis-à-vis Minorities After the Enlargement Decade' (2006) 15 *EUI Working Papers*.

[54] See for instance, Open Society Institute: EU Accession Monitoring Program, *Monitoring the EU Accession Process: Minority Protection—An Assessment of Selected Policies in Candidate States (Bulgaria, Czech Republic, Estonia, Hungary, Latvia, Lithuania, Poland, Romania, Slovakia, Slovenia)*, Open Society Institute (ed), vol 1, (Budapest, Open Society Institute, 2002); and Open Society Institute: EU Accession Monitoring Program, *Monitoring Minority Protection in EU Member States*, Open Society Institute (ed), vol 2 (Budapest, Open Society Institute, 2002).

[55] It is equally doubtful whether the recently established network of institutions and scholars in Europe dealing with the protection of national minorities (with centres such as the European Academy in Bolzano (EURAC) or the European Centre for Minority Issues (ECMI) in Flensburg) will be able to prevent the minority issue from dozing off.

[56] See the quotation from De Witte, n 40 above.

[57] See n 42 above.

(ii) Although the fifth accession wave is now complete, the external part of the story is far from over. The EU continues to use its leverage to make non-Member States comply with European minority protection standards. Notably vis-à-vis the Western Balkan States the Union employs an enhanced conditionality ('second generation conditionality'[58]) in the Stabilisation and Association Agreements, which basically means that the conditions are spelled out, monitored, and implemented more strictly.[59] The criticism voiced at the occasion of enlargement (double standards) is now taken into account by statements of commitment to internal minority protection.[60] But the Union does not only use its leverage vis-à-vis its neighbours. The method of setting minority protection as a condition to be fulfilled to receive certain benefits is also employed elsewhere, although in a much more indirect way: access to the EU's amended general system of preferences[61] is made subject to, inter alia, respect of human rights as laid down in the Civil Rights Covenant,[62] ie also Article 27 devoted to minority rights.[63, 64]

The EU's two-sided approach to minority protection, of course, raises legitimacy and credibility issues. But one has to bear in mind that the conditions imposed on countries applying for a certain benefit (be it accession or tariff reductions) are

---

[58] Toggenburg, n 53 above, 3.

[59] See for instance on minority protection: Commission, Croatia 2007 Progress Report, 2007, SEC(2007)1431, pp 12–15, issued in the framework of the Stabilisation and Association Agreement between the European Communities and their Member States, of the one part, and the Republic of Croatia of the other part, 29 October 2001 [2005] OJ L26/3 (28.01.05).

[60] See Toggenburg, n 53 above, 5. Toggenburg concludes from this that 'after eastward enlargement the Union's *minority momentum* has—with respect to the Union's external sphere—not only been upheld but increased and improved.' (p 5, italics in original). Similar also, see Smith, n 51 above, 105, at 120: '... admittedly the minority protection regime [of the European Union] is gradually strengthening.'

[61] Council Regulation EC 980/2005 applying a scheme of generalised tariff preferences, 27 June 2005 [2005] OJ L169/1 (30.06.05).

[62] See n 15 above.

[63] Article 9(1)(a) of Council Regulation EC 980/2005.

[64] Note that the WTO Appellate Body in Case WT/DS246/AB/R *EC—Tariff Preferences* stroke down the previous General System of Preferences (GSP) of the EU: *European Communities—Conditions for the Granting of Tariff Preferences to Developing Countries* [2004]. It held that access to the GSP could in principle be made subject to the fulfilment of certain objective standards, such as agreed in the WTO Agreement or other multilateral instruments (at 163: '... an *objective* standard. Broad-based recognition of a particular need, set out in the *WTO Agreement* or in multilateral instruments adopted by international organizations, could serve as such a standard'), and hence presumably the Civil Rights Covenant (though the Appellate Body did not rule on that specific point). But it found that the GSP was discriminatory, because access was not granted based on such an objective standard (at 188 and 189). However, note also that despite the Appellate Body ruling the amended GSP is still in WTO-legal limbo, because the Appellate Body did not rule on whether the GSP 'respond[ed] positively to the development, financial, and trade needs of developing countries' (paragraph 3(c) of the Enabling Clause, see *EC—Tariff Preferences,* at 179). In fact, there are strong doubts as to the legality of the amended GSP in this regard: see L Bartels, 'The WTO Legality of the EU's GSP+ Arrangement', (2007) 10 JIEL (4) 874–877; on *EC—Tariff Preferences*, see also M Irish, 'GSP Tariffs and Conditionality: A Comment on *EC—Preferences*', (2007) 41 J World Trade (4). For further reading in this regard, see L Bartels, *Human Rights Conditionality in the EU's International Agreements* (OUP, 2005).

at all times heavily influenced by the prevailing political climate. The flexibility of the *acquis communautaire,* respect of which is a condition for accession (and with it minority protection), is well known. It expands or contracts depending on whether the Union wants an accession process to move forward or not. Hence, minority protection in this regard should be seen as a vector carrying a political message rather than as a plain, 'black or white' legal criterion. The Copenhagen criteria therefore seem to be of a less legal nature than a first glance at them would suggest.

Finally, what about national minorities that are affected by runaway integration, the 'classical' national minority issue?[65] Does the EU address this issue at all? No explicit Community dictum can be found in this regard.[66] Obviously, Member States enjoy wide autonomy here—although not an absolute autonomy, as the Union's competences, especially those relating to the internal market, are of a functional nature and hence need to be reckoned with in any domain. In saying this, we shift our attention to obstacles to trade. This is the traditional domain of the Court of Justice and hence the subject of section V. But first, we shall examine the WTO's (non-)approach to minority issues.

IV. The WTO's (Non-)Approach to Minority Issues

The WTO does not approach national minorities. It stays as far away as possible from them. The organization is driven by its members:[67] Member States, not other entities, direct the WTO and determine its actions. Moreover, each of these Members is perceived as a monolithic bloc. In the WTO, only the government represents a Member State.[68] Its voice is the only one that is heard in the WTO. Any issue that is raised in the WTO is basically perceived as an *inter*-State issue. The *intra*-State dimension of the issue is left to each Member State. Hence, the two forms of discrimination in the WTO are centred on the State: 'Most-Favoured-Nation' (Article I of the General Agreement on Trade and Tariffs (GATT)) actually means 'most-favoured *State*' and 'National Treatment' (Article III of GATT) basically means that a *State* must treat products from other

---

[65] See section 2 of this article.

[66] For the scarce general references to national minorities, see n 42 above. It should also be noted that the Community competences in the domain of culture are very limited, because the Community may only 'adopt incentive measures' and 'recommendations' (Article 151(5) of the ECT).

[67] It is usually said to be a 'member-driven' organisation. See among many, E Petersmann, 'From "Member-driven governance" to constitutionally limited "multi-level trade governance" in the WTO', in G Sacerdoti, A Yanovich, and J Bohanes (eds), *The WTO at Ten—The Contribution of the Dispute Settlement System* (Cambridge University Press, 2006) 86.

[68] Weiler calls this the 'Government-is-the-State fallacy' (JHH Weiler, 'The Rule of Lawyers and the Ethos of Diplomats: Reflections on Internal and External Legitimacy of WTO Dispute Settlement' (2000) 9/00 *Jean Monnet Working Paper* 5).

States in the same way as its own. Thus, we can say that one should not refer to an approach of the WTO to national minority issues, but rather to a *non*-approach.

But there are other, less restrictive views. The role and nature of the WTO is often considered to be going beyond the one of a classical international organization. In fact, constitutional language is increasingly being used to analyse and describe the WTO.[69] A discourse about the WTO and human rights has been led for some years,[70] regardless of the fact that the typical framework for such a discourse is the nation State. However, these contributions are often normatively tinged and not so much anchored in positive law.[71] But it must also be noted that the WTO Agreement itself does not completely ignore the sub-State level. Article 3 of the Technical Barriers to Trade (TBT), for instance, deals with technical measures taken by *local* governments or non-governmental entities.[72] Article XXIV(12) of GATT addresses compliance by sub-State level governments.[73] And the 'domestic industry' plays an important role in many anti-dumping proceedings.[74]

Yet, the relevance of these references for our purposes is limited. Some of the references, although pertaining to the structure of the State in layers (Article 3 of the TBT or Article XXIV(12) of GATT), only illustrate the fact that in some States the central authorities may not have the necessary competences or means to ensure compliance by all sub-State entities with an agreement. In other words, these references can be seen as best effort clauses.[75] Other references are simply

---

[69] See for instance the twin articles in the EJIL by Trachtman and Dunoff (JP Trachtman, 'The Constitutions of the WTO' (2006) 17 EJIL (3); JL Dunoff, 'Constitutional Conceits: The WTO's 'Constitution' and the Discipline of International Law' (2006) 17 EJIL (3)).

[70] See most recently, C Kaufmann, *Globalisation and Labour Rights: the Conflict Between Core Labour Rights and International Economic Law* (Hart Publishing, 2007).

[71] See eg Krisch's (normative) discussion of three primary constituencies of the international order (the national, the international, and the cosmopolitan constituency): N Krisch, 'The Pluralism of Global Administrative Law' (2006) 17 EJIL (1). Interestingly, Krisch could also think of 'subnational groups as additional constituencies' (274, fn 118).

[72] Article 3 of the TBT on 'Preparation, Adoption and Application of Technical Regulations by Local Government Bodies and Non-Governmental Bodies'.

[73] Article XXIV(12) of GATT: 'Each contracting party shall take such reasonable measures as may be available to it to ensure observance of the provisions of this Agreement by the regional and local governments and authorities within its territories.' On Article 8.1(b) of the Subsidies and Countervailing Measures (SCM), which addresses 'assistance to disadvantaged regions', see T Cottier and C Germann, 'The WTO and EU Distributive Policy: the Case of Regional Promotion and Assistance', in J Scott and G De Búrca (eds), *The EU and the WTO: Legal and Constitutional Issues* (Hart, 2001), 185, at 200.

[74] See the 'domestic industry' in Article 4 of the ADA, and, more specifically, the 'domestic industry' as the 'producers in a certain area' in Article 4.2 of the ADA (the latter referring to the 'isolated market' as defined in Article 4.1(ii) of the Anti-Dumping Agreement (ADA)). On the 'domestic industry', see for instance Case WT/DS141/AB/R, *EC—Bed Linen* [2001] or Case WT/DS184/AB/R, *US—Hot-Rolled Steel* [2001]. See also the 'domestic industry' in Article 4 of the Agreement on Safeguards (AS) (see Case WT/DS177,178/AB/R, *US—Lamb* [2001] on Article 4:1(c) of the AS). On the role of private firms in domestic proceedings leading to the imposition of anti-dumping duties, see J Paul Lindeque, 'A Firm Perspective of Anti-dumping and Countervailing Duty Cases in the United States' (2007) 41 J World Trade (3) (regarding the USA).

[75] On this 'federal clause' (Article XXIV(12) of GATT) and the related case law, see Cottier and Germann, n 73 above, at 205.

part of a system that is set up to determine whether an exemption from standard WTO obligations is applicable ('domestic industry' in the ADA or the SA).

It thus remains a fact that the WTO Agreement does not address sub-State level entities, let alone national minorities, directly. National minorities, like individuals, are to the largest extent ignored by the WTO Agreement,[76] and so are the issues we identified above (runaway integration, lack of integration, issues faced by autonomous minorities). Hence, the means of national minorities are very limited: they can only exercise political influence from outside the WTO through non-governmental organizations (NGOs) or take influence via the State government. The former—*NGO influence*—is partly regularized in the case law. The latter—*mediated influence*—is visible in the case law. Both will be examined in section VI.

V. The European Court of Justice and Minority Issues

Language is the vector that carries national minority issues to the Court of Justice: national minority issues arise mainly when the Court deals with language questions. Not surprisingly, the Court sees language from an economic angle. It considered in *Parliament v Council* (linguistic diversity):

As regards marginalisation of the languages that remain excluded from the information society, [...], it is not a risk of a specifically cultural nature. Marginalisation of languages may be understood as the loss of an element of cultural heritage, but also as the cause of a difference of treatment between economic operators in the Community, who enjoy greater or lesser advantages depending on whether or not the language they use is widespread.'[77]

Language in that context is seen not as an element of cultural heritage but rather as an object or instrument of economic activity.'[78]

This economic perspective on language, contestable as it is, is not exceptional for the Court. With the Court essentially being an offspring of the economy, it is in its nature to analyse cases from an economic angle (that of the market freedoms). This economic perspective not only prevails in the domain of language issues, but also when the Court considers national minority issues as such: the Court sees

[76] See E Petersmann, 'European and International Constitutional Law: Time for Promoting 'Cosmopolitan Democracy' in the WTO', in J Scott and G De Búrca (eds), *The EU and the WTO: Legal and Constitutional Issues* (Hart, 2001) 81, at 107, who identifies a '[n]eed for Advisory Parliamentary and Civil Society Institutions in the WTO so as to Promote Better Representation of Citizen Interests' (capitals in original).
[77] Case C-42/97 *European Parliament v Council (linguistic diversity)* [1999] ECR I-869, at 50. Note that the case is not about linguistic diversity as such in the Community, but rather about the legal basis (and the corresponding powers of the Parliament) for a decision on a 'programme to promote the linguistic diversity of the Community in the information society' (at 1) ('centre of gravity' doctrine, at 54).
[78] Ibid, at 53.

the protection of national minorities (and of human rights) as a mere excuse not to follow business as usual. In legal terms, the protection of national minorities could be a ground to justify obstacles to trade.

A. *Bickel and Franz* and *Mutsch*

There are two cases in which the Court handled the protection of national minorities as such a 'mandatory requirement'[79] that could possibly justify an obstacle to a market freedom: *Mutsch*[80] and *Bickel and Franz.*[81] *Mutsch* was decided in 1985 and *Bickel and Franz* in 1998. In both cases the Court had to consider similar facts: A person, who was criminally prosecuted, asked for the criminal process to be conducted in its mother tongue. The link to national minorities was in both cases that national law reserved this right to nationals residing in the territory normally inhabited by a national minority and restricted it to their language: in *Mutsch* Belgian nationals living in the small German-speaking part of Belgium had the right to ask for processes to be conducted in German (but not Mr Mutsch who was German-speaking, but had Luxembourg nationality); in *Bickel and Franz* Italian nationals living in the Italian Province of South Tyrol, a majority of the population of which is German-speaking, could ask for a process to be conducted in German (but not Mr Bickel and Mr Franz, both German-speaking foreigners). Accordingly, in both cases the question was raised before the Court whether it was contrary to EC law to reserve this right to nationals and, consequently, to exclude nationals of other Member States from the scope of this right.

In both cases the Court ruled in favour of the market freedoms: in *Mutsch* the Court held that Mr Mutsch, as a worker benefiting from free movement, must be granted a process in German language;[82] in *Bickel and Franz* the Court ruled that Mr Bickel and Mr Franz were service receivers and as such entitled to a process in German language. Both rulings were based on the reasoning that nationals of the EU may not be discriminated against.

Only in *Bickel and Franz* the Court explicitly referred to the protection of minorities as a possible ground for justification.[83] However, the Court found that it did not justify the restriction *in concreto*:

The Italian Government's contention that the aim of those rules is to protect the ethno-cultural minority residing in the province in question does not constitute a valid justification in this context. *Of course, the protection of such a minority may constitute a legitimate*

---

[79] Case 120/78 *Rewe-Zentral v Bundesmonopolverwaltung für Branntwein (Cassis de Dijon)* [1979] ECR 649, at 8.

[80] Case 137/84 *Ministère Public v Mutsch* [1985] ECR 2681 (henceforth *Mutsch*).

[81] Case C-274/96 *Bickel and Franz* [1998] ECR I-7637 (henceforth *Bickel and Franz*).

[82] *Mutsch,* ibid, at 18.

[83] For 'justification' in *Mutsch*, see A Arnull, 'Social advantages and the language barrier' (1985) 10 EL Rev (5) 348.

aim. It does not appear, however, from the documents before the Court that that aim would be undermined if the rules in issue were extended to cover German-speaking nationals of other Member States exercising their right to freedom of movement.[84]

In neither one of the cases did the Court impose an excessive burden on the national courts, because they were all well equipped to handle cases in German due to their experience with cases involving members of the German-speaking minority. And of course, no Member State is obliged to offer more to free moving persons than it offers to its own nationals (ie a process in its recognized national languages).[85] But that is only half of the issue at stake. While it is true that the extension of the benefit *in concreto* to Mr Bickel and Mr Franz does not as such undermine the autonomy regime in South Tyrol, the same is not necessarily true if multiple such cases occur. In saying this, we point at broader considerations of justice. If we take them into account, the anatomy of an autonomy regime becomes important: it is a fact that most autonomy regimes that were established to the benefit of a minority, even more than States as such, represent a compromise that is essentially based on the population ratio between the different groups at the time when the compromise was concluded.[86] The effects of this balance between the groups can be felt in the most delicate neurones of the autonomy system, such as in the very procedural questions at hand in *Mutsch* and *Bickel and Franz*. Not to decide such questions in the light of the initial compromise can threaten the balance of the whole system. If *Mutsch* and *Bickel and Franz* were to be interpreted in a way that, for instance, Germans and Austrians must be treated in all circumstances in the same way as German-speaking inhabitants of South Tyrol, this could lead to an increased influx of Germans and Austrians into South Tyrol. It is clear that this could undermine the balance reached in the initial compromise. The backbone of the autonomy regime would then be at stake.

These considerations show that some friction occurs between regimes for autonomous minorities and free movement under the EC Treaty. One would not go as far as saying that they are incompatible. Yet, as the case law stands now, the EC trade regime certainly has a serious effect on autonomy regimes that protect national minorities. But neither the Court nor the Advocate General addressed

---

[84] *Bickel and Franz,* n 81 above, at 29 (emphasis added). In *Mutsch* the justification and proportionality test was not yet so explicit; the lack of justification is therefore only implicit. This can be seen from the argument of the Italian government (which submitted observations): *Mutsch*, n 80 above, at 9.

[85] S Kadelbach, 'Union Citizenship', in A Von Bogdandy and J Bast (eds), *Principles of European Constitutional Law* (Hart, 2006) 453, at 479: 'With regard to minority rights, there is no reason for assuming a general claim to the use of one's mother tongue before national courts of other Member States.'

[86] In De Witte's words: '"part of the package" of measures adopted to settle the South Tyrol minority dispute' (B De Witte, 'Free Movement of Persons and Language Legislation of the Member States of the EU—Some Reflections after the Recent Judgement in Bickel and Franz' (1999) 18 Academia—The Science Magazine of the European Academy of Bolzano (March–June) 4) (in this case this is the Gruber-De Gasperi Agreement of 5 September 1946 between Austria and Italia (relating to the status of South Tyrol)).

these broader issues in *Mutsch* or *Bickel and Franz*—though certainly not out
of a lack of awareness. Rather, the two cases, like many others, should be seen
as a non-outspoken, but still conscious preference for the economic approach.
Indeed, this preference is not, in principle, objectionable, and especially not in
light of the diminishing role of the State[87] and of the corresponding ever increasing role of the EU.

B. Other Language Cases

Mutsch and *Bickel and Franz* are about minority protection as a 'mandatory
requirement'.[88] They mostly concern autonomous minorities and, to a lesser
extent, issues of runaway integration. Does the Court address any of the other
issues we identified? Again case law of the Court relating to language is indicative.
In *Groener*[89] the Court upheld an Irish legal requirement for a Dutch teacher to
pass an Irish language exam in order to be allowed to give art lessons in Dublin.
In *Konstantinidis*[90] the Court ruled that a Greek national could ask the German
authorities to spell his name in a specific, authentic way in the registers. And in
Garcia Avello[91] the Court ruled that Community law obliged Belgian authorities
to grant the registration of the Spanish dual surname to the children of a Spanish
and a Belgian citizen (while the children both had the Belgian as well as the
Spanish nationality). In all three cases, citizens of the EU, who were making use
of their freedoms, challenged national rules that were applicable throughout the
recipient Member State. One could call these groups of moving Union citizens
intra-Community immigrant minorities. In a sense, the creation of such minorities is the very point of Community law. However, in our initial analysis of the
definition of national minorities we concluded that such groups would not be
national minorities in the sense of this paper. Suffice it to observe therefore that

---

[87] See D Halberstam, 'The bride of Messina: constitutionalism and democracy in Europe' (2005)
30 EL Rev (December) 801: 'In many ways, then, the story of European constitutionalism is one
about freedom: [...] the freedom generated by lifting the individual out of the confines of Member
State political processes. The latter is not a radical freedom intended to dissolve the Member States by
creating a singular demos or aimed at establishing a federal system *à l'américaine*. Instead, it is an idea
of freedom based on the dispersion of power away from a monopoly of decision-making previously
held by the Member States' (emphasis in original; footnotes omitted).
[88] See Case 120/78 *Rewe-Zentral v Bundesmonopolverwaltung für Branntwein (Cassis de Dijon)*
[1979] ECR 649, at 8. Of course, there are other aspects to the two cases. In particular in *Bickel and
Franz* there were issues of service freedom and citizenship (for further details, see P Eeckhout, 'The
EU Charter of Fundamental Rights and the Federal Question' (2002) 39 CML Rev (5), at 960, and
M Bultermann, 'Comment on Case C-274/96, Criminal proceedings against Horst Otto Bickel and
Ulrich Franz, Judgment of the Court of 24 November 1998' (1999) 36 CML Rev (6)). However,
these issues are of little importance to our concerns.
[89] See Case C-379/87 *Groener v Minister for Education and others* [1989] ECR 3967.
[90] See Case C-168/91 *Konstantinidis* [1993] ECR I-1191 (on the case and a 'droit à l'identité',
see D Gaurier, 'EuGH, URT. v. 30.3.1993—Rs C 168/91 (Christos Konstantinidis) [case note in
French]' (1995) 3 ERPL 490).
[91] See Case C-148/02 *Garcia Avello v Belgium* [2003] ECR I-11613.

the issues that these minorities face and that are partly addressed in the case law are largely different to the national minority issues we deal with in this paper. It will thus be up to later studies to examine whether or not any experience from the case law dealing with intra-Community migrant minorities can be transposed to national minorities. Remember, however, that it is the fact that these intra-Community immigrant minorities come into contact with national minorities that in the end brings the cases, which are relevant for this paper, to the Court (eg *Bickel and Franz*).

C. *Gouda*

Apart from the language cases, case law of the Court concerning national minorities is scarce. The *Gouda*[92] case arguably has a certain impact on regimes protecting cultural pluralism. In *Gouda*, Dutch authorities refused to allow foreign companies to broadcast their programmes in the Netherlands, because they did not fulfil the conditions set by Dutch media law. These conditions pertained to the structure of the Dutch media system (namely regarding the structure of broadcasting companies and regarding the advertisements they were broadcasting) and, hence, could hardly ever be fulfilled by companies from other Member States. This structure (and as a part of it the conditions in question) was established to guarantee pluralism in the media. As Advocate General Tesauro put it:

In order to ensure that *the range of broadcasts reflects various political, social and religious components of Dutch society* most of the national air time is distributed among the 'omroepverenigingen' [...] which are associations of listeners or viewers with legal personality, consisting of at least 150 000 members. In addition, a limited amount of air time (about 8%) is allotted to political parties, religious groups and *cultural minorities*.[93]

The Court found that the conditions imposed on foreign broadcasting companies were restrictions of their freedom to provide services that could not be justified, mainly because they are not necessary.[94] Even though the Court acknowledged, in a similar way as in *Bickel and Franz* with minority protection, that ' [a] cultural pluralism understood in that sense may indeed constitute an overriding requirement relating to the general interest which justifies a restriction on the freedom to provide services',[95] the rules could not be justified in the case at hand. Of course, as in many services cases, in *Gouda* the dual burden problem was lurking in the

[92] See Case C-288/89 *Stichting Collectieve Antennevoorziening Gouda and Others v Commissariaat voor de Media* [1991] ECR I-4007.

[93] Opinion of the Advocate General in *Gouda,* ibid, at 4022–4023 (emphasis added). See also the argument of the Netherlands: *Gouda*, at 22.

[94] *Gouda*, ibid, at 24 (note that the 'conditions relating to advertising' were not justified, because the objective of the rule could not justify them (at 29)). On *Gouda*, see J Art, 'Legislative Lacunae, the Court of Justice and Freedom to Provide Services', in D Curtin and D O'Keeffe (eds), *Constitutional Adjudication in European Community and National La*w (Butterworth, 1992) 121.

[95] *Gouda,* ibid, at 23.

background: upholding the Dutch media law would have required foreign companies to fulfil both the Dutch as well as the home State criteria. In this sense, the wider issue of policy export was also on the table in *Gouda*. But despite these broader implications, we can retain that the Court in *Gouda*, as in *Mutsch* and in *Bickel and Franz*, ruled against a structural regime protecting pluralism and that, in all these instances, the Court gave preference to economic considerations.

D. Sub-State Entities and Case Law

Besides these cases involving national minority issues, it is noteworthy that sub-State entities very often play a significant role in cases reaching the Court of Justice. In fact, whenever a measure, of which the validity is disputed before the Court, emanates from a sub-State entity (such as a regional or local authority), the structure of the State is to a certain extent co-affected by the Court's decision. In this sense, it can be said that a multi-level governance aspect is inherent in the judicial system of the EC. Think only of *Belgium v Commission (Walloon waste)*[96] where the Commission brought an infringement action against Belgium because of the Walloon waste decree. Such a multi-level governance aspect can, of course, also concern sub-State minority regimes, as that of South Tyrol in the preliminary ruling in *Angonese*.[97] However, apart from the structural *per se* concern of the authorities of a minority protecting autonomy regime (ie apart from the fact that they are a party in, or at least concerned by the case before the Court), the minority dimension in these cases is usually rather limited. In *Angonese*, for instance, one could see a national minority trait in that such measures are probably typically adopted in the environment of an autonomy regime—*in casu* a sort of local grab measure on persons which requires that the language certificate needed for a job application must have been passed in South Tyrol. However weak such links to national minority issues may be, it should not be forgotten that the system of the EU provides a regular judicial mechanism that takes the concerns of sub-State entities into account. In other words, there are judicial ways of making the concerns of national minorities visible, although they may be indirect.

In a similar vein, it is interesting to note that Member States frequently defend the interests of sub-State entities before the Court of Justice (be it as plaintiffs or defendants). In *Belgium v Spain (Rioja)*,[98] for instance, Spain essentially defended the interests of a Spanish region (the province Rioja where the wine that was the subject of the preceding case, *Delhaize*,[99] was produced). Under Community law

---

[96] See Case C-2/90 *Commission v Belgium (Walloon waste)* [1992] ECR I-4431.

[97] Case C-281/98 *Angonese v Cassa di Risparmio di Bolzano* [2000] ECR I-4139. For a case note on *Angonese*, see R Lane and NN Shuibhne, 'Case C-281/98, Roman Angonese v. Cassa di Risparmio die Bolzano SpA, Judgment of 6 June 2000, not yet reported' (2000) 37 CML Rev (5).

[98] See Case C-388/95 *Belgium v Spain* [2000] ECR I-3123.

[99] See Case C-47/90 *Delhaize and others v Promalvin and others* [1992] ECR I-3669. Note that *Belgium v Spain (Rioja)*, ibid, was on the question whether Spain failed to fulfil its treaty obligations

this may be an aspect of the judicial system that has little connexion to national minorities. However, attention is drawn to it here, because under the WTO judicial system, examined below, the parallel occurrence is more important.

What do we retain from our analysis of the case law of the Court of Justice? The cases examined almost exclusively relate to the issues faced by autonomous minorities. The cases address issues of runaway integration only marginally. Lack of integration issues only come up in the case law of the Court in relation to EU citizens who reside in another Member State than their home State (intra-Community immigrant minorities), but not in relation to national minorities in the sense of this paper. However, we must remember that the protection of national minorities is considered by the Court as a potential reason to justify obstacles to trade—obstacles that become the subject of discussion, because the worker or service provider/receiver (or even the EU citizen) that moves freely within the Union brings along his or her culture, in particular his or her language. Hence, together with the moving person always comes along a risk of discrimination. Apart from that, the structure of the judicial system of the Union guarantees that a certain minimal attention is given to sub-State entities, which potentially includes autonomous minorities. As a final aspect of the Court's national minority case law we retain that it relates exclusively to the internal side of the EU. This is, of course, because the external side of the Union (*in concreto* conditions imposed on accession candidates or third countries) is basically not subject to the jurisdiction of the Court.

VI. Minority Issues and Dispute Settlement in the WTO

WTO dispute settlement is a *res publica:* it is an affair between States. The dispute settlement bodies of the WTO have never explicitly addressed national minority issues. Substantive issues, such as the WTO-legality of a national minority regime, have never been dealt with. One cannot even find the term 'minority' in the sense of a national minority in the WTO case law. In light of the scarcity of provisions in the WTO Agreement, noticed above, this is not surprising. However, this does not mean that national minorities do not have an interest in WTO cases. It simply means that the normal State sovereignty façade is upheld before the judicial bodies. But behind this façade a national minority may be active and take influence on the government of its State. The minority then has an influence on the case that is *mediated* by the State (section A). And on rare occasions, the façade is pierced and one catches a glimpse of a minority directly at work in the case law. This happens when NGOs informally join in a proceeding

by not changing the legislation that was found to be incompatible with Community law in *Delhaize*. In *Delhaize* the Court answered the preliminary question by saying that the limitation of exports of bulk Rioja wine established under this national legislation could not be justified.

before the judicial bodies (section B). We will see these two mechanisms (sections A and B) by means of a discussion of *EC—Asbestos*[100] (section A) and of the *Softwood Lumber* disputes[101] (section B).

A. EC—Asbestos

EC—Asbestos is well known for addressing the issues of 'like products' (Article III(4) of GATT)[102] and of the justification of trade restricting measures for reasons of protecting 'human life or health' (Article XX(b) of GATT),[103] rather than for raising national minority issues. Nonetheless, *EC—Asbestos* reveals a number of important elements. In the case, Canada brought an action against the EC, after France had banned imports of asbestos and all products containing asbestos[104] due to the carcinogenic properties of asbestos. Asbestos containing products from Canada were mainly produced in Quebec.[105] This points at a first important element: in *Asbestos*, Canada fought for and represented mainly the interests of Quebec and Quebecois companies.[106] The rest of Canada or the federal government itself did not have much interest in the dispute as such. One could say that the Canadian authorities in *Asbestos* were Quebec's agents—the agents of a national minority—before the judicial bodies. In a similar way, Quebecois interests were at stake before the Appellate Body in *Canada—Autos*,[107] as well as before a Panel in *Canada—Aircraft credits and guarantees*.[108] Quebec is obviously

---

[100] Case WT/DS135/AB/R *EC—Asbestos, above,* note 13 (henceforth either *EC—Asbestos* or *Asbestos*).

[101] The *Softwood Lumber* disputes, n 112 below.

[102] *EC—Asbestos,* n 100 above, at 87 *et seq.*   [103] *EC—Asbestos,* ibid, at 155.

[104] By 'décret no 96–1133 relatif à l'interdiction de l'amiante, pris en application du code de travail et du code de la consommation' (*EC—Asbestos,* n 100 above, at 1).

[105] See R Howse and E Tuerk, 'The WTO Impact on Internal Regulations—A Case Study of the Canada-EC Asbestos Dispute', in J Scott and G De Búrca (eds), *The EU and the WTO: Legal and Constitutional Issues* (Hart, 2001), 283, at 291: 'In Canada, asbestos is manufactured exclusively in Quebec. Partly for national unity reasons, but also because of the importance of support from Quebec to any political party in Canada that seeks to form a majority government, Quebec has frequently been the beneficiary of many industrial assistance and protective measures by the Canadian government; this trend has been exacerbated by persistently high unemployment rates in the province, which is home to many of Canada's 'sunset' or troubled industries.'

[106] See T Kelly, *The Impact of the WTO—The Environment, Public Health and Sovereignty,* (Cheltenham, Edward Elgar, 2007), 92, for details on the political situation regarding asbestos products and on representation of Quebec by Canada.

[107] Case WT/DS139/AB/R, WT/DS142/AB/R *Canada—Certain Measures Affecting the Automotive Industry* [2000]. See JD Krikorian, 'Canada and the WTO: Multilevel Governance, Public Policy Making and the WTO *Auto Pact Case*', in P Gallagher, P Low, and AL Stoler (eds), *Managing the Challenges of WTO Participation—45 Case Studies* (Cambridge University Press, 2005), 134, at 143: 'There was a widespread belief that auto manufacturers would take the government's defence of the Auto Pact as a sign of good faith and maintain facilities such as the one in Sainte-Thérèse, Quebec, that were facing likely closure.'

[108] Case WT/DS222/R *Canada—Export Credits and Loan Guarantees for Regional Aircraft* [2002], at 7.316 *et seq.* on the question whether equity guarantees by the Investissement Québec to the aircraft industry constituted prohibited export subsidies under Article 3.1(a) of the SCM.

an exemplary case for our purposes, as it is a very strong and prominent national minority. But in my view these cases show a general point: minorities, even if they are not as prominent as Quebec, can put pressure on the government of their State to make it bring a case to the WTO or simply to have it defend their interests before the dispute settlement bodies. The other party in *Asbestos*, the EC, further illustrates this: the EC exclusively defended the interests of one sole Member State, France, and not necessarily of the whole EC.[109]

Admittedly, in many WTO cases a State party merely defends the partial interests of one constituent entity or of a part of the economy (see only the vast anti-dumping case law). Hence, the features of *Asbestos* identified above are as such not particularly pertinent to national minorities. One could also argue that not many national minorities may have the necessary weight to have a case launched in the WTO: not only does this require extensive resources,[110] it also depends on *intra*-State relations, the structure of the State, and not least the goodwill of the majority—again similar to the EC where the Commission enjoys discretion whether or not to bring a case to a WTO dispute settlement.[111]

Undoubtedly, whether or not a national minority has access to the WTO judicial bodies and thus can argue its cause, strongly depends on its political and financial leverage. *Ergo*, the dispute settlement system of the WTO is highly exclusive, and, if open at all, then to autonomous minorities. But my point is not that the WTO judicial system integrates minorities. The point is rather that there may be some space, even though limited, for the concerns of national minorities to be brought in, when settling disputes in the WTO; that there may be some channels that are open for the influence of national minorities; and that national minorities are not entirely excluded from the WTO judicial system. On the whole, one could say that States have a *mediate* position between national minorities and the WTO.

B. *Softwood Lumber* Disputes

A more direct glimpse of national minorities in WTO proceedings can be caught, when they submit *amicus curiae* briefs. Such a glimpse of national minorities is

---

[109] This is not to say that France is a national minority within the EC—even though such an idea is not as exotic as it once used to be: B De Witte, 'Politics Versus Law in the EU's Approach to Ethnic Minorities' (2000) 4 *EUI Working Papers* 16, at 14, examines the thought that Member States have become EC national minorities, but dismisses it. See also N Krisch, 'The Pluralism of Global Administrative Law' (2006) 17 EJIL (1), at 258, who treats the EU as a national constituency (but see fn 40).

[110] See D Tussie and V Delich, 'Dispute Settlement between Developing countries: Argentina and Chilean price Bands', in Gallagher, Low and Stoler, n 107 above, at 22 (on case WT/DS207/AB/R *Chile—Price Band System and Safeguard Measures Relating to Certain Agricultural Products* [2002]), in particular the interesting '[L]essons for others' at 36.

[111] However, there may be some possibilities to have this discretion reviewed by the Court of Justice: see Case C-70/87 *FEDIOL v Commission* [1989] ECR 01781, at 13–23 (on admissibility).

rare, though: the *Softwood Lumber* disputes[112] are the only known instances. The Appellate Body set the benchmark for *amicus* briefs in *US—Shrimp/Turtle*,[113] after environmental NGOs had submitted briefs. It ruled that it was basically left to the discretion of the Panel whether it would take *amicus* briefs into account or not.[114] Seemingly, however, a Panel must take a brief into account, when a party to a dispute explicitly adopted a position expressed in the brief.[115]

This approach was applied in the *Softwood Lumber* disputes. *Softwood Lumber* was a long and complex affair between the United States and Canada. At the heart of the affair were the low, subsidy-like fees the Canadian provincial governments (mainly British Columbia and, behold, Quebec) charged on harvested trees, the timber of which was exported to the US market.[116] US authorities used an entire arsenal of trade measures against these imports (countervailing measures under SCM and anti-dumping duties under ADA). The whole affair is important for our purposes, because Canadian indigenous peoples—national minorities in our sense—were involved. These Indian peoples basically argued that the Canadian logging system infringed their rights. Using its discretion, the Panel in *Softwood Lumber III* accepted an *amicus* brief submitted by Interior Alliance Indigenous Nations and asked parties to comment on it.[117] This was widely acclaimed for being a major development.[118] In *Softwood Lumber IV*[119] the Appellate Body received a brief from, among others, the Indigenous Network on Economies and Trade and noted that it raised issues not addressed by the

---

[112] The *Softwood Lumber* disputes consist in a row of disputes before WTO Panels and the Appellate Body (and in a number of disputes under the NAFTA dispute settlement system and before US authorities). The cases are DS236, DS247, DS257, DS 264, DS277, DS311. All case materials can be found on the webpage of the WTO website (see: <http://www.wto.org> under the heading 'dispute settlement'). A mutually agreed solution between the US and Canada was reached on 12 October 2006, ending all the *Softwood Lumber* disputes.

[113] Case WT/DS58/AB/R *US—Shrimp/Turtle, United States—Import Prohibition of Certain Shrimp and Shrimp Products* [1998].

[114] *US—Shrimp/Turtle*, ibid, at 108.

[115] The US partly adopted a position expressed in a brief: *US—Shrimp, above*, note 113, at 99–100. Basically the same seems to apply to the Appellate Body itself: see the question-answer in *US—Shrimp*, ibid, at 84–86 (but see AE Appleton, 'Shrimp/Turtle: Untangling the Nets' (1999) 2 JIEL (3) 487–488, who doubts the legal capacity of the Appellate Body to accept directly submitted briefs; for the complete picture; see B Stern, 'The Emergence of Non-State Actors in International Commercial Disputes through WTO Appellate Body Case-law', in G Sacerdoti, A Yanovich, and J Bohanes (eds), *The WTO at Ten—The Contribution of the Dispute Settlement System* (Cambridge University Press, 2006) 372, at 375–378).

[116] See for more details on the facts: G Gagné, 'Policy Diversity, State Autonomy, and the US-Canada Softwood Lumber Dispute: Philosophical and Normative Aspects' (2007) 41 J World Trade (4) 708 *et seq*.

[117] Case WT/DS236/R *Softwood Lumber III, United States—Preliminary Determination with Respect to Certain Softwood Lumber from Canada* [2002], at 7.2.

[118] See among many: 'WTO Member Comment On Indigenous Amicus Brief In Lumber Dispute', International Center for Trade and Sustainable Development, (16 May 2002) 2 Bridges Trade BioRes (9).

[119] Case WT/DS257/AB/R *Softwood Lumber IV, United States—Final Countervailing Duty Determination With Respect to Certain Softwood Lumber from Canada* [2004], at 9.

parties. After having received an *amicus* brief (from an environmental organization) in *Softwood Lumber VI*, the Panel decided 'in light of the absence of consensus among WTO Members on the question of how to treat amicus submissions, [...] not to accept unsolicited amicus curiae submissions in the course of this dispute'.[120] Hence, the initial euphoria has died down after the last dispute in the *Softwood Lumber* affair.[121]

While these submissions of *amicus* briefs as such show the interests national minorities may have in the WTO (and in trade regimes in general), it is important to put them in the right perspective: whereas the dispute settlement bodies acknowledged the receipt of the briefs, they never relied on them in their reasoning. In *Softwood Lumber III* the implications of the brief were not addressed at all. In *Softwood Lumber IV* the Appellate Body 'did not find it necessary to take the two *amicus curiae* briefs into account in rendering its decision'.[122] In *Softwood Lumber VI* the briefs as such were rejected.[123]

Arguably, the indigenous NGO's attempted to bring a wholly internal policy issue (their relations to the Canadian authorities) before the dispute settlement bodies. They initially succeeded, because their claims supported the US position: not the position of the indigenous peoples' own State, but of its opponent who had an interest in gathering their support and who is in general very open to *amicus* briefs. But even though these aspects are interesting from a general point of view, the implications of the whole *amicus curiae* system remain negligible—not only for national minorities but also for NGO's in general: any direct involvement is subject to the discretion of the Panels—a discretion that is exercised in an very restrained way—and all other gates are guarded by the State parties (briefs as appendices to the States' submissions or, in general, the position of the Member State as a *mediator* for national minorities).[124]

Dispute settlement in the WTO therefore remains a highly exclusive process. National minorities, especially autonomous minorities as Quebec in *Asbestos* or the Canadian indigenous peoples in the *Softwood Lumber* disputes (the latter probably also suffering from a lack of integration), may have an interest in a WTO dispute, but their legal means are controlled by the States and, to a lesser extent, by the Panels. Having an interest in a dispute, but no legal means to articulate it, is disastrous—or, at the very least, it shows a flaw in the law.

---

[120] Case WT/DS277/R *Softwood Lumber VI, United States—Investigation of the International Trade Commission in Softwood Lumber from Canada* [2004], at fn 75.

[121] In fact, it had already died down after the imbroglio created by the communication of the Appellate Body in Case WT/DS135/AB/R *EC—Asbestos* had been settled, because the Appellate Body rejected all 17 requests to submit briefs (see JL Dunoff, 'Constitutional Conceits: The WTO's 'Constitution' and the Discipline of International Law' (2006) 17 EJIL (3) 660).

[122] *Softwood Lumber IV,* n 119 above, at 9.

[123] See ibid, the quote in the preceding paragraph and n 120.

[124] On the involvement of private parties in general, see RJ Zedalis, 'When Do the Activities of Private Parties Trigger WTO Rules?' (2007) 10 JIEL (2) (in particular p 347 on Case WT/DS255/R *Argentina—Measures Affecting the Export of Bovine Hides and the Import of Finished Leather* [2000]).

VII. Perspectives

Our analysis of the EC- and the WTO-trade regimes yielded a number of results. It revealed that the EC addresses national minority issues in different ways. Externally, the EC uses its leverage to impose on third States measures protecting national minorities. Internally, the EC follows a limited, individualist approach, which also shows systemic elements, and otherwise relies on the Council of Europe. The WTO does not follow any approach towards national minorities. On the contrary, it hides them behind the façade of States.

We therefore observe considerable differences in the two trade regimes. Certainly, these differences are partly explained by the distinct nature of the two entities: the EC gradually developed into an organism of integration,[125] whereas the WTO simply claims to regulate inter-State trade. Only with integration, it seems, issues relating to sub-State entities, and in particular national minorities, arise naturally. And only for integration a possibility to harmonize the legal orders of the constituent entities is indispensable. It is not surprising then that harmonization is infinitely more difficult in legal terms in the WTO than in the EC, as it is only possible by an amendment of the WTO Agreement.[126]

The picture may look different before the courts though, as courts are notoriously difficult to control. They may well develop into an engine of integration, although this was not the intention at the outset. This leads back to our main argument: in the beginning we contended that it was *possible,* though *unlikely,* that national minority issues as the Court of Justice had to address them arise in the future before the WTO dispute settlement bodies. Let me explain this argument.

Why is it *possible* that national minority issues arise in the future before a Panel? Did we not observe that national minorities had interests in WTO dispute settlement but no legal means? So we did and we also noticed that States kept the gates to the WTO judicial system. The analysis of the case law of the Court of Justice, however, revealed an intrinsic feature: national minority issues typically arise, when persons move and with them their distinctive characteristics (typically their language). Now, while the conventional WTO clearly is about moving goods, a new concept of trade slowly materializes: world trade in services. The Appellate Body has already decided the first true services case in *US—Gambling.*[127] The

---

[125] P Trachtman, 'The Constitutions of the WTO' (2006) 17 EJIL (3), at 634: 'It is striking that both the US and the EC began with emphases on commercial relations, and developed broader capacities over time.'

[126] But see the (limited) possibility to adopt 'interpretations' by a 'three-fourths majority of the Members' in Article IX:2 of the WTO Agreement (see M Matsushita, T Schoenbaum, and PC Mavroidis, *The World Trade Organization: Law, Practice, and Policy* (2nd edn, OUP, 2006) 804).

[127] Case WT/DS285/AB/R *United States—Measures Affecting the Cross-Border Supply of Gambling and Betting Services* [2005].

General Agreement on Trade in Services (GATS) makes authors think whether it could be 'a vehicle for international migration'.[128] Indeed, the notion of service is broad under the GATS.[129] Mode 4 of the GATS[130] even allows the movement of natural persons under a service cloak. This means that part of the workers' freedom as it is known in the EC has found its way into the WTO via the GATS.[131] Hence, it seems that national minority issues could in the future arise before the WTO dispute settlement organs: it is *possible* that a Quebecois *Bickel and Franz*[132] will be decided by a Panel.[133]

This is, however, *unlikely* for a number of reasons. First, GATS, mode 4 is the most heavily restricted. Very often members made exemptions to commitments regarding mode 4 in the schedules to the GATS.[134] And it seems doubtful whether WTO members are prepared to substantively liberalize mode 4 in the near future. Second, the limited number of GATS cases decided by WTO dispute settlement organs shows that members are reluctant to bring service cases.[135] Probably, they are themselves afraid of the vast potential of the GATS. And third, we have seen that WTO members avidly guard the gates to dispute settlement. Most of them want to prevent minorities from raising national policy issues before Panels, as is illustrated by the *Softwood Lumber* disputes.[136]

But what if a case such as *Bickel and Franz* would be brought to a Panel nevertheless? Would it decide the case in a similar way as the Court of Justice? The Appellate Body showed considerable flexibility in handling reasons to justify obstacles to trade, when it construed the 'conservation of exhaustible natural resources'[137] as mostly encompassing environmental protection in general in

---

[128] P Eeckhout, 'Constitutional Concepts for Free Trade in Services', in J Scott and G De Búrca (eds), *The EU and the WTO: Legal and Constitutional Issues* (Hart, 2001) 211, at 222.

[129] Eeckhout, ibid, 228. See also EH Leroux, 'Eleven Years of GATS Case Law: What Have We Learned?' (2007) 10 JIEL (4) 751–755.

[130] Article I:2(d) of GATS: '[...] trade in services is defined as the supply of a service [...] by a service supplier of one Member, through presence of natural persons of a Member in the territory of any other Member.'

[131] Note also that most of the relief to tensions between national minorities and States in Europe is brought by the Council of Europe and the High Commissioner on National Minorities (see n 30 above). The EC therefore does not have to cope with tensions alone, whereas the WTO does not benefit from a similarly effective 'safety valve'.

[132] Case C-274/96 *Bickel and Franz* [1998] ECR I-7637.

[133] A serious possibility in light of the proposed 'Quebec Identity Act' (Bill 195) (see A Égré, 'Just Sign on the Dotted Line... (Interview with Daniel Turp, Member of Quebec Parliament)' (2008) 46 Academia—The Science Magazine of the European Academy of Bolzano (1) 31).

[134] M Trebilcock and R Howse, *The Regulation of International Trade* (3rd edn, Routledge, 2005) 376: 'A particular concern of many developing countries is the liberalization of Mode 4 service provision, ie the movement of persons into the consumer country for purposes of the delivery of services. This is an area where many developed countries have been unprepared to make bold liberalization commitments, because of the issues raised for immigration policy [...].'

[135] See Grynberg and Qalo who argue that there are strong indications that workers are covered by mode 4 and that this issue is highly sensitive (R Grynberg and V Qalo, 'Migration and the World Trade Organization', (2007) 41 J World Trade (4) 779).

[136] *Softwood Lumber* disputes, n 112 above.   [137] Article XX(g) of GATT.

US—Shrimp/Turtle[138] and when it read an element of justification for reasons of public health into the likeness of a product under Article III(4) of GATT in *EC—Asbestos*.[139] It cannot be excluded therefore that a Panel or the Appellate Body would deal with 'the maintenance of public order'—justification[140] in a creative way.[141] Again however, it is unlikely that the WTO judicial organs avail themselves of the same liberty as the Court of Justice in finding 'mandatory requirements'.[142] After all, the Panels and the Appellate Body have always stuck much more to the wording of the WTO Agreement than the Court of Justice with the Treaties. Hence, for national minorities the WTO picture will probably remain bleak for the future. It seems that the Appellate Body will not break the tabu of national minorities soon. But maybe this paper attracts attention to this tabu and thus leads the way to breaking it on the long run.

---

[138] Case WT/DS58/AB/R *US—Shrimp/Turtle*, at 129 *et seq.*; note in particular the reference to the preamble of the WTO Agreement.

[139] Case WT/DS135/AB/R *EC—Asbestos,* at 113.

[140] Article XIV(a) of GATS.

[141] M Matsushita, T Schoenbaum, and PC Mavroidis, *The World Trade Organization: Law, Practice, and Policy* (2nd edn, OUP, 2006) 638: '[. . .] the (probably narrow) term *public morals*, but also the wider term *public order*' (emphasis in original). But see fn 5 to Article XIV(a) of GATS: 'The public order exception may be invoked only where genuine and sufficiently serious threat is posed to one of the fundamental interests of society.' Lamy, probably writing colloquially, does not seem to have a particularly restrictive approach to exceptions in general: '[. . .] Art. XX of GATT provides that nothing prevents a Member from setting aside market access obligations when a Member decides, unilaterally, that considerations other than those of trade must prevail.' (See P Lamy, 'The Place of the WTO and its Law in the International Legal Order' (2006) 17 EJIL (5) 978).

[142] *Cassis de Dijon* [1979] ECR 649, at 8. See M Irish, 'GSP Tariffs and Conditionality: A Comment on *EC—Preferences*', (2007) 41 J World Trade (4), at 696: 'GATT Article XX is directed at exemptions from trade obligations, not at creating an extra enforcement mechanism for other areas of public international law.'

Monitor and Manage: MiFID and Power in the Regulation of EU Financial Markets

*Larry Catá Backer**

Abstract: MiFID, the Market in Financial Instruments Directive, came into force on 1 November 2007, and is hailed as the next great step toward market integration within the European Union (EU). It is grounded in two key traditional policies of market regulation: surveillance and management. MiFID will exact a greater degree of transparency—paralleling American principles of market regulation. It will also require adherence to a 'best execution' standard for all clients. Most analyses have focused on the costs and implementation of these requirements. Transparency is viewed as either a burden (or opportunity) because of the need to produce, keep, and manage more data. Markets in information will surely grow. The 'best execution' standards provide a greater means of standardizing industry practices—with the potential benefit to regulators to which power over market behavior should flow. This article will focus on the potential ramifications of the surveillance and regulatory aspects of MiFID in terms of the nature of the character of the regulatory power in the financial products sector. Specifically the article examines the effects of the creation of the markets for information elaborated or augmented through MiFID in terms of the regulation of the behavior of participants in financial markets and the entities they serve. Particular attention will be paid to the effects of MiFID on public and private anti-corruption campaigns, the use of these regulations to influence the behavior of issuers and market middlemen, and the potential utility of these regulations to elements of civil society and the media in their campaigns for corporate and capital social responsibility.

* Professor of Law, Pennsylvania State University; Director, Coalition for Peace and Ethics (see: <http://www.peaceethics.org>), visiting Professor of Law, Tulane University Law School 2007–08 (where much of the work on this article was completed). The author may be contacted at: lcb11@psu.edu. An earlier version of this paper was presented at the Conference: EU Financial Services Regulation: Completing the Internal Market. Institute of Advanced Legal Studies, London, United Kingdom, 26 October 2006 (organized by the Academy of European Law and the Centre for Commercial Law Studies, Queen Mary, University of London). My thanks to my research assistant, Nicholas Fernez, and to the conference participants for their very helpful comments and suggestions.

I. Introduction

The Market in Financial Instruments Directive (MiFID),[1] came into force on 1 November 2007,[2] replacing the Investment Services Directive (ISD).[3] The European Commission has proclaimed, 'MiFID and its implementing measures together establish a comprehensive legislative framework at European level relating to the establishment and conduct of investment firms, multilateral trading facilities and regulated markets.'[4] As the Financial Service Authority (FSA) explains it to its Internet audience, 'MiFID extends the coverage of the current ISD and introduces new and more extensive requirements that firms will have to adapt to, in particular for their conduct of business and internal organisation.'[5] MiFID's implementation, businesses are warned, 'will significantly alter financial services regulation in the UK, how firms operate their businesses, and the way they interact with their clients.'[6]

MiFID is meant to accomplish several goals. Among the most important is to broaden the market for financial services across the territories of EU Member States by extending the range of core financial services subject to 'passporting' rules,[7] principally by introducing the Multilateral Trading Facility (MTF) as a core cluster of services subject to passporting.[8] The requirements of the Capital Requirements Directive[9] will be extended to firms that fall within the scope of

---

[1] Directive 2004/39/EC of the European Parliament and of the Council of 21 April 2004 on markets in financial instruments amending Council Directives 85/611/EEC and 93/6/EEC and Directive 2000/12/EC of the European Parliament and of the Council and repealing Council Directive 93/22/EEC, ([2004] OJ L145/1 (30.04.04)), available at: <http://europa.eu.int/eur-lex/pri/en/oj/dat/2004/l_145/l_14520040430en00010044.pdf> (hereafter 'MiFID').

[2] Directive 2006/31/EC of the European Parliament and of the Council amending directive 2004/39/EC on markets in financial instruments, as regards certain deadlines, at Article 1(4).

[3] Directive 93/22 ([1993] OJ L141/27). The Commission has published a report on transposition. See European Commission, Internal Market, Securities and Investment, Investment Services and Regulated Markets, MiFID Transposition State of Play, last updated 23 April 2008, available online at: <http://ec.europa.eu/internal_market/securities/isd/mifid_implementation_en.htm>.

[4] European Commission, Internal Market, Securities and Investment, Investment Services and Regulated Markets (MiFID), Your Questions on MiFID, Markets in Financial Instruments Directive and Implementing Measures, available online at: <http://ec.europa.eu/internal_market/securities/isd/questions/index_en.htm>.

[5] FSA, Markets in Financial Instruments Directive (MiFID), available online at: <http://www.fsa.gov.uk/Pages/About/What/International/EU/fsap/mifid/index.shtml>.

[6] FSA, Planning for MiFID, November 2005, available online at: <http://www.fsa.gov.uk/pubs/international/planning_mifid.pdf>, at 3.

[7] On passporting under MiFID, see The Committee of European Securities Regulators (CESR), Public Consultation, The Passport Under MiFID, Ref 06–669 (December 2006), available online at: <http://www.mifidconnect.org/content/1/c4/81/67/cesr_passport.pdf>.

[8] See, eg MiFID, Art 31. For a discussion, see, eg E Avgouleas, 'A Critical Evaluation Of The New EC Financial-Market Regulation: Peaks, Troughs, And The Road Ahead' 18 Transnational Law (2005) 179, 193–195.

[9] The Capital Requirements Directive is comprised of two Directives: Directive 2006/48/EC ([2006] OJ L177/1) (available online at: <http://eur-lex.europa.eu/LexUriServ/site/en/

MiFID.[10] MiFID will also exact a greater degree of transparency in the operation of financial markets—echoing American principles of market regulation.[11] These include the generation of pre- and post-trade data, the extension of transparency, and reporting requirements for 'Systematic Internalisers' (SI).[12] It will also require adherence by investment firms to a 'best execution' standard for all clients.[13]

MiFID is one of a batch of harmonizing legislation growing out of the Financial Services Action Plan[14] and the associated 'Lamfalussy process'.[15] The

oj/2006/l_177/l_17720060630en00010200.pdf>) and Directive 2006/49/EC ([2006] OJ L177/201) (available online at: <http://eur-lex.europa.eu/LexUriServ/site/en/oj/2006/l_177/l_17720060630en02010255.pdf>).

[10] See, eg FSA, Markets in Financial Instruments Directive (MiFID), available online at: <http://www.fsa.gov.uk/Pages/About/What/International/EU/fsap/mifid/index.shtml>.

[11] Compare the American effort legislated as Reg NMS, Securities and Exchange Commission, Final Regulation: Regulation NMS, Release No 34–51808; File No S7–10-04 (2005). This focus on transparency extends from earlier regulatory efforts on disclosure by companies seeking to participate in the financial markets such as the Prospectus Directive 2003/71 ([2003] OJ L345/64), the Prospectus Regulation Commission Regulation 2004/809 ([2004] OJ L149/1), and the Transparency Directive 2004/109 ([2004] OJ L390/38). Harmonization in communication within financial markets has been advanced through efforts of the International Accounting Standards/International Financial Reporting Standards (IAS/IFRS) to harmonize financial reporting through, for example, IAS Regulation 1606/2002 ([2002] OJ L243/1)).

[12] Systematic internalisers are defined in MiFID as 'investment firms which, on an organized and frequent basis, deals on own account by executing client orders outside a regulated market or an MTF': MiFID, Art 4(7). 'Firms that routinely cross buy and sell orders are deemed to be "systematic internalisers" and must provide definite bid and offer quotes in liquid shares for orders below 'standard market size': A Jenkins, 'Preparing for MiFID: On Your Marks! Get Se! Go!, Bearing Point, Inc.', White Paper: Strategy, Process and Transformation (July 2005, updated March 2006) available online at: <http://www.bearingpoint.fr/media/Library/MIFID_PREP.pdf>.

[13] MiFID, Arts 19(1) and 21(1).

[14] Financial Services Action Plan (FSAP), Commission Communication of 11 May 1999 entitled 'Implementing the framework for financial markets: action plan' (COM(1999) 232 final—not published in the Official Journal), available online at: <http://europa.eu/scadplus/leg/en/lvb/l24210.htm> (including progress reports from 1999). 'Disparities between Member States' rules on corporate governance can give rise to legal and administrative barriers which hinder the efficient operation of the EU financial market. However, the term "corporate governance" covers a wide range of issues whose ramifications for the single financial market are at present unclear. Any Community initiative in this area should therefore initially be confined to reviewing national codes of corporate governance applied in the different Member States in order to identify any barriers which could frustrate the development of a single EU financial market.' Ibid, at General Conditions.

[15] 'The core of the EC's regulatory and supervisory approach in financial services is now founded on the 4-level Lamfalussy process.': Commission of the European Communities, White Paper: Financial Services Policy 2005–2010, SEC(2005) 1574, COM(2005) 629 FINAL, Brussels, 1 December 2005, 3.1, at 9. For a general description, see Financial Markets: Commission Welcomes Parliament's Agreement On Lamfalussy Proposals For Reform IP/02/195, Brussels, 5 February 2002 available online at: <http://europa.eu/rapid/pressReleasesAction.do?reference=IP/02/195&format=HTML&aged=1&language=EN&guiLanguage=en>. For a more detailed discussion, see EC Commission, Commission Staff Working Document The Application of The Lamfalussy Process To EU Securities Markets Legislation—A Preliminary Assessment by the Commission Services SEC(2004) 1459 (15 November 2004). Available online at: <http://ec.europa.eu/internal_market/securities/docs/lamfalussy/sec-2004–1459_en.pdf>. As the UK Government explained:
'Given the scale of the task involved in adopting and implementing such a large programme of FSAP Regulations and Directives, ECOFIN decided in July 2000, as its top priority, to complete a

process involves the enactment of framework legislation (Level 1) to be followed by more detailed implementing legislation based on the framework adopted (Level 2). This is eventually to be followed by a comitological process among regulators for greater integration in fact (Level 3)[16] and strengthening enforcement (Level 4). MiFID, the core of the framework provisions in this aspect of financial services integration, and constituting the 'Level 1' text, came into force on 30 April 2004.[17] Level 2 legislation has started coming down the regulatory pike in the form of an Implementing Regulation[18] and an additional Directive.[19] Level 3 will focus on implementation and enforcement of Levels 1 and 2 requirements through 'supervisory convergence' among the regulatory authorities of the Member States and has been advanced in two influential reports of the EU's Financial Services Committee.[20]

This article considers MiFID in the context of the EU's regulatory project for markets, specifically, and for the 'single market' in general. The paper starts with a view of MiFID from the inside. It lays out MiFID's complexity, order, comity, and direction in the context of the substantive policy advanced and the methodology embraced.[21] That substantive policy is grounded in the value of

single EU capital market by 2003. A Committee of Wise Men chaired by Baron Alexandre Lamfalussy was appointed. The Lamfalussy Committee recommended a new decision-making procedure for the adoption of EU legislation affecting the securities markets, which was endorsed by the Stockholm European Council in March 2001.' (HM Treasury, FSA and the Bank of England, The EU Financial Services Action Plan: A Guide (31 July 2003), at p 12, 16, available online at: <http://www.fsa.gov. uk/pubs/other/fsap_guide.pdf>.)

[16] See G Ferrarini, 'The Harmonisation of Capital Markets Law in the EU: Assessments and Prospects,' paper presented at the Conference: EU Financial Services Regulation: Completing the Internal Market (London, 27 October 2006).

[17] Directive on Markets and Financial Instruments 2004.

[18] See Commission Regulation (EC) No 1287/2006 of 10 August 2006 implementing Directive 2004/39/EC of the European Parliament and of the Council as regards record-keeping obligations for investment firms, transaction reporting, market transparency, admission of financial instruments to trading, and defined terms for the purposes of that Directive ([2006] OJ L241/1 (09.02.06)), available online at: <http://ec.europa.eu/internal_market/securities/isd/mifid2_en.htm>, (hereafter 'Implementing Regulation 2006'). This Regulation focuses on investment firm record keeping obligations, transaction reporting rules, market transparency requirements, rules for the admission of financial instruments to trading, and deferred terms.

[19] See Commission Directive 2006/73/EC of 10 August 2006 implementing Directive 2004/39/ EC of the European Parliament and of the Council as regards organisational requirements and operating conditions for investment firms and defined terms for the purposes of that Directive ([2006] OJ L241/26 (09.02.06)), available online at: <http://ec.europa.eu/internal_market/securities/isd/ mifid2_en.htm> (hereafter 'Implementing Directive 2006').

[20] See, Financial Services Committee (FSC) (2006), Report on Financial Supervision ('Francq Report II'), February 2006; and Financial Services Committee (FSC) (2005), Report on Financial Supervision ('Francq Report I'), July 2005.

[21] That complexity has generated enough confusion to produce a Commission document organizing and answering the most commonly put to it, a document weighing in at 135 pages. More will likely be generated. See European Commission, Internal Market, Securities and investment, Investment in Services and Regulated Markets, Your Questions on MiFID, available online at: <http://ec.europa. eu/internal_market/securities/docs/isd/questions/questions_en.pdf> (last updated 23 April 2008).

surveillance for controlling behavior and in an understanding of an objective of control as focused on the management of a situation rather than on the eradication of a problem.

With the surveillance and reporting aspects of MiFID firmly in mind, this article then turns to a consideration of the most interesting ramifications of MiFID raised within the context of the broader issues with respect to which MiFID appears to be largely concerned. These ramifications can be divided into seven broad but related themes that MiFID raises, and that will be worth sustained review as this new broad attempt at regulating financial markets is implemented. Together, these themes suggest both the power and limits of regulatory attempts like MiFID to control markets, or to privatize monitoring and redirect it for the benefit of the political community, or to reinforce the State system in the context of behavior that jumps borders, or to achieve broader policy goals, principally criminal enforcement and control of political activity.

II. MiFID From the Inside and on its Own Terms

MiFID presents an institutionally complex set of modifications of the Financial Services Directive.[22] As a regulatory document, MiFID is divided into five main components. The first sets forth key definitions and the regulatory scope of MiFID. Its provisions are to a substantial extent, also framed by an Annex to the Directive. The second sets out substantive requirements for authorization and operating conditions. The third focuses on rules governing regulated markets. The fourth lays out the public institutional framework for regulation within the multi-tiered structure of the EU. The last includes a variety of important house-keeping provisions. The requirements of MiFID are further elaborated in both an implementing directive[23] and an Implementing Regulation.[24] The complexity of its provisions is matched only by that of the justifications advanced for its structure and limitations.

This section is divided into two parts. The first untangles the regulatory framework, at least in broad strokes. The second considers the web of justification of that structure and the administrative response of the UK public authorities. Both serve as the foundation for the analysis that follows in section III.

The document is important if only to suggest the difficulties, even for the Commission, of understanding the important of this regulatory scheme. See, ibid, at 45 (question 167) (providing a modified answer to definition of the term 'money market instrument' in Article 4(1)(19) of MiFID).

[22] Investment Services Directive 93/22 ([1993] OJ L141/27).
[23] See Implementing Directive 2006, n 18 above.
[24] See Implementing Regulation 2006, n 17 above.

A. The Regulatory Framework of MiFID

MiFID applies fully to 'investment firms'[25] and 'regulated markets'[26] to which separate but related authorization regimes are applied.[27] It is only partially applicable to credit institutions otherwise authorized to provide one or more investment services or activities.[28] MiFID provides the by now standard list of exemptions from regulation,[29] and permits Member States the authority to exempt further classes of investment actors.[30] The most important scope additions that MiFID makes to its predecessor are regulation of investment advice and the operation of multilateral trading facilities as a specific component of 'regulated markets'.[31] Covered investment firms are subject to regulation with respect to their investment services and activities. Investment services and activities are defined as those services and activities listed in MiFID's Annex I.[32] Annex I lists eight covered services or activities in its scope provision, including investment advice and operation of multilateral trading facilities.[33] Investment advice is defined as 'the provision of personal recommendations to a client, either upon its request, or at the initiative of the investment firm'.[34] But that advice must be given 'in respect of one or more transactions relating to financial instruments'.[35] Multilateral trading facilities is defined as a multilateral *system* 'operated by an investment form

---

[25] MiFID, Title I, Art 1(1). An investment firm is defined as 'any legal person whose regular occupation or business is the provision of one or more investment services to third parties and/or the performance of one or more investment activities on a professional basis'. Ibid, at Title I, Art 4(1)(1).

[26] Ibid. A regulated market is defined in MiFID, Art 4(13).

[27] The authorization requirements scheme for investment firms is set forth in Title II (Arts 5–35) and the regulated markets authorization requirements scheme is set forth in Title III (Arts 36–47) of MiFID.

[28] MiFID, Title I, Art 1(2).

[29] MiFID, Title I, Art. 2. Noteworthy, though, is the exception for certain firms engaged in commodities transactions through other financial intermediaries. See MiFID, Art 2(1)(i) and 2(1)(k).

[30] MiFID, Title I, Art 3. The exemption covers a variety of financial services intermediaries. The exemption provided is important for two reasons. The first is that it covers a large number of market participants. The second is that the exemption may significantly affect the harmonization of the regulatory framework.

[31] HM Treasury, Consultation Document: UK Implementation of the EU Markets in Financial Instruments Directive (Directive 2004/39/EC) (December 2005), available online at: <http://www.hm-treasury.gov.uk/media/2E0/CA/ukimplementationeumarkets151205.pdf>, at 10. 'Regulated markets' are defined as 'a multilateral system operated and/or managed by a market operator, which bring together or facilitates the bringing together of multiple third party buying and selling interests in financial instruments': MiFD, Title I, Art 4(1)(14). The market operator itself 'may be the regulated market itself.': MiFID, Title I, Art 4(1), (13).

[32] MiFID, Title I, Art 4(1)(2). The Commission is given some latitude with respect to derivatives, otherwise covered as a financial instrument subject to regulation. See ibid. The Implementing Regulations added a bit of detail to trading in derivatives on regulated markets. See Implementing Regulation 2006, Arts 37–39.

[33] MiFID, Annex I, Section A(1)–(8). Annex A also provides a list of covered 'ancillary services' (ibid, at Section B) and forms of covered 'financial instruments' (ibid, at Section C).

[34] MiFID, Title I, Art 4(1)(4),

[35] Ibid. Financial instruments are limited to those described in MiFID, Annex I, Section C. See, MiFID, Title I, Art 4(1), (17). The kinds of financial instruments now included within the regulatory

or a market operator' which essentially operates like a 'regulated market' as that term is itself defined in MiFID.[36] The Commission may clarify, but not change, the scope definitions of Article 1.[37]

Like the prior rules, a central element of MiFID consists of the vesting, in the governmental apparatus of each Member State, of authority to authorize the provision of 'investment services' by those eligible to engage in such a business, in accordance with the framework specified in MiFID.[38] That framework builds on the good practices and governance frameworks of the ISD.[39] These provisions are meant to provide protection to investors by maintaining a basic system of harmonized good governance standards. These include initial capital endowment,[40] organizational requirements,[41] and qualifications for owners and operators of investment firms.[42] Additional rules are provided for the governance, trading practices and finalization of transactions of operators of multilateral trading facilities,[43] and in the relationship between registered investment forms and third countries.[44]

The core of the governance provisions of MiFID center on the conduct of the business of regulated firms.[45] Member States are required to monitor for compliance.[46] The conflict of interest rules represent a significant expansion over the old rules.[47] Title II, Chapter II, Section 2 of MiFID sets out the core of investor protection provisions.[48] The investor protection measures are more extensively developed than under the old ISO and cover a number of important areas, including conduct of business obligations,[49] the provision of services through

---

ambit include non-financial derivatives (principally commodity and more exotic derivatives). See MiFID , Annex I, Section C (4)–(10).

[36] MiFID, Title I, Art 4(1), (15).   [37] MiFID, Art 4(2).

[38] See MiFID, Title II, Arts 5–10.   [39] See MiFID, Arts 11–15.

[40] See MiFID, Arts 11–12. Minimum capital requirements are only indirectly regulated by MiFID. The actual mandatory levels are set forth as a specific part of the general Capital Requirements Directive. See Capital Requirements Directive (Directive 2006/48/EC and Directive 2006/49/EC), adopted on 14 June 2006. It will apply to all credit institutions and investment firms in the EU.

[41] MiFID, Art 13. MiFID's governance provisions are more extensive than those in ISD. These provisions were extensively fleshed out in the MiFID Implementing Directive. See Implementing Directive 2006, Arts 5–25. The record keeping requirements are specified in the Implementing Regulation. See Implementing Regulation 2006, above note [18] at Arts 7–8. The organizational and good governance provisions of MiFID and in the Implementing Directive and Implementing Regulation are worth study in their own right, but that analysis is beyond the scope of this article.

[42] MiFID, Arts 9–10.

[43] MiFID, Art 14. These requirements are meant to bring MTF practice into conformity with those of other regulated markets. The focus of these rules is on transparency (Article 14(2) and (4)), issuer information (Article 14(6)), and regulatory compliance with State agents (Article 14(7)).

[44] MiFID, Art 15.   [45] MiFID, Arts 16–35.   [46] MiFID, Arts 16–17.

[47] See especially MiFID, Art 18(2). The 2006 Implementing Directive specifies the development and publication of conflict of interest rules appropriate to the nature of the business of the regulated entity. See Implementing Directive 2006, Art 22. These provisions are also meant to expand and harmonize investor protection.

[48] MiFID, Arts 19–24.

[49] MiFID, Art 19. Firms are required to 'act honestly, fairly and professionally in accordance with the best interests of its clients' (ibid). Minimum requirements for investor communication are also

the medium of another investment firm,[50] best execution policies,[51] client order handling rules,[52] tied agents,[53] and eligible counterparties rules.[54]

Title II, Chapter II, Section 3, sets forth an expanded group of market transparency and integrity rules.[55] This is another section in which the prior rules have been substantially expanded. Investment forms 'which execute transactions in any financial instruments admitted to trading on a regulated market must report details of such transactions' to Member State regulatory agencies within a working day of execution.[56] The most important set of innovations involve pre-trade transparency rules.[57] One set of these new rules applies only to transactions in shares by systemic internalisers and requires them to 'publish a firm quote in those shares admitted to trading on a regulated market for which they are systemic internalisers, and for which there is a liquid market'.[58] Investment firms have a

specified, focusing on conveying an understanding of the nature and risks of the investment service and the specific instruments offered to clients (Article 19(3)). The Directive also provides for obtaining client information and experience relevant to the investment (Article 19(4) and (5)) recordkeeping (Article 19(7)) and reporting (Article 19(8)). The 2006 Implementing Directive fleshed out these requirements. See Implementing Directive 2006, Arts 24, 26–45.

[50] MiFID, Art 20. This provision establishes rules for liability in the context of the appropriateness and accuracy of information, and for proper performance of the services rendered.

[51] MiFID, Art 21. MiFID, Art 21(1) imposes on Member States the obligation to require investment firms to take all reasonable steps to obtain 'the best possible result of their clients taking into account price, costs, speed, likelihood of execution and settlement, size, nature or any other consideration relevant to the execution of that order'. These rules apply in the absence of specific instructions from clients. Still, the best execution policies under which such efforts are to be undertaken is framed as a general obligation, rather than one that requires modification with respect to each individual order (Articles 21(2) and (3)). However, best execution criteria are elaborated in the Implementing Directive. See Implementing Directive 2006, Art 44. The criteria focus more precisely on client characteristics.

[52] MiFID, Art 22. This is essentially an equal treatment rule for clients. But the rule is targeted for the small order client. Larger clients with larger orders may be exempted from these provisions at the option of any Member State (Article 22(2)) and a Member State may determine that transmission to a regulated market or MTF satisfies the requirements of the rule (ibid).

[53] MiFID, Art 23. MiFID imposes a rule of unconditional responsibility. Id.

[54] MiFID, Art 24. The rules provide an exception to the investor protection rules where the counterparty is otherwise responsible.

[55] MiFID, Arts 25–30. These provisions are to be implemented without prejudice to the allocation of responsibility under the Market Abuse Directive, Commission Directive 2003/6/EC ([2003] OJ L96/16 (04.12.03)). In December 2006, the FSA published FSA 2006/70 Transparency Obligations Directive (Disclosure and Transparency Rules) Instrument 2006, which amended the FSA's rules and implemented the TD in the UK, effective from 20 January 2007. See FSA 2006/70, available at <http://www.fsa.gov.uk/pages/handbook>.

[56] MiFID, Art 25(3). The Implementing Regulation defines 'the most relevant market in terms of liquidity' for purposes of making such reports. See Implementing Regulation 2006, Arts 9–10. It also fleshes out a number of other reporting requirements (ibid, at Arts 11–14).

[57] MiFID, Art 27.

[58] MiFID, Art 27(1). These provisions do not apply where there is no liquid market (in which case the systemic internaliser must disclose quotes to clients on demand) or when dealing 'in sizes above standard market size' (Article 27(1)). The market for each share is measured against all orders executed in the EU (Article 27(1)). These quotes are to be made public 'in a manner which is easily accessible to other market participants on a reasonable commercial basis' (Article 27(3)). Systemic internalisers are bound by these quotes on orders they receive from retail clients and professional clients with an exception for orders larger than one of a size larger than one 'customarily undertaken by a retail

post-trade transparency obligation with respect to 'shares admitted to trading on a regulated market, outside a regulated market or MTF'.[59] Another set imposes similar rules on MTF transactions.[60] The Implementing Regulation provides criteria for determining whether an investment firm is a systematic internaliser (and thus subject to the reporting and transparency rules).[61]

The cross-border trading provisions of MiFID were meant to clarify the establishment rules of the ISD. Article 31 permits an investment firm authorized in one Member State to provide investment services in other Member States on compliance with certain notification rules.[62] Branches may be established without having to proceed with additional authorization procedures in the host State.[63] And investment firms are granted access to regulated markets established in the territory of any Member State.[64] Similar rules apply to regulated markets and MTFs.[65]

Regulated markets themselves are the regulatory subject of the comparatively less extensive Title III of MiFID. Paralleling the regulatory framework applied to investment firms, MiFID seeks to create a harmonized approach to principles of regulating markets while allowing a certain measure of flexibility in the implementation of those principles. 'The provisions governing regulated markets are aimed at providing high-level principles of regulation in order to allow for flexibility in the development of such markets.'[66] MiFID provides for a public

investor' and may execute orders for professional clients at prices different from their quoted ones (Article 27(3)). The Implementing Regulations specify the manner of determining market liquidity for purposes of the application of MiFID, Art 27. See Implementing Regulation 2006, Art 22. The Implementing Regulation also elaborates a number of other requirements with respect to systematic internaliser pre transaction transparency. See Implementing Regulation 2006, at Arts 23 (standard market size definition), 24 (maintenance of record of quotes reflecting prevailing market conditions), 25 (order execution), and 26 (retail size).

[59] MiFID, Art 28. Systematic internalisers thus have an obligation to make public the details of transactions in shares as if they had been traded in regulated markets.
[60] MiFID, Arts 29–30. The Implementing Regulation describes the sort of information that an investment firm or market operator operating an MTF (or a regulated market pursuant to the requirements of MiFID, Art 44) must make public. See Implementing Regulation 2006, Arts 17 (information to be provided) and 18 (waiver criteria). Private transaction waivers are also treated (MiFID, Art 19).
[61] See Implementing Regulation 2006, Art 21. Investment firms who deal on their own account outside a regulated market or MTF will be treated as a systematic internaliser if such trading takes on the characteristics of a market. The Implementing Regulation specifies three criteria in that respect: (1) activity that has a material commercial role for the firm that is carried out under an institutionalized set of procedures, (2) the activity is carried out through an automated technical system, and (3) the activity is regularly and continuously available to clients of the firm (ibid).
[62] MiFID, Art 31 (imposing State-to-State system of notification).
[63] MiFID, Art 32. The provisions do give host State authorities some leeway where there may be evidence of inadequacy. See, eg MiFID, Art 32(3).
[64] MiFID, Art 33. No additional regulatory requirements can be imposed if the investment firm chooses to gain access by becoming a remote member of or having remote access to the regulated market, or otherwise by setting up a branch in the host State (Article 33). Investment firms are also provided with access to central counterparty, clearing, and settlement facilities (Article 34).
[65] MiFID, Art 35.
[66] HM Treasury, Consultation Document: UK Implementation of the EU Markets in Financial Instruments Directive (Directive 2004/39/EC) (December 2005), available online at: <http://www.hm-treasury.gov.uk/media/2E0/CA/ukimplementationeumarkets151205.pdf>, at 16.

registration of regulated markets, and prohibits the operation of unauthorized markets.[67] Authorization requires 'good reputation' and 'sufficient experience' requirements for operators.[68] 'The Commission shall publish a list of all regulated markets in the Official Journal of the European Union.'[69] MiFID imposes organizational requirements,[70] rules relating to admission of financial instruments to trading,[71] access to regulated markets,[72] the implementation of monitoring systems,[73] and provisions for pre- and post-trade transparency.[74] The transparency rules are fleshed out in the 2006 Implementing Regulation.[75]

The Implementing Regulations under MiFID elaborated rules with respect to the publication and availability of pre- and post-trade information applicable to the transparency obligations of regulated markets, MTFs and systematic internalisers.[76] The regulation emphasizes a focus on real time publication as the standard, with necessary modifications depending on transaction type.[77] Of great importance are the rules for channels of publication. The Implementing Regulation

[67] MiFID, Title III, Art 36(1). Ownership information, among other things, would be public (Article 38(2)(a)), and ownership transfers would be subject to public approval (Article 38(3)).

[68] MiFID, Art 37(1). The standard for refusal to approve authorization is 'objective and demonstrable grounds' (Article 37(1)). In addition, people who 'are in a position to exercise, directly or indirectly, significant influence over the management of the regulated market to be suitable' (Article 38(1)).

[69] MiFID, Art 47 (to be updated once a year).

[70] MiFID, Art 39. These include managing potential adverse consequences of conflicts of interest (Article 39(a)), managing significant operational risk (Article 39(b)), developing sound management of technical operations (Article 39(c)), development of 'transparent and non-discretionary rules and procedures that provide for fair and orderly trading' and the establishment of objective criteria for efficient execution of orders (Article 39(d)), effective arrangements to facilitate finalization of transactions (Article 39(e)), and to ensure that the regulated market to have 'sufficient financial resources to facilitate its orderly functioning' (Article 39(f)).

[71] MiFID, Art 40 (requiring the development of 'clear and transparent rules regarding the admission of financial instruments to trading'). Financial instruments admitted are subject to a 'fair, orderly and efficient' trading standard and that such instruments are freely negotiable. Derivatives are also subject to an 'orderly pricing' and 'effective settlement' standards (Article 40(2)). Suspension and removal of instruments is treated at Article 41 of MiFID.

[72] MiFID, Art 42. The access rules are subject to transparency and non-discrimination standards (Article 42(1)), specify who, beside investment firms, may be admitted (Article 42(3)), and to provide 'appropriate arrangements on their territory so as to facilitate access to and trading on those markets by remote members or participants established in their territory' (Article 42(6)).

[73] MiFID, Art 43 ('regulated markets shall monitor the transactions undertaken by their members or participants under their systems in order to identify breaches of [regulated market] rules, disorderly trading conditions or conduct that may involve market abuse'). Significant breaches must be reported to the State (Article 43(2)).

[74] MiFID, Arts 44 (current bid and offer prices and the depth of trading interests at those prices) and 45 ((price, volume and time of transactions executed in respect of shares). Member States may waive the publication of pre-trade information under certain circumstances (Article 44(2)). Member States may also provide for deferred publication of post trade information (Article 45(2)).

[75] See Implementing Regulation 2006. For example, see at Article 27, which elaborates MiFID's post-trade transparency rules to investment forms and regulated markets and operators of MTFs, specifies the sort of information that must be made public with respect to transactions in shares admitted to trading on regulated markets and MTFs.

[76] Implementing Regulation 2006, Arts 29–34.

[77] See Implementing Regulation 2006, Art 29.

permits public dissemination within the meaning of the relevant provisions of the information if 'investors located within the Community' may obtain the information from one of three sources: (1) the facilities of a regulated market or MTF, (2) the facilities of a third party (whether or not located within the Community), and (3) other proprietary arrangements otherwise unspecified.[78]

MiFID also touches on the regulatory structure within the legal orders of the Member States. Article 48 of MiFID requires each Member State to designate a 'competent authority' in which the administrative requirements of MiFID will fall,[79] and to cooperate with peer authorities.[80] MiFID encourages the resolution of consumer complaints by non-judicial alternatives.[81] Finally, in a series of transitional provisions, the ISD[82] is repealed and minimum capital rules are provided for firms which would be exempt from MiFID under Article 3's optional exemption provisions.[83]

B. The Framework of Regulatory Justification

The EU has portrayed MiFID as a multi-objective innovation in legislation. In a June 2006 press release, Internal Market Commissioner Charlie McCreevy was quoted describing MiFID as 'a ground-breaking piece of legislation. It will transform the landscape for the trading of securities and introduce much needed competition and efficiency.'[84] Its virtues for investors rested on the provision of greater protection for investors and greater choice.[85] All this choice and protection pro-

---

[78] Implementing Regulation 2006, Art 30. Arrangements to make information public must satisfy an additional three conditions under the Implementing Regulation. First, there is a reliability assessment, continuous monitoring and correction standard imposed on such arrangements. Second, the arrangement 'must facilitate the consolidation of data with similar data form other sources'. And lastly, information generated through such arrangements must be made available on a 'non-discriminatory commercial basis at a reasonable cost' (Article 32).

[79] MiFID, Art 48. These entities must be public authorities, but 'without prejudice to the possibility of delegating tasks to other entities where that is expressly provided for' (Article 48(2)). Delegations are possible with respect to Articles 5(5) (delegation of administrative, preparatory and ancillary tasks relating to the granting of authorization of investment forms providing only advice or transmission services), 16(3) (same with respect to initial authorization), 17(2) (same with respect to monitoring), and 23(4) (allowing collaboration with investment firms and credit institutions in registering and monitoring tied agents). Designated authorities must be vested with certain powers, sufficient to carry out the requirements of MiFID and its Implementing Directive and regulation. See Article 50. These powers are extensive, touching on broad authority to gain access to information, to suspend trading, and to ensure compliance by elements to the regulated industries. These powers are coupled with extensive sanctioning powers (Articles 51–52).

[80] MiFID, Arts 49, 62. In addition, Member States may conclude cooperation agreements with non-EU States. The focus is on the exchange of information (Article 63(1)), but only to the extent protected by the professional secrecy rules in MiFID. See MiFID, Art 54.

[81] MiFID, Art 53.　　[82] MiFID, Art 69.　　[83] MiFID, Art 67.

[84] See EC Commission, Markets in Financial Instruments Directive ('MiFID'): Implementing Measures Close to Adoption, Brussels, 26 June 2006 (IP/06/846), available online at: <http://europa.eu/rapid/pressReleasesAction.do?reference=IP/06/846&format=HTML&aged=0&language=EN&guiLanguage=fr>.

[85] Ibid.

duced an additional benefit: It should drive down the cost of capital, generate growth and boost our competitiveness.'[86]

'The implementing (or 'level 2') measures develop a number of the provisions set out in the framework (or 'level 1') Directive adopted in April 2004. Having emerged from a lengthy consultation and negotiation phase, they are balanced, proportionate and sensible. They will protect investors and consumers without imposing unnecessary compliance burdens on firms.'[87]

The EC Commission offered seven reasons for pushing MiFID as a necessary replacement to the Investment Services Directive (ISD).[88] The Commission argued that ISD: (1) failed to provide sufficient harmonization to prevent dual/ multiple regulation of firms doing cross-border business; (2) offered little consumer protection with respect to business models and market structures that emerged after adoption of ISD; (3) failed to regulate the full range of investment services; (4) did not provide a satisfactory framework for competition between exchanges and other marketplaces; (5) fragmented liquidity and created barriers to cross border transactions through its failure to adequately harmonize the regulation of exchanges and other marketplaces; (6) failed to provide an adequate level of supervisory cooperation within and between Member States; and (7) was generally otherwise out of date and inflexible.[89] But the FSA remained dubious of the financial integration potential of MiFID, especially in light of the uneven application of its rules to investment firms, markets and financial instruments.[90]

Of special concern was the perceived need to control and harmonize regulation of alternative markets, and in particular: (i) multilateral trading facilities (MTF), (ii) other over the counter facilities and particularly systematic internalisers (SI), firms executing orders from their own account. 'The MiFID requirements on transaction reporting aim to ensure that firms report details of transactions in any financial instruments admitted to trading on a regulated market quickly and accurately to the appropriate competent authority.'[91]

With respect to MTFs, the Treasury had this to say in its December 2005 Report: 'Since the mid-1990s there has been a growth in organised marketplaces

---

[86] Ibid. For the Commissioner, there were additional benefits to the MiFID system: 'MiFID will remove obstacles to firms' use of the EU-wide investment "passport", foster competition and a level playing field between Europe's trading venues, and ensure a high level of protection for investors across Europe.'

[87] Ibid.

[88] Investment Services Directive, Commission Directive 93/22/EEC repealed by MiFID, Art 69, as amended by Directive 2006/31/EC of the European Parliament of the Council ([2004] OJ L114/60 (27.04.04)), Art 1(1).

[89] HM Treasury, Consultation Document: UK Implementation of the EU Markets in Financial Instruments Directive (Directive 2004/39/EC) (December 2005), available online at: <http://www.hm-treasury.gov.uk/media/2E0/CA/ukimplementationeumarkets151205.pdf>, at 2.2 (at 9).

[90] 'The linking of MiFID to the benefits of financial integration also begs the question of how the directive is likely to facilitate greater financial integration.' (HM Treasury, ibid, at 7.17 (at 61)).

[91] FSA, Implementing MiFID for Firms and Markets (July 2006), CP06/14, available online at: <http://www.fsa.gov.uk/pubs/cp/cp06_14.pdf>, at 17.1 (at 119) (hereafter 'FSA 2006').

which have not sought designation as exchanges. These have been run by investment firms and banks using a wide variety of business models and trading a wide variety of financial instruments. MiFID defines such markets as MTFs and establishes a EU-wide set of regulatory standards for them. The purpose is to help facilitate competition between venues for the execution of orders, at the same time as guaranteeing that all market places are governed by standards which seek to protect market integrity.'[92] Some commentators have agreed that MiFID will contribute to increasing competition among exchanges, for example, as competitive markets are changed as a result of regulation of this type on both sides of the Atlantic, but remain sceptical that the additional competition is entirely to the better.[93]

The Treasury report extracts two objectives that may not be as compatible as one might like. The setting of uniform regulatory standards is not necessarily competition enhancing, especially if regulatory competition has economic and market efficiency effects. If one views the development of off regulatory markets as evidence of the opinion of the markets on the efficacy of the current regulatory framework (and its potential privileging of some forms of market making over others), then the effort may well have perverse effects. Moreover, the elaboration of a vast system of private information gathering, storage, and retrieval systems is not cheap, and may have the effect of limiting rather than increasing competition, as the costs of compliance reduce the profitability of the industry.[94] Moreover, expansion of coverage to 'investment advice' was meant to serve consumer protection concerns, rather than market efficiency concerns. Indeed, there was a sense that efficiency might have to take a back seat to consumer protection to enhance the integrity of the markets.[95] Yet, MiFID also permits Member States to exempt financial services intermediaries from MiFID coverage, even those who provide 'investment advice'.[96]

[92] FSA, Consultation Document: UK Implementation of the EU Markets in Financial Instruments Directive (Directive 2004/39/EC) (December 2005), available online at: <http://www.hm-treasury.gov.uk/media/2E0/CA/ukimplementationeumarkets151205.pdf>, at 10.

[93] See, eg I Kokkoris and R Olivares-Caminal, *Some Issues on Cross Border Stock Exchange Mergers*, 29 U Pa J Int'l L 455 (2007) ('Some permutations of mergers may induce competitive harm and thus lead to a post-merger market characterized by a lower degree of competition. This would lower the degree of innovation as well as the improvement of exchange services' (ibid, at 526).

[94] The views from industry are well known and were widely published through trade media in the years leading up to the effective date of MiFID. See, eg, Steve Ranger, MiFID: Cheat Sheet: Banks Get Miffed at New Regulation, Silicon.com, Financial Services (31 October 2005), available online at: <http://www.silicon.com/financialservices/0,3800010322,39153793,00.htm>.

[95] See FSA, Consultation Document: UK Implementation of the EU Markets in Financial Instruments Directive (Directive 2004/39/EC) (December 2005), available online at: <http://www.hm-treasury.gov.uk/media/2E0/CA/ukimplementationeumarkets151205.pdf>, at 10. A recent Commission Green Paper emphasized the value of consumer protection in the construction of integrated markets for financial services in its ongoing regulatory efforts. See EC Commission, Green Paper on Retail Financial Services in the Single Market, COM(2007) 226 Final (Brussels, April 30, 2007) (emphasizing lower prices and more choices for consumers, at 19–23). The Green Paper suggested that MiFID's foundational objective 'is to protect consumers by enhancing responsible behaviour by firms.' (ibid, at 33).

[96] MiFID, Art 3(1).

Like MTFs, SIs present a unique regulatory opportunity from which MiFID does not shy. And indeed, the case of the SI is emblematic of the overarching purposes of MiFID, which is to construct a comprehensive regulatory regime over markets as they have metastasized since the good old days of markets as physical spaces in which people (licensed by the State) traded specific instruments (controlled by the State). The FSA agreed in its July 2006 Report about this aspect of the MiFID regulatory scheme, an aspect it sought to embrace.[97] Referring to MiFID, the FSA was quick to agree with it EU counterparts about the theoretical extent of the scope of MiFID: 'It creates a new, comprehensive EU-wide pre- and post-trade transparency regime for trades in any share admitted to trading on an EU RM, whether those trades are executed on an RM, an MTF or by an investment firm operating outside those systems—ie Over-the-Counter (OTC).'[98] And it agreed that MiFID ended the sort of discretionary loopholes that had made harmonization difficult under the old ISD.[99] Still, the FSA was also quite aware of the limitations built into that comprehensiveness. 'The details of the pre-trade requirements differ according to type of trading venue and trading methodology. They will apply to transactions on RMs and MTFs and also to trading undertaken by investment firms—designated as "systematic internalisers" (SIs)—which, on an organised, frequent and systematic basis, deal on own account by executing client orders outside RMs and MTFs. The details of the post-trade transparency requirements are the same across all trading venues.'[100]

Yet no amount of regulatory enthusiasm can cover the difficulties and contradictions of the actual regulatory scheme. Comprehensiveness might well be an object—but the universe within which comprehensiveness is sought is quite constructed indeed. Thus for example, this wholly regulated world (at least for the moment) is restricted to financial instruments admitted for trading on an EU regulated market (including MTFs). While those financial instruments are broadly defined for purposes of admission to trading, the actual scope of reporting is much more severely limited to equity securities. Thus though regulated markets are indeed regulated, the extent of the regulation is neither uniform nor complete as to the securities admitted to trading. There are good and sufficient reasons for these limitations, but they produce consequences in the aggregate. Among the most important are the creation of incentives to trade in forms that might reduce the compliance costs of the regulatory scheme to the operators of

---

[97] 'The main purpose of these changes is to help regulators uphold the integrity of markets by enabling them to obtain a more complete picture of their firms' trading activities than they can at present.' (FSA 2006, n 91 above.)

[98] FSA 2006, n 91 above: 'MiFID ends the discretion which Member States had under the ISD to require certain transactions to be executed on an RM (the so-called "concentration" rule). The UK had not exercised this discretion.'

[99] 'MiFID ends the discretion which Member States had under the ISD to require certain transactions to be executed on an RM (the so-called "concentration" rule). The UK had not exercised this discretion.' (FSA 2006, n 91 above.)

[100] FSA 2006, n 91 above.

regulated markets as well as to investment firms. That there appears to remain a large unregulated space still in the securities markets suggests the contours of the space within which these changes in behavior will occur.

Lastly, it is clear to all regulators, at least in Britain, that the new transparency obligations can lead to new markets in the provision of information. With respect to the growth industry in private information services that MiFID creates, the FSA appears eager to facilitate growth on a robust global market. In a widely circulated document, the FSA proposed that MiFID firms be permitted to use their choice of 'FSA-approved Trade Data Monitor/s (TDM) to meet their MiFID post-trade publication obligations. Firms could choose on a per trade basis which TDM they want to use.'[101] But more importantly, the FSA announced an intention to refrain from regulating 'the number of TDMs. RMs, MTFs, data publishers and new service providers could choose to be TDMs and be admitted to our list of approved entities. This could include non-UK RMs and other non-UK entities.'[102]

It is possible that some TDMs may choose to outsource some of their services. It is important to note that TDMs would still remain ultimately responsible for meeting their obligations irrespective of whether there are separate outsourcing or other agreements in place (FSA 2006, at 107).

MiFID thus appears to serve as both a market creating and a market regulating vehicle.

In addition, MiFID carries over certain ISD exemptions under MiFID, Art 3,[103] that permit Member States to exempt investment firms providing only investment advice and/or receiving and transmitting orders otherwise brought within the scope of the regulation for the first time. Exemptions are only available where those firms are otherwise regulated at the national level, are not allowed to hold clients' funds or securities, and only transmit orders to a limited list of entities. Moreover, there is a significant consequence to exemption: Where a Member State exercises this exemption the exempted firm cannot take advantage of the free movement provisions in MiFID. It cannot provide cross-border services or establish a branch in another Member State without applying for separate authorizations in the country or countries concerned.

With the possible exception of the new markets in information, the U.K. Treasury's response to MiFID has been guarded. It has expressed the view that:

1.7 The Treasury and FSA have both committed to only go beyond the minimum necessary in implementing EU financial services directives where this is consistent with better regulation. This means where there is a market failure which requires correcting and the benefits of doing so demonstrably exceeds the costs. This approach will be applied to the implementation of MiFID.[104]

---

[101] FSA 2006, n 91 above, at 106. FSA indicated that it 'would publish a list of TDMs on our website so data consolidators would know where to source the trade information' (n 91 above, at 107.)

[102] FSA 2006, n 91 above, at 107.   [103] MiFID, Art 3.

[104] FSA, Consultation Document: UK Implementation of the EU Markets in Financial Instruments Directive (Directive 2004/39/EC) (December 2005), available online at: <http://www.hm-treasury.gov.uk/media/2E0/CA/ukimplementationeumarkets151205.pdf>, at 4.

The FSA has taken a similar approach. In a 2005 speech, posted to the FSA website, Hector Sants, then Managing Director, Wholesale and Institutional Markets at the FSA stated its position as follows: 'Our approach to implementation is intelligent "copy-out" of the MiFID text, with requirements tougher than the Directive only where this can be justified by on cost benefit analysis.'[105] Commentators, like Niamh Maloney, have picked up on this language, describing the FAS's approach as a 'light touch' method of transposition.[106]

The enthusiasm of HM Treasury and the FSA for MiFID and the regulatory project to be undertaken in light of the need to transpose MiFID into national law might be explainable. Other than a change in vocabulary, and perhaps the form of certain processes, MiFID does little violence to the normative regulatory universe within which the FSA has been comfortable and UK financial services sector regulation has developed. And MiFID offers a bonanza of sorts to the industry facilitators—at least from a cynical perspective. It will take a tremendous amount of effort to learn and incorporate the new vocabulary and make the dozens of small but significant changes to operations that the new MiFID language might require.

So there you have it. From the EU's perspective, the MiFID solves any number of problems. Even problems that are essentially conflicting in nature—for example consumer protection, efficiency, and competitiveness within Europe. From the UK's perspective, there is little to MiFID that is earth shattering—the vocabulary is different but the changes might be more or less marginal. It is hard to believe that either institution has it quite right. The EU may overestimate the aggregate benefits of MiFID in particular. It is possible to see in MiFID not so much the solution of old problems as the crafting of categories of new problems (or perhaps better put—of new opportunities for making money from regulatory market distortions) it creates or at least facilitates.[107] And the FSA might

---

[105] See Hetor Sants, Speech by Hector Sants, FSA Annual Public Meeting, 21 July 2005, available online at: <http://www.fsa.gov.uk/pages/Library/Communication/Speeches/2005/0721_hs.shtml>.

[106] N Maloney, 'Financial Market Regulation in the Post-Financial Services Action Plan Era' 55 Int'l & Comp LQ 982 (2006). The article suggests:

'It appears that the new agenda will be characterized by: consolidation and reflection; greater transparency and market consultation; limited legislative intervention; a focus on cost-benefit analysis and more "joined-up" regulation; reliance on softer techniques such as investor education and the integration of market mechanisms and self regulation; and, most importantly, a driving concern to ensure effective implementation and robust supervision of the new regulatory regime in the post-FSAP environment.' (Ibid, at 985.)

Id., at 985.

[107] For example, Compliance LLC offers, through its website, packages for training in financial service sector compliance, including MiFID compliance, and developing methods for taking strategic advantage of the provisions of these new regulations starting at about $10,000. See Compliance LLC, available at: <http://www.mifid-training.net/>. 'SunGard is a global leader in software and processing solutions for financial services, higher education and the public sector' (Sungard, About Sungard, available online at: <http://www3.sungard.com/sungard/default.aspx?id=4>) offers a number of products and facilities to aid its customer base in MiFID compliance. See Sungard, The Markets in Financial Instruments (MiFID) and Sungard, available online at: <http://www3.sungard.com/financial/default.aspx?id=272>.

have to deal with many more changes that are more than skin deep. Both points appear to be at the heart of the financial services sector's reaction to the impending changes to be brought on by MiFID, at least in the UK.[108]

Looking at the totality of that extremely complex project that is MiFID, it is possible to discern two very broad issues with which the entire project is effused. The first is the relationship between regulating States and markets. MiFID broadens the definition of markets (this is a key objective of the new framework) by including two substantially new players in cross-border market regulation: the MTF (multilateral trading facility), and SI (systematic internalisers). MiFID looks to the creation of (or more complete correspondence between) markets and regulators or regulatory units. But at the same time it preserves the EU traditional segmentation approach to markets and securities regulation (one not unknown in the United States).

This focus on the connection between States, markets, and regulation serves to reinforce the policy of functional differentiation among segments of the financial markets—markets or trading in different forms of securities merit distinct regulatory frameworks. The issue is only in conceptualizing the differences and constructing the categories. But there is controversy with respect to both. In the case of MiFID, that means that MiFID regulation is substantially limited to markets in equity securities. Coupled with a willingness in the statutory framework to consider extension to other forms of securities markets after a trial run in equities regulation.

But the embrace of functional differentiation, while segmenting aggregate regulation, tends also to increase the scope and breadth of regulation within each regulated segment. MiFID, within the scope of its regulatory reach thus imposes a more focused regulatory regime targeting information generation and an enhanced power in the State (and its regulators) to intervene in the management of covered markets. The basic objective is to broaden and deepen governmental power to directly intervene in the functioning of capital markets through the medium of 'transactions in shares.'

---

[108] Parsing through the websites of stakeholders in the financial services sector this conclusion becomes more rather than less apparent. Thus, for example, MiFID Connect, a joint program established by The Association of British Insurers (ABI), The Association of Private Client Investment Managers and Stockbrokers (APCIMS), Association of Foreign Banks (AFB), The Bond Market Association, the British Bankers' Association (BBA), Building Societies Association (BSA), the Futures and Options Association (FOA), The International Capital Market Association (ICMA), Investment Management Association (IMA), The International Swaps and Derivatives Association (ISDA) and the London Investment Banking Association (LIBA), has created an extensive network of information for the purpose of 'reducing the legal risk and simplifying the implementation of' MiFID. See MiFID Connect, About MiFID Connect, available online at: <http://mifidconnect. com/bba/jsp/polopoly.jsp?d=569&a=7552>. They argue that MiFID 'will have a major impact on current market and trading practice as well as upon the way in which the financial service sector is currently regulated'. Id. And so have 'embarked on a five-stage programme of work for establishing an industry approach towards implementing MiFID'.

Most analyses have focused on the costs and implementation of these requirements.[109] Transparency is viewed as either a burden (or opportunity) because of the need to produce, keep, and manage more data.[110] Markets in information will surely grow. The 'best execution' standards provide a greater means of standardizing industry practices—with the potential benefit to regulators to which power over market behavior should flow. The focus of this article lies in an equally important but more often neglected aspect of financial services regulation: the potential ramifications of the surveillance and reporting aspects of MiFID as a critical aspect of the character of regulatory power in the financial products sector.[111] Specifically the analysis here will concentrate on the effects of the creation of the markets for information created or augmented through MiFID in terms of the regulation of financial markets and the entities they serve. Particular attention will be paid to the effects of MiFID on consequences in terms of public and private anti-corruption campaigns, the use of these regulations to influence the behavior of issuers and market middlemen, and the potential utility of these regulations to elements of civil society and the media in their campaigns for corporate and capital social responsibility.

III. The Consequences of Monitoring and Managing Markets; Seven Variations on a Theme

The picture presented by MiFID, complexity, order, comity, and direction, all grounded in a proper and legitimate substantive policy, transparency and equality of opportunity for all participants in the regulated market, is what those

---

[109] For some interesting efforts, see, eg E Avgouleas, 'A Critical Evaluation Of The New EC Financial-Market Regulation: Peaks, Troughs, And The Road Ahead' 18 Transnational Law, 179, 188–199 (2005); Mark Tilden et al., MiFID Implementation: Cost Survey of the UK Investment Industry (LECG Ltd, 31 October 2005) available online at: <http://www.fsa.gov.uk/pubs/interna­tional/mifid_cost_survey.pdf>. LECG describes itself as 'a global expert services firm, provides independent expert testimony and analysis, original authoritative studies, and strategic consulting services to clients including Fortune Global 500 corporations, major law firms, and local, State, and federal governments and agencies around the world.' LECG, *About LECG*, available online at: <http://www.lecg.com/website%5Chome.nsf/OpenPage/AboutLECG>.

[110] FSA reports that UK financial services providers already subject to FSA transparency and best execution rules tend to welcome the harmonization provisions of MiFID because they see these changes as bringing continental firms up to UK standards. However, the UK financial sector was less sure of aggregate benefits through this form of harmonization. 'Though great majority of companies thought that the best execution requirement in MiFID will level the playing field in terms of reputation costs and costs of execution, only about two fifths thought that this would create material new opportunities for them as compared to current UK supply.' See FSA, The Overall Impact of MiFID (November 2006), App 2 at 77, available online at: <http://www.fsa.gov.uk/pubs/international/mifid_impact.pdf>.

[111] For a discussion of the character of surveillance as governance, see LC Backer, 'Global Panopticism: Surveillance Lawmaking by Corporations, States, and Other Entities' 15 Indiana Journal of Global Legal Studies (forthcoming, 2008).

who develop, implement, oversee, monitor, and critique, these regulatory frameworks have grown to expect. The quibbles, even the major critiques, as has been suggested, all accept the foundational assumptions on which MiFID is built—information and management overseen by the State. Yet MiFID is far more than that, and its consequences beyond the obvious, might be worth a bit of exploration. This section suggests seven broad but related consequences that MiFID raises, and that will be worth sustained review as this new broad, if segmented, attempt at regulating financial markets is implemented. Together, these themes suggest both the power and limits of regulatory attempts like MiFID to control markets, or to privatize monitoring and redirect it for the benefit of the political community, or to reinforce the State system in the context of behavior that jumps borders, or to achieve broader policy goals, principally criminal enforcement and control of political activity.

A. The Ability of the Private Sector to Organize Markets Beyond the Regulatory Powers/Purview of the State will always Outpace the Ability of the Regulating Entity (the State/EU/etc) to Extend its Regulatory Matrix

The move over 15 years or so from the ISD to MiFID provides a template for the future. The regulation of securities, whether at the framework or detail level, will remain incomplete as long as the markets to be regulated operate beyond the regulatory reach of the State. Market regulation tends to serve as a partial intervention in an area of economic activity that is inherently dynamic and that develops along the lines of its own logic. Regulation, then, is not market defining. Rather, it tends to reduce itself to another factor affecting a dynamic equilibrium to which the market tends.[112]

   Given this essential character of the relationship between public regulation private markets, in which no single State (or grouping of States) can contain capital flows and transactions, MiFID itself must be understood as both partial and temporary. There is likely to be a MiFID II in the next decade.[113] This is something that ought to be well understood by regulators.[114] MiFID itself recognises

---

[112] For a useful discussion, see AM Corcoran, 'The Future is Now—Are We Ready?', 26 No 10 Futures & Derivatives L Rep 1 (November 2006) ('Technology typically precedes the law, but technology should not get so far ahead of the authorities that they are without the resources (either in-house or through contract) to deliver on the financial integrity/customer protection mandate delegated to them. Regulators must recognize when the structure of regulation itself may also need to evolve', ibid).

[113] Already in 2005, the Commission 'identified two areas where carefully targeted, evidence-based initiatives might bring benefits to the EU economy: investment funds and retail financial services'. (EC Commission, White Paper: Financial Services Policy 2005–2010 COM(2005) 629 final, at para 4.4.)

[114] Indeed, the FSA continues to commission studies of future behavior from significant regulatory stakeholders. See, eg KPMG, Financial Advisory Services, The future of advice A report for the

the need for further study and elaboration built into the Directive itself. Still, this is not an argument against MiFID's project. It merely reminds that law, in this case certainly, is attempting the control of a moving target. Regulatory efforts will always inevitably lag behind actual practice, in part because the pace of regulation is generally slower than that of market or individual behavior, and in because individuals (and markets) will tend to change their behavior in light of perceived costs of compliance with regulatory efforts and availability of substitutes or alternatives. Regulation and market behavior thus produce a synergy in which regulation sometimes acts as a catalyst for innovation—if only to avoid or profit, from regulation.[115] MiFID will not deviate form this pattern, and its most interesting consequences may well be the way it forces innovation in markets for financial instruments and in the structure of markets for such instruments in a global context.

The partial and temporary nature of MiFID as currently enacted can be understood in three aspects. First, MiFID is structurally partial. It does not purport to regulate the entire field in which the market understands itself as operating. Second, even in those areas of market activity it does purport to regulate, MiFID does not regulate completely. Because markets tend to change over time, it is possible that MiFID might actually regulate itself either into irrelevance or obstruction. Third, MiFID is geographically partial. MiFID cannot reach related activity outside of the enforcement territory of the European Union and does not seek to prevent the free movement of capital abroad. The first two aspects are discussed below. The last is taken up in the following section.

The structural partiality of MiFID is both deliberate and well understood. It represents both a political compromise and a realization that a more comprehensive regulatory structure might have been institutionally impossible to implement. The segmentation of regulation takes two forms with respect to MiFID. First, MiFID carves out a number of financial instruments and transactions from its coverage, and applied unevenly to those financial instruments or transactions covered by the regulatory scheme. Thus, for example, MiFID's critical

FSA—GI personal lines (May 2006), available online at: http://www.fsa.gov.uk/pubs/other/future_advice_gi.pdf> ('Mindful of its statutory goals and concerned to minimise risk of future regulatory failures, the FSA asked KPMG to build scenarios of what the retail landscape might look like in five or more years time', ibid, at 3). The purpose of these efforts are well known to regulators and stakeholders. 'Like any business, the Regulator plans to use the scenarios to stimulate internal and external debate on the future of retail distribution and use this to inform development of its own regulatory strategy' (ibid, at 3). For the justification in theory, see eg, R Baldwin and M Cave, *Understanding Regulation: Theory, Strategy, and Practice* (OUP, 1999).

[115] For a discussion of this synergy in the context of a discussion of self regulation, from an American perspective, see eg, OH Dombalagian, 'Self And Self-Regulation: Resolving the SRO Identity Crisis' 1 Brook J Corp Fin. & Com L 317 (2007) ('there are many SROs that provide the critical infrastructure needed to ensure fair and efficient markets while sparing the SEC and the public the cost of securities oversight. SROs are also best positioned to debate and promulgate the ethical norms that govern the industry, as long as such responsibilities are confined to those spheres of activity where they work best', ibid, at 318).

transparency rules were drafted to initially concentrate on equities markets, the EU signaling early an unwillingness to extend the transparency regimes even to bonds.[116] Moreover, certain commodities and exotic derivatives, and certain investment firms fall within regulatory exemptions that can be tricky to apply.[117] This may result in market distortion (or at least have a market effect). It may create incentives to other forms of financial instruments by people seeking to avoid regulatory burdens of MiFID, or even by States.[118] But that is unlikely, given the size and centrality of equity markets in global finance. Or it may induce changes in investment firm behavior in light of the form of regulatory exemptions for firms, instruments, or transactions. Still, at the margin, it may increase incentives to innovate in financial instrument products, at least at the margin—producing potential new sources of regulatory interest.[119]

Second, MiFID represents only a partial attempt to regulate the new forms of market internalization in the hands of brokers and other market participants. As Andrea Corcoran rightly notes, broker market internalization initiatives:

have the potential to fundamentally alter market structure in as yet unforeseen ways. To some it may seem as if brokers are purchasing a new governance stake in markets to address their previous concerns about equitable representation within the typical exchange structure. If successful, the apparent consequence could be a "remutualization", around an intermediary, investment bank user base. Whether these changes will result in fragmentation, more or less transparency, or consolidation, depends on their success and collateral effects, as do any regulatory implications.[120]

MiFID thus can change character entirely, from a process-oriented scheme to a scheme with significant substantive value.

---

[116] See eg, EU's McCreevy Rules Out Mandatory Bond Transparency, Reuters, available online at: <http://about.reuters.com/productinfo/compliance/MiFID/news/mandatory_bond_transparency.aspx>. But Member States remain free to regulate in this area. On the FSA's consideration of transparency in secondary bond trading, see eg, FSA, Trading Transparency in the UK Secondary Bond Markets, DP05/5, available online at: <http://www.fsa.gov.uk/pubs/discussion/dp05_05.pdf>.

[117] For an example of the approach of the FSA to this complexity in exemption regimes, see FSA, MiFID and Commodity Derivatives: Update on Scope and Exemption Issues (presentation by Nick Bertram, 26 April 2007), available online at: <http://www.fsa.gov.uk/pubs/international/26apr07_mifid.pdf>, with further guidance to follow.

[118] Consider, at its extreme, the for the moment abortive efforts by elements of the US Government to create a virtual futures market in the likelihood of terror attacks. See M Spann and B Skiera, 'Taking Stock of Virtual Markets' OR/MS Today (October 2003), available online at: <http://www.lionhrtpub.com/orms/orms-10–03/frfutures.html>.

[119] It is no surprise, then, that regulators and the primary stakeholder communities, view extension of transparency rules as troubling. In considering an extension of transparency rules to secondary trading in bonds, the FSA concluded that 'Extreme caution would need to be exercised in mandating greater transparency in the UK and Europe. In particular, we agree with many respondents, and with the conclusions of the CEPR research, that mandating pre-trade transparency is likely to impact on the existing complex market structures, in potentially significant but unknown ways.' (FSA, Trading Transparency in the UK Secondary Bond Markets, Feedback on DP05/5, DP06/04, available online at: <http://www.fsa.gov.uk/pubs/discussion/fs06_04.pdf>, at 5.)

[120] AM Corcoran, 'The Future is Now—Are We Ready?' 26 No 10 Futures & Derivatives L Rep 1 (November 2006).

There are parallels with similar American efforts in this regard. Compare, for example, the recent American efforts in regulation through Regulation NMS;[121] another attempt to recapture regulatory monopoly over markets by extending traditional forms of market regulation to markets that have evolved to avoid either the inefficiencies of those forms of markets or the burdens of the regulations over them. Like its EU counterparts, American regulators are seeking to recapture regulatory control of markets that have evolved beyond the forms reflected in traditional regulatory regimes. As one market analyst suggested in the American context: 'connectivity providers, such as extranet, direct market access, and FIX engine vendors, are the biggest beneficiaries of Reg NMS. Connectivity becomes increasingly important as the markets become more electronic and more formally linked. While the SEC's intention was for investors to reap the biggest benefits, this unfortunately is not the case. The typical retail investor will likely see no difference in the way he or she participates in the equity markets, and the typical institutional investor's job just got harder.'[122] It is possible that a similar result will be produced through MiFID.[123]

The partial nature of MiFID is not merely formal and structural, but is temporally partial as well. Because the market is a moving target, even that portion of it that MiFID purports to regulate will not likely remain regulated to the extent supposed for very long. MIFID does little (nor could it without actually co-opting the market itself) to prevent a market reaction to its rules that produces changes in market focus, norms or structures. It is possible for the market to move beyond MIFID by developing mechanisms not covered by the current regulatory reach. Indeed, it is already possible to point to those areas in which the market has already seeped beyond MIFID and with respect to which regulatory action is likely in the future. Two examples can be illustrated:

---

[121] See Securities and Exchange Commission, Regulation NMS (effective 29 August 2005), Release No 34–51808; File No. S7–10-04, RIN 3235-AJ18, available online at: <http://www.sec.gov/rules/final/34–51808.pdf>.
[122] See Celent Communications, Press Release: Regulation NMS: One Rule to Bind Them All, Report Published by Velent, New York, 18 April 2005, available online at: <http://www.celent.com/PressReleases/20050418/RegulationNMS.htm>. The American approach to alternative trading systems (ATS) generally has been subject to some criticism:
'[T]he American approach is both incremental and bifurcated, building on the existing regulatory framework for brokers and exchanges. This approach has been broadly criticized as insufficiently cognizant of the unique characteristics of an ATS, and as an attempt to pigeonhole ATSs as enhanced brokers or exchanges that merely delays the acceptance of new understandings of the ATS. [fn 47] Commentators have also criticized the Regulation for allowing ATSs to self-identify as either brokers or exchanges, as those that register as exchanges may then regulate the brokers against whom they are competing. Moreover, many ATSs lack the requisite size and depth to register as exchanges, and must thus adopt the broker regime.'
See I H-Y Chiu, 'Securities Intermediaries In The Internet Age And The Traditional Principal-Agent Model Of Regulation: Some Observations From European Union Securities Regulation' 2 Va L & Bus Rev 307, 321 (2007).
[123] See C Kentouris, 'Regulations Rule: Despite Differences Reg. NMS and MiFID Converge on Best Execution and Require Metrics' Security Industry News (4 September 2006), available online at: <http://www.rblt.com/documents/SIN09–06-06.pdf>.

The first focuses on the evolution of over and under thresholds markets. SI markets below current trading thresholds (this one is particularly interesting for the politics it has generated on the eve of the transposition of MiFID). In 2005, there were press reports of the problems to be created when the EC Commission indicated a desire to set the SI threshold at trading 15% of their own shares, with predictions of the addition of 400 new 'markets' adding an additional compliance burdens in the tens of billions of Euro.[124] By the summer of 2006, the Commission had retreated: 'However, the European Commission dropped the 15% rule in early September. As a result, the compliance costs of MiFID for European securities firms have reduced significantly to a total spending of $1 billion, estimates TowerGroup.'[125]

The second focuses on the evolution of non-traditional markets and market mechanisms. These include virtual markets,[126] and Internet markets (including games and simulations, virtual securities and the like).[127] These venues essentially obsolete a regulatory framework grounded in investment firms trading securities invariably authorized for sale on a regulated market in the traditional sense.

Moreover, and quite perversely, the regulatory framework—comprehensiveness within a limited universe of market trading in securities—invites avoidance to the extent that transactions costs are raised by the regulations and cheaper substitutes are available.[128] The hunt for these cheaper (and perhaps more efficient alternatives will likely shape the character of the market and market behavior to some extent. MiFID will increase incentives for the creation of additional new forms of investment vehicles. More importantly, it may adversely affect competitiveness by enhancing incentives for the creation of new (unregulated or differently regulated) fora in which to trade regulated and unregulated (or differently regulated) securities. At the same time, regulatory fragmentation encourages an appetite for expansion, even as the objects of regulation scurry elsewhere.[129]

---

[124] See City Compass, 'Estimates of 400 new Exchanges from Brussels for MiFID' (27 July 2005), available online at: <http://www.citycompass.org/newsarchivefullarticle.asp?msg=41>.

[125] See FinExtra, 'MiFID Compliance Bill Could Reach $1 billion' (4 October 2006), available online at: <http://www.finextra.com/fullstory.asp?id=14339>.

[126] See SL Murphy, 'Momentum Takes Trading Into Virtual Market Setting' Austin Business Journal (13 March 1998), available online at: <http://www.bizjournals.com/austin/stories/1998/03/16/focus6.html> (describing programs developed by Momentum Securities Management Corp that allows consumers to seek the best execution price themselves. See generally, HG Manne, 'Insider Trading: Hayek, Virtual Markets, and the Dog that Did Not Bark' (2005) 31(1) Journal of Corporation Law 167–185, available at SSRN: <http://ssrn.com/abstract=679662>, but see GL Clark, London's Place in the World of Finance: A Supply-side Approach' (25 October 2001), *Working Paper No 01–17*, available at SSRN website: <http://ssrn.com/abstract=288388>.

[127] See eg, P Eckersley, 'Virtual Markets for Virtual Goods', available online at: <http://www.cs.mu.oz.au/~pde/writing/virtualmarkets-revised.pdf> (on virtual markets and copyright).

[128] This point is elaborated at section IV of this article.

[129] Article 65(1) of MiFID, requires the Commission to report on the adequacy of the level of pre- and post-trade transparency in classes of financial instrument other than shares. See eg, European Commission, Internal Market and Services DG, Markets in Financial Instruments Directive (MiFID), Public Hearing on Non-equities Markets Transparency, Brussels, Background Paper (11 September 2007), available online at: <http://ec.europa.eu/internal_market/securities/

The partial nature of MiFID is to be understood both in terms of its comprehensiveness (a point well illustrated above) but also in terms of its geographical limitations. At the margin, it may create incentives for moving markets abroad. As the Americans learned after the paroxysm of burdensome regulation from Sarbanes-Oxley through the terrorism and surveillance provisions post 11 September 2001, markets are global and securities (and capital generally) easily translatable.[130] As a consequence, capital may be hard to regulate from within one territorial space. This is a lesson that American market regulators have been learning, as they discover the difficulties of applying provisions of the Sarbanes-Oxley Act fully, that is, to the actions of firms and their agents without the territory of the United States.[131]

B. Governmental Regulatory Systems Remain Inefficient and Incapable of a Comprehensive Extension of their Control/Coercion Frameworks as Long as Regulation is Limited by the Territorial Principle—However Broadly Applied

Regulation works best when the object regulated is wholly contained within the territorial jurisdiction of the political community seeking to assert regulatory authority. This is the core of arguments that have been asserted for centuries to justify transfers of power from a more local to a more general level of government.[132] It is at the heart of the American constitutional Commerce Power,[133]

docs/isd/hearing_en.pdf>. The most recent report was published as European Commission, Internal Market and Services DG, Markets in Financial Instruments Directive (MiFID), Report on Non-Equities Market Transparency Pursuant to Article 65(1) of the Directive 2004/39/EC on Markets in Financial Instruments ('MiFID'), Brussels (3 April 2008), available online at: <http://ec.europa.eu/internal_market/securities/docs/isd/nemt_report_en.pdf>. The Commission concluded that while there was not yet a need for Community regulation of all such instruments, there might well be a need for transparency regulation 'in the context of retail access to the market prices of bind' (ibid, at 6, p 12).

[130] See R Karmel, 'Reform of Public Company Disclosure in Europe' (2005) 26 University of Pennsylvania Journal of International Economics Law 379.

[131] On the extraterritorial application of the Sabanes Oxley Act of 2002 and its travails, see eg, MD Vancea, 'Exporting U.S. Corporate Governance Standards through the Sarbanes-Oxley Act: Unilateralism or Cooperation?' 53 Duke LJ (2003). See also E Greene and P Boury, 'Post-Sarbanes-Oxley Corporate Governance in Europe and the USA: Americanisation or Convergence?' (2003) 1(1) International J of Disclosure & Governance 21–34.

[132] See eg, the essays in R Howse and K Nicolaidis (eds), *The Federal Vision: Legitimacy and Levels of Governance in the United States and the European Union* (OUP, 2001). The modern criticisms of this sort of centralization are of long pedigree in the United States. See eg, W Thompson, *Federal Centralization: A Study and Criticism of the Expanding Scope of Congressional Legislation* (Harcourt Brace and Company, 1923). For a discussion of federalism and the construction of new centralizing global communities, see eg, essays in R Gibbins and SJ Randall (eds), *Federalism and the New World Order* (University of Calgary Press, 1994). Cf F Beasley, *Power in Business and the State: An Historical Analysis of Its Concentration* (Routledge, 2001).

[133] For a critical analysis, see RH Bork and DE Troy, 'Locating the Boundaries: The Scope of Congress's Power to Regulate Commerce' 25 Harvard Journal of Law & Public Policy (2002).

as well as the internal market of what has become the European Union,[134] and underlies the limiting policy of Subsidiarity as both a principle of EU law[135] and as a generalized principle of governance.[136]

MiFID is based on the same sorts of regulatory justifications: the directives are meant to respond to a problem for which individual Member States cannot adequately regulate, and so regulation (in this case by means of directives functioning as framework regulation) at the more general level of governance is appropriate to resolve the problem. And so it may be, centering on 'yardstick competition' that may lead to harmonization.[137]

Still, while the efficiencies of breaking through Member State regulatory barriers are positive, capital is no longer confined, even within the borders of the EU[138] And so, what appears at first blush to be an attempt at comprehensiveness, may actually also point to the limitations of the regulatory framework. As academic commentators have recently rightly argued:

> the traditional methods that the SEC and its foreign counterparts use to oversee cross-border market activity have lost some of their historical efficacy. Our markets are now interconnected and viewing them in isolation—as we have for so long—is no longer the best approach to protecting our investors, promoting an efficient and transparent U.S. market, or facilitating capital formation for U.S. issuers.'[139]

Territoriality tends to foster the sort of regulatory competition that also can also impede harmonization beyond borders, a problem especially where the reality of economic activity belies the limits of territory.[140]

---

[134] See Commission of the European Communities, Completing the Internal Market: White Paper from the Commission to the European Council, COM (85) 310 Final (June 1985).

[135] See eg, A Estella, *The EU Principle of Subsidiarity and Its Critique* (2002).

[136] See eg, Y Blank, 'Localism in the Legal Global Order' (2006) 47 Harv Int'l LJ 263.

[137] See, eg, P Salmon, 'Political Yardstick Competition and Corporate Governance', in G Ferrarini and E Wymeersch (eds), *The European Union, in Investor Protection in Europe: Corporate Law Making, the MiFID and Beyond* (2006) 31, 41–44.

[138] See EF Greene, 'Beyond Borders: Time To Tear Down The Barriers To Global Investing' (2007) 48 Harv Int'l LJ 85 ('There can be no argument that the securities markets are now global and that the dominance of the United States as the leading player in the global marketplace is being challenged' ibid, at 85). The author, General Counsel, Citigroup Corporate & Investment Banking in 2007, makes a point that can be generalized. For just as the global nature of securities markets challenges the dominance of the Americans, it will challenge the power of the EU to create a contained regulatory framework through MiFID.

[139] E Tafara and RJ Peterson, 'A Blueprint for Cross-Border Access to U.S. Investors: A New International Framework' (2007) 48 Harv Int'l LJ 31, 32.

[140] 'Since the SEC's Concept Release discussing foreign exchange access, the problems involved in allowing foreign exchanges into the United States have become even more intractable because the SEC has passed Regulation NMS, and the EU has passed the Markets in Financial Instruments Directive (MiFID).' (R Karmel, 'The Once and Future New York Stock Exchange: The Regulation of Global Exchanges' (2007) 1 Brook J Corp Fin & Com L 355, 370–371. The problem is not merely one of the arrogance of territorially based power but of ideas. 'Although both laws are to some extent aimed at enforcing best execution obligations in the face of the threat of internalization and fragmentation of securities price discovery mechanisms, they are based on different legal systems, and they are not necessarily compatible' (ibid). Clearly, this poses the traditionally central problem of legal

Considered in this light, the nature of MiFID as both expansive within the scope of its regulatory mandate but limiting in the scope of that mandate becomes clearer. The FSA was clear that the MiFID would apply broadly even if only to a limited universe of financial instruments. They offered as an example the execution of a trade of a share traded on both the London and New York markets. Even if the trade was effected in New York, if the shares were also listed in London, MiFID would apply. However, if the shares are listed only abroad, MiFID might not extend to domestic execution.

As a consequence, MiFID's broadly stated principles are substantially reduced in scope in the application of its technical provisions. And, indeed, what MiFID produces is a host of technical questions on the extent of the limitations to the broad application promised in its purpose. There will be much work for lawyers and regulators with respect to these technical limitations. Here is but one example: will shares traded only by EU MTFs and SIs now qualify as shares admitted to trading on EU regulated markets, including covered MTFs? Or better put, will such shares if not otherwise registered for trading on regulated markets now be required to so register? The effects on trading may be significant.

And more importantly, the constraints of territorially based regulation might create certain perverse incentives. First, is outsourcing. Outsourcing of trading, and the constriction of complex multinational corporate trading enterprises to take advantage of territorially distinct trading environments. Second is emigration of 'citizenship'. If simple emigration is possible and reduces the regulatory burden without affecting business, emigration of 'citizenship' of trading vehicles might prove a hard incentive to resist under the right circumstances, with a consequential incentive to move capital transactions outside the EU. Third, is intensification of a certain drift toward a *movement to a global free movement of capital model*. In this effort the Europeans will be aiding efforts already (inadvertently enhanced by American regulatory effects). Firms may seek to lower transaction costs in trading within unregulated (or differently regulated) global markets (or national markets) beyond the reach of EU regulators and MiFID. This effect may be especially useful with respect to multi-listed shares when regulatory transaction costs are lower elsewhere.

There is an irony here: to the extent that MiFID does not apply to certain investment advisors (because they may be exempted), certain financial instruments (because the transparency rules do not apply to them, for example, or because they are not described in the descriptive Annexes), and certain markets (because they remain unnamed or exempted) regulatory authority remains with the Member States to the extent authorized in their national legal orders.[141] In this

harmonization, a problem has proven increasingly less intractable over the last century. But for all that, it remains a potent force, especially in cases, such as this, where territory may reinforce tendencies to divergence rather than harmonization.

[141] See eg, MiFID, Art 3.

sense, MiFID also compounds the problems of territorially induced regulatory fracture downward as well as upward. This may enhance regulatory competitive-ness[142] but works against market transactional efficiencies.[143]

The limits of territorial jurisdiction is a hard lesson for any State. It is, perhaps, a harder one for a supra-national quasi constitutional entity like the EU. It follows, that MiFID will not be able to reach all activity with effects in the EU, or worse, coerce appropriate behavior from actors who might, instead, respond by moving. These constraints have been recognized in the legal academic literature, which increasingly calls for the adoption of frameworks to avoid the limits of territorially based rules.[144]

C. MiFID Builds in a Certain Tension Between the Traditional Regulatory Approach, which Focuses on Transactions, and the Policy Focus of the Regulatory Framework, which Focuses on Consumers

MiFID essentially attempts that old legislative trick—new wine in old bottles. But it manages to perpetuate the foundational regulatory difficulty of the American approach (an approach that made sense perhaps in the 1930s but that increasingly appears more of an impediment than an enhancement to the attainment of policy goals in a global environment), which focuses on securities transactions and not on consumers. From the perspective of protecting markets, the American approach, now three quarters of a century old, makes a certain amount of sense. Focusing on transparency and equal access to information, it leaves every person free to engage in market activities with whatever intelligence and resources she might have. This system might be optimal in a market populated by a set of relatively equally endowed individuals. But financial markets have been substantially segmented

---

[142] See the essays in W Bratton, J McCahery, S Picciotto, and C Scott (eds), *International Regulatory Competition and Coordination: Perspectives on Economic Regulation in Europe and the United States* (OUP, 1996).

[143] For an interesting reflection on a related issue, see C Bradley, 'Private International Law Making for the Financial Markets' 29 Fordham Int'l LJ 127 (2005) ('International banking organ-izations need to focus not only on the Basel committee's work on capital adequacy, but on the EU's implementation of the Basel standards—in addition to domestic implementation in the different jurisdictions where they are licensed. Some lobbying energy is focused on persuading harmonizers to use the same approaches to particular issues that have been adopted elsewhere. For example, in commenting on CESR proposals, the SIA has urged CESR to copy the approach of U.S. regulators.' (Ibid, at 152–153.)

[144] See eg, E Tafara and RJ Peterson, 'A Blueprint for Cross-Border Access to U.S. Investors: A New International Framework' (2007) 48 Harv Int'l LJ 31, 45 (proposing a system of substituted compliance with SEC registration and reporting rules); EF Greene, 'A Blueprint for Cross-Border Access to U.S. Investors: A New International Framework' (2007) 48 Harv Int'l LJ 85 (arguing that 'SEC should also pursue a substituted compliance framework for issuers. A non-U.S. issuer subject to a robust offering registration regime in its home jurisdiction … should not also be required to comply with U.S. securities registration requirements if it wishes to sell securities to U.S. investors' and vice versa (ibid, at 97)).

for a while.[145] More importantly, securities regulatory agencies have increasingly focused on substantive issues—from shareholder rights,[146] to the composition of the board of directors of public companies[147]—that depart substantially from the no-substance foundation of the traditional securities informatics regime.

The approach confirmed by MiFID does not advance consumer protection beyond the framework adopted nearly a century ago in the United States, but does contribute to the costs of corporate and governmental compliance. It reinforces a managerial relationship between the State and the market for management's sake (that is, for the purpose of keeping active the practice of exercising authority). It increases the costs of business but may also facilitate avoidance through a strategy of careful compliance with increasingly complex statutory norms. MiFID may thus unintentionally provide the appearance of protection but avoids its substantive effects to any appreciable degree.

The transactions approach additionally spawns a related and quite troublesome issue: the resulting complexity of regulation appears to create the sort of markets in avoidance that tends to benefit the middleman classes—principally lawyers and regulators. It is thus possible to characterize MiFID as a regulator's scheme rather than a consumer or market efficiency program. There is a sense that MiFID, like the earlier MAD (the Market Abuse Directive),[148] is a regulator's undertaking.[149] This sense is deepened by the nature of MiFID itself. MiFID is nothing if not (perhaps necessarily) complex. Complexity requires interpretation and usually increases the need for further regulation. The cycle, and the necessary dependency it creates, is well understood.[150]

---

[145] For a discussion in the context of the construction of a global economic order, see H Siebert, *The World Economy* (Routledge, 1999).

[146] For a discussion in the American context, see LA Bebchuk, 'The Myth of the Shareholder Franchise' (2007) 93 Va L Rev 675.

[147] For a critical commentary in light of the changes to US law after the enactment of the Sarbanes Oxley Act of 2002, see R Romano, 'The Sarbanes-Oxley Act and the Making of Quack Corporate Governance' (2005) 114 Yale Law Journal.

[148] Commission Directive 2003/6/EC [2003] OJ L96/16 (12.04.03). There were a number of implementing provisions as well. See Commission Directive 2003/124/EC [2003] OJ L339/70, (24.12.03); Directive 2003/125/EC [2003] OJ L339/73 (24.12.03); Directive 2004/72/EC, [2004] OJ L162/70 (30.4.04); Commission Regulation (EC) No 2273/2003 [2003] OJ L336/33, (23.12.03), 33. For the response of the UK, see discussion in FSA, UK Implementation of the EU Market Abuse Directive (Directive 2003/6/EC): A Consultation Document, June 2004, available online at: <http://www.hm-treasury.gov.uk/media/1/B/market_abuse_parts1and2_180604.pdf>.

[149] See JA Gomez-Ibanez, *Regulating Infrastructure: Monopoly, Contracts, and Discretion* (2003) ('the effort to substitute competition for regulation may actually increase the complexity and importance of the regulator's task', ibid, at 249). Regulators are said to be subject to certain institutional incentives, which to some extent, affects the nature of their relationship, as a class, to regulation and its implementation. Thus, for example, regulators may prefer a regulatory stance that increases their independence from direct and substantial legislative control, and that requires substantial specialization (thus making regulators more remote from both the class of people affected by regulation and the public in general). See eg, WA Niskanen, Jr, *Bureaucracy And Representative Government* (1971); JQ Wilson, *Bureaucracy: What Government Agencies Do And Why They Do It* (1989) 244–48.

[150] See, M Moran, *The British Regulatory State: High Modernism and Hyper-Innovation* (OUP, 2003).

MiFID benefits the *political classes* as well.[151] Regulatory complexities in the purported service of the populace increase the modalities of popular dependence on regulators and other professional classes of 'protectors'.[152] A cynical interpretation, perhaps, this sort of dependency analysis is not less potent for that. In some respects, MiFID joins those large framework regulations that draw power from private relations or other communities, and redirect it to the State (or in this case, a supra-national entity). The dependency model of the relationship of individuals to the State has only increased in the last century.[153] This is not to suggest that the regulatory thrust of MiFID is necessarily wrong, or that regulation will inevitable morph into an uncontrolled complexity.[154] It does suggest, however, that the movement of regulation from private to public, from industry to the State, from providers (or consumers) to political organizations, does tend to shift power generally, and that power concentrations can tend to produce a certain dependency among those regulated.

This last point is not necessarily a policy objective that has been fully aired or resolved. For some, MiFID might suggest another step in the construction of a new sort of feudalism, grounded in dependencies based on regulatory power and complexity. Indeed, Level 3 of the Lamfalussy Process[155] is substantially focused on regulator interaction. Its term of art 'supervisory convergence' appears as the 'great buzzword of all Level 3 Committees, and also of the European Commission White Paper on the post FSAP [Financial Services Action Plan]',[156] though its precise parameters have yet to be determined.

---

[151] Peter Schuck's observations on power incentives in legislation may be useful here: 'Legislators and Their Staff. Legislators might prefer legal complexity for four self-interested, electorally related reasons. Complexity can help them to (1) confer divisible policy benefits on constituents; (2) confer divisible non-policy benefits; (3) enhance their power over bureaucrats; and (4) ease the legislature's collective action problem.' See PH Schuck, 'Legal Complexity: Some Causes, Consequences and Cures' (1992) 42 Duke LJ 1, 27.

[152] At its worst, and following Weberian theories of bureaucratization, see M Schulz, 'Limits To Bureaucratic Growth: The Density Dependence Of Organizational Rule Births' Administrative Science Quarterly (December 1998): 'Bureaucratization is regarded as a rule generation process turned loose. Bureaucracy theorists—as well as much of the general public, including government officials who promise to reinvent government—assume that bureaucracies frantically breed rules, and frequently they imply that rule breeding intensifies as bureaucratization proceeds.' And this process suggests a shift of authority from networks of private organizations (economic, religious, social, ethnic and the like) to a consolidating set of public networks.

[153] For the classic statement, see M Weber, Economy and Society (University of California Press, 1978); M Weber, *The Protestant Ethic and the Spirit of Capitalism* (Peter Smith, 1988).

[154] See eg, B Levitt and JG March, 'Organizational Learning' (1988) 14 Annual Review of Sociology 319–340 (bureaucratization as an aggregation of rules that represent organizational learning); X Zhou, 'The Dynamics Of Organizational Rules' (1993) 98 American Journal of Sociology 98: 1134–1166 (organic theory of bureaucratization and rule growth).

[155] See EC Commission, Commission Staff Working Document, The Application Of The Lamfalussy Process To EU Securities Markets Legislation: A Preliminary Assessment by the Commission Services (SEC(2004) 1459, 15 November 2004), available online at: <http://ec.europa. eu/internal_market/securities/docs/lamfalussy/sec-2004–1459_en.pdf>.

[156] See K Lannoo, 'European Financial Systems Governance' *CEPS Policy Brief* 106:1–7. Brussels: Centre for European Policy Studies Paper (July 2006), available online at: <http://shop.ceps.be/

Still, these observations ought not to be read as any sort of endorsement for a redirection of regulatory focus from transactions to consumer protection by the State and its apparatus. Even a focus on consumers would not necessarily produce perfect, or even perfectly targeted, regulation. This appears to be an unavoidable difficulty of protection based on consumer education in markets characterized by a drive toward perfect information, a point elaborated below.

D. The Transaction Costs of Regulation Create Great Incentives to Avoidance as Capital Seeks its Most Efficient Modality on a Global Basis

As anyone engaged in economic criminal activity can attest, governmental regulation is sometimes best understood as a sort of tax on the activity subject to regulation. Its effects are rarely as straightforward as the thrust of a statute might suggest. Regulation, then, is sometimes better understood as a cost of production, rather than as a normative framework within which human activity occurs. MiFID is, to a large extent, something like a large set of transaction costs, as well as the expression of policies designed to change substantive behavior norms.

The 'tax' or 'transaction' costs of regulation cannot be understated. It is a necessary result of attempted regulatory monopoly (at least within a political territory); though on a global scale segment market monopolies (to the extent that regulatory monopolists compete) disfavors monopolist power. The generated costs of these effects are inevitably reflected in the market and the pricing of its products. If these costs generate comparative inefficiencies they can: (a) reduce profits on an individual or aggregate scale or at the limit; (b) reduce the size and power of the market.

There are several important considerations in this context. In the context of enforcement, the issue of domestic bias arises. MiFID presents large issues of enforcement across borders, not just within the EU but beyond as well. As American commentators have noted in respect of the extra-territorial enforcement of American securities laws against foreign issuers seeking funds in American securities markets, there might well be a domestic bias in enforcement.[157] For one, such enforcement is easier, requires less bargaining with other sovereigns and strengthens domestic institutional power within the borders of its jurisdiction. Still, American commentators have suggested MiFID's traditionally European mutual recognition mechanism as a valuable platform for integration of American and European financial services.[158]

downfree.php?item_id=1340> See generally, T Padoa-Schioppa, *Regulating Finance: Balancing Freedom and Risk* (OUP, 2004) ('a market-friendly response to the globalisation of financial markets calls for closer cooperation between banking, insurance, and securities supervisors.' (ibid, at 2).

[157] See eg, DC Langevoort, 'Structuring Securities Regulation in the European Union: Lessons from the U.S. Experience', *in* G Ferrarini and E Wymeersch (eds), *Investor Protection in Europe: Corporate Law Making, the MiFID and Beyond* (2006) 485, 496–501.

[158] See EJ Pan, 'A European Solution to the Regulation Of Cross-Border Markets' (2007) 2 Brook J Corp Fin & Com L 133, 138.

But the most important effect, in the case of MiFID, might well be the character of the 'leakages' it produces. In this case the leakages work principally to the benefit of middlemen including the usual cast of characters—lawyers, information purveyors, and consulting firms. In this sense, the institutional mechanics of MiFID themselves serve as a market regulator in the sense that the complexity of those mechanics makes it difficult for any investment firm or regulated market to operate without hiring specialists.[159] And to the investor, the system remains substantially opaque—giving rise to another set of specialists who target the consumer end of the regulatory scheme for when 'things go wrong'. But regulatory leakage may extend the application of MiFID beyond its mandatory scope. For example, the FSA has indicated that its particular approach to the transposition of the Directive will likely bring firms within the ambit of MiFID's requirements that otherwise would fall wholly or partially outside the scope of that Directive.[160]

Still, it is unclear if aggregate welfare is increased. Substantial empirical study is required.[161] Thus, for example, if the bulk of the costs of compliance are front loaded, and continuous compliance can take advantage of economies of scale or regularization and routinization of compliance actions, then compliance costs may actually help current players by acting as a regulatory barrier to entry of competitor firms.[162] On the other hand, this regulatory barrier may send more innovative firms unable to successfully compete to other, unregulated markets.

---

[159] Regulatory complexity has spawned a rich area of research in law. See eg, PH Schuck, 'Legal Complexity: Some Causes, Consequences and Cures' (1992) 42 Duke LJ 1. He notes, rightly, that:
'Complexity-induced costs can be both inefficient and unfair. In fields as diverse as agency regulation, trusts and estates, and torts, complexity can inhibit beneficial transactions, impose dead-weight losses, create frustrating delays, consume the energies of talented individuals, breed new and difficult-to-resolve disputes, and discourage compliance. Promoting passivity and entrenching the status quo, legal complexity can stultify a society that often depends on vigorous action in solving problems. Complexity's costs, moreover, impose disproportionate burdens on the poor by raising prices and necessitating the services of lawyers and other professionals trained in the management of complexity.' (Ibid, at 19 (footnotes omitted.)
[160] See FSA, Planning for MiFID (November 2005), at 5 (identifying operators of collective investment schemes, occupational pension scheme firms, life companies and friendly societies, financial advisors that do not hold client assets ands authorized professional firms).
[161] The FSA has considered undertaking some research in this area, especially with respect to transparency and consumer protection. The FSA has proposed a study to 'investigate ways of understanding the market impact of measures used to disclose the price of retail investment products'. See FSA, The Effect of Transparency of Charges on Consumer Welfare, 21 February 2007, available online at: <http://www.fsa.gov.uk/Pages/Library/research/economic/interest/transparency.shtml>. There are additional avenues from the theoretical literature that may prove useful here—for example, complexity theory. See DT Hornstein, 'Complexity Theory, Adaptation and Administrative Law' (2005) 54 Duke LJ.
[162] For example, the FSA, in its popularizing literature speaks of the changes as essentially front loaded in terms of costs. It suggests, for example, to businesses, that '[o]rganization structure, governance oversight, policies and procedures and trading and infrastructure are of critical importance, but MiFID will have an impact on many other functions in firms.' (FSA, Planning for MiFID (November 2005), at 7 (identifying the need to consider institutional and operational changes in IT systems, client services, client management, data capture and retention, branch structure, legal, internal audit, trading execution, compliance, risk management, marketing and human resources recruitment and

E. The Greatest Effect of MiFID is the Creation (Potentially at Least) of Robust Markets in Information

Like many recent legislative efforts, MiFID produces unanticipated regulatory consequences. In this case one such consequence is particularly interesting from a markets point of view. MiFID's legislative requirements effectively advance the creation of a new and potentially large contribution to a dynamic market—the market for information. More specifically, MiFID may serve to invigorate markets in the information required to be produced by the legislation.

In this regard, consider, for example, the new Trade Data Monitoring regimes described in the FSA 2006 report.[163] The FSA was concerned about the effect of the new rules on its regulatory framework.[164] As a consequence of MiFID's flexibility rules, 'the number of providers of trade processing services for transactions executed away from RMs and MTFs is likely to increase. While we recognise the benefits and opportunities that competition could bring in this area, it also poses risks for the overall quality of market data.'[165] Among the greatest risks, the FSA feared data fragmentation as a consequence of the 'ability for firms to assert ownership rights over their trade data' in more fractured markets,[166] and a deterioration of the integrity of market data.[167] The solution might be more regulation,[168] a regulated market in data in which approved trade data monitors (TDMs) 'would check the trade publications in real-time for potential inaccuracies and arrange for the information to be made publicly available in a way that facilitates its consolidation with similar data from other sources'.[169] The FSA's proposal is meant to recognize both the commercial value of trade information, and to manage a market in such information consistent with its traditional regulatory goals and the framework rules of MiFID.[170]

MiFID's new regime will thus produce significant competitive pressure on traditional information sources—especially on traditional regulated markets,

---

training.) But these changes tend to be of a type that requires a large initial investment of resources, the marginal cost of compliance with which will decrease over time as changes become routinized and internalized within firm culture. Indeed, the FSA has estimated a broad range of costs, from small to fairly significant to both the State and affected firms depending on the extensiveness of the transposition necessary. See HM Treasury, Consultation Document: UK Implementation of the EU Markets in Financial Instruments Directive (Directive 2004/39/EC) (December 2005), at 7.59–7.99, available online at: <http://www.hm-treasury.gov.uk/media/2E0/CA/ukimplementatio-neumarkets151205.pdf>.

[163] See FSA, Implementing MiFID for Firms and Markets (July 2006), CP06/14, available online at: <http://www.fsa.gov.uk/pubs/cp/cp06_14.pdf>.

[164] 'MiFID allows investment firms a choice over the means by which they make public their post-trade information. In principle, this creates a risk of fragmentation of post-trade data, which could undermine the efficiency of UK equity markets.' (Ibid, 13.10, at 74.)

[165] Ibid, 16.64 at 105.   [166] Ibid, 16.65 at 105.   [167] Ibid, 16.66 at 105.

[168] Ibid, 16.69, at 105–106.   [169] Ibid, 16.71, at 106.

[170] 'We recognise there may be commercial value in trade information, and investment firms would be entitled to realise that value. This is in keeping with the overall objective of enhancing competition in the provision of trade information.' (Ibid, 16.74, at 106.) For an elaboration of the proposal itself, see ibid, 16.71–16.87.

which had enjoyed substantial information monopolies. And here is a potential perversity of MiFID, by extending regulation of securities markets in traditional form it may hasten the elaboration of nontraditional market structures for securities. Adding a layer of regulation and transaction (information) costs within a structure in which the markets affected may not be able to capture the income from the added transactions (in information), may substantially and negatively affect those markets. Might it be relevant to ask now: are the Exchanges now closer to obsolescence? The recent merger activity among traditional exchanges suggests that they are conscious of this effect.

The extent of the effect will be a function of the success of MiFID in *disaggregating* markets in transactions for securities (the traditional primary activity of markets) from markets for information on transactions in securities (a new product that MiFID enhances). Disaggregation is the key here to industry creation (information) and regulatory segmentation.

Lastly, it will be important to remember that the emerging *markets for information on transactions in securities* will generate its own regulatory distortions and interventions. The FSA's 2006 Report already points in that direction.[171] And one of those distortions may well affect the character of fiduciary duty standards in Europe.[172] Another suggests that the devolution of mandatory disclosure and publication requirements effects a privatization of public functions that both co-opts the regulated to some extent, and devolves sovereign authority as well.[173] The issue of managed self-regulation on the fundamental character of private enterprises has still to be satisfactorily explored. But its implications for both public and private governance may be significant.[174]

It is also important to remember that even robust markets in information would not necessarily guarantee any level of the sort of consumer protection heralded by the drafters of MiFID.[175] This complicates any effort to reform the focus of markets regulation.[176] Gabaix and Laibson argue that 'informational shrouding flourishes even in highly competitive markets, even in markets with costless advertising, and even where the shrouding generates allocational inefficiencies.'[177]

---

[171] See discussion, at nn 152–159 above.

[172] See AF Loke, 'From the Fiduciary Theory to Information Abuse: The Changing Fabric of Insider Trading Law in the U.K., Australia and Singapore' (2006) 54 Am J Comp Law 123 (examining the way in which a 'parity of information norm' grounding securities regulation in the UK has substituted for traditional fiduciary theory).

[173] For an elaboration of this argument, see I H-Y Chiu, 'Delegated Regulatory Administration In Mandatory Disclosure—Some Observations From EU Securities Regulation' (2006) 40 Int'l Law 737.

[174] For a discussion in the context of corporate social responsibility, see LC Backer, 'Multinational Corporations, Transnational Law: The United Nation's Norms on the Responsibilities of Transnational Corporations as a Harbinger of Corporate Social Responsibility as International Law' (2006) 37 Columbia Human Rights Law Review 287.

[175] See X Gabaix and D Laibson, 'Shrouded Attributes, Consumer Myopia, and Information Suppression in Competitive Markets' (2006) 12 The Quarterly Journal of Economics 505–540.

[176] See discussion, above, at text and nn 145–156.

[177] Ibid.

These tendencies are especially apparent where product markets have close sub-stitutes. The securities markets of course are replete with substitutes. In the case of MiFID, the focus on equities within a larger but less comprehensive regulatory framework provides venues for the development of regulation avoiding substitute markets and instruments.

F. MiFID Deepens a Surveillance Culture in the Construction of Governance Institutions

MiFID continues and deepens a global process of privatizing surveillance. In this sense, MiFID may be not only a regulators' undertaking, but also more pre-cisely an undertaking for the benefit of the police authority of the State.[178] As government power has become more total, as it has asserted a superior authority and the right to govern in those areas once left to other social, cultural, and eco-nomic communities within the State, the nature of governance has had to evolve to fit the new boundaries of governance. Government power has evolved from limited scope statutes to vast amorphous systems of governance mimicking the complex web of relations once evolving outside of its control.[179] With respect to the governance of economic activity in particular, that broadening has sought to mimic within governmental functions the networks of regulation once asserted by self-regulating stakeholders (for their own benefit).

Since the last quarter of the twentieth century, the State (at least in the West) has sought to do two things simultaneously. First, it has sought to gather more and more information on all operations within its territory (and beyond to the extent relevant). The information has a variety of uses. Information is a critical component of law enforcement. Information is also vital to the ongoing develop-ment of policy. Its availability also benefits the various sectors of the stakeholders in the particular market for information (the disclosure regimes of the American Securities laws for the benefit of the investor class is a classic example). At its

---

[178] See LC Backer, 'Surveillance and Control: Internal, External and Governmental Monitoring of Corporate Insiders After Sarbanes-Oxley' (2004) Michigan State Law Review 327.

[179] Thus, for example, I have explained how recent American securities law changes memorialized in the Sarbanes-Oxley Act of 2002:

'sought to legislate an architecture of corporate discipline, and from that discipline, to develop and impose substantive behavior norms tied to the forms of externally imposed self-discipline. That architecture of corporate discipline—essentially hierarchical, continuous, and integrated within the core of the institutional governance architecture, like Jeremy Bentham's Panopticon, defines a structure of information gathering centrally focused on corporate directors who are required to "see" everything. Yet these seers are themselves "seen" by the ultimate regulator. That ultimate regulator, the federal government, selects the data to be gathered, deploys corporate outsiders to monitor inter-nal surveillance efficiencies, defines the boundaries of effective analysis (that is of analysis with legal effects), and selects the judgment to be made from certain clusters of information, but not from oth-ers.' (LC Backer, 'Global Panopticism: Surveillance Lawmaking by Corporations, States, and Other Entities' 15 Indiana Journal of Global Legal Studies (forthcoming, 2008), citing in part, J Bentham, *Panopticon, or, The Inspection House, & C* (1787), reprinted in Miran Bozovic (ed), *The Panopticon Writings* (1791) (Verso 1995) 29–95.

broadest scope, information can serve in the development and influence on (in totalitarian regimes control of) political, social, economic, and other respects of culture (that is information gathering has normative consequences well exploited by the State).[180]

Second, States have sought to privatize information gathering for its own use in the disciplining of social organization. Government has sought to make surveillance a reflex. It is organized as a 'multiple, automatic and anonymous power; for although surveillance rests on individuals, its functioning is that of a network of relations from top to bottom, but also to a certain extent from bottom to top and laterally; this network "holds" the whole together and traverses it in its entirety with effects of power that derive from one another: supervisors, perpetually supervised.'[181]

MiFID represents another step in the implementation of systems of '[h]ierarchized, continuous and functional surveillance'[182] through which 'disciplinary power became an "integrated" system, linked from the inside to the economy and to the aims of the mechanism in which it was practiced.'[183] To a great degree, MiFID is about the spreading of information. But not all information, just those pieces of information selected by the government (and by that selection privileged) required to be gathered, dispersed, by whom, to whom and when. The system has the benefit of being driven by those who are meant to be regulated by it, with the State sitting in the background monitoring the monitors.

The nature of the information to be gathered itself will produce both compliance and reaction. The population itself embraces systems through which it serves as the very instrument of its discipline, but with a twist—resistance to participation in surveillance itself becomes a transgression. The emphasis is so great because the stakes have become so high—stability and the management of the State and its relations both domestic and international. This leads to the last point.

G. MiFID Adds another Element to the Global Efforts to Manage Conflict and Crime

MiFID is important not only in its own right, but also in its role as an element in the global efforts to manage conflict and crime. It serves as a nexus point for the regulation of economic activity, crime, and political conflict. MiFID's multiple objectives thus add a layer of additional complexity, the resolution of which is deferred.

---

[180] See M Foucault, *Discipline and Punish: The Birth of the Prison* (A Sheridan, trans) (Vintage Books, 1977), at 170–177; M Foucault, T*he History of Sexuality; Vol I: An Introduction* (R Hurley, trans) (Random House, 1978), at 89–91.

[181] M Foucault, *The History of Sexuality; Vol I: An Introduction* (R Hurley, trans) (Random House, 1978), at 176–177.

[182] M Foucault, *Discipline and Punish: The Birth of the Prison* (A Sheridan, trans) (Vintage Books, 1977), at 176.

[183] Ibid.

While the direct objectives of MiFID are to benefit consumers and the market (efficiency, competitiveness, protection), its more potent beneficiaries may be the police, military, and secret service sectors of governments. Information, like munitions in an earlier age, appears to have become among the most important components of war. And war, like any other activity, is difficult enough to maintain without capital. In this case, information gathering both shapes the nature of efforts to produce it (thus privileging those matters with respect to which information is gathered) and suggests the diffusion of power among the State and those who are responsible for gathering these goods. Where markets become part of the battlefield (in this case against the financing of illegal activity, whether political or economic) both direct regulation, and the co-opting of private entities in the war effort follow. But this suggests a distortion of purpose (no longer fixated on consumer protection directly) and those distortions (or expansions of purpose) will affect the utility of the regulation for all of its beneficiaries. Confusion in this case is likely to follow as stakeholders compete for maximization of benefit from the regulatory scheme. MiFID, in this sense, evidences the move to governmentality nicely described by Foucault.[184] 'One of the most notable features of governmentality research has been its investigation of power "beyond the state," that is, with the tactics, techniques and technologies which configure apparently "non-political" sites like the firm or the school as spaces of power.'[185] And so it is with MiFID.

Market regulation, of which MiFID is representative, also can be understood as a method for the management of crime in three respects. First, it serves in the expanding global movement to identify and suppress corruption. Anti-corruption campaigns have become a focal point of global governance efforts in hard and soft law. For example, both the World Bank and the Chinese Communist Parties are at the forefront of these at the moment.[186] Related to anti-corruption campaigns are efforts to prevent organized money laundering. Governments, in particular, have been targeting criminal gang activity because of its use as a principal form of banking for political and military campaigns waged by insurgent and anarchist groups. Third, and more generally, are efforts against financial fraud. This

---

[184] See M Foucault, 'Governmentality', in G Burchell, Colin Gordon, and P Miller (eds) *The Foucault Effect: Studies in Governmentality* (1991) 87.

[185] M Foucault, 'Security, Territory, and Population', in M Foucault, *Ethics: Subjectivity and Truth* (P Rabinow, ed) (1997) 67–71.

[186] The World Bank has 'identified corruption as among the greatest obstacles to economic and social development. It undermines development by distorting the rule of law and weakening the institutional foundation on which economic growth depends.' See World Bank, Anti-Corruption, available online at: <http://web.worldbank.org/WBSITE/EXTERNAL/TOPICS/EXTPUBLICSECTORANDGOVERNANCE/EXTANTICORRUPTION/0,,menuPK:384461-pagePK:149018-piPK:149093-theSitePK:384455,00.html>. The Chinese Government's increased emphasis on anti-corruption campaigns was nicely expressed in a January 2007 speech by Chinese President Hu Jintao. See 'Hu Charts Path in Anti-Corruption Drive' *People's Daily Online* 10 January 2007, available online at: <http://english.peopledaily.com.cn/200701/10/text20070110_339797.htm>.

reflects what appears to be a growing conflation between banditry and politically motivated violence.[187] Consider the reluctance of the House of Lords to approve the extradition treaty with the United States[188] in the wake of the use of anti-terrorism based extradition powers on English bankers and other financial types for violation of US financial fraud or securities laws.[189]

Market regulation that is, the management and control of the vehicle through which vast amounts of wealth are negotiated, has acquired a military and national defense character as well, especially as a weapon in the political and economic aspects of modern warfare. These include the financing of terrorist or politically violent movements,[190] attempts at market disruptions as a tactic of war by combatant organizations,[191] and criminal financial activity with politically destabilizing effects. Where these activities are conflated there is a necessary convergence of the need for market surveillance and for the use of markets as a source for data gathering and the needs of the police and military wings of the State apparatus.

Putting all of this together, the fundamental character of MiFID might be better understood. Indeed, it is impossible to understand MiFID except in its broader context. MiFID is at once about market regulation, the creation of new industry (information production), the privatization of governmental functions (surveillance and data gathering), and also the management of crime and of political conflict. Ironically, as a means of subsidizing traditional exchanges (by bringing competitors within the regulatory matrix within which they operate), MiFID's utility is doubtful at best. Yet, it will have substantial effect. And perhaps there is a substantial sort of utility in that.

---

[187] See eg, MG Manwaring, *Street Gangs: The New Urban Insurgency* (Strategic Studies Institute, 2005) ('more than half of the countries in the world are struggling to maintain their political, economic, and territorial integrity in the face of diverse direct and indirect non-state—including criminal gang—challenges').

[188] In 2006, the UK House of Lords in 'a vote of 189–152, Parliament's upper house approved a measure demanding an end to the streamlined extraditions to the United States. By a vote of 171–138, the Lords backed another measure which would restrict the ability to extradite to America if the alleged offense was partly committed in Britain.' See House of Lords Vote Against British-US Extradition Rules, San Diego Union Tribune, 1 November 2006, available online at: <http://www.signonsandiego.com/news/world/20061101-1527-britain-us-extradition.html>. The House of Lords later relented. See 'House of Lords Backs Down in Amending US Extradition Treaty' Islamic Republic News Agency, 25 August 2007, available online at: <http://www.irna.ir/en/news/view/line-20/0611083829182031.htm>.

[189] 'Three British bankers have already been extradited under the treaty to face fraud charges in the US connected to the collapse of Enron, while two Muslims are in the process of appealing against being sent to face US trials on alleged terrorism charges.' ('House of Lords Backs Down in Amending US Extradition Treaty', ibid.)

[190] See eg, B Zagaris, 'The Merging of the Counter-Terrorism and Anti-Money Laundering Regimes' (2002) 34 Law and Policy in International Business 45; Z Abuza, 'Funding Terrorism in Southeast Asia: The Financial Network of Al Qaeda and Jemaah Islamiya' (2003) 25(2) Contemporary Southeast Asia 169; Cf S Biddle, *Afghanistan and the Future of Warfare: Implications for Army and Defense Policy* (Strategic Studies Institute, 2002).

[191] See eg, J Robb, *Brave New War* (Wiley, 2007).

IV. Conclusion

MiFID presents an interesting picture. On the whole it represents a positive development for Europe; it is a signal that Europe is ready to compete on an equal basis with the United States for control of the cultural understanding of the norms applicable to transactions in securities from which global harmonization will eventually arise. Yet it is not without certain peculiarities consonant with the form of regulation undertaken. On the one hand, it ties in nicely with current common understandings of the most appropriate communal approaches to the regulation of securities markets. That common understanding increasingly emphasizes surveillance and monitoring as both enforcement technique and substantive objective. But it also accepts, to some extent, the imperfect nature of regulation. And thus MiFID tends to focus regulation on problem management rather than on their control or eradication. But partial regulation will produce other than the intended effect. That is the nature of markets—in this case markets for regulation. Where MiFID fails to regulate, others will step in, and States will eventually follow. This article examines the potential consequences of MiFID in this regulatory context. It has suggested that MiFID may be as important for the markets in information that it spawns than for the market defects it seeks to manage.

Political Path Dependency in Practice: the Takeover Directive

*Beate Sjåfjell**

I. Introduction[1]

Unlike much that has been written about the Takeover Directive,[2] where the focus has been on the technicalities of its provisions, and its implementation in the laws of the Member States, this paper looks at the Directive from a bird's-eye perspective before exploring the three issues set out below.

Firstly, taking the implied and express premises of the Directive as read, we attempt to assess the Directive on its own terms. Taking a step back, we then consider whether these same premises form a sound basis for legislative action. Finally, we take an even bigger step back and consider the Directive's overall perspective. Is this perspective, which forms the basis of the Directive's premises and provisions, sufficiently wide and is the Directive's scope sufficiently all-encompassing?

II. The Directive on its Own Terms

A. The Terms

The main idea underpinning the Directive is that of the market for corporate control.[3] The Directive seeks to promote the market for corporate control because

* Dr juris and postdoctoral research fellow at the Department of Private Law, Faculty of Law, University of Oslo, email: b.k.sjafjell@jus.uio.no (comments are welcome). This paper was written in the stimulating environment of the Centre for European Law at the Faculty of Law in Oslo, during the author's research fellowship there.

[1] I am grateful to Professor Takis Tridimas for inviting me to present this paper at the CCLS/ERA conference 'EU Financial Services Regulation: Completing the Internal Market' in London, October 2006. I would also like to thank the participants at the conference for a stimulating discussion, and Professor Hans Petter Graver, and most especially Professor Ola Mestad, for insightful comments to an early draft of this paper, as well as Professors Luca Enriques and Steef Bartman for inspiring feedback to a later version. The usual disclaimers apply.

[2] Directive 2004/25/EC on takeover bids ([2004] OJ L142/12–23).

[3] The term was coined in an article in 1965, see H.G. Manne 'Mergers and the Market for Corporate Control' (1965) 73 The Journal of Political Economy, 110–120, but apparently the theory

it is assumed that its intended dual effect—disciplining managers and facilitation of restructuring—will be beneficial for European businesses.

The market for corporate control is said to have a disciplining effect because it is thought to lead to the most efficient use of company resources, both preventively (the board/management will be kept on their toes for fear of a takeover that will lead to their replacement) and curatively (takeovers will ensue where the board/management is not up to scratch, and those replacing them will do a better job). This is clearly linked to the original principal-agent issue, where managers are seen as agents for the shareholders (the principals) and the problem to be addressed is managers' unwillingness to act wholly in the shareholders' interests. This issue is regarded as most relevant to companies with dispersed shareholders, as it is seen as difficult for dispersed shareholders to coordinate their efforts to monitor and discipline managers themselves.[4]

Further, the market for corporate control is supposed to have a positive effect on resource allocation, contributing to a necessary restructuring of businesses by channelling capital from stagnating areas to areas that are new and innovative. Here the rationale is that managers are not necessarily the first to (want to) realise that their company needs to be restructured, relocated, or even shut down. Takeovers therefore have a beneficial effect of 'creative destruction'.[5]

The Commission-appointed High Level Group of Company Law Experts (known as the Winter Group)[6] emphasizes the view that 'actual and potential takeover bids are an important means to discipline' management and facilitate restructuring.[7]

One might therefore assume that the main goal of the Takeover Directive is to maximize takeovers—ie facilitate as many takeovers as 'the market' desires.[8]

---

itself was first presented by R Marris, see the chapter on 'A Theory of Take-over', in R Marris, *The Economic Theory of 'Managerial' Capitalism* (Macmillan, 1964) 29 *et seq*. It was to take several decades and a takeover wave in the 1980s in the USA before the market for corporate control became a commonly used term in company law debates.

[4] Because of the so-called free-rider problem, leading to rational apathy.

[5] RG Rajan and L Zingales, *Saving Capitalism from the Capitalists. Unleashing the Power of Financial Markets to Create Wealth and Spread Opportunity* (Crown Business, 2003) 1, using the term generally about the process that 'vibrant, innovative' financial markets keep alive.

[6] The Winter Group was given the difficult task of finding a way out of the deadlock after the compromise proposal adopted by the Conciliation Committee on 6 June 2001 failed to obtain the required majority in the European Parliament on 4 July 2001. The full text of the Winter Takeover Report may be found at: <http://ec.europa.eu/internal_market/company/docs/takeoverbids/2002-01-hlg-report_en.pdf>.

[7] Together with the possible synergy effect of takeovers, see the Winter Takeover Report, p 19. Due to time and space constraints, the focus is here on the alleged disciplining and restructuring effect.

[8] This is not said explicitly in the preamble of the Directive, which focuses rather on the protection of especially the minority shareholders, see inter alia Recitals 2, 9, and 25, although some indication may be found in Recital 3: '... to prevent patterns of corporate restructuring within the Community from being distorted by arbitrary differences in governance and management cultures', and Recital 19: 'Member States should take the necessary measures to afford any offeror the possibility of acquiring majority interests in other companies and of fully exercising control of them'. The focus on protection in the preamble may at least partly be explained by reference to the legal basis of the Directive,

The intended result of the supposedly beneficial dual effect of the market for corporate control on European businesses, as outlined above, is that businesses will become more competitive and in general promote the objectives of the Lisbon agenda: a vibrant economy, more jobs and so on. As such, this attempt to complete the integration of the financial market through the Takeover Directive, which has been characterized as 'the missing plank',[9] may be seen as a part of the EU's general goal of economic development.[10]

B. The Main Tools of the Directive

(i) An Overview

The Takeover Directive contains a number of presumably sensible provisions that we will not go into here. These concern: rules on cooperation between Member States in the case of cross-border takeovers regarding supervisory authorities and choice of law;[11] requirements for all Member States to have various rules regulating the bid process;[12] and rules on information and transparency in takeover attempts.[13] Our assessment of the Directive instead focuses on its three main substantive provisions: board neutrality, breakthrough, and the mandatory bid.[14]

(ii) The Board Neutrality Rule

The board neutrality rule, contained in Article 9(2)–(4) of the Takeover Directive, requires the board of the target company to remain passive during a takeover attempt.[15] That is, the target board is not allowed—without the consent of the shareholders—to do more than inform the shareholders about the bid and its merits. Article 9(5) provides details of the opinion that the board must give concerning the bid and also imposes a requirement that employees must be included in this process. It is not sufficient for the board simply to have the consent of the last shareholders' general meeting to the taking of defensive action at the board's discretion if a takeover attempt should occur. The consent of the shareholders

Article 44(2)(g) of the European Community Treaty (EC Treaty), which focuses on the protection of shareholders 'and others' (typically creditors and employees); see Recital 1 of the Directive.

[9] Proposal for a Directive on Takeover Bids, Frequently Asked Questions (MEMO/02/201) 2 October 2002, p 2, characterizing the Directive as necessary to achieve 'a truly integrated EU capital market'—without the Directive a 'huge plank of the Internal Market would be missing'.

[10] See Article 2 of the EC Treaty.

[11] Takeover Directive, Art 4. However, whether the choice of law rules are precise and appropriate enough to fulfil their role, is an open question.

[12] Takeover Directive, Arts 7 and 13.

[13] Article 6 on information concerning the bid including the bidder's intentions; Article 8 on disclosure of the bid; and Article 9(5) requiring the target board to make public its opinion on the bid, with a right for the employees of the target company to make their view known.

[14] Takeover Directive, Arts 9, 11, and 5, respectively.

[15] And refrain from 'taking any action [...] which may result in the frustration of the bid and in particular before issuing any shares which may result in a lasting impediment to the offeror's acquiring control of the offeree company' (Takeover Directive, Article 9(2)).

must be given in a general meeting after the bid has been announced, the rationale being that shareholders can only consider an actual bid and will be unable to
make prudent decisions concerning hypothetical takeover attempts.[16] The only
exception to this passivity rule is that the board may actively go out and seek to
bring other bidders to the table. The permissible actions on the part of the target
board are therefore mainly intended to ensure that the target shareholders get as
high a price—if they decide to sell—as possible.

The board neutrality rule is obviously designed to make takeovers easier in principle, as defensive actions by the board might make takeovers impossible, more
expensive or at least more time-consuming. The rule goes straight to the heart
of one of the biggest and oldest controversies in European company law, which
concerns diverging views regarding the purpose of the company and the role of
the board. This meant it was impossible to garner sufficient political support to
make this rule obligatory and, to bring an end to the Directive's long and tortuous
negotiating history, an optionality clause was introduced.[17] Per September 2007,
it appears that seven Member States will opt out (Belgium, Denmark, Germany,
Italy, Luxembourg, The Netherlands, and Poland), while the rest opt in.[18]

(iii) The Breakthrough Rule

The breakthrough rule contained in Article 11 of the Takeover Directive allows
acquirers to break through certain control structures, such as the system of A/B
shares typical, for example, in Sweden,[19] while leaving others, such as the pyra-
mid structures typical of Italian companies,[20] untouched.[21] The main condition

---

[16] The Winter Takeover Report, pp 27–28.   [17] Takeover Directive, Art 12.
[18] Commission Staff Working Document: Report on the Implementation of the Directive on
Takeover Bids, SEC(2007)268, Ann 1, p 12; giving the details regarding 17 Member States that had
implemented the Directive and the eight others that had made clear their plans to do so per January
2007 (the report is based on the Member States' answers to a Commission questionnaire regarding
the transposition of the Directive). Since the report was published, also Belgium and The Netherlands
have transposed the Directive, leaving per 26 September 2007, Italy and Poland as the opt-out countries that have not yet finished the transposition process (personal information from the Commission,
notes on file with the author). The three EFTA States, Norway, Iceland, and Liechtenstein are not
included in the Commission's overview, although all three states are obliged to implement the Takeover
Directive in accordance with the EEA agreement. Norway has opted out of the board neutrality rule,
not because of an objection to a board neutrality rule in principle, but because of a sceptical attitude
as regards the wisdom of the Directive's far-reaching neutrality rule with no general exception for
decisions that are part of the natural day-to-day business of the company such as the Norwegian rules
have; see B Sjåfjell 'Report from Norway' (2006) 3 (issue 1) European Company Law 35–39 [as in the
printed version], regarding the then proposal for implementation, since adopted in *Lov om verdipapirhandel* (The Norwegian Securities Trading Act) (29 June 2007 No 75).
[19] R Skog 'The Takeover Directive, the "Breakthrough" Rule and the Swedish System of Dual
Class Common Stock' (2004) 15 European Business Law Review 1439–1451.
[20] M Bianchi, M Bianco, and L Enriques, Pyramidal Groups and the Separation between
Ownership and Control in Italy (Working Paper, 12 July 1999), available online at: <http://ssrn.
com/paper=293882>.
[21] The rule was proposed by the Winter group in a more extensive version, encompassing, inter
alia, 'golden shares' in privatized enterprises (specifically excluded in the Takeover Directive, see
Article 11(7)); the Winter Takeover Report, pp 29–36.

for breakthrough is that the acquirer must have purchased 75% of capital with voting rights.[22] The breakthrough lasts for the duration of the takeover process, including a general meeting of shareholders that the acquirer may convene to amend the articles of association[23] or to replace the board, thereby enabling the acquirer to achieve control.

This rule is even more controversial than the board neutrality rule. Its formulation is highly complex and unclear—both with regard to the conditions for breakthrough (how is '75% or more of the capital carrying voting rights' to be interpreted in a company with A/B shares?) and to its consequences. To mention just two examples, Article 11(5) stipulates that 'equitable compensation' is to be provided to shareholders whose rights are broken through.[24] Although it may be inferred through the application of logic and by reference to Article 6(3)(e) that such compensation is to be paid by the acquirer,[25] it is symptomatic of the Directive's lack of clarity and precision that this is not explicitly stated. Secondly, how is the level of compensation to be fixed? The Directive leaves this entirely to the individual Member States, meaning that the rules will vary from country to country, with many (if not all) Member States choosing to leave the whole issue to be decided by the courts, or by the companies themselves through the inclusion of opting-in clauses in their articles of association.

This rather impotent attempt at levelling the playing field by attacking a section of the vast variety of control structures in Europe—and leaving the rest unchanged[26]—never had a chance politically of being adopted as an obligatory rule. The optionality clause contained in Article 12 therefore also applies to the breakthrough rule, and with the exception of the Baltic States, it seems that all Member States will opt out.[27]

Theoretically, this rule should make takeovers easier, by facilitating the takeover of formerly impregnable companies. However, that only holds true if the rule is taken in isolation and viewed in a positive light.[28] Even in countries that

---

[22] Takeover Directive, Art 11(4).   [23] Making the breakthrough permanent.
[24] Specifically advised against by the Winter group, except in 'exceptional cases', see the Winter Takeover Report, p 35.
[25] A question raised by SM Bartman 'Analysis and Consequences of the EC Directive on Takeover Bids' (2004) 1 (issue 1) European Company Law 5–8 [as in the printed version], on p 8.
[26] In fairness to the Winter group, it should be added that they suggested that control structures outside the scope of the breakthrough rule should be revised and possibly dealt with in general company or contract law; the Winter Takeover Report, pp 36–39.
[27] Commission Staff Working Document: Report on the Implementation of the Directive on Takeover Bids, SEC(2007)268, Ann 1, p 12. The information regarding the Baltic States is still valid, and the four Member States that have confirmed their transposition of the Directive after the report was published (Belgium, Cyprus, The Netherlands, and Spain) have stuck to their opt-out choice regarding the breakthrough rule; status per 26 September 2007, according to personal information from the Commission; notes on file with author. Norway has also opted out, see B Sjåfjell, 'Report from Norway' (2006) 3 (issue 1) European Company Law 35–39 [as in the printed version].
[28] See inter alia, R Skog 'The Takeover Directive, the "Breakthrough" Rule and the Swedish System of Dual Class Common Stock' (2004) 15 European Business Law Review 1451 stating that

opt in to this rule (or where market forces prevail on companies to choose to do so, see below), it is very likely that those wishing to have control will simply choose other forms of corporate structure exempt from the breakthrough rule. The effect of the rule on the cost of a takeover, considering the compensation to be paid to those who have their rights broken through, and the impact of this on the enthusiasm of potential acquirers, is also unclear.

The introduction of the breakthrough rule illustrates the Commission's drive towards a system that it perceives as exhibiting the ultimate sign of good corporate governance: 'one share one vote'. The revision clause contained in Article 20 has been read as containing an underlying threat: if the individual Member States (or at least the companies based in them, see below) do not voluntarily go along with the 'best' solution for the European economy, mandatory rules may follow.[29] It seems somewhat paradoxical that, rather than first considering rationally the pros and cons of the existing systems of corporate governance in Continental Europe, the Commission tries through the Takeover Directive to facilitate simultaneously the introduction of the Anglo-American shareholding structure and the solution to the problems that this very system is perceived to entail.[30] A prize-winning research paper gives substance to these misgivings, stating that 'one share one vote' is a 'suboptimal corporate voting mechanism that compromises economic efficiency and distorts the incentives of corporate constituencies'.[31] This clearly illustrates the lack of any consensus in Europe in favour of this system,[32] and the long anticipated study into this issue on behalf of the Commission gave not quite the result the Commission appears to have anticipated.[33]

---

the assumption that A/B shares are a major obstacle to takeovers 'lacks theoretical as well as empirical support'.

[29] See Commission Staff Working Document: Report on the Implementation of the Directive on Takeover Bids, SEC(2007)268, pp 10–11, where it is stated that the number of Member States implementing the Takeover Directive 'in a seemingly protectionist way is unexpectedly large', and that the result of a further evaluation of the situation in the Member States may be that 'the revision of the Directive scheduled for 2011' is brought forward.

[30] The market for corporate control is supposed to mitigate the perceived main principal/agent issue in dispersed shareholdings.

[31] A Khachaturyan, The One-Share-One-Vote Controversy in the EU (European Capital Markets Institute (CEPS) Paper No 1/August 2006), available online at: <http://ssrn.com/abstract=908215>.

[32] At the ECGI Transatlantic Corporate Governance Conference in June 2006, the last item of the conference was an Oxford Union-Style debate over the motion: 'This House believes it is acceptable to vest different classes of shares with different voting rights' (see: <http://www.ecgi.org/tcgd/2006/programme.php>). The motion was carried by a clear majority.

[33] See 'Commission publishes external study on proportionality between capital and control in EU listed companies', Brussels, 4 June 2007 (IP/07/751), p 1: 'The study finds that, on the basis of the academic research available, there is no conclusive evidence of a causal link between deviations from the proportionality principle and either the economic performance of listed companies or their governance.' The study itself, which was carried out by Institutional Shareholder Services (ISS), the European Corporate Governance Institute (ECGI), and the law firm Shearman & Sterling, is available at: <http://ec.europa.eu/internal_market/company/shareholders/indexb_en.htm>.

(iv) Faith in Market Forces

As mentioned above, both the board neutrality and breakthrough rules are optional. Article 12 of the Takeover Directive provides that Member States who wish to do so can opt out of the rules, but legislation in such Member States must provide companies with the possibility of opting in to either rule, a choice that must be reversible.[34] Further, opt-out Member States must decide whether they wish to give their potentially opting-in companies the opportunity of not being bound by the neutrality and breakthrough rules where takeover attempts are made by bidders who are not themselves bound to these rules: the reciprocity twist.[35] Sounds complicated? It is worse than it sounds: unanswered questions regarding interpretation of the reciprocity clause abound.[36]

Of the 25 Member States that have transposed the Directive or made clear their choices in their plans to do so, 11 have said no to reciprocity and 14 have said yes—although in the case of France, only with regard to the board neutrality rule.[37]

The point of including these optional rules in the Directive at all, when the Commission must have known that many Member States would opt out, particularly in the case of the breakthrough rule, lies in the Commission's belief in market forces. The hope is that the market will punish those companies that do not opt in, that shareholders will push for changes in companies' articles of association and that we will see a gradual move in Europe towards a harmonized corporate control structure.[38] However, the costs may very well outweigh the benefits.

---

[34] Takeover Directive, Art 12(2) and Recital 21.

[35] As the reciprocity option contained in Article 12(3) according to Recital 21 is open only for Member States that opt out, this may be seen as an incentive to do exactly that, as that would give the companies that do opt in to the rules on a voluntary basis an even more flexible position, compared to the companies of opt-in Member States.

[36] See eg, J Rickford 'The Emerging European Takeover Law from a British Perspective' (2004) 15 European Business Law Review 1401–1409.

[37] Commission Staff Working Document: Report on the Implementation of the Directive on Takeover Bids, SEC(2007)268, p 12, confirmed still valid per 26 September 2007 (personal information from the Commission; notes on file with author). As regards the inclusion of the reciprocity option in the Member States' implementation of the Directive, the report's characterization of this is that it 'may hold back the emergence of an active takeover market, as opposed to the original objective of the Directive' (p 7, regarding the board neutrality rule). Norway seems to have chosen not to allow opt-in companies to apply the reciprocity exception; albeit not expressly regulated it is implicit in the formulation specifying that the companies can choose to opt in to the board neutrality and breakthrough rules of the Directive, with reference to Article 12(2) (and not Article 12(3)) of the Directive, in *Lov om verdipapirhandel* (The Norwegian Securities Trading Act) (29 June 2007 No 75) Section 6–17.

[38] Eagerness may be perceived amongst the most ardent supporters of the Directive: the journal European Company Law in August 2006 used the editorial to launch a competition with the title 'Crack the OOC-Code!' (OOC being Opt-Out Companies) with prizes for the best idea for getting companies to opt in and stay opted-in; see SM Bartman 'Crack the OOC-Code!' (2006) 3 (issue 4) European Company Law 162–163 [as in the printed version].

(v) The Mandatory Bid Rule

Many contributions to the discussion on the Takeover Directive focus on the mandatory bid rule contained in Article 5, so we will not go into this rule in detail here.[39] This rule, which provides that a potential acquirer must bid for all the shares of the target company once a certain threshold (to be determined by the individual Member States) has been passed, although well-known in Europe, has a questionable place in the Directive. The motivation for making the rule, which supposedly protects the interests of minority shareholders, obligatory on an EU level is unclear.[40] Its effect on the making of takeover bids is presumably that of a deterrent:[41] if an acquirer has to be prepared to pay for 100% of the shares when the initial aim was to buy only, say, 35%, this obviously greatly increases the potential cost of a takeover.[42] If one regards takeovers as beneficial for society, as does the Winter group,[43] this should be a cause for concern.[44] It is not merely a question of a trade-off between the facilitation of takeovers and the protection of minority shareholders, as the mandatory bid rule may also function to the detriment of this latter group.[45] If it was thought possible to design

[39]   See, inter alia, L Enriques 'The Mandatory Bid Rule in the Takeover Directive: Harmonization without Foundation?' (2004) 4 European Company and Financial Law Review 440–457; J Lau Hansen 'When Less Would be More: The EU Takeover Directive in its Latest Apparition' (2003) 9 The Columbia Journal of European Law 275–298; B Sjåfjell, 'The Golden Mean or a Dead End? The Takeover Directive in a Shareholder versus Stakeholder Perspective', in SM Bartman (ed), *European Company Law in Accelerated Progress* (Kluwer Law International, 2006) 107–144; MJ Sillanpää, 'Enhancing Shareholders' Equality by a Takeover Bid Rule in the Articles of Association', in M Suksi (ed), *Law under Exogenous Influences* (Turku Law School, 1994); R Skog, *Does Sweden Need a Mandatory Bid Rule? A Critical Analysis* (Juristförlaget, 1995); and also an early contribution by a later member of the Winter group: J Schans Christensen, *Contested Takeovers in Danish Law: A Comparative Analysis Based on a Law and Economics Approach* (GEC Gads Forlag, 1991) 226–231.

[40]   The grounds for including the rule are not discussed at all in the Winter Takeover report. For a discussion of some possible motivations for the mandatory bid rule, see B Sjåfjell, 'The Golden Mean or a Dead End? The Takeover Directive in a Shareholder versus Stakeholder Perspective', in SM Bartman (ed), *European Company Law in Accelerated Progress* (Kluwer Law International, 2006) 124–132.

[41]   There is 'broad consensus in the literature' that the mandatory bid rule 'inevitably reduces the number of value-increasing control acquisitions'; L Enriques 'The Mandatory Bid Rule in the Takeover Directive: Harmonization without Foundation?' (2004) 4 European Company and Financial Law Review 448.

[42]   See the Winter Takeover Report, p 49: 'It is indeed *a major disincentive to the acquisition of control* if such acquisition imposes an obligation to bid but the price to be paid is not predictable' (emphasis added). The disincentive effect of a *higher* price for the acquisition of control induced by a mandatory bid rule is however not discussed. Further, the rule may exacerbate the free-rider problem in dispersed shareholdings, see also M Burkart and F Panunzi, Takeovers (ECGI Working Paper Series in Finance, Paper No 118/2006), available online at: <http://ssrn.com/abstract_id=884080>, pp 12–14.

[43]   Winter Takeover Report, p 19.

[44]   See also E Berglöf and MC Burkart, 'European Takeover Regulation' (2003) 18 Economic Policy 208: The mandatory bid rule 'goes against both objectives set up by the Commission: improved contestability and a "level playing field". The rule lowers contestability in firms with controlling shareholders, and since it has a differential impact depending on the structure of the ownership and control, the rules make the playing field less levelled.'

[45]   Although minority shareholders in an actual takeover may profit *ex post* from the mandatory bid rule, the *ex ante* effect may be to reduce the number of takeovers, which will also affect minority

the mandatory bid rule to function as a greater deterrent against value-reducing takeovers than value-increasing, this should have been properly discussed, along with the threshold appropriate for achieving such an effect.[46]

Since the Directive is intended to facilitate the making of takeovers, it is ironic that its main obligatory rule acts as a deterrent. On the other hand, such rules already exist in most Member States,[47] so the Directive's mandatory bid rule may not make so much difference in practice—except, of course, in that it prevents Member States from freely revising their company law. Changing a rule at the EU level is, to put it mildly, a much more complicated process.

C. The Overall Effect of the Main Substantive Rules

The optional neutrality and breakthrough rules are controversial and in part very complex. They open up the way for market-driven changes, but the consequences for control structures and corporate governance in general in Europe, are impossible to predict. Even taking the most optimistic view, there is a risk that the costs will outweigh the benefits. The obligatory mandatory bid rule can hardly be seen as facilitating takeovers and, although it is not a new rule within Europe, it will now be obligatory in all the 30 countries that have to apply EU company law.

The overall effect of the Directive is therefore at best unclear, and we may safely conclude that, assessed on its own terms, the Directive is not a success.

We will now move on to the second and third issues outlined above, taking a closer look at the terms of the Directive and then considering the perspective from which it has emerged.

III. Questioning the Terms

Taking a closer look at the premises of the Directive, one might be tempted to ask whether they are really based on generally accepted and substantiated economic theories, supported by unequivocal empirical evidence,[48] or whether they

---

shareholders. See also L Enriques 'The Mandatory Bid Rule in the Takeover Directive: Harmonization without Foundation?' (2004) 4 European Company and Financial Law Review 448–449, and M Burkart and F Panunzi, Takeovers (ECGI Working Paper Series in Finance, Paper No 118/2006), available online at: <http://ssrn.com/abstract_id=884080>, p 14.

[46] This possibility may appear to be indicated by J A McCahery et al., 'The Economics of the Proposed European Takeover Directive', in G Ferrarini et al. (eds), *Reforming Company and Takeover Law in Europe* (OUP, 2004) 621–622, whilst M Burkart and F Panunzi, Takeovers (ECGI Working Paper Series in Finance, Paper No 118/2006), available online at: <http://ssrn.com/abstract_id=884080>, pp 14–15 seem to dismiss this possibility.

[47] This may be in part because the Member States anticipated such an obligatory EU rule, see B Sjåfjell 'The Golden Mean or a Dead End? The Takeover Directive in a Shareholder versus Stakeholder Perspective', in SM Bartman (ed), *European Company Law in Accelerated Progress* (Kluwer Law International, 2006) 123–124.

[48] The Winter group merely refers to 'available economic evidence': Winter Takeover Report, p 19.

actually rest on unfounded postulates that have been repeated so many times that we believe them to be true. At the very least, there is reason to question whether the Directive is based on theories derived from economic models with overly narrow assumptions.

We saw above that the theoretical basis for the Takeover Directive is that of the market for corporate control, with its alleged dual beneficial disciplining and restructuring effect.

Let us consider the disciplining effect first. There is reason to doubt the assumptions on which the belief in this effect is founded. To begin with, takeovers are not always rationally (economically) motivated.[49] Research indicates that the underperforming companies are not particularly targeted for takeover: size may be a more important factor.[50] Further, there is very little clear indication of improved performance among firms that have been taken over.[51] Even when taking into consideration the possibility that the disciplining effect may materialize mainly in companies that are not taken over, this raises serious questions.

The theory of the market for corporate control is also based on the assumption that the share price reflects the value of the company and the quality of its management (this is questionable)[52] and that the shareholders' opinion as to what the company should do and how it should be run is the benchmark that companies should be measured against. This is a cue to discuss the nature and purpose of a company, but space and time do not permit such a discussion here.[53]

---

[49] See in general on the possible motivations for takeovers, E Berkovitch and MP Narayanan 'Motives for Takeovers: An Empirical Investigation' (1993) 28 The Journal of Financial and Quantitative Analysis 347–362; and based on a review of the empirical evidence, M Martynova and L Renneboog, Takeover Waves: Triggers, Performance and Motives (ECGI Finance Working Paper No 97/2005), available online at: <http://ssrn.com/abstract:_id=820984>, p 36.

[50] J Franks and C Mayer, 'Hostile Takeovers and the Correction of Managerial Failure' (1996) 40 Journal of Financial Economics 163–181, leading the authors to conclude that the 'market for corporate control does therefore not function as a disciplinary device for poorly performing companies' (at 180). See also M Burkart and F Panunzi, Takeovers (ECGI Working Paper Series in Finance, Paper No 118/2006), available online at: <http://ssrn.com/abstract_id=884080>, pp 4–5 with references to other studies.

[51] See for an analysis based on qualitative case studies of takeovers in the UK in the mid-1990s, S Deakin et al, Implicit Contracts, Takeovers, and Corporate Governance: In the Shadow of the City Code (ESRC Centre for Business Research, University of Cambridge, Working Paper 254/2002), available online at: <http://www.cbr.cam.ac.uk/pdf/WP254.pdf>. See also M Burkart and F Panunzi, Takeovers (ECGI Working Paper Series in Finance, Paper No 118/2006), available online at: <http://ssrn.com/abstract_id=884080>, pp 4 and 6–7 with further references.

[52] S Deakin and G Slinger, 'Hostile Takeovers, Corporate Law, and the Theory of the Firm' (1997) 24 Journal of Law and Society 132; MM Blair, 'Shareholder Value, Corporate Governance, and Corporate Performance', in P Cornelius and B Kogut (eds), *Corporate Governance and Capital Flows in a Global Economy* (OUP, 2003) 59 with further references. On the other hand, JN Gordon, Independent Directors and Stock Market Prices: The New Corporate Governance Paradigm (ECGI Law Working Paper No 74/2006), available online at: <http://ssrn.com/paper=928100>, is more optimistic and points to several arguments in favour of the increased accuracy of share prices.

[53] For an analysis of fundamental questions in company law, see B Sjåfjell, *Rules, Values & Takeovers* (University of Oslo, 2007) Part II. A revised version of this doctoral thesis is forthcoming as *Towards a Sustainable European Company Law* (Kluwer Law International, 2009).

Suffice it to say that companies are legal entities in which a number of parties, internal and external, have an interest. And although the so-called market for corporate control might function in the sense that it disciplines boards and managers to focus more narrowly on the current shareholders' interest, specifically their assumed interest in achieving a greatest possible profit should they sell their shares, this does not mean that the market for corporate control leads to companies being run in a manner beneficial to the companies themselves or to society.

Most empirical studies looking at the effect of takeovers focus primarily on the short-term effect on the target company shares.[54] A rise in the target company share price around the time of the takeover, which is what such studies generally show,[55] is seen as beneficial. In other words, a profit made by target shareholders that sell[56]—and thereafter have no relationship with the target company—is interpreted as being beneficial for the company that is taken over.[57] The fact that the acquirer shareholders generally fare much worse, in the same short-term perspective,[58] is often overlooked, and the long-term effects and the implications for society in general are ignored.

Those studies that do look at the long-term effects show inconclusive or negative results, implying that the anticipated gains from takeovers, which spark the rise in target share price, turn out to be on average either non-existent or overstated.[59] Although there have been some studies that indicate positive results, this is not

---

[54] M Martynova and L Renneboog, Takeover Waves: Triggers, Performance and Motives (ECGI Finance Working Paper No 97/2005), available online at: <http://ssrn.com/abstract:_id=820984>, p 17, showing the highest results at the beginning of a takeover wave—towards the end, even target shareholders lose out.

[55] Inter alia, M Burkart and F Panunzi, Takeovers (ECGI Working Paper Series in Finance, Paper No 118/2006), available online at: <http://ssrn.com/abstract_id=884080>, p 5.

[56] Those who remain shareholders of the target company do not profit by the higher share price *per se*; their position depends on the future development of the company.

[57] See inter alia, M. Martynova and L. Renneboog, The Performance of the European Market for Corporate Control: Evidence from the 5th Takeover Wave (ECGI Finance Working Paper No 135/2006), available online at: <http://ssrn.com/abstract=941731>, p 3, regarding 2,419 European mergers and acquisitions in the period 1993–2001, where it is stated that these were 'expected to create takeover synergies, since their announcements trigger substantial share price increases. However, most of the takeover gains are captured by the target firm shareholders.'

[58] M Martynova and L Renneboog, Takeover Waves: Triggers, Performance and Motives (ECGI Finance Working Paper No 97/2005), available online at: <http://ssrn.com/abstract:_id=820984>, pp 20–21 and M Burkart and F Panunzi, Takeovers (ECGI Working Paper Series in Finance, Paper No. 118/2006), available online at: <http://ssrn.com/abstract_id=884080>, pp 5–6.

[59] M Martynova and L Renneboog, 'Takeover Waves: Triggers, Performance and Motives' (ECGI Finance Working Paper No 97/2005), available online at: <http://ssrn.com/abstract:_id=820984>, pp 22–25 with further references, stating at pp 22–23 that the long-term wealth effects (ie effect on share price) demonstrates that 'takeovers lead to a decline in share prices several years following the transaction', while at p 24 it is stated that 14 out of 25 studies regarding the operating performance 'report a post-merger decline in the profitability of the merging firms', while 6 show insignificant changes and 5 show a 'significantly positive increase in operating returns'. The authors add at p 25 that both types of studies 'suffer from measurement errors and statistical problems' and that the results should be interpreted with caution.

the main conclusion of a recent study of the long-term operating performance of companies after European mergers and acquisitions.[60] The study has investigated the long-term performance of companies following 155 European mergers and takeovers completed between 1997 and 2001.[61] Although the authors emphasize the difficulty in finding clear results, the general conclusion for the companies involved in the investigated European mergers and acquisitions is a significant decrease in profitability. This decrease becomes insignificant when controlled for the performance of 'peer companies', chosen to control for 'industry, size and pre-event performance', suggesting that the decrease is caused by unrelated 'macroeconomic changes'. However, the study also shows that the long-term performance of these companies deteriorates following 'hostile bids and tender offers', as compared to 'friendly' takeovers and negotiated deals,[62] indicating that uninvited ('hostile') takeovers generally speaking have a negative effect on long-term company performance.

It has been maintained that the aggregated results cover up the fact that there are both good and bad takeovers and that the market eventually disciplines the actors behind the bad takeovers.[63] But especially as the aggregated result seems to be negative, this seriously calls into doubt the suitability of uninvited takeovers as a mechanism for controlling the management of companies.

Now for the restructuring effect: Will takeovers lead to corporate restructuring that is good for the European economy? Some probably will, while some will not.[64] Once we have established that size may factor heavily in the motivation behind a takeover, we can also see that takeover bids may be motivated not through the implementation of a rational business strategy, but through fear of becoming a target. There is a further risk of takeovers being motivated by empire-building or simply pure miscalculation. It may be posited that the narrower and shorter-term the focus of those involved is, the higher the risk of mistakes. The fact that the UK's takeover-friendly regime seems to have worked well for the London market, in terms of facilitating a very liquid capital market, does not

---

[60] M Martynova, S Oosting, and L Renneboog, The Long-Term Operating Performance of European Mergers and Acquisitions (ECGI Finance Working Paper No 137/2006), available online at: <http://ssrn.com/abstract=944407>, giving an overview of prior research which at pp 3–4 shows that former empirical studies can be evenly divided into three groups: reporting respectively positive, negative, and insignificant change in performance, with recent US studies as the most positive, and the UK studies as the more contradictory.

[61] The selection is explained at ibid, pp 6–7 where we also see that the authors' definition of 'long-term' may be as short as one year. Although obviously more interesting than just registering the change in share price immediately around the takeover, it may be queried whether the full effect (positive or negative) is captured if only the first-year results are investigated.

[62] Ibid, p 19.

[63] ML Mitchell and K Lehn 'Do Bad Bidders Become Good Targets?' (1990) 98 The Journal of Political Economy 372–398.

[64] See also E Berglöf and MC Burkart 'European Takeover Regulation' (2003) 18 Economic Policy 171–213 referring to 'hostile takeovers (as) a rather blunt instrument for achieving desirable contestability of control'.

mean that this regime will be beneficial for Continental European businesses and their societal role.[65] Doubts have even been cast on whether this regime is optimal for business and society in the UK.[66]

The Winter report does not enter into this discussion or attempt to assess the empirical research on the effect of takeovers. Instead the report merely refers to the alleged disciplining and restructuring effects as unequivocally and undisputedly beneficial (which is clearly not the case)—claiming that this is 'in the long term in the best interests of all stakeholders, and society at large'.[67] The Winter report offers no substantiation of this claim.

In general we may ask whether the increased focus on share price and short-term profits for target shareholders, which seems to be an inevitable consequence of a vibrant market for corporate control, is good for European business. The answer seems to be no, not necessarily. Research has indicated that the consequences include the risk of negative effects on long-term investments such as those relating to research and development,[68] and on the trust necessary in long-term implicit contracts, such as those with core employees and suppliers.[69] However, empirical studies are not conclusive here. Further research has found it difficult to substantiate the hypothesis of direct appropriation of rent from employees to shareholders through takeovers; ie for example, a wage cut transfer to higher share price.[70] Whether future empirical research will confirm or reject such a direct connection, the argument remains that there is a risk of an active market for corporate control undermining the trust that long-term relationships, such as

---

[65] The UK City Code was a major source of inspiration for early Takeover Directive proposals.

[66] Inter alia, S Deakin and G Slinger, 'Hostile Takeovers, Corporate Law, and the Theory of the Firm' (1997) 24 Journal of Law and Society 124–151.

[67] The Winter Takeover Report, p 19.

[68] See M Burkart and F Panunzi, Takeovers (ECGI Working Paper Series in Finance, Paper No 118/2006), available online at: <http://ssrn.com/abstract_id=884080>, p 11, and WN Pugh and JS Jahera Jr, 'State Anti-takeover Legislation and Firm Financial Policy' (1997) 18 Managerial and Decision Economics 681–692. Although one may query then why US companies outdo their European counterparts in research and development, and especially the reasons for Germany's poor performance in this regard, see 'US Widens Gap with Europe on R&D' Financial Times, 30 October 2006, front page, first section.

[69] A Shleifer and L Summers, 'Breach of Trust in Hostile Takeovers', in AJ Auerbach (ed), *Corporate Takeovers: Causes and Consequences* (University of Chicago Press, 1988).

[70] From an early, US perspective, see C Brown and JL Medoff 'The Impact of Firm Acquisitions on Labor', in AJ Auerbach (ed), *Corporate Takeovers: Causes and Consequences* (University of Chicago Press, 1988) who state at p 11 that they found 'small (and sometimes positive) changes in wages and employment following an acquisition'. Note should however be made of A Shleifer and L Summers 'Breach of Trust in Hostile Takeovers', in AJ Auerbach (ed), ibid, warning at p 48 about not distinguishing between uninvited takeovers and voluntary mergers in this respect; stating that the study by Brown and Medoff probably only has voluntary mergers as its empirical material. A more recent review from a US perspective states that available studies show the measurable effect on employees, customers, and suppliers to be 'generally small and often statistically insignificant', but there apparently is no study that has attempted to address these issues with a 'consistent sample', see S Bhagat and R Romano, 'Empirical Studies of Corporate Law', in A Mitchell Polinsky and S Shavell (eds), *Handbook of Law and Economics* (Elsevier, 2007) 946–1012, quotes from 987.

typically that of the employees with the company in which they are employed, is based on.[71]

It is only possible to pin-point some of the uncertainties here. Overall we may conclude that there are too many questions and too few answers. A study on the then takeover proposal, presented to the European Parliament in 2002, made exactly this point when it stated that the 'very foundations' of the Takeover Directive could be disputed—but this does not seem to have been followed up at all during the legislative process.[72]

IV. Questioning the Perspective

As touched upon earlier, the Directive's perspective is defined by the goal of economic development. Sustainable development is the EU's fundamental and overarching goal, as set out in Article 2 of the EC Treaty and emphasized in a number of high level policy documents.[73] Sustainable development entails balancing economic and environmental and social interests. The integration of the sustainable development objective in 'the Community policies and activities referred to in Article 3' (the internal market) is a general principle of EC law, see Article 6 of the EC Treaty. This principle, 'fundamental to the concept of sustainable development',[74] is not just a guideline, but a central element of Community law that constitutes a vital part of the European Union's fulfilment of its international obligations.[75]

We need not go further than to the company law-related area of accounting law to find efforts at integrating the objective of sustainable development into internal market policies; see, for example, the Commission Recommendation on including environmental issues in the annual accounts and reports of companies.[76] With reference to Article 6 of the EC Treaty and various programmes,

[71] As already pointed out from an early US perspective by JC Coffee, Jr, 'Regulating the Market for Corporate Control: A Critical Assessment of the Tender Offer's Role in Corporate Governance' (1984) 84 Columbia Law Review, stating at 1223 that a higher frequency of takeovers may 'result in both demoralization costs and increased opportunistic behaviour by employees who come to see their tenure in office as no longer predictably related to their own performance'.

[72] B Dauner Lieb and M Lamandini, Report to the European Parliament on the Commission's New Proposal of a Directive on Company Law Concerning Takeover bids (Study No IV/2002/06/01). No reference to this part of the report has been found in the subsequent preparatory work (notably the Winter report). Further, Professor Lamandini has confirmed that, as per 3 November 2006, the authors had not received any comment or question regarding the first part of their study, where these issues were discussed (email on file with author).

[73] The EU sustainable development strategy has led to the original Lisbon strategy of jobs and growth being extended to encompass the recognition that 'economic growth, social cohesion and environmental protection must go hand in hand': A European Union Strategy for Sustainable Development (Luxembourg, European Commission, 2002), p 21; see also, inter alia, Presidency Conclusions of the Brussels European Council 15 and 16 June 2006 (10633/1/06 REV 1).

[74] PGG Davies, *European Union Environmental Law* (Ashgate Dartmouth, 2004) 32.

[75] Ibid, at 32–33 and 28 (the latter on the EC being a signatory to the Rio Declaration).

[76] Commission Recommendation 2001/453/EC on the recognition, measurement and disclosure of environmental issues in the annual accounts and annual reports of companies ([2001] OJ L156/33–42).

strategies, and communications regarding the 'integration of environmental objectives into all Community policies and actions',[77] the recommendation focuses on the 'ways and means used by companies to report on financial aspects relating to the environment' with the following motivation:

An enhanced attention to financial aspects could contribute to achieving the goals of the programme;[78] ensuring that environmental expenditures and risks are taken into account could increase the company's awareness of environmental issues.[79]

The Takeover Directive regulates changes of control that could lead to correspondingly abrupt changes of policy in—as the case often is—very large companies with activities in several countries. The Directive might therefore seem to be a natural legislative initiative within which the further integration of the sustainable development objective could have been considered. Instead, not only is there no indication of any such integration in the Takeover Directive, the notion does not even feature at any stage of the legislative process. The Directive is clearly both too narrow and too shallow in its perspective, which leads us to this paper's conclusion.

V. Conclusion

A. Political Path Dependency in the Narrow and Wide Sense

The Takeover Directive is an example of political path dependency in both the narrow and the wider senses of the term.[80]

To take the narrow sense first, returning to the topic of the Directive assessed on its own terms: it would seem that those involved in the legislative process lost sight of the reasons for starting the whole project. The adoption of a Directive on takeover bids became an end in itself, regardless of the number of political compromises necessary to achieve this and regardless of whether the final result was anywhere near suitable to promote the original objective of the legislative initiative. It is no wonder that Commissioner Bolkestein was frustrated: so much so that he declared the Takeover Directive not to be worth the paper on which it was written.[81] Bolkestein was probably trying to realize a particular vision, and

---

[77] Ibid, Recitals 1, 2, and 3.   [78] Ie, sustainable development.

[79] Commission Recommendation 2001/453/EC on the recognition, measurement and disclosure of environmental issues in the annual accounts and annual reports of companies ([2001] OJ L156/33–42), Recital 1.

[80] 'Path dependency' is used as a metaphor in this paper, rather than introducing the discussion of a specific legal-economic term.

[81] See eg, F Bolkestein 'The Capital Markets Directives' (2005) 2 (issue 1) European Company Law 4–8 [as in the printed version], on p 7, where he declares the Takeover Directive a failure '—a step backwards in terms of economic reform. It is no secret that I would have preferred a much more ambitious Directive. Instead, we are faced with the result of political arbitrage—a half-hearted compromise that does little to promote a level playing field.'

although the above discussion may show that there are grounds to question its premises; one can certainly sympathize with his frustration.

Also the questions raised above regarding the premises of the Directive illustrate the path-dependency picture of the Directive: Even if the Directive had been a success in the eyes of Bolkestein, ie clearly takeover-facilitating, doubts have been raised as to whether that would then have had the anticipated beneficial effect for European business and economic development in general. This was pointed out during the legislative process[82] but appears to have been totally ignored—staying on the same track was apparently a more comfortable choice.

In the wide sense of the term, returning to the question of the Directive's perspective, the Takeover Directive is a striking example of political path dependency in practice. It is symptomatic of a general legislative failure: the lack of a comprehensive approach. In view of the global challenges we face and current awareness of the interrelationship and interdependence between the different areas of law and policy, there is an emphasis at the highest level in the EU on overarching aims, notably that of sustainable development. The integration of sustainable development into all Community policies and areas, including the internal market, is mandated by Article 6 of the EC Treaty. In the legislative process leading to the Takeover Directive, this could have led to a discussion of whether facilitating takeovers is at all compatible with the sustainable development objective. At the very least, the Treaty-mandated integration should have been discussed within the realms of the Takeover Directive. This could for example have led to the possible environmental effect of a planned takeover being included together with effects on employment in the obligations of the bidder and the board of the target company, respectively, to make clear their opinions on the effect of the takeover on the interests of the company.[83] As far as the core internal-market areas of company and securities law are concerned, however, everything has instead continued along the same tracks.

B. A Call for a Proper, Comprehensive Debate

The debacle of the Takeover Directive illustrates the need for a thorough and comprehensive debate to identify Europe's higher goals in a global perspective and establish a strategy for obtaining them. Briefly, the toughest challenge we face is the implementation of strategies into all areas of policy to save the very basis of our existence and tackle other global issues, such as the grave injustice of approximately 50,000 people dying every day of poverty-related causes.[84] Obviously, we

---

[82] In B Dauner Lieb and M Lamandini, Report to the European Parliament on the Commission's New Proposal of a Directive on Company Law Concerning Takeover Bids (Study No IV/2002/06/01) (see n 72 above).

[83] Articles 6(3)(i) and 9(5) of the Takeover Directive.

[84] J Dine, *Companies, International Trade and Human Rights* (Cambridge University Press, 2005) 1, with reference to the World Health Report 2001.

should not attempt to solve every problem through company and securities law, but we have to move away from the other extreme view, which is that none of these matters should be considered in the context of traditional economic areas of the law. The aggregated economic, social, and environment impact, in Europe and globally, of our public companies is so great that we cannot exclude their regulation from a discussion of how to face the global challenges of our time.

Failure to consider legislation in its overall context leads to the risk of, for example, company law, on the one hand, and environmental and development law on the other being mutually counterproductive. The danger that vital areas, such as global development, will suffer because of segregated legislative and policy systems has been recognized, inter alia, in the formulation of the principle of 'policy coherence for development'. This principle has been affirmed by the EU, its Member States and a number of international institutions, including the OECD, as vital for achieving more effective development cooperation.[85]

In the area of company and securities law we need a thorough debate based on serious research—not unfounded postulates—about what works in Continental Europe and what should be changed. This needs to replace the current trend of trying to change things on the basis of a preconception of the ultimate solution, which, if it exists at all, does so in the same parallel universe as the perfect market. Further, the debate must be comprehensive in that it must place the goal of European economic development in the larger, global picture of balancing economic, environmental, and social interests to achieve a sustainable development.

We may do well to remember as we go into to these highly necessary debates that any simple answer to an economic question is wrong.

---

[85] L van Schaik et al., Policy Coherence for Development in the EU Council: Strategies for the Way Forward (Centre for European Policy Studies), available online at: <http://shop.ceps.be/BookDetail.php?item_id=1356>, p 1.

The Changing Payments Landscape of Europe: Issues of Regulation and Competition

*René Smits**

I. Introduction

The European Central Bank (ECB) is intimately entwined with the single financial market in the EU and, thereby, with the changes taking place on that market, notably in the area of payments. The establishment of the ECB, as the monetary authority for the single currency, was the culmination of a process of law-making and policy coordination based on a completion of the internal market which has continued to be perfected ever since. After all, Economic and Monetary Union (EMU) consists of three elements:

(1) the substratum of a 'completed' single financial market, epitomized by directly effective Treaty provisions on capital and payment;

(2) an economic union characterized by coordination of State economic policies within a Community framework which includes several prohibitions of certain State economic behavior, notably in respect of budgets; and

(3) a monetary union characterized by a single currency and a single monetary authority, and by the transfer of sovereignty from State to Community level in this field.

Not only can the ECB be placed at the end of the process of integration leading to EMU, it is also deeply involved in efforts to make the single financial market more complete than it was at EMU's inception. Furthermore, internal market rules apply to the functioning of the ECB.

This article, based on a presentation before a two-day seminar on 'EU Financial Services Regulation: Completing the Internal Market', held at Queen Mary,

* Jean Monnet Professor of the Law of Economic and Monetary Union, *Universiteit van Amsterdam*, Amsterdam (NL)—Visiting Professorial Fellow, Queen Mary, University of London, London (GB)—Chief Legal Counsel, *Nederlandse Mededingingsautoriteit* (Netherlands Competition Authority), The Hague (NL)—Research assistance by Denis Barunovic (legal trainee at *NMa* in 2007 and by Tim Staal (paralegal at *NMa* in 2008) is gratefully acknowledged. This article states the law as at 25 July 2008.

University of London, on 26–27 October 2006, focuses on a topical element of the connection between the ECB and the single market, namely payments regulation and supervision. It also discusses competition issues in the changing European landscape which form the focus of attention of the competition authorities and the ECB. After a brief discussion of some other issues in section II, namely so-called 'remote access' in monetary policy operations, compliance with internal market rules in respect of bank note production, and the ECB's involvement in the general thrust towards completion of a single financial services market, I focus on payments systems. Section III discusses the issues of oversight of the payment systems. It is followed by an extensive discussion of SEPA, the acronym for the Single Euro Payments Area. Section IV outlines the concept of SEPA and the concerns, notably from a competition viewpoint, relating to its structure and establishment. A single payments area is underpinned by a new set of rules, initially boldly labeled 'New Legal Framework' by the European Commission. After setting out the main features of this framework as laid down in the Payment Services Directive (PSD) in section V, criticism of this regulatory environment for SEPA is developed in section VI. This criticism includes alternative proposals for regulation which could have been followed and may still, at a future time, show the way for efficient and effective payment rules in Europe. Conclusions and recommendations are summed up in section VII.

II. The ESCB, the Eurosystem, and the Single Market: Overview

A. The Institutional Setup

By way of reminder, it is recalled that the European System of Central Banks (ESCB) consists of legal entities established under national law, the National Central Banks (NCBs), and an entity established under Community law, the ECB. The ESCB is governed by the EC Treaty and the ESCB Statute, annexed to the latter, and by national law in so far as the NCBs are concerned.[1] National law has been made compatible with Community law as a precondition for the adoption of the single currency (the so-called fifth, legal, 'Maastricht' criterion for entry into the euro zone).[2]

---

[1] Furthermore, the ESCB Statute refers to national law in respect to the NCBs' liability. See Article 35.3.
[2] See Articles 109 and 121(1) of the EC Treaty. These provisions may become Articles 131 and 140(1) of the Treaty on the Functioning of the European Union (TFEU), ie the EC Treaty, as amended by the Treaty of Lisbon amending the Treaty on European Union and the Treaty establishing the European Community, signed at Lisbon, 13 December 2007 [2007] OJ C 306/01. See: Consolidated versions of the Treaty on European Union and the Treaty on the Functioning of the European Union [2008] OJ C 115/01. In a referendum in June 2008, Ireland voted against ratification of the Lisbon Treaty, making its actual coming into force uncertain at best.

The ESCB is governed by the ECB's decision-making bodies, the Governing Council and the Executive Board. The latter consists of six members appointed at EU level, the former consists of the members of the Executive Board and the Governors of the NCBs of Member States that have adopted the euro.[3] These governors are appointed and dismissed[4] at national level. Since not all Member States have adopted the single currency, the ESCB performs functions both for the 'in' States, acting as the Community's (the euro area's) monetary authority, and for the EU as a whole. In order to distinguish between the two functions, the ESCB has adopted the name 'Eurosystem' to indicate the ECB and the NCBs of the States fully participating in monetary union. This self-styled term will not be found in the EC Treaty or the Statute but is made official by the Lisbon Treaty.[5] Apart from the two above-mentioned decision-making bodies, the ECB has a third such body, the General Council.[6] This consists of the President and the Vice-President of the ECB plus the Governors of *all* NCBs. It performs functions in respect of both 'ins' and 'outs' and, thus, for the entire ESCB, not 'just' for the Eurosystem.

B. The ESCB and the Single Market

There are several internal market issues of direct relevance for the EU's monetary authority. Let me confine myself to mentioning the following.

(i) 'Remote Access' to Monetary Policy Operations

Even before the establishment of the ESCB, an issue could be discerned which is a direct consequence of the idea of a single market. When preparing access to its lending facilities the ESCB, operating through the NCBs, had the option (some, including this author, would argue that it was under an obligation) to enter into direct relationships with credit institutions irrespective of the latter's place of establishment. Thus, credit institutions might have accessed the monetary authority's window through any of its 'operational arms', ie NCBs. I have argued for such 'remote access' to be applied in monetary policy operations.[7] In practice, the Eurosystem has opted for a less far-reaching solution. Instead of applying no division whatsoever along national lines of access to central bank money, as a consequence of the Treaty's freedom to provide (and receive) services,[8] it thus far only offers credit institutions access to 'their' local central bank on the basis of

---

[3] Article 10.2 of the ESCB Statute provides that each member of the Governing Council has one vote and further specifies voting rights for NCB Governors once the number of Governors exceeds 15 or reaches 22.

[4] Although the independence requirements of the Treaty and the Statute do not allow dismissal on policy grounds. See, notably, Article 14.2 of the ESCB Statute.

[5] Article 282(1) of the TFEU.

[6] Article 47 of the ESCB Statute (renumbered Article 46 under the Lisbon Treaty).

[7] See thesis by R Smits, *The European Central Bank—Institutional Aspects* (The Hague/London/Boston, 1997) 242–260.

[8] Article 49 of the EC Treaty (renumbered Article 56 under the Lisbon Treaty).

collateral from anywhere in the Eurozone. The so-called Correspondent Central
Banking Model (CCBM) allows banks to use their collateral held in one State to
obtain central bank credit in another, 'their' State.[9] A new CCBM2 is about to
be developed with the intention of overcoming some of the shortcomings of the
'interim solution' to the pan-European use of collateral for access to central bank
money.[10] Nevertheless, this CCBM2, whilst providing a single IT platform for
domestic and cross-border use of collateral for central bank credit, still seems to
be based on what is euphemistically called 'the principle of decentralization of
access to credit'.[11] Just as with TARGET2 (see below), CCBM2 will be provided
by a number of NCBs (the NCBs of Belgium and the Netherlands), so that a
trend towards specialization for specific central banking functions may be discerned within the Eurosystem. On the issue of 'remote access', the Eurosystem
and the commercial banks might argue that there is no market demand for access
to central bank money on a 'remote access' basis. Even so, organizing core operations of the EU's monetary authority in a manner that prolongs national borders
instead of abolishing them would not seem to be compatible with the requirements of the internal market. To be fair, mention should be made of the fact
that in another area of Eurosystem operations, that of NCB cash services, remote
access has been achieved in the entire euro area as from June 2007.[12] The general
question whether organizing one's business along State lines is compatible with
internal market law goes beyond the present article.

(ii) *Public Procurement of Goods and Services*

For the procurement of services by third parties, the ESCB follows public procurement rules. This has been confirmed by an ECB Decision[13] setting out the
rules for public procurement which the ECB will follow with the exception of
contracts in the context of the fulfillment of the Eurosystem's or the ESCB's public tasks. For the procurement of bank notes, a separate decision has been taken.
In 2004, the Governing Council adopted a guideline[14] pursuant to which a common Eurosystem competitive approach to tendering will apply to the procurement of euro banknotes at the latest as from 1 January 2012. It seeks to ensure
an open, competitive bidding process that, at the same time, respects the special

---

[9] See: <http://www.ecb.int/paym/coll/coll/ccbm/html/index.en.html>.
[10] See ECB Press Release, Launch of the CCBM2 project (17 July 2008), available online at:
<http://www.ecb.eu/press/pr/date/2008/html/pr080717_1.en.html>.
[11] See: <http://www.ecb.int/paym/coll/coll/ccbm2/pdf/070516_CCBM2_presentation.pdf>.
[12] See ECB, Single Euro Payments Area (SEPA) from Concept to Reality—Fifth Progress Report
(July 2007) (hereafter: Fifth Progress Report of the Eurosystem on SEPA), available online at: <http://
www.ecb.int/pub/pdf/other/singleeuropaymentsarea200707en.pdf>, p 22.
[13] Decision of the European Central Bank of 3 July 2007 laying down the Rules on Procurement
(ECB/2007/5) (2007/497/EC) [2007] OJ L184/34. See online at: <http://www.ecb.int/ecb/legal/
pdf/l_18420070714en00340048.pdf>.
[14] Guideline of the European Central Bank of 16 September 2004 on the Procurement of Euro
Banknotes (ECB/2004/18) (2004/703/EC), OJ [2004] L 320/21. See online at: <http://www.ecb.
int/ecb/legal/pdf/l_32020041021en00210033.pdf>.

nature of bank notes whose production is subject to secrecy requirements to prevent counterfeiting and whose wide use by the public requires that environmental and health standards be upheld.

(iii) Completing the Internal Market in Financial Services

Another aspect of the interplay between of the Eurosystem and the internal market concerns the continuous pressure by Europe's monetary authority for the completion of the single financial services market. In its 'advocacy role', the ECB is a constant factor clamoring for measures to complete the internal market. This is evident from speeches by Governing Council members and from ECB Opinions. The ECB monitors financial integration, acts as a catalyst for change and integration and participates in financial markets regulatory and supervisory committees, such as the Committee of European Banking Supervisors[15] and the European Banking Committee.[16] At an international level, the ECB participates in the Basle Committee on Banking Supervision.[17]

(iv) Prudential Supervision

This brings me to the issue of prudential supervision. The Eurosystem has been given a contributory task in the field of prudential supervision and financial-system stability. In spite of the limited assignment of competences and the convoluted wording of the relevant provisions,[18] I

---

[15] See Article 3, sub (c) of Commission Decision of 5 November 2003 establishing the Committee of European Banking Supervisors (2004/5/EC) [2004] OJ L3/28. See further: <http://www.c-ebs.org/>.

[16] See Article 3 of Commission Decision of 5 November 2003 establishing the European Banking Committee (2004/10/EC) [2004] OJ L3/36.

[17] See: <http://www.bis.org/bcbs/>.

[18] Article 105(5) of the EC Treaty (to which Article 3.3 of the ESCB Statute corresponds) reads as follows:

'The ESCB shall contribute to the smooth conduct of policies pursued by the competent authorities relating to the prudential supervision of credit institutions and the stability of the financial system.'

Article 105(6) of the EC Treaty (to which Article 25.2 of the ESCB Statute corresponds) reads as follows:

'The Council may, acting unanimously on a proposal from the Commission and after consulting the ECB and *after receiving the assent* of the European Parliament, confer upon the ECB specific tasks concerning policies relating to the prudential supervision of credit institutions and other financial institutions with the exception of insurance undertakings.' (Emphasis added.)

If the Lisbon Treaty enters into force, Article 105(5) and (6) of the EC Treaty will be replaced by Article 127 (5) and (6) of the TFEU. The latter provision amends the procedure for activating operational supervisory functions for the ECB:

'The Council, acting by means of regulations in accordance with a special legislative procedure, may unanimously, and *after consulting* the European Parliament and the European Central Bank, confer specific tasks upon the European Central Bank concerning policies relating to the prudential supervision of credit institutions and other financial institutions with the exception of insurance undertakings.' (Emphasis added.)

have argued that the ECB and the ESCB had a wider ambit than usually thought.[19]

The Eurosystem's efforts to promote effective and efficient prudential supervision and to foster the stability of the financial system can all be seen in the context of both its monetary and financial stability mandate and of the completion of the internal market. The Eurosystem has to strike a balance between its stability orientation and the promotion of free markets. The developments toward convergence of prudential standards and the creation of a truly level playing field for the financial industry against a backdrop of a large number of national supervisory authorities, the emergence of players that are truly cross-border in nature and the lack of a single EU-wide financial authority are also beyond the scope of the present contribution.

III. The ESCB and Payments Systems Oversight

A. The Legal Framework

The legal framework for the Eurosystem's role in the area of payment systems, although not much more extensive than that in respect of its prudential role, is far more straightforward.

Article 105(2) (4th indent) of the European Community Treaty (EC Treaty)[20] and the corresponding provision in the ESCB Statute (Article 3.1, 4th indent) read as follows:

The basic tasks to be carried out through the ESCB shall be:
[...] to promote the smooth operation of payment systems.

Chapter V of the ESCB Statute, devoted to Prudential Supervision, consists of a single provision, Article 25, the second paragraph of which corresponds to Article 105(6) of the EC Treaty (Article 127(6) of the TFEU) and the first paragraph of which reads as follows:
'25.1 The ECB may offer advice to and be consulted by the Council, the Commission and the competent authorities of the Member States on the scope and implementation of Community legislation relating to the prudential supervision of credit institutions and to the stability of the financial system.'
Article 105(5) of the EC Treaty is not applicable in Member States with a derogation (Article 122(3) of the EC Treaty; see Article 139(2) of the TFEU), nor is Article 3 ESCB Statute (Article 43.1 [42.1 after ratification of the Lisbon Treaty] ESCB Statute). Articles 25.1 and 25.2 of the ESCB Statute are applicable. Pursuant to its Opt-out Protocol, Denmark is treated as a Member State with a derogation. The UK's Opt-out Protocol specifies, in Paragraph 3, that Article 105(5) does not apply to the UK. Paragraph 5 does not mention Article 25 of the ESCB Statute which, therefore, does apply in the UK, as it does in Member States with a derogation and Denmark.

[19] See, most recently, 'The Role of the ESCB in Banking Supervision', in *Liber Amicorum Paolo Zamboni Garavelli: Legal Aspects of the European System of Central Banks*, (ECB, 2005), 199–212. See: <http://www.ecb.int/pub/pdf/other/legalaspectsescben.pdf>.
[20] Article 127(2) of the TFEU under the Lisbon Treaty.

Furthermore, Article 22 of the ESCB Statute provides as follows:

Clearing and payment systems

The ECB and national central banks may provide facilities, and the ECB may make regulations, to ensure efficient and sound clearing and payment systems within the Community and with other countries.

The regulatory power referred to in Article 22 of the ESCB Statute is laid down in Article 110 of the EC Treaty and Article 34 of the ESCB Statute. In the context of the internal market, the prescription for the ESCB to act in accordance with open market and free competition principles is relevant. It is contained in Article 105(1) of the EC Treaty, last sentence,[21] and the corresponding last sentence of Article 2 of the ESCB Statute, which read as follows:

The ESCB shall act in accordance with the principle of an open market economy with free competition, favouring an efficient allocation of resources, and in compliance with the principles set out in Article 4 [of this Treaty].

It should be noted that Article 105(1) and (2) of the EC Treaty do not apply to Member States with a derogation,[22] nor to those with an opt out (ie, UK and Denmark).[23] Article 2 of the ESCB Statute does apply to Member States with a derogation and to the UK,[24] even though the corresponding Article 105(1) of the EC Treaty does not. As to the applicability of Article 22 of the ESCB Statute, see section 6(a)(*i*) below.

B. Payments Oversight Function

(i) General

The EC Treaty has provided for an oversight function in respect of payments systems as these are closely related to monetary policy: it is through the payment system that monetary policy decisions translate into the real economy. Traditionally, central banks have had a function in overseeing payment systems. Contrary to monetary policy, where decisions are taken centrally and execution is largely decentralized, payment systems oversight is predominantly decentralized in policy-setting and implementation. The predominant role for NCBs is due to the fact that payment systems are still organized along national lines. The opaqueness of competences in this field also plays a role here. It is unclear from

---

[21] Article 127(1) of the TFEU if the Lisbon Treaty enters into force.
[22] Article 122(3) of the EC Treaty (Article 139(2) of the TFEU if the Lisbon Treaty enters into force).
[23] Paragraph 5 of the UK Opt-out Protocol (not amended by the Lisbon Treaty in this respect) and Paragraph 2 of the Danish Opt-out Protocol (similarly unchanged in this respect by the Lisbon Treaty) in conjunction with Article 122(3) of the EC Treaty (Article 139(2) of the TFEU), respectively.
[24] Because Article 43.1 (42.1 after ratification of the Lisbon Treaty) of the ESCB Statute does not mention Article 2 as not applying to Member States with a derogation and because Paragraph 8 of the UK Opt-out Protocol does not mention Article 2 as not applying to the UK.

an academic viewpoint and, as far as one can say from the outside, an issue of discussion within the Eurosystem, how far the ESCB competences in respect of payments stretch.

(ii) ESCB Statements

A first sort of guidance has been given by the Eurosystem itself in a policy statement of June 2001.[25] In respect of retail payment systems, it contains the following statement concerning Eurosystem intervention:

In respect of retail payment arrangements, such systems handle large volumes of payments of relatively low value and generally carry little, if any, systemic risk. As a rule, the definition of the oversight of retail payment systems will continue to be performed by the relevant NCBs. However, where new developments occur or where retail schemes would have potential cross-border implications, general policy lines for oversight are defined at the Eurosystem level.

As this statement makes clear, the Eurosystem had systemic risk clearly in mind when setting out how it would make use of its competences in the area of payment systems. This 'systemic risk' from payment systems has been internationally recognized in the early 1990s, when the Lamfalussy Report on interbank netting schemes was drawn up in the context of the G10.[26]

In the area of retail payments, a more recent statement by the Eurosystem sets out its involvement with the retail payment systems.[27] As we will see, the introduction of a Single Euro Payments Area (SEPA) has drawn the Eurosystem far more into the supervision of payment systems.

In July 2008, in its Payment Systems and Market Infrastructure Oversight Report 2007, the ECB summed up its involvement with oversight of payment and settlement systems—'basic infrastructures needed for the proper functioning of market economies'.[28] It stated that 'their smooth functioning is crucial for the practical implementation of the central bank's monetary policy and for maintaining the stability of and the confidence in the currency, the financial system and the economy in general.' The ECB's oversight function 'aims to ensure the safety and efficiency of payment and settlement systems and central counterparties operating in euro, by applying, inter alia, appropriate minimum

[25] Role of the Eurosystem in the Field of Payment System Oversight, Policy Statement of 21 June 2000, available online at: <http://www.ecb.int/pub/pdf/other/paysysoveren.pdf>.

[26] Bank For International Settlements, Report of the Committee on Interbank Netting Schemes of the Central Banks of the Group of Ten countries, November 1990, available online at: <http://www.rba.gov.au/PaymentsSystem/Publications/BISCommitteeOnPaymentAndSettlementSystems/lamfalussy.pdf>.

[27] See: Central Banks' Provision of Retail Payment Services in Euro to Credit Institutions, Policy Statement, 19 August 2005, available online at: <http://www.ecb.int/pub/pdf/other/policystatementretailpaymentservicesen.pdf>.

[28] ECB, Payment Systems and Market Infrastructure Oversight Report 2007, published 11 July 2008, available online at: <http://www.ecb.int/pub/pdf/other/paymentsystemsandmarketinfrastructureoversightreport2007en.pdf>.

standards and requirements to them'. Although acknowledging that the EC Treaty only explicitly mentions the smooth operation of *payment* systems, the ECB relies on the possibility that *securities and derivatives clearing and settlement* systems—again 'an important component of the domestic and global financial infrastructure'—are 'a source of systemic disturbance' (with such disturbance possibly spilling over to payment systems via delivery versus payment (DvP) settlement methods) for claiming competence to oversee these other systems, as well. Relying for now primarily on standards, minimum requirements, and expectations, rather than on regulations, the ECB expects its oversight to evolve over time. The Eurosystem intends to publish 'a comprehensive overview of its oversight framework in a dedicated oversight policy statement', covering the legal basis, rationale, scope, methods and organization of the oversight function. After all, the oversight activities are carried out in an evolving business and legal environment, characterized by the emergence of pan-European retail payment infrastructures, linkages between 'national' retail payment infrastructures and new SEPA payment infrastructures.

The attribution of competences to the centre (ECB) or the periphery (NCBs) within the Eurosystem is specifically mentioned. It is said that the central bank 'best placed to do so' undertakes oversight of individual systems.[29] '(E)ither because of its proximity to the overseen entity or because of national laws that establish an oversight obligation', a specific entity is charged with 'a leading role' in oversight. Note that the Eurosystem relies on national law attributing (payment systems) oversight for the division of labour among its constituent parts. This 'national' responsibility is 'typically' seen in case of 'systems with a clear national anchorage'. The ECB further specifies that '[f]or systems that have no clear national anchorage, the body entrusted with oversight responsibility is the central bank where the system is legally incorporated unless the Governing Council of the ECB decides to assign the oversight responsibilities to the ECB.'

Another interesting statement made in the Report, from the point of view of the operation of the internal market, concerns the establishment of infrastructures settling payment transactions in euro. Elaborating a previously adopted policy,[30] the ECB adopted a further set of principles[31] in 2007 making a matter of principle of the location within the euro area of 'the main payment infrastructures

[29] Note the similarity of wording with the allocation of cases within the European Competition Network. The Commission Notice on cooperation within the Network of Competition Authorities (2004/C 101/03) [2004] OJ C101/43, mentions the conditions for an authority to be 'well placed' to pursue a case (notably, in paragraph 8). Allocating the handling of individual cases to enforce compliance with competition law differs, of course, from establishing permanent oversight relationships in the performance of the supervisory function of oversight.

[30] ECB Press Release, 'Policy Statement on Euro Payment and Settlement Systems Located Outside the Euro Area', 3 November 1998, available online at: <http://www.ecb.int/press/pr/date/1998/html/pr981103_3.en.html>.

[31] ECB, The Eurosystem Policy Principles on the Location and Operation of Infrastructures Settling Euro-denominated Payment Transactions, 19 July 2007, available online at: <http://www.ecb.europa.eu/pub/pdf/other/eurosystem_policy_principlesen.pdf>.

for euro transactions'. This apparent deviation from the freedom of establishment enshrined in Article 43 of the EC Treaty,[32] is given the following rationale: 'particularly because this would put the Eurosystem's control over the euro at risk'. Even though in line with policies of central banks in the past, which wished to see the main infrastructures for transactions in their currencies established on 'national soil', and which even opposed placement of securities in their currency outside their sphere of influence, this somewhat power-based rationale seems in need of further legal backing.

C. TARGET

In line with the central banks' traditional concerns for systemic risk, the Eurosystem's earliest involvement in payments has been in the context of the establishment of TARGET, the Trans-European Automated Real-time Gross settlement Express Transfer system. It is a *Real-T*ime, *Gross Settlement* (RTGS) system, linking the RTGS systems of the NCBs with that of the ECB and providing a mechanism for the transfer of large value transactions in euro. An RTGS system allows money to be transferred on an order-by-order basis and in real time. This avoids exposure to a counterparty in case of netting at the end of the day when a counterparty failure would lead to the unwinding of all transactions considered complete. RTGS provides for 'immediate finality'. The EU has adopted legislation to underpin this finality.[33] In 2008, the Eurosystem is in the process of migrating[34] towards TARGET2, providing a single shared platform (SSP) to be provided by three NCBs, Banque de France, Bundesbank, and Banca d'Italia.[35]

A further development is the preparation of a platform for post-trading securities settlement (TARGET2Securities, or T2S).[36] This service would bring the ECB and the NCBs involved (those providing TARGET2 plus de Banca de España) into a field hitherto untouched by central banks: the settlement of

---

[32] Article 49 of the TFEU if the Lisbon Treaty is ratified.

[33] Directive 98/26/EC Directive of the European Parliament and of the Council of 19 May 1998 on settlement finality in payment and securities settlement systems [1998] OJ L166/45.

[34] See: <http://www.ecb.int/paym/t2/migration/html/index.en.html>.

[35] See: <http://www.ecb.int/paym/t2/features/html/index.en.html>. Note the tendency towards specialization mentioned above in the context of CCBM2.

[36] T2S is a 'platform for the cross-border and domestic settlement of securities against central bank money [...] serving the Central Securities Depositories (CSDs)', says the ECB on its website. See: <http://www.ecb.int/paym/t2s/html/index.en.html>. See, also: <http://www.ecb.int/press/pr/date/2007/html/pr070308_2.en.html>. See, further, 'The ECB steels itself for a leap outside the realm of rates—A project to set up a single settlement platform for securities holds risks for Europe's central bank', in Financial Times, 17 April 2007, p 9. For an overview of the issues on this initiative, see P Norman, 'T2S: The Next Big Challenge', in SPEED (Settlement • Payment • E-money & E-trading • Development), Vol 2, No 1, Summer 2007, pp13–18. See, finally, ECB Press Release, 'Launch of the TARGET2—Securities project', 17 July 2008, available online at: <http://www.ecb.eu/press/pr/date/2008/html/pr080717.en.html> and the 'T2S User Requirements Management Summary', available online at: <http://www.ecb.europa.eu/paym/t2s/pdf/T2S_URD_V4_080717.pdf>.

securities trading in central bank money, a function now performed by Central Securities Depositories (CSDs). T2S evokes a host of questions on the legal authority of the central banks to undertake this function and on competition aspects, which it is not be possible to dwell on in this context.[37]

All this is background to the creation of the Single Euro Payments Area in which the ECB and the NCBs will be seen to play a dominant role fostering its introduction, guiding its set-up, and overseeing its implementation.

IV. SEPA

A. An Outline of SEPA

The monetary division of the EU between the euro area and the Member States that have not yet adopted the single currency is clearly illustrated by an initial lack of agreement on the exact meaning of SEPA. To some, this acronym stands for: *Single European Payments Area* whereas, for others, it stands for: *Single Euro Payments Area*. So, the question arises whether it is an EU-wide payment system that is the objective, or a euro area-wide one. By now, it is clear that the intention is to establish an integrated market for payment services in euro across the entire EU and the three countries which, together with the EU, constitute the European Economic Area (EEA), plus Switzerland.[38]

The ECB and the European Commission define SEPA as follows:[39]

an integrated market for payment services which is subject to effective competition and where there is no distinction between cross-border and national payments within the euro area—the removal of all technical, legal and commercial barriers between the current national payment markets'.

The same statement contains the following description of the payment structure:

[...] when consumers, businesses and governments are able to make cashless payments throughout the euro area from a single payment account anywhere in the euro area using a single set of payment instruments as easily, efficiently and safely as they can make payments today in the domestic context.

---

[37] These aspects have been extensively discussed in R Smit's presentation 'Towards a Borderless Market in Securities Post-trading: Issues of Competence and Competition' before the Joint ECB-Commission Conference on 'The Safety and Efficiency of Post-Trading Arrangements in Europe', Frankfurt am Main, 21–22 April 2008, available online at: <http://www.ecb.europa.eu/events/pdf/conferences/septa/smits.pdf>.

[38] See the ECB brochure on SEPA, available at the website of the European Payments Council (EPC), at: <http://www.europeanpaymentscouncil.eu/documents/ECB%20SEPA%20Brochure%202006.pdf>.

[39] See the Joint statement from the European Commission and the European Central Bank, 4 May 2006—Single Euro Payments Area, online at: <http://www.ecb.int/press/pr/date/2006/html/pr060504_1.en.html>.

Thus, 'a single domestic payments market in which citizens and economic actors will be able to make payments as easily and inexpensively as in their hometown'[40] will be created. The market players brought together within the European Payments Council (EPC) work together to establish schemes, set frameworks, and adopt standards. Thus, SEPA is by and large an industry-driven process with important impetus from the authorities and underpinned by legislation, to be discussed below.

B. Dateline

The aforementioned Joint Statement from the ECB and the European Commission contains two major dates for the introduction of SEPA:

(1) 1 January 2008, when EU citizens, enterprises and public administrations should be (rather, should have been; see below) able to use both the SEPA credit transfer and the SEPA direct debit payment instruments, technical barriers to cross-border acceptance at the point of sale and cash withdrawals for card payments in euro should also have been removed and interoperability ensured and the necessary conditions for infrastructures to become SEPA-scheme compliant should have to be in place;

(2) 31 December 2010, on which date a critical mass of national credit transfers, direct debits, and card payments should have migrated to SEPA payment instruments.

The changeover originally planned could not be completely implemented in time. As the ECB's Fifth Progress Report on SEPA of July 2007 already made clear a lot of work needed to be done before the 28 January 2008 deadline, a date itself set four weeks later in order not to coincide with end-of-year routines.[41] The availability of a SEPA-compliant direct debit instrument has been delayed,[42] with the effective date now being the transposition date of the PSD, ie 1 November 2009.

C. Some Characteristics of SEPA

SEPA will be characterized by several aspects, which can be summed up as follows:

(1) self-regulation by the industry, which organizes the changeover and sets the standards;

---

[40] Quote from the website of the EPC; see: <http://www.europeanpaymentscouncil.eu/content.cfm?page=sepa_vision>.

[41] And with the changeover to the euro in Cyprus and Malta. See ECB's Fifth Progress Report of the Eurosystem on SEPA, July 2007, p 5, and passim.

[42] See the *SEPA Core Direct Debit Scheme Rulebook* adopted by the EPC on 24 June 2008, available online at: <http://www.europeanpaymentscouncil.eu/documents/EPC016-06%20Core%20SDD%20RB%20V3%201%20Approved.pdf>.

(2) standardization of euro payments across the euro area and beyond;

(3) the intended service level should be at least as good as existing national instruments, but preferably better;

(4) public authorities should take the lead with changeover to SEPA-compliant payments;

(5) effective competition should be ensured; this requires open access and non-discriminatory conditions to join SEPA-compliant payment schemes;

(6) in spite of the previous aspect, there are still concerns by European competition authorities on the effect for consumers and competition, concerns which the ECB has come to endorse more and more;

(7) SEPA will be based on necessary payments legislation, proposed by the European Commission in the context of the 'New Legal Framework', to be discussed below.

SEPA includes common standards for credit transfers, direct debits, and credit and debit card transactions.

D. Competition Concerns

(i) General

The introduction of SEPA takes place at a time when the industry is under scrutiny by the European Commission in the context of its sector inquiry into the retail banking sector. Also, the National Competition Authorities (NCAs) have expressed concerns about the SEPA project. At a relatively late stage in the process towards SEPA, the ECB has added its voice to the chorus of authorities expressing competition concerns. Recently, one NCA scrutinized the national changeover plans towards SEPA and warned of anti-competitive behaviour in the transition process.

(ii) European Commission

In the context of a more general focus on the financial services industry, the European Commissions Directorate General on Competition (DG Comp) notably investigated the retail banking sector on the basis of Article 17(1) of Regulation 1/2003.[43] In its Final Report,[44] the Commission:

• finds symptoms suggesting that competition may not function properly in certain areas of retail banking;

---

[43] Council Regulation (EC) No 1/2003 of 16 December 2002 on the implementation of the rules on competition laid down in Articles 81 and 82 of the Treaty [2003] OJ L1/1, available online at: <http://eur-lex.europa.eu/LexUriServ/LexUriServ.do?uri=OJ:L:2003:001:0001:0025:EN:PDF>.

[44] DG Comp, Communication from the Commission—Sector Inquiry under Art 17 of Regulation 1/2003 on retail banking (Final Report), COM(2007) 33 final, 31 January 2007, available at: <http://eur-lex.europa.eu/LexUriServ/LexUriServ.do?uri=COM:2007:0033:FIN:EN:PDF>.

- considers that the conjunction of sustained high profitability,[45] high market concentration and evidence of entry barriers raises concerns about banks' ability to exploit market power over consumers and small firms;
- notes the existence of entry barriers: both network and standardization requirements and the regulatory environment provide scope for formal cooperation among market players;
- finds substantial discrepancies in merchant, cardholder and inter-bank fees (so-called multilateral interchange fees, or MIFs) across Member States which highlight market fragmentation;
- questions the necessity of MIFs, without already deciding on the acceptability under competition law of these;[46]
- notes that payment systems in some Member States (eg Belgium, Denmark, and Finland) impose particularly high joining fees, thus directly dissuading new entrants to join the circle of members;
- considers that high switching costs lead to low customer mobility.

The full report elaborates these concerns, and others, which have been summarized above on the basis of the executive summary of the Final Report. It notably also devotes passages to the governance structure of the major card issuing schemes, an issue that is of special importance in the context of the transition towards SEPA.

(iii) ECA

Apart from the federal competition authority's investigation, the State authorities together with the latter have issued a report on Competition Issues in Retail Banking and Payments Systems Markets in the EU. This report by the European Competition Authorities, an informal grouping of all EU/EFTA competition authorities, including the European Commission and the EFTA Surveillance Authority, sets out general and SEPA-specific concerns.[47]

The ECA's *general concerns* relate to:

(a) non-discriminatory access rules to payment schemes as incumbents decide on access of newcomers;
(b) the separation between management and ownership of access rules to payment systems;
(c) the lack of consultation of customers on access rules.

[45] Note that this Report dates to early 2007, which is seven months before the start of the credit crisis which has led to enormous losses for financial institutions worldwide.

[46] The Commission notes that: 'most domestic debit card domestic networks set significantly lower (or even zero) interchange fees than international networks on debit card transactions, resulting in generally lower merchant fees' (at p 4).

[47] ECA Financial Services Subgroup, Competition Issues in Retail Banking and Payments Systems Markets in the EU (public version), adopted in Nice (F) on 18–19 May 2006, available online at: <http://www.nmanet.nl/Images/ECA%20FINAL%20REPORT%20PUBLIC%20VERSION_tcm16-89513.pdf>.

The ECA's more *SEPA-specific concerns* are the following:

(a) '[it is] not clear to NCAs that the current process towards SEPA will lead to more competition, lower prices and better services for end users. More consultation is needed on SEPA';

(b) customer mobility becomes especially important in SEPA; there may be cause to establish a European switching facility;

(c) transparent and non-discriminatory terms of access for services provided by infrastructure providers should be guaranteed; the ECA calls for a strengthening of (what was then) Article 23 of the 'New Legal Framework'[48] (see below).

(iv) NCAs

It may be noted that at least one NCA has reviewed the national transitional measures from the introduction of SEPA. After receiving replies to a consultation, the Netherlands Competition Authority, *NMa*, in a document on SEPA,[49] warned banks not to collude on the withdrawal from the market of efficient and user-friendly payment instruments currently in use,[50] announcing that it would scrutinize such behaviour against competition rules.[51] This sits uncomfortably with calls by the Dutch central bank, *DNB*, for an agreed timing-out of non-SEPA-compliant instruments.[52] One can only sympathize with the Dutch credit institutions for being caught between such conflicting demands: although the call for keeping intact safe and efficient payment instruments is understandable from a consumer's perspective, advanced by *NMa*, an agreed timing-out of such instruments seems the option most conducive to the transition to SEPA-compliant instruments, as put forward by *DNB*. In this respect, the public utterance of Competition Commissioner Neelie Kroes on the requirement of SEPA compliance, implying that only technical compliance is needed (instruments should be

---

[48] Currently, Article 28 of the Payment Services Directive (PSD) on access to payment systems.

[49] *NMa*, SEPA vision document 'A Single Payments Market, Increasing Competition?', 29 May 2008, available at: <http://www.nmanet.nl/Images/SEPA%20Vision%20document%20NMa_tcm 16-116625.pdf>.

[50] This refers notably to the PIN payments scheme according to which customers pay through a debit card system, giving the payee a right to collect from the customer's bank through the 'payment chain' including a transactions processor (Interpay). PIN stands for Personal Identification Number. The system is owned by Currence Holding BV, established by the eight major banks in The Netherlands. See: <http://www.currence.nl/PIN.uk/index.html>.

[51] '*Eén betaalmarkt, meer concurrentie?*' ('A single payments market, more competition?'), speech by Pieter Kalbfleisch, Chairman, *NMa*, at the 9th yearly conference on the future of payment systems, 29 May 2008, available online at: <http://www.mededingingsautoriteit.eu/Images/Speech%20 Pieter%20Kalbfleisch%20betalingsverkeer%20290508_tcm16-115835.pdf>.

[52] '*Hoe zorgen we voor een maatschappelijk verantwoorde implementatie van SEPA, naar aanleiding van de zorgpuntennota?*' ('How to ensure a socially acceptable implementation of SEPA on the basis of points of concern raised?'), speech by Flip Klopper, then Director, *DNB*, at the 9th yearly conference on the future of payment systems, 29 May 2008, available online at: <http://www.dnb.nl/dnb/home/ nieuws_en_publicaties/nieuwsoverzicht_en_archief/speeches_2008/nl/46-176507.html>.

so devised as to be technically ready for use across Europe) and not actual usabil-
ity (instruments can, indeed, already be used everywhere in the internal market),
may be relevant for determining which path to follow.[53]

(v) ECB

Even though issues relating to market access and transparency have always figured in the mind of the ECB, it has become more and more focused on effective
market functioning in the context of SEPA. The first major expression of concern
was the publication of *The Eurosystem's view of a 'SEPA for cards'*,[54] in November
2006. In this document, the Eurosystem elaborates its views on how SEPA could
be structured in a manner which 'maximises benefits for Europe's citizens'. It
describes SEPA's characteristics for cards as follows:

(1) consumer's choice among competing payment card schemes without a pre-
    assigned priority in use at point-of-sale terminals;
(2) a competitive, reliable and cost-efficient card market;
(3) no obstacle for merchants to accept any payment cards compliant with the
    SEPA Cards Framework.

The Eurosystem continues with a sketch of the possible options for adopting the
latter Framework. A card scheme may either replace the national scheme by an
international one which is SEPA-compliant (1), it may enter into alliances with
other card schemes or expand throughout the entire euro area (2) or, as a third
option, (3) it may co-brand with an international card scheme. Although all three
options ensure SEPA compliance, the Eurosystem confesses to be 'deeply concerned about a possible evolution whereby the two international card schemes
progressively become the only providers of card payment services offered by
banks in the euro area'.[55] These concerns are based on the fact that international
card schemes typically apply higher interchange fees, leading to an increase in
fees paid, and on retaining the valuable experience of national card schemes in
Europe. Thus, 'the Eurosystem expects at least one European card scheme to

---

[53] In a speech at the ERRT Conference (European Retail Round Table) in Brussels, 14 January
2008, titled 'Europe's Payment Systems after the MasterCard decision', Neelie Kroes, the European
Commissioner for Competition Policy said: 'It is clear that SEPA compliance cannot be interpreted
in a way that a scheme has to cover all the 31 SEPA states. Banks must be able to decide for themselves
whether joining one or other card scheme represents a good business case to them. In other words:
market forces alone shall decide which SEPA states and how many of the SEPA states should actually
be covered by a particular payment scheme. The EPC has just recently confirmed this interpretation.' She further remarked: 'This obviously means that there is no need for national systems to
be replaced by the existing international schemes because of SEPA. And this obviously also means
that new schemes are guaranteed a real chance to enter the markets.' See: <http://europa.eu/rapid/
pressReleasesAction.do?reference=SPEECH/08/9&format=HTML&aged=0&language=EN&guiL
anguage=en>.
[54] ECB, The Eurosystem's View of a 'SEPA for Cards', available online at: <http://www.ecb.int/
pub/pdf/other/eurosystemsviewsepacardsen.pdf>.
[55] Ibid, p 2.

emerge in the coming years.' This means that co-branding (option 3) cannot be the only solution for SEPA, or even the main long-term solution for SEPA in respect of cards. Although the ECB and the NCBs of the euro area accept that co-branding may help banks to fulfill their SEPA datelines they argue that, in the long run, the commercial banks should establish a European card scheme.

Fostering competition is also what the Eurosystem aims at in the remainder of the report setting out its viewpoint on a SEPA for cards. Europe's monetary authority invites Europe's federal competition authority to decide on the acceptability with a view to antitrust law of interchange fees, so that banks have clear guidance in developing their business model for SEPA. The Eurosystem calls for alignment of the position in this respect between the European Commission and NCAs, knowing that both DG Comp and several NCAs (notably the OFT) have (had) cases at hand on MIFs, further discussed in section (*iv*) below. Also in respect of other practices, the Eurosystem would like the competition authorities to clarify whether these MIFs can be accepted. There is a strong preference for standards to ensure open and fair competition. SEPA should not be just a patchwork of national schemes accepting cards from other Member States but should evolve into a truly innovative system of payment providers benefiting from EU-wide economies of scale.

In its Fifth Progress Report on SEPA[56] the Eurosystem again very clearly calls for the creation of an additional European debit card scheme. This time, it openly acknowledges that such a scheme, equivalent to those originating in the USA, Japan or China, is 'a largely political objective, which the Eurosystem invites the banks to share'.[57] Concerning the issue of interchange fees, the European Commission is again called upon to reach a decision on current cases so that the market can establish 'future-proof scheme rules'. The Eurosystem itself professes neutrality in respect of the issue of MIFs but strongly argues that geographical differentiation of interchange fees (if any) is incompatible with SEPA in the long-term. After all, an integrated domestic Euro area market is the objective. Both in respect to card schemes and infrastructures, the Eurosystem lists the requirements for SEPA compliance.

There are four further elements of the involvement of the Eurosystem that merit mentioning here. First, the measure of detail in which the ECB's latest document specifies its views concerning the creation of SEPA means that the industry-led standardization[58] is minutely scrutinized and, if necessary, corrected

---

[56] See ECB, Single Euro Payments Area (SEPA) from Concept to Reality—Fifth Progress Report (July 2007) (hereafter: Fifth Progress Report of the Eurosystem on SEPA), available online at: <http://www.ecb.int/pub/pdf/other/singleeuropaymentsarea200707en.pdf>, p 22.

[57] ECB, Fifth Progress Report of the Eurosystem on SEPA, p 12.

[58] Industry-led standard setting is in itself suspect from a competition law viewpoint. In a different context (of Microsoft setting the standard by being the dominant provider of certain software and hardware), the Court of First Instance, in its judgment of 17 September 2007 in Case T-201/04 *Microsoft/Commission* [2007] ECR II-3601), remarked: 'Although, generally, standardisation may effectively present certain advantages, it cannot be allowed to be imposed unilaterally by

by the EU's monetary authority. Second, the Eurosystem seems to be fully convinced of the merits of free competition. The benefits for the end consumer and
the requirements of effective market functioning are the general themes on which
its involvement with SEPA is described. On the highly-contested issue of the
openness of the payments market for non-banks, the Eurosystem supports initiatives from outside the EPC, the main bulwark of banks promoting SEPA.[59]
The evolution of card fees and prices 'is a very sensitive issue for the Eurosystem',
as it considers that 'SEPA cannot in any circumstances be used as an excuse to
increase the general price level'. '[T]he high efficiency and low fee levels currently
offered by card payment schemes and processors' in several States should be continued under SEPA.[60] Innovation and transparency are catchwords in this Fifth
Progress Report.[61] In it, the Eurosystem even goes so far as to argue for account
number portability, a long-term consumer demand in respect of banks.[62] Third,
the issue of data protection, already mentioned in the Eurosystem's view of a
'SEPA for cards',[63] is again given prominence, doubtless in connection with
the vexed issue of data protection and US anti-terrorist measures in which the
SWIFT scheme was embroiled.[64] The Eurosystem requires card schemes 'to
avoid any transfer of personal data in a non-aggregated form to countries that are
not compliant with the EU's data protection rules'.[65] Fourth and finally, apart
from other issues such as fraud and the speed with which Member States should

an undertaking in a dominant position by means of tying' (paragraph 1152). See for a recent policy
statement on standards: Neelie Kroes, European Commissioner for Competition Policy, 'Being Open
about standards', speech before the OpenForum Europe—Breakfast seminar in Brussels on 10 June
2008, available online at: <http://europa.eu/rapid/pressReleasesAction.do?reference=SPEECH/08/3
17&format=HTML&aged=0&language=EN&guiLanguage=en>.

[59] ECB, Fifth Progress Report of the Eurosystem on SEPA, pp 21–22.
[60] Ibid, p 16.
[61] The Fifth Progress Report of the Eurosystem on SEPA mentions 'innovation' 9 times, 'transparency' 14 times and 'competition' 16 times.
[62] ECB, Fifth Progress Report of the Eurosystem on SEPA, p 19: '[. . .] the Eurosystem would like
to repeat its request for the EPC to devise a long-term solution to provide a more user-friendly account
identifier than the IBAN. While elaborating a long-term solution, the concept of account number
portability should be reviewed.' In this respect, it must be noted that the use of the International
Bank Account Number or IBAN does nothing to promote cross-border bank account portability
as the Member State of establishment and a code for identifying the bank (branch) are included in
this number. For more on account number portability, see Expert Group on Customer Mobility in
Relation to Bank Accounts—Report, Brussels, 5 June 2007; available online at: <http://ec.europa.
eu/internal_market/finservices-retail/docs/baeg/report_en.pdf>, and <http://www.finextra.com/
finextra-downloads/newsdocs/ECaccountswitch.pdf>.
[63] ECB, The Eurosystem's View of a 'SEPA for cards', November 2006, p 13.
[64] See 'ECB Rapped by EU Privacy Regulator over SWIFT', *CentralBankNews.com*, 2 February
2007, and 'Commission Starts Data Transfer Talks with the US', *European Voice*, 1 February 2007.
See also, ECB press release, 'Remarks by the European Central Bank on the Oversight of SWIFT',
1 February 2007, available online at: <http://www.ecb.int/press/pr/date/2007/html/pr070201.
en.html>, and 'Remarks by the European Central Bank on a Resolution Passed by the European
Parliament Relating to the Operations of SWIFT', 15 February 2007, available online at: <http://
www.ecb.int/press/pr/date/2007/html/pr070215.en.html>.
[65] ECB, Fifth Progress Report of the Eurosystem on SEPA, p 15.

implement the necessary legislation supporting SEPA, it is worth mentioning that the Eurosystem, itself relying on data for a proper underpinning of its policies, calls for an increase in the balance-of-payment reporting threshold for euro payments. Reiterating a similar call in 2005, the Eurosystem calls for a revision of the relevant regulation[66] and welcomes national decisions to raise the reporting threshold 'without waiting for European decision'.

(vi) Specific issue: MIFs

The specific issue of MIFs merits a brief interlude.[67] Four-party[68] payment card systems often work on the basis of multilateral interchange fees. These are fees normally paid by the so-called acquiring bank, ie the bank that contracts merchants for card acceptance, to the bank issuing cards to consumers. Card schemes argue that MIFs are crucial for their operations because of imbalances between costs associated with issuing and acquiring services. In its Visa card decision of 2002,[69] the European Commission[70] accepted a modified MIF scheme applicable to cross-border transactions because they cover certain costs in the operation of the Visa card scheme, such as the cost of processing transactions, the cost of providing a so-called payment guarantee to the merchant (who is assured of payment by the credit card issuer) and the cost of the period during which the cardholder does not have to repay his or her debt. In its MasterCard/Europay UK Decision of 2005,[71] the OFT accepted that a collective agreement on an appropriate level

---

[66] Regulation (EC) No 2560/2001 of the European Parliament and of the Council of 19 December 2001 on cross-border payments in euro [2001] OJ L344/13.

[67] For a discussion of MIFs, see: H Leinonen, 'On the Efficiency of Multilateral Interchange Fees (MIFs)—How to Price Cash and Cards in Order to Promote Payment Efficiency?' BoF Online 2007, No 4, Bank of Finland Financial Markets and Statistics, 6 June 2007, Suomen Pankki/Finlands Bank, available online at: <http://www.suomenpankki.fi/NR/rdonlyres/C0528167-B9EA-4E40-A784-EA246FAE8D6E/0/BoF_Online_4_2007_Leinonen.pdf>. Another central banker's view is: SE Weiner (Federal Reserve Bank of Kansas City), 'Interchange Fees in Various Countries: Developments and Determinants', in *Review of Network Economics*, Vol 4, Iss 4, December 2005, available online at: <http://profile.nus.edu.sg/fass/ecsjkdw/weiner_RNE_dec05.pdf>.

[68] The card issuing bank, the bank acquiring merchants who accept card payments, the cardholder, and the card-accepting merchant.

[69] Commission Decision of 24 July 2002 relating to a proceeding under Article 81 of the EC Treaty and Article 53 of the EEA Agreement (Case No COMP/29.373—Visa International—Multilateral Interchange Fee) (2002/914/EC), available online at: <http://eur-lex.europa.eu/LexUriServ/site/en/oj/2002/l_318/l_31820021122en00170036.pdf>.

[70] The Commission had already acted in respect of other aspects of the Visa system. See the its Decision of 9 August 2001 relating to a proceeding under Article 81 of the EC Treaty and Article 53 of the EEA Agreement (Case No COMP/29.373—Visa International) [2001] OJ L293/24, available online at: <http://eur-lex.europa.eu/LexUriServ/site/en/oj/2001/l_293/l_29320011110en00240041.pdf>.

[71] Decision of the Office of Fair Trading, No CA98/05/05, 6 September 2005, Investigation of the multilateral interchange fees provided for in the UK domestic rules of Mastercard UK Members Forum Limited (formerly known as MasterCard/Europay UK Limited), available online at: <http://www.oft.gov.uk/shared_oft/ca98_public_register/decisions/mastercard.pdf>, and the companion paper to the decision, Case CP/0090/00/S, available online at: <http://www.oft.gov.uk/shared_oft/ca98_public_register/decisions/oft811.pdf>.

of MIF could, in principle, benefit consumers and satisfy the exemption conditions of Article 81 and the Chapter I prohibition of the UK Competition Act, but not in the case at hand. Other competition authorities, among whom those in Germany,[72] Poland,[73] the Netherlands,[74] Switzerland,[75] and Australia[76] have also issued decisions on the acceptability of elements of card schemes.[77] The general thrust of the competition law enforcement agencies has been to scrutinize the acceptability of MIFs without going so far as to declaring them incompatible with the law, with the clear exception of Poland's *UOKIK*'s strong stance. The enormous financial interests at stake for the incumbent card schemes and for consumers,[78] and the technicalities of the operation of card systems may explain the fact that protracted proceedings have not led to an overall negative or positive stance towards MIFs.[79] Considering the changes to be effected in card schemes

---

[72] On the involvement of the *Bundeskartellamt* (Federal Competition Office) with inter-bank interchange fees, see A Mundt and M Buch, '*Die Vereinbarkeit von kollektiven Interbankenentgelten in bargeldlosen Zahlungssystemen mit dem Kartellverbot des Art. 81 EGV und Paragr. 1 GWB*' ('The compatibility of collective inter-bank fees in cashless payment systems with the cartel prohibition of Article 81 EC and section 1 of the German Competition Act'), in *Wertpapiermitteilungen*, Vol 55 (2001), No 45, pp 2142–2154. Currently, the *Bundeskartellamt* investigates a case concerning MIFs in Germany.

[73] On 4 January 2007, the Polish Office for Competition and Consumer Protection (*UOKIK*) prohibited the use of interchange fees and imposed fines totalling PLN 164 million (on current exchange rates (July 2008) around EUR 50 million) on the banks concerned. See: <http://www. uokik.gov.pl/en/press_office/press_releases/art72.html>.

[74] The Netherlands Competition Authority (*NMa*) has imposed a fine of slightly more than EUR 30 million on Interpay, the then common enterprise of the major banks in the Netherlands providing payment services, for charging excessive rates for the provision of network services for debit-card transactions (Case 2910/Interpay), at: <http://www.nmanet.nl/engels/home/News_and_ publications/News_and_press_releases/2004/04_10.asp>. On review, this fine was revoked. The fine imposed on the banks that had eliminated competition by setting up Interpay as a central sales office was maintained albeit at a reduced level (from EUR 17 to EUR 14 million). See: <http://www. nmanet.nl/engels/home/News_and_Publications/News_and_press_releases/2005/NMa_Reviews_ Fines_Imposed_on_Banks_and_Interpay.asp>.

[75] Where the competition authority took the position that an MIF was only permitted if 'the advantages of the multilateral procedure outweigh the disadvantages only if the fixing of the [MIF] is objectively limited to the cost elements that are necessarily linked to the functioning of the network', which proved not to be the case in its investigation concluded in 2005. See: <http://www.weko. admin.ch/publikationen/pressemitteilungen/00235/Zusammenfassung-KK-E.pdf?lang=en&PHPS ESSID=803e870c884cfaf0ddf17e90260c17a3>.

[76] The Reserve Bank of Australia (RBA) has also played a major role in reducing MIFs in Australia. For information about the Australian central bank's close involvement in the setting of interchange fees, see: its press release No 2006–08 of 29 September 2006 'Interchange Fees for the Mastercard and Visa Schemes', available online at: <http://www.rba.gov.au/MediaReleases/2006/mr_06_08. html>. The RBA's website contains a host of further information on its oversight of transparent and cost-based fees in the card industry. For the latest policy statement, see: P Lowe, Assistant Governor (Financial System), RBA, 'The Preliminary Conclusions of the Payments System Review', address to the Visa Forum 2008, Hamilton Island, Queensland, 4 June 2008, available online at: <http://www. rba.gov.au/Speeches/2008/sp_ag_040608.html>.

[77] For an extensive and informative overview, see: PVF Bos, 'International Scrutiny of Payment Card Systems', in Antitrust Law Journal, Vol 73, Issue 3, 2006, pp 739–777.

[78] See the website 'stopunfaircardfees' of the EU's retailers' organization Eurocommerce at: <http://www.stopunfaircardfees.eu/index.php?page=home>.

[79] The Commission Decision and the OFT Decision referred to before contain extensive reasoning on the acceptability of the cross-border and domestic interchange fee schemes, respectively. See,

across Europe ahead of SEPA, and in the light of the ECB's insistence that at least one European card system emerges, the ECB's appeal to the competition authorities for clear guidance on the acceptability of MIFs was well-timed.[80] In its MasterCard decision of December 2007, the European Commission concluded that MasterCard's cross-border MIFs inflated the cost of card acceptance for both merchants and shoppers, 'without leading to objective efficiencies or related benefits to consumers'.[81] By making it virtually impossible to negotiate a price 'below the invisible floor of the MIF', MasterCard has created 'an instrument that has the effect of restricting price competition between acquiring banks' that infringes Article 81(1) of the EC Treaty.[82] MasterCard has lodged an appeal with the Court of First Instance.[83] Meanwhile, MasterCard has temporarily repealed its cross-border MIFs as from 21 June 2008.[84]

After the Commission's decision in MasterCard case, the onus is on the card industry to prove why MFIs are necessary and conducive to consumer welfare rather than a commercial choice that comes at a cost to consumers and other economic operators. If MFIs are to be accepted in principle, the card industry should prove why a certain level is acceptable from the viewpoint of competition law.

V. A 'New Legal Framework': The Payment Services Directive

A. Legislative History

The European Commission set out the work on new EU-wide regulations concerning payments by publishing a consultation paper.[85] After a round of

---

also, the European Commission's Interim Report I, Payment Cards, Sector Inquiry under Article 17 Regulation 1/2003 on retail banking, 12 April 2006, available online at: <http://ec.europa.eu/comm/competition/sectors/financial_services/inquiries/interim_report_1.pdf>.

[80] For a critical view of the Commission's approach to MIFs, see J Ordover, M Guerin-Calvert, and P Jones, 'Credit Card Multilateral Interchange Fee Regulation: The Wrong Strategy', draft, 5 January 2005, available online at: <http://www.europeancardreview.com/interchange.pdf>.

[81] L Repa, A Malczewska, AC Teixeira, and EM Rivero, 'Commission Prohibits MasterCard's Multilateral Interchange Fees for Cross-border Card Payments in the EEA', in *Competition Policy Newsletter*, 2008 nr 1, pp 1–7, available online at: <http://ec.europa.eu/comm/competition/publications/cpn/cpn2008_1.pdf>. This article also refers to the previous decision of the Commission in the VISA case.

[82] Ibid, at p 2. See also EC Press Release, 'Antitrust: Commission Prohibits MasterCard's intra-EEA Multilateral Interchange Fees', 19 December 2007, available online at: <http://europa.eu/rapid/pressReleasesAction.do?reference=IP/07/1959>.

[83] Case T-111/08 (*MasterCard and others*, pending) [2008] OJ C116/47.

[84] EC Press Release, 'Antitrust: Commission Notes MasterCard's Decision to Temporarily Repeal its Cross-border Multilateral Interchange Fees within the EEA', 12 June 2008, available online at: <http://europa.eu/rapid/pressReleasesAction.do?reference=MEMO/08/397&format=HTML&aged=0&language=EN&guiLanguage=en>. According to this EU press release, MasterCard repealed the cross-border MIFs because it 'failed to come forward with an alternative MIF that could be justified'.

[85] Communication from the Commission to the Council and the European Parliament concerning a New Legal Framework for Payments in the Internal Market (Consultative Document)

consultations, the Commission submitted a proposal for a Directive on payment services in the internal market.[86] The ECB issued an extensive opinion,[87] welcoming the initiative and suggesting that parts of the legislative texts that are crucial to SEPA should be separated from the more controversial aspects concerning the access to the payment systems for a new class of payment institutions. Consequently, this part could be carved out. As an alternative, the ECB proposed adopting the rules most closely connected to SEPA in an ECB regulation. See paragraph 7.2 of its Opinion, which reads as follows:

7.2 Another possibility might be for the Governing Council of the ECB to adopt an ECB regulation under Article 105 (2) of the Treaty and Article 22 of the Statute which would govern the specific SEPA related provisions of the proposed directive that fall within the ESCB's fields of competence, while recognising, however, that not all provisions facilitating SEPA could be adopted on this basis.

The European Parliament's Committee on Economic and Monetary Affairs issued a report on 20 September 2006, setting out a whole range of technical issues and touching, just as the ECB before it, on the status of payment institutions and their regulation.[88] On the issue of the supervision of the latter, the European Parliament's *rapporteur* argued that payment institutions be subject to the overview of authorities entrusted with prudential banking supervision. The ECB, for its part, had argued in its Opinion that the supervisory competences should be clarified and that the competences of the ECB and the NCBs should be respected. The European Parliament further argued that a three-day execution time for payment orders could be accepted until 1 January 2012 and not, as originally proposed 2010, whereas the normal execution time should be one working day. The *rapporteur* supported the choice of legal basis for the proposal.

B. Payment Services Directive

(i) Overview

After a lot of wrangling, especially on the status of payment institutions and the extent of their regulatory burden, agreement was reached between the Council

---

Document COM(2003) 718 final, available online at: <http://eur-lex.europa.eu/LexUriServ/site/en/com/2003/com2003_0718en01.pdf>. For a summary of the responses, see: <http://ec.europa.eu/internal_market/payments/docs/framework/2004-contributions/annex-02_table.pdf>.

[86] Proposal for a Directive of the European Parliament and of the Council on payment services in the internal market and amending Directives 97/7/EC, 2000/12/EC, and 2002/65 (Document COM(2005) 603 final), December 2005, available online at: <http://eur-lex.europa.eu/LexUriServ/site/en/com/2005/com2005_0603en01.pdf>.

[87] Opinion of the European Central Bank of 26 April 2006 on a proposal for a directive on payment services in the internal market (ECB/2006/21) (2006/C 109/05) [2006] OJ C109/10, available online at: <http://www.ecb.int/ecb/legal/pdf/c_10920060509en00100030.pdf>.

[88] At: <http://www.europarl.europa.eu/omk/sipade3?PUBREF=-//EP//NONSGML+REPORT+A6-2006-0298+0+DOC+WORD+V0//EN&L=EN&LEVEL=1&NAV=S&LSTDOC=Y>.

and the European Parliament on the Payment Services Directive. The European Parliament's position[89] of 24 April 2007 led to agreement with the Council on 13 November 2007.[90] The PSD,[91] as it is known, has a lengthy preamble and is divided into six titles, as follows:

Title I   Subject-matter, scope, definitions
Title II   Payment service providers
          Chapter 1—Payment institutions
          Chapter 2—Common provisions

Title III   Transparency of conditions and information requirements for payment services
          Chapter 1—General rules
          Chapter 2—Single payment transactions
          Chapter 3—Framework contracts
          Chapter 4—Common provisions

Title IV   Rights and obligations in relation to the provision and use of payment services
          Chapter 1—Common provisions
          Chapter 2—Authorisation of payment transactions
          Chapter 3—Execution of payment transactions
          Chapter 4—Data protection
          Chapter 5—Out-of-court complaint and redress procedures for the settlement of disputes

Title V   Implementing measures and Payments Committee
Title VI   Final provisions

The PSD does not contain a precise definition of 'payments'.[92] 'Payment services' are defined as business activities listed in the Annex to the PSD (see below). The closest the Directive comes to defining 'payments' is the terms in which a 'payment transaction' is described: 'an act, initiated by the payer or by the payee, of

---

[89] Position of the European Parliament adopted at first reading on 24 April 2007 with a view to the adoption of Directive 2007/…/EC of the European Parliament and Council on payment services in the internal market and amending Directives 97/7/EC, 2000/12/EC and 2002/65/EC. See: <http://www.europarl.europa.eu/sides/getDoc.do?type=TA&reference=P6-TA-2007-0128&language=EN&ring=A6-2006-0298#BKMD-64>.

[90] On the website mentioned in n 89 above, it says that '(a)s an agreement was reached between Parliament and Council, Parliament's position at first reading corresponds to the final legislative act, Directive 2007/64/EC'. See also, for the adoption by the Council of Directive 2007/64/EC, 2823rd Council meeting General Affairs and External Relations, EN13900/07 (Presse 236) Press Release, Luxembourg, 15 October 2007, available online at: <http://register.consilium.europa.eu/pdf/en/07/st13/st13900.en07.pdf>.

[91] Directive 2007/64/EC of the European Parliament and of the Council of 13 November 2007 on payment services in the internal market amending Directives 97/7/EC, 2002/65/EC, 2005/60/EC, and 2006/48/EC and repealing Directive 97/5/EC [2007] OJ L319/1.

[92] For a discussion of the state of payment regulation in the EU before SEPA and the PSD, see M van Empel, 'Retail Payments in the EU', in (2005) 42 CML Rev 1425–1444.

placing, transferring or withdrawing funds, irrespective of any underlying obligations between the payer and the payee'.[93] Questions on the nature of payments and the nature of money are avoided: the PSD clearly regulates payments in 'fiduciary' money, ie book money, and not in bank notes or coins.[94]

Title II includes a new class of players in the area of payments, payment institutions. Title III contains rules on consumer protection, whereas Title IV sets out rules on authorization, execution, and value date of a payment. The scope of the PSD extends to all payment services provided within the Community, but 'Titles III [Transparency of conditions and information requirements] and IV [Rights and obligations in relation to payment services] shall apply only where both the payer's payment service provider and the payee's payment service provider are, or the sole payment service provider in the payment transaction is, located in the Community'.[95] These Titles III and IV apply to payment services made in euro or the currency of a Member State outside the euro area.[96] National law is to be made compliant with the PSD by 1 November 2009 at the latest.[97]

(ii) Some Issues

The PSD raises a number of questions from both a legal and a policy perspective. These issues are mentioned here before a closer look is taken at the Directive to see whether and, if so, how, it solves these questions.

First, the question arises whether payments law is to be harmonized completely or just partially. Is the PSD's coverage of payments law so encompassing that questions of civil law concerning payments within the EU can be settled finally on the basis of its provisions? Complete coverage of payments law seems warranted but is not likely to have been achieved. The PSD is based on Articles 47(2) and 95 of the EC Treaty:[98] the former provision concerns harmonization, through the adoption of *directives*, of rules relating to the pursuit of business activities in the context of the right of establishment and the freedom to provide services[99] and the latter is the basis for the adoption of '*measures*' (ie, *regulations or directives*) harmonizing rules in the context of the establishment and functioning of the internal market. The contents of the PSD could thus have been adopted in two separate acts: one relating to the licensing criteria and further standards

---

[93] Article 4(5) of the PSD.

[94] These 'cash transactions' are excluded in Article 3(a) of the PSD if directly effected between payer and payee. Cheques are also outside the scope of the PSD. On this, see D Mavromati, *The Law of Payment Services in the EU: The EC Directive on Payment Services in the Internal Market* (European Monographs No 60, Kluwers Law International, 2008) 141–149 and 154–156.

[95] Article 2(1) of the PSD.

[96] Article 2(2) of the PSD. Please, note the extensive list of 'negative scope' in Article 3.

[97] Article 85 of the PSD.

[98] Article 47 of the EC Treaty will become Article 53 of the TFEU, and Article 95 of the EC Treay will become Article 114 of the TFEU if the Lisbon Treaty is ratified.

[99] Article 47 of the EC Treaty also applies to matters regulated in the EC Treaty Chapter on services: Article 55 of the EC Treaty.

for payment institutions and their supervision and another one concerning the regulation of payment services (Titles III and IV of the PSD).[100] As will be discussed below, a threesome of legal instruments—with some of the technical rules pertaining to execution time and value dates enshrined in an ECB regulation— might have been possible or even commendable, even though the applicability of these rules outside the euro area would have posed problems.[101]

Second, the extent of national exemptions (and party exemptions) is an issue. The PSD, although containing a provision entitled 'Full harmonization',[102] is rife with exceptions and exemptions which will make the regulation of payment services differ among the 27 Member States.[103] Some of these exceptions even

---

[100] D Mavromati makes the same point, n 94 above, at 256–257.

[101] As Articles 22 and 34 of the ESCB Statute do not apply in States with a derogation or an opt-out, as will be discussed in section VI.A(ii) below.

[102] See Article 86 of the PSD which states that 'full harmonization' is intended except in respect of 12 specified provisions *insofar* as the PSD contains harmonized provisions.

[103] Without trying to be complete, the following *overview of exemptions and derogations* may be given.

Article 86(1) of the PSD reads as follows: 'Without prejudice to Article 30(2), Article 33, Article 34(2), Article 45(6), Article 47(3), Article 48(3), Article 51(2), Article 52(3), Article 53(2), Article 61(3), and Articles 72 and 88 insofar as this Directive contains harmonised provisions, Member States shall not maintain or introduce provisions other than those laid down in this Directive.' The provisions referred to concern the following issues:

Article 30(2): **Precedence for 1987 Consumer Credit Directive** (CCD)—arguably, also for 2008 CCD.

Article 33: **Member State option** on burden of proof on information requirements lying with the payment service provider.

Article 34(2): **Member State option** to vary threshold amounts for application of party derogations from information requirements for low-value payment instruments and electronic money.

Article 45(6): **Member State option** for more favourable provisions for payment service users in respect of the termination of a framework contract.

Article 47(3): **Member State option** to require payment service providers to provide information on paper once a month free of charge whereas the main rule on information for the pay*er* on individual payment transactions allows digital information ('in an agreed manner which allows the payer to store and reproduce information unchanged').

Article 48(3): Similar **Member State option** in respect of information for the pay*ee* on individual payment transactions.

Article 51(2): **Member State option** not to apply Article 83's option of out-of-court redress procedures between payment service users and their payment service providers to consumers.

Article 52(3): **Member State option** to forbid or limit, with a view to the need to encourage competition and promote the use of efficient payment instruments, the payee from requesting from the payer a charge or from offering him a reduction for the use of a given payment instrument.

Article 53(2): **Member State option** to vary threshold amounts for the application of derogations from certain rules concerning obligations between payment service providers and their payment service users.

Article 61(3): **Member State option** to reduce the payer's liability for unauthorised payment transactions.

Article 72: **Member State option** to require shorter execution times for national payment transactions.

Article 88: **Member State option** to permit legal persons who began their activities of payment institutions before 25 December 2007 to continue without authorisation until 30 April 201; **Permanent exemption** from the authorisation requirement for financial institutions that started business listed as activity no. 4 (Execution of payment transactions where the funds are covered by a

allow different treatment of 'purely national' transactions, reintroducing a concept which is entirely alien to a Single Euro Payments Area (SEPA). This feature has led one author to qualify the PSD as an instrument prescribing 'mixed
harmonization'.[104] Note that these exceptions are not restricted to States outside
the euro area.

Third, the question remains whether the adoption of a directive on issues of a
technical nature concerning payments does not infringe the regulatory competences of the ECB itself. In its Opinion, the ECB argued that it was competent to

credit line for a payment service user) before 25 December 2007, provided the financial institution is
included in the consolidated supervision of the parent.

Moreover, the following Member State options can be distinguished:

Article 2(3): **Member State option** to waive application of the PSD to institutions exempt from
the Consolidated Banking Directive pursuant to Article 2 thereof (with the exception of the central
banks of Member States and post office giro institutions).

Article 7(3): **Conditional Member State option** not to apply the calculation of own funds to
payment institutions included in the consolidated supervision of the parent under the Consolidated
Banking Directive.

Article 8(1): **Member State option** to choose one of three methods for the calculation of own
funds.

Article 9: **Member State (or competent authorities') option** to choose safeguarding requirements
against commingling of funds from payment services with those from other activities.

Article 22(3): **Member State option** to apply the requirement of professional secrecy taking into
account the relevant provisions on professional secrecy in the Consolidated Banking Directive.

Article 26: **Member State (or competent authorities') option** to waive part of the authorisation
procedure in respect of small payment institutions (which apparently may also be natural persons),
subject to certain conditions.

Article 30(1): **Member State option** to apply Title III to micro-enterprises in the same way as to
consumers.

Article 53(3): **Member State option** to limit the derogation from Articles 60 and 61 (payment
service provider's and payer's liability for unauthorised payment transactions) for e-money institutions to payment accounts or payment instruments of a certain value.

And the following **party derogations** are possible:

Article 32(2): Agreement between payment service provider and payment service user on charges
for additional or more frequent information or communication other than specified in framework
contract.

Article 34(1): Party derogations possible from information requirements for low-value payment
instruments and electronic money.

Article 53: Party derogations possible from certain rules in Title III Chapter 2 (Authorisation of
payment transactions).

Article 62: Parties may agree that the payer is entitled to a refund from his payment service provider in a direct debit even though the PSD's normal conditions for this are not met.

Article 65: Party option to include in a framework contract a charge for a notification of a payment
order by a payment service provider to the payments service user if the refusal is objectively justified.

Article 67: Party option to agree that the payment service provider deducts charges from an amount
to be transferred.

Article 68(2): Party option on the scope of application of Section 2 (execution time and value date)
to other payment transactions than those specified in Article 68(1), ie payment transactions in euro,
in another Member State currency or involving only one currency conversion between the euro and
another Member State currency (but Article 73 on value date is 'not at the disposal of the parties').

[104] D Mavromati, *The Law of Payment Services in the EU: The EC Directive on Payment Services in
the Internal Market* (2008).

issue regulations under the ESCB Statute for some of the more technical aspects, closely linked with the establishment of SEPA.

Fourth, the 'light' supervisory regime for payment institutions, which was heavily fought by incumbents (ie, existing credit institutions and e-money institutions) and their spokespersons in the Council and the European Parliament raises the issue of a level playing field in the payment services industry. We will have to wait and see the implementation of the Directive to establish whether the PSD will succeed in creating such a competitive environment. In a point made by another author,[105] different Member States may rely on different sets of exemptions. This is even rather likely as these possible deviations have been included in order to accommodate different concerns by different States. Thus, a real patchwork of rules will be created instead of a single rulebook for payment transactions across Europe.

Fifth, on a more legalistic tone, there is the question whether only legal entities can become payment institutions, or also natural persons. This is important for the separation of funds between payments services and other activities. The proposal was equivocal on this point. The PSD has opted for a definition of a payment institution as a legal persons,[106] although it permits natural persons to be registered as payment institution, by way of exception for small enterprises that will then not be granted the right to establish or provide services in other Member States.[107]

This issue is closely linked to a sixth one, namely that of other activities than payments services which payment institutions may engage in. As will be discussed briefly below, the PSD does not restrict payment institutions to payment services but contains guarantees in case they venture out into other business.[108]

Another more legal issue, the seventh, concerns the question whether payment accounts held at payment institutions constitute 'deposits or repayable funds' and would thereby make payment institutions credit institutions. The PSD specifically provides that 'any funds received by payment institutions from payment service users with a view to the provision of payment services shall not constitute a deposit or other repayable funds within the meaning of Article 5 of Directive 2006/48/EC, or electronic money within the meaning of Article 1(3) of Directive 2000/46/EC.'[109]

---

[105] B Lyddon, 'Europe's Patchwork Directive—Uneven Implementation of the New Directive means Europe's Payments Project May Come Apart at the Seams', in *SPEED*, Vol 3, No 1, 2008, 31–35, at 34.

[106] Article 4(4) of the PSD defines a 'payment institution' as: 'a legal person that has been granted authorisation in accordance with Article 6 of this Directive to provide and execute payment services throughout the Community'.

[107] See Articles 26–27 of the PSD ('Waiver'). See also, Article 13 of the PSD on 'Registration'.

[108] See Article 16 of the PSD. See also, Article 17 of the PSD on (the oversight of) outsourcing of payment services.

[109] Article 16(2) of the PSD. Directive 2006/48/EC of the European Parliament and of the Council of 14 June 2006 relating to the taking up and pursuit of the business of credit institutions (recast) [2006] OJ L177/1, is the Consolidated Banking Directive. Directive 2000/46/EC is the

The eighth issue is whether the competent authorities supervising payment institutions may be distinct from the prudential supervisory authorities for the banking industry. It seems hardly efficient to organize a split. The related question of how to involve NCBs in the supervision of payment institutions brings into focus the long-standing discussion about the allocation of prudential supervisory authority to central banks or to separate agencies. This point is also taken up further below (under *(v)*).

A ninth issue concerned execution time: was this to be day + 1, or will there be exemptions? The PSD has opted for the more efficient (almost) 24-hour approach by regulating that payments should be completed by the end of the business day following that of the payment order. Yet, a temporary derogation (up to three days until 2012) and a special rule for paper-based transactions apply, as well as a national option to shorten the execution time for purely domestic payments.[110]

Finally, a tenth issue is that of implementation once the legal instrument of a directive had been chosen. It is, after all, the timely implementation without infusion of national specificities which determines the level of harmonization achieved. The measure in which Member States make use of the option to invoke exemptions is also relevant here. On top of this, the possibility of divergent transposition dates may make the PSD's rules difficult to apply in practice. When one supposes that one Member State adopts the relevant legislation well in time and another does so only after the ultimate date set for implementation, payment transactions between these States may be subject to different rules as to the rights and obligations of payment services providers, which may even be established in a third State. The idea of adopting the same changeover date, suggested by an author on the PSD,[111] may help solve this problem. Moreover, as the same author on the PSD has argued,[112] the possibility that one State applies PSD rules in areas which do not have to be covered, strictly speaking, whereas another State does not, may also make for 'skewed' applicability of the norms adopted. A case in point is the application of national rules which reflect the PSD to a transaction in dollars between payment service providers in two Member States: Titles III and IV of the PSD do not apply to transactions not in euro or another Member State currency. Likewise, transactions which do not 'end' in the EU may be subject to different regimes, depending on whether the implementing State extends

Directive of the European Parliament and of the Council of 18 September 2000 on the taking up, pursuit of and prudential supervision of the business of electronic money institutions [2000] OJ L275/39, or E-money Directive. The E-Money Directive has been subject to a consultation with a view to its review. See Commission Staff Working Document on the Review of the E-Money Directive, SEC(2006) 1049, 19 July 2006, available online at: <http://ec.europa.eu/internal_market/bank/docs/e-money/working-document_en.pdf>. For more information on the review of the E-money Directive, see: <http://ec.europa.eu/internal_market/bank/e-money/index_en.htm>.

[110] Article 69–72 of the PSD.

[111] B Lyddon, n 105 above, 32, argues for a 'consistent go-live date' for the PSD's implementing legislation.

[112] B Lyddon, n 105 above, 33–34.

the PSD rules to such transactions to which the PSD, strictly speaking, does not apply.[113]

(iii) Different Classes of Payment Service Providers

The PSD distinguishes between different classes of payment service providers. 'Payment services' are those that have been listed in the Annex to the PSD, namely:

(1) Services enabling *cash to be placed on a payment account* as well as all the operations required for operating a payment account.
(2) Services enabling *cash withdrawals from a payment account* as well as all the operations required for operating a payment account.
(3) *Execution of payment transactions, including transfers of funds on a payment account with the user's payment service provider or with another payment service provider*:
    (a) execution of direct debits, including one-off direct debits,
    (b) execution of payment transactions through a payment card or a similar device,
    (c) execution of credit transfers, including standing orders.

(4) *Execution of payment transactions where the funds are covered by a credit line for a payment service user*:
    (a) execution of direct debits, including one-off direct debits,
    (b) execution of payment transactions through a payment card or a similar device,
    (c) execution of credit transfers, including standing orders.

(5) *Issuing and/or acquiring of payment instruments*.
(6) *Money remittance*.
(7) *Execution of payment transactions where the consent of the payer to execute a payment transaction is given by means of any telecommunication*, digital or IT device and the payment is made to the telecommunication, IT system or network operator, acting only as an intermediary between the payment service user and the supplier of the goods and services. (Emphasis added.)

Apart from credit institutions, which have traditionally been the most active players in the field of payments, there will now be a new class of payment institutions but, also, the electronic money institutions, covered by the E-money Directive. Despina Mavromati[114] distinguishes even more payment service providers as regulated by the PSD.[115] For a level playing field for all payment service providers,

---

[113] Article 2(1) and (2) of the PSD.

[114] D Mavromati, *The Law of Payment Services in the EU: The EC Directive on Payment Services in the Internal Market* (2008), at 264.

[115] The ECB and the NCBs, post office giro institutions and Member States or their regional or local authorities.

their access to payment systems is crucial: it is of no use to allow newcomers onto the market without ensuring their ability to offer payment services through existing or newly established payment systems.

(iv) Access to Payment Systems

Thus, the issue of access to payment systems was a crucial one: only if access conditions are clear, non-discriminatory, and unequivocally guaranteed by oversight of their application would the introduction of payment institutions as a new class of entrants into the payment market 'pay off' in terms of better and cheaper service for consumers. Article 28 of the PSD regulates access to payment systems[116] as follows. Payment service providers that are legal persons shall have access to payment systems on the basis of 'objective, non-discriminatory and proportionate' rules. These rules 'shall not inhibit access more than is necessary to safeguard against specific risks such as settlement risk, operational risk and business risk and to protect the financial and operational stability of the payment system'. The same provision further provides that 'payment systems may not impose on providers, users or on other payment systems' (a) 'restrictive rules on effective participation in other payment systems', or (b) 'a rule which discriminates between authorised payment service providers or between registered payment service providers in relation to the rights, obligations and entitlements of participants', or (c) 'any restriction on the basis of institutional status'.

(v) Payment Institutions and their Supervision

The PSD introduces a system of authorization which closely resembles that for credit institutions under the Consolidated Banking Directive.[117] Home State control and mutual recognition have been provided for[118] and a system of notification for out-of-State establishment and the cross-border provision of services.[119] Payment institutions are to have sound and prudent management and should have robust corporate governance,[120] whereas any non-payment services should be conducted through a separate entity if they would otherwise impair (or would be likely to impair) the institution's financial soundness or its supervision by the competent authorities.[121] The suitability of shareholders with qualifying holdings in a payment institution is to be verified.[122]

Initial and permanent capital requirements vary according to the type of business conducted. Initial capital is set at €20,000 for an institution only engaging in money remittance, at €50,000 for an institution whose business consists of

---

[116] Defined as 'a funds transfer system with formal and standardised arrangements and common rules for the processing, clearing and/or settlement of payment transactions' (Article 4(6) of the PSD).

[117] See the Consolidated Banking Directive (n 109 above).

[118] Articles 10(9) and 20–21 of the PSD.   [119] Article 25 of the PSD.

[120] Article 10(4) of the PSD.   [121] Article 10(5) of the PSD.

[122] Article 10(6) of the PSD.

money remittance and acting as an intermediary, and at €125,000 for an entity offering payment services 1–5 in the Annex to the PSD.[123] The minimum own funds[124] required may be calculated by one of three methods among which States may choose:

(1) a method which requires a payment institution to hold own funds of at least 10% of its fixed overheads in the preceding year; or

(2) another method under which a payment institution must have own funds equal to the sum of several amounts resulting from applying a scaling factor *k*—variable according to the payment institution's activities—to 'payment value', ie one-twelfth of the total amount of payment transactions in the preceding year; or

(3) a third method under which a payment institution must have own funds equal to the sum of interest income, interest expense, commissions and fees received, and other operating income, multiplied by a multiplication factor and scaled by a scaling factor *k*. This scaling factor *k* is higher the more activities the payment institution undertakes.[125]

Further safeguards can be found in the requirements of no commingling of funds for other activities with those for payment services and the insulation thereof or, alternatively, their insurance.[126] Other permitted activities for payment institutions are: ancillary services, the operation of payment systems and 'business activities other than the provision of payment services, having regard to applicable Community and national law'.[127] In a further specification[128] of application of relevant laws, the PSD declares the 1987 Consumer Credit Directive[129] to prevail.[130]

The PSD regulates the allocation of supervisory authority. It makes clear that several authorities may be so designated within one Member State, and that these do not have to be those entrusted with prudential supervision of credit institutions. In such cases, cooperation between the various authorities is required, as well between competent authorities of payment institutions as with those

---

[123] Article 6 of the PSD.
[124] As defined in Articles 57 to 61, 63, 64, and 66 of the Consolidated Banking Directive (n 109 above). See Article 7 of the PSD.
[125] Article of the 8 PSD.   [126] Article 9 of the PSD.   [127] Article 16 of the PSD.
[128] Apart from distinguishing payment accounts from deposits or other repayable funds held by credit institutions; see text accompanying n 109 above.
[129] Council Directive 87/102/EEC of 22 December 1986 for the approximation of the laws, regulations and administrative provisions of the Member States concerning consumer credit [1987] OJ L42/48. The PSD does not mention Directive 2008/48/EC of the European Parliament and of the Council of 23 April 2008 on credit agreements for consumers and repealing Council Directive 87/102/EEC, [2008] OJ L133/66. My reading is that the PSD intends to give precedence to Directive 2008/48/EC, as well, with effect from 12 May 2010, when Directive 87/102/EEC shall be repealed.
[130] See Articles 16(5), 30(3), and 51(4) of the PSD.

supervising credit institutions.[131] NCBs are mentioned as potential designees.[132] For effective supervision, close cooperation among the Member States' authorities is crucial. The unpleasant prospect of several competent authorities within a single State may materialize if separate financial supervisory authorities and central banks are each given competences, possibly with the competition authority overseeing compliance with access to payment systems. If even a few States were to opt for several authorities, cross-Union collaboration among them may become very difficult indeed, based on the sheer number of overseers.[133] Supervisory enforcement tools[134] and professional secrecy and exchange of information,[135] including mandatory exchange of information between supervisory authorities of payment institutions with the ECB and NCBs ('in their capacity as monetary and oversight authorities') and with other authorities, is provided for.[136]

(vi) *Transparency of Conditions and Information Requirements for Payment Services*

With the focus of this contribution on the role of the ECB and NCBs in the payments area, the consumer provisions of the PSD will not be discussed at length. Thus, the influence of harmonizing provisions in this area will be briefly sketched, also with a view to assess whether some of these rules might have been adopted by the ECB under its own regulatory powers.

The PSD distinguishes *single payment transactions* from *framework contracts*. For both types of instruments, the PSD sets out extensive information and conditions to be notified to the payment service user.[137] Also, information to be given to the payer and to the payee on transactions is specified.[138] Party autonomy prevails if the payment service user is not a consumer.[139] The PSD protects the parties to a framework contract against early termination.[140] This is subject to a one-month notice, but a two-months notice applies if the contract has been concluded for an indefinite period of time, and, also, if agreed in the framework contract. Also, the costs of termination are regulated: termination shall be free

---

[131] Article 20(3) of the PSD.   [132] Article 20(1) of the PSD.

[133] If 'only' two agencies were entrusted with (various aspects of) the supervision of payment institutions in each State, this would lead to 54 agencies which have to cooperate EU-wide. This is assuming that these agencies include those responsible for the supervision of credit institutions. If the latter were to be separate from those responsible for the supervision of payment institutions, their mutual cooperation would further increase the group of agencies.

[134] Articles 21 and 25(2)–(5) of the PSD.

[135] Article 22 of the PSD, with a Member State option referring to Articles 44–52 of the Banking Directive 2006/48/EC.

[136] Articles 24 and 25 of the PSD.

[137] Articles 37 (single payment transactions) and 42 (framework contracts) of the PSD.

[138] Articles 38–39 (single payment transactions) and 47–48 (framework contracts) of the PSD.

[139] Article 30(1) of the PSD. Note that Article 30 of the PSD, setting out the scope of application of Title III, is one of the provisions giving precedence to the 1987 Consumer Credit Directive, as noted previously.

[140] Article 45 of the PSD.

of charge if the contract was concluded for a fixed period exceeding 12 months or for an indefinite period of time after the expiry of 12 months; in other cases 'charges for the termination shall be appropriate and in line with costs'.

(vii) Title IV—Rights and Obligations in Relation to the Provision and Use of Payment Services

This Title is important for the actual handling of payment transactions. It regulates consent and withdrawal of payment instructions, liability for use of payment instruments and such important issues as execution time and value dates.

Title IV applies to consumers and others but party autonomy prevails in respect of specified obligations when the payment service user is not a consumer.[141] Consent to a payment transaction is required. Consent may be withdrawn but not after the payment order has become irrevocable.[142] The obligations of the payment service user and the payment service provider in relation to payment instruments are regulated[143] and the payment service provider's liability for unauthorised payment transactions is set out. Article 59 distributes the burden of proof in respect of evidence for transactions allegedly unauthorized. Article 60 provides that '[. . .] in the case of an *unauthorised payment transaction*, the payer's payment service provider *refunds* to the payer immediately the amount of the unauthorised payment transaction and, where applicable, *restores the debited payment account to the state in which it would have been had the unauthorised payment transaction not taken place* (emphasis added).' The payer's liability for unauthorized payment transactions is set out in Article 61, which provides: 'the payer shall bear *the losses* relating to any unauthorised payment transactions, *up to a maximum of EUR 150*, resulting from the use of *a lost or stolen payment instrument* or, if the payer has failed to keep the personalised security features safe, from the *misappropriation of a payment instrument* (emphasis added)'. So, if a user has failed to keep safe his PIN or other security features, his protection is the same as when he has been the subject of theft or has lost a payment instrument. However, fraud is punished since 'the payer shall bear *all the losses* relating to any unauthorised payment transactions if he incurred them by acting *fraudulently* or by *failing to fulfil one or more of his obligations* under Article 56[144] *with intent or gross negligence* (emphasis added).'

Receipt, refusal, and irrevocability of a payment order are regulated. As a general rule, the payment service user may not revoke a payment order once it has been received by the payer's payment service provider. Yet, special rules apply for

---

[141] Article 51 of the PSD. Thus, the Title does not contain mandatory rules in respect of others than consumers.

[142] Article 54 of the PSD.   [143] Articles 56–57 of the PSD.

[144] Ie, '(a) to use the payment instrument in accordance with the terms governing the issue and use of the payment instrument; and (b) to notify the payment service provider, or the entity specified by the latter, without undue delay on becoming aware of loss, theft or misappropriation'.

payment orders initiated by or through the payee, for direct debits, and in respect of agreed-date payment orders.[145]

The PSD's rules on execution time and value date (Article 69) are applicable to transactions in euro, to national payment transactions in the currency of a non-euro area State, and to single-conversion (between the euro and the currency of a Member State outside the euro area) payment transactions. The rule is that execution should take place *at the latest by the end of the next business day*. However, this is subject, until 1 January 2012, to a payer and his payment service provider agreeing on a period no longer than three business days whereas, for paper-initiated payment transactions, these periods may be extended by a further business day. Also, a different execution time may be agreed between the parties as Article 68 (1) PSD makes clear: party autonomy prevails.[146]

VI. Payment Services Directive: Criticism[147]

A. Choice of Legal Instrument

(i) General Issue

A single market with a single currency needs a single set of rules concerning this currency. This means that a regulation rather than a directive would have been the correct legal instrument. A directive with national exemptions and variations, some even to be agreed by parties, will not succeed in bringing about a clear-cut set of rules regulating payments within the EU. There will be a patchwork of different legal regimes concerning euro payments, something which is to be deplored. The author's preference would have been for a regulation based on Articles 95(1)[148] and 123(4), last sentence, of the EC Treaty.[149] Even in times when subsidiarity prevails, it would have been appropriate to adopt a directly

---

[145] Article 66 of the PSD.

[146] Except in respect of the value date rule: credit value must be given to an amount credited to the payee's payment account on the business day at which the payee's payment service provider's account has been credited; debit value may not arise before the amount is debited from the payment account (Article 73 of the PSD). Another exception to party autonomy is that parties may not agree on execution time exceeding 4 business days from the receipt of a payment order (Article 68(2) in connection with Article 64 of the PSD).

[147] For a previous critique of the PSD, see R Smits, 'What is Wrong with the Payment Services Directive?', in *SPEED*, Vol 1, No 3, Winter 2006–07, 20–24.

[148] Article 95 of the EC Treaty provides the legal basis for adopting 'measures [ie directives or regulations] for the approximation of the provisions laid down by law, regulation or administrative action in Member States which have as their object the establishment and functioning of the internal market'. If the Lisbon Treaty is ratified, Article 95 of the EC Treaty becomes Article 114 of the TFEU.

[149] Article 123(4) of the EC Treaty concerns the transition to the third stage of EMU. It contains the following passage:

The Council, acting by a qualified majority of the said Member States [i.e. the Member States without a derogation], on a proposal from the Commission and after consulting the ECB, shall take the

effective legal instrument in the area of euro payments. This might also have been achieved if recourse had been had to Article 22 of the ESCB Statute. The prerogatives of the ECB would then have been respected whilst, at the same time, a single set of rules would have applied, at least across the euro area.

(ii) Applicability of a Euro Payments Regulation

The latter restriction is due to the fact that Article 123(4) of the EC Treaty and Article 22 of the ESCB Statute do not apply across the entire EU. Pursuant to Article 43 of the ESCB Statute, Article 22 does not apply in States with a derogation, ie Sweden and all newly acceded States except Slovenia, Malta, and Cyprus and, as from 1 January 2009, Slovakia.[150] Denmark, a Member State with an opt-out, is equated to a State with a derogation.[151] Although Article 122(3) of the EC Treaty does not exclude applicability of Article 123(4) of the same Treaty in States with a derogation, the situation is different for the UK. Pursuant to its Opt-out Protocol, not only Article 22 of the ESCB Statute but, also, Article 123(4) does not apply to the UK.[152] Therefore, should the Council have adopted a regulation based on Article 123(4), this regulation might not have applied in the UK.[153] Should the ECB have made use of its regulatory competences and have adopted a regulation on the more technical aspects of payments services pursuant to Article 22 of the ESCB Statute, this ECB regulation would

other measures necessary for the rapid introduction of the ecu as the single currency of those Member States.

Assuming that the Council can continue to make use of this provision, adoption of a regulation on the introduction of the euro (which the Treaty still calls the ecu) in payments could be based on this provision. The Member States with a derogation (Article 122(5) of the EC Treaty) and the UK (Paragraphs 7 and 5, respectively, of the UK Opt-out Protocol) do not have the right to vote on such measures. Article 123(4) of the EC Treaty does not reappear in the TFEU (supposing ratification of the Lisbon Treaty). Article 133 of the TFEU contains a specific competence to legislate on the euro, which reads as follows: 'Without prejudice to the powers of the European Central Bank, the European Parliament and the Council, acting in accordance with the ordinary legislative procedure, shall lay down the measures necessary for the use of the euro as the single currency. Such measures shall be adopted after consultation of the European Central Bank.' Article 133 of the TFEU would not apply in Member States with a derogation (Article 139(2)(f) of the TFEU), nor in the States with an opt-out due to the Opt-out Protocols of the UK (Paragraph 4 of which, in the post-Lisbon version (Protocol No 15), excludes Article 133 of the TFEU) and Denmark (Protocol No 16 continues the situation under which Denmark, as long as it exercises its opt-out is treated as a Member State with a derogation).

[150] See Council Decision of 8 July 2008 in accordance with Article 122(2) of the Treaty on the adoption by Slovakia of the single currency on 1 January 2009 [2008] OJ L195/24. See also, Council Regulation (EC) No 693/2008 of 8 July 2008 amending Regulation (EC) No 974/98 as regards the introduction of the euro in Slovakia [2008] OJ L195/1, and Council Regulation (EC) No 694/2008 of 8 July 2008 amending Regulation (EC) No 2866/98 as regards the conversion rate to the euro for Slovakia [2008] OJ L195/3.

[151] Paragraph 2 of the Danish Opt-out Protocol.

[152] Paragraphs 8 and 5, respectively, of the UK Opt-out Protocol (Paragraphs 4 and 7 in the post-Lisbon version).

[153] Unless the legal basis would have included Article 95 of the EC Treaty which does apply in the UK.

not have applied in the UK either. Moreover, the ECB regulation would not have applied in all other Member States that have not yet adopted the single currency.[154] Furthermore, it may be argued that an ECB regulation would have to be confined to euro payments and could not extend to payments in the currencies of other Member States.

Nevertheless, it is argued that there are ways around these limitations. The most obvious ones are the adoption of the single currency by the Member States that have not yet done so or the amendment of the EC Treaty and the ESCB Statute so as to make it possible for the Council and the ECB to regulate on euro payments across the European Union.[155] The latter amendment is logical in view of the European sovereignty over its currency yet seems unattainable in the present mood concerning EU competences. Two other methods to extend regulation on euro payments to the 'out' States are the following. The UK, Denmark, and the Member States with a derogation could 'adopt' an ECB payment regulation or a Council payment regulation by specifically allowing their provisions to govern euro payments, or even payments in their national currencies, within their territories. The regulations should provide for this. There is a precedent for this in the option in Regulation No 2560/2001 on cross-border euro payments,[156] which allows an extension of the scope of applicability. It may also 'apply to cross-border payments made in the currency of another Member State when the latter notifies the Commission of its decision to extend the Regulation's application to its currency'.[157] Another, less 'intrusive' method of extending the application of euro payment regulations would be the 'reception' of such rules by declaring them applicable in contracts and other legal instruments in Member States outside the euro area. Although referring to the euro rules as applicable to private law on euro payments outside the euro area would not provide the same legal security, it would certainly go some length towards unifying the law of Europe on euro payments.

B. Necessity of Introducing a New Class of Payment Service Providers

The introduction of a new class of payment service providers, next to credit institutions and e-money institutions, ie the payment institutions, is to be welcomed from a competition point of view. Only if incumbents are kept alert by newcomers who may innovate and raise service levels in the payments industry may the consumer

---

[154] Since Article 43.1 (42.1 in the post-Lisbon version) of the ESCB Statute excludes application of Article 22 to Member States with a derogation.

[155] Beyond the possibility of adopting regulations on the basis of Article 95 of the EC Treaty.

[156] Regulation (EC) No 2560/2001 of the European Parliament and of the Council of 19 December 2001 on cross-border payments in euro [2001] OJ L344/13.

[157] Article 9 of Regulation (EC) No 2560/2001. See the Communication from the Commission pursuant to Article 9 of Regulation (EC) No 2560/2001 of the European Parliament and of the Council (2002/C 165/08) in [2002] OJ C165/36, in which the Commission mentions the notification that Sweden extends the application of this regulation to the Swedish *krona*.

expect benefits from SEPA and its legal underpinnings. Nevertheless, it has to be acknowledged that this issue has prevented a speedy adoption of the PSD.

C. Legal Standards

The draft Directive was certainly not a model of clarity or good drafting. The compromises achieved did not raise the standard on either score. In an area of the law that is not only characterized by its technicalities but also by its immense importance for the daily life of ordinary citizens and economic operators, a legal result more readable and clearer in its intentions would have been very welcome. It may well be that the lack of uniformity achieved by the PSD and the absence of clarity in payment systems rules require new legislation at any early stage. From this point of view, the review clause of Article 87 of the PSD, even though specifically addressing issues of its scope, seems too limited.[158]

D. No Unequivocal Rules on Time of Payment and Execution Time

In line with the preceding remark, the rules on the execution time of payment orders and on value dates seem less clear-cut than they might have been. Acknowledging the technical difficulties of regulating for various types of payments across an entire continent, it has to be admitted that simple short rules on the time of payment would have been preferable. Furthermore, the rules on execution time and on value date are not innovative and may constitute a step backwards for some Member States.[159] In view of the modern mass payment instruments developed in East Asia, SEPA should provide Europe with a chance to catch up. The EU's revelatory environment should be conducive to this rather than protecting, at least temporarily, slack transactions effected by unwieldy incumbents in several Member States.

E. Access for Newcomers

Because SEPA is being established on the basis of standard setting by the payment industry itself, clear access rules and close supervision of their application are of the essence in order to foster increased competition. As it stands, Article 28 of PSD seems to be a sufficient basis for that. Especially, the specification that the 'objective, non-discriminatory and proportionate' access rules 'do not inhibit

---

[158] It refers to specific elements of the PSD which may need to be revised subject to a review by 1 November 2012.

[159] For this reason, Article 72 of the PSD allows Member States to provide for shorter maximum execution times for 'national payment transactions'. This would undermine the territorial scope of the rule and potentially continue national markets which SEPA and the PSD intended to merge into a single pan-European market for payments.

access more than is necessary to safeguard against specific risks', with a further specification of such risks,[160] is useful. It is now up to national legislatures and supervisors to make sure that SEPA's promise to open hitherto national markets is delivered, and to DG Comp and NCAs to ensure that payment systems are indeed open to all relevant players.[161]

F. Competences of the ESCB

Mention has been made several times of the possible interference with the competences of the ESCB. This relates both to the regulatory competence of the ECB pursuant to Article 22 ESCB Statute and to the competences of the NCBs which may have a right to be designated as supervisor of payment institutions.

VII. Conclusion and Recommendations

The introduction of SEPA and the adoption of the PSD mark major steps towards the completion of the monetary union and towards a true internal market for payments. The enhanced scope for competition in the payments industry raises the prospect of payment services at lower prices for the majority of European consumers. Nevertheless, it is sad to see that the completion of the monetary union in the area of payments fulfils the potential of the single currency more than 10 years late: the euro was introduced in 1999 and the PSD and SEPA will not be fully effective before 2010. Better late than never...Additionally, there are several reasons for concern. In order for consumer welfare to be enhanced, it is important that competition, price transparency, and service levels increase everywhere in the EU and do not lead to a deterioration in the position of some Member States with advanced payment systems. The issue of non-discriminatory and transparent access to payment systems on the basis of adequate technical and legal requirements that do not go beyond what is strictly necessary, is of prime importance. The ECB's concerns on competition and on the establishment of a European card scheme reflect challenges of the project which have been highlighted by the completion authorities, as well. A lot of work still needs to be done, not only in the technical area[162] and in respect of communications towards the

---

[160] Mention is made of 'settlement risk, operational risk and business risk and to protect the financial and operational stability of the payment system' but this is not intended to be exhaustive.

[161] The Commission has shown vigilance in respect of access rules when it acted in respect of anti-competitive behaviour in the card industry. See Press Release IP/07/1436, 'Antitrust: Commission Fines Visa €10.2 million for Refusing to Admit Morgan Stanley as a Member', 3 October 2007, available online at: <http://europa.eu/rapid/pressReleasesAction.do?reference=IP/07/1436&form at=HTML&aged=0&language=EN&guiLanguage=en>, and Decision COMP/37.860 (Morgan Stanley/Visa International and Visa Europe), provisional non-confidential version, available online at: <http://ec.europa.eu/comm/competition/antitrust/cases/decisions/37860/en.pdf>.

[162] On the state of the payments industry, the prospects of compliance with the PSD and SEPA and the costs of transition, as well as profitability trends, see the World Payments Report

public and major players in the payments process, but also as regards clarity of rules. As I have argued, the legislative underpinning of SEPA will probably be a patchwork of national laws, more or less harmonized along the same lines. I say 'more or less' as 'goldplating', ie the practice of adding national specialties to the ingredients of EU law when transposing directives, will take its toll. The openness of the implementation process is important in this respect: the better interested parties and outsiders in general can assess the likely rule-making in implementation of the PSD, the greater the chance that they may detect this tendency.[163] Praise should be given to the UK for its unparalleled openness in this respect: it has taken a most active stance in the preparation of the PSD and its implementation.[164]

Even more worrying than divergent implementation is the fact that these somewhat diverging national laws will then be applied by national supervisors most probably—as in the banking industry—in a manner which belies the unity of the market and the singleness of the currency. This could have been prevented, and might still in the future be remedied, by the adoption of a single regulatory framework in the form of a regulation. Either the Council or the ECB might act to replace a continued patchwork of national rules based on a flawed directive by directly effective regulations covering the core issues of payments law. These rules should be forward-looking and stimulate innovation and modernization. For the moment, it is imperative that Member States move fast ahead with implementation of the PSD.[165] Ideally, they should involve the ESCB closely in payment systems supervision as the central banks have core competences in the area which are crucial to an effective implementation of

2007, published on 13 September 2007 by Capgemini, ABN AMRO, and the European Financial Management & Marketing Association (EFMA), available online at: <http://www.capgemini.com/resources/thought_leadership/world_payments_report_2007/>. See the press release at: <http://www.capgemini.com/m/en/doc/World_Payments_Report_2007-PR.pdf>.

[163] Even though it should be acknowledged that this may also lead, perversely, to greater chances for influencing the national legislative process with a view to maintaining national specificities or safeguarding vested interests.

[164] HM Treasury issued a consultation document on the PSD as early as July 2006 (see: <http://www.hm-treasury.gov.uk/media/5/1/payments_condoc040706.pdf>. See also, The Payment Services Directive: A Revised Regulatory Impact Assessment, December 2006, available online at: <http://www.hm-treasury.gov.uk/media/A/8/paymentservices_ria_151206.pdf>. Further documents issued were: Implementation of the Payment Services Directive: A Consultation Document, December 2007, available online at: <http://www.hm-treasury.gov.uk/media/3/7/consult_paymentservice181207>.pdf; HM Treasury Press notice 151/07, 'Treasury Launches Consultation on the Implementation of the Payment Services Directive', 19 December 2007, available online at: <http://www.hm-treasury.gov.uk/newsroom_and_speeches/press/2007/press_151_07.cfm>; Implementation of the Payment Services Directive: A Summary of Consultation Responses, June 2008, available online at: <http://www.hm-treasury.gov.uk/media/1/0/consult_paymentservicesdirective_response170608.pdf>; and Implementation of the Payment Services Directive: A Consultation on the Draft Legislation, July 2008, available online at: <http://www.hm-treasury.gov.uk/media/A/1/consult_paymentservices-draftleg210708.pdf>.

[165] See the Ecofin Council conclusions on SEPA, Press Release, 2844th Council meeting Economic and Financial Affairs, Brussels, 22 January 2008, available online at: <http://www.europeanpaymentscouncil.eu/documents/ECOFIN%20Conclusions%2022%20January%202008.pdf>.

the single monetary policy.[166] From a legal perspective, both the legislation and its implementation through supervision should respect the central banks' autonomous powers. This means that they should have a role in the supervision of payment institutions.

It is not only in the area of payments that law and practice do not fully match the potential of the monetary union in Europe. Its economic union should be better governed, as well.[167] Not only have Member States established a bad record in abiding by the budgetary rules of Article 104 of the EC Treaty[168] and the Stability and Growth Pact, they also lose no chance for bickering about policies instead of aligning them forcefully. A united stand on the international scene is sorely lacking,[169] even whilst monetary and exchange-rate policies have become exclusive Community competences since 1999.[170] It is not only for the sake of Europe and its position in the world, or for European consumers and citizens, that the argument is made that Europe should get its house in order, both in respect of payment services and of economic governance. Only if the EU is able to achieve good regulation and proper governance on the basis of streamlined decision-making, is it free to devote its energies to the major challenges ahead and around. These global challenges include the pressing needs of addressing climate change, energy conservation and supply, the achievement of the Millennium Development Goals,[171] peace (Darfur, Middle East, …) and inspiring answers to the perceived threats of economic and cultural globalization, which require communication of economic and social successes and involvement in inter-faith and inter-cultural dialogue.[172] Clear rules and a well governed integrated open market should provide a solid internal basis for Europe's outward-looking contributions to the world.

[166] See the ECB's reasoning underpinning oversight activities in its July 2008 Payment Systems and Market Infrastructure Oversight Report 2007 (see n 28 above).

[167] See R Smits, 'Some Reflections on Economic Policy', in *Legal issues of economic integration* 34(1): 5–25, 2007.

[168] Article 126 of the TFEU if the Lisbon Treaty is ratified.

[169] As rightly advocated by the European Commission ('The most effective way for the euro area to align its influence with its economic weight is by *developing common positions and by consolidating its representation, ultimately obtaining a single seat* in the relevant international financial institutions and fora', (emphasis in the original) in its Communication EMU@10: Successes and Challenges after 10 years of Economic and Monetary Union (Document COM(2008) 238 final), 7 May 2008, available online at: <http://ec.europa.eu/economy_finance/emu10/com2008_238en.pdf>, and the report with the same title, at: <http://ec.europa.eu/economy_finance/publications/publication12682_en.pdf>. See, also, L Bini Smaghi, 'A Single EU Seat in the IMF 'Journal of Common Market Studies 2004, Vol 42, No 2, 229–248, and R Smit's thesis (n 7 above), ch 6.

[170] Or from later dates for Member States that adopted the single currency after the euro's launch (Greece: 2000; Slovenia: 2007; Cyprus and Malta: 2008; Slovakia: 2009). Of course, the 'out' Member States retain their competences in the monetary field.

[171] See <http://www.un.org/millenniumgoals/>.

[172] See Decision No 1983/2006/EC of the European Parliament and of the Council of 18 December 2006, concerning the European Year of Intercultural Dialogue (2008) [2006] OJ L412/44. See also: <http://www.tv1111.eu>.

Legal and Economic Appraisal of the 'More Economic Approach' to Unilateral Exclusionary Conduct: Regulation of Loyalty-Inducing Rebates (Case C-95/04P)

*Leonardo Borlini**

Abstract: The European Court of Justice (ECJ) judgment in the *British Airways* case has settled the treatment of targeted and loyalty-inducing rebates/commissions confirming the legal test being applied to assess exclusionary unilateral conduct. The timing of the decision, issued after the publication of DG Discussion Paper on the Application of Article 82 of the Treaty to Exclusionary Abuses, makes it necessary to appraise it within the context of the 'more economic approach' orientating the review process of abuse doctrine. This article approaches the issue by first summarizing the various phases of the *British Airways* case in the light of the relevant legal precedents. Thereafter, the main arguments advanced against the European Courts' pronouncements from a legal viewpoint are assessed. The article suggests that such criticism calls for a dramatic change in the 'structionalist test' adopted by the European institutions. That course would be of primary relevance: not only would it plainly conflict with the teleological interpretation of Article 82 of the European Community Treaty (EC Treaty) vis-à-vis exclusionary conduct, but it would entail a shift to analysis centred mainly (when not only) on the effects produced over the *short run*. The article goes on to weigh the treatment of exclusionary rebates as shaped by the recent case law against the *economic approach* set out by the DG Discussion Paper. The focus is on the economic standards suggested therein, alongside their implications and drawbacks. Finally, assuming a strictly economic viewpoint, the article explores the 'more economic approach' both towards retroactive rebates, and, more generally, exclusionary conduct. By bringing into play the insights provided by information economics, behavioural

* PhD Candidate in International Law and Economics, Bocconi University, Milan. LLM Cantab, Researcher for the Paolo Baffi Centre on Central Banking and Financial Regulation, Bocconi University. Earlier drafts of the article have benefited from invaluable input by Professor Giorgio Sacerdoti and Professor Rodolfo Jannaccone Pazzi. The author would also like to thank Professor Piet Eeckhout and Professor Takis Tridimas: without their encouragement this publication would not have been possible. The views expressed are personal.

economics, and dynamic economic theories, the article suggests that relevant aspects of the 'more economic approach' which should orientate the review process the abuse doctrine is undergoing are far from being uncontroversial. In light of the above, we argue that, first, the European Courts' late decisions mirror a stance of truly *juris-prudentia*, and, secondly, the advocated role of economics for the European Competition policy ultimately represents a crucial *political* choice.

I. Introduction

On 15 March 2007, the ECJ dismissed British Airways' (hereinafter: BA) appeal[1] against the judgment of the European Court of First Instance (CFI),[2] which, in turn, had upheld the Commission's decision finding that the BA's loyalty-inducing targeted scheme for travel agents infringed Article 82(b), and (c) of the EC Treaty.[3] Unsurprisingly, despite the ECJ judgment settling the legal proceeding once for all, it mitigates neither the ongoing debate on the regulation of discounts and rebates applied by dominant firms—including commission schemes on the buying side—nor the more general dispute on the role of sound economics in applying Article 82 to exclusionary conduct. Whereas some have captioned the meaning of the ruling 'good news for small competitors',[4] other reactions seem quite hostile towards the ECJ stance, describing the judgment under examination as a transitional and ill-founded ruling.[5] For we are not in front of pretentious arguments of lawyers who will bring in just 'any case that makes money',[6] and this seminal case deals with issues of wider relevance concerning the scope of Article 82,[7] alongside its enforcement to exclusionary abuses of dominant

---

[1] Case C-95/04P Judgment of the Court (Third Chamber) of 15 March 2007—*British Airways plc v Commission of the European Communities, Virgin Atlantic Airways Ltd,* (Rec.2007,p.I-2331).

[2] Case T-219/1999 Judgment of 17/12/2003, *British Airways/Commission,* (Rec.2003, p.II-5917).

[3] 2000/74/EC: Commission Decision of 14 July 1999 relating to a proceeding under Article 82 of the EC Treaty (IV/D-2/34.780—*Virgin/British Airways*) (OJ [2000] L 30/1).

[4] J McDowell and D Hendry, 'A Victory for the Little Guy. The European Court of Justice Dismisses BA Loyalty Rebates' (2007) 6(4) Competition Law Insight 3 *et seq.* For a comprehensive reconstruction and detailed analysis of the case under discussion, see O Odudu, 'Annotation of Case C-95/04 P, British Airways plc v Commission, judgment of the Court of Justice (Third Chamber) of 15 March 2007' (2007) 44 CML Rev 1781–1815.

[5] See, for instance, B Allan, 'Virgin-v-British Airways: Orthodoxy Prevails', available online at: <http://www.globalcompetitionpolicy.org>. Needless to emphasize that the Commission welcomed the ECJ judgment; see Competition: Commissions welcomes European Court of Justice in the Virgin/ British Airways case, Brussels, 15 March 2007, available online at: <http://www.europa.eu.int>.

[6] Perils of this sort are put forward by R Pitofsky, in the Panel Discussion, 'Policy, Objectives, Enforcement Tools and Actors, Types of Abuses, The Case of Excessive Pricing', in CD Ehlermann, and I Atanasiu (eds), *European Commission Law Annual: 2003. What Is an Abuse of Dominant Position?* (Hart, 2006), at 35.

[7] Amongst the most renowned EC competition law (and EU law) textbooks, which address the case at hand, see R Whish, *Competition Law* (5th edn, Oxford University Press, 2006) 695–698; A Jones and B Sufrin, *EC Competition Law. Text, Cases; and Materials,* (2nd edn, Oxford University Press, 2004) 440 *et seq;* A Arnull, A Dashwood, M Dougan, M Ross, S Spaventa, and D Wyatt,

position,[8] the judgment is analysed along with the European Commission's process of internal review concerning that sort of conduct. The latter was announced in June 2003 by Mario Monti, the then competition Commissioner,[9] and led to the publication of the European Commission DG Discussion Paper on the Application of Article 82 of the Treaty to Exclusionary Abuses (hereinafter, the DP) on 19 December 2005.[10] This process seems far from being completed.[11] Nonetheless, the DP (the only tangible result thus far) presents a quite neat economic and effect-oriented framework.[12] Thus, 'the timing of the judgment is...somewhat ironic as it essentially reinforces the Commission's traditional enforcement practice at time when' it seems 'to move towards a more effect-based approach'.[13] The ECJ ruling in *British Airways* represents a fundamental precedent for the treatment of loyalty-inducing rebates. What is more, the analysis of the case, its judicial solution, and the criticism it has been facing allow us

Wyatt & Dashwood, European Union Law (5th edn, Sweet & Maxwell, 2006) 1066–1068; G Monti, 'Competition Law and Policy', in D Chalmers, C Hadjiemmanuil, G Monti, and A Tomkins, *European Union Law* (Cambridge University Press, 2006) 1050–1051; M Dabbah, *EC and UK Competition Law: Commentary, Cases and Materials* (Cambridge University Press, 2004) 368; D Chalmers and G Monti, *European Union Law. Updating Supplement*, (Cambridge University Press, 2008) at 171–174. For an energetic critique of the CFI's ruling, see J Kallaugher and B Sher, 'Rebates Revisited: Anticompetitive Effects and Exclusionary Abuses under Article 82' (2004) 25(5) ECLR 263 *et seq.* An opposite view is taken by L Gyselen, 'Rebates: Competition on the Merits or Exclusionary Practice?', in Ehlermann and Atanasiu, n 6 above, 287 *et seq.*, especially 312–314. For further considerations on the application of Article 82 of the EC Treaty to the granting of rebates by dominant firms, as substantiated by the CFI decisions in *British Airways* and *Michelin II*, see HG Kamann, E Bergmann, 'The Granting of Rebates by Market Dominant Undertakings under Article 82 of the EC Treaty' (2005) 26(2) ECLR 83–89.

  [8] For ease of reference abusive conduct is usually declined in two categories: exploitative abuses (including those which aim to harm the customer of the dominant firm); and exclusive abuses (ie behaviours designed to impact negatively on rivals). See, *ex multis*, G Monti, n 7 above, at 1048.

  [9] At the 8th Competition Law and Policy Workshop in Fiesole, Florence, June 2003. To appreciate the various nuances this process entails see, *ex multis*, M Monti, in Ehlermann and Atanasiu, n 6 above, at 7, and P Lowe, Director-General, DG Competition Speech at 30th Annual Fordham Corporate Law Institute Conference, 23 October 2003.

  [10] DG Discussion Paper on the Application of Article 82 of the Treaty to Exclusionary Abuses, available online at: <http://europa.eu.int/comm/competition/antitrust/others/discpaper 2005.pdf>.

  [11] Suffice it to highlight that by the established deadline for comments (31 March 2006), over 120 responses from a wide range of commentators were generated. That bears stark testimony to the difficulty of finding common ground on some crucial issues concerning exclusionary abuses. See DG Competition website for discussion paper, results of consultations and hearings, online at: <http://ec.europa.eu/comm/competition/antitrust/art82/index.html>. After having convened a hearing on the Discussion Paper on 14 June 2006, the senior officials made numerous speeches outlining the DG Competition's reaction to the comments; see J Kallaugher and A Weitbracht, 'Article 81 and 82 EC in 2006 – The Year in Review' (2007) 28 ECLR 316–324, at 320.

  [12] V Mertikopoulou, 'DG Competition's Discussion Paper on the Application of Article 82 to Exclusionary Abuses: the Proposed Economic Reform from a Legal Point of View' (2007) 28 ECLR 241–251, at 241, remarks that 'emphasis on economics, akin to the common law approach, is the basic characteristic of the review, and a manifestation of the ever-expanding institutional dynamics inherent to the European Community'. On the convergence between *law* and *economics*, as a constituent element of the current education of lawyers see AT Kronman, *The Lost Lawyer. Failing Ideals of the Legal Profession* (Harvard University Press, 1993) 166 *et seq.*

  [13] McDowell, and Hendry, n 4 above, at 4 *et seq.*

to consider a more general and basic issue, that is the role of economics for the current and future enforcement of Article 82 of the EC Treaty. In other terms, the treatment of exclusionary retroactive rebates constitutes the *fil rouge* of our work. Eventually, it permits us to leave the analysis of the specific case at hand, and to turn to the process of reorientation of the treatment of *general* exclusionary conduct by dominant undertakings under Article 82. This inductive operation is facilitated by the very fact that makes the case at issue rather controversial: rebates represent a peculiar form of price competition.[14] As such their treatment entails issues which go to the very heart of any anti-trust policy, and inevitably involves economic considerations.

II. General Framework

Three lines of reasoning should be developed in order to appraise the ECJ ruling in *British Airways* and the criticism it has raised. First, the ECJ judgment (particularly its most criticized passages) is read following an essentially legal viewpoint, in light of the applicable precedent under Community competition law. Secondly, the chronological circumstance that the DP is published *after* the CFI and *before* the ECJ have handed down their respective judgments explains part of the criticism against the ruling of the latter. Therefore, the above mentioned case law is weighed against the relevant aspects of the *likely* reorientation in the application of Article 82 of the EC Treaty to exclusionary rebates. Finally, we question whether 'sound economics' *alone* can lead this process of reviewing, without altering the very nature of the EC competition regulation of dominant undertakings' conduct as expressed by a teleological interpretation of Article 82. Such a three-fold analysis allows us to highlight the intricacy of the subject under consideration, and, at the same time, to show that rulings, as the one being discussed, do not necessarily mirror a misunderstanding of the microeconomic analysis of the competitive process. Rather, they address the need of safeguarding primary legal values and the pragmatic aim of permitting the enforcing authorities (the European Commission and the national authorities of the 27 Member States) an expeditious intervention according to sound principle of administration of justice. In addition, they may be seen as safeguards for a specifically *European* perspective of anti-trust law. The remainder of the article follows the analytical framework just sketched out. We first summarize the *British Airways* case, taking into due account both the European Courts' rulings and the treatment of retrospective discounts in some of the cases decided under Article 82. The second part of this article contains a legal appraisal of the criticism the case at hand has triggered out. The essence of our analysis is that the main critiques raised against

---

[14] Note that 'fidelity rebates' represent 'a topic with which Community law has always had particular difficulty'; see Allan, n 5 above.

the ECJ's ruling should be read as *more general* arguments in favour of a changed competition *policy* concerning exclusionary abuses of dominant position. On the whole, such critiques seem to advocate a reading of the 'protection of competitive structure' aim which appears rather different from that implied by the teleological interpretation the ECJ gives to Article 82. The third part turns to the DP's approach in assessing rebates, ie 'retroactive discounts applicable where a customer exceeds a specified target for sales in a defined period'.[15] To consider the settled case law in the light of the positions expressed in the DP makes it easier to show how difficult it can be to reconcile encouraging *prima facie* efficient pricing behaviour, while, at the same time, ensuring that dominant firms do not foreclose efficient rivals.[16] While assessing the DP's approach to retroactive rebates we mention how the main economic literature underpinning EC competition law addresses this conduct. In the final part we attempt to explore the (current and potential) role of economics and its implication for the ongoing review process towards unilateral exclusionary conduct.

III. The British Airways Case

Let us start with a summary of the *British Airways* case.

A. The Commission's Decision

Following a complaint lodged by Virgin Atlantic Airways—(Virgin) the then new entrant—about agreements between BA and travel agents relating to commissions and other financial incentives for the sale of BA tickets,[17] the Commission decided to initiate a proceeding in relation to BA's marketing agreements with United Kingdom travel agents and adopted a statement of objections against BA on 20 December 1996. The BA's bonus schemes provided travel agents with a basic commission for the sale of BA tickets and a separate additional performance bonus calculated by reference to the increase in sales compared to individualized volume targets. In other words, BA compared the

---

[15] Kallaugher, and Sher, n 7 above, at 263.

[16] Or, in Judge Richard Posner's pithy terms, '"the exquisite problem" of dealing with conduct that is both exclusionary and efficient'; cited, *ex multis*, by P Marsden, 'Art 82 Review. DG-Comp Officials Now Need to Set Out a Convincing Theory of Likely Harm to Consumer', in (2006) 5(11) Competition Law Insight 3.

[17] In detail, BA concluded agreements with travel agents established in the United Kingdom and accredited by the International Air Transport Association (IATA) entitling them to a basic standard commission on their sales of BA air tickets. Between 1996 and 1997, that commission amounted to 9% on sales of international tickets and 7.5% for ticket sales on domestic flights. In addition to that basic commission system, BA concluded agreements with IATA travel agents comprising three distinct systems of financial incentives: marketing agreements, global agreements and, finally, a performance reward scheme. For further details as to the running of each agreement and scheme see *British Airways plc v Commission*, n 2 above, paras 6–14; Gylesen, n 7 above, at 312 *et seq*.

travel agents' sales during the yearly, quarterly, or monthly reference period with its sales in, respectively, the previous year, the corresponding quarter in the previous year, or the corresponding month of the previous year. What is more, the performance bonus was payable on *all* BA tickets sold, not just those above the target sales threshold (so called *rolled back* payments).[18] As Gylesen remarks, BA 'rewarded customers meeting the volume targets with rebates which were calculated on the basis of these customers' total sales and not just on the basis of the incremental sales (ie, sales exceeding the volume target)'.[19] On 17 November 1997, BA adopted a third type of incentive scheme, consisting of a new system of performance rewards, applicable from 1 January 1998 (the new system of performance rewards), the main difference with the previous bonus scheme being that the travel agent's performance was measured by comparing its sales in a given month with those of the same month in the previous year.[20] Virgin made a complaint to the Commission concerning this revised system of financial incentives as well. Interestingly, in *Virgin/British Airways* the Commission for the first time dealt with a loyalty-inducing scheme in the services sector and on the buying side. By a decision of 14 July 1999, it condemned incentive schemes established by BA as an abuse of its dominant position on the UK market for air travel agency services, and fined it Euro 6.8 m. According to the Commission, both BA performance bonus schemes amounted to an abuse of its dominant position by rewarding travel agents' loyalty *and* discriminating against some travel agents with the object and effect of excluding BA's competitors from the UK market for air transport.[21]

---

[18] Jones, and Sufrin, n 7 above, at 440.

[19] Gylesen, n 7 above, at 313.

[20] The essential features of the changed system of performance rewards are the following: (1) 'In addition to the new basic flat commission rate of 7% to be applied thenceforth to all tickets sold in the United Kingdom, each travel agent could earn an additional commission of up to 3% for international tickets and up to 1% for domestic tickets. The size of the additional variable element for domestic and international tickets depended on the travel agents' performance in selling BA tickets. The agents' performance was measured by comparing the total flown revenue arising from the sales of BA tickets issued by an agent in a particular calendar month with that achieved during the corresponding month in the previous year.' (2) '... every percentage point of improvement in performance level over a benchmark of 95% earned the travel agent an additional variable element of 0.1% by way of extra commission on the sale of international tickets and in addition to the basic commission of 7%. For sales of domestic tickets, the variable element was 0.1% for every 3% increase in sales over the 95% benchmark. The maximum variable element payable to travel agents under the new performance rewards system was 3% for international tickets and 1% for domestic tickets for a performance level of 125% or above in both cases.' See Case T-219/1999 *British Airways plc v Commission*, n 2 above, paras 15–16.

[21] *Virgin/British Airways*, n 3 above, Recitals 96–111, and Article 1 of the contested Decision: '[BA] infringed Article 82 [EC] by operating systems of commission and other incentives with the travel agents from whom it purchases air travel agency services in the United Kingdom, which, by rewarding loyalty from the travel agents and by discriminating between travel agents, have the object and effect of excluding BA's competitors from the United Kingdom markets for air transport.' See also G Monti, n 7 above, at 1051.

B. The CFI's Judgment

BA appealed this decision to the CFI in 2003. In support of its appeal, BA submitted eight pleas in law (ranging from alleging that the Commission lacked competence to those which, on various grounds, claimed that there was no abuse of a dominant position). Each plea was, however, rejected by the CFI, which, therefore, upheld the Commission's decision that BA had breached Article 82. In particular, regarding whether there was an abuse of a dominant position, the CFI maintained that:

- the Commission was correct to define the relevant market as air ticket distribution services in the UK;[22]
- BA held a dominant position in this market;[23]
- BA had applied dissimilar conditions to equivalent transactions given that different agents would receive different levels of commission for exactly the same level of revenue;[24]
- the loyalty enhancing scheme limited the access of BA's competitors;[25] and
- there was no economic justification to the exclusionary practice.[26]

Before turning our attention to the appeal brought before the ECJ, it is worth considering these findings closely, given that some of them were appealed and gave rise to severe critiques by renowned commentators.[27] First, the CFI found that the Commission was right in taking the view that BA was in a dominant position by defining a market consisting of air travel agency services in the UK where BA was the dominant *buyer*.[28] Secondly, the Commission held that BA occupied a

---

[22] As to the definition of the relevant product and geographic market, see Case T-219/1999 *British Airways plc v Commission*, n 2 above, respectively, paras 94–100 and 110–116. The contested decision supported that the product market to be taken into consideration, for the purposes of establishing the dominant position of BA, is comprised by the services which airlines purchase from travel agents for the purposes of marketing and distributing their airline tickets, *Virgin/British Airways*, n 3 above, Recital 72. The issue of market definition under EC competition law cannot be suitably addressed here. Suffice it to remember that it should be looked at as a means to an end. As G Monti, n 7 above, at 1035 highlights: 'To an economist market definition is a way to determine whether the undertaking has market power.' See also M Monti, Market Definition as a Cornerstone of EU Competition Policy Workshop on Market Definition, 5 October 2001, available online at: <http://europa.eu.int.comm/competition/index.en.html>.

[23] See *British Airways plc v Commission*, n 2 above, paras 189–197.

[24] Ibid, paras 233–240.   [25] Ibid, particularly, paras 270–278.

[26] Ibid, paras 279–293.

[27] See, among the others, Kallaugher and Sher, n 7 above, at 264 *et seq*; and R O'Donoghue, 'Over-Regulating Lower Prices: Time for a Rethink on Pricing Abuses under Article 82 EC', in Ehlermann and Atanasiu, n 6 above, at 388–399.

[28] BA argued that the market identified by the Commission did not really exist and that even if it did, the Commission had incorrectly considered the relevant market: it should have looked instead at the position of BA on the air transport market. The CFI upheld the Commission's definition of the relevant market and its finding of dominance, making it clear that it is possible for a buyer to be in a dominant position. See Arnul, Dashwood et al, n 7 above, at 1043: 'Although much of the case law concerns dominance held by producers or suppliers... *buyer* power may also lead to abuses under

dominant position within the relevant market even though BA's market share for some of the relevant period was less than 40%. Some commentators maintain that this figure is very low for a finding of dominance.[29] However, as it is apparent from the relevant passage of the CFI judgment, a number of special factual circumstances led the Commission and the CFI itself to hold that BA was dominant with such a relatively low market share, notably: (a) BA's share was significantly greater than the share of any other individual competitor and, indeed, of the next five competitors combined; (b) it had been at or above that level for the preceeding 10 years; (c) BA's position was reinforced by considerable barriers to entry (notably its slot holding at Heathrow).[30] Needless to say that this finding represents a remarkable case for the relevance of factors other than market share to assess dominance.[31] Whilst it is evident from the scope and the terms of BA's appeal to the CFI that the company disagreed both with the Commission's assessment of the relevant market and its finding of dominance, this part of the decision was not subject to appeal, since appeals to the ECJ may be made only in relation to matters of law, and not in relation to matters of fact and evidence. Thus, BA was likely to have considered that it had little chance of persuading the ECJ that an incorrect legal test had been applied. Thirdly, the CFI upheld the Commission's finding that BA's schemes were abusive on *two grounds*: not only were they designed to obtain the loyalty of the distributors (and hence to foreclose distributors' market to competitors), but they were also discriminatory in that the different commissions paid to travel agents distorted competition between them.[32] Indeed, The BA's performance reward schemes 'could result in different rates of commission being applied to an identical amount of revenue generated by the sale of BA tickets by two travel agents, since their respective sales figures, and hence their rates of growth, would have been different during the previous reference period'.[33] Therefore, according to the CFI, BA's performance

---

Article 82.' Kamann, and Bergmann, n 7 above, at 83–84, point out the BA practices 'constituted an abuse of the market dominant position on the market for air transport. This was even though the conduct had direct effects only on the travel agency services market. However, a *nexus* between these markets existed: due to the services of the travel agents a high number of BA tickets were sold.' See *British Airways plc v Commission*, n 2 above, at paras 127–135.

[29] See, among the others, S Lawrence, 'Taking a Tough Line on Fidelity Rebate' (2007) 5 Competition Law Insight, 6 *et seq*.

[30] See *British Airways plc v Commission*, n 2 above, at paras 190–225. O'Donoghue, n 27 above, at 388, argues: 'The Commission focused on BA's market share (42% of the market at the date of the introduction of the rebates, compared to 5.8% for the next-largest supplier and less than 4% each for all the others).'

[31] In commenting the case at hand, Jones and Sufrin, n 7 above, at 347, point out that: 'The lower is the market share of the undertaking, the greater the significance which attaches to other factors indicating dominance.' See also G Monti, n 7 above, at 1043–1045.

[32] To this extent, BA's conduct was contrary to subparagraph (c) of the second paragraph of Article 82 of the EC Treaty.

[33] See *British Airways plc v Commission*, n 2 above, para 235. This mechanism entails, for example, that Agent X who sold tickets worth £100,000 in Year 1 and £200,000 in Year 2, received a greater commission than Agent Y who sold tickets worth £ 200,000 in both years.

reward scheme, 'by remunerating at different levels services that were nevertheless identical and supplied during the same reference period', distorted 'the level
of remuneration which the parties concerned received in the form of commissions paid by BA'.[34] Since the ability of agents to compete highly depended on
their financial resources, this distortion eventually could alter the very process
of competition among them.[35] To put it differently, those discriminatory conditions of remuneration affected the competition in supplying air travel agency
services to travellers and stimulation of the demand from competing airlines for
such services. Fourthly, having highlighted that, BA's performance reward system was found discriminatory and, thus, contrary to Article 82(2)(c) of the EC
Treaty, it is to make clear that the main complaints by BA (and the critiques commentators have raised) were against the CFI upholding of the Commission's decision in relation to the exclusionary effect on airlines competing with BA caused
by the 'fidelity-building' nature of BA's incentive.[36] The CFI deemed, as the
Commission had done, the retroactive structure of the commissions paid by BA
to be the very cause of their exclusionary effect. As such it was capable of hindering maintenance of the existing level of competition or the development of such
competition on that market.[37] A passage of the CFI's analysis about this central issue deserves to be entirely quoted as it effectively illustrates the European
Courts' approach to the issue. In paragraph 293 the CFI stated:

... for the purpose of establishing an infringement of Article 82 EC, it is *not* necessary to
demonstrate that the abuse in question had a *concrete effect* on the markets concerned. It
is *sufficient* in that respect to demonstrate that the abusive conduct of the undertaking in
the dominant position tends to restrict competition or, in other words, that *the conduct is
capable* of having, or *likely to have*, such an *effect*.[38]

---

[34] Ibid, para 236.   [35] Ibid, paras 237–238.

[36] See, for instance, Kallaugher, and Sher, n 7 above, at 263 *et seq*; Jones, and Sufrin, n 7 above, at
442, observed that 'much of this part of the judgment follows very closely the *Michelin II* judgment.
In particular paragraphs 241–7 are almost identical to paragraphs 54–9 of *Michelin II* ...'. See Case
T-203/01 *Manufacture Français des Pneumatiques Michelin* [2003] ECR II- 4071. On this aspect of
the CFI judgment, see Kamann and Bergmann, n 7 above, at 83. See also B Sher, *Price Discounts and
Michelin II; What Goes Around Comes Around* (2002) 10 ECLR 482 *et seq.*, at 483–485.

[37] In particular, the CFI rejected the BA's objections which deny the fidelity-building nature of
the system. Given the specific factual circumstance of the case—'the rival undertakings were not in
a position to attain in the United Kingdom a level of revenue capable of constituting a sufficiently
broad financial base to allow them effectively to establish a reward scheme similar to BA's in order to
counteract the exclusionary effect of that scheme against them on the United Kingdom market for air
travel agency services.' See *British Airways plc v Commission*, n 2 above, paras 272–278.

[38] Ibid, para 293, italics added. Note, however, that the CFI found the disputed practices were
not only 'indeed likely to have a restrictive effect on the United Kingdom markets for air travel agencies and air transport, but also that such an effect has been demonstrated in a concrete way by the
Commission' (para 294). See also paras 295–296. Furthermore, it maintained in para 297 that: '...
where an undertaking in a dominant position actually puts into operation a practice generating the
effect of ousting its competitors, the fact that the hoped-for result is not achieved is not sufficient to
prevent a finding of abuse of a dominant position within the meaning of Article 82 EC.'

Borlini

Finally, the CFI admitted that loyalty-inducing rebates infringe Article 82 unless they are based on 'economically justified considerations'.[39] This implies that, according to the CFI, not all loyalty-inducing rebates are abusive. Thus, the CFI suggests a two-step test to draw the line between legitimate and abusive rebates. First, it must be assessed whether the rebate scheme is capable of producing foreclosure effects. Secondly, if competition may be foreclosed, it must be considered whether the undertaking offering the rebates has any objective economic justification for its conduct.[40] For this, it has to be determined whether the exclusionary effect may be compensated, or outweighed, by advantages in terms of efficiency which also benefit the consumer. If not, that system must be regarded as an abuse. The CFI concluded that BA had failed to show such justification.[41]

C. The Appeal to the ECJ

Following the CFI's decision, BA appealed to the ECJ. However, only the seventh plea was brought before the ECJ:

claiming that there was no abuse of a dominant position, BA challenged the Commission's assertion that the bonus schemes at issue engendered discrimination between travel agents established in the United Kingdom or produced an exclusionary effect in relation to competing airlines.[42]

In support of its appeal, BA raised five pleas in law, alleging that the CFI erred in law respectively:

• by applying the wrong test in assessing the exclusionary effect of the bonus schemes at issue and concluding that they had no objective economic justification;

[39] *British Airways plc v Commission*, n 2 above, para 271.
[40] See *ex multis* Jones and Sufrin, n 7 above, at 445; Whish, n 7 above, at 701. This approach is in line with the settled case law and the Commission's practice as well. Incidentally, the two-step process—(i) Is there a *prima facie* abuse?—(ii) Is it nonetheless objectively justified?—was authoritatively questioned by Advocate General Jacobs in his opinion in *Syfait*. The Advocate General seemed to suggest a one-step analysis, combining the two into a single question: 'I would add that the two-stage analysis . . . is to my mind somewhat artificial. Art.82 EC, by contrast with Art.81 EC, does not contain any explicit provision for the exemption of conduct otherwise falling within it. Indeed, the very fact that conduct is characterised as an "abuse" suggests that a negative conclusion has already been reached, by contrast with the more neutral terminology of "prevention, restriction, or distortion of competition" under Art.81 EC. In my view it is therefore more accurate to say that certain categories are types of conduct on the part of a dominant undertaking do not fall within abuse at all.' Opinion of Advocate General Jacobs, Case C-53/03 *Synetairismos Farmakopoion Aitolias & Akarnanias (Syfait) and others v Glaxosmithkline AEVE*, delivered on 28 October 2004, available online at: <http://curia.europa.eu/>, para 72. See also Mertikopoulou, n 7 above, at 247 and *contra* Gyselen, n 7 above, at 291: '. . . the circumstance that Article 82, unlike Article 81, lacks a provision which provides dominant companies with an explicit legal basis for invoking objective justifications for their market behaviour is immaterial since the purpose of Article 82 cannot be to deprive companies of the possibility to out-come their rivals with lawful means'.
[41] *British Airways plc v Commission*, n 2 above, paras 279–285.
[42] Case C-95/04P *British Airways plc v Commission*, n 1 above, para 15.

- by disregarding evidence that BA's commissions had no material effect on its competitors;
- by failing to consider whether there was prejudice to consumers under sub-paragraph (b) of the second paragraph of Article 82 of the EC Treaty;
- by wrongly concluding that the new performance reward scheme had the same effect as the marketing agreements, despite the difference relating to the duration of the respective reference periods, and by not analysing or quantifying the effects of that scheme on BA's competitors;
- by misapplying subparagraph (c) of the second paragraph of Article 82 of the EC Treaty in assessing the discriminatory effect of the bonus schemes at issue in relation to United Kingdom travel.

All of the five grounds of appeal were rejected, as being inadmissible or lacking in foundation, in accordance with the Advocate General Kokott's recommendation.[43] Looking more closely at the substantive findings, the ECJ rejected BA's argument that the CFI (and the Commission) had made use of the wrong test in assessing the exclusionary effects of the bonus schemes and concluding that they had no objective economic justification. Unsurprisingly, the ECJ rejected the argument that the CFI should have based its findings on the practices specifically listed in Article 82, confirming that such practices do not represent an exhaustive list. The ECJ also maintained that the bonuses and discounts schemes considered in the cases of *Michelin*[44] and *Hoffman-La Roche*[45] are only examples of anti-competitive rebates/discounts and not exhaustive:[46] When applying Article 82, the Commission and the national authorities of the Member States should consider that new types of conduct constantly evolve.[47] Turning to the essence of BA's first plea, the company had argued that the test used by the CFI does not distinguish between schemes which build/enhance customer loyalty by legitimate price competition and those which exploit unlawful exclusionary tactics. In all likelihood, this was the central plank of the appeal and needs to be deepened. According to BA, Article 82(b) entails unlawful foreclosure only where the disputed conduct limits rivals' sales to the prejudice of consumers. That would occur, BA argued, only if incentives are conditioned upon exclusive dealing or where the sales outlet cannot choose freely between the dominant firm and its competitors (as would be the case, for instance, where the outlet could only make profits by dealing exclusively or mainly with the dominant firm or where the dominant firm's prices are predatory). Thus, incentives which do not have

---

[43] Case C-95/04P *British Airways plc v Commission, Opinion of Advocate General Kokott*, of 23 February 2007, respectively, paras 40–63; 70–83; 84–91; 92–102; and 104–134.

[44] Case *Michelin II*, n 38 above, at 98 *et seq*.

[45] Case 85/76 *Hoffman-La Roche v Commission* [1979] ECR 461.

[46] See Case C-95/04P *British Airways plc v Commission*, n 1 above, especially paras 57–60. Gyselen, n 7 above, at 296–305, considers also *European Sugar Industry; Hoffman-La Roche; Hilti; British Plasterboard; Solvay; and ICI* as examples of cases concerning rebates linked to exclusive dealing. See also Jones and Sufrin, n 7 above, at 411–429 and Whish, n 7 above, at 695–703.

[47] See *Opinion of Advocate General Kokott*, n 43 above, paras 37–39.

that quality constitute legitimate price competition to the benefit of the consumers. The ECJ rejected this argument, confirming the CFI conclusion as to the legal test being applied. In considering whether a system of discounts or bonuses constitutes an abuse, it first has to be determined whether those discounts or bonuses can produce an exclusionary effect. The relevant questions, according to the Court, are whether the discounts or bonuses are capable, firstly, of making market entry very difficult or impossible for competitors of the dominant undertaking and, secondly, of making it more difficult or impossible for its customers to choose between various sources of supply or commercial partners.[48] If this first condition is fulfilled, consideration must then be given to whether there is an objective economic justification for the discounts/bonuses granted.[49] Applying this to the facts of the case, the ECJ held that the CFI was right to examine that BA's bonus schemes had a loyalty enhancing effect capable of producing an exclusionary effect[50] and was without objective economic justification.[51] In particular, it observed in respect of the 'exclusionary effect' condition that the CFI had correctly considered the following three features:

(i) The schemes were based on *individual* targets, dependent on growth in turnover of individual agents over a particular period.[52]
(ii) The schemes were *retroactive*: they rewarded the entire turnover achieved from BA sales, not just the incremental turnover (ie the part above the performance threshold). As a result, even small changes in sales could have a disproportionate effect and this provided a strong incentive not to switch.[53]
(iii) Other airlines would have to offer disproportionately higher rebates to outbid BA's rebates. Given the structure of the market and BA's position, other competitors were not able to do so.[54]

Following Advocate General Kokott's recommendations, the Court deemed that both BA's allegations, concerning its competitors financial capability of making competitive counter-offers to travel agents and the CFI's over-estimation of the very noticeable effect at the margin of the bonus schemes at issue were matters of interpretation of facts and, as such, not matters for reconsideration in the context of an appeal on questions of law.[55] Coming to the possibility of the dominant undertaking showing that it had objective economic justification for offering

---

[48] See Case C-95/04P *British Airways plc v Commission*, n 1 above, para 69. J Temple Lang, 'Fundamental Issues Concerning Abuse Under Article 82 EC', Regulatory Policy Institute, Oxford, July 2005, Annual Competition Policy Institute, available online at: <http://www.rpieurope. org/2005%20Conference/Temple_Lang_under-Article-82EC.pdf>, proposes the following definition for exclusionary/anti-competitive abuse: 'conduct which limits the production, marketing or technical development of competitors of the dominant enterprise, to the prejudice of consumers, by creating handicaps, difficulties for competitors which would otherwise exist or be as serious. Such conduct may lead to change in the market structure, but can be illegal whether or not it does so.'
[49] Ibid, para 70.   [50] Ibid, para 77.   [51] Ibid, para 90.
[52] Ibid, para 72.   [53] Ibid, paras 73–74.   [54] Ibid, paras 75–76.
[55] Ibid, paras 78–79.

rebates, the ECJ confirmed that the decisive question is 'whether the exclusionary effect arising from such a system, which is disadvantageous for competition, may be counterbalanced, or outweighed, by advantages in terms of efficiency' which, demonstrably, also benefit consumers.[56] The BA's argument was found to challenge the assessment of facts and evidence made by the CFI, hence, to go beyond ECJ's limited jurisdiction to assess errors of law.[57] The second ground of appeal was, therefore, dismissed in its entirety. Before entering into the analysis of the remaining pleas, let us distil two points of the ECJ's assessment:

(i) The European Courts emphasize that proof of *potential* foreclosure is a *necessary* condition for the application of Article 82.[58]

(ii) Thus, the three features taken into account by the Courts in order to assess the *potential* exclusionary effects of the BA's scheme should be considered merely *indicative*: since demonstration of appreciable potential effects is necessary, the anti-trust authority concerned (*in casu*, the Commission) 'must always assess the allegedly abusive practices in their market context'.[59]

As to the second plea, BA also argued that the CFI had erred in law by disregarding evidence which BA claimed to show that there was no material effect on its competitors. The CFI was held not to have committed any error of law in concluding that the bonus schemes had a fidelity-building effect. It had examined the schemes by, for instance, emphasizing the very noticeable effect at the margin, (ie for those sales which agents needed to make in order to reach the target level). As such, BA could not claim that the CFI did not examine the probable effects of those schemes on its competitors.[60] The ECJ was also satisfied that the CFI did take into account all relevant circumstances, reiterating that it cannot substitute its appraisal of market conditions and the competitive situation for that of the CFI.[61] Pursuant to the third plea, the CFI had made an error in law by not examining whether BA's conduct involved a prejudice to consumers within the meaning of subparagraph (b) of the second paragraph of Article 82 of the EC Treaty. The ECJ dismissed BA's argument that the CFI did not properly take

---

[56] Ibid, para 87. See also *Opinion of Advocate General Kokott*, ibid, n 43 above, para 86.

[57] See Case C-95/04P *British Airways plc v Commission*, n 1 above, paras 87–89.

[58] Gyselen, n 7 above, at 292–295, groups several foreclosure scenarios. According to the conceptual framework he suggests, in the first scenario there is evidence of *exclusionary intent*, which, although forensically useful for the anti-trust authority, is a sufficient, not necessary condition for the application of Article 82 of the EC Treaty. By contrast, the empirical evidence that the dominant undertaking behaviour's has *actually* produced foreclosure effects to the detriment of the competitive process constitutes a sufficient, but not a necessary condition. The third scenario is the one at issue, where only a *potential foreclosure* effect can be shown.

[59] Ibid, at 294. The issue of the standard of proof needs to be systemically addressed. Indeed, it is highly questionable if the specified 'possible' foreclosure standard ought to be replaced by a 'likely' or even an 'actual' standard. See Kallaugher, and Sher, n 7 above, at 273; and see section III (A), (C)(i) and IV (D) of this article.

[60] See Case C-95/04P *British Airways plc v Commission*, n 1 above, paras 96–100.

[61] Ibid, para 101.

account of whether consumers suffered prejudice as a result of the schemes. In another rather critical passage it stated:

> Article 82 EC is aimed not only at practices which may cause prejudice to consumers directly, but also at those which are *detrimental to them through their impact on an effective competition structure*, such as is mentioned in Article 3(1)(g) EC that Article 82 is designed to *protect the structure of the market*.[62]

This excerpt is extremely suggestive of the EC Courts' approach on abusive conduct. Predictably, it has been widely criticized. The issue will be dealt with thoroughly below;[63] here suffice to remark that the CFI was found right in not examining whether 'BA's conduct had caused prejudice to consumers within the meaning of subparagraph (b) of the second paragraph of Article 82 EC'—which explicitly refers to prejudice to consumers—and, instead, examining whether the bonus schemes in question 'had a restrictive effect on competition and to conclude that the existence of such an effect had been demonstrated by the Commission in the contested decision'.[64] To us, the ECJ's stance on the issue could not have been stated more clearly. BA's third plea was therefore rejected. The fourth ground of appeal was in two parts. The first involved the differences between the marketing agreements and the performance reward scheme BA had adopted in 1998, while the second turned once again to the requirements for proving the foreclosure effect of these commission schemes. As to the first, BA complained that the CFI had erred in ascribing the same effects to the marketing agreements and the performance reward scheme, whereas each was subject to separate conditions and that at least the performance reward scheme could not have had foreclosure effect primarily on account of its short reference periods. The ECJ first confirmed that the CFI had pointed out the differences between that scheme and those agreements in relation to the duration of the periods under consideration and had ascribed, irrespective of this difference, decisive importance to the fact that: (i) both those agreements and that scheme could have resulted in exponential increases in commission rates from one period to another by reason of their very noticeable effect at the margin; and (ii) BA's competitors were not in a position, given their much smaller market share, to offset the overall effect of those agreements and that scheme with counter-offers.[65] Thereafter, the ECJ dismissed this part of the plea on the ground that the assessment of these factual circumstances fell entirely within the jurisdiction of the CFI and it was not for the Court of Justice, on an appeal, to substitute its own assessment of the same facts.[66] As

---

[62] Ibid, para 106, italics added.   [63] See section IV below.

[64] Case C-95/04P *British Airways plc v Commission*, n 1 above, para 107.

[65] Ibid, para 113.

[66] Ibid, para 114. The possible impact of the duration of the reference period on the exclusionary effect of *retroactive* rebate/bonus scheme is another rather disputed point. We refer to the results of the recent study of FP Maier-Rigaud, 'Switching Costs in Retroactive Rebates—What's Time got to do with it?' (2005) 26(5) ECLR, 272–276. In contrast to the traditional literature, it maintains that 'the length of the reference period in rebate schemes is *irrelevant* for the economic assessment of switching

regards the second part of the fourth plea, the ECJ, contrary to what BA had argued, found the CFI's analysis of the effects of the bonus schemes at issue sufficiently quantified.[67] Finally, BA claimed that the CFI had misapplied Article 82(c) which forbids dominant undertakings from applying dissimilar conditions to equivalent transactions with other trading parties, thereby placing them at a competitive disadvantage. BA argued that the CFI was in error to assume that certain travel agents sales could be seen as equivalent transactions and not to give detailed finding as to the existence of competitive disadvantage. The ECJ rejected these arguments, holding that it was appropriate for the CFI to find that the schemes resulted in different travel agents receiving different rewards in return for the sale of an identical number of tickets (depending on whether the sales targets were met and exceeded).[68] The ECJ went on to say that the CFI had been justified in concluding that, for there to be abusive discrimination, the abuse must hinder the position of business partners of the dominant undertaking, with 'no requirement of actual quantifiable deterioration in the competitive position of *individual* companies'.[69] Therefore, it held that the CFI did not err in law in concluding (without further analysis) that agents' ability to compete had been affected by the schemes due to discriminatory treatment of equivalent transactions.[70]

IV. Legal Appraisal and Criticism

Overall, the ECJ dismissed BA's appeal without much ado. The judgment was quite predictable and in line with the case law on retrospective and loyalty inducing rebates. Moreover, most of the pleas were rejected because of the limited jurisdiction of the ECJ on the assessment of the facts and related evidence. Thus, one may wonder why it has been slated as an ill-founded judgment challenging the hard task of those who are willing to *develop* European Competition law in recent years.[71] The critics of the ECJ's ruling essentially argue that: 'the judgment contains an unqualified restatement of the old orthodoxy with its emphasis on structured-based standards that attach decisive importance to the form of the conduct under examination',

costs and a potential foreclosure effect' because switching costs are 'an increasing function of the rebate percentage and the amount of units already bought from the dominant firm;' (ibid, at 272). The DG Discussion Paper, n 10 above, paras 160–161, seems to accept this thesis, explicitly recognizing that in most cases the length of the reference period has no bearing on the loyalty enhancing effect. The exception is where the dominant company is no longer an unavoidable trading partner. See *contra* Kallaugher and Sher, n 7 above, at 267, who, in their thorough critical assessment of Gyselen's paper (see Gyselen, n 7 above) maintain that the reference period plays a crucial role in determining the switching costs for customers. The latter would increase during the reference period up to prohibitive levels towards the end of it (so called 'suction effect'). As a consequence, 'uncertainty is, at best, a secondary factor in assessing the extent of switching costs'.

[67] Case C-95/04P *British Airways plc v Commission*, n 1 above, para 123.
[68] This part of the plea was, therefore, deemed inadmissible; see ibid, para 137.
[69] Ibid, para 145, italics added.   [70] Ibid, paras 148–149.
[71] Allan, n 5 above.

and 'the Court reached a conclusion of *per se* prohibition subject only to the possibility of objective economic justification'.[72] In the eyes of other commentators, as a consequence of the approach adopted by the European Courts in *British Airways*, firms 'which offer loyalty schemes in a number of markets may need to adapt their commercial offering in those markets' where they are dominant.[73] A further portrait of the judgment at issue is worth recalling: 'the clarity given … will not only be good news for smaller airlines which are trying to target new markets or new routes dominated by one or two incumbents, but will also be good news for any smaller player faced with a dominant company that is using its discount or rebate structure to protect its market power'.[74]

Our analysis of the case and the criticism it has raised proceeds as follows:

(a) Some premises are taken in order to cast light on the lively debate about this ruling. These preliminary considerations regard: first, the necessity of distinguishing the limited jurisdiction of the ECJ on several pleas against the CFI's judgment from what they might conceal, that is criticism directed to some of the basic principles, which govern the treatment of exclusionary rebates, and the judgment at stake upheld. Secondly, a certain misconception of basic notions of legal and economic competition theory, which, likewise appears to have played a relevant role within the ongoing debate upon alleged exclusionary rebates. Finally, the stark contrast between the outcome of the *Virgin/BA* case within the EC and US legal system.[75]

(b) After having outlined the likely impact of the circumstances just mentioned, we attempt to show that the debate about the ECJ's position on loyalty-inducing rebates/commissions hides more fundamental issues regarding the underlying objectives pursued by applying Article 82 to exclusionary abuses. In the light of this thesis, we assess the two main critiques against the judgment at stake concerning, respectively, the relative weight being attributed to the protection of the competitive structure, and the supposed too formalistic

---

[72] Allan, n 5 above. Similar stances have been put forward in several legal newsletters published right after the ECJ's ruling. See, for instance, R Grasso, *Servizi di agenzia di viaggi aerei: la Corte di giustizia conferma che per accertare l'abuso di posizione dominante è sufficiente l'idoneità della condotta a determinare effetti anticompetitivi. Le nuove guidelines sono più lontane?*, available online at: <http://www.freshfields.com/onlinenewsletters/newslettergiuridica/newspage/giuridica.asp?newsitem=300#D>.

[73] Lawrence, n 31 above, at 8 *et seq.*, although we do not really see the 'number of difficulties' this can create, those dominant firms' management might happen to face.

[74] J McDowell and D Hendry, n 4 above, at 3.

[75] Rather ironically, the two rival airlines involved in the disputes started both in the EU and the US have recently been the central characters of another anti-trust case: According to the Britain's Office of Fair Trading and the America's Department of Justice, on this occasion their behaviour has been that of allied players rather than competitors. See 'Flying in Formation. It Takes Two to Fix prices', in *The Economist*, 2 August 2007: 'A clearer example of illegal price-fixing than that between BA and Virgin would be hard to imagine. The two firms discussed "fuel surcharges" at least six times between August 2004 and January 2006, during which time they rose from £5 to £60 on a return ticket. […] Although the fines closed the civil case against BA, a criminal investigation is taking place as well, and the OFT refuses to say whether charges will be brought against individuals.'

connotation of the current enforcement practice, both eventually crystallized by the ECJ in *British Airways*.

(c) Finally, we weight the ECJ's explicit position on the function of the 'protecting of competition' goal against the two main current (and diverging) doctrinal approaches.

A. Preliminary Considerations

(i) *The Respective Roles of the ECJ and the CFI*

Coming to the first premise, we have seen that the ECJ dismissed the *main part of BA's appeal* on the grounds that *it involved issues that went beyond its limited jurisdiction to review errors of law*. The ECJ thus fully respects the division of competence set out by Article 225 of the EC Treaty, and Article 58, first paragraph, of its Statute.[76] With regard to this aspect, some of the criticism towards the ECJ's ruling appears, to say the least, ungenerous. Either of two: The respective roles of the ECJ and the CFI are not sufficiently clear yet, or some arguments raised against the ECJ ruling conceal (or misuse) the considerable dissatisfaction (also) eminent scholars had expressed towards the CFI's judgment.[77] We are inclined to support the latter idea. The ECJ, inter alia, *explicitly* confirmed some extremely relevant principles on the treatment of fidelity enhancing rebates (and other exclusionary conduct as well), namely that: (i) the *capability* of producing an exclusionary effect is *sufficient* to establish an abusive conduct, save the possibility of proving an objective economic justification; (ii) the individualized and retroactive nature of the rebates at stake, along with the impossibility for competitors to outbid the dominant firm's offer, constitute *indicators* of an abusive scheme; (iii) Article 82 is also aimed at catching conduct which is *indirectly* detrimental to consumers through its impact on an *effective competition structure*.

[76] The abovementioned provisions clearly establish that the scope of the appeal before the ECJ must be limited to questions of law. Assessment of the facts does not, save where there may have been distortion of the facts or evidence, constitute a question of law submitted as such for review by the Court of Justice. To that effect, see for example Case C37/03 P *P BioID v OHIM* [2005] ECR I-7975, paras 43 and 53; Case C113/04 P *Technische Unie v Commission* [2006] ECR I-0000, para 83, and *ex multis*, Arnull, Dashwood et al., n 7 above, at 389–399, especially 397–399; M Condinanzi, 'Art. 225', in A Tizzano (ed) *Trattati dell'Unione Europea e della Comunità Europea* (Giuffrè, Milan, 2004) 1041–1042; A Tizzano, 'La Cour de justice après Nice: le transfert de competénces au Tribunal de première instance', in *DUE*, 2002, 587 *et seq.*; G Tesauro, *Diritto Comunitario* (4th edn, Cedam, Padova, 2005) 53, and 261–270, especially, 261–263. As to the substantial contribution of the creation of the CFI in 1999 to the specific field of competition law, M Monti, in Ehlermamn, and Atanasiu, n 6 above, at 8, asserts: '... Both the economic and legal aspects of the Commission's decisions are now subject to intense judicial scrutiny, which gives the Commission "a clear incentive for deep analysis".' 'For further considerations, see M Moavero Milanesi, 'La tutela della concorrenza tra poteri regolativi delle Autorità indipendenti e controlli giurisdizionali. Il contesto comunitario', in Studi di integrazione europea (2007) 3, 724–746.

[77] See, among the others, Kallaugher, and Sher, n 7 above, at 263 *et seq.*, and, with less intensity, G Monti, n 7 above, at 1051.

The latter principles mirror *choices* of legislative policy, as such subject to recurrent criticism. More generally, they reflect the peculiar 'identity' of the European competition law regarding exclusionary abusive conduct covered by Article 82.[78] Some of those fiercely criticized rulings such as the one at issue, often—in a more or less manifest fashion—desire a drastic change of this 'identity'.[79] Incidentally, the latter was described by Professor Giuliano Amato in 1999 in terms of application of competition rules to achieve, along with economic efficiency, the protection of foundations of liberal democracy by precluding the creation of excessive private power.[80]

(ii) *Some Theoretical Misconceptions*

The latter remark leads us to the second introductory consideration. Even though we submit that it is in the natural course of things that choices underlying whatever legal system are subject to periodical reviews, and, notwithstanding the

[78] See DJ Gerber, *Law and Competition in Twentieth Century Europe: Protecting Prometheus* (Oxford University Press/Clarendon Press, Oxford, 1998) *passim*, especially 5–51. The author, a comparative lawyer, remarks that there is a rich tradition of thought in Europe about what we currently call 'competition law', which has given European domestic competition laws, as well as EC competition law, a distinctive nature. Therefore, Gerber asserts that EC competition law is not just a counterpoint to the US system. On this aspect, see also L Brittan, *European Competition Policy: Keeping the Playing-Field Level* (Brassey's for CEPS, 1992), 3. The Former Commissioner emphasizes that the combined aims of achieving an internal market and promoting competition create a form of *sui generis* competition law, which does not fit with any particular school of economic analysis used in other jurisdictions. Noteworthy, he goes on to state that Chicago thinking is not directly relevant to EC competition policy since 'Chicago does not need to worry about creating a single market. Rather, it presupposes the existence of an integrated market.'

[79] In our view this identity is directly descended from the very idea of Europe, to which D Chalmers, in Chalmers, Hadjiemmanuil et al, n 7 above, at 2–6 dedicates extremely meaningful passages. The author recalls the marvellous essay of J Habermas, and J Derrida, 'February 15, or What Binds Europeans Together: Plea for a Common Foreign Policy in Core Europe', in D Levy et al., *Old Europe, New Europe, Core Europe: Transatlantic Relations after the Iraq War* (Verso, 2005) 5 *et seq.*, at 10–12, a short excerpt of which is worth quoting even for the limited purposes of our work: '... the triumph of capitalism was bound up with sharp class conflicts, and this fact has hindered an equally positive appraisal of free markets. That differing evaluation of politics and markets may explain *Europeans' trust* in the *civilizing power of the state* and their expectations for it to *correct market failures*'.

[80] G Amato, *Antitrust and the Bounds of Power* (Oxford University Press, 1999) 3–4, emphasizes this feature of the anti-trust law: 'Antitrust law ... was ... desired by politicians and (in Europe) by scholars attentive to the problem of the democratic systems, who saw it as an answer (if not indeed "the" answer) to a crucial problem for democracy, the emergence from the company or firm, as an expression of the fundamental freedom of individuals, of the opposite phenomenon of private power.' Note, however, that Amato does not hide that in Europe, and particularly, in some States characterized by a strong national protectionism, anti-trust law has been shaped as an embankment to the excessive power of the State; see G Amato, *Il potere e l'antitrust,* (Il Mulino, Bologna, 1998) 17. With different intonations and starting his reasoning from the specific assessment of the Italian anti-trust law 10 years after its entry into force, G Rossi, in F Rampini (ed), *Capitalismo Opaco* (Editori Laterza, Rome-Bari, 2005) 79–84, supports similar ideas, by arguing that, since the free market is never self-regulating, but, rather, tends to create monopolies and monopolizations, it is a specific duty of policy to provide the market with an appropriate regulation. Professor Rossi goes on stating that: 'Adam Smith's invisible hand can create much wealth, not democracy.' Translated from Italian by the author of the present paper.

significant commitment and effort put in by the European and national institutions, academe, and business world, we would hazard at saying that the debate upon the EC Competition regulation of certain abusive exclusionary conduct still seems to linger on an immature phase. This statement might appear severe, but, judging from certain puzzling comments upon the case at hand, some basic concepts are frequently misconceived. Indeed, it cannot be contested that notions such as 'harm to consumers', 'objective economic justification', and 'degree of likeness sufficient to establish a foreclosure effect' are in the need of a further and decisive clarification by the European judicature and enforcing authorities.[81] Yet, acknowledging (as the ECJ did in the case at hand) that three particular features enable a court to identify when a rebate/bonus schemes *can* have a foreclosure effect is quite different from arguing that the Court reached a conclusion of a *per se* prohibition of them. Again, even though virtually nobody (for sure not the European institutions) denies that *one* of the governing aims of any system of competition law is *consumer welfare*,[82] to us, it is tendentious to state that the ECJ's ruling protects competitors *instead of* competition.[83] As we look more closely in the last part of this work at whether neo-classical microeconomics still makes sense (and represents the economic theoretical basis of EC competition policy), it is more precise to assert that the protection of the competition process—which, understood as a process of rivalry, ceases to exist, at least for a certain time, in the absence of (efficient) competitors[84]—is a strong means (if not the strongest) to

---

[81] The Commission and the European Courts are not oblivious of the issue. The very statement that indirect harm to consumers can be brought about by possible impacts on effective competition, enshrined in paragraph 106 of the BA Appeal (n 62 above), shows that the European Courts do not ignore the issue, taking (at least) an incipient position on it. As to the Commission, the analysis contained in the DG Discussion Paper must be welcome as a promising *first step*; see section V of this work.

[82] For an accurate analysis of the notion of consumer surplus/welfare see, *ex multis*, P Krugman and R Wells, *Microeconomics* (Worth, 2005) 136–147. In short, *consumer welfare* is usually defined as the difference between what a person is willing to pay for a certain commodity and the price he is actually required to pay. The sum of the *consumer welfare* and the *producer surplus* (ie the differences between the price at which producers are willing to supply a product and the price they actually receive) represents the *total welfare*. For a comprehensive review of the main competing arguments see, eg, S Bishop and B Walker, *The Economics of EC Competition Law: Concepts, Application and Measurement* (2nd edn, Sweet & Maxwell, 2002) 23 *et seq.*; and M Motta, *Competition Law. Theory and Practice* (Cambridge University Press, 2003) 18 *et seq.*

[83] See, for instance, E Rousseva, 'Modernizing by Eradicating: How the Commission's New Approach to Article 81 dispenses with the Need to Apply Article 82 EC to Vertical Restraints' (2005) 42 CML Rev 587 *et seq.*, at 592: 'The emphasis on changes of market structure and reduction of consumer choice actually disguised a policy of protecting competitors.'

[84] See, for instance, W Wurmnest, 'The Reform of Article 82 EC in the light of 'Economic Approach', in MO Mackenrodt, B Conde Gallego, and S Enchelmaier (eds), *Abuse of Dominant Position: New Interpretation, New Enforcement Mechanisms?* (Springer, Berlin/Heidelberg, 2008) 15; and Mertikopoulou, n 12 above, at 242: '… the case law states that protecting competitors is important where those competitors are vital for a competitive market structure'; and the Opinion of Advocate General Kokott, n 43 above, citing as for this fundamental issue: Case 85/76 *Hoffmann-La Roche v Communities*, n 44 above, at 44; Case 322/81 *Michelin v Commission (Michelin I)* [1983] ECR 3461, at 91; Case 31/90 *L'Oréal v De Nieuwe AMCK* [1980] ECR 3775, at 27; Case C-62/86 *AKZO v Commission* [1991] ECR I-3359, at 69. Further, Advocate General Kokott at para 68

guarantee, inter alia, consumer welfare.[85] While discussing this point, Professor Eleanor Fox reminds us that 'the enterprise to protect the competition process and the openness of market has a well respected pedigree, from Friedrich von Hayek to Michael Porter.'[86] Finally, it is quite inaccurate both from a legal and an economic viewpoint to make competition *merely* based on price utterly equivalent to a competitive strategy based on a scheme of individualized and, above all, retroactive rebates/bonuses. We risk stating the obvious, but there is a dramatic difference between the former behaviour—indeed, one of the basic means of competition—and the second *structured* strategy, which is likely to bind the counterparts for a certain time, affecting their possibility to change supplier (or buyer, as in the *BA* case). A word of caution here: we do not argue that such a

remarks: '... Article 82 EC, like the other competition rules of the Treaty, is not designed only or primarily to protect the immediate interests of individual competitors or consumers, but to protect the structure of the market and thus competition as such (as an institution), which has already been weakened by the presence of the dominant undertaking on the market. In this way, consumers are also indirectly protected. Because where competition as such is damaged, disadvantages for consumers are also to be feared.' It should be noted that an uncontroversial definition of competition still seems to be lacking. According to O Black, *Conceptual Foundations of Antitrust* (Cambridge University Press, 2005) at 6: 'It's a scandal of antitrust that neither its practitioners nor its theorists agree—*in so far as they consider the question at all*—on what competition is'; a similar view is expressed by RJ Van den Berg, and PD Camescasca, *European Competition Law and Economics: A Comparative Perspective* (2nd edn, Sweet & Maxwell, 2006) at 6. Cf, the seminal work of J Vicker, 'Concepts of Competition', in (1995) 47 Oxford Economic Papers, 1–23. L Gyselen, Abuse of Monopoly Power Within the Meaning of Article 86 of the EEC Treaty: Recent Developments, in 1989 Fordham Corporate Law Institute (B Hawk (ed), 1990), pp 597–650, at 600 defined competition as 'a *process* in which a multitude of competitors rival one another to court consumer's favour' and contrasted this concept of competition with the perfect competition model. In the following we refer to competition as here described.

[85] Cf, *ex multis*, Whish, n 7 above, at 1–17 and 19–20. While discussing the function of competition law, Professor Whish deals specifically with the issue of 'protecting competitors' and the historical influence of the so-called 'Freiburg School' of ordoliberalism. See also Jones and Sufrin, n 7 above, at 2–30. On the influence of the Freiburg ordoliberalism on European Competition Law see, *ex multis*, Gerber, n 78 above, at 232 *et seq.*; DJ Gerber, 'Constitutionalizing the Economy: German Neo-liberalism, Competition Law and the "New" Europe' (1995) 42 American Journal of Competition Law, 23 *et seq.*; W Möschel, 'Competition Policy from an Ordo Point of View', in A Peacock and H Willgerodt (eds), *German Neo-Liberals and the Social Market Economy* (Palgrave Macmillan, 1989) 146 *et seq.* We cannot even attempt to explore the foundations of this School of economic and legal thinking. For the limited purposes of our work suffice it to remember that the Freiburg School, composed of economists and lawyers, was establish in the 1930s at the University of Freiburg. Its members supported a new form of liberal thought which was rooted in the belief that a competitive economic system was necessary for a free trade and equitable society. Strongly influenced by the intellectual tradition of German philosophy, particularly by Immanuel Kant, the ordoliberal thinkers saw the need to protect the economic freedom and the market players to enable them to engage actively in the competitive process. For a critical analysis of the ordoliberal competition policy in relation to Article 82 cases, see Kallaugher, and Sher, n 7 above, at 268–269.

[86] EM Fox, 'Abuse of Dominance and Monopolisation: How to Protect Competition Without Protecting Competitors', in Ehlermann, and Atanasiu, n 6 above, at 73. See also FA Von Hayek, 'Competition as a Discovery Procedure', in *New Studies in Philosophy, Politics, Economics and the History of Ideas* (University of Chicago Press, 1978) at 179–190; ME Porter, 'Towards a Productivity-based Approach of Evaluating Mergers and Joint-ventures' (2001) 33 UWLA Law Review, 17 *et seq.*

strategy is to be considered *per se* abusive;[87] what we would like to stress is simply that *pure* price competition, on the one hand, and an individualized and retroactive rebate/bonus scheme, on the other, might end up having a common result (ie a lower price for the final consumer *in the short run*), but their *effects* on the *structure* of the relevant market could be like chalk and cheese.

(iii) The Different Outcome in the US

As to the third and the last premise, it cannot be ignored that the different approach to discounts and rebates by US courts applying Section 2 of the Sherman Act has recently been vividly illustrated 'by the fact that Virgin brought an action in the US against BA's commission scheme at the same time as its complaint to the Commission under EC Law'.[88] As Jones and Sufrin remarked, the trial court in the US 'granted summary judgment in favour of BA' and this ruling was upheld on appeal by the Second Circuit Courts of Appeal, on the ground that 'Virgin had failed to show that BA's incentive schemed harmed consumers.'[89] Without questioning the appropriateness of either ruling, we would like to emphasize that the very divergence between Article 82 of the EC Treaty and Section 2 of the Sherman Act is deeply rooted in the European and American distinctive historical, legal, and cultural traditions.[90] Arguably the different results the cases ended

---

[87] *Per se* rules are to be intended as *ex ante* descriptions of what is banned. An excellent discussion of an effect-based rules rather than a form-based approach to can be found in J Gual, M Hellwig, A Perrot, M Polo, P Rey, K Schmid, R Stenbacka, Report to the European Commission by the European Advisory Group for Competition Policy (hereinafter: EAGCP) An Economic Approach to Article 82, available online at: <http://www.ec.europa.eu/dgs/competition/economist/eagcp_july_21_05.pdf>, p 6 *et seq.* The Report is also published in (2006) 2 Competition Policy International 111 *et seq.*

[88] Jones and Suffrin, n 7 above, at 449.

[89] Ibid. Cf *Virgin Atlantic Airways Ltd v British Airways plc*, 257 F.3d 256 (2nd Cir 2001).

[90] A comparison between the structural differences of the EC and US anti-trust law even focuses 'only' on Art 82 of the EC Treaty and Section 2 of the Sherman Act is evidently beyond the scope of our work. For our purposes it is sufficient to point out that: first, Section 2 of the Sherman Act prohibits: (a) monopolization; or (b) attempts to monopolize; or (c) combinations or conspiracies to monopolize; and, secondly, traditionally, the US legal system, above all under the influence of the Chicago School, has shown a substantial confidence in the robustness of the market to withstand and correct monopolistic distortion, and scarce faith in the ability of governments to intervene in a way that improves upon market. Although the post-Chicago thinking is prone to acknowledge adverse effects that might derive from monopolistic behaviour, it remains the case that US courts and regulators are typically less willing than European counterparts to intervene in such scenario. See for example, the recent US Supreme Court's judgment in *Verizon v Trinko* (2004) 124 S Ct 872. By contrast, European authorities have traditionally shown greater scepticism about robustness of market and a greater trust in the capabilities of regulators to intervene to correct market failures. To put it another way, the relative weights of false positive (intervention in circumstances where it is actually not justified) and false negative (non-intervention in circumstances where it is in fact justified) errors tend to assume opposite positions within the two legal systems. As regards the US legal system and the debate between Chicago and Harvard Schools see, H Hovenkamp, *Federal Antitrust Policy—The Law of Competition and its practice* (West Information Publishing Group, 1999) 10 *et seq.*; H Hovenkamp, 'Antitrust Policy After Chicago' (1985) 84 University of Michigan Law Review 213 *et seq.*, especially 226–229; MS Jacobs, 'An Essay on Normative Foundations of Antitrust Economics' (1995) 74 North Carolina Law Review 219 *et seq.*, especially 222–225; RH Bork, *The Antitrust Paradox: A Policy at War with Itself* (Basic Books Inc, 1978) 90–91, 426–429; EM Fox and LA Sullivan , 'Antitrust-Retrospective and

up with in the EU and US had some influence upon those who commented on the ECJ's decision in *British Airways*, and advocated a general less intervening approach regarding certain exclusionary conduct susceptible to be caught by Article 82. However, authors who seriously argue such an approach do not ignore that, as a matter of fact, 'legal transplanting' operations are extremely delicate, with scarcely any chance to succeed without properly weighing the inherent differences between the legal systems at stake. Moreover, it seems to us that in so far as the basic object of consumer welfare and the means to achieve it are concerned, the divergences between the US and EC anti-trust legal traditions are getting thinner. For instance, one can compare what is stated at paragraph 54 of the DP,[91] and the drastic change of mind of Professor Richard Posner, one of the leading representatives of—to borrow Paul Krugman's words—'the Temple of free-market theory, the University of Chicago'.[92] In contrast with his past firm statement that consumer welfare is the only and ultimate goal of anti-trust analysis, Posner suggestively argued in 2001 that:

[e]fficiency is the ultimate goal of anti-trust, but competition a mediate goal that will often be close enough to the ultimate goal to allow to look no further.[93]

B. On the ECJ's Reading of the 'Protection of Competition' Aim and its Alleged Excessively Formalistic Approach

We can now turn to the very core of our argument. The ECJ's judgment has triggered such a debate because something more than the mere treatment of

Prospective: Where Are We Coming From? Where Are We Going?' (1987) 62 New York University Law Review 936 *et seq.*

[91] DG Discussion Paper, n 10 above, para 54: 'The essential objective of Article 82 when analysing exclusionary conduct is the protection of competition on the market as a means of enhancing consumer welfare and of ensuring an efficient allocation of resources.' See also N Kroes, Preliminary Thoughts on Policy Review of Article 82, Speech at the Fordham Corporate Law Institute, New York, 23 September 2005, available online at: <http://europa.eu/pol/comp/index_en.htm>.

[92] P Krugman, *The Accidental Theorist. And Other Dispatches from the Dismal Science* (Penguin, 1999) at 170. Interestingly, some Chicagoans happened to confusingly label 'consumer welfare' the total welfare, which, according to this School of economic thought, should serve as a yardstick for US anti-trust law.

[93] RA Posner, *Antitrust Law* (2nd edn, University of Chicago Press, 2001) at 29, cited also by ILO Schmidt, 'The Suitability of the More Economic Approach for Competition Policy: Dynamic v. Static Efficiency' (2007) 28 (1) ECLR 408, adding: 'His distinction between *mediate* and *ultimate* goal correspond exactly to the position of the Harvard School. A good performance is of course the ultimate goal of competition policy but, in an individual case, it is not suitable to adopt a decision.' Interestingly, also the current Commissioner of the US Federal Trade Commission, JT Rosch, in commenting on the DG Discussion Paper, emphasizes the recent progressive 'transatlantic convergence...occurred on the basic theoretical principle underlying analysis if single-firm (or unilateral) conduct ...'. Having pointed this out, Rosch asserts that 'notwithstanding the increasing convergence, I concluded that we in the United States can learn from the experience of the EC'. See JT Rosch, Reflections on the Discussion Paper on the Application of Article 82 to Exclusionary Abuses, available online at: <http://www.ftc.gov/speeches/rosch/060511RoschStGallenRemarks.pdf>, p 1 *et seq.*

retrospective rebates/bonuses is at stake. In other words, the debate about the treatment of any knotty exclusionary conducts under Article 82 of the EC Treaty, 'is not new and has been going for many years but the latest case law and the modernisation program, in force since 1 May 2004, has intensified' it,[94] remaining to add that it has been strengthened even further by the publication of the Discussion Paper.[95] Yet, what seems to be vigorously testified to by the case at hand is that several critical comments on judgments about allegedly exclusionary conduct—such as the BA's loyalty-inducing commissions—cover, beneath the surface, a specific vision of the underlying objectives of Article 82. Once the various positions for or against the ruling on a specific exclusionary conduct are identified, it may not be long before the underlying stances about the general criteria to be applied in order to assess dominant undertakings' conduct can be detected. In sum, two main theoretical approaches currently seem to face each other. Critics of the present enforcement practice argue that it overestimates the *form* of an allegedly anti-competitive behaviour and it lacks a clear and coherent economic basis. Further, it is maintained that the *effects* of the alleged competitive practice on the specific market are not sufficiently considered. As a result, the current enforcement practice (and the case law upholding it) might chill competition by banning pro-competitive conduct.[96] In contrast, sceptics of the advocated new approach claim that, inter alia, legal certainty and a workable and expeditious handling of competition cases call for clear rules. They further point out that an excessively ponderous economic analysis might impede or delay the enforcing authority in deciding, and, likely, bring about a 'war of experts'.[97] This would fatally hamper both the enforcing action and the judiciary settling of the cases

[94] LL Gormsen, 'Art. 82 EC: Where Are we Coming from and Where Are We Going to?' (2006) 2(2) The Competition Law Review, 2, fn 6.

[95] Marsden, n 16 above, at 3, goes even further: The Discussion Paper 'certainly did its job. It generated an incredible debate about what kind of competition we want in Europe …'

[96] See, eg, Kallaugher and Sher, n 7 above, at 263 *et seq.*; J Temple Lang, 'Defining Legitimate Competition on the Merit: How to Clarify Pricing Abuses under Article 82 EC' (2003) 26 Fordham International Law Journal 83–162, especially at 86 *et seq.*; D Waelbbroeck, 'Michelin II: A Per Se Rule Against Rebates by Dominant Companies?' (2005) 1 Journal of Competition Law and Economics 149 *et seq.*; Gormsen, n 94, 1 *et seq.*; D Rynar, 'Exclusionary Pricing and Price Discrimination Abuses Under Article 82—An Economic Analysis' (2002) ECMLR, 286 *et seq.* See also O'Donaghue, n 29, p 371 *et seq.*; and J Ratliff, 'Abuse if Dominant Position and Pricing Practices: A Practitioner's Viewpoint', in Ehlermann, and Atanasiu, n 6 above, at 427 *et seq.*

[97] See, eg, Wurmnest, n 84 above, at 4 *et seq*; Schmidt, n 93 above; Mertikopoulou, n 12 above, at 241 *et seq.* Some commentators go even further and reject the legitimacy of an economic assessment in competition cases, cf L Boy, 'Abuse of Market Power: Controlling Dominance or Protecting Competition', in H Ullrich (ed), *The Evolution of European Competition Law: Whose Regulation, Which Competition?* (Edward Elgar Publishing, 2006) 291 *et seq.* In order to appraise how harmful and pointless (in terms of waste of human energy, material, technical, and intellectual resources) the peril of a 'war of experts' can be, we refer the reader to what Konrad Lorenz asserts regarding intraspecific competition (*Embittered competition among human beings*) in his marvellous 'Civilized Man's Eight Deadly Sins'. In our opinion, this essay could be extremely useful for anybody who approaches the issue of competition, no matter from what perspective. See L Lorenz, 'Die acht Todsünden der zivilisierten Menschheit' (1973), in L Bioccia Marghieri and LF Lindner (trans), *Gli otti peccati capitali della nostra civiltà* (27th edn, Adelphi, 2003) 43–50.

according to sound principle of administration of justice. Finally, they argue that protecting the competition process is, at the *status quo*, the most accurate way to achieve the aims a correct interpretation of Article 82 envisages. By taking those competing visions into consideration, we now examine the main arguments raised against the ECJ's ruling in *British Airways* and show how they fit with the thesis we have put forward.

(i) *The Protection of the Competitive Structure*

As mentioned, the ECJ judgment in *British Airways* has been criticized for confirming that Article 82 of the EC Treaty is not only concerned with practices that cause direct harm to consumers 'but also reaches conduct that is indirectly detrimental to them through its impact on an effective competitive structure'.[98] That is to say, according to European Courts, the BA bonuses schemes do not directly affect consumers, but they are nonetheless deemed abusive for their effects on the relevant market structure. Unsurprisingly, the critics themselves of the judgment under examination submit that 'all anti-trust systems have to determine the relative importance that they attach to the promotion of, respectively, *a competitive structure* and *competitive behaviour*. In particular, they have to decide how far to constrain competitive behaviour over the short term to avoid the possibility of prejudice to the competitive structure over the long term.'[99] This is precisely the point. We suggest another reading of the same position: the legal assessment of whatever *commercial* sensible practice of a dominant undertaking, which can foreclose rivals (particularly, efficient rivals), significantly depends on how much weight an anti-trust legal system gives to the goal of protecting competition *over the mid-long period*.[100] This stance needs to be spelled out. Before claiming that the effects of BA's bonus schemes—as well as effects of any other allegedly exclusionary conduct by dominant undertakings—on the relevant market have not been accurately appreciated, one has to address a more basic and radical issue. That is the actual interpretation of the word *effect* within the relevant legal system. In detail, it should always be clear whether the relevant notion of *effects* includes only or mainly those brought about *in the short run*, or it also embraces the *structural consequences* on the specific market, which, by definition, can be

---

[98] Allan, n 5 above. Similar positions had been expressed by other eminent scholars in commenting the CFI's ruling. See, eg, Kallaugher and Sher, n 7 above, at 305 *et seq.*

[99] It is admitted that 'European competition law has consistently attached a great importance to the maintenance of a competitive structure. There is no disagreement between the Court and the Commission as to this point.' Cf Allan, n 5 above.

[100] In his fundamental study R Kahn, *The Economics of the Short Period*, (Macmillan, 1989), at 22–26 draws the contours of the notion 'short period', and, symmetrically, of 'long period'. Accordingly, the short period for an industry is one in which 'the fixed plant and organisation of all, or nearly, all the firms can be assumed to remain constant'. Furthermore, the Author outlines the implications for the anti-trust theory of such definitions. For an effective analysis of the distinction between *short run* and *long run*, and its implication in terms of economies and diseconomies of scale, see Krugman and Wells, n 82 above, at 182 *et seq.*, especially, 197–201.

appreciated only *over the mid-long term*. To claim any position with respect to certain conduct, without addressing this issue, is captious. What is more, such an attitude can be legitimately interpreted as an indirect critique to the relative weight assigned to the protection of competition aim within the legal system under consideration. It can be easily shown that the analyses of those who openly criticize the European institutions' approach towards retroactive and loyalty-inducing rebates, lately crystallized in *British Airways*, entail a notion of *effect* definitely similar to the former outlined above. By the same token, the second reading, which accords definitely better with neoclassical economics, being also supported by the European Courts, has been maintained by authors who argue that the *main objective* of competition policy and law is and will remain 'the *maintenance of a competitive structure* which automatically leads—at least as a pattern of prediction—to a good performance and an increase in consumers' welfare';[101] and, hence, manifest a certain scepticism towards any legal and/or economic approach which tends to diminish the relative relevance of the *effects* over *the mid-long run*. However, even once having addressed this basic issue, it remains difficult to design a consistent competition policy which should shape the enforcement activity. Indeed, some conduct, such as retroactive rebates, are characterized by an inherent complexity, whereby clear-cut rules can hardly be conceived. What invariably remains important is clarifying the relevant concept of *effect*, and, thereafter, assessing the allegedly exclusionary conduct through an inherently consistent conceptual framework. We propose two theoretical approaches to the issue, which aptly exemplified the latter assertion. First, we consider the stance of those who argue that by protecting freedom of competition, although individual economic freedom should be 'guaranteed as a human right', 'advancing consumer welfare in economic terms' cannot be granted.[102] This doctrinal position entails some of the recurrent specious arguments in favour of a less intervening enforcement policy, supposed to accord with the modernization process and be supported by economics. Quite the opposite, in highlighting this trade-off between individual economic freedom and consumer welfare, what *neo-classical microeconomics*[103] tells us is contested. It is argued that 'while the move to protect suppliers may increase choice and potentially improve allocative

---

[101] Schmidt, n 93 above, at 410, italics added. The author stresses that 'in order to avoid any misunderstanding, competition . . . must be well founded in general'. See also, with different intonations, Gyselen, n 7 above, at 290–292; and Mertikopoulou, n 12 above, at 241–244, especially at 242. This philosophy is often labelled as 'structionalist test', for its mediate objective is to impede abusive practice which brings about an alteration of the competition structure. More straightforwardly, in order to safeguard consumer welfare the direct goal is to protect 'the structural process of rivalry' competition consists of. Cf Kallaugher and Sher, n 7 above, at 276.

[102] Gormsen, n 94 above, at 15.

[103] Ibid; the author summarizes what standard microeconomics asserts as follows: 'protecting the competitor through an act of curtailing the power of the near monopolist, the consumer may benefit through increased choice and reallocation of profits from the monopolist to alternative competitors. As these competitors will not have the ability to reap monopoly profits, we would then expect these profits to be passed back to the consumer through reduced prices. If these effects outweigh the value

efficiency' this outcome '*is not guaranteed. Nor is it guaranteed* that dynamic movements towards productive efficiency' will be attained more easily in this way.[104] Accordingly, a more precise methodology would be one where unilateral behaviour is assessed on the basis of its actual or likely effect in the market.[105] Yet, in economics (as in life) *nothing is guaranteed*. Economic models, such as standard approaches which currently explain competition policy *and* those which could be proposed alternatively, by their nature, are grounded on a number of assumptions. Their *predicted* (not *guaranteed*) outcomes derive from the elaboration of these assumptions. On the one hand, this does not lessen the insights they carry over the more complex and unpredictable real world. On the other, changing the model likely entails changing assumptions. Therefore, if, under *certain* assumptions, it might be true that whilst 'in some circumstances it is *plausible* that the protected competitors will become efficient over time . . . it is also *possible* that the most *productive* way of supplying customers will be through one *single supplier*',[106] it appears too simplistic to support that 'depending on which of these effects is the greatest the consumer could then actually gain or lose from such measures'. Indeed, this position seems to pay no heed to two very basic issues: (i) monopolists (or, in other words, *single suppliers*) over the mid-long run are likely to be high cost producers to the detriment of the consumers;[107] (ii) EC competition policy pursues multiple goals, among which *productive efficiency*, although it stands as one of the foremost, is not exclusive. Even though the contingent conditions are such that *the most productive way of supplying customers will be through one single supplier*,[108] at least a further trade-off should be taken into due account. Indeed, having an efficient monopolist on the market can significantly reduce *dynamic efficiency*.[109] In sum, clear-cut solutions, such as that under discussion, can hardly be delineated. Even assuming that they can be figured out, it still

---

of any above-cost discount offered by the near monopolist, consumers could gain from overall price reductions.'

[104] Ibid. Italics added.   [105] Ibid.

[106] Ibid, adding: ' . . . especially when economies of scale are great', italics added.

[107] This constitutes the well-known problem of the 'deadweight loss' of monopoly, whereby, the monopolist being a price maker and absent competitive restraints, in the mid-long run, he is able to earn the largest profits by refraining from expanding its production to the maximum extent possible. As a consequence, consumers will be deprived from goods or services that they would have been prone to pay for at the competitive market price, outcome known as *allocative inefficiency*. 'The extent of this loss is sometimes referred to as the 'deadweight loss' attributable to monopoly ; the loss itself is known as the 'social welfare cost of monopoly'. See Whish, n 7 above, at 5. For an accurate economic analysis of the matter we refer the reader to the fundamental essay by L Cowling and DC Müller, 'The Social Cost of Monopoly' (1978) 88 Economic Journal 727–748. For an updated insight of the issue, see Motta, n 82 above, at 40–45.

[108] Otherwise the monopolist would be 'X-inefficient'. For an ample study of the notion of 'X inefficiency', see H Leibenstein, 'Allocative Efficiency v. X-Efficiency' (1966) 56 American Economic Review 392–415, cited also by Whish, n 7 above, at 5.

[109] See, for instance, Whish, n 7 above, at 3–6, especially at 5: ' . . . the monopolist may not feel the need to innovate, because he does not experience the constant pressure to go on attracting custom by offering better more advanced product.'

appears that the essential decision about the relative importance to assign to the 'protecting competitive structure' aim cannot be circumvented. As an example of analysis, which neither eludes the inherent complexity of the matter, nor is inconsistent with its own economic assumptions, we propose Gyselen's, here recalled in its essential passages. At first, he emphasizes the difficulties of dealing with practices through which dominant firms seek to exclude competitors from the market (or to contain their growth) by tending to make their customers (and possibly also their downstream clients) happy with low prices.[110] Furthermore, he admits that 'the enforcer's intervention in these cases is—conceptually speaking—far trickier than in case of excessive pricing' since it is 'inspired by faith in competition as a process of rivalry between competitors *and* in this process contribution to customer and consumer welfare in the longer run'.[111] Thus, ultimately it would be a matter of faith: a 'faith' not of a religious kind, but grounded on neoclassical microeconomic theory, according to which competition process should benefit final consumers *over the mid to long run*. Any different legal assessment should be grounded on a different 'faith', that is on different readings of neoclassical microeconomic theories, or different economic theories and, in turn, assumptions; most likely, a heavier relative weight allocated to consumers' benefit *in the short run* and, consequently, a diminished relevance of the social benefit over the mid/long run. To conclude this point, the shift from an economic theory which favours the mid-long perspective to an approach that, on the contrary, focuses on the effects in the short run seems to be the common premise of most of those criticize jurisdictional positions as ECJ's in *British Airways* from a strictly legal viewpoint. It remains in question whether this shift might be justified on some reliable economic theory and, provided that such a theory exists, how far it complies with EC rules on exclusionary conduct.[112] For the moment, it seems that our effort to show that specific critiques against the ECJ ruling under discussion are disguised corollaries of a different reading of EC competition policy's fundamental objectives has found a first robust case.

(ii) A Truly Excessively Formalistic Approach?

We now try to establish whether our thesis gets through the other main argument raised against the ECJ's ruling in *British Airways*, that is its excessive reliance on the *form* of the conduct in order to determine whether or not it had exclusionary effects. This approach of the ECJ, in turn, would end with shaping a *per se* prohibition of the fidelity-inducing rebates/bonuses which would not consider market-specific factors. Unquestionably, distinguishing pro-competitive from anti-competitive exclusionary practices turns on 'fine distinctions capable

---

[110] See Gyselen, n 7 above, at 290, who adds: 'the trouble with these exclusionary pricing practices is that they may foreclose business opportunities for the dominant company's competitors' and, consequently, it 'may harm the competitive process'.

[111] Ibid.   [112] We explore these issues below, especially in section VI.

of graduation', and also entails 'a very fact-specific endeavour'.[113] However, precisely because of the fact-specific nature of pricing conduct and, pursuant to the European Courts' consistent jurisprudence, since proof of the appreciable potential foreclosure is a *sine qua non* condition for the application of Article 82 of the EC Treaty, the Commission (and the Member States' national authorities when enforcing Article 82) must always assess the alleged abusive conduct in the specific market conditions. In this sense, 'one could perhaps say that there are no *per se* rules'.[114] As seen in *British Airways*, the ECJ deemed that the CFI had not erred in law in assessing the bonus schemes in view of the specific factual circumstance. To us, the ECJ did not uphold a *per se* prohibition. Rather, it judged that the CFI had first looked at three *formal* features of the BA schemes (retroactivity, individuality, and the economic impossibility of being outbid by BA's competitors) as *potential indicators* of a specific *worked out* sort of fidelity rebates. Then, the CFI, by weighing these formal features of BA's schemes against the *specific factual circumstances* of the case (and the evidence provided by the parties) had showed that BA's commissions were capable, firstly, of making market entry very difficult or impossible for BA's competitors and, secondly, of making it more difficult or impossible for its customers to choose between various sources of supply or commercial partners.[115] Does the second critique regarding the alleged too formalistic approach of the ECJ fit with our starting thesis? The answer is yes, but less plainly than the first critique does. This one time commentators put forward a trade-off between the reliance on form on the one hand, and the assessment of the *actual effects* of the alleged exclusionary conduct on the other. Accordingly, an allegedly *firmly formalistic* approach followed by the Commission and European Courts would go hand in hand with the emphasis on the *likely* effects on the *structure* of the relevant market. Yet, as illustrated above, the argument itself of an excessive formalistic approach can be reasonably contested.[116] Moreover, although an

---

[113] Wurmnest, n 84 above, at 9. See also M Monti, n 9 above, at 7, and Gyselen, n 7 above, at 320, who argues: 'It is not enough to point at some theoretical or entirely negligible potential foreclosure problem. This means that the litmus test for any target rebate system depends on the outcome of *evidentiary exercise*', (emphasis added).

[114] Gyselen, n 7 above, at 294. Similarly E Paulis, in the Panel Discussion, 'Policy, Objectives, Enforcement Tools and Actors, Types of Abuses, The Case of Excessive Pricing', in Ehlerman and Atanasiu, n 6 above, at 26–27.

[115] Similar arguments could answer also to those positions claiming that, by upholding the CFI's decision, the ECJ would establish a de facto per se rule, because it did not take in to account the fact that Virgin Atlantic had continued to increase its market shares during the operative period of BA's scheme. Cf, authoritatively, B Allan, 'Art. 82: A Commentary on DG Competition Discussion Paper' (2006) 2(1) Competition Policy International 43 *et seq.*, at 47, according to whom the CFI found 'an anticompetitive effect on the basis of a factual assumption that, absent the incentive schemes employed by BA, rival airlines would have expanded more vigorously that they did'; *contra* M Dreher and M Adam, 'Abuse of Dominance Under Reform—Sound Economics and Established Case Law' (2007) 4 ECLR at 281: '... In fact the CFI had indeed taken account of the effects of the rebate. It merely reached a different conclusion by following the Commission's argument that Virgin in the absence of the loyalty schemes would have had even more success...'

[116] As Dreher and Adam, ibid, at 281 stress: 'The dispute is at heart more about the question what effects are actually generated by a certain conduct than it is about the query whether such effects should be considered at all.'

analysis of the actual effects of the specific conduct in the marketplace would allow showing *also* those benefits/harms in terms of the consumer welfare, which are immediately noticeable in the short run, nothing demonstrates that these effects outweigh the structural impact of the alleged exclusionary conduct over the mid/long period. Again, the main objection remains; it would seem that the criticism on the specific ruling at hand hides scepticism on the necessity/opportunity to protect the competitive structure in the first place.

C. What does the EC Treaty Protect?

Leaving aside for the moment what the DG Discussion Paper says on the matter (Part V) and what a *truly* 'modern economic approach' would suggest (Part VI)—thereby remaining a little longer within strictly legal borders—we ought to question what the European Courts' interpretation of the EC Treaty tells us on the issue. At this point, it should be clear that the key question, on which any doctrinal interpretation seems to converge, regards what EC competition law in general, and Article 82, in particular, ought to protect. As stressed elsewhere,[117] despite the fact that the opposite is occasionally argued,[118] the settled case law of the ECJ is rather clear in articulating the aims of Article 82, and stating that the latter provision should be read as an application of the general objective of the Community's activities laid down by Article 3(1)(g) of the EC Treaty, that is, the 'institution of a system ensuring that competition is not distorted'.[119] As a result, Article 82 is designed to protect the intensity of competition, of which the competitive structure of the relevant market is the best approximation, and through it, the interests of consumers. In the EU, the prominent position of the consumer welfare aim is inferred by the wording of the Treaty and the types of forbidden conduct referred to in Article 82(a), and (b).[120] As pertinently stressed by Gerber, in Community law, the decision in *Continental Can* to interpret the concept of 'abuse' teleologically (ie by reference to the fundamental objectives of the Community) had a feed-back effect on the system in 'determine(ing) the structure and the development of the abuse law' by 'establishing the concept of

---

[117] Wurmnest, n 84 above, at 13.
[118] See, for instance, R O'Donoghue and AJ Padilla, *The Law and Economics of Article 82 EC* (Hart Publishing, 2006) 4.
[119] See Case 6/72 *Continental Case v Commission* [1973] ECR 215, para 23; Case 85/76 *Hoffmann-La Roche v Commission,* n 45 above, para 38. Particularly, the latter judgment at 125 (amended to reflect the new numbering of Treaty articles) states that: 'The prohibitions contained in Article 81 and Article 82 must be interpreted and applied in the light of Article 3(1)(g) of the Treaty which provides that the activities of the Community shall include the "institution of a system ensuring that competition in the common market is not distorted" and Article 2 of the Treaty which gives the Community the task of promoting "throughout the Community a harmonious development of economic activities". By prohibiting the abuse of a dominant position within the market in so far as it may affect trade between Member States, Article 82 therefore *covers not only abuse which may directly prejudice consumers but also abuse which indirectly prejudices them by impairing the effective competitive structure as envisaged by Article 3(1)(g) of the Treaty.*' (Emphasis added.)
[120] Mertikopoulou, n 12 above, at 242–243.

competitive distortion as the analytical starting point'.[121] The definition of 'abuse'
in *Hoffman La Roche*,[122] and the explicit assigning of a 'special responsibility'
to dominant undertakings in *Michelin I*[123] provide further strong cases for this
reading. What the ECJ have most recently stated in *British Airways*[124] is utterly
consistent with the previous settled case law. To sum up, Article 82 aims at protecting the structure of the market and, as a consequence, competition. Even so,
the latter must not be read as an end in itself. Quite the contrary, it represents
the means envisaged by the Member States—which signed the EC Treaty—and
by the European institutions—created with that Treaty—to enhance consumer
welfare, ensure an efficient allocation of resources, and prevent welfare reducing
behaviours.[125] It can be argued that the echo of the Ordo-liberal school reverber-
ates within this interpretation.[126] Yet, like it or not, what the ECJ has lately stated
in *British Airways,* does not allow a *duplex interpretatio.* The achievement of the
fundamental goals mentioned (consumers' welfare at the front) can hardly be
attained over the short term; on the contrary 'the protection of the competitive structure' is, a goal being preserved *in the mid to the long run.* Formulated
differently, the protection of competition over the mid-long run (or, in other
terms, the safeguarding of the competitive structure of the relevant market)

[121] DJ Gerber, 'Law and the Abuse of Economic Power in Europe', (1987), 62, Tulane Law
Review 57, 100–105; emphasis added. The same excerpt is cited and analysed by G Monti, n 7 above,
at 1065–1066.
[122] Case 85/76 *Hoffmann La Roche v Commission,* n 45 above, para 6: '...an objective concept
relating to the behaviour of an undertaking in a dominant position which is such as to influence the
structure of a market where, as a result of the very presence of the undertaking in question, the degree
of competition is weakened and which, through recourse to methods different from those which
condition normal competition in products or services on the basis of the transactions of commercial
operators, has the effect of hindering the maintenance of the degree of competition still existing in
the market or the growth of that competition'. This interpretation is referred also by M Monti, in
Ehlerman and Atanasiu, n 6 above, at 5, who points out: 'It became progressively clear that a dominant firm should not be prohibited from competing on the merits with its rivals, or from engaging in
behaviour which is otherwise objectively justified.'
[123] Case 322/81 *NV Nederlandse Banden-Industrie Michelin v Commission,* n 89 above, para 57.
[124] Case C-95/04P *British Airways plc v Commission,* n 1 above, para 106. 'Article 82 EC is aimed
not only at practices which may cause prejudice to consumers directly, but also at those which are
detrimental to them through their impact on an effective competition structure, such as is mentioned
in Article 3(1)(g) EC that article 82 *is designed to protect the structure of the market*' (emphasis added),
excerpt already quoted in section III of our article. See also Advocate General Kokott, Opinion of 23
February 2007, n 43 above, para 68.
[125] Mertikopoulou, n 12 above, at 242, stresses that ' competition law in the EU and the Member
States has traditionally incorporated (mostly concurrent) goals along with the protection of competition...specifically the freedom of competition such as fairness, economic equity, single market
integration, liberalisation.'
[126] See Kallaugher, and Sher, n 7 above, at 271 *et seq.*; J Vickers, 'Abuse of Market Power', European
Association for Research in Industrial Economics, Berlin, 3 September 2004, available online at:
<http://www.oft.gov.uk/NR/rdonlyres/948b9FAF-B83C-49F5-B0FA-B25214DE1999/0/
spe9394/.pdf>, at 5 who stresses that for the ordoliberal school 'where market power could not be eliminated, the favoured competition law standard was that dominant firms should act as *if* constrained by
competition. That would allow "performance competition" (Leistungswettbewerb)—to offer better
deals to customers. But it would disallow "impediment competition" (Behinderungswettbewerb)—
hindering rivals' ability to offer better deals to customers.'

constitutes the strongest means (or the necessary immediate goal) to strike the balance between the different objects which EC competition policy pursues. More precisely, Article 82(b) does not protect competitors, but only competition, since it outlaws interference with the competitors' ability to rival, without protecting them from competition on the merits. Thus, if correctly interpreted, it represents a very strong guiding tenet in itself.[127] This should happen without penalizing *consumer welfare*, accurately perceived as an object being assessed in the mid to the long run. The interpretation of the text and the spirit of Article 82 require that 'the competitive structure of the market and the economic freedom of market agents are preserved, for the benefit of consumers'.[128] With regards to this reading, the textual reference contained in Article 82(b) 'to the prejudice of consumers' provides us with another interpretative key. A reading of this element consistent with the ECJ teleological interpretation of Article 82 demands an assessment of exclusionary conducts' possible harm to consumers in a market where competition has been already weakened by the presence of the dominant firm. Accordingly, the possible harm to consumers has to be assessed over the mid-long run. Eventually, our thesis should emerge clearly: criticism about the alleged too formalistic approach of the European Courts, and the substantial lack of an accurate analysis of the effects of BA behaviour can be read as directed to the interpretation the ECJ has consistently given to Article 82.

D. Interim Conclusion

The European Courts' stress on the market structure has provoked harsh criticism, which has often been condensed in the assertion that the current treatment of dominant firms' exclusionary conduct tends *to protect competitors instead of competition*. On the contrary, 'this is an empty slogan. It goes without saying that competition law should not protect competitors. The crucial problem is that in cases of market dominance it is often too difficult to draw the line between the protection of competitors and the protection of competition.'[129] This position is

---

[127] Mertikopoulou, n 12 above, at 242: 'In the EU the notion of harm to consumers should hence be read with that of harm competition, although the two notions are quite distinct. Moreover, consumer welfare is an aim which should be viewed dynamically, ie, by examining also its dimension on a mid and long-term basis.'

[128] Mertikopoulou, n 12 above, at 242. See also Mertikopoulou, at 243–244, who, explaining the *ratio* of Article 82 and the notion of competition on the merit, points out that the scope of the limits on dominant firms' behaviour must be read in light of the circumstance that 'dominance not only signifies a state of poor competition: because of dominance, the impact of the firm's conduct both on the remaining competition in the market, and on the consumer, is exponentially greater.'

[129] Wurmnest, n 84 above, at 14. See also EM Fox, 'What is Harm to Competition?' (2002) 70 Antitrust Law Journal, fn 371, 395: 'The principle by which European Court condemns exclusionary practices by dominant firms, unless justified, is often phrased as a dynamic one: the right of market actors to enjoy access to the market on the merits. It is a principle of freedom of non-dominant firms to trade without artificial obstacles construed by dominant firms, and carries an assumption

further elaborated by Professor Mario Monti, who, in identifying the policy goal and the inherent difficulties of EC competition regulation on abusive exclusionary behaviours, indicates:

> ... to protect competition and consumers, not competitors as such; but there are certainly circumstances where the protection of competition requires that efficient competitors are not excluded from the market.... The crucial question is thus whether the practice may be justified by a positive reason based on competition by better performance, or whether it constitutes a simple attempt to exclude competitors.[130]

The *British Airways* case represents a telling example of dispute where clear-cut rules cannot be adopted. To that extent we agree with commentators who highlight the hard task of distinguishing beneficial over pernicious effects on competition of exclusionary conduct, and, warn against the perils of chilling pro-competitive behaviours by a rough application of Article 82 of the EC Treaty.[131] Nonetheless, in *British Airways* the ECJ seems to have respected the approach suggested by Monti. Indeed, if a '*per se* prohibition' means that certain forms of competitive conduct are not allowed to dominant firms, no matter the specific conditions of the market under consideration, neither the CFI, nor the ECJ in upholding the CFI's decision established such a prohibition with regards to the BA's retrospective commissions. Finally, it must be emphasized that both the European Courts adopted the two-step approach for assessing of allegedly abusive behaviours, by leaving the dominant firms the chance to show that *prima facie* exclusionary rebates/bonuses are *objectively economically justified*. This last principle can play a key role in *future* disputes regarding exclusionary abuses for it constitutes the judicial statement that enforcement of Article 82 cannot deprive dominant companies of the possibility to compete with their rivals by lawful means, that is to say, 'by better performance', or in Monti's words, 'on the merits'.[132] To conclude, we believe that what Fox and Sullivan assert in analysing the basic theoretical divergences between Chicagoans and traditionalists in the US, *mutatis mutandis*, suitably describes what has been happening in Europe lately. The basic difference between those who support the ECJ's treatment of exclusionary abuses, and those who criticize it, 'is a difference of vision about

---

that preserving freedom is important to the legitimacy of the competition process and is likely to inure to the benefit of all market players, competitors, and consumers.'

[130] M Monti et al., n 6 above, at 7.

[131] 'This concern is well articulated, for instance, by Vickers, n 126 above, at 1 *et seq*, who stresses the need for an effect-based rather than formalistic approach. See also Kallaugher, and Sher, n 7 above, at 265 *et seq*.; Kamann and Bergmann, n 7 above, at 83 *et seq*.; Mertikopoulou, n 12 above, at 244.

[132] A substantial application of the second part of the test would address also part of the criticism raised by those who strongly argue that the overall test is unduly interventionist and inconsistent with a competition policy based on sound economic principles. See Kamann, and Bergmann, n 7 above, at 83; *contra* Kallaugher and Sher, n 7 above, at 265 *et seq*.; especially the part of their work titled 'Business Justifications, Efficiency Defences and Rebate Systems under Article 82', at 281–285.

what kind of society we are should strive to be'.[133] As Goyder aptly points out, within the European context, the relevance of an effective system of competition law is *political*, not only economical.[134] However, criticism has the merit to bring to light the complex dynamic relations between recent high-profile pronouncements of the Luxemburg-based Courts, the incipient process of review on the application of Article 82 to exclusionary practices (of which the DP is, for the time being, the only tangible result),[135] and the 'more economic approach' for the same sort of conduct.[136] As stressed at the outset of our work, the publication of the DP between the CFI and ECJ rulings in *British Airways*, and, more generally, the ongoing debate about the suitable role of economics for the assessment of alleged violations of Article 82 cannot be ignored in any attempt to outline comprehensive and balanced evaluations of the most recent case law. Thus, in the remaining two parts of our work we attempt to shed some light upon these dynamics.

---

[133] Fox and Sullivan, n 90 above, at 959.

[134] DG Goyder, *EC Competition Law* (Oxford European Community Law Library Series) (Paperback, 1996) at 16: 'if the Common market was to be . . . a market where economic progress would result from the efforts of independent undertakings, large and small, from any of the Member States, then the individual territorial markets of Member States had to be made open and kept available to them . . . The aim of integrating national markets therefore became a necessity, and not just an optional extra, in Community competition policy.' This line of thought is also shared by the former Commissioner Mario Monti. Some of his considerations on the issue are particularly enlightening: 'I personally believe that *this principle of an open market economy does not imply an attitude of unconditional faith with respect of the operation of market mechanisms. On the contrary, it requires a serious commitment as well as self restraint by public powers, aimed at preserving those mechanisms . . .*'. Monti goes on to state 'I consider all' the 'legal instruments' set out by the EC competition law 'as different tools at our disposal to achieve a single aim: to maintain a vibrant and competitive economy in Europe'; M Monti, 'European Competition for the 21st Century', in The Fordham Corporate Law Institute— Twenty-eighth Annual Conference on International Antitrust Law and Policy (2001) (New York City), pp 257–258; italics added. Finally, we refer the reader to the insightful essay of N Irti, *L'ordine giuridico del mercato* (3rd edn, Editori Laterza, Rome-Bari, 2004) 73–79.

[135] Allan, n 5 above, commenting on the ECJ ruling in *British Airways* clearly states: 'The judgment is written as if the Discussion Paper did not exist'. McDowell, and Hendry, n 4 above, at 4 *et seq*, express, through less harsh comments though, a similar position in the conclusion of their paper.

[136] The recent judgment of the CFI (Grand Chamber) in *Microsoft* neatly exemplify these dynamic relations. Cf Case T-201/04 *Microsoft Corp v Commission of the European Communities*, judgment of 17 September 2007, (Rec.2007,p.II-3601). For the official comments of the current Commissioner Neeliee Kroes, see eg, 'The EU v Microsoft. A Bittersweet Win over Microsoft', from *The Economist. com*, 17 September 2007. The President of the European Commission Josè Manuel Barroso praised the relevance of judgment for the 'legal certainty and the authority of the Commission's competition policy', echoed by Mario Monti, the Competition Commissioner at time of the fining, who stressed the importance of the CFI's ruling as a precedent which increases the legal certainty for the several cases about similar practice within the information technology industry; see, for instance, 'Il caso Microsoft. La vittoria dell'UE', in *Il Sole 24 ore*, 18 September 2007. Rossi, n 86 above, at 80, maintained that the case shows how the giants of *new economy* tend to protect themselves against rivals by extremely powerful obstacles. Note that, at the time, Microsoft was only under investigation by the Commission. In Rossi's opinion the thesis of the temporary nature of the monopolistic positions is not consistent with the aim of promoting innovation of products and technologies. On the contrary, the Microsoft case would show that the abuse of dominant position aims at discouraging innovations which threaten monopolistic power.

V. Retroactive Rebates in the DG Discussion Paper

In this section we mainly focus on the DG DP's passages directly relevant to the regulation of exclusionary rebates. At the outset, some of the main features of the document are spelled out as they are strictly related to the issue at hand. Particularly, the legal value and the guiding philosophy of the DP need to be addressed. Thereafter, the DP's assessment of *retroactive rebates/commissions* (such as those employed by BA) is illustrated. Finally, we attempt to appraise the differences (as well as eventual convergences) between the Commission's approach in the DP and the European Courts' rulings in *British Airways*. In analysing the subject, we take into due account that the ECJ's judgment in *British Airways* is the last on this specific issue, a chronological element relevant on its own right, which, ultimately, helps us to consider the ECJ's stance towards the reorientation process of the application of Article 82 of the EC Treaty to exclusionary abuses. A position, we deem of truly *juris-prudentia*, which accords with the teleological interpretation of Article 82, and, arguably, with neo-classical economic tenets.

A. The DP's Legal Value and its Foremost Features

There is no doubt as to the need of guidelines on the application of Article 82 of the EC Treaty for a number of reasons. Not only is such a document of great interest to the business community. It would be essential in coordinating and guiding national authorities and courts when applying EC competition rules as well. Indeed, since the coming into force of Regulation 1/2003, national authorities are *obliged* to apply Articles 81 and 82 of the EC Treaty when trade between Member States is affected.[137] Moreover, at approximately the same time as the DP, the Commission presented a Green Paper on Damages Actions for the Breach of the EC Anti-trust Rules.[138] This paper represents a relevant step in order to strengthen the so-called 'private enforcement' of the EC Competition law: '... the Commission intends to enable victims to invoke EC Competition Law as a "sword", and to obtain damages from, or injunctions against, cartels or

---

[137] Cf Article 3 of Regulation 1/2003 on The Implementation of the Rules on Competition Laid Down in Articles 81 and 82 of the Treaty [2003] OJ L1/1. For a further analysis see, *ex multis*, Jones and Sufrin, n 7 above, at 1050–1188, specifically at 1051–1057; Whish, n 7 above, at 75–77; A Riley, 'EC Antitrust Modernisation: The Commission does very well—Thank You! Part Two: Between the Idea and the Reality: Decentralisation under Regulation 1' (2003) ECLR 657 *et seq.*; C Rizza, 'The Duty of National Competition Authorities to Disapply Anti-Competitive and the Resulting Limitations on the Availability of the State Action Defence (Case C-198/01)' (2004) 25 (2) ECLR 126 *et seq.*; G Tosato, 'Il processo di modernizzazione', in G Tosato and L Bellodi (eds), *Il Nuovo diritto eurpeo della Concorrenza. Aspetti Procedurali* (Giuffrè, Milan, 2004) 25–47. For a comprehensive analysis of the modernization process of the EC anti-trust policy, see CD Ehlermann, 'The Modernization of EC Antitrust Policy: a Legal and Cultural Revolution' (2000) 37 CML Rev 537–590; and R Wesseling, *The Modernisation of EC Antitrust Law* (Hart Publishing, 2000), *passim*, specifically at 5–49.

[138] Wurmnest n 84 above, at 7.

dominant companies.'[139] Also the European Competition Network, the aim of which is to 'ensure close cooperation among national authorities, and between the national authorities and the Commission'[140] calls for clear guidelines on the matter. The DP represents a *first* tangible basis upon which to build up the future Guidelines; the effort of the Commission with this respect has to be uncondi-tionally commended. However, one has to remember that the DP has not been converted into guidelines yet, and, the Commission chose a clear non-committal title to its project: not 'Guidelines', not even 'Draft Guidelines', but *'Discussion paper.'*[141] What is more, the very text of the DP stresses that '...it cannot create any legitimate interest nor can it be relied upon to provide guidance to current Commission enforcement policy'.[142] Even assuming that Guidelines on exclu-sionary rebates had *already* been published, as the Advocate General Kokott emphasized in her Opinion in *British Airways*, '(a)ny reorientation in the applica-tion of Article 82 EC' could have been 'of relevance only for the future decisions of the Commission, not for the legal assessment of a decision already taken'.[143] This latter statement accords perfectly with the analogue documents *already* published by the Commission, respectively, on vertical restraints, and horizontal cooperation agreements.[144] The Advocate General goes on to say that 'even if

---

[139] Green Paper of 19 December 2005 on Damages Actions for the Breach of the EC Antitrust Rules, COM (2005) 672 Final.

[140] Wurmnest, n 84 above, at 7. On these aspects, cf Article 11, especially paragraphs (1), (3), (4), (6), and Recital 15 of Regulation 1/2003, n 131 above. For an analysis of the emergence of the EU network, the Commission's position within the network, and the relationship within members of the network and their national governments, see, respectively, DJ Gerber, 'The Evolution of a European Competition Law'; M Siragusa, 'The Commission's Position within the Network. The Perspective of the Legal Practitioners'; and G Tesauro, 'The Relationship between the National Competition Policies and Their Respective Governments in the Context of the Modernisation Initiative', in CD Ehlerman and I Atanasiu (eds), *European Competition Law Annual 2002: Constructing the EU Network of Competition Authorities*, available online at: <http://www.iue.it/RSCAS/Research/Competition/2002(papers)shtml>.

[141] Italics added. See D Hull, 'In Drawing up Possible Guidelines the Commission has to Negotiate the Narrow Gap between Precedent and Reform' (2007) 6(2) Competition Law Insight, 3 *et seq.*

[142] See DG Discussion Paper, n 10 above, Recital 7. Soft law, which undeniably represent an effective means of convergence, should never used to introduce unwarranted restriction to the scope of the relevant rule and their deterring effect. See Mertikopoulou, n 12 above, at 244.

[143] Opinion of Advocate General Kokott, n 43 above, para 28.

[144] Cf Commission Notice on Guidelines on Vertical Restraints (2000 C291/01), Recital 1 and 6, and Guidelines on the Applicability of Article 81 of the EC Treaty to Horizontal Cooperation Agreements ([2001] OJ C3/02), Recital 1 and 6: '(t)he guidelines set out the principles for the assess-ment of', respectively, 'vertical agreement under Article 81 EC Treaty' and 'horizontal cooperation under Article 81 EC Treaty'. We find the same statement in Recital 7 of the DG Discussion Paper, n 10 above. Some of the reasons which can explain the Commission's caution in promulgating Guidelines on Article 82 are to be recalled. This operation allows one to differentiate the case of the Guidelines published for matters related to Article 81 of the EC Treaty over the as yet unpublished guidelines on Article 82 practices: indeed, the two cases are often inaccurately made equal. Hull, n 141 above, at 3 *et seq.*, aptly points out the Commission's caution 'is understandable for a number of rea-sons...'. Above all, the fact that 'in promulgating the guidelines on the application of Article 82, the Commission will be entering a territory that is largely uncharted in terms of articulat-ing a coherent set of guiding principles. In contrast, when it issued the various sets of guidelines

its administrative practice were to change, the Commission will still have *to act within the framework prescribed for it by Article 82 EC as interpreted by the Court of Justice*.'[145] Thus, it is clear that guidelines themselves are not legally binding on the courts. However, it is probably safe to say that 'any guidelines will amount to more than mere statements of principle in that they are likely to constrain the Commission and may well be hard for courts to ignore if companies rely upon them to their detriment'.[146] To us, it is likewise safe to assert that such likely effects can hardly be assigned to the DP, at least, in its present form. Further, it is worth pointing out that, since at the time of both the Commission's contested decision (July 1999) and the CFI's judgment (December 2003) the DP did not even exist, BA could not rely upon it. In view of the above, it is easier to ponder some of the critiques raised against the ECJ judgment in *British Airways*,[147] and, more generally, to assess the ever-rising institutional dynamics inherent to the European Community. Finally, by taking into due account the legal value and the prospective role the DP is nonetheless likely to play for the *future* Commission's enforcing activity, we can drop our legal analysis into the mutable scenario the regulation of exclusionary abuses is currently experiencing. A comprehensive evaluation of the DP is evidently beyond the scope of our work.[148] Nevertheless, some of its general features must be recalled in order to appraise the elements introduced by the DP about the treatment of exclusionary rebates. First, the orientation of the DP is declared in the introduction:

With regard to exclusionary abuses the objective of Article 82 is the *protection of competition* on the market as a means of *enhancing consumer welfare* and of *ensuring an efficient allocation of resources*... In applying Article 82, the Commission will adopt an approach which is based on the *likely effects on the market*.[149]

The primary aim of Article 82 of the EC Treaty vis-à-vis exclusionary abuses would be *consumer welfare*.[150] However, that principle is not without qualifications. Indeed, the primary goal of enhancing *consumer welfare* is juxtaposed to

---

dealing with restrictive agreements covered by article 81 ... the Commission had the benefit of having had corresponding block exemption regulation in place for a number of years.'

[145] Opinion of Advocate General Kokott, n 43 above, para 28.

[146] Hull, n 141 above, at 3 *et seq.*

[147] Allan, n 5 above, asserts that: 'The judgment is written as if the Discussion Paper did not exist... although the Court speaks the language of the market effect.'

[148] We refer the reader to Allan, n 115 above, at 43 *et seq.*; Rosch, n 93 above, at 1 *et seq.*; Wurmnest, n 84 above, at 8 *et seq.*; Marsden, n 16 above, at 3 *et seq.*

[149] Cf DG Discussion Paper, n 10 above, para 4, italics added.

[150] It is noteworthy that, while for some commentators, the Commission departs neatly from the traditional view of European competition policy, as *consumer welfare* would represent the 'guiding star' for it—see eg, Competition Law Forum's Article 82 Review Group, 'The Reform of Article 82' (2006) 2 *European Competition Law Journal*, at 169—according to Wurmnest, n 84 above, at 18, the German *Bundeskartellamt* understands the proclamation enshrined in paragraph 4 of the DP to say that the traditional objectives of Article 82 have not changed. Cf the Written Statement of the German Bundeskartellamt and the Germany Ministry of Economy and Technology on the DG Discussion Paper on the Application of Article 82 of the Treaty to Exclusionary Abuses, at 5 (Bonn, 2006).

allocative efficiency, a fact worth being considered when assessing behaviours of dominant firms which seek to foreclose competitors from the market (or to contain their growth) by trying to make their customers happy with low prices *in the short run*.[151] What is more, the *protection of competition on the market* is mentioned *as the means*—we would say 'the immediate goal'—to achieve the abovementioned fundamental aims. Again, the very fact that the Commission concedes that Article 82 may also aim to protect 'not yet as efficient' competitors when the dominant company benefits from, for instance, economies of scale and scope, learning curve effects, or first mover advantages that later entrants can not be expected to match,[152] is hardly reconcilable with a inflexible consumer welfare standard, at least, if understood as an exclusive goal to be attained *in the short term*.[153] Secondly, the DP entrenches an effect-based approach,[154] which is elaborated in Section V describing the general framework for the analysis of exclusionary abuses. After citing the definition of abuse provided by the Court in *Hoffman-La Roche*,[155] the DP goes on to state:

... the conduct in question must in the *first* place have *the capability*, by *its nature, to foreclose competitors from the market*. To establish such capability it is in general sufficient to *investigate* the *form* and *nature* of the conduct in question. It *secondly* implies that, in the *specific market context*, a *likely* market distorting *foreclosure effect* must be established.[156]

Four brief notes on this excerpt: (a) it is consistent with both the opinion of Advocate General Kokott and the ECJ judgment in *British Airways*;[157] (b) the Commission *literally* makes reference to the *capability* of the conduct at issue 'by its nature, to foreclose competitors from the market', and suggests that this capability

[151] More generally, the excerpt is consistent with the letter and the spirit of Article 82, as interpreted by the ECJ. As Mertikopoulou, n 12 above, at 243 points out: 'Promoting efficiency (in the sense of aggregate welfare is a distinct concept in relation to increasing consumer surplus. In this context it should be clear that a practice reducing the level of competition in the marketplace, if increasing efficiency for the benefit of the undertaking exercising the practice without transferring benefits to the consumers, is caught by the prohibition of Art. 82 EC.'

[152] Cf DG Discussion Paper, n 10 above, para 67.

[153] Interestingly, pundits, who have rather different opinions on the general role economics should play in the future European competition policy, agree on this point. See, eg, Allan, n 115 above, at 46 *et seq.*, and Wurmnest, n 84 above, at 19.

[154] Allan, n 115 above, at 48, who, commenting the general objectives of the DP, emphasizes a certain tension between the central aim of *consumer welfare* and 'its dominant philosophy', which 'may be described as a precautionary principle under which any threat to the long-term competitive structure of the market is sufficient to justify intervention ...'. As to the actual scope of the effect-based approach other commentators are rather sceptical. See eg, Marsden, n 16 above, at 3 *et seq.*: 'But what effect are they looking for?' The DP's '... initial analytical framework section spelled out the focus on consumer harm in detail ... Unfortunately, the drafters took a huge step back in the Discussion Paper's implementation sections, analysing business practices only by reference to the Commission's much longer-held concern about foreclosure of competitors (see DP para 162, in particular)'.

[155] Cf DG Discussion Paper, n 10 above, para 57; Case 85/76 *Hoffman La Roche,* cited above at n 122.

[156] Cf DG Discussion Paper, n 10 above, para 58.

[157] Cf, respectively, Opinion of Advocate General Kokott, n 43 above, para 45, and Case C-95/04P *British Airways plc v Commission*, n 1 above, paras 69 and 85.

should be first assessed by investigating 'the form and nature of the conduct'; (c) the stress on the foreclosure *effect* on the market seems to mark a noticeable departure from the widely criticized strictly formalistic approach articulated by the CFI in *Michelin II*.[158] By way of corollary, it would seem that the ECJ in *British Airways* takes a certain distance from that approach as well;[159] (d) the very fact that the DP uses the qualification *likely* to indicate the type of effect on the market to be established is another meaningful point. Irrespective of the (current or future) legal value of the DP, as a general rule, no requirement of proving an *actual* foreclosure effect is set out. Thirdly, the framework itself of the DP, along with its position in respect of specific exclusionary practices reveals the Commission's intent to rationalize the matter of exclusionary conduct by embracing a 'more economic' approach to the abuse doctrine.[160] Considering the general aim of refining the existing established rules vis-à-vis exclusionary abuses, this general character of the document is not without shades. Indeed, by trying to bring the EC law in line with modern economic thinking, it seems that the Commission implicitly deems part of the existing case law outdated. However, in weeding out inconsistencies of the previous practice, the need of clear and logical guidelines should not have been lost: '[t]he proposed changes with regard to the existing case enforcement practice should be duly highlighted. In this regard the Discussion Paper falls short.'[161] A more narrative style could have better highlighted any deviations of the wished-for changes from the existing enforcement practice. Moreover, a plain distinction was needed between the current state of the law, the reasons and the extent to which a more economic analysis was called for, and the final description of the outcomes of the advocated adjustments in contrast with existing standards. The DP lacks such a clear analysis, 'as even an informed reader needs to study certain passages carefully to spot the exact change'.[162] Finally, considerable room is given both within the general framework,[163] and the single sections on specific practices[164] to economic justifications and efficiencies. In drawing the general outline of the possible economic justification, the DP distinguishes between two types of

---

[158] Cf Case T 203/01 *Michelin II*, n 38 above, paras 239 and 241. Allan, n 115 above, at 43 points out how the formalistic approach in *Michelin II* '... evoked a strong reaction from those whom it gave primacy to form over substance and, in so doing, produced results that lack economic logic'.

[159] See *contra* Allan, n 115 above, at 47.

[160] See M Dreher and M Adam, 'The More Economic Approach to Article 82 EC and the Legal Process', in (2006) Journal of Competition Law, at 259. Implications, objectives, consequences of such an approach are exposed in the Report by the EAGCP, n 87 above, at 2–12.

[161] Wurmnest, n 84 above, at 4.

[162] See Wurmnest, n 84 above, at 5, who recalls the critique about the Section on *Dominance*, voiced by M Monti, 'The Concept of Dominance in Article 82'(2006) 2 *The European Competition Journal* 31 *et seq.*, at 51.

[163] Cf DG Discussion Paper, n 10 above, Section 5.5: *Possible defences: objective justifications and efficiencies.*

[164] Cf DG Discussion Paper, n 10 above, Sections 6.2.5, 7.2.5, 8.2.4, 9.2.1.3, 9.2.2.5, and 10.2.4, dealing with, respectively possible defences and efficiencies for predatory pricing, tying and bundling, refusal to supply relationship, refusal to start supplying an input, and issues of abuses in aftermarkets (or secondary markets).

possible objective justifications, and the efficiencies defence.[165] As to the objective justifications, the DP draws a line between the *objective necessity defence*—'where the dominant company is able to show that the otherwise abusive conduct is actually a necessary conduct on the basis of objective factors external to the parties involved, and in particular external to the dominant company'—and the *meeting competition defence*—'where the dominant company is able to show that the otherwise abusive conduct is actually a loss minimising reaction to competition from others'.[166] On balance, 'the net effect of such conduct is to promote the very essence of the competitive process, namely to win customers by offering better products or better prices than those offered by rivals.'[167] The efficiency defence is conditioned upon four cumulative elements: (1) that efficiencies are realized or likely to be realized as a result of the conduct concerned;[168] (2) that the conduct concerned is indispensable to realize these efficiencies;[169] (3) that the efficiencies benefit consumers;[170] (4) that competition in respect of a substantial part of the products concerned is not eliminated.[171] In our mind, the most remarkable move of the DP towards a coherent system of modern economics is contained in the proposed objective economic justifications and efficiencies defence.[172] This point should not

[165] Cf DG Discussion Paper, n 10 above, para 77: 'Exclusionary conduct may escape the prohibition of Article 82 in case the dominant undertaking can provide an objective justification for its behaviour or it can demonstrate that its conduct produces efficiencies which outweigh the negative effect on competition…'

[166] Cf DG Discussion Paper, n 10 above, para 78. See, respectively, paras 80 and paras 81–83, for a more accurate analysis of the two types of objective justification. See Dreher and Adam, n 115 above, at 278–280, and D Slater and D Waelbroeck, 'Meeting Competition: Why is not an Abuse under Article 82?', College of Europe, in (2004) 3 Research Papers in Law, available online at: <http://www.coleurop.be>.

[167] Ibid.

[168] The dominant company must in the first place be able to show that the conduct is undertaken to contribute to improving the production or distribution of products or to promote technical or economic progress, for instance by improving the quality of its product or by obtaining specific cost reductions or other efficiencies.…'. Cf DG Discussion Paper, n 10 above, para 85.

[169] '…It is for the dominant company to demonstrate that there are no other economically practicable and less anticompetitive alternatives to achieve the claimed efficiencies, taking into account the market conditions and business realities facing the dominant company. The dominant company is not required to consider hypothetical or theoretical alternatives.… The dominant company must explain and demonstrate why seemingly realistic and less restrictive alternatives would be significantly less efficient.' Cf ibid, para 86.

[170] '…This will be the case when the Commission on the basis of sufficient evidence is in a position to conclude that the efficiencies generated by the conduct are likely to enhance the ability and incentive of the dominant company to act pro-competitively for the benefit of consumers …'. Cf ibid, para 87.

[171] '…This requires that the pass-on of benefits must at least compensate consumers for any actual or likely negative impact caused to them by the conduct concerned. If consumers in an affected relevant market are worse off following the exclusionary conduct, that conduct can not be justified on efficiency grounds.' Cf ibid, para 88. This latter condition is further spelled out in paragraphs 89–91, which lists the relevant principle the Commission should pursue in analysing the challenging issue of passing on the efficiencies benefits to consumers.

[172] This position is supported also by Wurmnest, n 84 above, at 6; *contra* Allan, n 115 above, at 53: 'the strength of the precautionary principle is also demonstrated by the narrow scope given to the concept of objective justifications'.

be underestimated; it accords with the positions of eminent scholars and practitioners who, when advocating a modern approach towards exclusionary abuses, stress that the crucial issue for shaping a *balanced policy* in exclusionary cases is to assess whether there are positive reasons, grounded on competition on the merits, which may justify an otherwise foreclosure practice.[173] This latter feature of the DP seems to suggest that economic objective justifications and efficiency defences could be the guiding yardsticks for the enforcing authorities in order to appropriately consider economics when dealing with exclusionary conduct.[174]

B. The DP's Approach to Retroactive Rebates

(i) General Principles of the DP's Section on Rebates

One of the most original contributions of the DP is in the area of rebates. At the outset of the Seventh Section (*Single branding and rebates*) the DP points out that: 'Rebate systems can be formulated and modulated in many ways and it is therefore not possible to provide an exhaustive list.'[175] Thereafter, it highlights the basic distinction between unconditional rebates—which 'while granted to certain customers and not to others, are granted for every purchase of these particular customers, independently of their purchasing behaviour'—and conditional rebates—'granted to customers to reward a certain (purchasing) behaviour of the customers themselves'.[176] At the outset of its analysis, the Commission also feels the need to explicitly point out that a supplier can use rebates (as single branding) both for efficiency enhancing reasons and for anti-competitive reasons, and that rebates may have efficiency enhancing effects and anti-competitive effects.[177] A further noticeable element consists of the DP's emphasis on the fact that, foreclosure aside, 'another possible negative effect of rebate systems is price discrimination between the different buyers'.[178] Yet, as Allan emphasizes, what makes the Section under discussion innovative is mainly the circumstance that, for the first time, the DP introduces an element of

---

[173] See, for instance, what is maintained by M Monti in the excerpt referred to above in section IV D.

[174] See section V (C)(iii) in this article.

[175] DG Discussion Paper, n 10 above, para 136.

[176] Ibid, para 137, adding: 'The latter type of rebates may depend on a number of aspects of the customer's behaviour, such as the amount purchased in a preceding period from the same supplier or the percentage of total requirements purchased in a preceding period from the same supplier or the supply of a certain service by the customer.' Since this work primarily regards loyalty-inducing rebates, our analysis is focused solely on the DP's treatment of conditional rebates.

[177] Ibid, para 138.

[178] Ibid, para 140. As to this point the DP (in fn 88) refers explicitly to the established case law, particularly to the CFI's judgment in *British Airways*. However, the DP considers discriminatory rebates only to the extent they foreclose rivals; cf ibid, para 141. The mere exploitative intent and/or effect is beyond the object of the DP in its present form.

predation pricing analysis to the assessment of rebates.[179] This orientation would manifestly represent a material change in case of a future systematic application by the enforcing authorities. Nonetheless, it makes the DP's approach to rebates less clear than it looks at first, since it refers to the assessment of predation, being the latter a conduct based on pricing strategies, the assessment of which is still rather controversial, as the debate on the DP's analysis itself confirms.[180] Therefore, in order to make the DP's approach towards *retroactive rebates* clear, we outline the principles asserted by the Commission as regards predatory pricing. We finally describe how the DP uses the elements of predation analysis for retrospective rebates.

(ii) Elements of Predation Theory

Without going into details, predation is defined by reference to the conventional notion of a *deliberate sacrifice*, that is to say 'incur(ing) in losses or forego(ing) profits...in the short run that enables a dominant firm to eliminate or discipline one or more rivals, or to prevent entry by one or more potential rivals, thereby hindering the maintenance or the degree of competition still existing in the market or the growth of that competition'.[181] The DP stresses the need of making a distinction between price reductions, which form part of an ordinary competitive process (explicitly labelled as 'an essential element of competition'), on the one hand, and predation, on the other.[182] Subsequently, the Commission proposes a litmus test which follows the standard cost-based model developed from the settled case law,[183] the only relevant difference being the replacement of the average variable cost (AVC) standard stated in *AZKO*[184] by the average avoidable cost (AAC) standard.[185] To sum up:

---

[179] See Allan, n 115 above, at 60, and the DG Discussion Paper, n 10 above, para 146.

[180] For an insightful assessment of this method see eg, Allan, n 115 above, at 56 *et seq.*, and Wurmnest, n 84 above, at 9 *et seq.* Interestingly, despite some common critiques raised against the DP's assessment of specific exclusionary conduct, and a manifest dissatisfaction towards the general orientation of the Document, the two authors maintain quite opposite views about the path the Commission should follow in drawing the future guidelines.

[181] DG Discussion Paper, n 10 above, para 93.

[182] Ibid, para 94. See also para 95.

[183] Ibid, paras 100–112. See also Allan, n 115 above, at 56–59.

[184] Cf Case C-62/86 *AKZO Chemie BV v Commission* [1991] ECR I-3359.

[185] Pursuant to para 108 of the DG Discussion Paper, n 10 above, the reference to avoidable costs compared to variable costs is more accurate (and practical) for it focuses on the ability of the (dominant) firm to change its cost base over the period under examination. The underlying rationale is spelled out in para 106. According to para 105 the relevant period 'over which to measure the costs will be in principle be the time period in which the alleged predatory pricing has taken place or, if still continuing, is expected to take place' save the possibility to choose different periods when appropriate in particular cases. See also paras 103–104 for the criteria the Commission follows in order to choose certain cost benchmarks, and to apply them from the available data in the relevant market.

(i) prices below average avoidable costs (AAC) are presumed exclusionary, unless a credible explanation is offered;[186]
(ii) prices between AAC and average total costs (ATC) are presumed exclusionary if a predatory intent, that '. . . objectively speaking is part of a strategy or plan to predate', may be established;[187]
(iii) price above ATC may be predatory only in extreme circumstances.[188]

As to the recoupement of the losses incurred, despite the DP's general definition of predation being grounded on sacrifice and recoupement, 'two complementary elements of seemingly equal standing,'[189] its analysis of the evidence for predation envisages recoupement as a possible, but non-necessary element.[190] The Commission concludes that, in general, proof of dominance is sufficient to establish the likelihood of recoupement.[191] 'So, the notion of recoupement appears to progress from an element that it is important to prove independently to an element that is assumed to exist by virtue of the proof of dominance.'[192]

(iii) *Assessment of Exclusionary Retroactive Rebates*

Coming back to rebates, the DP distinguishes between *retrospective rebates* offered in respect of *total sales* (that is rebates granted on all purchases during that period), and those offered in respect of *incremental sales* (that is rebates granted only on incremental purchases above a certain threshold, known as *prospective rebates*).[193] The gist of the DP's theory is that a rebated price is

---

[186] Cf DG Discussion Paper, n 10 above, paras 109–110. As an example of a possible explanation, the DP mentions 'the case where the low price is part of a one-off temporary promotion campaign to introduce a new product and where the duration and extent of the campaign are such that exclusionary effects are excluded'.

[187] Ibid, para 112. The DP thoroughly illustrates different elements that, directly or indirectly, may be used to show such an intent at paras 113–123.

[188] Ibid, para 127. 'An example of such an exceptional situation is where companies in a collective dominant situation apply a clear strategy to collectively exclude or discipline a competitor by selectively undercutting the competitor and thereby putting pressure on its margins, while collectively sharing the loss of revenues' (ibid, para 123).

[189] Allan, n 115 above, at 56

[190] DG Discussion Paper, n 10 above, para 115.

[191] Ibid, para 122. That outcome is consistent with the position traditionally taken by the ECJ as regards predation, being unnecessary, according to EC competition law, to prove the recoupement (ie the fact that the predatory strategy has succeeded). Cf Case T-83/91 *Tetra Pak v Commission* [1994] ECR II-755, [1997] 4 CMLR 726 (CFI), and on appeal, Case C-334/94P [1996] ECR I-5951, [1997] 4 CMLR 662 (ECJ).

[192] Allan, n 115 above, at 56.

[193] DG Discussion Paper, n 10 above, para 151. Given the focus of this work on retrospective rebates, we refer to paragraphs 166–169. The essence of the method proposed by the Commission is a straightforward application of the predation theory, whereby a rebate is presumed abusive if the rebated price for the purchases above the threshold does not cover the dominant undertaking's ATC. Incidentally, the DP, in para 151, stresses the relevance of the terms in which the threshold is formulated: 'for instance as a percentage of total requirements of the buyer, as an individualised volume target or as a standardised volume target'.

prima facie abusive unless either it covers the dominant firm's ATC, or there is no evidence of possible foreclosure.[194] The intrinsic rationale of the theory is that '[t]he rebate system should not hinder *as efficient competitors*' (ie smaller rivals already active in the market and potential entrants) 'to expand or enter'.[195] In the case of *retrospective rebates*, the DP proposes a standard under which a rebate is *prima facie* deemed to create a market distorting foreclosure effect (and, hence, it is presumed abusive). In essence, if the share of the market at which the rebated price covers the dominant firm's ATC is greater than the share an efficient entrant can reasonably be expected to capture, then the retroactive rebate scheme is presumed abusive.[196] In such a case, 'the strength of the inducement to purchase more from the dominant supplier, ie the loyalty enhancing effect, will depend, amongst other things, on the level of the rebate percentage and on the level of the threshold'.[197] Indeed, 'the higher the rebate percentage and the higher the amount that needs to be purchased before the rebate kicks in', and 'the stronger the inducement just below the threshold'. This approach to *retroactive rebates* is explained by the circumstance that 'exceeding the threshold' allows the dominant firm to reduce not only 'the price for all purchases above the threshold, but also for all previous purchases during the reference period'. This effect is known as 'suction' effect. In other terms, 'the rebate enables the dominant supplier to use the inelastic or "non contestable" portion of demand of each buyer, ie the amount that would anyhow be purchased by the buyer, as leverage to decrease the price for the elastic or "contestable" portion of demand, ie the amount for which the buyer may prefer and be able to find substitutes'.[198] The Commission's suggested test is a rather complex application of the predation theory, based on the comparison of two market shares:

(1) The *commercially viable share* (CVS), that is the share of the market that an efficient entrant can reasonably be expected to capture.[199]

---

[194] In the case of retroactive rebates, the latter condition is likely to occur when: (a) the rebate scheme does not affect a substantial part of the market demand; (b) the threshold is set substantially below the level of indications that customers would expect to buy from the dominant firm in any event; or (c) there are clear indications of a lack of foreclosure effect such as aggressive and significant entry and/or switching of customers. See the summary of the test, ibid, at para 162.

[195] Ibid, para 154, which explicitly refers to retroactive rebates, emphasis added. The rationale is the same also for the prospective rebates, the DP deals with thereafter; cf paras 166–169.

[196] Cf ibid, paras 152–166. See the summary at para 162.

[197] Ibid, para 153.   [198] Ibid.

[199] Cf ibid, para 152: '... the dominant position will in general ensure that most buyers will anyhow purchase most of their requirements from the dominant supplier, for instance because its brand is a "must stock item" preferred by many final consumers or because the capacity constraints on the other suppliers are such that a good part of demand can only be provided by the dominant supplier.' See also para 143.

(2) The *required share* (RQS), which is the share of customers' requirements the entrant should at least capture such that 'the effective price be at least as high as the average total cost of the dominant company', where:[200]

(a) the effective price (Pe) is the rebated price for the buyer over the commercially viable share 'in case this share would allow the buyer to benefit from the rebate on the purchases *below the threshold*';[201]

(b) while the average total cost (ATC) is calculated on the basis of a volume equal to the threshold specified in the rebate scheme of the dominant firm.[202]

Once the required share is determined, some cases are easier than others, as they do not require the Commission to assess the CVS. For instance, when 'the shares of the customers' requirements purchased from actual rivals are smaller than the required share, the rebate scheme is likely to have a foreclosure effect where there is in addition no indication that these rivals are less efficient'.[203] Another situation when it is sufficient comparing the required share to the actual shares of the competitors occurs when the market share of each competitor is much bigger than the required share. In such a case, 'the rebate system is unlikely to have a foreclosure effect that hinders competition.'[204] In contrast, '... in case it is not clear from the required share itself whether or not the rebate system is likely to have a foreclosure effect, the Commission will endeavour to assess the commercially viable share an efficient competitor or entrant can be expected to supply and to compare this with the required share.'[205] The assessment of the CVS is not an automatic operation at all. Quite the opposite, it entails a detailed and very fact-specific analysis which should consider the particular features of the market and sector context at issue.[206] According to the DP, the Commission should 'in particular be attentive that the rebate system does not foreclose *potential* competitors'.[207] This entails that the Commission starts its analysis with estimation of the rebate's effect on an entrant that 'would enter at *minimum efficient scale* and which would sell the same percentage to each customer in the market'.[208] The DP further establishes

---

[200] Ibid, para 155: 'The required share (RQS) is calculated as follows: $RQS = R \times P/(P - ATC)$.' Where: (i) R is the rebate percentage customers obtain once they have purchased more than the threshold; (ii) P is the (list) price without the rebate; and (iii) ATC is the average total cost of producing the product of the dominant company.

[201] Ibid, para 154, especially the exemplification proposed in the relative box. Emphasis added.

[202] Cf ibid, para 154: 'The main reason to take ATC as the cost benchmark below which the rebate system is considered to lead to an exclusionary effective price is that the leveraging between the 'non-contestable' and the 'contestable' portion of demand allows the rebate system to operate without a profit sacrifice and thus to operate for a long time. The customer may not derive a direct benefit from the rebate system as the rebate may only bring the average price down to the level existing without the rebate system.'

[203] Ibid, para 155, that goes on to say that 'in such a situation a rival would have to more than double its sales to these customers to overcome the foreclosure effect.'

[204] Ibid.   [205] Ibid, para 156.   [206] Ibid, para 157.

[207] Ibid, emphasis added.   [208] Ibid.

that the CVS determined as just illustrated may be adjusted when it is too low.[209] The possible results of the comparison between the required share and the commercially viable share can be summarized as follows:[210]

Box: comparing commercially viable share and required share

If CVS = RQS and thus CVS = R × P/(P −ATC), then Pe = ATC
If CVS < RQS and thus CVS < R × P/(P −ATC), then Pe < ATC
If CVS > RQS and thus CVS > R × P/(P −ATC), then Pe > ATC

Thus, if the *commercially viable share* exceeds the *required share*, the retroactive rebate scheme is presumed to be *non-exclusionary*. On the contrary, if the *required share* exceeds *commercially viable share* the scheme is *prima facie exclusionary*.

(iv) Other Relevant Elements: Efficiency Defences

The Commission put forward some additional indications in order to further improve the application of the predation theory to the analysis of retroactive rebates. A first group regards relevant elements related to the threshold. More precisely, for the assessment of the rebate scheme, it is crucial *in what terms* the threshold is formulated. Indeed, pursuant to the Commission, it is materially different whether the threshold is devised, on the one hand, by reference to a percentage of the total requirements of the buyer or as an individualized volume target, and, on the other hand, as a standardized volume threshold.[211] In the first two cases the dominant firm can set 'the threshold at which the rebate kicks in at such a level as to create a maximum loyalty enhancing effect'.[212] The Commission further denotes that 'setting the threshold in terms of a percentage of total requirements of the buyer *is most straightforward* in order to enhance loyalty', and that '*individualised volume targets* allow the dominant supplier to create *the same loyalty enhancing effect*'.[213] To exemplify the latter case, it makes explicit reference, inter alia, to the CFI's ruling in *British Airways*.[214] A second material element for assessing

---

[209] '... because entry is likely to occur at a larger scale than the minimum efficient scale, because other incumbent competitors are likely to expand at a larger scale or because entrants are likely to concentrate sales on a limited number of customers to whom they can sell more per customer...', ibid.

[210] Source: ibid, para 154, Box at p 46.

[211] Cf ibid, para 158. In the case of standardized volume threshold, the loyalty inducing effect would be less likely; cf para 159.

[212] Ibid, para 160, adding: 'Such uncertainty may, where the customers want to minimise the risk of not obtaining the rebate, induce further loyalty.'

[213] Ibid, emphasis added.

[214] Ibid, and especially fn 10. More straightforwardly, at the end of the same paragraph the DP reads: 'In case the threshold(s) is (are) formulated in terms of ... an individualised volume target, the Commission will normally presume that it (they) is (are) set at such level(s) as to hinder customers to switch to and purchase substantial additional amounts from other suppliers and thus enhance loyalty.'

the loyalty-enhancing effect of a retroactive rebate scheme regards whether the customers are left in *uncertainty* as to the level of the target threshold or the level of the rebate.[215] Thirdly, the Commission indicates specific elements concerning *lato sensu* the actual effect of the scheme on the specific market a dominant firm may rely on in order to rebut a presumption that the scheme at hand creates a distorting foreclosure effect.[216] To conclude the DP's assessment of *retroactive rebates*, efficiency defences must be addressed. A first case could be that the rebate system 'is indispensable to obtain cost advantages and pass them on to the customers'.[217] The efficiency defence at hand is limited in that such cost savings: (i) need to be substantiated; (ii) may require a rebate system using a (grid of) standardized volume target(s); but (iii) are unlikely to require and are unlikely to be efficiently achieved with a rebate system where the threshold is set in terms of a percentage of total requirements of the buyer or an individualized volume target.[218] A second possible defence is represented by a rebate system which 'is indispensable to incite the customers to purchase and resell a higher volume and avoid double marginalisation.'[219] Also this defence is not unconditional. Indeed, the dominant firm must show that the rebate scheme will lower the retail price in case the customer has considerable market power. Regarding the type of rebate, this may require conditional rebates on incremental purchases, but, according to the Commission, it is unlikely to be efficiently achieved with retroactive rebates. The last defence, explicitly envisaged by the DP, occurs when the rebate scheme is 'indispensable to provide the incentive for the dominant supplier to make certain relationship—specific investments in order to be able to supply a particular customer'.[220] In this latter case, 'it must be shown that the relationship-specific investment is a significant long-term investment' (ie the investment is irrecoverable in the short term) and that 'the investment is asymmetric, ie that the supplier invests more than the buyer'.[221]

C. The ECJ's Judgment in British Airways and the Commission's Analysis of Retroactive Rebates in the DP: Dynamics Inherent to the European Institutions

By comparing the ECJ's judgment in *British Airways* with the DP's analysis of retroactive rebates, we can show that, even though the two approaches diverge

---

[215] Cf ibid, para 160.

[216] For instance, the dominant firm can show that the individualized or standard volume targets are set particularly low compared to the buyers' total purchases from the dominant company, and, consequently, they have no perceptible effect on customers switching. By the same token, the dominant firm can show that entry or expansion of competition is actually possible to a larger scale than that assessed by the Commission as the commercially viable share. Cf ibid, para 163.

[217] Ibid, para 173.   [218] Ibid.   [219] Ibid, para 174.

[220] Ibid, para 175; 'An investment is considered relationship-specific if, after termination of the supply contract with that particular customer, the investment cannot be used by the supplier to supply other customers and can only be sold at a loss.'

[221] Ibid.

as the ECJ makes no use of the predation theory to assess BA's appeal, their con-
verging traits are more (and more material) than can be imagined after reading
certain comments on the ruling under discussion. Our last remarks on this comparison address efficiency defences. Our take is that an appropriate consideration
of these defences can represent a valuable *trait d'union* between, on the one hand,
a treatment of alleged exclusionary price conduct consistent with the teleological
interpretation of Article 82 of the EC Treaty, and, on the other, the advocated
sound economic approach.

(i) An 'Unavoidable Divergence'

In *British Airways*, the ECJ does not apply any criterion based on the 'predation
theory' that the DP introduced in order to assess conditional rebates. Indeed,
there is no reference to the calculation of the *required share* and the *commercially viable share*. To us, this choice is perfectly comprehensible for a number of
reasons. Let us begin with our *interim* conclusion about the accordance of the
ECJ's decision in *British Airways* with the teleological interpretation of Article
82 of the EC Treaty.[222] Not to mention the likely procedural mistake the Court
would have made, had it developed, in lieu of the CFI, an analysis inspired by
the predation theory as the DP proposes, it is plain that, by confirming the CFI's
conclusion on the *exclusionary* nature of BA's schemes, the Court does not dramatically depart from its settled case law. In so doing, the ECJ makes it clear
what should be undisputed, that is the Commission has not *'carte blanche* to
abolish unwanted case law with a *soft law instrument!'*.[223] Secondly, it has to be
considered that the DP's approach to predation is at an incipient state. It has
been widely criticized both by scholars who seem to fear more a less intervening
enforcing policy resulting from the eventual application of the DP, and authors
who advocate an approach similar to that adopted in the US, by including sacrifice, exclusion, *and recoupement* in order to determine whether a certain conduct
does indeed display the features of a predatory strategy.[224] By the same token,
even an author such as Rosch, who enjoys the privilege to comment the DP from
a rather neutral position—being the current Commissioner of the US Federal
Trade Commission (FTC)—is sceptical about the accuracy of the DP's proposed analysis.[225] All those positions converge in questioning the elaborated cost
benchmark introduced by the Commission. Whereas Allan contests the universal use of the average total cost (ATC), proposing, alternatively, the average avoidable cost (AAC) of the dominant firm,[226] Rosch and Wurmnest draw attention

[222] See section IV(C) and (D) of this article.
[223] Wurmnest, n 84 above, at 29; on this aspect, see section V(A) of this article. As stressed by
Mertikopoulou, n 12 above, at 244, although soft law represents a powerful means of convergence,
'it should not be used in such a way to introduce unwarranted restriction to the scope' of Art 82, thus
'disrupting the letter and the spirit of the law'.
[224] See, respectively, Wurmnest, n 84 above, at 9, n 120 above, pp 14–15, and EAGCP, n 87
above, at 52.
[225] Rosch, n 93 above, at 7–9.   [226] Allan, n 115 above, at 71.

to the circumstance that economists themselves doubt whether it is possible in practice to built up benchmarks, as those proposed by the Commission, starting from such measures of costs, since the collecting process is far from being easy and costless.[227] More remarkably, Rosch questions the extent to which the legality of single-firm conduct should depend on accounting cost analysis. He first points out that, whereas the US Supreme Court 'has left up in the air' the issue of what measure of costs is appropriate for the predatory analysis, the DP appears more precise, by identifying five possible measures of costs.[228] Rosch then highlights that 'the discussion of the correct measure of costs may miss an important point',[229] namely, the fact that debate among economic experts 'sometimes pale in comparison with the debates between experts about cost principle'. Thus, the trier of the fact 'may not be able to decide one way or the other' and, in turn, 'the plaintiff won't be able to carry its burden of proof. Hence, the defendant wins.'[230] This argument is evidently strong, logically leading to the radical conclusion that 'this debate makes one wonder whether requiring cost-based analysis is really a prescription for doing nothing.'[231] Rosch's thesis is even more suggestive if one considers that it has been elaborated by an American expert of anti-trust law, who had worked for decades as a private lawyer (mostly for defendants, according to his explicit statement), before being recently appointed as Commissioner for the US FTC. While Rosch put forward such arguments, some European scholars call for an adjusted version of the costs benchmark proposed in the DP, which arguably would remarkably diminish the possibility of intervention by the European Commission.[232] Thirdly, the DP's proposed approach for retroactive rebates (as well as for other unilateral conduct) widely relies on the *'as efficient competitor'* test, first elaborated by Richard Posner, who asserted that an exclusionary conduct is one that is 'likely in the circumstances to exclude from the defendant's market an equally or more efficient competitor'.[233] Yet, this test is affected by considerable flaws.[234] Applicative problems aside,[235] the 'as efficient

---

[227] See Wurmnest, n 84 above, at 20, 23–24; Rosch, n 93 above, at 7. Motta, n 82 above, at 413–415 points out the difficult task of finding a convincing economic theory of predation.

[228] Cf DG Discussion Paper, n 10 above, paras 64–65 and 106–110.

[229] Rosch, n 93 above, at 9.

[230] Ibid. By the same token, some economists doubt that it is possible in practice to measure with any precision the elaborated cost-benchmark proposed in the DP to refine the European Courts' case law.

[231] Ibid. As Rosh himself recalls, Professor Andy Gavil remarks that, in the US, the defendant always prevails when the legal test for exclusionary conduct is predatory pricing, no matter what exact cost measure is employed. See AI Gavil, Are the Antitrust Rules for Monopolists Really 'Unclear' or 'In Flux'?', Before the American Bar Section of Antitrust Law, Fall Forum (15–16 November 2005).

[232] See eg, Allan, n 115 above, at 58–59.

[233] Posner, n 98 above, at 196.

[234] See, *ex multis*, Vickers' deep analysis on the issue, n 126 above, at 18–21. See also G Monti, n 7 above, at 1067, and Wurmnest, n 84 above, at 23.

[235] See, for instance, Wurmnest, n 84 above, at 23 *et seq.*, who highlights the difficulties in obtaining reliable information on pricing conduct and costs of the dominant company (regarded in many national laws as business secrets). Thus, the practical application of the 'as efficient' competitor test would involve 'a great deal of guesswork diminishing its practical value'.

test' may be overly narrowly focused. Indeed, it would not catch anti-competitive conduct in a number of important cases. Particularly, it would fall short in those 'markets prone to monopolisation' which 'exhibit significant economies of scale or scope, or bottlenecks', and 'can exclude equally efficient competitors'.[236] As a result of such contingent conditions of the relevant market, a dominant firm with high market share has significant cost advantages over the potential entrants. Indeed, since it always produces at larger scale than its competitors, its average costs are lower than those of the latter. If so, conduct that would not exclude an 'as efficient' firm can in fact exclude the only actual rivals the dominant firm is ever likely to face.[237] Finally, also the alternative tests with some pedigree in the economic literature are not without problems.[238] As to the *'sacrifice test'*, it assists to explain the illegality of a predatory-like pricing. Indeed, sales at a loss are only rational when the dominant firm expects to recover losses after the rivals having abandoned the market. Yet, this test, while explaining the motivation for the exclusionary conduct, does not explain whether there is 'harm to competition', and, more fundamentally, what 'harm to competition' means.[239] A third possibility is declaring abusive those practices which foreclose rivals whose presence enhance *consumer welfare*. The test evidently accords with the prevailing aims (and, hence, orientation) the contemporary European competition policy pursues. However, as Vickers asserts, 'this standard of anti-consumer effect, stated as a *necessary condition* for a finding of unlawful exclusion would place a more or less *strict limiting principle on anti-trust intervention* against firms with market power.'[240] That partly depends on the standard of proof required to establish the anti-consumer effects in term of higher price and lower output, as one first needs to establish if those effects must be actual or probable, or it is sufficient for the conduct under question 'to have the tendency, a reasonable capability, or merely a possibility of causing them'.[241] A further relevant shortcoming of the standard is related to the limited *concept* of competition it entails. Indeed, *competition* is potentially far broader than what can be measured by assessing the negative output and price effects resulting from dominant firms' behaviours. Finally, by recalling Fox's arguments, Vickers questions if *harm to competition* should include harm to the *dynamic process* of competition, and, if so, what that means in practical terms.[242] In view of the above, we believe that the DP's analysis of *retroactive rebates*, which is largely influenced by the predation theory, cannot represent, at this state of the affairs, a safe starting point for the development of a coherent and effective competition policy. Our take is that the inherent problems, which still

---

[236] Ibid, at 24; See also G Monti, n 7 above.

[237] H Hovenkamp, *The Antitrust Enterprise: Principle and Execution* (Harvard University Press, 2005) at 153.

[238] See eg, Vickers, n 126 above, at 17 *et seq*.

[239] See ibid, at 18, cited also by G Monti, n 7 above, at 1066–1067.

[240] Vickers, n 126 above, at 22, emphasis added.

[241] Ibid, at 22.   [242] Ibid, at 22 *et seq*.

affect the solution proposed by the Commission in the DP, have made the ECJ's pronouncement *unavoidable*. In making no reference to the predatory theory, the ECJ did pronounce a relevant word of caution with respect to an extremely controversial field. A field where modern economics itself, at least the modern economic approach underlying the DP, still seems too fragile for representing a firm starting point to depart from the settled case law. In this sense, the divergence between the last ECJ's pronouncement in the field of exclusionary retroactive rebates, on the one hand, and the DG Commission Discussion Paper's proposed solution, on the other, exemplifies the inherent dynamics between these institutions.[243]

(ii) Substantial Convergences

Notwithstanding the lack of any reference to the predation theory in the ECJ's judgment in *British Airways,* the pronouncement shares (as the CFI's ruling does) certain relevant elements with the approach proposed by the DP, regarding both the central aim of Article 82 of the EC Treaty, and the role of the further indications for the treatment of retroactive rebates. A first assonance between what concluded by, respectively, the European Courts in *British Airways,* and the DP, can be found considering the additional elements the latter indicates for the assessment of alleged exclusionary retroactive rebates. Particularly, the setting of *individualized volume targets* and the *uncertainty* in which customers may be left as to the level of the rebate/commission played a considerable role in the CFI's ruling on BA's schemes.[244] It is perhaps pleonastic to stress that, insofar as these elements are concerned, the position of those who claim that the ECJ's judgment in *British Airways* is written as the DP did not exist should be reconsidered, although, admittedly, 'it is unclear whether these features... supplement or replace the price/cost model' proposed by the DP itself.[245] As to the 'protection of competition' goal, the ECJ's position in *British Airways* is extremely clear and accords neatly with the teleological interpretation developed in the Court's previous case law.[246] As widely illustrated in the final part of this work, this reading has been criticized by some of the authors who advocate an approach more straightforwardly led by economics.[247] Yet, the DP itself, despite its neater economic and effect-based framework, does not seem to take a dramatically changed stance on the issue.[248] Indeed, in spite of 'a certain amount of "Chicago-style" semantics

---

[243] This dynamic relationship is now particularly evident in the field of abusive exclusionary conduct. With respect to it, indeed, the modernization process of EC competition law still needs to achieve material and reliable results as with Article 81 practices and mergers.

[244] See, respectively, section IV(A) and section V(B)(iv) of this article.

[245] Allan, n 115 above, at *et seq.*

[246] Cf Case C-95/04P *British Airways plc v Commission*, n 1 above, para 106, and section IV(B) and (D) of this article.

[247] See section VI(A) of this article.

[248] See section V(A) of this article.

in the DP',[249] it is reasonable to think that the European competition policy will not inevitably pursue the same orientation the US anti-trust law adopted 'a quarter of a century ago'.[250] On the one hand, the ECJ has confirmed, in its recent case law, an unequivocal choice with respect to the dilemma regarding how far to constrain competitive behaviour over the short term to avoid detrimental effects to the competitive structure over the long term:[251] According to the Court, the European perspective is a long-run perspective. On the other, the DP's guiding philosophy, even if admittedly articulated less clearly, does not seem that far. Its guiding principles are consistent with the protection of competition as a structural phenomenon.[252] Thus, there is a remarkable convergence between the ECJ and the Commission's DP on how the aim of safeguarding *effective competition structure* is to be interpreted. It represents the means (or the immediate goal) the European institutions envisage in order to protect, inter alia, *consumer welfare*, seen as the primary (but not the only) object of EC competition policy. Arguably, the main object of safeguarding competition as delineated by the Commission in the DP is not in the need to be neatly distinguished from how it is interpreted by the European Courts. Rather, this policy goal should be discerned from the *attractiveness* of its underpinning philosophy. Eminent commentators, while conceding that 'DG COMP's vision for the future of Article 82 is based on the laudable policy of promoting consumer welfare through an effect-based analytical model', point out that there is a material peril that 'its precautionary principle will lead the European Commission to place undue weight on the assumed gains from long-term improvements in structure as the expense of the arguably more tangible gains from short term dynamism'.[253] Some of the arguments raised by authors maintaining such positions are rather suggestive and depict effectively the main issues the ongoing debate on treatment of exclusionary abuses (and, especially, pricing practices) is focus on.[254] However, the same positions make us glimpse a certain attraction to the old Chicagoans' views. Particularly, we refer to the scarce attention paid to *dynamic efficiency*; an uneasy attitude towards the social cost of the so-called 'false positives' or 'type I errors', and, consequently, a certain underestimation of risks of the opposite sort (ie 'false negatives');[255] and, a rather short-sighted belief that a competition policy shaped by these features *will*

---

[249] Wurmnest, n 84 above, at 26.   [250] Ibid.

[251] This theme is widely addressed, see section IV(B)–(D) of this article.

[252] See section V(A) of this article.   [253] Allan, n 115 above, at 49.

[254] See, for instance, Allan, n 115 above, at 49, especially fn 20, and at 50, according to whom an alternative and less precautionary approach, might better consider, at least in some specific situation, certain gains in productive efficiency, that, pursuant to the European contested approach, are retained as part of the producer surplus. More noticeably, Allan stresses how relevant a precise indication of the two elements that the DP designs can be in order to 'decide the level of foreclosure that engages Article 82', namely, 'the level of competitive harm and the degree of probability that that will occur', ibid, at 52–53.

[255] The social cost of the so-called 'false positives' or 'type I errors' should not be underestimated. Yet, reducing at the minimum margin the scope for intervention available to the enforcing authorities—as some seem to advocate—would expose the European market to exaggerated perils of 'type II errors'. In any case, this approach would rebut the traditional orientation of EC competition policy.

be, in the end, to the benefit of consumers (although we must concede that it can likely end up with benefiting firms with market power). In the light of the drawbacks of such views *and* the principles confirmed in the recent ruling in *British Airways*, we join Wurmnest's optimistic thesis that 'it can be predicted that the ECJ will accept a more nuanced abuse control' without going 'as far as to depart radically from its settled case jurisprudence'.[256]

(iii) *The Different Treatment of Efficiency Defences*

The extent to which efficiency defences are actually taken into consideration in the European Courts' rulings in *British Airways* needs to be examined closely. In section III of our work, we describe how the CFI admitted that loyalty-inducing rebates infringe Article 82 of the EC Treaty, unless they are based on 'economically justified considerations'.[257] Remarkably, this part of the CFI's judgment had been not subject to appeal; the ECJ, hence, had not had to rule on the issue. However, although the concerned passages of the CFI's decision, accepted at face value, show a sympathetic attitude towards economic efficiency in general, we agree with Dreher and Adam, according to whom, 'the *British Airways* judgment…does not make any' substantial 'reference to the notion of economic efficiency'.[258] More generally, even though the European Courts' case law explicitly addresses the possibility of abusive conduct being justified on objective economic grounds,[259] as a matter of fact, in no case concerning pricing conduct has either Court applied this defence in favour of a dominant undertaking.[260] The inherent ambiguity of the efficiency defence may explain why the European Courts have constantly refrained from applying it in its pure form.[261] In detail, an accurate application of this defence needs to establish how far the justification on objective economic base may include elements of efficiency. *Legitimate objectives* can be pursued in an *efficient* manner:[262] this should no doubt be considered when assessing alleged exclusionary conduct. Yet, since in the case of targeted loyalty rebates, the fidelity enhancing effect itself is deemed *illegitimate*,

---

[256] Wurmnest, n 84 above, at 26.

[257] See section III(B) of this article. Cf *British Airways plc v Commission*, n 2 above, para 271.

[258] Dreher and Adam, n 115 above, at 279, adding that the CFI merely spells out 'what is long-established case law, namely that a volume rebate based on an economically justified consideration will not infringe Art. 82 EC, if it does not tend to prevent customers buying from rival producers'.

[259] Cf, for instance, Case 27/76 *United Brands* (1978) ECR 297, at 152–160. See Case T–65/89 *BPB Industries* (1993) ECR-II-389, at 117; *British Airways plc v Commission*, n 2 above, at 246–247; *Manufacture Français des Pneumatiques Michelin*, n 38 above, at 98, 108–109.

[260] According to PJ Lowenthal, 'The Defence of Objective Justification in the Application of Art. 82' (2004) 28 World Competition 444 *et seq.*, specially at 456, 464, in no cases *at all* has either Court applied this defence in favour of a dominant undertaking. In this sense, the *British Airways* case does not represent an exception. See also Dreher and Adam, n 115 above, at 279, and fn 13, and G Monti, n 7 above, at 1066; Gyselen, n 7 above, at 290 *et seq.*

[261] Dreher and Adam, n 115 above, at 279.

[262] Ibid, and also T Eilmansberger, 'How to Distinguish Good from Bad Competition Under Art. 82: In Search of a Clearer and More Coherent Standards for Anti-Competitive Abuses' (2005) 42 CMLR, at 133, 136.

it remains that an illegitimate aim can never be justified by efficiencies.[263] In contrast, the Commission's DP appears to depart from the existing case law in that the factual assessment, and possible application, of efficiency defences are envisaged as an essential moment in considering the foreclosing *effect* of any alleged exclusionary behaviour.[264] We maintain that the stringent conditions set out in case of *retroactive rebates*,[265] not only aim at restricting the access to such defences, but also represent the attempt to draw a clear line between legitimate and illegitimate objectives, which may be pursued through the rebate scheme. The innovative treatment of efficiency defences, which arguably represents the DP's most remarkable shift towards an effective more economic approach, is to be welcomed with no hesitation. An objective and detailed consideration of these defences can properly address the need to *refine* the European bodies' approach in setting the role of economics as regards exclusionary cases (especially, in the likely case the DP leads to Guidelines). Within the two-step analysis set out by the European Courts' case law to assess alleged exclusionary abuses, the weighing of possible efficiency justifications can be chosen as the appropriate moment for the deployment of modern economic instruments. In this way, for instance, most of the material issues brought about by the application of predation theory to retroactive rebates can be bypassed without excluding relevant economic aspects from the whole analysis.

VI. A Sensible Consideration of Economics within the Review Process on Abuse of Dominant Position

Several arguments advanced by authors who have energetically denounced a substantial lack of economic analysis in the European Courts' precedent on retroactive rebates seem to assume that there exists no dispute as to which set of economic theories should remodel the application of Article 82 of the EC Treaty vis-à-vis exclusionary conduct. What is more, many commentators who submit these arguments do not directly question the extent to which economic insights should be employed. In the final part of this work, we attempt to show that relevant aspects of the 'more economic approach' called for orientating the review process the abuse doctrine is undergoing are far from being uncontroversial.[266] We first address the treatment of retroactive rebates from an economic angle by considering specific models

---

[263] Dreher and Adam n 115 above, at 279. 'This would lead to the efficient achievement of an undesired aim, and, in the end, to an unwarranted result.'

[264] See section V(A) of this article.   [265] Cf section V(B)(iv) of this article.

[266] According to G Monti, n 7 above, at 1066, two basic questions regarding the economics-oriented shift of the competition policy's focus are to be addressed: first, its desirability and legitimacy and, secondly, once agreed that this reorientation is desirable, the way to implement it. In the remaining part of this article, we focus on issues inherent to the economic shift, which should be preliminarily discussed.

put forward by scholars who have severely criticized the European Courts' case law on target and retroactive rebates. In so doing, we highlight their common assumptions and the policy implications they entail. This leads us to critically consider the current role of economics within the context of competition policy with regard to allegedly unilateral foreclosing conduct. Accordingly, we examine the economic theoretical basis of EC competition policy and the primary goals the Commission has recently indicated as yardsticks for the ongoing economic-oriented review. The result of this analysis is somewhat counter-intuitive. Despite the apparent clearness of the Commission's policy declarations, the foremost aims it explicitly pursues (ie consumer welfare and allocative efficiency) might be competing. This possible conflict among aims being pursued is not the only ambiguous outcome: even the expression 'more economic approach' is susceptible to various interpretations which do not necessarily fit with one another. Thirdly, even though the current economic models, which, according to some commentators, should ground EC Competition policy, are supposed to represent a reasonably solid anchor for the future application of Article 82 to exclusionary conduct, they still present inherent problematic aspects renowned economists and legal scholars have systematically highlighted.[267] Therefore, the final section of our work aims at outlining the main methodological issues intrinsic to the 'modern economic approach'.[268] Our analysis is carried out keeping in mind what sometimes seems to be, at best, implied, that is the economic paradigms supposed to underpin the review process of abuse doctrine are not the *most modern*.[269] Finally, we ponder whether the 'more economic approach' orientating the review process of the abuse doctrine can be properly integrated with basic legal values and the peculiar aims assigned to competition policy by the EC Treaty. In other terms, we question whether the privileged position lately accorded to (a certain meaning of) economic efficiency and consumer welfare can be conciliated with

---

[267] See, among others, D Schmidtchen, M Albert, and S Voigt (eds), *The More Economic Approach to European Competition Law* (Mohr Siebeck, 2007), especially at 7–216; 22–36, 37–58, 59–64, 65–97, and the ample literature referred to therein; Dreher , and Adam, n 115 above, at 278–282; R Smith, S King, 'Does Competition Law Adequately Protect Consumers?' (2007) 28 ECLR 408–424; Schmidt, n 93 above, at 412 *et seq.*

[268] This article does not claim originality for several of the arguments advanced. There is, for instance, a parallel discussion in WH Roth, 'The More Economic Approach and the Rule of Law', in Schmidtchen, Albert, Voigt, n 267 above, at 57 *et seq.*; and S Voigt, 'More Economic does not Necessarily Means "Better"—Perils and Pitfalls of the More Economic Approach as Recommended by the European Commission', in ibid, at 97 *et seq.*; Schmidt, n 93 above, at 408–412. For further insights of the pervasive issue of "missing economics" within the "more economic" process, see, among others, JE Stiglitz, 'Competition and Competitiveness in a New Economy', in H Handler and C Burger (eds), *Competition and Competitiveness in a New Economy* (Austrian Minister for Economic Affairs, Vienna, 2002) at 11–22,; Smith and King, n 267 above, at 408–412; S Bowles, *Microeconomics: Behaviour, Institutions, and Evolution* (Princeton University Press, 2003) especially at 95 *et seq.*

[269] Incidentally, multiple-game models have recently shown how some of the shortcomings of the 'more economic approach' could have a direct bearing on the inter-institutional dynamics which currently characterize EC competition policy. See C Kirchner, 'Goal of Antitrust and Competition Law Revisited', in Schmidtchen, Albert, Voigt, n 267 above, at 11 *et seq.*

a richer synthesis between Community policies and legal principles preserved by the European Courts.[270] As a matter of clarification, we should also like to note that it goes beyond the scope of this work to propose definitive solutions as to what extent economic analysis should be employed and which shape it could end up taking. Nonetheless, we aim at making it clear that any argument in favour of 'the more economic approach' is remarkably vulnerable insofar as it does not explicate how it solves the inevitable trade-offs it faces. For instance, assuming when consumer welfare as a guiding objective, any model has to show how regularly (and a standard length of the period over which) firm surplus is expected to be attained without affecting consumer welfare.[271] Hardly any relevance can be attributed to arguments against the treatment of alleged foreclosing conduct by the Commission and European Courts in contexts where competent authorities are left without any solid parameter for orientating their activity. This holds true irrespective of how well articulated the *pars destruens* is. Our take is that any economic theory, which aims at orienting the revision of abuse doctrine, reflects a particular viewpoint of competition policy, and, ultimately, represents a peculiar *political* choice. Formulated in slightly different words, the positivistic view of thinkers who deny an inherent and natural character of the marketplace, considering it as a result of particular legislative policies, permeates our study.[272]

A. Modern Economic Approaches to Retroactive Rebates

We now illustrate specific applications of the 'more economic approach' to retroactive and targeted rebates in order to weigh them against the treatment of the same sort of conduct as delineated in the recent European Courts' case law and the DP (respectively, dealt with in the second and third part of this work). The starting point of our analysis is the general framework provided by the Report to the European Commission by the European Advisory Group in 2005 (hereinafter: EAGCP). We then explore four specific models put forward by scholars and practitioners shortly before and after the publication of the DG Commission DP. All the models under discussion are rather critical towards the Commission's practice (and the European Courts' pronouncements upholding it) for it would

---

[270] See Gerber, n 78 above, at 100–105. According to P McNutt, *Law, Economics, and Antitrust. Towards a New Perspective* (Edward Elgar, 2006) at 346, it is even harder to draw a comprehensive synthesis of values and objectives when considering the global anti-trust system, being 'not at all clear to law and economic scholars how to read the move towards a global competition law'.

[271] The latter explanations represent the minimal contents of any system claiming to constitute the orientating paradigm even within the borders of traditional microeconomics.

[272] This thesis is subtly illustrated by Irti, n 134 above, *passim*, and, especially at XII, 3–15, 47–51, 97–110. Incidentally, this view alone can explain a great deal of the current debate on Article 82. From an economic viewpoint, Stiglitz authoritatively denies the natural character and the infallible normative power of the market as described by traditional models. See, for instance, JE Stiglitz, 'Information and the Change in the Paradigm of Economics' Prize Lecture, 8 December 2001, available online at: <http://www.nobelprize.org>, 482–486.

lack a consistent economic analysis assume alterations of the market structure over the mid-long period as a parameter to assess the effects on competition of the rebate scheme at issue, and, as a consequence, lead to *per se* or *de facto per se* rules. By contrast, modern applications of economics to rebates would allow assessment of the actual effect on competition of the particular conduct at stake. In the end, our analysis permits us to spell out the main assumptions and policy implications of the models at issue. Without discussing their internal consistency, we will show that they are grounded on assumptions which are as subjective as those characterizing the methods they criticize. Moreover, they do not solve the main dilemmas and technical drawbacks inherent to 'the more economic approach'.

Coming to the general framework proposed by the EAGCP, against which we will weigh each of models considered below—when the rebate scheme comes in the forms of retroactive rebates it applies to the whole quantities bought by the customer, and amounts to switching to a new price scheme as soon as the threshold is achieved.[273] On the other hand, fidelity rebates are conditional on the client buying all its quantities, or at least a given percentage of them, from the firm. In most cases, rebates imply some form of discrimination between customers.[274] At any rate, one should always distinguish potential anti-competitive over effects *pro-competitive effects* and *efficiency considerations*. The modern economics, which should inspire the enforcement of EC competition law, thus, relies heavily on an effect-based approach and is suspicious of any form-oriented approach.[275] It is maintained that certain types of rebates deployed by dominant firms should be carefully monitored because of their *exclusionary potential*.[276] Indeed, rebates can exclude actual or potential competitors from the market on which the firm is dominant. This is the case, for example, for selective rebates offered to those of the dominant firm's customers that would switch to a new entrant were the rebate not offered (in this case, predatory pricing take the form of selective rebates targeted at the rival's prospective customers), or of retroactive schemes insofar as a certain threshold is achieved and the rebate applies to all quantities bought by the customer from the dominant firm. Economists highlight that, like predatory prices, rebates induce short run sacrifices and may have exclusionary effects either by inducing exit or by discouraging entry. Thus, the main anti-competitive effect

---

[273] See EAGCP, n 87 above, at 34; Kamann, and Bergmann, n 7 above, at 83 *et seq.*, especially at 86, fn 40.

[274] For an analysis of how a discriminatory pricing strategy may operate in an anti-competitive way, see Motta, n 82 above, at 498–499. See also Krugman, and Wells, n 82 above, at 352–357. For a further assessment of the discriminatory effects of rebates, see EAGCP, n 87 above, at 30–33.

[275] In relation to Article 82 cases, the above mentioned policy implication is clearly asserted by the EAGCP, n 87 above, at 5–7: it 'would start out from the effects of anticompetitive conduct, such as exclusion of competitors in the same market or in a horizontally or vertically related market one, and consider the competitive harm that is inflicted on consumers. Adopting such an effects-based approach would ensure that these various practices are treated consistently when they are adopted for the same purpose.'

[276] Motta, n 82 above, at 499; EAGCP, n 87 above, at 34. We refer to the EAGCP Report for a first assessment of rebates' potential horizontal and vertical foreclosure.

of retroactive rebates is to try and induce the customer not to buy from rivals in a fashion extremely similar to exclusive dealing. When assessing rebate schemes implemented by a dominant firm, pro-competitive effects and efficiency considerations should obviously be regarded as well. Efficiencies may be either a cause or a consequence of rebates. With regards to this element of the assessment, some noticeable points are to spelled out. First, efficiency may be either a cause or a consequence of rebates. It is suggested that a general way of assessing the prevalence of pro-competitive effects over anti-competitive ones is to check whether total output has increased or not. Secondly, pro-competitive effects of rebates may occur in a range of circumstances. Since rebates allow high and low demand elasticity consumers to be treated differently, elastic demand segments tend to generate lower margins. Therefore, consumers with a high elasticity of demand benefit from the practice, although consumers with a low elasticity may suffer from it. As a result, the overall effect on consumer welfare is a priori ambiguous.[277] Third, notwithstanding the above, pursuant to the Ramsey pricing model,[278] rebates of this sort may also allow for the recovery of fixed costs, and possibly encourage R&D investments that involve such large fixed costs. Thus, in accordance with the EAGCP Report, rebates are more likely to have a pro-competitive effect when high fixed costs are involved. In terms of consumer welfare, rebates that are targeted to those consumers who are more likely to switch to competitors imply a more intense competition for this group of consumers, who would thus benefit from this situation. The other consumers may indirectly benefit from an increased pressure on the price they face.[279] Rebates may also generate efficiency gains in terms of economies of scale for the dominant firm, or economies of transaction costs for its customers (the buyer concentrates its purchase on a single seller). Finally, rebate schemes can enhance efficiency by solving adverse selection or moral hazard problems.[280] Kamann and Bergmann point out that the consideration of all the aspects just outlined leads to the general intuition that rebates that take the form of pure quantity rebates are more likely to be motivated by efficiency considerations than fidelity rebates, whilst retroactive and loyalty-inducing rebates are more likely to have anti-competitive effects, being motivated by exclusionary considerations. However, the weighing of efficiency aims is a rather complex assessment susceptible to different approaches. Some authors refer to peculiar aspects of the scheme at stake (such as the relevante period of reference; rebate rates/rebate scale; product and personal point of reference) to differentiate between quantitative discounts and fidelity rebates, since both are bound to the purchased amount in a certain period.[281] By contrast,

---

[277] EAGCP, n 87 above, at 36.

[278] As widely known, Ramsey pricing is concerned with prices that maximize the sum of industry profits and consumer surplus. Cf F Ramsey, 'A Contribution to the Theory of Taxation' (March 1927) Economic Journal 37, 47–61.

[279] Kamann and Bergmann, n 7 above, at 86.

[280] EAGCP, n 87 above, at 36.   [281] Ibid, 86–87.

others assert that the mere form of the rebate may not even constitute an orientating indicator.[282] Accordingly, to deal with an alleged story of anti-competitive
rebates, the competition authority should follow an effect-orientated analysis.
For example, it should first identify the kind of exclusionary strategy at work,
and look for possible pro-competitive effects of the practice.[283] The model proposed by the EAGCP seeks to establish whether as efficient competitors would
be kept out from the market by the penalty imposed by the incumbent through
the rebate scheme on new entrants. In a second phase, efficiency effects have to be
carefully assessed: 'among the critical factors are the ability of downstream firms
to pass on a reduction in their own input prices and the incentives given to these
downstream firms to exert effort'.[284] The view of rebates prevailing in several
contemporaneous approaches recognizes that the anti-competitive effects of this
practice may indeed dominate; hence the rebate scheme should be prohibited.
That typically occurs where a supplier uses rebates so as to impose a penalty on
new entrants. A rational customer will switch to a new supplier only when the
latter offers a price that is lower than the price charged by the incumbent supplier
minus the rebate. Therefore, the rebate would be 'analogous to a penalty paid by
the entrant', playing the role of an 'entry fee, designed to extract some of the efficiency gains of new entrants'.[285] In other terms, it would create a barrier to entry
for efficient entrants or impair efficient competitors.[286] In short, the rebate clause
can be compared to an *external effect* imposed on potential entrants, as it is this
externality that makes the rebate scheme profitable for the incumbent supplier.
According to the standard models, consumers are harmed because the probability of entry/expansion of efficient rivals is reduced and prices are likely to be
raised over the mid-long period. Following this framework, in dealing with real
cases, competition authorities should proceed by first identifying such an external effect. Then, they should ponder the magnitude of the penalty imposed on
the entrant.[287] Finally, the likely or actual foreclosing effect should be addressed,
and, in case the competition authority deems this effect has occurred, efficiencies
have to be carefully weighed. Since it is a possibility for consumers to switch to
new entrants competitors may be at stake when a rebate scheme is run, economic
theory stresses the need to quantify the switching costs of the customers, and the
possible transactions costs in case of switching to competitors. It is worth noting

[282] Ibid, at 37.
[283] Ibid. This is also the approach suggested by G Federico, 'When are Rebates Exclusionary?'
(2005) 26(9) ECLR 477 *et seq.*, who remarks that part of the attractions of a form-based approach lies
in the fact that it can provide legal certainty.
[284] EAGCP, n 87 above, at 37–38.
[285] Ibid. It is relevant for the purpose of the present work to stress that this analysis accords in
many of its central passages with Gylesen's; see section IV(B)(i) of this article.
[286] EAGCP, n 87 above, at 37, noting that 'the entrant will enter only if its costs are so low that
entry remains profitable despite the entry fee generated by the rebate'.
[287] This can be approximated by computing the reduction in price that the entrant should offer in
order to be able to enter the market at various quantity levels; cf EAGCP, n 87 above, at 37.

that several approaches grounded on traditional microeconomics do not take into consideration other specific costs, such as costs related to incomplete information which in real life are likely to play a central role.[288] What is more, they do not pay substantial attention to the dynamic effects on the market of the rebate scheme at issue. Quite the contrary, they widely rest on static analyses.

Turning to the first of the considered models put forward by scholars who energetically argue the need of a consistent economic analysis in this field, let us start with the approach proposed by Kallaugher and Sher. The central question 'should be whether the conduct is *likely* to lead to anti-competitive effects, mainly in the form of higher prices or reduced choice *in the short to the medium run*'. Accordingly, they suggest a three-step test. First, it should be questioned whether the system generates *high* switching costs, assuming the latter essentially as a function of the reference period. Secondly, one should determine whether any substantial switching costs identified under the first phase do create material barriers to entry (in the sense of reduced sales opportunities) for existing competitors. Thus, the causal link between high switching costs and barriers to entry/expansion is not taken as a given. Rather, the factors relevant within the second step are the following: the number and size of customers participating in the programme, the proportion of their sales that is shifted to the dominant firm as a result of the rebate scheme, the cost base of the potential entrants, and duration of the reference period of the scheme.[289] Finally, the competition authority should consider whether these barriers to entry are *likely* to lead to an anti-competitive harm, which must not be equated with a change in the structure of the relevant market. Quite the opposite, it is whether the conduct *is likely to harm consumers* in terms of higher prices or reductions in real consumer choice that really matters. Kallaugher and Sher argue that 'only an abuse test with sound economic underpinning can ensure that Community law protects the "competition process" and not competitors'.[290] What it is not plainly stated, but can be easily inferred inter alia from the previous parts of their work, is that the competition process inherent to the model is exhausted by a process of rivalry considered in a static perspective, and, arguably, *over the short term*. To recap, according to the three-step test devised, each likely effect is to be assessed over this limited period of time. If this model may facilitate examining the overall actual or likely effect, it evidently runs the risk of leaving out any dynamic consideration. For example, according to this test, it does not matter if the temporary gains in consumer welfare can be outweighed by the entrance/expansion of efficient rivals which, in a

---

[288] Stiglitz, n 272 above, at 482 *et seq.*

[289] Kallaugher and Sher, n 7 above, at 282. For a critical discussion on the relevance of the reference period, see n 66 above.

[290] Ibid, at 281. On the contrary, Wurmnest n 84 above, 14 claims that: 'this is an empty slogan. It goes without saying that competition law should not protect competitors. The crucial problem is that in cases of market dominance it is often too difficult to draw the line between the protection of competitors and the protection of competition.' This stance is further elaborated, *ex multis*, by Fox, n 129 above, 395 *et seq.*

reasonable period of time, will be able to offer high-quality products at competitive prices. Aside from the limitation of the relevant effects to those consequences produced in the short period, one might argue that positions such as the one under discussion, which openly criticize the European institutions' structionalist approach towards retroactive and loyalty-inducing rebates (lately crystallized in the ECJ pronouncement in *British Airways*), imply a *static* notion of *effect*. In the same way, the main competing reading, which accords more with neoclassical economics and dynamic theories, has been maintained by authors who argue that the *main objective* of competition policy and law is and will remain 'the *maintenance of a competitive structure.* This argument automatically leads (at least as a pattern of prediction) to good performance and an increase in consumers' welfare,[291] and, hence, manifests a certain scepticism towards any legal and/or economic approach which tends to diminish the relative relevance of the *dynamic effects* being necessarily assessed over *a mid-long run perspective*. Again, it is worth stressing that according to Kallaugher and Sher's model, the foreclosing *likely* effect is not deemed abusive in or of itself, but needs to create *high* barriers to entry, which, in turn, should result in higher prices or reduced choice of products and/or services in the short run. We do not question the consistency of this model with its own assumptions. However, it seems that each of the formulated hypotheses leads to a progressive and substantial restriction of the scope of Article 82 of the EC Treaty to exclusionary rebates. On the other hand, this result accords neatly with the arguments advanced by the two scholars, whereby the approach devised by the Commission and further developed by the European Courts is 'unduly interventionist'.[292]

The second model we consider was put forward by Federico in 2005. In order to assess the impact of rebates over competition, Federico proposed an alternative approach, widely grounded on traditional microeconomics. In view of the pervasive deployment of retroactive rebates in the business practice and the efficiencies they might result in over the short term, Federico attempts to distil the range of circumstances and conditions under which retroactive rebate schemes might consist in efficient pricing behaviours and the exclusionary risk is minimum.[293] According to his analytical framework, in the case of retroactive rebates applied by the dominant firm, the rival would suffer a loss as soon as its sales go above the difference between the total consumer demand and the volume threshold under the rebate scheme. When this level is overcome, the unit price that a rival would need to offer to be competitive should compensate the consumer for the loss of the retroactive discount that would have been granted by the dominant firm over the entire quantity of purchases. However, Federico goes on to state that, as volumes purchased by the rival increase, the loss of the retroactive rebate suffered by the customer, as a result of purchases made out of the retroactive rebate

---

[291] Schmidt, n 93 above, 419, italics added.   [292] Ibid, at 265.
[293] Cf Federico, n 283 above, at 478–480.

scheme offered by the dominant firm, would be absorbed over a larger volume base. That would allow 'the price offered by the rival to converge back towards the discounted price charged by the dominant firm'.[294] Here again, the model seems not to take into due account the dynamic scenario. Suffice to stress that it can hardly be taken for granted that the rival could be able to keep up the strategy of the dominant firm over the medium period. Formulated it another way, the whole model presents a rather static perspective. Furthermore, the consequent introduction of elements of predation theory suffers from all the drawbacks we have examined above.[295]

In his critical study towards *per se* rules prohibiting otherwise pro-competitive loyalty-inducing and retroactive rebates, O'Donoghue argues that real concern should only arise in the following rather limited circumstances: (1) the dominant firm's non-contestable base of sales covers a significant portion of buyers and buyers needs; (2) it is unlikely that new buyers emerge; (3) the dominant firm is using loyalty rebates or targeted discounts to price below average variable costs the contestable segment of buyers. In other words, a rebate scheme of this sort could have a foreclosure effect only 'if the dominant firm can 'leverage' sales from its assured base across to all or nearly all of customers' requirements'.[296] Not even the minimum critical entry scale is left to rivals. Leaving aside the lack of dynamic perspective, the emphasis on the length of the reference period, and the consideration of short-run effects, this approach can paradoxically introduce *per se* allowed 'safe harbours' for dominant firms. According to O'Donoghue, indeed, it seems unlikely that rebate schemes which do not entail 'rollback discounts' should attract the scrutiny of the competition authorities.[297]

More recently Allan, arguing that the DP approach is unduly hostile towards prospective rebates and overstates the differences between the prospective and retrospective rebate schemes, has designed an alternative approach. In Allan's view the challenge remains to consider whether a rebate scheme that produces an effective price below the ATC ought to be held to have an anti-competitive effect.[298] In this respect, he maintains the predation elements introduced by the DP and argues that a retrospective rebate structure with large value of initial rebate relative to the customer's total purchase might act as a strong competitive constraint. In more detail, he points outs that a structure similar to that formulated by the DP would probably be necessary for modification to: (a) substitute AAC for ATC; (b) clarify the assessment of a commercially viable share;[299] (c) consider the degree of correlation between the initial threshold and increments in

---

[294] Ibid, at 479.   [295] Cf section V(B)(ii) and (iii) of this article.
[296] O'Donoghue, n 29 above, at 373. See *contra* Kallaugher and Sher, n 7 above, at 283, and n 18 who argue that a quantity rebate (ie a contractually binding commitment to purchase a large volume of products) 'can impose far greater switching costs on a customer and create higher potential barriers to entry than a target rebate scheme'.
[297] O'Donoghue, n 29 above, at 378.
[298] Allan, n 115 above, at 65 and section V(B)(ii) and (iii) of this article.
[299] Cf section V(B)(ii) and (iii) of this article.

efficiency, the format of the rebate scheme, and other possible evidence of predation intent. It is noteworthy that Allan maintains the two-step test devised by the
European Courts' case law and finally adopted by the DP. Nonetheless, he explicitly points out that the DP places undue weight on the assumed gains from long-
term improvements in the competitive structure. To conclude, the models just
described have the merit highlighting the perils of *per se* rules and to point out
the need to take into due account economic efficiencies and other factual aspects
when assessing retroactive rebates. Yet, they all explicitly, or by way of implication, choose the short period as the reference horizon to assess the effects on the
competitive process of the schemes at hand. This choice, of course, is far from
being without *economic* and *legal* implications. Again, they seem to overestimate
the actual possibility for anti-trust authorities and judges to establish in real cases
whether efficient competitors would be excluded or impeded to enter the market.
Whereas to reduce the period for assessing the consequences of the price conduct
might simplify the task of those bodies, this cannot exclude a remaining amount
of discretion in order to foresee the dynamic evolution of the market even within
the short period. Finally, where the models adopt some of the tests discussed at
length above (ie, *as efficient, sacrifice,* and *harm to competition* tests) the material
shortcomings of the latter still affect the accurateness of their results.[300]

B. Economic Foundations of EC Competition Policy on Abuse of Dominant Position

The relevance of economics in anti-trust enforcement was acknowledged decades
ago.[301] If the need to translate economic insights into legal proceedings represents
a hard technical task for anti-trust authorities, judges, scholars, and practitioners,
the existence of different schools of thought applying various and competing models to a particular setting is not less troublesome.[302] Therefore, before questioning
the suitability of the more economic approach to the abuse doctrine, it seems
useful to briefly delineate the economic models and assumptions which currently
seem to prevail within the EC anti-trust system. European competition policy
assumes as its *economic* theoretical foundations neoclassical microeconomic equilibrium models, industrial organization, and game theory. Even though these

---

[300] Cf section V(C)(i) of this article, and, especially, the shortcomings highlighted by Vickers, n
126 above, at 17 *et seq.*

[301] See O Williamson, 'Economies as an Antitrust Defence: The Welfare Trade-Off', (1968) 58
American Economic Review 18 *et seq.*; C Kaysen and DF Turner, *Antitrust Policy: An Economic and
Legal Analysis* (Harvard University Press, 1965) especially at XVI *et seq.*; LA Sullivan, *Handbook Of
The Law Of Antitrust* (1977) 2 *et seq.* More recently see, *ex multis,* U Böge, The Role of Economics in
Antitrust Enforcement. A German and European Approach, speech at the Antitrust Reform in Europe:
A Year in Practice, hosted by the International Bar Association and European Commission, DG
Competition, 10 March 2005, available online at: <http://www.oecd.org/dataoecd/7/13/35911017.
pdf>.

[302] Roth, n 268 above, at 57.

foundations are widely recognized,[303] certain aspects concerning the specific policy objectives and enforcing guiding criteria are still debated within the context of the reorientation process which, at last, has involved Article 82 cases. In detail, the ongoing debate's focus has shifted on:

- consumer welfare as the foremost goal of competition policy alongside allocative efficiency;
- the length of the reference period over which to assess unilateral exclusionary conduct;
- the extent of the role being assigned to economic analysis within this process.

As to the first point, the Commission, as several commentators do, calls for an effect-oriented approach to assess exclusionary unilateral conduct which may increase *consumer welfare.* The latter would be the main goal of competition policy alongside allocative efficiency.[304] Being that this is the Commission's view expressed in the DP, it should be questioned if a material disagreement exists with reference to the recent European Courts' pronouncements. The ECJ seems to have embraced a more nuanced and comprehensive idea of the foremost aims pursued through Article 82 by the EC Treaty.[305] Thus, if an issue exists regarding the main goals that current and future competition policy shall pursue, it is not due to a divergence between what was officially declared by the Commission and what has lately been affirmed by the European Courts. Rather, issues arise since the Commission has so far not been able to clearly remove persistent tensions between the main goals of competition law.[306] As a result, the hierarchy it has lately sketched out in the DP might happen to be unclear for practitioners and judges. This state of affairs has been exploited by those who strive to give 'business' (and not 'economics') the status of anti-trust defence and reduce the material scope of Article 82. In view of the above, one might well understand readings such as the one advanced by Van Den Bergh, who asserts that the resulting ambiguity 'increases the discretionary power of the European Courts in the law-making game by bringing legal certainty into play'.[307] In other words, a firm and

---

[303] See, *ex multis*, Whish, n 7 above, at 5 *et seq.*; O'Donoghue, and Padilla, n 118 above, at 5 *et seq.*; Motta, n 82 above, at 39 *et seq.*

[304] Kroes, n 93 above. See also Report by EAGCP, n 87 above, at 15, G Monti, n 7 above, at 1066; Allan, n 115 above, at 49, stresses that the DP makes a precise choice focusing on 'consumer welfare in preference to total welfare under which little or no value appears to be assigned to gains in productive efficiency that are retained as part of the product surplus'. Thus, it should be clear that in the context above depicted a practice reducing the level of competition in the relevant market, where it increases efficiency for the benefit of the undertaking exercising the practice without transferring benefits to the consumers, is caught by the prohibition of Article 82.
Note that Motta, n 82 above, at 19, points out that it is a hard to assess whether competition authorities and courts favour *in practice* a consumer welfare or a total welfare aim. See, ibid, 20–21.

[305] Cf section IV(C) of this article, and Mertikopoulou, n 12 above, at 243–245.

[306] RJ Van Den Bergh, *The More Economic Approach and the Pluralist Tradition*, in Schmidtchen, Albert, Voigt, n 268 above, at 28; see section VI(C)(ii) of this article.

[307] Van Den Bergh, n 306 above, at 28.

clear position of the Commission with regard to the actual meaning of *consumer welfare* would eradicate much of the uncertainty within the business community on this crucial point. The central question regards how consumers welfare standard relates to allocative efficiency. Consumer welfare may be interpreted in different ways depending on the economic criterion deployed. Under the Pareto criterion, the goal at issue requires that changes improving individual welfare of producers also improve welfare of individual consumers. This interpretation does not entail any conflict between allocative efficiency and consumer welfare. Yet, it puts heavy limitations on the scope of competition policy. Indeed, policy decisions which make producers better off without making any consumer worse off are exceptions rather than rules.[308] In a second interpretation, consumer welfare is defined as the maximization of the consumer surplus, particularly by reducing consumer prices. There is no basis in welfare economics for this definition. It neither produces Pareto improvements (as policy intervention reducing prices for consumers invariably worse off producers), nor does it satisfy the alternative Kaldor-Hicks criterion, which aims at maximizing total welfare, since it requires that consumers would result in being better off without accepting gains that benefit producers only.[309] Moreover, the very fact that the Kaldor-Hicks criterion of total welfare is rejected by the Community law implies that the relevance given to competitive prices for consumers prevails over the cost savings for efficient firms or profits from their shareholder which cannot be passed on to customers. Accordingly, wealth transfers, and not efficiency considerations, seem to orientate the rule-formulating process.[310] A first inherent limit of the more economic approach towards EC competition policy is now manifest. It cannot alter the necessity to assess in real-life cases whether consumers receive a fair share of the efficiency savings stemming from a certain business conduct. Despite the Commission's policy declarations, non-efficiency considerations seem to prevail and 'the European Court still has the final say on the interpretation of the criterion of distributional justice'.[311] Arguably, the European Courts have followed this line of reasoning in *British Airways* by deeming that the retroactive nature of rebates could not be justified by incremental cost savings associated with higher sales. Considerations of distributional justice have prevailed over the efficiencies the dominant firm could have realized.[312] Coming to the length of the reference period, a weighing of the restraint on the competitive process and efficiencies would take place in each individual case in order to assess the final effects on consumer welfare.[313] To our mind, it cannot be questioned, especially within the

---

[308] Ibid, at 29.

[309] Ibid. For a further analysis of consumer and total welfare standards in different jurisdictions, see Motta, n 82 above, at 19–22.

[310] Van Den Bergh, n 306 above, at 30.   [311] Ibid.

[312] See, for example, paras 282–284 of the CFI decision on British Airways, and Kamann and Bergmann, n 7 above, at 86 fn 40.

[313] Cf DG Discussion Paper, n 10 above, paras 77 *et seq.*; Schmidt, n 93 above, at 408; EAGCP Reports, n 87 above, at 8 *et seq.*

context of EC competition policy, that this goal is to be assessed *over the mid-long run*.[314] Only such an analysis permits inter alia to: (a) realistically assume that firms are willing and able to adjust their fixed costs in order to minimize average total costs for each level of output; (b) take into account that the number of the firms in the industry is not fixed; (c) consider the '"competition" aspects of the monopolistically competition' which, by definition come 'into play when we move from the short to the long run';[315] (d) most remarkably, assess effects on *dynamic efficiency*. Admittedly, this option entails a resolute choice among possible competition policies.[316] As widely illustrated, when dealing with allegedly exclusionary conduct, the European Courts take into account effects over the mid-long period in the form of alterations of the market structure (so called 'structionalist test'). Here, what seems contested by the critics of the Courts' approach is not a departure from the Commission's recent practice. Rather, it is the economic nature itself of this test alongside its suitability to assess dynamic effects under discussion.[317] Quite the opposite, renowned economists consider the analysis of the (actual or foreseeable) alterations of the market structure being the appropriate starting point of economic analysis being developed on a case-by-case basis in order to assess long-term dynamic effects.[318] To conclude the point: once again, we argue that the adoption of such a test stems from a precise *political* choice, as well as the use of one of the alternative models proposed in literature.[319] Of course, the inherent attitude towards exclusionary abuses is different and is likely to lead to different results. However, this does not deprive the structionalist approach of its economic nature. Turning, finally, to the role of economic analysis, the two-fold test shaped by the case law in order to assess alleged exclusionary abuses is not likely to be altered. However, different attitudes should guide the two different phases. As regards the assessment of conduct's capability of having,

[314] Cf Report by EAGCP, n 87 above, at 9: 'The term "consumer welfare" conceal the fact that we are really talking about a multi-facetted concern.... In many cases, it is also necessary to think about consumers' welfare in the future, as well as today.'

[315] Krugman and Wells, n 82 above, respectively at 197–201; 221–226; 391–397, especially at 395. Note this reading not only accords with fundamental notions of neo-classical microeconomics, but it also fits the ECJ exegesis of Article 82 grounded on teleological and systematic criteria; cf Mertikopoulou, n 12 above, at 242.

[316] EAGCP, n 87 above, at 11.

[317] This position is authoritatively voiced by Kallaugher and Sher, n 7 above, at 276 *et seq.*

[318] Gyselen, n 7 above, at 290 –292; Schmidt, n 93 above, at 408; and Kirchner, n 269 above, at 22–25. The EAGCP Reports, n 87 above, at 10–12, describes the intertemporal trade-off between short-term consumer welfare (ie more favourable prices or conditions at present) and long-term consumer welfare, based on the expectations that the profits of a monopolist today may attract competitors to enter the market, thereby creating competition in the future and enhancing consumer welfare over the long run. Pursuant to the Report, given the extreme difficulties in foreseeing the possible evolutions in cases involving market foreclosure, the use of *structural aspects of the market,* is justifiable as a proxy for the explicit assessment of consumer welfare in future markets. This process can *also* call for a policy intervention designed to prohibit exclusionary practices and to keep markets open for competition. Examples of structural aspects of markets being taken into account include traditional notions of market structure and potential for entry by new competitors.

[319] See the models described at section VI(A) of this article.

or being likely to have, an exclusionary effect, both the Commission and the ECJ in its latest decisions have been stressing the need of adopting a fact-specific approach. Nonetheless, the DP takes a step further in that, for the assessment of specific kinds of alleged foreclosing practice (such as, exclusive dealing, predation pricing, rebates), it envisages a systematic deployment of specific economic models.[320] By contrast, the issue of efficiency defences and economic objective justifications marks the main divergence between the approach suggested by the Commission and the latest case law.[321] The DP seems to follow closely the course suggested by economists and scholars of industrial organizations in favour of a more consistent and ample framework for considering pro-competitive effects of potential exclusionary conduct.

C. Methodological Issues

In the preceding discussion, we have outlined the main assumptions and features of the 'more economic approach' to Article 82 cases, as it is presented by the Commission, several economists, and legal scholars. We have also attempted to show that material parts of the DP and relevant principles affirmed in the latest European Courts' pronouncements adhere to some degree to the cause of a more consistent use of economic insights when dealing with alleged unilateral exclusionary conduct. Indeed, it is not disputed that the assessment of each specific case shall be undertaken on the basis of the consideration of its anti- and pro-competitive effects, rather than *only* on the form or the intrinsic nature of particular practices. The question to be asked, therefore, is not *whether* economic analysis has to be employed, but regards the *intrinsic limits* of the advocated/ adopted economic approach, and, the *extension to which* economic analysis should be employed. A further important point we deal with is related to other economic theories, which might contribute to shape competition law enforcement vis-à-vis Article 82 cases, being plain that the so-called 'more economic approach' is not to be seen as the only possible model.[322] Since the revision of EC competition policy aims at developing an *inherently consistent* and *truly modern* system, we feel it necessary to indicate the main pitfalls and the trade-offs intrinsic to the prevailing models. In the following, we show the main methodological issues of the current model, which a *truly* modern economic analysis should solve to safely anchor the review process EC competition policy is undergoing, especially in relation to abusive conduct.

---

[320] That approach is not without theoretical and practical shortcomings, as the case of retroactive rebates plainly shows. Cf section V(C)(i) of this article.

[321] Cf section V(C)(iii) of this article.

[322] See, for instance, Van Den Bergh, n 306 above, at 28; R Kirstein, '"More" and "Even More" Economic Approach "'in Schmidtchen, Albert , Voigt, n 267 above, at 59–64; Schmidt, n 93 above, at 408.

(i) Different Meanings of 'More Economic Approach'

A first point for clarification regards the meaning itself of the 'more economic approach'. With reference to Article 82 cases, it may be briefly defined as an approach which attempts to replace a mechanical legal formalism to the interpretation of 'abuse of dominant position' for a method oriented towards a careful assessment of how competition works in a specific market and how certain business conduct of the dominant firm may affect the competitive process and thereby consumer welfare.[323] However, if this definition delineates what is usually referred to as 'more economic approach', there are at least two other meanings this expression may imply.[324] Less legalistic method aside, 'more economic' might refer to an economic use of resources. From this viewpoint, one ought to consider the resources the various competition agencies need in order to implement the approach, as well as those spent by the private actors.[325] As highlighted elsewhere, the interpretation of 'more economic' just sketched out conflicts with what the Commission has in mind, since it can reasonably be assumed that the less legalistic approach will increase the resources spent on most competition cases.[326] Somewhat related to the second interpretation though, a third way which makes sense out of the qualification 'more economic' is possible. This interpretation takes into account that in real markets reliable information is scarce and this state of affairs, in turn, affects the possibility of each actor (no matter whether competition authorities or firms) to predict the actions of others. As a consequence, shorter planning horizons are likely to come along with sub-optimal investments and, thus, negative consequences on allocative efficiency. Accordingly, a more economic approach would aim at increasing predictability and, thereby, allocative efficiency. The European Commission has its primary focus only on the first interpretation, whereas economists have recently shown that there are good reasons for claiming that a 'truly' economic approach should strive to strike the balance between the three aspects just illustrated.[327]

(ii) Remaining Tensions between Different Goals

According to recent policy declaration (and the DP framework), the aim of European competition policy 'is *simple*: to protect competition in the market as a means of enhancing consumer welfare and ensuring efficient allocation of

---

[323] Roth, n 258 above, at 37; EAGCP, n 87 above, at 2.

[324] S Voigt, '"More Economic" Does not Necessarily Mean "Better"—Perils and Pitfalls of the "More Economic Approach" as Recommended by The European Commission', in Schmidtchen, Albert, Voigt, n 267 above, at 97.

[325] Ibid, at 99; and Schmidt, n 93 above, at 411. These resources include the opportunity costs of in-house counsel, as well as money spent for legal and economic external advice.

[326] Voigt, n 324 above, at 99. Accordingly, 'the improvement in Commission decisions that could be the consequence of the first interpretation ought to outweigh the additional costs that need to be incurred to carry out this "more economic" approach'.

[327] Ibid, at 97–100.

resources...'.[328] Unfortunately, the European Commission's aim is far from being simple. We have already shown the tensions which might remain between consumer welfare and allocative efficiency, and the primary relevance of distributional issues enforcing authorities and judges could face when applying Article 82 of the EC Treaty.[329] Here, it remains to consider whether competition policy *alone* is actually the best means to safeguard consumers, and, then, whether consumer welfare and allocative efficiency compete with *other* policy goals. As to the first issue, substantial parts of consumer protection currently rest on competition law. This approach finds its theoretical basis in standard market models which attribute consumer risk to market failure, mainly in the form of lack of competition. More recently, the latter models have been integrated with neo-classical consumer theories,[330] pursuant to which systematic market failures are brought about by imperfect information issues.[331] Since neo-classical economics sees consumer harm as the result of conditions on the *supply side* of the market, 'consumer policy and competition policy are logically intertwined'.[332] Yet, recent studies which deeply make use of behavioural economics' insights for the understanding of consumers' behaviour show that, under certain circumstances, the two aims of increasing competition and benefiting consumers may conflict with each other.[333] Smith and King argue that policy prescriptions from behavioural economics may differ from prescriptions based on neo-classical consumer theories.[334] As yet the two approaches have not been combined to any appreciable extent or in a way that may materially contribute to policy making.[335] However, the study under discussion would show that, as a matter of perspective, a future integration of the two approaches may result in more precise policy responses. For present purposes, it should be highlighted that the perspective just outlined shows that competition law should not shoulder the full burden of protecting

---

[328] Kroes, European Competition Policy: Delivering Better Markets and Better Choices, available online at: <http://europa.eu.int/comm/competition/index-en.html>.

[329] See section VI(B) of this article.

[330] See, *ex multis*, NW Averit and RH Lande ande, 'Consumer Sovereignty: A Unified Theory of Antitrust and Consumer Protection Law' (1997) 65 Antitrust Law Journal 713 *et seq*; M Waterson, 'The Role of Consumers in Competition and Competition Policy' (2001) 607 Warwick Economic Research Paper 2 *et seq*.

[331] The latter theories are specific application of information economics which assign primary importance to elements like search costs and transactions costs, adverse selection, information externalities, incomplete contracts, and related behaviour. Cf, for instance, the seminal studies of KJ Arrow, 'Uncertainty and Economics of Medical Care' (1963) 53 American Economic Review 941 *et seq*.; S Salop and JE Stiglitz, 'Bargains and Ripoffs: A Model of Monopolistically Competitive Price Dispersions' (1977) 44 Review of Economic Studies 493–510; G Akerlof, 'The Market of "Lemons": Quality Uncertainty and the Market Mechanism' (1970) 84 Quarterly Journal of Economics 488–500, at 499 *et seq*.

[332] J Vickers, in OECD conference papers, Paris, October 2005, available online at: <http://www.oecd.org/dataoecd/31/46/36581073.pdf>.

[333] L Sylvan, 'Activating Competition: The Consumer-Competition Interface' (2004) 12 Competition and Consumer Law Journal 191, at 192, and Bowles, n 208 above, at 95, cited also by Smith and King, n 267 above, at 419.

[334] Smith and King, n 267 above, at 420–424.   [335] Ibid, at 421–424.

consumers.[336] Regarding the existence of remaining inconsistencies within the 'more economic approach', one has first to consider the interface between static and dynamic efficiencies. It goes without saying that a truly economic approach must consider a dynamic concept of efficiencies. If dynamic efficiencies are realized, the scope for conflicts between efficiency goals pursued by the dominant firm and consumer welfare is likely to be smaller, for consumers will also benefit from product innovation.[337] Moreover, potential tensions between efficiency goals and the non-economic objectives remain. The view that competition law represents a powerful instrument to curb private initiatives against the process of market integration has left European competition policy with a heavy legacy.[338] Furthermore, as Roth highlights, 'European competition policy is instrumental' insofar as according to Article 3(g) of the EC Treaty, 'it is meant to serve the more general objectives as set forth in Article 2 EC..., besides all the other policies listed in Article 3 EC'.[339] Again, a number of so-called integration clauses in the EC Treaty[340] demand that certain non-competition aims shall be taken into account when pursuing other Community policies. Here, it seems that the advocators of the 'more economic approach' do not adequately consider the inevitable tensions between the strictly effect-based rules and the broader political design European competition policy has to be collocated into. If it might be argued that the market integration aim is losing importance,[341] a full move towards a 'more economic approach' would require a dramatic change in the case law that can be mainly if not only explained from a social, distributional, or industrial viewpoint. Yet, the 'inconsistencies' brought about by the pursuit of non-efficiency goals are an integral part of the European policy tradition and European Court's case law. It seems highly questionable that they can be passed over simply by implementing the 'more economic approach' in the different fields of competition law.[342] As it happens in the case of the basic freedoms of the EC Treaty, when public policy objectives are at issue, the enforcing authorities cannot avoid the weighing process between these objectives and the economic goals.

---

[336] Ibid, at 424.

[337] A similar argument is advanced by Van Den Bergh, n 306 above, at 30, by considering the rejection of a Williamsonian trade-off in a merger case.

[338] See, *ex multis*, ibid, at 31, Whish, n 7 above, at 20–21; Motta n 82 above, at 20; Amato, n 80, at 3 *et seq*.

[339] Roth, n 268 above, at 41. See also Whish, n 7 above, at 22 *et seq*.

[340] Articles 6, 127(2), 151(4), 153(2), 157(3) of the EC Treaty.

[341] Van Den Bergh, n 306 above, at 32; Gerber, n 78 above, at 391. See also Case T-41/96 *Bayer AG v Commission* (2000) ECR II-3383, upheld by the ECJ in Joined Cases C-2/01P and C-3/01P *Commission v Bayer* (2004) ECR I-23.

[342] According to Roth, n 268 above, at 42: 'The point to be made is the following: a "more economic approach" that excludes the relevant public policy considerations from its agenda will only deal with half of the story and to the extent the integration clauses have to be applied as part of competition law'. See also Mertikopoulou, n 12 above, at 243 who aptly remarks that: 'The EC Treaty is a comprehensive set of rules with its own dynamics; it creates a *sui generis* legal order...the socio-political principles and values which the latter promotes are not always quantifiable in terms of efficiency.'

(iii) *The 'Missing Economics' within the 'More Economic Approach'*

Let us refer again to the European Commissioner Kroes' declaration in 2005, frequently recalled by the advocators of the 'more economic approach' to Article 82 of the EC Treaty. After having stressed the primary importance of consumer welfare and allocative efficiency for the European Competition Policy, the current Commissioner went on to say: 'An effect-based approach, *grounded in solid economics*, ensures that citizens enjoy the benefits of a competitive dynamic market'.[343] Here again, there is room for remarkably diverging interpretations as to what is intended for 'solid economics'. In other terms, the problem of 'omitted economics is pervasive', and it is particularly evident when considering the economic-oriented approach which should re-orientate the abuse doctrine for which binding guidelines are still lacking.[344] Three points are to be made. First, as stressed in many parts of this work, if the concept of 'solid economics' is meant to correspond with a static assessment of effects in the market place, nothing guarantees that dynamic competition will improve. Besides, one should be aware that under a dynamic view, X-inefficiency in the sense of Leibenstein can result from the lack of competition in the marketplace. Yet, traditional economic analyses still seem to be largely dominated by static and pure game theoretic approaches.[345] With reference to this aspect, several economists agree that the modern economic approach should strive for a *dynamic* and not primarily static efficiency.[346] Dynamic theories of competition[347] should, thus, contribute to shape the European competition policy as regards Article 82 cases. According to Van den Bergh, when approaching competition problems in the new economy, 'the key issue is whether a particular business practice or amalgamation may affect the pact of innovation in the long run, rather than if it produces identifiable efficiencies increasing consumer welfare in the present time'.[348] However, since dynamic competition is a process with uncertain results (Von Hayek) and we still lack a convincing dynamic theory to which to anchor competition law enforcement, 'the only way to promote dynamic efficiency is to maintain effective competition' over the mid-long run.[349]

[343] Kroes, n 327 above, italics added.

[344] Van Den Bergh, n 306 above, at 33–36. Note that we do not linger upon well-known pitfalls common to any economic approach to competition law enforcement. Here suffice to remind that, for instance, Sullivan, n 301 above, at 2 et *seq*, long ago remarked that any deployment of economics for the application of antitrust rules substantially relied on the need to have trustworthy data of the relevant market. Again, the risks of unduly delay by the European Commission and National Authorities associated to elaborated economic analysis should not be underestimated.

[345] Van Den Bergh, n 306 above, at 33.

[346] This position is voiced, among the others, by Schmidt, n 93 above, at 408; Kirchner, n 269 above, at 12.

[347] See, for instance, DB Andretsch, WJ Boumol, and AE Burke, 'Competition Policy in Dynamic Markets' (2001) 19 International Journal of Industrial Organization 613–634; J Elling and D Lin, 'Introduction', in J Elling (ed), *Dynamic Competition and Public Policy: Technology, Innovation, and Antitrust Issues* (Cambridge/New York, 2001) 1–15; Stiglitz, n 268 above, at 11–22.

[348] Van Den Bergh, n 306 above, at 34.

[349] Schmidt, n 93 above, at 409. Van Den Bergh, n 306 above, at 34 points out that although 'over the last year there has been an expansion of economic research inspired by evolutionary thinking and

Secondly, many of the models put forward by pundits, who claim a more material and consistent use of economics when dealing with allegedly abusive conduct, hardly consider the profound insights information economics can bear for a far deeper understanding of how the *real* and *different* markets work.[350] In more detail, the existence of incomplete and asymmetric information, and relevant information or transaction costs may render inefficient the outcomes of free competition.[351] Yet, transaction and information costs are completely neglected in traditional models which assume that markets work smoothly and costless.[352] A final area where truly modern economics may affect the traditional analysis is behavioural economics. To assume bounded rationality both of consumers[353] and of organizations may cast a different light on the welfare impact of dominant firms' behaviour.[354] To conclude the point, the important message is that the so-called 'more economic approach' is not 'that modern'. It is largely based on static models and does not pay sufficient attention to insights from dynamic theories on competition, nor does it recognize that legal uncertainty is an economic cost, neglecting the material results of information economics. Moreover, it largely ignores possible insights from modern economic theories such as 'New Institutional Economics' and behavioural economics. In light of the above, it should be clear that a sufficiently convincing model, to which to anchor the future enforcement of Article 82, still needs to be drawn. Overall, the modernization process has been obtaining material results in shaping a sound economic framework for competition policy. However, this process must not be hastened; otherwise, as we have attempted to show, the whole system runs substantial risks of being inherently inconsistent and, ultimately, *inefficient*. What is even worse, without solving the main dilemmas we have shown the 'more economic approach' is susceptible to being misused: the model being elaborated should avoid *any business* practice being disguised as an *economic* defence.

D. Legal Issues Concerning the Applicability of the More Economic Approach

Despite their structural differences, the normative and economic approaches to competition law are intimately connected. However, as stressed in several parts of our work, there exist wide studies which have systematically considered

innovation economics, the latter theories have not yet received sufficient attention and their normative implications have not been fully drawn.' Wurmnest, n 84 above, at 22 argues that any attempt to measure the result of the dynamic competitive process in advance should be seen 'to quote *Van Hayek*, as "pretence of knowledge"'.

[350] Note that the models analysed, in section VI(A) of this article do ignore the insights of information economics. For a comprehensive illustration of this theory's objectives and results, see Stiglitz, n 272 above, at 482 *et seq.*, and, more recently, Stiglitz, n 268 above, at 11 *et seq.*

[351] According to Stiglitz, n 272 above at 483, 'the long standing presumption that in competitive equilibrium price equals marginal costs *cannot* be true in the markets with imperfect information' at 483.

[352] Kirstein, n 322 above, at 60. On this aspect, see Wurmnest, n 84 above, at 22.

[353] See section VI(C)(ii) of this article.   [354] Kirstein, n 322 above, at 60.

the suitability of the 'more economic approach' to European competition law, and pointed out the material issues of a downright application of economics to Article 82 cases. Some prominent aspects are in the need of a further word. First, when considering 'the more economic approach', at least encompassed by the DP, one could question how far the needs of *legal certainty* and *predictability* are satisfied. Indeed, various sets of presumptions (always rebuttable by dominant firms) are envisaged for each abusive conduct. Although, admittedly, such an approach could allow a certain degree of *flexibility*, in the eyes of some authors an excessive fragmentation of the economic tests might endanger the unity of the judiciary protection.[355] *De lege ferenda*, a second relevant aspect regards the required standard of proof. Indeed, were it only *actual* effects to count (as many critics of the current structionalist model advocate), the relevant conduct could be judged on the market only on an *ex post* basis. It does not take much imagination to see that such a prerequisite would entail remarkable consequences in the enforcing activities, 'by putting an enormous burden on competition authorities and private complaints which may turn out to be disproportionate'.[356] Moreover, an *ex post* evaluation entails a huge change from the current interpretation of the letter and the spirit of Article 82. Indeed, European competition law requires only that productive and dynamic efficiencies shall *possibly* or *likely* arise, thus taking an *ex ante* perspective. It is noteworthy that the DP confirms the latter approach.[357] Thirdly, the issue of the standard of proof is even more complex, depending also on *who* has the burden: when facts become relevant, it is decisive *what* standard of proof will be applied with reference to single issues (eg questions of causation, economic defence). As Schmidt has recently stressed, the more articulated the standard is (also in terms of economic analysis), the more likely a 'war of experts', and the less likely the chance that small and medium-sized firms in the position to actively take part in law suits.[358] Moreover, extensive economic studies and thorough adoptions of articulated economic tests may end up with lengthy administrative procedures of dubious result, while during the period at issue, competition may be impaired in a permanent and irreversible way.[359] Finally, one has also to keep in mind the so-called 'tertiary costs', that is to say costs for the parties involved associated with the time and effort required to enforce the rule.[360] In view of the above, an inflexible application of the 'more economic approach' to unilateral exclusionary abuse is highly questionable. Open-ended and effect-based rules accord with the teleological interpretation of Article 82. In order to promote predictability, reduce discretionary decisions and alleviate

---

[355] Wurmnest, n 84 above, at 9; Schmidt, n 93 above, at 410; Mertikopoulou, n 12 above, at 245, Roth, n 268 above, at 38.

[356] Roth, n 268 above, at 52.   [357] Cf section V(A) of this article.

[358] Schmidt, n 93 above, at 411–412.   [359] Mertikopoulou, n 12 above, at 251

[360] Mertikopoulou, n 12 above, at 250; Schmidt, n 93 above, at 411; Roth, n 268 above, at 60, who remarks: 'the higher is the standard of proof required for pursuing a legal right, the higher the tertiary costs in a case, and the less useful is a protection from the viewpoint of a plaintiff'.

'private enforcement' they should be supplemented as far as possible by more concrete rules, standards, and/or guidelines reflecting comprehensive economic theories based on empirical data.[361] Furthermore, legal concepts, intrinsic to the European legal tradition and acknowledged by EC legal system long ago, such as for example, *necessity* and *proportionality*, might come into play when increasing consumer welfare conduct has to be assessed with regard to its impact on actual and potential competition.[362]

VI. Conclusions

The controversial aspects of the 'more economic approach' which should orientate the review process the abuse doctrine is undergoing are not few and immaterial. Therefore, the energetic insistence on *hastening* the application of such an approach to guide the current re-orientation of competition policy can endanger the *inherently valuable contribution* of a sensible use of economic insights for shaping a *truly* modern competition policy. Whereas it is undeniable that economics provides precious analytical tools to assess the effects of unilateral conduct on welfare over the mid–long run, a *single* sufficiently comprehensive and solid *economic* theory, to which to safely anchor the legal appraisal of the extreme variety of potentially abusive conduct, still needs to be developped. Furthermore, there is much work to do in order to ease the inherent tension between fundamental legal values and a downright application of economics to competition policy. In the light of the above, pronouncements like the ECJ's in *British Airways*, and the CFI's in *Microsoft*[363] may be looked at as a word of caution, a signal of '*juris-prudentia*' against hurried positions ultimately advocating a restriction to the scope of Article 82 of the EC Treaty with respect to practices that certainly make *business* sense,[364] but do not necessarily stimulate competition over the mid-long run, and hence produce an *ambiguous economic* effect. A final remark: our essay starts from the *legal* appraisal of the last ECJ pronouncement on foreclosing rebates to conclude with the assessment of the *economic* approach to abuse doctrine. Throughout sections IV–VI of our work we have attempted to make as evident as possible that a key issue is at stake: the (restriction of the) scope of Article 82 vis-à-vis exclusionary conduct. No matter whether the analysis moves from law to economics (as in our case) or vice versa; eventually they both refer to a

---

[361] Wurmnest, n 84 above, at 9 *et seq.*; Schmidt, n 93 above, at 411; Mertikopoulou, n 12 above, at 250; Roth, n 268 above, at 55.

[362] Roth, n 268 above, at 60.

[363] For the official comments of the current Commissioner Neelie Kroes, see eg,' The EU v. Microsoft', available online at: <http//:The Economist.com>.

[364] How can a loyalty-inducing discount scheme be *commercially* unsound from the viewpoint of a dominant firm?

political decision, that is to say an act of will in relation to the interests at issue.[365] We believe it is of primary importance to recall that the review process Article 82 is undergoing follows a *political* design. Similarly, positions for or against an extensive and inflexible deployment of 'the more economic approach' at its current state are (consciously or not) *political* positions.[366] Of course, the same is true for a sensible use of the economic insights provided by modern theories which would acknowledge that for the European Commission and national authorities a sound technical choice of intervening on the market (as well as of not intervening) is still a policy choice grounded on solid economics, sound statutory interpretation, and jurisprudence.

[365] Irti, n 134 above, at XII, who recalls Carl Schmitt's well-known objection to the Walter Rathenau argument that nowadays faith is no longer politics, but economy. Schmitt replies that it would be more accurate to say that faith keeps on being represented by politics, but economy has become political, and thereby faith itself.

[366] On the intrinsic political nature of the process being discussed see, *ex multis*, the arguments advanced by Fox and Sullivan, n 90 above, at 959; Amato, n 80 above, at 3 *et seq.*; Fox, n 86 above, at 73; Von Hayek n 86 above 179 *et seq.*

SURVEY

EC Competition Law 2005–2006

Ian S Forrester, QC, Jacquelyn F MacLennan, and
Assimakis P Komninos*

I. Introduction

We were able to introduce our last contribution to the Yearbook of European Law[1] with the claim that EC competition law developments of that period had been of 'profound importance'. The years 2005 and 2006 represent the first period of enforcement after the *annus mirabilis* 2004, when the modernization/decentralization of EC competition law was finally put into effect. This has been a period of significant activity by the European Commission, in terms of both decisions and policy guidelines; and so again, we can characterize these developments as particularly interesting. The aim of the Commission with the modernization reforms was to refocus its work and deal with the most serious competition law infringements. This seems to have been successfully managed during these two years: certainly the cartel enforcement record and impressive totals in the fines imposed, and attention to the behaviour of Microsoft under Article 82 of the European Community Treaty (EC Treaty) bear witness to that. At the same time, the modernization approach inherently involved a shift toward a more economic approach in the enforcement of competition law, and this can be seen particularly in some of the legislative and 'discussion paper' policy developments. The decentralization thrust was most evident in the publication of the Commission's long awaited, highly controversial, Green Paper on damages actions for anti-trust violations that was followed by the publication of a White Paper in April 2008. As expected, this has provoked substantial interest and comment. The Commission accompanied its tough stance on cartels with a new Leniency Notice and new Fining Guidelines, designed to work together so as to invite companies to assess the risk of infringement of EC competition law, and conclude that confession rather than confrontation is the best option.

* The authors practise European law with White & Case in Brussels. Warm thanks are expressed to many of our colleagues at White & Case, who provided precious assistance in gathering and summarizing very extensive materials to produce this article. Ian Forrester particularly wishes in this review, which covers the 25th year after the first survey appeared in 1981, to salute the diligence and insights of his colleagues in contributing to these surveys of competition law developments.
[1] (2005) 24 YEL 511.

Meanwhile, the Community Courts were particularly productive. In the cartel area, they produced a record number of judgments which clarified many questions, particularly as regards the discretion of the Commission in imposing fines—although they did not provide the judicial counterbalance that some commentators have sought to the power of the Commission as prosecutor and decision-maker in these complex cases. As the fines imposed by the Commission reach ever higher levels, and the risk of consequential direct actions rises, the procedures leading up to findings of guilt and the imposition of penalties must be rigorous, and rigorously followed. Proper standards of due process and the rights of the defence must be fully respected. This, in our view, is likely to be fertile ground for appeals in years to come, and for reforms at the initiative of the Commission's services. The Courts were also active in the areas of the application of Article 81 of the EC Treaty to horizontal and vertical agreements, where a new approach to analysis under Article 81(1) is discernible, Article 82 of the EC Treaty and mergers, where the celebrated criticism by the CFI of the Commission's theories and procedures continued in a number of cases. Guidance was provided in a number of areas, such as the definition of 'economic activity' which underpins the application of Article 81, and key procedural issues regarding access to file.

EC competition law is now a booming area of administrative enforcement and policy, Community and national case law, legal practice and academic work. For a system which is only 40 years old, this is a remarkable achievement. The increased overall awareness of the competition rules in Europe must be credited to the officials, judges, practitioners, and academics who dedicated themselves to this initially 'exotic' field and made the whole system the success it is. Fifty years after the Treaty of Rome came in effect and 45 years after the first procedural rules led to the first administrative and judicial practice in this area, the time is right to take stock and conclude that the high profile of EC competition law, and the influence it plays on the global stage, is a tribute to those who have created, developed, enforced, and challenged it over those years.

II. Legislative and Policy Developments

A. Legislative Changes in the Transport Sector

The period covered by this survey saw some important changes in the application of the competition rules to air and maritime transport. In the past, these sectors have often benefited from special treatment in competition law terms, but this is now ceasing to be the case. Indeed, the legislative changes are a prelude to a concentrated effort by the Commission to introduce competition law disciplines to the area.

(i) Air Transport

On 28 September 2006, the Commission adopted Regulation 1459/2006,[2] phasing out the exemption from Article 81 of the EC Treaty for the International Air Transport Association (IATA) consultations on passenger tariffs, scheduled air services, and slot allocation at airports. The new Regulation replaces Regulation 1617/93[3] of 25 June 1993, which allowed airlines to discuss interlining prices set at IATA conferences and expired on 30 June 2005.

In 2004, the Commission began consultations in the sector which showed that slot allocation and scheduling conferences were compatible with the competition rules in their present form, so there was no need to prolong the block exemption. The Commission decided there were insufficient grounds to continue the exemption in relation to tariffs, as its benefits to passengers were not demonstrated. Less restrictive means than price-fixing might be available, as shown by the existing alternative interlining systems, so there were not sufficient guarantees that the benefits for consumers would continue to outweigh the restriction of competition, and continuing the block exemption might therefore no longer be justified.

However, to give the airlines sufficient time to adapt to the new situation and enable them to assess the compatibility of their agreements with the competition rules for themselves, Regulation 1459/2006 was adopted to cover a transitional period. For consultations on tariffs and slot allocation in the EEA and Switzerland, the exemption expired on 1 January 2007. For flights between the EU and the US or Australia it ran until 30 June 2007, coinciding with the likely end of the review of those authorities' antitrust policies in this respect. For routes between the EU and other third countries an exemption was granted until 31 October 2007, as interlining remained appreciably more important on those routes.

The Commission invited the IATA and the airlines to provide sufficient data to allow a detailed review of the situation in 2008 and a possible renewal of the block exemption. However, the case for renewal seems weak, and this exceptional block exemption relating to a retail price agreement, normally a hardcore infringement, is likely to disappear along with the liner shipping conference block exemption.[4]

---

[2] [2006] OJ L272/3.

[3] Commission Regulation 1617/93 of 25 June 1993 on the application of Article 85(3) of the Treaty to certain categories of agreements and concerted practices concerning joint planning and coordination of schedules, joint operations, consultations on passenger and cargo tariffs on scheduled air services and slot allocation at airports [1993] OJ L155/18.

[4] In June 2007, the Commission decided not to renew the Regulation, as the IATA had not provided sufficient proof of its benefits to passengers to justify a further extension. The IATA is now working on a new interlining system, compatible with the competition rules, to replace the tariff conferences.

(ii) Maritime Transport

Liner Conferences

Since the nineteenth century, shipping companies have come together in liner conferences to fix prices and regulate capacity—clear cartel-like behaviour—but Block Exemption Regulation 4056/86[5] allowed companies to set common rates and take joint decisions concerning limitation of supply. The exemption was initially deemed necessary to ensure the provision of reliable services and price stability. Exceptionally, it was open-ended in terms of duration and as such was not regularly reviewed.

However, after extensive consultations lasting three years, three independent studies, and the circulation of a White Paper,[6] the Commission concluded that the four cumulative conditions of Article 81(3) of the EC Treaty were no longer fulfilled. First, the alleged causal link between the restrictions (price-fixing and supply regulation) and the claimed efficiencies (reliable services) was deemed too tenuous, as tariffs could not be enforced and most cargo was not carried under this tariff, but under confidential individual agreements. Secondly, liner conferences did not result in clear, identifiable consumer benefits, particularly as price-fixing is a hardcore restriction and transport users considered the exemption benefited the least efficient members. Thirdly, less restrictive means of ensuring the same benefits were available in the form of consortia and individual service agreements, which were becoming more and more important in the sector. Moreover, regularity of services was not affected on trade routes where there were no conferences. The complex question of the fourth condition of Article 81(3) was left open, as the other three cumulative conditions were not fulfilled.

Since it was apparent that the industry no longer needed protection from competition, the Competitiveness Council decided on 26 September 2006 to adopt a new Regulation 1419/2006[7] repealing the block exemption from October 2008 onwards, thus giving the companies time to adapt to the new situation. The Regulation also extends the scope of the procedural framework laid down in Regulation 1/2003 to cabotage and international tramp vessel services. These sectors had previously been exempted from the normal competition law rules, but there seemed to be nothing to justify maintaining the

---

[5] Council Regulation 4056/86 of 22 December 1986 laying down detailed rules for the application of Articles 85 and 86 of the Treaty to maritime transport [1986] OJ L378/4, adopted shortly after the *Nouvelles Frontières* judgment (Joined Cases 209–213/84, *Ministère Public v Lucas Asjès*, [1986] ECR 1425) in which the Court held that the transport sector was subject to the fundamental and general Treaty rules, including the competition provisions.

[6] COM(2004) 654 final, 13 October 2004.

[7] Council Regulation 1419/2006 of 25 September 2006 repealing Regulation (EEC) No 4056/86 laying down detailed rules for the application of Articles 85 and 86 of the Treaty to maritime transport, and amending Regulation (EC) No 1/2003 as regards the extension of its scope to include cabotage and international tramp services.

exemption. The procedural rules will apply to all sectors of the economy, enabling the Commission, national courts, and competition authorities to enforce the competition rules in full. To ease the transition to a fully competitive regime, the Commission announced that before the end of the transitional period it would adopt guidelines on the application of the competition rules, particularly regarding exchange of information.[8]

It should be noted, particularly in light of the sector's international dimension, that liner conferences are exempted from the competition law rules in several other jurisdictions, despite a 2002 OECD call to its members to end their immunity. The EU is the first jurisdiction worldwide to respond.[9] However, a conflict of laws is unlikely to arise, as no jurisdiction considers conferences to be mandatory. Moreover, the abolition of the block exemption does not prevent companies from conferring with regard to non-EU routes.

Liner Consortia

Notwithstanding the repeal of the liner conferences exemption, shipping operators may still maintain cooperation within liner consortia. Block Exemption Regulation 823/2000[10] for maritime consortia, covering transport of cargo (not passengers) to or from one or more EU ports, allows shipping lines to engage in joint operational cooperation (vessel-sharing, coordination of routes and schedules). This exemption was recently reviewed, and has been extended to 25 April 2010 by Commission Regulation 611/2005.[11]

The review found that joint cooperation in liner consortia results in rationalization of activities and economies of scale, and improves productivity and quality of services. Hence the consortia benefit consumers through the exporting firms, provided there is sufficient competition on the market. To adjust the Regulation appropriately to current practice, the requirement of sufficient competition has been amended to allow individual confidential contracts to be taken into account. Another amendment relates to the 'non-withdrawal' clause, which now allows a member to withdraw from a consortium agreement after an initial period of up to 24 months without having to pay a financial penalty, rather than 18 months as before. This initial period now also applies to agreements under which the parties will make a substantial new investment.

---

[8] Guidelines were adopted after the period covered by this survey, which are also of interest to the analysis of information exchanges in general.

[9] OECD Secretariat: 'Discussion document on regulatory reform in international maritime transport', DSTI/DOT/MTC(99)8, 19.5.1999.

[10] Commission Regulation 823/2000 of 19 April 2000 on the application of Article 81(3) of the Treaty to certain categories of agreements, decisions and concerted practices between liner shipping companies (consortia) [2000] OJ L100/24.

[11] Commission Regulation 611/2005 of 20 April 2005 amending Regulation (EC) No 823/2000 on the application of Article 81(3) of the Treaty to certain categories of agreements, decisions and concerted practices between liner shipping companies (consortia) [2005] OJ L 101/10.

B. Procedural Changes

(i) Notice on Access to the File

The Commission finally issued its revised Notice on access to the file in competition law cases,[12] 'codifying' what has become its standard practice, and taking account of the revisions to the Merger Regulation and Regulation 1/2003. This replaces the previous 1997 Notice. Access to the Commission's file is one of the procedural guarantees necessary for the effective exercise of defence rights, in particular the right to be heard.[13] The Commission has 'an obligation to make available to the undertakings involved in Article [81(1)] proceedings all documents, whether in their favour or otherwise, which it has obtained during the course of the investigation'.[14] These principles are set out in Regulations 1/2003 and 773/2004 as well as in the Commission Notice, which states that 'the parties must be able to acquaint themselves with the information in the Commission's file, so that, on the basis of this information, they can effectively express their views on the preliminary conclusions reached by the Commission in its objections. For this purpose they will be granted access to all documents making up the Commission file.'[15] The exceptions to this rule concern business secrets and other confidential information, and internal documents of the Commission or national competition authorities ('NCAs'), including correspondence between the Commission and NCAs, or between NCAs.

The new Notice specifies the practical arrangements for giving the parties access to the Commission's file and the classification of the documents for disclosure purposes, and provides guidance on how to resolve disputes over confidentiality claims, and on balancing such claims with defence rights. The Notice confirms that the Commission may grant access either in electronic format (CD-ROMs, DVDs etc) or on paper.

The Notice appears to define 'business secrets' more narrowly than before, as information where disclosure 'could result in serious harm to the same undertaking', ie the company whose business activity is described in the information.[16] It makes a clear distinction between business secrets and 'other confidential information', which is defined as information whose disclosure would 'significantly harm a person or undertaking'. According to the Notice, information that may qualify as business secrets includes technical and/or financial information relating to a company's know-how, methods of assessing costs, production secrets and

---

[12] Commission Notice of 13 December 2005 on the rules for access to the Commission file in cases pursuant to Articles 81 and 82 of the EC Treaty, Articles 53, 54 and 57 of the EEA Agreement and Council Regulation (EC) No 139/2004 [2005] OJ C325/7.

[13] Joined Cases T-10/92 to T-12/92 and T-15/92 *Cimenteries CBR SA et al. v Commission* [1992] ECR II-2667, para 38.

[14] Case T-7/89 *Hercules Chemicals NV v Commission* [1991] ECR II-1711, para 54.

[15] Ibid, para 10.

[16] Case T-353/94 *Postbank NV v Commission* [1996] ECR II-921, para 87.

processes, supply sources, quantities produced and sold, market shares, customer and distributor lists, marketing plans, cost and price structure, and sales strategy. The category of 'other confidential information' includes information about companies which are able to put very considerable economic or commercial pressure on their competitors or their trading partners, customers, or suppliers. Thus this notion may include information that would enable the parties to identify complainants or other third parties who have a justified wish to remain anonymous. A document which is more than five years old will be presumed to be non-confidential.

According to the Commission, access to the file must only be granted to addressees of a Statement of Objections (SO), and only after the SO is sent out. A separate right of more limited access exists for complainants and other 'involved parties'. If the Commission proposes to reject a complaint, the complainant will be given access to the documents on which the Commission based its assessment. The Notice specifies that parties may also obtain access to the file via the general rules contained in the Transparency Regulation.[17] In practice, the rules on access to file remain unclear in places, and the Commission's practice varies considerably from case to case and in response to the dictates of administrative convenience.

(ii) Revised Leniency Notice

In December 2006, the Commission issued the latest revision of its Leniency Notice, first published in 1996 and previously revised in 2002.[18] Leniency aims to provide cartel participants with an incentive to blow the whistle on a cartel by providing evidence to the relevant competition authority. Applicants are offered either total immunity from fines or a reduction in the amount they would otherwise have been fined, in relation to both previously undetected infringements and ongoing investigations. The Leniency Notice has become a key element of the Commission's cartel armoury; it is indicative of this success that in the years 1996–2006 only 12 cartels were discovered without leniency, while 32 cartels were brought to light by leniency applications. Fines on participants in the first 12 cartels totalled EUR 439 million, while fines on participants in the leniency-discovered cartels totalled EUR 5,740 million.[19]

A successful legal system for tackling cartels is considered to depend on three factors: a high risk of detection by the authorities through pro-active investigations

---

[17] European Parliament and Council Regulation 1049/2001 of 30 May 2001 regarding public access to European Parliament, Council and Commission documents [2001] OJ L145/43. The first case in which this Regulation was successfully invoked, *VKI v Commission,* is reported in the section of this survey dealing with procedural matters.

[18] Commission Notice on immunity from fines and reduction of fines in cartel cases [2006] OJ C298/17.

[19] See Anderson and Heimler, 'What has Competition Done for Europe? An Inter-Disciplinary Answer', *Aussenwirtschaft*, No 4, 2007, available online at SSRN: <http://ssrn.com/abstract=1081563>, Table 2.

and enforcement in the absence of a leniency application; significant penalties for cartelists who fail to confess, so that the cost of getting caught outweighs the value of the cartel to the participants; and a leniency procedure which guarantees transparency and predictability in the treatment of applicants, together with the certainty of unpleasant consequences if leniency is not sought.

The reality in the EU these days is that the risk of detection of a cartel is low. One of the ironies of Regulation 1/2003 is that although the Commission fought for additional powers of investigation, and was granted the power to search the private homes of company directors, it hardly ever uses these new powers; instead it relies on a company's calculation that the risk of a fine (particularly with the increased level of fines resulting from the Fining Guidelines adopted in 2006) and of private damages claims will outweigh the benefits of cartel activity, and that it will decide to seek immunity or at least leniency under the Leniency Notice. There was an exponential rise in the number of leniency applications to the Commission after the adoption of the 2002 Notice, and the new Notice was intended to provide further encouragement to applicants. It therefore mainly sets out to:

• clarify the information required for an applicant to benefit from immunity;
• introduce a 'marker system' for immunity applicants;
• clarify the conditions for immunity/fine reductions, in particular the obligation of genuine and 'continuous' cooperation and the need to supply 'contemporaneous, incriminating evidence' or 'compelling evidence';
• clarify the procedure applicable to protect corporate statements made by immunity seekers from discovery in civil damages actions (these may be made in oral form);
• increase use of the procedure by making it clearer and more transparent.

The Notice maintains the principle that there should be only one immunity beneficiary per cartel. To assist in the race for leniency it introduces a new but discretionary marker system. The Commission gives little practical guidance on what will be needed to qualify for a marker, except to state that decisions will be made on a case-by-case basis, taking into account the specificities of each situation and the particular justifications. The marker system is really intended to enable the Commission to give a place in the queue in the absence of detailed evidence, but only after complete disclosure of the company's name and the market concerned. It will clearly allow coordination between various competition agencies when multiple filings are being made. In addition to the marker system, the Notice allows for a 'hypothetical application for immunity', which allows a company to discuss the possibility of immunity without disclosing its identity or the infringement.

The Notice has had a significant impact. The Commission has a substantial backlog of leniency applications to be processed and cases to be initiated. Once a case has been opened in a sector, it may safely be assumed that many companies will rush for leniency by giving the Commission evidence for a number of 'follow on' cases in the sector.

(iii) New Fining Guidelines

As reported later in this survey, the Commission's 1998 Fining Guidelines[20] met with a critical reception from Advocate General Tizzano when they were first subjected to judicial scrutiny in *Dansk Rørindustri*.[21] His comments were no doubt among the factors which led the Commission to issue revised Guidelines.[22] The 2006 Fining Guidelines introduce some important changes in the Commission's method of calculating fines. While the 1998 Guidelines used a four-step procedure, the new method involves a simplified two-step procedure, using a basic amount and adjustments to that amount.

The Commission has radically changed the factors it takes into account to calculate the basic amount of a fine.[23] The key factor now is the value of a company's sales of goods or services directly or indirectly related to the infringement in the relevant European Economic Area (EEA) geographical area. This is a return to the method used before the introduction of the 1998 Guidelines, which was also based mainly on sales values. The Commission also gives important new guidance on interpreting terminology which was not sufficiently explained in the 1998 Guidelines. Thus it explains that it will establish sales values using the best available figures for sales made by a company during the last full business year when it took part in the infringement; if the figures are incomplete or unreliable, it will use partial figures or any other relevant information. The sales value will not take VAT or other related taxes into account. Moreover, the Commission says it will treat infringements with a very wide geographic scope differently, by taking into account the relevant sales in a wider market than the EEA market.[24]

The most problematic issue is the assessment of gravity, ie the percentage of the sales value corresponding to the gravity of the infringement. The Commission will set this factor on a case-by-case basis, taking account of all the relevant circumstances, with a ceiling of 30%. The circumstances to be taken into account include the nature of the infringement, the combined market share of all companies concerned, the infringement's geographic scope, and whether or not it was implemented. Secret cartels are likely to attract the highest percentage, sometimes even the upper limit of 30%.

---

[20] Guidelines on the method of setting fines imposed pursuant to Article 15(2) of Regulation No 17 and Article 65(5) of the ECSC Treaty [1998] OJ C9/3.

[21] Joined Cases C-189/02 P, C-202/02 P, C-205/02 P to C-208/02 P and C-213/02 P, *Dansk Rørindustri et al. v Commission* [2005] ECR I-5425.

[22] Guidelines on the method of setting fines imposed pursuant to Article 23(2)(a) of Regulation No 1/2003, OJ [2006] C210/2.

[23] The 1998 Guidelines used a different method, for which the main criteria were the nature of the offence, its impact on the market and the size of the relevant geographical market. Considerable discretion remained in the calculation.

[24] Para 18 of the 2006 Guidelines.

Once calculated, the sales value will be multiplied by the number of years the infringement lasted. The Commission will not apply this duration increase if it lasted exactly one year or less.[25] The aim is to make long-lasting infringements very costly by punishing them with draconian fines.

Paragraph 25 of the Guidelines introduces a new concept in the Commission's fining policy, the 'entry fee', which will punish infringements considered as very serious by an increase of 15 to 25% of the basic sales value.[26]

The new Guidelines state explicitly that companies of a similar size will be grouped so that the Commission imposes the same fine on companies with similar shares in the market concerned, using rounded figures.

The basic amount of the fine will be adjusted to take into account aggravating and mitigating circumstances, the specific deterrent increase, the legal maximum, the Leniency Notice and the ability to pay. The Commission will decide whether aggravating and mitigating circumstances warrant an increase or reduction in the basic fine. Refusal to cooperate with the Commission during the investigation and playing a leading role in the infringement will qualify as aggravating circumstances and lead to an unspecified increase. Recidivists will pay a heavy penalty—the basic fine for companies previously fined by the Commission or a national competition authority will be increased by 100% for each past infringement. The Commission will take into account mitigating factors which include providing evidence of the early ending of the infringement, committing infringements as a result of negligence, cooperating with the Commission outside the scope of the Leniency Notice, taking part in infringements promoted or encouraged by public authorities or legislation, and playing a limited part in the infringement. This last is a new factor which replaces two mitigating factors in the 1998 Guidelines, a passive role in the infringement and not implementing the agreement. The list of adjustment factors is not exhaustive. A specific increase for deterrence will be applied to companies whose turnover is larger than the sales or services to which the infringement relates and those whose accountable profits are greater than the amount of the fine. Reductions or immunity will be granted using the Leniency Notice rules.

If the final fine is higher than 10% of the company's turnover, the Commission will apply the ceiling foreseen by Article 23(2) of Regulation 1/2003 and reduce it to exactly 10% of the company's turnover in the year preceding the decision.

If requested, the Commission will assess whether, in the specific and economic context, the undertaking cannot pay the fine, but will only grant a reduction on the basis of objective evidence that imposing the initial fine would irretrievably jeopardize the economic viability of the company concerned and deprive

---

[25] In the 1998 Guidelines no duration increase was applied for infringements lasting less than one year, but it was applied to infringements lasting exactly one year. In the 2006 Guidelines the duration increase only applies to infringements lasting over one year.

[26] The Commission refers mostly to cartels, but other infringements such as blatant abuse of a dominant position will also be subject to the increase.

its assets of all their value. The Commission also states that in special circum-stances it will impose symbolic fines, but while the 1998 Guidelines set a sym-bolic fine of EUR 1,000, the 2006 Guidelines do not specify an amount. Finally, the Commission states rather ominously that if the normal procedure under the Guidelines is not a sufficient deterrent, other methods may be applied. Thus the 10% ceiling is the Commission's only limit when fining large undertakings with very high turnovers. It remains to be seen whether the new Guidelines will enable fines to be predicted with a degree of certainty previously impossible in light of the Commission's intrinsically discretionary methods, or reduce the appeals focusing on fine issues. It is regrettable that the Commission did not include guidance on how it will deal with parent–subsidiary liability in cases where a parent company is found liable for having decisively influenced its subsidiary's commercial activities. In practice, even before the formal introduction of the new Fine Guidelines, the Commission's fines increased substantially, predicting the approach to be applied under the Guidelines.

C. Major Policy Developments

(i) Green Paper on Actions for Damages

Perhaps the most important policy development of these two years was the publication in December 2005 of the Commission's Green Paper on Damages Actions.[27] It was subsequently followed in 2008 by the publication of a White Paper.[27a] The Commission had already embarked on the ambitious project of fur-thering private antitrust enforcement in Europe after the modernization reforms of 1999–2004. In this task it received the full support of the Court of Justice, which in 2001 delivered a landmark ruling in *Courage*[28] that set out the basis for a system of individual civil liability for breach of the EC competition rules.

Although the modernization reforms opened the way for the full applica-tion of Articles 81 and 82 of the EC Treaty by national courts, it was still felt that modernization by itself could not enhance private antitrust enforcement in Europe. Thus, soon after the *Courage* ruling,[29] the Commission commissioned a study on the conditions for claiming damages in the Member States for infringe-ments of the EC competition rules. The results of that study were published on

---

[27] See generally on EC private enforcement and on the Green Paper, AP Komninos, *EC Private Antitrust Enforcement, Decentralised Application of EC Competition Law by National Courts* (Hart Publishing, 2008).

[27a] The present contribution was written before the publication of the White Paper, which falls outside the time period covered by the present survey. See Commission White Paper on Damages Actions for Breach of the EC Antitrust Rules, 2 April 2008, COM(2008) 165.

[28] Case C-453/99 *Courage v Crehan* [2001] ECR I-6297. On this ruling see Komninos, 'New Prospects for Private Enforcement of EC Competition Law: *Courage* v *Crehan* and the Community Right in Damages', (2002) 39 CMLR 447.

[29] *Courage*, ibid.

the Commission's website in 2004.[30] Predictably, they showed an 'astonishing diversity and total underdevelopment' of civil antitrust actions in the Member States. Up to mid-2004 there were apparently around 50 judged cases for damages actions (12 on the basis of EC law, around 32 on the basis of national law, and 6 on both). Only 28 of these judgments had resulted in a damages award (8 on the basis of EC competition law, 16 on national law, and 4 on both).[31]

After digesting the results of the Study and reflecting further on the appropriate way to move forward, the Commission published on 19 December 2005 for public consultation a Green Paper and a Commission Staff Working Paper on damages actions for breach of the EC antitrust rules.[32] The purpose of the Green Paper, which sets out a number of possible options to facilitate private damages actions, is to stimulate debate and facilitate feedback from stakeholders. The public consultation ran until 21 April 2006 and all comments received were posted on the Green Paper's webpage.[33]

The Commission is in favour of increased private enforcement, which it believes would have a number of advantages for private parties, in particular:

(a) compensating victims of illegal anti-competitive behaviour for loss suffered;
(b) increasing deterrence of antitrust infringements and compliance with the law;
(c) further development of a competition culture among market participants, including consumers, and greater awareness of the competition rules;
(d) the Commission and the national competition authorities do not have sufficient resources to deal with all cases of anticompetitive behaviour, and in any event administrative authorities have discretion to pursue other priorities.

The Green Paper lists in some detail a variety of options for encouraging private actions and establishing a more litigation-based system of private antitrust enforcement in Europe. It starts from the premise that the role of private enforcement of EC Treaty competition rules should be complementary to public enforcement. The Commission makes clear that it is keen to see increased private enforcement of the full range of competition infringements under EC law, and not just additional enforcement in cases already dealt with by the public

---

[30] The study is made up of a comparative report (Waelbroeck, Slater, and Even-Shoshan, 'Study on the Conditions of Claims for Damages in Case of Infringement of EC Competition Rules: Comparative Report', 31 August 2004), a report on economic models for the calculation of damages and 25 national reports.

[31] These statistics are only indicative, since not all judgments are published in some Member States and the comparative report necessarily relies on the national reports, whose quality varies. It should also be borne in mind that these statistics do not include cases that were settled with significant damages awards to the plaintiffs.

[32] Commission Green Paper on Damages Actions for Breach of the EC Antitrust Rules, COM(2005) 672 final. The Green Paper is accompanied by a Commission Staff Working Paper, Annex to the Green Paper on Damages Actions for Breach of the EC Antitrust Rules, SEC(2005) 1732, which sets out the various options more discursively.

[33] See: <http://ec.europa.eu/comm/competition/antitrust/others/actions_for_damages/index_en.html>.

authorities (so-called 'follow-on actions'). In other words, private enforcement would also aim to facilitate 'stand-alone' actions in cases with which public enforcement agencies could not or did not wish to deal.

The Green Paper acknowledges that one of the major obstacles to damages actions for private litigants is obtaining evidence of an alleged antitrust infringement, particularly when there is no prior decision by a competition authority establishing the infringement. Furthermore, proof and quantification of the actual damage can be very difficult in competition cases. Evidence is often held by the alleged infringer. This is why the question of discovery of evidence is considered to be of particular importance. Several options designed to deal with problems faced by a potential claimant are put forward for debate. They involve obligations for the defendant to turn over certain documents to the claimant. The Green Paper recognizes the difficulties of introducing pre-trial discovery, and emphasizes effective case management by the national courts through the organization of case management conferences or pre-hearing reviews. One possibility it examines is a form of court-ordered discovery based on fact-pleading, whereby the plaintiff sets out the relevant facts in detail and presents reasonably available evidence in support of his allegations. Also, the burden and standard of proof required could be adapted to the information imbalance between the claimant and the defendant. One option considered is to make decisions by national competition authorities that establish an infringement of the Treaty competition rules binding on civil courts in follow-on actions.[34]

One particularly controversial issue is the possible introduction of class actions in Europe. The Green Paper does not advocate the introduction of opt-out class actions, but rather refers to 'collective claims'. It gives thought to whether a form of collective consumer redress should be available, such as a right of action for consumer associations, and makes a useful distinction between: (a) 'representative claims' brought by a representative natural or legal person such as a consumer organization on behalf of a group of identified individuals, and aimed at protecting the individual rights of those represented; (b) 'collective claims' brought on behalf of a group of identified or identifiable individuals and aimed at protecting the interests of those represented; and (c) 'public interest litigation' aiming to benefit the public at large and resulting in an award to the natural or legal person who brought the action or to those who suffered the damage.

Another controversial issue is the impact of private enforcement on the EU leniency programme. The Commission believes that private damages claims and leniency programmes share the common aim of preventing cartels from being formed in the first place. Companies understand that anticompetitive agreements are illegal under EC and national competition law, and that infringing these rules carries great risks in terms of both fines and civil liability. The leniency

---

[34] For arguments against this proposal see Komninos, 'Effect of Commission Decisions on Private Antitrust Litigation: Setting the Story Straight' (2007) 44 CMLR 1387.

programme is part of this system of deterrence, as it makes the discovery of secret cartels more likely (for Commission views, see IP/02/247 and MEMO/02/23). However, the possibility of damages actions might affect the operation of leniency programmes. In this respect the Green Paper puts forward several options. One is to make leniency applications non-discoverable; by making sure they do not have to be turned over to claimants in jurisdictions where disclosure requirements exist, this option would ensure the confidential nature of the leniency programme. Another possibility is to reduce a leniency applicant's civil liability, while leaving unchanged the civil liability of the other cartel members, who would be jointly and severally liable for the entirety of the loss suffered.

An even more controversial issue, raising many eyebrows, is the possible introduction of punitive damages.[35] In the US, damages awards based on infringement of US federal anti-trust law are automatically trebled; a jury first decides on the award itself, and at a later stage the court trebles the award as found by the jury. The Commission does not put forward the option of introducing treble damages, but it does suggest, for debate, the option of introducing double damages, either automatically or at the discretion of the court hearing the case.

Finally, the Green Paper includes interesting options on two of the most characteristic legal questions that arise in private antitrust actions, those of the 'passing-on' defence and 'indirect purchaser' standing. The passing-on defence refers to the situation where a defendant claims the plaintiff has passed on his losses to his customers and perhaps ultimately to consumers, so an award for damages would amount to unjustified enrichment. If read broadly, this defence can strike a fatal blow at any private antitrust enforcement action,[36] and some competition laws have adopted the policy of disallowing or restricting it. This has been the case in the US[37] and recently in German law, although the German position is more nuanced. The Green Paper considers various options, but it is fair to say that basically it accepts that Community law does not in principle prohibit defences based on unjustified enrichment. On the standing of indirect purchasers, again, many options are considered, but a certain preference can be discerned for a rule of broad standing, as is in any event required by the Court of Justice's rulings in

---

[35] A recent judgment of the UK High Court stated that in an action following an infringement decision of the Commission, a claimant is only entitled to claim compensatory damages, and not exemplary (ie intended to punish and deter), restitutionary damages or an account for profits. The court observed that in some Member States, notably Germany, an award of exemplary or punitive damages is regarded as contrary to public policy (*Devenish Nutrition Ltd et al. v Sanofi-Aventis SA (France) et al.* [2007] EWHC 2394 (ChD), see comment by Dawes, *e-Competitions*, January 2008-II, No 15157 p 1.)

[36] For recent French examples where follow-on civil actions failed at first instance because of the passing-on defence and its rather broad reading by the courts, see T Com. Paris, 26.1.07, *Sté Laboratoires Juva Production and Sté Laboratoires Juva Santé—SED v SAS Roche and Sté Roche Vitamins Europe Ltd*, No RG 2003048044; T Com. Nanterre, 11.5.06, *Arkopharma v Roche SA and Hoffmann La Roche SA*, No RG 2004F02643.

[37] See the US Supreme Court's landmark judgment in *Hanover Shoe v United Shoe Machines Corp* 392 US 481 (1968).

Courage and *Manfredi*.[38] It is nevertheless true that some form of compromise can be attained so as to avoid a multiplicity of actions and plaintiffs, thus safeguarding the efficiency of the whole system.[39] The Green Paper seems conscious of this and stresses *de lege ferenda*: 'It is suggested that the determining factor could be the effective enforcement of Community law. If limiting the rights of certain individuals to claim is necessary to ensure a system which is more effective in safeguarding the enforcement of Articles 81 and 82, then it is submitted that such limitations should be acceptable under Community law. Therefore, it might be necessary to determine what rights must be facilitated to ensure an effective enforcement system rather than insisting on the absolute protection of all private rights. For the protection of the rights of consumers, a specific small claims procedure or collective action might be an efficient form of redress given the very low level of individual damage suffered in many of the cases.'[40]

The Competition Commissioner announced the preparation of a White Paper on antitrust damages actions as a follow-up to the Green Paper, in order 'to take the debate forward with some concrete ideas on follow-up'.[41] However, there has not yet been any official indication as to more concrete steps and the Commission insists it has not yet decided how to proceed. It has three possible alternatives:

(a) not to propose or take any action at all and defer to the laws of the Member States, while hoping that the Green Paper will encourage national initiatives;

(b) to adopt a 'soft law' Community instrument that is not legally binding, such as a notice, a communication, or guidelines;

(c) to propose Community legislation ('hard law'), in the form of a regulation or a directive (or both).

It seems the Commission will probably propose a legislative measure, most likely a directive, perhaps coupled with a more general regulation. It has not indicated what legal basis it might use to implement its proposal: this could be

---

[38] Joined Cases C-295 to C-298/04 *Vincenzo Manfredi et al. v Lloyd Adriatico Assicurazioni SpA et al* [2006] ECR I-6619, reviewed later in this survey.

[39] See for example Oliver, 'Le règlement 1/2003 et les principes d'efficacité et d'équivalence' (2005) 41 CDE 351, at 385, according to whom one solution would be to accept indirect purchasers' standing as a matter of principle but interpret the causation requirements strictly, thus essentially blocking most such claims.

[40] Staff Working Paper, para 180.

[41] See Commissioner Kroes, 'Competition Policy and Consumers', Speech Made at the General Assembly of Bureau Européen des Unions de Consommateurs (BEUC) (Brussels, 16 November 2006), available online at: <http://ec.europa.eu/comm/competition/speechesindex_2006.html>. In early January 2007, the Commission published a call for tenders to provide a study related to the economic and social impact assessment of the envisaged White Paper. The Green Paper was received favourably by the European Economic and Social Committee (EESC) (see Opinion INT/306 of the European Economic and Social Committee on the Green Paper—Damages actions for breach of the EC antitrust rules COM(2005) 672 final, Brussels, 26 October 2006) and by the European Parliament (see European Parliament Resolution of 25 April 2007 on the Green Paper on Damages Actions for Breach of the EC Antitrust Rules, 2006/2207(INI)).

either Article 83(2) of the EC Treaty, which concerns measures to give effect to the Treaty's competition law provisions, or Article 65(c) of the EC Treaty, which concerns measures in the field of judicial cooperation in civil matters having cross-border implications.

Whatever the Commission's next moves, the Green Paper has certainly created a fruitful and at times heated discussion as to the desirability of private actions for damages in Europe. Most of its critics refer to the US excesses and warn against a wholesale importation of the US system. It is indeed true that class actions, coupled with pre-trial discovery and contingency fees, have led to excesses in the US. They can result in effective blackmail and extortion of huge sums by class action lawyers from companies wanting to avoid the costs and uncertainties (not least because of the jury trial system) of protracted litigation. There is no doubt that such a development in Europe must be avoided at all costs. It is thus encouraging that the Commission has made clear in its Green Paper that 'the ultimate objective should be to foster a competition culture, not a litigation culture'.[42]

(ii) Discussion Paper on the Application of Article 82 EC to Exclusionary Abuses

In December 2005, DG COMP, published a Staff Discussion Paper[43] describing a general framework for analysing abusive exclusionary conduct by a dominant company. (Another paper on exploitative abuses was announced at the time but has not been published yet.) The Commission's goal of launching a public debate on the enforcement of Article 82 of the EC Treaty was achieved: numerous comments were submitted, a hearing was held and debate was fostered in academic circles. Interestingly, this renewed interest in unilateral conduct has now gone global, with papers by the ICN and the US Antitrust Modernization Commission.

As the Discussion Paper correctly points out, Article 82 aims to protect not competitors but competition itself, and hence consumers. The main change proposed in the Paper is the introduction of more economic reasoning, with a view to maximizing consumer welfare and protecting the competitive process. However, while the goal of a more economics-based approach is to be applauded, the Paper nevertheless continues to rely heavily on a number of negative presumptions inherited from the previous approach.

The Paper is well-structured. It begins with the concept of dominance and goes on to describe a common framework for analysis, before reviewing some specific types of abuse. This brief summary aims to highlight its major features.

---

[42] Green Paper, para 12.
[43] For the text of the Discussion Paper in pdf format, see <http://ec.europa.eu/comm/competition/antitrust/art82/index.html>.

Defining dominance. The Paper clarifies that a company may only be found dominant if it has 'substantial market power'. However, beyond this grand declaration, the Commission continues to rely heavily on market shares to establish dominance, and is prepared to consider a company with only a 40% market share as dominant.

Framework for analysis. The common framework proposed in the Paper for analysing all exclusionary abuses of a dominant position has three stages: (i) assessing whether the form of the conduct indicates that it is capable of having restrictive effects, (ii) establishing likely or actual foreclosure effects, and (iii) considering possible defences. This third stage constitutes a major innovation.

Foreclosure. The Commission's main concern is foreclosure which hinders competition and thereby harms consumers. It is careful to emphasize that dominant companies remain free to compete on their merits: Article 82 of the EC Treaty only prohibits exclusionary conduct that produces actual, indirect, or long-term anticompetitive effects. When deciding whether there is foreclosure, the Commission takes into account the form, nature and incidence of the conduct. Equally efficient competitors constitute the benchmark. However, the standard for foreclosure sometimes seems rather too lax to be in line with the allegedly more economics-based approach.

Defences. The Paper innovates by proposing three possible defences a dominant company may offer. First, it may invoke factors such as health and safety requirements which apply to all companies active on the market to demonstrate that its conduct is objectively necessary for the production or distribution of the products concerned (the 'objective necessity' defence). Secondly, it may respond proportionately to low pricing by competitors (the 'meeting competition' defence). Thirdly, it may, on the model of Article 81(3) of the EC Treaty, prove the existence of efficiencies which outweigh the negative effects created (the 'efficiency' defence). The introduction of these three defences is to be welcomed, but their very narrow scope may be regretted. Moreover, an integrated analysis would have fitted the framework of Article 82 better than the proposed two stages of first finding foreclosure and then assessing possible defences, which seem to place the burden of proof entirely on dominant companies.

Predatory pricing. The Discussion Paper has little new to offer with regard to predatory pricing, apart from introducing avoidable average costs (AAC) as the new cost benchmark. The Commission also helpfully recognizes that pricing between AAC and average total costs is not in itself abusive when there is no other evidence of a predatory strategy. However, it refuses to consider it necessary to prove recouping. Similarly, the Paper remains essentially based on formal price/costs tests inherited from the previous formal approach, and could have gone further in acknowledging that dominant companies may have legitimate justification for their pricing behaviour.

Single branding. Single-branding clauses oblige buyers to purchase all or at least a significant proportion of their requirements from the same supplier. The analysis of them in the Paper does not depart substantially from a *per se* approach: the Commission continues to use presumptions and to assume that such clauses have an anti-competitive effect by their nature. A genuine economic approach would also have considered the importance of the barriers to entry beyond the percentage of the market that is tied.

Rebates. The Paper goes in the right direction by recognising that rebates should not be condemned as abusive *per se*, since dominant companies may use them to improve efficiency as well as for anticompetitive reasons. To assess foreclosure, the Commission proposes focusing on the suction effect of the conduct and the amount that equally efficient competitors could supply to the same customers (the commercially viable share). The use of such an effect-based assessment is welcome, especially in light of recent cases such as *British Airways*[44] which followed a pure 'old school' approach. However, the system described in the Paper is extremely complex, making it very difficult for companies to assess the legality of their behaviour *ex ante*. At present, the paper's approach and the law as declared by the European Courts is divergent.

Tying and bundling. The possible exploitative and discriminatory effects of tying and bundling fall outside the Paper's scope. The Commission recognizes the ambivalent nature of the practices. It repeats the four-prong test: (i) distinct products, where it considers that independent demand for the tied product suffices to demonstrate the existence of two products (this approach was upheld by the Court of First Instance (CFI) in *Microsoft*);[44a] (ii) foreclosure, where a more economic approach looking at long-term incremental costs is adopted; (iii) dominance in the tying product; and (iv) justifications. However, it still relies on a number of presumptions which shift the burden of proof to the dominant company, especially when the Commission lacks sufficient data.

Refusal to supply. This section of the Paper focuses on refusals to supply leading to vertical foreclosure. The Commission alludes to adopting a rule of reason whereby improving the competitive process in the downstream market ('allocative efficiency') would be balanced against safeguarding the incentives to invest upstream ('dynamic efficiency'), based on the specifics of each case, Overall this method deserves praise, but because it presumes competitors have incentives to invest, it risks automatically tipping the balance in favour of antitrust intervention. The Paper examines several types of refusals to supply.

Discontinuation of supply. The Paper distinguishes between discontinuing supplies and refusal to supply from the outset. According to the Commission, in the

---

[44] Case T-219/99 *British Airways plc v Commission* [2003] ECR II-5917, upheld on appeal in Case C-95/04 P, *British Airways plc v Commission* [2007] ECR I-2331.
[44a] Case T-201/04 *Microsoft v Commission* [2007] ECR II-3601.

case of discontinuation there would be no need to prove the input was indispensable. Such watering down of the standard risks discouraging firms from entering into commercial agreements in the first place, lest they are unable to stop supplying later. Moreover, the loose definition used in the Paper comes close to transforming the indispensability requirement into a mere convenience test. The four other common conditions are (i) a termination/refusal, (ii) dominance, (iii) negative effects on competition (rather than elimination of all competition), and (iv) absence of justification.

IPR and interoperability. The Commission also deals separately with refusals to license intellectual property rights. The Paper adopts the five conditions for refusals to supply and adds that the refusal must prevent the development of the market for which the licence is an indispensable input. It would have been better to refer to preventing the appearance of a new product. Lastly, the Commission has devised a special category for refusal to supply information needed for interoperability.

The Discussion Paper was intended as a basis for public consultations,[45] and the most important matters raised by contributors to the consultations were the subject of a public hearing in June 2006.[46] The Commission has since applied the principles set out in the Discussion Paper in the *Prokent/Tomra* Decision,[47] which is examined later in this survey.

III. Important European Court Judgments and Commission Decisions

A. The Scope of the Competition Rules

(i) Non-Competition Concerns

Meca-Medina[48]

Mr Meca-Medina and Mr Majcen were two professional athletes who competed in long-distance swimming contests. During the World Cup in that sport they tested positive for Nandrolone, an anabolic substance. The International Swimming Federation (FINA) suspended them under the Olympic Movement's Anti-Doping Code for four years, a term subsequently reduced to two years by the Court of Arbitration for Sport. The two athletes complained to the Commission, alleging that the International Olympic Committee's rules on doping control

---

[45] For the contributions submitted, see <http://ec.europa.eu/comm/competition/antitrust/art82/contributions.html>.

[46] For the presentations at the public hearing, see: <http//ec.europa.eu/comm/competition/antitrust/art82/ hearing.html>.

[47] Commission Decision of 29 March 2006 (*Prokent/Tomra*).

[48] Case C-519/04 P *David Meca-Medina and Igor Majcen v Commission* [2006] ECR I-6991.

were not compatible with the Community rules on competition and freedom to provide services. Following the Commission's rejection of their complaint, they brought an action before the CFI to have that Decision set aside. The CFI dismissed their action and held that the rules on doping control did not fall within the scope of Community competition law or of the Treaty provisions on freedom to provide services.[49]

On appeal, the Court of Justice held that sport is subject to Community law insofar as it constitutes an economic activity. The Court disagreed with the CFI that Articles 39, 48, 81, and 82 of the EC Treaty do not affect rules concerning questions which are of purely sporting interest and, as such, have nothing to do with economic activity. With particular reference to competition law, the Court held that the CFI had erred in law in considering the specific sporting rules on doping control as lying outside the scope of Articles 81 and 82, since it had not first determined whether those rules fulfilled the specific requirements of Community competition law.[50] The Court therefore set aside the CFI judgment and proceeded to rule itself on the application for annulment of the Commission's decision.

The Court held that the penal nature of the rules at issue and the magnitude of the penalties applicable if they were breached were capable of producing adverse effects on competition. Rules of that kind could indeed prove excessive, owing both to the way in which the circumstances in which penalties for doping might be imposed were distinguished from those in which they were not, and to the severity of those penalties.[51] To escape the prohibition on distortion of competition laid down by the Treaty, the restrictions imposed by those rules must be limited to what is necessary to ensure the proper conduct of competitive sport. *In casu* it did not appear that these restrictions went beyond what was necessary to ensure that sporting events took place and functioned properly. Finally, the Court rejected arguments based on Article 49 of the EC Treaty as misplaced: this case was about the legality of a Commission Decision taken pursuant to Regulation 17,[52] so judicial review must be limited to competition law grounds. The Court therefore upheld the Commission's rejection of the complaint.

This case must be seen in the context of the earlier ruling by the ECJ in *Wouters*,[53] where the Court, perhaps for the first time, was openly confronted with anti-competitive conduct which, however, was justified or justifiable on

---

[49] Case T-313/02 *David Meca-Medina and Igor Majcen v Commission* [2004] ECR II-3291.
[50] ECJ judgment, para 33.   [51] Ibid, para 48.
[52] Council Regulation No 17 of 6 February 1962: First Regulation implementing Articles [81] and [82] of the Treaty, OJ, English Special Edition 1959–1962, p 87.
[53] Case C-309/99 *JCJ Wouters et al. v Algemene Raad van de Nederlandse Orde van Advocaten* [2002] ECR I-1577. On this judgment, see Forrester, 'Where Law Meets Competition: Is *Wouters* like a *Cassis de Dijon* or a Platypus?', in Ehlermann and Atanasiu (eds), *European Competition Law Annual 2004: The Relationship between Competition Law and (Liberal) Professions* (Hart Publishing, 2006), 271 *et seq.*

non-economic or non-competition grounds.[54] There the Court had followed a proportionality approach borrowed from the case law on the four freedoms. *Meca-Medina* confirms this approach. It further shows the differences that may arise between the CFI, a court more attuned to competition law litigation, which thus prefers a more purist approach (hence its findings that the specific rules in question did not pertain to competition law), and the European Court of Justice (ECJ), a court much more accustomed to dealing with conflicts of legal principles and rights based thereon, as well as with difficult questions of delineation of competences and legal principles. This judgment is also a confirmation of the proposition that *Wouters* was not a one-off case, but rather an important precedent dealing with the outer limits of competition law.

(ii) *The Concept of 'Undertaking'*

FENIN[55]

In July 2006, the ECJ rejected the appeal by FENIN, the Spanish association of marketers of medical goods and equipment, against the CFI's dismissal[56] of its action for annulment of a 1999 Commission Decision.[57] FENIN had complained to the Commission that 26 public bodies which ran the Spanish national health system, including three ministries ('SNS'), were abusing their dominant position by delaying payment for medical goods and equipment, without their creditors being able to exert any commercial pressure to make them put an end to the practice. The Commission rejected FENIN's complaint on the grounds that the SNS were not acting as undertakings when they participated in the management of the public health service, and that their demand-side activities could not be dissociated from the subsequent supply-side activities which they provided. The Decision was upheld on appeal by the CFI, which agreed that the SNS were not undertakings for the purposes of application of Article 82 of the EC Treaty.

FENIN appealed the CFI judgment on the sole ground that the CFI had misinterpreted the definition of 'undertaking' as set out in the case law of the Community Courts. Its plea had two limbs. Firstly, FENIN argued that the CFI had incorrectly failed to consider whether the SNS's purchasing activity in itself constituted an economic activity. Alternatively, it argued that the SNS's purchasing activity was economic in nature and therefore subject to the competition rules, since their subsequent activity, namely the provision of medical treatment, was an activity of an economic nature.

---

[54] On this question, see generally Komninos, 'Resolution of Conflicts in the Integrated Article 81 EC', in Ehlermann and Atanasiu (eds), *European Competition Law Annual 2004, The Relationship Between Competition Law and the (Liberal) Professions* (Hart Publishing, 2006) 451 *et seq*.

[55] Case C-205/03 P *Federación Española de Empresas de Tecnología Sanitaria ('FENIN') v Commission* [2006] ECR I-6295.

[56] Case T-319/99 *FENIN v Commission* [2003] ECR II-357.

[57] See Forrester, MacLennan, and Komninos, 'EC Competition Law Developments 2003–2004', (2005) 24 YEL 511, at 553.

The ECJ rejected the second part of the plea as inadmissible since FENIN had only raised it on appeal,[58] and dismissed FENIN's arguments in relation to the first part of the plea. It recalled its judgments in *Höfner and Elser*,[59] *Commission v Italy*,[60] and *AOK-Bundesverband and Others*[61] that 'the definition of an undertaking covers any entity engaged in an economic activity, regardless of the legal status of that entity and the way in which it is financed',[62] and that 'it is the activity consisting in offering goods and services on a given market that is the characteristic feature of an economic activity'. On the basis of this case law, the ECJ considered the CFI was right to conclude that the Commission did not have to dissociate the SNS's activity of purchasing goods from the subsequent use to which the goods were to be put in order to determine the nature of the purchasing activity. Rather, the ECJ confirmed that the Commission and the CFI were correct in holding that the nature of the purchasing activity must be determined according to whether or not the SNS's subsequent use of the purchased goods amounted to an economic activity.[63] Thus the Court dismissed FENIN's appeal.

This judgment is interesting in that it contains a short but strong reaffirmation of the Community Courts' case law that whether an entity is classified as an undertaking depends on the economic nature of its activities. Each activity should be analysed separately, so that '[i]t is quite possible for an entity to be treated as an undertaking as regards some of its activities, while others fall outside the sphere of competition law.'[64] Thus when a public body carries out both economic and non-economic activities, only its activities which are economic in nature fall within the scope of EC competition law.

However, the terseness of the ECJ's reasoning also misses the opportunity to bring together and synthesize the Community Courts' now voluminous case law on this topic.[65] Furthermore, by rejecting as inadmissible the second limb of FENIN's appeal, contrary to the Advocate General's Opinion,[66] the judgment leaves open the question of whether public health services may be considered as undertakings when they provide similar services to private patients. By analogy with the case law regarding medical activities in the context of freedom to provide

---

[58] Judgment, paras 21–22.
[59] Case C-41/90 *Höfner and Elser v Macrotron* [1991] ECR I-1979, para 21.
[60] Case C-35/96 *Commission v Italy* [1998] ECR I-3851, para 36.
[61] Joined Cases C-264/01, C-306/01, C-354/01, and C-355/01, *AOK-Bundesverband et al. v Commission* [2004] ECR I-2493, para 46.
[62] Judgment, para 25.   [63] Ibid, para 26.
[64] Opinion of Advocate General Poiares Maduro in *FENIN*, para 10.
[65] Apart from *Höfner and Elser* and *AOK-Bundesverband*, the criteria for defining what constitutes an undertaking arose in several other cases during the 1990s: see Joined Cases C-159/91 and C-160/91 *Poucet and Pistre* [1993] ECR I-637; Case C-364/92 *SAT Fluggesellschaft* ('*Eurocontrol*') [1994] ECR I-43; Case C-244/94 *FFSA and Others* [1995] ECR I-4013; Case C-343/95 *Diego Calì & Figli* [1997] ECR I-1547; Cases C-67/96, C-115/97 to C-117/97, and C-219/97 *Albany* [1999] ECR I-5751; Case C-475/99 *Ambulanz Glöckner* [2001] ECR I-8089; Joined Cases C-180/98 to C-184/98 *Pavlov and Others* [2000] ECR I-6451.
[66] Opinion of Advocate General Poiares Maduro in *FENIN*, para 37.

services,[67] it could be argued that medical activities should also fall within the scope of Articles 81 and 82 of the EC Treaty, and that a body involved in financing medical benefits should be classified as an undertaking in that context, even if it is a State body. However, as we argued in our last survey of competition law developments,[68] such a solution is not necessarily desirable, as it would mean distinguishing between purchases by a public health service depending on whether they were for publicly or privately funded patients, some being subject to EC competition law and others not, with all the practical and legal difficulties this would entail.

SELEX Sistemi Integrati[69]

In *SELEX* the CFI upheld a Commission Decision to reject a complaint lodged by SELEX, a company operating ATM systems, against Eurocontrol, an international organization established by European States to promote cooperation in the field of aviation and a uniform system of air traffic management (ATM). Essentially the complaint alleged that Eurocontrol's management of intellectual property rights in the context of development and acquisition of ATM software and hardware created factual monopolies in the production of systems that were subsequently standardized by Eurocontrol. SELEX complained in particular of three areas of Eurocontrol's activities: (1) the adoption and implementation of common technical standards; (2) coordination of national research and development activities, in particular the acquisition of prototypes and the management of the related intellectual property rights; and (3) providing assistance to national administrations in the planning, specification and creation of ATMs.

The Commission rejected the complaint, reasoning that although in principle the Community competition rules apply to international organizations, the relevant activities of Eurocontrol were not of an economic nature, so that Eurocontrol could not be considered as an undertaking for the purpose of applying Article 82 of the EC Treaty. The CFI upheld the Commission's Decision. The Court began by noting the ECJ case law according to which the concept of an 'undertaking' may apply to any entity, regardless of its legal status and the way in which it is financed.[70] It was true that the ECJ had ruled in another case[71] that Eurocontrol was not an undertaking, but that was not decisive, as it had not then considered whether the activities of Eurocontrol which were at stake were economic activities for the purpose of applying EU competition law.[72] The CFI reasoned that as the activities in which an entity such as Eurocontrol engages as a public authority

---

[67] See for the most recent reaffirmation Case C-372/04 *The Queen, on the application of Yvonne Watts v Bedford Primary Care Trust, Secretary of State for Health* [2006] ECR I-4325.

[68] Forrester, MacLennan, and Komninos, n 57 above, at 553.

[69] Case T-155/04 *SELEX Sistemi Integrati v Commission* [2006] ECR II-4797.

[70] *Höfner and Elser*, para 21; *Pavlov and Others*, para 74.

[71] *SAT Fluggesellschaft (Eurocontrol)*, paras 30, 31.

[72] *SELEX*, para 54.

can be severed from its other activities for the purpose of applying the EU competition rules, its various activities must be examined individually, and the fact that some may be non-economic activities of a public authority does not prevent others from being considered as economic in nature.[73]

The CFI went on to determine that Eurocontrol's standardization activities, acquisition of prototypes of ATM systems and management of intellectual property rights could not be described as economic activities. The participating States themselves developed common technical standards in the context of international cooperation through Eurocontrol, and subsequently adopted the standards acting though the Council of Eurocontrol. The results of the development activity stayed within the organization itself, which meant there was no market for technical standardization services.[74] Relying on *FENIN*, the Court reasoned that 'economic activity consists of the offer of goods and services on a given market and not the acquisition of such goods and services' and that 'the nature of the purchasing activity must [...] be determined according to whether or not the subsequent use of the purchased goods amounts to an economic activity.'[75] An organization purchasing goods for non-economic activities does not act as an undertaking simply because it is a purchaser in a given market.[76] Consequently, the Court reasoned that Eurocontrol's acquisition of prototypes in the context of standardization was not an economic activity because its standardization activity was not an economic activity. Neither its acquisition of prototypes in the context of its R&D activities nor the management of the related intellectual property rights made Eurocontrol's R&D an economic activity, since these activities did not involve offering goods or services on a given market.[77] Eurocontrol distributed public funds to promote R&D in the sphere of ATM equipment. Although it acquired ownership of the prototype and the related intellectual property rights under subsidy contracts, the acquisition was not an end in itself and did not enable it to exploit those rights for commercial purposes, but was 'merely one element in the legal relationship between the body granting the subsidy and the organization receiving it'.[78]

Unlike the Commission, the CFI found that when Eurocontrol assisted national administrations in drafting the contract documents for calls for tenders or selecting undertakings to participate in calls for tenders, it did act as an undertaking, since private entities could also provide such services.[79] Although the fact that Eurocontrol's provision of assistance was not remunerated and was carried out in pursuit of a public service objective indicated that it was non-economic, that did not entirely rule out the existence of an economic activity.[80] However,

---

[73] Ibid.   [74] Ibid, para 61.   [75] Ibid, para 65, citing *FENIN*, para 36.
[76] Ibid, paras. 67–68, discussing *FENIN*, para 37.   [77] Ibid, para 75.
[78] Ibid, para 76. An additional argument supporting this reasoning was that Eurocontrol made these intellectual property rights available to interested undertakings free of charge (para 77).
[79] Ibid, para 88, citing Case T-128/98 *Aéroports de Paris v Commission* [2000] ECR II-3929, para 124, upheld in Case C-82/01 P *Aéroports de Paris v Commission* [2002] ECR I-9297, para 82.
[80] Ibid, para 90.

the Court found that SELEX had not provided sufficient evidence of a breach of Article 82 with regard to that activity.

B. Cartels

As noted above, the Commission continued during the period covered by this survey to pursue cartels with unabated zeal, and there was an equally zealous pursuit of leniency by companies hoping to escape or reduce the increasingly harsh penalties imposed on cartel members. As many of the cases examined in this survey show, the main goal of companies accused of cartel activities now seems not to be exculpation but a reduced fine by applying for leniency, or at least attempting to disprove the Commission's findings on the duration or degree of their cartel participation. An almost automatic series of appeals seems to have followed cartel decisions. Clearly the soft law on leniency and fine-setting is having a major effect in the establishment of new cartels; and although judging by the number of cartels that are still coming to light, the Commission's crackdown is not acting as a total deterrent, a cartel participant's cost benefit analysis has to be tempered by the knowledge that previous notions of loyalty owed by one cartel member to another have now gone for good. Indeed, modern corporate notions of risk management include competition law compliance among the matters upon which management systems must keep an eye.

We feel it right to observe that the current levels of fines imposed by the Commission are astonishing. They are often far above the penalties imposed in national law for the gravest offences. While there is no doubt that cartels can have pernicious economic effects upon their victims, who ultimately include all consumers, the current levels of fines are plainly criminal in severity, and very severe indeed. The Commission's procedures for taking decisions do not satisfy the standards of rigour by which a criminal prosecution should be governed. The decision-maker is a college of political leaders, which decides without having seen or participated in the hearing of the accused party. The hearing does not afford an effective opportunity for the testing of contested facts, and the Hearing Officer (despite excellent legal and personal qualities) has little share in the taking of the ultimate decision by the College of Commissioners. This is not to criticize the officials, who do the best that the inadequate system permits. These procedural weaknesses reinforce doubts as to the legitimacy of imposing gigantic fines at the end of the process. The institution and the interested parties deserve better.

(i) Judgments

Dansk Rørindustri[81]

This appeal in the long-running pre-insulated pipes cartel saga was the first case in which the ECJ was asked to consider the legality of the Commission's 1998

---

[81] *Dansk Rørindustri*, n 86 below.

Guidelines on the method of setting fines.[82] It also gave the ECJ an opportunity to apply the twin principles of legitimate expectations and non-retroactivity to the Commission's increasing use of soft law guidelines. Finally, the case will be remembered for Advocate General Tizzano's strong criticisms of the 1998 Fining Guidelines, which arguably contributed to the Commission's revision in 2006.[83]

Following a complaint lodged in January 1995 by the Swedish company Powerpipe AB, the Commission adopted a Decision in October 1998[84] imposing fines of over €92 million on 10 companies involved in a cartel in the market for pre-insulated pipes.[85] It calculated the fines on the basis of the then novel 1998 Fining Guidelines, giving greater importance to the gravity of the infringement than to the turnover of each company on the market where the infringement took place. This was allowed by the Guidelines, but the Commission had allegedly told the companies it would not be applied. As a result, many of the smaller companies involved in the cartel were fined much larger amounts than if their fine had been based solely on their turnover. They therefore appealed the level of the fines to the CFI, alleging that the Commission had breached the principle of legitimate expectations.

However, the CFI dismissed all the appeals.[86] First, as regards the argument that the Guidelines were illegal in that the basic amounts they set for calculating fines were so high as to deprive the Commission of the discretion conferred on it by Article 15 of Regulation 17, the CFI found that the Commission was 'not required, when assessing fines in accordance with the gravity and duration of the infringement in question, to calculate the fines on the basis of the turnover of the undertakings concerned, or to ensure, where fines are imposed on a number of undertakings involved in the same infringement, that the final amounts of the fines resulting from its calculations for the undertakings concerned reflect any distinction between them in terms of their overall turnover or their turnover in the relevant product market'.[87]

The CFI further held that the Commission had not infringed the principles of proportionality and equal treatment in setting the fines, as 'the Commission is not required to ensure that the final amounts of the fines for the undertakings concerned to which its calculations lead reflect every difference between them in terms of turnover, the applicant[s] cannot criticize the Commission because the

---

[82] 1998 Fining Guidelines, above.   [83] 2006 Fining Guidelines, above.

[84] Commission Decision of 21 October 1998 (*Pre-Insulated Pipe Cartel*) [1999] OJ L24/1.

[85] Pre-insulated pipes are used in district heating systems to transport water heated in a central site to the premises to be heated. Since they carry water or steam at a very high temperature, they must be insulated to ensure economic, risk-free distribution.

[86] Case T-21/99 *Dansk Rørindustri v Commission* [2002] ECR II-1681; Case T-9/99 *HFB et al. v Commission* [2002] ECR II-1487; Case T-17/99 *KE KELIT v Commission* [2002] ECR II-1647; Case T-23/99 *LR AF 1998 v Commission* [2002] ECR II-1705; Case T-15/99 *Brugg Rohrsysteme v Commission* [2002] ECR II-1613; Case T-16/99 *Lögstör Rör v Commission* [2002] ECR II-1633; and Case T-31/99 *ABB Asea Brown Boveri v Commission* [2002] ECR II-1881.

[87] CFI judgment, paras 286–290.

starting point taken for [them] resulted in a fine higher, in percentage of total turnover, than the fine imposed on ABB'.[88]

Third, the CFI rejected the alleged breach of the principle of non-retroactivity because the Guidelines were applied to conduct which took place before they had entered into force, pointing out that the application of the Guidelines did not in fact breach the principle of non-retroactivity, because the method they laid down for calculating fines was based on the two principles set out in Article 15(2) of Regulation 17, namely the gravity and duration of the infringement, and the maximum turnover percentage of each undertaking.[89]

Fourth, the CFI rejected the alleged breach of the principle of the protection of legitimate expectations, and found that the Commission was entitled to raise the general level of fines within the limits laid down in Regulation 17 if that was necessary to ensure the implementation of competition policy.[90]

Finally, the CFI rejected the applicants' claims that their defence rights had been infringed[91] and that the contested Decision did not contain an adequate explanation of the method used to set the amount of the fines.[92]

On appeal, while the ECJ upheld the CFI's judgments, it did so on the basis that the changes in the Commission's fining policy were reasonably foreseeable, rather than on the premise that use of the Guidelines was not contrary to the principle of non-retroactivity. While a change in the Commission's general competition policy regarding fines may have an impact in terms of the principle of non-retroactivity, especially when it comes about as a result of the adoption of rules such as the Guidelines,[93] the Commission must be allowed to adjust the level of fines at any time in order to ensure the proper application of the Community competition rules. Consequently, companies cannot claim a legitimate expectation that the level of fines previously imposed or the method of calculating fines may not change during the course of administrative proceedings:[94] '[t]raders cannot have a legitimate expectation that an existing situation which is capable of being altered by the Commission in the exercise of its discretionary power will be maintained'. The ECJ therefore considered it reasonable for companies, 'at the time when the infringements concerned were committed',[95] to take into account that the Commission might choose to change its fining guidelines during the course of proceedings and apply the new guidelines to infringements committed before they were adopted.

However, the ECJ did accept that companies could have a legitimate expectation that their fine would be reduced if they cooperated with the Commission under the terms of the Leniency Notice: 'It is apparent that the legitimate expectation that traders are able to derive from the notice is limited to an assurance that their fines will be reduced by a certain percentage, but that the notice does not

---

[88] Ibid, paras 295–298. [89] Ibid, para 231. [90] Ibid, paras 241–243.
[91] Ibid, paras 202–207. [92] Ibid, para 384. [93] ECJ judgment, para 222.
[94] Ibid, para 227. [95] Ibid, paras 231, 232.

extend to the method of calculating fines or, a fortiori, to a specific level of the fine capable of being calculated at the time when the trader decides to implement his intention to cooperate with the Commission.'[96]

The case, like the *Archers Daniels Midland* appeal,[97] confirms that the Commission is entitled to exceed the level of fines imposed in previous cases and to change the method of calculating fines. The judgment gains added relevance in light of the harsher penalties under the 2006 Fining Guidelines.[98] Companies currently under investigation by the Commission now face the risk of being subject to these harsher penalties, even if the alleged infringements had already ceased when the new Guidelines were adopted.

The case is also interesting for Advocate General Tizzano's criticisms of the fairness of the 1998 Fining Guidelines. He described as 'not without foundation' the claim that 'whenever the Commission exceeded the 10% limit during the calculation procedure, it was not possible for any adjustment of the calculation (by reference to the duration of the infringement, mitigating circumstances, and so forth) made above that threshold to have any specific repercussions on the final amount of the fines.'[99] He also considered that 'the calculation method used by the Commission is not without risk as far as the fairness of the system is concerned. It does not seem to me to be fully consistent with the requirements of individualization and progressiveness of the penalty—two principles of cardinal importance in any punitive system.'[100] He recommended that the Commission should attempt to 'steer a slightly different course' as regards its fining policy, in order to ensure 'reasonableness and fairness'[101] in the future.

Archer Daniels Midland (ADM)[102]

The judgment on ADM's appeal brought to an end the proceedings resulting from a 2000 Commission Decision fining five companies, ADM (US), Ajinomoto Co and Kyowa Hakko Kogyo (Japan), and Daesang-Sewon and Cheil Jedang (Korea) a total of €1,100 million for instigating and participating in a worldwide lysine cartel.[103] On appeal to the CFI[104] by all the companies except Ajinomoto,

---

[96] Ibid, para 188.

[97] Case C-397/03 P *Archer Daniels Midland Company and Archer Daniels Midland Ingredients v Commission (ADM)* [2006] ECR I-4429.

[98] In paragraph 3 of the 2006 Guidelines the Commission explains that during the eight years of implementing the 1996 Guidelines it 'acquired sufficient experience to develop further and refine its policy on fines'.

[99] Advocate General's Opinion, para 119.

[100] Ibid, paras 129, 130.   [101] Ibid, para 133.

[102] Case C-397/03 P *Archer Daniels Midland Co. and Archer Daniels Midland Ingredients Ltd v Commission* [2006] ECR I-4429.

[103] Commission Decision of 7 June 2000 (*Amino Acids*) [2001] OJ L152/24.

[104] Case T-220/00 *Cheil Jedang Corp v Commission* [2003] ECR II-2473; Case T-223/00 *Kyowa Hakko Kogyo Co Ltd and Kyowa Hakko Europe GmbH v Commission* [2003] ECR II-2553; Case T-224/00 *Archer Daniels Midland Company and Archer Daniels Midland Ingredients v Commission* [2003] ECR II-2597; and Case T-230/00, *Daesang Corp and Sewon Europe v Commission* [2003] ECR II-2733.

the fines were slightly reduced, as the CFI disagreed with the Commission's assessment of the existence and degree of certain aggravating and mitigating factors. The CFI also made a number of interesting statements on the appropriate method for calculating fines.[105] Only ADM appealed the CFI judgment, on six grounds, the two main ones being that the judgment infringed the principles of: (a) non-retroactivity and equality by upholding the Commission's retroactive application of the 1998 Fining Guidelines;[106] and (b) a corollary of the *non bis in idem* principle, by holding that the Commission was not required to offset or take into account fines imposed by other authorities in respect of the same actions.

The ECJ dismissed the first of these grounds, adopting the same reasoning as in the *Dansk Rørindustri* judgment:[107] while a change in the Commission's fining policy resulting from the adoption of new guidelines might have an impact in terms of the principle of non-retroactivity, the Commission must be able to adjust the level of fines at any time to ensure the proper application of the Community competition rules. Consequently, undertakings cannot claim a legitimate expectation that the level of fines previously imposed or the method of calculating fines may not vary during the course of administrative proceedings.[108] The ECJ therefore considered it was reasonable for undertakings, 'at the time when the infringements concerned were committed',[109] to take into account that the Commission might choose to change its fining guidelines during the course of proceedings and apply the new guidelines to infringements committed before they were adopted.

The second main ground of the appeal concerned whether the Commission was required to make allowances for fines imposed by other authorities to penalize the effects of the same anticompetitive conduct in other jurisdictions. ADM presented this argument as a 'corollary to the principle of non bis in idem, namely that concurrent penalties concerning the same facts should be taken into account'.[110] The ECJ acknowledged that the EC legal order recognizes the principle as regards both decisions by Member States' authorities[111] and those of authorities in third countries, but stressed that it only applied if the actions investigated by those various authorities were identical.[112] In this case it upheld the CFI's finding that ADM's conduct assessed by the Commission was not identical to its conduct assessed by the US and Canadian competition authorities.

Although the judgment confirms that the Commission should take concurrent penalties imposed by third country authorities concerning the same facts into account when determining the level of a fine, it also severely circumscribes the possibility for undertakings to rely on that principle by clarifying that 'where the sanction imposed in a non-member country covers only the applications or effects of the cartel on the market of that State and the Community sanction covers only

---

[105] Forrester, MacLennan and Komninos, n 57 above, at 558–561.
[106] [1998] OJ C9/3.   [107] *Dansk Rørindustri*, paras 170–172.
[108] *ADM*, paras 20–22.   [109] Ibid, para 25.   [110] Ibid, para 46.
[111] Case 7/72 *Boehringer v Commission* [1972] ECR 1281.   [112] *ADM*, para 52.

the applications or effects of the cartel on the Community market, the facts are not identical'.[113] This statement seems to close the door almost entirely on the use of the principle in cartel cases, except in the narrow circumstances when the sanctions imposed by a third State also cover the application or effects of the cartel in the EU. It is not clear whether the principle extends equally to damages awards in third countries which also cover the harm caused in the EU,[114] as the judgment only refers to 'authorities of a non-member country'.

Graphite Cartel Cases—Showa Denko and SGL Carbon[115]
Over the last few years, students of competition law have become familiar with various forms of graphite, owing to its popularity as a subject of cartel activity. Graphite electrodes are used in the recycling of scrap steel into new steel in electric arc furnaces. The Commission found in 2001 that eight companies had been involved in a worldwide price-fixing cartel in the graphite electrodes sector.[116] Seven of the companies appealed the Decision but the CFI broadly upheld it, although it reduced the fines imposed.[117] Some of the companies appealed to the ECJ, whose findings in *Showa Denko* and *SGL Carbon* are analysed together here because they both deal in detail with the application of the *non bis in idem* principle to sanctions imposed outside the EU when the Commission and third country authorities charge an undertaking with the same facts. (The US DOJ and the Canadian authorities had also investigated the case and imposed penalties.) The Court held for the first time that the principle was not necessarily applicable, and that the Commission was not required to take into account the fines previously imposed by non-EU authorities—a similar result to that in the *ADM* case where a 'corollary' of the principle was before the Court.[118]

The ECJ recognized that *non bis in idem* constitutes a fundamental principle of EU law,[119] but considered that although the Commission and the other authorities had prosecuted the same international cartel, they had pursued different goals, as each authority was seeking to safeguard competition within its own jurisdiction.[120] The Court pointed out that the authorities acted under their own enforcement power within their jurisdictions, and that their assessments could

---

[113] *ADM*, para 69.

[114] The possibility for foreign purchasers to claim treble damages under the US anti-trust laws for injuries sustained in foreign commerce when the underlying anticompetitive conduct also caused effects in the US marketplace was limited by the US Supreme Court in *Hoffmann-La Roche, Ltd v Empagran SA* 542 US 1 (2004). Foreign purchasers are now precluded from bringing suit in US courts when their foreign injuries are 'independent of any adverse domestic effect'.

[115] Case C-289/04 P *Showa Denko v Commission* [2006] ECR I-5859; Case C-308/04 P, *SGL Carbon v Commission* [2006] ECR I-5977.

[116] Commission Decision of 18 July 2001 (*Graphite electrodes*) [2002] OJ L100/1.

[117] Joined Cases T-236/01, T-239/01, T-244/01 to T-246/01, T-251/01, and T-252/01 *Tokai Carbon et al. v Commission* [2004] ECR II-1181.

[118] *Showa Denko*, paras 51, 56, 60; *SGL Carbon*, paras 27, 32, 36.

[119] *Showa Denko*, para 50; *SGL Carbon*, para 26.

[120] *Showa Denko*, para 55; *SGL Carbon*, para 31.

diverge considerably.[121] It added that public international law did not prevent authorities of different countries from convicting the same person on the basis of the same facts.[122] Similarly, neither the agreement concluded with the US, which is limited to procedural questions, nor any other convention binding on the Community required the application of *non bis in idem* to facts like those at issue.[123] Thus although the Commission could take foreign fines into account, it was not required to do so, not even by the principles of proportionality and equity.[124] In the absence of any global competition regime or convention, this ruling flows logically from the mere application of the concept of State sovereignty in the international sphere. If there were a common international framework, the solution would be completely different. This could be clearly illustrated by the situation where a cartel is simultaneously identified within the territorial scope of application of the EU legal system by both Community law and the law of one or more Member States.[125]

Besides this major clarification, the two rulings shed light on various interesting issues regarding the setting of fines. Regarding the calculation of the basic fines, the Court confirmed that the Commission may divide undertakings into several categories, provided they are assigned to a category in a consistent and coherent manner.[126] When this is the case, grouping them on the basis of turnover and market share and applying different basic amounts to each category neither violates the principle of equal treatment nor exceeds the discretion enjoyed by the Commission.[127]

The Court confirmed that warning fellow conspirators of the risk of inspections by the Commission could constitute an aggravating circumstance.[128] It also emphasized that the Commission is entitled to apply a deterrence multiplier, as fines are designed not only to punish unlawful acts, but also to act as a deterrent against infringing the competition rules.[129] In this regard the Commission enjoys a particularly wide discretion as to the choice of factors to be taken into account.[130] In any event, the worldwide turnover and size of an undertaking are relevant factors that may justify the application of a deterrence multiplier.[131] The Court also stressed that some elements such as the actual intensity of the undertaking's participation do not affect the gravity of the cartel and may be taken into account at a later stage in the calculation of the fine.[132] It went on to hold that the 10% of turnover cap only applies to the final amount of the fine, and a fine may

---

[121] *Showa Denko*, paras 55–56; *SGL Carbon*, paras 31–32.

[122] *Showa Denko*, para 57; *SGL Carbon*, para 33.

[123] *Showa Denko*, paras 58–59; *SGL Carbon*, paras 34–35.

[124] *Showa Denko*, para 60; *SGL Carbon*, para 36.

[125] The Court expressly contrasted the international situation with the internal EU situation: *Showa Denko*, para 54; *SGL Carbon*, para 30.

[126] *SGL Carbon*, para 54.   [127] Ibid, paras 50, 51, 56.   [128] Ibid, para 69.

[129] *Showa Denko*, para 16.   [130] Ibid, para 36.

[131] Ibid, paras 17–18, 29, 42.   [132] Ibid, para 37.

exceed this 10% limit at intermediate stages of the calculation, provided the final amount complies with it.

With regard to defence rights, the Court recalled that the Commission's failure to communicate a document may only constitute a breach of defence rights if the Commission relied on the document and it was the only means of proving the objections. The undertaking must also show that the result would have been different if the document was removed from the file.[133] The Court also considered that the right to be heard was satisfied as soon as the Commission defined in the SO the matters of facts and law it would take into account to set the fines, including deterrence.[134]

The Court rejected the argument that a company's poor financial situation should be taken into consideration in setting the amount of the fine, because that would unjustifiably protect the least adapted undertakings. However, the consequences on unemployment and on upstream and downstream sectors may be taken into account, as provided in the 1998 Fining Guidelines, which allow the adjustment of the fine in light of the 'specific economic and social context'.[135]

Lastly, the Court confirmed that the Commission has discretion to set a default interest rate higher than the market rate if the fine is not paid in time, in order to discourage dilatory behaviour.[136]

SGL Carbon[137]

This case too was an appeal arising from the CFI's judgments in the graphic electrodes cartel,[138] but here the—successful—appellant was the Commission. One contested issue in the CFI cases concerned the scope of an undertaking's obligations when answering a request for information. SGL Carbon relied on the right not to incriminate oneself to contend that it was under no obligation to submit documents such as minutes of the meetings of the cartel. As SGL had applied for leniency, an ancillary question was whether providing such documents could lead to a reduction in the fine. The CFI rejected SGL's broad assertion of its right to remain silent, but found on the facts of the case that SGL was not obliged to provide preparatory documents for the meetings, because that would amount to requiring it to admit to infringing the competition rules. As SGL was not compelled to provide the documents, the CFI concluded that its decision to do so nevertheless should be regarded as voluntary collaboration justifying a reduction of the fine, in application of the 1996 Leniency Notice.[139]

The Commission successfully appealed this ruling. The ECJ strongly reaffirmed the principles it had previously developed in *Orkem*,[140] according to which the addressee of a request for information is compelled to cooperate actively, which

---

[133] *SGL Carbon*, paras 97–98.   [134] *Showa Denko*, para 70.
[135] *SGL Carbon*, paras 105–106.   [136] Ibid, paras 113–116.
[137] Case C-301/04 P *Commission v SGL Carbon and others* [2006] ECR I-5915.
[138] Case C-308/04 P *SGL Carbon v Commission* [2006] ECR I-5977.
[139] CFI judgment, para 409.   [140] Case 374/87 *Orkem v Commission* [1989] ECR 3283.

implies providing the Commission with all information and documents relating to the subject matter of the investigation. The ECJ considered it irrelevant that the documents might be used later to establish the existence of an anticompetitive violation.[141] It contrasted the production of existing documents with the provision of narrative responses in which an undertaking would be forced to admit its participation to an infringement.[142] Only in this latter case could the undertaking successfully invoke the right to remain silent; in the former case, the Court concluded that the undertaking could still exercise its defence rights effectively by contesting the Commission's interpretation of the documents during the administrative or judicial proceedings.[143] Since providing the documents fell within SGL's obligations, it could not benefit from a fine reduction on that ground.

This judgment resolves the previous uncertainties in the case law. Post-*Orkem* the Court had seemed ready to take a more lenient stance, as evidenced in its *PVC II* judgment, where it noted that the European Court of Human Rights (ECHR) case law had evolved since *Orkem*.[144] The CFI in *Tokai Carbon* followed the same line of reasoning. In *SGL Carbon*, however, the ECJ reverted to its previous position as expressed in *Orkem*. The strict approach it adopted is not inconsistent with existing general principles of law. The ECHR case law is far from unequivocal; one of the latest Strasbourg cases dealing with the issue held that the right not to incriminate oneself did not apply to the obligation to hand over pre-existing documents to the authorities.[145] Moreover, the scope of defence rights for legal entities is often narrower than for individuals.

Interestingly, the Court also extended the scope of the right to remain silent to elements leading to the establishment not only of an infringement, but also of aggravating circumstances. SGL had informed some of its co-conspirators of the Commission's investigations. Following the Advocate General, the Court held that the Commission could not force SGL to disclose the names of the undertakings it had warned, because this conduct could lead to an increased fine, thus implicitly recognizing that it would violate the right of non-self-incrimination.[146] In theory, the fact that SGL chose to reveal the requested names without being legally compelled to do so could have led to a fine reduction for voluntary cooperation under the leniency programme, but the Court also held that the leniency programme presupposes a 'genuine spirit of cooperation' which cannot be satisfied by incomplete or misleading replies.[147] The company was free not to answer, but once it had decided to reply, the response submitted should be complete and

---

[141] *Commission v SGL Carbon*, n 137 above, paras 40–41, 44.
[142] Ibid, para 42.   [143] Ibid, para 49.
[144] Joined Cases C-238/99 P, C-244/99 P, C-245/99 P, C-247/99 P, C-250/99 P to C-252/99 P, and C-254/99 P *Limburgse Vinyl Maatschappij et al. v Commission* [2002] ECR I-8375, para 274.
[145] ECHR judgment of 17 December 1996 in *Saunders v United Kingdom* [1996] Rec VI-2064.
[146] *Commission v SGL Carbon*, paras 66–67, 69; Opinion of Advocate General Geelhoed, paras 76–78.
[147] *Commission v SGL Carbon et al.* paras 68–69.

not misleading. The ECJ therefore overturned the CFI judgment and held that SGL could not benefit from a further fine reduction on that ground.

Finally, it may be noted that the Court decided to give final judgment rather than refer the case back to the CFI. In light of the circumstances explained above, it halved the fine reduction the CFI had granted SGL, from 8 to 4% of the fine.[148] This cases shows the risk for companies in any appeal to the ECJ that a gain at CFI level can be annulled. It also shows the Court taking a hard line approach to the rights of cartel defendants. An issue unresolved by the case, and arising in subsequent proceedings, is the right of the Commission to require information to be provided from companies located outside the EU.

Tokai Carbon[149]

The detection of one cartel may lead its members to reveal another, in the hope of thereby winning immunity or leniency. During the Commission's investigation into the graphite electrodes cartel, UCAR, one of the companies involved, applied for leniency in connection with a cartel which covered two neighbouring markets, the speciality markets for isostatic graphite and extruded graphite. In December 2002,[150] the Commission found that eight companies had participated in the cartel on the speciality graphite market between July 1993 and February 1998 and imposed fines totalling €60.6 million. UCAR, although one of the largest producers, obtained immunity for its whistle-blowing. Not very surprisingly, some of the other producers, Tokai Carbon Co Ltd, Intech EDM BV, Intech EDM AG and SGL Carbon, challenged the Decision and sought reductions of their fines. For the most part, the CFI confirmed the Decision and the calculation of the fines. However, it reduced the fine imposed on SGL from EUR 27.75 million to EUR 18.45 million, and that fine imposed on Intech EDM AG from EUR 980,000 to EUR 420,000.

The CFI found that the starting amount for SGL Carbon determined by the Commission was manifestly incorrect. To calculate the fines the Commission had relied on figures provided by the undertakings themselves. In its response to the Statement of Objections, SGL pointed to certain qualifications it had made regarding its turnover figures of EUR 80.4 million, stating that some of the figures concerned sales from outside the isostatic graphite market. SGL provided amended figures which referred exclusively to isostatic graphite, and concluded on that basis that its worldwide turnover in 1997 from isostatic graphite was EUR 45.6 million. The Decision ignored the amended figures and found that SGL's worldwide turnover in 1997 from sales of isostatic graphite was EUR 80.4 million. The CFI held that in so doing the Commission 'committed a manifest error of assessment. Although it expressly claimed that it based its decision

---

[148] Ibid, para 76.
[149] Cases T-71/03, T-74/03, T-87/03, and T-91/03 *Tokai Carbon et al. v Commission* [2005] ECR II-10.
[150] Commission Decision of 17 December 2002 (*Speciality Graphite*) [2006] OJ L180/20.

in respect of isostatic graphite solely on figures provided by the undertakings themselves, in SGL's case, the Commission took account of figures which, according to the express statements which the applicant had sent to it within the time-limit, included products other than isostatic graphite.'[151] Consequently the CFI reduced the starting amount used in calculating the fine from EUR 20 million to EUR 11.3 million—and it did not stop there, but went on to award SGL a further reduction relating to the 50% increase in its basic amount. SGL had explicitly admitted during the administrative procedure that in substance the Commission's allegations against it were true, including the fact that it was a ringleader of the cartel, and it was therefore in principle estopped from disputing those facts before the CFI. However, the CFI held that 'there is no bar to SGL challenging the increase of the basic amount as being excessive merely because it did not challenge the finding that it was a ringleader. In any event, the Court may, in its unlimited jurisdiction, review whether the 50% uplift was appropriate by assessing the respective roles played by the undertakings involved in the infringement.'[152] The CFI went on to find that since the behaviour of other members of the cartel, especially LCL and Tokai, was not readily distinguishable from that of SGL, a 50% increase in SGL's fine could not be justified, and therefore reduced it to 35%. Consequently, taking into account the reductions already granted by the Commission, the final amount of SGL's fine for its participation in the isostatic graphite cartel was reduced to EUR 9,641,970. With the fine imposed for participating in the extruded graphite cartel, this reduced SGL's total fine to EUR 18,451,970.

The CFI also reduced the fine of €980,000 imposed jointly on Intech EDM AG and Intech EDM BV. Intech argued that the Commission had breached the rule under Article 15(2) of Regulation 17 (now Article 23(4) of Regulation 1/2003) that a fine may never be more than 10% of the worldwide turnover of the company concerned. The worldwide turnover of Intech EDM BV in 2001 was EUR 11.3 million, and that of Intech EDM AG was EUR 4.2 million. The CFI observed that the 10% ceiling aims to protect undertakings 'against excessive fines which could destroy them commercially'. Thus the turnover refers not to the period of the infringements, but to a period closer to the imposition of the fine, the financial year preceding imposition.[153] When the Decision was adopted Intech EDM BV was no longer the parent company of Intech EDM AG, although both companies belonged to the same holding company. The Commission had not established that under these circumstances the companies formed part of one undertaking. Consequently the CFI limited the joint and several liability of Intech EDM AG to EUR 420,000 and reduced the fine imposed on it to that amount.[154] The effect of this ruling is that if companies which previously formed

---

[151] Judgment, para 251.　　[152] Ibid, para 327.
[153] Ibid, para 389.　　[154] Ibid, para 392.

a single economic unit have separated before the Decision is issued, each company is entitled to have the 10% ceiling applied to it individually.

The Court also clarified the question of which undertaking is the 'first' to provide the Commission with decisive evidence within the meaning of Section B(b) of the 1996 Leniency Notice. Tokai Carbon had challenged the Commission's finding that UCAR was the first such undertaking, arguing that it too had provided decisive evidence and deserved a fine reduction for doing so. The CFI found that the Commission enjoys broad discretion in determining which undertaking is the first to provide decisive evidence; it is not for the Courts to intervene unless that discretion is 'manifestly exceeded'.[155] In the CFI's view, neither Tokai nor SGL qualified as the 'first' undertaking, and the Commission's conclusion in that regard was correct.

Vitamins Cartel Appeals[156]

The Vitamins Cartel Decision[157] imposed record fines of EUR 850 million on eight companies, only two of which appealed, BASF and Daiichi. The CFI reduced BASF's fine from EUR 296.16 to EUR 236.845 million and Daiichi's from EUR 23.4 to EUR 18 million, on the basis of the Commission's misinterpretation of concepts such as 'instigator', 'leader', or 'decisive evidence'. However, the importance of the judgments is that they constitute a sort of limiting benchmark on appeals, as the CFI gave out a strong signal by blessing the Commission's argumentation of the case almost in its entirety.

The Court gave an interesting analysis of the slight nuance which differentiates the role of a cartel instigator from that of the leader in a cartel. It defined the instigator of a cartel as the company which persuades or encourages other companies to establish or join it. It is not merely a founding member, but must take the initiative by offering competitors an opportunity to collude or trying to persuade them to do so. The leader of the cartel, on the other hand, is the company which first decides to implement the agreement and thus gives it a voluntary boost by making sure it will have an effect on the market. The mere fact that the cartel members decide jointly at their meetings on price increases, including their amount, their timing and how they are implemented, cannot obscure the special responsibility of the first company to implement the agreement. However, the Court added that the first company to announce a new price or a price increase will not necessarily be regarded as the cartel leader when the price or increase has been fixed in advance by agreement with the other cartel members, who have also agreed which of them should be the first to announce it. These definitions may be key in cases where companies are challenging the treatment given by the Commission to immunity/leniency applicants.

---

[155] Judgment, paras 358–366.
[156] Case T-15/02 *BASF v Commission* [2003] ECR II-213, and Case T-26/02 *Daiichi Pharmaceutical v Commission*, [2003] ECR II-713.
[157] Commission Decision of 21 November 2001 (*Vitamins*) [2003] OJ L6/1.

The Court also clarified some terms used in the 1996 Leniency Notice,[158] explaining that 'decisive evidence'[159] is not the same as 'sufficient information'[160] to establish the cartel's existence, although it should be decisive for that purpose. It should consist of elements which could be used directly as the main evidence to support the finding of an infringement, rather than merely indicating what direction the Commission's investigation should take.[161] The Court also considered whether it is possible to provide decisive evidence orally,[162] and concluded that oral evidence, which is normally provided at a hearing, should in principle be regarded as a lower means of cooperation than the disclosure of information in writing. An undertaking which chooses to wait for the hearing and then disclose information orally must bear in mind that it runs the risk that another undertaking may provide the Commission with decisive written evidence of the cartel's existence before the hearing takes place.

Much of the above analysis applies equally to the following judgment, in which similar issues were raised by the parties and examined by the Courts.

Sodium Gluconate Cartel Appeals[163]

In these three judgments[164] the CFI upheld the Commission's Decision,[165] the first in which a fine reduction was granted under the 1996 Leniency Notice. The case is an example of the increasing cooperation between the EU and US anti-trust authorities, as it was the US Department of Justice which informed the Commission in March 1997 of a possible worldwide cartel in the sodium gluconate market.

The Decision[166] fined six producers or former producers of sodium gluconate[167] a total of €57 million for their participation in a worldwide price-fixing and market-sharing cartel between 1987 and 1995. To ensure the fines had a sufficiently deterrent effect, further upward adjustments of the starting amount were made in the case of Archer Daniels Midland (ADM) and Akzo, on the grounds that 'large undertakings have legal and economic knowledge and infrastructures which enable them more easily to recognize that their conduct constitutes an infringement and be aware of the consequences stemming from it under

---

[158] Notice on the non-imposition or reduction of fines in cartel cases [1996] OJ C207/4.
[159] Leniency Notice, Section B(b).   [160] Ibid, Section B(a).
[161] Judgment, para 493.   [162] Ibid, paras 503–506.
[163] Case T-314/01 *Avebe v Commission* [2006] ECR II-3085; Case T-322/01 *Roquette Frères SA v Commission* [2006] ECR II-3137, and Case T-329/01 *Archer Daniels Midland Company v Commission* [2006] ECR II-3255.
[164] All references are to Case T-329/01 unless otherwise stated.
[165] ADM has appealed the CFI's judgment to the ECJ in Case C-510/06 P, pending.
[166] Commission Decision of 2 October 2001 (*Sodium Gluconate*).
[167] Sodium gluconate is a chelating agent which de-activates metal ions in industrial processes used inter alia in industrial cleaning (bottle-washing, utensil-cleaning), surface treatment (de-rusting, degreasing, aluminium etching) and water treatment. Chelating agents are thus used in a wide range of industries. Sodium gluconate is sold worldwide and the competing undertakings have a worldwide presence.

competition law'.[168] The basic fine imposed on Jungbunzlauer was also increased by 50% on the ground that it had acted as ringleader of the cartel. However, the Commission also granted reductions to all the undertakings involved in the cartel, although it refused to grant the first company to come forward with information a 100% reduction in its fine[169] because it only approached the Commission after receiving a request for information.

Three of the six members of the cartel appealed the level of their fines but not their actual participation in the cartel. They put forward several pleas, the two main ones being effectively those made by ADM in the lysine cartel appeal reported above, ie that the Decision infringed the principles of non-retroactivity and equality by applying the 1998 Fining Guidelines; and that of *non bis in idem*, by holding that the Commission was not required to offset or take into account fines imposed by other authorities in respect of the same actions.

The ECJ dismissed the first of these grounds, using the same reasoning as in *Dansk Rørindustri* and the *Vitamins* appeals:[170] a change in the Commission's fining policy resulting from the adoption of new guidelines might have an impact in terms of non-retroactivity, the Commission must be able to adjust its fining policy at any time to ensure the proper application of the Community competition rules.[171] Consequently, undertakings cannot claim a legitimate expectation that the level of fines previously imposed or the method of calculating fines may not change during the course of administrative proceedings.[172] Undertakings engaging in cartel activities should bear in mind that the Commission might choose to change its fining guidelines during the course of proceedings and apply the new guidelines to infringements committed before they were adopted.

The second main ground of the appeal concerned whether the Commission was required to make allowances for fines imposed by other authorities to penalize the effects of the same anticompetitive conduct in other jurisdictions. The CFI found that those fines in fact related to other cartels in the lysine and citric acid markets, and that in any case, the principle of territoriality allows both the Commission and third country competition authorities to impose fines on undertakings which infringe their respective competition rules. The Commission was therefore not required by the principle of *non bis in idem* to take account of other fines.[173]

However, in Case T-322/01 the CFI both reduced and increased the fine imposed on Roquette. It reduced the fine because it decided the Commission had not established that one of the products made by Roquette was included in the cartel,[174] but then increased it because it found Roquette had been negligent in providing information to the Commission.[175]

---

[168] CFI judgment, para 18.
[169] Under the 1996 Notice the first undertaking to come forward was not guaranteed immunity automatically, but only at the Commission's discretion.
[170] *Dansk Rørindustri*, paras 222–232.   [171] Ibid, paras 170–172.
[172] CFI judgment, paras 53 and 79.   [173] Ibid, para 292.
[174] CFI judgment in Case T-322/01, para 55.   [175] Ibid, para 313.

Belgian Beer Cartel[176]

In this judgment the CFI lowered the fine imposed on Danone by about €2 million, but dismissed the remainder of the company's appeal against the Commission's Decision of December 2001 on cartel behaviour in the Belgian beer market.[177] The Commission had found that between 1993 and 1998, several brewers colluded illegally with a view to partitioning the Belgian beer market and fixing prices there. The Decision distinguished between two cartels, one in the so-called 'Horeca' sector (hotels, restaurants, catering), and one in the retail sector (supermarkets and other food shops), including the sale of private label beers. It was the first of a series of Decisions condemning cartels in national beer markets.[178] Fines were imposed on the largest and second-largest operators in the Belgian beer market, Interbrew and Alken-Maes, the latter as a subsidiary of Danone. Alken-Maes was found to have committed both infringements, while Danone was only held responsible for the infringements in the Horeca market. The companies were fined about EUR 45 million each. Danone appealed, requesting the annulment of the Commission decision or at least a reduction of the fine.

Danone claimed the Commission had infringed defence rights and the principle of sound administration by not giving it access to the file. The CFI recalled that the Commission is under a duty to make available to the companies concerned all documents, whether in their favour or otherwise, which it has obtained during the course of the investigation, except if confidential information is involved.[179] If the Commission is found to have relied on incriminating documents that were not in the investigation file and were not disclosed to the companies concerned, those documents should be excluded as evidence.[180] On the other hand, if documents which might have contained exculpatory evidence are not in the investigation file, the applicant must expressly ask for access to those documents. If it fails to do so during the administrative procedure, its rights in that respect will be barred in any action for annulment which may be brought against the final decision.[181]

The CFI reduced the increase in the fine for aggravating circumstances (on the basis of the 1998 Fining Guidelines) from 50% to 40%.[182] The Court agreed with the Commission that Danone had exercised coercion on Interbrew by threatening to destroy it on the French market if it refused to grant Danone a certain sales quota in the Belgian market. However, the Court also found that Interbrew

---

[176] Case T-38/02 *Groupe Danone v Commission* [2005] ECR II-4407. The ECJ has since dismissed Danone's appeal against the CFI judgment in Case C-3/06 *Groupe Danone v Commission* [2007] ECR I-1331.

[177] Commission Decision of 5 December 2001 (*PO/Interbrew and Alken-Maes*) [2003] OJ L200/1.

[178] Commission Decision of 5 December 2001 (*Luxembourg Brewers*) [2002] OJ L253/21; Commission Decision of 29 September 2004 (*Brasseries Kronenbourg—Brasseries Heineken*) [2005] OJ L184/57; Commission Decision of 18 April 2007 (*Dutch Beer Market*).

[179] *Danone*, para 33 *et seq.*   [180] Ibid, para 35.

[181] Ibid, para 37.   [182] Ibid, para 313.

had played a more active role than that described by the Commission, and that the Commission had not proved the causal link between Danone's coercion and Interbrew's extended cooperation.

The CFI confirmed the Commission's analysis of another aggravating circumstance, ie Danone's recidivism. Danone was involved in cartel cases in 1974 (glass containers)[183] and 1984 (flat glass Benelux).[184] The ruling clarifies that the concept of recidivism is not limited to any period, market or company name, and also applies to multinational and multi-product groups like Danone.[185] Neither Regulation 17[186] nor the 1998 Fining Guidelines impose a limit on how far back in time the Commission can go to take account of recidivism.[187] The principle of legal certainty remains untouched as long as an undertaking which committed an infringement is subsequently found to have committed a similar one.[188] The decisive argument for the Court was that antitrust penalties must have a deterrent effect.

Danone argued that its cooperation efforts were underestimated, and that it had been treated less favourably in that regard under the 1996 Leniency Notice[189] than Interbrew.[190] Danone only won a 10% reduction, whereas Interbrew received a 30% reduction as its cooperation was seen to be more decisive for the establishment of the infringement and, unlike Danone, it did not contest the facts after receiving the SO. In the Commission's view Danone's declaration in response to the SO, in which it did not specifically contest the facts but did add a series of observations to clarify the significance of some facts, in fact amounted to contesting those facts. The CFI upheld this part of the Decision.[191]

Interestingly, the CFI found that the Commission had misapplied the 1998 Fining Guidelines, as it had applied the percentage figure for aggravating circumstances (now +40%) to the basic amount, and then applied the percentage figure for attenuating circumstances (now –10%) to the resulting figure. The CFI ruled that according to the 1998 Guidelines, both the 40% increase and the 10% reduction (in total +30%) had to be applied to the basic amount.[192] The result was a slight increase in the total fine. This part of the judgment confirms the full jurisdiction of the CFI, as it adjusted the fine on the basis of an argument not raised by any of the parties to the procedure. It also shows that an appeal to the CFI can result in a less favourable outcome for the applicant than the appealed Decision.

---

[183] Commission Decision of 15 May 1974 (*Agreements between manufacturers of glass containers*) [1974] OJ L160/1.

[184] Commission Decision of 23 July 1984 (*Flat Glass Benelux*) [1984] OJ L212/13.

[185] *Danone*, para 345 *et seq.*   [186] See n 52 above.   [187] *Danone*, para 353.

[188] See Case T-203/01, *Manufacture française des pneumatiques Michelin v Commission* [2003] ECR II-4071.

[189] 1996 Leniency Notice, *op. cit.*   [190] *Danone*, para 464 et seq.

[191] Ibid, para 515.   [192] Ibid, paras 519–525; Case T-220/00 *Cheil Jedang*, n 104 above.

Acerinox[193]

The ECJ's judgment in *Acerinox* ended the long-running litigation resulting from the Commission's 1998 *Stainless Steel* Decision,[194] which imposed on six producers of stainless steel flat products, including Acerinox, fines ranging from ECU 810,000 to ECU 8,100,000. Acerinox was fined ECU 3,530,000. Acerinox, ThyssenKrupp Acciai speciali Terni, and ThyssenKrupp Stainless Steel all brought actions before the CFI for annulment of the Decision or, alternatively, a substantial reduction of their fines.[195] While the CFI largely upheld the Decision, it did find that the Commission had infringed the principle of equal treatment in concluding that the three undertakings had not produced any new information within the meaning of the 1996 Leniency Notice,[196] although they had admitted the existence of the founding meeting of the cartel. The CFI therefore reduced the fine imposed on Acerinox to EUR 3,136,000. Acerinox appealed the CFI's judgment to the ECJ, alleging a number of defective statements of reasoning and errors of assessment.

The ECJ agreed that the CFI's statements of reasoning were defective, as it had failed to reply to an argument concerning Acerinox's participation in a cartel in Spain.[197] The ECJ therefore annulled that aspect of the CFI's judgment,[198] but went on to find that the Commission was entitled to conclude, without committing any error of assessment, that Acerinox had participated in the agreement in all the Member States concerned.[199] Assessing the alleged lack of evidence of Acerinox's participation in the infringement in the Spanish market, the Court considered the Commission had been entitled to conclude that Acerinox had indeed participated in the cartel in Spain, and had given full reasons for its conclusion. It therefore found that the CFI had correctly applied the rule governing the burden of proof for establishing the participation of undertakings in manifestly anticompetitive meetings.[200]

The ECJ went on to reject Acerinox's plea that the Commission's refusal to grant it as substantial a fine reduction as that granted to the other cartel members on the ground that Acerinox had contested the allegations against it, even though its cooperation with the Commission was comparable to that of the other undertakings, was discriminatory and constituted a breach of Acerinox's fundamental defence rights.[201] The ECJ found that the type of cooperation which may qualify an undertaking for a fine reduction is not limited to admitting the nature

---

[193] Case C-57/02 P *Compañía española para la fabricación de aceros inoxidables SA (Acerinox) v Commission* [2005] ECR I-6689.

[194] Commission Decision of 21 January 1998 (*Alloy surcharge*) [1998] OJ L100/55.

[195] Case T-48/98 *Acerinox v Commission* [2001] ECR II-3859, and Joined Cases T-45/98 and T-47/98 *Krupp Thyssen Stainless and Acciai speciali Terni v Commission* [2001] ECR II-3757.

[196] 1996 Leniency Notice, n 158 above.   [197] *Acerinox*, para 37.

[198] Ibid, para 38.   [199] Ibid, para 107.

[200] Case C-199/92 P *Hüls v Commission* [1999] ECR I-4287, para 155; Case C-235/92 P, *Montecatini v Commission* [1999] ECR I-4539, para 181.

[201] *Acerinox*, para 82.

of the facts, but also involves admitting participation in the infringement.[202] To qualify for a further reduction, an undertaking must behave in such a way as to enable the Commission to establish the infringement more easily, and not merely respond to a statement of objections by denying any participation in the infringement.[203] This finding infringes neither an undertaking's defence rights nor the principle of equal treatment.

The judgment thus confirms the Community Courts' settled case law on the burden of proof when an undertaking's participation in cartel activities is established. It also clearly reinforces the incentives for companies to admit expressly[204] that there was a cartel and that they took part in it, as this may earn them a larger fine reduction than a company which merely does not dispute the main factual allegations in the statement of objections.

Degussa[205]

In this judgment the CFI reduced the fine imposed on Degussa AG[206] for participation in a price-fixing and information-sharing cartel concerning methionine, an amino-acid used in the production of animal feed, whose other members were Nippon Soda, Aventis (formerly Rhône-Poulenc) and its subsidiary Aventis Animal Nutrition. Degussa advanced four arguments: (a) a challenge to the legality of the fine, (b) an error in the Commission's consideration of the continuous nature and duration of the infringement, (c) Commission errors of fact and law in setting the level of the fine, and (d) breach of professional secrecy.

Degussa began by challenging the legality of Article 15.2 of Regulation 17 under Article 241 EC, claiming that it did not set out in sufficient detail what the Commission's decisional practice should be, and thus infringed the principle of legal certainty. The CFI rejected Degussa's arguments, finding in particular that Article 15.2 specified a ceiling for fines (10% of turnover), that the Commission had to respect the principles of equal treatment and proportionality, and that it had established a legal fining practice. Degussa also raised Article 7(1) of the ECHR, but this was held to be irrelevant given the non-criminal nature of the Commission proceedings.

Secondly, Degussa admitted participating in the infringement from 1986 to 1988 and 1992 to 1997, but denied participating throughout the period from 1986 to 1999 as asserted by the Commission. Degussa argued that the Commission had failed to consider that there were no unlawful agreements between 1988 and 1992 and that the agreements were terminated in 1997; indeed, it had failed to prove that any unlawful conduct took place during those periods. However, the CFI found that although the Commission had not presented any evidence to suggest a price-fixing agreement between 1988 and 1992, there was evidence

---

[202] Ibid, para 91.   [203] Ibid, para 94.   [204] Ibid, para 93.
[205] Case T-279/02 *Degussa v Commission* [2006] ECR II-897.
[206] Commission Decision of 2 July 2002 (*Methionine*) [2003] OJ L255/1.

that sensitive commercial information was discussed during that period and that members had not distanced themselves expressly from the cartel. The Court also found that despite the withdrawal of one member, there was a single continuous infringement, and that there was evidence that the members of the cartel still met between 1997 and 1999.

Degussa had more success with its arguments regarding the level of the fine imposed. Although the CFI rejected its argument that the Commission had failed to provide sufficient reasoning when setting the level of the fine and had wrongly characterized the cartel as worldwide in scope, it accepted its submission that the Commission had incorrectly assessed the effect on the market. In particular, the CFI found that the Commission should have taken into account that there had been disagreements between the cartelists and that prices had fallen during certain periods. The CFI therefore reduced the basic fine by EUR 5 million, to EUR 30 million.

Degussa further argued that the Commission had considered incorrect turnover figures when setting the fine. It claimed the Commission should only have included the figures for SKW Trostberg from 1 July 2000, when it merged with Degussa-Hüls, and should have excluded turnover from sectors that were abandoned in 2001. The CFI rejected the latter claim but accepted the former one, although finding it insufficient grounds to annul the Decision. However, it was relevant for evaluating whether the Commission had breached its equal treatment obligation, and in light of the new turnover figure, there had been a breach. The CFI thus considered that the basic fine should only have been increased by 80%, and not 100% as in the Decision. Degussa also submitted that the Commission had not taken its level of cooperation sufficiently taken into account. The Court disagreed, finding that Degussa had not unambiguously accepted the findings in the Statement of Objections.

Finally, the Court rejected Degussa's arguments that the Commission had breached the principle of professional secrecy under Article 287 of the EC Treaty by leaking the contents of its Decision to the press, as Degussa had failed to prove that the Commission had in fact leaked any documents.

Degussa therefore lost all its arguments except that relating to the Commission's mis-assessment of the effects on the market, and succeeded only in reducing its fine from EUR 118 million to EUR 91.125 million.

Austrian Banks[207]

In June 2002, the Commission found that eight Austrian banks had participated in a hard-core cartel to fix prices for certain banking services.[208] Seven of the banks concerned appealed the Decision. The CFI's judgment contains at least four interesting points.

---

[207] Joined Cases T-259/02 to T-264/02, and T-271/02 *Raiffeisen Zentralbank Österreich AG et al. v Commission* [2006] ECR II-5169.
[208] Commission Decision of 11 June 2002 (*Austrian Banks – Lombard Club*) [2004] OJ L56/1.

First, the banks claimed the Commission was incorrect in finding that each so-called 'round table' meeting between the cartel participants was not a separate infringement of Article 81 of the EC Treaty, but a single, complex and continuous cartel arrangement between the members. They argued that each round table acted autonomously and there was no coordination between the different round tables by the Lombard Club.[209] The CFI agreed with the Commission's interpretation of the facts, finding that it was plain from the case law that an infringement of Article 81 could arise from either a single act or a combination of a number of acts. This was the case even when each separate meeting, agreement or concerted practice could on its own constitute an infringement of Article 81. When the evidence demonstrated that the individual anticompetitive acts taken together could be said to be part of an overall plan which could distort competition, the Commission was entitled to consider the infringement as single, complex, and continuous.[210]

Second, the banks claimed that the cartel was purely national in nature and could therefore have had no effect on intra-Community trade. The Court referred to the settled case law on the effect on trade between Member States,[211] holding that the Commission was correct to consider the cumulative potential effect of agreements (in this case, between the cartel's participants) to establish an effect on intra-Community trade. When an anticompetitive agreement extends throughout one Member State, this reinforces the compartmentalization of markets on a national basis and obviates the Treaty objective of market integration. Moreover, when a cartel covers the whole of a Member State, there is a strong presumption that it will assist in partitioning markets and disrupting intra-Community trade. The banks had failed to rebut this presumption, particularly because certain documents suggested that the cartel arrangements were far-reaching.[212] In the Court's view the cartel arrangements probably assisted the retention of market structures in the Austrian market, and may have reinforced certain barriers to entry to that market which the applicants had actually described in detail in their pleadings.

Third, the banks challenged the classification of the infringement as very serious, but the CFI once again upheld the Commission on this point. The Court stressed that the Commission was correct to designate price-coordination cartels as very serious infringements by their nature. For the CFI this classification

---

[209] The terms of the anticompetitive agreement between the eight banks were allegedly set out in a document known as 'Lombard 8.5', hence the use of the expression 'Lombard Club' to designate the cartel and the important judgments to which it gave rise.

[210] The Court referred to Joined Cases C-204/00 P, C-205/00 P, C-211/00 P, C-213/00 P, C-217/00 P, and C-219/00 P *Aalborg Portland A/S et al. v Commission* [2004] ECR I-123, para 258.

[211] Joined Cases C-215 and 216/96 *Carlo Bagnasco et al. v Banca Popolare di Novara soc coop arl (BNP) and Cassa di Risparmio di Genova e Imperia SpA (Carige)* [1999] ECR I-135.

[212] The Decision cited a document from one bank which claimed the arrangements extended across Austrian territory 'down to the smallest village'. Commission Press Release IP/06/492 of 14 December 2006.

was supported by the importance of the banking sector and the scale of the anticompetitive arrangements. The banks also argued that Austria's small size meant the arrangements could not be classified as very serious. The Court disagreed, holding that the limited size of the geographic market concerned was irrelevant for classifying an infringement as very serious or otherwise. In any event, the Court held that the territory of one Member State or part of one Member State may be considered a substantial part of the common market, and referred persuasively to the *Luxembourg Brewers* case[213] as evidence that the size of a Member State is not a relevant factor for assessing the gravity of an infringement.

Finally, one applicant argued that the Commission had relied on insufficiently reliable documents to establish its market share, and as a result had erred in calculating the starting point for its fine. The Commission categorized the banks by way of their market share in order to establish the starting points for fines. For one bank it had relied on a document relating to a different case, ie a confidential document produced in the context of the merger of Bank Austria and Creditanstalt.[214] The confidential version of this document revealed higher market shares for Österreichische Postsparkasse than the non-confidential version. In this case the CFI concluded that the Commission could only use the limited data set out in the non-confidential version to establish the starting point for Österreichische Postsparkasse's fine, and therefore reduced its fine by around EUR 3 million.

This appeal was not the first appearance of the Austrian Banks cartel before the European Courts; the cartel investigation had already given rise to another important procedural cases which is reported below.

Peróxidos Orgánicos[215]

The main interest of this case is that it gave the CFI an opportunity to reiterate clearly the rules concerning the limitation of proceedings. It arose following a Commission Decision[216] condemning a cartel in the European market for organic peroxides, chemicals used in the plastics and rubber industry, involving inter alia Akzo, Atofina, and Peroxid Chemie. The cartel was implemented in Spain in a sub-arrangement which involved the applicant and, either directly or indirectly, the other companies listed above. Peróxidos Orgánicos, a Spanish company active in the chemical industry, participated only in the Spanish sub-arrangement.

Peróxidos Orgánicos did not deny its participation in the cartel, but claimed it should not have been fined because the proceedings were time-barred under

---

[213] Case T-49/02 *Brasserie National et al. v Commission* [2005] ECR II-3033.
[214] Case IV/M.873—*Bank Austria/Creditanstalt.*
[215] Case T-120/04 *Peróxidos Orgánicos v Commission* [2006] ECR II-4441.
[216] Commission Decision of 10 December 2003 (*Organic peroxides*) [2005] OJ L110/44.

the Regulation on Limitation Periods,[217] as more than five years had passed between its alleged final involvement in the Spanish sub-arrangement and the Commission's first enquiry measures. According to Peróxidos Orgánicos, the cartel lasted until 20 March 1997. The Commission denied that a time-bar applied, arguing that Peróxidos Orgánicos knew about the main agreement, and that it was not clear exactly when it finally ceased taking part in the Spanish sub-arrangement, although in the Commission's view its involvement in the cartel had ended on 31 December 1999.

According to Article 1.1(b) of the Regulation on Limitation, the Commission's power to impose fines for infringements of competition law is limited to 'five years in the case of all . . . infringements [other than those of provisions concerning applications or notifications of undertakings or associations of undertakings, requests for information, or the carrying out of investigations]'. Article 1.2 specifies that this period begins 'upon the day on which the infringement is committed. However, in the case of continuing or repeated infringements, time shall begin to run on the day on which the infringement ceases.' Article 2 of the Regulation on Limitation Periods lays down that the limitation period may be interrupted by '[a]ny action taken by the Commission . . . for the purpose of the preliminary investigation or proceedings in respect of an infringement', including 'written requests for information'. The interruption takes effect 'from the date on which the action is notified to at least one undertaking or association or undertakings which have participated in the infringement', and each such interruption 'shall start time running afresh'.

The Court pointed out that Peróxidos Orgánicos had admitted at the hearing that the sending on 20 March 2002 of a request for information to undertakings which had participated in the Spanish sub-arrangement was an action capable of interrupting the limitation period under the terms of Article 2 of the Regulation on Limitation Periods, and that the interruption would apply to Peróxidos Orgánicos as a participant in that sub-arrangement.[218] The Court went on to consider the date on which the company's involvement in the Spanish sub-arrangement ceased, and the probative value of the evidence on which the Commission had based its assessment that Peróxidos Orgánicos had continued to take part in the Spanish sub-arrangement until at least 20 March 1997. The CFI stressed in this context that it is normally for the Commission to prove the duration of an infringement, which entails knowing the date on which it ended, irrespective of whether or not the duration is disputed as part of a defence of limitation or for other reasons. However, the 'apportionment of the burden of proof is likely to vary, . . . , inasmuch as the evidence on which a party relies may be of such a kind as to require the other party to provide an explanation or justification, failing which

---

[217] Council Regulation 2988/74 of 26 November 1974 concerning limitation periods in proceedings and the enforcement of sanctions under the rules of the European Economic Community relating to transport and competition [1974] OJ L319/1.
[218] Judgment, para 47.

it is permissible to conclude that the burden of proof has been discharged' by examining the apportionment of the burden of proof between the company and the Commission.[219]

After a careful review of the evidence, the Court concluded that 'the Commission had sufficient indicia to support the assessment in the contested decision that the Spanish sub-arrangement operated, in any event, until the end of March 1997, and did so with the participation, at least indirectly, of the applicant. Further, the applicant has been unable to dispute specifically, with supporting evidence, those indicia in such a way as to cast doubt on their probative value, or to provide an alternative convincing explanation as to why such indicia existed, in accordance with the case law. As the Commission had established the above evidence corroborating the applicant's continued participation in the Spanish sub-arrangement beyond 20 March 1997, it was for the applicant to provide an alternative explanation or justification capable of contradicting the interpretation given to that evidence, failing which it is permissible to conclude that the burden of proof borne by the Commission has been discharged.'[220]

The Court therefore concluded that as it was established that Peróxidos Orgánicos had continued to participate in the Spanish sub-arrangement until at least 20 March 1997, and the limitation was interrupted on 20 March 2002 at the latest, the proceedings against the company and the imposition of a fine were not time-barred.

Nederlandse Federatieve Vereniging voor de Groothandel op Elektrotechnisch Gebied (FEG)[221]

This case arose from a Commission Decision condemning the FEG for restrictive practices, but the main point on which the ECJ was asked to rule was the consequences of excessively lengthy Commission proceedings. The Commission had eventually found that the FEG had violated Article 81 of the EC Treaty by entering into a collective exclusive dealing arrangement, and by restricting the freedom of its members to determine their selling prices independently. However, it took 102 months—63 months, including 36 months of inaction, to complete its investigations and notify the Statement of Objections, then another 39 months (16 months before the hearing and 23 months afterwards)—to reach this conclusion. The Commission itself admitted that the proceedings had dragged on, acknowledged its partial responsibility, and consequently reduced the fine imposed by EUR 100,000.

FEG's appeal aimed to obtain the annulment of the Decision on the ground of excessive duration, or alternatively a further reduction of the fine. The CFI dismissed both pleas. It recalled that although the Commission is bound to

---

[219] Ibid, paras 51–54.   [220] Ibid, para 71.
[221] Case C-105/04 P *Nederlandse Federatieve Vereniging voor de Groothandel op Elektrotechnisch Gebied et al. v Commission* [2006] ECR I-8725.

give a decision within a reasonable period, the excessive length of proceedings only entails the annulment of the decision if it adversely affects the ability of the undertakings concerned to defend themselves.[222] The CFI distinguished two phases, before and after the Statement of Objections had been notified. It held that the length of the first phase was not relevant in itself because no formal accusations had been made at that stage.[223] It also considered that although the 23 months subsequent to the hearing were excessive, the delay had not affected FEG's defence rights.[224] It therefore upheld the Decision and refused to reduce the fine, as the Commission had already taken the excessive delay into account.[225] FEG appealed to the ECJ.

The ECJ first confirmed the CFI's distinction between the investigative phase and the remainder of the procedure following the notification of a statement of objections.[226] It also confirmed that the excessive duration of proceedings may only lead to annulment if it compromises defence rights.[227] However, unlike the CFI, both the Advocate General and the ECJ considered that an excessively lengthy first phase might affect the ability of the undertakings concerned to defend themselves in the second phase of the procedure.[228] They pointed out that the more time passes between investigative measures and the notification of a statement of objections, the more difficult it will become to obtain exculpatory evidence, especially with respect to defence witnesses, owing to management and staff changes.[229] It is therefore the total duration following the first investigative measure that must be taken into account, even though defence rights are only exercised during the second phase of the procedure.[230] The Advocate General proposed to set the judgment aside and refer the case back to the CFI, but the ECJ decided to rule on the merits.[231] It considered that the arguments put forward by FEG were *'abstract and imprecise'*,[232] and concluded that FEG failed to adduce sufficient evidence that its defence rights had actually been breached, in particular by not specifying persons whom it could not contact, when they had left FEG and what hoped-for information it had no longer been able to obtain.[233]

After recalling the limited scope of its review, the ECJ also confirmed the CFI's refusal to grant a further reduction in the fine, on the ground that the Commission had already on its own initiative reduced the fine by EUR 100,000.[234] In so doing it departed significantly from Advocate General Kokott's conclusions. She found that the CFI had committed a manifest error of law by focusing solely on the

---

[222] Joined Cases T-5/00 and T-6/00 *Nederlandse Federatieve Vereniging voor de Groothandel op Elektrotechnisch Gebied et al. v Commission* [2003] ECR II-5761, paras 73–74.

[223] Ibid, paras 78–79.   [224] Ibid, paras 85–93.

[225] Ibid, para 438.   [226] ECJ judgment, para 37.

[227] Ibid, para 43.   [228] Ibid, para 49; Opinion of AG Kokott, para 128.

[229] ECJ judgment, para 49.   [230] Ibid, para 50; Opinion of AG Kokott, paras 112, 132.

[231] CFI judgment, para 54; Opinion of AG Kokott, para 133.

[232] ECJ judgment, para 56.   [233] Ibid, paras 57–59.   [234] Ibid, paras 217–219.

second procedural phase and totally failing to consider the excessive duration of the first phase.[235] She concluded that the judgment should be set aside in its entirety and referred back to the CFI,[236] or alternatively that the ECJ should give a €50,000 reduction per year of inaction during the first phase, and a further €50,000 for the excessive duration of the second phase, leading to a total fine reduction of €200,000.

This judgment should be welcomed for recognizing, for the first time with respect to cartel investigations, that the excessive duration of either of the two procedural phases may adversely affect the defence rights of the undertakings concerned. However, it is disappointing in that the ECJ laid on the undertakings concerned the heavy burden of proving that their defence had actually been negatively affected. Moreover, the total discretion left to the Commission to assess the appropriate amount of a reduction can be criticized when the Commission itself is recognized as responsible for dragging out the proceedings.

ThyssenKrupp Stainless AG (Alloy Surcharge)[237]

This case shows the Commission's readiness to correct its mistakes following an adverse judgement by the Community courts, and thereby ensure that companies do not escape cartel fines for procedural reasons. It did so by re-adopting an original 1998 Decision concerning a cartel fixing an important part of the price of stainless steel (the 'alloy surcharge') between 1993 and 1994, in violation of Article 65 of the Treaty establishing the European Coal and Steel Community (ECSC Treaty). The original Decision had been challenged before both Community Courts, and was partly annulled insofar as it found ThyssenKrupp liable for its subsidiary Thyssen Stahl GmbH,[238] as the Commission had committed a procedural error by not explicitly inviting the parent company in the Statement of Objections to give its views on the cartel behaviour of its subsidiary. The Commission subsequently decided to re-open the procedure against ThyssenKrupp, and on 5 April 2006 it issued a new Statement of Objections correcting this error. The Commission fined ThyssenKrupp Stainless AG a total of EUR 3.168 million, applying a 20% reduction instead of the original 10% reduction, as the CFI had granted another company in comparable circumstances a 20% reduction on appeal.[239]

---

[235] Opinion of AG Kokott, para 143.   [236] Ibid, para 144.

[237] Commission Decision of 20 December 2006 (*Alloy Surcharge—re-adoption*) [2007] OJ L182/31.

[238] *Krupp Thyssen & Acciai Terni*, n 195 above; Joined Cases C-65/02 P and C-73/02 P, *ThyssenKrupp Stainless GmbH und ThyssenKrupp Acciai speciali Terni SpA v Commission* [2005] ECR I-6773.

[239] CFI judgment, para 246: the extent of their cooperation had to be 'regarded as comparable in so far as those undertakings provided the Commission, at the same stage of the administrative procedure and in similar circumstances, with similar information concerning the conduct imputed to them'.

German Banks[240]

Connoisseurs of competition law may particularly appreciate this case, with its unusual procedural elements and its exceptional concluding knock-out defeat of the Commission.

In 1999, the Commission began a cartel investigation against approximately 150 banks established in seven Member States,[241] which it suspected of having agreed to fix the prices of currency exchange services for Euro-zone Member States' currencies between 1999 and 2002. The investigation led inter alia to a Decision[242] which imposed fines on several German banks[243] for concluding an illegal agreement on currency exchange services. The banks maintained that there been no such cartel, and appealed both the substance of the Decision and the fines. The Commission failed to submit a defence to this application by the requisite deadline, due to human error when faxing the defence to the Court.

In October 2004, the CFI handed down judgment by default, annulling the Decision solely on the basis of the arguments made by the applicants.[244] The Court found the banks had shown that the Commission had not proved the existence of an agreement to the requisite legal standard. The Commission subsequently applied to have the judgment by default set aside. In September 2006 the CFI rejected the application, but decided that an applicant is in principle free to develop arguments in an application to set aside a default judgment, and may therefore comment on pleas by the respondent which the Court did not consider in the default judgment. The Court was therefore required to render a full judgment in such a case.

In its judgment the Court found the Commission's application admissible, and then re-examined the substance of the case on the basis of the arguments raised by the Commission and the submissions by the banks. With regard to the evidence of the meetings between the banks, it concluded that the Commission had not established to the requisite standard that there was an agreement between the alleged participants on the commission charges. In particular, the Court held that the Commission had erred in finding[245] that the banks had concluded a prohibited agreement or concerted practice at a specific meeting on 15 October 1997 in Frankfurt, where they agreed on a commission rate of about 3% for the buying and selling of Euro-zone banknotes during the transitional period (ie from the inception of the Euro as the European currency in 1999 until the date of its introduction in January 2002). The CFI concluded that the main reason for the meeting in question was the legal uncertainty prevailing as to whether fees could

---

[240] Joined Cases T-44/02 OP, T-54/02 OP, T-56/02 OP, T-60/02 OP, and T-61/02 OP *Dresdner Bank et al. v Commission (German Banks)* [2006] ECR II-3567.

[241] Belgium, Germany, Ireland, the Netherlands, Austria, Portugal, and Finland.

[242] Commission Decision of 11 December 2001 (*Bank charges for exchanging Euro-zone currencies—Germany*), [2003] OJ L15/1.

[243] Commerzbank, Dresdner Bank, HVB, DVB, and VUW.

[244] Under Rule 122 of the CFI's Rules of Procedure.   [245] Decision, para 2.

be charged for such exchange operations. The Commission had not taken this factor into account in its market analysis, nor provided sufficient direct evidence from which it could be concluded without any doubt that the banks had entered into an agreement. Although the Commission had shown that the banks had referred during meetings to approximate levels of commissions (which were in any case known throughout the industry), it had failed to show the existence of a concurrence of wills between them.

Interestingly, the judgment sheds light on the rather opaque subject of the standard of proof to which the Commission must adhere in its presentation of arguments and use of evidence in cartel proceedings. The Court stated: 'None the less, the direct evidence relating to the meeting of 15 October 1997 is not sufficient for it to be considered, *without any reasonable doubt remaining on that point*, that the banks present concluded such an agreement. Although the elements cited by the Commission demonstrate that some of the banks present referred to the approximate level of commissions—which were in fact a matter of public knowledge—during the meeting, those indicia do not suffice to support to the requisite standard of proof the theory that there was a concurrence of wills on the common fixing of those prices'[246] (emphasis added).

On the basis that there was no agreement between the parties for the purposes of Article 81(1), it was not necessary for the CFI to consider any other pleas. Accordingly, the Commission had not produced sufficient evidence to justify modifying the judgment by default, and its application was dismissed.

There was no further appeal by the Commission in this case. The principles established by the CFI can be expected to be tested by defendants in other, more 'mainstream' appeal procedures.

French Beef[247]

In December 2006, the CFI dismissed an action brought by four French federations of farmers and one French federation of slaughterers, and in essence upheld a widely publicized Commission Decision[248] which imposed substantial fines on the federations for concluding a minimum price agreement and agreeing to suspend or at least limit beef imports into France from other Member States. The circumstances of the case were exceptional, as the agreement was concluded in an

---

[246] Judgment, para 145.

[247] Joined Cases T-217/03 and T-245/03 *Fédération Nationale de la Coopération Bétail et Viande (FNCBV) v Commission* and *Fédération nationale des syndicats d'exploitants agricoles (FNSEA) Fédération nationale bovine (FNB), Fédération nationale des producteurs de lait (FNPL) and Jeunes agriculteurs (JA) v Commission* [2006] ECR II-4987. An application by the Fédération Nationale de l'Industrie et des Commerces en Gros de Viandes (FNICGV), a federation representing slaughterers, which sought only the annulment or reduction of its fine under Article 229 of the EC Treaty was declared inadmissible by Order of 9 November 2004, as the time limit of two months laid down in Article 230 of the EC Treaty had expired. The CFI stated that an autonomous proceeding under Article 229 of the EC Treaty was not possible and was as such subject to the limitations on control of legality.

[248] Commission Decision of 2 April 2003 (*French Beef*) [2003] OJ L209/12.

atmosphere of crisis and tension due to widespread demonstrations by farmers, and were even supported by the French government.

The pleas of law put forward by the applicants related to the specific nature of the agricultural sector. First, on the material scope of application of the competition rules, the CFI qualified the federations as associations of undertakings grouping farmers together.[249] Since farmers incontestably engage in an economic activity and thus qualify as undertakings, the claim by some of the applicants that they were in fact trade unions rather than undertakings was unsurprisingly rejected. In substantive terms the applicants denied that the agreement was restrictive, but the CFI, following settled case law, found that it constituted a restriction by object and rejected attempts by the parties to invoke the exceptional circumstances of the case.[250] Equally, the CFI refused to accept that 'the freedom of trade unions to protect their collective interests' justified conduct which infringed Article 81(1) of the EC Treaty.[251]

The applicants went on to argue that the agreement should benefit from the exemption in Regulation 26/62[252] for activities related to production of and trade in agricultural products which are necessary for realizing the objectives of the common agricultural policy. The Court rejected this argument, as the agreement did not stabilize the market or aim to ensure a fair standard of living for the agricultural community, two objectives of the common agricultural policy set out in the Treaty.

A third plea disputed the duration of the infringement. As the agreement was entered into by local federations, the national federations claimed that the Commission should not have taken that agreement into account. The CFI upheld the Commission's finding that the local federations were members of the national federations and had been called on by the national federations to implement the agreement. The Commission found that the cartel had lasted beyond the written agreement (24 October–30 November 2001), despite its warning that the agreement was unlawful, and claimed that a secret oral agreement had existed until 11 January 2002. The Court confirmed the Commission's conclusion, referring to the substantial body of evidence supporting it.[253]

Alternatively, the applicants asked for a substantial reduction of the fines imposed by the Commission. Here the Court obliged: it increased the 60% reduction granted by the Commission to a 70% reduction due to the specific economic context, which was an objective factor to be taken into account under point 5(b) of the 1998 Fining Guidelines. The exceptional circumstances arising

---

[249] Judgment, para 48.

[250] Ibid, paras 81–94, including the regulated character of the market, ministerial support, and the background of the crisis.

[251] Ibid, para 101.

[252] Regulation No 26 of 4 April 1962 applying certain rules of competition to production of and trade in agricultural products, OJ (English Special Edition Series I-1959–1962), 129.

[253] Judgment, para 189.

from the mad cow crises in the beef sector and the fact that the agreement was exclusively between federations dealing with two levels of the production chain of a basic agricultural product justified this reduction.[254]

Importantly, the CFI made some interesting statements on the calculation of fines, notably on the legal ceiling of 10% of turnover.[255] The Court criticized the Commission for failing to explain how it had calculated the ceiling: when the Commission fines an association of undertakings and calculates compliance with the 10% ceiling on the basis of the turnover achieved by the members, it is obliged to state this expressly in its decision and set out the reasons justifying that approach.[256] However, this failing had no consequences. Moreover, the Court stated that the 10% ceiling must not be calculated by reference to the turnover of the federations, but to that of each undertaking belonging to the association of undertakings, provided it was active on the affected market. The previous case law required an association to be able to bind its members by virtue of its internal rules, but the Court believed its solution was justified in this case, as the infringements bore on the activities of its members and benefited them. This method of calculation does in fact reflect more appropriately the association's economic power and influence on the market, an essential element in the deterrent character of the fine.

(ii) Commission Decisions
Rubber chemicals[257]
In December 2005, the Commission decided that four producers of rubber chemicals had entered into a cartel agreement which covered at least the EEA from 1996 to 2001. Rubber chemicals are used in the tyre industry to improve the performance or the production process of rubber. The investigation started in 2002 following Flexsys' application for leniency, which led to dawn raids on the premises of Crompton, Bayer, and General Química. All the cartel members filed for leniency during the proceedings.

The cartel was a classic price-fixing and information exchange agreement. The parties coordinated their price increases, including amounts, markets targeted, and announcements. They also monitored their respective market shares and set up a means of compensating important shifts from the agreed allocation. The Commission recalled that it is up to a company which attends manifestly anticompetitive meetings to rebut the presumption that it tacitly approved the unlawful agreement, by proving that it either distanced itself sufficiently or reported the cartel to the authorities.

---

[254] Ibid, paras 299–334.
[255] Article 15(2) of Regulation 17, modified by Article 23(2) of Council Regulation 1/2003 of 16 December 2002 on the implementation of the rules on competition laid down in Articles 81 and 82 of the Treaty [2003] OJ L1/1.
[256] Judgment, paras 233–245.
[257] Commission Decision of 21 December 2005 (*Rubber chemicals*) [2006] OJ L353/50.

With regard to duration, the Commission could only prove the existence of the cartel from 1996 to 2001. The continuous nature of the infringement was not contradicted by periods of conflict and temporary returns to more competitive prices, especially given the continuous effect of the cartel and the fact that the parties continued to communicate with each other.

The Commission found Repsol liable for the involvement of its subsidiary General Química, on the basis that a parent company may be presumed liable for illegal conduct by a wholly-owned subsidiary unless it can reverse this presumption by showing that it did not in fact exercise a decisive influence over the subsidiary's general commercial policy. There is no need in such cases to show that the parent company encouraged the illegal behaviour or was even involved in the daily management of the subsidiary, but the fact that the parent was the sole shareholder for a long period is relevant.

The Commission concluded that the cartel constituted a very serious infringement, and that as cartels *ipso facto* seek to restrict competition, it was irrelevant that this particular one had been 'largely ineffective'. To determine the respective weight of each cartel participant, the Commission relied on worldwide market shares because the cartel was in fact global, but it also took into account the value of the product market in the EEA. Applying differential treatment, the Commission considered that to ensure each individual fine acted as an effective deterrent, it should be proportionate to the size of the undertaking concerned.

The Commission reduced General Química's fine by 50% due to its passive role in the cartel, which was limited to being informed of and accepting the agreements reached by the other members. Its participation in the collusive contacts was also significantly more sporadic than that of the other members of the cartel. However, the Commission did not accept that because Crompton did not act as a leader of the cartel, this meant that it was only a passive or minor participant.

The Commission refused to reduce the fines because the infringement had been terminated immediately and voluntarily before an investigation was opened. It took the view that this would be grounds for a reduction only if the conduct was not manifestly anticompetitive; moreover, it had taken the voluntary termination of the infringement sufficiently into account when calculating the duration of the cartel. The Commission also refused to reduce the fines for companies which had implemented a compliance programme, pointing out that this did not change the fact of the infringement and the need to penalize it. However, Flexsys won full immunity for being the first company to disclose the existence of the cartel and provide the Commission with sufficient evidence to carry out dawn raids. Crompton challenged Flexsys' privileged status, alleging that it had not disclosed all available materials, had coerced other companies and had continued the infringement after applying for leniency. The Commission concluded that these very serious allegations were not supported by the evidence. With regard to the evidence Flexsys had provided, the Commission added that if there were no weaknesses or uncertainties in the case after the first leniency application, there would be no scope left for subsequent leniency applications to fulfil the requirement of 'significant added value'. Lastly, the Commission repeated that the possible withdrawal of the first conditional immunity would in no way affect the position of the subsequent applicants.

The Commission emphasized that companies which seek leniency must cooperate fully, which entails assuming their responsibilities and not hiding behind individual employees who are not forthcoming. The Commission also warned leniency applicants that the strategy (adopted by Bayer) of attempting to weaken the Commission's case with regard to each piece of evidence and each event showing the existence of the cartel prior to a certain date cast serious doubt on the extent and continuity of its cooperation.

Copper Fittings[258]

In September 2006, the Commission fined 30 companies belonging to 11 different corporate groups a total of EUR 314.76 million for taking part in an illegal price-fixing cartel in the copper fittings sector. This was then the fifth largest set of fines ever imposed on a cartel. Copper fittings, which include copper alloy fittings such as gunmetal, brass, and other copper-based alloys), are used in plumbing and sanitary applications to connect tubes carrying water, air, or gas. The various forms of fittings, such as end-feed, solder ring, compression, press, and push-fit, were all covered by the cartel. The EEA market in these products is estimated to be worth around EUR 550 million. The Commission found that between 1988 and 2004 the companies had fixed prices, price increases, discounts and rebates, allocated customers, and exchanged commercially sensitive information at a number of meetings, handwritten notes of which were used as evidence against the members. The cartel was found to constitute a single, complex and continuous infringement, which started as an arrangement between the UK manufacturers and grew to include European companies as their operations spread to continental Europe.

Mueller was the first company to come forward under the Commission's leniency programme, and for this and for continuing to cooperate with the Commission investigation it received full immunity, thus avoiding a fine which would otherwise have been over €10 million. Its leniency application in January 2001 was followed by a number of dawn raids. The fines of IMI, Delta and Frabo were also reduced by 50%, 20%, and 20%, respectively for their assistance under the leniency programme.

The Commission increased by 60% the fines on four of the groups, Aalberts, Delta, Advanced Fluid Connections, and Legris, because it found they had continued their illegal arrangements even after the Commission's initial investigations. Advanced Fluid Connections' fine was increased by a further 50% because it provided the Commission with misleading information during the investigation.

Appeals by some of the companies concerned are pending.

---

[258] Commission Decision of 20 September 2006 (*Fittings*) [2007] OJ L283/63.

Industrial Bags[259]

In November 2005, the Commission fined 16 companies in the market for industrial plastic bags used to pack products such as animal feed, fertilizers, and building materials a total of €290.71 for operating an illegal cartel.

Following a tip-off from one of the cartel members, the Commission carried out dawn raids in June 2002. It claimed to have found evidence that the cartel had been active for over 20 years. Participants had fixed prices in Germany, Belgium, the Netherlands, Luxembourg, France, and Spain, agreed sales quotas by geographic area, shared orders from large customers, exchanged information on their sales volumes, and organized collective bidding in response to invitations to tender. The agreements were allegedly made in the course of meetings of the Valveplast trade association and were arranged by the companies' senior management. The Commission claimed to have written evidence of its findings and referred to documents instructing the destruction of incriminating evidence, indicating that the companies knew their activities were illegal. In light of the nature and duration of the infringement and the wide area affected, the Commission characterized the cartel as a very serious infringement.

In deciding the amount of the fines, the Commission took account of the firms' differing economic weight. Thus because of its size and economic strength, UPM-Kymmene's fine was doubled, to EUR 56.55; moreover, its basic fine was increased by 50% for recidivism, as it had previously taken part in the Cartonboard cartel.[260] The Commission also took account of the aggravating factor that during the inspections a Bischof + Klein employee had destroyed a document which Commission officials had indicated they wanted to see, and increased that firm's basic fine by 10%. For a number of firms the fine reached the maximum of 10% of their turnover. However, the firm which blew the whistle on the cartel, British Polythene Industries (BPI), escaped a fine of EUR 56.95 million by receiving full immunity under the Commission's 1996 Leniency Notice. Six other firms provided the Commission with information and therefore enjoyed fine reductions ranging from 30% to 10%.

Appeals were lodged with the CFI in February 2006.[261]

---

[259] Commission Decision of 30 November 2005 (*Industrial bags*) [2007] OJ L282/41.
[260] Commission Decision of 13 July 1994 (*Cartonboard*) [1994] OJ L243/1.
[261] Case T-26/06 *Trioplast Wittenheim (TW) v Commission*; Case T-40/06 *Trioplast Industrier AB v Commission*; Case T-43/06 *Cofira SAC v Commission* (removed from the register on 6 July 2006); Case T-51/06 *Fardem Packaging v Commission*; Case T-53/06 *UPM-Kymmene (UPM) v Commission*; Case T-54/06 *Kendrion v Commission*; Case T-55/06 *RKW v Commission*; Case T-59/06 *Low & Bonar (LB) and Bonar Technical Fabrics (BTF) v Commission*; Case T-64/06 *FLS Plast (FLSP) v Commission*; Case T-65/06 *FLSmidth (FLS) v Commission*; Case T-66/06 JM *Gesellschaft für industrielle Beteiligungen (JMG) v Commission*; Case T-68/06 *Stemphe and Koninklijke Verpakkingsindustrie Stempher (Stempher) v Commission*; Case T-72/06 *Groupe Gascogne v Commission*; Case T-76/06 *Plásticos Españoles (Aspla) v Commission*; Case T-78/06 *Armando Álvarez v Commission*; Case T-79/06 *Sachsa Verpackung v Commission*.

C. Vertical Agreements

(i) *GlaxoSmithKline Services (GSK Spain)*[262]

This was by far the most important case of the last years in the area of distribution agreements and parallel trade. In *GSK Spain*, a Community Court dealt for the first time with the substantive question of whether a pharmaceutical company may, without infringing Article 81 of the EC Treaty, establish different regimes for selling its products, depending on whether the reseller's intention was to deliver them under the mandatory state public health system or was to deliver them on the open market. The CFI upheld GSK's challenge to the Commission's refusal of an exemption in a Decision which had improperly disregarded GSK's submissions on the realities of the pharmaceutical industry.

GSK notified to the Commission its 'General Sales Conditions' for wholesalers of pharmaceutical products, whereby its medicines were to be sold to Spanish wholesalers at prices differentiated according to whether or not they were reimbursable under the Spanish health insurance scheme. In practice, medicines intended to be reimbursed in other Member States were to be sold at a higher price than those intended to be reimbursed in Spain, where the Spanish government had set prices at a quite low level, reflecting its budgetary constraints. The Commission considered that the sales conditions had the object and effect of restricting competition and that GSK had not shown they contributed to the promotion of technical progress, the first condition for exemption under Article 81(3) of the EC Treaty.[263] The case is known as the 'dual pricing' case, but this is something of a misnomer, as in reality GSK had agreed only one price with its wholesalers, the price which referred to medicines not reimbursable under the Spanish legislation. There was another, much lower, price for medicines reimbursable in Spain under the national legislation, but this was a price set by the Spanish State and not by GSK. In addition, the Spanish legislation expressly intended that State-set price to be confined to Spanish territory, for products reimbursable under the Spanish legislation.

The CFI's most interesting findings clearly refer to Article 81(1). Thus it found that the applicability of Article 81(1) cannot depend merely on whether an agreement may limit parallel trade, but must also depend on whether its object or effect may limit competition, to the detriment of the *final consumer*:[264] 'Consequently, while it is accepted that an agreement intended to limit parallel trade must in principle be considered to have as its object the restriction of competition, *that applies in so far as the agreement may be presumed to deprive final consumers of*

---

[262] Case T-168/01 *GlaxoSmithKline Services Unlimited v Commission*, [2006] ECR II-2969. Two of the authors of this survey represented GSK before the CFI and represent the company in the appeals.

[263] Commission Decision of 8 May 2001 (*Glaxo Wellcome*) [2001] OJ L302/1.

[264] Judgment, para 119.

those advantages... However, if account is taken of the legal and economic context in which GSK's General Sales Conditions are applied, it *cannot be presumed that those conditions deprive the final consumers of medicines of such advantages.* In effect, the wholesalers, whose function, as the Court of Justice has held, is to ensure that the retail trade receives supplies with the benefit of competition between producers are economic agents operating at an intermediate stage of the value chain and may keep the advantage in terms of price which parallel trade may entail, in which case that advantage *will not be passed on to the final consumers*' (emphasis added).[265]

The CFI further noted that the price of pharmaceuticals, set by national ministries in function of their own choices concerning budget, public health, encouragement of investment and other public policy considerations, lies 'structurally outside the play of supply and demand and is established at structurally different levels throughout the Community'.[266] This meant, according to the CFI, that '[a]s the prices of the medicines concerned are to a large extent shielded from the free play of supply and demand owing to the applicable regulations and are set or controlled by the public authorities, it cannot be taken for granted at the outset that parallel trade tends to reduce those prices and thus to increase the welfare of final consumers'.[267]

According to the Court, the specific context of the pharmaceutical sector made it necessary for the Commission to undertake an effects-based analysis under Article 81(1) EC.

Ultimately the Court upheld the Commission's subsidiary conclusion under Article 81(1) and found that the notified agreement restricted competition by effect, albeit only slightly. However, it annulled those parts of the Decision that rejected GSK's request for an exemption under Article 81(3), because the Commission had not appropriately addressed GSK's 'relevant, reliable and credible' arguments about the effects of parallel trade on its research and development in perhaps the most innovation-driven of industries.[268]

The Court's judgment relies heavily on the special characteristics of the pharmaceutical sector to reach its conclusions. It notes, in particular, the importance of competition by innovation. The Court accepted that a pharmaceutical company's return on investment is highly dependent on a limited number of products which are increasingly costly to develop and enjoy less and less time on the market before patent expiry. Parallel trade represents a clear reduction of the possibility of pharmaceutical companies to invest more in research and development. At the same time, it was clear that no significant added value flows from parallel trade for the final consumer. The largest beneficiaries of parallel trade, the parallel traders themselves, contribute nothing to patient welfare or medical/pharmaceutical innovation. They generate exceptional profits which are lost from

---

[265] Judgment, paras 121–122.   [266] Judgment, para 141.
[267] Judgment, para 147.   [268] Judgment, para 263 *et seq.*

the productive process of the industry. If GSK were allowed to impose certain limitations on parallel trade, that would be beneficial for innovation: 'The fact that the profit is retained by the producer will in all likelihood give rise to a gain in efficiency by comparison with the situation in which the profit is shared with the intermediary, because a rational producer which is able to ensure the profitability of its innovations and which operates in a sector characterised by healthy competition on innovation has every interest in reinvesting at least a part of its surplus profit in innovation.'[269]

GSK,[270] the Commission[271] and two of the interveners, EAEPC[272] and Aseprofar,[273] have all appealed the CFI's judgment in *GSK Spain*. However, notwithstanding these pending appeals, it is already possible to identify a number of positive effects from the CFI ruling on the interpretation of Article 81.

In Community law certain restrictions systematically qualify as 'restrictions by object', in particular naked price-fixing, customer allocation or output restrictions; or minimum resale price maintenance. This is because such restrictions are considered to be always detrimental to consumers and to have no redeeming social value; hence their condemnation in the EU as restrictions 'by object' (and in US anti-trust law as *per se* restrictions).[274] Restrictions of parallel trade, in particular, have usually been viewed with suspicion.

In *GSK Spain* the CFI found that while a restriction 'by object' must by its nature incontrovertibly have serious negative anticompetitive consequences for consumers, and this must be apparent from the nature of the restriction itself with no need for any further examination of its actual effects, this assumption simply cannot work in the pharmaceutical sector because of its special characteristics. The CFI was particularly concerned that no evident harm was caused to consumers by a limitation on parallel trade in pharmaceuticals. It is this fact that formed the basis of the CFI's ruling that there was no restriction of competition 'by object'.

Some commentators start from these premises to state that 'until recently market integration and economic freedom seemed to have overshadowed efficiency considerations in the objectives of European competition policy'.[275] Others note that along with other recent CFI judgments,[276] *GSK Spain* emphatically reminds us that consumer welfare should be the ultimate aim of EC competition law.[277]

---

[269] Judgment., para 274.   [270] Case C-501/06 P.   [271] Case C-513/06 P.
[272] Case C-515/06 P.   [273] Case C-519/06 P.
[274] See, however, recently *Leegin Creative Leather Prods, Inc v PSKS, Inc* 551 US (2007), where the US Supreme Court overruled its 100 year-old legal precedent (*Dr Miles Medical Co v John D Park & Sons Co*, 220 US 373), which had held that resale price maintenance is *per se* illegal. Under US anti-trust law, such arrangements should now be examined pursuant to a rule of reason analysis.
[275] See Cseres, 'The Controversies of the Consumer Welfare Standard', (2006) 3(2) CompLRev 121, at 151.
[276] See *O2 (Germany)* (n 333 below) and *Austrian Banks* (n 208 above), reviewed elsewhere in this survey.
[277] See Nikpay, Kjølbye, and Faull, 'Article 81', in Faull and Nikpay (eds), *The EC Law of Competition* (Oxford, 2007) 260.

While not agreeing or disagreeing with these commentaries, we wish to stress that in our view, the CFI rejected the argument that market integration and consumer welfare are antithetical aims; it did no more than underline the importance of consumer harm as a necessary element of restriction of competition. A restriction of competition 'by object' would require a judgment or presumption based on a shared consensus of economic opinion that a particular contractual provision or agreement (the best known example being a cartel) always reduces consumer welfare by its very nature. Indeed, this was implicit in *Consten & Grundig*,[278] as the CFI explained in *GSK Spain*: '[I]n *Consten and Grundig v Commission*...the Court of Justice, contrary to the Commission's contention in its written submissions, *did not hold that an agreement intended to limit parallel trade must be considered by its nature, that is to say, independently of any competitive analysis, to have as its object the restriction of competition.* The Court of Justice...carried out a competitive analysis, abridged but real, during the course of which it held, in particular, that the agreement in question sought to eliminate any possibility of competition at the wholesale level in order to charge prices which were sheltered from all effective competition, considerations which led it to reject a plea alleging that there was no restriction of competition' (emphasis added).[279]

In other words, while Community competition law has shown a certain predisposition to protect the single market, it has not done so without paying attention to the ultimate goal of consumer welfare. Rather, the protection of parallel trade and the single market imperative have been seen as a proxy for safeguarding consumer welfare. This means that in exceptional cases where parallel trade and the resulting intra-brand competition offer no substantial benefits to consumers, while at the same time negatively affecting inter-brand competition, parallel trade as such should not merit protection by the competition rules. Exactly as the CFI held, *Consten & Grundig* is no less a case about consumer welfare than is *GSK Spain*.

Indeed, this approach is not unknown to the Commission, whose Article 81(3) Guidelines stress that 'the objective ... is to protect competition on the market as a means of enhancing consumer welfare and of ensuring an efficient allocation of resources'.[280] Further, the Article 81(3) Guidelines note that competition and market integration 'serve these ends since the creation and preservation of an open single market promotes an efficient allocation of resources throughout the Community for the benefit of consumers.'[281] In other words, the Commission sees market integration not as an aim in itself, but rather as a proxy (an indicator) of consumer welfare, exactly as the CFI viewed it in referring to *Consten &*

---

[278] Joined Cases 56/64 and 58/64 *Établissements Consten SARL and Grundig-Verkaufs-GmbH v Commission* [1965] ECR, English special edition, p 299, at 342.

[279] Judgment, para 120.

[280] Commission Notice—Guidelines on the Application of Article 81(3) of the Treaty [2004] OJ C101/97, para 13.

[281] Ibid.

Grundig. Viewed in this way, the Spanish *GSK* case is not a revolution, but rather a sensible confirmation of a long-standing truth. It remains to be seen whether this approach will be followed by the Court of Justice.

(ii) CEPSA[282]

In this reference for a preliminary ruling by the Spanish *Tribunal Supremo*, the Court was asked to consider the fuel distribution agreements concluded between CEPSA and a number of service station operators in Spain, which allegedly gave rise to practices restricting competition. The *Tribunal Supremo*'s question related to whether certain clauses contained in those agreements, classified as commission or agency contracts, came under a block exemption relating to motor vehicle and other fuels.

The Court began by considering its jurisdiction and the admissibility of the request, as the Commission and CEPSA (the defendant in the main proceedings) both submitted that no reply should be given to the question referred by the Spanish court. CEPSA argued that the matter concerned domestic law as the European Regulation in question had been incorporated into domestic law, and thus the Court had no jurisdiction. CEPSA also argued that there was no effect on trade between the Member States, so that Article 81(1) of the EC Treaty was not applicable in the main proceedings. The Court rejected these arguments, stating that where 'in regulating internal situations, domestic legislation adopts the same solutions as those adopted in Community law in order, as in the case in the main proceedings, to avoid any distortion of competition, it is clearly in the Community interest that, in order to forestall a risk of future differences of interpretation, provisions or concepts taken from Community law should be interpreted uniformly, irrespective of the circumstances in which they are to apply'.[283] The Commission, on the other hand, argued that the factual context of the dispute in the main proceedings was not described in sufficient detail for a useful answer to be provided. The Court recognized that some relevant information had not been included in the reference, but found that despite the gaps it was still possible to determine the scope of the question referred.

The Court then considered the main substantive issue, namely whether exclusive fuel distribution contracts with characteristics described by the Spanish court fell within the scope of Article 81 and Regulation 1984/83. It recalled that vertical agreements such as those concerned in these proceedings were covered by Article 81 only when the operator was regarded as an independent economic operator and there was therefore an agreement between two undertakings. In this context the Court also noted that for the purposes of determining whether two

---

[282] Case C-217/05 *Confederación Española v Compañía Española de Petróleos SA* [2006] ECR I-11987.
[283] Judgment, para 20.

entities constituted two 'undertakings', the decisive test was the unity of their conduct on the market, not their formal separation. By way of example, the relationship between principal and agent could be characterized by such economic unity.

The Court stated that to determine whether a service-station operator was an independent economic operator, it was necessary to consider the agreement concluded with the principal, particularly the clauses (both express and implied) relating to financial and commercial risks associated with the sales of goods to third parties. The Court agreed with the Commission that 'the question of risk must be analysed on a case-by-case basis, taking account of the real economic situation rather than the legal classification of the contractual relationship in national law.' The Court then set out the criteria to be considered by a national court when assessing the actual allocation of risk, including the risks linked to the sale of the goods and those linked to investments specific to the market, ie the investments enabling the service-station operator to negotiate or conclude contracts with third parties. It stated that when those risks are negligible Article 81 is not applicable, but only in respect of the obligations imposed on the intermediary in the context of the sale of goods to third parties. Indeed, when agents can be considered to be acting as independent operators, agency contracts may contain exclusivity and non-competition clauses which relate to the relationship between agent and principal. These types of provisions could infringe the competition rules insofar as they entailed locking up the market concerned.

Finally, the Court noted that Regulation 1984/83 did not list the imposition of a retail price as an obligation that could be imposed on a reseller. CEPSA's stipulations as to price would therefore constitute a restriction on competition not covered by the block exemption. The Court's answer to the question referred was summarized as follows: '[...] Article [81] of the Treaty applies to an agreement for the exclusive distribution of motor-vehicle and other fuels, such as that at issue in the main proceedings, concluded between a supplier and a service-station operator where that operator assumes, to a non-negligible extent, one or more financial and commercial risks linked to the sale to third parties.'

This judgment essentially confirms the Court of Justice's case law regarding the exclusion of agency agreements from the scope of Article 81. However, the Court stressed that this exclusion only applies to obligations that relate to the sale of goods to third parties on behalf of the principal, and that other obligations which may affect the commercial freedom of agents (such as exclusivity and non-competition provisions) must still be analysed under Article 81 EC.

D. Motor Vehicle Cases

No survey of EC competition law developments would be complete without a few cases involving motor vehicle distribution, which has been so much a focus of Commission activity over the years.

(i) Vulcan Silkeborg[284] and Brünsteiner[285]

Both these cases dealt with the entry into force of the new Motor Vehicle Block Exemption Regulation (MVBER),[286] which allows a supplier to terminate a distribution agreement by giving the distributor two years' notice. Article 5(3) of the old MVBER[287] provided for a shortened notice period of one year in cases 'where it [was] necessary to reorganise the whole or a substantial part of the [distribution] network'. The automotive suppliers in these two cases sought to take advantage of that provision in order to adapt their distribution networks to the requirements of the new MVBER, including the novel prohibition of combining exclusive and selective distribution. Some terminated distributors with whom the suppliers did not enter into a new agreement challenged the legality of the one-year notice period before national courts. Following a preliminary reference, the ECJ shed some light on the necessary substantive conditions for making use of the Article 5(3) exception, and on the consequences of the entry into force of the new MVBER in that regard.

The ECJ first emphasized that the reduced notice provided by Article 5(3) constituted a derogation and must thus be construed strictly.[288] The terms 'reorganization of the whole or a substantial part of the network' meant a change to a supplier's distribution structure that was both substantively and geographically significant.[289] While it was not for national courts to question the economic and commercial considerations governing a supplier's decision to reorganize its network, because the provision in Article 5(3) constituted an exception, the need for the reorganization was not simply a matter for the supplier's discretion.[290] It must be convincingly justified on grounds of economic effectiveness, based on objective circumstances within or outside the supplier's company which would affect the supplier if he had to respect the two-year notice period when terminating the agreement.[291]

Applying these principles, the Court held that the entry into force of the new MVBER did not automatically make the reorganization of distribution

---

[284] Case C-125/05 *VW Audi Forhandlerforeningen (Vulcan Silkeborg) v Skandinavisk Motor* [2006] ECR I-7637.

[285] Joined Cases C-376/05 and C-377/05 *Brünsteiner and Autohaus Hilgert v Bayerische Motorenwerke* [2006] ECR I-11383.

[286] Commission Regulation 1400/2002 of 31 July 2002 on the application of Article 81(3) of the Treaty to categories of vertical agreements and concerted practices in the motor vehicle sector [2002] OJ L203/30.

[287] Commission Regulation 1475/95 of 28 June 1995 on the application of Article 85(3) of the Treaty to certain categories of motor vehicle distribution and servicing agreements [1995] OJ L145/25.

[288] *Vulcan Silkeborg*, para 27.

[289] Ibid, paras 29–30. For instance, a change relating to the nature or form of the structures, their subject matter, the allocation of internal duties within the structures, how the goods and services in question are supplied, the number or quality of the participants in the structures or their geographical coverage.

[290] Ibid, para 36.   [291] Ibid, paras 37–38.

networks necessary.²⁹² In particular, it pointed out that suppliers could adapt existing distribution agreements during the transitional period, without being forced to terminate them immediately.²⁹³ However, the Court also acknowledged that the entry into force of the new MVBER might, owing to the particular nature of an individual distribution network, require changes significant enough to be considered as amounting to a reorganization within the meaning of Article 5(3).²⁹⁴ This could be the case if a supplier who had previously combined exclusive and selective distribution decided to adopt a selective distribution system or an exclusive distribution network for sales, with a selective system for after-sales services.²⁹⁵ Moreover, while immediate reorganization to comply with the new MVBER was not compulsory during the transitional period, it was not forbidden either, if it could be convincingly justified on grounds of effectiveness.²⁹⁶

Whether the supplier decides to modify its distribution network immediately or wait until the transitional period has ended, the new MVBER applies to all existing distribution agreements in force at the end of the transitional period.²⁹⁷ Hence agreements not brought into conformity with the new MVBER, such as agreements containing provisions listed as hardcore restrictions under the new MVBER although they were lawful under the old one, would fall outside the safe harbour of the new MVBER and be subject to Article 81(1) and (3) of the EC Treaty.²⁹⁸ In that regard, national law was entitled to provide that such agreements containing one of the listed hardcore restrictions were invalid in their entirely.²⁹⁹

(ii) Peugeot³⁰⁰

In October 2005, the Commission adopted a Decision condemning Peugeot SA and its Dutch subsidiary for implementing a rebate system, backed up by direct pressure, to hinder exports from the Netherlands to other Member States. The infringement was two-fold. First, Peugeot introduced a bonus system which basically excluded cars sold to non-resident buyers when assessing whether distributors had reached their sales target. Secondly, only cars registered in the Netherlands were taken into account to calculate the amount of bonus paid.

The Commission refused to characterize the measures as merely unilateral, and found an agreement within the meaning of Article 81 of the EC Treaty between Peugeot (and its Dutch subsidiary) and its individual dealers (through the association of Dutch dealers VDPN). Referring to previous case law, the Commission recalled that tacit acquiescence by the retailers might be sufficient to prove the

---

²⁹² Ibid, para 58.   ²⁹³ Ibid, para 61.   ²⁹⁴ Ibid, para 62.
²⁹⁵ Ibid, para 63.   ²⁹⁶ Ibid, para 35.   ²⁹⁷ Ibid, para 44.
²⁹⁸ Ibid, para 46.   ²⁹⁹ Ibid, para 50.
³⁰⁰ Commission Decision of 5 October 2005 (*SEP et al./Peugeot*).

existence of an agreement.[301] In this case it contended that the admission of the dealers to the distribution network implied that they expressly or tacitly accepted the policy pursued by Peugeot. Moreover, the dealers' cooperation was indispensable for achieving Peugeot's objective of slowing down parallel imports of new cars. The Commission also argued that whenever the dealers filed a purchase order for a vehicle, they implicitly accepted Peugeot's circulars defining the conditions for earning bonuses. Thus the circulars constituted an agreement, as they formed part of a set of continuous business relations governed by a general agreement drawn up in advance and were tacitly accepted by the authorized dealers. The existence of an agreement was further evidenced by a system of monitoring and penalties intended to ensure compliance with the conditions laid down by Peugeot. Lastly, the Commission noted that the remuneration system was the result of long discussions between Peugeot and the VDPN, which sent dealers clear information reiterating the contents of the circulars, especially the limits on exports. The remuneration system was therefore clearly an integral part of the distribution contract and thus an agreement caught by Article 81(1).

The violations were considered to be restrictions by object. The Commission stressed that it objected to the fact that a bonus was only paid for cars registered in the national market, and not to the fact that only sales within a geographically limited territory were taken into account to calculate the sales target. The system was complemented by systematic ex-post checks. The Commission also found that the system had other restrictive effects. Firstly, the dealers needed the bonus to earn a profit. Secondly, they used part of the bonus to grant discounts to their clients, meaning that they had less flexibility to offer discounts on cars sold to non-resident clients unless they were prepared to accept a lower profit margin than for cars sold to domestic consumers. Thirdly, the Commission noticed that exports declined during the infringement period, though the price differential, albeit decreasing, remained significant during that period.

Moreover, Peugeot put direct pressure on its distributors. Peugeot and its Dutch subsidiary repeatedly drew dealers' attention to the need to reduce exports. Peugeot also delayed deliveries of exported cars during periods of shortage and introduced special promotion lines for which exports were forbidden. The Commission also received complaints from consumers who had suffered from delayed deliveries.

The Commission found the infringements to be very serious and imposed a EUR 49.4 million fine in light of their gravity and duration. It commented that Peugeot's in-house legal department was fully aware of the situation and could have advised on the competition law problems. Further, neither Peugeot nor its subsidiary had contacted the Commission with a view to clarifying the question.

---

[301] Case T-41/96 *Bayer v Commission* [2000] ECR II-3383, confirmed on appeal in Joined Cases C-2/01 P and C-3/01 P *Bundesverband der Arzneimittel-Importeure v Bayer and Commission* [2004] ECR I-23.

The Decision reaffirms the principles distinguishing unilateral conduct from vertical agreements. Because a contractual link between a supplier and its distributors is not sufficient to establish an agreement within the meaning of Article 81, the Commission was careful to adduce evidence that the dealers had tacitly accepted the circulars sent by Peugeot. The key factor in the case was the intermediary role played by the dealers' association, which negotiated with Peugeot and passed on its recommendations to the individual dealers. It is also worth noting that the Commission limited its objections to the method used to calculate how the bonus was paid, leaving car manufacturers free to use reward programmes to encourage dealers to increase sales within the territory allocated to them. However, they could not seek to prevent exports and parallel trade as Peugeot had done. Finally, it should be noted that the Commission assessed the effects of the practice despite characterizing it as a restriction by object.

(iii) Volkswagen[302]

In this judgment the ECJ once again rejected a Commission attempt to stretch the concept of the notion of an agreement under EC law in order to prohibit certain behaviour under Article 81(1) of the EC Treaty. The judgment also clarifies the circumstances in which a distributor's tacit consent to the apparently unilateral conduct of a manufacturer may be inferred.

During the 1990s, Volkswagen (VW) put in place an EU-wide distribution network of authorised dealers. Each dealership agreement stated that the dealer would comply with all instructions issued for the purposes of the agreement regarding the distribution of new VW cars, and that VW would issue non-binding recommendations concerning retail prices and discounts. In 1996 and 1997 VW realized that some of its German dealers were selling vehicles below its non-binding price recommendations. In response it sent three circulars in September 1996 and April and June 1997, and five letters to some of them in September and October 1996, April 1997 and October 1998, 'exhorting' them to grant customers limited discounts or no discounts at all on the non-binding price recommendations. In July 1997 and October 1998, following a buyer's complaint, the Commission opened investigations into these 'exhortations', and in 2001 it adopted a Decision[303] finding they were illegal under Article 81 and imposing a EUR 31 million fine on VW.

VW appealed the Decision to the CFI,[304] which in December 2003 annulled it on the ground that the Commission had failed to establish the existence of a concurrence of wills between VW and its dealers, and that there was therefore no agreement. The CFI found the Commission had been wrong to assert that the dealers' signature of the dealership agreement involved acceptance on their part

---

[302] Case C-74/04 P *Commission v Volkswagen,* [2006] ECR I-6585.
[303] Commission Decision of 29 June 2001 (*Volkswagen*) [2001] OJ L262/14.
[304] Case T-208/01 *Volkswagen v Commission* [2003] ECR II-5141.

of the contents of all subsequent circulars and letters issued by VW. Instead the Commission should, at least in the case of selective distribution systems such as this one, examine the dealer's conduct to see whether it displayed acquiescence to such 'exhortations' by a manufacturer; and acquiescence could not be regarded as established *ipso facto* simply because the dealer had entered the distribution network.[305]

The Commission appealed the CFI judgment to the ECJ, which found that Article 81(1) 'does not imply that any call by a motor vehicle manufacturer to dealers constitutes an agreement within the meaning of Article 81 and does not relieve the Commission of its obligation to prove that there was a concurrence of wills on the part of the parties to the dealership agreement in each specific case'.[306] Rather, in establishing the existence of an agreement under Article 81(1), 'the will of the parties may result from both the clauses of the dealership agreement in question and from the conduct of the parties and in particular from the possibility of there being tacit acquiescence by the dealers in a call from the manufacturer.'[307]

The ECJ did, however, annul the CFI's finding that 'an unlawful contractual variation could be regarded as having been accepted in advance, upon and by the signature of a lawful distribution agreement.'[308] According to the ECJ, 'a call which is contrary to the competition rules may be regarded as being authorized by seemingly neutral clauses of a dealership agreement'.[309] This must be assessed by 'examining the clauses of the dealership agreement individually, taking account where applicable of all other relevant factors, such as the aims pursued by that agreement in the light of the economic and legal context in which it was signed'.[310] Nevertheless, the ECJ found that this error did 'not affect the soundness of the conclusion reached by the Court of First Instance, to the effect that the calls at issue in the present case cannot be regarded as constituting an "agreement" within the meaning of Article 81'.[311] The ECJ therefore upheld the CFI's finding and confirmed the annulment of the Commission's decision and the fine imposed on Volkswagen.

Once again, the ECJ has clearly disapproved of the Commission's attempts to extend the boundaries of the definition of an 'agreement'. The *Volkswagen* judgment is in line with previous judicial pronouncements where the Community Courts have rejected the Commission's expansive (and expanding) interpretation of the notion of an agreement.[312] As a result, unilateral conduct by an undertaking will continue to fall outside the scope of the EC competition rules unless the company in question is dominant, in which case certain types of unilateral conduct may constitute abuses of a dominant position.[313]

---

[305] Ibid, paras 45–47.   [306] ECJ judgment, para 36.   [307] Ibid, para 39.
[308] Ibid, para 18.   [309] Ibid, para 46.   [310] Ibid, para 45.   [311] Ibid, para 54.
[312] For previous attempts, see *Bayer v Commission* and *Bundesverband der Arzneimittel-Importeure and Commission v Bayer AG*, n 301 above, and *DaimlerChrysler*, n 314 below.
[313] *Bayer v Commission*, para 176.

The judgment also helpfully clarifies the circumstances in which a distributor's tacit consent to apparently unilateral conduct by a manufacturer can be inferred, ie both from the wording of the agreement itself, and from the intent of the parties and their subsequent actions. As a result, though an agreement may appear neutral, it may still be possible to infer that it has an anticompetitive purpose if, taking into account all other relevant factors such as the aims pursued by it in light of the economic and legal context in which it was signed, there is evidence that a distributor has consented to subsequent unilateral anticompetitive measures adopted by a manufacturer.

(iv) DaimlerChrysler[314]

In its judgment in *DaimlerChrysler,* the CFI took a more liberal stance towards agency agreements under EC competition law than the Commission. The Court's approach is more consistent with the previous case law.

In the Decision[315] which was appealed to the CFI, the Commission fined DaimlerChrysler AG and its legal predecessors Daimler-Benz AG and Mercedes-Benz AG for agreeing with Mercedes-Benz's German dealers to prevent parallel trade. The Commission rejected the argument that the dealers were agents: 'In the statement of objections (point 152), the Commission indicated that the Mercedes-Benz agents have to bear a number of commercial risks inextricably linked to their function as agent which result in Article 81 being applicable to the agreements between Mercedes-Benz and the agents in the same way as with regard to dealers.'[316]

The Commission then examined the argument that the agents did not bear the same risks as dealers, as they did not bear any of the contractual risks associated with new vehicle business such as the risks of marketing, transport, storage, price, guarantee, or default. It rejected this argument, as the agents bore a considerable share of the price risk (discounts came out of their commission), as well as the transport and transport cost risks in respect of new vehicles. Moreover, they had to use their own resources for promotional activity. In addition, to become a Mercedes-Benz agent it was necessary to comply with a number of commercial conditions which the Commission viewed as risks to be borne by the agent. They included obligations to carry out repairs under guarantee (paid at standard rates and with the agent required to keep tools to carry out repairs), set up a workshop for repairs at the agent's own expense, and keep a stock of spare parts for the agent's own account. Further, an agent's revenues from activities pursued on a self-employed basis were many times greater than those from negotiating new-vehicle sales contracts. The Commission therefore rejected the agency defence: 'In view of the number and quantitative scope of the risks that Mercedes-Benz

---

[314] Case T-325/01 *DaimlerChrysler AG v Commission* [2005] ECR I-3319.
[315] Commission Decision of 10 October 2001 (*Mercedes-Benz*) [2002] OJ L257/1.
[316] Decision, para 53.

agents have to bear, DaimlerChrysler's argument that the risks borne by agents are typical of those borne by a genuine commercial agent cannot be accepted. The position would be different only if the agent could choose whether to assume in particular the considerable risks connected with demonstration and business vehicles, carrying out guarantee work, setting up maintenance and repair facilities and supplying spare parts, or simply to negotiate new-vehicle sales contracts. This is, however, not the case.'[317]

The second sentence quoted above seems odd: why should it make a difference if the agent was forced to do one thing or chose to do another? Moreover, the Commission expressly rejected (for theoretical reasons) the argument that the agents formed an integral part of Daimler and were therefore genuine commercial dealers, as '[t]he criterion of integration is, unlike risk allocation, not a separate criterion for distinguishing a commercial agent from a dealer.'[318]

However, the Decision did not stand the test before the CFI. The Court recalled that while the EC Treaty prohibits coordinated anticompetitive conduct by two or more undertakings, the unilateral conduct of a manufacturer is not covered by that prohibition: 'It is clear from the wording of that article that the prohibition thus laid down concerns exclusively conduct that is coordinated bilaterally or multilaterally, in the form of agreements between undertakings, decisions by associations of undertakings and concerted practices. It follows that the concept of an agreement within the meaning of Article 81(1) EC, as interpreted in case-law, centres around the existence of a joint intention between at least two parties [...] It follows that, where a decision by a manufacturer constitutes unilateral conduct of the undertaking, that decision escapes the prohibition laid down in Article 81(1) EC.'[319]

The CFI thus found that Daimler had acted unilaterally,[320] and that the German agents had to be assimilated to employees of Daimler and regarded as integrated into that undertaking and forming an economic unit with it: 'the relationship between the agents and the applicant is such that the former sell Mercedes-Benz vehicles in all material respects under the direction of the applicant, with the result that they should be treated in the same way as employees and considered as integrated in that undertaking and thus forming an economic unit with it.'[321]

Neither their activity of soliciting orders with a view to transmitting them to Daimler, nor the other services they supplied for Daimler, ie repair and after-sales services, were held by the Court to be associated with a commercial risk which could allow the agents to be classified as independent operators. Moreover, 'the categorization of the status of the German Mercedes-Benz agent under Article 81(1) EC set out in paragraph 102 above is not undermined by the fact that the German Mercedes-Benz agents are required to undertake certain activities

---

[317] Ibid, para 160.   [318] Ibid, para 163.
[319] *DaimlerChrysler*, paras 83 and 84.   [320] Ibid, para 119.   [321] Ibid, para 102.

and assume certain financial obligations under the agency agreement. It should also be noted that the activities are carried out on markets other than the market at issue in the present case. Even if it must be recognized that those obligations expose the agent to certain limited risks, they do not of themselves operate to affect the relationship between the applicant and its agents under competition law as regards the market at issue in these proceedings.'[322]

The CFI's judgment thus takes a more liberal stance with regard to agency agreements than the Decision, and rejects the Commission's approach of concentrating primarily on the allocation of financial risk and downplaying the test of whether the agent is an 'auxiliary organ forming an integral part of the principal's undertaking'. The Commission's emphasis on risk rather than the notion of integration is not really consistent with the ECJ's position since *Consten and Grundig*, which seems to centre more on whether the agent is an integral part of the principal.[323] By contrast, the CFI reaffirms the test of whether the agent is an 'auxiliary organ forming an integral part of the principal's undertaking', which the Commission expressly rejected in its Decision.

The judgment at least partly contradicts the statements made in the Vertical Guidelines. On a more general note, it may lead to a change in the Commission's practice with regard to agency agreements, which could have significant repercussions for undertakings and how they decide to distribute their products. If the agent forms an integral part of the principal's undertaking, there is no agreement between undertakings within the meaning of Article 81(1) of the EC Treaty, whereas if the agent bears a (significant) commercial risk, he may be classified as an independent operator falling under the scope of Article 81(1) EC. However, when the risk he bears is only limited, that risk cannot in itself permit classifying the agent as an independent operator falling within the scope of Article 81(1).

(v) *General Motors Nederland and Opel Nederland*[324]

This ECJ judgment brought to an end the long-running litigation which followed the Commission's 2000 Decision[325] fining Opel Nederland EUR 43 million for entering into agreements with Opel dealers in the Netherlands which aimed at restricting or prohibiting export sales of Opel vehicles to end users resident in other Member States and Opel dealers established in other Member States. The Decision found that Opel's general strategy included a restrictive bonus policy which excluded export sales to final consumers from bonus campaigns. This finding was appealed to the CFI[326] on the ground that the policy on bonuses was not

---

[322] Ibid, para 113.

[323] See also Commission Notice: Guidelines on Vertical Restraints [2000] OJ C291/1, paras 13 and 15.

[324] Case C-551/03 P, *General Motors Nederland and Opel Nederland v Commission* [2006] ECR I-3173.

[325] Commission Decision of 20 September 2000 (*Opel*) [2001] OJ L59/1.

[326] Case T-368/00 *General Motors Nederland and Opel Nederland v Commission* [2003] ECR II-4491.

intended to restrict competition. On the contrary, its objective was stated to be to stimulate sales in the Netherlands, while not providing an additional stimulus for exports; this, it was argued, was very different from aiming to restrict exports.

Although the CFI found that the Commission had erred in its conclusion that Opel had implemented a policy of restricting supplies,[327] it nevertheless concluded that Opel's bonus system was likely to inhibit export sales. According to the CFI, as bonuses were no longer granted for export sales, the dealers' margin of economic manoeuvre to carry out such sales was reduced compared with domestic sales.[328] They were therefore obliged either to apply less favourable conditions to foreign customers than domestic customers, or be content with a smaller margin on export sales. The withdrawal of bonuses for export sales made such sales less attractive to foreign customers and dealers. The measure was therefore by its nature likely to inhibit export sales, even without any restriction on supply.[329] The CFI also took into account the fact that the measures adopted by Opel were actually prompted by the increase in export sales and were designed to reduce them.

On further appeal, the ECJ found that 'as bonuses were no longer granted for export sales, the margin of economic manoeuvre which dealers had to carry out such sales was reduced in comparison with that which they had to carry out domestic sales.'[330] The ECJ also stated that 'an agreement concerning distribution has a restrictive object for the purposes of Article 81 EC if it clearly manifests the will to treat export sales less favourably than national sales and thus leads to a partitioning of the market in question. [. . .] such an objective can be achieved not only by direct restrictions on exports but also through indirect measures, such as those at issue in this case, since they influence the economic conditions of such transactions.'[331]

The case serves as a further warning that marketing arrangements which reward and motivate sales by dealers to domestic customers more generously than sales to customers residing in other Member States are at risk under EC law. We would welcome a recalibration of the Commission's traditional preoccupation with facilitating parallel trade in the motor vehicle sector. The manufacturer wishes to motivate its dealer network to promote sales on the domestic market, which the dealer can serve best. Sales in other Member States may be more lucrative as well as being a lot easier to achieve. It is not the case that competition is equally well-promoted by 'free-rider' sales into a higher-priced distant territory as by domestic sales. We are unpersuaded that competition at grassroots level is best enhanced by ruling that a dealer who sells ten cars to customers far away deserves identical participation in incentive trips and other rewards to a dealer who has sold ten cars on the tough domestic market. For the moment, however, the law takes a different view. Agreements which clearly aim to treat parallel trade unfavourably will continue to be regarded in principle as having the object of

---

[327] Ibid, paras 88 and 89.   [328] Ibid, para 100.   [329] Ibid.
[330] ECJ judgment, para 74.   [331] Ibid, paras 67 and 68.

restricting competition when, in view of the legal and economic context in which they operate, they are presumed to deprive final consumers of the advantages of effective competition in terms of supply or price.[332]

E. Horizontal Agreements

(i) O2[333]

If *GSK Spain* was one of the most important judgments rendered in the last years in the area of vertical agreements, certainly the same can be said of *O2* with regard to horizontal agreements. The judgment of the CFI in *O2* confirms the importance of carefully analysing agreements under Article 81(1) of the EC Treaty in light of their individual factual and economic circumstances. It also seems part of a new approach to Article 81(1) by the CFI.

In 2002 the Commission dealt with two cooperation agreements[334] between T-Mobile and O2 which concerned infrastructure sharing and national roaming on the UK and German markets for 3G mobile telecommunications networks.[335] In both agreements the parties divided British and German territory into different areas in which they respectively agreed on limited reciprocal site-sharing not involving the core network or frequencies, or national roaming on each other's networks in areas where only one had a 3G network. The agreements also included some other restrictive clauses. The parties requested either negative clearance under Article 81(1) of the EC Treaty, or alternatively an exemption under Article 81(3) EC.

In its Decisions the Commission found that with regard to the market for sites and site infrastructure the agreements did not restrict competition. By contrast, the Commission found that on the market for wholesale access to national 3G roaming, the agreements constituted a restriction under Article 81(1), due to the parties' market power at both the wholesale and retail levels. However, they were exempted under Article 81(3). In more highly populated areas where incentives to roll out the 3G networks were high, the Commission granted only a brief exemption, while in less densely populated areas with lower economic incentives to roll out networks it granted a slightly longer exemption period.[336]

---

[332] *GlaxoSmithKline Services v Commission*, n 262 above.

[333] Case T-328/03 *O2 (Germany) v Commission* [2006] ECR II-1231.

[334] Network-sharing agreements involve the sharing of network components or sites where the components are physically installed. The degree of cooperation depends on the networks' level of integration and increases from sites to base stations, radio network controllers (RNC), core networks (intelligent part) and frequencies. National roaming involves not the sharing of infrastructure, but the use of each other's networks to provide services to each other's customers.

[335] Commission Decision of 16 July 2003 (*T-Mobile Deutschland/O2 Germany*) [2004] OJ L75/32; Commission Decision of 30 April 2003 (*O2 UK Limited/T-Mobile UK Limited*) [2003] OJ L200/59. Although both Decisions aimed to apply the same competition policy approach, they were not identical due to the significant factual and regulatory differences.

[336] In both Decisions, the Commission exempted roaming agreements in rural areas until 31 December 2008. They were not exempted for a longer period because the markets concerned were

The German network-sharing Decision was appealed by the exemption beneficiary, O2. In its judgment the CFI held that in finding the agreement was caught
by Article 81(1) EC, the Commission had failed to analyse its actual effects on
competition, preferring instead to make 'broad and general statements which
[we]re unsupported'.[337] In a strongly-worded judgment, the CFI concurred with
O2 and partially annulled the Decision insofar as it concluded that the agreements fell within the scope of Article 81(1). In particular, the CFI stressed that:

> where it is accepted that the agreement does not have as its object a restriction of competi-
> tion, the effects of the agreement should be considered and for it to be caught by the pro-
> hibition it is necessary to find that those factors are present which show that competition
> has in fact been prevented or restricted or distorted to an appreciable extent. *The competi-
> tion in question must be understood within the actual context in which it would occur in the
> absence of the agreement in dispute*; the interference with competition may in particular be
> doubted if the agreement seems really necessary for the penetration of a new area by an
> undertaking [...]
>
> Such a method of analysis, as regards in particular the taking into account of the com-
> petition situation that would exist in the absence of the agreement, does not amount to
> carrying out an assessment of the pro- and anticompetitive effects of the agreement and
> thus to applying a rule of reason, which the Community judicature has not deemed to
> have its place under Article 81(1) EC.[338]

Rather, the CFI stated, 'the examination required in the light of Article 81(1) EC
consists essentially in taking account of the impact of the agreement on existing
and potential competition ... and the competition situation in the absence of the
agreement [...] those two factors being intrinsically linked.'[339]

Applying these criteria, the CFI found the Commission had failed to substantiate its claim that in the absence of the agreement O2 would have been present
on the 3G market. The Court also criticized the Decision for failing to evaluate
specifically the amendments to the German agreement which related to roaming in urban areas, both in space and time. The CFI considered it possible that
instead of restricting competition between network operators, a roaming agreement could in some circumstances enable the smallest market operator to compete with the major players. As a result, and in light of the specific characteristics
of the relevant emerging market, O2's competitive situation on the 3G market
would probably not have been secure without the agreement, and might even
have been jeopardized. The CFI strongly rebuked the Commission for its weak
analysis: ' ... *the Decision*, in so far as it concerns the application of Article 81(1)
EC and Article 53(1) of the EEA Agreement, *suffers from insufficient analysis, first,
in that it contains no objective discussion of what the competition situation would
have been in the absence of the agreement*, which distorts the assessment of the
actual and potential effects of the agreement on competition and, second, in that

emerging markets on which it was difficult to evaluate the likely effects of the restrictions much more
than five years ahead.

[337] Judgment, para 81.   [338] Ibid, paras 68 and 69.   [339] Ibid, para 71.

it does not demonstrate, in concrete terms, in the context of the relevant emerging market, that the provisions of the agreement on roaming have restrictive effects on competition, *but is confined, in this respect, to a petitio principii and to broad and general statements*[340] (emphasis added).

Finally, the CFI confirmed that even though Regulation 17 under which the agreements had been notified to the Commission had expired, the Commission was still under an obligation to adopt a decision on the legality of the agreements under Article 81(1), due to the retroactive effect of the judgment.

Thus the judgment confirms the importance for both the Commission and parties to analyze agreements carefully under Article 81(1) in light of their individual factual and economic circumstances.[341] It clearly establishes that a counter-factual method should be used, comparing the future degree of market competition with and without the agreement. The judgment has thus been said to represent a rejection of the 'ordoliberal' approach to what constitutes a restriction of competition in EC law.[342] It also, with *Austrian Banks*[343] and *GSK Spain,* seems to indicate a new trend in the CFI's approach to Article 81(1) EC. Under its previous approach the CFI would probably have limited itself to considering whether the agreement was necessary for an undertaking to penetrate a new area. In *O2* it seems to have gone further and considered under Article 81(1) whether, in the absence of the agreement, O2 would have been a less effective competitor; in other words, it examined the pro-competitive effects of the agreement, which is traditionally done only under Article 81(3). It remains to be seen whether this trend will continue in the future.

Similarly, the Article 81(3) EC Guidelines stress that 'the objective...is to protect competition on the market as a means of enhancing consumer welfare and of ensuring an efficient allocation of resources'.[344] Commissioner Kroes has also stated publicly that 'consumer welfare is now well established as the standard the Commission applies when assessing mergers and infringements of Articles 81 and 82'.[345]

---

[340] Ibid, para 116.

[341] Kuik, 'The Quest for Legal Certainty—The EC Competition Law Approach to Horizontal Co-operation Agreements', in Amato and Ehlermann (eds), *EC Competition Law, A Critical Assessment* (Hart Publishing, 2007) 143–172.

[342] Robertson, 'What is a Restriction of Competition? The Implications of the CFI's judgment in *O2 Germany* and the Rule of Reason', (2007) ECLR 28(4) 252, at 256.

[343] See *Austrian Banks*, n 208 above: 'The ultimate purpose of the rules that seek to ensure that competition is not distorted in the internal market is to increase the well-being of consumers [...] Competition law and competition policy therefore have an undeniable impact on the specific economic interests of final customers who purchase goods or services. Recognition that such customers—who show that they have suffered economic damage as a result of an agreement or conduct liable to restrict or distort competition—have a legitimate interest in seeking from the Commission a declaration that Articles 81 EC and 82 EC have been infringed contributes to the attainment of the objectives of competition law.'

[344] Guidelines on the Application of Article 81(3) of the Treaty, n 280 above, para 13.

[345] 'European Competition Policy—Delivering Better Markets and Better Choices', Speech on 15 September 2005 at the European Consumer and Competition Day, London, available online at: <http://ec.europa.eu/comm/ competition/speeches/index_2005.html>.

(11) *Asnef-Equifax*[346]

In this important ruling the ECJ provided guidance on the assessment of information exchange schemes under Article 81(1) of the EC Treaty. Asnef-Equifax, a group of financial organizations, set up a system for exchanging solvency and credit information about customers, in order to evaluate the risks undertaken when engaging in credit or lending activities. A decision condemning the system as anticompetitive was appealed up to the Spanish Supreme Court, which referred questions relating to the assessment of this arrangement under the competition rules to the ECJ.

Although the case primarily involved the application not of Article 81 but the equivalent provisions of Spanish law, the ECJ decided to hear it on the ground that the Supreme Court considered the appealed decision was founded on the legal principles of Spanish competition law and the application of EC competition law, and that the aim of the request for a preliminary ruling was to preclude contradictory or divergent interpretations.[347] The issue of effect on trade between Member States was irrelevant for determining whether the request was admissible, as it concerned the substance of the case.[348]

Assessing the system under Article 81(1), the Court observed that its primary purpose was to diminish the risks of lending by reducing the disparity between the information available to credit institutions and that held by potential borrowers. Similar systems existed in numerous countries and they contributed to the functioning of the credit supply system;[349] their main objective was not to restrict or distort competition; although it was for the Supreme Court to determine whether this particular system had such an effect.

The ECJ clarified that information exchange systems have the effect of restricting competition if they reduce or remove the degree of market uncertainty.[350] It stressed that the compatibility of an information exchange system with the EC competition rules cannot be assessed in the abstract; it depends on the economic conditions in the relevant markets and the specific characteristics of the system concerned.[351] Among relevant factors the Court listed: (1) market concentration (information exchange on a highly concentrated market is more likely to enable companies to be aware of the market position and commercial strategy of their competitors, thus distorting competition in the market and increasing or facilitating the probability of collusion); (2) the nature of the information exchanged (it should be anonymous to reduce the risk of anticompetitive effects); and (3) the conditions of access to the information, which should be objective and nondiscriminatory.[352]

The Court specifically rejected the argument that the existence of an information exchange system would necessarily lead to collective anticompetitive

---

[346] Case C-238/05 *Asnef-Equifax, Servicios de Información sobre Solvencia y Crédito, SL, Administración del Estado v Asociación de Usuarios de Servicios Bancarios* [2006] ECR I-11125.
[347] Judgment, paras 17–21.   [348] Ibid, para 22.   [349] Ibid, paras 46–47.
[350] Ibid, para 51.   [351] Ibid, para 54.   [352] Ibid, paras 58–60.

conduct such as a boycott of potential borrowers. It could not be inferred that because the system was able to reduce the risk that applicants for credit would default, it would also reduce uncertainty as to the risks of competition.[353] If a national court found that the system did actually restrict competition, it should then consider the effects of Article 81(3). The Spanish court's questions related to the Article 81(3) requirement that consumers must be allowed a fair share of the resulting benefit. The ECJ focused on whether that requirement is satisfied when, owing to the existence of an information exchange system, some consumers may be faced with increased rates or even refused credit.[354] It reasoned that under Article 81(3) the beneficial nature of the effect on all consumers in the relevant market must be taken into consideration, as opposed to the effect on each member of that category of consumers.[355] The Court concluded that exchanges of information between financial institutions on the solvency of customers are likely to benefit all consumers, as they prevent situations of over-indebtedness for consumers of credit and should in principle lead to greater overall availability of credit.

(iii) The Cannes Agreement[356]

The interesting point with this case is that while it is one of a number of cases relating to agreements between collecting societies where the Commission has raised competition concerns, it is the first in which binding commitments have been accepted.

In October 2006, the Commission made commitments given in respect of the Cannes Extension Agreement by the five major music publishers, BMG, EMI, Sony, Universal, and Warner and 13 European collecting societies, legally binding, thereby closing its investigation into potential Article 81 infringements by the parties to the Agreement. The Cannes Extension Agreement related to 'Central Licensing Agreements', whereby a record company can conclude a single licensing agreement with a collecting society covering all or part of the EEA. The record company pays all royalties due, and the collecting society distributes them to the relevant artists. Although the Commission recognized in its Decision that these types of agreements benefit competition, they could also lead to conflict between right-holders and collecting societies. The Agreement was an attempt at resolving such conflicts and at laying down terms for administering mechanical copyright for the reproduction of sound recordings.

In February 2003, Universal International Music BV filed a complaint alleging that Clause 9(a) of the Cannes Extension Agreement was contrary to Article 81 of the EC Treaty. In January 2006, the Commission informed the parties of its concerns regarding the Agreement, particularly Clause 9(a) relating to the granting of rebates to record companies, and Clause 7(a)(i) which related to the

---

[353] Ibid, para 62.　　[354] Ibid, paras 66–68.　　[355] Ibid, para 70.
[356] Commission Decision of 4 October 2006 (*Cannes Agreement*) [2007] OJ L296/27.

possibility of collecting societies engaging in commercial publishing or record-producing activities.

In respect of the rebates clause, the Commission found that in the market for licensing music copyright; 'there is currently very little scope for price competition among collecting societies', and that 'the only element of price competition among collecting societies in the framework of Central Licensing Agreements appears to be the granting of rebates'. Although the Commission accepted that Clause 9(a) did not contain an express prohibition of rebates paid out of administration fees, it found that the conditions it imposed made such rebates highly impracticable for collecting societies. On the non-compete Clause 7(a)(i) which prohibited collecting societies from undertaking commercial publishing or record publishing activities, the Commission commented that it appeared 'to have the object and may have the effect of crystallizing the current structure of the industry by fending off any potential competition among collecting societies, publishers and record companies in the future'.

In February 2006, all the parties to the Agreement proposed two commitments within the meaning of Article 9(1) of Regulation 1/2003, which were accepted by the Commission in its Decision. They proposed to delete Clause 7(a)(i) from the Agreement, and not to enter into an agreement with a similar effect in the future. With respect to Clause 9(a), they offered an amended version which allowed collecting societies to grant rebates to record companies if approved by a competent body of that society. These rebates would be paid out of the administrative fees retained from the royalties.

(iv) De Beers[357]

This case gave the Commission another opportunity to make use of the new powers granted to it under Article 9 of Regulation 1/2003 to accept commitments offered by undertakings and make them binding, instead of adopting a decision requiring an infringement to be brought to an end. It concerned the worldwide market for the production and supply of rough diamonds, on which De Beers and Alrosa respectively occupied the leading and second positions. In 2002, they notified to the Commission a five-year trading agreement whereby Alrosa undertook to supply De Beers with rough diamonds worth up to USD 800 million a year. Following the notification the Commission initiated two sets of proceedings, one based on Article 81 of the EC Treaty against both companies, and the other based on Article 82 of the EC Treaty against De Beers alone.

With the entry into force on 1 May 2004 of Regulation 1/2003 the notification lapsed, but the procedural steps already taken continued to be effective for the purpose of applying Regulation 1/2003. In December 2004 De Beers and Alrosa responded to the Commission's Statements of Objections by proposing joint commitments which were deemed to constitute a preliminary assessment

---

[357] Commission Decision of 22 February 2006 (*De Beers*).

within the meaning of Article 9(1) of Regulation 1/2003. They provided for a progressive reduction in the value of Alrosa's sales of rough diamonds to De Beers from USD 700 million in 2005 to USD 275 million in 2010, with a subsequent cap at that level. These commitments were the subject of a notice in the Official Journal[358] which prompted 21 interested third parties to submit comments to the Commission.

In January 2006, De Beers individually offered new, more onerous commitments in the proceedings initiated under Article 82, providing for the definitive cessation of all purchases of rough diamonds from Alrosa with effect from 2009, following a period of progressive reduction in purchases between 2006 and 2008. The Commission invited Alrosa to state its position on the commitments proposed by De Beers, and at the same time sent it a non-confidential copy of the comments by the 21 interested third parties relating to the joint commitments of December 2004.

In February 2006, the Commission adopted, pursuant to Article 9(1) of Regulation 1/2003, a formal Decision[359] making the individual commitments proposed by De Beers in January 2006 binding and bringing the Article 82 proceedings against the company to an end. However, the Decision did not give the Commission's reasons for preferring to accept De Beers's more onerous commitments rather than the less onerous joint commitments initially proposed by Alrosa and De Beers in 2004. It was therefore arguable that the Commission's conduct was contrary to the principle of proportionality, as it was under a duty to examine whether the less onerous joint measures initially proposed by Alrosa and De Beers were capable of addressing any competitive concerns it may have had, before adopting the more onerous commitments proposed individually by De Beers. The CFI has since confirmed this in its July 2007 judgment following Alrosa's appeal of the Commission's Decision.[360]

(v) Bundesliga and FAPL

Of particular interest are two more commitment Decisions, both dealing with joint selling arrangements of TV rights to football games. In *Bundesliga* and *FA Premier League*, the rights were sold exclusively by associations of clubs. As the Commission has applied the competition rules to professional sports since the *Bosman* case,[361] the respective associations had notified their rules and regulations to obtain ITS approval.[362] In *Bundesliga*[363] the German football league

---

[358] [2004] OJ C289/10.   [359] [2006] OJ L205/24.

[360] Case T-170/06 *Alrosa v Commission* [2007] ECR II-2601.

[361] Case C-415/93 *Union Royale Belge des Sociétés de Football Association ASBL v Jean-Marc Bosman, Royal Club Liégeois SA v Jean-Marc Bosman et al.* and *Union des Associations Européennes de Football (UEFA) v Jean-Marc Bosman* [1995] ECR I-4921.

[362] Notification took place before May 2004, ie when the prior authorization system was still in place.

[363] Commission Decision of 19 January 2005 (*Joint selling of the media rights to the German Bundesliga*) [2005] OJ L134/46.

offered up-front commitments that were sufficient to offset any competition concerns. The Commission's position can be summarized as follows: the rights must be separated, offered in different packages and attributed for a limited period (generally no more than three seasons) through a non-discriminatory and transparent procedure. Football clubs must be allowed to exploit deferred TV rights or unused live TV rights to their own games. Under certain conditions (after a delay), the clubs can also exploit their rights on new media (Internet, UMTS). The Commission has become wary of licence agreements entered into by an exploiter who has acquired several centrally marketed packages with exclusive exploitation rights.

Similarly, in FAPL,[364] the English Football Association Premier League (FAPL), whose shareholders are the clubs participating in the Premier League, had exclusive power to sell the rights to broadcast Premier League matches. The Commission raised objections. It argued that joint and exclusive sale of large packages of media rights created barriers to entry, that various restrictions on the output of the FAPL limited the development of products and markets and, generally, that the sales policy led to foreclosure on downstream markets.

The Commission required commitments, and the FAPL agreed to set up an open and transparent bidding procedure to attribute the rights for a limited period, ie no more than three seasons. Rights were to be offered in several packages, one of them being available to free-to-air broadcasters only. In accordance with the Commission's policy of encouraging the development of new media, the FAPL agreed that both it and the clubs would have the right to provide video content on the Internet and via UMTS services after a certain period. In reaction to BSkyB's successful bid for all the TV rights packages in 2003, the FAPL specified that starting with the rights for the 2007 season, no one buyer would be able to acquire exclusive rights to all the centrally marketed live rights packages. In addition, for the seasons prior to 2007, BSkyB agreed with the Commission in 2003 to sub-license some of the rights to competitors.

However, in May 2004, BSkyB announced that it had not received any offers matching the reserve prices it had set in agreement with the EU. The Commission expressed disappointment. In November 2005, following increasing pressure from the Commission, the FAPL presented revised commitments which addressed the concerns raised during the consultation process following the publication of the initial commitments. They included specifying the precise terms of the 'no single buyer' rule and the conduct of the auction process, creating more evenly balanced packages of rights and increasing the availability of rights to broadcast via mobile phones.[365] On this basis the Commission adopted in March 2006 an Article 9

---

[364] Commission Decision of 22 March 2006 (*The Football Association Premier League Limited (FAPL)*), a summary of which was published at [2008] OJ C7/18.
[365] Press Release IP/05/1441.

decision which made the revised commitments legally binding[366] on the FAPL until 30 June 2013. If the FAPL breaks the commitments during that period, the Commission can impose a fine amounting to 10% of its total worldwide turnover, without having to prove any violation of the competition rules.

The *Bundesliga* and *FAPL* commitment Decisions offer a model for dealing with joint selling cases. The Commission consistently finds that while joint selling of football rights restricts competition under Article 81(1) of the EC Treaty,[367] substantial commitments by the parties enable the case to be closed with an Article 9 decision concluding that there are no longer grounds for action, without any finding on the existence or otherwise of an infringement, and with no analysis of the conditions for an exemption under Article 81(3).[368]

F. Article 82 EC Cases

(i) *AstraZeneca*[369]

The first EU case relating to patent 'evergreening', and one of the few cases involving alleged misuse of patent procedures and acquisition of an intellectual property right, rests on allegations that AstraZeneca ('AZ') illegally extended patent protection for omeprazole, the active substance in Losec, AZ's best-selling anti-ulcer drug. After defining the relevant product market as omeprazole and omeprazole-like products, the Commission found that AZ was dominant on this market,[370] and that it had infringed Article 82 of the EC Treaty by misusing the patent system and the procedures for marketing pharmaceuticals to block or delay market entry of generic versions of Losec.

According to the Commission, AZ illegally obtained supplementary protection certificates (SPCs) for Losec by giving misleading information to several national patent offices in the EU. SPCs extend basic patent protection for active substances in pharmaceutical products; their duration depends on the date of 'the first authorization to place the product on the market in the Community'. The notion of 'first authorization' is not clearly defined in the SPC Regulation.[371] To maximize the length of patent protection, AZ assumed that it referred to

---

[366] See: <http://ec.europa.eu/comm/competition/antitrust/cases/decisions/38173/commitments. pdf>.

[367] These arrangements involved entities with a particular market power. The Commission's more permissive policy vis-à-vis joint selling by competing SMEs can be illustrated by Commission Decision of 16 December 1971 (*SAFCO*) [1972] OJ L13/44.

[368] Recital 13 of Regulation 1/2003, n 255 above.

[369] Commission Decision of 19 July 2005 (*AstraZeneca*), a summary of which was published in the OJ at [2006] OJ L332/24.

[370] Notably, IP rights played an important part in the finding of AZ's dominance, as they gave it the power to control competitive threats from original medicine manufacturers, generic producers and parallel importers (Decision, paras 517–540).

[371] Council Regulation 1768/92 of 18 June 1992 concerning the creation of a supplementary protection certificate for medicinal products [1992] OJ L 182/1. Only in 2003 did the ECJ rule (in Case C-127/00 *Hässle AB v Ratiopharm GmbH* [2003] ECR I-14781) that the relevant date for

the publication of a decision on price approval, reasoning that only after that decision can a pharmaceutical product be placed on the market in the EU.[372] Consequently, in its SPC applications for omeprazole AZ referred to the date of publication of a price list featuring Losec in Luxembourg, but did not reveal the dates of prior marketing authorizations by the competent medicinal authorities in France and Luxembourg. The Commission considered that AZ had not acted in good faith, since it did not advocate its theory consistently and did not have sufficient evidence to claim that the publication of the price list was a condition for putting Losec on the market.[373] Moreover, when national patent offices rejected AZ's reasoning and requested it to provide the date of the first national marketing authorization, AZ referred to the Luxembourg authorization rather than the earlier French authorization. As a result AZ obtained SPCs for omeprazole in three Member States where it was not eligible for protection, and extended the duration of protection in other Member States.

The Commission concluded that AZ engaged in abusive conduct by giving misleading representations 'as part of its SPC Strategy for omeprazole during two stages with a view to preventing, or at least delaying generic entry',[374] and concealing information in proceedings before national patent offices.[375] The Commission stressed that to establish an abuse it did not need to show that the patent offices actually relied on the misleading information;[376] if a dominant company misuses regulatory procedures with exclusionary intent, it is not necessary to prove that the conduct had actual anticompetitive effects.[377] Given that the SPC abuse bears some resemblance to the US *Walker Process* line of case law,[378] it is worth noting that the requirements for a *Walker Process* claim are much stricter: an antitrust violation is established only if the plaintiff can demonstrate fraud on the patent office (defined as 'knowingly and wilfully misrepresenting facts to the Patent Office')[379] and that the patent would not have been issued but for the patentee's misrepresentation or omission.[380]

The Decision delivers a final blow to the exercise/existence dichotomy.[381] The Commission flatly rejected the contention that merely acquiring a patent cannot as a matter of principle violate Article 82, because it relates only to the existence rather than the exercise of the patent right.[382] It asserted that national IP laws are not affected by the application of EU competition law to misleading

---

the purpose of the SPC Regulation should be the date of authorization by a competent medicinal authority.

[372] Decision, paras 633–634.   [373] Ibid, paras 657–663.   [374] Ibid, para 773.
[375] Ibid, paras 666–667 and 677.   [376] Ibid, paras 764–765.   [377] Ibid, para 758.
[378] *Walker Process Equipment v Food Machinery & Chemical*, 382 US 172 (US 1965).
[379] *Walker Process*, 382 US at 177–178.
[380] See eg *CR Bard, Inc v M3 Sys, Inc*, 157 F.3d 1340, 1365 (Fed Cir 1998), and *Nobelpharma Ab v Implant Innovations*, 141 F.3d 1059, 1071 (Fed Cir 1998). A finding of *Walker Process* fraud must be based on '*clear showing of reliance, i.e., that the patent would not have issued but for the misrepresentation or omission*'.
[381] Decision, para 738.   [382] Ibid, para 741.

representations made in the context of applications for IP rights,[383] and that the bundle of rights forming part of the subject matter of an SPC does not include a right to make misleading representations.[384]

The Commission also found that AZ had infringed the competition rules by withdrawing the marketing authorizations it held for Losec capsules in various Member States. Medicinal products may only be placed on the market in any Member State after being granted a marketing authorization by a competent national medicinal authority. Once the so-called data exclusivity period has ended, generic drug manufacturers and parallel importers may rely on the safety and efficacy data submitted by the original manufacturer, as long as the product they want to place on the market is 'essentially similar' to the original pharmaceutical product.[385] AZ replaced its Losec capsules (the original formulation) with a tablet formulation in several Member States and asked the national medicinal authorities to deregister the market authorizations for the capsules. The deregistration of the capsules created legal hurdles for generic manufacturers and parallel importers whose market authorizations relied on AZ's reference market authorization. In some Member States the parallel trade licences for Losec capsules were revoked and market authorizations for generic versions of Losec capsules were denied.

In the Commission's view, AZ's deregistration of the capsules violated Article 82 because its aim was to impede parallel trade, delay generic entry and thereby preserve AZ's dominant position on the market. Although the deregistration was not *per se* objectionable under the applicable pharmaceutical regulations, those rules did not give the holder of a marketing authorization 'any right to prevent other parties from entering the market'.[386] The deregistration of the capsules was not justified by public health concerns; moreover, it was not a standard procedure, as it would have been more usual for the marketing authorization for the old formulation to co-exist with a marketing authorization for the new one. Importantly, the Commission did not allege misrepresentation by AZ, and did not challenge the launch of the new formulation of Losec or the withdrawal of Losec capsules as such. Its finding of an abuse was based on the theory that the special responsibility of a dominant company requires it to use its public entitlements reasonably, and not 'with the clear purpose of eliminating competition'.[387]

---

[383] Ibid, para 741.   [384] Ibid, para 742.

[385] These basic principles were established by Council Directive 65/65/EEC of 26 January 1965 on the approximation of provisions laid down by law, regulation or administrative action relating to proprietary medicinal products (OJ, English Special Edition 1965–1966 (I), p 17), which was in force when AZ engaged in the allegedly abusive conduct. It has now been replaced by Directive 2001/83/EC of the European Parliament and of the Council of 6 November 2001 on the Community code relating to medicinal products for human use [2001] OJ L311/67.

[386] Decision, paras 840–843.

[387] Ibid, para 820 and note 616. The Commission relied on the judgments in Joined Cases T-24/93, T-25/93, T-26/93 and T-28/93 *Compagnie Maritime Belge Transports SA et al. v Commission* [1996] ECR II-1201, para 108; Case 226/86 *British Leyland v Commission* [1986] ECR 3263, paras 21–24, and Case T-30/89 *Hilti AG v Commission* [1991] ECR II-1439, para 99.

The Commission assumed that it was not necessary to show the conduct actually had anticompetitive effects in order to establish an Article 82 violation.[388] The Article 82 Discussion Paper sheds more light on the Commission's reasoning: it seems that merely showing an exclusionary intent creates a presumption that the conduct had an exclusionary effect and shifts the burden of proof to the dominant company. The presumption of an abuse can be rebutted if the company offers evidence that its conduct 'does not and will not have the alleged likely exclusionary effects, or that the conduct is objectively justified'.[389]

The *AZ* Decision is the first in which the Commission has extensively addressed the issue of antitrust immunity for 'government petitioning'. In the US, use of regulatory procedures is normally considered 'government petitioning' under the terms of the *Noerr-Pennington* doctrine, which shields the act of petitioning governmental agencies from antitrust liability, even if it has anticompetitive aims or effects.[390] The immunity extends to false statements made in the course of government petitioning,[391] provided the act of petitioning itself is not sham.[392] To date the case in which this has been discussed most comprehensively is *Compagnie Maritime Belge*,[393] where one of the elements of abusive conduct was the enforcement of a cooperation agreement between shipping companies and Ogefrem, the (then) Zairean shipping authority which gave the shipping companies exclusive rights to shipments between certain sea ports. According to the Commission, the insistence on strict enforcement of the arrangement constituted an abuse of dominance within the meaning of Article 82. The shipping companies relied on the *Noerr-Pennington* doctrine, arguing that 'the mere inducement of government action cannot constitute an abuse within the meaning of Article 82'.[394] The CFI found that the *Noerr-Pennington* defence was inapplicable,[395] and reasoned that a dominant company which enjoys an exclusive right, with an entitlement to waive that right, is under a duty to make reasonable use of the right of waiver in respect of third parties' access to the market. The ECJ confirmed that *Noerr-Pennington*

---

[388] Decision, paras 758, 848.

[389] DG Competition Discussion Paper on the application of Article 82 of the Treaty to exclusionary abuses, (reviewed earlier in this survey).

[390] See *Eastern RR Conference v Noerr Motor Freight*, 365 US 127, 135–38 (1961) l; *United Mine Workers v Pennington*, 381 US 657, 670 (1965). Noerr-Pennington immunity applies to 'petitions' before legislatures, administrative agencies, and courts: *Otter Tail Power Co v United States*, 410 US 366, 379–80 (1973) and *California Transp Co v Trucking Unlimited*, 404 US 508, 510 (1972).

[391] *Pennington*, 381 US, at 670.

[392] This is understood as petitioning that is objectively baseless and intended only to burden a rival with the governmental decision-making process itself. See *City of Columbia v Omni Outdoor Adver, Inc*, 499 US 365, 380 (1991).

[393] Commission Decision of 23 December 1992 (*Cewal, Cowac and Ukwal*), [1993] OJ L34/20, upheld in *Compagnie Maritime Belge*, n 387 above, and Joined Cases C-395/96 P and C-396/96 P *Compagnie Maritime Belge Transports SA et al. v Commission* [2000] I-1365, paras 84–86, which upheld the substance of the Commission's original decision, but annulled most of the fines on a procedural technicality.

[394] CFI judgment in *Compagnie Maritime Belge*, para 88.

[395] Ibid, para 110.

was inapplicable,[396] observing that activity designed to influence a public authority in the exercise of its discretion is different from a request to a governmental
entity to comply with a contract whose purpose is to 'enforce legal rights which
the authority concerned is, by definition, bound to observe'.[397]

The Commission relied on this reasoning in the Decision, asserting that AZ's
deregistration of Losec capsules was not government petitioning, since it did not
amount to 'requests addressed to the public authorities in the framework of an
overtly political process or an attempt to influence decisions taken in a field where
such authorities have a margin of discretion, or in general in order to receive an
independent review of the merits of the petition'.[398] The Commission's definition
of government petitioning seems rather narrow, as although the national authorities had to comply with AZ's request to deregister Losec, the consequences of
deregistration for generic drug manufacturers and parallel importers were unclear
and depended on the interpretation of the relevant pharmaceutical regulations by
the competent national authorities.

AZ has, perhaps not surprisingly, appealed.

(ii) Prokent/Tomra[399]

Although the published version of the Commission's Decision fining Tomra EUR
24 million for infringing Article 82 of the EC Treaty was not available when this
part of the survey was written, the information publicly available indicates that
it raises interesting issues, as it is the first to implement the new economics-based
approach presented in the Article 82 Discussion Paper reviewed earlier in this
survey.

Tomra manufactures and sells reverse-vending machines which collect empty
drink containers. Taking into account its high market share (above 80% on
several national markets), the weak position of its rivals and the lack of countervailing buyer power, the Commission found Tomra to be dominant despite
the apparent lack of barriers to entry. The abuse consisted of entering into three
types of agreements which allegedly foreclosed competition: (i) single-branding
agreements with discounts conditional on maintaining exclusivity, (ii) individual
quantity requirements for all or nearly all a customer's demand, and (iii) a retroactive rebate scheme conditional on reaching an individual target threshold.

The Commission claimed to have investigated the likely anticompetitive
effects of the practice fully, even though the case law only required it to show that
'the conduct is capable of having that effect'.[400] This was a response to criticism

---

[396] ECJ judgment in *Compagnie Maritime Belge*, paras 84–86. For comments on the case, see
eg, Treacy and Feaster, *Compagnie Maritime Belge Transports SA v Commission of the European
Communities* (T24/93) [1997] 4 CMLR 273 (CFI)', (1997) 18 ECLR 467, and Preece, '*Compagnie
Maritime Belge*: Missing the Boat', (2000) 21 ECLR 288.
[397] Ibid.   [398] Decision, para 819.
[399] Commission Decision of 29 March 2006 (*Prokent/Tomra*), a summary of which was published
in the OJ at [2008] OJ C219/11.
[400] *Michelin v Commission*, n 188 above, para 239.

of its actions with respect to past decisions. Thus it pointed to market developments which evidenced the exclusionary effect of the practice. First, it showed that there had been no new entrants on the market, despite the lack of major barriers to entry and the continuously weak position of Tomra's rivals. Second, it noted that Tomra was able to increase its sales, as the majority of total market demand was covered by the agreements. The Commission distinguished between non-contestable market share, ie the part of demand covered by the exclusionary practices and closed to competition, and contestable market share, ie the part of total market demand open to competition between the dominant undertaking and its rivals. On the basis of its market data, it concluded that when the non-contestable market share was larger Tomra's market share increased, which tended to show foreclosure.

Tomra denied that any of its agreements were exclusionary, and in particular that its rebate scheme was loyalty-inducing. It produced an economic study demonstrating that although its customers sometimes purchased more than the quantity required to get the rebate, the 'suction effect' alleged by the Commission would only exist if a customer decided to buy its products specifically to qualify for the rebate. Beyond that point, a customer was totally free to choose whatever product he preferred, and he might continue to buy the dominant product because he thought it was the best option, perhaps even below the threshold. The Commission rejected this argument, wondering why Tomra would voluntarily fix the target threshold below demand, as this would necessarily reduce the usefulness of such a rebate scheme. Moreover, if Tomra actually set the target threshold at expected demand, and this happened to correspond to the quantity actually bought by the customer at the end of the period, there was a 'suction effect'.

Tomra also calculated the price an equally efficient competitor would have to charge to compete with it, noting that this price was above cost regardless of whether such a competitor competed only for the part of demand above the target threshold, or for both that part and the last unit necessary to obtain Tomra's rebate. In addition, the larger the part of demand above the target threshold, the higher the price an equally efficient competitor could fix to meet Tomra's conditions. In light of this, Tomra submitted that its scheme could not be abusive, as an equally efficient competitor could viably remain on the market. The Commission disagreed, observing that a competitor's profit would decrease if it chose also to compete for the last unit necessary to obtain the threshold, and that it was not individually rational to forego profit voluntarily. The Commission therefore concluded that an equally efficient competitor would avoid competing for that last unit and limit its action to the part of demand above the target threshold. It thus found that the rebate scheme had an exclusionary effect.

The Decision can be criticized. It may be clothed in economic reasoning, but in essence it departs little from the old mantra that retroactive rebate schemes are illegal by nature. The Commission merely referred to theoretical 'individual rationality' to rebut Tomra's arguments. It would have done better to carry out a full assessment of the market situation, as the theory underlying exclusionary abuses mainly applies to near-monopolies, making it crucial to determine how strong the dominance is, the size of the contestable market share, and the degree of foreclosure (for instance, by taking possible alternative marketing routes into account). In sum, while the Commission's adoption of more effect-based reasoning is welcome, it might have been expected to base its *Tomra* Decision on a more thorough economic analysis than that indicated by the publicly available information.

(iii) Microsoft: Developments in 2005 and 2006

As reported in the previous edition of this survey, in March 2004 the Commission adopted a Decision[401] finding that Microsoft had abused its dominance by: (i) refusing to supply competitors with 'interoperability information' regarding its work group server operating systems, and (ii) tying Windows Media Player with its Windows PC operating system. To remedy the abuses, Microsoft had to: (i) prepare and then license a detailed description of the functioning of part of its server operating system, and (ii) bring out a special version of Windows without media player functionality. Microsoft also had to submit a proposal for a monitoring system, including the appointment of a Trustee with the power to conduct proactive investigations. Finally, the Commission imposed what was then the largest fine ever on a single company, namely EUR 497,196,304. Predictably, Microsoft sought the annulment of the Decision,[402] and also sought its suspension pending the outcome of the main appeal. However, the President of the CFI rejected the latter request in December 2004.[403]

During the period covered here the oral hearing in the action for the annulment of the Decision took place (on 24–28 April 2006), and there were also interesting developments in the parallel proceedings regarding Microsoft's compliance with the 2004 Decision. One concerned the requirement for Microsoft to propose a monitoring system and Trustee. The Commission and Microsoft initially disagreed on the terms describing the Trustee's mission. When they finally reached agreement, the Commission adopted a Decision in July 2005 which implemented the 2004 Decision and precisely defined the method of appointing the Trustee and his role and mandate.[404] In particular, it reiterated that the Trustee would have access to Microsoft's documents, premises, personnel and source code, and emphasized his independence and ability to behave proactively. In October 2005 the Commission, in accordance with the procedure laid down in the Decision, appointed Neil Barrett as Monitoring Trustee, with two technical advisers.

[401] Commission Decision of 24 March 2004 (*Microsoft*) [2007] OJ L 32/23.
[402] Case T-201/04 R *Microsoft v Commission* [2004] ECR II-4463. The CFI's judgment, rendered on 17 September 2007, upheld all aspects of the Decision except the appointment of a Trustee.
[403] Order of 22 December 2004 in Case T-201/04 R *Microsoft v Commission* [2004] ECR II-4463.
[404] Commission Decision of 28 July 2005 (*Microsoft*), available online at: <http://ec.europa.eu/comm/competition/antitrust/cases/decisions/37792/trustee.pdf>.

Secondly, a dispute arose as to whether Microsoft had complied with its obligations under the 2004 Decision. This led to the application of Article 24 of Regulation 1/2003, which empowers the Commission to impose a daily penalty payment of up to 5% of average daily turnover on an undertaking which fails to comply with an infringement decision. The procedure has two stages: the Commission first takes an Article 24(1) decision threatening to impose the daily penalty payment if the undertaking is still defaulting on a determined date; and if that is the case, and after consulting the Advisory Committee, it then takes an Article 24(2) decision fixing the definitive amount of the penalty and the duration of the non-compliance (the starting date being the date mentioned in the Article 24(1) decision). In its Article 24(2) decision the Commission may impose a reduced penalty. In this case the Commission considered that Microsoft had failed to comply with its obligations in two ways, and on 10 November 2005 it adopted a Decision pursuant to Article 24(1) of Regulation 1/2003 which threatened Microsoft with a EUR 2 million daily penalty payment if it did not comply by 15 December 2005.[405]

Firstly, the Commission found that the Technical Documentation supplied by Microsoft was insufficient to discharge its obligation to supply *'complete and accurate specifications'* for all the relevant Protocols to perform file/print and user administration services in Windows work group servers. Relying on its experts' opinion, the Commission held that the Technical Documentation was difficult to use and lacked essential information for licensees to develop work group server operating systems which could interoperate with Microsoft's. Secondly, it took issue with the substantial level of royalties requested by Microsoft, noting that the royalties should not reflect the strategic value stemming from Microsoft's market power: they could only be more than nominal if: (i) the protocols were Microsoft's own creation, (ii) they were innovative, and (iii) the remuneration was in line with a market valuation for comparable technologies. After a detailed analysis, including an assessment of the innovativeness of the information provided, the Commission concluded that Microsoft had failed to provide the interoperability information on reasonable and non-discriminatory (RAND) terms.

The dispute regarding the licensing terms was not resolved during the period covered by this survey. However, in December 2005, the Commission sent Microsoft a Statement of Objections regarding the aspect of the dispute relating to the Technical Documentation. Although Microsoft had revised the interoperability information it had supplied, the Commission considered that by 15 December 2005 it had still not fully complied with its obligations. It based its position on reports from the Monitoring Trustee that the Technical Documentation was flawed in its conception and its level of explanation and detail. Microsoft disagreed with these criticisms and claimed that the latest version complied with its obligations. Microsoft also submitted further revised technical information which was examined by the Commission and the Trustee, and which the Commission again

---

[405] Commission Decision of 10 November 2005 (*Microsoft*).

found to be unsatisfactory. After a hearing in March 2006, the Commission, again relying on reports from the Trustee and its own technical experts, adopted on 12 July 2006[405a] a Decision under Article 24(2) of Regulation 1/2003 fining Microsoft EUR 280.5 million for non-compliance from 16 December 2005 to 12 July 2006. In substance, the reports pointed out that even the most recent version of the Technical Documentation still lacked information on, in particular, the required properties, some definitions of important terms, and a proper index, and required too much prior knowledge, and could therefore not be used by licensees to develop interoperable products. The Commission rejected Microsoft's contention that the Technical Documentation satisfied the industry practice, and concluded that throughout the relevant period it had been incomplete and inaccurate to such an extent that it was not a suitable basis for an interested undertaking to start developing work group server operating systems which would interoperate with Microsoft's products, as envisaged by the 2004 Decision. However, because the Commission had left open the question of Microsoft's compliance regarding the licensing terms, it reduced the final daily penalty payment from EUR 2 million to €1.5 million, to cover only the aspect of the dispute relating to the documentation, while retaining the possibility to impose the remaining EUR 0.5 million penalty with regard to the licensing terms.

Interestingly, in the same Decision the Commission amended its November 2005 Article 24(1) Decision by increasing the periodic penalty payment to €3 million from 31 July 2006. The increase would apply to both the failure to provide complete and accurate technical documentation and the unreasonable licensing terms. The Commission justified the increase by Microsoft's failure to comply for such a long time and the need to ensure its compliance. Thus the July 2006 Decision is 'mixed', as it is both an Article 24(2) Decision fixing the definitive amount of the penalty payment, and an Article 24(1) Decision notifying an increased penalty payment from a future date. Microsoft lodged an action for annulment of this Decision.[406]

A third dispute arose with regard to the licensing terms. This time the issue was not the remuneration as in the RAND aspect of the dispute discussed above, but the contractual terms on which Microsoft could license. In June 2005, the Commission informed Microsoft by letter that it was under an obligation to permit the distribution of software developed by its licensees to third parties in source code form, unless the software included an invention by Microsoft which satisfied the patentability criteria of novelty and inventiveness. Microsoft lodged an action for annulment against the letter,[407] arguing that this open source approach would unnecessarily disclose and nullify its trade secrets protection.

[405a] Commission Decision of 12 July 2006 (*Microsoft*) available online at: <http://ec.europa.eu/comm/competition/antitrust/cases/decisions/37792/art24_2_decision.pdf>.

[406] Case T-271/06, *Microsoft v Commission*. Microsoft eventually decided to discontinue these proceedings.

[407] Case T-313/05 *Microsoft v Commission*. Microsoft eventually decided to discontinue these proceedings.

(iv) Coca Cola Commitment Decision[408]

This was an investigation that resulted in the first commitment decision under Article 82 of the EC Treaty. In June 2005, the Commission adopted an Article 9 decision that renders commitments offered by the Coca-Cola Company and three major bottlers (together, 'Coca-Cola') concerning the carbonated soft drinks ('CSDs') market, legally binding. As a consequence of the commitments offered, the Commission closed its investigations, one of the longest to date, into Coca-Cola's sales practices in the CSD market.

The commitments cover all EEA countries and remain in force until 2010. They are binding on Coca-Cola in all markets where it holds a market share above 40% which is more than twice the share of its nearest competitor. In terms of content, they apply to a broad range of sales practices in the CSD market.

First, exclusivity arrangements are prohibited. Coca-Cola customers must remain free to buy and sell carbonated soft drinks from any supplier of their choice. The only exception concerns cases where Coca-Cola wins an open and competitive tender by providing the best offer; in all other negotiations, Coca-Cola may not condition advantages on obtaining exclusivity. Special rules apply to private tender and sponsorship agreements.

Second, target and growth rebates are forbidden. Coca-Cola may no longer offer any rebates that reward its customers purely for purchasing the same amount as or more of its products than in the past. The absence of any individual or growth target should make it easier for Coca-Cola's customers to purchase from other CSD suppliers if they so wish. At the same time, volume-based rebates based on standardized purchase thresholds available to all similarly situated customers are allowed.

Third, the commitments prohibit tying and bundling. Coca-Cola may not force a customer of one of its best-selling brands (eg regular Coke or Fanta Orange) to purchase additional products such as its Sprite. Similarly, it may no longer offer a rebate conditional on commitments by customers to purchase additional products together with its best-selling brands, or to reserve shelf space for the entire group of products.

Fourth, with regard to cooler space, the commitments require 20% of Coca-Cola's coolers to remain free for other products. In particular, when Coca-Cola provides a free cooler to a retailer and there is no other chilled beverage capacity in the outlet to which the consumer has direct access and which is suitable for competing CSDs, the retailer is free to use at least 20% of the cooler provided by Coca-Cola for any product it chooses. In addition, Coca-Cola may not preclude retailers from acquiring their own coolers.

Fifth, the commitments limit the contractual clauses in financing agreements in the on-premises channel. It is common industry practice for beverage suppliers to make loans to bars and restaurants. Coca-Cola may not condition such

---

[408] Commission Decision of 22 June 2005 (*Coca-Cola*) [2005] OJ L 253/21.

financing agreements on an obligation to purchase a specific range of its products. Restaurants and bars must also retain the opportunity to terminate the agreement without being subject to any penalty.

In addition to the above, Coca-Cola agreed to further commitments aimed at facilitating the implementation of the settlement. They include publicity obligations on its website and invoices, as well as annual reporting obligations to the Commission. Any breach of the commitments could lead the Commission to fine Coca-Cola a fine 10% of its total worldwide turnover.

More than any other of the recent commitment decisions, the Coca-Cola decision shows the usefulness of Article 9 of Regulation 1/2003 in attaining very efficient, prompt, and far-reaching remedies in the market-place. It thus proves to be an excellent enforcement tool, far preferable to an infringement decision imposed unilaterally on a company. If a company instead succeeds in reaching a settlement, the Commission is *de facto* in a strong position to achieve the remedies it considers necessary, while at the same time the company concerned plays a full part in the process of specifying and describing the remedies. The Commission should, on the basis of this very successful example, give serious weight to the superiority of the Article 9 mechanism over infringement decisions, particularly with regard to Article 82 of the EC Treaty and to related remedies.

G. Select Procedural Matters

(i) *Access to the File and Transparency*

Austrian Banks—Lombard Club[409]

Before the Austrian banks themselves came to judgment in their appeal against a condemnation for cartel activities, the CFI had already ruled on two procedural cases arising from the Commission's investigations into their cartel. Both arose from a Commission Decision concerning access by third parties to its file on the case, but while the Court's ruling in each case was similar, the Decisions in question were very different. As will be analysed below, they indicate an important development in the Commission's view of what the goals of competition law should be.

While the Commission was investigating the cartel, the consumer organization Verein für Konsumenteninformation (VKI) requested access to the Commission's administrative file in the case, as it was engaged in proceedings before the Austrian civil courts to assert certain financial claims assigned to it by consumers against one of the cartel participants, the Bank für Arbeit und Wirtschaft AG (BAWAG). When the Commission rejected VKI's request, VKI sought annulment of this Decision.

---

[409] Case T-2/03 *Verein für Konsumenteninformation (VKI) v Commission*, [2005] ECR II-1121.

The CFI obliged. The Court held that in such cases the Commission must examine each document requested to see whether partial access could be given, and that it had failed both to examine and give reasons for refusing access to each of the requested documents, and to assess whether partial access could be given. It examined the Commission's application of the exceptions relating to investigations, commercial interests, court proceedings and the privacy and integrity of the individual under the Transparency Regulation, and concluded that they did not necessarily apply to the whole of the administrative file, and that even where they might apply, they concerned only certain passages in certain documents. In the Court's view, it was not apparent that the Commission had 'considered specifically and exhaustively the various options available to it in order to take steps which would not impose an unreasonable amount of work on it but would, on the other hand, increase the chances that the applicant might receive, at least in respect of part of its request, access to the documents concerned'.[410]

The Court held that the concrete, individual examination of the documents referred to in a request for access was one of an institution's elementary duties in response to such a request. It emphasized that exceptions to the principle of access to documents must be interpreted particularly strictly.[411] To rely on an exception to the principle of disclosure under Article 4(2) of the Transparency Regulation, the document must actually undermine the protected interest rather than simply concern that interest; the risk of a protected interest being undermined must be reasonably foreseeable and not purely hypothetical; there must be no overriding public interest; and the concrete examination must be carried out in respect of each document requested in order to assess the extent to which an exception to the right of access was applicable and the possibility of partial access. The Court acknowledged that such an examination might not be necessary when, due to the particular circumstances of the individual case, it was obvious that access must be refused or granted. However, it held that only in exceptional cases where the administrative burden of a concrete, individual examination would be particularly heavy, thereby exceeding the limits of what might reasonably be required, would it be permissible to derogate from the obligation to examine each document individually to determine whether any exception applied or whether partial access was possible. Moreover, even when an institution considered the burden to be unreasonable, it must still consult the applicant and try to have him state his request more specifically.

This was the first case won by an applicant against the Commission following the entry into force of the Transparency Regulation in December 2001. It places on Community institutions the heavy burden of fully justifying any rejection of a request for access to documents. The judgment thereby hands a helpful tool to applicants claiming damages in national proceedings, who might not otherwise have an automatic right of access to a Commission competition file.

---

[410] Judgment, para 126.   [411] Ibid, para 106.

Further consideration of the Transparency Regulation:
Yves Franchet and Daniel Byk[412]

Before going on to the second case in which a third party successfully sought access to the Lombard Club file, it may be interesting to examine a 2006 case in which the Transparency Regulation was also considered. Although *Franchet and Byk v Commission* was not in the field of competition law (it was brought in the context of anti-fraud investigations), it nevertheless builds on the *VKI* judgment and adds clarification which is relevant to a request for access to information, whether or not in the context of a competition case. It therefore seems appropriate to draw attention to it in this survey of competition law developments.

The case concerned an application for annulment of Decisions by the European Anti-Fraud Office (OLAF) and the Commission refusing access to certain documents relating to an enquiry into accounting irregularities in Eurostat, where both applicants were high-ranking officials. The applicants sought access to certain correspondence sent by OLAF to the Luxembourg and French judicial authorities and communications from OLAF to the Commission. OLAF formally rejected these requests in October 2003 ('the first contested Decision'), stating that the documents were covered by the exceptions in Regulation 1049/2001 relating to inspections, investigations, and audits, and to court proceedings. A second request by the applicants to obtain the annexes to a report which they had received was rejected by the Commission on 19 December 2003 ('the second contested Decision').

The Court started by recalling previous case law which held that the exceptions contained in the Transparency Regulation had to be construed and applied restrictively.[413] It then considered the protection of court proceedings exception on which OLAF had relied. The Court recalled that it had already[414] interpreted the expression 'documents drawn up solely for the purposes of specific court proceedings', in the context of a previous Commission Decision concerning public access to Commission documents,[415] to mean 'the pleadings or other documents lodged, internal documents concerning the investigation of the case, and correspondence concerning the case between the Directorate-General concerned and the Legal Service or a lawyer's office'. The CFI also recalled that the exception does not apply to documents drawn up in connection with a purely administrative matter, and that the competent national authorities are solely and entirely responsible for any action they take in response to reports and information forwarded by OLAF.

---

[412] Joined Cases T-391/03 and T-70/04 *Yves Franchet and Daniel Byk v Commission* [2006] ECR II-2023.

[413] Judgment, para 84.   [414] Case T-92/98 *Interporc v Commission* [1999] ECR II-3521.

[415] Commission Decision 94/90/ECSC, EC, Euratom on public access to Commission documents—Decision refusing access to documents—Protection of the public interest (court proceedings) [1994] OJ L46/58.

In this case the CFI held that OLAF's communications to national authorities would not necessarily lead to the opening of national judicial proceedings (or administrative or disciplinary proceedings at Community level), and it could therefore not be said that these documents came under the court proceedings exception: 'To find under these circumstances that the various documents sent by OLAF were drawn up solely for the purposes of court proceedings would not correspond to the interpretation given by the case law to that exception, and runs counter to the obligation to construe and apply the exceptions restrictively.'[416] OLAF should only have refused access if the national courts had been consulted and had objected to the disclosure. The first contested Decision was thus held to be vitiated by an error insofar as it relied on this exception.

The Court then considered the second exception, based on the protection of the purpose of inspections, investigations and audits. It accepted that all the documents requested related to such activities, but held that this was not enough in itself to justify the application of this exception. The test was whether inspections or investigations were in progress at the time of the requests and would have been jeopardized by the requested disclosures. The Court also stated, referring to *VKI*, that 'the examination which the institution must undertake in order to apply an exception must be carried out in a concrete manner and must be apparent from the reasons for the decision.'[417] Such an examination was required for each document referred to in a request for access.

In summary, it was necessary to assess, first, whether the documents requested fell within one of the exceptions; second, if so, whether the need for protection under the exception was genuine; and, third, whether it applied to the whole of each document. In terms of the first contested Decision, the Court found that disclosure of documents sent to the national authorities could prevent any procedures or investigations the national authorities might decide to initiate from being conducted efficiently, and the Commission had therefore not erred in invoking the investigations and audits exception concerning those documents. The Court reached similar conclusions regarding the report which was the subject-matter of the second contested Decision and one of the communications from OLAF to the Commission. However, it found that it had not been demonstrated that investigations would have been threatened by the disclosure of the other communications from OLAF to the Commission, as OLAF had based its assessment on the nature of the documents rather than on any particular information they contained. This was an error of law, and the Court therefore partially annulled the first contested Decision.

Finally the Court addressed the question of the existence of an overriding public interest. It held that the Commission had not erred in finding that the right to a fair hearing invoked by the applicants as an overriding interest was in this case a

---

[416] Judgment, para 96.   [417] Judgment, para 115.

private interest, and not an overriding public interest justifying disclosure of the requested documents.

While the applicants therefore obtained access to some of the requested documents, and the Court obliged the Commission to reassess its blanket refusal of access, this case nevertheless sets a limit on the greater transparency suggested in *VKI*. The Commission may as a result be encouraged to rely more often on the exception based on the protection of the purpose of inspections, investigations and audits in order to refuse access to documents. Third parties seeking access to documents will need to check the justifications provided by the Commission if they wish to challenge such a refusal.

FPO's Request for Access to the Lombard Club File[418]

In the second case regarding access to the *Lombard Club* file, the CFI upheld the Commission's novel Decision that it had the power to disclose a non-confidential copy of a Statement of Objections sent to an undertaking in the course of a cartel investigation to the undertaking's final customer. The Court also made a number of welcome comments regarding the link between EC competition law and consumer welfare.

In June 1997, during the Commission's investigations into the Austrian banks' cartel activities, an Austrian political party, the Freiheitliche Partei Österreichs (FPO) asked the Commission to commence proceedings under Article 81 of the EC Treaty, and sent the Commission a copy of the 'Lombard 8.5' document referred to earlier in this survey. In September 1999, the Commission sent the banks in question Statements of Objections setting out its initial conclusion that they had entered into anticompetitive agreements concerning the fees and conditions applicable to their customers. In November 2000, the Commission sent each bank a supplementary Statement of Objections alleging that they had also entered into agreements relating to fees for national currency to Euro exchange transactions. The FPO requested copies of all the Statements of Objections, claiming that as a customer of the banks under investigation it had suffered economic harm as a result of the alleged anticompetitive practices. The Commission informed the banks that it intended to grant the FPO's request under Article 6 of Regulation 2842/98.[419] Although two of the banks objected on the ground that the FPO was not a complainant with a 'legitimate interest' under Article 3(2) of Regulation 17, the Commission Hearing Officer decided in August 2001 (ie before the Transparency Regulation entered into force in December 2001, though by then it was certainly clear in which direction the wind of disclosure was blowing) to disclose non-confidential versions of the original and supplementary Statements of Objections to the FPO. In December 2001, the President of the

---

[418] *Austrian Banks*, n 208 above.
[419] Commission Regulation 2842/98 of 22 December 1998 on the hearing of parties in certain proceedings under Articles 85 and 86 of the EC Treaty [1998] OJ L354/18.

CFI dismissed an application for interim measures to suspend the Commission's Decision or restrain it from disclosing the Statement of Objections, concluding that the requirement of urgency was not fulfilled and the balance of interests was not in favour of suspending the operation of the contested Decision.[420]

The CFI rejected all the banks' claims. It considered that neither Regulation 17 nor Regulation 2842/98 required an applicant's complaint to be at the origin of Commission infringement proceedings,[421] and that the Commission was not required to state expressly its reasons for finding that the FPO had a legitimate interest in all the banking markets affected by the case.[422] Furthermore, when an applicant has proved that it has a legitimate interest, the Commission is not obliged to verify whether it may have other motives for obtaining the Statement of Objections,[423] and is entitled to disclose a non-confidential version of it to the applicant.[424] The CFI added that any confidentiality concerns an undertaking under investigation might have as regards disclosure of its identity or the extent of its participation in the alleged agreement could not affect this conclusion.[425]

The judgment is important because, like the ruling in *VKI v Commission*, it indicates a clear policy choice by the CFI to give greater importance to the increased involvement of private parties in EC competition investigations than to the protection of certain confidential information. The CFI clearly takes the view that final customers who purchase goods or services have a legitimate interest in ensuring that the Commission can establish infringements of Articles 81 and 82 of the EC Treaty, as this helps to achieve the objectives of EC competition law, including that of consumer benefit.[426] These statements build on the ECJ's judgments in *Courage*[427] and *Manfredi*,[428] and are in line with the Commission's renewed emphasis on the desirability of increased private enforcement of EC competition law. The judgment confirms the importance the Community institutions now give to private enforcement, and indicates that when there is a conflict between the protection of information in a non-confidential Statement of Objections which potentially incriminates certain undertakings, and the need to ensure greater private enforcement of EC competition law, the latter interest will prevail over the former.

(ii) Article 86 EC Complaints—T-Mobile Austria[429]

In this case, the ECJ quashed the CFI judgment and confirmed the Commission's discretion not to bring proceedings under Article 86(3) of the EC Treaty following a complaint. It also rejected the more lenient approach taken by the CFI and the Advocate General regarding the right of the complainant to appeal such a

---

[420] *Austrian Banks*, para 83.   [421] Ibid, para 91.   [422] Ibid, para 131.
[423] Ibid, para 118.   [424] Ibid, para 107.   [425] Ibid, para 206.
[426] Ibid, para 115.   [427] *Courage v Crehan*, n 28 above.
[428] *Vincenzo Manfredi*, n 38 above (see further below).
[429] Case C-141/02 P *Commission v T-Mobile Austria* [2005] ECR I-1283.

decision. Finally, it ruled on the admissibility of an appeal lodged by a privileged applicant which was successful at first instance.

Max.mobil (now, T-Mobile Austria) complained to the Commission that it had had to pay the same fee for its GSM licence as the public operator Mobilkom. Max.mobil argued that Austria had granted an unlawful advantage to a state-owned undertaking, contrary to Articles 82 and 86 of the EC Treaty, and requested the Commission to act. The Commission decided not to bring proceedings under Article 86(3). Max.mobil challenged this refusal before the CFI.

The CFI interpreted Article 86(3) by analogy with the other EC competition law provisions, in particular Articles 81, 82, 87, and 88 of the EC Treaty, which grant procedural rights to complainants.[430] The CFI also noted that the discretion enjoyed by the Commission under Article 86 EC was more limited than under Article 226 of the EC Treaty, given the difference in wording ('must where necessary' instead of 'may').[431] Consequently the Commission was under an obligation to undertake a diligent and impartial examination of complaints. Moreover, a decision on whether to start proceedings was subject to judicial review,[432] although the review must be limited to verifying the appropriateness of the statement of reasons provided by the Commission.[433] However, the CFI eventually found the action unfounded.

On appeal, the ECJ rejected the CFI's reasoning. The Court recognized that individuals may be entitled to challenge a decision not to bring proceedings under Article 86(3), but only in exceptional circumstances and when they were directly and individually concerned.[434] The need to comply with these requirements could not be circumvented by invoking the principle of sound administration or any other general principle of EC law.[435] The Court also dismissed the analogy with the procedural rights under the Regulation implementing Articles 81 and 82,[436] and found that the letter sent to max.mobil could not constitute a challengeable act because it did not produce binding legal effects.[437] Beyond the admissibility issue of the challenge, the ECJ held that the Commission was under no obligation to start proceedings following a complaint, and that individuals may not force the Commission to take a position.[438] The Court thus found the action inadmissible in the first place and did not have to rule on the substance.

This ruling can be criticized. First, as Advocate General Poiares Maduro rightly observed, Article 86 grants the Commission a supervisory power comparable to the other Treaty competition provisions,[439] and it thus has a duty to carry out a diligent and impartial examination of complaints.[440] Furthermore, when the Commission has a direct power of decision having effects on the market, the case law requires legal protection to be given to individuals particularly affected

---

[430] Case T-54/99, *max.mobil v Commission* [2002] ECR II-313, paras 49–51.
[431] Ibid, para 54.   [432] Ibid, paras 55–57.   [433] ECJ judgment, para 21.
[434] Ibid, para 68.   [435] Ibid, para 72.   [436] Ibid, para 70.
[437] Ibid, para 70.   [438] Ibid, para 69.
[439] Opinion of Advocate General Maduro in *T-Mobile Austria*.   [440] Ibid, para 56.

by the decision in question, regardless of the absence of any obligation for the Commission to act on a specific case.[441]

Second, the Advocate General pointed out that the Commission's letter stating its intention not to bring proceedings constituted a Decision which produced binding legal effects for both the Member State concerned and the complainant, even though neither of them qualified as its addressee.[442] The letter actually set out an objective situation of law relating to the applicability of certain Treaty provisions;[443] it neither closed a procedure conferring procedural rights on the parties as in Articles 81 and 82,[444] nor formed part of an exclusive dialogue with the Member State as in the framework of Article 88 EC.[445] However, it must be open to challenge by affected individuals fulfilling the criteria laid down by Article 230(4) of the EC Treaty.[446] The Advocate General concluded that max. mobil was directly and individually concerned, as the Commission took its specific situation into consideration in the Decision by making a comparison between the fee paid by max.mobil and its competitor Mobilkom.[447] The Court's decision ignored these strong arguments of principle.

The Court also ruled on a procedural issue concerning appeals by the EU institutions. It accepted as admissible the Commission's appeal against the CFI's rejection of a plea of inadmissibility, even though the CFI had subsequently dismissed the action as unfounded.[448] The Advocate General reached the same conclusion, but his reasoning was more detailed. He noted that while privileged applicants are not required to show interest to lodge an appeal,[449] they must still identify a decision subject to appeal[450] and are not entitled to appeal solely in the interest of the law.[451] Besides practical justifications, he recalled that the nature of the ECJ's review function is to verify the correct interpretation and application of Community law in a specific case. The AG concluded that in this case the express rejection of the inadmissibility plea constituted an intermediate finding open to appeal, because it was the consequence of a dispute and was connected with the operative part of the CFI's judgment.[452]

(iii) Syfait—The Position of National Competition Authorities under Article 234 EC[453]

This case raised a key question of importance: whether a dominant pharmaceutical undertaking is under a duty to supply unlimited quantities of prescription medicinal products to wholesalers. The ECJ's judgment proved in the end to be something of a damp squib as to Article 82 of the EC Treaty, but provides

---

[441] Ibid, para 35.   [442] Ibid, para 45.   [443] Ibid, para 43.
[444] Ibid, para 38.   [445] Ibid, para 42.   [446] Ibid, para 46.
[447] Ibid, paras 66–67.   [448] *T-Mobile Austria*, para 50.
[449] Advocate General's Opinion, para 17.   [450] Ibid, para 19.
[451] Ibid, para 21.   [452] Ibid, para 22.
[453] Case C-53/03 *Synetairismos Farmakopoion Aitolias & Akarnanias (Syfait) et al. v Glaxosmithkline AEVE and GlaxoSmithKline plc* [2005] ECR I-4609.

Forrester, MacLennan, and Komninos

invaluable guidance on the criteria an authority must fulfil in order to make referrals to the Community Courts. The case reached Luxembourg through a preliminary reference from the Greek Competition Authority, the *Epitropi Antagonismou*. The Court considered the reference inadmissible on the ground that the Authority was not a 'court or tribunal' in the sense of Article 234 of the EC Treaty. This finding on the inadmissibility of preliminary references by national competition authorities (NCA) will have important repercussions of an institutional and procedural nature in view of the decentralized system of anti-trust enforcement which came into force in May 2004.

The substance of the case had to do with the extent to which a dominant pharmaceutical undertaking may implement unilateral policies making supplies to wholesalers contingent upon demand in the Member State concerned. Although the ECJ did not rule on this question, pharmaceutical companies have grounds for satisfaction with Advocate General Jacobs's Opinion, which recognized the specificity of the industry owing to the extent of state intervention involved, notably with regard to product prices, and concluded that a refusal by a dominant pharmaceutical company to meet all its customers' orders does not automatically constitute abuse of a dominant position.[454]

Whether an NCA can be considered a court or tribunal in the sense of Article 234 EC has always been a matter for debate. There were precedents where the ECJ had admitted references from bodies resembling the Greek Authority, but while the Authority has some of the characteristics of a judicial body, in other respects it is more of an independent administrative authority. Advocate General Jacobs's Opinion on this point was finely balanced, making it clear that he had doubts but thought that as a matter of efficiency and economy the Court should admit the reference. The Court, however, preferred to take a narrow view of what constitutes a court or tribunal. It noted that there were no particular safeguards in respect of the dismissal or termination of the appointment of members of the Authority, and that it was not sufficiently independent of the public administration. Interestingly, the ECJ also recalled that pursuant to Article 11(6) of Regulation 1/2003, the Commission has the power to relieve NCAs of their competence by initiating its own proceedings.[455] A body may refer a question to the ECJ only if there is a case pending before it, and if it is called upon to give judgment in proceedings intended to lead to a decision of a judicial nature. In the ECJ's view, whenever the Commission relieves an NCA of its competence, the proceedings initiated before that authority will not lead to a decision of a judicial nature.

---

[454] In fact the ECJ had the opportunity to pronounce on the substance of the case, as the Athens Civil Court of Appeal referred the same questions as those referred by the Greek Competition Authority in the context of a number of national proceedings brought by Greek wholesalers against GlaxoSmithKline AEVE. See now Judgment of 16 September 2008 in Joined Cases C-468/06 *Sot. Lelos Kai Sia et al. v Glaxosmithkline AEVE Farmakeftikon Proionton,* not yet reported.

[455] See in particular on this point Komninos, 'Article 234 EC and National Competition Authorities in the Era of Decentralisation', (2004) 29 ELRev 106, at 110 *et seq.*

The Court's ruling deserves particular attention in the new era of decentralized enforcement. It is true that since the form and organization of NCAs vary considerably between Member States, it is not easy *a priori* to determine their qualification under Article 234 EC. Generally speaking there are two prevailing models. One is what might be called a 'monist' model where the NCA is an integrated independent administrative body, such as the German *Bundeskartellamt*, the Italian *Autorità garante della concorrenza e del commercio*, the Greek *Epitropi Antagonismou*, the Dutch *Nederlandse Mededingingsautoriteit*, the Portuguese *Autoridade da concorrência*, the UK Office of Fair Trading, or (recently) the Spanish *Comisión Nacional de la Competencia*. These integrated authorities are given full powers to hear, decide, and impose penalties, while their decisions are reviewed by national administrative, special, or ordinary civil courts, depending on the legal system in question. However, the administrative appearance of such authorities, notwithstanding their quasi-judicial nature and their functional separation from the public administration, appears to be an obstacle to the admissibility of their preliminary references.

The second model for NCAs is a 'dualist' one, with on the one hand a specific authority in charge of investigations which forms part of the public administration, and on the other an independent body with powers of decision which may be administrative or judicial, although its exact nature may vary from case to case and may present distinctive features that make its categorization difficult. This model has been adopted by Member States such as Austria, Belgium, Finland, France, Ireland, and Sweden. Ireland is unique in having no specialized authority or 'cartel' or 'market' court to take decisions, cases being decided by the ordinary courts. This type of administrative or judicial body with powers of decision seems to fit the criteria of Article 234 and the pertinent case law better; indeed, the Court accepted a preliminary reference from the old Spanish *Tribunal de defensa de la competencia* in the *Spanish Banks* case.[456]

Thus it may be concluded that the Court could not *a priori* have adopted the position that all NCAs qualify as a court or tribunal under Article 234, since their respective characteristics, in particular their dependence on or independence of the administration, vary and can only be judged *ad hoc*. This may be regrettable from the point of view of uniformity and equal treatment, but it is merely a consequence of the Member States' institutional and procedural autonomy, which is also recognized by Article 35 of Regulation 1/2003. In our view the Court showed its awareness of the problem of equal treatment/uniformity, while feeling bound by earlier restrictive case law on what constitutes a court or tribunal under Article 234. It resolved the issue by implicitly making a U-turn and holding that few if any NCAs would qualify as 'courts' or 'tribunals' in the Article 234 sense.

---

[456] Case C-67/91 *Dirección General de Defensa de la Competencia v Asociación Española de Banca Privada et al. (Spanish Banks)* [1992] ECR I-4785.

The about-turn is not highlighted. Indeed, in paragraphs 30 to 33 of its judgment the Court engages in an *ad hoc* examination of the particular characteristics of the Greek NCA which might give the impression that in some circumstances it would still be ready to admit preliminary references from certain NCAs. However, paragraphs 34 to 36 resolve any doubts by making it clear that bodies which can be relieved of their competence under Article 11(6) of Regulation 1/2003 by the Commission, an administrative authority, cannot be considered as judicial bodies. In other words, the Court saw the Article 11(6) possibility as an obstacle to the Article 234 preliminary reference procedure. Presumably Article 11(6) and the other mechanisms for cooperation between administrative authorities in the context of the European Competition Network could not be reconciled with the more specific mechanism of judicial cooperation in Article 234 EC. To admit preliminary references from NCAs would have meant moving from an administrative system based on the discretionary powers of administrative authorities to an anticipated or even premature 'judicialization'.

The Court's approach therefore seems to be that it will no longer admit preliminary references from NCAs, whether of a 'monist' or a 'dualist' structure, when those authorities form part of the ECN and the Commission therefore theoretically retains the power to relieve them of their competence by initiating proceedings. In this sense the Court has implicitly departed from its earlier more permissive approach in *Spanish Banks,* and the absence of any reference to that case is indicative of its about-face. This restrictive approach is likely to disappoint many competition law specialists, who would prefer it if all NCAs presenting certain minimum judicial characteristics were equally entitled to submit references to Luxembourg, especially following the decentralization of EC competition law enforcement. On the other hand, the ECJ's position is understandable, since a more liberal approach might not be fully compatible with long-standing case law declaring references coming from various administrative bodies or parts of national authorities to be inadmissible. In the Court's mind, the ECN appears a more appropriate context than Luxembourg to provide support to NCAs when they are dealing with Community competition law. The Court may also have feared that an 'exception' for the competition field would open the floodgates to hundreds of references by an incalculable number of administrative authorities in a Union of 27 Member States.

(iv) Damages Actions—Manfredi

If *Courage* was the ruling where the Court of Justice consecrated the existence of a Community law right in damages when an individual is harmed by a violation of EC competition law, *Manfredi*[457] is where the Court went on to deal

---

[457] *Vincenzo Manfredi*, n 38 above.

further with the specific conditions of this Community right in damages.[458] This was a preliminary reference case from Italy, where insurance companies had been sued for damages by Italian consumers for prohibited cartel behaviour previously condemned by the Italian competition authority.[459] The ECJ was basically asked to decide:

(a) whether consumers enjoy a right to sue cartel members and claim damages for harm suffered when there is a causal relationship between the agreement or concerted practice and the harm;

(b) whether the starting date of the limitation period for bringing an action for damages is the day on which the agreement or concerted practice was put into effect or the day when it came to an end;

(c) whether a national court should also of its own motion award punitive damages to an injured third party, in order to make the compensable amount higher than the advantage gained by the infringing party and discourage the adoption of agreements or concerted practices prohibited under Article 81 of the EC Treaty.[460]

The Court, building on *Courage*, and after making it clear that the basis for individual civil liabilities deriving from a violation of Article 81 does indeed lie in Community law, made a fundamental distinction between the *existence* and *exercise* of the right in damages. That the *existence* of the right is a matter of Community law is obvious from the fact that the Court solemnly reiterated the most important pronouncements of *Courage*.[461] This was also clearly the context in which the Court proceeded to define, as a matter of Community law, the basic

---

[458] See also De Smijter and O'Sullivan, 'The *Manfredi* Judgment of the ECJ and How it Relates to the Commission's Initiative on EC Antitrust Damages Actions', (2006–3) *EC Competition Policy Newsletter* 23, p 24, according to whom 'the judgment in *Manfredi* has now crystallised—and effectively harmonised—the law on a number of salient points'.

[459] Italian courts had earlier sent similar preliminary references to Luxembourg, but the ECJ had held them to be inadmissible because it thought that the referring courts had not included enough information on the purpose of and need for the references: Case C-425/03 *Provvidenza Regio v AXA Assicurazioni SpA*, Order of 19 October 2004, unpublished; Joined Cases C-438/03, C-439/03, C-509/03 and C-2/04 *Antonio Cannito et al. v Fondiaria Assicurazioni SpA et al.*, Order of 11 February 2004, [2004] ECR I-1605.

[460] The Court was also asked to decide whether the nullity of agreements contrary to Article 81 of the EC Treaty can be relied on by third parties (its answer was yes), and whether Community law is contrary to a national rule which provides that plaintiffs must bring actions for damages for infringing Community and national competition rules before a court other than that which usually has jurisdiction in actions for damages of similar value, thereby involving a considerable increase in costs and time. Another preliminary question sent to Luxembourg in this case related to the applicability of *Community* competition law to the anti-competitive conduct at issue.

[461] Judgment, paras 60, 61, 63, 89–91, citing paras 25–27 of *Courage*. In particular, paragraph 91, quoting paragraph 27 of *Courage*, stresses that 'the *existence* of such a right strengthens the working of the Community competition rules and discourages agreements or practices, frequently covert, which are liable to restrict or distort competition. From that point of view, actions for damages before the national courts can make a significant contribution to the maintenance of effective competition in the Community' (emphasis added).

conditions of the right in damages: 'It follows that any individual can claim compensation for the harm suffered where there is a causal relationship between that harm and an agreement or practice prohibited under Article 81 EC.'[462]

In other words, the right in damages is open (a) to 'any individual', as long as there is (b) 'harm', (c) a competition law violation, and (d) a 'causal relationship' between that harm and that violation. In thus defining the Community law conditions of the right in damages, the Court has produced a broad rule of standing, while at the same time omitting the requirement of fault.

To mark the distinction between the *existence* of the right and its basic conditions, governed by Community law, and its *exercise* and the more specific conditions, governed by national law, the Court stressed again that 'any individual...can claim compensation for [harm causally related with an Article 81 EC violation]', but 'in the absence of Community rules governing the matter, it is for the domestic legal system of each Member State to prescribe the detailed rules governing the *exercise* of that right, including those on the application of the concept of "causal relationship", provided that the principles of equivalence and effectiveness are observed' (emphasis added).[463] Thus the Court deferred to national law for the specific questions pertaining to the causal relationship between harm and antitrust violation, and the availability of punitive damages,[464] and questions on limitation of actions and competent national tribunals.

The most important contribution of *Manfredi* is clearly its recognition of a broad rule of standing, by referring to 'any individual' and by explicitly recognizing that consumers enjoy standing to sue for compensation for harm caused to them by anticompetitive conduct.[465] Such a principle therefore seems to exclude the unqualified application in Europe of the US limitations with regard to indirect purchasers' standing. Another contribution of *Manfredi* is in the area of the nature and extent of damages, in particular whether loss of profit and interest can be separate grounds for damages. Although the Court was not specifically requested by the referring courts to pronounce on this particular issue, it held: 'It follows from the principle of effectiveness and the right of any individual to seek compensation for loss caused by a contract or by conduct liable to restrict or distort competition that injured persons must be able to seek compensation not only for actual loss (damnum emergens) but also for loss of profit (lucrum cessans) plus interest...Total exclusion of loss of profit as a head of damage for which compensation may be awarded cannot be accepted in the case of a breach of Community law since, especially in the context of economic or commercial litigation, such a total exclusion of loss of profit would be such as to make reparation of damage practically impossible...As to the payment of interest,...an

---

[462] Judgment, para 61.   [463] Judgment, paras 63–64.
[464] Judgment, paras 64 and 92 *et seq.* as to causal relationship and punitive damages respectively.
[465] Judgment, paras 60, 61, 63.

award made in accordance with the applicable national rules constitutes an essential component of compensation.'[466]

It is also interesting that the Court did not exclude the possibility of awarding punitive damages but rather deferred on this issue to national law. Indeed, it stressed that 'as to the award of damages and the possibility of an award of punitive damages, *in the absence of Community rules governing the matter*, it is for the domestic system of each Member State to set the criteria for determining the extent of the damages, provided that the principles of equivalence and effectiveness are observed' (emphasis added).[467]

Another important contribution of *Manfredi* is with regard to limitation periods, which vary considerably between the Member States. More important than the period itself, however, is its starting point.[468] The Court held that 'a national rule under which the limitation period begins to run from the day on which the agreement or concerted practice was adopted could make it practically impossible to exercise the right to seek compensation for the harm caused by that prohibited agreement or practice, particularly if that national rule also imposes a short limitation period which is not capable of being suspended.'[469] According to the Court, when there are continuous or repeated infringements, such a limitation period might expire even before the infringement was brought to an end, in which case it would be impossible for any individual who had suffered harm after the expiry of the limitation period to bring an action. It is noteworthy that the Commission's December 2005 Green Paper on Actions for Damages[470] identified this particular problem, and went even further by including an option to suspend the limitation periods from the date when the Commission or national competition authorities institute proceedings,[471] precisely in order to facilitate follow-on civil claims for damages.

It is expected that the forthcoming Commission White Paper on Damages Actions[471a] will certainly build on *Manfredi*. Both *Manfredi* and its predecessor *Courage* make it possible now to speak of an *acquis communautaire* on this matter, which any initiative by the Commission must respect and on which it must build.

---

[466] Judgment, paras 95–97. On the requirement to include compensatory interest in the damages award, see also paras 122–124 of the Commission's Staff Working Paper.

[467] Judgment, para 92.   [468] See Staff Working Paper, para 261 *et seq.*

[469] Judgment, para 78.   [470] Examined earlier in this survey.

[471] Option 36 of the Green Paper. Compare also section 33(5) of the German Competition Act, as recently amended, which provides that the initiation of public proceedings automatically suspends the running of prescription for private claims. It is noteworthy that under US law a plaintiff must commence proceedings within four years after the cause of action accrued, but if any civil or criminal proceeding is instituted by the US government, the running of the statute of limitations is suspended during the pendency of that proceeding and for one year thereafter. See sections 4B and 5(i) of the Clayton Act.

[471a] The White Paper was published in April 2008, but falls outside the scope of this survey.

H. Merger Control

(i) Important Judgments

General Electric and Honeywell Appeals[472]

During the period covered by this survey, the Community Courts were once again asked to review a number of prominent merger decisions. While their judgments were less dramatic than in earlier cases, they nevertheless constituted at least partial reverses for the Commission, whose findings were again heavily criticized.

The judgments of the CFI in both *Honeywell* and *General Electric* were the culmination of one of the most heavily politicized merger cases in recent years, in which the Commission infamously prohibited the merger between GE and Honeywell after the transaction had been approved by the US authorities. The *General Electric* judgment, while not annulling the Decision, is similar to the Court's three other renowned merger judgments in *Airtours, Schneider,* and *Tetra Laval,*[473] in that the CFI once again criticized broad aspects of the Commission's substantive reasoning.

The Commission[474] had found that the merger would result in the creation or strengthening of dominant positions in three different ways: (i) vertical effects: the Commission found that GE's existing dominant position on the market for large commercial jet aircraft engines would be strengthened owing to the vertical effects of the merger resulting from the integration of GE's activity as a manufacturer of the engines with Honeywell's activity as a manufacturer of starters for those engines;[475] (ii) conglomerate effects: the Commission also concluded that dominant positions would be created on various world markets for avionics and non-avionics products where Honeywell already enjoyed strong positions prior to the merger, as a result of two types of conglomerate effects;[476] and (iii) simple horizontal overlaps on markets where both companies were already active.[477]

In the *General Electric* judgment the CFI overturned the Commission's assessment of the potential vertical and conglomerate effects of the merger, while upholding in part its findings on a horizontal anticompetitive effect. The Decision was thus upheld, but on substantially reduced grounds. As regards vertical anticompetitive effects, the CFI dismissed the Commission's claims that if the merger had taken place there would be post-merger vertical foreclosure of the engine starter market, as GE would be the sole effective supplier of engine starters. Instead the CFI found that foreclosure could only come about if GE selectively

---

[472] Case T-209/01 *Honeywell v Commission* [2005] ECR II-5527, and Case T-210/01 *General Electric v Commission* [2005] ECR II-5575.

[473] Case T-342/99 *Airtours v Commission* [2002] ECR II-2585; Case T-310/01 *Schneider Electric v Commission* [2002] ECR II-4071; Case T-5/02 *Tetra Laval v Commission* [2002] ECR II-4381, confirmed on appeal in Case C-12/03 P, *Commission v Tetra Laval* [2005] ECR I-987 (examined below).

[474] Case COMP/M.2220 – *General Electric/Honeywell* [2004] OJ L48/1.

[475] Ibid, paras 419–427.   [476] Ibid, paras 342–411.   [477] Ibid, paras 428–477.

refused to supply rival engine manufacturers. In line with the *Tetra/Laval*[478] judgment, such an 'extreme form of conduct' would be sufficiently 'visible and obvious' to be penalized under Article 82 of the EC Treaty. The Commission's failure to take into account the deterrent effect of Article 82 was sufficient to vitiate its conclusions.[479] However, the judgment has been criticized as seeking merely to criticize the Commission for not having evaluated the potential deterrent effect of Article 82,[480] and resulted in comments that the Court was 'trying to be Solomonic, to give something to everyone'.[481]

As regards conglomerate anticompetitive effects, the CFI found that the Commission had not adduced convincing evidence to show with a sufficient degree of probability that GE's financial strength and vertical integration (ie its aircraft-leasing subsidiaries) would help the merged entity to achieve dominance in a number of markets for various avionics and non-avionics products.[482] The CFI also overturned the Commission's three 'bundling' findings (pure, technical, and mixed bundling). It found that the Commission had failed to show either that the merged entity would have had the capability to engage in bundling or, on the basis of convincing evidence, that it would be likely to do so and that as a result a dominant position would be strengthened or created.[483] As the Commission had failed to meet this standard as regards all three types of bundling, the CFI concluded that its conglomerate effects analysis was wrong.

However, the CFI did partly uphold the Commission's horizontal overlap findings, although it once again found some errors in the Commission's analysis. In particular, the CFI was persuaded by the Commission's finding that GE was dominant in the market for engines for large commercial aircraft, stating that its consistently high (and increasing) market share was a 'particularly convincing' element of the analysis of dominance.[484] As a result, and on these limited grounds, the final Decision was upheld—although many commentators have referred to the judgment as a pyrrhic victory for the Commission.[485]

Both judgments clarify a number of procedural aspects of the EC merger control rules. In *Honeywell* the CFI highlighted the need for applicants to ensure that the pleas they submitted, were, if well-founded, sufficient 'to invalidate the operative part of the contested decision and could therefore support an action that might be capable of resulting in the annulment of that decision'.[486] Thus

---

[478] CFI judgment in *Tetra Laval*.　　[479] *General Electric*, paras 305–312.

[480] Killick and Schulz, 'Horizontal and Vertical Mergers in the Reformed EC Merger Control', in Amato and Ehlermann (eds), *EC Competition Law, A Critical Assessment* (Oxford/Portland, 2007), at 491.

[481] See Fox, 'The European Court's Judgment in *GE/Honeywell*—Not a Poster Child for Comity or Convergence' (2006) 20(2) Antitrust 77.

[482] *General Electric*, paras 335–362.

[483] Ibid, para 405.　　[484] Ibid, paras 149–151.

[485] See Killick, 'The *GE/Honeywell* judgment—in Reality another Merger Defeat for the Commission' (2007) 28 ECLR 52.

[486] *Honeywell*, para 51.

in this case Honeywell's pleas should have been able to overcome all three findings of the Commission's Decision ie the horizontal, vertical, and conglomerate
anticompetitive effects of the merger.[487] However, Honeywell had only contested
the Commission's findings concerning the conglomerate effects of the merger,
ie essentially bundling, and this was insufficient to justify the annulment of the
Decision. In this regard the CFI rejected the possibility that any deficiencies in an
applicant's pleas could be remedied by way of a reference to pleadings in another
case[488] or by joining two cases brought by different applicants.[489]

General Electric clearly establishes that in merger proceedings undertakings
cannot have access to the Commission's file before the Statement of Objections
is served,[490] or to observations by third parties which the Commission receives
after the deadline for submitting commitments. 'In view of the strict timetable
laid down by Regulation No 4064/89, and given the necessity for speed which
characterizes procedures governed by that regulation, the imposition of such an
obligation after the last date for the submission of commitments would be likely
to deny the Commission a sufficient period of reflection to analyse the case-file as
a whole and draft its final decision.'[491]

Finally, the *General Electric* judgment confirms that the same principles of
access to the file and protection of defence rights apply to merger proceedings as
to other competition proceedings, with the proviso that 'their application may
reasonably be adapted to the necessity for speed, which characterizes the general
scheme of that regulation'.[492] The CFI therefore rejected General Electric's claim
that the deadline set for its response to the SO was unacceptably short in light of
the late provision of access to the file, the volume of materials to be reviewed and
the scope of the case. The Court admitted an 'adverse effect on the conditions
under which all the parties to the proceedings must work', but pointed out that
'the gain in terms of the speed of the proceedings as a whole was regarded by the
legislature as justifying those sacrifices, particularly in order to take account of
the commercial interest of the parties to a merger in completing their proposed
merger as quickly as possible.'[493]

Tetra Laval Appeal to the ECJ[494]

In summarily rejecting as inadmissible the Commission's appeal against the
CFI's[495] finding that it was wrong to have blocked Tetra Laval BV's proposed
acquisition of Sidel SA on the ground that it would result in the creation of a
dominant position,[496] the ECJ made a number of interesting remarks regarding the standard of proof required when the Commission assesses conglomerate
effects. The Court was to some extent prompted by the Opinion of Advocate
General Tizzano, who had pointed out that the CFI judgment could not have

---

[487] Ibid, paras 102–104.   [488] Ibid, para 67.   [489] Ibid, para 75.
[490] Ibid, para 693.   [491] *General Electric*, para 684.   [492] Ibid, para 631.
[493] Ibid, para 701.   [494] *Commission v Tetra Laval*, n 473 above.
[495] Ibid.   [496] ECJ judgment, paras 143–146.

the result of requiring the Commission to establish the anticompetitive nature of a transaction with absolute certainty. For the Advocate General, it was sufficient if, 'on the basis of solid elements gathered in the course of a thorough and painstaking investigation, and having recourse to its technical knowledge, the Commission is persuaded that the notified transaction would very probably lead to the creation or strengthening of such a dominant position'.[497] However, the Advocate General considered that when it was difficult to foresee the effects of a transaction, the Commission should allow it.[498] These statements appear to relax the strictness of the test laid down by the CFI. The Advocate General also distinguished between findings of fact, where the standard of judicial review is higher, and complex economic assessments, where the Court's review of the Commission's findings is necessarily more limited. In this regard he noted: 'The rules on the division of powers between the Commission and the Community judicature, which are fundamental to the Community institutional system, do not however allow the judicature to go further, and particularly [. . .] to enter into the merits of the Commission's complex economic assessments or to substitute its own point of view for that of the institution.'[499]

The ECJ's judgment also appears to criticize the language of the CFI, albeit not overtly.[500] Although the Court found that the CFI committed no errors in the exercise of its power of review, it stated that the prospective analysis the Commission is required to carry out must constitute 'an examination of how a concentration might alter the factors determining the state of competition on a given market in order to establish whether it would give rise to a serious impediment to effective competition. Such an analysis makes it necessary to envisage various chains of cause and effect with a view to ascertaining which of them are the *most likely*' (emphasis added).[501]

This can be contrasted with the language of the CFI, which spoke of the need for the Commission to establish that 'a dominant position would, in all likelihood, be created or strengthened in the relatively near future.'[502] The ECJ therefore seems to have implicitly re-interpreted the text of the first instance ruling, although without attempting to develop a more refined test along the lines suggested by the Advocate General.

Impala[503]

The judgment of the CFI in *Impala* was the first in which a Community Court annulled an unconditional clearance decision after the Commission had undertaken a full Phase II investigation, and thus raises concerns over the legal certainty

---

[497] Opinion of Advocate General Tizzano, paras 73–74.
[498] Ibid, para 77.   [499] Ibid, para 89.
[500] However, for a contrary opinion, see Nicholson, Cardell, and McKenna, 'The Scope of Review of Merger Decisions under Community Law' (2005) European Competition Law Journal 139.
[501] ECJ judgment, para 43.   [502] CFI judgment, para 153.
[503] Case T-464/04 *Impala v Commission* [2006] ECR II-2289.

of Commission clearance decisions.[504] It also signals an apparent loosening of
the three cumulative conditions set out by the CFI in *Airtours*[505] for a finding of
collective dominance.[506]

In July 2004, after provisionally concluding that a joint venture between the
recorded music divisions of Sony Corporation and Bertelsmann AG (BMG) was
incompatible with Community law, in particular because it would reinforce a
collective dominant position on the market for recorded music, the Commission
finally authorized the transaction.[507] It considered that the concentration would
not create or reinforce a dominant position for the firms involved, alone or
collectively with the other music majors (Universal, Warner, and EMI).

In December 2004 the Commission's clearance of the merger was challenged by the Independent Music Publishers and Labels Association (Impala),
an international association of 2,500 independent music production companies. Although Impala's request that the action should be dealt with under the
expedited procedure set out in Article 76a of the CFI Rules of Procedure was
granted, it still had to wait 19 months for the CFI's judgment, which annulled
the Decision on the grounds that the Commission had not demonstrated to the
requisite legal standard either the non-existence of a collective dominant position
before the concentration, or the absence of a risk that such a position would be
created as a result of the concentration. It did so using the same *Tetra Laval*[508]
standard of review as that used by the Community Courts when reviewing prohibition decisions.[509]

Regarding the substance of the Decision, the CFI first analyzed whether the
major record companies enjoyed a pre-existing situation of collective dominance, stating *obiter dicta* that the three cumulative *Airtours* conditions necessary to establish collective dominance may also be met 'on the basis of what
may be a very mixed series of indicia and items of evidence relating to the signs,
manifestations and phenomena inherent in the presence of a collective dominant position'.

Thus, in particular, close alignment of prices over a long period, especially
if they are above a competitive level, together with other factors typical of a
collective dominant position, might, in the absence of an alternative reasonable explanation, suffice to demonstrate the existence of a collective dominant

---

[504] Although the Commission re-approved the joint venture in October 2007 after conducting a
renewed investigation (see IP/07/1437).
[505] *Airtours*, n 473 above, paras 62, 195.
[506] First, the market must be transparent enough for the undertakings which coordinate their
conduct to be able to monitor sufficiently whether the rules of coordination are being observed.
Second, there must be some form of deterrent mechanism in the event of deviant conduct. Third,
the reactions of undertakings which do not participate in the coordination such as current or future
competitors, and also the reactions of customers, should not be able to jeopardize the results expected
from the coordination.
[507] Commission Decision of 19 July 2004 (*Sony/BMG*) [2005] OJ L62/30.
[508] *Tetra Laval*, n 473 above.   [509] *Impala*, paras 327–329.

position, even where there is no firm direct evidence of strong market transparency, as such transparency may be presumed in such circumstances.'[510]

Despite these statements, however, the CFI then went on to examine whether the Commission had correctly applied the traditional *Airtours* criteria. It focused on two main aspects of the Decision: the degree of price transparency of the record market in light of the significance of campaign discounts; and the necessary existence of a retaliation mechanism (the third *Airtours* condition).

As regards the significance of campaign discounts for market transparency, the CFI rebuked the Commission's 'vague assertions'[511] as 'imprecise, unsupported, and indeed contradicted by other observations in the decision',[512] and thus insufficiently reasoned. The CFI conducted a detailed review of the whole body of evidence before it, and criticized the Commission heavily for the formal and substantive manner in which it had conducted its investigation. The body of evidence contained 'a great number of errors'[513] and did not support the conclusions the Commission drew from it,[514] and the Commission had failed to carry out a 'serious examination' into campaign discounts either before or after the oral hearing[515] or in the SO.[516] Similarly, as regards the existence of a retaliation mechanism, the CFI found that the Commission was 'not in a position to indicate the slightest step which it had completed or undertaken' to assess whether retaliation had occurred in the past.[517]

The CFI also rejected, using strong language, the Commission's finding that the concentration would not create a collective dominant position. It described the Commission's 'extremely succinct'[518] analysis as 'superficial, indeed purely formal', especially in the case of a concentration that 'raises serious problems'.[519] The CFI was equally critical of the Commission's analysis of the existence of deterrent mechanisms, highlighting the inadequacies of its backward-looking analysis of whether retaliation had occurred in the past, when merger control requires a prospective analysis. Rather, the CFI concluded: 'it follows moreover, from the Decision and from the case-file that such credible and effective deterrent measures do actually appear to exist in the present case and, in particular, the possibility of sanctioning a deviating major by excluding it from compilations. In the statement of objections, moreover, the Commission had clearly found that that deterrent measure was effective and the Decision provides no explanation of the reasons why it would not ultimately be effective.'[520]

The judgment has been criticized for seemingly lowering the *Airtours* bar for the Commission to intervene on the basis of coordinated effects. It 'represents a possible bright spot for future intervention on the basis of coordinated effects,

---

[510] Ibid, paras. 251–252.
[511] Ibid, para 289.
[512] Ibid, para 320.
[513] Ibid, para 425.
[514] Ibid, para 434.
[515] Ibid, paras 398, 45.
[516] Ibid, para 451.
[517] Ibid, para 471.
[518] Ibid, para 525.
[519] Ibid, para 528.
[520] Ibid, para 538.

even though the Commission lost the particular case in court'.[521] The CFI has in effect created a presumption that the mere presence of indicia of coordinated effects now allows the Commission, absent 'an alternative reasonable explanation', to conclude that a dominant position already exists. The judgment has also set alarm bells ringing in European industry because of its potential to encourage disgruntled third parties to challenge merger clearances adopted by the Commission after an extended Phase II investigation. By stating that the Community Courts will use the same standard of judicial review when evaluating a clearance decision as in reviewing a prohibition decision, it 'creates the spectre of increased ex post intervention against already closed deals, and creates unhealthy incentives for complainants'.[522]

Moreover, the fact that it took the CFI 19 months to hand down its judgment[523] despite recourse to the expedited procedure, again raises the question of whether a new specialist judicial panel or chamber with jurisdiction over merger cases should be established within the CFI to speed up challenges. This proposal was recently examined by the European Union Committee of the House of Lords,[524] which concluded that the creation of a new court or a specialist panel or chamber within the CFI was unnecessary and would not significantly reduce the duration of proceedings in merger cases.

Finally, there is a certain irony in the outcome of the recent series of merger appeals which the CFI has recently had to decide: while *General Electric* is widely regarded as a pyrrhic victory for the Commission, the same qualification may equally be attributed to the Commission's defeat in *Impala* from the perspective of merging parties who share an overarching wish for legal certainty. It will be interesting to see whether the CFI's findings on collective dominance are upheld on appeal by the ECJ.[525]

(ii) Select Commission Cases

MAN/Scania[526]

In December 2006, the Commission approved the proposed acquisition by the German truck maker and engineering conglomerate MAN AG of its Swedish rival Scania AB. After investigating all the markets affected by the proposed

---

[521] See Weitbrecht , 'EU Merger Control in 2006—the Year in Review' (2007) 28 ECLR 125.

[522] See Völcker and O'Daly, 'The Court of First Instance's *Impala* Judgment: a Judicial Counterreformation in EU Merger Control?' (2006) 27 ECLR 589.

[523] Although the delays in *Impala* were due largely to the applicant's behaviour: see paras 546–553 of the judgment.

[524] House of Lords European Union Committee, 15th Report of 2006/7, HL Paper 75, available online at <http://www.publications.parliament.uk/pa/ld200607/ldselect/ldeucom/75/75.pdf>.

[525] See now Judgment of 10 July 2008 in Case C-413/06 P, *Bertelsmann and Sony Corporation of America v Impala*, not yet reported.

[526] Commission Decision of 20 December 2006 (Case COMP/M.4336 – *MAN/Scania*), available online at: <http://eur-lex.europa.eu/LexUriServ/LexUriServ.do?uri=CELEX:32006M4336:EN:HTML>.

transaction between two of the largest European truck and bus manufacturers, the Commission concluded in its unconditional clearance Decision that the acquisition would not significantly impede effective competition in the EEA or a substantial part of it.[527]

The Commission noted that to some extent competition for the sale of buses and trucks is still national in scope, for reasons including different purchasing patterns and specific technical requirements. It therefore examined a large number of national markets in the EEA where both MAN and Scania were active. The investigation indicated that European bus and truck markets would remain competitive even after the proposed transaction. Clearance was also favoured by lack of customer concern and of any evidence pointing to a risk of uncoordinated or coordinated effects post-merger.

The Commission concluded that the merged entity would still face strong competition from a number of other important market players, such as DaimlerChrysler, Volvo, Iveco, and DAF, as well as smaller competitors in some national markets. It also noted that some of the affected product markets, such as the Swedish market for city buses, were bidding markets characterized by 'lumpy orders', where the respective shares of the different players sometimes varied significantly and might therefore be exaggerated at a given point in time. In the Spanish and Portuguese markets for inter-city buses and tourist coaches, where the merged entity would also have high market shares, the Commission's investigation was complicated by the existence of local bus manufacturers who bought ready-made chassis, built the bus bodies themselves, and sold the finished buses to end-customers. The presence of such local 'body-builders' combined with that of large integrated manufacturers allowed the Commission to conclude that the proposed transaction would not impede competition in these markets.

Despite this, however, the merger had not yet been implemented at the end of 2007. MAN initially launched a hostile takeover bid of EUR 10.2 billion for Scania in November 2006, but its takeover plans faced persistent resistance from Scania and its second largest shareholder, a Swedish investment company controlled by the renowned Wallenberg family. MAN later withdrew its bid and the two companies, together with Volkswagen AG, which is the biggest shareholder in both MAN and Scania, have since been trying to reach an amicable solution for a tie-up.

Lufthansa/Swiss[528]

In a further consolidation of European airlines after the merger of Air France and KLM in 2004,[529] the Commission cleared the planned acquisition of Swiss International Airlines Ltd by Lufthansa AG, subject to certain conditions

---

[527]   Ibid. See also Commission Press Release of 20 December 2006, IP/06/1868.
[528]   Commission Decision of 4 July 2005 (Case COMP/M.3770—*Lufthansa/Swiss*).
[529]   See Commission Decision of 11 February 2004 (Case COMP/M.3280—*Air France/KLM*).

under which the merging airlines agreed to scale back their activities in several European airports. In light of these concessions, the Commission concluded that the proposed acquisition would not significantly impede effective competition in the EEA and Switzerland.[530]

In line with the earlier *Air France/KLM* Decision, the Commission defined the relevant market for scheduled passenger air transport services on a 'point of origin/point of destination' (O&D) basis, which considered every combination of a point of origin and a point of destination as a separate market from a demand substitutability point of view. This approach allowed it to conclude that the proposed acquisition would eliminate or significantly impede competition on a number of intra-European routes, most importantly Zurich-Frankfurt and Zurich-Munich, and on certain long haul routes to the US, South Africa, Thailand and Egypt. In reaching this conclusion the Commission took into account a variety of factors in addition to the parties' market shares, such as slot and capacity constraints at the relevant airports, substitutability of direct and indirect flights, the availability of alternative passenger transport such as rail transport on the affected routes, the specific needs and preferences of 'time-sensitive' passengers, and the impact of Lufthansa's close cooperation with members of the Star Alliance.

In response to the Commission's concerns, the merging parties offered a comprehensive package of commitments to mitigate the harmful effects on competition. They undertook to make a certain number of slots available for an unlimited period on six long-haul routes and on the routes to and from Zurich, Frankfurt, Berlin, Munich, Düsseldorf, Vienna, Stockholm, and Copenhagen, in order to enable one or more new entrants to operate non-stop frequencies on those routes. The commitments package also contained a new element, the granting of so-called 'grandfather rights' over the slots obtained for the Zurich-Frankfurt and Zurich-Munich routes. The idea of grandfather rights is to offer an additional incentive to an operator which services the route for at least three years, thereby encouraging market entry and increasing the value of the slots. The commitment to surrender slots was accompanied by measures requiring Lufthansa not to increase its planned offer of flights on the affected routes, so that a new entrant would have a fair chance to gain sufficient scale and establish itself as a credible competitor.

The Commission considered the remedy package sufficient to make potential competition effective, as the concessions would make it possible to strike a fair balance between allowing potential competition on the affected routes and ensuring that the efficiencies the parties could derive from their network were not compromised, thus harming consumers' interests. In particular, the Commission regarded the granting of grandfather rights for the Frankfurt and Munich slots as sufficient to mitigate the concerns expressed by some competitors.

---

[530] Ibid. See also Commission Press Release of 5 July 2005, IP/05/837.

Johnson and Johnson/Pfizer Consumer Healthcare[531]

In this Decision the Commission approved, subject to conditions, the acquisition by Johnson & Johnson (J&J) of Pfizer's consumer healthcare business (PCH).

The Commission's investigation revealed that while the transaction as initially notified would not significantly modify the structure of most of the markets concerned, it would give rise to competitive concerns in relation to three product markets: dermatological antifungals in Italy, daily-use mouthwash in Greece, and nicotine replacement therapy (NRT) products. In the first two of these product markets there would be horizontal overlaps between J&J and PCH's activities, while as regards NRT products, the transaction raised the issue of the potential vertical relationship between J&J's nicotine patch manufacturing activities and PCH's NRT business. However, after J&J offered to divest the overlapping activities in Italy and Greece and all or part of its global nicotine patch manufacturing business, the Commission concluded that the proposed transaction would not significantly impede effective competition in the EEA or a substantial part of it.

Reuters/Telerate[532]

One of the innovations of the 2004 Merger Regulation was the pre-notification referral system provided for by Article 4(5). When a concentration does not satisfy the criteria for Community dimension but is capable of being reviewed under the merger control rules of at least three Member States, the parties can refer the case to the Commission. Unless the relevant national authorities object, the operation then enjoys a 'deemed Community dimension'. This mechanism has proved remarkably popular: at the time of writing 125 requests for the august status of Community dimension had been made since the system was introduced, making up 10% of all Commission notifications during that time.

The mechanism was used successfully in Reuters's acquisition of Telerate, an operation which was reviewable in 12 Member States but did not satisfy the criteria for Community dimension. Reuters, a UK company, is one of the two main global providers of financial market data and multimedia news tailored for finance and corporate professionals. Telerate, a US company, also provides financial market data and news worldwide, focusing on the distribution of real-time market data from many different sources.

Two areas of concern for the Commission were the supply of real-time market data and financial market data platforms (MDPs), the technological means that enable customers of real-time market data to integrate and deliver information from various sources. Regarding the former, the Commission concluded that the market would remain fiercely competitive post-acquisition. However, it also found that the two parties were the only major providers of MDPs worldwide,

---

[531] Commission Decision of 11 December 2006 (Case COMP/M.4314—*Johnson & Johnson/ Pfizer Consumer Healthcare*), a summary of which can be found at [2007] OJ C39/5.

[532] Commission Decision of 23 May 2005 (Case COMP/M.3692—*Reuters/Telerate*) [2005] OJ C154/05.

and that the combination of their proprietary platforms would lead to a nearly uncontested market position in the provision of MDPs. To allay these concerns, the parties undertook to provide a perpetual exclusive global licence for Telerate's MDP product to Hyperfeed Technologies, a US provider of financial market data technology. This would allow Hyperfeed to be able to establish itself as a viable and effective competitor to Reuters. Satisfied with this commitment, the Commission granted the transaction conditional approval.

Tesco/Carrefour (Czech Republic and Slovakia)[533]

This was the first merger case to be referred to the competition authority of a Member State which joined the EU in 2004. Tesco is a major UK company active in food and non-food retailing, with over 2,300 stores worldwide, including 31 in Slovakia and 27 in the Czech Republic. Carrefour, the major French retailer, has over 11,000 stores worldwide, including 11 supermarkets in the Czech Republic and four in Slovakia. Tesco intended to acquire ownership of Carrefour's stores in the Czech Republic and Slovakia, as well as Carrefour's interest in a shopping centre in Prague.

Although the merger was notified to the Commission, the Slovak Antimonopoly Office requested under Article 9(2)(b) of the Merger Regulation to be referred those parts of the transaction which would affect competition in three local markets in the cities of Bratislava, Kosice, and Zilina. The Slovak NCO argued, and the Commission agreed, that these markets 'did not constitute a substantial part of the Common Market'.[534] The Commission did, however, clear the part of the proposed acquisition relating to the Czech market. It considered that in the Czech Republic the merged entity would still only be the fourth largest retailing group nationally. Even in the individual local markets, the parties would still face competition from a number of other strong retailers.

In the event, in February 2007 the Slovak Antimonopoly Office refused to clear the concentration, despite a number of proposals by Tesco (such as the sale of some of its business) to allay concerns about the anticompetitive impact of the transaction. The Office did not accept these proposals, and concluded that the 'change of the market originating from the transaction would be against consumers'.

Omya/Huber[535]

This Decision originated from a referral request to the Commission by the Finnish Competition Authority under section 22 of the Merger Regulation.

---

[533] Commission Decision of 22 December 2005 (Case COMP/M.3905—*Tesco/Carrefour*) [2006] OJ C52/6.

[534] This is not the first time the Commission has referred the acquisition of supermarkets where the geographic market was found to be local to NCAs: see for instance *Promodes/S21/Gruppo GS* (M.1086).

[535] Commission Decision of 19 July 2006 (COMP/M.3796—*Omya/J.M. Huber PCC*) [2007] OJ L72/24.

Finland's request was subsequently seconded by the competition authorities of Sweden, France and Austria, and the Commission accepted jurisdiction in May 2005. Its Phase I investigation revealed serious doubts as to the compatibility of the transaction with the common market and it therefore initiated a Phase II investigation. A Statement of Objections was sent to Omya on 2 May 2006 and an oral hearing followed. Finally the Commission approved Omya's purchase of Huber's on-site precipitated calcium carbonate (PCC) business in July 2006, subject to divestment commitments. Omya and Huber undertook to divest a precipitated calcium carbonates (PCC) plant in Finland and PCC coating technology developed by Huber.

Omya is active in the production of PCC and ground calcium carbonates (GCC) for applications in the paper industry. Calcium carbonates (CC) are an important part of paper production, bought in bulk by paper mills and added to paper to improve its texture, brightness and printability. Omya sought clearance from the Commission to acquire the on-site PCC business of its rival Huber. This involved Huber's sale to Omya of twelve PCC production facilities, six of them in the EEA.

The Commission thoroughly examined the market for CCs in the paper industry. It found that the market could be further sub-divided into coating applications (use of CCs for coating paper) and filling applications (use of CCs in the production of the paper itself), which it found to be two distinct markets.[536] The Commission also distinguished merchant supply of CCs, where paper mills purchase CCs from independent suppliers, from on-site supply, where paper manufacturers have CCs produced by a partner company on-site at their paper factory; on-site supply capability significantly reduces the costs of CCs for paper mills. Lastly, paper mills which opt for merchant supply solutions can be characterized as 'on-siteable'—those who could use an on-site supplier but choose not to—and those not 'on-siteable', who have no option but to use merchant supplies.[537]

The result of the different supply solutions available to paper mills is that the geographic market varies: for on-siteable paper mills it will be at least EEA-wide, as a CC manufacturer may come from far away to establish itself for a number of years as the on-site supply partner at a mill. For merchant customers, however, the market is reduced to a relatively small radius around the paper mill, since transport costs become prohibitive after a certain distance.[538]

The Commission assessed the potential anticompetitive effects of the transaction in Sweden, Austria, France, and Finland. It found a competition concern only in relation to the market for coating CCs in southern Finland.[539] The Commission found that Huber had been planning to enter the coating CC

[536] Decision, para 136. This was due to lack of demand-side substitutability. This finding is reiterated more specifically at paragraph 152 in relation to filling PCC and coating PCC.

[537] Ibid, para 205. This would be the case if the paper mill was not suited to accommodating an on-site CC facility.

[538] Ibid, para 239.   [539] Ibid, para 269.

market in a 'timely manner', ie within six months of the time when the deal was agreed, and would have been a significant competitive constraint on Omya.[540] Huber had been developing a GCC/PCC coating blend, allegedly with this aim, shortly before the takeover deal was formalized. It would have had every reason to compete for Omya's customers and, unlike other competitors, would have represented significant competition in the south of Finland.[541] The Commission found that the elimination of this potential competition would leave Omya with fewer incentives to innovate, or at least less incentive to pass on innovation to customers.[542] It also concluded that but for the merger, Huber was likely to grow into a significant competitor in the coating CC market, and that there were not enough actual or potential customers in southern Finland to maintain sufficient competitive pressure following the merger.[543]

In response Omya claimed that it could have constrained Huber's ability to compete in any case, as the technology Huber was developing was a blend which relied on Omya's GCC as an essential component, and Omya could therefore simply have raised the price of the GCC supplied to Huber, which would be passed on to customers in higher prices for Huber's blended technology.[544] However, the Commission rejected this argument, pointing out that Omya would have difficulty in identifying exactly which of its products were being used for blending. To support this finding it added that Omya had not managed to raise its price of GCC to customers of SMI, a supplier of coating PCC for blends in central Finland.[545]

The Commission cleared the merger with divestment undertakings, namely the sale of Huber's on-site PCC plant in Kuusankoski, Finland and the divestment of Huber's PCC coating and PCC coating additive technology.[546]

Inco/Falconbridge[547]

The Merger Regulation and the Guidelines on the Applicability of Article 81 to Horizontal Cooperation Agreements[548] both make it clear that if a concentration produces efficiencies which are merger-specific, timely, verifiable, and benefit consumers, those efficiencies can be an important factor in lessening its adverse competitive effects. Merging parties anxious to obtain the green light from the Commission have increasingly sought to underline the possible efficiencies of their transactions. One case in which the Commission paid particular attention to an efficiency claim was the acquisition of Falconbridge by Inco.

Falconbridge and Inco were both Canadian companies active in the mining, processing and refining of nickel and other metals. The proposed acquisition was

---

[540] Ibid, paras 394 and 408.   [541] Ibid, para 425.   [542] Ibid, para 441.
[543] Ibid, para 440.   [544] Ibid, para 439.   [545] Ibid, para 435.
[546] These divestment undertakings formed the subject of litigation between Omya and the Commission in Case T-275/06, but Omya eventually withdrew its action for annulment.
[547] Commission Decision of 4 July 2006 (Case COMP/M.4000—*Inco/Falconbridge*) [2007] OJ L72/18.
[548] [2001] OJ C3/2.

set to create the world's largest nickel company. The Commission found that the merger would significantly impede effective competition in three markets: the EEA-wide market for the supply of nickel to the plating and electroforming industry, the worldwide market for the supply of high purity nickel to produce super-alloys, including super-alloys used in safety-critical parts, and the world-wide market for the supply of high-purity cobalt for the production of super-alloys in safety-critical parts.

The new entity would have become by far the largest supplier in the EEA of nickel products to the plating and electroforming industry, and the almost mon-opolist supplier of high purity nickel used in super-alloys and high purity cobalt for super-alloys used in safety-critical applications (eg in aircraft engines). The Commission's investigation showed that in addition to having very high market shares in all three markets (respectively 70%, 90%, and 95%), the parties would be able to raise prices in all three markets after the merger.

The parties claimed, however, that the proposed transaction would generate significant operating efficiencies, due to the proximity of their mining and pro-cessing operations in the Sudbury basin in Canada. This, they argued, would result in increased production at a lower cost, which would benefit all nickel con-sumers and offset any anticompetitive effects of the transaction. The Commission acknowledged that the merger was likely to bring about these efficiencies, but questioned whether they were merger-specific, since most of them could be achieved by creating a mining and processing joint venture in the Sudbury basin, leaving Inco and Falconbridge free to compete in refining and marketing. The Commission also considered that these efficiencies, which arose upstream in the nickel production chain, were unlikely to be passed on to consumers in the three relevant downstream markets, where the merged entity would have an almost monopolistic position. In the event, the Commission was not convinced that the efficiency gains would outweigh the likely anticompetitive effects in the relevant identified end-nickel product markets, and on that basis declined to clear the transaction.

The case is also interesting for the commitments the Commission eventu-ally accepted in order to clear the takeover. It is perhaps an indication of the Commission's evolving practice since its Merger Remedies Study in 2005[549] that it required not only an upfront purchaser, but also that the divestment should be completed before the merger was implemented. The parties offered to divest Falconbridge's sole nickel refinery and related assets and sell these assets to LionOre, an international mining company. In June 2006 Falconbridge and LionOre concluded a binding agreement for the sale of the divested business, subject to the completion of the Inco/Falconbridge merger and the Commission's approval of LionOre as a suitable purchaser. However, in the event the takeover fell through, as Inco had not acquired the majority of the shares of Falconbridge when the bid expired.

---

[549] See: <http://ec.europa.eu/comm/competition/mergers/legislation/remedies_study.pdf>.

Finmeccanica/Alcatel Alenia Space and Telespazio[550]

In this Decision the Commission cleared two joint ventures resulting from the merger of Alcatel's and Finmeccanica's space activities. Alcatel Alenia Space, held 67% by Alcatel and 33% by Finmeccanica, combines Alcatel Space and Alenia Spazio's activities. It designs, develops, and manufactures space systems, satellites, payloads, instruments, and associated ground systems for civilian and military applications. Telespazio, held 67% by Finmeccanica and 33% by Alcatel, combines Telespazio and Alcatel Space's services and operations activities. It handles operations and services for satellite solutions, including control and exploitation of space systems, as well as value-added services for networking, multimedia, and earth observation.

Following an initial investigation, the Commission raised concerns regarding the risk of market foreclosure affecting the Telemetry Tracking and Control (TTC) and radar altimeters satellite subsystems. The parties responded by offering commitments concerning the two subsystems, including the licensing of certain rights to competitors, and price monitoring for telemetry tracking and control. Specifically, the commitments included the granting of licences for TTC equipment and radar altimeters on terms approved by the Commission. The parties also undertook to submit any dispute relating to the obligations to supply competitors or charge reasonable prices to arbitration. However, they undertook unconditionally to license command receivers and radar altimeters.

Given that commercial satellite systems and subsystems are sourced either globally or at European level, the Commission investigated whether the proposed combination might exclude competing satellite prime contractors and integrators from their respective markets or negatively affect users. The investigation showed that there was no reason for concern.

It is interesting to note that while the Commission had no competition concerns with respect to the military satellite market, it observed that it may reconsider its approach to market definition in future cases. In previous decisions military satellites and subsystems have been held to constitute national markets when the provider is national, but otherwise the market has been considered as worldwide in geographical scope.

The Decision is of wide general interest in presenting a good deal of information and analysis concerning the space sector (as regards commercial, institutional, and military satellites), a complex sector of great commercial, scientific and political importance. It also constitutes an illuminating case study showing how the Commission sets about giving effect to the Merger Regulation. The combination involved the bringing together of horizontally and vertically related activities.

---

[550] Commission Decision of 28 April 2005 (Case COMP/M.3680—*Finmeccanica/Alcatel Alenia Space and Telespazio*).

T-Mobile Austria/tele.ring[551]

In what is commonly called the first 'gap case' since the ECMR was recast and the so-called SIEC test was implemented, the Commission conditionally cleared T-Mobile Austria's proposed acquisition of the Austrian mobile phone operator tele.ring. The case demonstrates that what was perceived (principally by Anglo-Saxons) as an enforcement gap under the old ECMR did indeed exist. However, the recast ECMR now enables the Commission to take control over such cases. As this merger did not create a dominant position for the merged entity or result in the creation of collective dominance, the Commission would previously have had great difficulty in dealing with such an arguably problematic transaction, as it could not be dealt with under the concept of individual/collective dominance.

The merger reduces the number of main players in the Austrian retail market for the provision of mobile telephony services to end-customers from four to three by combining the number two player, T-Mobile Austria, with the number four player, tele.ring. The merged entity has a market share of 30–40%, with the market leader Mobilkomm retaining its position post-merger (35–45%). Other players in the market are ONE (15–25%), and H3G (less than 5%). The market will become more symmetrical post-merger owing to the presence of two large operators of a similar size, giving rise to uncoordinated effects. As the merged entity did not reach the level normally considered to constitute dominance (in terms of market share), the Commission could not adopt its traditional unilateral effects approach.

In its analysis the Commission focused on the particular role and features of tele.ring, which it qualified as a maverick, a term usually used in the context of coordinated effects.[552] The Commission's price comparison and switching behaviour analysis showed that tele.ring was the most active player on the market, charging the most advantageous prices, and that over 50% of customers moving from the two largest operators switched to tele.ring. Tele.ring thus exerted considerable competitive pressure on the two largest operators, as shown by its continuously growing market share, which had more than doubled in the last three years, to the detriment of T-Mobile and Mobilkomm. The elimination of the operator which charged the most competitive prices and pursued the most aggressive strategy to win new customers would clearly be to the disadvantage of Austrian consumers and significantly impede effective competition.

The Commission then examined how far the other small players on the market might be able to take over tele.ring's maverick role post-merger. The H3G network only covers 2 to 8% of Austrian territory and about 50% of the population. For areas not covered by its own network it relies on a national roaming contract

---

[551] Commission Decision of 26 April 2006 (Case COMP/M.3916—*T-Mobile Austria/Tele.ring*) [2007] OJ L88/44.

[552] Horizontal Guidelines [2004] OJ C31, para 37. Mavericks are usually aggressive smaller players which do not play along with the oligopoly and thus exert considerable pressure on it.

with Mobilkomm. This makes it dependent on variable per minute costs rather than a high proportion of fixed costs like other network operators, and reduces its possibilities of making economies of scale. The Commission therefore concluded that despite an aggressive pricing strategy in the past, H3G would not be able to replace tele.ring as a maverick.

The Commission also considered the characteristics of service provider YESSS!, the low-cost variant of network operator ONE. As YESSS! only issued prepaid cards with limited services and it was uncertain whether the parent company ONE, a rather passive player on the market, would reposition its low-cost brand and rethink its pricing strategy post-merger in order to win customers, the Commission did not consider YESSS! a likely new maverick.

The Commission took the view that the merger would produce uncoordinated effects and have a significant effect on prices. The removal of tele.ring as an independent operator would not necessarily result in price increases, but it was deemed sufficient that without the merger, price reductions would be significantly higher so as to attract new customers, owing to tele.ring's aggressive price strategy. This shows that the finding of uncoordinated effects can go beyond the most likely scenario, where the merging parties are each other's closest competitors.[553] However, the Commission did not rule out that those uncoordinated effects could give rise to coordinated effects, thereby confirming that the two types of effect are not mutually exclusive and may be argued in parallel.

The Commission did not assess whether the *Airtours* criteria were fulfilled, as the proposed remedies would also eliminate any coordinated effects the merger might produce. In a somewhat complex high-tech market characterized by fierce competition, parallel pricing was highly unlikely, and the situation could be described as a non-collusive oligopoly where the Commission could intervene without having to carry out a coordinated effects analysis.

To remedy the Commission's concerns regarding the anti-competitive effects likely to arise from the merger, the proposed commitments had to create a market situation that would permit the emergence of a new maverick which could act as a similar competitive constraint on the two main players. T-Mobile committed to divest tele.ring's two packages of UMTS frequencies, one to H3G, the upfront buyer, and one to a smaller competitor. T-Mobile also undertook to divest a large number of the mobile telephony pylon sites currently operated by tele.ring, mainly to H3G and some to ONE (if interested). T-Mobile entered into a legally binding framework agreement with H3G to achieve upfront implementation. The upfront buyer mechanism was thus used to facilitate H3G's extension of its network in the near future, so that it could quickly become a full network operator likely to follow a price strategy similar to that followed by tele.ring in the past. This attempt to strengthen competitors can be questioned, as it should not be the objective of competition policy, and in

---

[553] Horizontal Guidelines, para 37.

some circumstances consumers may benefit from a certain asymmetry, as larger firms can act more efficiently. However, after a thorough investigation, including a Statement of Objections, the Commission finally cleared the transaction, subject to the commitments.

Telefónica/O2[554]

In January 2006, the Commission issued a Phase I Decision with commitments clearing Telefónica SA's acquisition of control of O2 plc by way of a public bid announced in October 2005. In its competitive assessment, the Commission delineated the following relevant markets: (1) wholesale call termination services on fixed and mobile networks; (2) wholesale international roaming services; (3) retail fixed-line communication services; (4) retail mobile telecommunications services; and (5) an emerging market for advanced seamless pan-European mobile telecommunication services for multinational corporations. The Commission also identified competition concerns in the areas of: wholesale call termination services and international roaming services, particularly in the UK.[555]

Regarding call termination services, despite its concerns, the Commission did not identify any way in which the transaction could lead to foreclosure effects on call termination services in the Czech Republic or Spain, where Telefónica had a 100% share of call termination services, or in Germany, Ireland, or the UK, where O2 had a similar share. The Commission reasoned that it would be extremely difficult for the merged entity to engage in price discrimination against foreign telecommunication operator customers on these national markets. Even if there were price or other discrimination, those customers would be able to detect and retaliate against it, as there were few obstacles in this market to switching to other international carriers.

However, the Commission did identify serious concerns in relation to the wholesale provision of international roaming services. Roaming is a service which enables a domestic subscriber to a mobile telephony network to make calls in other countries where the operator has no coverage but has concluded agreements with network operators in those countries for the use of their mobile telephony network services. Effectively, domestic network operators buy wholesale international roaming services from their counterparts in other countries for service fees, which are then passed on to their customers by way of a higher per call (or subscription) charge. The Commission's concerns centred on the way in which the various alliances of network operators created to improve the provision of international roaming services across EEA Member States operated. At the

---

[554] Commission Decision of 10 January 2006 (Case COMP/M.4035—*Telefónica/O2*).

[555] The Commission also raised some issues in relation to the emerging market for advanced seamless pan-European mobile telecommunication services for multinational corporations. However, these competition concerns were alleviated by the application of the remedy regarding the wholesale provision of international roaming services.

time of the Decision, Telefónica was a member of the FreeMove alliance, with France Télécom, Telecom Italia, and Deutsche Telekom. O2 was a member of the Starmap alliance, a similar but less formal framework in which a number of smaller telecommunications companies from EEA Member States cooperated. The Commission predicted that as a consequence of this alliance structure and given its ownership by Telefónica, O2 would either move from the Starmap to the FreeMove alliance after the transaction, or at least align its behaviour closely with the FreeMove alliance or its members. As a result of this change in the structure of the European alliances, O2 would have little incentive to provide wholesale international roaming services to or source them from non-FreeMove operators, which would thus be likely to incur cost increases and pass them on to their customers. In the UK, where only the fully vertically integrated Vodafone Group would have remained as a non-FreeMove supplier of wholesale international roaming services following the transaction, its anticompetitive effects would be particularly serious.

The parties proposed two remedies to alleviate the Commission's concerns. The first was that O2 would undertake to remain in the Starmap alliance for two years following the transaction, and would also set up a 'roaming committee' to decide its roaming strategies independently of Telefónica, while Telefónica would erect an ethical screen to prevent commercially sensitive information on roaming services from spilling over to it from O2. The second proposed remedy was that Telefónica would exit the FreeMove alliance and undertake not to re-enter it without the Commission's consent before 2011.

The Commission dismissed the first proposed remedy as unworkable and insufficient to resolve the competition concerns presented by the transaction. If O2 remained in Starmap and Telefónica in FreeMove, a structural and effective link between the two organizations would be constituted and approved. Accordingly, the Commission accepted the second proposed remedy, which fully removed its concerns as to the parties' membership of the two alliances.

Honeywell/Novar[556]

In March 2005, the Commission conditionally cleared the US company Honeywell International Inc's acquisition of all the outstanding shares of the UK company Novar plc ('Novar'), by way of a public bid announced in December 2005. Following its first phase investigation, the Commission concluded that the parties' activities in Italy overlapped horizontally to a significant extent in relation to commercial building security systems (fire and intrusion alarms), and commercial building control systems,[557] specifically for the supply of packaged fire alarm solutions to third-party installers. The parties had submitted in their

---

[556] Commission Decision of 30 March 2005 (Case COMP/M.3686—*Honeywell/Novar*).
[557] Decision, para 9.

notification that concerns would not arise in the market in Italy because: (1) there were a large number of competitors with an established track record of supplying Italian customers; (2) barriers to entry to the Italian market were low and it was possible to sell equipment manufactured in any Member State in Italy without seeking domestic Italian certification; (3) installers had significant buyer power and were able to play the manufacturers off against each other to increase pressure on prices; and (4) the nature of the bidding procedures in the market for the installation of fire alarm systems accentuated and exacerbated the market's competitive intensity.

The Commission's investigation did not support these arguments. First, sales figures collected from third-party market participants demonstrated that the merged entity's position would be significantly stronger than envisaged in the notification. Third parties described the total value of the Italian market as around EUR 75, million, rather than the EUR 100 million the parties had proposed in their notification. This led the Commission to conclude that the merged entity would have a market share of around 55–60% in the national market (the parties estimated their combined market share in their notification in the region of 30–40%). It would therefore hold more than half the market in Italy, and would be over twice as large as the second biggest player, Siemens, which had a share of around 20–30%.

Second, the parties characterized the market for the installation of fire alarm systems to end-consumers (the downstream installation market) as a bidding market. They submitted a few requests for quotes as evidence of this market feature, but the Commission was not persuaded by the limited evidence in the notification. In the market investigation, third party respondents stated that the market was not a bidding market. Price lists were set for a given period and could be informally renegotiated between manufacturers and installers from time to time. The Commission also held that in any event, even when bidding procedures are used in a downstream market, their presence does not necessarily reflect the competitive situation in the market under scrutiny, in this case the upstream sales of fire alarm systems to installers.

Third, in respect of new entry, many major European players were already present in Italy but with notably lower market shares than those they held in other countries, and than those of the merged entity.

The Commission could therefore not conclude that the presence of other strong players on the market, the potential for new entry, or the bidding activities were viable competitive constraints on the merged entity's clear incentive to increase prices on the Italian market. To address the Commission's concerns, Honeywell undertook to divest its entire Italian fire alarm systems business, which traded under the brand name of ESSER Italia, to a third party purchaser. This structural remedy satisfied the Commission's concerns, resulting in the merger's clearance.

Ineos/BP Dormagen[558]

On 10 August 2006, after a Phase II investigation, the Commission cleared an asset purchase transaction by which the Ineos Group acquired control of British Petroleum plc's (BP) Ethylene Oxide (EO) and Ethylene Glycols (EG) businesses based at its production facility in Dormagen, Germany.[559] The Commission's preliminary market investigation found that the proposed transaction could have generated competition concerns, as Ineos would acquire a very strong position on the EO market where the parties were direct and horizontal competitors. The Commission calculated that Ineos's and BP's share of the total EEA merchant market for EO was in the region of 55–60%, with Ineos's closest post-transaction competitor having less than a 30% share. Other players were much smaller, with generally less than 10% shares in the EEA. The transaction combined two of the three largest EO manufacturers in the EEA and would make Ineos substantially the largest supplier of EO to the EEA merchant market. The relative and absolute size of Ineos's post-acquisition market share on the EEA merchant market for EO led the Commission to open a Phase II investigation, but the acquisition was finally cleared with no undertakings or commitments. Ineos/BP Dormagen is therefore an example of a rather rare type of Phase II decision, without commitments.[560] Such decisions represent less than 1% of total decisions taken to date and less than a quarter of total Phase II decisions to date.[561] Put another way, the Commission is more than twice as likely after a Phase II investigation to render a decision requiring additional commitments to restore competition post-transaction than a decision requiring no such additional steps.

The Decision was based on the fact that competitors would have an incentive to react to supra-competitive price increases or other anticompetitive conduct by Ineos post-acquisition, and Ineos's customers would have sufficient ability to switch suppliers in response to such behaviour. The Commission's reasoning largely ran as follows. EG is a derivative product of EO. EG production takes up around 42% of total EEA capacity for EO production. Many EO producers are vertically integrated to EG production and divert relatively little of their EO to the EO merchant marketplace. However, the Commission learned from its market investigation that at the time of the transaction, substantial new capacity for EG was being commissioned by manufacturers in the Middle and Far East. It concluded that in the near future these new facilities would produce EG at substantially lower cost than in Europe, before importing them for sale into the

---

[558] Commission Decision of 10 August 2006 (Case COMP/M.4094) [2007] OJ L69/40.

[559] In December 2005, the Commission cleared Ineos's acquisition of certain of BP's other olefins and chemicals businesses: see Commission Decision of 9 December 2005 (Case COMP/M.4005— *Ineos/Innovene*) [2006] OJ C11/10.

[560] An Article 8(2) clearance under the old Merger Regulation or an Article 8(1) clearance under the new one.

[561] As at end November 2007, see: <http://ec.europa.eu/comm/competition/mergers/statistics.pdf>.

EEA. This would cause EG production in the EEA to decrease, with the effect that vertically integrated manufacturers of EGs would have spare EO capacity to divert to the merchant market. This spare capacity, which would be free to be sold on the merchant market, would constrain any price increases, supra-competitive pricing, or other anticompetitive conduct Ineos might undertake on the EEA merchant market for EO.[562] The Commission therefore cleared the acquisition unconditionally.

---

[562] A significant number of strong players also remained on the market for EO, notwithstanding the difference in market shares between Ineos and the remaining market participants.

REVIEWS OF BOOKS

EU Consumer Law and Policy by Stephen Weatherill (Edward Elgar, 2005), 253 pages, £25, ISBN 9781843769637

I. Introduction

Is European consumer protection an anomaly in this globalizing economy, particularly in light of its counterpart in the US? How are we to understand the new 'Consumer Policy Strategy'[1] and the recent call from the European Commission ('EC') for 'Better Regulation'?[2] Stephen Weatherill's book, a second and more comprehensive edition of his previous *EU Consumer Law and Policy*, answers these and other questions.[3] The book presents an accurate institutional account of European Union (EU) consumer law and policy, an approach that is both the strength and the weakness of the volume. Weatherill offers a clear and thorough analysis of EU consumer law and policy, beginning with the creation of the European Economic Community in the mid-1950s and finishing with the draft Constitutional Treaty rejected by the French and Dutch referenda in 2005. There is hardly anyone better placed than Professor Weatherill to explain the evolution of EU law in light of the major institutional challenges, constitutional compromises and federal tensions of the last 50 years of the common market. Though this institutional perspective is meticulously constructed through insightful analyses and future predictions, some blind spots remain. As a result, at the end of the book the reader is left with some important unanswered questions, such as: Does the European trend reflect a global consumerist perspective? Or is the European

---

[1] See Communication from the Commission to the Council, the European Parliament and the European Economic and Social Committee, EU Consumer Policy Strategy 2007–2013 Empowering Consumers, Enhancing their Welfare, Effectively Protecting Them, COM(2007) 99 final (13 March 2007) (hereinafter Policy Strategy), available online at: <http://ec.europa.eu/consumers/overview/cons_policy/doc/EN_99.pdf>.

[2] See Commission Green Paper on the Review of the Consumer Acquis: Better Regulation (Presented by the European Commission), COM (2006) 744final, (8 February 2007), available online at: <http://ec.europa.eu/consumers/cons_int/safe_shop/acquis/green-paper_cons_acquis_en.pdf> (listing relevant harmonizing legislation in matters of contract law).

[3] S Weatherill, *EU Consumer Law and Policy* (Edward Elgar, 2005).

model substantively different from its US counterpart? And, ultimately, what is happening to consumer protection in the West?

By adopting a merely institutional approach, the book does not address the ideological and social context in which EU consumer protection emerges. For instance, a reader would like to know what were the salient ideological, economic, and social tensions which European federalism sought to resolve through its institutional compromises.[4] While Weatherill analyses the federal tensions arising between the Member States and Brussels, he purposely omits other key players such as national bureaucracies, big businesses, social movements, and civil society.[5]

While this book is in itself a valuable contribution, my sense is that two other perspectives, one comparative and the other historical, would have both enriched Weatherill's analysis while allowing a broader audience, perhaps including non-Europeans and non-lawyers, to appreciate his work. From a comparative standpoint, for example, the US consumer protection experience would have revealed federal tensions similar to those experienced by Brussels and Luxembourg, thus offering a valuable insight into the interaction between courts, different levels of government and society in a federal polity.[6] Moreover, a comparative perspective could have revealed key ways in which European and US approaches to consumer protection are radically different. For instance, several authors have analysed the 'varieties of capitalism' in Western economies, which emerge within Europe itself.[7] Recently, James Whitman has defined the consumerism versus producerism distinction as being key to understanding the cultural as well as the ideological divide between Europe and the US.[8] Such cultural and social cleavages divergences *between* the EU and the US or even *within* Europe itself never emerge in the volume.

Similarly, as to the historical perspective, Weatherill's analysis does not take into account some of the major socio-cultural and ideological transformations that have accompanied the institutional and doctrinal changes in EU consumer law and policy in last fifty years. While Ralph Nader in the late 1960s was promoting consumer protection in the United States as a civil struggle for consumer

---

[4] See P Kurzer, *Markets And Moral Regulation: Cultural Change In The European Union* (Cambridge University Press, 2001).

[5] See P Bourdieu, *Les Structures Sociales de L'Economie* (Le Seuil, 2000).

[6] See WT Vukowich, *Consumer Protection in the 21st Century: A Global Perspective* (Transnational Publishers, 2002); see also JHH Weiler, 'The Transformation of Europe' (1991) 100 Yale LJ 2403.

[7] See PA Hall and D Soskice (eds), *Varieties of Capitalism: The Institutional Foundations of Comparative Advantage* (OUP, 2001); see also G Teubner, 'Legal Irritants: Good Faith in British Law or How Unifying Law Ends Up in New Differences' (1998) 61 MLR 11 (offering a comparison of different market economies within Europe).

[8] See JQ Whitman, 'Consumerism Versus Producerism: A Study in Comparative Law' (2007) 117 Yale LJ 340, 354 (analysing the profound cultural divide between the European market ideology of producerism and the US ideology of consumerism).

rights,[9] who were the main proponents of consumer rights in Europe and where did European consumerist ideologies came from? Were the Brussels technocrats or the members of the European Parliament the major proponents of consumer rights and were they inspired by John F Kennedy's speech in 1962?[10] What was happening at the national level of Member States with respect to consumer ideology and what was the purpose, in terms of integration strategy, of introducing 'consumer rights' throughout the EU in the late 1980s?

Finally, comparative and historical perspectives would have provided a deeper understanding as to how the form and substance of EU consumer law and policy are inevitably intertwined.[11] For instance, they would have provided an explanation as to why United States legal thought, in particular law and economic analyses rather than other approaches, was received largely by European legal elites in order to regulate consumer contracts and other private law rules.[12] Moreover, these perspectives could have revealed why the EC, in contrast to the Federal Trade Commission (FTC), is increasingly regulating consumer protection through a mix of soft law and hard law tools, as well as new governance and comitology techniques, all of which are rooted in the need to address the complexity of the European social-market economy.[13]

This essay analyses the chapters of Weatherill's book by dividing them into five parts. Part II addresses the well-known narrative of European integration in terms of positive and negative integration. Part III demonstrates how a comparative perspective could enrich the current debate on judicial federalism in European consumer law.[14] Part IV focuses on private law aspects of consumer law and policy while Part V adopts an historical viewpoint to understand the legal reception and the legal resistance, which took place in European consumer law (the reception and resistance of law and economics in European consumer law).

---

[9] See R Nader, *Unsafe At Any Speed: The Designed-In Dangers Of The American Automobile* (Grossman, 1965); see also H Mantel and S Skrovan, *An Unreasonable Man* (2006) (a film documentary on Ralf Nader, available online at: <http://www.imdb.com/title/tt0492499/awards>).

[10] See M Everson, 'Legal Construction of the Consumer 99–121', in F Trentmann (ed), *The Making of the Consumer: Knowledge, Power and Identity in the Modern World* (Berg, 2007).

[11] See generally, D Kennedy, 'Form and Substance in Private Law Adjudication' (1976) 89 Harv L Rev 1685.

[12] See U Mattei and Fernanda Nicola, 'A "Social Dimension"', in 'European Private Law? The Call for Setting a Progressive Agenda' (2006) 41 New Eng L Rev 1.

[13] See C Joerges and J Neyer, 'From Intergovernmental Bargaining to Deliberative Political Processes: The Constitutionalization of Comitology' (1997) 3 Eur LJ 273; J Scott and DM Trubek, 'Mind the Gap: Law and New Approaches to Governance in the European Union' (2002) 8 Eur LJ 1; see also G de Burca and J Scott (eds), *Law and New Approaches to Governance in the EU and US* (Hart Publishing, 2006).

[14] See F Cafaggi (ed), T*he Institutional Framework of European Private Law* (OUP, 2006); C Poncibò, *The Challenges of EC Consumer Law* (2007), available online at: <http://cadmus.eui.eu/dspace/handle/1814/7359>; L Antoniolli, 'Consumer Law as an Instance of the Law of Diversity' (2006) 30 VT L Rev 855–882.

II. Negative and Positive Consumer Law for Market Integration

The first chapter of the book offers an historical account of the evolution of EU consumer policy by bringing to the forefront the enduring federal tension between the regulation of the internal market and the domestic social policies of the Member States. According to Weatherill, the European Community has addressed these tensions through processes and institutional changes rather than through the construction of a typical federal State. For instance, the Maastricht Treaty[15] broadened the scope of consumer policy by adding a positive commitment in the text of the Treaty in the form of an explicit consumer protection Title.[16] This positive commitment to market re-regulation is generally acclaimed as a counterpart to the negative integration of the market, simply aimed at deregulating inter-State trade.[17] However, Weatherill highlights that, despite this codification in the EU Treaty, there has been prodigious and persistent ambiguity and disagreement over the institutional competences of the different levels of government to regulate or deregulate consumer protection in the internal market. Similarly, the subsidiarity principle and Community power to harmonize laws to promote the functioning of the internal market have heightened federal tensions rather than promoting stable solutions. In this uncertain constitutional milieu, the Treaty for a European Constitution (TEC) signaled some important changes by committing the EU to a high level of consumer protection.

While EU consumer law developed through changes in law and the integration of consumer protection norms into the Treaty, Weatherill highlights that consumer policy supplemented slow institutional changes, such as those resulting from the 'constitutionalization' of consumer protection or through landmark European Court of Justice (ECJ) cases, via two important routes. First, soft law resolutions by the Council and the Commission Action Plans helped to strengthen the importance of EU consumer law. In fact, soft law initiatives launched by the institutions in Brussels often preceded the adoption of consumer protection laws at the European level. This was true even where there was a possible 'competence creep', meaning the Community did not have full competence to

---

[15] Treaty on European Union, 7 February 1992 [1992] OJ C 224/1, reprinted in (1992) 31 ILM 253.

[16] See Treaty Establishing the European Community, 24 December 2002 [2002] OJ C325/65, Art 153(1)–(2) ('1. In order to promote the interests of consumers and to ensure a high level of consumer protection, the Community shall contribute to protecting the health, safety and economic interests of consumers, as well as to promoting their right to information, education and to organise themselves in order to safeguard their interests. 2. Consumer protection requirements shall be taken into account in defining and implementing other Community policies and activities ...').

[17] See F Scharpf, *Governing Europe: Effective and Democratic?* (OUP, 1999) at 45 (discussing the connection between negative integration and market deregulation).

regulate a particular issue.[18] Secondly, the harmonization of national consumer laws at the Community level became a powerful instrument to enable the adoption of narrowly tailored measures to create common obligations for the Member States in order to achieve similar goals despite divergent regulatory approaches.

In Weatherill's narration of the evolution of EU consumer law, the legal, policy and institutional perspectives are constantly intertwined. His narrative adopts the perspective of the European institutions as he aims to show how each of them had a particular vision of EU consumer law and policy that was integral to the construction of a common market. In each historical phase, each institutional compromise reflected the new equilibrium of a multilevel system of governance, which, as Weatherill puts it, is 'more than a market, but less than a state'.[19] Well aware of the ambiguities and tensions that EU consumer protection brings with it, Weatherill offers a meticulous analysis of its evolution and some cautionary remarks about its future: 'Here too examination of consumer policy opens a window on a broader landscape marked by conundrums about the shape the European Union should assume in [the] future if it is to live up to the motto allocated it by the draft Constitutional Treaty signed in 2004—"united in diversity".'[20]

The second and the third chapters of the book tackle some of the most important topics of EU consumer protection and address the notions of negative and positive integration, respectively. In the second chapter, the author offers a detailed analysis of the role of the European Court of Justice in striking a balance between the market liberalization of products and services under Articles 28 and 49 of the TEC and the protective measures of the Member States. In explaining the principle of *Cassis de Dijon*[21] put forward in a landmark ECJ decision, the author offers an in-depth analysis of the doctrinal implications and the critiques which emerged from this case.[22] On the one hand, the case has been interpreted through the principle of 'mutual recognition',[23] which enables diverse national products to circulate freely within the internal market. Thus, the institutional implication of *Cassis* is that it 'substantially reduced the Commission's workload',[24] by reinforcing the strong supranational ties between the Court and the Commission. On the other hand, Weatherill notes that *Cassis* sparked several critiques on the 'deregulatory impulse'[25] of EC law. Moreover, commentators speculate that such cases could create a 'regulatory gap' by striking down national

---

[18] See Weatherill, n 3 above, at 14; see also MA Pollack, 'Creeping Competences: The Expanding Agenda of the European Community' (1994) 14 J Pub Pol'y 95.

[19] See Weatherill, n 3 above, at 5.   [20] Ibid, at 3.

[21] See Case 120/78 *Rewe-Zentral AG v Bundesmonopolverwaltung für Branntwein* [1979] ECR 649 [1979] OJ C256/2.

[22] See Weatherill, n 3 above, at 44.

[23] See KA Armstrong, 'Mutual Recognition', in C Barnard and J Scott (eds), The Law of the Single European Market (Hart Publishing, 2002) at 225 (defining three dimensions of policy evolution of the concept of mutual recognition).

[24] See Weatherill, n 3 above, at 46.   [25] Ibid, at 47.

legislation in a particular field while, at the same time, no Community legislative action fills the gap.[26]

Weatherill avoids taking sides in the debate while skillfully casting light on the gaps, conflicts, and ambiguities that emerge from the ECJ jurisprudence on free movement. The author shows how the ECJ carefully evaluated each national measure obstructing free movement in light of the Member States' interest in keeping the protectionist measure in place. Weatherill demonstrates how the attitude of the ECJ has shifted over time from relying on a 'reasonably circumspect consumer'[27] who is well aware of the consequences of her choices, to having 'less faith'[28] that the market is protective of consumer interests. By surveying the case law on consumer protection, the author effectively demonstrates that *Cassis* creates 'non-absolute mutual recognition'[29] which does not completely harmonize the market through negative integration but rather allows Member States to justify before the ECJ why protective national regulations of unfair practices should remain in place.

The third chapter casts light on positive integration through legislative harmonization, namely European Directives adopted by the Community legislature and transposed by the Member States into their national legal systems. According to the author, the two main functions of harmonization have been, firstly, creating common rules for the internal market, and, secondly, establishing an 'appropriate standard' of consumer protection that will apply across the EU.[30] In his discussion of the *Tobacco Advertising* ruling,[31] in which the Court made clear that '[t]he Treaty confers no competence to harmonize per se,'[32] the author explains what he views as the 'dark side' of harmonization.[33] Through judicial scrutiny the *Tobacco Advertising* judgment revealed the limits of the Community's power to adopt legislation. In this context Weatherill suggests that a 'competence anxiety'[34] currently pervades the Commission's regulatory agenda.

III. A Comparative Perspective for EU Consumer Law and Policy

The first chapters of the book immediately confirm the author's impressive mastery of the field. Weatherill offers a subtle institutional analysis of the interaction between the Brussels-based supranational institutions and the Member States. However, by referring, for instance, to United States Supreme Court

[26] See ibid at 47, and see also D Caruso, 'Limits of the Classic Method: Positive Action in the European Union after the New Equality Directives' (2003) 44 Harv Int'l LJ 331.

[27] Weatherill, n 3 above, at 54 (quoting Cases C-267 and 268/91 *Keck and Mithouard* [1993] ECR I-6097).

[28] See ibid, at 55.   [29] Ibid, at 55.   [30] See ibid, at 63.

[31] See Case C-376/98 *Germany v Parliament and Council* [2000] ECR I-8419 (hereinafter *Tobacco Advertising* ruling).

[32] Weatherill, n 3 above, at 73.   [33] Ibid, at 73–77.   [34] Ibid, at 75.

Jurisprudence interpreting the Necessary and Proper Clause,[35] the Dormant Commerce Clause,[36] and the Federal Common Law,[37] the author could have highlighted how ECJ jurisprudence has innovatively mediated a number of socio-economic tensions in the European quasi-federal model.[38]

In this regard, Professor Joseph Weiler has shown how, although the expansion of Community jurisdiction through the implied power doctrine is similar to the American Necessary and Proper Clause, neither the expansion of the former nor the application of the latter has 'ignite[d] major "federal" political disputes between the actors',[39] despite increased judicial federalism. Similarly, through a comparative analysis of the dormant commerce clause, Donald Regan has explored the different approach of the ECJ and its United States counterpart.[40] Regan shows that, in assessing the mandatory requirement and the proportionality of a given domestic consumer protection measure, the proportionality test adopted by ECJ is not merely an anti-protectionism device.[41] Rather, the proportionality test as interpreted by the ECJ has become an innovative approach to maintaining national regulatory diversity while assessing alternative regulatory paths for consumer protection.

In addition to these insights, an historical perspective on consumer policy would have shown how, at different times, ferocious attacks from the Right and the Left marked a shift in regulatory approaches adopted by federal agencies.[42] For instance, in different periods both the FTC and the EC have entered into a transatlantic dialogue and have adopted similar legal tools and similar policy strategies such as economic analysis and empirical data collection that inform their regulatory approaches.[43] Thus, historical and comparative inquiries can

[35] US Constitution, art I, section 8, cl 18 (vesting Congress with the power 'to make all Laws which shall be necessary and proper for carrying into Execution the foregoing Powers, and all other Powers vested by this Constitution in the Government of the United States, or in any Department or Officer thereof').

[36] See, eg, *S Pac Co v Arizona ex rel Sullivan* (1945) 325 US 761, 769 ('For a hundred years it has been accepted constitutional doctrine that the commerce clause, without the aid of Congressional legislation, thus affords some protection from state legislation inimical to the national commerce, and that in such cases, where Congress has not acted, this Court, and not the state legislature, is under the commerce clause the final arbiter of the competing demands of state and national interests') (citations omitted).

[37] See K Lenaerts and K Gutman, '"Federal Common Law" in the European Union: A Comparative Perspective from the United States' (2006) 54(1) Am J Comparative L 1–121.

[38] See, eg, M Poiares Maduro, *We the Court: The European Court of Justice and the European Economic Constitution* (Hart Publishing,1998).

[39] Weiler, n 6 above, at 2447.

[40] See DH Regan, 'The Supreme Court and State Protectionism: Making Sense of the Dormant Commerce Clause' (1986) 84 Mich L Rev 1091.

[41] See ibid, at 1179–1182.

[42] See R Nader, *Unsafe At Any Speed: The Designed-In Dangers Of The American Automobile* (Grossman, 1972) (providing critiques from the Left); R Posner, 'The Federal Trade Commission' (1969) 37 U Chi L Rev 47, 61–78 (offering critiques from the Right).

[43] See GA Bermann, 'Regulatory Cooperation between the European Commission and U.S. Administrative Agencies' (1996) 9 Admin LJ Am U 933.

shed light on whether a given consumer protection regulation has been influenced by certain ideologies rather than others[44] and whether there is a continental divide in the way consumer policy is formulated by federal agencies as well as politicians.[45] Finally, such an approach could show if consumer advocates on both sides of the Atlantic are engaging in a global dialogue on the ideologies, legal tools,[46] and policy strategies[47] leading to similar regulatory reforms in a context of federal experimentalism.[48]

IV. Private Law Aspects of EU Consumer Law and Policy

In chapter four, Weatherill tackles regulatory techniques and reforms aimed at addressing market transparency and consumer protection regarding consumer credit, doorstep selling, package-travel, and time-shares. Weatherill shows that choosing particular EC regulatory techniques, such as the pre-contractual disclosure of information concerning a contemplated transaction, is a type of protection which minimizes interference with private autonomy. According to the author, this approach aims to promote informed consumer choice without replacing private choice with public decision-making about the content of contracts. Thus, efficiency depends on the capacity of the consumer to process the information that is supplied and to act rationally in response. Without rational behavior, regulatory intervention will not have its intended effect. Weatherill examines how, over time, the consumer credit Directives have favored transparency in order to allow the consumer to be more fully aware of the costs of credit while also permitting the Member States to impose stricter standards, as long as they do not impede Community goals.

Weatherill analyses the issue of minimal and maximal harmonization of European Directives as another area that is creating enormous institutional as well as federal tensions.[49] Minimal harmonization determines the floor of the

---

[44] See J Whitman, n 8 above; see also F Nicola, 'Constitutional Asymmetry in the Formation of European Private Law' (2008) 16:1 Cardozo J Int'l & Comp L 87–154.

[45] See J Whitman, n 8 above; see also J Rosen, 'Continental Divide', *Legal Affairs*, Sept–Oct 2004, available online at: <http://www.legalaffairs.org/issues/September-October-2004/review_rosen_sept-oct04.msp>.

[46] See F Nicola, 'Another View on European Integration: Distributive Stakes in the Harmonization of European Law' in *Progressive Lawyering, Globalization and Markets: Rethinking Ideology and Strategy* (C Dalton, ed) (William S Hein & Co, 2007) 233–260.

[47] See G de Búrca and J Scott (eds), *Law and New Governance in the EU and the US* (2006); see also G de Búrca and J Scott, 'Narrowing the Gap? Law and New Approaches to Governance in the European Union: Introduction' (2007) 13 Colum J Eur L 513, at 513–517.

[48] See D Kennedy, 'Three Globalizations of Law and Legal Thought: 1850–2000' in DM Trubek and Alvaro Santos (eds) *The New Law and Development: A Critical Appraisal* (Cambridge University Press, 2006) 19–73.

[49] See generally, M Dougan, *National Remedies before the Court of Justice: Issues of Harmonisation and Differentiation* (Hart Publishing, 2004).

preemption of national measures by European Directives, so that Member States may provide additional consumer protection if they like. Differently, maximal harmonization contained in a European Directive establishes both a floor and ceiling for domestic regulations.[50] Minimal harmonization that has brought fragmentation rather than harmonization of legal regimes is one of the main concerns both driving the Commission's consumer credit reforms and, more generally, causing European contract law to lean toward maximum harmonization approaches. However, Weatherill points out how the fact that there is no uniform duration of post-agreement cooling off periods might 'make sense' and how a 'sophisticated analysis' on the impact of diverse legislation ought to be undertaken at the EU level.[51]

Chapter five analyses consumer contracts by introducing the debate on imposing limits on contractual freedom. By introducing the Unfair Terms Directive[52] and the Sales-Warranties Directive,[53] Weatherill points out that the focus of the Community legislature has not always been on party autonomy and market information, but rather on unequal bargaining power and mandatory contract terms. This approach to consumer contracts has marked a major ideological shift in the history of private law in Europe in the last 50 years.[54] In fact, most of the domestic private law regimes have introduced either good faith or mandatory provisions to limit contractual freedom in the realm of consumer and standardized contracts. Rather than addressing the different national legal traditions, Weatherill analyses the regulatory choices present at the European level by demonstrating that the process of creating a 'European private law'[55] has been characterized at the same time by the regulatory choices of the Commission as well as by ECJ interpretation of private law Directives. While the ECJ has not shied away from setting aside national civil procedure laws limiting consumers' access to the protections guaranteed by the Unfair Terms Directive,[56] the judges in Luxembourg have refused to determine unfairness based on a specific contract term, instead relying only on 'general criteria'.[57] Weatherill shows that, despite the activism of the ECJ in interpreting the Directives, the Court has called on the national courts to interpret the unfairness of a contractual term in some particular circumstances.

[50] See ibid, at 83 (Weatherill points out that both the Court and the Commission recently adopted a problematic maximal or full harmonization approach, which eliminates the diversity among national regulatory approaches, thus furthering market integration).

[51] Weatherill, n 3 above, at 112.

[52] Council Directive 93/13/EEC on Unfair Terms in Consumer Contracts [1993] OJ L095/29 (EC).

[53] Council Directive 1999/44/EC on certain aspects of the sale of consumer goods and associated guarantees [1999] OJ L171/12.

[54] See F Wiacker, Giuffre (ed) *Storia del diritto privato moderno: con particolare riguardo alla Germania* (1980).

[55] See Weatherill, n 3 above, at 149.

[56] See Joined Cases C-240/98 to C-244/98 *Océano Grupo Editorial AS v Murciano Quintero* and *Salvat Editores SA v JM Sánchez Alcon Prades and Others* [2000] ECR I-4941 (ECJ).

[57] See Weatherill, n 3 above, at 125.

Moreover, the Commission has emphasized the different domestic implementation among the Member States of the Unfair Terms Directive, which has become discernible through a database of domestic cases created by the Commission.[58]

Chapters six and seven are the last two chapters on European private law. Very early on, in the mid-1980s, the Community adopted the Product Liability Directive,[59] which Weatherill points out was a highly contested measure. The author shows that, despite implementation by the Member States, interpretation by the Court and revision by the Commission, the Products Liability Directive failed to create a harmonized strict liability regime. In fact, when a producer is able to show that a given product defect was unknown or unknowable when the product was first placed on the market, the allocation of risk 'is shifted back on to the shoulders of the unlucky consumer.'[60] After this attack on this provision of the Directive and the fact that it has yet to be revised, Weatherill develops the chapter by addressing one of the leitmotifs of his book, namely the preemption of national product liability laws through maximum harmonization and how the *Tobacco Advertising*[61] ruling played a significant role in the ECJ's interpretation of the Directive. Weatherill's emphasis on the political climate of suspicion and the new attitude towards competences,[62] which surrounds Community initiatives, is an interesting way through which the author interprets the new regulatory shift of the Commission and the ECJ. Rather than heightening socio-economic tensions arising in EU consumer law, Weatherill sees the new cautionary strategy of the Commission, in adopting new legislation with less ambitious goals, as a way to limit federal anxiety emerging between the EU and its Member States.

In chapter seven Weatherill offers a deeper sense of the current debate on a very controversial topic—the adoption of a European civil code—or, as he puts it, how 'harmonization has bitten deep into private law'.[63] Weatherill first describes how the broad consultation launched by the Commission on this issue attracted widespread scholarly interest as well as fierce criticisms of Commission initiatives. Then he points out that the private lawyers who primarily addressed their national legal orders until the adoption of the Unfair Terms Directive[64] in 1993 had not realized the impact that the harmonization had on their domestic private law regimes. Only by the turn of the century were private lawyers ready to voice their skepticism to the Commission. As a result, the Commission, according to Weatherill, became more cautious and tried to address the critiques in future legislation.

---

[58] See the European Database on Case Law Concerning Unfair Contractual Terms, at: <https://adns.cec.eu.int/CLAB/SilverStream/Pages/pgHomeCLAB.html>.

[59] See Council Directive 85/374/EEC on the approximation of the laws, regulations and administrative provisions of the member states concerning liability for defective products [1985] OJ L210/29.

[60] Weatherill, n 3 above, at 139.

[61] *Tobacco Advertising* ruling, n 31 above.

[62] See Weatherill, n 3 above, at 157.   [63] Ibid, at 169.

[64] Council Directive 93/13/EEC on Unfair Terms in Consumer Contracts [1993] OJ L095/29.

According to Weatherill, the Europeanization of private law is the most evident example of how private and constitutional legal orders are entangled in European integration. Behind the reform of the contract law *acquis* lurks the specter of the *Tobacco Advertising*[65] ruling. In fact, after *Tobacco Advertising*, the Commission has taken more seriously the question of whether diversity among national contract law regimes creates obstacles to trade. For this reason, the Commission now requires hard data for new Community legislation on European contract law. Weatherill analyses both economic and cultural critiques put forward by European jurists on the Commission reform agenda. These critiques of the harmonization of private law have, in turn, affected the Commission proposal to adopt by 2009 a Common Frame of Reference, a controversial 'soft' law tool for the drafting and interpretation of European contract law.

Finally, even if the mainstream economic argument in favor of harmonization has been the elimination of transaction costs, Weatherill points out two equally potent criticisms put forth by lawyers. First, there is the claim that the Commission needs to demonstrate whether legal diversity really distorts competition. Under this claim, future harmonization would be a matter of impact assessment and sector-specific inquiry. The second criticism points out how harmonization suppresses regulatory competition, thus preventing market actors from choosing the most efficient legal regime. Even though Weatherill's account of the different arguments is very accurate, in his account, the economic approach to harmonization has no ideological component. However, most of the law and economics arguments put forward by jurists in this debate have been shaped by transatlantic legal ideas coming from the mainstream of American law and economics. Moreover, even when the Commission adopts the vocabulary of regulatory competition and transaction costs as a merely descriptive category, in reality this demonstrates a 'selective reception' of U.S. law and economics arguments.[66]

Chapter eight addresses a central issue on EU consumer policy—namely, advertising law. The author casts light on federal tensions, mediated by ECJ jurisprudence, arising between the national regulation of advertising and the free movement of goods. This negative consumer law approach has been coupled with a positive harmonization in the field. The Community has adopted Directives, some more controversial than others, regulating misleading and comparative advertisement, television broadcasting, and tobacco advertising. Once again, according to Weatherill, the *Tobacco Advertising*[67] judgment is a lesson to the Community legislature for future harmonization, in so far as 'the EC must shape its strategy on the regulation of advertising with more careful regard for its absence of any general legislative competence.'[68]

---

[65] *Tobacco Advertising* ruling, n 31 above.
[66] See Nicola, n 12 above.
[67] *Tobacco Advertising* ruling, n 31 above.
[68] Weatherill, n 3 above, at 187.

V. An Historical Perspective: Legal Resistance and Legal Reception in European Private Law

The author's analysis of European private law in chapters four through seven provides a good example of the second type of blind spot characterizing the volume. By examining the intellectual history of contract law, the author could have offered a more comprehensive analysis of the changing ideas of the lawyers, technocrats, and judges shaping EU consumer law and on the impact of US ideologies on such developments. For instance, the idea of freedom of contract, whose popularity rose and fell throughout the twentieth century, has been supported by shifting rationales, ranging from the will-theory to unequal bargaining power, the latter of which prompted mandatory terms in consumer contracts. In the US, however, the Chicago law and economics movement succeeded in shifting the debate back towards market efficiency and consumer choice in private law.[69] This return to freedom of contract and private autonomy has been highly contested in the US by scholars adopting a non-mainstream law and economics approach[70] and by those adopting law and society or social psychology approaches to private law.[71]

An analysis of why the Community chose to adopt a good faith clause and a black list of mandatory terms to protect consumers from unfair contractual terms would have shed light on how national private law regimes have historically developed a social approach to contract law.[72] In particular, it is worth noting that in the European context, ideas of resistance to Community initiatives have been associated with national and more social approaches to consumer law.[73] Only recently has a social perspective on European private law been put forward by scholars resisting the Commission agenda from different perspectives.[74] Even

[69] See R Posner, *Economic Analysis of Law* (5th edn, Aspen Law & Business, 1998) 86–129; R Cooter and T Ulen, *Law & Economics* (Pearson Addison Wesley, 2000).

[70] See D Kennedy, 'Distributive and Paternalist Motives In Contract and Tort Law, with Special Reference To Compulsory Terms and Unequal Bargaining Power' (1982) 41 Md L Rev 563, at 563–611; see also R Craswell, 'Passing on the Costs of Legal Rules: Efficiency and Distribution in Buyer-Seller Relationships' (1991) 43 Stan L Rev 361; C Jolls, 'Accommodation Mandates', (2000) 53 Stan L Rev 223.

[71] See RW Gordon, 'Maccaulay, Macneil, and the Discovery of Solidarity and Power in Contract Law' (1985) Wis L Rev 565; see also J Hanson and D Yosifon, 'The Situational Character: A Critical Realist Perspective on the Human Animal' (2004) 93 Geo LJ 1.

[72] See Section 9 of the AGBG Gesetz zur Regelung des Rechts der Allgemeinen Geschäftsbedingungen (Act on General Terms and Conditions of Trade) of 9 December 1976 [BGBl. I 3317], as amended, now Section 307 of the German Civil Code; L Raiser, *Das Recht der allgemeinen Geschäftsbedingungen* (1935), HOLLIS number [005138771]; see also C Joerges, 'History as Non-History: Points of Divergence and Time Lags Between: Friedrich Kessler and German Jurisprudence' (1994) 42 Am J Comp L 163, at 163–193.

[73] See H Collins, 'European Private Law and the Cultural Identity of States' (1995) 3 Eur Rev Private L 353.

[74] See Hans W. Micklitz, 'Principles of Social Justice in European Private Law' (2000) 19 YB Eur L 167; see also the Study Group on Social Justice in European Private Law, 'Social Justice in European Contract Law: A Manifesto' (2004) 10 Eur LJ 653, at 653–674.

though the term 'social' has been frequently used in the European discourse as a synonym for resistance, its significance is utterly vague and does not properly reflect what type of resistance against European integration should be advanced through EU law.[75]

Thus, another effective way to show the changing legal ideas among European lawyers would have been to tackle the ideologies characterizing the 'legal resistance' to European private law from its inception.[76] Among other benefits, this would have offered an important explanation to the escalating tensions over the Product Liability Directive[77] and its interpretation before the ECJ. For example, in the mid-1980s, the Directive was adopted as a barrier to the spillover effect of US class action litigation, but in the last twenty years it has triggered wide resistance in domestic courts, national legislatures, and scholarly communities.[78]

For instance, in *Commission v France*[79] the Commission challenged the French Government for non-conformity in transposing the Product Liability Directive. Among other claims, the French Government argued that such transposition would have infringed upon Article 6(1) of the European Convention on Human Rights by denying a fair trial to plaintiffs, who, under the Product Liability Directive, were left in a situation of *damnum absque injuria*. The ECJ decided that European law preempted those French product liability provisions, which were incompatible with the Directive and more favorable to consumers. Thus, the Court condemned France for not implementing the same liability standards imposed by the Product Liability Directive.[80]

---

[75] See Mattei and Nicola, n 12 above; see also A Verbeke, Negotiating in the Shadow of the Ius Commune, Key-Lecture, 12th Ius Commune Congress, Liège, November 2007.

[76] See D Caruso, 'The Missing View of the Cathedral: The Private Law Paradigm of European Legal Integration' (1997) 3 Eur LJ 3 (showing how the implementation of the Product Liability Directive had important distributive consequences with which the French Parliament, and in particular national politicians, were not equipped to deal).

[77] Council Directive 85/374/EEC on the approximation of the laws, regulations and administrative provisions of the member states concerning liability for defective products, see n 59 above.

[78] See similar cases Case C-52/ 00 *Commission v France* [2002] ECR I-3827; Case C-152/00 *Commission v Greece* [2002] ECR I-3879; Case C-183/00 *Gonzaléz Sanchez* [2002] ECR I-3914; Case C-402/03 *Skov Æg v Bilka Lavprivarehus A/S* [2006] ECR I-199; see also C Joerges, 'The Challenges of Europeanization in the Realm of Private Law: A Plea for a New Legal Discipline' (2005) 24 Duke J Comp & Int'l L 149, 173 (offering an important scholarly contribution and explaining that '[g]iven that the Product Liability Directive is based upon now outdated Treaty provisions, the chances for a more prudent exercise of judicial powers seems likely, although such comments cannot explain, let alone justify, the Court's revival of the language of orthodox supranationalism').

[79] See Case C-52/00 *Commission v France* [2002] ECR I-3827.

[80] See ibid, at 49 ('. . . by including damage less of EUR 500 in Article 1384–2 of the Civil Code;

– by providing in the first paragraph of Article 1386–7 thereof that the supplier of a defective product is to be liable in all cases and on the same basis as the producer, and

– by providing in the second paragraph of Article 1386–12 thereof that the producer must prove that he has taken appropriate steps to avert the consequences of a defective product in order to be able to rely on the grounds of exemption from liability provided for in Article 7(d) and (e) of the Directive, the French Republic has failed to fulfil its obligations under Articles 9(b), 3(3) and 7 of the aforementioned directive.').

In the aftermath of this judgment, France did not change one of the provisions of its *Code Civil* that was in conflict with the EC Products Liability Directive. This provision of the French Civil Code, in conflict with the Directive, considered the supplier of a defective product liable on the same basis as the producer when the producer could not be identified. Thus, the French consumer could freely decide to bring a torts suit against a producer or supplier even though the supplier had informed the injured person within a reasonable time of the identity of the producer. In March 2006, the ECJ held that France was in breach of Community law not only by not correctly transposing the Directive but also by not complying with the previous judgment of the ECJ. Thus, the French Republic was commanded to pay 'a penalty payment of EUR 31,650 for each day of delay in taking the necessary measures to comply fully with the judgment in Case C-52/00 *Commission* v *France* [...]'.[81] Though the initial resistance to the Product Liability Directive was a result of nationalist and welfarist views rejecting *in toto* the European dimension, today different forms of resistance are being levied against European private law by both social justice advocates unhappy with the ECJ's conservative interpretation of the Directive,[82] and by neoliberal lawyers who favor regulatory competition rather than less efficient European-wide standards.[83]

More and more significant in the European private law discourse is the adoption of law-and-economics analyses and the European 'legal reception' of different American schools of thought.[84] When Weatherill mentions that 'contractual freedom cannot be viewed in the same light today as it was 50 or more years ago',[85] he describes the transition to information and party autonomy in European consumer credit regimes without stating why this shift in legal ideas contrasts starkly to the one adopted by the Community in the Unfair Terms Directive. By pointing out which strands of law and economics were received by European lawyers, the author could have demonstrated that the focus on efficient information represented only one of the possible law-and-economics approaches addressing consumer protection in the United States literature. Moreover, in explaining the switch from standards to rules and the turn towards private autonomy and

---

[81] See Case C-177/04 *Commission v France* [2006] ECR I-2461, [2006] OJ C131 (holding that 'the French Republic has failed to take the necessary measures to comply fully with the judgment in Case C-52/00 *Comm'n v France* as regards the transposition of Article 3(3) of Council Directive 85/374/EEC of 25 July 1985 [...]'). See n 60 above.

[82] See G Howells and T Wilhelmsson, *EC Consumer Law: Has it Come of Age?* (2003) 28 Eur L Rev 370.

[83] See R Van den Bergh, 'Forced Harmonisation of Contract Law in Europe: Not to be Continued', in S Grundman and J Stuyck (eds), *An Academic Green Paper on European Contract Law* (Kluwer Law International, 2002).

[84] The reception of legislation or legal ideas is part of the inquiry of comparative lawyers. See M Graziadei, 'Comparative Law and the Study of Transplants and Receptions', in M Reimann and R Zimmermann (eds), *The Oxford Handbook of Comparative Law* (2007) (providing an overview); see *also* Nicola, n 13 above.

[85] Weatherill, n 4 above, at 115.

consumer choice, Weatherill could have highlighted the relevance of legal formalism to the process of replacing national regimes with European consumer credit legislation.[86]

VI. Regulatory Tools in EU Law: Product Safety and
Access to Justice

In chapter nine, Weatherill analyses different types of regulatory tools used to implement the Product Safety Directive,[87] which differs from the Product Liability Directive[88] in that it does not create liability in private litigation, but instead imposes a general prohibition on manufacturers and retailers from putting unsafe products on the market.[89] The Product Safety Directive creates a system of information exchange regarding dangerous products and risk assessment among national and sub-national authorities and coordinated by the Commission. However, Weatherill casts light on 'softer patterns of coordination and information sharing'[90] among national administrative agencies which have developed as a 'bottom-up' initiative, often bypassing the Commission and even the central governments of the Member States. The author embraces these forms of cooperation which are driven by local knowledge and practical problem-solving approaches, since this 'system reflects desirable features of the notion of subsidiarity.'[91]

In chapter ten, Weatherill analyses the importance of securing consumers' access to justice and the current limits thereof. Access to justice is a key issue also tackled by the Commission in its new Consumer Policy Strategy for 2007–2013.[92] The Commission initiative resonated widely because of its proposal to create a stronger system for redress and enforcement by considering new strategies other than alternative dispute resolution (ADR), as well as actions on collective redress mechanisms for consumers which should entail a similar outcome to the well-known US class actions.

Weatherill superbly masters both the constitutional as well as the practical perspective by showing where the limits of the current European consumer protection regime lie. In analysing the avenues of reform, the author surveys both soft law initiatives such as education policies to raise consumer awareness of legal rights as well as hard law initiatives such as Regulation 2006/2004

---

[86] See D Caruso, 'Private Law and State-Making in the Age of Globalization' (2006) 39:1 NYU J Int'l L & Pol.

[87] Council Directive 92/59 on general product safety [1992] OJ L228/24, amended by Council Directive 2001/95 on general product safety [2001] OJ L11/4.

[88] Council Directive 85/374/EEC on the approximation of the laws, regulations and administrative provisions of the member states concerning liability for defective products; see n 59 above.

[89] See Weatherill, n 3, at 200.   [90] Ibid, at 216.

[91] Ibid, at 224.   [92] See Policy Strategy, n 1 above.

which regulates the cooperation between national authorities on the enforcement of consumer protection rules. But Weatherill can also be critical of some
Community initiatives. For instance, he shows that Directive 98/27 on injunctions for the protection of consumer interests, rather than preventing violations
of consumer rights, provides a remedy only when an abuse has been committed. Thus, as Weatherill points out, the Directive 'is in a sense an admission of
failure'.[93] But in his hope for a 'trustworthy European Union'[94] the author ends
the chapter by outlining possible avenues of reform: soft law initiatives to educate
consumers, cross-border public enforcement mechanisms, and full recognition
by the ECJ of the horizontal direct effect of Directives, since this current denial
of the Court 'robs the Directive of some of its vitality as a method of creating
consumer rights within national systems'.[95] However, by mentioning the US side
of the same story, such as regarding public enforcement mechanisms, the author
could have educated the reader as to whether the ADR approach is a desirable
one, whether the Commission is really looking across the Atlantic, and if so, what
the main criticisms of using ADR in the realm of consumer protection disputes
have been.[96]

The book ends with a general evaluation of European consumer policy over
the last 20 years. Among the lines of inquiry Weatherill puts forward, are the variety of regulatory tools, the struggles concerning harmonization through minimal and maximal approaches, and the question of 'competence sensitivity'[97] as it
reappeared in the aftermath of the *Tobacco Advertising*[98] ruling. In this respect,
the book presents a valuable contribution to the field of EU law. Furthermore, the
book organizes and gives an excellent overview of consumer law and its underlying debates, critiques, and avenues for reform, through various institutional
lenses.

Finally, in discussing the combination and scholarly classification of regulatory
techniques that EU consumer protection entails, the author suggests that such
classifications are valuable because they can 'provide a thematic framework,'[99]
but warns that 'their danger lies in the risk that they may lead one to overstate an
academically attractive thematic order where there is in practice none.'[100]

In addition to summarizing Weatherill's view, this book review has put forward two perspectives—one historical and the other comparative—which illustrate that EU consumer protection policy can benefit from classifications of
regulatory techniques as long as such classifications include a discussion of the
ideas underlying the form and substance of the selected lawyering tools. Even

---

[93] Weatherill, n 3, at 242.   [94] Ibid, at 244.
[95] Ibid, at 234. In reality, the issue of the 'complete denial' of the horizontal direct effect by the
ECJ is a more complex one that has also been addressed through the notion of 'Incidental Horizontal
Effect.' See P Craig and G De Burca, *EU Law: Text, Cases, and Materials* (3rd edn, OUP, 2003) 220.
[96] See Mattei and Nicola, n 12 above, at 57.
[97] See Weatherill, n 3, at 249.
[98] See *Tobacco Advertising* ruling, n 31 above.
[99] Weatherill, n 3, at 247.   [100] Ibid, at 247.

though conceptualizing legal tools, theorizing about the underlying ideologies and uncovering the genealogies of legal doctrines might not directly influence the agenda of the EC, these avenues are worth exploring, especially in the context of an increasingly globalized legal discourse. In particular, for consumer protection, which has a long tradition in the US and, in some respects, an even longer one in Europe, it is worth inquiring into the potential of new and old ideas, of the taxonomies created by professional projects and of the academic debates taking place on both sides of the Atlantic and, indeed, around the world.

*Fernanda Nicola**

* The author would like to thank Peer Zumbansen, Gráinne De Búrca, Daniela Caruso, Christian Joerges, and Michele Graziadei for their insightful comments on this essay.

Constitutionalism, Multilevel Trade Governance and Social Regulation by Christian Joerges and Ernst-Ulrich Petersmann (eds) (Hart Publishing Ltd, 2006), 554 pages, £75, ISBN 9781841136653

The book under review is an impressive collection of reflections on currently topical themes in law and political science. Edited by two distinguished law professors then at the European University Institute in Florence, the group of 19 scholars, many of whom are affiliated with the Transformations of the State research centre at the University of Bremen, offer a great variety of perspectives on the interrelated paradigms of constitutionalism, multilevel trade governance, and social regulation. The essays differ not only in their approaches, but also in the degree of analytical depth. But the common premise on which all the authors build their analyses, as Ernst-Ulrich Petersmann points out in the Introduction, is the shared constitutional value that 'respect for human rights, private and democratic self-government and social justice requires more transparent, participatory and deliberative forms of transnational "cosmopolitan democracy", as well as more legal coherence in multilevel trade governance' (at p xxi).

This direct reference to respect for human rights as the main benchmark against which the democratic nature of any national and transnational regime is judged and assessed, is familiar in the work of Petersmann for those who are acquainted with his scholarship. It has elicited praise and criticism on numerous occasions and thus will not be dealt with here (see, for example, the contribution by Nickel, at p 165 in this volume). According to Petersmann, the national constitutions are incomplete and partial in that full respect for constitutional rights and freedoms provided therein cannot be achieved without cooperation with other States and participation in international organizations and respect for the international rule of law (including the respect for human rights required by the UN Charter). For Petersmann, freedom of trade should not be seen as a mere policy instrument, but indeed as an individual—and thus protectable—right. And this is where one of the main World Trade Organization (WTO) problems lies, for its members do not (yet) see the ultimate objective of the WTO as the protection of freedom to trade as a fundamental human right. This protection can only be achieved with the full synergy of domestic and international (including trade) constitutionalisms.

Against this background, Christian Joerges in his contribution (Section IV, Epilogue), which closes the book, offers a different approach to explaining the process of constitutionalization of the global trade regime. According to him, at the heart of the process of the constitutionalization of global governance lie the same forces as those which prompted the emergence of the theory of conflict of law in the domain of private law. Thus he approaches the analysis of transnational governance from the perspective of private, comparative, and European law, in contrast to Petersmann's starting point in human rights and constitutional law. Inspired by the draft EU Constitution, he maintains that 'supranational constitutionalism' has to create a type of unity which maintains diversity, or, as the draft Constitution declared, '*Unitas in pluralitate*', 'a constitutional conflict-of-laws paradigm' (p 494). According to Joerges, democratic failure is an inherent feature of the WTO. The 'mutual recognition' of these deficits, he argues, can be conceptualized as a modern type of conflict-of-laws theory, where such a conceptualization may be perceived as a key to 'constitutionalisation'.

The contributions in between the two editors' opening and concluding essays are divided into three main sections. It should be emphasized that given that trade governance forms a big part of the global governance agenda, the authors concentrate their attention on the WTO and its legal regimes. The first section is titled 'International Trade Law: Constitutionalisation and Judicialisation in the WTO and Beyond'. Patrizia Nanz clarifies the theoretical basis for the analysis of democratic legitimacy of transnational trade governance from the point of view of political theory. She concentrates, among other subjects, on sources for normative legitimacy in international decision-making and on explaining the reasons for the *problematique* of transnational governance, judged in light of the involvement of private actors and the inter-relationship between the judicial and political decision-making processes in the WTO. Achim Helmedach and Bernhard Zangl examine change in the GATT/WTO adjudication process, which has become more judicialized in recent years. In the authors' view, this judicialization of dispute adjudication is a mere prerequisite for the emergence of an international rule of law in international trade: '[i]f, in practice, conflicting parties do not use the dispute settlement procedures, one cannot meaningfully speak of an emerging international rule of law' (p 92). Christiane Gerstetter continues this analysis of dispute settlement body (DSB) jurisprudence. She argues that the appellate body is increasingly using the technique of 'balancing', refusing to embark solely on strictly textual interpretations of governing law (this is, the WTO Agreement itself), but instead trying to arrive at decisions on the basis of impartial and comprehensive consideration of all the legally relevant interests at stake—that is, on the basis of equity.

Rainer Nickel expounds on whether there can be a 'global law' without constituencies, ie, whether global law can be adopted without the engagement of national Parliaments. He argues that one of the consequences of the loss of the governmental control over a growing number of transnational issues is the shift of the law-production process from the nation-State to international level. As a result, 'governmental actors create regulations without the direct involvement of constituencies, and without complementary courts that control exercise of authority' (p 163). This is what he terms 'legal globalisation'. After criticizing as incomplete different theories explaining the challenges of a transnational legal orders and how these should be faced, he proposes his own concept of participatory transnational governance, the major component of which is the acknowledgement of the specific nature of law. This law (in its 'concrete' shape) should not be confined just to the list of constitutional fundamental rights, but should embed 'the procedural fine print of civil society involvement' (p 179). Failure to legitimize transnational civic participation brings with it a danger of 'benevolent and enlightened absolutism' of governments and powerful private players at the expense of 'good' transnational governance (p 190). The need for a greater civic participation is further explained in the contribution by Jens Steffek and Claudia Kissling.

The question Joost Pauwelyn tries to answer is whether the WTO is 'missing the boat' by adhering to the main postulates of international public law, ie by applying hard law to the exclusion of soft law norms, and only involving States to the exclusion of other subjects. He points to the eminent danger of marginalization of the WTO as an appropriate forum for the settlement of complex trade disputes if other important social questions, governed by distinct (binding and not on the parties) legal instruments, are ignored. Interestingly, he argues that the interpretation of the phrase 'any relevant rules of international law applicable in the relations between the parties' (Article 31(3)(c) of the Vienna Convention) should not be constrained to norms legally binding upon the WTO members, but should rather be seen as a reflection of a common understanding between them (p 217). Using the example of standards-setting practices, which are often delegated to NGOs and MNCs, and which, similarly to States, can be driven by protectionist motives, he further argues that such trade-distorting practices by non-State actors should also fall within the purview of the WTO.

Section II of the book is entitled 'Transnational Governance Arrangements for Product Safety', and offers insight into the SPS and TBT agreements and related instruments by five authors. Thorsten Hüller and Matthias Leonhard Maier explore the claims for regulatory authority of the Codex Alimentarius Commission, analysing the nature of tension between rich and poor countries and the participation of NGOs in the work of the Commission. Alexandra Herwig argues that the precautionary principle should not be applied formalistically, in that the precautionary principle affirms that 'the lack of scientific proof *alone* shall not be used as a justification for not responding to feared, but poorly corroborated, hazards' (p 306). As main reference cases she uses *EC-Hormones* and *Japan-Apples*. Elizabeth Fisher in her turn argues that it is misguided to oppose 'democratic' national risk regulation standards to 'undemocratic' SPS requirements for national measures to be based 'on scientific principles'. She argues that, given that public administration deals with standard-setting on risk regulation, it follows that the SPS Agreement covers regulating the administrative action. As a result, 'debate and dispute over the SPS Agreement are essentially an extension of national debates over administrative constitutionalism and risk regulation' (p 28).

Damian Chalmers starts his article by stressing the apparent inconsistency in the current debate over global governance. Some argue that there is a big potential for self-government, but others stress ever-growing administrative density. He then explains certain concerns about global governance, and concludes that global governance is acquiring normative structures that act as powerful sources of legitimation and emancipation. He rejects the idea of opposition to globalization and global governance as naïve and counter-productive.

In his very informative analysis, Robert Howse speaks of the 'extraordinary' mechanism set up by the TBT Agreement, in that it elevates existing 'relevant international standards' into the ranking of binding norms of international law. Drawing largely on the *Sardines* decision, he points to the imbalance created by the TBT itself, which, contrary to the general WTO principle of taking decisions by consensus, automatically accords the status of a binding international norm to standards set by other (mostly non-statal) organizations who do not take decisions by consensus. Their decisions can therefore become binding even on members that voted against a particular standard. Harm Schepel continues this discussion. He points out that ISO—the mother of all standards organizations— is not mentioned in the TBT, which indicates the deliberate intention of the drafters of the Agreement to omit mention of the ISO due to its private character. 'Negotiating parties were reluctant to grant a private organization the same kind of normative competence that they delegated to public organizations under SPS' (p 403). Thus, the intergovernmental symmetry preserved in the SPS Agreement is compromised in the case of the TBT Agreement.

Finally, Section III—'WTO and Transnational Environmental Governance'— contains contributions from three authors, Christine Godt, Ulrike Ehling and Oren Perez. Analysing global environmental governance using the Convention on Biological Diversity (CBD) as a case study, Godt concludes that global environmental governance theory 'challenges the central concept of intergovernmental policy which is conceived to safeguard (democratic) sovereignty' (p 433). Ehling argues that the WTO Committee on Trade and Environment has failed on all accounts, and that it is 'basically just another institution of highly formalized discussions among the WTO members, and is not a forum of extraordinary expertise or of special democratic legitimacy' (p 455).

This cursory *expose* of some of the essays included in *Constitutionalism, Multilevel Trade Governance and Social Regulation* shows that the treatise under review provides a myriad of approaches to the seemingly few issues which are spelled out in the title of the book. However, all the contributions argue for more legitimate, democratic, participatory, open, and transparent trade governance, in which human rights are observed and which ensures functioning social regulation. This book is destined to be one of the main reference books for researchers who work on constitutionalization and governance, but probably less so for lawyers who have to deal with WTO law on a daily basis. Still, even practitioners have to see the WTO in the broader context. As Mike Moore, a former WTO Director-General, has put it:

The WTO is a powerful force for good in the world. Yet we are too often misunderstood, sometimes genuinely, often wilfully. We are not a world government in any shape or form. People do not want a world government, and we do not aspire to be one. At the WTO, governments decide, not us.

But people do want global rules. If the WTO did not exist, people would be crying out for a forum where governments could negotiate rules, ratified by national parliaments, that promote freer trade and provide a transparent and predictable framework for business. And they would be crying out for a mechanism that helps governments avoid coming to blows over trade disputes. That is what the WTO is. We do not lay down the law. We uphold the rule of law. The alternative is the law of the jungle, where might makes right and the little guy doesn't get a look in.[1]

This is exactly what *Constitutionalism, Multilevel Trade Governance and Social Regulation* does: it frames the debate around the legitimacy of the supranational trade policies in the broader context of global governance.

Galina Zukova

[1] DG Mike Moore, Speech 'The Backlash against Globalization? Liberal International', Ottawa, 26 October 2000, available online at: <http://www.wto.org/english/news_e/spmm_e/spmm39_e.htm>.

European Administrative Law
by Jürgen Schwarze (rev edn, Sweet & Maxwell, 2006), 1,562 pages, £211, ISBN 9780421965607

When, almost 20 years ago, 'Europäisches Verwaltungsrecht' (Nomos, 1988) appeared in German, it pioneered new ground. With the idea of a European administrative law only about to be established, the book became an 'instant classic'. Swift translations into a number of European languages followed. The English edition appeared as 'European Administrative Law' in 1992.

The structure of the original monograph was interesting. Its first chapter investigated the idea of a 'Community of administrative law' (p 3), the concept of administration and sources of EC administrative law. However, more importantly, it analysed the 'emergence of a European administrative law through comparative method' (p 76). This meant an immense undertaking in Chapter 2: the analysis of the essential characteristics of the administrative law of all of the then EC Member States. Each of the substantive chapters that followed paid homage to this comparative dimension. Thus, in addition to providing a compendium of *European* administrative law, the book was equally a compendium of *comparative* administrative law.

Five substantive chapters provided the heart of the book: Chapter 3 looked at the 'legal constraints and the freedom of decision of the administration', that is, mainly at the principle of legality. Chapter 4 concentrated on the principle of equality and the prohibition of discrimination, Chapter 5 focused on the principle of proportionality and Chapter 6 dealt with the principles of legal certainty and the protection of legitimate expectations. Finally, Chapter 7 investigated the procedural aspects of the administrative law of the European Community.

Twenty years on, it was high time for a new compendium on the state of administrative law of the European Community (EC) and a re-evaluation of the general principles that inform and structure that sub-discipline of European law. Since the first edition, the EC has created or improved its own institutional administrative structures and an impressive body of academic literature on European administrative issues has emerged. Very significant judicial and academic developments were also waiting in the wings of the twelve national administrative orders originally investigated. And not to forget: since 1988, 15 new legal orders

have entered into the European administrative circle. All these legal riches provided a goldmine worth exploiting; yet, they equally posed a formidable barrier
to the task of thoroughly updating the book along the lines of its original structure. Perhaps unsurprisingly, but sadly nonetheless, the author has shied away
from this titanic task. Instead he decided 'to leave the book and its key reference
marks unchanged, but add an extended introduction to the reprinted version'.
'The crucial changes which have occurred in European administrative law in the
past 15 years will be described and evaluated in th[e] introduction' (cix–x). This
added introduction comprises 121 pages and has five substantive parts.

Part B investigates the subsequent evolution of the Community's general principles. What are the principal innovations identified? Firstly, '[v]arious already-
established general principles of law which are important for administrative law
have since been transferred into primary law by the Treaties of Maastricht or
Amsterdam' (cxv). (Within the list of such principles, Schwarze mentions the
principle of proportionality. Is this supposed to imply that the principle of proportionality was not a constitutional principle before Maastricht?) Second, a strong
and debateable claim follows: '[a]n overview reveals that the judiciary has put less
emphasis on developing major new legal principles and has focused instead on
clarifying the existing established principles and developing them further' (cxix).
The remainder of this section provides an in-depth analysis of the development
of the major general principles of European administrative law: legality, equality, proportionality, protection of legitimate expectations and legal certainty, and
due process of law.

Let us briefly discuss the author's discussion of the first principle: the principle
of legality. Schwarze defines it as follows (cxx): 'The principle of the legality of
administration, which in the meaning of the liberal State under the rule of law is
meant to limit the exercise of powers by the State and therefore protect civil liber-
ties, is a cornerstone of the constitutions of all Member States.' He moves on to
claim that '[e]ven in the early days, the ECJ had established the applicability of
the principle of the legality of administration in its various manifestations such
as the principle of the hierarchy of norms or the principle of the priority of laws
in the sphere of Community law' (ibid). Has it? If so, why has the Community
legal order since 1996 bemoaned the absence of a clear hierarchy of norms that
would allow it to sharpen the separation of powers within the EC? Who exactly is
the Community 'legislator'? Who is the Community 'executive'? What are their
distinct legal instruments? In a word: what will the constitutional equivalent of
the (German) 'state' principle of 'legality of administration' (*'Gesetzmäßigkeit der
Verwaltung'*) in the EC legal order? Schwarze identifies the principle with the
'requirement of a legal base' (cxx). However, this is a *constitutional* requirement for
all legal actions of the Community. It can hardly characterize the Community's
executive function.

Part C concerns the codification of European administrative law. The anticipated conclusion here is as follows: '[e]ven half a century after the entry into force

of the first Community treaty there is no coherent and uniform codification of the principles of administrative law' (clxii–iii). Yet, there are important exceptions to this rule. Regulation 1/2003 represents such 'a very significant example of secondary administrative procedural law' (clxv). For the indirect implementation of Community law, there has 'also been a noticeable trend for some time to create at least certain uniform legal standards for the implementation of administrative law by enacting written law in specific areas of the law' (clxvii). The 1992 Customs Code is mentioned.

Part D looks at the important structural changes in the administrative organization of the European Union. This is arguably the most intriguing dimension. Institutionally, the establishment of the Court of First Instance has undoubtedly 'been a factor in making possible increased levels of judicial control over legal and factual aspects in each individual case' (cxviii). In a similar vein, various Community agencies have been established and thus increased the potential for a direct Community administration. More important still is another change. 'The original description of the then legal *status quo* was, by and large, limited to the differentiation between direct Community administration implemented by the administrative bodies of the Community and indirect administration, which as a rule leaves the implementation of Community law to the authorities of the Member States ... To a great extent, clear separations of duties have been superseded by forms of *administrative co-operation between administrative bodies of the Community and the Member States*' (cxii–iii, emphasis added). Cooperation may take place horizontally, that is: between individual national authorities; and vertically, that is: between the national and European administration. The various forms of cooperation are said to 'include the exchange of information and date, control mechanisms on the basis of report and notification duties, official assistance and assistance in implementation as well as the co-operation in the taking of decisions' (clxxvi). A major application is found in the reformed implementation regime of EC Competition law and its 'network' of competition authorities.

Part E looks at the changes in the interaction between national and European administrative law. The comparative law perspective of the 1988 edition had been able to show various impulses of national administrative law on the European administrative legal system. French law had proved particularly influential early on, followed by German and British law. Scandinavian countries added their impact after their accession. Still, Schwarze rightly observes that the issue of which legal tradition has prevailed 'is not helpful for a fundamental understanding of the evolution of European administrative law'. It would be 'much more important to realise and accept that European law evolves from discourse between the various legal orders and from a unique synthesis of different legal ideas in which it is unthinkable that one specific national legal order can constantly gain the upper hand' (clxxxv).

But has European administrative law, in turn, influenced the national administrative systems? It is argued that 'the reverse trend, ie the fact that there is now a system of mutual interaction, has only come to the fore of public opinion slowly' (clxxxvii). In this section, Schwarze looks at various impulses of European secondary law and case law on national law and find a number of examples—such as the possibility of injunctive relief in Great Britain—for a 'process of mutual cross-fertilisation' (cci). Finally, the seeds of a *ius commune Europaeum* are broached. While national administrative law will retain its characteristics, the author believes it 'unlikely that in the long run there will continue to be two separate legal regimes for the indirect implementation of Community law and the purely national application of administrative law which exists alongside each other' (ccii). Thus, 'States which have an existing strong tradition of administrative law are decidedly more sceptical (although not pessimistic) as far as the future prospects of developing an administrative *ius commune* in Europe are concerned' (cxxiii).

Part F focuses on the 'changes in the parameters for European administrative law due to the extension of the EU and the adopted Treaty establishing a Constitution for Europe'. In line with his interaction thesis, expansions of the European membership may have a mutual impact. In fact, the author identifies 'a process of reform from the mid-nineties which predominantly centred in the approximation of the national legal rules to the EU and the reform of the national administrative structures of the acceding states'. Here Europe as well as the legal orders of Western Europe served as models (ccix). The second section moves to an analysis of the Treaty establishing a Constitution for Europe. This may now have only historic interest. However, Schwarze makes a number of interesting points. Article III-285 of the Treaty establishing a Constitution for Europe is said to be 'a long way from being a possible future legal base for the creation of a comprehensive European administrative law or even just serving as a tool for the development of a general administrative procedural code' (ccxix). Still, 'it might be worthwhile to regulate in written law at least the basic principles of European administrative law' (ccxx).

A résumé follows these five substantive sections (Part G). How does the author systematize and summarize the administrative development of the EC in the past two decades? 'If one should attempt to summarise and characterise the more recent legal developments, there has been a further clarification and detailed classification of the general principles of law. In that way, a more dense and multilayered net of administrative legal rules has been created.' (ccxxii). There has also been a gradual shift from 'the classic principle of separating between the implementation of European administrative law by the Commission (as an exception) and the implementation of Community law by national authorities (as the rule) on the one hand and the principle of co-operation between member State[s] and European authorities on the other hand'. Third, while the influence of (Western) national administrative orders on the European order continues, 'the administrative laws of the new Member States in central and eastern Europe are likely to have less of an influence on the legal development at European Union level' (ccxxiv).

Do these three (major) conclusions necessitate modifying the final hypothesis of the original edition? The original hypothesis had been as follows: 'As regards the future perspectives for the completion of E.C. administrative law, at present and for the foreseeable future, all hopes, with the exception of partial and sectoral legislative codifications, rest upon a gradual, cautious and pragmatic further development of case law in the Community.' And Schwarze 'would still subscribe to that view' (ccxxvii–iii).

In sum, the revised edition of Schwarze's *European Administrative Law* is a dual package. It contains the classic original 1992 English edition and, as such, is already worth buying for those European lawyers, like myself, that are interested in the historical evolution and evaluation of the European legal construct. On the other hand, European lawyers that expect a comprehensive monograph dealing with the present structure and content of Europe's administrative legal order will be disappointed. The added introduction may succeed in *sketching* '[t] the crucial changes which have occurred in European administrative law in the past 15 years'. However, in the light of these truly *crucial* changes during this time, this welcome introduction was not a substitute for complete rewriting. The author has deliberately opted against undertaking this enormous task. The result is a reprint of a praiseworthy 'classic', but not a book that describes or explains the European Union's administrative law of the first decade of the twenty-first century. That latter task is now left to another book: PP Craig's *EU Administrative Law* (OUP, 2006).

Robert Schütze

EU Intervention in Domestic Labour Law
by Phil Syrpis (OUP, Monographs on
Labour Law, 2007), 177 pages, £55,
ISBN 9780199277209

In this Oxford Monograph on Labour Law, Phil Syrpis invites the reader to a challenging and stimulating analysis of the rationales for European Union (EU) intervention in domestic labour law. At a time when fundamental principles of domestic labour laws are increasingly put under pressure by EU intervention, as recently illustrated in the *Viking* and *Laval* cases, the author provides us with a very useful set of analytical tools to better understand the variety of policy options available at EU level.

As is made clear in the introduction (Chapter 1), the intention of the author is not to provide an exhaustive review of interventions by the Court of Justice of the European Communities (Court of Justice) and the EU political institutions (ie the European Council, Council of Ministers, European Parliament, Commission, social partners, and advisory committees). Rather, it is to provide a theoretical framework for the analysis of the evolution of EU intervention in labour law and, as far as possible, to suggest directions for future action. The author questions the assumption that disparities between the labour laws of the Member States are incompatible with the European project. The impact of the EU on disparities between domestic labour laws is therefore the recurrent theme throughout the monograph which makes its reading particularly interesting and dynamic. The author first provides a theoretical framework (Chapters 2 and 3) for the analysis of EU intervention in domestic labour law that follows (Chapters 4 and 5).

Drawing inspiration from the Preamble to the Treaty on European Union, Syrpis identifies three rationales for EU intervention in labour law (Chapter 2): integrationist, economic, and social. Although the rationales are not always easy to distinguish in practice and may also conflict with one another, they constitute useful analytical tools with which to appraise EU intervention in the field of labour law. The main focus of the monograph is on the integrationist rationale. Indeed, as the author could perhaps have made clearer in the introduction, integration is not an end in itself but ultimately aims at the promotion of economic and social progress; the integrationist rationale is therefore the most complex and deserves specific attention. This rationale lies behind EU labour law intervention which aims to establish and improve the functioning of the European market through the elimination of barriers to the free movement of factors of production and distortions of competition. In particular, and this is the keystone and the most useful input of this monograph, the author points out that different definitions of barriers to free movement and distortions of competition may lead to distinct conclusions on the need for EU intervention in the field of labour law.

Firstly, as regards barriers to free movement, the view that currently prevails in the case law of the Court of Justice is that almost any disparity between national rules may affect access to the labour market of another Member State and therefore constitutes a barrier to free movement that should either be justified or be eliminated (*Dassonville* test). Syrpis argues however that disparities between domestic labour laws or practices need *not* be understood as constituting barriers to free movement, and need *not* be eliminated, *unless* they actually prevent access to national markets or are discriminatory in law or in fact along the lines of the *Keck* test.

Second, as far as distortions of competition are concerned, the author distinguishes between five possible definitions of distortions of competition among which he favours the following three. The first approach assumes that the functioning of the unregulated market is beneficial as long as free movement is ensured. Therefore, there is no need to regulate the EU market and mere differences between the laws of the Member States are not capable of distorting competition *so long as* free movement is possible and ensures competition between legal systems on the market (a). The two other approaches supported by the author illustrate a lesser degree of confidence in the autonomous functioning of the market and suggest that EU institutions can act to ensure that competition will be beneficial. It can, on the one hand, be argued that divergences in the standards guaranteed by domestic law may constitute distortions of competition but *only* where standards in certain Member States are 'unacceptably low' in which case it is appropriate that minimum standards be set (b). An alternative view is that disparities between national labour law regimes *only* lead to distortions of competition if there is a risk that regulatory competition will lead Member States to search for competitive advantages through the adoption of sub-optimal standards ('race to the bottom') (c). This risk may exist even if no State has 'unacceptably low' standards. If such a threat can be established, EU intervention should respect the disparities between domestic standards but set basic parameters. These perspectives on the notions of barriers to free movement and distortions of competition are particularly interesting in that they provide strong arguments in support of the view that, analysed from an integrationist perspective, EU intervention could or should be tolerant to the disparities between domestic labour laws unless specific conditions are met.

The analysis of the integrationist rationale is followed by a shorter overview of the economic and social rationales for EU intervention in the field of labour law. Although these two rationales are less complex, their presentation illustrates that they may be relied upon to pursue the economic and social meta-objectives of the EU without recourse to the integrationist argument. It also usefully introduces the reader to the tensions that may arise from the co-existence of three different rationales for EU intervention. The economic rationale underlies EU intervention which aims to improve the performance of the European economy. This rationale may apply, for instance, to measures adopted on the basis of the Employment Title of the Treaty establishing the European Community (EC). The social rationale, by contrast, explains EU intervention aimed at the improvement of the position of workers. It is illustrated by reference in particular to the Social Chapter of the EC Treaty. Specific attention is devoted to pointing at the independence of the social rationale from the economic rationale, the former constituting a distinct objective in itself.

Having introduced the reader to the three main rationales for EU intervention in domestic labour law, the author turns to the analysis of the competences of the EU to take action on the basis of each of these rationales. Although Chapter 3 is more traditional in substance, it is an important step for the analysis that follows in the subsequent chapters. As the Community is bound to act within the limits of the powers and objectives conferred upon it by the EC Treaty, intervention at European level must have an adequate legal basis in the Treaty. EC intervention must also comply with two crucial principles. The principle of subsidiarity, first, governs the level—whether Member State or EC level—at which action should be taken in cases of shared competences. It must be shown not only that Member States cannot sufficiently achieve the objective of EC intervention but also that EC intervention would actually better achieve it. Second, in all cases where the need for EC intervention is established, it will have to comply with the principle of proportionality. The measure adopted at EC level must be both suitable and necessary to achieve its objective. The author, with whom I can only agree, argues that, as guardians of the Member States' autonomy, the principles of subsidiarity and proportionality should be applied strictly to preserve national diversity and ensure the legitimacy of EU intervention. The Court of Justice is therefore invited to adopt a more stringent approach to these principles against which the validity of EU intervention can be tested. When EU intervention in labour law is motivated by an integrationist rationale, the subsidiarity test is likely to be easy to pass since it may be more adequate to shape the EU market at EU level than at national level. National legitimate interests could however be protected through a stringent application of the proportionality test. To the extent that the Court of Justice may review the validity of the EU intervention motivated by economic and social rationales, it is the subsidiarity test that should be given particular attention. Indeed, it is not always obvious that EU level intervention is more adequate than national intervention to pursue economic or social objectives.

Within the theoretical framework sketched out here of both the three rationales for EU intervention and the issue of EU competence, the book moves on to analyse the case law of the Court of Justice on the elimination of barriers to free movement, which provides a clear illustration of the tension between the three rationales. Chapter 4 builds upon the idea that, as analysed from an integrationist perspective, disparities between domestic labour laws do not *per se* constitute barriers to free movement. It is therefore argued that the Court of Justice should substitute the *Keck* approach to barriers to free movement for the *Dassonville* test described in Chapter 2; this would ensure greater respect for national autonomy in labour law not only in relation to the free movement of goods but also the free movement of workers, services, and establishment. Although the author touches upon it, one could have hoped for a more detailed analysis of the practical consequences which adoption of the *Keck* test would entail. Indeed, as the author acknowledges, this remains an obscure aspect of the case law of the Court after *Keck*. Syrpis however recalls that even within the previous understanding of barriers to free movement, ie under the *Dassonville* approach, the Court of Justice has been tolerant of the disparities in national labour laws in two ways. Where a national measure raises concerns from the point of view of the integrationist rationale, it may be flexible in accepting justifications submitted by Member States, as was done in *Rush Portuguesa*. The Court of Justice may also adopt a lower degree of scrutiny of the proportionality of national measures, in particular when they are justified by socio-economic objectives or the protection of fundamental rights. Both the flexible acceptance of justifications and the lower proportionality test constitute tools with which the Court of Justice can allow the Member States a measure of autonomy. These techniques however crystallize a tension between the integrationist, economic, and social rationales at the stage of justifications and proportionality. According to the author, this could be avoided by the adoption of the *Keck* test, which is less suspicious of domestic labour laws in the first place.

The author then turns to an analysis of the interventions of EU political institutions (Chapter 5). The strains imposed by EU political institutions on domestic labour laws, and their relationship with the Court of Justice are analysed in three stages.

First, it is pointed out that political institutions should have a leading role in defining the approach to be adopted at EU level in relation to the integrationist rationale for intervention. In particular, when political institutions intervene for integrationist reasons to serve the single market and if the resulting measure is brought for review before the Court of Justice to ensure that it actually contributes towards serving the single market, the Court of Justice should allow political institutions a degree of discretion. Indeed, this situation must be distinguished from that analysed earlier in relation to competences where it was suggested that the Court should control the conformity of EU intervention with the principles of subsidiarity and proportionality in a stringent way so as to ensure respect for national interests. The same observation applies when the Court of Justice reviews EU intervention motivated by social and economic ends since in both cases the measure should not only contribute to the given aims but also refrain from compromising the market. In other words, it is advocated that the Court of Justice should allow political institutions a degree of discretion when deciding on market-making. Conversely, when faced with questions related to the adequate balance to be found between the three rationales for EU intervention, the Court of Justice should draw inspiration from existing interventions by political institutions on similar issues. Such a dialogue between the various EU institutions is illustrated by reference to the case of posted workers which has triggered important case law and legislation.

Second, the author points out that it is possible to read the attitude of EU political institutions as expressing a different understanding of barriers to free movement than that adopted by the Court of Justice in the *Dassonville* test. If indeed political institutions considered disparities between domestic labour laws to be problematic from the point of view of market integration, they could have sought to intervene on the basis of the integrationist rationale. Syrpis points out that political institutions have not attempted to do so, either because they do not consider that disparities between domestic labour laws constitute barriers to trade or because no agreement could be reached on harmonization. This therefore casts doubt on whether political institutions actually have the same understanding as the Court of Justice about what constitutes a barrier to trade and about how to approach disparities in labour laws. As this argument is particularly interesting and is relied upon later on to support the author's view that the Court of Justice should change its approach to barriers to free movement, it is regrettable that this point was not treated in more depth.

Third, although harmonization of domestic labour laws has not been pursued by the EU political institutions for integrationist reasons, and since as the author argues that there is no legal basis to harmonize either for economic or for social reasons, EU intervention by political institutions has taken other forms. EU political institutions have in particular had recourse to the setting of minimum standards and to the open method of coordination. Interestingly, both techniques are therefore scrutinised in light of the three rationales for EU intervention and the principles of subsidiarity and proportionality.

The adoption of minimum standards of labour law may be justified under the integrationist rationale. Indeed, although allowing Member States to adopt different measures above the minimum agreed at EU level might raise concerns in relation to free movement, according to conceptions (b) and (c) of distortions of competition, as described above, the diversity of domestic labour law above a minimum level is compatible with the single market. The onus would however be on the EU institutions to show that the adoption of minimum standards is necessary either because certain Member States have excessively low standards which prevent the market from functioning correctly (conception (b)) or because there is a risk of race to the bottom (conception (c)). By contrast, justifying the adoption of minimum standards of labour law on the basis of the economic or social rationales might be more difficult. In particular it is not clear that the EU is in a better position than Member States to adopt minimum social standards with a social or economic rationale. The Working Time Directive is taken as an example to show how difficult it is to assess the social and/or economic effects of a measure. The author supports the view that a vigorous scrutiny of the conformity of that Directive with the principles of subsidiarity and proportionality could have led to its annulment.

The open method of coordination (OMC) is also scrutinized in light of all three rationales for intervention by EU political institutions in domestic labour law. The OMC, as it exists in the framework of the European Employment Strategy for instance, can first be justified by reference to the integrationist rationale. More specifically, it can be explained by reference to conception (c) of distortions of competition. Indeed, market integration through the creation of the European Monetary Union and the coordination of economic policies create pressures on Member States to deregulate their labour market, thus creating a risk of a race to the bottom. Alternatively, the OMC could be justified by reference to a social rationale to the extent that it seeks to preserve the European social model; or an economic rationale to the extent that it pursues the improvement of European economy. For the OMC to pursue either of these rationales however, specific attention should be devoted to actually ensuring that the OMC does not lead to deregulation or to less social protection as may be feared from its content. From that perspective, Syrpis proposes a clearer assertion of the social objective of the OMC and suggests coupling the OMC with minimum standard-setting (accompanied by non-regression clauses) and/or asserting fundamental social rights. Such a 'hard' OMC, with precise guidelines to meet the objectives of any of the three rationales, should however be carefully scrutinized in light of the proportionality principle. Alternatively, a 'soft' OMC, with a less normative character could be contemplated.

Overall, this monograph offers a thought-provoking perspective on EU intervention in the field of domestic labour law, and its rationales. The text is dense, concise and very well thought through. The author is well aware of the specificity of the theoretical approach that he develops; he therefore does so progressively and justifies each stage of the reasoning. This makes the reading both accessible and strongly argued. Syrpis achieves his aim by indeed casting doubt on the assumption that disparities between domestic labour laws run counter the EU project of market integration. He skillfully argues that the EU political institutions and, mostly, the Court of Justice could increase EU legitimacy by developing mechanisms which are more respectful of Member State autonomy in labour law. The author also succeeds in demonstrating that the EU can legitimately ensure that Member States remain within permissible bounds designed in particular to preserve the social meta-objective of the EU that tends to be neglected. Syrpis' suggestion that the integrationist rationale first be re-defined, and secondly that the three rationales for EU intervention be re-balanced is therefore convincing.

The only regret this reviewer would express, as already indicated above, is that the practical consequences of the adoption of the *Keck* test and the divergences of views between the Court of Justice and EU political institutions on the notion of barriers to free movement are not subject to a more developed analysis.

The book provides a good overview of EU intervention in the field of labour law. Further added value might have been provided by a more developed discussion of fundamental social rights. Although the monograph points in this direction, it does not, for instance, expand on the relationship between the OMC and EU fundamental social rights. EU anti-discrimination law also constitutes an increasingly important lever for EU intervention in domestic labour laws that receives little attention in the book. That said, it is only because the analysis is particularly stimulating that this reviewer would have hoped for it to be developed further.

Elise Muir

European Security Law
by Martin Trybus and Nigel D White
(eds) (OUP, 2007) 365 pages, £65,
ISBN 9780199218622

The book represents one of the rather rare attempts to analyse the development of the European Security and Defence Policy (ESDP) from a legal perspective. While much emphasis is commonly placed on the lack of political will and scarce European defence budgets to explain why the EU is still considered an infant security actor, this valuable collective work demonstrates that an adequate and consistent legal framework may significantly contribute to tackle the European and global security challenges ahead.

While the analysis is driven by the legal perspective, it is embedded in the relevant political science and international relations literature on ESDP, which allows this book to be considered as a 'bridge-builder' between disciplines. *European Security Law* may therefore be of great value for both lawyers with an interest in European security policy and policy analysts with an interest in international law.

The book is structured in three sections. The first section (Chapters 2 and 3) is about the past and the uncertain future. Chapter 2 offers, within the limits set by a book chapter, a very interesting overview of the ill-fated European Defence Community (EDC), a complete stranger despite being often referred to in the history of European integration. It is surprising to discover at the outset that the EDC was mainly a supranational organization, including a court with a substantial role. This is difficult to believe in the Cold War context, where the entire emphasis could be expected to be placed on military force and collective defence. Chapter 3 outlines the main relevant provisions of the now abandoned 2004 Constitutional Treaty. In this respect, and in contrast with other expected institutional reforms that are on 'stand-by', ESDP does not seem to depend on new constitutional developments. In any event, these early chapters have in common that they deal with major European treaty projects which did not become a reality. But they provide an excellent starting point to outline the legal issues at stake.

The second section (Chapters 4–9) discusses various aspects of ESDP such as crisis-management operations, the anti-terrorism dimension, armaments policy,

and collective defence. The reader might perhaps miss an introductory chapter
in this section analysing the ESDP's institutional backbone, composed by the
Council and a number of Council-controlled bodies, and commenting inter alia
on the limited role of the EU High Representative—the perennial Mr Solana—
the fragmented command and control of peacekeeping operations or the fact
that military and civilian operations—those involving the deployment of police
or judicial experts—are handled completely separately. The EU prides itself on
its special ability to combine civilian skills and resources for reconstruction and
development with military force for security. It makes no sense to separate the
two in the planning and management of operations. The description of legal
instruments, although comprehensive across the different chapters, is somehow
fragmented.

The analysis in this part reveals however several important issues and findings. Chapter 4 offers a comprehensive analysis of the legal framework (mandate,
legal status, and applicable law) of ESDP missions conducted at the time of writing, and clearly demonstrates the growing geographical and functional reach of
ESDP missions. However, the reader may miss some more comment on the fact
that there is little evidence of any coherent plan underlying the EU's interventions. Though the European Security Strategy provides a good set of general set
of principles of objectives, this does not explain why, for example, five out of the
nearly 20 operations have been in the Congo. Chapter 5 includes a (short) discussion of the applicability of humanitarian and human rights law to EU-led operations, a topic which, to the reviewer's knowledge, had previously received very
little attention. The contribution on ESDP's anti-terrorism aspects (Chapter 6)
correctly identifies the growing contribution envisaged for ESDP in this field
while making equally clear that ESDP is not at the centre of the EU's counter-
terrorism efforts. The chapter analysing the compatibility of ESDP and NATO
(Chapter 8) may, despite its interest, be somewhat puzzling. Its main argument is
that 'the EU should not pursue the idea of creating a traditional defence alliance'
(p. 174). However, it does not seem that this is a core issue at stake in any event
at present. Chapter 9 focuses on an examination of the emerging institutional
framework of a European armaments policy in the light of recent developments
in the field, namely the establishment of the European Defence Agency and the
initiatives of the European Commission which is attempting to play a helpful role
in practice.

The third section (Chapters 10–14) tackles the problem of the coherence and
effectiveness of European security policy. A connecting thread between the
authors in this and also in other sections is that the close cooperation and desirable consistency between the EU and other international organizations (beginning with the UN) would be convenient, but not indispensable: it is suggested
that, legally and politically, the EU can act more independently.

Chapter 10 analyses different forms of flexibility and differentiation in the second pillar. This is a very useful contribution because of the underlying tension

between an alleged increase in effectiveness as a result of differentiation and the potential threat to the coherence of EU policy and legal order that such differentiation might cause. The author rightly concludes his chapter by stating that current forms of flexibility 'do not seem to be a threat to consistent external action' (p 248). Although somehow disappointing for supporters of European integration, it is perhaps time to move on from the traditional 'convoy' approach to accept the reality of multi-speed Europe. This is followed, in Chapter 11, by an informative treatment of ESDP in the context of EU external relations. The last three chapters in this section deal with the coherence of EU security policy with other international security frameworks, namely NATO, the OSCE, and the UN. The analysis in Chapter 14 of the relationship between the ESDP and Chapters VII and VIII of the UN Charter is of particular interest, especially its discussion on the hierarchy between the two systems and on the room for autonomous action on the part of the EU.

On the substance, and without ignoring the problems and failures of the ESDP, the book generally takes an unashamedly 'glass half-full' approach and provides a more promising picture than many current analysts. If the authors' call to ensure that ESDP is both supported and guided by the rule of law is heeded, it is likely that the ESDP will be a stronger instrument as a result.

Tony Fernández Arias

Tables of Cases

COURT OF FIRST INSTANCE

EUROPEAN COURT OF JUSTICE

Alphabetical

EUROPEAN COURT OF JUSTICE OPINIONS

NATIONAL CASES

Denmark

Eire

France

Germany

Netherlands

EUROPEAN COURT OF HUMAN RIGHTS ECHR

Tables of Legislation

Decisions

NATIONAL LEGISLATION

Italy

France

EUROPEAN TREATIES AND CONVENTIONS

INTERNATIONAL CONVENTIONS
AND AGREEMENTS

Index